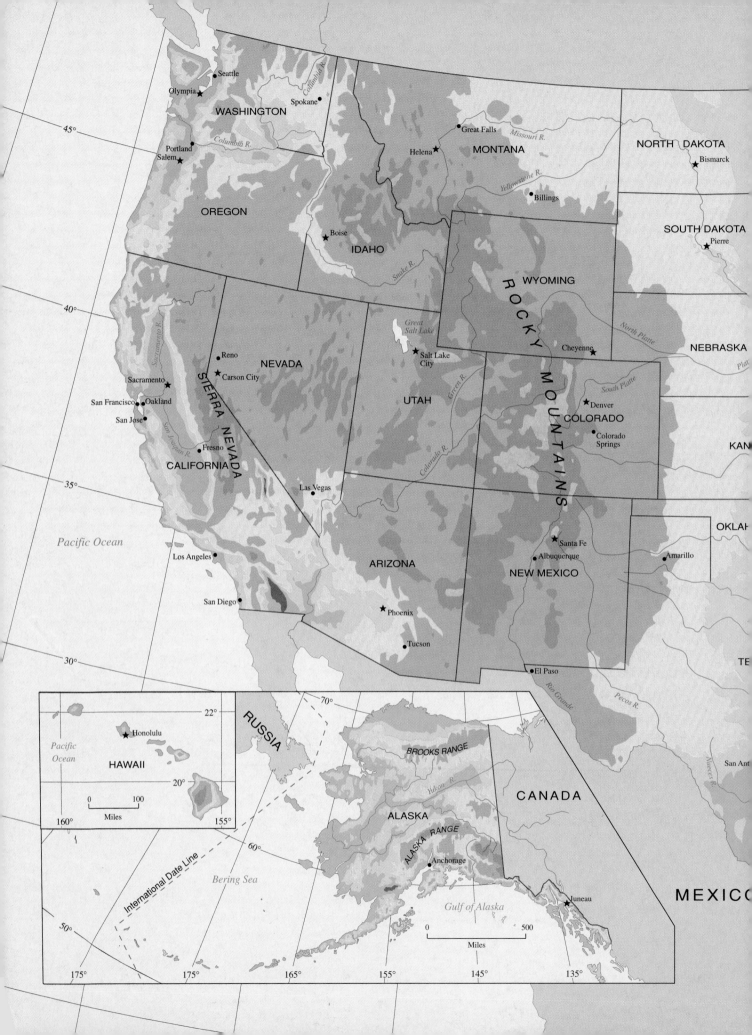

Seattle •
Olympia ★
WASHINGTON
Spokane •

45°

Portland •
Salem ★
Columbia R.

OREGON

Great Falls •
Helena ★ MONTANA
Missouri R.
Yellowstone R.
Billings •

NORTH DAKOTA
Bismarck ★

Boise ★
IDAHO
Snake R.

SOUTH DAKOTA
Pierre ★

40°

R O C K Y   M O U N T A I N S
WYOMING

Great
Salt Lake

Reno •
Carson City ★
NEVADA

Salt Lake
City ★

Cheyenne ★
North Platte

NEBRASKA

Plat

Sacramento ★
San Francisco • Oakland
San Jose •

SIERRA NEVADA

UTAH
Green R.

South Platte

Denver ★
COLORADO
Colorado
Springs •

KAN

35°

San Joaquin R.
Fresno •

CALIFORNIA

Las Vegas •

Colorado R.

Pacific Ocean

Los Angeles •

San Diego •

ARIZONA
Phoenix ★

Tucson •

Santa Fe ★
Albuquerque •
NEW MEXICO

El Paso •

OKLAH

Amarillo •

TE

Rio Grande

Pecos R.

San Ant

Nueces R.

30°

70°
22°
Honolulu ★
Pacific
Ocean
HAWAII
20°
160°   155°
0   100
Miles

RUSSIA

BROOKS RANGE

Yukon R.

CANADA

ALASKA

ALASKA RANGE

Anchorage •

International Date Line

60°

Bering Sea

50°

Gulf of Alaska

Juneau ★

0   500
Miles

MEXICO

175°   175°   165°   155°   145°   135°

CANADA

MINNESOTA
Duluth
St. Paul
Minneapolis
Falls

IOWA
Des Moines
maha
In

MISSOURI
Kansas City
St. Louis
Jefferson City

MISSISSIPPI R.
ARKANSAS
Little Rock
ma City
adian R.
na City

LOUISIANA
Baton Rouge
New Orleans
Houston
Trinity R.
Sabine R.
Red R.

L. Superior
WISCONSIN
Madison
Milwaukee
Chicago
Gary

MICHIGAN
L. Michigan
Lansing
Detroit

L. Huron

L. Ontario

ILLINOIS
Springfield

INDIANA
Indianapolis
Cincinnati
Louisville
KENTUCKY
Frankfort
Ohio R.
Nashville
Knoxville
TENNESSEE
Memphis
Tennessee R.
Birmingham
ALABAMA
Montgomery
Jackson
Chattahoochee R.
Altamaha R.
Alabama R.
GEORGIA
Atlanta
Tallahassee

MISSISSIPPI

Wisconsin R.
Mississippi R.

Missouri R.
Illinois R.
Wabash R.

OHIO
Columbus
Cleveland
Wheeling

WEST
VIRGINIA
Charleston

Cumberland R.

APPALACHIAN MOUNTAINS

VIRGINIA
Richmond
Norfolk
Roanoke R.

NORTH CAROLINA
Raleigh
Charlotte
Cape Fear R.
SOUTH
CAROLINA
Columbia
Santee R.
Charleston

L. Erie
Buffalo
Allegheny R.

PENNSYLVANIA
Harrisburg
Pittsburgh
Potomac R.

St. Lawrence R.

MAINE
Augusta
Portland

Burlington
Montpelier
VT.
N.H.
Concord
Manchester
Albany
NEW YORK
Hartford
CONN.
MASS.
Boston
Providence
R.I.

Newark
New York
Trenton
NEW JERSEY
Philadelphia
Hudson R.

Baltimore
MD.
Dover
DELAWARE
Annapolis
WASHINGTON D.C.

FLORIDA
Jacksonville
Miami

Gulf of Mexico

Atlantic Ocean

BAHAMAS

CUBA

Elevation

Feet	Meters
9,843	3,000
6,562	2,000
3,281	1,000
1,640	500
656	200
0	0
Below sea level	Below sea level

67°   66°
Atlantic Ocean
San Juan
PUERTO RICO
Ponce
18°
Caribbean Sea
0   50
Miles

200   400
Miles

95°   90°   85°   80°   75°

GREENLAND
(KALAALIT-NUNAAT)
(DEN.)

Arc

ICELAND

ALASKA
(U.S.)

CANADA

IREL

UNITED STATES

*Atlantic
Ocean*

PORTU

AZORES
(PORT.)

MEXICO

MADEIRA IS.
(PORT.)

CANARY IS. (SP.)

Tropic of Cancer

BAHAMAS

WESTERN
SAHARA
(MOR.)

20°

HAWAII (U.S.)

CUBA

DOMINICAN
REPUBLIC

PUERTO RICO (U.S.)

MAURITAN

HAITI

ANTIGUA AND BARBUDA

BELIZE

JAMAICA

DOMINICA

CAPE
VERDE

HONDURAS

ST. KITTS-NEVIS

ST. VINCENT AND
THE GRENADINES

SENEGAL

GUATEMALA

NICARAGUA

GRENADA

GAMBIA

GUINEA

EL SALVADOR

BARBADOS

GUINEA-
BISSAU

COSTA RICA

TRINIDAD AND TOBAGO

GUYANA

SIERRA
LEONE

PANAMA

VENEZUELA

SURINAME

LIBERIA

COLOMBIA

FRENCH GUIANA (FR.)

D'I

Pacific Ocean

Equator

ECUADOR

GALAPAGOS
IS.
(ECU.)

KIRIBATI

PERU

BRAZIL

WESTERN
SAMOA

AMERICAN
SAMOA (U.S.)

FRENCH
POLYNESIA

BOLIVIA

TONGA

20°

Tropic of Capricorn

CHILE

PARAGUAY

*Atlan.
Ocea*

URUGUAY

40°

ARGENTINA

FALKLAND IS. (U.K.)

60°

Antarctic Circle

80°

Political divisions as of September 1996

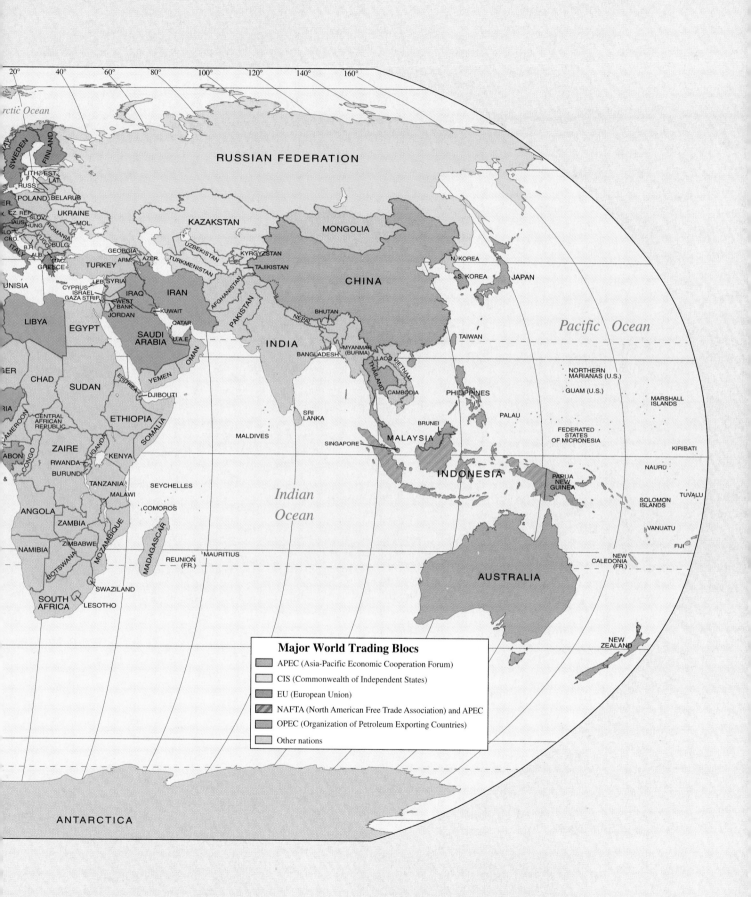

Major World Trading Blocs

- APEC (Asia-Pacific Economic Cooperation Forum)
- CIS (Commonwealth of Independent States)
- EU (European Union)
- NAFTA (North American Free Trade Association) and APEC
- OPEC (Organization of Petroleum Exporting Countries)
- Other nations

Michael P. Conzen
University of Chicago

Advisory Editor for Cartography

America's History

Volume 2 SINCE 1865

John Sloan (1871–1951), a leader of the Ashcan school of art, began his career as a staff artist for the Philadelphia *Inquirer*. He moved to New York in 1904, where his newspaper illustrations often satirized the foibles of the wealthy. Sloan's sympathies lay with ordinary people—he briefly joined the Socialist party—and in his paintings he sought to capture the drama in scenes of everyday life.

Six O'Clock, Winter is one such scene, depicting a rush hour crowd of shop girls, clerks, and workingmen, who seem unaware of the elevated subway train hovering menacingly above them.

John Sloan *Six O'Clock Winter*, 1912
Oil on canvas, 26 x 32". The Phillips Collection, Washington, D.C. Acquired 1922.

THIRD EDITION

America's History

Volume 2 SINCE 1865

James A. Henretta
University of Maryland

W. Elliot Brownlee
University of California, Santa Barbara

David Brody
University of California, Davis

Susan Ware

Marilynn S. Johnson
Boston College

Worth Publishers

America's History, Volume 2: Since 1865, *Third Edition*

Copyright © 1997 by Worth Publishers, Inc.

All rights reserved.

Manufactured in the United States of America

Library of Congress Catalog Card Number: 96-060600

ISBN: 1–57259–214–1

Printing: 2 3 4 5 — 01 00 99 98 97

Executive editor: Paul Shensa

Development editor: Jennifer E. Sutherland

Design: Malcolm Grear Designers

Art director: George Touloumes

Production editor: Laura Rubin

Production supervisor: Stacey B. Alexander

Layout: Fernando Quinones

Picture editor: Deborah Bull/Photosearch

Picture researcher: Joanne Polster/Photosearch

Line art: Demetrios Zangos

Cartography: Mapping Specialists, Ltd.

Composition and separations: TSI Graphics

Printing and binding: R.R. Donnelley & Sons Company

Cover: John Sloan, *Six O'Clock, Winter*, 1912
Oil on canvas, 26 × 32″. The Phillips Collection, Washington, D.C.
Acquired 1922 (detail)

Worth Publishers
33 Irving Place
New York, NY 10003

For our families

Contents in Brief

Contents

★   ★   ★

★ ★ ★

Documents D–1

★ ★ ★

Appendix A–1

★ ★ ★

Illustration Credits IC–1

★ ★ ★

Index I–1

Chapter Features

★   ★   ★

TABLES

AMERICAN LIVES

Preface

★   ★   ★

We live in troubled intellectual times. Political turmoil in the academic world and in the wider culture has forced close scrutiny of established beliefs and methods. These "culture wars," as they have been called, have had a direct impact on the interpretation and teaching of history. The debate over the *National Standards for History* provided a forceful reminder that historians assume a great social responsibility when they define the content, structure, and meaning of the nation's past.

We welcome this challenge. From the very inception of *America's History*, we set out to write a *democratic* history, one that would convey the experiences of ordinary people even as it recorded the accomplishments of the great and powerful. We focused not only on the rich diversity of peoples who have become Americans but also on the institutions—political, economic, and social—that forged a common national identity. And we presented political and social history in an integrated way, using each perspective to make better sense of the other. The recent debates over the purposes and meaning of history have confirmed our belief that this is the right approach, and we have therefore continued and improved upon it.

The Third Edition of *America's History* remains committed to presenting a balanced and comprehensive narrative of our nation's past. In our discussion of government and politics, diplomacy and war, we show how they affected—and were affected by—ethnic groups and economic conditions, intellectual beliefs and social changes, and the religious and moral values of the times. Just as important, we place the American experience in a global context. We trace aspects of American society to their origins in European and African cultures, consider the American Industrial Revolution from the perspective of the world economy, and plot the foreign relations of the United States as part of an ever-shifting international system of imperial expansion, financial exchange, and diplomatic alliances.

Organization

As historians explore ever more diverse aspects of the American experience, the need to organize this disparate material for the student becomes more and more imperative. We have therefore given *America's History* a clear chronology and a strong conceptual framework. Volume 2 is divided into three Parts, with each Part corresponding to a distinct phase of development. Each Part begins at a crucial turning point, such as the Cold War, and emphasizes the dynamic forces that it unleashed and that symbolized the era. To aid student comprehension, each Part begins with a two-page overview: first, a **Thematic Timeline** highlights the key developments in government, the economy, society, culture, and foreign affairs; then these themes are summarized in a brief **Part essay**. Each Part essay focuses on the crucial engines of historical change—in some eras primarily economic, in others political or diplomatic—that created new conditions of life and transformed social relations. The essays and the Part organization help students understand the major themes and periods of American history, to see that bits and pieces of historical data acquire significance as part of a larger pattern of development.

In telling this complex story, we give equal attention to historical actors and to historical institutions, customs, and forces—writing what the historian Lawrence Stone has called "the new narrative history." At the center of our narrative are the actions of individual Americans: we show how people of all classes and groups make their own history. But we also make clear how people's choices are influenced and constrained by circumstances: the customs and institutions inherited from the past and the distribution of power in the present. Such a presentation not only conveys the diversity of the American experience but also helps students understand their own potential for purposeful action as responsible citizens.

Changes in the Third Edition

Those acquainted with the Second Edition will find much that is familiar and many changes as well. The most important change is the addition of a new author, Professor Marilynn S. Johnson of Boston College. The author of the prize-winning monograph, *The Second Gold Rush: Oakland and the East Bay in World War II,* Dr. Johnson now shares with Susan Ware the major responsibility for twentieth-century America and has used her specialized knowledge to augment our treatment of California and the western United States.

Other changes have resulted from the extraordinarily helpful suggestions of instructors who have used *America's History.* Responding to their concerns, we have made major changes in many chapters. Chapter 17 has been extensively revised to show more clearly the differing patterns of settlement on the Great Plains and in the Far West. The three chapters devoted to the pivotal 1960–1980 period have been substantially rewritten and reorganized. Chapter 30, "The Ascent of Liberalism," integrates the stories of the civil rights movement and domestic politics in the 1960s. Chapter 31, "The Vietnam Experience," brings together the entire history of the war in a single chapter. Chapter 32, "The Lean Years," presents the social and economic changes and national politics of the 1970s. In addition, Chapter 33 has been significantly revised and updated to provide an integrated analysis of domestic and global changes and trends in the 1980s and 1990s.

Reflecting newly published scholarship, we have significantly revised many sections of the text. Reflecting recent work on gender, we have sharpened our analysis of men's as well as women's lives. We have drawn on the new western history to enrich the coverage of Spanish- and English-speaking settlers in Texas and the Southwest in the nineteenth century. We tell the story of cultural interaction in the West from the perspective of all participants—the resident native Americans as well as incoming groups: Mormons, miners, ranchers, and farm families. Our analysis of late nineteenth-century politics incorporates recent scholarship on the New South, while the chapter on the city includes new materials on popular culture and sexuality.

In the twentieth century we have included additional coverage of Mexican-American workers during the Great Depression, new insights from Soviet archives on the cold war era, and an expanded discussion of cultural dissent in United States during those years. Drawing on yet another emergent field of scholarship, the Third Edition of *America's History* incorporates more material on the role of the state throughout American history, including recent challenges by Christian groups and New Right activists to the system of national government created during and after the New Deal.

Features

The Third Edition of *America's History* contains a wealth of special features, all closely tied to the main text. We have expanded our much-hailed **American Lives** feature so that every chapter now includes an incisive biography of an important individual or group. Among the new Lives are studies of newspaper mogul William Randolph Hearst, rock music idol Elvis Presley, environmental activist Lois Marie Gibbs, and Bill Gates, the founder of Microsoft.

We have also expanded our coverage of the lives of ordinary Americans and, to enhance their presence in the historical record, we have refined our **American Voices** feature. Each chapter contains two or three contemporary first-person accounts from the letters, diaries, autobiographies, and public testimony of ordinary Americans that paint a vivid portrait of the social or political life of the time. Finally, recognizing the challenge of technological change in the present, we have deepened our discussion of **New Technology** in the past; major essays focus on the technical aspects of innovations and how they affected everyday life. Taken together, these documents and essays provide instructors with a range of teaching materials and assist students to enter the life of the past and see it from within.

At the beginning of each chapter, we have added a brief **outline** to provide students with an overview of the main themes. Then, at the end of the chapter, we reiterate the themes in an analytic **Summary** and remind students of important events in an expanded **Timeline.** The annotated **Bibliography** that follows every chapter now begins with a general section containing two or three books of general interest or particular importance.

We have improved and expanded our illustration program. Professor Michael R. Conzen, our advisory editor for cartography, has prepared five entirely new maps, including the Western mining frontier in the late nineteenth century and the military-industrial complex in Los Angeles during the Cold War. In addition, each chapter includes around fifteen photographs, carefully selected to enhance a particular aspect of the text. To help students understand and remember complicated sequences of events we have added new tables listing, for example, the key legislation of the Reconstruction and Progressive eras and the major initiatives of President Johnson's Great Society program.

Supplements

Student Guide

by Thomas R. Frazier (Baruch College, emeritus)

The *Student Guide* is designed to help students improve their performance in the course. Not only will their comprehension of the textbook and their confidence in their abilities be advanced through its conscientious use, but they will develop better learning skills and study habits. The guide begins with an introduction by Gerald J. Goodwin (University of Houston) on how to study history. Each chapter includes a summary of the essential facts and ideas of the text chapter, with fill-in questions; the timeline from the textbook with short explanations of the significance of each event; a glossary; skill-building exercises based on a map, table, or figure from the textbook; exercises for the American Voices documents and the American Lives and New Technology essays; and a self-test.

Instructor's Resource Manual

by Thomas R. Frazier (Baruch College, emeritus), Stephen J. Kneeshaw (College of the Ozarks), and Linda Moore (Eastern New Mexico University)

The *Instructor's Resource Manual* contains an abundance of materials to aid instructors in planning the course and enhancing student involvement. For each chapter of the textbook the resources include chapter themes, a brief summary, the timeline from the textbook with additional details, lecture suggestions, class discussions starters, topics for writing assignments, and topics for research. In addition, the manual includes nine historiographic essays on a variety of topics by outstanding scholars in these fields. For courses with a topical focus, special documents sets (modules) are provided for constitutional, southern, and diplomatic history, as well as the history of African-Americans, Latinos, native Americans, and women. The *Instructors Resource Manual* also includes a guide to writing about history by Gerald J. Goodwin, a guide to the use of computers and the Internet in teaching history by James B. M. Schick (Pittsburg State University), and a film and video guide by Stephen J. Kneeshaw.

Test Bank

by Thomas L. Altherr and Adolph Grundman (Metropolitan State College of Denver), and James Miller

The test bank provides 120 to 150 questions for each chapter, including multiple-choice questions, fill-ins, map questions, and short and long essay questions. Computerized test-generation systems are also available for IBM-compatible and Macintosh platforms.

Documents Collection

by Douglas Bukowski, Stephen J. Kneeshaw (College of the Ozarks), and Louis S. Gerteis (University of Missouri, St. Louis)

The *Documents Collection*, containing approximately 170 key documents, is packaged with the textbook (if required) or available separately. Each document is preceded by a brief introduction and followed by questions to help students understand its context and significance.

Transparencies

A set of 56 full-color acetate transparencies reproduces maps, figures, and fine art from the textbook, along with teaching suggestions.

Lecture Presentation CD-ROM Archive

New for the Third Edition, the presentation CD-ROM software will make it easy for instructors to include multimedia in classroom lectures. An exciting resource to introduce multimedia into your lectures. The disk, available in Mac and Windows formats, includes electronic lecture outlines and digital images of maps, figures, and fine art from the textbook.

Acknowledgments

We are extremely grateful to the many scholars and teachers who reported on their experiences with the Second Edition or reviewed manuscript chapters of the Third Edition. Their comments often challenged us to rethink or justify our interpretations and always provided a check on accuracy down to the smallest detail.

Paula Baker, University of Pittsburgh

Michael C. Batinski, Southern Illinois University

Roger Biles, East Carolina University

Frederick Blue, Youngstown State University

Jonathan M. Chu, University of Massachusetts–Boston

Doug Clark, Linn-Benton Community College

Martin B. Cohen, George Mason University

George Daniels, University of South Alabama

Ronald L. F. Davis, California State University, Northridge

William Deverell, California Institute of Technology

Melvyn Dubofsky, Binghamton University

Keith Edgerton, Montana State University–Billings

Mario T. Garcia, University of California, Santa Barbara

Esther S. Goldberg, Las Positas College, Livermore

Janettte Thomas Greenwood, Clark University

Adolph H. Grundman, Metropolitan State College of Denver

Robert L. Harris, Jr., Africana Studies and Research Center, Cornell University

Benjamin T. Harrison, University of Louisville

Colette A. Hyman, Winona State University

Joy E. Ingram, Pellissippi State Technial Community College

Elizabeth Jameson, University of New Mexico

John Jameson, Kent State University

Robert David Johnson, Williams College

Howard Jones, University of Alabama

K. Austin Kerr, Ohio State University

Tracy K'Meyer, University of Louisville

Thomas J. Knock, Southern Methodist University

George S. McCowen, Williamette University

Dr. Lee Augustus McGriggs

Robert C. McMath, Jr., Georgia Institute of Technology

María E. Montoya, University of Michigan

Linda Ann Moore, Eastern New Mexico University

David M. Pletcher, Indiana University

Glenda Riley, Ball State University

Leanne Sander, University of Colorado

David F. Schmitz, Whitman College

Bruce J. Schulman, Boston University

Kathryn Kish Sklar, Binghamton University

Melvin Small, Wayne State University

Judith M. Stanley, California State University, Hayward

Susan Williams, Fitchburg State College

Laura Matysek Wood, Tarrant County Junior College, Northwest

Randall Bennett Woods, University of Arkansas

Peter M. Wright, Oklahoma City Community College

Mitch Yamasaki, Chaminade University of Honolulu

As the authors of *America's History*, we know better than anyone else just how much of this book is the work of other hands and minds. We are grateful to R. Jackson Wilson, who conceived the intellectual scaffolding of the project, and to David Follmer, who in various guises as our editor, publisher, and agent, has helped us to create it. We are equally appreciative of the assistance provided by three very special people at Worth Publishers: Bob Worth gave us the resources and the incentive to develop the full potential of *America's History*. Paul Shensa provided us with constant stimulation and extraordinarly helpful advice. And Jennifer Sutherland held us to the highest scholarly standards as she masterfully edited our text.

Special thanks are also due to many other individuals: Deborah Bull and the staff of Photosearch; the fine assistant editors who worked closely with us on the Third Edition—Jeannine Ciliotta, Phyllis Fisher, Barbara Gerr, and Debra Osnowitz; our project editor, Laura Rubin; and the Worth production and editorial staff: Stacey Alexander, George Touloumes, Demetrios Zangos, Brad A. Fox, and Yuna Lee.

We also want to express our thanks for the valuable research assistance provided by Andrew Laas, University of Maryland, Amy Richter of New York University, and Beverly Bastian and Michael Adamson of the University of California, Santa Barbara.

From the very beginning we have considered this book as a joint intellectual venture and with each edition our collaborative effort has grown. We are proud to acknowledge our collective authorship of *America's History*.

James A. Henretta
W. Elliot Brownlee
David Brody
Susan Ware
Marilynn S. Johnson

About the Authors

★   ★   ★

James A. Henretta is Priscilla Alden Burke Professor of American History at the University of Maryland, College Park. He received his undergraduate education at Swarthmore College and his Ph.D. from Harvard University. He has taught at the University of Sussex, England; Princeton University; UCLA; Boston University; as a Fulbright lecturer in Australia at the University of New England; and in 1991–92 at Oxford University as the Harmsworth Professor of American History. His publications include *The Evolution of American Society, 1700– 1815: An Interdisciplinary Analysis*; *"Salutary Neglect": Colonial Administration under the Duke of Newcastle*; *Evolution and Revolution: American Society, 1600–1820*; *The Origins of American Capitalism*; and important articles in early American and social history. He recently completed a fellowship at the Woodrow Wilson Center working on a study of *The Transformation of the Liberal State in America, 1800–1970*.

W. Elliot Brownlee is Professor of History at the University of California, Santa Barbara. He is a graduate of Harvard University, received his Ph.D. from the University of Wisconsin, Madison, and specializes in U.S. economic history. He has been awarded fellowships by the Charles Warren Center, Harvard University, and the Woodrow Wilson International Center for Scholars. He has been a visiting professor at Princeton and was Bicentennial Lecturer at the U.S. Department of the Treasury. His published works include *Dynamics of Ascent: A History of the American Economy*; *Progressivism and Economic Growth: The Wisconsin Income Tax, 1911–1929*; *Women in the American Economy: A Documentary History, 1675–1929* (with Mary M. Brownlee); *The Essentials of American History* (with Richard N. Current, T. Harry Williams, and Frank Freidel); *Funding the Modern American State: The Rise and Fall of the Era of Easy Finance, 1945–1995*; and *Federal Taxation in America: A Short History*.

David Brody is Professor Emeritus of History at the University of California, Davis. He received his B.A., M.A., and Ph.D. from Harvard University. He has taught at the University of Warwick in England, at Moscow State University in the former Soviet Union, and at Sydney University in Australia. He is the author of *Steelworkers in America*; *Workers in Industrial America: Essays on the 20th Century Struggle*; and *In Labor's Cause: Main Themes on the History of the American Worker*. He has been awarded fellowships from the Social Science Research Council, the Guggenheim Foundation, and the National Endowment for the Humanities. He is past president (1991–92) of the Pacific Coast Branch of the American Historical Association. His current research is on industrial labor during the Great Depression.

Susan Ware specializes in twentieth-century U.S. history and the history of American women. From 1986 to 1995 she taught at New York University and is now an independent scholar based in Cambridge, Massachusetts. She received her undergraduate degree from Wellesley College and her Ph.D. from Harvard University. Ware is the author of *Beyond Suffrage: Women in the New Deal*; *Holding Their Own: American Women in the 1930s*; *Partner and I: Molly Dewson, Feminism, and New Deal Politics*; *Modern American Women: A Documentary History*; and *Still Missing: Amelia Earhart and the Search for Modern Feminism*. She serves on the national advisory boards of the Franklin and Eleanor Roosevelt Institute and the Schlesinger Library of Radcliffe College and has been a historical consultant to numerous documentary film projects.

Marilynn S. Johnson is Assistant Professor of History at Boston College, where she teaches American urban and social history. She received her B.A. degree from Stanford University and her M.A. and Ph.D. from New York University. She is the author of *The Second Gold Rush: Oakland and the East Bay in World War II* and is currently working on a study of urban police violence in the late nineteenth and twentieth centuries. Her articles and reviews have appeared in *Pacific Historical Review*, *Journal of American History*, *Journal of Urban History*, and *Labor History*. She recently served on the editorial board of *Pacific Historical Review*.

America's History

Volume 2 SINCE 1865

Robert B. Elliott

Robert B. Elliott (1842–1884) was born in Boston and educated there and in Jamaica and England. After studying law and serving in the navy during the Civil War, he moved to Charleston and served in the state legislature (1868–1870), Congress (1871–1874), and as speaker of the South Carolina house (1874–1876). This 1874 lithograph, *The Shackle Broken by the Genius of Freedom*, shows him addressing state legislators on civil rights. After Reconstruction he left politics and practiced law in New Orleans.

CHAPTER **16**

The Union Reconstructed

1865–1877

★   ★   ★

When the Confederacy collapsed in the spring of 1865, President Lincoln hoped that he could achieve a swift reconciliation between the triumphant North and the shattered South. In his second inaugural address Lincoln had spoken of the need to "bind up the nation's wounds." But many questions remained unanswered. Who would control the rebuilding of the Union—the president or Congress? How long should the rebuilding last? How far should it go: should it exclude former Confederates from politics and reward freedmen with land confiscated from their former masters?

At the end of the war most Republican leaders defined the task of rebuilding simply as a matter of *restoration*. These moderates wanted to establish loyal, pro-Union state governments and restore the southern states' representation in Congress. But freedmen, former abolitionists, and some Republican politicians favored a more radical plan—one requiring a degree of *reconstruction* of the South. In their view, steps should be taken to ensure a measure of political and even economic equality for the freed slaves and to prevent the return to power of unrepentant planters. For radicals, the key to reconstructing the South was to make the Republican party dominant there.

When northern Republicans adopted a policy of radical reconstruction in 1867, ex-Confederates and their Democratic sympathizers in the North maintained that their goal should be the *redemption* of the South. They claimed that the Union victory had defeated democracy in the South, depriving southerners of control over their economic, social, and political systems. The Union would be rebuilt, the redeemers claimed, only when white southerners regained power over their states and their own affairs.

The Reconstruction Era—the years from 1865 to 1877—was shaped by continuous struggles among the groups holding these differing views. It was a time of

485

unparalleled peacetime turmoil and violence. In the struggles, every kind of tactic was brought to bear: the assassination of one president and the impeachment of another; the adoption of three amendments to the Constitution and a welter of new legislation; the use of violence, including nighttime terrorism by robed whites in the South; the creation of new institutions by African-Americans; and conventional compromises and deals by politicians on all sides.

Presidential Restoration

Lincoln and his successor, Andrew Johnson, took the initiative in rebuilding the Union. Both believed that the southern states had never legally left the Union, that rebuilding the nation was simply a process of restoring state governments loyal to the Union, and that this political process could take place quickly, largely under presidential direction. This moderate approach put the presidents on a collision course with those Republicans in Congress who sought a reconstruction of southern society.

Restoration under Lincoln

The process of rebuilding had actually begun during the war as Lincoln tried to subvert the southern war effort. Lincoln thought that a policy of moderation and reconciliation in the portions of the South occupied by federal troops would induce the Confederates to abandon the rebellion. In implementing his restoration plan, Lincoln relied on his power as military commander in chief. He assumed that states could not legally secede and that reorganizing the Union was purely an administrative mat-

ter. (In 1869, in *Texas v. White*, the Supreme Court accepted Lincoln's constitutional interpretation, ruling that secession was impossible under the Constitution.)

Lincoln's Plan. In December 1863 Lincoln announced his restoration plan. He offered a general amnesty to all Confederate citizens except high-ranking civil and military officials. Citizens of states seeking to reconstitute their governments would have to take an oath pledging their *future* loyalty to the Union and accepting the Union's wartime acts and proclamations concerning slavery. When 10 percent of the number of voters in 1860 had taken the loyalty oath, those individuals could organize a new state government.

Lincoln aimed his plan at former southern Whigs, many of whom he had known well as former political allies. Under his plan they would step forward, declare allegiance to the Union, and take charge of southern state governments. That is what happened in three states under military occupation: Louisiana, Arkansas, and Tennessee. The former Whigs who organized loyal governments under Lincoln's supervision often retained their economic power. In Louisiana, for example, Whig sugar planters who declared their loyalty to the Union received help from Generals Benjamin F. Butler and Nathaniel P. Banks, who used their troops to enforce labor discipline, transforming slaves into wage laborers and enabling the former Whigs to save their plantations.

Radical and Moderate Republicans. Many members of his own party, including some of his fellow moderates, disapproved of Lincoln's plan. Their opposition was based in part on a different constitutional interpretation. They argued that the southern states *had* left the Union and were now the equivalent of conquered provinces with territorial status. As such, they were subject to Congressional rule rather than executive authority.

Radical Republicans

Lincoln's readmission plan was harshly criticized by radical Republicans. One of their leaders was Thaddeus Stevens (front row, second from left), pictured here with fellow members of Congress in a photograph by Mathew Brady. Stevens outlined a radical economic plan that called for a redistribution of land in the South. He believed that the former slaves needed more than the vote to control their fate—they needed land. He was unable to muster support for this radical plan.

The most strenuous criticism came from a group of radical Republicans, some of whom had abolitionist backgrounds. Led by Senator Charles Sumner of Massachusetts and Representative Thaddeus Stevens of Pennsylvania, the radicals wanted a harder, slower peace. In Stevens's words, the federal government should "revolutionize Southern institutions, habits, and manners." He declared that "the foundations of their institutions . . . must be broken up and relaid, or all our blood and treasure will have been spent in vain."

Stevens, Indiana Congressman George W. Julian, and African-American leaders, including Frederick Douglass, staked out the most radical definition of what reconstruction should mean. The core of their program was an economic one: confiscation and redistribution of southern plantations to the freed slaves and to white farmers who had been loyal to the Union. The program was meant to fulfill the dreams of the former slaves, whose expectations had been raised by emancipation, and of the poor white farmers of the South. To the former slaves, emancipation and freedom meant control over their lives. But to control their fate in an agricultural economy, they knew they needed to own land. But Stevens and Julian were unable to recruit other members of Congress to support a large-scale redistribution of land in the South. The majority of radical Republicans regarded such a plan as a violation of the Constitution's protection of property rights and a threat to the capitalist order.

The radical Republicans did agree on three key points: (1) The leaders of the Confederacy should not be allowed to return to power in the South, (2) steps should be taken to establish the Republican party as a major, even dominant, force in southern political life, and (3) the federal government should ensure that African-Americans participated in southern society with full *civil* equality by guaranteeing their voting rights. The last point was especially important. As Frederick Douglass declared in May 1865, "Slavery is not abolished until the black man has the ballot."

Moderate Republicans in Congress shared the radicals' view that Lincoln's program was too lenient, and they endorsed the first two points of the radical program. But as a group they hesitated to go further and support black suffrage and civil equality. Like virtually all conservative Republicans and Democrats, some moderates were profoundly racist and believed that African-Americans could never become responsible citizens. Like Lincoln, other moderates had confidence in blacks' abilities. But they wanted to avoid the violent resistance that southern whites might mount in response to drastic changes in the relationship between the races.

The Wade-Davis Bill. In 1864 the radical and moderate Republicans in Congress devised an alternative to Lincoln's program that was based on the two reconstruction principles on which they could agree. In the Wade-Davis bill, passed by Congress on July 2, 1864, they set harsher conditions for former Confederate states to rejoin the Union. A *majority* of a state's adult white men would have to swear an oath of allegiance to the Union. The state could then hold a constitutional convention, but no one could vote in the election for delegates or serve as a delegate unless he swore that he had never carried arms against the Union or aided the Confederacy in any way. Requiring this pledge, which became known as the *ironclad oath*, would exclude most southern whites, therefore leaving the task of constitution making to those white men who had overtly opposed the Confederacy. Finally, the bill required that slavery be prohibited and that Confederate civil and military leaders be permanently disfranchised.

The Wade-Davis bill proposed going further than Lincoln's plan in punishing ex-Confederates, especially those who had led the rebellion. Despite this difference, Lincoln seemed ready to compromise with the Congressional Republicans. Rather than openly challenging Congress by vetoing the Wade-Davis bill, he executed a "pocket" veto by not signing it before Congress adjourned. At the same time he initiated informal talks with members of Congress aimed at producing a compromise solution when the war ended. He even suggested that he might support the radical program of establishing federal control over race relations in the South and guaranteeing the vote to African-Americans there. In the last speech he ever delivered, on April 11, 1865, Lincoln demonstrated that he was moving pragmatically to endorse freedmen's suffrage, beginning with those who had served in the Union army and those who were educated.

The Assassination of Lincoln. Whether Lincoln and his party could have forged a unified approach to reconstruction is one of the great unanswered questions of American history. On April 14, 1865—Good Friday—Lincoln was shot in the head at Ford's Theater in Washington by an unstable actor named John Wilkes Booth. Ironically, Lincoln might have been spared if the war had dragged on longer, for Booth and his Confederate associates had originally plotted to kidnap the president to force a negotiated settlement. After Lee's surrender, Booth became desperate for revenge. In the middle of the play he entered Lincoln's box, shot him at close range, stabbed a member of the president's party, and fled. Booth was hunted down and killed by Union troops. Eight people were eventually convicted as accomplices by military courts, and four of them were hanged.

Lincoln never regained consciousness and died on April 15. The Union—and the hundreds of thousands of African-Americans for whom his name had become synonymous with freedom—went into profound mourning. Even Lincoln's critics suddenly conceded his greatness. Millions of Americans honored his memory by waiting in silence to watch the train carrying his body back to Illinois for burial.

Lincoln's death dramatically changed the prospects for a moderate reconstruction. At one stroke John Wilkes Booth had sent Lincoln to martyrdom, convinced many northerners that harsher measures against the South were necessary, and forced the presidency into the hands of Vice-President Andrew Johnson.

Restoration under Johnson

Andrew Johnson was a self-made man and former slaveholder from the hills of eastern Tennessee. A Jacksonian Democrat, he saw himself as the champion of ordinary white people. He hated what he called the "bloated, corrupt aristocracy" of the Northeast, and he blamed southern planters for the Civil War. His political career had led from the Tennessee legislature and governorship to the U.S. Senate, where he remained, loyal to the Union, after Tennessee seceded. He served as military governor of his home state after federal forces captured Nashville. In 1864 the Republicans nominated him as vice-president in an effort to promote wartime political unity and to court the support of southern Unionists.

Like Lincoln, Johnson believed that the southern states had retained their constitutional status and that reunification was exclusively an executive matter. During the summer of 1865, when Congress was not in session, Johnson unilaterally executed his own plan for restoration. He insisted only that the states revoke their ordinances of secession and ratify the Thirteenth Amendment, which abolished slavery. He offered amnesty and a return of all property except slaves to almost all southerners if they took an oath of allegiance to the Union. Southerners who were excluded from amnesty—high-ranking Confederate military officers and civil officials and persons with taxable property of more than $20,000—could petition Johnson personally. By December 1865 all the former Confederate states had functioning governments and had met Johnson's requirements for rejoining the Union.

Johnson's plan would not become complete until Congress accepted the senators and representatives from the former Confederacy. Under the Constitution, Congress is "the judge of the elections, returns and qualifications of its own members" (Article I, Section 5), and it would not convene again until December 1865. This step need not have been a problem for Johnson. Whereas most moderate Republicans in Congress hoped to make changes in Johnson's program to bring it closer to the Wade-Davis bill, they supported the basic outline of his program. Perhaps most important, they agreed with Johnson that the federal government should not protect African-American suffrage or civil equality. Even most radicals were optimistic. They liked the stern treatment of Confederate leaders, and they hoped that the new southern governments would respond positively to Johnson's conciliatory attitude and offer the vote at least to African-Americans who were literate and owned property (probably no more than 10 percent of adult black men).

During the summer and fall, however, Johnson lost the support of radical Republicans. They first became angered over a telegram that Johnson had sent in August to the provisional governor of Mississippi, who was presiding over the state's constitutional convention. Johnson urged that the vote be given to literate African-Americans on the grounds that "the radicals, who are wild upon negro franchise, will be completely foiled." The telegram also embarrassed Republican moderates, who had hoped to win the support of the radicals as well as that of Johnson for a compromise program.

In the fall of 1865 news reports of conditions in the South alarmed the moderates and further outraged the radicals. They learned that ex-Confederates were frequently attacking freedmen and white Union supporters, that the new provisional governments were making

Andrew Johnson
The president was not an easy man. This photograph of Andrew Johnson (1808–1875) conveys some of the personal qualities that contributed so centrally to his failure to reach an agreement with Republicans on a program of moderate reconstruction.

no effort to enfranchise African-Americans, and that ex-Confederates had taken control of southern governments. Southern voters elected to Congress nine men who had served in the Confederate Congress, seven former officials of Confederate state governments, four generals and four colonels from the Confederate army, and even the vice-president of the Confederacy, Alexander Stephens. It turned out that Johnson had been exceedingly liberal in pardoning ex-Confederate leaders. He seemed less interested in punishing them than in humbling them by making them submit to his personal power.

As radical Republicans increased their attacks on Johnson, he shifted away from his strongly bipartisan stance. He began to believe he could build a coalition of white southerners, northern Democrats, and conservative Republicans to support the creation of a democracy for white southerners. To avoid embarrassing potentially supportive Republicans or ex-Whigs in the South, his banner would be "National Union." Democrats in both the North and the South praised Johnson as the leader they needed to restore their party on a national basis. As the president warmed to Democratic applause, he granted more and more pardons to wealthy southerners—an average of a hundred a day in September.

The president's movement toward the Democrats further agitated radical Republicans and dismayed the moderates. By December 1865, when Congress convened, the moderates had become convinced that they had to join the radicals in order to protect the Republican party. It would be necessary, they concluded, to take action to guarantee the civil rights of former slaves and establish the Republican party in the South.

The Republican party acted quickly to reject the newly elected southern representatives and proposed that Johnson work with Congress on a new program for reconstructing the South. A House-Senate committee—the Joint Committee on Reconstruction—was formed to develop that program in cooperation with the president.

The Joint Committee conducted public hearings on conditions in the former Confederacy and publicized alarming reports from army officers, federal officials, and white and black southerners. The testimony augmented the newspaper reports by revealing an astonishing level of violence and providing disturbing details on how southern planters and legislatures were attempting to resubjugate the freed slaves. Although most moderates were still not ready to impose black suffrage on the South, almost all of them were shocked by what they regarded as a movement to circumvent the Thirteenth Amendment.

Acting on Freedom: African-Americans in the South

While congressmen discussed conditions in the South, African-Americans were already far advanced in acting on their idea of freedom. They were exultant and hopeful; their main concern was economic independence, which they assumed was necessary for true freedom. During the Civil War they had acted on this assumption throughout the South whenever Union armies drew near. But many officers actively sympathized with the planters, allowing those who expressed loyalty to the Union to retain control of their plantations and their former slaves. Other officers wished to destroy the power of the planters but preserve a class system in the South. In 1863, General Lorenzo Thomas, for example, devised a plan to lease plantations in the Mississippi Valley to loyal northern men who would hire African-American laborers under conditions set by the army.

During the final months of the war, when the Union directed its military operations against civilians, freedmen found greater opportunities to win control of land. Most visibly, General William T. Sherman reserved vast tracts of coastal lands in Georgia and South Carolina—the Sea Islands and the abandoned plantations within 30 miles of the coast—for black settlers and gave them

Schoolhouse, Port Hudson, Louisiana
This was probably the first schoolhouse built for freedmen by Union forces. In front, African-American soldiers from the Port Hudson "Corps d'Afrique" pose with their textbooks. In 1865 and 1866 most new schools in the South were established by blacks forming societies and raising money among themselves.

Eliphalet Whittlesey

Report on the Freedmen's Bureau

In October 1865, Colonel Eliphalet Whittlesey, an assistant commissioner for the Freedmen's Bureau in North Carolina, wrote the following report on the activities of the Bureau. He was later promoted to general and served as a trustee of the national Freedman's Savings Bank in Washington, D.C. He was typical of many Freedmen's Bureau officials in that he saw his role as one of mediating between two worthy groups: former slaves and former masters.

On the 22d of June I arrived at Raleigh with instructions . . . to take the control of all subjects relating to "refugees, freedmen, and the abandoned lands" within this State. I found these subjects in much confusion. Hundreds of white refugees and thousands of blacks were collected about this and other towns, occupying every hovel and shanty, living upon government rations, without employment and without comfort, many dying for want of proper food and medical supplies. A much larger number, both white and black, were crowding into the towns, and literally swarming about every depot of supplies to receive their rations. My first effort was to reduce this class of suffering and idle humanity to order, and to discover how large a proportion of these applicants were really deserving of help. . . .

It was evident at the outset that large numbers were drawing rations who might support themselves. . . . orders were issued that no able-bodied man or woman should receive sup-

plies, except such as were known to be industrious, and to be entirely destitute. . . . The homeless and helpless were gathered in camps, where shelter and food could be furnished, and the sick collected in hospitals, where they could receive proper care. . . .

Suddenly set free [the freedmen] were at first exhilarated by the air of liberty, and committed some excesses. To be sure of their freedom, many thought they must leave the old scenes of oppression and seek new homes. Others regarded the property accumulated by their labor as in part their own, and demanded a share of it. On the other hand, the former masters, suddenly stripped of their wealth, at first looked upon the freedmen with a mixture of hate and fear. In these circumstances some collisions were inevitable. . . .

. . . [M]any freedmen need the presence of some authority to enforce upon them their new duties. . . . The efforts of the bureau to protect the freedmen have done much to restrain violence and injustice. Such efforts must be continued until civil government is fully restored, just laws enacted, or great suffering and serious disturbance will be the result. Contrary to the fears and predictions of many, the great mass of colored people have remained quietly at work upon the plantations of their former masters during the entire summer. . . . In truth, a much larger amount of vagrancy exists among the whites than among the blacks. . . .

The report is confirmed by the fact that out of a colored population of nearly 350,000 in the State, only about 5,000 are now receiving support from the government. . . . Our officers . . . have visited plantations, explained the difference between slave and free labor, the nature and the solemn obligation of contracts. The chief difficulty met with has been a want of confidence between the two parties.

. . . Rev. F. A. Fiske, a Massachusetts teacher, has been appointed superintendent of education, and has devoted himself with energy to his duties. . . . the whole number of schools . . . is 63, the number of teachers 85, and the number of scholars 5,624. A few of the schools are self-supporting, and taught by colored teachers, but the majority are sustained by northern societies and northern teachers. The officers of the bureau have, as far as practicable, assigned buildings for their use, and assisted in making them suitable; but time is nearly past when such facilities can be given. The societies will be obliged hereafter to pay rent for school-rooms and for teachers homes. The teachers are engaged in a noble and self-denying work. They report a surprising thirst for knowledge among the colored people—children giving earnest attention and learning rapidly, and adults, after the day's work is done, devoting the evening to study. . . .

Source: Report of the Joint Committee on Reconstruction, 39th Cong., 1st sess. (Washington, D.C.: U.S. Government Printing Office, 1866), II: pp. 186–192.

"possessory titles" to 40-acre tracts. Sherman had little use for radicals and freedmen; he only wanted to relieve the pressure that African-American refugees were placing on his army as it marched across the Lower South. But the freedmen assumed that Sherman's order meant

that the land would be theirs—a reasonable expectation after one of Sherman's generals told a large group of freedmen "that they were to be put in possession of lands, upon which they might locate their families and work out for themselves a living and respectability."

The Freedmen's Bureau. The resettlement of freedmen was organized by the Bureau of Refugees, Freedmen, and Abandoned Lands, which Congress created in March 1865. Known as the Freedmen's Bureau, it was charged with feeding and clothing war refugees of both races, renting confiscated land to "loyal refugees and freedmen," and drafting and enforcing labor contracts between freedmen and planters. The Freedmen's Bureau also worked with the large number of northern voluntary associations that sent missionaries and teachers to the South to establish schools for former slaves (see *American Voices*, page 490).

By the end of the war the army and the Freedmen's Bureau had resettled about 10,000 families on half a million acres of "Sherman" land in Georgia and South Carolina. Reports of such actions inspired many African-American families to stay on their old plantations in the hope that they would own some of the land after the war. When the South Carolina planter Thomas Pinckney returned home, his freed slaves told him, "We ain't going nowhere. We are going to work right here on the land where we were born and what belongs to us." One Georgia freedman offered to sell to his former master the share of the plantation he expected to receive after the federal redistribution.

Johnson's amnesty plan allowed pardoned Confederates to recover their land if Union troops had confiscated or occupied it. In October, Johnson ordered General Oliver O. Howard, head of the Freedmen's Bureau, to tell Sea Island blacks that they did not hold legal title to the land and that they would have to come to terms with the white landowners. When Howard reluctantly obeyed, the dispossessed farmers protested: "Why do you take away our lands? You take them from us who have always been true, always true to the Government! You give them to our all-time enemies! That is not right!" When some of the Sea Islanders refused to deal with the restored white owners, Union soldiers forced them to leave or work for their old masters.

The former slaves resisted efforts to remove them. Often led by African-American veterans of the Union army, they fought pitched battles with plantation owners and bands of ex-Confederate soldiers. Whenever possible, landowners attempted to disarm and intimidate the returning black soldiers. One soldier wrote from Maryland: "The returned colard Solgers are in Many cases beten, and their guns taken from them, we darcent walk out of an evening. . . . they beat us badly and Sumtime Shoot us." In this warfare federal troops often backed the local whites, who generally prevailed in recapturing their former holdings.

A New Labor System. Throughout the South high postwar prices for cotton prompted returning planters not only to reclaim land but also to establish a labor system that was as close to slavery as they could make it. On paper, emancipation had cost the slave owners about $3 billion—the value of their capital investment in former slaves—a sum that equaled nearly three-fourths of the nation's economic production in 1860. The *real* losses of planters, however, depended on whether they lost control of their former slaves. Planters attempted to reestablish that control and to substitute low wages for the food, clothing, and shelter that their slaves had previously received. They also refused to sell or rent land to blacks, hoping to force them to work for low wages.

The freedmen resisted the new wage system as well as the loss of land. During the growing seasons of 1865 and 1866 thousands of former slaves abandoned their old plantations and farms. Many freedmen sought better lives in the towns and cities of the South. Those who remained in the countryside either refused to work in the cotton fields or tried to reduce the amount of time they worked there. When they could, freedmen developed their own garden plots, guaranteeing themselves a subsistence level of rations during the postwar disruptions. Freedmen who did return to work in white-owned cotton fields refused to submit to the grueling gang system that had been the major tool of economic exploitation under slavery. Now they wanted a pace of work and independence that reflected their new status. What was freedom all about if not to have a bit more leisure time, to work less intensely than they had as slaves, and to work for themselves and their families?

Wage Labor of Ex-Slaves
This photograph, taken in South Carolina shortly after the Civil War, shows former slaves being led from the cotton fields. Although they now worked for wages, they were probably organized into a gang not far removed from the earlier slave gangs. Their plug-hatted crew leader is dressed much as his slave-driving predecessor would have been.

The Black Codes. The efforts of former slaves to control their own lives ran counter to deeply entrenched white attitudes. Emancipation had not destroyed the racist assumptions and fears that the planters had fostered in order to maintain and defend slavery. Former slave owners and many poorer whites who looked to them for leadership attempted to maintain the South's caste system. Beginning in 1865, southern legislatures enacted laws—known as Black Codes—that were designed to keep African-Americans in a condition close to slavery.

The codes varied from state to state, but virtually all required the arrest of blacks for vagrancy if they were found without employment. In most cases they could not pay the fine, and the county court would then hire them out to an employer, who could hold them in slaverylike conditions. Several state codes established specific hours of labor, spelled out the duties expected of laborers, and declared that any laborer who did not meet those standards was a vagrant. The codes usually restricted black employment opportunities outside agriculture by requiring licenses for those who wished to pursue skilled work or even "irregular job work."

The state legislatures went even further, sanctioning the efforts of local governments to circumscribe the lives of blacks. Localities set curfews, required black agricultural workers to obtain passes from their employers, insisted that blacks who wanted to live in town obtain white sponsors, and, in an effort to prevent political gatherings, sharply regulated meetings of blacks, including those held in churches. Fines and forced labor were the penalties for violators.

Congressional Initiatives

Reports of southern repression aroused moderate Republicans in Congress, who decided to provide some guarantees of the civil rights of freedmen. The moderates first drafted a bill to extend the life of the Freedmen's Bureau and enlarge its powers, including the authority to establish courts to protect the freedmen's rights.

The news from the South had not, however, convinced Republicans that they should confiscate land and give it to the freedmen. A large majority of Republicans voted down an amendment to the Freedmen's Bureau bill proposed by Thaddeus Stevens that would have made "forfeited estates of the enemy" available to freedmen. Still, Republicans were now willing to go further in creating opportunities for land ownership. Thus the Freedmen's Bureau bill countermanded Johnson's order to Howard to evict the freedmen from the confiscated lands on the Sea Islands. Also, two days after the bill's passage, the House passed another bill, sponsored by George Julian, that became the Southern Homestead

Act of 1866. It designated about 45 million acres of public land in Alabama, Arkansas, Florida, Louisiana, and Mississippi for 80-acre grants to settlers who cultivated the land for five years. Congress prohibited anyone who had supported the Confederacy from filing a claim until 1867. Although Republicans were unwilling to violate planters' property rights, they offered freedmen the same chance to acquire land that northerners had enjoyed since the passage of the Homestead Act of 1862.

Republicans approved the Freedmen's Bureau bill almost unanimously, but in February 1866 Johnson vetoed it. The bill was unconstitutional, he argued, because the Constitution did not authorize a "system for the support of indigent persons" and because the states most directly affected by its provisions were not yet represented in Congress. His veto, implying that *any* Reconstruction legislation passed without southern representation was unconstitutional, enraged moderate Republicans. They tried to override the veto but failed, just barely, to hold the votes of enough conservative Republicans to collect the necessary two-thirds majority.

Democrats applauded Johnson's firmness. To celebrate the veto and Washington's birthday, a group of Democrats went to the White House to serenade him. The president emerged to deliver an impromptu, impassioned speech that suggested to many listeners that he was drunk. Accusing the radical Republicans of being traitors, he likened Stevens and Sumner to Confederate leaders because they all were "opposed to the fundamental principles of this Government." He mentioned himself two hundred times in the speech and suggested that the radicals were plotting to assassinate him.

The First Civil Rights Bill. Johnson's veto and his Washington's birthday speech pushed the moderate Republicans close to a complete break with him. But they still expected his cooperation on their second major piece of legislation, a civil rights bill. Passed in March 1866, it defined the citizenship rights of freedmen—for example, the rights to own and rent property, make contracts, and have access to the courts. And it authorized federal authorities to bring suit against anyone who violated those rights and guaranteed that appeals in such cases could be heard in federal courts. The moderate Republicans were prepared to expand federal protection of civil rights, though they were still not ready to guarantee black suffrage.

Against the advice of his cabinet, Johnson vetoed the civil rights bill. He restated his constitutional point about absent southern representation and added a new objection, with the votes of Democratic wards in the large cities in mind. The bill, he argued, discriminated against whites by providing immediate citizenship for newly freed slaves. Under federal law, he pointed out, immigrants had to wait five years.

Johnson's veto was the last straw for almost all moderate Republicans. They now agreed with the radicals that Congress must take charge of Reconstruction. In April moderates engineered an override of Johnson's veto, and in July—after watering down the Freedmen's Bureau bill by requiring freedmen to buy the confiscated land on the Sea Islands—they won the votes of enough conservative Republicans to pass the Freedmen's Bureau bill over a second veto.

The Fourteenth Amendment. The central part of the independent plan that moderates and radicals now undertook was to provide freedmen with constitutional as well as legislative protection. In April the Joint Committee on Reconstruction drafted and submitted to Congress a proposal for a fourteenth amendment to the Constitution. It did not provide what the radicals wanted—a guarantee of black suffrage—but it went beyond the Civil Rights Act of 1866.

Section 1 declared that "all persons born or naturalized in the United States" were citizens. No state could abridge "the privileges or immunities of citizens of the United States," deprive "any person of life, liberty, or property, without due process of law," or deny anyone "the equal protection of the laws." The drafters intended these phrases to be vague but hoped that their force would increase over time, especially since Section 5 gave Congress the power to enforce the amendment. Section 2 penalized any state that denied suffrage to any adult male citizen. A state's representation in the House of Representatives would be reduced by the percentage of adult male citizens who were denied the vote.

Rising violence against African-Americans throughout the South clinched the support of moderates for the amendment. Most dramatic were three days of race rioting in Memphis in May. Forty-six blacks and two whites were left dead, and hundreds of black houses, churches, and schools were looted and burned. In June 1866 Congress forwarded the Fourteenth Amendment to the states for ratification.

President Johnson attacked the Fourteenth Amendment. Even its moderate provisions went too far in protecting African-Americans for his taste, and he wanted to create an issue for the 1866 elections. At his urging, ten ex-Confederate states, joined by Delaware and Kentucky, turned it down, denying the amendment the necessary approval of three-fourths of the states. Among the former states of the Confederacy, only Tennessee approved the amendment, and it was formally readmitted to the Union in July 1866.

The Congressional Elections of 1866. Johnson planned to attack the Fourteenth Amendment and advance his National Union movement during the Congressional elections of 1866. In July a National Union Convention met to unite his supporters from around the nation. But

Resistance in the South

The engraving, subtitled "Verdict, 'Hang the D---Yankee and Nigger,'" appeared in *Harper's Weekly* in March 1867. It may have led readers to recall the killing of the Republicans who attended the black suffrage convention in New Orleans the previous summer. There are no reliable estimates of the number of Republicans, white and black, killed by ex-Confederates during Reconstruction.

the Republican and Democratic politicians in attendance were unwilling to share power across party lines, and the convention did not attempt to create a new national party. Another problem for Johnson's movement was a major race riot in the South just two weeks before the convention assembled. A white mob in New Orleans attacked the delegates to a black suffrage convention and, aided by the local police, killed forty people, including thirty-seven blacks. Popular support in the North for radical Reconstruction seemed to grow instantly.

In August and September Johnson tried to win back support in a disastrous "swing around the circle"—a railroad tour from Washington to Chicago and St. Louis and back. It was unprecedented for a president to campaign personally, and Johnson made matters worse by engaging in shouting matches with hecklers and insulting members of the hostile crowds. His message was consistent: Congress had acted illegally by approving the Fourteenth Amendment without the participation of all the southern states, southerners were now loyal to the Union, and the real traitors were the radical Republicans who were delaying restoration of the Union.

Moderate and radical Republicans responded by escalating their attacks on Democrats. They charged that ex-Confederates wanted to resume the Civil War and, in a practice that became known as "waving the bloody shirt," charged that the Democratic party had caused the Civil War and then sided with the traitors. Indiana's Republican governor, Oliver Morton, described the Democratic party as "a common sewer and loathsome receptacle, into which is emptied every element of treason North and South, every element of inhumanity and barbarism which has dishonored the age."

The 1866 Congressional elections brought a humiliating defeat for the president, who still had two years left to serve. The Republicans won a three-to-one majority in Congress (margins of 42 to 11 in the Senate and 143 to 49 in the House) and gained control of the governorship and legislature in every northern state, as well as West Virginia, Missouri, and Tennessee. The moderate Republicans interpreted the election results as a clear call for radical Reconstruction rather than mere restoration of the South. The most important policy shift was the moderates' acceptance of the radicals' proposition that the federal government must guarantee the vote for black men, at least in the South.

Radical Reconstruction

In the months following the 1866 elections, moderates and radicals in Congress joined together to take control of Reconstruction. They agreed on a more radical program than even the one proposed in the Wade-Davis bill. Congressional Reconstruction began by treating the South as conquered territory. It proceeded to protect the civil rights of former slaves through the Fourteenth Amendment to the Constitution, protect their suffrage through the Fifteenth Amendment, and establish state governments in the South in which former slaves played important roles.

The Congressional Program

In March Congress passed the Reconstruction Act of 1867, designed to implement the radical plan. It organized the South as a conquered land, dividing it (with the exception of Tennessee) into five military districts, each under the command of a Union general. Each commander was ordered to register all adult black men in his district but was given considerable discretion in registering former Confederates. After the registration, the commander was to supervise the election of a convention to write a state constitution and make certain that the constitution included guarantees of black suffrage. Congress would readmit the state to the Union if its voters ratified the new constitution, if that document proved acceptable to Congress, if the new state legislature approved the Fourteenth Amendment, and if enough states had already ratified the Fourteenth Amendment to make it part of the Constitution. Johnson vetoed the act, but Congress overrode the veto. In 1868 six states—North Carolina, South Carolina, Florida, Alabama, Louisiana, and Arkansas—met the requirements and were readmitted to the Union. (See Table 16.1 for a summary of the Reconstruction laws and constitutional amendments.)

Such measures were radical, but a few radical Republicans argued that even more dramatic steps were needed to guarantee racial equality. They pressed for the distribution of land to former slaves, federal support for black schools, and disfranchisement of ex-Confederates. Congressman George Julian warned that "the power of the great landed aristocracy in these regions, if unrestrained by power from without, would inevitably assert itself." But even the most extreme radicals accepted the new Reconstruction policies as all they could get in 1867.

The Tenure of Office Act. Republicans also acted to check the power of President Johnson to undermine their Reconstruction plan. At the same time the Reconstruction Act of 1867 became law, Congress passed the Tenure of Office Act, which required Senate consent for the removal of any official whose appointment had required Senate confirmation. Congress chiefly wanted to protect Secretary of War Edwin M. Stanton, a Lincoln appointee and the only member of Johnson's cabinet who favored radical Reconstruction. In his position Stanton could do much to prevent Johnson from frustrating the goals of Reconstruction. Congress also required the president to issue all orders to the army through its commanding general, Ulysses S. Grant, who was also a supporter of radical Reconstruction. In effect, Congress was attempting to reconstruct the presidency as well as the South.

Johnson appeared to cooperate with Congress at first, appointing generals recommended by Stanton and Grant to command the five military districts in the South. But he was just biding his time. In August 1867, after Congress had adjourned, he "suspended" Stanton until Congress reconvened and replaced him with Grant on a temporary basis, believing that Grant would act like a good soldier and follow orders. Next Johnson replaced four Republican generals who commanded southern districts, including Philip H. Sheridan, Grant's favorite cavalry general.

TABLE 16.1

Primary Reconstruction Laws and Constitutional Amendments

Law (Date of Congressional Passage)	Key Provisions
Thirteenth Amendment (January 1865*)	Prohibited slavery
Civil Rights Act of 1866 (April 1866)	Defined citizenship rights of freedmen Authorized federal authorities to bring suit against those who violated those rights
Fourteenth Amendment (June 1866†)	Established national citizenship for persons born or naturalized in the United States Reduced state representation in House of Representatives by the percentage of adult male citizens denied the vote
Reconstruction Act of 1867 (March 1867‡)	Divided the South into five military districts, each under the command of a Union general Established requirements for readmission of ex-Confederate states to the Union
Tenure of Office Act (March 1867)	Required Senate consent for removal of any federal official whose appointment had required Senate confirmation
Fifteenth Amendment (February 1869)	Forbade states to deny citizens the right to vote on the grounds of race, color, or "previous condition of servitude"
Ku Klux Klan Act (April 1871)	Authorized president to use federal prosecutions and military force to suppress conspiracies to deprive citizens of the right to vote and enjoy the equal protection of the law

*Ratified by three-fourths of all states in December 1868.
†Ratified by three-fourths of all states in July 1868.
‡Ratified by three-fourths of all states in March 1870.

Johnson, however, had misjudged Grant, who wrote a letter protesting the president's thwarting of Congress and then deliberately leaked it to the press. When the Senate reconvened in the fall, it intensified the political drama by overruling Stanton's suspension. Grant increased the pressure on Johnson by resigning so that Stanton could resume his office. Johnson overreacted, publicly protesting Grant's resignation. Grant responded by becoming an open enemy of the president.

The Impeachment of Johnson. Johnson decided to challenge the constitutionality of the Tenure of Office Act. In February 1868 he formally dismissed Stanton. This time Stanton barricaded the door of his office and refused to admit the replacement Johnson had appointed. Three days later, on February 24, the House of Representatives lashed out at Johnson by using the power granted by the Constitution to impeach—to charge federal officials with "Treason, Bribery, or other high Crimes and Misdemeanors." The House overwhelmingly (128 to 47) brought eleven counts of criminal misconduct, nine of which dealt with violations of the Tenure of Office Act, against the president.

The trial in the Senate, which the Constitution empowers to act as a court in impeachment cases, lasted eleven weeks and was presided over by Chief Justice Salmon P. Chase. On May 16 thirty-five senators voted for conviction, one vote short of the two-thirds majority required. Seven moderate Republicans had broken ranks, voting for acquittal along with twelve Democrats. The reluctant moderates were overwhelmed by the drastic nature of impeachment and conviction; Congress had removed federal judges from office, but never before had it seriously considered removing a president. Whereas these moderates agreed that Johnson had broken the law, they felt that the real issue was a disagreement between Congress and the president over a matter of policy. They feared that a conviction based on a policy dispute would establish a dangerous precedent and undermine the presidency. The Civil War had demonstrated to them the need for a strong federal government administered by a powerful executive. These moderates doubted that the nation could preserve internal unity, advance the Republican economic program, and defend itself against foreign enemies without a strong presidency.

The radical Republicans had failed to convict Johnson, but they had defeated him politically. For the remainder of his term Johnson was forced to allow Reconstruction to proceed under Congressional direction.

The Elections of 1868. The impeachment controversy made Grant, already the North's most popular war hero, a hero of Reconstruction as well, and he easily won the Republican presidential nomination. In the fall campaign he supported radical Reconstruction and "waved the bloody shirt," but he also urged reconciliation between the sections. His Democratic opponent was Horatio Seymour, a former governor of New York and a Peace Democrat who almost declined the nomination, certain that Grant would win. In the face of rising violence in the South, Seymour and the Democrats received little support for their claim that the government should let southern state governments reorganize on their own. Grant won about the same share of the northern vote (55 percent) that Lincoln had in 1864, collected a majority of the national popular vote, and received 214 of 294 electoral votes, including those of six of the eight reconstructed states. The Republicans also retained two-thirds majorities in both houses of Congress. The Republicans were convinced they had a strong popular mandate for their program of radical Reconstruction.

The Fifteenth Amendment. The Republicans quickly produced the last major piece of Reconstruction legislation—the Fifteenth Amendment. Intended to guarantee black male suffrage, the amendment forbade states to deny their citizens the right to vote on the grounds of race, color, or "previous condition of servitude."

Some radical Republicans would have preferred more aggressive protection of black citizenship such as prohibiting state governments from using property ownership or literacy tests to disqualify blacks as voters. But Republican moderates did not want to ban tactics that northern and western states might want to employ to deny immigrants the vote. Massachusetts and Connecticut used literacy as a requirement for voting, as did California, which sought to deny the vote to Chinese immigrants. Even though it failed to prohibit such tactics, the Fifteenth Amendment was much more effective than the Fourteenth in promoting African-American suffrage. The amendment was passed in February 1869, and Congress required the unreconstructed states of Virginia, Mississippi, Texas, and Georgia to ratify it before they were readmitted to the Union.

The Issue of Suffrage for Women

Radical Reconstruction could have changed the legal status of women. Instead, by referring to adult "male citizens," the Fourteenth Amendment wrote the term "male" into the Constitution for the first time and, in effect, sanctioned the denial of suffrage for women. Under the Fourteenth Amendment, suffrage limitations

based on gender—alone among all the possible restrictions on suffrage—would not reduce a state's representation in Congress.

Former abolitionists such as Elizabeth Cady Stanton and Susan B. Anthony were deeply disappointed. They had organized a massive petition drive that had collected almost 400,000 signatures in support of the Thirteenth Amendment; they believed that their male collaborators would reciprocate by supporting universal suffrage. In fact, many did, but most assumed that the public was not ready for the idea. As Wendell Phillips told women leaders, "One question at a time. This hour belongs to the Negro."

The leaders of the women's movement did not oppose ratification of the Fourteenth Amendment. They accepted defeat at the federal level and focused on the reform of state constitutions. Through a new organization, the American Equal Rights Association—which they formed in 1866 at the first women's rights convention since the Civil War—they launched a campaign to win *universal* suffrage at the state level.

The Fifteenth Amendment wounded those who sought the vote for women even more deeply; it made no reference to gender and thus permitted states to deny

A Woman Suffrage Quilt Made around 1875
Homemade quilts provided funds and a means of persuasion for the temperance and antislavery movements. But woman suffrage quilts, such as this detail from "The Suffragette Quilt" (circa 1860–1880), picturing a women's rights lecturer, were rare. The leaders of the woman suffrage movement usually regarded quilts and needlework as representing the domestic subjugation of women.

suffrage to women. In response, Stanton and Anthony concluded that feminists should develop a program independent of any political party. They broke with Republican abolitionists and refused to support the Fifteenth Amendment unless it was accompanied by a new amendment enfranchising women. Stanton argued that ratification of the Fifteenth Amendment alone would create an "aristocracy of sex." She declared, "All manhood will vote not because of intelligence, patriotism, property or white skin, but because it is male, not female." In promoting a new amendment she made a special appeal to women of the business class:

> American women of wealth, education, virtue and refinement, if you do not wish the lower orders of Chinese, Africans, Germans and Irish, with the low ideas of womanhood to make laws for you and your daughters . . . to dictate not only the civil, but moral codes by which you shall be governed, awake to the danger of your present position and demand that woman, too, shall be represented in the government!

Other advocates of woman suffrage, including Lucy Stone and Frederick Douglass, saw the politics of suffrage differently. The Fifteenth Amendment had opened up a schism in the ranks of the women's movement. In 1868 Stone and Douglass broke with the American Equal Rights Association of Stanton and Anthony and formed a new group, the New England Woman Suffrage Association. Their goal was to maintain an alliance with Republicans and support the Fifteenth Amendment. They believed that this was the best way to enlist Republican support for women's suffrage after Reconstruction issues had been settled.

The differences between the two groups increased in the postwar years. In 1869 the American Equal Rights Association renamed itself the National Woman Suffrage Association and elected Stanton as its first president. It concentrated on mobilizing local suffrage societies in communities around the country. Meanwhile, the New England Woman Suffrage Association reorganized itself as the American Woman Suffrage Association. Its members elected Henry Ward Beecher, a prominent Brooklyn minister, as its president and cultivated strong ties with Republicans and men who had been abolitionists.

For twenty-one years the two national organizations competed for the leadership of the women's movement. The "American" association tended to focus on suffrage, whereas the "National" association developed a more comprehensive reform posture. While the split weakened the movement in the short run, the formation of the "National" association meant that a major part of the women's movement had broken away from abolitionism and Republicanism and was free to develop independent political strategies.

The South during Radical Reconstruction

Between 1868 and 1871 all the southern states met the Congressional stipulations and rejoined the Union. The Reconstruction governments under Republican control remained in power for periods ranging from a few months in Virginia to nine years in South Carolina, Louisiana, and Florida. African-Americans were at the center of forming and maintaining these Republican governments. In Alabama, Florida, South Carolina, Mississippi, and Louisiana they constituted an outright majority of registered voters. They provided the votes for Republican victories there and in Georgia, Virginia, and North Carolina as well, where they accounted for nearly half the registered voters. But the Republican governments were more than African-American regimes; they also drew support from whites who had not owned slaves and from white northerners who had moved south after the war (see Map 16.1).

Democratic ex-Confederates satirized and stereotyped the Republicans who dominated the reconstructed state governments. They mocked and scorned black

The First Vote
This lithograph appeared in *Harper's Weekly* in November 1867. The voters represent elements of African-American political leadership: an artisan with tools, a well-dressed member of the middle class, and a Union soldier.

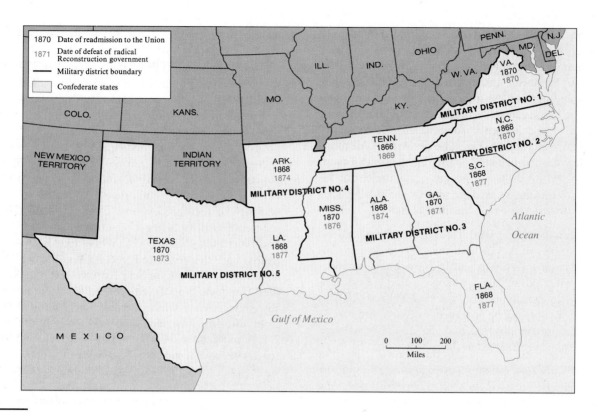

MAP 16.1

Reconstruction
The federal government organized the Confederate states into five military districts during radical Reconstruction. For each state the first date indicates when that state was readmitted to the Union; the second date shows when radical Republicans lost control of the state government. All the ex-Confederate states rejoined the Union from 1868 to 1870, but the periods of radical rule varied widely. Radicals lasted only a few months in Virginia; they held on until the end of Reconstruction in Louisiana, Florida, and South Carolina.

Republicans as ignorant field hands who could only play at politics, and they referred to whites who became Republicans as *scalawags*—an ancient Scots-Irish term for underfed, runty, worthless animals. White settlers who had come from the North were denounced as *carpetbaggers*—transient exploiters who carried all their property in cheap suitcases called carpetbags. Carpetbaggers held more than half the Republican governorships in the South and almost half of the southern seats in Congress.

Actually, few southern Republicans conformed to these stereotypes. Some carpetbaggers had come south to seek personal profit, but they also brought capital and skills to invest in the region's future. Most were former officers of the Union army who had fallen in love with the South—its climate, people, and economic opportunities. Many carpetbaggers were professionals and college graduates. The scalawags were even more diverse. Some were wealthy ex-Whigs and even former slave owners. Some of these groups saw Republicanism as the best way to attract northern capital to southern railroads, mines, and factories. Immigrant workers and

farmers were often found among the Republicans. The largest such group were the Germans in southwest Texas. They sent to Congress Edward Degener, an immigrant and a San Antonio grocer whom Confederate authorities had imprisoned and whose sons had been executed for treason. But most numerous among the scalawags were yeomen farmers from the backcountry districts who wanted to rid the South of its slaveholding aristocracy. Scalawags had generally fought against, or at least refused to support, the Confederacy; they believed that slavery had victimized whites as well as blacks. "Now is the time," a Georgia scalawag wrote, "for every man to come out and speak his principles publickly and vote for liberty as we have been in bondage long enough."

African-American Political Leadership. The Democrats' stereotypes of black political leaders were just as false. Until 1867 most African-American leaders in the South, attracted to the movement for black suffrage, came from the elite that had been free before the Civil War. When Congress began to organize Republican governments in 1867, this diverse group of ministers, artisans, shopkeepers, and former soldiers reached out to the freedmen. African-American speakers, some financed by the Republican Congressional Committee, fanned out into the old plantation districts and drew ex-slaves into political leadership. Still, few of the new leaders were field hands; most had been preachers or artisans. The literacy of one ex-slave, Thomas Allen, who was a Baptist minister and shoemaker, helped him win election to the Georgia legislature. "In my county," he recalled, "the colored people came to me for instructions, and I gave them the best instructions I could. I took the *New York Tribune* and other papers, and in that way I found out a great deal, and I told them whatever I thought was right."

Many of the African-American leaders who emerged in 1867 had been born in the North or had spent many years there. They moved south when Congressional Reconstruction began to offer the prospect of meaningful freedom. Like white migrants, many were veterans of the Union army. Some had fought in the antislavery crusade, some were employed by the Freedmen's Bureau or northern missionary societies, and a few were from free families and had gone north for an education. Others had escaped from slavery and were returning home. One of these was Blanche K. Bruce, who became one of two black U.S. senators from Mississippi. He had received tutoring on the Virginia plantation of his white father. During the war Bruce escaped to Kansas from Missouri, where his father had moved, and then returned to Missouri, establishing a school for African-Americans in Hannibal. He arrived in Mississippi in 1869 and entered politics; in 1874 he became the second African-American elected to the Senate and the first elected to a full term until 1966.

Although the number of African-Americans who held office during Reconstruction never reflected the black share of the electorate, they held positions of importance throughout most of the South, and their significance increased in every state under Republican rule. Sixteen African-Americans served in the U.S. House of Representatives in the Reconstruction Era. In 1870 Mississippi sent Hiram Revels, a minister born in North Carolina, to the Senate as its first African-American member. In 1868 African-Americans won a majority in one house of the South Carolina legislature; subsequently they won half the state's eight executive offices, elected three members of Congress, and won a seat on the state supreme court. Over the entire course of Reconstruction twenty African-Americans served as governor, lieutenant governor, secretary of state, treasurer, or superintendent of education, and more than six hundred served as state legislators. Almost all the African-Americans who became state executives had been freemen before the Civil War, whereas most of the legislators had been slaves. Because these African-Americans

represented districts that large planters had dominated before the Civil War, they embodied the potential of Reconstruction for revolutionizing class relationships in the South.

The Radical Program. Southern Republicans believed that the South needed to be fundamentally reconstructed. They wanted to end its dependence on cotton agriculture and unskilled labor and create an economy based on manufacturing, capital investment, and skilled labor. Southern Republicans fell far short of making this vision a reality, but they accomplished much more of it than their critics gave them credit for.

Southern Republicans made their societies more democratic. They repealed Black Codes and rejected new proposals for enforcing labor discipline. They modernized state constitutions, extended the right to vote, and made more offices elective. They established hospitals, penitentiaries, and asylums for orphans and the insane. South Carolina purchased medical care for poor people, while Alabama provided them with free legal counsel. Republican governments built roads in areas where roads had never existed. They supervised the rebuilding of the region's railroad network and subsidized investment in manufacturing and transportation. They undertook major public works programs. And they did all this without federal financing. To pay for their ambi-

Hiram R. Revels

In 1870 Hiram R. Revels (1822–1901) was elected to the U.S. Senate from Mississippi to fill Jefferson Davis's former seat. Revels was a free black from North Carolina who had migrated to the North and attended Knox College in Illinois. He recruited blacks for the Union army and as an ordained Methodist minister served as chaplain of a black regiment in Mississippi, where he settled after the war.

tious programs they introduced the taxes that northern states had relied on since the Jacksonian period. These were general property taxes that taxed not only real estate but the trappings of wealth—personal property such as furnishings, machinery, tools, and even cash. The goal was to force planters to pay their fair share of taxes and to force uncultivated land onto the market. In many plantation counties, especially in South Carolina, Louisiana, and Mississippi, former slaves served as tax assessors and collectors, administering the taxation of their onetime owners.

The most important accomplishments of the southern Republicans came in education. Republican state governments viewed schooling as the foundation for a democratic order in the South. Led by both black and white superintendents of education, many of whom had served in the Freedmen's Bureau, the Reconstruction governments built public schools that served more people, black and white, than had ever been reached by free education in the South. African-Americans of all ages rushed to attend the newly established schools, even when they had to pay tuition. An elderly man in Mississippi explained his desire to go to school: "Ole missus used to read the good book [the Bible] to us . . . on Sunday evenin's, but she mostly read dem places where it says, 'Servants obey your masters.' . . . Now we is free, there's heaps of tings in that old book we is just suffering to learn." By 1875 about half of all the children in Florida, Mississippi, and South Carolina were enrolled in school.

Virtually all the new schools were segregated by race; only Louisiana attempted to establish an integrated system. But most African-Americans seemed to agree that segregation was an issue for a later day; most shared Frederick Douglass's judgment that what was

most important was the fact that separate schools were "infinitely superior" to no schools at all.

Social Institutions in Freedom.   The building of schools was part of a larger effort by African-Americans to fortify the institutions that had sustained their spirit during the days of slavery. Most important, they strengthened family life as the cornerstone of new communities. Families moved away from the slave quarters, usually building homes scattered around or near their old plantations and farms. Sometimes they established entirely new all-black villages. Husbands, wives, and children who had been separated by the slave trade often reunited, sometimes after journeys of hundreds of miles. Couples stepped forward to record marriages that had not been recognized under slavery. As slavery crumbled, mothers rescued their children from the control of planters and overseers. Many women refused to work in the fields. Instead, they insisted on tending gardens, managing households, and bringing education and religion to their children. Wives asserted their independence, opening individual bank accounts, refusing responsibility for their husbands' debts at country stores, and bringing complaints of abuse and lack of child support to the Freedmen's Bureau.

Christianity had played a central role in nineteenth-century slave society, and freed slaves buttressed their new communities by founding their own churches. They rejected participation in biracial congregations, which usually accorded blacks only second-class status, requiring them to worship in segregated balcony pews and denying them rights in church ownership or governance. Instead, they purchased land and built their own churches. These churches joined together to form African-American versions of the Southern Methodist

A Freedmen's School
An 1866 sketch from *Harper's Weekly* of a Vicksburg, Mississippi, school run by the Freedmen's Bureau illustrates the desire for education by ex-slaves of all ages. Because most southern blacks were farmers, schools often offered night classes that left students free for field work during the day.

and Southern Baptist denominations. The largest new denominations were the National Baptist Convention and the Colored Methodist Episcopal Church. The vigorous new churches served not only as places of worship but as schools, social centers, and political meeting halls. The ministers were community leaders and often held political office during Reconstruction. Charles H. Pearce, a Methodist minister in Florida, declared, "A man in this State cannot do his whole duty as a minister except he looks out for the political interests of his people." The religious message of black ministers, who called for a recognition of the brotherhood of man and a special destiny like that of the "Children of Israel," provided a powerful religious bulwark for the Republican politics of their congregations.

The Planters' Counterrevolution

Even if radical Reconstruction had been adopted right at the end of the Civil War, it would have sparked southern resistance to federal power. But coming after Johnson's lenient policy of restoration, which had enabled ex-Confederates to regain control of the South, the reaction was especially intense. Former slave owners were the most bitter opponents of the Republican program, especially the effort to expand political and economic opportunities for African-Americans, because it threatened their vested interest in traditional agriculture and their power and status in southern society. Led by former slave owners, the ex-Confederates staged a massive counterrevolution—one designed to "redeem" the South by regaining control of its state governments.

The former slave owners united under the Democratic banner to oppose the Republicans. In the eight southern states where whites formed a majority of the population—all except Louisiana, Mississippi, and South Carolina—planters sought to return ex-Confederates to the rolls of registered voters. They appealed to racial solidarity and southern patriotism, and they attacked black suffrage as a threat to the social status of whites. Relying primarily on conventional, albeit unsavory, means of political competition, Democrats recovered power in Tennessee in 1869 and Virginia in 1870.

But the Democrats were prepared to go far beyond conventional techniques. Throughout the Deep South and almost everywhere that Republicans and Democrats were nearly equal in number, planters and their supporters engaged in terrorism against people and property. They organized secret societies to frighten blacks and Republican whites from voting or taking other political action.

The Ku Klux Klan. The most widespread of these groups, the Ku Klux Klan, was organized in Tennessee in 1865 and quickly spread throughout the South. The

Klan's first leader was Nathan Bedford Forrest, a former Confederate general. A skilled and ferocious leader, Forrest was notorious in the North for an incident at Fort Pillow, Tennessee, in 1864, when his troops killed African-American soldiers holding the fort after they had surrendered. Forrest based the initial organization of the Klan on Confederate army units and openly threatened to kill Republicans if they tried to suppress the Klan.

By 1870 the Klan was operating almost everywhere in the South as a military force serving the Democratic party. The Klan murdered and whipped Republican politicians, burned black schools and churches, and attacked party gatherings. In October 1870 a group of Klansmen assaulted a Republican rally in Eutaw, Alabama, killing four African-Americans and wounding fifty-four. For three weeks in 1873 Klansmen laid siege to the small town of Colfax, Louisiana, which was defended by black veterans of the Union army who were holding the county seat after a contested election. On Easter Sunday, armed with a small cannon, the whites overpowered the defenders and slaughtered fifty blacks and two whites after they had surrendered under a white flag. Such terrorist tactics enabled the Democrats to seize power in Georgia and North Carolina in 1870 and make substantial gains elsewhere. An African-

Klan Portrait, 1868
Two armed Klansmen from Alabama pose proudly in their disguises. Northern audiences saw a lithograph based on this photograph in *Harper's Weekly* in December 1868.

Harriet Hernandes

The Intimidation of Black Voters

The following testimony was given in 1871 by Harriet Hernandes, a black resident of Spartanburg, South Carolina, to the Joint Congressional Select Committee investigating conditions in the South. The terrorizing of black women through rape and other forms of physical violence was among the means of oppression used by the Ku Klux Klan.

Question: How old are you?

Answer: Going on thirty-four years. . . .

Q: Are you married or single?

A: Married.

Q: Did the Ku-Klux come to your house at any time?

A: Yes, sir; twice. . . .

Q: Go on to the second time. . . .

A: They came in; I was lying in bed. Says he, "Come out here, sir; come out here, sir!" They took me out of bed; they would not let me get out, but they took me up in their arms and toted me out—me and my daughter Lucy. He struck me on the forehead with a pistol, and here is the scar above my eye now. Says he, "Damn you, fall." I fell. Says he, "Damn you, get up." I got

up. Says he, "Damn you, get over this fence!" and he kicked me over when I went to get over; and then he went on to a brush pile, and they laid us right down there, both together. They laid us down twenty yards apart, I reckon. They had dragged and beat us along. They struck me right on top of my head, and I thought they had killed me; and I said, "Lord o' mercy, don't, don't kill my child!" He gave me a lick on the head, and it liked to have killed me; I saw stars. He threw my arm over my head so I could not do anything with it for three weeks, and there are great knots on my wrist now.

Q: What did they say this was for?

A: They said, "You can tell your husband that when we see him we are going to kill him. . . ."

Q: Did they say why they wanted to kill him?

A: They said, "He voted the radical ticket [slate of candidates], didn't he?" I said, "Yes," that very way. . . .

Q: When did [your husband] get back home after this whipping? He was not at home, was he?

A: He was lying out; he couldn't stay

at home, bless your soul! . . .

Q: Has he been afraid for any length of time?

A: He has been afraid ever since last October. He has been lying out. He has not laid in the house ten nights since October.

Q: Is that the situation of the colored people down there to any extent?

A: That is the way they all have to do—men and women both.

Q: What are they afraid of?

A: Of being killed or whipped to death.

Q: What has made them afraid?

A: Because men that voted radical tickets they took the spite out on the women when they could get at them.

Q: How many colored people have been whipped in that neighborhood?

A: It is all of them, mighty near.

Source: Report of the Joint Select Committee to Inquire into the Condition of Affairs in the Late Insurrectionary States, House Reports, 42d Cong., 2d sess. (Washington, D.C.: U.S. Government Printing Office, 1972), Vol. 5, South Carolina, December 19, 1871.

American politician in North Carolina wrote, "Our former masters are fast taking the reins of government" (see American Voices, above).

Congress responded to the Klan-led counterrevolution by passing the Force Acts in 1870 and 1871, which included the Ku Klux Klan Act (1871). The acts authorized the president to use federal prosecutions, military force, and martial law to suppress conspiracies to deprive citizens of the right to vote, hold office, serve on juries, and enjoy equal protection of the law. For the first time, the government had made private criminal acts violations of federal law. Federal agents penetrated the Klan and gathered evidence that provided the basis for thousands of arrests, and federal grand juries in-

dicted more than 3,000 Klansmen. In South Carolina, where the Klan was most deeply entrenched, federal troops occupied nine counties, made hundreds of arrests, and drove as many as 2,000 Klansmen from the state. The U.S. attorney general brought several dozen notorious Klansmen to trial and sent most to jail. Elsewhere, victories were only temporary. Justice Department attorneys usually faced all-white juries, and the department lacked the resources to prosecute effectively. Only about 600 Klansmen were convicted under the Force Acts, and only a small fraction of them served significant prison terms.

The Grant administration's war against the Klan raised the spirits of southern Republicans, but if they were going to prevail, they required what one carpet-bagger described as *"steady, unswerving power from without."* In particular, to defeat the well-armed paramilitary forces of the ex-Confederates, they needed sustained federal military aid. However, after seeming to defeat the Klan, northern Republicans increasingly lost enthusiasm for fighting—let alone enlarging—what amounted to a guerrilla war. Republican leaders continued to "wave the bloody shirt," but with each election it had less appeal to voters. Northerners grew weary of the financial costs of Reconstruction and the continuing bloodshed it seemed to produce. Moreover, they became preoccupied with the severe economic depression that began in 1873. Conservative and even moderate Republican leaders began to regard southern Republican governments as too radical and to conclude that they had much in common with southern economic elites. Racism played a role as well; many moderate Republicans in the North began to conclude that Republican defeats in the South reflected the incompetence of black politicians. Because of diminishing federal help, Republican governments in the South eventually found themselves overwhelmed by ex-Confederate politicians during the day and by terrorists at night. Democrats overthrew Republican governments in Texas in 1873, in Alabama and Arkansas in 1874, and in Mississippi in 1875.

The defeat in Mississippi demonstrated the crucial role of federal aid. As elections neared in 1875, paramilitary groups such as the Rifle Clubs and Red Shirts operated openly. Often local Democratic clubs paraded armed, as if they were militia companies. They identified black leaders in assassination lists called "deadbooks," broke up Republican meetings, provoked rioting that left hundreds of African-Americans dead, and threatened voters, who still lacked the protection of the secret ballot. Mississippi's Republican governor, Adelbert Ames, a Congressional Medal of Honor winner from Maine, appealed to President Grant for federal troops, but Grant refused, fearing damage to Republicans in northern elections and lacking the heart for more bloodshed. Ames then contemplated organizing a state militia but ultimately decided against it, believing that only blacks would join. Rather than escalate the fighting and turn it into a racial war, he conceded victory to the terrorists.

By 1877 Republican governments, along with token U.S. military units, remained in only three states: Louisiana, South Carolina, and Florida. Southern Republicans had done their best to reconstruct southern society, but the ex-Confederates had exhausted northern Republicans. They even won some sympathy from the northern Republicans, who finally abandoned the southern members of their party (see American Lives, pages 504–505).

The Economic Fate of the Former Slaves

The greatest failure of radical Reconstruction lay in not redistributing land, along with the resources required to cultivate it, from planters to former slaves. The only major federal program enabling freedmen to obtain land, the Southern Homestead Act, turned out to provide little assistance. Although the land was free, very few freedmen had the capital to move their families and buy the necessary seeds, tools, and draft animals to get in their first crop. Fewer than 7,000 ex-slaves claimed land, and only about 1,000 eventually qualified for ownership, most of them in sparsely populated areas of Florida. Compounding the problem, state governments rarely had the resources to help freedmen buy and settle land. Alone among the Republican state governments, South Carolina purchased land from planters and resold it to former slaves on long-term credit. Between 1872 and 1876 the South Carolina land commission enabled more than 14,000 African-American families (accounting for about one-seventh of the state's black population) to purchase homesteads.

Without guaranteed economic independence, the content of freedom depended largely on thousands of conflicts between freedmen, acting individually and collectively, and the planter class. Here too the federal government failed to assist the freedmen in a significant way. The vast majority of army officers and federal marshals held the racist assumption that had been behind the Black Codes—that former slaves were suited only for agricultural labor. If these agents of the federal government had different ideas at first, they usually came to support the economic interests of the planters. A Louisiana freedman described the process as follows: "Whenever a new Provost Marshall comes he gives us justice for a fortnight or so; then he becomes acquainted with planters, takes dinners with them, receives presents; and then we no longer have any rights, or very little." In disputes between employers and laborers, federal marshals generally sided with the planters and sustained their authority. Army commanders complied with the requests of planters for help in forcing African-Americans to work. They expelled former plantation workers from towns and cities and punished them for disobedience, theft, vagrancy, and erratic labor.

Even agents of the Freedmen's Bureau often supported the planters. Many Bureau officials interpreted their mandate to promote a transition to free labor as meaning that they should teach former slaves to be industrious, reliable agricultural workers. They preached the gospel of work to African-Americans. To discourage labor violence, they warned that it was better "to suffer wrong than to do wrong." They urged former slaves to vindicate the cause of abolition by staying at home and working even harder than they had under slavery.

Nathan Bedford Forrest: A Violent Defender of Honor

There was much violence in the life of Nathan Bedford Forrest (1821–1877). Most of the violence was focused on the protection of slavery during the Civil War and on the defeat of radical Reconstruction afterward. More than any other white southerner, Forrest was responsible for defeating Reconstruction governments and efforts to extend democracy to African-Americans.

At the age of twenty-four Forrest demonstrated his readiness to use violence when he leapt to the defense of his family's honor. Armed with only a pistol and a bowie knife, he fought off four men who had a grudge against his uncle, a merchant in the hamlet of Hernando, Mississippi. The uncle died from a bullet meant for his nephew, but young Forrest had shown that he could meet violence with violence. He became a local hero and soon used his pistol again, facing down a well-armed planter who had just killed a friend of his. The local citizens rewarded Forrest's courage by making him town constable and county coroner, and a respectable young woman from Hernando agreed to marry him.

Forrest's father had been a yeoman farmer and blacksmith who followed the frontier from North Carolina to Tennessee, where Bedford, the oldest child of eleven, was born. His family moved to northern Mississippi in 1834, but three years later, when he was only sixteen, his father died, leaving Bedford the primary breadwinner. He had no more than six months of schooling but supported the family, working on its small farm and then joining an uncle's horse-trading business. At the age of twenty-one, when his mother remarried, he left home for Hernando.

Recognized and respected in Hernando, the hard-driving young Forrest was able to scratch his way up the social ladder in the booming cotton economy. He took over his uncle's store, ran a stagecoach service between Hernando and Memphis, opened a brickyard, again traded horses and cattle, and then turned to buying and selling slaves. By 1850 he owned three of his own. In 1851 Forrest's ambition took him and his family to nearby Memphis, Tennessee. In that Mississippi River town he became one of the largest interstate slave traders and entered the ranks of the planter class. He

Nathan Bedford Forrest
In his often violent career Forrest was a farmer, slave trader, planter, politician, cavalry general, Grand Wizard of the Ku Klux Klan, and railroad entrepreneur. This portrait was done by Nicola Marshall, circa 1866. (Collection of the Tennessee State Museum)

purchased large land holdings, including a Mississippi plantation of more than 3,000 acres worked by dozens of slaves. He even entered politics, winning election to the Memphis Board of Aldermen in 1857.

The Civil War created new opportunities for Forrest. His reputation for boldness and shrewdness, as well as his riding and shooting skills, won him an appointment from the governor of Tennessee as a lieutenant colonel. He organized a cavalry regiment and, after distinguishing himself at Shiloh, was promoted to brigadier general in July 1862. In the course of the war he became the premier cavalry officer of the Confederacy, perhaps the best on either side. The Confederate government failed to make the best use of Forrest and his troops, but he almost always carried out his missions with dramatic success, protecting Confederate armies in retreat, raiding Union lines of communications, and attacking Union posts, often deep behind enemy lines.

Forrest's intimate knowledge of the countryside and the people of the Mississippi, Tennessee, and Cumberland river valleys, superb organizational skills, powerful tactical sense of when to use bluff and deception, sobriety, and ability to inspire his troops served him well. He had a ferocious temper and used it to good advantage in combat, turning a zest for fighting into enraged fury whenever his honor or the honor of his troops seemed to be at stake. He counted thirty Union soldiers that he had killed personally—one more than the number of horses shot out from under him. And he was wounded by saber cut or gunfire several times, including once by a junior Confederate officer whom Forrest quickly stabbed to death.

Forrest's code of honor, readiness for violence, racism, and commitment to slavery, all honed and hardened by war, have suggested to many that Forrest played a role in the slaughter of black troops at Fort Pillow, Tennessee, on April 12, 1864. Forrest approached the assault on the fort with a combination of anger and contempt for the garrison there—largely white pro-Union Tennesseans and former slaves. The war in western Tennessee had taken a bitter turn in 1864, involving civilians more directly in combat, and Forrest was outraged at rumors that the garrison had been harassing local whites loyal to the Confederacy. Although Forrest's direct role in the slaughter remains uncertain, it is clear that his troops believed that they were acting as he wished, that they experienced the same fury he usually displayed in battle, and that he accepted the outcome with equanimity.

The war left Forrest exhausted but determined to recreate as much of his old life as possible. That meant adapting to the new economic system and, when necessary, to the reality of Union victory. In 1866, to restore his plantation labor force, he rented his Mississippi land to seven former Union officers and worked closely with the Freedmen's Bureau, writing some of the highest-wage contracts. He drew on some of his old slave-trading skills to bring in workers from as far away as Georgia. At the same time he moved into new enterprises: provisioning the reorganized plantations, selling fire and life insurance, and contracting for paving the streets of Memphis and for laying railroad track. In building the Memphis and Little Rock Railroad, Forrest used labor supplied by the Freedmen's Bureau. Meanwhile, he sought a pardon from President Johnson, which was granted in 1868.

But Forrest was determined to oppose a radical Reconstruction. As conflicts between ex-Confederates and coalitions of former Unionists and freedmen intensified, Forrest's ambition, racism, and loyalty to his comrades—a sense of honor defined by shared wartime experiences—led him to support the effort to restore the social world of 1860. In 1867 he joined secret organizations in Memphis and Nashville that became chapters of the Ku Klux Klan. He soon became the Klan's Grand Wizard and turned the organization into a major force throughout most of the South. Under cover of his insurance business Forrest corresponded with perhaps thousands of Confederate veterans and traveled to neighboring states to confer with other ex-generals.

In 1868 the Republican governor of Tennessee, "Parson" William G. Brownlow, threatened to organize a militia of eastern Tennessee Unionists to root out the Klan. Forrest told his former troops to prepare for civil war, warning a reporter from the Cincinnati *Commercial* that he could "raise 40,000 men in five days, ready for the field." Forrest's intimidation worked, as it had so often in the past. Brownlow resigned early in 1869 to take a seat in the U.S. Senate, and his replacement sought to appease the Democrats and the Klan. Victorious in Tennessee and hoping to reduce pressure from Washington on the Klan, Forrest ordered its members to destroy their regalia and moderate their excesses, such as whippings and jailbreaks. Forrest knew full well that he had no power to implement such an order.

Forrest might have continued a secret life within the Klan, but after his political victory he appeared to devote his full attention to his businesses. He tried to combine northern capital with new sources of cheap labor. Marketing bonds in New York, he established the Selma, Marion, and Memphis Railroad. He promoted Chinese immigration to the South and made extensive use of convict labor on his railroad and plantation crews. But he achieved only modest success in the depression of the 1870s and became embroiled in complicated, massive litigation. In 1877 he died of a debilitating intestinal illness that might have been related to his wartime wounds.

One Bureau official told some freedmen that their former master "is not able to do without you, and you will . . . find him as kind, honest, and liberal as other men" and that "you can be as free and as happy in your old home, for the present, as anywhere else in the world." The agents of the Freedmen's Bureau who did side with African-Americans were stymied by northern racism, lack of funds, understaffing, poor coordination within the Bureau, and uncooperative military authorities.

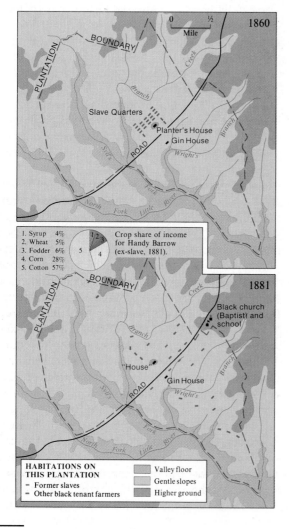

MAP 16.2

The Barrow Plantation

Comparing the 1860 map of this central Georgia plantation with the 1881 map reveals the changing patterns of black residence and farming. In 1860 the slave quarters were clustered near the planter's house, which sat on a small hilltop. The free sharecroppers of 1881 built cabins along the spurs or ridges of land between the streams, scattering their community over the plantation. A black church and school were built by this date. A typical sharecropper on the plantation earned most of his income from growing cotton.

Sharecropping. The Freedmen's Bureau did help change, however, the way planters controlled the labor of their former slaves. It encouraged, even compelled, planters and freedmen to agree on written contracts through a formal bargaining process. The labor contract system was a poor substitute for land ownership, but it assisted the freedmen in attaining something else they greatly desired: the elimination of gang labor.

As early as 1865 written contracts between freedmen and planters provided that the former slaves would work for wages. But the contracts also provided for less supervision, a slower pace of work, and more free time than had been typical under slavery as well as the elimination of drivers and overseers. By 1866 the process of bargaining between planters and freedmen had become more difficult, partly because a shrinking money supply had reduced the amount of cash available to pay wages. To resolve the growing number of conflicts over labor contracts, Freedmen's Bureau agents introduced a form of compensation that was common, though not typical, in northern agriculture: payment of agricultural workers in shares of the crop rather than in wages. This system was known as *sharecropping*. While it came to involve many poor whites in the South, it was far more important for blacks. For them, sharecropping became the dominant mode of agricultural labor (see Map 16.2).

At first freedmen were enthusiastic about sharecropping. It increased their control over working conditions and allowed them to improve their standard of living. Under typical sharecropping contracts, sharecroppers turned over half to two-thirds of their harvested crops to their landlord. The owner's share was not necessarily excessive, because the landlord commonly provided land, seed, fertilizer, tools, and assistance in marketing.

The sharecropping system joined laborers and the owners of land and capital in a common sharing of risks and returns. But it produced little upward mobility. By the end of Reconstruction only a fraction of sharecroppers, no more than one-quarter of the total, had managed to save enough to rent land with cash payments, as most landless whites did. Even though these so-called tenant farmers could take their crops directly to market, they remained impoverished.

Land Ownership. Virtually all African-American farmers struggled long and hard to buy the land they tilled, and some of the cash renters gradually succeeded. They were willing to pay exorbitant prices for land just for the sake of being independent. But the system was stacked against them. African-American renters had far less access to land ownership than did their white counterparts. Planters made agreements among themselves to drive up the price of land to blacks or even refuse to sell to them. Some planters used the Ku Klux Klan to intimi-

Sharecropping
This sharecropping family seems proud of its new cabin and crop of cotton, which it planted in every available bit of ground. But the presence of the white landlord in the background suggests the forces that led families like this one into debt peonage.

date blacks who tried to buy land. Despite the adversity, by 1910 black farmers owned nearly a third of the land they cultivated. But black farm owners usually occupied marginal land—in the coastal swamps of Georgia and South Carolina, for example—and the land usually cost far more than its productivity warranted.

Debt Peonage. The financial condition of all African-American farmers was extremely difficult. Sharecropping, cash renting of land, and land ownership enabled former slaves to raise their incomes but also increased their financial needs. They wanted more food and better clothing than they had received under slavery; they often needed more farm supplies than their landlords were willing to provide; and renters and owners had to purchase all their seed, fertilizer, and equipment. The purchase of major farm supplies almost always required borrowing, but southern banks were reluctant to lend money to black farmers, whom they saw as bad risks, and cash was generally in short supply.

The owners of country stores stepped in. Eager to lend money, they furnished everything black farmers needed and extended credit for the purchases. The country merchants took advantage of the weak bargaining power of the former slaves, especially the sharecroppers, by charging unusually high prices and interest rates. In effect, these storekeepers became rural loan sharks. Once sharecroppers accepted credit from country merchants, high interest rates made it difficult for them to settle their accounts. At best they broke even after paying their debts. Most sharecroppers fell deeper and deeper into debt.

Throughout the South, when Democrats regained

control of state governments, they passed laws that gave force to this economic system by providing merchants with the right to take liens on crops. Merchants could seize crops to settle sharecroppers' debts and seek criminal prosecution of sharecroppers who could not pay the full amount of the interest they owed. Indebted African-American farmers faced imprisonment and forced labor unless they toiled on the land according to the instructions of the merchant-creditor. Increasingly, merchants and landlords cooperated to maintain this lucrative system, and many landlords became merchants. The former slaves had become trapped in the vicious circle of *debt peonage*, which tied them to the land and robbed them of their earnings.

In sum, despite the odds against them, the freedmen won some modest economic gains. But the gains came only within the restrictions of the system of debt peonage that replaced slavery. Thus, most African-Americans and many whites remained mired in an agricultural poverty created by racism and economic forces.

The North during Reconstruction

Although the Republicans in Congress failed to break the hold of the planter elite on the South, they did reconstruct the economy of the North. They enacted nearly all of their nationalizing economic program—national banking, tariff protection, and subsidies for internal improvements—despite resistance from the Democrats. The Republican program promoted unprecedented economic growth and industrial development.

A Dynamic Economy

The Civil War disrupted the nation's economic life, yet by the 1870s Americans had become more productive than ever before. Northeastern industry led the way. Production of iron more than doubled between the end of the Civil War and 1870 and doubled again by 1880. Steel production grew even more rapidly, increasing fivefold between 1865 and 1870 and then nearly twenty times by 1880. The era began an *age of capital*—a period that lasted until World War I and was marked by great increases in investment in factories and railroads. It also began the era of big business, which was characterized by the rise of giant corporations.

The Republican Economic Program. During Reconstruction, Republicans expanded the ambitious economic program they had enacted during the war. The broad support middle-class northerners gave to the program indicated that they now largely shared business-class values.

The scope of the program was vast. Republicans strengthened government regulation of the banking system, winning praise from investors who appreciated a more predictable economic environment. Republican Congresses expanded subsidies to national rail systems and chartered new railroads, expanded the national postal system, and financed major river and harbor development throughout the North. They also funded the cavalry forces that fought the nation's wars against the Indians in the Great Plains (see Chapter 17). In fact, military spending accounted for 60 percent of the federal budget by 1880. Republicans also used the Homestead Act of 1862 to subsidize the settling of the Great Plains.

Revenues raised from the Civil War tax system paid for those programs. Postwar Congresses kept the high tariffs, which had proved lucrative and appealed to average Republicans because they seemed to provide protection against foreign workers. Congress also retained the "emergency" wartime taxes on alcohol and tobacco, which were popular among many Republicans because they taxed "sin."

The tariffs and "sin" taxes not only funded programs but also provided money to pay back Americans who had bought Union bonds during the war. Because the taxes increased the cost of everyday items, average Americans were paying a far higher share of their income for debt repayment than were the wealthy. Moreover, the repayment was going largely to the wealthy, who owned a disproportionate share of Civil War bonds. Republicans were intentionally redistributing wealth from the poor to the rich, who were more likely to save and invest, as a way of increasing the supply of capital and accelerating the rate of economic growth.

The most popular Republican economic program was the Civil War pension program, which the government extended and broadened virtually every year. It provided disabled veterans and the widows and children of Union veterans with generous benefits, which were particularly welcome during the severe depressions of the 1870s and 1890s. At the same time, the pensions solidified the Republican loyalty of the families of men who had served in the Union army.

An ideological shift also contributed to the Republicans' success in enacting their economic program. The Civil War had led many Americans to relax their traditional suspicion of concentrations of power in both business and government. This was particularly true of the men and women who had served in the Union army and the Sanitary Commission. The war had given them their first direct experience of living and working within modern bureaucracies—elaborate hierarchies that imposed a high degree of job specialization and rigorous discipline. Wartime service also had taken them, usually for the first time, far from home and placed them in intimate contact with people who came from distant places but served in the same cause. And the Union had won the war. This disciplined, collective, national—and successful—experience predisposed northerners to accept American business, the Republican party, and the federal government as the central agencies of national economic development.

Republican Foreign Policy

Some Republican leaders were alert to new possibilities for expansion abroad. The most important advocate of expansion was William H. Seward, Lincoln and Johnson's secretary of state. Believing in the importance of foreign commerce to the long-term health of the republic, Seward promoted the acquisition of colonies that could be used as trading bases in the Caribbean and the Pacific. But Seward was ahead of his time. During the Reconstruction Era most Americans wanted to concentrate on developing their own territory.

Seward inherited his most pressing foreign policy issues from the Civil War. In Mexico, Napoleon III's puppet government under Archduke Maximilian was still in power; the threat this European regime posed to American interests in the Southwest was especially great since it might draw die-hard Confederate soldiers to its support. "On to Mexico," Grant only half jokingly told an aide just a day after he accepted Lee's surrender at Appomattox. It was a good guess as to where the next war might take place. Within a year President Johnson and Seward sent General Philip Sheridan with 50,000 battle-hardened Union veterans to the Mexican border, while Seward negotiated the withdrawal of French troops. The threat of force worked. The French left in 1867, abandoning Maximilian to a Mexican firing squad.

The American government was also troubled by another Civil War issue: Great Britain's allowing the *Alabama* and other Confederate cruisers to sail from British shipyards to raid Union commerce. Seward claimed that Britain had violated international laws of neutrality and owed compensation for damages. Britain, fearing that Americans might build ships for British enemies in a future war, accepted Seward's legal analysis and agreed to submit the *Alabama* claims to arbitration. However, Charles Sumner, chairman of the Senate Foreign Relations Committee, insisted that the compensation cover "indirect" damages. Including lost shipping revenue and the costs of Britain's prolonging the war, his estimates reached more than $2 billion. Sumner was angry over British aid to the Confederacy during the war and wanted to acquire Canada as part of the financial deal with Britain. In 1866 Congress restricted Canadian trade and fishing privileges in an attempt to force Canadians to support annexation. However, with the stakes so high, the British refused to agree to a settlement during Johnson's presidency.

Meanwhile, American expansionist ambitions in the Caribbean and the Pacific met with only mixed success. Supporting the U.S. Navy's demands for a base in the Caribbean, Seward negotiated a treaty with Denmark to purchase the Virgin Islands, but the Senate rejected the $7.5 million price. The Senate also turned down his proposal to annex Santo Domingo (the present-day Dominican Republic), which had won independence from Spain in 1865. Seward did persuade Congress to annex the small Midway Islands west of Hawaii after his effort to acquire the Hawaiian Islands had failed. Most important, in 1867 Seward persuaded the Senate to ratify a treaty to buy Alaska from Russia and to appropriate the $7.2 million for the purchase. Critics referred to Alaska as "Johnson's Polar Bear Garden" and "Seward's Folly," but its acquisition promised to obstruct British ambitions in North America. Also, the price was reasonable when weighed against even the low estimates that Congress made of Alaska's fish, fur, lumber, and mineral resources.

When Ulysses S. Grant became president in 1869, he took up the cause of expansion in the Caribbean. He was influenced by American investors and adventurers in Santo Domingo, including Orville E. Babcock, his former military aide, who became his personal secretary in the White House. Grant proposed a treaty to annex

the country as a colony for freed slaves dissatisfied with Reconstruction. The Senate defeated Grant's imperial ambition in 1870. Leading the attack was Charles Sumner, who feared that annexation would threaten the independence of the neighboring black republic of Haiti. "These islands by climate, occupation, and destiny . . . belong to the colored people," he declared.

Grant's secretary of state was the genteel Hamilton Fish, a former Whig who had been governor of New York and a U.S. senator. Fish had less interest than Seward in acquiring new territory and concentrated on settling differences with Britain. Part of his goal was to strengthen the ties of capital and commerce between the two nations. Interest in annexing Canada still remained high, but Fish finally persuaded Grant that the British North America Act of 1867, uniting Canada in a confederation (the Dominion of Canada) and providing for greater self-government, had removed any serious Canadian interest in annexation. Fish then quickly negotiated the Treaty of Washington in 1871, which submitted for arbitration all the outstanding issues between the two countries, including the *Alabama* claims. In 1873 the British government obeyed the ruling of an international tribunal established under the treaty and presented a $15.5 million check to the U.S. government. A period of unprecedented goodwill between America and Britain followed.

The Politics of Corruption and the Grant Administration

During the Grant administration the Democratic party, seeking to reestablish its national base of power, made the Republican economic program its primary target. Since the key elements of Republican policy had wide support, the Democrats avoided attacking specific programs. Instead, they renewed their traditional assault on "special privilege."

Democrats warned that Republican programs were creating islands of privilege, enabling wealthy individuals to buy favors from the federal government and allowing the Republicans to buy support from the people that their programs served. The result, Democrats charged, was an increasing concentration of wealth and power in the hands of the wealthy and a corruption of the republic. By stressing corruption, the Democrats tried to appeal to Americans who valued honesty and still cherished the Jeffersonian ideal of a society composed of independent and virtuous farmers, artisans, and small entrepreneurs. The Democrats claimed they would restore the competitive economy that had been lost during the Industrial Revolution and the Civil War.

"Grantism"

Grant was lampooned on both sides of the Atlantic for the scandalous behavior of his administration. The British magazine *Puck* showed Grant only barely defying gravity in protecting corrupt members of his administration. Despite the scandals, the British public welcomed Grant with admiration on his triumphal foreign tour in 1877.

Dissident Republicans. Some Republicans joined the Democratic chorus condemning Grant's policies. The dissidents included radicals on Reconstruction such as Charles Sumner, but most numerous and influential were men such as Charles Francis Adams—wealthy, well-educated members of established northeastern families—who resented the critical role professional politicians had come to play in the party. They attacked Grant for turning the Republican party into a self-serving bureaucracy with too many professional politicians in executive positions, especially cabinet posts. And they faulted their party for requiring government workers to pay a portion of their salaries into the party's treasury.

The dissidents coined the term *Grantism* to describe this new system of party patronage. To counter it they endorsed a program of civil service reform, beginning

with a *merit system* to replace the spoils system established under Jackson. A civil service commission would administer competitive examinations as the basis for appointments.

The Liberal Republicans and the Election of 1872. When the dissident Republicans failed to replace Grant as the party's nominee in 1872, they called themselves the Liberal Republicans and formed a new party. The name reflected their commitment to liberty, competition, and limited government. Their platform emphasized civil service reform and—in an appeal for Democratic support—amnesty for all former Confederates and removal of troops from the South. For president they nominated Horace Greeley, the influential editor and publisher of the New York *Tribune*. In an attempt to steal the Liberals' thunder, the Democrats nominated Greeley too, but with little enthusiasm. Although Greeley supported reconciliation with ex-Confederates, he had earlier favored a radical approach to Reconstruction, and he supported high tariffs, which conflicted with the views of the Democrats.

In the election of 1872 Grant won an even larger percentage of the popular vote—56 percent—than he had in 1868. In fact, this was a higher percentage of the popular vote than any candidate had won since Andrew Jackson in 1828. Grant carried every northern state and, because of support for him among African-American voters and the distaste of ex-Confederates for Greeley, Grant also carried all the states of the former Confederacy except Tennessee, Georgia, and Texas.

Crédit Mobilier and the Whiskey Ring. During Grant's second term the issue of corruption in the Republican party erupted again. In 1873 a Congressional committee confirmed newspaper reports of a complicated deal in which high-ranking Republicans appeared to have cheated the taxpayers. The scandal centered on Crédit Mobilier, a construction company that contracted for work on the Union Pacific Railroad. It turned out that Crédit Mobilier was a dummy corporation. Union Pacific stockholders had formed it and made enormous purchases from it, sometimes for services that were never delivered, and paid for those purchases with Union Pacific stock and federal subsidies. In an attempt to prevent a Congressional investigation, the insiders had sold Crédit Mobilier stock at a discount to several members of Congress.

An even more dramatic scandal, which reached into the White House itself, involved the Whiskey Ring, a network of large whiskey distillers and Treasury agents who defrauded the Treasury of millions of dollars of excise taxes on liquor. The ring was organized by a Union general, John A. McDonald, whom Grant had appointed to the post of supervisor of internal revenue in St. Louis. Grant's private secretary, Orville Babcock, kept a protective eye on McDonald's activities and funneled some of the spoils into the campaign chests of the Republican party. The game was up in 1875 when Benjamin Bristow, an upright and ambitious secretary of the treasury, exposed the ring and brought indictments against more than 350 distillers and government officials. Babcock was later acquitted, but more than a hundred men, including McDonald, went to prison.

The Whiskey Ring scandal ruined Grant's second term and crushed whatever prospects he might have had for a third. Grant had ordered Bristow to "Let no guilty man escape," but Grant protected his good friend Babcock with extraordinary measures, possibly even perjuring himself in a deposition he gave in the presence of Chief Justice Morrison Waite.

The Depression of 1873–1877. These scandals occurred in the midst of the worst depression the nation had ever endured. By 1876 nearly 15 percent of the labor force was unemployed, and thousands of farmers had gone bankrupt. The precipitating event was the Panic of 1873, which involved the bankruptcy of the Northern Pacific Railroad and its major investor, Jay Cooke. Both Cooke's privileged role as a financier of the Civil War and the extensive Republican subsidies to railroads suggested to many suffering Americans that Republican financial manipulations had caused the depression.

To Americans who had suffered economic loss or even ruin, the Grant administration seemed unresponsive. Especially troublesome was the important issue of how much paper money should be in circulation. Rapidly falling prices hurt small farmers and all others who were heavily in debt. Forced to repay debts with dollars that were swiftly increasing in value, they called on the federal government to increase the nation's money supply, an action that they hoped would stop prices from falling. The Grant administration ignored the debtors' pleas for relief and further angered them by insisting that Civil War bondholders be fully repaid in gold, even though they had bought their bonds with greenbacks and had received only the guarantee that the interest on the bonds would be paid in gold. In 1874 the Democrats gained sufficient support from Republicans to push through Congress a bill that would have increased the number of greenbacks in circulation and eased the money pinch. But President Grant vetoed it, fueling Democratic charges that Republicans served only the special interests of capitalists. In the election of 1874 the Democrats rode their criticism of Grant's leadership to gains in both houses of Congress and a majority in the House of Representatives—for the first time since secession.

Before the new Congress met, however, the lame-duck Republicans passed the Specie Resumption Act of 1875. This law provided that the federal government would exchange gold for greenbacks, thus making federal paper money as "good as gold." It put the nation's money supply squarely on the gold standard, a step that increased the confidence of investors in the economy and helped foreign trade. But by increasing the value of greenbacks the act induced wealthy Americans to hoard them, reducing the amount of money in circulation, pushing prices up more sharply, and increasing still more the burden of carrying debts. The severe financial pain felt by many Americans worsened even further the political prospects of the Grant administration.

The Political Crisis of 1877

Republican leaders approached the 1876 presidential campaign with a sense of foreboding. If they were to thwart the Democrats, they had to shake themselves free of the atmosphere of scandal and special privilege that had come to surround President Grant. They turned to the electoral-vote-rich state of Ohio for a candidate— Governor Rutherford B. Hayes, who had won three closely contested races. His scandal-free terms had won him a reputation for honesty, he had a good Civil War record, and he was a supporter of civil service reform. He was a moderate on Reconstruction and a former Whig whose election strategy included an appeal to southern conservatives, especially former southern Whigs.

The Democrats concentrated on the Grant scandals. They nominated Governor Samuel J. Tilden of New York, a well-known fighter of corruption who had helped break the control of the infamous Tweed Ring over New York City politics. Their platform emphasized reform, especially of the civil service, promising to save the nation from "a corrupt centralism which has honeycombed the offices of the Federal government itself with incapacity, waste, and fraud."

The Election of 1876. On election night the outcome seemed clear; headlines announced that Tilden had won. The Democrats celebrated, and the Republicans were plunged into gloom. In Ohio, Hayes went to bed convinced that he had been defeated. Tilden had won a bare majority of the popular vote—51 percent. The Democrats had made deep inroads in the North, carrying New York, New Jersey, Connecticut, and Indiana, and had apparently swept the southern states (see Map 16.3).

But by dawn two or three sleepless politicians at Republican headquarters in New York City had woven a daring strategy. Republicans still controlled election procedures in three southern states: Louisiana, South

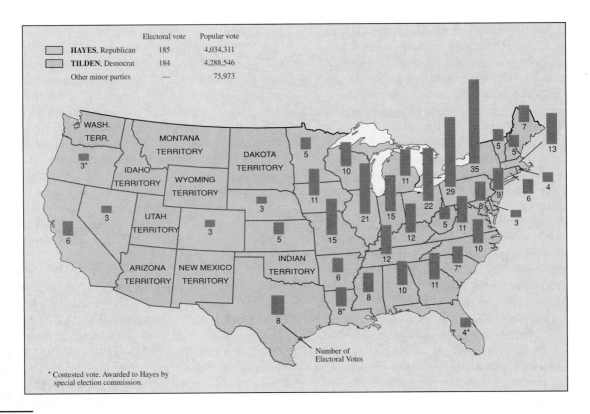

MAP 16.3

The Election of 1876
Tilden made such large inroads in northern states that Hayes could not win without the contested votes of three states in the Deep South. (Hayes also needed to defeat the efforts of the governor of Oregon to replace a Republican elector from that state with a Democrat.)

Carolina, and Florida. If they could argue that Democratic fraud and intimidation had affected the election results in those states, they could certify Republican victories and report Republican electoral votes. Of course, newly elected Democratic officials in the three states would send in electoral votes for Tilden. As a result, there would be two sets of electoral votes from those states when Congress counted them early in 1877. If Congress accepted all the Republican votes, Hayes would have a one-vote electoral majority. The audacious announcement came: Hayes had carried the three southern states and won the election.

The Compromise of 1877. The Constitution had not established a method to resolve this unprecedented dispute over the validity of electoral votes, and the long period of uncertainty between the election in November and the inauguration the following March was filled with rumors: There might be a violent coup by Democrats if the Republicans tried to steal the election; Presi-

dent Grant might use the military to prevent Tilden from taking office; there might be a new election or even a new civil war. The commander of the army, General William T. Sherman, believed that he might be the only person able to preserve the peace, and he deployed four artillery companies in Washington. While the rumors flew, various interests tried to gain advantage from the situation. Railroad promoters jockeyed for new federal subsidies, promising to deliver blocs of support in Congress to the party that made the best promises. Politicians on all sides flirted with the opposition, hoping for rewards.

In the end, political compromise and accident won out. Congress decided to appoint an electoral commission to settle the question. The commission included seven Republicans and seven Democrats. The fifteenth and deciding vote would go to Justice David Davis of the Supreme Court, a man with a reputation for being free of party loyalty. But Davis resigned from the Court at the crucial moment to accept election to the Senate

Anti-Republican Sentiment, 1876

This Democratic cartoon portrays Union soldiers, with bayonets fixed, coercing African-Americans to vote Republican. The carpetbag in the foreground identifies the politics of the civilian at the voting table. To the far left, the individual casting a watchful eye on the proceedings is probably an ex-planter, supposedly powerless in the new politics of the South.

from Illinois, and the deciding vote fell to Joseph P. Bradley, a lifelong Republican. When the commission completed its careful investigation of the election results in Florida, Louisiana, and South Carolina, the decision on each state was made by a straight party vote of eight to seven.

It remained to be seen whether Congress would accept the result. The Senate was controlled by the Republicans, and the House by the Democrats. Southern Democrats held the balance of power, and Hayes's representatives sought their support. Some of those southerners were convinced that Hayes had made various promises to the "negotiators"—to confine federal troops to their barracks throughout the South, appoint Democrats to major offices, and support the construction of a railroad across Texas to the Pacific. Whether or not such promises were actually made, enough southerners in the House accepted the commission's findings to make Hayes president.

This sequence of events is often referred to as the Compromise of 1877, but historians remain uncertain about whether any kind of deal was really struck. Dur-

ing his campaign Hayes had promised to end the military occupation of the South. He had also planned to appoint a few Democrats to his cabinet. And his faction of the Republican party did not support the Texas railroad scheme. The alleged compromise might have been a fiction created by southern Democrats to justify their votes for Hayes.

The End of Reconstruction. The only thing known for certain was that Reconstruction had ended. The outcome was mixed and unclear; no single position had emerged triumphant. In 1877 political leaders on all sides were ready to say that what Lincoln had called "the work" was complete. But for many Americans, especially the freed slaves, the work had clearly not been completed. To be sure, they had won three amendments to the Constitution, established public schools for African-American children, and gained some access to land for former slaves. But any work toward further improvement in the condition of African-Americans had been abandoned and left to the slow, frustrating, and imperfect processes of history.

Summary

In 1865, after the Civil War ended, President Abraham Lincoln's plan for quickly restoring the Union encountered opposition from radical Republicans in Congress, who believed that freedmen must have the vote, and moderate Republicans, who wished to punish the South and establish their party there. Lincoln was assassinated before he could negotiate a unified Republican position.

Possibilities for a swift sectional reconciliation continued into the administration of Andrew Johnson, but he could not satisfy both moderate Republicans and the defeated Confederacy. His difficulties in working with Congress deepened the contest for the control of Reconstruction and resulted in an erratic policy that intensified the South's resistance to federal power.

Congressional Reconstruction extended the civil rights of former slaves through the Fourteenth Amendment, protected their suffrage through the Fifteenth Amendment, and encouraged the formation of southern state governments in which freedmen played crucial roles. Republicans, however, failed to equip those governments to defeat the old planter elite, which managed to regain control through political appeals to racial solidarity and by means of terror and intimidation. Northern Republican leaders tired of the conflict and began to doubt the abilities of African-American political leaders. During the economic depression of the 1870s they increasingly concluded that they had substantial interests in common with white Southern elites.

By 1877 all the Reconstruction state governments had been ousted. The freedmen won some modest economic gains during Reconstruction, but without access to land ownership they became ensnared in a system of debt peonage and again found themselves dependent on the planters, who were now their landlords.

The Republicans proved to be more successful in consolidating the power of industrial capitalism than in reconstructing the South. Democrats attacked the Republican economic program with a Jacksonian critique of "special privilege," but most northerners came out of the Civil War more receptive to concentrations of power and to the values of the business class. Many believed that the Republican program was necessary for sustained prosperity and a strong nation. Although scandals inflamed opposition to the Grant administration, the Republicans took the election of 1876 by capitalizing on the South's hunger for an end to Reconstruction and for some influence in national politics. What is sometimes called the Compromise of 1877 kept the Republicans in control of the federal government by cementing an alliance between the northern business class and southern economic elites.

TIMELINE

1863	Lincoln announces his restoration plan
1864	Wade-Davis bill passed by Congress Lincoln gives Wade-Davis bill a "pocket" veto
1865	Freedmen's Bureau established Lincoln supports limited suffrage for freedmen Lincoln assassinated; Andrew Johnson succeeds as president Johnson implements his restoration plan Joint Committee on Reconstruction formed
1866	Republicans fail to override Johnson's veto of Freedmen's Bureau bill Civil Rights Act passes over Johnson's veto Memphis and New Orleans riots Johnson makes disastrous "swing around the circle" American Equal Rights Association founded Johnson defeated in Congressional elections
1867	Reconstruction Acts Tenure of Office Act Purchase of Alaska
1868	Impeachment crisis Fourteenth Amendment ratified Ulysses S. Grant elected president
1869	*Texas v. White*
1870	Ku Klux Klan at peak of power First Force Act passed by Congress Fifteenth Amendment ratified
1871	Ku Klux Klan Act passed by Congress Treaty of Washington
1872	Grant's reelection as president
1873	Panic of 1873 ushers in depression of 1873–1877 Crédit Mobilier scandal breaks
1874	Democrats win majority in House of Representatives
1875	Whiskey Ring scandal undermines Grant administration
1877	Compromise of 1877 Rutherford B. Hayes becomes president Reconstruction ends

BIBLIOGRAPHY

Among the best general studies are three older works: W. E. B. Du Bois, *Black Reconstruction* (1935), the first book to challenge traditional racist interpretations of Reconstruction; John Hope Franklin, *Reconstruction: After the Civil War* (1961); and Kenneth M. Stampp, *The Era of Reconstruction, 1865–1877* (1965). More modern studies are Eric Foner, *Reconstruction: America's Unfinished Revolution, 1863–1877* (1988), currently the best survey of Reconstruction, and James M. McPherson, *Ordeal by Fire: The Civil War and Reconstruction* (1993).

Presidential Restoration

For important studies of presidential efforts to rebuild the Union, see the books on Abraham Lincoln listed in Chapter 15 and the following works on Andrew Johnson: Albert Castel, *The Presidency of Andrew Johnson* (1979); Eric L. McKitrick, *Andrew Johnson and Reconstruction* (1960), which initiated scholarly criticism of Johnson; and James Sefton, *Andrew Johnson and the Uses of Constitutional Power* (1979). Books that focus on Congress include LaWanda Cox and John H. Cox, *Politics, Principle, and Prejudice, 1865–1867* (1963); David Donald, *The Politics of Reconstruction, 1863–1867* (1965); and William B. Brock, *An American Crisis: Congress and Reconstruction, 1865–1867* (1963). For insight into developments in the South, see Dan T. Carter, *When the War Was Over: The Failure of Self-Reconstruction in the South, 1865–1867* (1985). Michael Perman, *Reunion without Compromise: The South and Reconstruction, 1865–1868* (1973), analyzes how the South manipulated Johnson.

Radical Reconstruction

For studies of Congress's role in radical Reconstruction, see Michael Les Benedict, *A Compromise of Principle: Congressional Republicans and Reconstruction* (1974); William Gillette, *Retreat from Reconstruction, 1863–1879* (1979); and Hans L. Trefousse, *Impeachment of a President: Andrew Johnson, the Blacks, and Reconstruction* (1975). William S. McFeely, *Grant: A Biography* (1981), deftly explains the politics of Reconstruction. Also helpful is Brooks D. Simpson, *Let Us Have Peace: Ulysses S. Grant and the Politics of War and Reconstruction, 1861–1868* (1991). Study of the South during radical Reconstruction should begin with the wealth of literature on the experience of blacks. Among the most useful works are Ira Berlin et al., *Freedom: A Documentary History of Emancipation, 1861–1867: The Wartime Genesis of Free Labor: The Lower South* (1990); Robert Cruden, *The Negro in Reconstruction* (1969); Jacqueline Jones, *Labor of Love, Labor of Sorrow: Black Women, Work, and the Family from Slavery to the Present* (1985); and Leon F. Litwack, *Been in the Storm So Long: The Aftermath of Slavery* (1979). The economic condition of the freedmen and the postwar South is the focus of Robert Higgs, *Competition and Coercion: Blacks in the American Economy, 1865–1914* (1977); Jay Mandle, *The Roots of Black Poverty: The Southern Plantation Economy after the Civil War* (1978); Roger L. Ransom and Richard Sutch, *One Kind of Freedom: The Economic Consequences of Emancipation* (1977); Jonathan M. Wiener, *Social Origins of the New South: Alabama, 1860–1885* (1975); and Gavin Wright, *The Political Economy of the Cotton South* (1978). Specialized studies of African-Americans and race relations, often focusing on particular states, include John Blassingame, *Black New Orleans, 1860–1880* (1973); Barry A. Crouch, *The Freedmen's Bureau and Black Texans* (1992); Barbara Fields, *Slavery and Freedom on the Middle Ground: Maryland during the Nineteenth Century* (1985); Thomas Holt, *Black over White: Negro Political Leadership in South Carolina during Reconstruction* (1977); Peter Kolchin, *First Freedom: The Responses of Alabama's Blacks to Emancipation and Reconstruction* (1972); Howard N. Rabinowitz, *Race Relations in the Urban South, 1865–1890* (1977); Willie Lee Rose, *Rehearsal for Reconstruction: The Port Royal Experiment* (1964); and Joel Williamson, *After Slavery: The Negro in South Carolina during Reconstruction, 1861–1877* (1965). Other state studies of Reconstruction politics appear in Richard Lowe, *Republicans and Reconstruction in Virginia, 1856–1870* (1991), and Otto Olsen, ed., *Reconstruction and Redemption in the South* (1980). The best study of carpetbaggers is Richard N. Current, *Those Terrible Carpetbaggers: A Reinterpretation* (1988). On yeomen farmers, consult Steven Hahn, *The Roots of Southern Populism: Yeoman Farmers and the Transformation of the Georgia Upcountry, 1850–1890* (1983). The most thorough study of the Ku Klux Klan is Allen W. Trelease, *White Terror: The Ku Klux Klan Conspiracy and Southern Reconstruction* (1972). Biographies of Nathan Bedford Forrest include Brian S. Wills, *A Battle from the Start: The Life of Nathan Bedford Forrest* (1992), and John A. Wyeth, *That Devil Forrest: A Life of General Nathan Bedford Forrest* (1989). To survey Reconstruction politics in the South, consult Michael Perman, *The Road to Redemption: Southern Politics, 1869–1879* (1984).

The North during Reconstruction

On state politics in the North, see Eugene H. Berwanger, *The West and Reconstruction* (1981), and James Mohr, ed., *The Radical Republicans in the North: State Politics during Reconstruction* (1976). Studies on national politics that extend beyond Reconstruction include Paul H. Buck, *The Road to Reunion, 1865–1900* (1937), and Morton Keller, *Affairs of State: Public Life in Late Nineteenth-Century America* (1977). The best studies of classical liberalism and liberals during the Reconstruction Era are John G. Sproat, *"The Best Men": Liberal Reformers in the Gilded Age* (1968), and Robert Kelley, *The Transatlantic Persuasion: The Liberal-Democratic Mind in the Age of Gladstone* (1968). On political corruption, see Mark W. Summers, *The Era of Good Stealings* (1993). On the monetary difficulties of the 1870s, see Walter T. K. Nugent, *The Money Question during Reconstruction* (1967). On the Compromise of 1877, see K. I. Polakoff, *The Politics of Inertia: The Election of 1876 and the End of Reconstruction* (1973), and C. Vann Woodward, *Reunion and Reaction* (1956).

P A R T **4**

A Maturing Industrial Society

1877–1914

THEMATIC TIMELINE

	Economy	Politics	Society	Culture	Diplomacy
	The Triumph of Industrialization	**From Inaction to Progressive Reform**	**Racial, Ethnic, and Gender Divisions**	**The Rise of the City**	**An Emerging World Power**
1877	Carnegie launches modern steel industry Knights of Labor becomes national movement (1878)	Election of Rutherford B. Hayes ends Reconstruction	Defeat of the struggle for black equality End of nomadic Indian life	National League founded (1876) Dwight L. Moody pioneers urban revivalism	U.S. becomes a net exporter
1880	Gustavus Swift pioneers vertically integrated firm American Federation of Labor founded (1886)	Ethnocultural issues dominate state and local politics Civil service reform (1883)	Chinese Exclusion Act (1882) Dawes Severalty Act divides tribal lands (1887)	Electrification transforms city life First *Social Register* defines high society (1888)	Diplomacy of inaction Naval buildup begins
1890	U.S. surpasses Britain in iron and steel output Economic depression (1893–97) Era of farm prosperity begins	Populist party founded (1892) William McKinley wins presidency; defeats Bryan's free silver crusade (1896)	Black disfranchisement and racial segregation in the South Immigration from southeastern Europe rises sharply	Settlement houses spread progressive ideas to cities Hearst's *New York Journal* pioneers yellow journalism	Social Darwinism and Anglo-Saxonism promote expansionism Spanish-American War (1898–99); conquest of the Philippines
1900	Great merger movement Immigrants dominate factory work Industrial Workers of the World founded (1905)	Progressivism in national politics Theodore Roosevelt attacks the trusts Hepburn Act enforces government's regulation of railroads (1906)	Women take leading roles in social reform Revival of the struggle for civil rights Immigration restriction movement launched	Dreiser's *Sister Carrie* (1900); triumph of literary naturalism Muckraking journalism Movies begin to overtake vaudeville	Panama cedes Canal Zone to United States (1903) Roosevelt Corollary to Monroe Doctrine (1904) Root-Takahira agreement (1908)
1910	Ford builds first automobile assembly line	Election of Woodrow Wilson (1912) New Freedom legislation creates Federal Reserve, FTC	NAACP founded (1910) Women win the right to vote in western states World War I ends the great European migration	Urban liberalism	Taft's Dollar Diplomacy promotes American business Woodrow Wilson proclaims U.S. neutrality in World War I

While the nation's attention was focused on the political drama of Reconstruction, few people noticed an equally momentous watershed in American economic life. For the first time, as the decade of the 1870s passed, farmers no longer constituted a majority of working Americans. Henceforth, America's future would be linked irrevocably to its development as an industrial society.

The effects of accelerating industrialization were felt, first of all, on the manufacturing sector itself. As heavy industry emerged and the railroad system was completed, the modern techniques of industrial management took shape and big, nationwide firms began to dominate American enterprise. The modern labor movement became firmly established, and, as immigration surged, the foreign-born and their children became America's workers. What had been partial and limited changes became general and widespread as America turned into a land of factories, great corporate enterprise, and restless workers.

Second, the demands of industrialism largely drove the final surge of settlement across the Great Plains and the Rockies. Cities called for new sources of food, and industry needed the Far West's mineral resources. In the struggle for their way of life, western Indians were ultimately defeated not so much by the rifles of army troopers as by events taking place far away in the nation's industries and cities. These same economic forces set in motion the Asian, Mexican, and European migrations that made for a multiethnic western society. Rural America was likewise locked into the advancing Industrial Revolution. The distress American farmers experienced in this period resulted from their imperfect integration into the modern industrial order. They remained small-scale operators in an economic world increasingly dominated by far-flung railroads and giant corporations.

Third, industrialization transformed the physical and human makeup of the nation's cities. By 1900 one in five Americans lived in cities. That was where the jobs were—as workers in factories; as clerks and salespeople in offices and department stores; as members of a new salaried middle class of managers, engineers, and professionals; and, at the apex, as a wealthy elite of property owners and entrepreneurs. But the city was more than just a place to make a living. It provided a setting for an urban way of life unlike anything seen before in the United States.

Fourth, politics marched in step with the industrial order. In the years of unprecedented economic expansion between 1877 and 1893 there seemed little need for government intervention. The major parties were robust and active, but their vitality stemmed from a political culture of popular participation, from ethnocultural conflicts linked to party loyalties, and from the informal functions political parties performed as highly organized machines. Economic crisis during the 1890s triggered a major challenge to the political status quo, first by distressed farmers active in the Populist party and then, as economic troubles spread, by the divisive campaign for free silver. The election of 1896 turned back that challenge. Still unresolved, however, was another economic concern: the enormous concentration of business power that had accompanied the nation's corporate development. This issue dominated national politics during the Progressive Era. In those years, too, the nation belatedly began to address its social ills. Women progressives took the lead in the struggle to make life better for America's urban masses. African-Americans, victimized by disfranchisement and segregation, found allies among white progressives and launched a new drive for racial equality.

Fifth, the dynamism of America's economic development forced a decisive shift in the country's foreign relations. In the decades after the Civil War, America had been inward-looking, its indifference to global affairs reflected in an inactive diplomacy and a neglected navy. The economic crisis of the 1890s, however, brought home to American leaders the need for secure access to overseas markets for the nation's surplus products. In short order the United States fought a brief war with Spain, acquired an overseas empire, and asserted its national interests in Latin American and Asia. There was no mistaking America's standing as a Great Power, and as World War I approached, no evading the responsibilities and entanglements that came with that elevated status.

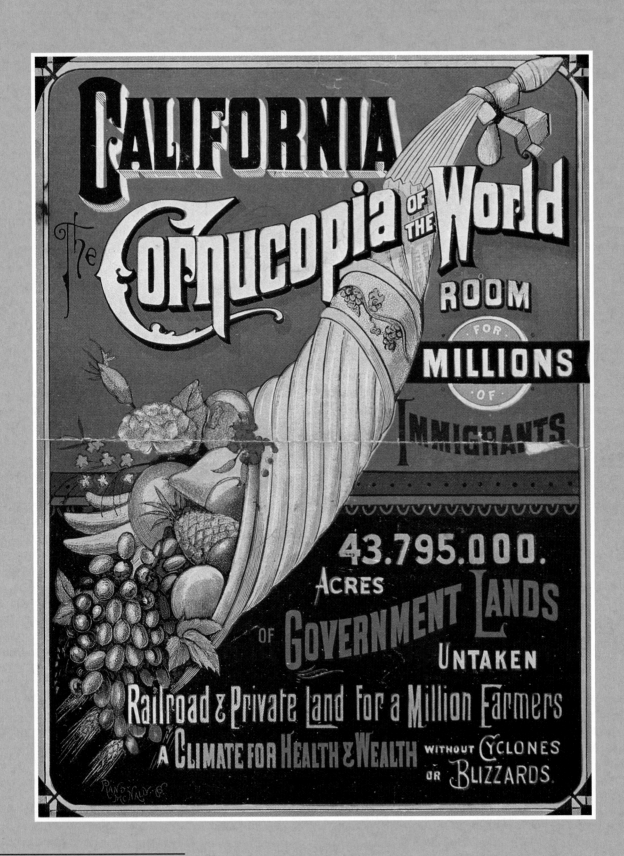

California: Cornucopia of the World

In the 1880s there was a burst of publicity about the charms of southern California. Eager for business, the Southern Pacific Railroad was especially responsible for this promotion.

The American West

★   ★   ★

During the last decades of the nineteenth century, American society seemed to be at odds with itself. From one angle the nation looked like an advanced industrial society, with great factories and mills and enormous, crowded cities. But from another angle America still seemed to be a frontier country, with pioneers streaming onto the Great Plains, repeating the old dramas of "settlement" they had been performing ever since Europeans had first set foot on the continent. Not until the census of 1890 did the federal government declare that a "frontier of settlement" no longer existed: the country's "unsettled area has been so broken into . . . that there can hardly be said to be a frontier line."

That same year, 1890, the country surpassed Great Britain in the production of iron and steel. Newspapers reported Indian wars and labor strikes in the same edition. The last tragic episode in the suppression of the Sioux, the massacre at Wounded Knee, South Dakota, occurred only eighteen months before the great Homestead steel strike of 1892. This alignment of events from the distant worlds of factory and frontier was not accidental. The final surge of settlement across the Great Plains and the Far West was powered primarily by the dynamism of American industrialism.

The Industrial Revolution likewise shaped the history of agricultural America in these years. Farmers had one foot in the Jeffersonian past and the other in the industrial age. They remained small-scale operators in an economic world increasingly dominated by far-flung railroads and giant corporations. They were producing for international markets but thinking like family farmers. Rural America could no longer be understood on its own terms. Its history had become linked ever more tightly to the larger industrial society.

The Great Plains

During the 1860s agricultural settlement reached the western margins of the high-grass prairie country. Beyond, roughly at the 98th meridian, stretched vast semi-arid lands that were uninviting to farmers accustomed to woodlands and ample rainfall. They saw it much as did the New York publisher Horace Greeley on his way to California in 1859: "a land of starvation," "a treeless desert," with a "terrible" climate of baking heat in the daytime and "chill and piercing" cold at night.

Greeley was describing the Great Plains. The geologic event that created this wide, dry expanse occurred 60 million years ago when the Rocky Mountains had

been thrust up out of the ocean covering western North America. With no outlet, the shallow inland sea to the east dried up, forming a hard pan on which sediment washing down from the mountains built up a loose, featureless surface layer. The mountain barrier also made for a dry climate because the moisture-laiden winds from the Pacific spent themselves on the western slopes. The weather pattern, moreover, was extremely unstable because of the convergence on the plains of major weather systems blowing in from the Pacific, the Arctic, and the Gulf of Mexico. Only vegetation capable of withstanding the periodic cycles of severe drought and bitter winters could take hold on the plains. This meant a virtually treeless landscape except along the river bottoms. Short grasses dominated, especially the gramma, or buffalo

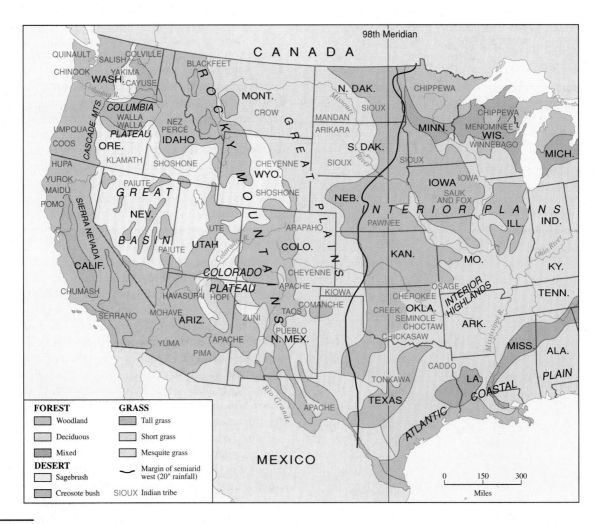

MAP 17.1

The Natural Environment of the West
As settlers pushed into the Great Plains beyond the line of semiaridity, they sensed the overwhelming power of the natural environment. In a landscape without trees for fences and barns and without adequate rainfall, ranchers and farmers had to relearn their business. The native Americans peopling the plains and mountains had in time learned to live in this environment, but this knowledge counted for little against the ruthless pressure of the settlers to domesticate the West.

grass, variety. The short grass was the linchpin of the fragile plains ecosystem, matting the easily blown soil into place and sustaining a rich wildlife dominated by large grazing animals: pronghorn antelope in the sparser regions and buffalo on the central plains. What the dry short-grass country had not sustained, until quite recent times, was human settlement (see Map 17.1).

Indians of the Great Plains

Probably a hundred thousand native Americans lived on the Great Plains at mid-nineteenth century. They were a diverse people, divided into six linguistic families and at least thirty tribal groupings. The Mandan, Arikara, and Pawnee were mostly agriculturalists, planting maize and beans and living in permanent villages on the eastern margins and along the Missouri River. Relatively concentrated and sedentary, these tribes were ravaged by smallpox and measle epidemics brought by Europeans. Increasingly dominant were the hunting tribes that had migrated onto the Great Plains since the seventeenth century: Kiowa and Comanche in the southwest; Arapaho and Cheyenne on the central plains; and, to the north, Blackfeet, Crow, Cheyenne, and the great Sioux nation.

The Teton Sioux. Originally the Sioux had been eastern prairie people occupying semipermanent settlements in the lake country of northern Minnesota. Under pressure from the better-armed Ojibwa and with dwindling sources of fish and game, some Sioux tribes drifted westward during the early eighteenth century. Around 1760 they began to cross the Missouri River into the vast short-grass country. These Sioux became a nomadic people, living in portable skin tepees and relying on the hunt for survival. From tribes to the south and west they acquired horses. Now mounted, the Sioux became splendid hunters and formidable fighters, claiming the entire Great Plains north of the Arkansas River as their hunting grounds. By the early nineteenth century they had built an essentially new and robust culture based on the horse, the buffalo, and the open land.

The westernmost Sioux—they called themselves the Teton people, or Lakotas (meaning "allies")—made up a loose confederation of seven tribes. In the winter months the tribes broke up into small bands, but each spring they assembled and prepared for the summer hunt. Summer was also the season for making war. Mostly, raiding parties of thirty or forty warriors went forth intent on capturing ponies and taking scalps, but occasionally larger, well-organized territorial campaigns were mounted against rival tribes. The Sioux, it must be remembered, were an invading people. Warfare was the means by which they drove out or subjugated longer-settled tribes and made themselves the dominant power on the northern Great Plains.

A society that celebrates the heroic virtues is likely to define gender roles sharply. Before the Sioux got horses, chasing down the buffalo had been a group enterprise. The entire community—women as well as men—worked collectively to construct a "pound" and channel the herds in the right direction. Once on horseback, the male

Teepee Liner
For the Plains Indians, tribal life revolved around the buffalo hunt and the battleground. So these were the themes with which an unknown Indian artist decorated this dewcloth, which was hung inside a teepee to shield the occupants and provide some insulation from the cold.

buffalo hunters were on their own, and gender roles became more distinct. For the women, success at the hunt meant many more buffalo skins to prepare. This was laborious, painstaking work, increasing the wealth of the tribe but also heavily burdening Sioux women. Fanny Kelly, who had been a Sioux captive, considered their life "a servitude"; but she also noticed that they were "very rebellious, often displaying ungovernable and violent temper." Subordination to men was not how native American women understood their unrelenting labor; this was their allotted share in a partnership on which the proud nomadic life of the Teton Sioux depended.

Teton Religion. Living so close to nature and depending on its bounty for survival, the Sioux saw sacred meaning in every manifestation of the natural world. Unlike Europeans, they conceived of God not as a supreme being but, in the words of the ethnologist Clark Wissler, as "a controlling power or series of powers pervading the universe." The most sacred of those powers were the *wakan tanka*. First came the sun, Wi; then came Skan, the sky; Maka, the earth; and Inyan, the rock. Below these came the moon, wind, and buffalo, down through a hierarchy embodying the natural order. The central experience of Sioux religion was to establish a bond with these mysterious powers through visions induced by prayer and fasting in an isolated place. Medicine men provided instruction, but the religious experience was essentially an individual matter and open to both women and men. The vision, when a supplicant achieved it, attached itself to an object—a feather, the skin of an animal, or a shell—which was tied into a sacred bundle and became that person's lifelong talisman. For the tribe as a whole, Sacred Pipe bundles served as the symbolic and ceremonial core of Sioux religion. In the Sun Dance, the entire tribe engaged in the rites of coming of age, fertility, and the hunt and combat, followed by four days of fasting and dancing in supplication to Wi, the sun.

The world of the Teton Sioux was not self-contained. From the start of their westward trek, they had been traders, exchanging pelts and buffalo robes for the agricultural products of the sedentary Plains Indians. The Sioux soon extended these exchanges to include the white traders who had appeared on the upper Missouri River during the eighteenth century, and a substantial commerce in furs developed. Although the buffalo provided most of the essentials of life—not only food but clothing, shelter, fuel, carrying bags, and a variety of bone implements—the Sioux came to rely as well on the traders' pots, kettles, blankets, knives, and firearms. The trade system they had entered was linked to the Euro-American market economy, yet it was also integrated into the Sioux way of life. Everything depended on the survival of the Great Plains as the Sioux had found it—wild grassland on which the antelope and buffalo ranged free.

Intruders

On first encountering it, Americans themselves saw no better use for the Great Plains. After exploring a drought-stricken stretch in 1820, Major Stephen H. Long declared it "almost wholly unfit for cultivation, and of course uninhabitable by a people depending upon agriculture for their subsistence."

For years thereafter maps marked the plains region as the Great American Desert. And with that notion in mind, Congress formally designated the Great Plains in 1834 as permanent Indian country. The army general in charge, Edmund Gaines, wanted the border forts stretching from Lake Superior to Fort Worth, Texas, to be constructed of stone because they would be there forever. Trade with the Indians would continue, but it would be closely supervised and licensed by the federal government, with the Indian country otherwise off limits to white intrusion.

Events swiftly overtook the nation's solemn commitment to the native Americans. During the 1840s settlers began a massive movement westward to Oregon and California. Instead of serving as a buffer against the British and Mexicans, the Indian country became a bridge to the Pacific. The first wagon train headed west for Oregon from Missouri in 1842. Thousands of emigrants then traveled the Oregon Trail to the Willamette Valley or, cutting south beyond Fort Hall, down into California. Approaching that juncture in 1859, it seemed to Horace Greeley as if "the white coverings of the many emigrant and transport wagons dott[ing] the landscape" gave "the trail the appearance of a river running through great meadows, with many ships sailing on its bosom." However, these "ships" left behind not a trailing wake of foam but a rutted landscape devoid of grass and game and littered with abandoned wagons and rotting garbage.

The Railroads. Talk about the need for a railroad to the Pacific soon began to be heard in Washington. How else could the distant territories formally acquired from Mexico and Britain in 1848 be firmly linked to the Union? The settlers bound for California and Oregon themselves clamored for relief from the ordeal of the overland journey by wagon train. For nearly twenty years, however, the project languished while the North and the South argued over the terminus for the route to the Pacific. Meanwhile, the Indian country was crisscrossed by overland freight lines and Pony Express riders and, in 1861, by the telegraph lines that brought San Francisco into instant communication with the East. The next year, with the South in rebellion and no longer a political factor, the federal government finally moved forward with the transcontinental project.

No private company could be expected to foot the bill by itself. The construction costs were staggering, and earnings were likely to be limited in the short run.

Beyond the well-populated states bordering the Mississippi, railroads would have to be built mostly in advance of the economic demand for them. In addition to generous land grants along the right-of-way, the federal government offered millions of dollars in public loans to the two companies that undertook the transcontinental project: the Union Pacific and the Central Pacific. Even so, raising private capital proved hard, requiring bonds at very high interest rates and a flood of stock with little underlying value. On top of that, the railroad promoters plundered shamelessly, diverting into their own pockets over half the construction costs.

The Union Pacific, building westward from Omaha, made little headway until the Civil War ended but then advanced rapidly across Indian country, reaching Cheyenne, Wyoming, in November 1867. It took the Central Pacific nearly that long moving eastward from Sacramento to cross the crest of the Sierra Nevada. Both then worked furiously—since the government subsidy was based on miles of track built—until, to great fanfare, the tracks met at Promontory Point, Utah, in 1869. The transcontinental link was actually a pretty rickety affair, capable of moving people but not a lot of freight. It would eventually have to be wholly rebuilt. None of the other land-grant railroads made it as far as the Rockies before the Panic of 1873 hit, throwing them into bankruptcy and bringing work to an abrupt halt.

By then, however, railroad tycoons had changed their minds about the Great Plains. No longer did they see it through the eyes of the Oregon-bound settlers—as a place to be gotten through en route to the Pacific. Rail transportation, they realized, was laying the basis for the economic exploitation of the Great Plains. This calculation spurred the railroad boom that followed economic recovery in 1878. Construction soared. During the 1880s, 40,000 miles of track were laid west of the Mississippi. There were new routes to southern California via the Southern Pacific from New Orleans and the Santa Fe from Kansas City and to Portland, Oregon, via the Northern Pacific from St. Paul, Minnesota, plus feeder lines and regional systems that crisscrossed the interior West.

The Cattle Kingdom. Of all the opportunities beckoning on the Great Plains, the most obvious was cattle raising. All prospective ranchers had to do was to observe the great herds of grazing buffalo to imagine the plains as cow country. And now, just as the ranchers stood poised to move in, those herds disappeared. A small market for buffalo robes had existed for years. Then, in the early 1870s, eastern tanneries discovered how to cure the hides, and a huge demand developed among shoe and harness manufacturers. Parties of professional hunters with high-powered rifles swept across the plains and began a systematic slaughter of the buffalo (see American Lives, pages 524–525). The great

Killing the Buffalo
This woodcut shows passengers shooting buffalo from a Kansas Pacific Railroad train. . . . A small thrill added to the modern convenience of traveling west by rail.

herds, already diminished by disease and shrinking pasturage, almost vanished within ten years. Many people spoke out against this mass killing, but no way existed to stop people bent on making a quick dollar. Besides, as General Philip H. Sheridan pointed out, exterminating the buffalo would starve the Indians into submission and open up the feeding grounds for a more valuable commodity, the Texas longhorn.

Bred from Spanish stock on Mexican ranchos since the eighteenth century, these tough cattle had spread across the Rio Grande and been acquired by Anglo ranchers. About 5 million head roamed south Texas in 1865, hardly worth bothering about because they could not be profitably marketed. That year, however, the Missouri Pacific Railroad reached Sedalia, Missouri. At that terminal, which connected to hungry eastern markets, a $3 longhorn might command $40. With this incentive, Texas ranchers inaugurated the famous Long Drive as cowboys herded the longhorn cattle hundreds of miles north to the railroads that were pushing west across Kansas.

At Abilene, Ellsworth, and, beginning in 1875, Dodge City, ranchers sold their cattle, and trail-weary cowboys went on a binge. These wide-open cattle towns captured the nation's imagination as symbols of the Wild West. The reality was much more ordinary. The cowboys, many of them blacks and Hispanics, were in fact farmhands on horseback, working long hours under harsh conditions for small pay. Colorful though it seemed, the Long Drive was actually a makeshift method of bridging a gap in the developing transportation system. As soon as railroads reached the Texas range country during the 1870s, ranchers abandoned the hazardous and wasteful Long Drive.

Buffalo Bill and the Wild West

Scott County, Iowa, was still frontier country when William F. Cody was born there on February 26, 1846. Kansas, where his family moved in 1854, was even wilder, for it not only was frontier country but was racked by bloody conflict between proslavery and free-soil settlers. Bill's father, Isaac Cody, was active on the free-soil side, serving in the Topeka legislature and frequently in harm's way from neighboring southern sympathizers and marauding border ruffians. One of Bill's first exploits was a wild gallop, with proslavery men in hot pursuit, to warn his father of a trap set for him near the family farm. Isaac Cody was less an idealist, however, than a typical enterprising westerner on the lookout for the main chance. He had been an Indian trader, a farm manager, a stagecoach operator, and, in Kansas, a land speculator around Grasshopper Falls. When he died suddenly in 1857, Cody left the family with a pile of land titles but little money.

Bill, never much for schooling anyway, had to find work. Only eleven, he was taken on by Majors and Waddell, the firm that transported goods from Fort Leavenworth to army posts west of the Missouri River. Bill worked as a messenger boy, livestock herder, and teamster helper on the freight wagons. When his employers (now Russell, Majors, and Waddell) organized the short-lived Pony Express in 1860, Cody became a stocktender and occasional rider in the Colorado-Nebraska division. Most of this was hard and tedious labor, but there were flashes of excitement—scrapes with Indians and bandits (at fifteen, Bill killed one), buffalo stampedes, and brief encounters with Wild Bill Hickock and other tough western characters on whom Bill could model himself. In the early part of the Civil War, Cody was at loose ends. Among other things he engaged in horse thieving disguised as guerrilla activity in Missouri, and he became a heavy drinker. After a stint in the Seventh Kansas Cavalry and a halfhearted effort to settle down after the war (and an unhappy marriage), Cody got his lucky break in 1867.

The Kansas Pacific Railroad was building a line through Indian country to Sheridan, Kansas. To provision the work crews, the contractors hired Cody at

Buffalo Bill Cody

$500 a month—excellent pay—to bring in twelve buffalo a day for the cooks. Cody was a crack shot and an excellent horseman, and he knew buffalo hunting. This assignment was duck soup for him, and the aplomb with which he carried it off soon gave him the name "Buffalo Bill."

The next summer, 1868, Indian war broke out in Kansas, and Cody got his second claim to fame when he was hired as chief scout for the U.S. Fifth Cavalry. Cody knew the Kansas landscape intimately, seemed to have a remarkable instinct for following a trail, and was intrepid in the face of danger. At the height of the fighting in 1868–1869 Cody saw repeated action. In the climactic Battle of Summit Springs, his scouting played a decisive role and he himself shot the Cheyenne chief, Tall Bull. Although the legends later built up around Buffalo Bill (and the claims of others) have inclined scholars to be skeptical, Buffalo Bill was in fact an authentic hero. Perhaps the best testimony was the extra $100 awarded him by the normally tightfisted army "for extraordinarily good services as a trailer and fighter in the pursuit of hostile Indians."

Out of these promising materials there began to emerge a mythic figure. In July 1869 the dime novelist Ned Buntline (Edward Zane Carroll Judson) came through Kansas, met Cody, and, after returning to New York, wrote *Buffalo Bill, the King of the Border Men*—the first of some 1,700 potboilers to feature Cody's name and exploits. Then there were the buffalo-hunting parties of the rich and famous that Cody periodically led, including a royal hunt in 1872 with the Grand Duke Alexis of Russia that had the entire country agog. With his white horse, buckskin suit, crimson shirt, and broad sombrero, Buffalo Bill began to play his part to the hilt. "He realized to perfection the bold hunter and gallant sportsman of the plains," wrote one appreciative participant. In 1872 Cody was persuaded to appear as himself in a play Buntline proposed to put on in New York. Buntline was said to have dashed off *The Scouts of the Prairie* in four hours, and critics pronounced it "execrable." But Buffalo Bill, who mostly ad-libbed, was a great hit, and so was the production. Cody was launched on his career as a showman.

From then on the lines between reality and make-believe began to blur. Not only did Buffalo Bill draw on his past exploits when he went on stage, but he had the stage in mind when he returned to the real world. During the Sioux wars of 1875–1876 Cody was again out in the field as an army scout. (Fortunately, the fighting took place during the theatrical off-seasons in the East.) Shortly after the annihilation of Custer's troops at Little Big Horn, Cody gained a measure of vengeance in a famous skirmish in which he killed and scalped a Sioux chief named Yellow Hand. Cody rode into that engagement wearing his stage *vaquero* outfit—black velvet and scarlet with lace—so that when he reenacted the mayhem on stage, he could say that he was wearing the very clothes in which he had seen action. Over time, with some help from Cody, the fight with Yellow Hand assumed legendary proportions, becoming a formal duel, with a challenge laid down by the Indian chief, and troopers and Indian warriors lined up on opposing sides to watch Buffalo Bill and Yellow Hand fight it out.

The mythic West Cody was creating became full-blown in his Wild West Show. Modeled on the circus and rodeo, it was first staged in 1883. It was an open-air extravaganza with displays of horsemanship, sharp-shooting by Little Annie Oakley, real Indians (in one season Chief Sitting Bull toured with the company), and reenactments of stagecoach robberies and great events such as Custer's Last Stand. The Wild West toured the country every year and was a smashing success in Europe as well.

Buffalo Bill had been keen enough to see the hunger of city people for a legendary West. He traded on his talents as a showman, but he relied as well on his grasp of the authentic world behind the make-believe. When Cody died in 1917, that world had long gone, but his Wild West Show kept it alive in legend, where it still remains in the mythic figures of cowboys and Indians that populate our movies and television screens.

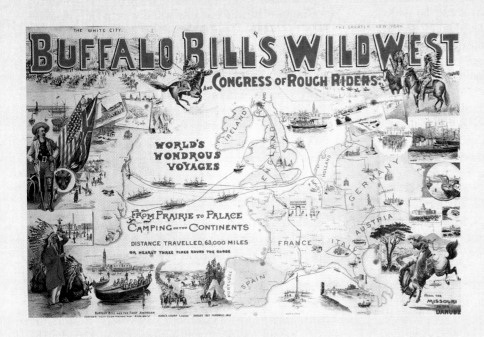

Buffalo Bill's Wild West Show
The Wild West Show had worldwide appeal. This poster celebrates one of Buffalo Bill's European tours. (Buffalo Bill Historical Center)

The Cowboy at Work
Open-range ranching, in which cattle from different ranches grazed together, gave rise to distinctive traditions. At the roundup, cowboys separated the cattle by owner and branded the calves. The cowboy, traditionally a colorful figure, was really a farmhand on horseback, with the skills to work on the range. He earned twenty-five dollars a month, plus meals and a bed in the bunkhouse, in return for long hours of grueling, lonesome work.

Others, meanwhile, introduced longhorns to the northern ranges and found that the cattle could survive the harsh winters. In Texas ranchers owned or leased the land they used, sometimes in huge tracts. But what legal basis did they have for grazing cattle north of Texas? If the land was controlled by Indians, ranchers believed no one owned it. And if it was controlled by the federal government, then it was beyond reach, since government policy reserved the public domain for family-sized farms. So entering cattlemen simply helped themselves, treating the land as a free commodity for anyone who seized it and put it to use. Hopeful ranchers would spot a likely area along a creek and claim as much land as they could qualify for as settlers under federal homesteading laws, plus what could be added through the fraudulent claims made by one or two ranch hands. By a common usage that quickly became established, ranchers had a "range right" to all the adjacent land rising up to the divide—the point where the land sloped down to the next creek.

News of easy money traveled fast: calves at $5, steers at maybe $60 on the Chicago market. Rail connections were in place or coming in, and the grass was free. Profits of 40 percent per annum were a sure thing. The rush was on, drawing from as far away as the East Coast and Europe both the smart money and the romantics (like the recent Harvard graduate Teddy Roosevelt), eager for a taste of the Wild West. By the early 1880s the plains were overflowing with cattle; as many as 7.5 million head were decimating the grass and trampling the water holes.

A cycle of good weather only postponed, and made worse, the inevitable disaster. When it came—a hard winter in 1885, a severe drought the following summer, and then record blizzards and bitter cold—cattle died by the hundreds of thousands. An awful scene of rotting carcasses greeted the cowhands riding out onto the range the following spring. The recent slaughter of buffalo had produced equally ghastly sights, but no one owned the buffalo (and horror at their fate was therefore regarded as "sentimental") whereas every dead steer represented some rancher's investment. On top of that, beef prices collapsed when hard-pressed ranchers dumped the surviving cattle on the market. The boom had turned into a financial disaster, and investors fled, leaving behind a more enduring ecological disaster: the native grasses never recovered from the relentless overgrazing during the drought cycle.

Open-range ranching came to an end. Ranchers fenced their land and planted hay for the winter. No longer would cattle be left to fend for themselves on the open range. The crucial adaptation was to shift from reliance on wild vegetation to the cultivation of feed crops. Elsewhere, Hispanic grazers from New Mexico brought sheep in to feed on the forbs and woody plants that had replaced the native grasses. Sheep raising, previously scorned by ranchers as unmanly and resisted as a threat to cattle, became a major enterprise in the sparser high country after the beef debacle of the mid-1880s. Some ranchers even sold out to the despised "nesters"—those who wanted to farm the Great Plains.

Homesteaders. The movement of farmers onto the plains was not exactly spontaneous. Powerful interests devoted themselves to overcoming the notion of a Great American Desert. Foremost were the railroads, which were eager to sell the public land they had been granted—180 million acres of it—and develop traffic for their routes. They advertised aggressively, offered cut-rate tickets, and sold their land holdings at bargain prices. Land speculators, steamship lines, and the western states and territories did all they could to encourage settlement. And so did the federal government, with its offer under the Homestead Act (1862) of 160 acres of public land to settlers.

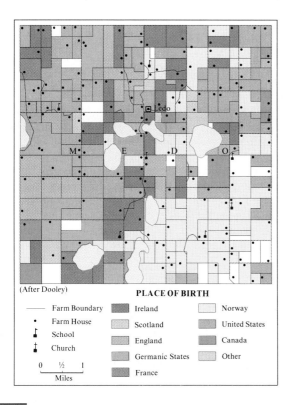

(After Dooley)

PLACE OF BIRTH

— Farm Boundary
• Farm House
School
Church

0   ½   1
Miles

Ireland
Scotland
England
Germanic States
France

Norway
United States
Canada
Other

MAP 17.2

The Rural Ethnic Mosaic: Blue Earth County, Minnesota, 1880
What could have been more natural for emigrants such as Ida Lindgren (see American Voices, page 528) than to settle next to others sharing common ties to a homeland. This map of Medo township reveals that in rural America, no less than in the cities, ethnicity strongly influenced where people lived.

"Why emigrate to Kansas?" asked a testimonial in *Western Trail*, the Rock Island Railroad's gazette. "Because it is the garden spot of the world. Because it will grow anything that any other country will grow, and with less work. Because it rains here more than any other place, and at just the right time." Too boastful, a prospective settler might think, but surely holding a grain of truth. Besides, the climate might improve. "Why may we not suppose that the genial influences of civilization—that extensive cultivation of the earth—might contribute to the multiplication of showers?" asked Josiah Gregg, an early traveler on the plains. Might not "these sterile regions . . . be thus revived and fertilized, and their surface covered one day by flourishing settlements to the Rocky Mountains?" Over time Gregg's vision became an article of faith among boosters of the plains. As if to confirm that optimism, an exceptionally wet cycle occurred between 1878 and 1886. "As the plains are settled up we hear less and less of drouth, hot winds, alkali and other bugbears that used to hold back the adventurous," remarked a Nebraska man. Some settlers attrib-

uted the increased rainfall to soil cultivation and tree planting. Others credited God. As a settler on the southern plains remarked, "The Lord just knowed we needed more land an' He's gone and changed the climate."

No amount of optimism, however, could dispel the pain of migration. "That last separating word *Farewell*! sinks deeply into the heart," one pioneer woman recorded in her diary, thinking of family and friends left behind. Emigrants had always seen parting as a kind of death, with reunion unlikely "on this side of the dark river." But then came the treeless land, an alien and frightening place to a Swedish emigrant such as Ida Lindgren (see Map 17.2 and American Voices, page 528). "Such an air of desolation," wrote another Nebraska-bound woman; and, from the Texas plains, "such a lonely country." One old hand likened these despairing feelings to an illness. "A stranger travelling on the prairie would get his hopes up, expecting to see something different on making the next rise." But all he found was "grass and then more grass—the monotonous, endless prairie! . . . To him the disappointment and monotony were terrible. 'He's got loneliness,' we would say of such a man."

For women, this hard experience had a liberating side to it. Prescribed gender roles broke down as women shouldered men's work on new farms and gained a heightened sense of self-reliance in the face of danger and hardship. When husbands died or got sick, their wives took up the reins and operated farms on their

Buffalo Chips
With no trees around for firewood, settlers on the plains had to make do with dried cow and buffalo droppings. Gathering the "buffalo chips" must have been a regular chore for Ada McColl on her homestead near Lakin, Kansas (1893).

AMERICAN VOICES

Ida Lindgren

Swedish Emigrant in Frontier Kansas

Like many emigrants, Ida Lindgren did not find it easy to adjust to the harsh new life on the frontier. Her diary entries and letters home show that the adjustment for the first generation was never complete.

May 15, 1870 [Lake Sibley, Nebraska]
What shall I say? Why has the lord brought us here? Oh, I feel so oppressed, so unhappy! Two whole days it took us to get here and they were not the least trying part of our travels. We sat on boards in the work-wagon packed in so tightly that we could not move a foot, and we drove across endless, endless praries, on narrow roads; no, no, not roads, tracks like those in the fields at home when they harvested grain. No forest but only a few trees which grow along the rivers and creeks. And then here and there you see a homestead and pass a little settlement. The Indians are not so far away from here, I can understand, and all the men you see coming by, riding or driving wagons, are armed with revolvers and long carbines, and look like highway robbers.

No date [probably written July 1870]
Claus and his wife lost their youngest child at Lake Sibley and it was very sad in many ways. There was no real cemetery but out on the prairie stood a large, solitary tree, and around it they bury their dead, without tolling of bells, without a pastor, and sometimes without any coffin. A coffin was made here for their child, it was not painted black, but we lined it with flowers and one of the men read the funeral service, and then there was a hymn, and that was all.

August 25, 1874 [Manhattan, Kansas]
It has been a long time since I have written, hasn't it? . . . When one never has anything fun to write about, it is no fun to write. . . . We have not had rain since the beginning of June, and then with this heat and often strong winds as well, you can imagine how everything has dried out. There has also been a general lamentation and fear for the coming year. We are glad we have the oats (for many don't have any and must feed wheat to the stock) and had hoped to have the corn leaves to add to the fodder. But then one fine day there came millions, trillions of grasshoppers in great clouds, hiding the sun, and coming down into the fields, eating up *everything* that was still there, the leaves on the trees, peaches, grapes, cucumbers, onions, cabbage, everything, everything. Only the peach stones still hung on the trees, showing what had once been there.

July 1, 1877 [Manhattan, Kansas]
. . . It seems so strange to me when I think that more than seven years have passed since I have seen you all. . . . I can see so clearly that last glimpse I had of Mamma, standing alone amid all the tracks of Eslov station. Oliva I last saw sitting on her sofa in her red and black dress, holding little Brita, one month old, on her lap. And Wilhelm I last saw in Lund at the station, as he rolled away with the train, waving his last farewell to me. . . .

Source: H. Arnold Barton, ed., *Letters from the Promised Land.* (Minneapolis: University of Minnesota Press, 1975), 143–145, 150–156.

own. Under the Homestead Act widows and single women had as heads of households the same rights as men; according to land-office records, women filed 12 percent of the claims in Colorado and Wyoming. "People afraid of coyotes and work and loneliness had better leave ranching alone," advised one woman homesteader. "At the same time, any woman who can stand her own company . . . and is willing to put in as much time at careful labor as she does at the washtub, will certainly succeed; will have independence, plenty to eat all the time, and a home of her own in the end."

The vision of new land to be farmed drove men and women onto the plains. By the 1870s the midwestern states had filled up, and farmers looked hungrily westward. "Hardly anything else was talked about," recalled the short story writer Hamlin Garland about his Iowa neighbors. "Every man who could sell out had gone west or was going. . . . Farmer after farmer joined the march to Kansas, Nebraska, and Dakota. . . . The movement . . . had . . . become an exodus, a stampede."

The same excitement took hold in northern Europe. Not only Germans came; for the first time Russians, Norwegians, and Swedes arrived in large numbers. At the peak of the "American fever" in 1882, over 105,000 Scandinavians emigrated to the United States. Swedish and Norwegian became the primary languages in parts of Minnesota and the Dakotas. Roughly a third of the farmers on the northern plains were foreign-born (see Map 17.2).

The Exodusters. The motivation for most settlers, American or European, was prosaically economic, but for some southern blacks Kansas briefly represented something more precious—the modern land of Canaan. Blacks from Kentucky and Tennessee had been migrating to Kansas all through the 1870s. Then, in the spring

Exodusters
Driven from their homes by terror raids, these southern
blacks camped out on a Mississippi levee on the way to
Kansas.

of 1879, with Reconstruction over and federal protection withdrawn, black communities fearful of white vengeance were swept by religious enthusiasm for Kansas. Within a month or so some 6,000 blacks from Mississippi and Louisiana arrived via St. Louis, most of them with nothing more than the clothes on their backs and faith in the Lord. How many of these Exodusters remained is hard to say, but the 1880 census reported 40,000 blacks in Kansas, by far the largest African-American concentration in the West aside from Texas, whose expanding cotton frontier attracted hundreds of thousands of black migrants during the 1870s and 1880s.

No matter where they came from (except perhaps for emigrants from the Russian steppes), homesteaders had seen nothing like the plains before. A cloud of grasshoppers might descend and destroy a crop in a day; a brushfire or hailstorm could do the job in an hour. What forested land had always provided—springs for water, lumber for cabins and fencing, ample firewood—was absent. Water had to be hauled long distances or collected in rain cisterns, fuel came from cow chips and hay twisted into "cats," and shelter took the form of dugouts cut into hillsides and, after a season or two, sod houses built of turf cut from the ground. The absence of trees, on other other hand, meant that far less labor was needed for clearing the land for the first crop. New technology and better seed overcame obstacles once thought insurmountable: steel plows enabled homesteaders to break the tightly matted ground; barbed wire, invented in 1874 by Joseph F. Glidden, an Illinois farmer, provided cheap, effective fencing against roaming cattle; and strains of hard-kernel wheat that could tolerate the extreme temperatures of the plains came in from Europe. The open, level land was ideal for grain crops. Homesteaders had good crops while the wet cycle held and began to anticipate the wood-frame house, deep well, and full coal bin that might make life tolerable on the plains.

Then, in the later 1880s, the dry years came and silenced those hopeful calculations. "From day to day," reported the budding novelist Stepher Crane from Nebraska, "a wind hot as an oven's fury . . . raged like a pestilence," destroying the crops and leaving farmers "helpless, with no weapon against this terrible and inscrutable wrath of nature. . . . It was as if upon the massive altar of the earth, their homes and their families were being offered in sacrifice to the wrath of some blind and pitiless deity." Recently settled land emptied out, as homesteaders fled in defeat. The Dakotas lost 50,000 settlers between 1885 and 1890, and comparable departures occurred up and down the drought-stricken plains.

Others held on grimly. Stripped of the illusion that rain followed the plow, the survivors came to terms with the semiarid climate prevailing west of the 98th meridian. The Mormons in the area near the Great Salt Lake had demonstrated how irrigation could turn a wasteland into a garden. But the Great Plains mostly lacked the surface water needed for irrigation. The answer lay in dry-farming methods, which involved deep planting to bring subsoil moisture to the roots and quick harrowing after rainfalls to turn over a dry mulch that slowed evaporation. Dry farming produced a low yield per acre, however, and was not suited for the unequipped homesteader. Dry farming developed most fully on the corporate farms that covered up to 100,000 acres in the Red River Valley in North Dakota. But even family farms, which remained the norm elsewhere, could not operate with less than 300 acres of cereal crops and without machinery for plowing, planting, and harvesting. The McCormick reaper, although invented before the Civil War, began to be produced in quantity in response to the demand of western farmers.

By the turn of the century the Great Plains had fully submitted to agricultural development. About half the nation's cattle and sheep, a third of its cereal crops, and nearly three-fifths of its wheat came from the newly settled lands. In this process there was little of the "pioneering" that Americans associated with the westward movement. The railroads came before the settlers, eastern capital financed the ranching bonanza, and agriculture depended on sophisticated dry-farming techniques and modern machinery.

And where was the economic capital of the Great Plains? Far off in Chicago. There, at the hub of the nation's rail system, the wheat pit traded western grain and consigned it to world makets, the great packing houses slaughtered western cattle and supplied the nation with sausage, bacon, and sides of beef. In return, western ranchers and farmers received lumber, barbed wire, McCormick reapers, and Sears Roebuck catalogues. Chicago was truly "nature's metropolis."

The Impact on the Indians

What about the native Americans who had inhabited the Great Plains? Basically, their fate has been told in the foregoing account of western settlement. "The white children have surrounded me and have left me nothing but an island," lamented the great Sioux chief Red Cloud in 1870, the year after the completion of the transcontinental railroad. "When we first had all this land we were strong; now we are all melting like snow on a hillside, while you are grown like spring grass."

No matter that provision for a permanent Indian country had been written into federal law and ratified by treaties with various tribes. By 1860 all the resettled eastern tribes (see Chapter 11), treaties notwithstanding, had been forced to cede their lands and move farther west.

The nomadic tribes presented a more formidable barrier. As incursions into their lands increased from the late 1850s on, the Indians struck back all along the frontier: the Apache in the Southwest, the Cheyenne and Arapaho in Colorado, and the Sioux in the Wyoming and Dakota territories. Fighting ferociously between 1865 and 1867, the Sioux prevented a wagon road from being built through their prized Powder River hunting grounds to the booming mining town of Bozeman, Montana. The Indians hoped that if they resisted stubbornly enough and made the cost high enough, the whites would tire of the struggle and leave them in peace. This seemed not altogether fanciful in the weary aftermath of the Civil War. But the federal government did not give up; instead it formulated a new policy for dealing with the western Indians (see Map 17.3).

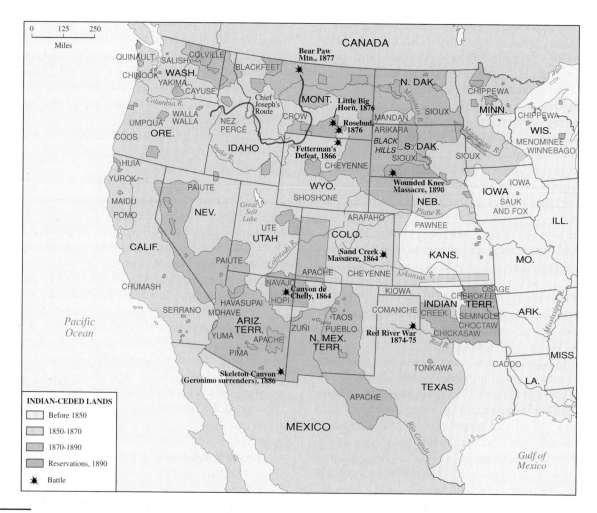

MAP 17.3

The Indian Frontier

As settlement pushed onto the Great Plains after the Civil War, the Indians put up bitter resistance, but ultimately to no avail. Over a period of decades they ceded most of their lands to the federal government, and by 1890 they were confined to scattered reservations where most could expect an impoverished and alien way of life.

The Reservation Solution. Few whites questioned the necessity of moving the native Americans out of the path of settlement and into reservations. This process had already begun, and now it would be pushed to a conclusion. And to it would be linked something new: a planned approach for weaning the Indians from their tribal way of life. Under the guidance of the Office of Indian Affairs, they would be wards of the government until they learned "to walk on the white man's road."

The government set aside two extensive areas for the Indians. It allocated the southwestern quarter of the Dakota Territory—present-day South Dakota west of the Missouri River—to the Teton Sioux tribes. And it assigned what is now Oklahoma to the southern Plains Indians as well as to the Five Civilized Tribes—the Choctaw, Cherokee, Chickasaw, Creek, and Seminole—and other eastern Indians who were already there. Scattered reservations went to the Apache, Navaho, and Ute in the Southwest and to the mountain Indians in the Rockies and beyond.

As in the past, land was transferred through the legal process of treaty making. And, as in the past, the white settlers bribed and tricked the Indian chiefs and in the end forced them to accept what they could not prevent. In 1868 the western Sioux tribes signed a treaty ceding all their land outside the Dakota reservation but explicitly retaining their hunting grounds in the Powder River country. "We have now selected and provided reservations for all, off the great road," concluded the western commanding general in September 1868. "All who cling to their old hunting-grounds are hostile and will remain so till killed off." That they would resist was inevitable. "You might as well expect the rivers to run backward as that any man who was born a free man should be contented when penned up and denied liberty to go where he pleases," said Chief Joseph of the Nez Percé, who, under his leadership, undertook in 1877 a remarkable 1,500-mile march from eastern Oregon almost to Canada trying to escape confinement in a small reservation.

The U.S. Army was thinly spread, having been cut back after the Civil War to a total force of 27,000. But these were veteran troops, including 2,000 black cavalrymen of the Ninth and Tenth regiments, whom Indians called with grim respect "buffalo soldiers." Technology also favored the army. Telegraph communications and railroads enabled the troopers to be quickly concentrated; repeating rifles and Gatling guns increased their firepower. As fighting intensified in the mid-1870s, a reluctant Congress made appropriations to augment the western troopers. Tribal rivalries meant that the army always had Indian allies; for example, the Kiowas and Pawnee could be counted on to fight the Sioux. But the worst disadvantages facing the Indians derived less from a formidable U.S. Army or their own disunity than from the overwhelming impact of white settlement.

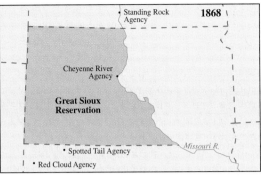

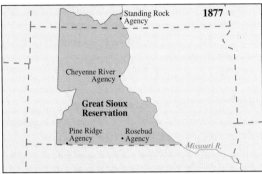

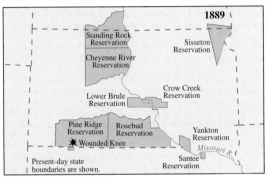

MAP 17.4

The Sioux Reservations in South Dakota, 1868–1890

In 1868, when they bent to the demand that they move onto the reservation, the Sioux thought they had gained secure rights to a substantial part of their ancestral hunting grounds. But as they learned to their sorrow, fixed boundary lines only increased their vulnerability to the land hunger of the whites and sped up the process of expropriation.

Resisting the reservation solution, the Indians fought on for years—in Kansas in 1868–1869, in the Red River Valley of Texas in 1874, and sporadically in New Mexico among the Apache until the capture of Geronimo in 1886. On the northern plains the crisis came in 1875, when the Indian Office—despite the treaty of 1868—ordered the Sioux to vacate their Powder River hunting grounds and withdraw to the reservation.

Led by Sitting Bull, Sioux and Cheyenne warriors gathered on the Little Big Horn River to the west of the

Powder River country. In a typical concentrating maneuver, army columns from widely separated forts converged on the Little Big Horn from three sides. The commanding general, Alfred H. Terry, sent Colonel George A. Custer ahead with a small force to locate the Sioux encampment, with orders to block the Indians from escaping into the Big Horn Mountains before the main army forces arrived. Instead, the reckless Custer sought out battle on his own. On June 25, 1876, he advanced on what he thought was a minor Indian encampment. This turned out to be the main force of 2,500 warriors, who surrounded and annihilated Custer and his 256 men. It was a great native American victory but not a decisive one. The day of reckoning was merely postponed.

Weakened by unrelenting military pressure and increasing physical privation, the Sioux bands one by one gave up and moved onto the reservation. The last to come in were Sitting Bull's followers. They had retreated to Canada, but in 1881, after five hard years, they recrossed the border and surrendered at Fort Buford, Montana.

By then the open plains were no more. Homesick bands of southern Cheyenne learned this bitter truth in 1878 when they escaped from their reservation in the Indian Territory of Oklahoma. Along the route to their native grounds in the Wyoming Territory lay three railroads, numerous telegraph lines, and ranchers and homesteaders eager to report the Cheyenne's movements. The Cheyenne made their way through Kansas and Nebraska, but the army eventually caught up and captured them. The survivors declared that they preferred death to returning to the reservation. The government relented and permitted them to stay on their native land.

It was not Indian resistance but relentless white pressure that wrecked the reservation solution. Prospec-tors began in the mid-1870s to dig gold in the Black Hills, sacred land to the Sioux and entirely inside their reservation. Unable to hold back the prospectors or buy out the Sioux, the government opened up the Black Hills to gold seekers at their own risk, and in 1877, after Sioux resistance had crumbled, forced the cession of the western third of their Dakota reservation (see Map 17.4).

The Indian Territory of Oklahoma met the same fate. Two million acres in the heart of the territory had not been assigned to any tribe, and white homesteaders coveted that fertile land. The "Boomer" movement, stirred up initially by railroads running across the Indian Territory during the 1880s, agitated tirelessly to open this so-called Oklahoma District to settlers. In 1889 the government gave in and placed the Oklahoma District under the Homestead Act. On April 22, 1889, a horde of claimants rushed in and staked out the entire district within a few hours. Two tent cities—Guthrie with 15,000 people and Oklahoma City with 10,000—were in full swing by nightfall.

Severalty. The completion of the land-grabbing process was hastened, ironically, by the avowed friends of the native Americans. The Indians had never lacked sympathizers, especially in the East. After the Civil War reformers created the Indian Rights Association. The movement got a boost from Helen Hunt Jackson's powerful book *A Century of Dishonor* (1881), which told the story of the unjust treatment of the Indians. The reformers, however, had little sympathy for the tribal way of life. They could think of no future for the Indian other than assimilation into white society.

During the 1870s the Office of Indian Affairs had developed a program to train Indian children for farming and manual work and prepare them for citizenship.

The Cherokee Strip

This photograph captures the wild race into the Cherokee Strip in the northern part of Oklahoma Territory on September 16, 1893, the second such "run" that opened the region to white settlement. The winners staked out their claims under the Homestead Act and looked forward to a prosperous future on some of the richest farmland in America. Those who lost out hoped for better luck as other parts of the territory opened up. The Indians who had lived on the land had nothing to hope for because this process spelled the end of their way of life.

Some attended reservation schools, while the less lucky were sent to boarding schools distant from family and home. The reformers approved of this educational program and favored the efforts by the Indian Office to undercut tribal authority. In particular, they highly esteemed private property as a "civilizing" force.

The resulting policy was called *severalty*—the division of reservation lands into individually owned parcels. Even though private ownership was a concept repugnant to the Indians and earlier experiments with land allotments had failed dismally, the reformers remained unshaken in their faith that private property would transform the native Americans into prudent, hardworking members of white society. With their blessing, the Dawes Severalty Act of 1887 authorized the president to divide tribal lands, giving 160 acres to each family head and smaller parcels to other individuals. The land would be held in trust by the government for twenty-five years, and the recipients would become U.S. citizens. The remaining reservation lands would be sold off, with the proceeds placed in an Indian education fund.

The Last Battle: Wounded Knee. The Sioux were among the first to feel the full effect of the Dawes Act. According to the proposed allotments, roughly half their Dakota lands would become "surplus" and available for white settlement. The government drew up a plan to divide the Sioux reservation into six smaller ones (see Map 17.4) and again began the familiar process of negotiating assent from the unwilling Indians.

On February 10, 1890, the federal government announced that it had gained the required number of Sioux signatures (three-quarters of the population) and opened the ceded land to white settlement. But no surveys had been made of the reservation boundaries, nor any provision for land allotments for Indians living in the ceded areas. On top of these signs of bad faith, drought wiped out the Indians' crops. It seemed beyond endurance. The Sioux had lost their ancestral lands and faced a future as sedentary farmers that was alien to

their traditions. And immediately confronting them was a hard winter of starvation.

But news of salvation had also come. An Indian messiah, a holy man who called himself Wovoka, was preaching a new religion on a Paiute reservation in Nevada. In a vision, Wovoka had gone to heaven and received God's word that the world would be regenerated. The whites would disappear, all the Indians of past generations would return to earth, and life on the Great Plains would go back to the time of the roaming buffalo. All this would come to pass in the spring of 1891. Preparatory to that great day, the Indians should follow Wovoka's commandments and practice the Ghost Dance. That daylong ritual of dancing and praying sent participants into trancelike states during which their spirits rose to heaven.

Wovoka's teachings were nonviolent and not specifically antiwhite, but among Wovoka's Sioux adherents the new religion took a belligerent and increasingly threatening turn against white settlers. As the frenzy of the Ghost Dance swept through some Sioux encampments in the fall of 1890, resident whites became alarmed and called for army intervention.

When Indian police backed by federal troops tried to arrest Sitting Bull on December 14, a gun battle broke out, killing the old chief and at least twelve others. Worse was to come. Within the Minneconjou tribe, the medicine man Yellow Bird had stirred up a fervent Ghost Dance following. But with their chief, Big Foot, desperately sick with pneumonia, the tribe had given up and come in under military escort to an encampment at Wounded Knee Creek on December 28. The next morning, when the soldiers attempted to disarm the Indians, a battle exploded in the encampment. In American Voices (page 534) Black Elk describes what happened. Twenty-five U.S. troopers died, and among the Indians 146 men, women, and children perished, many of them shot down as they fled.

Wounded Knee was the final episode in the long war of suppression of the Plains Indians, but it was not the

The Dead at Wounded Knee
In December 1890 U.S. soldiers massacred about 146 Sioux men, women, and children in the Battle of Wounded Knee in South Dakota. It was the last big fight on the northern plains between the Indians and the whites. Black Elk, a Sioux holy man, related that "after the soldiers marched away from their dirty work, a heavy snow began to fall . . . and it grew very cold." The body of Yellow Bird lay frozen where it had fallen.

Black Elk

Wounded Knee: "Something terrible happened . . ."

Black Elk, an Oglala Sioux holy man, was at Wounded Knee when the killing occurred. This is his account, as he recollected the event forty years later.

It was in the evening when we heard that the Big Foots were camped over there with the soldiers. . . . In the morning [December 29, 1890] I went out after my horses, and while I was out I heard shooting off toward the east, and I knew from the sound that it must be wagon guns [cannon] going off. The sounds went right through my body, and I felt that something terrible would happen. . . .

A little way ahead of us, just below the head of the dry gulch, there were some women and children who were huddled under a clay bank, and some cavalrymen were there pointing guns at them. . . .

I had no gun, and when we were charging, I just held the sacred bow out in front of me with my right hand. The bullets did not hit us at all. . . .

After the soldiers marched away, I heard from my friend, Dog Chief, how the trouble started, and he was right there by Yellow Bird when it happened. This is the way it was:

In the morning the soldiers began to take all the guns away from the Big Foots. Soldiers were on the little hill and all around, and there were soldiers across the dry gulch to the south and over east along Wounded Knee Creek too. The people were nearly surrounded, and the wagon-guns were pointing at them.

Some had not yet given up their guns, and so the soldiers were searching all the tepees, throwing things around and poking into everything. There was a man called Yellow Bird, and he and another man were standing in front of the tepee where Big Foot was lying sick. They had white sheets around and over them, with eyeholes to look through, and they had guns under these. An officer came to search them. He took the other man's gun, and then started to take Yellow Bird's. But Yellow Bird would not let go. He wrestled with the officer, and while they were wrestling, the gun went off and killed the officer. As soon as the gun went off, Dog Chief told me, an officer shot and killed Big Foot who was lying sick inside the tepee.

Then suddenly nobody knew what was happening, except that the soldiers were all shooting and the wagon-guns began going off right in among the people.

Many were shot down right there. The women and children ran into the gulch and up west, dropping all the time, for the soldiers shot them as they ran. There were only about a hundred warriors and there were nearly five hundred soldiers. The warriors rushed to where they had piled their guns and knives. They fought soldiers with only their hands until they got their guns. . . .

It was a good winter day when all this happened. The sun was shining. But after the soldiers marched away from their dirty work, a heavy snow began to fall. The wind came up in the night. There was a big blizzard, and it grew very cold. The snow drifted deep in the crooked gulch, and it was one long grave of butchered women and children and babies, who had never done any harm and were only trying to run away.

Source: John G. Neihardt, ed., *Black Elk Speaks: The Legendary "Book of Visions" of an American Indian* (1932; rpt. New York: Washington Square Press, 1971), 216–223.

---

end of their story. The process of severalty then proceeded without hindrance. On the Dakota lands the Teton Sioux fared relatively well, and many of the younger generation settled down as small farmers and stock grazers. Ironically, the more fortunate tribes were probably those occupying reservation lands that did not attract white settlement and thus were bypassed by the severalty process. The flood of whites into South Dakota and Oklahoma, on the other hand, left the Indians as small minorities in lands that were once wholly theirs— 20,000 Sioux in a South Dakotan population of 400,000 in 1900 and 70,000 members of various tribes in a population of a million when Oklahoma became a state in 1907.

Even so, tribal identities survived until, with the restoration of the reservation policy in 1934, they once again rested on a communal territorial basis. All along, native American cultures had been adaptive, some of them, for example, developing written languages during the nineteenth century. This cultural resilience would persist—in religion, in tribal structure, in crafts—but the fostering native American world was gone, swept away, as an Oklahoma editor put it in the year of statehood, by "the onward march of empire."

California and the Far West

On the western edge of the Great Plains, the Rocky Mountains rise up to form a great barrier between the flat eastern two-thirds of the country and the rugged Far West (see Map 17.1). Beyond the Rockies lie two vast plateaus: on the north side the Columbia plateau, extending into eastern Oregon and Washington, and flanking the southern Rockies, the Colorado plateau. Where they break off, the plateaus carve out the desert-like Great Basin that covers eastern Utah and all of Nevada. The Great Basin gives way southeastwardly to plains and mountain ridges that are equally rainless but are drained by the rivers of lower Arizona and New Mexico. Separating this arid interior from the Pacific are two great mountain ranges—the Sierra Nevada and, to the north, the Cascades—beyond which lies a coastal region that is cool and rainy in the upper corner but increasingly dry as one proceeds southward until, in southern California, rainfall becomes almost as sparse as it is in the interior.

What most impressed Americans about this far western country was its sheer inhospitability. "Who are to go there?" asked Senator George McDuffie in 1843 when the nation was preparing to seize this land. "The territory consists of mountains almost inaccessible, and low lands . . . where rain never falls, except during spring; and even on the [part of the territory fit for occupation—the part lying on the seacoast] no rain falls from April to October, and for the remainder of the year there is nothing but rain. Why, sir, sir, of what use will this be for agricultural purposes? I would not, for that purpose, give a pinch of snuff for the whole territory."

Too grim, perhaps, but with enough truth to it to explain why the Far West could not be occupied in standard American fashion—that is, by a multitude of settlers moving westward along a broad front, blanketing the land and bringing it under cultivation homestead by homestead. The wagon trains moving to Oregon's Willamette Valley adopted an entirely different strategy of occupation—the planting of distant oases in a vast, mostly barren landscape. This was the strategy pursued by New Spain ever since it had sent the first wagon trains 700 miles northward from Mexico into the upper Rio Grande Valley in 1598. When the Southwest was taken from Mexico by the United States 250 years later, major Hispanic settlements existed in New Mexico and California, and lesser settlements—some of them, like Tucson, little more than *presidios,* or fortified towns—were scattered along the borderlands into south Texas. At that time, aside from Oregon, the only significant Anglo settlement was around the Salt Lake in Utah, where Mormons had moved to escape persecution and plant a New Zion. Fewer than 100,000 Euro-Americans—roughly

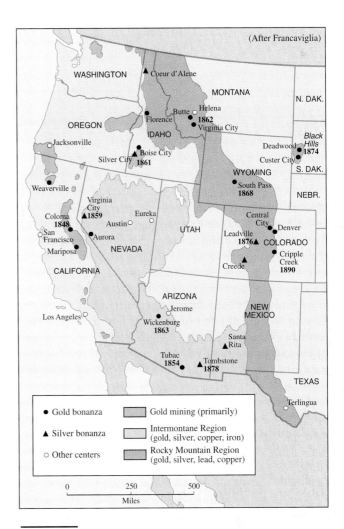

MAP 17.5

The Mining Frontier

The Far West was America's gold country because of its geological history. Veins of gold and silver form when molten material from the earth's core is forced up into fissures caused by the tectonic movements that create mountain ranges, such as the ones that dominate the far western landscape. It was these veins, the product of mountain-forming activity many thousands of years earlier, that prospectors began to discover after 1848 and furiously exploit. Although widely dispersed across the Far West, the lodes that they found followed the mountain ranges, bisecting the region and bypassing the great plateaus not shaped by the ancient tectonic activity.

25,000 of them Anglo and the rest Hispanic—lived in the entire Far West in 1848.

More emigrants would be coming in, certainly, but Senator McDuffie's slight valuation of the nation's newly acquired western territory seemed about right. California was "hilly and mountainous," noted a U.S. naval officer in 1849, too dry for farming and surely not "susceptible of supporting a very large population."

But the naval officer had not taken into account the recent discovery of gold in the Sierra foothills. California would indeed support a very large population, drawn, however, not by the lure of arable land but by dreams of gold. Extraction of mineral wealth became the basis for the Far West's development, and that meant, first of all, explosive growth. By 1860, when the Great Plains was still Indian country, California was a booming state with 300,000 residents. There was also a burst of city building. Overnight San Francisco became a bustling metropolis—it had 57,000 residents by 1860—and was the hub of a mining empire that stretched to the Rockies. For the mining camps on the eastern slope, it was Denver that became the metropolis. In its swift urbanization, the Far West resembled gold-rush Australia much more than it resembled the American Midwest; like San Francisco, Melbourne was a city incongruously grand amid the empty spaces and rough mining camps of the Australian "outback." Finally, the distinctive pattern of nucleated settlement persisted, driven now, however, by a proliferation of mining sites and by people moving not east to west, but coming mainly from California and moving west to east.

The Mining Frontier

By the mid-1850s, as easy pickings in the California gold country rapidly diminished, disappointed prospectors began to pull out of the region and spread across the West in hopes of striking it rich elsewhere. Gold was discovered on the Nevada side of the Sierras, in the Colorado Rockies, and along the Fraser River in British Columbia. New strikes occurred in Montana and Wyoming during the 1860s, in the Black Hills of South Dakota a decade later (an anomalous outcropping du-

plicating on the Great Plains the mineral geology otherwise found only in the mountainous Far West), and in the Coeur d'Alene region of Idaho during the 1880s.

As the news of each gold strike spread, a wild, remote area turned almost overnight into a mob scene of prospectors, traders, gamblers, prostitutes, and saloon keepers. At least 100,000 fortune seekers flocked to the Pike's Peak area of Colorado in the spring of 1859. Trespassers on government or Indian land, the prospectors made their own law. The mining codes devised at community meetings limited the size of a mining claim to what a person could reasonably work. This kind of informal lawmaking also became an instrument for excluding or discriminating against Mexicans, Chinese, and African-Americans in the goldfields. And it turned into hangman's justice for the many outlaws who infested the mining camps.

The heyday of the prospectors was always brief. They were equipped only to skim gold from the surface of the earth and from streambeds. Extracting the metal locked in underground lodes required mine shafts and crushing mills, which took capital, technology, and business organization. The original claim holders quickly sold out after exhausting the surface gold or when a generous bidder came along. At every gold-rush site prospecting soon gave way to entrepreneurial development and large-scale mining. Rough mining camps turned into big towns.

Virginia City. Nevada's Virginia City started out as a bawdy, ramshackle mining camp. But with the opening of the Comstock silver lode in 1859, it soon boasted a stock exchange, five newspapers and, in short order, ostentatious mansions for the mining kings, fancy hotels, opera, even Shakespearean theater. The underlying characteristics of a boomtown persisted, however. Vir-

Virginia City, Nevada
This undated photograph shows a mature Virginia City, taken around the mid-1870s, when the Comstock lode was yielding 500 tons of ore per day. The industrial face of the city can be seen on the upper left, where on the outskirts of town a processing mill crushed the ore and extracted the silver. Virginia City gave the appearance, with its churches and fine public buildings, of a place destined to last forever. But in fact, when the Comstock lode played out in the early 1880s, Virginia City quickly declined and, in a fate all too common in bonanza mining, became a ghost town.

ginia City was a magnet for job seekers of both sexes: men laboring as miners for $4 a day, and many of the working-class women becoming dance-hall entertainers and prostitutes because that was the best chance offered them by the city's bonanza economy. In 1870 the ratio of men to women was two to one, and children made up only 10 percent of the population. There were a hundred saloons, and brothels lined D Street.

When James Galloway arrived from California looking for work on February 4, 1875, however, he brought his family with him, as did many other miners. By 1880 there were as many women and children as men in Virginia City. Galloway's diary describes a family life that was not out of the ordinary—churchgoing, picnics, the purchase of a lot for a small house. But Galloway was infected by Virginia City's pervasive gambling fever: he speculated regularly in mining stock and always lost money. In the end he fell victim to the extraordinary hazards of hard-rock mining. He was killed when his sleeve got caught in the gears of a mine machine. He might have survived if he had permitted rescuers to hack off his arm, but he took a long chance on being cut loose and coming out whole, and lost.

Industrialization of Western Mining. In its final stage the mining frontier passed into the industrial world. At some sites gold and silver proved less important than the more common metals—copper, lead, zinc—for which there was a huge demand in eastern manufacturing. Beginning in the mid-1870s, copper mining thrived in the

Butte district of Montana, especially after the opening of the fabulous Anaconda mine, and also flourished in the Globe and Copper Queen fields of New Mexico and Arizona. In the 1890s, after earlier finds at Leadville, Colorado, the Coeur d'Alene silver district became the nation's main source of lead and zinc.

Entrepreneurs raised capital, built rail connections, devised the technology for treating the lower-grade copper deposits, constructed smelting facilities, and recruited a labor force. As elsewhere in American industry, trade-union organization appeared among the miners (see Chapter 18). And as elsewhere in corporate America, the western metal industries went through a process of consolidation. The Anaconda Copper Mining Company and other Montana mining firms came under the control of the Amalgamated Copper Company in 1899. That same year, the American Smelting and Refining Company brought together the bulk of the nation's lead-mining and copper-refining properties. Blackfeet and Crow country in the 1860s, the Butte copper district was a center of industrial capitalism barely thirty years later.

The Pacific Slope. If the Far West had lacked mineral wealth, its history would certainly have been very different. Before the discovery of gold at Sutter's mill, it was Oregon's Willamette Valley, not dry California, that mostly attracted westward-bound settlers. And had it not been for the gold rush, California likely would have remained like the Willamette Valley—an economic back-

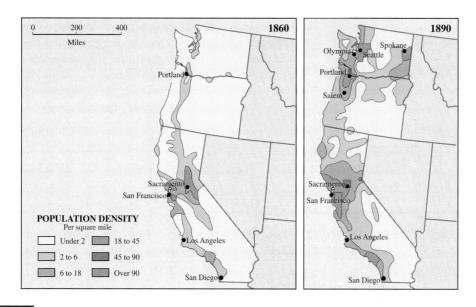

MAP 17.6

The Settlement of the Pacific Slope
In 1860 the settlement of the Pacific slope was remarkably uneven—fully under way in northern California, scarcely begun anywhere else. By 1890 a new pattern had begun to emerge, with the swift growth of southern California already foreshadowed and the settlement of the Pacific Northwest well launched.

water lacking markets for its products and slow to build its population. In 1860, although already a state, Oregon had scarcely 25,000 inhabitants, and its principal city, Portland, was little more than a village. It was booming California (see Map 17.6) and the mining country tributary to it that pulled Oregon from the doldrums by creating a market for the Willamette farms and for the state's fisheries and timber. North of Oregon, territory very thinly settled into the 1870s, the arrival of rail transportation in the early 1880s had an equally tonic effect. The development of Washington on the Pacific side largely duplicated Oregon's experience, but east of the Cascades, on the fertile, semiarid Columbia plateau, a rich grain-producing region also sprang up.

During the 1880s Oregon and Washington (which became a state in 1889) grew prodigiously. Where scarcely a hundred thousand settlers had lived twenty years earlier, by 1890 there were nearly three-quarters of a million. Portland and, even more dramatically, Seattle had blossomed into important commercial centers, both prospering from a robust mixed economy of farming, ranching, logging, and fishing.

California's fertile central valley and forested north coast experienced a comparable development, as did the irrigated valleys of Utah, which by 1890 had over 200,000 people. At a certain point, especially as railroads opened up eastern markets, this diversified growth became self-sustaining. But what had triggered it, what had provided the first markets and underwritten the service infrastructure, was the bonanza mining economy, at the hub of which stood San Francisco, metropolis for the entire Far West.

Hispanics, Chinese, Anglos

The Hispanic Southwest. California was the anchor of two distinct far western regions. First, it joined with

Oregon and Washington to form the Pacific slope. Second, by climate and Hispanic heritage, it was linked to the Southwest, which today includes Arizona, New Mexico, and Texas. Here, along a 1,500-mile borderland, settlements had been planted over many years by the viceroys of New Spain and had formed, after the 1821 revolution, the northernmost provinces of Mexico. Most populous and best established were the settlements along the upper Rio Grande Valley in New Mexico; the main town, Santa Fe, over 200 years old, contained 4,635 residents in 1860. Farther down along the Rio Grande was El Paso, nearly as ancient but much smaller, and, as the Rio Grande emptied into the Gulf of Mexico, newer towns such as Laredo. A grazing economy spread up to the Nueces River. Beyond lay San Antonio, which had been founded to establish Spain's claim to central Texas. At the other end, in California, a Hispanic population was spread thinly in presidio towns along the coast and in great ranchos in the countryside.

The economy of this Hispanic crescent was pastoral, consisting primarily of cattle and sheep ranching. In south Texas there were family-run rancheros. Everywhere else the social order was highly stratified. At the top stood an elite, beneficiaries of royal land grants, proudly Spanish, and devoted to the traditional life of a landed aristocracy. Below them, with little in between, was a laboring population of servants, artisans, *vaqueros* (cowboys), and farm workers.

In New Mexico there was a large *mestizo* population, a peasantry of mixed Hispanic and Indian blood. Although Spanish-speaking and faithfully Catholic, in their village life and farming methods these New Mexicans bore the marks of their Pueblo Indian origins more than their Hispanic heritage. The Indian population, although reduced from the golden age of the Pueblo civilization before the arrival of the Spaniards, still occupied much of the Rio Grande Valley, living in the old ways in adobe villages and making the New Mexico countryside

Vaqueros *in a Corral*
On California cattle ranches owners relied on Mexican cowhands—*vaqueros*—whose skills as riders and rope handlers were unexcelled. This striking painting was done in 1877 by James Walker, who came from New York City but had a special enthusiasm for southwestern scenes. (Thomas Gilcrease Institute)

a patchwork of Hispanic and Pueblo settlements. And to the north a vibrant new people, the Navajo, had appeared, warriors like the Apache from which they had sprung but also skilled at crafts and living as sheep-raising pastoralists. New Mexico was one place where European and native American cultures managed a successful, if uneasy, coexistence and where the Indian inhabitants were equipped to hold their own against the Anglo challenge.

In California, by contrast, the Hispanic occupation was harder on the indigenous hunter-gatherer peoples, inevitably undermining their tribal structure, reducing them to coerced labor, and making them easy prey for the aggressive Anglo miners and settlers, who, in short order, nearly wiped out California's once numerous Indian population.

The fate of the Hispanic Southwest after its incorporation into the United States depended on the rate of Anglo immigration. In New Mexico, which remained off the beaten track even after the arrival of railroads in the 1880s, the Santa Fe elite more than held its own, incorporating the Anglo newcomers into Hispanic society through intermarriage and business partnerships. In California, on the other hand, the expropriation of the great ranchos was relentless even though the 1848 peace treaty with Mexico had recognized the property rights of the *californios* and had made them U.S. citizens. The fact that they actually won most of the lawsuits challenging their Mexican land grants did not matter very much. Burdened by huge legal expenses, rising taxes, and the costs of removing squatters, the dons saw their ranchos auctioned off or lost in swindles by Yankees swarming in with business deals. Around San Francisco the rancho system disappeared almost in a puff of smoke. Farther south, where Anglos were slow to arrive, the dons held on longer. By the 1880s just a handful of the original families still retained their Mexican land grants.

The New Mexico peasants found themselves similarly embattled. Crucial to their livelihood were their grazing rights on communal lands. But these were customary rights that could not withstand legal challenge when Anglo ranchers established title and began putting up fences. The peasants responded resiliently. Their subsistence economy relied on a division of labor that gave women a central productive role in the village economy. Women raised much of the family food in small gardens, engaged in the village bartering trade, made the clothes, and plastered the adobe houses. With the loss of the communal lands, the men began to leave the villages seasonally to work on the railroads or in the Colorado mines and sugar-beet fields, earning crucial dollars while leaving the village economy in their wives' hands.

Elsewhere, hard-pressed Hispanics struck back for what they considered rightfully theirs. In El Paso the fighting issue was control over nearby salt beds. Salt was always a precious commodity, sometimes serving in ancient times as money; *sal* is the Latin root of the word *salary*. So El Pasoans rose in revolt when title to their communal salt beds passed into private hands in 1879. When Anglo ranchers began to fence in communal lands in San Miguel County, the New Mexicans long settled there, *los pobres* (the poor ones), organized themselves into masked night-riding raiders and in 1889 and 1890 mounted an effective campaign of harassment against the interlopers. After 1900, when Anglo farmers swarmed into south Texas bent on exploiting new irrigation methods, the displaced *Tejanos* responded with sporadic but persistent night-riding attacks. Much of the raiding by Mexican "bandits" from across the border in the years before World War I was really a civil war fought by embittered *Tejanos* who had lived north of Rio Grande for generations.

But they, like the New Mexico villagers who became seasonal wage laborers, could not avoid being driven into the ranks of a Mexican-American working class as the Anglo economy developed. The same development, however, also began to attract increasing numbers of immigrants from old Mexico.

Mexican Immigrants. All along the southwest borderlands, economic activity was picking up in the late nineteenth century. Railroads were being built, copper mines were opening in Arizona, cotton and vegetable agriculture was being developed in south Texas, and fruit growing was introduced in southern California. There is no way of knowing how many Mexicans migrated to the work thus created, since the borders were open until 1917 and few bothered to register when they entered the United States. In Texas the Hispanic population increased from about 20,000 in 1850 to 165,000 in 1900. Some came as contract workers for railway track gangs and harvest labor; virtually all were relegated to the lowest-paying and most backbreaking work; and everywhere they were discriminated against and reviled by higher-status Anglo workers.

Mostly the Mexicans came as short-term and casual workers, not as permanent settlers, but some remained and swelled the numbers and resources of established Mexican-American communities. In Tucson, a Mexican elite dominated the expanding local economy. But most Mexican urban dwellers were poor laboring people segregated in what was already identifiably the *barrio*—the Mexican ghetto—of the southwest borderland cities.

What stimulated the Mexican migration, of course, was the enormous demand for workers by a region undergoing explosive economic development. Hence the exceptionally high numbers of immigrants in the California population of that era: between 1860 and 1890 roughly one-third were foreign-born, more than twice the level for the country as a whole. Many came from Europe; most numerous were the Irish, followed by the

Germans and British. But there was also another group that was unique to the West—the Chinese.

The Chinese Migration. Attracted first by the California gold rush of 1849, 200,000 Chinese came to the United States over the next three decades. In those years they constituted a considerable minority of California's population—around 9 percent—and because virtually all were actively employed, they represented a much larger proportion of the state's labor force—probably a quarter. Elsewhere in the West, at the crest of mining activity, their presence could surge remarkably, for example, to over 25 percent of Idaho's population in 1870.

The coming of the Chinese to North America was not an isolated event, but part of a worldwide Asian migration that began in the mid-nineteenth century. Driven by poverty from their overpopulated lands, the Chinese went to Australia, Hawaii, and Latin America; Indians moved to Fiji and South Africa; and Javanese immigrated to Dutch colonies in the Caribbean. Most of these Asians migrated under the system of indentured servitude, which in effect made them the property of others. That was not true of the Chinese who came to America. Contrary to the stubborn image of a "coolie trade," they came as free workers, their passage financed by a *credit-ticket system.* Under that system migrants merely borrowed passage money from a broker; unlike indentured servants, they retained their personal freedom and the right to choose their employers.

Once they arrived, however, Chinese immigrants normally entered the orbit of the Six Companies—a powerful confederation of Chinese merchants in San Francisco's Chinatown. Most of the arrivals were unattached males eager to earn a stake and return to their native Cantonese villages. The Six Companies not only acted as an employment agency but provided them with the social and commercial services they needed to survive in an alien world. The few Chinese women—the male/female ratio was thirteen to one—worked mostly as servants and prostitutes, sad victims of the desperate poverty that drove the Chinese to America. Some were sold by impoverished parents; others had been enticed into fraudulent marriages or kidnapped by procurers and transported to America.

Until the early 1860s, when surface mining played out, Chinese men labored mainly in the California goldfields—as prospectors where the white miners permitted it, as laborers and cooks where they did not. Then, when construction began on the transcontinental railroad, the Central Pacific hired Chinese workers. Eventually they constituted four-fifths of the railroad's labor force, doing most of the pick-and-shovel labor laying the railroad tracks across the Sierras. The Central Pacific perfected a system of contract labor for employing the Chinese. Many were recruited directly from around Canton by labor agents and worked in labor gangs

Building the Central Pacific
Chinese laborers at work on the great trestle spanning the canyon at Secrettown in the Sierra Nevada.

under the control of "China bosses," who not only supervised but fed, housed, paid, and often cheated them.

When the transcontinental railroad was completed in 1869, the Chinese scattered. Some continued to work in construction gangs for the railroads, while others labored on swamp-drainage and irrigation projects in the Central Valley and then became agricultural workers and, if they were lucky, small farmers and orchardists. The mining districts of Idaho, Montana, and Colorado also attracted large numbers of Chinese, but according to the 1880 census nearly three-quarters remained in California. In San Francisco many of them became factory workers. The Chinese were excluded from higher-wage trades, but they soon dominated certain industries—such as cigar making—that competed with eastern products and could survive only with cheap labor. "Wherever we put them, we found them good," remarked Charles Crocker, one of the promoters of the Central Pacific. From the standpoint of employers, "their orderly and industrious habits make them a very desirable class of immigrants."

The Anti-Chinese Agitation. White workers, however, did not share this enthusiasm for Chinese labor. Why they should have taken so venomous a view of the Chinese has never been easy to explain. It involved, most certainly, a sense of unfair economic competition that pitted them against "Chinamen's wages" and "Chinamen's living conditions." But the hatred clearly went deeper. In other parts of the country, racism was directed against African-Americans; in California, where there were few blacks, it found a target in the Chinese. They were "an infusible element" who could not be assimilated into American society, wrote the young journalist Henry George in a famous 1869 letter that made his reputation as a spokesman for California labor. "They practice all the unnameable vices of the East. [They are] utter heathens, treacherous, sensual, cowardly and cruel." Sadly, this vicious racism was intertwined with labor's republican ideals. The Chinese, argued George, would drive out free labor, "make nabobs and princes of our capitalists, and crush our working classes into the dust . . . substitut[ing] . . . a population of serfs and their masters for that population of intelligent freemen who are our glory and our strength."

The anti-Chinese agitation climaxed in San Francisco in the late 1870s when mobs ruled the streets, at one point threatening to burn the docks of the Pacific Mail Steamship Company at which the Chinese arrivals landed. The fiercest agitator, an Irish teamster named Denis Kearney, quickly became a dominant figure in the California labor movement. Under the slogan "The Chinese Must Go!" Kearney led a Workingmen's party that strongly challenged the state's major parties. Democracts and Republicans, however, jumped on the bandwagon, joining together in 1879 to write a new state constitution replete with anti-Chinese provisions and pressuring Washington to take up the issue. Finally, after renegotiating the Burlingame Treaty (1868) that had granted China most-favored-nation trade status, Congress in 1882 passed the Chinese Exclusion Act, which barred the further entry of Chinese laborers into the country.

Chinese immigration effectively came to an end, but not the job opportunities that had attracted the Chinese in the first place. If anything, the West's agricultural development intensified the demand for cheap labor, especially in California, which was shifting from wheat, the state's first great cash crop, to fruits and vegetables.

This intensive agriculture required lots of workers: stoop labor, meagerly paid and mostly seasonal. This was not, as one San Francisco journalist put it, "white men's work." That ugly phrase serves as a touchstone for California agricultural labor as it would thereafter develop—a kind of caste labor system, always drawing some downtrodden, footloose whites into it, yet basically defined along color lines. But if not the Chinese, then who? First, Japanese immigrants, who came in increasing numbers and by the early twentieth century constituted half of the state's agricultural labor force. Then, when anti-Japanese agitation closed off that population flow in 1908, Mexico became the next, essentially permanent, provider of migratory workers for California's booming commercial agriculture.

The irony of the state's social evolution is painful to behold. Here was California, a land of limitless opportunity, boastful of its democratic egalitarianism. Yet simultaneously, and from its very birth, it was a racially torn society, at once exploiting and despising the Hispanic and Asian minorities whose hard labor helped make California the enviable land it was.

The Golden West

The hundreds of thousands of fortune seekers who descended on California changed everything. Mineral wealth poured in, first from the gold country, then from Nevada's Comstock lode, and finally from mining sites up and down the Far West. Railroad building accelerated and agriculture boomed. California counted over a million residents by 1890, fully a quarter of them living in San Francisco.

Life in California contained all that the modern world of 1890 had to offer—a cosmopolitan city, com-

Market Scene, Sansome Street
This exuberant painting by William Hahn captures downtown San Francisco as he saw it in 1872, a veritable boiling pot of races (note the black woman at left and the Chinese group at right) and classes (note, in the middle of the market bustle, the proper lady at far left with her Lord Fauntleroy son). It was its role as metropolis for the entire Far West that gave San Francisco the great vitality conveyed in this painting. (Crocker Art Museum)

fortable travel, a high living standard, colleges and universities, and even resident painters and writers. Yet California was still remote from the rest of America, still a long journey away and, of course, differently and spectacularly endowed by nature. Location, environment, and history all conspired to set California somewhat apart from the American nation. And so, in certain ways, did the Californians.

California Culture. What Californians yearned for was a cultural tradition of their own. Closest to hand was the bonanza era of the Forty-Niners. California had the great good fortune of attracting to its parts one Samuel Clemens. Clemens arrived in the Nevada Territory in 1861, did a bit of prospecting, became a reporter in Nevada City, and adopted the pen name Mark Twain. In 1864 he left for San Francisco, where he became a newspaper columnist writing about what he pronounced "the livest, heartiest community on our continent."

Exiled briefly in 1865 to Angel's Camp in the Sierra foothills because his sharp pen had made him dangerous enemies, Twain listened to the tales of the old miners from the neighborhood. One he jotted in his notebook, as follows:

> Coleman with his jumping frog—bet stranger $50—stranger had no frog, and C. got him one:—in the meantime stranger filled C's frog full of shot and he couldn't jump. The stranger's frog won.

In Twain's hands this fragment was transformed into a tall tale that caught the imagination of the country and made his reputation as a humorist. What "The Celebrated Jumping Frog of Calaveras County" had somehow encapsulated was the entire world of make-or-break optimism in the mining camps.

In short stories such as "The Luck of Roaring Camp" and "The Outcasts of Poker Flat," Twain's fellow San Franciscan Bret Harte developed this theme in a more literary fashion and firmly implanted it in California's memory. Other writers—among them the amateur historian Charles Howard Shinn in his *Mining Camps: A Study in American Frontier Government* (1885)—gave a more serious gloss to California's bonanza origins. Even so, this past was too raw, too suggestive of the tattered beginnings of so many of the state's leading citizens—in short, too disreputable—for an up-and-coming society.

Then, in 1884, Helen Hunt Jackson published her novel *Ramona*. In this story of a half-caste girl caught between two cultures, Jackson intended to advance the cause of the Indians, but she placed her tale in the evocative context of Old California, and that rang a bell. By then the Spanish missions—disestablished by the Mexican government in 1833, long before the influx of Yankees—had fallen into total disrepair and the padres were wholly forgotten, their Indian acolytes scattered and in dire poverty. Now that lost world of "sun, silence and adobe" became all the rage. Sentimental novels and histories appeared in abundance, and there was a movement to restore the missions. The Spanish-Mexican dons of the great ranchos became larger in death than they had ever been in life. Many communities began to stage Spanish fiestas, and the mission style of architecture enjoyed a great vogue among developers.

In its Spanish past California found the cultural traditions it needed. The same kind of discovery was taking place elsewhere in the Southwest, although in the case of Santa Fe and Taos there were live Hispanic roots to celebrate.

Land of Sunshine. All this enthusiasm was of course strongly tinged with commercialism, as was a second distinctive feature of California's development. The southern part of the state was neglected, thinly populated, and too dry for anything but grazing and some chancy wheat growing. What it did have, however, was an abundance of sunshine. At the beginning of the 1880s there burst upon the country amazing news about the charms of southern California. "There is not any malaria, hay fever, loss of appetite, or languor in the air; nor any thunder, lightning, mad dogs . . . or cold snaps." This publicity was mostly the work of the Southern Pacific Railroad, which had reached Los Angeles in 1876 and was eager for business. When the Santa Fe arrived in 1885, a furious rate war broke out and it became possible to travel from Chicago or St. Louis to Los Angeles for $25 or less. Thousands of people, mostly midwesterners, poured in; a dizzying real estate boom developed, along with the frantic building of resort hotels such as San Diego's opulent Hotel del Coronado. Los Angeles County had less than 3 percent of the state's population in 1870; it had 12 percent by 1900. Although the real estate bubble burst at the end of the 1880s, by then southern California had firmly established itself as the land of sunshine and orange groves. It had found a way to translate climate into riches.

The Great Outdoors. That California was specially favored by nature some Californians knew even as the great stands of redwoods and sugar pine were being hacked down, the soil depleted by the relentless cycle of wheat crops, the streams polluted, and the hills torn apart by reckless mining techniques. Back in 1864 influential Americans who had seen it prevailed on Congress to grant to the state of California "the Cleft, or Gorge in the granite peak of the Sierra Nevada Mountain, known as Yosemite Valley," which would be reserved "for public pleasuring, resort, and recreation." When the young naturalist John Muir arrived in California four years later, he headed straight for Yosemite. Its "grandeur . . . comes as an endless revelation," he

Kitty Tatch and Friend on Glacier Point, Yosemite
From the time the Yosemite Valley was set aside in 1864 as a place for "public pleasuring, resort, and recreation," it attracted a stream of tourists eager to experience the grandeur of the American West. As is suggested by this photograph taken sometime in the 1890s, the magic of Yosemite was enough to set even staid young ladies dancing.

wrote. Muir, and others like him, became devoted to studying the High Sierras and protecting them from "despoiling gain-seekers . . . eagerly trying to make everything immediately and selfishly commercial." One result was the creation of California's national parks in 1890—Yosemite, Sequoia, and King's Canyon. Another was the formation in 1892 of the Sierra Club, which became a powerful voice of the defenders of California's wilderness.

They won some and lost some. In particular, there was an uphill battle against the advocates of water-resource development, who insisted that California's irrigated agriculture and thirsty cities could not grow without tapping the abundant snowpack of the Sierras. By the turn of the century, Los Angeles faced a water crisis that threatened its growth. The answer was a 238-mile aqueduct to the Owens River in the southern Sierras. A bitter controversy blew up over this immense project, driven by objections by local residents and

preservationists to the damming up of the beautiful Owens Valley. More painful was the defeat suffered by John Muir and his allies in their battle to save the Hetch Hetchy gorge north of Yosemite National Park. In 1913, after years of controversy, the federal government approved the damming of Hetch Hetchy to serve the water needs of San Francisco.

When the development stakes became high enough, nature lovers like John Muir generally came out on the short end. Even so, something original and distinctive had been added to California's heritage—the linking of a society's well-being with the preservation of its natural environment.

The Agricultural Interest

In certain grain-growing areas, such as California's Central Valley until the 1890s, farmers might be large-scale and even corporate operators. In the South after Reconstruction the typical farmer was a tenant or sharecropper. Elsewhere, and most commonly, farmers were independent freeholders operating family farms. The freeholder tradition was deeply rooted in the Jeffersonian ideal of a country of independent farmers, an ideal enshrined in the national policy of providing land from the public domain for homesteaders. In an age of trusts and corporations, farmers succeeded as did no other group in retaining the *forms* of economic independence. But their *functions* took them far from the self-sufficient yeoman farmer tradition of Jeffersonian America. American farmers had, for better or worse, been fully inducted into the modern economic order.

The Farming Business

With the settlement of the Great Plains, the regional patterns of American agriculture (see Map 17.7) became well defined. The wheat belt lay on the western edge of the Midwest, from North Dakota down to Kansas and into northern Texas. Wheat had always been a virgin crop, the first to be planted when new land opened up. As the frontier moved on, wheat growing moved steadily westward. It settled on the Great Plains, where hardy European strains resisted the harsh climate and produced a bread flour superior to that from the soft-kerneled wheat of milder regions. On the wheat-producing Columbia plateau in the Northwest, Spanish and Australian varieties did best. In the Midwest the main crop was corn—feed for the nation's livestock. North of the corn belt, dairy farming stretched from Minnesota as far east as New York and New England. In California wheat growing gave way to orange groves, fruit orchards, vineyards, and vegetable crops. Cotton

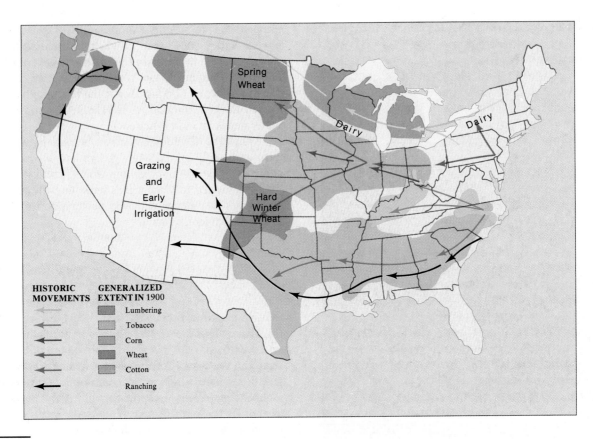

MAP 17.7

Agricultural Regions, 1900
The development of agricultural regions reflected the commercial bent of American agriculture—that is, farmers raised crops for market rather than for home consumption. Regional specialization matched climate and soil to the most suitable crops. The westward movement carried crops westward, of course. Wheat, generally a first crop choice in frontier areas, was concentrated finally on the northern and central plains and in the Northwest. By 1900 the basic pattern of crop specialization was well established in the United States.

dominated southern agriculture, spreading during the last third of the nineteenth century westward from the old Cotton Kingdom into Texas and northward into Oklahoma and Arkansas.

General farming, in which no crop represented as much as 40 percent of a farm's total production, was still common; and so was subsistence farming in areas, such as New England and the southern Appalachians, where the terrain was hilly and infertile. But a cash crop was what farmers wanted, and that preference made for the remarkable regional specialization of American agriculture. "The old rule that a farmer should produce all he required is part of the past," remarked one farm journal. "Agriculture, like all other business, is better for its subdivisions, each one growing that which is best suited for his soil, skill, climate and market, and with its proceeds purchasing his other needs."

Specialization in cash crops was one manifestation of the commercial bent of American farmers. Another was their attitude toward land. Americans had little of

the passionate identification with the soil that tied European peasants to their inherited plots. In 1910 more than half of American farmers had moved within the previous five years. Farmers saw their acreage as a commodity. In frontier areas, where newly developed land appreciated rapidly, they anticipated as much profit, if not more, from the land's value as from the crops it produced. Nor were farmers averse to borrowing money. In boom times they rushed into debt to buy more land and better farm equipment. They relished the innovations of the industrial age, especially the railroad. They happily supported whatever inducements that might be necessary, such as the public purchase of railway bonds, to lure a line to their towns. All these enthusiasms—for cash crops, land speculation, borrowed money, and new technology—bore witness to the conviction that farming was a business, "like all other business."

The bedrock of their commercial identity was the larger economic system in which they were situated: farmers stood at the center of a vast and complex network of trade and industry. A sophisticated array of commodity exchanges determined prices and found buyers throughout the country and beyond. Great processing industries turned wheat into flour, livestock into dressed meat, and fruits and vegetables into canned goods. Entire rail systems, port facilities, and fleets of ships were devoted to moving the products of American farmers. All this activity gave farmers access to the expanding urban markets in the United States and overseas; about 20 percent of American agricultural production went abroad during the late nineteenth century. American farmers were likewise abundantly supplied with modern goods and services. The capital they needed came, via mortgage companies and banks, from distant eastern and European lenders. The McCormick Reaper Company, John Deere, and other manufacturers sold them labor-saving farm machinery that cut production costs for the leading crops by about half between 1850 and 1900.

No one could deny that the result was an agricultural system of amazing abundance; farm output more than tripled between 1860 and 1900. To an Austrian observer reflecting on the scarcity that had always been humankind's lot, the surplus produced by American agriculture seemed "the greatest event of modern times."

Agrarian Distress

Somehow this triumph of American agriculture as a productive system did not translate into good times on the farm. On the contrary, the late nineteenth century was a time of deep agricultural discontent.

Farm Life. The grievances of farmers stemmed partly from the harshness of rural life. No one labored longer or harder. Farmers worked an average of sixty-eight hours a week in 1900, twelve hours longer than industrial workers; in 1850 the difference had been only six hours. Mechanization did not actually reduce the workload on farms, as it generally did in factories. Crop acreage tended to increase in step with more efficient planting and harvesting machinery. Most other chores remained on the farmer's shoulders.

For women, too, farming demanded unrelenting labor. Like other work in America, farm work was sextyped. Except under dire necessity, northern farm women did not labor in the fields after the pioneering days. It was true that substantial numbers of widows and single women ran farms on their own—300,000 were recorded in the 1900 census—but the evidence suggests that these women mostly relied on hired hands for the heavy field work. In the South, especially among poor tenant farmers, it was different; wives, both black and white, commonly went into the fields, making "a full hand at whatever the occasion demands—plowing, hoeing, chopping, putting down fertilizer, picking cotton."

Even without working in the fields, however, farm women contributed crucially to the farm enterprise. Farming could be thought of as a "dual economy" in which men's labor brought in the big payment at season's end while women's labor provisioned the family day by day and produced a steady bit of money for groceries. And if the crop failed, it was women's labor that carried the family through. No wonder rural society placed a high premium on marriage: a mere 2.4 percent of Nebraska women in 1900 had never married. The western farmer was well advised to take a wife for the "pecuniary advantage in the domestic economy of his household."

Throughout rural America, children, as soon as they were old enough, pitched in with the farm chores and field work. "Many a time a shudder has passed through the mother heart of me," said a Missouri woman, "at the sight of some little fellow struggling with the handles of a plow, jerking and stumbling over cloddy ground from daylight till dark. Boys 'making a full hand,' 'helping Pa.'" Farm children in 1900 attended school only two-thirds as many days as did city children, and they left school at an earlier age. In an era of rapidly advancing urban education farm children still attended gloomy, ungraded one-room schools—hardly the little red schoolhouses of popular mythology.

Rural Schooling

In one-room schoolhouses, such as this one, probably in Colorado, farm children got the rudiments of an education. Teaching offered one of the few opportunities for rural women to support themselves and obtain a paying job, albeit for very skimpy wages.

Farm families might have accepted how hard they labored, how the men and women were worn out and the children sacrificed, for the living they wrested from the soil. It was harder to swallow the widening discrepancy in the quality of life between farm and city. Electricity, indoor plumbing, and paved roads had not yet come to the farm. Work in the kitchen remained almost unaffected by appliances that were already commonplace in many urban homes. Laundry was "the most trying" of all household chores, involving long hours spent lugging and boiling water, bent over washtubs and rubbing boards. Even on well-equipped farms, a Michigan woman observed, "the women must still do the work much as their mothers did before." "I have in mind a small, delicate woman," wrote another woman from Pennsylvania, "with a family of small children who does all her own housework, milks four or five cows, cooks for extra help, carries from the spring all the water—no time to read a paper or book. . . . Yet neither [her husband] nor she has any idea they could make her burden easier."

The isolation of homesteading was most severely felt on the Great Plains, with its cruel winters and long, empty distances. Farm life everywhere, however, tended to be lonely and circumscribed. Rural neighborhoods, even in long-settled areas, totaled 3 or 4 square miles where perhaps a dozen families lived. As one writer remarked, "the end of the neighborhood was almost the end of the world." Hamlin Garland and other authors of the late nineteenth century wrote powerfully about the dullness of the countryside and the lure of the city. "I hate farm life," grumbled one of Garland's heroines. "It's nothing but fret, fret and work the whole time, never going any place, never seeing anybody but a lot of neighbors just as big fools as you are. I spend my time fighting flies and washing dishes and churning. I'm sick of it all."

Understandably, when farmers formed organizations they provided for social activity first of all. This was true of the National Grange of the Patrons of Husbandry, whose local granges spread by the thousands across rural America in the early 1870s. The Grange became the social center for farm families through its fraternal ceremonies and its dances, picnics, and lectures. Women and men joined on an equal footing. Oliver H. Kelley, the government clerk who founded the Grange in 1867, hoped that participation by "the young folks of both sexes . . . will have a tendency to instill in their minds a fondness of rural life, and prevent in great measure so many of them flocking to the cities."

Economic Problems. The hunger for social activity cemented organizational ties, but the dynamism of agrarian movements came from economic grievances. The

farmers' basic problem was their imperfect participation in the economic transformations of the late nineteenth century. They remained individual operators in a business world that was becoming ever more complex and highly organized. And they were, in certain ways, acutely aware of their predicament. They understood, for example, the disadvantages they faced as individuals dealing with the big businesses that supplied them with machinery, arranged their credit, and marketed their products.

Farmers had first formed cooperatives, mostly stores and creameries, before the Civil War. The Grange took up the cooperative idea in a big way by purchasing in bulk from suppliers and by setting up cooperative banks, insurance companies, grain elevators, and processing plants. The Iowa Grange even started to manufacture farm implements in 1873.

Unfortunately, opposition by private business was too unrelenting, cooperative managers too unskilled, and the pooled resources of the farmers too thin. Most of the Grange cooperatives eventually failed. The cooperative idea, however, was highly resilient and would be revived by every successive farmers' movement. Ultimately, in the twentieth century, rural cooperatives of many kinds—marketing unions, stores, grain elevators, telephone exchanges—would dot the countryside. The farmers' hostility to middlemen also left as a legacy the great mail-order house of Montgomery Ward, which had been founded in 1872 to serve Grange members. As a solution to the organizational weakness of the farmer in the marketplace, however, cooperative movements had to be accounted a failure.

The power of government, however, might be enlisted to do for farmers what they could not do for themselves. The Grange was itself a social-educational organization, but in the early 1870s it encouraged the formation of independent political parties that ran on antimonopoly platforms. The main targets were grain elevator companies and railroads that routinely cheated farmers (so they felt) on storage charges, wheat grading, and freight rates. In a number of prairie states these agrarian parties won control of the legislature and passed so-called Granger laws regulating grain elevators, fixing maximum railroad rates, and prohibiting discriminatory practices against small and short-haul shippers. Constitutional difficulties arose, however, over the question of whether the states were exceeding their police powers when they tried to regulate interstate commerce. In *Wabash v. Illinois* (1886) the Supreme Court decided that they were, voiding an Illinois law that prohibited long- and short-haul rate discrimination and putting all the Granger laws in jeopardy. By then, however, a movement had started for federal regulation of the railroads. The Interstate Commerce Act (1887) created the Inter-

TABLE 17.1

Freight Rates for Transporting Crops

	Grand Island to Omaha (150 miles)				Grand Island to Chicago (650 miles)		
Date effective	Corn	Wheat (in cents per hundredweight)	Oats	Date effective	Corn	Wheat (in cents per hundredweight)	Oats
January 1, 1883	18	19½	18	January 7, 1880	32	45	32
April 16, 1883	15	16½	15	September 15, 1882	38	43	38
January 10, 1884	18	19½	18	April 5, 1887	34	39	34
March 1, 1884	17	19½	17	November 1, 1887	25	30	25
August 25, 1884	20	20	20	March 21, 1890	22½	30	25
April 5, 1887	10	16	10	October 22, 1890	22	26	22
November 1, 1887	10	12	10	January 15, 1891	23	28	25

Source: Sigmund Diamond, ed., *The Nation Transformed* (New York: George Braziller, 1963), p. 352.

state Commerce Commission—the first federal regulatory agency—and made railroad regulation a permanent part of national public policy, although not with much practical effect for the next twenty years.

Farmers turned to cooperatives and government regulation out of a deep sense of organizational disadvantage. But that disadvantage, real as it was, did not really account for the unprofitability of farming in these years. Manufacturers and banks lacked the degree of market control ascribed to them by angry farmers. The much-maligned mortgage companies actually could not rig credit markets in the western states; their interest rates matched those in the rest of the country. Nor, for the period 1865–1890, could manufacturers establish a relative price advantage over agriculture. In fact, the wholesale prices of all commodities fell at a slightly faster rate than did farm prices during these years. And on the railroads, freight rates fell steadily and East-West differentials narrowed as improved technology reduced operating costs and the volume of western traffic increased (see Table 17.1).

The Wheat and Cotton Belts. The impact of the general fall in prices, or *deflation*, did have dire consequences for certain kinds of farmers, however. First, there were those whose crops were subject to wider, more unpredictable price swings—namely, cotton and wheat. The second category of farmers at risk in deflationary periods were those in debt, since falling prices forced them to pay back more in real terms than they had borrowed. And who was most deeply in debt? The same two groups: cotton and wheat farmers.

The nature of their indebtedness was different. Tenant farmers growing cotton normally got credit from the local furnishing merchant to carry them through the growing season, with the crop serving as collateral. The debt was short-term but nevertheless painfully hard if they had to repay with earnings reduced by falling cotton prices. For wheat farmers, indebtedness was a more deep-seated and entangling problem because, in the nineteenth century, wheat was characteristically a virgin-land crop. Settling new land meant going into debt to start up—to pay for machinery, fencing, a new house, and so on. So wheat farmers were frequently debtors. And if, as commonly occurred in frontier areas, a speculative spirit took hold and land prices were bid up, the debt burdens of newly mortgaged farmers could become insupportable when prices dropped.

This happened, for example, in Harrison Township, Nebraska, which was first settled in 1872. Land that sold for $8 an acre in 1880 brought $25 and up a few years later. Given wheat prices in the late 1880s, an investigator noted, no one taking out a mortgage to buy land at $25 an acre could hope to meet the payments at 6 percent interest. "One is almost tempted to draw the moral that the would-be purchaser . . . had almost better throw his money away than invest it in farming operations in Nebraska."

In the 1870s the major wheat-growing states had been Illinois, Wisconsin, and Minnesota. Those states had been at the center of the Granger agitation of that decade. By the 1880s wheat had moved on to the Great Plains. Among the indebted wheat farmers of Kansas, Nebraska, and the Dakotas, along with the cotton farmers of the South, the deflationary economy of the 1880s made for stubbornly hard times. All it would take was a sharp drop in world prices for wheat and cotton to bring on a real crisis.

Summary

In 1860 the Great Plains were still the ancestral home of nomadic Indian tribes that had built a vibrant society based on the horse and the buffalo. By 1890 the Indians had been crowded onto reservations and forced to abandon their tribal way of life. With railroads leading the way, cattle ranchers and homesteaders in short order displaced the Indians and domesticated the Great Plains. Beyond the Rockies, a different pattern of settlement occurred. Because so much of this region was arid and uninhabitable, occupation took the form of oases of settlement rather than the progressive occupation along a broad frontier that had prevailed east of the Rockies. And while arable land had been the lure for settlers up to that point, what drove settlement beyond the Rockies was the discovery of mineral wealth. For the entire trans-Mississippi West, the pace of occupation was accelerated by the nation's economic development. Industry needed the West's mineral resources; the cities demanded agricultural products; and, from railroads to barbed wire, the industrial economy provided the means for a swift and decisive conquest of the West.

By population, economy, and strategic position, California was the regional power dominating the Far West in the late nineteenth century. It was the anchor both of a crescent of Hispanic settlement to the southwest and of the Pacific slope region stretching up to the Canadian border. The discovery of gold had set off a huge migration that overwhelmed the thinly spread Hispanic inhabitants and swiftly transformed California into a populous state with a large urban sector. California developed a distinctive culture that capitalized on its rediscovered Hispanic heritage and its climate and natural environment. The treatment of the Chinese, Japanese, and Mexicans who provided the state with cheap labor, however, infused a dark streak of racism into its society.

The settlement of the West completed a national agricultural development characterized by regional crop specialization. American farming became integrated into the modern industrial order. However, that integration was imperfect, in particular because farming remained a family operation in an economy increasingly dominated by large-scale enterprise. Most aggrieved, and most prepared to protest, were the cotton farmers of the South and the wheat farmers of the Great Plains.

TIMELINE

1849	California Gold Rush Chinese migration begins
1862	Homestead Act
1864	Yosemite Valley reserved as public park
1865	Long Drive of Texas longhorns begins
1867	Patrons of Husbandry (the Grange) founded U.S. government adopts reservation policy for Plains Indians
1868	Indian treaty confirms Sioux rights to Powder River hunting grounds
1869	Union Pacific–Central Pacific transcontinental railroad completed
1874	Barbed wire invented
1875	Sioux ordered to vacate Powder River hunting grounds; war breaks out
1876	Battle of Little Big Horn
1877	San Francisco anti-Chinese riots
1879	Exoduster migration to Kansas
1882	Chinese Exclusion Act
1884	Helen Hunt Jackson's novel *Ramona*
1886	Dry cycle begins on the Great Plains *Wabash v. Illinois*
1887	Dawes Severalty Act Interstate Commerce Act
1889	Oklahoma opened to white settlement
1890	Indian massacre at Wounded Knee, South Dakota U.S. census declares end of the frontier

BIBLIOGRAPHY

Western history has become a bitterly contested ground in recent years. The fountainhead of the voluminous traditional scholarship is Frederick Jackson Turner's famous essay "The Significance of the Frontier in American History" (1893), reprinted in Ray A. Billington, ed., *Frontier and Section: Selected Essays of Frederick Jackson Turner* (1961). The most comprehensive recent Turnerian history is Ray A. Billington and Martin Ridge, *Westward Expansion: A History of the American Frontier*, 5th ed. (1982). The "new" western history is critical of Turnerian scholarship for being "Eurocentric"— for seeing this history only through the eyes of frontiersmen and settlers—and for masking the rapacious and environmentally destructive underside of western settlement. Patricia N. Limerick's skillfully argued *The Legacy of Conquest: The Unbroken Past of the American West* (1987) opened the debate. Richard White, *"It's Your Misfortune and None of My Own": A New History of the American West* (1991), provides the fullest synthesis of the new scholarship. For an authoritative, balanced treatment of the main themes of western history, see the essays in Clyde A. Milner II et al., *The Oxford History of the American West* (1994). On women's experience—another primary concern of the new western history—the starting point is Susan Armitage and Elizabeth Jameson, eds., *The Women's West* (1987). There are incisive environmental essays in Donald Worster, *Under Western Skies: Nature and History in the American West* (1992). For the period covered by this chapter, see Rodman Paul, *The Far West and the Great Plains in Transition, 1859–1900* (1988).

The Great Plains

The classic book, stressing the settlers' adaptation to climate and environment, is Walter P. Webb, *The Great Plains* (1931). There is an excellent chapter on the ecological history of the southern plains in Donald Worster, *The Dust Bowl* (1979). Robert M. Utley, *The Indian Frontier of the American West, 1846–1890* (1984), is a good introduction and Robert H. Lowie, *Indians of the Great Plains* (1954), is a classic anthropological study. On the religious life of the Plains Indians, see Howard L. Harrod, *Renewing the World: Plains Indians Religion and Morality* (1987). The best study of white attitudes is Richard Drinnon, *Facing West: The Metaphysics of Indian-Hating and Empire-Building* (1980). On phases of plains settlement see Oscar Winther, *The Transportation Frontier: The Trans-Mississippi West, 1865–1890* (1964); Lewis Atherton, *The Cattle Kings* (1964); Everitt Dick, *Sod-House Frontier* (1954); and Mary W. M. Hargreaves, *Dry-Farming in the Northern Great Plains* (1954). The peopling of the plains can be explored in Craig Miner, *West of Wichita: Settling the High Plains of Kansas 1865–1890* (1986); Frederick C. Luebke, ed., *Ethnicity and the Great Plains* (1980); Nell Irvin Painter, *Exodusters: Black Migration to Kansas after Reconstruction* (1976); Julie Roy Jeffrey, *Frontier Women: The Trans-Mississippi West, 1840–1880* (1979); and Glenda Riley, *The Female Frontier: A Comparative View of the Prairie and the Plains* (1988). On the integration of the plains economy with the wider world, an especially rich book is William Cronon, *Nature's Metropolis: Chicago and the Great West* (1991). Richard Slotkin, *The Fatal Environment: The Myth of the Frontier in the Age of Industrialization, 1800–1890* (1985), deals with the process by which Americans translated the hard realities of conquering the West into a national mythology.

California and the Far West

The best book on western mining is Rodman Paul, *Mining Frontiers of the Far West: 1848–1880s* (1963). An important case study of women in a mining town is Paula Petrik, *Women and Family on the Rocky Mountain Frontier: Helena, Montana, 1865–1900* (1987). On western miners the standard book is Mark Wyman, *Hard Rock Epic: Western Miners and the Industrial Revolution, 1860–1910* (1979). Two valuable regional histories are Carlos A. Schwantes, *The Pacific Northwest: An Interpretive History* (1989), and Donald W. Meinig, *Southwest: Three Peoples in Geographical Change, 1600–1970* (1971). A very imaginative recent treatment of the New Mexico peasantry is Sarah Deutsch, *No Separate Refuge* (1987). On Hispanic Texas an important book is David Montejano, *Anglos and Mexicans in the Making of Texas* (1987). Leonard Pitt, *The Decline of the Californios: A Social History of the Spanish-Speaking Californians, 1846–1890* (1960), offers a narrative history of that subject, with an emphasis on the fate of the large ranchers. Important local studies of laboring Hispanics and their communities are Mario T. Garcia, *Desert Immigrants: The Mexicans of El Paso, 1880–1920* (1981), and Richard Griswold del Castillo, *The Los Angeles Barrio, 1850–1890* (1979). On the Asian migration to America, the best introduction is Ronald Takaki, *Strangers from a Different Shore: A History of Asian Americans* (1989), which can be supplemented with Gunther Barth, *Bitter Strength: A History of the Chinese in the United States, 1850–1870* (1964), and Sucheng Chan, *This Bittersweet Soil: The Chinese in California Agriculture, 1860–1910* (1986). Labor's opposition to the Chinese is skillfully treated in Alexander Saxton, *The Indispensable Enemy: Labor and the Anti-Chinese Movement in California* (1971). Kevin Starr, *California and the American Dream, 1850–1915* (1973), provides a comprehensive account of the emergence of a distinctive California culture. On John Muir and the California wilderness, see Michael L. Smith, *Pacific Visions: California Scientists and the Environment, 1850–1915* (1987).

The Agricultural Interest

The standard works are Fred A. Shannon, *The Farmer's Last Frontier, 1860–1897* (1945); Gilbert Fite, *The Farmer's Frontier, 1865–1900* (1966); and Allan G. Bogue, *From Prairie to Corn Belt: Farming on the Illinois and Iowa Prairies in the Nineteenth Century* (1963). Most helpful on cotton farmers are the relevant chapters in Gavin Wright, *Old South, New South: Revolutions in the Southern Economy since the Civil War* (1986), and Edward L. Ayers, *The Promise of the New South: Life after Reconstruction* (1992). On farm women, see Deborah Fink, *Agrarian Women: Wives and Mothers in Rural Nebraska, 1880–1940* (1992), and Elaine Lindgren, *Land in Her Own Name: Women as Homesteaders in North Dakota* (1991). The flavor of farm life can best be captured in fiction: Hamlin Garland, *Main-Travelled Roads* (1891); Willa Cather, *My Antonia* (1918); and Ole E. Rölvaag, *Giants in the Earth* (1927).

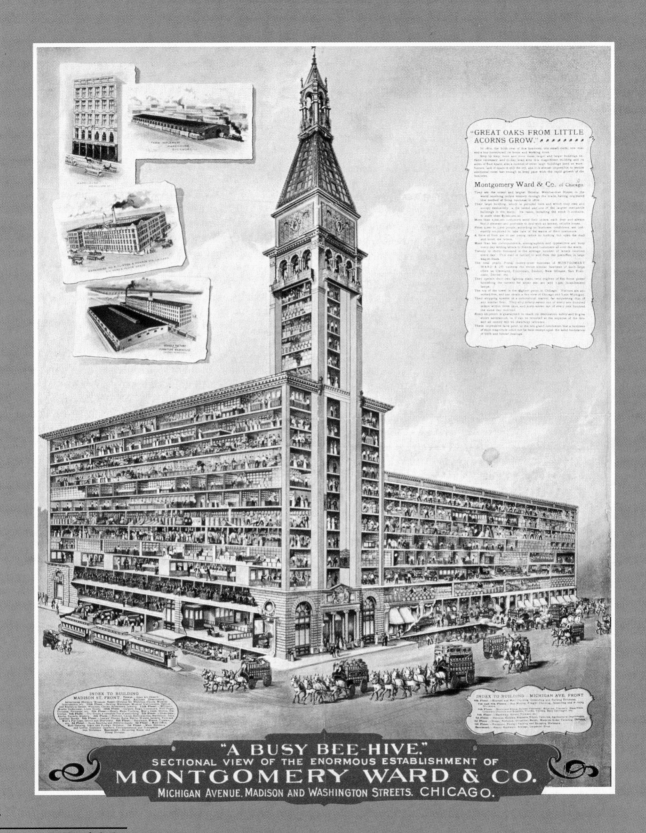

"A BUSY BEE-HIVE."
SECTIONAL VIEW OF THE ENORMOUS ESTABLISHMENT OF
MONTGOMERY WARD & CO.
MICHIGAN AVENUE, MADISON AND WASHINGTON STREETS, CHICAGO.

Montgomery Ward & Co.

In 1872 Aaron Montgomery Ward began selling goods to
rural customers through mail-order catalogues. Montgomery
Ward, along with Sears, Roebuck & Co., represented one
part of a revolution in American retailing, which included
department stores and chain stores as well as the great mail-
order houses.

Capital and Labor in the Age of Enterprise

1877–1900

★   ★   ★

Reconstruction ended in 1877. That year also marked the end of the first great crisis in America's emerging system of industrial capitalism. In 1873, four years earlier, the major banking house Jay Cooke & Co. had failed, triggering a financial panic. In the economic depression that followed, 47,000 firms went under. Wholesale prices fell about 30 percent, railroad building almost ground to a halt, and orders for industrial goods disappeared. And with unemployment running as high as 25 percent, hundreds of thousands of workers lost their jobs. Suffering was widespread. Across the country workers demanded "bread for the needy, clothing for the naked, and houses for the homeless." Before long the foundations of the social order began to shake.

On July 16, 1877, railroad workers in West Virginia went on strike against the Baltimore and Ohio system to protest wage cuts. In railway towns along the B&O tracks crowds cheered as the strikers attacked company property and prevented trains from running. The strike spread quickly to other lines. In Pittsburgh the Pennsylvania Railroad roundhouse went up in flames on July 21, followed by the Union Depot the next day. Rioters and looters roamed freely. For nearly a week violent strikes swept other cities, including San Francisco, St. Louis, Omaha, and Chicago. President Rutherford B. Hayes called up the National Guard, which gradually restored order. On August 15, the president wrote in his diary: "The strikers have been put down *by force*." The Great Strike of 1877 had been crushed, but never had the nation edged so close to social revolution.

And then recovery came. Within months the economy was booming again. The march toward industrial power resumed. The physical output of manufactured goods increased over 150 percent between 1877 and 1890. The vitality of industrial capitalism renewed America's confidence in the future. "Can there be any doubt that cheapening the cost of necessaries and conveniences of life is the most powerful agent of civilization and progress?" asked a railroad president in 1888. "History and experience demonstrate that . . . material progress must come first and . . . upon it is founded all other progress."

Industrial Capitalism Triumphant

Economic historians speak of the late nineteenth century as the age of the Great Deflation. Prices fell steadily worldwide, including in the United States. Following a brief upturn after 1877, wholesale prices declined by almost 30 percent between 1880 and 1892. Normally, falling prices are a sign of economic stagnation: there is not enough demand for the available goods and services. But that was not America's experience in these years. Because of increasing efficiencies in production and distribution, manufacturers were able both to cut prices *and* to earn profits and invest in better equipment. So that while in England, which was a mature industrial power, the Great Deflation did indeed signal economic decline, in the United States it was associated with dramatic industrial expansion (see Figure 18.1).

Basic Industry

By the 1870s manufacturing already had a long history in America. But the early factories were really appendages of the larger agricultural economy. They processed farm and forest products and, as in preindustrial times, relied on hand labor and water wheels for power. The goods they produced—textiles, boots and shoes, paper and furniture—were primarily consumer goods that replaced existing homemade or artisan-made products. Gradually, however, a different kind of demand developed. This was the result of the surging economic growth of the country. Railroads needed locomotives, new factories needed machinery, and the expanding cities needed vast quantities of building materials for trolley lines, sanitation systems, and commercial buildings. Locomotives, machinery, and construction materials were *capital goods*—that is, goods that themselves added to the productive capacity of the economy. While consumer goods remained very important, it was the manufacture of capital goods that became the core of America's industrial economy.

Iron and Steel. Central to this development was the shift from iron making to the manufacture of steel. An extensive metal-making industry already produced large quantities of wrought iron, whose malleability made it ideally suited for use by country blacksmiths and farmers. But wrought iron was expensive—it was produced in small batches by skilled puddlers and rollers—and did not stand up under heavy use as railway track. In 1856 the British inventor Henry Bessemer perfected a new process for refining iron. Unlike the puddling furnaces that made wrought iron, Bessemer converters produced steel—a harder, more durable metal—and did so in large amounts with little labor (see New Technology, page 553). Others took up this invention, but it was Andrew Carnegie who demonstrated its revolutionary importance.

Carnegie had arrived from Scotland in 1848 at the age of twelve with his poverty-stricken family. He became a telegraph operator and then went to work for the Pennsylvania Railroad and rapidly climbed the managerial ladder. Having become wealthy from a series of successful speculations, Carnegie resigned in 1865 to become an iron manufacturer. His main customers were his former associates in the railroad business.

Keenly aware of the possibilities of the Bessemer converter, Carnegie embarked in 1872 on a venture aimed at the fullest exploitation of the new refining

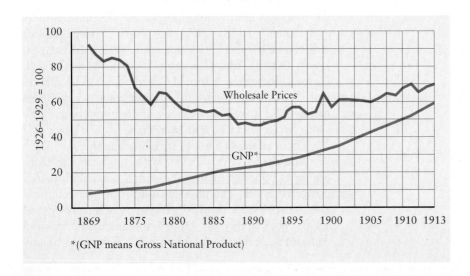

FIGURE 18.1

Business Activity and Wholesale Prices, 1869–1913
This graph shows the key feature concerning the performance of the late nineteenth-century economy: namely, that while output was booming, the price for goods was falling.

Iron and Steel

Iron was not a product new to the nineteenth century in the sense that plastic is new to the twentieth century. Early Europeans made iron tools and weapons at least a thousand years before Christ. Since those remote times the underlying processes have not changed, for these are dictated by the nature of iron metallurgy. What did change were the techniques for carrying out those processes.

The first break from ancient methods came when blast furnaces appeared in Belgium around 1340. Ore was melted in a charcoal-burning furnace to which limestone had been added. A blast of air then set off a combustion process that combined carbon from the charcoal with the molten iron while the impurities combined with the limestone to form a slag. The slag was drawn off from the top while the molten iron was tapped from the bottom into sand forms resembling piglets feeding from a sow—hence the term "pig iron."

By the late eighteenth century Great Britain was running out of wood for charcoal. The substitution of coke, made by superheating coal, saved the industry and gave Britain the competitive edge it needed to launch the Industrial Revolution. Endowed with ample forests, the United States was slow to adopt coke-using furnaces, but by 1860 it had caught up with Britain technologically.

The search for a metal harder and more durable than wrought iron resulted in the invention in 1856 of an entirely different refining process by the Englishman Henry Bessemer. The Bessemer converter was a pear-shaped vessel that was open at the top and had a bottom perforated by many holes. Molten pig iron flowed into the top while the converter was tilted on its side. Air was blasted through the perforated bottom with great force, and the converter then swung back to its upright position. The resulting combustion set off a spectacular display of flame and smoke. Within fifteen minutes, the impurities in the molten iron burned off and the flames died down. The converter was again tilted on its side, and after manganese and other chemicals had been added, the purified iron was emptied into ingot molds. The refined metal, called steel, was ideally suited for use as railroad track.

Bessemer's device, although invented primarily with the aim to gain a more durable metal, also proved vastly more efficient than the hand-operated puddling furnaces that produced wrought iron. The Bessemer converter turned out great quantities of steel with virtually no labor, and this forced changes up and down the line. To feed the converters' appetite for pig iron, blast fur-

The Bessemer Steel Furnace

naces were built larger and, with the introduction of the hot blast, became much faster. To handle the flow of steel from the converters, rolling mills became increasingly mechanized and automatic. The stages of production became integrated, which made the integrated steel plant of 1900—capable of producing 2,500 tons or more a day—a voracious consumer of ore and coal.

The commanding lead the United States had built up by 1900 rested on the world's best reserves of coking coal in western Pennsylvania and the vast ore deposits in Minnesota's Mesabi Range, northern Michigan's older fields, and Alabama.

The geographical face of American industrialism changed as the places best located in relation to raw materials, transportation, and markets—Pittsburgh, the steel towns along the Great Lakes, and Birmingham, Alabama—became the great centers of steel production. American cities relied on steel for the construction of skyscrapers, trolley lines, subways, and the vast underground complexes of pipe that supplied the urban millions with water and gas and carried away their sewage. Without steel, the emerging automobile industry would not have grown, nor would a host of other industries.

It is no wonder that historians have called the last decades of the nineteenth century America's Age of Steel. What was overlooked at the time and for long afterward was the fact that the nation's natural resources were not inexhaustible. It is the exhaustion of the great Mesabi Range that has leveled the playing field among global competitors and helped trigger the recent decline of the American steel industry.

process. He built a massive steel mill outside Pittsburgh that utilized the most advanced equipment of the day. Equally important, the mill integrated all the stages of production—smelting, refining, and rolling—into a single operation that began with iron ore and ended with finished steel rails. Carnegie's mill, which he named the Edgar Thompson Works after his admired former boss at the Pennsylvania Railroad, repaid its investment in a few years and became a model for the modern steel industry.

Large, integrated steel plants swiftly replaced the older blast furnaces and puddling mills. At first steel went mostly into railroad building; rails made up nearly three-quarters of the total output of steel in 1885. But thereafter, as railroad building slowed, the demand became more diversified. More and more steel went into bridges, skyscrapers, machinery, and a host of other industrial uses, such as pipes and tubing, sheet steel and wire, and armor for the nation's new navy.

Expanding the Industrial Base. The production of copper and other nonferrous metals went through a similar development. Before the Civil War, copper had been employed mainly in the manufacture of kettles, pots and pans, and other household products. Now it became a key ingredient in oil-refining equipment, electric generators, and other new products such as telephone cable. Copper output grew at a phenomenal rate, increasing from 14,000 tons in 1870 to 130,000 tons in 1890.

The growth of the metal industries depended on the intensive exploitation of the country's mineral resources. Major discoveries of rich iron ore deposits occurred from the 1850s onward, first in upper Michigan and then in the huge Mesabi Range of Minnesota. The Mesabi ore was shipped down the Great Lakes to the growing steelmaking centers in Pennsylvania, Ohio, and Illinois, giving the nearest lakeshore points, such as South Chicago and Gary, Indiana, a competitive advantage and contributing to the westward shift of the industry (see Map 18.1).

Coal mining, a minor enterprise before 1850, grew rapidly, first in the anthracite region of eastern Pennsylvania and then in the bituminous (soft coal) fields of western Pennsylvania and Ohio. The production of bituminous coal, the primary industrial fuel, doubled every decade after 1870 (see Table 18.1) and exceeded 400 million tons by 1910.

It was the insatiable energy needs of American industrialism that spurred this remarkable expansion in coal mining. Carnegie's blast furnaces and Bessemer converters burned prodigious amounts of coal. Coal-burning steam engines drove locomotives and ships and increasingly became the power source for factories. As much machinery was powered by steam engines as by water wheels by 1880; steam was six times as important twenty years later.

At the Philadelphia Centennial Exhibition of 1876 visitors gazed in wonder at the enormous Corliss reciprocating engine, which had a flywheel 30 feet in diameter and could drive all the other exhibits in Machinery Hall. The reciprocating engine, however, was superseded by the steam turbine in the 1880s. The turbine was an inherently superior design because it utilized continuous rotation rather than the back-and-forth motion of the reciprocating engine. These advances in turn

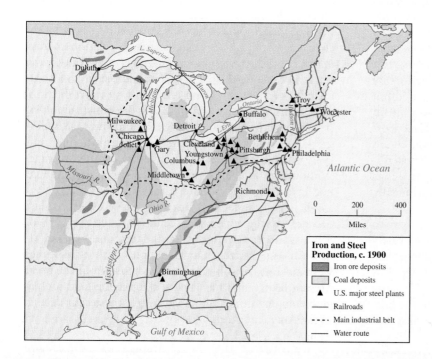

MAP 18.1

The Westward Movement of Iron and Steel Production

Before the Civil War, the iron industry was concentrated in eastern Pennsylvania and northern New Jersey. With the shift to steel and the westward movement of population and industry, production moved first to western Pennsylvania, and then to Ohio, Indiana, and Illinois and southward into Alabama. The specific locations—Pittsburgh, Youngstown, Chicago, Birmingham—were dictated by the rail network, new sources of coal and iron ore, and markets for steel.

TABLE 18.1

Increasing Output of Heavy Industry, 1870–1910

	Bituminous Coal (thousands of tons)	Rolled Iron and Steel (thousands of tons)	Copper (tons)	Industrial Machinery (millions of dollars)
1870	20,471	850*	14,112	110.4†
1880	50,757	3,301	30,240	98.6‡
1890	111,302	6,746	129,882	185.6
1900	212,318	10,626	303,059	347.6
1910	417,111	24,216	544,119	512.4

*Approximate total.
†Data for 1869.
‡Data for 1874.

The Corliss Engine
The symbol of the Philadelphia Centennial in 1876 was the great Corliss engine, which towered over Machinery Hall and powered all the equipment on exhibit there. Yet the Corliss engine also signified the incomplete nature of American industrialism at that time; it soon became obsolete. Westinghouse turbines generating electricity would be the power source for the nation's next great World's Fair in Chicago in 1893.

laid the basis for the next major innovation: the coupling of the steam turbine to the electric generator. After 1900 factories rapidly converted from steam to electric power.

Thus, in the decades after the Civil War the modern metal-producing industries were established, the nation's mineral resources came under intensive exploitation, and energy was harnessed to the manufacturing system. All these basic elements of modern industrialism—steel, coal, and energy output—grew after 1870 at rates far exceeding that of manufacturing production itself.

The Railroads

Much the largest demand for the capital goods mentioned in the previous section came from the railroads. They were the best customers for iron and steel, made the heaviest demands on the nation's machine-building capacity, and consumed a big portion of the coal it produced. Americans never doubted that they wanted railroads. Water transportation had developed impressively before the Civil War. But canal barges and riverboats, while good for carrying bulky raw materials, could not provide the year-round, on-time service demanded by the growing industrial economy.

Railroads had started in the 1830s as feeders linking river and canal traffic to inland towns and cities but quickly grew into a system that rivaled water transportation. By 1860, with a network of tracks already covering the states east of the Mississippi, the railroad clearly was going to be industrial America's mode of transportation (see Map 18.2).

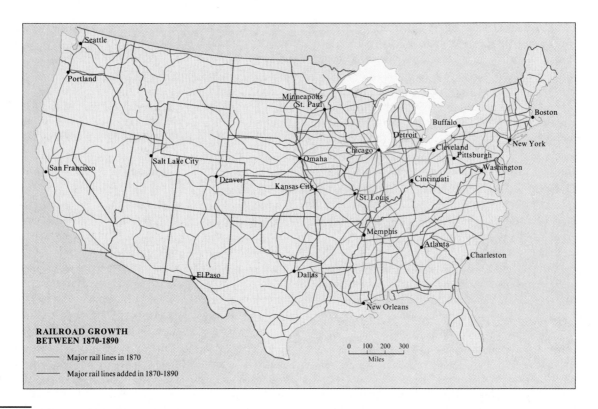

MAP 18.2

The Expansion of the Railroad System, 1870–1890

In 1870, the nation had 53,000 miles of rail track; in 1890, 167,000 miles. That burst of construction essentially completed the nation's rail network, although there would be additional expansion for the next two decades. The main areas of growth were in the South and west of the Mississippi. The Great Plains and the Far West accounted for over 40 percent of all railroad construction in this period.

The question was: Who would pay for railroad development? Two options were available. Railroads could be state enterprises, as the canals had been, supported by public funding as an internal improvement that would benefit the entire community. Or, alternatively, they could be treated as private enterprises financed by investors trying to make money.

The United States—unlike most European countries—chose to leave railroads to private enterprise, but there was no avoiding a big role for the government because of the huge public interest in getting the railroads built. Many towns and cities, for example, offered financial aid, mostly by subscribing for bonds, to attract railroads. States gave similar financial help, especially in the devastated South, where during Reconstruction railroads were seen as essential to economic recovery. States that had public domains, such as Texas and Maine, offered land grants to railroads. And land grants were the principal means by which the federal government encouraged interregional railroads, beginning in 1850 with the Illinois Central, which linked Chicago to the South, and culminating with huge grants to the transcontinental railroads because of the national inter-

est in tying the Far West to the rest of the country. Altogether, some 180 million acres were conveyed to the railroads from the state and federal domains.

The most important boost that government gave the railroads, however, was not money or land but a legal form of organization—the *corporation*—that enabled them to raise private capital in prodigious amounts. Those who bought stock in the railroads—and thus became their legal owners—enjoyed *limited liability*: they risked only the money they had invested; their personal assets could not be seized to pay the corporation's debts. A corporation also could borrow money by issuing interest-bearing bonds. Most of the money raised by the railroads came from bond issues; that is, it was borrowed money. Stock became a debased financial instrument, often given away to sweeten the sale of bonds or used by railroad promoters to gain control of other properties or reward themselves. Much of it represented no underlying value and was considered to be "watered."

The actual responsibility for railroad building generally was given over to a "construction company," which, despite the name, was really another part of the elaborate financing system. Hiring and compensating the contractors and suppliers—the formal job of the construction company—often involved persuading them to accept the railroad's bonds as payment and, when that failed, wheeling and dealing to raise cash by selling or borrowing on the bonds. Since the promoters of the railroad and the owners of the construction company were one and the same, the opportunities for plunder were enormous. In the case of the most notorious construction company, the Union Pacific's Crédit Mobilier, probably half the building costs ended up in the pockets of the promoters.

Railroad promotion was not for the faint of heart. Most successful were promoters with the best access to capital—their own or that of others. John Murray Forbes, a great Boston merchant in the China trade, recruited New England money to develop the Chicago, Burlington and Quincy Railroad into the preeminent midwestern system. Cornelius Vanderbilt, who left the steamboat business in 1863 to become a railroad tycoon, was essentially a consolidator, tying together previously independent lines up the Hudson River and across New York State to form the New York Central Railroad. Vanderbilt and his son William built the Central into a trunk line to Chicago that was rivaled only by the Pennsylvania Railroad. James J. Hill, who without federal subsidy made the Great Northern into the best of all the transcontinental railroads, was certainly the nation's champion railroad builder. In contrast, Jay Gould, who at one time or another controlled the Erie, Wabash, Union Pacific, and Missouri Pacific systems, always remained a stock-market speculator at heart. Whether he was a *robber baron*—someone who loots commerce and gives nothing in return—can be answered only by closer inspection of his career (see American Lives, pages 558–559).

Railroad development in the United States was often sordid, fiercely competitive, and subject to boom and bust. When the Panic of 1893 hit, a third of the industry (by track mileage) went bankrupt. Yet there was no denying what had been achieved. Vast sums of capital had been raised—well over $10 billion, probably a quarter of it attracted from Europe—and the network that was built exceeded the trackage of the rest of the world combined. By 1900 virtually no corner of the country lacked rail service.

The Railway System. Accompanying this physical growth was the rising efficiency of railway transportation. The early system, built by competing local companies, had been a jumble of discontinuous segments. Gauges of track—the width between the rails—varied widely, and at terminal points railroads were not physically connected. Many rivers lacked railroad bridges. Also, each railroad company reserved the use of its track exclusively for its own equipment. As late as 1880 goods could not be shipped through from Massachu-

setts to South Carolina. Eight times along the way, freight cars had to be emptied, with the contents physically moved and loaded onto new cars across a river or at the other side of a city.

Beginning with the Civil War years, however, pressure increased for integration of the railroads. Track was hastily laid through Philadelphia, Richmond, and other cities to speed the shipment of troops and equipment. The postwar economy, as it grew more complex and interdependent, demanded a better-organized rail system. Much railroad integration took place through the expansion of great trunk lines such as the Pennsylvania, New York Central, and Illinois Central to connect different regions of the country. By the end of the 1880s a standard track gauge (4 feet 8 1/2 inches) had been adopted across the country. In 1883 the railroads rebelled against the jumble of local times that made scheduling a nightmare and, acting on their own, divided the country into the four standard time zones that we still use. Fast-freight firms and standard accounting procedures enabled shippers to use the railroad network as if it were a single unit, moving their goods without breaks in transit, transfers between cars, or the other delays that had once bedeviled them.

At the same time, railroad technology was advancing. With more durable steel rails in place, locomotives became heavier and more powerful, freight cars progressively larger, and freight trains longer. The Consolidation-type locomotive, with four sets of driving wheels, nearly tripled the pulling power of freight trains. To control the great mass and length of the new freight trains, the inventor George Westinghouse perfected the automatic coupler, the air brake, and the friction gear for starting and stopping a long line of cars. Costs per ton-mile fell by 50 percent between 1870 and 1890, resulting in a steady drop in freight rates for shippers.

The railroads brilliantly met the transportation needs of the maturing industrial economy. However, this achievement did not stem from any orderly plan or design; it sprang from the competitive energy of a free-wheeling market economy. For the railroads, the costs of unrestrained growth were painfully high. On many routes there were too many railroads, and they fought for the available traffic by cutting rates to the bone. Many were saddled with huge bonded debt from the extravagant construction years; about a fifth of this volume of debt failed to pay interest even in a pretty good year such as 1889. So it was no wonder that when the economy turned bad, as it did in 1893, there were wholesale bankruptcies.

Out of the rubble, however, came a major railroad reorganization that was primarily the handiwork of Wall Street. Investment banking firms such as J. P. Morgan & Co. and Kuhn, Loeb & Co. had sprung up to feed the railroads' insatiable appetite for capital. Investment bankers performed the key middleman's role, taking the stocks and bonds issued by railroads and finding

Jay Gould:
Robber Baron?

... JAY GOULD was an operator pure and simple, although, in a general way of speaking, he was as far as possible from pure and as far as possible from simple. ... It would be at least very difficult to show that the Nation as a whole is a dollar richer by the existence of JAY GOULD, while he himself has become the richer ... from the expansion of the city and the Nation. He has simply absorbed what would have been made in spite of him.

Thus did the *New York Times* bid farewell to Jay Gould at his death on December 3, 1892. There was a name for the kind of businessman the *Times* thought Gould was: a robber baron—in the Middle Ages, the renegade knights who exacted tribute from all who passed by and in Gould's time, capitalists who extracted riches from, while adding nothing to, the economic system. By that definition, was Gould a robber baron? Yes, said historians for many years, following the thesis first advanced by Matthew Josephson in his book *The Robber Barons* (1934). Today, knowing a great more about Gould than Josephson ever did, historians are no longer so sure.

Jay Gould was born on May 27, 1836, in Roxbury, New York, in the mountainous Catskill region. John Gould wanted Jay, his only son, to take over the family farm, but the boy was small and sickly, and he detested farm work. By sheer tenacity Jay got more education than most farm boys, but tenacity could not get him to Yale, which had been his dream. At sixteen he became a surveyor, at nineteen he wrote a flowery history of Delaware County for money, and then at twenty he got a big break. An eccentric but wealthy tanner, Zadock Pratt, befriended Gould, taking him as a partner to set up a tannery in Pennsylvania, where Gould had located a rich new source of tanning bark. The venture succeeded thanks to Pratt's money and Gould's hard work, but after two years there was a falling out, and Pratt proposed terminating the partnership. He would buy Gould's share for $10,000 or sell out to the young man for $60,000. Gould found backers among the leather merchants who marketed the tannery's output and bought out the surprised Pratt. This was a typical Gould maneuver—bold, unexpected, and decisive. The new partnership quickly turned sour, primarily because

Jay Gould

of a collapse of the leather market. The damage to well-reputed merchants discredited Gould in the leather trade. He had made money amid the wreckage of other people's businesses, another Gould trademark. In 1860 he settled in New York, bent on satisfying what had become his obsession: he wanted to be rich.

Enlisting in the Union army probably never occurred to him; the Civil War was too good a chance for turning quick profits; and besides, Gould had no taste for fighting. He married the daughter of a wealthy New York merchant in 1863, sired six children in rapid succession, and became a devoted family man. These were, above all, schooling years for Gould. He learned about the railroads from a controlling interest he gained in a small Vermont road. And—no one knows exactly how—he developed a consummate mastery of the intricacies of Wall Street finance. Few could have been aware of this when Gould was elected in 1867 to the executive board of the Erie Railroad just as a titanic battle for control of the Erie was taking shape.

The protagonist was Cornelius Vanderbilt, who wanted to ally the Erie with his emerging New York Central system. Vanderbilt began secretly buying up Erie stock, a maneuver that had gained him control of other key railroad properties. This time, however, Erie stock mysteriously kept entering the market even though no more could legally be issued by the Erie. Gould was exploiting a dubious loophole: freshly minted convertible bonds that could be immediately converted to stock. Vanderbilt countered with court injunctions, forcing Gould and his confederates to decamp to New Jersey, and in Albany Vanderbilt lobbied to prevent legalization of the convertible bond gambit. A bidding war began for legislators' votes, which, with the Erie dollars overflowing his satchel, Gould finally won. To settle things, however, Vanderbilt and his allies had to be compensated for their losses, which Gould ingeniously arranged by spending $9 million from the Erie treasury to buy back their stock at inflated prices. The Erie was effectively bankrupted, but it was now firmly in Gould's hands.

Gould proceeded to show how money—lots of it—could be made from control of a large enterprise that was itself unprofitable and badly managed. The trick was to manipulate stock prices, buying and selling with an insider's advance knowledge. For example, Gould announced that he was replacing the United States Express Company, which operated on the Erie line, with a new company that he intended to form. United's stock dropped from 60 to 16, at which point Gould bought, renewed the contract, and sold on the stock's rebound. He walked away with a cool $3 million. Under Gould's rule, the Erie never earned enough to service its debt. Long-suffering European stockholders finally rebelled, forcing him out in March 1872, and charged him with criminal fraud. Resourceful as ever, Gould tied up the suit in the courts, finally persuading the plaintiffs to accept a settlement that was of little account.

Gould was never able to shed the unsavory reputation he acquired during the Erie years. But even in that buccaneering period there was another side to him as a railroad man. Indifferent to day-to-day operations, Gould had a brilliant strategic sense for how railroads should grow. The key, he knew, was integrated development, with trunk line service between major centers. Right off Gould moved to take over the local roads west of Pittsburgh and Buffalo, hoping to make the Erie the dominant system linking the Atlantic seaboard and the Midwest. But he lacked the resources, and the Pennsylvania and the New York Central, spurred by his challenge, beat him out, capturing the key western lines and leaving the Erie a weak secondary system.

Yet the vision had been Gould's, and ten years later he found greener fields for his strategic talents in the area west of St. Louis and southward into Texas. The railroads in this region were a jumble of incomplete, disconnected lines when Gould came on the scene in 1879. He began buying control, finishing the lines, and linking them into a regional system operating more than 5,000 miles of track under his parent company, the Missouri Pacific. He also moved aggressively in other parts of the country, challenging established railroads and cutting rates ruthlessly to take traffic from them. By 1882 he controlled 15 percent of the nation's entire trackage and Western Union and the New York Elevated besides.

The economic boom that fostered this empire building did not last, however, and after 1881 Gould found himself on the wrong side of the stock market, overextended in holdings that were falling in value. On the verge of ruin in early 1884, he managed to get a "corner" on the stock of the Missouri Pacific, forcing up its price and thus saving himself. But Gould was not the same man after that. He lost his iron nerve, and his health began to fail. He swore off speculation. His business dealings, while still far-flung, became more cautious and defensive. But to the end he remained a tough customer, never justifying himself, never cloaking himself in religious piety, not even seeking to make amends by a show of philanthropy. In death he thumbed his nose at the world: his entire fortune—$75 million—went in trust to his family.

A century later, historians can perhaps appreciate better than Gould's obituarists the positive side of Gould's amazing business career. The nation's railroad network bore in some considerable degree Gould's mark by virtue of his own system building and the spur he gave to others. Moreover, his forays into the territory of other railroads broke open monopoly markets and drove shipping prices down. Railroads might have made less money, but shippers and consumers benefited from cheaper transportation costs. Even Gould's purely speculative ventures might have contributed to the nation's economic growth. Economists say that money made in speculation is an especially efficient source of fresh capital, and that is what Gould's winnings were to America's capital-hungry railroads.

Let us suppose that Gould never understood this. Let us suppose further that he was motivated by greed, that his methods were unscrupulous, and that if he had lived at a later time, he probably would have ended up in prison. Are we justified in calling him a robber baron?

buyers among banks, insurance companies, and investors in this country and abroad. And when railroads fell into bankruptcy—or rather, into receivership, because they could not be permitted to stop operating—the investment bankers stepped in to pick up the pieces. They persuaded investors to help out by accepting lower interest rates or putting up more money. Railroads emerged healthier from receivership. Just as important, the competitive pressures on them eased. The investment bankers did this by consolidating rival roads or developing "communities of interest" among them. Through interlocking directorates orchestrated by J. P. Morgan, once-competing railroads ended up effectively sharing a common board of directors. By the early twentieth century, half a dozen great regional systems had emerged, and the nerve center of American railroading had shifted to Wall Street.

The Managerial Revolution

At one time, observed the railroad expert Marshall M. Kirkman in 1896, it had been thought "practically impossible to manage a great railway effectively." On the early railroads "management had been personal and autocratic; the superintendent, a man gifted with energy and clearness of perception, moulded the property to his own will. But as the properties grew, he found himself unable to give his personal attention to everything. Undaunted, he sought to do everything and do it well. He ended by doing nothing."

It is not hard to understand the mistake of the early railroad superintendent. Where in a world of small businesses could he find a model for running an enterprise that was too big for personal and direct control? No problem was harder to grasp, no solution harder to imagine.

As trunk lines moved westward from Baltimore, Philadelphia, and New York before the Civil War, they came up against a managerial crisis that had not troubled shorter railroads. In 1856 the Erie Railroad official Daniel C. McCallum offered a crucial insight into the problem. On a 50-mile railroad the superintendent could attend to every detail personally, "and any system, however imperfect, may prove comparatively successful." But not on 500-mile railroads: "I am fully convinced that in the want of a system lies the true secret of their failure." Thus, McCallum identified the need for a *system*—a formal administrative structure—for the successful operation of large-scale, complex enterprises. He knew he was working in the dark: "We have no precedent or experience upon which we can fully rely."

The railroads were the most complex form of nineteenth-century enterprise. They had to raise huge amounts of capital, and their properties stretched over ever-greater distances. They employed armies of workers—nearly 50,000 on the Pennsylvania system by 1890. And unlike the leisurely traffic on canals, trains had to be precisely scheduled and closely coordinated. Even with the use of telegraphic communication, train accidents took a heavy toll.

Step by step, always under the prod of necessity, the early trunk lines pioneered the main elements of modern business administration. They separated overall management from day-to-day operations and created departments along functional lines—maintenance of way, rolling stock, and traffic. Then they carefully defined the lines of communication from the operating divisions upward to the central office. When Albert Fink perfected his cost-accounting system for the Louisville and Nashville Railroad after the Civil War, managers at last had precise data with which to assess the performance of their railroads. By the end of the 1870s the managerial crisis of the railroads had been resolved.

As industrial enterprises became comparably complex, they confronted the same kind of managerial problems. However, manufacturers benefited from the experience of the railroads. Andrew Carnegie, for example, drew on his early career with the Pennsylvania Railroad. Whether by learning from the railroads or through trial and error, large companies moved toward a modern management structure and solved the problems of administering far-flung business empires.

Mass Markets and Large-Scale Enterprise

The railroads sparked a revolution in the distribution and marketing of goods. Until well into the industrial age, business firms were typically small. Most manufacturers produced goods in limited quantities, mainly for nearby markets, and left the marketing to wholesale merchants and commission agents. Products normally passed through numerous hands on their way from the factory to final sale to the consumer.

Then after the Civil War the scale of economic activity began to grow dramatically. "Combinations of capital on a scale hitherto wholly unprecedented constitute one of the remarkable features of modern business methods," the economist David A. Wells wrote in 1889. He could see "no other way in which the work of production and distribution can be prosecuted." The increasing scale of enterprise seemed "not voluntary on the part of the possessors and controllers of capital, but necessary or even compulsory." What was there about the nation's economic activity that led to Wells's sense of inevitability?

The dynamic features of American growth—availability of capital, receptivity to technology, and the emergence of an industrial base—certainly played a role. But the key to large-scale enterprise lay in the

American market. Immigration and a very high birth rate swelled the population from 40 million in 1870 to over 60 million in 1890. People flocked to the cities, and the railroads brought these dense consuming markets within the reach of distant producers. The telegraph, which was in widespread use by the Civil War, eliminated communication barriers. Unlike Europe, America was not carved up into many national markets; no political frontiers impeded the flow of goods across the continent. Meanwhile, high tariffs protected American industry from foreign competition. Nowhere else did manufacturers have so vast and accessible an internal market for their products.

Gustavus Swift and Vertical Integration. The meatpacking industry was a case in point. Before the Civil War, Cincinnati and Chicago had become great processors of preserved products such as salt pork and smoked beef. But fresh meat remained the province of local butchers and slaughterhouses whose practices had scarcely changed since the preindustrial era. Fresh meat was a luxury item, and the diet of city dwellers, especially the poor, depended heavily on salt pork.

The coming of the railroads brought big changes to the fresh-meat business. Cattle raising shifted to the grazing ranges of the Great Plains and the feedlots of the corn belt. Chicago, the rail terminal for the upper Midwest, became the hub of the American meat trade once the Union Stock Yards opened in 1865. Cattle were shipped by railroad from Chicago to eastern cities, where, as before, they were slaughtered in local "butchertowns." Nothing more was needed for the meat trade to service an exploding urban population indefinitely. In Europe no further development ever did occur.

But Gustavus F. Swift, a shrewd Massachusetts cattle dealer who settled in Chicago in 1875, saw the future differently. Processing fresh meat locally seemed inefficient to him. Livestock in cattle cars deteriorated en route to the East, and local slaughterhouses were too small to utilize waste by-products and cut labor costs. If a way could be found to keep the dressed beef fresh in transit, processing operations could be concentrated in Chicago. Primitive refrigeration already enabled Chicago pork-packing plants to operate year-round. The problem was how to apply this technology to a railroad

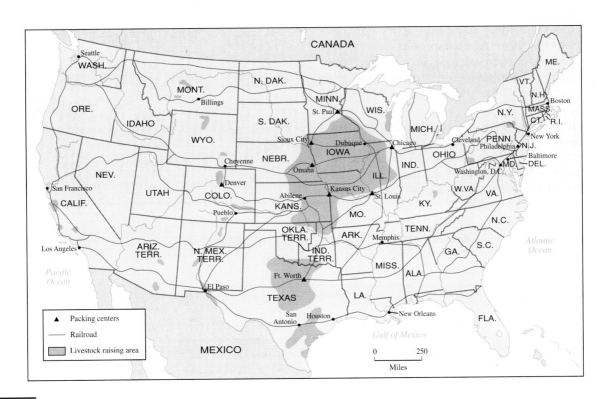

MAP 18.3

The Dressed Meat Industry

The meat-packing industry clearly shows how transportation, supply, and demand combined to foster the growth of the American industrial economy. The main centers of beef production in 1900—Chicago, St. Paul, Kansas City, Fort Worth—were great rail hubs with connections westward to the cattle regions and eastward to the great cities hungry for cheap supplies of meat. Vertically integrated enterprises sprang from these elements, linked together by an efficient and comprehensive railroad network.

freight car. After Swift's engineers figured out an effective system of air circulation, he built a fleet of refrigerator cars and constructed a central beef-processing plant at the Chicago stockyards.

This was only the beginning of Swift's innovations. Since no refrigerated warehouses existed in the cities to which he shipped chilled beef, Swift built his own network of branch houses. Next, he established a fleet of wagons to distribute his products to retail butcher shops. Swift constructed additional facilities to process the fertilizer, chemicals, and other usable by-products from his slaughtering operations. He also added to his line of business other perishable commodities, including dairy products, so that he could fully utilize his refrigerated cars and branch houses. As the demand grew, Swift built more packing houses in other stockyard centers, including Kansas City, Fort Worth, and Omaha.

Step by step, Swift created a new kind of enterprise, the *vertically integrated* firm—that is, a national company capable of handling within its own structure all the functions of an industry. In effect, Swift & Co. replaced a large number of small specialized firms operating in local markets. Several other Chicago companies that had started as preserved pork packers—Armour & Co. was the most prominent—followed Swift's lead. By the end of the 1890s five firms, all of them nationally organized and vertically integrated, produced nearly 90 percent of the meat shipped in interstate commerce. The entire geography of the meat industry had changed (see Map 18.3).

The Birth of Mass Marketing. The development of the refrigerator car had made all this possible in the fresh-meat trade. In most other fields no single event was so decisive. But other manufacturers did share Swift's insight that the essential step was to identify a mass market and then develop a national enterprise capable of serving it. In the petroleum industry John D. Rockefeller built the Standard Oil Company partly by taking over rival firms, but he also developed a national distribution system to reach the enormous market for kerosene to light and heat homes. The Singer Sewing Machine Company formed its own sales organization, using both retail stores and door-to-door salesmen. Through such distribution systems, manufacturers provided technical information, credit, and repair facilities for their products. Like the meat packers, these companies became vertically integrated firms that served a national market.

To gain the benefits of mass distribution, retail business went through comparable changes. Montgomery Ward and Sears, Roebuck developed into national mail-order houses for rural consumers. From Vermont to California farm families selected identical goods from mail-order catalogues and became part of the nation-

wide consumer market. In the cities, mass distribution followed different strategies. Department stores, a form of retailing pioneered by John Wanamaker in Philadelphia, spread to every large city. The most important innovators in this field were Jewish families such as the Strauses of New York, the Lazaruses of Columbus, Ohio, and the Mays of Colorado, most of whose founders had started as peddlers or small dry goods proprietors. An alternative route to urban distribution was provided by the establishment of chain store systems; this was the strategy of the Great Atlantic and Pacific Tea Company (A & P) and the F. W. Woolworth Company.

American society prepared its citizens to be consumers of the standardized goods produced by national manufacturers and sold by mass marketers. The high rate of geographical mobility broke down the local loyalties and regional identities that were so strong in Europe. And social class in America, though by no means absent, was blurred at the edges. Equally important, it did not call for distinguishing ways of dressing. Foreign

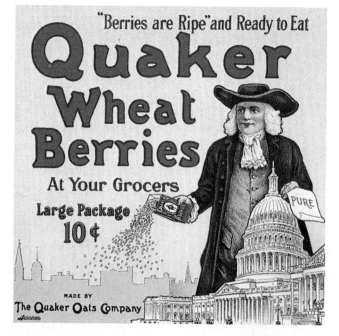

Quaker Oats

Like crackers, sugar, and other nonperishable foods, oatmeal had traditionally been marketed to consumers in bulk from barrels. In 1882 the grain merchant Henry P. Cowell completed the first continuous-process mill for oatmeal, cutting production costs and greatly increasing output. He also hit on the idea of selling oatmeal in boxes of standard size and weight to a national market. Broadsides showing the Quaker Oats man soon appeared in every American town, advertising a product of reliable quality and uniform price. (National Museum of American History, Smithsonian Institution) visitors often noted that ready-made clothing made it difficult to tell salesgirls from debutantes on city streets.

The American consumer's receptivity to standardized goods should not be exaggerated. Gustavus Swift, for example, encountered great resistance to his Chicago beef: How could it be wholesome weeks later in Boston or Philadelphia? Cheap prices helped, but advertising perhaps had a greater influence. Modern advertising was born during the late nineteenth century, bringing brand names and an urban landscape increasingly cluttered by billboards and signs. By 1900 advertisers were spending more than $90 million a year for space in newspapers and magazines. Advertisements urged readers to bathe with Pears' soap, eat Uneeda biscuits, sew on a Singer machine, and snap pictures with a Kodak camera. The active molding of demand for brand names became a major function of American business.

The New South

"Shall we dethrone our idols?" This was a question that southerners had to ask themselves as they enviously observed the burst of economic activity in the North. For many the answer was a resounding yes. Nostalgia for the glories of the Old South became the chief target of the advocates of southern economic development. The South, they argued, had always given "the places of trust and honor" to "warriors and orators," forgetting that "what it would most need was the practical wisdom of businessmen." Led by Henry W. Grady of the Atlanta *Constitution*, an influential group of publicists made the "practical wisdom of businessmen" the credo of a "New South."

Catching up with the North was no easy task. The plantation economy of the Old South had strongly im-

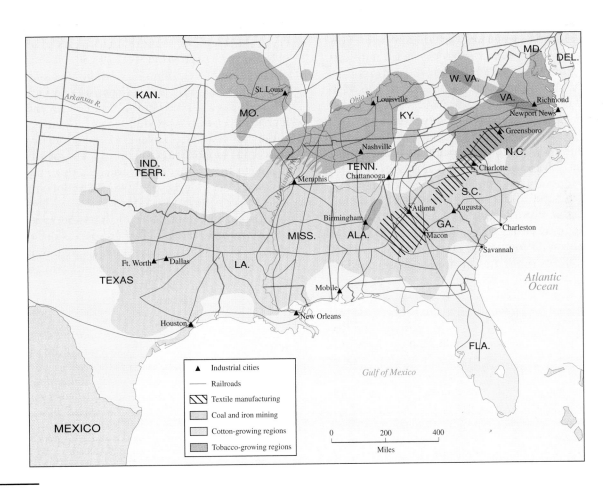

MAP 18.4

The New South, 1900
The economy of the Old South focused on raising staple crops, especially cotton and tobacco. In the New South staple agriculture continued to dominate but there was marked industrial development as well. Industrial regions developed, producing textiles, coal and iron, and wood products. By 1900 the South's industrial pattern was well defined.

peded industrial development. In 1860 railroad building lagged far behind; there were few cities, a primitive distribution system, and not much manufacturing. After the devastation of the Civil War this modest infrastructure was quickly restored. In 1877, with both Reconstruction and economic depression ended, outside capital flowed in and a railroad boom developed. Track mileage doubled in the next decade and, at least by that measure, the South became nearly competitive with the rest of the country (see Map 18.4).

But the South remained overwhelmingly an agrarian society; two of every three persons lived on the land. Farming and poverty are not necessarily linked, but in the South they were. Sharecropping, which required a cash crop (see Chapter 16), committed the South to cotton despite soil depletion and unprofitable prices. With leases on a year-to-year basis, neither tenant nor owner had an incentive to invest in long-term improvements. At a time of rapid advances in northern agriculture, cotton growing remained tied to the mule, the plow, and the hoe.

The result was a stagnant agricultural system. Low productivity and low cotton prices translated into low-wage agriculture. The price for southern farm labor fell steadily, until in South Carolina and Georgia it stood at scarcely half the national average by the 1890s—roughly 75 cents a day without board for a farm laborer.

Southern Industry. This low agricultural wage turned out to be the salvation of the South's hopes for industrialization. Consider, for example, how southern textile mills got started in the Piedmont upcountry of North Carolina, South Carolina, and Georgia in the mid-1870s. Capital was raised locally, subscribed in large amounts and small under a drumbeat of boosterism. Workers were recruited mostly from the surrounding

hill farms, where people struggled to make ends meet. To attract them, mill wages had to be higher than their farm earnings, but not much higher. And since the agricultural wage was so low in the South, the new mills had a great competitive advantage over the long-established New England industry—an estimated 40 percent in labor costs in 1897.

The labor system that evolved likewise reflected southern agrarian society. To begin with, it was a family system. "Papa decided he would come because he didn't have nothing much but girls and they had to get out and work like men," recalled one woman. It was not Papa, in fact, but his girls whom the mills wanted for work as spinners and loom tenders. But they could not be recruited individually: no right-thinking parent would have permitted that. There was, on the other hand, no objection to hiring by families; after all, everyone had been expected to work on the farm. And so the family system of mill labor developed, in which half or more of the operatives were women and the work force was very young. Fully a quarter of all southern textile workers in the 1880s were under fifteen years of age; three-quarters were twenty-four or younger.

The hours were long—twelve hours a day was the norm—but life in the mill villages was, in the words of one historian, "like a family." Employers tended to be highly paternalistic, providing company housing and a variety of services. The mill workers themselves built close-knit, supportive communities, but for whites only. Although they sometimes worked as day laborers and janitors, blacks hardly ever got jobs as operatives in the mills.

Cheap, abundant labor might have been termed the South's most valuable natural resource. But the South was rich in other natural resources as well. From its rich soil came tobacco, the region's second cash crop. When

The Industrial South

No development so raised the hopes of New South proponents as the success of the region's textile industry. After 1877 new mills had sprung up in South Carolina, North Carolina, and Georgia. Investors received a high rate of return—average profits ran at 22 percent in 1882—and publicists boasted that new jobs were being created for "the necessitous masses of poor whites." This 1887 engraving of a "model" mill at Augusta, Georgia, conveys the South's sense of pride in its new industrial prowess.

TABLE 18.2

Comparison of South and Non-South Value Added per Worker, 1910

Type of Industry	South	Non-South
Lumber and timber products	820	1020
Cotton goods	544	764
Cars and general shop construction by steam railroad companies	657	746
Turpentine and resin	516	—
Tobacco manufactures	1615	1394
Foundry and machine-shop products	1075	1307
Printing and publishing	1760	2100
Cottonseed oil and cake	1715	—
Hosiery and knit goods	461	724
Furniture and refrigerators	732	1052
Iron and steel	1182*	1433
Fertilizer	1833	1947

This table reveals the consistency with which northern industries (except tobacco manufactures) controlled the more skilled—and hence, more value-creating—processes of production.

*Partially estimated.

Source: Gavin Wright, *Old South, New South: Revolutions in the Southern Economy since the Civil War* (New York: Basic Books, 1986) 163.

cigarettes became fashionable in the 1880s, the young North Carolina entrepreneur James B. Duke seized the new market by taking advantage of a southern invention—James A. Bonsack's machine for producing cigarettes automatically. Blacks retained the manual tasks of stemming and stripping the leaf that they had always performed, but as in the textile mills, machine tending was restricted to white women.

Lumbering, by contrast, was largely integrated, with a labor force evenly divided between black and white men. The extensive pine forests of the South were rapidly—*heedlessly* is perhaps the better word—exploited in those years. Finally, the rich coal and iron ore deposits of Alabama were vigorously developed from the late 1870s onward, so that by 1890 nearly a million tons of pig iron were being produced in the Birmingham district.

Despite the South's high hopes, this burst of industrial development did not lift the region out of poverty. Industrial output increased more rapidly than in the North but not enough to make much headway against the dominant agricultural sector. In 1900 two-thirds of all southerners made their living from the soil, just as they had in 1870. Moreover, the industries that did develop were usually extractive, such as forestry and mining. Nearly two-thirds of the South's labor force worked in the production of raw materials, compared with hardly one-eighth in the Middle Atlantic and New England states. Processing rarely went beyond coarse, semifinished goods, even in textiles. Industry by indus-

try, the key statistic—the value added by manufacturing—showed the South lagging consistently behind the North (see Table 18.2).

Southerners tended to blame the North: the South was a "colonial" economy controlled by New York and Chicago. There was some truth to this charge. Much of the capital—by no means all—did come from the North, and the integrating processes of the economy did subordinate regional to national interests. When the railway network moved to a standard gauge, it was the southern railroads that were most out of line. In 1886, in one massive effort, the entire South converted to the 4 feet 8 1/2 inch standard of the North. Nor was there a lack of instances in which northern interests used their muscle to maintain the interregional status quo. Railroads, for example, varied freight rates so that it was cheap for southern cotton and timber to flow out and for northern manufactured goods to flow in.

Yet in the end the South's economic backwardness was mostly of its own making. The crowning irony was that the great advantage of the South—its cheap labor—kept it from developing a more technologically advanced economy. First, low wages discouraged employers from replacing workers with machinery. Second, low wages attracted labor-intensive industry, such as textiles. Third, a cheap labor market inhibited investment in education. (In its way, this was a rational choice: better-educated workers would flee to higher-wage markets, and the investment in them would be lost.)

What was special about the southern labor market was that it was *insulated* from the rest of the country: the normal flow of workers back and forth did not occur, and wage differentials did not narrow. So long as this condition persisted, the South would remain a tributary economy, a supplier on unequal terms to the advanced industrial heartland of the North.

The World of Work

In a free enterprise system profit drives the entrepreneur. But the industrial order is not populated only by profit makers. It includes—in vastly larger numbers—wage earners. What is done for profit always acts directly and powerfully on those who work for wages. Never did those actions have more profound consequences for working people than in the late nineteenth century.

Labor Recruits

Wherever in the world industrialism took hold, it set people in motion. Artisans moved into factories, farm folk migrated to manufacturing centers, an industrial labor force emerged. These events took place in all industrializing nations. But the United States built its

work force in a distinctive way. Unlike European countries, it could not rely primarily on its own population.

For one thing, the demand for labor was enormous. American industry required nearly three times as many workers in 1900 as it had in 1870 (see Figure 18.2). No less important, except in the South, native-born Americans could no longer be attracted into factories. Rural people, who still accounted for about 75 percent of the population in 1870, were certainly mobile, but the many who went westward remained farmers. About half of all farm migrants did move to cities, but not into the factories. The desirable jobs—those of puddlers, rollers, molders, and machinists—required industrial skills not held by rural Americans. But these people did have a basic education; they could read and calculate, and they understood American institutions and ways of doing things. City-bound white Americans found their opportunities in the multiplying white-collar jobs in offices and retail stores rather than in the nation's factories.

As for rural blacks, even the lowest factory job probably seemed better than sharecropping or day labor on a farm. Modest numbers of blacks began to migrate northward and westward—roughly 80,000 between 1870 and 1890 and another 200,000 from 1890 to 1910. Most of them settled in cities, but they encountered racial barriers as impenetrable as those in the South. The great majority of black men ended up as casual laborers and janitors, and black women worked as

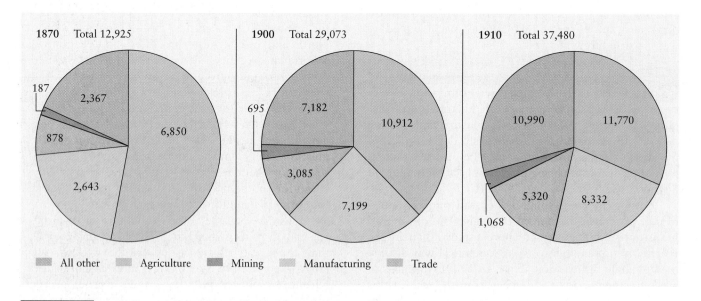

FIGURE 18.2

Changes in the Labor Force, 1870–1910
The numbers represent thousands of people (i.e., 12,925 = 12,925,000 workers).
They reveal both the enormous increase in the labor force between 1870 and 1910
and the dramatic shift from agriculture to industry and other nonagricultural jobs.

Ironworkers—Noontime
The qualities of the nineteenth-century craft worker—dignity, "unselfish brotherhood," a "manly" bearing—shine through this painting by Thomas P. Anschutz. *Ironworkers—Noontime* became a popular painting when it was reproduced as an engraving in *Harpers' Weekly* in 1884.

maids and laundresses. Only 7 percent of African-American men held factory jobs in 1890. Their opportunity had been preempted by another source of cheap labor. Blacks could be excluded because industrial employers had plenty of foreign workers.

Immigrant Labor. The exodus from the Old World had started in the 1840s when over a million Irish peasants fled the potato famine. In the following years, European agriculture became increasingly commercialized while peasant populations grew and outstripped the available land. The erosion of peasant economies struck first in Germany and Scandinavia. Then, later in the nineteenth

century, troubled times spread eastward into Austria-Hungary and Russia and southward into Italy and the Balkans. In the industrial districts of Europe the forces of economic change also cut loose many workers in the declining artisan trades and in obsolete occupations such as hand-loom weaving.

Ethnic origin largely determined the kind of work that the immigrants found in their new country. Seasoned artisans and industrial workers generally sought the same types of jobs that they had held in the Old World. The nineteenth-century occupational structure took on an ethnic character: the Welsh worked as tin-plate workers, the English as miners, the Germans as

Immigrant Workers
Many native-born Americans resented the influx of peasant immigrants from eastern and southern Europe that began in the 1880s. In fact, the newcomers, more than any other group, manned the machines, laid the railroad tracks, and performed the heavy construction labor that built the nation's cities. They were Europe's gift—its most vigorous and hardworking people.

machinists and traditional artisans, the Belgians as glass workers, and the Scandinavians as seamen on Great Lakes boats. For common labor, employers had long counted on the brawn of Irish rural immigrants.

As industrialization advanced, European craft skills became outmoded while the need for unskilled workers increased. As a result, immigration began to shift away from northern Europe during the 1880s (see Figure 18.3). More than 9 million people migrated to America from eastern and southern Europe between 1900 and 1914. Italian and Slavic immigrants without industrial skills flooded into the lowest rungs of American industry. Heavy, low-paid factory labor became the domain of the recent immigrants. Blast-furnace jobs, a job-seeking investigator heard, were "Hunky work," not suitable for him or any other American.

It was not only the skills they had that determined where immigrants ended up in American industry. The newcomers, although generally traveling on their own, moved within well-defined networks. They followed relatives or fellow villagers already in America, joined

their households as family members or boarders, and relied on them to find a job. A high degree of ethnic clustering resulted even within a single factory. At the Jones and Laughlin steel works in Pittsburgh, for example, the carpentry shop was German, the hammer shop Polish, and the blooming mill Serbian. Immigrants also had different job preferences. Men from Italy, for example, liked outdoor work better than factory labor. And, already accustomed to it, they worked in gangs under a *padrone* (boss), much as they had in Italy.

Immigrants entered a modern industrial order, but they saw their surroundings through peasants' eyes. With the disruption of the traditional rural economies of eastern and southern Europe, many lost their lands and fell into the class of dependent, propertyless servants. Peasants could avoid that bitter fate only if they had money to buy property. In Europe job-seeking peasants commonly tried seasonal agricultural labor or temporary work in nearby cities. America represented merely a larger leap, made possible by cheap and speedy steamship transportation across the Atlantic. The peasant immigrants, most of them young and male, came intending to earn enough money to buy land in their native villages. As many as half did return, departing from America in great numbers during depression years. No one knows how many saved enough money to achieve their peasant goals and how many left for lack of work. Their willingness to take the worst jobs and their tendency to leave in bad times clearly made them an ideal labor supply for the new industrial order.

A few fields, such as railroading, employed mostly native-born workers. Overall, however, immigrants manned American industry, constituting well over half the labor force of the nation's principal manufacturing and mining industries after the turn of the century.

Working Women

Between 1870 and 1900 the number of American women grew by half, but the number in wage-earning jobs jumped by almost two-thirds. Women became increasingly important to the industrial economy; by 1900 they made up more than a fourth of the total non-farm labor force. The role that they found as workers was shaped by their gender. Contemporary beliefs about womanhood largely determined which women entered the work force and how they were treated when they became wage earners.

Wives were not supposed to hold jobs. In 1890 fewer than 5 percent of married white women worked outside the home. Black married women had a much higher labor participation rate of over 30 percent. Except in affluent families, young women generally worked until they married. In most working-class

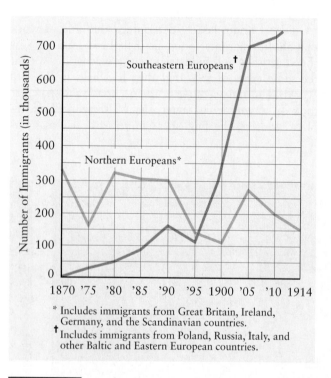

FIGURE 18.3

American Immigration, 1870–1914
This graph shows the surge of European immigration in the late nineteenth century. While northern Europe continued to send substantial numbers, it was overshadowed after 1895 by southern Europeans pouring into America to work in mines and factories.

Switchboard Operators
Telephone work offers a prime historical example of sex typing in American employment. When the first telephone exchange was set up in Boston in 1878, it was operated by teen-age boys, which followed the practice set in the telegraph industry. During the 1880s, however, young women increasingly replaced the boys, and by 1900 switchboard operation was defined strictly as women's work. In this photograph of a telephone exchange in Columbus, Ohio, in 1907, the older woman at left has risen to the position of supervisor, but it is the two men in the picture who are clearly in charge. The other major occupations in this new industry—telephone installation and line maintenance—were just as strictly male as switchboard operation was female, but of course on a much higher pay scale.

households, in fact, daughters had no choice because their earnings were needed by the family. The bulk of employed women therefore were young: the majority in 1890 were between sixteen and twenty-four years of age. When older women worked, one observer remarked, it "was usually a sign that something had gone wrong"—their husbands had died, deserted them, or stopped working.

Since women were held to be inherently different from men, it followed that they should not be permitted to do "men's work." And regardless of the value of their labor, they could not be paid a man's wage. The dominant view was that a woman did not require a "living wage" because, as one investigator reported, "it is expected that she has men to support her." Moreover, the occupation that served as the baseline for all women's jobs was domestic service, always very poorly paid or, in a woman's own home, not paid at all.

At the turn of the century women workers fell into three roughly equal numerical categories. A third worked as maids or other types of domestic servants. Another third held "female" white-collar jobs in teaching, nursing, sales, and office work. In industry, where the remainder worked, most women were classified as *operatives*—machine tenders and hand workers. They were heavily concentrated in the garment trades and textile mills but could be found throughout industry in "light" occupations—as packers, inspectors, assemblers, or sausage stuffers in packing houses. Few worked as supervisors, fewer in the crafts, and nearly none as day laborers.

Just how jobs came to be defined as male or female—in sociological lingo, the sex typing of occupations—is not easy to explain. Some jobs originally held by men, such as telephone operators and store clerks, had by the 1890s been taken over by women. In each case, as an occupation became feminized, it was redefined as having female attributes even though very similar or even identical work elsewhere was done by men. Once a job was identified as women's work, it became unsuitable for men. There were no male telephone operators by 1900.

Sex typing of work was legitimized by the sentimental view of women as the weaker sex, but powerful interests also played a role. Craft workers protected their male domain, and employers profited from cut-rate work. Wherever they worked, women earned less than did the least skilled males. At the turn of the century the weekly wage of women factory workers came to roughly $7, $3 less than that of unskilled men and $5 below the average for all industrial employees.

As with male workers, ethnicity and race played a big part in the distribution of women's jobs among particular groups. Exclusion from all but the most menial jobs applied as rigidly to black women as it did to black men. White-collar jobs were reserved for the native-born, although in the cities those people were often the second-generation daughters of immigrants. And as with men, ethnicity created clustering patterns in the jobs held by wage-earning women or, in the case of Italian families, restricted them to subcontracting tasks, such as sewing, that could be done at home.

But if ethnicity mattered in the workplace, gender mattered at least as much. Women's identity gave their work distinctive meaning. Department store clerks, for example, developed a work culture and language just as robust as that of the hard-drinking Danbury hatters described later in this chapter. Most important was the fact that wage-earning women were young and unmarried. For many, the first job was also an escape from family discipline. It represented an opportunity to gain some independence, form friendships with other young women, and experience, however briefly, a fun-loving time of nice clothes, dancing, and other "cheap amusements." Young male workers, by contrast, underwent a process of job socialization presided over by seasoned, older co-workers. Being young mattered to male workers, certainly, but did not define the work experience for them as it did for women.

To some degree, their youthful preoccupations made it easier for working women to overlook or accept the miserable terms under which they labored. But this did not mean that they lacked a sense of group solidarity and self-respect. Fashionable clothes might appear frivolous to the casual observer, but they also conveyed the message that the working girl considered herself to be as good as anyone. And there were occasions, as occurred with the Jewish garment workers of New York and the Irish-American telephone operators of Boston, when the rebellious youth culture united

with feelings of job grievance to produce astonishing strike movements among working women.

The Family Economy. Disapproval of wives working outside the home, although expressed in sentimental and moral terms, was based on solid necessity. From the standpoint of the labor market, the basic economic unit consisted of the individual employee. For workers, however, the family was the economic unit, to which the wife contributed crucially. Cooking, cleaning, and tending the children were not income-producing or reckoned in terms of money. But everyone knew that the family household could not function without the wife's contribution. Therefore, her place was in the home.

Working-class families, however, found the going hard on a single income. Only among highly skilled workers, wrote an investigator of the family budgets of miners and iron workers, "was it possible for the husband unaided to support his family." For most working-class families the hardest period came during the childbearing years, when there were many mouths to feed and only the earnings of the father. Thereafter, the family income began to grow. Not only unmarried sons and daughters but the younger children as well contributed their share. In 1900 one of every five children below the age of sixteen worked, including probably a quarter of a million younger than ten. "When the people own houses," remarked a printer from Fall River, "you will generally find that it is a large family all working together."

By the 1890s all the northern industrial states had passed laws prohibiting child labor and regulating work hours for teenagers. Most of those states also required children under fourteen years of age to attend school for a certain number of weeks each year. Working-class families continued to rely on a second income, but this money came more and more from the wife. After 1890 the proportion of working married women crept steadily upward. About a fifth of the wives of unskilled and semiskilled men in Chicago held jobs in 1920. Wage-earning wives, many with children, were on their way to becoming a primary part of America's labor force.

Autonomous Labor

No one supervised the nineteenth-century coal miner. He was a tonnage worker who was paid for the amount of coal he produced. He provided his own tools, worked at his own pace, and knocked off early when he chose. Such autonomous craft workers—almost all of them men—flourished in many branches of nineteenth-century industry. They were mule spinners in cotton mills; puddlers and rollers in iron works; molders in

Breaker Boys

In the anthracite districts of eastern Pennsylvania, giant machines called breakers processed the coal as it came out of the mines, crushing it and sorting it by size for sale as domestic fuel. The boys shown in this photograph had the job of picking out the slate and refuse as the processed coal came down the chutes, working long hours in a constant cloud of coal dust for less than a dollar a day. Breaker boy was the first job, often begun before the age of ten, in a lifetime in the mines. The photograph does not show any old men, but sick and disabled miners often ended their careers as breaker boys—hence the saying among coal diggers, "Twice a boy and once a man is the poor miner's life."

stove making; and machinists, glassblowers, and skilled workers of many other types.

In the shop they abided by the *stint*, a limit placed by themselves on the amount that they would produce each day. This informal system of limiting output infuriated efficiency-minded engineers. But to the worker it signified personal dignity and "unselfish brotherhood" with fellow employees. The male craft worker took pride in a "manly" bearing toward both his fellows and the boss. One day a shop in Lowell, Massachusetts, posted regulations requiring all employees to be at their posts in work clothes at the opening bell and remain, with the shop door locked, until the dismissal bell. A

machinist promptly packed his tools and quit, declaring that he had not "been brought up under such a system of slavery."

Underlying this ethical code was a keen sense of craft groups, each of which had its own history and customs. Hat finishers, masters of the art of applying fur felting to top hats and bowlers, had a language of their own. When a hatter was hired, he was "shopped"; if fired, he was "bagged"; when he quit work, he "cried off"; and when he took an apprentice, the boy was "under teach." The hatters, most of whom worked in Danbury, Connecticut, or Orange, New Jersey, formed a distinctive, self-contained community.

The craft worker's skills were crucial to nineteenth-century production. He was also valued for the responsibilities he assumed. He hired his own helpers, supervised their work, and paid them from his earnings. In an era when the scale of production was expanding, autonomous craft workers relieved their employers of the mounting burden of shop-floor management. Many factory managers tried to shift this responsibility to their employees. A system of inside contracting developed in metal-fabricating firms that did precise machining and complex assembling. Contractor-employees hired and paid their own men and supervised them.

The skilled worker was one central figure in nineteenth-century industry; the common laborer was another. Great numbers of laborers had been needed to dig canals, lay railroad tracks, and build cities. They were equally important in heavy industry. Until the last years of the century virtually all hauling of materials was done by hand. In the steel mills, a third or more of the workers shoveled coal and iron ore from freight cars, loaded the furnaces, and handled the tons of hot metal that passed through the mill daily. They worked in gangs, completely under the charge of the foreman or gang boss, who hired them, told them what to do, and disciplined and fired them.

Dispersal of authority was thus characteristic of nineteenth-century industry. The aristocracy of the workers—the craftsmen, inside contractors, and foremen—had a high degree of autonomy. However, their subordinates often paid dearly for that independence. The opportunities for abuse were endless. Any worker who paid his helpers from his own pocket might be tempted to exploit them. In the Pittsburgh area, foremen were known as "pushers," notorious for driving their gangs mercilessly. However, industrial labor in the nineteenth century was still on a human scale. People dealt with each other face to face and often developed cohesive ties within the shop. Striking craft workers commonly received the support of helpers and laborers, and labor gangs sometimes walked out on behalf of a popular foreman.

Systems of Control

As technology advanced and modern management emerged, controls over the work process intensified. Despite fierce resistance, workers increasingly lost the proud independence that had characterized nineteenth-century craft work.

When mine owners introduced undercutting machines in the 1880s, they deprived coal miners of the pick work that was their most prized skill. "Anyone with a weak head and a strong back can load machine coal," grumbled one Kentucky miner. "But a man has to think and study every day like you was studying a book if he is going to get the best of the coal when he uses only a pick." Similar complaints came from many other craft workers as their skills fell victim to machinery—from hand-loom weavers early in the nineteenth century to glassblowers a hundred years later.

The main source of this deskilling process was a new system that became known as *mass production.* The essential feature of this system was that it turned out standardized, high-volume products. Consider, for example, how work changed as a result of the creation of a national market for dressed beef in the 1870s. The huge packing houses that sprang up in Chicago shifted from the traditional reliance on skilled butchers to a highly specialized division of labor. At the Armour plant, workers performed seventy-eight distinct jobs, working efficiently and at high speed as the carcasses moved along, hooked to overhead conveyors. In a ten-hour day a gang of 157 workers could handle 1,050 head of cattle, many more per employee than was the case when one skilled butcher did everything. Machinery did not replace workers; rather, it was the division of labor that increased workers' output.

In most cases, however, the division of labor did lead to mechanization. This occurred because once jobs had been broken down into simple, repetitive tasks, it was generally possible to design machines that could do those tasks. The greatest opportunity came in the manufacture of products assembled from standardized, interchangeable parts, such as agricultural implements, sewing machines, typewriters, bicycles, and, after 1900, automobiles. In all these cases, machine tools that cut, drilled, and ground the metal parts had originally been manned by skilled machinists. But as machine tools became more specialized, they became *dedicated* machines—machines set up to do the same job over and

The Killing Floor
To the modern eye, the labor process depicted in this 1882 engraving of a Chicago meat-packing plant seems primitive and inefficient, but it contains the seeds of America's mass-production revolution. At the far left the steer has already been stunned by one specialist, killed by a second, and attached to a chain that will lift it onto the overhead conveyor. The division of labor is already in place (each of the workers on the line does a single repetitive task), and the process is continuous. It would be only a small step from the killing floors of the Chicago packing plants to Henry Ford's assembly line.

John Morison

The Impact of Mechanization

John Morison, a machinist, describes to a Senate investigating committee in 1883 what technological progress has meant to him and his fellow skilled workers.

Q. Is there any difference between the conditions under which machinery is made now and those which existed ten years ago?

A. A great deal of difference. . . . The trade has been subdivided and those subdivisions have been again subdivided, so that a man never learns the machinist's trade now. Ten years ago he learned, not the whole of the trade, but a fair portion of it. Also, there is more machinery used in the business, which again makes machinery. In the case of making the sewing-machine, for instance, you find that the trade is so subdivided that a man is not considered a machinist at all. Hence it is merely laborers' work. . . . Through this system of work, 100 men are able to do now what it took 300 or 400 men to do fifteen years ago.

Q. Have you noticed the effect upon the intellect of this plan of keeping a man at one particular branch?

A. Yes. It has a very demoralizing effect upon the mind throughout. The man . . . has got no chance whatever to learn anything else because he is kept steadily and constantly at that particular thing, and of course his intellect must be narrowed by it.

Q. And does he not finally acquire so much skill in the manipulation of his particular part of the business that he does it without any mental effort?

A. Almost. In fact he becomes almost a part of the machinery. . . . When I first went to learn the trade a machinist considered himself more than the average workingman; in fact he did not like to be called a workingman. He liked to be called a mechanic. . . . Today he recognizes the fact that he is simply the same as any other ordinary laborer, no more and no less.

Q. What is the social air about the ordinary machinist's house? Are there evidences of happiness, and joy, and hilarity, or is the general atmosphere solemn, and somber, and gloomy?

A. To explain that fully, I would state first of all, that machinists have got to work ten hours a day in New York, and that they are compelled to work very hard. In fact the machinists of America are compelled to do about one third more work than the machinists do in England in a day. . . . Of course when a man is dragged out in that way he is naturally cranky, and he makes all around him cranky; so, instead of a pleasant house it is every day expecting to lose his job by competition from his fellow workmen, there being so many out of employment, and no places for them, and his wages being pulled down through their competition, looking at all times to be thrown out of work in that way, and staring starvation in the face makes him feel sad, and the head of the house being sad, of course the whole family is the same, so the house looks like a dull prison instead of a home. . . .

Q. Where do you work?

A. I would rather not have it in print. Perhaps I would have to go Monday morning if I did. We are so situated in the machinist's trade that we daren't let them know much about us. If they know that we open our mouths on the labor question, and try to form organizations, we are quietly told that "business is slack," and we have got to go.

Source: U.S. Senate, Committee on Education and Labor, *Report on the Relations between Labor and Capital* (1885), I, pp. 755–759.

over—and the need for skilled operatives disappeared.

Technology took hold and set the pace of operations. The machine, not the worker, determined how fast production would go. "If you need to turn out a little more," boasted a superintendent at Swift & Co., "you speed up the conveyor a little and the men speed up to keep pace." Workers' frustrations and complaints about speedups were sure signs of the loss of control over their jobs.

"A man never learns the machinist's trade now," John Morison (see American Voices, above) complained in 1883. In the manufacture of sewing machines "the trade is so subdivided that a man is not considered a machinist at all. One man may make just a particular part of a machine and may not know anything whatever about another part of the same machine." Such a worker, noted an observer, "cannot be master of a craft, but only master of a fragment." The horror of what that meant is conveyed by one worker's description of another worker whose job at Western Electric was to cut rubber plates for ten hours a day. "When he talked to me he had to move his hand this way [indicating], as though he would take a piece of rubber plate and put it under the buzz saw. He has become a part of that machine. That machine is the means of his subsistence and that of his family."

Frederick W. Taylor and Scientific Management. The impact of machinery on labor was essentially unintentional. Employers recognized that mechanization would better enable them to discipline their workers, but that was only an incidental benefit of the efficiencies that came from the machinery itself. Gradually, however, employers came to realize that managing workers might itself be a way to reduce the cost of production.

The pioneer in this field was Frederick W. Taylor. Taylor had made a name for himself as an expert on metal-cutting methods. In 1895 he published a landmark essay, "A Piece-Rate System," that proposed a strategy for getting the maximum work from the individual worker. Taylor suggested two basic reforms. The first would eliminate the brain work from manual labor. Managers would assume "the burden of gathering together all of the traditional knowledge which in the past has been possessed by the workmen and then of classifying, tabulating, and reducing this knowledge to rules, laws, and formulae." The second reform, a logical consequence of the first, would deprive workers of the authority they had exercised on the shop floor. Workers would "do what they are told promptly and without asking questions or making suggestions. . . . The duty of enforcing . . . rests with the management alone."

Once they had the knowledge and the power, according to Taylor, managers would put labor on a "scientific" basis. That meant subjecting each task to a *time-and-motion study*, with an engineer analyzing and timing each job with a stopwatch. A personnel office would hire and train the right person for each job. Workers would be paid at a differential rate—that is, a certain amount if they met the stopwatch standard and a higher rate for additional output. Taylor claimed that his techniques would guarantee the optimum level of worker efficiency. His assumption was that only money mattered to workers and that they would automatically respond to the lure of higher earnings.

Taylor called his method *scientific management*. It was not in practice a roaring success. His reforms called for a total restructuring of factory administration. No company ever adopted Taylor's entire system, and the few that tried paid dearly for the effort. His job-analysis method, which was widely used, met with stubborn resistance. "It looks to me like slavery to have a man stand over you with a stopwatch," complained one iron molder. A union leader insisted that "this system is wrong, because we want our heads left on us." Far from solving the labor problem, as Taylor claimed it would, scientific management embittered relations on the shop floor.

Yet Taylor achieved something of fundamental importance. He was a brilliant publicist, and his teachings spread throughout American industry. Taylor's disciples moved beyond his simplistic economic psychology,

creating new professions of personnel administration and industrial psychology that purported to know how to extract more and better labor from workers. A threshold had been crossed into the modern era of labor management.

So the circle closed on American workers. With each advance, the quest for efficiency cut deeper into their cherished autonomy. Mechanization, scientific management, and the growing scale of industrial activity diminished workers and cut them down to fit the production system. The process occurred unevenly. For textile workers the loss had come early, but miners and ironworkers felt it much more slowly. Others, such as craft workers in the building trades, escaped the process almost entirely. But increasing numbers of workers found themselves in an environment that crushed any sense of mastery or even understanding.

The Labor Movement

Wherever industrialization has taken hold, workers have organized and responded collectively. However, the movements they built have varied from one industrial society to another. In the United States, workers were especially uncertain about the path they wanted to take. Only in the 1880s did the American labor movement settle into a fixed course.

Reformers and Unionists

In 1883 a New York wagon driver named Thomas B. McGuire testified before a Senate committee. He had saved $300 from his wages "so that I might become something of a capitalist eventually." But he soon failed. "A man in the express business today owning one or two horses and a wagon cannot even eke out an existence from the business," McGuire complained. "The competition is too great from the Adams Express Company and all those other monopolies." McGuire's prospects seemed no better in the hack (hired carriage) business:

> Corporations usually take that business themselves. They can manage to get men, at starvation wages, and put them on a hack, and put a livery on them with a gold band and brass buttons, to show that they are slaves—I beg pardon; I did not intend to use the word slaves; there are no slaves in this country now—to show that they are merely servants.

Slave or liveried servant, the symbolic meaning was the same to McGuire. He was speaking of the crushed aspirations of the independent American worker.

Labor Reform and the Knights of Labor. What would satisfy the Thomas McGuires of the nineteenth century? Only the restoration of a republican society in which all members were social and political equals and everyone might hope to become independent. Recapturing the republican virtues did not require returning to the agrarian past but, rather, moving beyond the selfishness of the existing industrial order to a future when no distinction would exist between capitalists and workers. All would be "producers" laboring together in what was commonly called the "cooperative commonwealth." This ideal inspired wave after wave of labor-reform movements going back to the workingmen's parties of the 1830s and culminating after the Civil War in the Noble and Holy Order of the Knights of Labor.

The Knights of Labor was founded in 1869 as a secret society of Philadelphia garment cutters. The organization gradually spread to other cities and by 1878 had become a national movement. Led by Grand Master Workman Terence V. Powderly, the Knights boasted an elaborate ritual and ceremony calculated to appeal to the fraternal spirit of nineteenth-century workers. They got from the Knights of Labor a sense of belonging very much like that offered by the Masons or Odd Fellows. For the Knights, however, fraternalism was harnessed to labor-reform advocacy. The goal was to "give voice to that grand undercurrent of mighty thought, which is today [1880] crystallizing in the hearts of men, and urging them on to perfect organization through which to gain the power to make labor emancipation possible."

But how was "emancipation" to be achieved? The Knights tried a number of solutions, including cooperation. Funds would be raised to set up cooperative factories and shops owned and run by the employees. As those cooperatives flourished and spread, American society would be transformed into a cooperative commonwealth. But little was actually done. In reality, the Knights concentrated mainly on "education." Powderly regarded the organization as a vast labor lyceum that almost anyone could join. The cooperative commonwealth would arrive in some mysterious way as more and more "producers" became members and learned the group's message from lectures, discussions, and publications. Social evil would not end in a day but "must await the gradual development of educational enlightenment."

Trade Unionism. The labor-reform movement expressed the higher aspirations of American workers. Another kind of organization—the trade union—tended to their day-to-day needs. Unions had long been central in the lives of craft workers. Apprenticeship rules regulated entry into a trade, and the *closed shop*—by reserving all jobs for union members—kept out lower-wage and incompetent workers. Union rules specified the terms of work, sometimes in minute detail. Above all, trade unionism defended the craft worker's traditional skills and rights.

The union also expressed the social identity of a craft. Hatters took pride in their drinking prowess, an on-the-job privilege that was jealously guarded, and their unions sometimes resembled drinking clubs. More often, however, craft unions had an uplifting character. A Birmingham iron puddler claimed that his union's "main object was to educate mechanics up to a standard of morality and temperance, and good workmanship." Because operating trains was a high-risk occupation, the railroad brotherhoods stressed mutual aid, providing ac-

A Railroad Brotherhood
Locomotive firemen, who fed the boilers on nineteenth-century steam engines, ranked below locomotive engineers but still considered theirs a privileged occupation. This union certificate conveys the respectable values to which locomotive firemen adhered and, as depicted in the scenes on the right-hand side, the need they felt to protect their families (through the affordable insurance provided by their union) in the event of accidents that were so much a part of the dangerous trade they followed.

cident and death benefits and encouraging members to assist one another. On the job and off, the unions played a big part in the lives of craft workers.

The earliest unions were local groups of workers in the same trade. Many of them, especially among German workers, were organized initially along ethnic lines. As expanding markets broke down their insularity, these unions began to form national organizations, starting with the International Typographical Union in 1852. By the 1870s molders, ironworkers, bricklayers, and about thirty other trades had formed national unions.

The protection of job interests might have seemed a far cry from the reform idealism of the Knights of Labor, but both motives arose from a single workers' culture. Seeing no conflict, many workers carried membership cards for both the Knights of Labor and a trade union. The careers of many labor leaders, including Powderly, likewise embraced both kinds of activity. For many years even the functional lines were indistinct. At the local level, little separated a trade assembly of the Knights from a local trade union; both engaged in fraternal and job-oriented activities.

Trade unions generally barred women, and so did the Knights until, in 1881, women shoe workers in Philadelphia struck in support of their male co-workers and won the right to form their own local assembly. By 1886 probably 50,000 women belonged to the Knights of Labor. Their courage on the picket line prompted Powderly's rueful remark that women "are the best men in the Order." For a handful, such as the hosiery worker Leonora M. Barry, the Knights provided a rare chance to take up leadership roles as organizers and officials. For many others the liberation was more modest but very real: "timid young girls—girls who have been overworked from their cradle—stand[ing] up bravely . . . swayed . . . by the wrongs heaped upon their comrades, talk[ing] nobly and beautifully of the hope of redress to be found in organization." Similarly, the Knights of Labor grudgingly expanded the opportunity for black workers to join, because of the need for solidarity and, just as important, in deference to the Order's egalitarian principles. The Knights could rightly boast that their "great work has been to organize labor which was previously unorganized."

The American Federation of Labor

In the early 1880s the Knights began to act increasingly like a trade union. Boycott campaigns against the products of "unfair" employers achieved impressive results. With the economy booming and workers in short supply, the Knights began to win strikes, including a major victory against Jay Gould's Southwestern railway sys-

tem in 1885. Workers flocked into the organization, and its membership jumped from 100,000 to perhaps 700,000 in less than a year. For a brief time the Knights stood poised as a potential industrial-union movement capable of bringing all workers into its fold.

The rapid growth of the Knights of Labor frightened the national trade unions. They tried to keep their local branches away from the Knights, but they met with little success. The unions then began to insist on a clear separation of roles, with the Knights confined to the field of labor reform. This was partly a battle over turf, but it also reflected a deepening divergence of labor philosophies.

This divergence is perhaps best seen in the debate over the shorter workday. For labor reformers, the need for more leisure arose from the duties workers had "to perform as American citizens and members of society." More free time for workers was a precondition for a healthy republican society. Increasingly, however, the issue was seized by trade unionists, who gave the demand for the eight-hour day a more practical bent: it would spread the available jobs among more workers, protect them against overwork, and (like higher wages) give them a better life. "Eight hours for work, eight hours for rest, eight hours for what we will" was the slogan of the trade unions, not the Knights of Labor.

The Haymarket Square Riot. The trade unions set May 1, 1886, as the deadline for achieving the eight-hour day. As that day approached, a wave of strikes and demonstrations broke out. In Chicago a battle on May 3 at the McCormick agricultural implement works resulted in the deaths of four strikers. Chicago was a hotbed of American *anarchism*—the revolutionary advocacy of a stateless society—and local anarchists, most of them German immigrants, called a protest meeting the next evening at Haymarket Square. The meeting went peacefully, but when police moved in at the end to break it up, someone threw a bomb and several policemen were killed or wounded.

The anarchist organizers of the rally were charged wih criminal conspiracy, a legal doctrine so broad that it required no proof of direct involvement in the bombing to justify a verdict of guilt. There was in fact no evidence linking them to the bombing. Four men were executed, one committed suicide, and the others received long prison sentences. They were victims of one of the great miscarriages of American justice.

Seizing on the antiunion hysteria set off by the Haymarket affair, employers took the offensive against the campaign for an eight-hour day. They broke strikes violently, compiled blacklists of strikers, and forced others to sign *yellow-dog contracts* guaranteeing that, as a condition of employment, they would not join a union. If trade unionists needed further confirmation of the

Abraham Bisno

Trade Unionist

Repeated strikes in Chicago caused a government commission to come to that city in 1900 to investigate the reasons for the labor troubles. Bisno, a garment worker and "walking delegate"—a local union agent—gives the trade-union side of the story.

Q. Present occupation.

A. Collecting fares on the loop here for the Union Elevated Railway Company.

Q. Former occupation.

A. I am a cloak maker by trade—made cloaks for some years—and I have had several occupations within the last few years. I have been walking delegate for our union.

Q. What union is that?

A. The Chicago Cloak Makers' Union. . . .

Q. Is the union to which you belong still in existence?

A. It is lately organized again; it was broken up after the defeat of the strike 2 years ago. . . .

Q. Are you a believer in the union of labor?

A. Yes. . . . Unless a firm recognizes the union and agrees to employ nobody except members of the union, the union cannot exist. In my own trade,

when our union was weak, our best men were victimized, and were out of a job most of the time; I mean our most intelligent men—men who do not want to put up with abuse easily. . . . So when these men demand that the union be recognized to the extent of not employing other people except members of their union, this is essential to the very existence of the organization. It is a life-and-death question with them. . . .

Q. You recognize that the strike is a coercive measure—an act of war [and] and an interference with the civil rights of a concern?

A. . . . Yes; but then the reduction in wages, or failing to raise the wages when conditions warrant, are acts of war and interference with my civil rights in a time of peace. It is the same thing. . . .

Q. What are the steps of persuasion brought into use to influence a man who has failed to yield to argument and has gone to work?

A. Well several. For instance, in one case we have alienated a man from the affections of his co-church members.

Q. That you call persuasion?

A. Yes; we went into the church and denounced the fellow as a traitor to

our interests, cutting our throats, sort of sinning against the religious laws, inflicting damage on so many families.

Q. That is one step?

A. That was one of the means; called him scab.

Q. Called him scab?

A. Yes; on the streets.

Q. To his face?

A. Yes. As I told you, it depends upon the temperament of the man. We would go after him in a hundred and one ways, if we can, to drive him out of the community.

Q. That you call persuasion?

A. Within the law; and I think under certain conditions it is right for a person to violate the law and take the consequences. Supposing I am fined for calling a man a scab. I am put into a fine, say, of $10 and have to go to jail for 20 days. The abuse I am suffering may be so great that I would take my medicine. I would tell a man he was a scab, and take my medicine for it and go to jail. . . .

Source: Report of the U.S. Industrial Commission (Washington, D.C.: U.S. Government Printing Office, 1901), VIII, pp. 53–58, 79–82.

---

tough world in which they lived, they found it in Haymarket and its aftermath.

Samuel Gompers and the AFL. In December 1886, having failed to persuade the Knights of Labor to desist from union activity, the national trade unions formed the American Federation of Labor (AFL). The AFL embodied the belief of the national unions that they constituted a distinctive movement. The Federation in effect locked into place the trade-union structure as it had evolved by the 1880s. Underlying this structure was the conviction that workers had to take the world as it was, not as they dreamed it might be.

The architect of the American Federation of Labor and its president for nearly forty years was Samuel Gompers. Gompers, a cigar maker from New York City, hammered out the philosophical position that would define American "pure and simple" unionism. First, the focus would be on concrete short-term gains. Second, unions would rely on economic power rather than politics. Third, they would limit their membership to workers organized along strictly occupational lines. Finally, the unions strongly rejected the theories and grand schemes that had excited the labor reformers. Gompers developed these views as general propositions, but they were grounded in the hard experience of

Samuel Gompers
This is a photograph of the labor leader in his forties taken when he was visiting striking miners in West Virginia, an area where mine operators resisted unions with special fierceness. The photograph was taken by a company detective.

unionists such as Abraham Bisno (see American Voices, page 577) who tried to organize their fellow workers and bargain collectively with employers. Bisno would have nodded in agreement with Gompers's assertion that "no matter how just . . . unless the cause is backed up with power to enforce it, it is going to be crushed and annihilated."

The steady growth of the trade unions seemed to justify Gompers's confidence that he had found the correct formula for the American labor movement. The Knights of Labor lost momentum. Hard hit by the anti-labor reaction to the Haymarket affair, the organization retreated from the trade-union field and returned to the rhetoric of labor reform. In many localities not yet reached by the AFL, Knights' assemblies for a time met the need for labor organization. But by the late 1890s the Knights of Labor had faded away.

Industrial War

The trade unions were conservative in that they accepted the economic order; all they wanted was a larger share of it for working people. This was, however, reason enough for employers to resist collective bargaining. In the 1890s the trade-union movement came under fierce attack.

The Homestead Strike. Among America's workers, few had more reason to be satisfied with their lives than the skilled steelworkers of Homestead, Pennsylvania. They earned good wages, lived comfortably, and generally owned their own homes. The town was very much their community, with a municipal government elected from their ranks. And in Andrew Carnegie the Homestead workers thought they had a truly sympathetic employer. For had not Good Old Andy said in a famous magazine article that the right of workers to combine was no less sacred than that of capitalists? or that workers held a moral claim on their jobs that forbade the use of strikebreakers by employers?

Carnegie, unfortunately, had other plans. In his view the union had become too expensive. It deprived his steel company of the full benefits of the advanced machinery he was introducing; and with that machinery, the skills of his workers counted for less. Lacking the stomach for the hard battle ahead, Carnegie hid himself in his remote castle in Scotland but left behind a second-in-command eminently qualified for the job at hand. This was Henry Clay Frick, a former coal baron with a fearsome reputation as an enemy of trade unionism.

After some perfunctory bargaining Frick announced that effective July 1, 1892, the company would no longer deal with the Amalgamated Association of Iron and Steel Workers. If the employees wanted to work, they would have to return on an individual basis. Frick's strategy was already clear. Preparations had been made to fortify the plant so that strikebreakers could be brought in to resume operations and defeat the union. At stake now was not just wage cuts but the defense of a way of life. To preserve their "workers' republic," Homesteaders thought they had the right to deny the company access to the plant, and town authorities turned away the county sheriff when he tried to take possession of the plant. The entire community— women no less than men—mobilized in defense of the union.

At dawn on July 6 two bargeloads of Pinkerton guards were seen approaching Homestead up the Monongahela River. Behind hastily erected barricades, the strikers opened fire, and a bloody battle ensued. When the Pinkertons finally surrendered, they were mercilessly pummeled by the enraged women of Homestead as they retreated to the railway station. Frick appealed to the governor of Pennsylvania, who called out the state militia. Homestead was placed under martial law; strike leaders and town officials were arrested on charges of riot, murder, and treason; and the great steel works was taken over and opened to strikebreakers.

The defeat at Homestead marked the beginning of the end for trade unionism in the iron and steel industry. Ended too were any lingering illusions about the sanctity of workers' communities such as Homestead. "Men talk like anarchists or lunatics when they insist that the workmen of Homestead have done right," asserted one conservative journal. Nothing could be permitted to interfere with private property or threaten law and order.

The Homestead strike ushered in an era of strife in which working people faced not only the formidable power of corporate industry but the even more formidable power of their own government.

The Great Pullman Boycott. The fullest demonstration of that hard reality occurred at a place that seemed an even less likely site for class warfare than Homestead. Pullman, Illinois, was a model factory town, famous for the amenities it offered to workers and the beauty of its landscaping and city plan. The town was named for its creator, George M. Pullman, who had made a fortune as the inventor and manufacturer of the Pullman sleeping cars that brought comfort and luxury to railway travel. Still, when the Panic of 1893 struck, business fell off and the Pullman Company cut wages. But the rents for company housing were not cut, and many workers' take-home pay shrank to a pitiful level.

When a committee finally called on him in May 1894 to present the workers' grievances, Pullman refused to budge. There was no connection between his roles as employer and landlord, he insisted. As for the

The Pullman Strike
Chicago was the hub of the railwork network and the strategic center of the battle between the Pullman boycotters and the trunk line railroads. For the strikers, the crucial thing was to prevent those trains with Pullman cars attached from running; for the railroads, it was to get the trains through at any cost. The arrival of federal troops meant that the trains would move and that the strikers would be defeated.

committee members who approached him, they were fired.

The strike that ensued might have become no more than a footnote in American labor history but for the fact that the Pullman workers belonged to the American Railway Union (ARU), a rapidly growing industrial union of railroad workers recently formed by the labor leader Eugene V. Debs. In response to the strikers' plea, the ARU directed its members not to handle Pullman sleeping cars, which were operated by the railroads but were owned and serviced by the Pullman Company. This was a classic example of a *labor boycott*, in which force is applied at a secondary point (the railroads) to put pressure on the primary target (Pullman).

Railroad officials, already fearful of the growing power of the ARU, saw the Pullman boycott as their chance to break the union. The General Managers' Association, which represented the railroads serving Chicago, insisted on running the Pullman cars. Since ARU members refused to operate trains with Pullman cars, a far-flung strike soon spread across the country and threatened to disrupt the entire economy.

Quite deliberately, the railroad managers maneuvered to bring the federal government into the dispute. Their hook was the U.S. mail cars, which they attached to every train hauling Pullman cars. When strikers tried to stop those trains, the General Managers' Association appealed to President Cleveland to send in troops to protect the U.S. mail and put an end to the growing violence. It so happened that in Attorney-General Richard Olney, a former railroad lawyer, the General Managers' Association had a direct link to the president. Overriding the protests of the liberal Illinois governor, John P. Altgeld, Cleveland sent federal troops. When this tactic failed to quell the popular resistance, Olney got court injunctions prohibiting the ARU leaders from conducting the strike. Debs and his subordinates refused to obey; they were held in contempt of court and jailed. Now leaderless and hopelessly uncoordinated, the strike quickly disintegrated.

No one could doubt why the great Pullman boycott had failed: it had been crushed by the naked use of government power on behalf of the railroad companies.

American Radicalism in the Making

Oppression does not radicalize all of its victims, but for some, it does. And when social injustice is most painfully felt, when the underlying power realities stand most clearly revealed, the process of radicalization speeds up. Such was the case during the depression years of the 1890s. Out of the industrial strife of that decade emerged the main forces of twentieth-century American radicalism.

Eugene Debs and American Socialism. Very little in Eugene Debs's background suggested that he would one day become the nation's preeminent socialist. Born in 1855 to middle-class French-Alsatian parents, Debs grew up believing in the essential goodness of American society as he found it in his hometown of Terre Haute, Indiana, a prosperous midwestern railroad center. Active in the Democratic party and very popular in the community, Debs might have made a career in politics or business. Instead, he returned to the railway yards where he had worked as a boy, got involved in the local labor movement, and in 1880, at the age of twenty-five, was elected national secretary-treasurer of the Brotherhood of Locomotive Firemen.

This was one of the craft unions that represented the skilled operating trades on the railroads. It was highly conservative, opposed to strikes, and indifferent to the well-being of low-paid track and yard laborers. This began to bother Debs, and in 1892 he unexpectedly resigned from his comfortable union post to devote himself to a new organization—the American Railway Union—that would organize all railroad workers irrespective of skill, that is, an *industrial union*.

The Pullman boycott, as it developed into a life-and-death struggle, visibly changed Debs. It had become "a contest between the producing classes and the money power of the country," he declared. Debs was sentenced to six months in the federal penitentiary not for violating any specific law but for refusing to obey court orders he knew to be trumped-up and prejudicial. He came out of jail an avowed radical, committed to a lifelong struggle against a system that enabled employers to enlist the powers of government to enforce their arbitrary rule over working people. Initially Debs identified himself as a Populist, but he quickly gravitated toward the socialist camp.

German refugees had brought the ideas of Karl Marx, the German radical philosopher, to America after the failed 1848 revolutions in Europe. Marx offered a powerful economic critique of capitalism. His prescription for revolution through class struggle inspired the most durable radical movements in the industrial world. Although little noticed in most parts of American society, Marxist socialism struck deep roots in the growing German-American communities of Chicago and New York. In 1877 the Socialist Labor party was formed, and from that time on Marxist socialism maintained a continuing, if narrowly based, presence in American politics.

When Eugene Debs appeared in their midst in 1897, the socialists were in a state of crisis. Their leader, Daniel De Leon, was a brilliant theorist but a poor political manager. He preferred an ideologically pure party to one that tried to win the popular vote. De Leon's rigid beliefs prompted a revolt within the Socialist Labor party, in which Debs joined. When the rival Socialist Party of America was formed in 1901, it was with the aim of building a broad-based political movement.

A spellbinding campaigner, Debs was a superb spokesman for his party. He had the common touch and attracted a devoted national following. Debs talked about socialism in a popular idiom, making Marxism understandable and persuasive to many ordinary Americans. Under him the new party began to break down ethnic barriers and attract American-born voters. Many trade unionists, disillusioned as Debs had been by the unsettling events of the 1890s, went through the same kind of radical evolution and joined the party in large numbers. In Texas, Oklahoma, and Minnesota socialism exerted a powerful appeal among cotton and wheat farmers. The party was also highly successful at attracting women activists. Inside of a decade, with a national network of branches and state organizations, the Socialist party had become a force to be reckoned with in American politics.

Western Radicalism. In the meantime, a different brand of American radicalism was taking shape in the West. After many years of mostly friendly labor relations, the situation in the western mining camps turned ugly during the 1890s. Powerful new corporations were taking over, and they wanted to get rid of the miners' union, the Western Federation of Miners (WFM). Moreover, silver and copper prices became increasingly unprofitable in the early 1890s, bringing pressure to cut miners' wages. When strikes resulted, they took a particularly violent turn.

In 1892 at Coeur d'Alene, a silver-mining district in northern Idaho, striking miners engaged in gun battles with company guards, sent a car of explosive powder careering into the Frisco Mine, and threatened to blow up processing plants. Martial law was declared, federal troops came in, the strikers were crowded into "bullpens" (enclosed stockades), and the strike was broken. Similarly violent strikes took place at Cripple Creek, Colorado, in 1894; at Leadville, Colorado, in 1896; and again in Coeur d'Alene in 1899.

In those western strikes government intervention was particularly naked and unrestrained. This was partly a reaction to the level of violence, but it stemmed also from the character of politics in the lightly settled western states: either the miners would dominate state politics—as they did in a coalition with the Populists during their successful strike at Cripple Creek in 1894—or, as was increasingly true, the mine owners would dominate, with disastrous consequences for the miners.

The union leaders—Ed Boyce, Charles Moyer, and "Big Bill" Haywood—all served time in the bullpens or on the barricades and drew the appropriately grim conclusions. Initially their radicalism led them, like Debs, into the Socialist party, but they were strongly inclined toward direct action. In 1897, WFM President Boyce called on all union miners to arm themselves with rifles, and his rhetoric—that the wage system was "slavery in its worst form"—had a hard edge. Any lingering faith in the political process died in the Colorado state elections of 1904, after the suppression of bitterly fought strikes across the state in the previous two years. The miners thought they had defeated their archenemy, the Republican governor James H. Peabody, only to have the Colorado Supreme Court overturn the election results and reinstall Peabody (who, by prearrangement, resigned in favor of his lieutenant governor).

In 1905 the Western Federation of Miners led the way in creating a new radical labor movement, the Industrial Workers of the World (IWW). Although the IWW initially had links to the Socialist party, it swiftly repudiated political action and settled on its own radical course. The Wobblies, as IWW members were called, fervently supported the Marxist class struggle—but strictly in the industrial field. Through action at the point of production and an unending struggle against employers—ultimately by means of a general strike—they believed that the workers themselves would bring about a revolution. A workers' society would emerge, run directly by the workers through their industrial unions. The term *syndicalism* describes this brand of workers' radicalism.

In both of its major forms—the politically oriented Socialist party and the syndicalist IWW—American radicalism flourished after the crisis of the 1890s, but only on a limited basis. Socialists and Wobblies lived, in a sense, on the tolerance of society. They would later be crushed without ceremony. Nevertheless, they served a larger purpose. American radicalism, by its sheer vitality, bore witness to what was exploitative and unjust in the new industrial order.

Summary

American industrialism took its modern shape during the last decades of the nineteenth century. Central to this development were the shift from iron making to the manufacture of steel, the great expansion of coal mining, and the technology for generating steam and electric power. These advances made possible the production of the capital goods and energy required by an expanding manufacturing economy. An efficient railway system provided access to national markets. A managerial revolution enabled entrepreneurs to master the complex business organizations they were building. The scale of enterprise grew very large, and the vertically integrated firm became the predominant form of business organization. Only in the South did prevailing conditions—in particular, its insulated, low-wage labor market—retard the growth of an advanced industrial economy.

In the North the enormous demand for labor led to a great influx of immigrants, making ethnic diversity a distinctive feature of the American working class. Gender also defined occupational opportunity. Women joined the labor force in growing numbers, but almost universally they were subjected to a sex-typing process that relegated them to "women's work," always at wage rates below those of men. Mass production—the high-volume output of standardized products—vastly improved the productivity of American manufacturing but also deskilled workers and mechanized their jobs. Scientific management, the brainchild of Frederick W. Taylor, cut further into the traditional autonomy of American workers by systematizing the labor process and shifting control into the hands of supervisors.

The late nineteenth century gave rise to the American labor movement in its modern form. In the Knights of Labor anticapitalist labor reform enjoyed one final surge during the mid 1880s and then succumbed to the "pure and simple" unionism of the American Federation of Labor. The AFL was conservative in that it accepted the economic order, but its insistence on a larger share of the benefits for working people guaranteed that the trade-union movement would be fiercely resisted by employers. The result was a series of bitter strikes: Homestead in 1892, the Pullman boycott of 1894, and, most violently, the series of metal miners' strikes in the Far West. The industrial warfare of the 1890s stirred new radical impulses, leading on the one hand to the political socialism of Eugene Debs and on the other to the industrial radicalism of the IWW.

TIMELINE

1869	Knights of Labor founded in Philadelphia First transcontinental railroad completed
1872	Montgomery Ward, first mail-order house, founded Andrew Carnegie starts construction of Edgar Thompson steel works near Pittsburgh
1873	Panic of 1873 ushers in economic depression
1875	John Wanamaker establishes first department store in Philadelphia
1876	Philadelphia Centennial Exhibition showcases Corliss steam engine
1877	Baltimore and Ohio workers initiate nationwide railroad strike
1878	Gustavus Swift introduces refrigerator car
1879	Jay Gould begins to build Missouri Pacific railway system
1883	Railroads establish national time zones
1886	Haymarket Square bombing in Chicago American Federation of Labor (AFL) founded
1890	U.S. surpasses Britain in producing iron and steel
1892	Homestead steel strike crushed Coeur d'Alene miners' strike inaugurates era of industrial warfare in western mining
1893	Panic of 1893 starts depression of the 1890s Wave of railroad bankruptcies; reorganization by investment bankers begins
1894	President Cleveland sends troops to break Pullman boycott
1895	Frederick W. Taylor explains scientific management in "A Piece-Rate System" Southeastern European immigration exceeds northern European immigration for the first time
1901	Eugene V. Debs helps found Socialist party
1905	Industrial Workers of the World (IWW) launched

BIBLIOGRAPHY

The most useful introduction to the economic history of this period is Edward C. Kirkland, *Industry Comes of Age, 1860–1897* (1961). A more sophisticated analysis can be found in W. Elliot Brownlee, *Dynamics of Ascent* (rev. ed., 1979). For essays on many of the topics covered in this chapter, consult Glenn Porter, ed., *Encyclopedia of American Economic History* (3 vols., 1980).

Industrial Capitalism Triumphant

On railroads a convenient introduction is John F. Stover, *American Railroads* (1970). The growth of the railroads as an integrated system has been treated in George R. Taylor and Irene D. Neu, *The American Railway Network, 1861–1890* (1956). Thomas Cochran, *Railroad Leaders, 1845–1890* (1953), is a pioneering study of the industry's entrepreneurs. Julius Grodinsky, *Jay Gould: His Business Career, 1867–1892* (1957), is a complex study that describes the contributions this railroad buccaneer made to the transportation system. Books such as Cochran's and Grodinsky's have gone a long way toward resurrecting Gilded Age businessmen from the debunking tradition first set forth with great power in Matthew Josephson, *Robber Barons: Great American Fortunes* (1934). Peter Temin, *Iron and Steel in the Nineteenth Century* (1964), is the best treatment of that industry. Joseph F. Wall, *Andrew Carnegie* (1970), is the definitive biography of the great steelmaker. Equally definitive in regard to the oil king is Allan Nevins, *A Study in Power: John D. Rockefeller* (2 vols., 1953). On the development of mass production the key book is David A. Hounsell, *From the American System to Mass Production, 1800–1932* (1984). Alfred D. Chandler, *The Visible Hand: The Managerial Revolution in American Business* (1977), is not an easy book but will amply repay the labors of interested students.

On the New South the standard work has long been C. Vann Woodward, *Origins of the New South, 1877–1913* (1951). Equally essential as a modern reconsideration is Edward L. Ayers, *The Promise of the New South: Life after Reconstruction* (1992). A brilliant reinterpretation of the causes of the South's economic retardation is Gavin Wright, *Old South, New South: Revolutions in the Southern Economy since the Civil War* (1986). Jacqueline Jones, *The Dispossessed: America's Underclasses from the Civil War to the Present* (1992), contains an excellent treatment of southern labor.

The World of Work

To understand the impact of industrialism on American workers, three collections of essays make the best starting points: Herbert G. Gutman, *Work, Culture and Society in Industrializing America* (1976); Michael S. Frisch and Daniel J. Walkowitz, eds., *Working-Class America: Essays on Labor, Community, and American Society* (1983); and Leon Fink, *In Search of the Working Class* (1994). On the introduction of Taylorism, the most useful book is Daniel Nelson, *Managers and Workers: Origins of the New Factory System* (1975). The impact of Taylorism on American workers is treated with insight in David Montgomery, *The Fall of the House of Labor: The Workplace, the State, and American Labor Activism, 1865–1925* (1987).

Two valuable collections of essays on immigrant workers are Richard Ehrlich, ed., *Immigrants in Industrial America* (1977), and Dirk Hoerder, ed., *American Labor and Immigration History, 1877–1920: Recent European Research* (1983). David Brody, *Steelworkers in America: The Nonunion Era* (1960), examines workers in a single industry. John Bodnar, *Immigration and Industrialization: Ethnicity in an American Mill Town* (1977), is an important case study of a single community. On women workers the best introduction is Alice Kessler-Harris, *Out to Work* (1982). Ava Baron, ed., *Work Engendered: Toward a New History of American Labor* (1991), is a rich collection of essays that apply gender analysis to the history of working people. On black workers useful introductions are William H. Harris, *The Harder We Run: Black Workers since the Civil War* (1982), and Philip S. Foner, *Organized Labor and the Black Worker* (1974). Walter Licht, *Getting Work: Philadelphia, 1840–1950* (1992), is a pioneering history of a labor market in operation.

The Labor Movement

The standard book on the struggle between labor reform and trade unionism is Gerald N. Grob, *Workers and Utopia, 1865–1900* (1961). For the Knights of Labor, it should be supplemented by Leon Fink, *Workingmen's Democracy: The Knights of Labor and American Politics* (1983), which captures the cultural dimensions of labor reform not seen by earlier historians. The place of labor in the political environment is the subject of David Montgomery, *Citizen Worker* (1993). Paul Krause, *The Battle for Homestead, 1880–1892* (1992), puts the great strike in a larger social context. The most recent survey, incorporating much of the latest scholarship, is Bruce Laurie, *Artisans into Workers: Labor in Nineteenth Century America* (1989).

The founder of the AFL is the subject of a lively brief biography by Harold Livesay, *Samuel Gompers and Organized Labor in America* (1978). Among the many books on individual unions, Robert Christie, *Empire in Wood* (1956), best reveals the way pure-and-simple unionism worked out in practice. On industrial conflict the most vivid book is Robert V. Bruce, *1877: Year of Violence* (1959). Stanley Buder, *Pullman: An Experiment in Industrial Order and Community Planning, 1880–1930* (1967), provides an informed account of the great Pullman strike and places it in its local context. The best book on the IWW is Melvyn Dubofsky, *We Shall Be All* (1969). On socialism, David Shannon, *The Socialist Party of America* (1955), remains the standard account. There is, however, a fine biography of that party's leader that supersedes previous studies: Nick Salvatore, *Eugene V. Debs: Citizen and Socialist* (1982). A dimension of American radicalism long neglected has received sensitive attention in Mari Jo Buhle, *Women and American Socialism, 1870–1920* (1982).

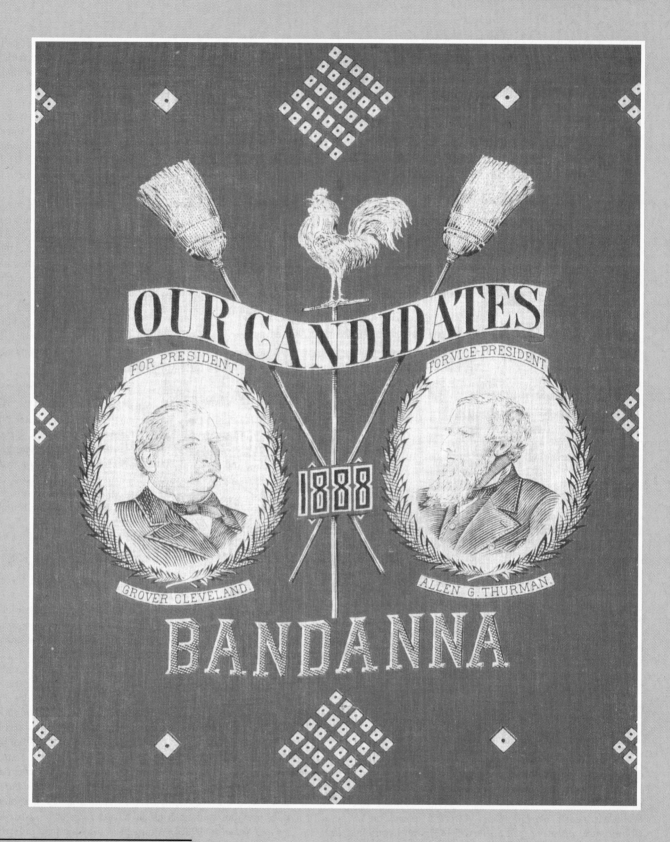

Bandanna, 1888 Election Memorabilia

During the late nineteenth century, politics became a vibrant
part of America's culture. Party paraphernalia, such as the
bandanna above, flooded the country. (Museum of American
Political Life)

CHAPTER 19

The Politics of Late Nineteenth-Century America

★   ★   ★

Ever since the founding of the republic, foreign visitors had been coming to America to study its political system. Most famous of the early observers was Alexis de Tocqueville, who wrote *Democracy in America* in 1832. When an equally brilliant visitor, the Englishman James Bryce, sat down to write his own account fifty years later, he decided that Tocqueville's great book could not serve as his model. For Tocqueville, Bryce noted "America was primarily a democracy, the ideal democracy, fraught with lessons for Europe." In his book, *The American Commonwealth* (1888), Bryce was much less rhapsodic. Democratic government as it existed in the America of the 1880s seemed to Bryce "a cause not so potent in the moral and social sphere as [Tocqueville] deemed it." The robust democracy celebrated by Tocqueville had devolved half a century later into the dreary machine politics of the Gilded Age.

Bryce was anxious that the European readers for whom he was writing not misunderstand him. His rigorously factual account of American politics contained "much that is sordid, much that will provoke unfavourable comment." Europeans should place those facts not in the context of their own countries, however, but in that of the United States. They needed to be aware of "the existence in the American people of a reserve of force and patriotism more than sufficient to sweep away all the evils now tolerated." Bryce was ultimately an optimist: "A hundred times in writing this book have I been disheartened by the facts I was stating; a hundred times has the recollection of the abounding strength and vitality of the nation chased away these tremours."

Just what it was that Bryce found so disheartening in the practice of American politics is the first subject of this chapter; the chapter will then discuss how the underlying vitality Bryce sensed began to reinvigorate the nation's politics by the start of the twentieth century.

The Politics of the Status Quo, 1877–1893

In times of national ferment, as a rule, public life becomes magnified. Leaders emerge. Electoral campaigns debate great issues. The powers of government expand. That had certainly been true of the Civil War era. During the crises of Union and Reconstruction the nation's public institutions had been tested to the utmost. The final crisis had occurred over the contested presidential election of 1876. In 1877, with the Republican Rutherford B. Hayes safely settled in the White House and the last federal troops withdrawn from the South, the era of sectional strife finally ended.

Political life went on, but it had been drained of its earlier drama. In the 1880s there were no Lincolns and no great national debates. Whereas defenders of the Union had once envisioned a social order and an economic system reshaped by an activist state, in the 1880s the nation's political leaders retreated to a more modest conception of state power. There remained an irreducible core of public functions—from managing the currency to crafting an Indian policy—and even, as on the question of railroad regulation, grudging acceptance of new governmental engagement. But the dominant rhetoric celebrated that government which governed least and as compared with the Civil War era, American government did govern less. In other ways, however, political life remained robust. The parties were highly organized and very active. And politics provided an arena in which the fierce cultural conflicts dividing Americans could be played out. But public policy itself seemed of no great moment; the nation's central concerns lay elsewhere.

The National Scene

There were five presidents from 1877 to 1893: Rutherford B. Hayes (Republican, 1877–1881), James A. Garfield (Republican, 1881), Chester A. Arthur (Republican, 1881–1885), Grover Cleveland (Democrat, 1885–1889), and Benjamin Harrison (Republican, 1889–1893). All were estimable men. Hayes, Garfield, and Harrison boasted distinguished war records. Hayes had served effectively as governor of Ohio for three terms, and Garfield had done well as a Congressional leader. Arthur, despite his reputation as a machine politician, had demonstrated fine administrative skills as head of the New York customs house. Cleveland had made his mark as reform mayor of Buffalo and governor of New York. None was a charismatic leader, and only Cleveland, the lone Democrat, was an assertive public figure. But circumstances more than personal qualities explain why these presidents did not make a larger mark on history.

Grover Cleveland
In the years after Reconstruction, Americans did not look for charismatic personalities or dramatic leadership in their presidents. They preferred men who accepted the limits of executive power, men of "sound conservatism." Grover Cleveland fitted the bill to perfection. For political reformers, Cleveland had the additional virtues of independence and personal integrity. He best represented the late nineteenth-century ideal of the American president.

Their biggest job was to dispense political patronage. Under the spoils system, government appointments were treated as rewards for those who had served the victorious party. Reform of this system became an urgent issue after President Garfield was killed in 1881. His assassin, Charles Guiteau, was a deranged religious fanatic, but advocates of civil-service reform managed to blame Garfield's death on the poisonous atmosphere of the spoils system. The resulting Pendleton Act of 1883 created a list of civil-service jobs to be filled on the basis of examinations administered by the new Civil Service Commission. The list originally included only 10 percent of all federal jobs, however, and patronage remained a preoccupation in the White House. When the Democrats won the presidency in 1884 for the first time in nearly thirty years, the pent-up hunger for jobs by the party faithful nearly overwhelmed Grover Cleveland. He was known to complain bitterly about the "damned, ever-lasting clatter for office." The standards of public administration did rise measurably, but there was no American counterpart to the elite professional civil services taking shape in Britain and Germany in these years.

Other than dispensing patronage, presidents did not have a lot to do. As late as 1897 the White House staff consisted of half a dozen assistants plus a few clerks, doorkeepers, and messengers. The president exerted little control over the federal bureaucracy. Budgetary matters were not his province but Congress's, and federal agencies accordingly paid much more heed to Capitol Hill and the key money-dispensing committees than to the White House.

The functions of the executive branch were, in any event, limited in these years. Of the 100,000 federal employees in 1880, fully 56 percent worked for the U.S. Post Office. During the 1880s the important government departments—Treasury, State, War, Navy, Interior—were sleepy places carrying on largely routine duties. Virtually all federal income came from customs duties and the excise tax on liquor and tobacco. These sources produced more money than the government spent. The question of how to reduce the federal *surplus* ranked as one of the most troublesome issues of the 1880s.

As for setting a national agenda, this was—unlike in Lincoln's day or our own—not to be looked for from the White House. "The office of President is essentially executive in nature," Cleveland insisted, not involving policy making. In fact, as a Democratic president facing a hostile Republican Senate, Cleveland did begin to assert himself on policy matters, but in a mostly negative way: in his first term he vetoed a record number of bills.

Congressional Government. On matters of national policy presidents took a back seat to Congress. But Congress was not well set up to do its work. Party discipline was weak, and procedural rules frequently stymied legislative business. Neither party ever stayed in power long enough to push through a coherent legislative program. From 1877 to 1893 neither Democrats nor Republicans controlled both houses for more than a single two-year term. Most of the time, the Democrats controlled the House and the Republicans ran the Senate.

Historically, the two parties represented somewhat different traditions. The Democrats favored states' rights and limited government whereas the Republicans were heirs to the Whig enthusiasm for publicly assisted economic development. After Reconstruction the Republicans backed away from that activist position and, in truth, neither party was eager to translate the remaining differences into well-defined positions. On most of the leading issues of the day—civil-service reform, the currency, and regulation of the railroads—the divisions occurred within the parties, not between them. The laws Congress passed could not be clearly identified as either Democratic or Republican.

Only the tariff retained its potency as a partisan issue. From Lincoln's day onward high duties protected American industry against imported goods. It was an article of Republican faith, as President Harrison said in 1892, that "the protective system . . . has been a mighty instrument for the development of the national wealth." The Democrats, free traders by tradition, regularly attacked Republican protectionism. In practice, however, the tariff was a negotiable issue like any other. Congressmen voted in accordance with their constituents' interests, regardless of party rhetoric. As a result, every tariff bill was a patchwork of bargains among special interests.

In 1887 President Cleveland cast off his reluctance to lead the nation and made the tariff a defining Democratic issue. Ardently opposed to protectionism, Cleveland devoted his entire annual message to Congress to tariff reform and campaigned on that basis for reelection in 1888. His narrow defeat seemed to confirm the political wisdom of evading big issues. "They told me it would hurt the party," he later wrote. "Perhaps I made a mistake from the party standpoint; but damn it, it was right. I had at least that satisfaction."

Campaign Politics. The major parties treated issues gingerly partly because they were so equally balanced. The Democrats, in retreat immediately after the Civil War, quickly regrouped and by the end of Reconstruction stood on virtually equal terms with the Republicans. Every presidential election from 1876 to 1892 was decided by a thin margin, and neither party gained command of Congress. Political caution seemed wise; any false move on national issues might tip the scales to the other side.

The Englishman James Bryce, accustomed to the ideological divisions between Tories and Liberals, grumbled about the indistinctness of American politics. "Neither party has any principles, any distinctive tenets," he wrote. Perhaps Bryce exaggerated when he added, "All has been lost, except office or the hope of it." But electoral success had unquestionably taken precedence over party principle.

This was evident in the way the Republican party treated its Civil War legacy. The major unfinished business after 1877 involved the needs of the former slaves in the South. The Republican agenda called for federal funding to combat illiteracy and, even more threatening to the South, federal protection for black voters in southern Congressional elections. Neither measure managed to make it through Congress, and both died during the Harrison administration. With little left to gain from Reconstruction politics, the Republicans backpedaled on the race issue and gradually abandoned the blacks to their fate.

The Republicans were not so willing to abandon their Civil War identification as saviors of the Union. In every election campaign Republican orators "waved the bloody shirt" against the "treasonous" Democrats. Service in the Union army gave candidates a strong claim to public office. One-third of Republican congressmen in the 1880s had a war record, and veterans' benefits always stood high on the Republican agenda. The Democrats played the same game in the South as the defenders of the Lost Cause. Bryce criticized American politicians for "clinging too long to outworn issues and neglecting the problems . . . which now perplex the country."

Alternatively, campaigns could descend into comedy. In the hard-fought election of 1884, for example, the Democrat Cleveland burst onto the scene as a reformer, fresh from his victories over corrupt machine politics as Buffalo mayor and New York governor. The Kansas editor William Allen White saw Cleveland as the champion of a people "sick with politics" and "nauseated at all politicians." But it turned out that years

The Plumed Knight
In the fierce party politics of the Gilded Age the political cartoon became a polished art form, and its high priest was Thomas Nast. In this cartoon Nast pillories James G. Blaine, celebrated as the "Plumed Knight" among his Republican supporters but fatally damaged in his ambitions to become president by reports that as Speaker of the House of Representatives he had taken bribes from an Arkansas railroad. Nast depicts the "knight" Blaine jousting in a tournament, with this ironic comment: "The 'Great American' Game of Public Office for Private Gain."

earlier Cleveland had fathered an illegitimate child, and throughout the campaign he was dogged by the ditty "Maw, Maw, where's Paw? He's in the White House, haw-haw-haw." His opponent, James G. Blaine, already on the defensive for taking favors from the railroads, got tangled up in the scandalous charge by a too ardent Republican supporter that the Democrats were the party of "Rum, Romanism and Rebellion." In the midst of all the mudslinging, the issues got lost.

The characteristics of public life in the 1880s—the inactivity of the federal government, the evasiveness of the political parties, and the absorption in politics for its own sake—derived ultimately from the conviction that little was at stake in public affairs. In 1887 Cleveland vetoed a small appropriation for drought-stricken Texas farmers with the remark that "though the people support the Government, the Government should not support the people." Governmental activity was itself considered a bad thing. All that the state can do, said Republican Senator Roscoe Conkling, "is to clear the way of impediments and dangers, and leave every class and every individual free and safe in the exertions and pursuits of life." Conkling was expressing the political corollary to the doctrine of *laissez-faire*—the belief that that government was best which governed least.

The Ideology of Individualism

In 1885, when the Knights of Labor were at their peak, the cotton manufacturer Edward Atkinson gave a talk to the textile workers of Providence, Rhode Island. They had, he told them, no cause for discontent: "There is always plenty of room on the front seats in every profession, every trade, every art, every industry. . . . There are men in this audience who will fill some of those seats, but they won't be boosted into them from behind." (There were certainly women as well in the audience—at least half the Rhode Island labor force was female—but, as was characteristic of the times, Atkinson assumed that economic opportunity was of interest only to men.) Every man, Atkinson continued, got what he deserved. For example, Cornelius Vanderbilt had amassed a fortune of $200 million by building the New York Central Railroad. Atkinson made some rapid calculations. Every person in the audience consumed about a barrel of flour a year. In 1865 it had cost $3.45 to ship that barrel from Chicago to Providence. In 1885 the New York Central carried it for 68 cents, taking 14 cents as profit, so that the workingman saved nearly $3. "Wasn't Vanderbilt a cheap man for you to employ as a teamster?" Atkinson asked. "Do you grudge him the fourteen cents?"

Atkinson's homely talk went to the roots of conservative American thought: any man, however humble, could rise as far as his talents would carry him; every

Facing the World

The cover of this Horatio Alger novel (1893) captures the myth of opportunity that Edward Atkinson extolled to his audience of textile workers. Our hero "Harry Vane" is a poor but earnest lad, valise packed, ready to make his way in the world and, despite the many obstacles thrown in his path, sure to succeed. In some 135 books Horatio Alger repeated this story, with minor variations, for an eager reading public that numbered in the millions.

person received his just reward, great or small; and the success of the individual, so encouraged, contributed to the progress of the whole. How persuasive the workers listening to Atkinson found his message we have no way of knowing. But the confidence with which Atkinson presented his case is evidence of the continuing appeal of the ideology of individualism in the age of industrial expansion.

A wide variety of popular writings trumpeted the individualist creed, from the rags-to-riches tales of Horatio Alger to the stream of success manuals with titles such as *Thoughts for the Young Men of America, or a Few Practical Words of Advice to those Born in Poverty and Destined to be Reared in Orphanages* (1871). It was a lesson celebrated in the lives of self-made men such as Andrew Carnegie, whose book *Triumphant Democracy* (1886) paid homage to a nation that had enabled a penniless Scottish child to rise from bobbin boy to steel magnate.

From the pulpit came the assurances of the Episcopal bishop William Lawrence of Massachusetts that "Godliness is in league with riches." Bishop Lawrence

was voicing a tradition in American Protestantism that went back to the Puritans: success in one's earthly calling signified the promise of eternal salvation. It was all too easy for a conservative ministry to make the furious acquisitiveness of industrial America morally reassuring. "To secure wealth is an honorable ambition," intoned the Baptist minister Russell H. Conwell in his lecture "Acres of Diamonds." "Money is power. Every good man and woman ought to strive for power, to do good with it when obtained." This notion of *stewardship*—the idea that wealth carried with it a social obligation—Andrew Carnegie elevated into a formal doctrine that he called "the gospel of wealth." Carnegie argued that it was the responsibility of the rich to put their money to good use. They should not coddle the less privileged but provide the libraries, education, and cultural and scientific institutions by which the worthy poor might prepare themselves for life's challenges.

Social Darwinism. American individualism drew strong intellectual support from the most important scientific theory of the age. In *The Origin of Species* (1859) the British naturalist Charles Darwin had presented a bold hypothesis to explain the evolution of plants and animals. In nature, Darwin wrote, all living things struggle and compete. Individual members of a species are born with characteristics that better enable them to survive in their particular environment: camouflage coloring for a bird, for example, or resistance to thirst in a desert animal. These survival characteristics, since they are heritable, become dominant in future generations, and the species evolves. This process of evolution, which Darwin called *natural selection*, created a revolution in biological science.

Although unintentionally, Darwin's theory made a big impact on the study of human society. Drawing on Darwin, the British philosopher Herbert Spencer developed an elaborate analysis of how society evolved through constant competition and "survival of the fittest." Social Darwinism, as Spencer's ideas became known, was championed in America by William Graham Sumner, a sociology professor at Yale. Competition, said Sumner, is a law of nature that "can no more be done away with than gravitation." Furthermore, "if we do not like the survival of the fittest, we have only one possible alternative, and that is the survival of the unfittest. The former is the law of civilization; the latter is the law of anti-civilization." And who are the fittest? "The millionaires. . . . They may fairly be regarded as the naturally selected agents of society. They get high wages and live in luxury, but the bargain is a good one for society."

Social Darwinists also argued against any interference with social processes. "The great stream of time and earthly things will sweep on just the same in spite of us," Sumner wrote in a famous essay, "The Absurd Attempt to Make the World Over" (1894). "That is why it is the greatest folly of which a man can be capable to sit down with a slate and pencil to plan out a new social world." As for the government, it had "at bottom . . . two chief things . . . with which to deal. They are the property of men and the honor of women. These it has to defend against crime." The political meaning of Social Darwinism was clear. As Sumner put it: "Minimize to the utmost the relations of the state and industry."

The Supremacy of the Courts. This antigovernment appeal not only paralyzed political initiative but also shifted power away from the executive and legislative branches. "The task of constitutional government," declared Sumner, "is to devise institutions which shall come into play at critical periods to prevent the abusive control of the powers of a state by the controlling classes in it." Sumner meant the judiciary. From the 1870s onward the courts increasingly accepted the role that he assigned to them, becoming the guardians of the rights of private property against abuse by an intrusive government.

The main targets of the courts were the states rather than the national government. This was the case because, under the federal system as it was understood in the late nineteenth century, the residual powers—those not delegated by the Constitution to the federal government—left to the states primary responsibility for social welfare and economic regulation. The basis for this authority was the *police powers* of the states to ensure the health, safety, and morals of their citizens. How to strike a balance between state responsibility for the general welfare and the liberty of individuals to pursue their private interests was the dominant legal issue of the era. The problem might have been harder except for the fact that most states, caught up in the conservative ethos of the day, were themselves cutting back on expenditures and public services. Even so, there were more than enough state initiatives to alarm vigilant judges. Thus, in the landmark case *In Re Jacobs* (1885), the New York Supreme Court struck down a state law prohibiting cigar making in tenements on the grounds that such regulation exceeded the police powers of the state. The 1880s saw a record number of laws declared unconstitutional by state courts.

Increasingly, however, it was federal judges who took up the battle against state activism. The Supreme Court's crucial weapon in this campaign was the Fourteenth Amendment (1868), which prohibited the states from depriving "any person of life, liberty, or property, without due process of law." The due-process clause had been adopted during Reconstruction to protect the civil rights of the former slaves. But due process protected the property rights and contractual liberty of any "person," and corporations counted as persons. So interpreted, the Fourteenth Amendment became by the

turn of the century a powerful means of restraining the states in the use of their police powers.

The Supreme Court erected similar barriers against the federal government through a narrow reading of the Constitution. In 1895 the Court ruled that the federal power to regulate interstate commerce did not cover manufacturing and struck down a federal income tax law. And in areas where federal power was undeniable—such as the regulation of railroads—the Supreme Court reserved for itself the oversight of decisions that invaded property interests, such as how much railroads could charge their customers. The courts in effect were claiming for themselves the power to shape public policy on economic affairs.

The preeminent conservative jurist of the day, Stephen J. Field, made no bones about the dangers he saw in the nation's headlong industrial development: "As population and wealth increase—as the inequalities in the conditions of men become more and more marked and disturbing—as . . . angry menaces against order find vent in loud denunciations—it becomes more and more the imperative duty of the court to enforce with a firm hand every guarantee of the Constitution."

Power conferred status. The law, not politics, attracted the ablest people and held the public's esteem. A Wisconsin judge boasted: "The bench symbolizes on earth the throne of divine justice. . . . Law in its highest sense is the will of God." Judicial supremacy reflected the degree to which the ideology of individualism had become dominant in industrial America; it also testified to the low esteem to which American politics had sunk after Reconstruction.

Cultural Politics

Yet for all the criticism leveled against it, politics figured centrally in the nation's life. Proportionately more voters turned out in presidential elections from 1876 to 1892 than at any other time in American history, and these voters showed the highest commitment to the party of their choice. People voted Democratic or Republican for a lifetime. Many participated actively. Among Republican voters in New York City, a fourth were dues-paying party members. National conventions attracted huge crowds. "The excitement, the mental and physical strains," remarked an Indiana Republican after the 1888 convention, "are surpassed only by prolonged battle in actual warfare, as I have been told by officers of the Civil War who later engaged in convention struggles." The convention he described had nominated the colorless Benjamin Harrison on a routine platform. What was all the excitement about? Why did politics mean so much to late nineteenth-century Americans?

For one thing, politics was a vibrant part of the nation's culture. The journalist George M. Towle told a

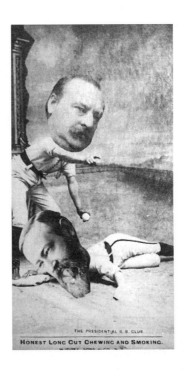

The Presidential B.B. Club (1888)
On the left, Grover Cleveland is the baseman; at center Benjamin Harrison is at bat; and on the right, Cleveland tags Harrison out—not, alas, the right prediction, since Harrison won the 1888 election.

British audience that America "is a land of conventions and assemblies, where it is the most natural thing in the world for people to get together in meetings, where almost every event is the occasion for speechmaking." Spellbinding orators such as Herbert G. Ingersoll drew enormous crowds at Republican rallies. During the election season the party faithful marched in impressive torchlight parades. Party paraphernalia flooded the country—handkerchiefs, mugs, posters, and buttons emblazoned with the Democratic donkey or the Republican elephant, symbols that had been adopted in the 1870s. In 1888 the presidential hopefuls were pictured on cards, like baseball players, in packs of Honest Long Cut tobacco. Campaigns had the suspense of baseball pennant races plus the excitement of the circus coming to town. In an age before movies and radio, politics ranked as one of the great American forms of mass entertainment.

Party loyalty was a deadly serious matter, however. Civil War emotions lasted a long time in both the North and the South. The Republican party, recalled the Cleveland reformer Brand Whitlock, was "a synonym for patriotism, another name for the nation. It was inconceivable that any self-respecting person should be a Democrat." In the North, Republicans had higher incomes and prided themselves on being the respectable elements of society. Senator George F. Hoar of Massachusetts described them as the people "who do the work of piety and charity in our churches . . . adminis-

ter the school systems, own and till their own farms . . . perform the skilled labor in the shops."

Ethnocultural Politics. More important than class, however, was religion and ethnic background. The two parties drew voters from different segments of society. Statistically, Democrats outside the South tended to be foreign-born and Catholic, whereas Republicans tended to be native-born and Protestant (see Figure 19.1). Among Protestants, the more pietistic a person's faith was—that is, the more personal and direct the believer's relationship to God—the more likely he or she was to be a Republican and to favor using the powers of the state to legislate public morality and regulate individual behavior. The Democrats, on the other hand, favored "the largest individual liberty consistent with public order."

During the 1880s ethnic tensions began to build in many cities. Education became an arena of bitter conflict. One issue was the place of foreign languages in the schools. Immigrant groups, especially the Germans, wanted their children taught in their own languages. However, native-born Americans passsed laws making English the language of instruction. In St. Louis, a heavily German city, the long-standing policy of teaching German to the entire student body was overturned after an acrimonious campaign.

Religion was an even more explosive educational issue. The use of the King James Version of the Bible in schools angered Catholics, who also fought a losing

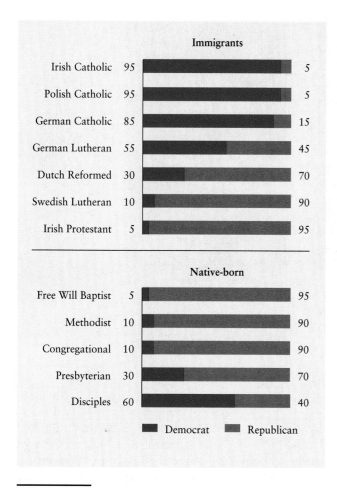

FIGURE 19.1

Ethnocultural Voting Patterns in the Midwest, 1870–1892

These figures demonstrate how voting patterns among mid-westerners reflected ethnicity and religion in the late nineteenth century. Especially striking is the overwhelming preference by immigrant Catholics for the Democratic party. Among Protestants there was an equally strong preference for the Republican party by certain groups of immigrants (Swedish Lutherans and Irish Protestants) and native-born (Free Will Baptists, Methodists, and Congregationalists), but other Protestant groups were more evenly divided in their party preferences.

battle over public aid for parochial schools. By 1900 such aid had been prohibited by twenty-three states. In Boston a furious controversy broke out in 1888 over the use of an anti-Catholic history textbook. When the school board withdrew the offending book, angry Protestants mounted a campaign to throw the moderates off the board and return the text to the curriculum.

Then there was the regulation of public morals. In many states so-called blue laws restricted activity on Sundays. When Nebraska banned Sunday baseball, the state supreme court approved the law as a blow struck in "the contest between Christianity and wrong." But

German and Irish Catholics, who saw nothing evil in a bit of fun on Sunday, considered blue laws a violation of their personal freedom.

The same kind of ethnocultural conflict flared over the liquor question. In a speech introducing the first constitutional amendment for national prohibition in 1876, Senator Henry W. Blair of New Hampshire laid down a challenge to his immigrant critics: "Upon discussion of this issue Irishman and German will in due time demonstrate that they are Americans." Although the Blair amendment languished, the antiliquor movement intensified. Many states adopted strict licensing and local-option laws governing the sale and consumption of alcoholic beverages. Indiana permitted drinking, but only joylessly in rooms containing "no devices for amusement or music . . . of any kind."

The hottest issues of the day—education, the liquor question, and observance of the Sabbath—were contested along ethnic and religious lines. Because they were also party issues—more so than tariffs, currency, and civil-service reform—they gave deep significance to party affiliation. Crusading Methodists thought of Republicans as the party of morality. For embattled Irish and German Catholics the Democratic party was the defender of their freedoms. The battles over public education and the liquor question were fought mostly at the state and local levels of northern politics. (The South, which received few immigrants, had a cultural politics driven by race rather than ethnicity.) In the North ethnocultural issues infused party affairs with a significance that would scarcely have been apparent to anyone looking only at the national scene.

Organizational Politics

Political life was also important because of the remarkable organizational activity it generated. By the 1870s both major parties had evolved a formal, well-organized structure. At the base lay the precinct or ward, where meetings could be attended by all party members. County, state, and national committees ran the ongoing business of the parties. Conventions determined party rules, adopted platforms, and selected the party's candidates for public office.

At election time the party's main job was to get out the vote. Wherever elections were close and hard-fought, the parties mounted intensive efforts organized down to the individual voter. In Indiana, for example, the Republicans appointed 10,000 "district men" in 1884, each responsible for turning out a designated group of voters. The Pennsylvania Republican party maintained a list of 800,000 voters classified by degree of voting reliability.

Only professionals could manage such a highly organized political system. The German sociologist Max Weber remarked that Americans regarded "politics as a

The Levi P. Morton Association
The top-hatted gentlemen in this photograph constituted the local Republican party organization of Newport, Rhode Island, named in honor of Levi P. Morton, Republican leader and vice-president during the Benjamin Harrison administration (1889–1893). The maleness of party politics leaps from the photograph and asserts more clearly than a thousand words why the suffragist demand for the right to vote was met with ridicule and disbelief.

vocation." This factor, above all else, gave American politics its special character. The distinguishing trait of American politicians, James Bryce observed, was "that their whole time is more frequently given to political work, that most of them draw an income from politics . . . that they . . . are proficient in the arts of popular oratory, of electioneering, and of party management." The party system required professionals, and professionalism created careers. Politics, like professional sports and trade unionism, served as an avenue of upward mobility for the many whose ethnic or class background barred them from the opportunities open to other Americans.

Machine Politics. Party administration seemed, on its face, highly democratic. In theory, all power derived from the party members in the precinct and ward organizations. In practice, however, the professionals ran the parties through unofficial internal organizations called *machines*, which consisted of insiders willing to accept discipline and do work in exchange for getting on the public payroll or pocketing bribes and other forms of "graft." The machines tended toward one-man rule, although the "boss" ruled more through the consent of the secondary leaders than through his own absolute power. Some bosses held public office. For state leaders, the U.S. Senate was preferred because, until the adoption of the Seventeenth Amendment in 1913, senators were chosen by state legislatures rather than by popular election. But public office was not necessary for the boss to run the show.

Absorbed in the tasks of power brokerage, machine bosses tended to see public issues as somewhat irrelevant. And the high stakes of money, jobs, and influence

made for intense factionalism. In New York, Manhattan's Tammany Hall was always at odds with the upstate Demcratic machine run by Senator David B. Hill. At the national level, Republicans fought bitterly among themselves after Ulysses S. Grant left the White House in 1877. For the next six years the party was divided into two warring factions—the Stalwarts, who followed Senator Roscoe Conkling of New York, and the Halfbreeds, who were led by James G. Blaine of Maine. The split was sparked by a personal feud between Conkling and Blaine, and it lasted because of a furious struggle over patronage. The Halfbreeds represented a newer Republican generation that was more inclined to pay lip service to political reform and less committed to the old Civil War issues. But issues had little to do with the war between Stalwarts and Halfbreeds. They were really fighting over the spoils of party politics.

And yet the record was not wholly negative. Machine politics raised the standards of government in certain ways. Disciplined professionals, veterans of machine politics, measurably improved the performance of state legislatures and Congress. More important, party machines filled a void in the nation's public life. They did informally much of what the governmental system left undone, especially in the cities (see Chapter 20).

The Mugwumps. But machine politics never managed to win public legitimacy. The social elite—intellectuals, well-to-do businessmen, and old-line families—deeply resented a politics that excluded people like themselves—the "best men." There was, too, a genuine clash of values. Political reformers called for "disinterestedness" and "independence"—the opposite of the self-serving careerism and party regularity fostered by the machine system. Many of them had earned their spurs as Liberal Republicans fighting the reelection of President Grant in 1872.

In 1884 Carl Schurz, Edwin L. Godkin, and Charles Francis Adams, Jr., split from the Republican party again because they could not stomach its presidential candidate, James G. Blaine, whom they associated with corrupt party politics. Mainly from New York and Massachusetts, these Republicans became known as Mugwumps—a derisive bit of contemporary slang, supposedly of Indian origin, referring to pompous or self-important persons. The Mugwumps threw their support to the Democrat Grover Cleveland and might have ensured his victory by giving him the votes by which he narrowly carried New York State. After the 1884 election, something of a national reform movement sprang up, spawning good-government campaigns across the country. Although they won some municipal victories, the Mugwumps achieved more as the nation's opinion molders. They controlled the respectable newspapers and journals and occupied a strategic place in the urban world.

Most of all, the Mugwumps defined the terms of debate over party politics by denouncing the machine system for its violation of American political values. The potency of this attack was most evident in their campaign for the secret ballot, which had been pioneered in Australia. Under this reform citizens would, in the privacy of a voting booth, mark an official ballot listing the candidates of all the parties instead of submitting in public view a party-supplied ticket at the polling place. The Australian ballot, which was adopted throughout the United States in the early 1890s, freed voters from party surveillance as they exercised the right to vote.

The Mugwumps were reformers, but not on behalf of social justice. The problems of working people did not evoke their sympathy, nor did they favor using the powers of the state to alleviate the suffering of the poor. As far as the Mugwumps were concerned, that government was best which governed least. Theirs was the brand of "reform" perfectly in keeping with a politics of the status quo.

Women's Political Culture

The young Theodore Roosevelt, an up-and-coming Republican state politician in 1884, referred to the Mugwumps contemptuously as "man-milliners." The sexual slur was not accidental. In attacking organizational politics, the Mugwumps were challenging one of the bastions of male society of the late nineteenth century. Party meetings and conventions were occasions not only for

carrying on the business of politics but also for performing the satisfying rituals of male sociability amid cigar smoke and whiskey. Moreover, politics was identified with manliness. It was brutally competitive. It dealt in the commerce of power. It was frankly self-aggrandizing. Party politics in short was no place for a woman.

So it was no wonder that the woman suffrage movement met with fierce opposition in those years. Susan B. Anthony succeeded in having a constitutional amendment introduced in 1878, but the cause of woman suffrage made little headway in Congress (see American Voices, page 595). Suffragists mounted campaigns at the state level, but before 1900 women gained the right to vote in only four western states: Wyoming, Idaho, Colorado, and Utah. In other states the most they could win was the right to vote for school boards or on tax issues. "Men are ordained to govern in all forceful and

Carry Nation Under Arrest

Opponents of alcohol had traditionally advocated temperance; that is, self restraint. The Woman's Christian Temperance Union took a more coercive approach. It demanded legal prohibition of alcohol. Some prohibitionists turned to direct action. Carry Nation became famous for her ax-wielding attacks on saloons. She meant to draw attention to the struggle, and so gladly went to jail—where she is headed in this photograph, taken in Enterprise, Kansas, in 1901.

Helen Potter

The Case for Women's Political Rights

In 1883 Helen Potter testified before the Senate Committee on Education and Labor about the sanitary conditions of the poor in New York City. But in the course of her testimony she delivered a powerful indictment of the unequal treatment of women that spoke volumes about the evolving women's political culture of the late nineteenth century.

The Witness. It is really an important question—this of the condition of women in our community. When I was a young girl I had some ambition, and when I heard a good speaker, or when I read something written by a good writer, I had an ambition to do something of that kind myself. I was exceedingly anxious to preach, but the churches would not have me; why, they said that a woman must not be heard. . . .

Q. I suppose you have an idea that women might abolish some of the tricks of the politician's trade?

A. Well, sir, it would take them a long time to learn to dare to do those things that men do in the way of politics—to sell and buy votes. . . .

Q. What would be the effect of conferring suffrage upon women? Would not the effect be injurious to the moral character and high influence of woman, if she should devote herself to the tricks of the politician's trade, which you very properly criticize so severely?

A. . . . I certainly think it would clean our streets, and I think it would purify politics, at least for the next two hundred years. It would take about that time to get women to understand the tricks of politicians as at present practiced. I do not think that women would be injured by it. . . . This Government is based upon the will of the people—women are "people," yet we have not a word to say about the laws. You will hear women in the course of your acquaintance say they wish they were men; I never heard a man say he wished he was a woman. . . .

Q. Why do you think that the suffrage is not extended to women by men— what is the true reason, the radical reason, why men do not give up one half their political power to women?

A. Well, it may arise from a false notion of gallantry. I think most men feel like taking care of, and protecting the ladies. . . . It would be all very well, perhaps, if all women had representatives, and if all had a generous, straightforward honorable man to represent them. But take the case of a good woman who has a drunken husband; how can he represent her? He votes for liquor and for everything he may happen to want, even though it may ruin her and turn her out of doors, and even though it may ruin her children. If the husband is a bad man would it not be better for that woman to represent herself?

Q. What effect do you think the extension of the suffrage to women would have upon their material condition, their wage-earning power and the like?

A. They would get equal pay for equal work of equal value. I do not think a woman ought to be paid the price of an expert, when she is not herself an expert, but I believe there would be a stimulus for a woman to fit herself for the very best work. What stimulus is there for woman to fit herself properly, if she never can attain the highest pay, no matter what sort of work she does? If women had a vote I think larger avenues of livelihood would be opened for them and they would be more respected by the governmental powers.

Source: U.S. Senate, Committee on Education and Labor, *Report upon Relations Between Labor and Capital* II, (1885), pp. 627, 629–632.

material things, *because they are men*," asserted an antisuffrage resolution, "while women, by the same decree of God and nature, are equally fitted to bear rule in a higher and more spiritual realm, where the strong frame and the weighty brain count for less"—that is to say, not in politics. Yet this invocation of the doctrine of "separate spheres"—that men and women had different natures, and that women's nature fitted them for "a higher and more spiritual realm"—did open a channel for women to enter public life.

"Women's place is Home," acknowledged the journalist Retha Childe Dorr. "But Home is not contained within the four walls of an individual house. Home is the community. The city full of people is the Family. . . . And badly do the Home and Family need their mother." So believing, women had engaged in charitable and reform activities since the early nineteenth century. Women's organizations fought prostitution, assisted the poor, agitated for the reform of women's prisons, and tried to improve educational and job opportunities for women. Since many of these goals required state intervention, women's organizations of necessity became politically active, but not, they stressed, out of any desire to participate in partisan politics or gain the ballot. Quite the contrary: women were bent on creating their own political sphere.

Thus, in 1869, Sorosis, a women's professional club in New York City, convened a Women's Parliament in the hope of launching a parallel government responsible for public matters that were of concern to women. Nothing came of the Women's Parliament, but it did indicate the degree to which the women's sphere could take a political form. If not a parallel government, the social activism of women certainly gave rise to a female political culture that made itself felt in the public life of late nineteenth-century America.

The Woman's Christian Temperance Union. No issue joined home and politics more poignantly than did the liquor question. Just before Christmas in 1873 the women of Hillsboro, Ohio, began to hold vigils and prayer meetings in front of the town's saloons, pleading with the owners to close down and end the suffering of families of hard-drinking fathers. Thus began a spontaneous uprising of women that spread across the country and, it was estimated, closed 3,000 saloons. The temperance movement had been inactive for twenty years. Now, from this groundswell of public agitation, came the Woman's Christian Temperance Union (WCTU), which after its formation in 1874 rapidly blossomed into the largest organization of women in the country.

The WCTU had a powerful consciousness-raising effect on its members and, because it excluded men, was the spawning ground for a new generation of women leaders. Under the guidance of Frances Willard, who became president in 1879, the WCTU moved beyond temperance and adopted a "Do-Everything" policy. Alcoholism, women recognized, was not simply a personal failing; it stemmed from larger social evils afflicting men. There was also an institutional reason for adopting a broader social vision. Willard's strategy would attract women who had no particular interest in the liquor question. Local bodies were encouraged to undertake causes that were important in their own communities. By 1889 the WCTU had thirty-nine departments concerned with labor, social purity, health, and international peace as well as temperance.

Most important, the WCTU was drawn to woman suffrage. This was necessary, Willard argued, "because the liquor traffic is entrenched in law, and law grows out of the will of majorities, and majorities of women are against the liquor traffic." Women needed the vote, said Willard, to fulfill their social responsibilities *as women*. This was very different from the claim made by the suffragists—that the ballot was an inherent right of all citizens *as individuals*—and was less threatening to masculine pride.

Not much changed in the short run. The WCTU was internally divided on the suffrage issue and did not become a major participant in the later struggles for women's right to vote. But by linking women's social concerns and women's political participation, the

Frances Willard
This photograph shows Willard at age thirty-three, when she was Dean of the Women's College of Northwestern University. A year later, she became corresponding secretary of the newly formed WCTU and embarked on her life's work as a temperance leader.

WCTU helped lay the groundwork for a fresh, broader-based attack on male electoral politics early in the twentieth century. And in the meantime, even without the vote, the WCTU demonstrated how potent a voice women could find in the public realm and how vibrant a political culture they could build.

The Crisis of American Politics: The 1890s

Ever since the end of Reconstruction in 1877 national politics had been stalemated by two evenly balanced parties. This equilibrium finally began to break down late in the 1880s. Benjamin Harrison's election in 1888 was the last of the cliff-hanger victories: the Democrat Grover Cleveland actually got a larger popular vote. Thereafter, the tide went heavily against the Republicans. In 1890 Democrats took the House of Representatives decisively, capturing 235 seats to the Republicans' 88, and won a number of governorships in normally Republican states. These losses can partly be explained by the lackluster performance of the Harrison administration and the success of the Democrats at tarring the protectionist McKinley Tariff of 1890 as a giveaway to the vested interests. Less visible but more ominous for the Republicans was an erosion of grass-roots ethnocultural support, with defections on the evangelical right to the Prohibitionist party and gains by the Democrats in local battles over education and public morality. In 1892 Cleveland regained the presidency by the largest margin in 20 years.

Had everything else remained equal, the events of 1890 and 1892 might have inaugurated a long period of Democratic supremacy. But everything else did not remain equal. By the time of Cleveland's inauguration, rising farm foreclosures and railroad bankruptcies signaled economic trouble. On May 3, 1893, the stock market crashed. Before the end of the year 16,000 firms and hundreds of banks had failed. In Chicago 100,000 jobless workers walked the streets; nationwide, the unemployment rate soared to over 20 percent. As always in hard times, suffering and unrest mounted alarmingly.

As the economic crisis of the 1890s set in, which party would prevail and on what platform became an open question. The first challenge arrived from the West and the South in the form of the Populist party.

The Populist Revolt

Farmers were of necessity joiners. They needed organization to overcome their social isolation and to obtain crucial economic services—hence the enormous appeal of the Patrons of Husbandry and, after its decline, of the farmers' alliances that began to spring up among southern and western farmers after 1877. From diffuse organizational beginnings, two dominant organizations emerged. One was the Farmers' Alliance of the Northwest, which was confined mainly to the midwestern states. More dynamic was the movement that originated in Texas. In the mid-1880s the Texas-based National (or Southern) Farmers' Alliance spread rapidly across the Great Plains and eastward into the cotton South as "travelling lecturers" extolled the virtues of cooperative activity and reminded farmers of "their obligation to stand as a great conservative body against the encroachments of monopolies and . . . the growing corruption of wealth and power." While thus recapitulating Granger resentment against railroads and merchants that had fueled earlier third-party movements, the alliances conceived of themselves as agents of social and economic reform rather than as incipient political parties.

How they were drawn into politics may be best seen in the experience of the Texas Alliance, which had established a massive cooperative, the Texas Exchange, that marketed the crops of cotton farmers and provided them with cheap credit. When cotton prices fell sharply in 1891, the Texas Exchange failed. The Texas Alliance then proposed a new scheme: a *subtreasury system* that would enable farmers to store their crops in public warehouses. Farmers would be able to borrow against those crops from a federally supplied fund at low interest rates until prices rose enough so their cotton could be marketed profitably. The subtreasury plan would provide the same credit and marketing functions as had the defunct Texas Exchange, but with a crucial difference: the federal government would play the key role. The subtreasury plan was thus a *political* proposal, and when it was rejected by the Democratic party as being too radical, the Texas Alliance decided to strike out in politics independently.

These events in Texas revealed, with special clarity, a process of politicization that went on throughout the Alliance movement. Rebuffed by the established parties, alliancemen more or less reluctantly abandoned their Democratic and Republican allegiances. Across the South and West, as they grew stronger and more impatient, state alliances began to field independent slates. In 1890 third parties won control of the Nebraska and Kansas legislatures and captured several governorships and eight state legislatures in the South. These successes led to the formation of the national People's (Populist) party. In the 1892 election, with the veteran antimonopoly campaigner James B. Weaver as their presidential

Mary Elizabeth Lease
As a political movement, the Populists were short on cash and organization, but long on rank-and-file zeal and tub-thumping oratory. No one was more rousing on the stump than Mary Elizabeth Lease, who came from a Kansas homestead and pulled no punches. "What you farmers need to do," she proclaimed in her speeches, "is to raise less corn and more *Hell!*"

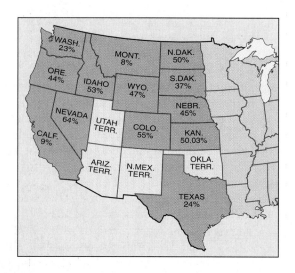

MAP 19.1

The Heyday of Western Populism, 1892
This map shows the percentage of the popular vote won by James B. Weaver, the People's party candidate, in the presidential election of 1892. Except for California and Montana, the Populists won broad support across the West and genuinely threatened the established parties in that region.

candidate, the Populists captured a million votes and carried four western states (see Map 19.1). For the first time agrarian protest truly challenged the national two-party system.

The challenge was driven as much by ideology as by the quest for political power. Populism contained a strong radical bent. The problems afflicting farmers, Populists felt, could stem only from some basic evil.

They identified that evil as the control of the "money power" over the levers of the economic system. "There are but two sides," proclaimed a Populist manifesto. "On the one side are the allied hosts of monopolies, the money power, great trusts and railroad corporations. . . . On the other are the farmers, laborers, merchants and all the people who produce wealth. . . . Between these two there is no middle ground."

By this reasoning, farmers and workers formed a single producer class. The Texas-based alliance renamed itself in 1889 the National Farmers' Alliance and Industrial Union. The title was not merely rhetorical. Organized in Knights of Labor assemblies, Texas railroad workers and Colorado miners cooperated with the farmers' alliances, got their support in strikes, and actively participated in forming state Populist parties. The platform of the national party contained strong labor planks, and party leaders earnestly sought the support of the labor movement. In its explicit class appeal—in recognizing that "the irrepressible conflict between capital and labor is upon us"—Populism differed fundamentally from the two mainstream parties.

Populism was also distinguished by the prominent role that women played in the movement. In the established parties the grass-roots organizations—the local political clubs—were for men only. Populism, on the other hand, arose from a network of suballiances that had formed for largely social purposes and welcomed women. "The Alliance has come to redeem woman from her enslaved condition," proclaimed a female member from Texas. "She is admitted into the organization as an equal to her brother" and is free of "the ostracism which has impeded her intellectual progress in the past." Although women participated actively and

En Route to a Populist Rally, Dickinson County, Kansas
Farm people traveled miles to rallies and meetings for the chance to voice their grievances and socialize with like-minded folks. This tradition infused Populism with a special fervor. Gatherings such as the one these Kansans were heading for were a visible sign of what Populism meant—a movement of the "people."

Lorenzo Dow Lewelling

Populist Confessional

In this 1894 speech given before a party gathering, the governor of Kansas, Lorenzo Lewelling, gives witness to the outrage at social injustice that animated the Populists and drove their crusade against the political status quo.

I have been asked why I was a Populist. I want to say to you, friends, that the same principles that made me a Republican in the early days, have today made me a populist, and I'll tell you what they are. I remember when I was a little boy my parents were the old line abolition kind of people that believed in equal rights for all and special privileges to none. God bless them for that sentiment, and don't you say so? Well, I remember . . . a picture of an African slave with his hands uplifted and in chains, and around the rim of the coin a motto "Am I not a man and Brother?" That made a wonderful impression on my mind. I was taught thus in my infancy to stand for . . . the weak against the strong, for

God knows the strong can take care of themselves. . . . The working men and women of this country, many of them, are simply in the shackles of industrial slavery.

. . . What is government to me if it does not make it possible for me to live? and to provide for my family! . . . If the Government don't do that, what better is the Government to me than a state of barbarism?

. . . The condition of the farmer is . . . about the same as that of the laborer. His earnings are naught. Add several ciphers together and you will have the sum of his profits this year and last. Take his wheat, which is worth twenty-five cents a bushel, and cost forty cents to raise it. How is he going to come out this year? I will tell you something: did you know that 43 percent of the homes in Kansas have already passed into the hands of landlords, who toil not neither do they spin? . . . We have got in the State of Kansas 10,000 people who are made homeless every year by the foreclosure

of mortgages and this has been going on for several years.

Call me calamity howler if you will. I wish I had the voice and pen and reputation of Jeremiah that I might howl Calamity until the people all over this broad land should hear me. It seems to me that the night of despair is really at hand. And I ask you who is to be responsible for our civil government, if you please, by which we are turned into beasts by conditions that the Government can and should prevent?

. . . The People's party has stepped into the breach between the classes to demand justice for the poor as well as to the rich and for every man. . . . I am willing, if you are willing, to place truth against the world. Truth is mighty and it will prevail.

Source: George B. Tindall, ed., *A Populist Reader* (New York, Harper & Row, 1966). pp. 148–159. Copyright George B. Tindall.

---

served prominently as speakers and lecturers, only a handful achieved high office in the alliances, and their role diminished once the Populist party entered politics. In deference to the southern wing, the Populist platform was silent on woman suffrage. Still, the major parties would scarcely have countenanced a spokeswoman such as the fiery Mary Elizabeth Lease, who became famous for calling on farmers "to raise less corn and more *Hell*." Lease insisted just as strenuously on Populism's "grand and holy mission . . . to place the mothers of this nation on an equality with the fathers."

In an age dominated by laissez-faire doctrine, what most distinguished Populism from the major parties was its positive attitude toward the state. The Populist platform declared: "We believe that the powers of government—in other words, of the people—should be expanded as rapidly and as far as the good sense of an intelligent people and the teachings of experience shall justify, to the end that oppression, injustice and poverty should eventually cease in the land." Populists such as

Lorenzo Dow Lewelling (see American Voices, above) considered it to be "the business of the Government to make it possible for me to live and sustain the life of my family."

The Populist program called for nationalization of the railroads and communications; protection of the land, including natural resources, from monopoly and foreign ownership; a graduated income tax; the creation of postal savings banks; the Texas Alliance's subtreasury plan; and the free and unlimited coinage of silver. From this array of issues, it was free silver that emerged as the overriding demand of the Populist party.

Free Silver. Cotton and grain farmers were especially vulnerable to falling commodity prices (see Chapter 17, page 547). In the early 1890s rock-bottom prices wreaked havoc among cotton, wheat, and corn growers and made them the core constituency of Populism. Inflationary solutions strongly attracted them. Increasing the money supply would raise farm prices and, since farmers would be paying back their loans in cheaper dollars, lighten the burden of farm debt. But how could the money supply be increased? One way was to get the government to issue paper dollars. This was the demand that had made the Greenbackers a robust third party in much of the South and West a decade earlier. And it was a key feature of the subtreasury plan: the funds lent to farmers on the collateral of their stored crops would be new money issued by the federal government.

But free silver—the expansion of the money supply by means of the unlimited coinage of silver—quickly became the more attractive alternative. For one thing, free silver was the simpler course and was more likely to be adopted than was the subtreasury plan. In addition, free silver would bring in hefty contributions to the Populist party from silver-mining interests. The mine operators, scornful though they might be of Populist radicalism, yearned for the day when the government would buy at a premium price all the silver they could produce, and to that end they were prepared to support the Populists.

Urban social democrats such as Henry Demarest Lloyd of Chicago and agrarian radicals such as Georgia's Tom Watson pleaded that free silver not be made the leading Populist issue. It would undercut the broader Populist program, they argued, and alienate wage earners, who had no enthusiasm for inflationary measures. Any chance of a farmer-labor alliance that might transform Populism into an American version of a social democratic party would be doomed. As Lloyd complained, free silver was "the cowbird of reform," stealing in and taking over the nest that others had built.

Although fiercely debated within the party, the outcome was never in doubt. The political appeal of free silver was simply too great. But once Populism made that choice, its capacity to maintain an independent existence was fatally compromised. For free silver was not an issue on which the Populists held a monopoly. Free silver was, on the contrary, a question at the very center of mainstream politics in the 1890s.

Money and Politics

In a rapidly developing economy such as nineteenth-century America's, the money supply is bound to be a big political issue. Money has to increase rapidly enough to meet the economy's needs or growth will be stifled. How fast the money supply should grow, however, is a question that creates sharp divisions. Debtors and victims of low prices want a larger money supply: more money in circulation inflates prices and reduces the real cost of borrowing. The "sound-money" people—creditors, individuals on fixed incomes, those in the slower-growing sectors of the economy—have the opposite interest. Touching people in the pocketbook as it does, the clash of interests can be explosive.

Before the Civil War the main source of the nation's money supply had been the banknotes circulated by several thousand local banks. Although more or less subject to state regulation, those banks issued notes in their private role as providers of credit to their customers. The banknotes they gave borrowers circulated as money until they were presented to the banks for redemption. Economists tell us that the burgeoning economy's need for money was amply met by the state banks, although the goodness of the banknotes—the ability of the issuing banks to stand behind their notes and redeem them at par—was always uncertain. During the Civil War this freewheeling system came to an end. Banknotes still existed, but the National Banking Act of 1863 required that they be backed by U.S. government bonds.

The effects of this action were threefold. First, the money supply became inadequate for the country's needs. Second, the ensuing economic troubles—the deflation of prices and the scarcity of credit—magnified public debate over the money question. Third, since solutions depended so heavily on what the federal government did, the money question became much more politicized.

The constitutional power of the federal government to issue money was in theory unlimited. The Lincoln administration had paid for the Civil War largely by printing paper money—greenbacks, so-called—backed by nothing more than the government's declaration that the greenbacks were legal tender. The prevailing policy, however, going back to the founding years of the republic, was to base the federal currency on the amount of *specie*—gold and silver—held by the U.S. Treasury.

Under the bimetallic standard, silver and gold were fixed in value at a ratio of sixteen to one: 16 ounces of silver equaled 1 ounce of gold. Silver, however, had become scarce relative to gold after mid-century. As silver rose in market price, it became more valuable as metal than as money, and it disappeared from circulation. In 1873 silver was officially dropped as a medium of exchange. Soon afterward great silver discoveries occurred in Nevada, Arizona, and elsewhere in the West. With this new supply, silver prices dropped swiftly. If the government resumed the coinage of silver at a ratio of sixteen to one, silver would flow into the Treasury and greatly expand the volume of currency. This would also, of course, greatly enrich the silver-mining interests.

With so much at stake for so many people, the currency question became one of the staple issues of post-Reconstruction politics. Twice the prosilver coalition in Congress won modest victories. First, under the Bland-Allison Act of 1878, the U.S. Treasury was required to purchase and coin between $2 million and $4 million worth of silver each month. Then, in the more sweeping Sherman Silver Purchase Act of 1890, 4.5 million ounces of silver bullion was to be purchased monthly to serve as the basis for new issues of U.S. Treasury notes.

These legislative battles, although hard-fought, cut across party lines in the characteristic fashion of post-Reconstruction politics.

But in the early 1890s silver suddenly became a defining issue between the parties; in particular, it had a radicalizing effect on the Democratic party.

The Cleveland Administration and the Silver Question. When the crash of 1893 hit, the Democrats were in power in Washington. The party in office usually gets blamed if the economy falters, but President Cleveland made things worse for the Democrats. When jobless marchers arrived in Washington in 1894 to appeal for federal relief, Cleveland's response was to disperse them forcibly and arrest their leader, Jacob S. Coxey. Cleveland's brutal handling of the Pullman strike further alienated the labor vote. Nor was he able to deliver on his campaign promise to reverse the protectionist McKinley Tariff of 1890. In a signal failure of presidential leadership, Cleveland lost control of the Congressional battle for tariff reform. The resulting Wilson-Gorman Tariff of 1894, which he allowed to pass into law without his signature, caved in to special interests and cut average rates only slightly.

Most disastrous, however, was Cleveland's rigidity on the silver question. Cleveland was a committed sound-money man who had repeatedly denounced "the dangerous and reckless experiment of free, unlimited, and independent silver coinage." Nothing that happened after the depression set in—not collapsing prices, not the suffering of farmers, not the groundswell of support for free silver in his own party—budged Cleveland from that position.

Economic pressures, in fact, soon pushed him in the opposite direction. The problem was a persistent drain on U.S. gold reserves caused partly by transfers of gold overseas due to an unfavorable balance of international payments and partly by redemptions of gold by holders of U.S. Treasury notes. To help stem the gold outflow, Cleveland persuaded Congress in 1893 to repeal the Sherman Silver Purchase Act, effectively sacrificing the country's painfully crafted effort at maintaining a partial bimetallic standard.

As his administration's difficulties deepened, Cleveland turned in 1895 to a syndicate of private bankers led by J. P. Morgan to finance the gold purchases needed to replenish the Treasury's depleted reserves. The administration's secret negotiations with Wall Street, once discovered, enraged Democrats and completed Cleveland's isolation from his party.

William Jennings Bryan and the Election of 1896. At their national convention in Chicago in 1896, the Democrats repudiated Cleveland and turned left. The leader of the triumphant silver Democrats was William Jennings Bryan of Nebraska. Bryan was a political phenom-

enon. Only thirty-six years old, he had already served two terms in Congress and had become a passionate advocate of free silver. He was a consummate politician and, no less important, an inspiring public speaker. Bryan, remarked the journalist Frederic Howe, was "pre-eminently an evangelist. . . . He was a missionary . . . the *vox ex cathedra* of the Western self-righteous missionary mind." Bryan spoke with a biblical fervor that swept up his audiences, and he did so again when he joined the debate on free silver at the Democratic convention. He had been quietly building up delegate support while distancing himself from convention politicking. Bryan locked up the presidential nomination when he electrified the convention with a stirring attack on the gold standard: "You shall not press down upon the brow of labor this crown of thorns, you shall not crucify mankind on a cross of gold."

Bryan's nomination meant that the Democrats had identified themselves as the party of free silver; his "cross of gold" speech meant that Bryan would turn the money question into a national crusade. No one could be neutral on this defining issue. Silver Republicans bolted their party; gold Democrats went for a splinter Democratic ticket or supported the Republican party; even the Prohibition party split into gold and silver wings. The Populists, meeting after the Democratic convention, accepted Bryan as their candidate. The free silver issue had become so vital that they could not do

William Jennings Bryan
As this ironic portrait of him suggests, Bryan's special genius as a politician was to place himself above politics and link his cause with moral values deep in the American psyche.

otherwise. Although they nominated their own vice-presidential candidate, the Georgian Tom Watson, the Populists found themselves for all practical purposes absorbed into the Democratic silver crusade.

The Republicans took up the challenge. Their key party leader was Mark Hanna, a wealthy Cleveland ironmaker, a brilliant political manager, and an exponent of the new industrial capitalism. He orchestrated an unprecedented money-raising campaign among America's corporate interests. Hanna's candidate, William McKinley of Ohio, personified the virtues of Republicanism, standing solidly for prosperity, high tariffs, and honest money. While Bryan broke with tradition and crisscrossed the country in a furious whistle-stop campaign, the dignified McKinley received delegations at his home in Canton, Ohio. As Bryan orated with passionate moral fervor, McKinley talked of industrial progress and a full dinner pail.

Lawyers March for the Gold Standard
Presidential campaigns of the late nineteenth century were always hard-fought, none more so than the 1896 election. Big issues were at stake: Would the country stay on the gold standard or drastically expand the money supply through the free coinage of silver? Lawyers paraded in the streets of New York City to demonstrate their conviction that the nation's fate hung on sound money and the election of the Republican William McKinley.

Not since 1860 had the United States witnessed such a hard-fought election over such high stakes. The nation's currency had exceptional social resonance in American life. For the middle class, sound money meant the soundness of the social order. With jobless workers tramping the streets and bankrupt farmers up in arms, Bryan's fervent assault on the gold standard struck fear in many hearts. Republicans denounced the Democratic platform as "revolutionary and anarchistic." They called Bryan's supporters "social misfits who have almost nothing in common but opposition to the existing order and institutions."

Although little noticed at the time, ethnocultural issues also figured strongly in the campaign. The Republicans had been the party of morality in the 1880s, appealing to supporters of temperance and Sunday laws but thereby alienating the foreign-born and Catholic vote. The Democrats had capitalized on these tensions in making their bid for electoral dominance in 1890 and 1892. Now, in 1896, the Republicans beat a strategic retreat from the politics of morality. McKinley himself had represented a mixed district in northeastern Ohio in Congress. In appealing to his immigrant and working-class constituents he had learned the art of easy tolerance, as expressed in his phrase "live and let live." Of the two candidates, the prairie orator Bryan, with his biblical rhetoric and moral righteousness, presented the more alien image to traditional Democratic voters in the big cities.

McKinley won handily, with 271 electoral votes to Bryan's 176 (see Map 19.2). He kept the Republican ground that had been regained in the 1894 midterm elections and pushed into Democratic strongholds, especially in the cities. Boston, New York, Chicago, and Minneapolis, all taken by Cleveland in 1892, went for McKinley in 1896. Bryan ran strongly only in the South, in silver-mining states, and in the Populist West. The gains his evangelical style brought in some Republican rural areas did not compensate for his losses in traditionally Democratic urban districts.

The paralyzing equilibrium of American politics ended in 1896. The Republicans prevailed through their skillful handling of both the economic and the cultural challenges. The Republicans persuaded the nation that they were the party of prosperity and reduced the liability of being perceived as the party of moral intolerance. In 1896, too, electoral politics regained its place as an arena for national debate, setting the stage for the reform politics of the Progressive Era after 1900.

The Decline of Agrarian Radicalism. As for Populism, it simply faded away. Fusion with the Democrats in 1896 deprived the People's party of its identity and undermined its organizational structure. After the election, the issue on which Populism had staked its fate—free sil-

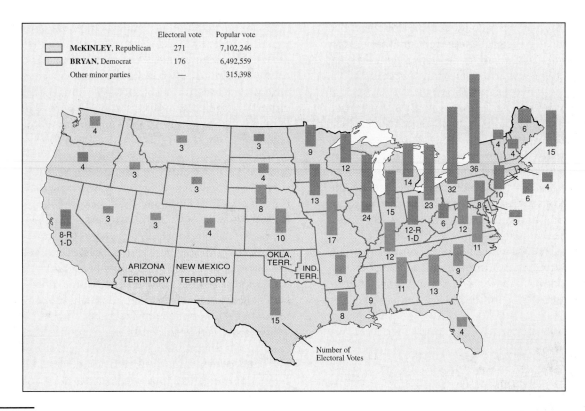

MAP 19.2

The Election of 1896

The 1896 election was one of the truly decisive elections in American history. The Republican party won by its largest margin since 1872. More important, the Republicans established a firm grip on the key midwestern and Middle Atlantic states— especially New York, Indiana, Ohio, and Illinois—that had been the decisive states in every national election since Reconstruction. The 1896 election broke a party stalemate of twenty years' duration and began a period of Republican domination that would last until 1932.

ver—vanished. During the 1890s gold was discovered in South Africa, Colorado, and the Yukon, while the new cyanide refining method greatly increased ore yields. The newly abundant gold supply took the sting out of the lost battle for free silver. At this point, moreover, the world market for agricultural commodities turned favorable. Wheat went from 72 cents a bushel in 1896 to 98 cents in 1909, corn rose from 27 cents to 57 cents, and cotton went from 6 cents to 14 cents a pound. Farm prices rose faster than did the prices of other products, and as a result, so did the real income of farmers. A new spirit of optimism took hold in the "golden age" of American agriculture before World War I.

The farmers' sense of inferiority and deprivation— that they were "rubes" and "hicks" and that life was inherently better in the city—began to subside after 1900. The new prosperity meant that more farmers could afford labor-saving home appliances and farm machinery

to lighten field work. New inventions eased the isolation and monotony of rural life. The telephone became commonplace, not so much because of the spread of commercial service but through the determined efforts of farmers themselves. Telephone cooperatives were the most common type of farm cooperative in the early twentieth century. The automobile, especially the Ford Model T, gave rural Americans a mobility they had never before known. The Country Life Commission, formed in 1908, took an optimistic view of farm society: "There has never been a time when the American farmer was as well off as he is today, when we consider not only his earning powers but the comforts and advantages he may secure."

The farmers' self-conception also changed irreversibly. In an agrarian nation, the distress of farmers could readily be regarded as a disorder of the entire country. Pushed far enough, farmers might mobilize to seize political power. In short, they could become Populists. But by the opening of the twentieth century farmers no longer constituted a majority of the population. In 1900 scarcely more than a third of the labor force earned a living from the soil; the proportion doing so would shrink in each succeeding census until, in our own time, fewer than 3 percent of the labor force is engaged in agriculture (see Appendix).

There would be times in the twentieth century when distressed farmers would turn again to insurgent politics, but never with the potency generated by the Populist party. It was as an organized interest group, not as a political movement, that farmers in the future would advance their cause.

Agriculture had long been at the heart of American life. In the twentieth century agriculture became just one more economic interest—important but subordinate in the larger scheme of the modern industrial order.

Race and Politics in the South

When Reconstruction ended in 1877, so did the hopes of African-Americans that they would enjoy the equal rights of citizenship promised them by the Fourteenth and Fifteenth amendments. Schools everywhere were strictly segregated. Access to jobs, justice, and social welfare was racially determined and unequal. And in 1883 the Supreme Court struck down the Civil Rights Act of 1875, exempting private citizens—owners of restaurants, theaters, and hotels—from the antidiscriminatory provisions of the Fourteenth Amendment. But southern state laws did not yet *require* that black pa-

trons be segregated in public accommodations, and practices varied a good deal across the South. The status quo was not stable, however, particularly when it came to railroad travel. As this became more common, whites demanded that blacks be excluded from first-class cars. By the late 1880s southern railroads were becoming the first public accommodation subject to segregation laws.

In politics the situation was even more fluid. Blacks had not been driven from politics. On the contrary, although varying from state to state, their turnout at elections was not far from that of whites in the early 1880s. But blacks did not participate on equal terms with whites. In the black belt areas, where African-Americans sometimes outnumbered whites, whites gerrymandered the districts to ensure that while blacks got some electoral representation, political control remained in white hands. Blacks, moreover, were routinely subject to intimidation and fraud at the polls—hence the large numbers whose votes were recorded as Democratic in those years. Even so, an impressive majority remained staunchly Republican, refusing, as the last black congressman from Mississippi told his House colleagues in 1882, "to surrender their honest convictions, even upon the altar of their personal necessities."

Whatever hope blacks entertained for better days, however, faded during the 1880s and then, in the next decade, expired in a terrible burst of racist terrorism. What made this outcome so tragic was that it coincided with a positive effort to overcome racial divisions. Black disfranchisement and rigid segregation stemmed directly from the crisis of the 1890s and, in particular, from a political upheaval that briefly challenged Democratic party rule in the South.

Disfranchisement

This political drawing that appeared in *Judge* magazine on July 30, 1892, shows members of the Ku Klux Klan barring black voters from the polls. By 1892, in fact, this drawing was behind the times. Literacy tests and poll taxes were beginning to disfranchise blacks with less menace and more likelihood of evading the constitutional requirement (note the sign behind the Ku Kluxers) under the Fifteenth Amendment that the right to vote not be denied "on account of race, color, or previous condition of servitude."

The Failure of Biracial Politics

No democratic society can survive if it does not enable competing economic and social interests to be heard. In the United States the two-party system performs that role. The Civil War crisis severely tested the two-party system because in both the North and the South political opposition came to be seen as treasonous. In the victorious North, despite the best efforts of the Republicans, the Democrats shed their disgrace and reclaimed their status as a major party. The South, however, was the defeated section. The scars of war went deep, and Reconstruction cut even deeper. The struggle for "home rule" empowered the Democrats. They had "redeemed" the South from black Republican domination—hence the name southern Democrats adopted: Redeemers. Cloaked in the mantle of the Lost Cause, the Redeemers claimed a monopoly on political legitimacy.

The Republican party did not fold up, however. On the contrary, it soldiered on, sustained by tenacious black loyalty, a hard core of white support, patronage from Republican national administrations, and a key Democratic vulnerability. This was the gap between the universality the Democrats claimed as the party of Redemption and the reality of who in fact controlled the party—a business elite of new entrepreneurs and older plantation owners indifferent to the plight of poor southerners.

Class antagonism, although often muted, was never absent from southern society. There had been long-smoldering differences between hill-country farmers and planters. Fresh sources of conflict now arose from the sharecropping system—which increasingly included whites as well as blacks—and from an emerging industrial working class. Unable to break the grip of the conservative elite, distressed southerners broke with the Democratic party in the early 1880s and mounted independent movements across the South. Most successful were the Readjusters, who briefly gained power in Virginia by opposing full repayment of Reconstruction debts that would enrich bond-holding speculators while leaving the state destitute. But conservative Democrats everywhere faced substantial challenges from disaffected farmers organized in Granges and acting through independent or greenback parties or, as in Tennessee, Louisiana, and Arkansas, by utilizing the Republican party. And then, after subsiding briefly, agrarian discontent revived with a vengeance, welling out of the farmers' alliances that sprang up across the South and spawning the formidable Populist challenge to Democratic rule.

What distinguished the South was not that it experienced intense agrarian protest—so, as we have seen, did the West—but that this agrarian challenge provoked a crisis in the southern party system. Refusing to countenance any opposition as legitimate, the ruling Democrats

stuffed ballot boxes, intimidated black voters, murdered opponents, and stirred up racial animosity by shouting "Negro domination!" If opposition was illegitimate, moreover, did it not follow that the incurably disloyal should be excluded from politics altogether? Exclusion had been the purpose behind the cumulative poll tax adopted by Georgia in 1877 and of South Carolina's "eight-box" law (1882), which made voting a nightmare for uneducated voters. It was clear, too, which voters these disfranchising measures mainly targeted: the blacks, whose political participation everywhere insulted southern sensibilities and, in black belt districts, made rule by white Democrats perpetually uneasy.

But Populists were themselves uneasy about black participation. Racism cut through southern white society and, so some thought, most infected the lowest rungs. "The white laboring classes here," wrote an Alabaman in 1886, "are separated from the Negroes, working all day side by side with them, by an innate consciousness of race superiority," which "excites a sentiment of sympathy and equality with the classes above them, and in this way becomes a healthy social leaven." Yet when times got bad enough, hard-pressed whites could also see blacks as fellow victims. "They are in the ditch just like we are," asserted one white Texan. Southern Populists never fully reconciled these contradictory impulses. They never questioned the conventions of social inequality: blacks had not been admitted to the sub-alliances. Nor were the economic interests of white landowning farmers and black tenants and laborers always in concert. But once agrarian protest turned political, the logic of racial solidarity became hard to deny.

Kept out of the Southern Alliance, black farmers had organized separately into the Colored Farmers' Alliance, giving them a certain amount of leverage with the emerging Populist movement. The Knights of Labor, which was open to blacks, also argued for interracial unity. The realities of partisan politics, once the alliances had taken that step, clinched the argument. In places where the Populists fused with the Republican party, such as North Carolina and Tennessee, they automatically became allies of black leaders and gained a black constituency. In areas where fusion did not happen, the Populists knew they needed to appeal to black voters. "The accident of color can make no difference in the interest of farmers, croppers, and laborers," argued the Populist leader Tom Watson. "You are kept apart that you may be separately fleeced of your earnings." By making this interracial appeal, even if not always wholeheartedly, the Populists put at risk the foundations of conservative southern politics.

The Repudiation of Racial Equality. The Populist challenge was put down, but at a frightful cost to racial justice in the South. In the contest for the black vote the conservative Democrats had many advantages: money, control of the local power structures, and a paternalistic relationship to the black community. They also played the race card to the hilt. The Democrats paraded as the "white man's party" while excoriating the Populists for courting "Negro rule." When all this did not suffice, mischief at the polls enabled the Democrats to beat back the Populists. Hence the Mississippian Frank Burkitt's bitter attack on the conservatives: they were "a class of corrupt office-seekers" who had "hypocritically raised the howl of white supremacy while they debauched the ballot boxes . . . disregarded the rights of the blacks . . . and actually dominated the will of the white people through the instrumentality of the stolen negro vote."

In the midst of these deadly struggles the Democrats decided to settle matters once and for all. Disfranchising the blacks, hitherto pursued hesitantly, now turned into a potent sectionwide movement. Florida adopted poll tax and multibox laws in 1889, but it was Mississippi's constitutional provision the next year for a literacy test that provided the foolproof device for driving blacks out of politics. The motives behind it were cynical, but the literacy test could be dressed up as a re-

form for Mississippians tired of the fraud and violence it took to maintain political control. "Their children and grandchildren," argued one, should not be left "with shotguns in their hands, a lie in their mouths and perjury on their lips in order to defeat the negroes." Better, a Mississippi journalist wrote, to devise "some legal defensible substitute for the abhorrent and evil methods on which white supremacy lies." This argument even persuaded some weary Populists: Frank Burkitt, for example, argued *for* the Mississippi literacy test in the words quoted in the previous paragraph. Other disfranchising methods—registration laws, property qualifications, the secret ballot (which demanded some basic literacy), and the already familiar poll tax—were also widely enacted during the 1890s, but none matched the literacy test as a flexible and efficient instrument for driving blacks from the polls (see Map 19.3).

The race issue had been instrumental in bringing down the Populists; now it helped reconcile them to defeat. Embittered poor whites, deeply ambivalent all along about interracial cooperation, turned their fury on the blacks. Insofar as disfranchising measures asserted militant white supremacy, poor whites approved. It was important, of course, that their own vulnerabilil-

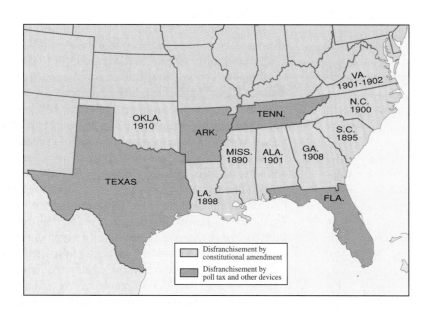

MAP 19.3

Disfranchisement in the South
In the midst of the Populist challenge to Democratic one-party rule in the South, a movement to deprive blacks of the right to vote spread from Mississippi across the South. By 1910 every state in the region except Tennessee, Arkansas, Texas, and Florida had made constitutional changes designed to prevent blacks from voting, and these four states accomplished much the same result through poll taxes and other exclusionary methods. For the next half century the political process in the South would be for whites only.

ity be partially protected by lenient enforcement and exemptions. The literacy test, for instance, was softened by Mississippi's understanding clause, which permitted illiterate voters to explain a constitutional passage that was read to them, and by Louisiana's grandfather clause, which exempted those entitled to vote on January 1, 1867, together with their sons and grandsons, from the test. But poor whites were not protected from property and poll-tax requirements, and many stopped voting. They might have objected more had they not been given a voice within the Democratic party.

From the 1890s onward a new brand of southern politician spoke for the poor whites, appealing not to their class interests but to their racial prejudices. Tom Watson, the fiery Georgia Populist, rebuilt his political career as a brilliant practitioner of race baiting. Starting in the early 1900s, he and other racial demagogues thrived throughout the South.

The Ascendancy of Jim Crow. The Populist struggle, tragically, produced a brand of white supremacy more virulent and impenetrable than anything blacks had faced since Emancipation. The color line, hitherto incomplete, became rigid and comprehensive. Segregated seating in trains, already in force generally since it was first enacted by Florida in 1887, provided a precedent for the legal separation of the races in public accommodations. Such racial legislation, known as Jim Crow laws, soon applied to every type of public facility—restaurants, hotels, streetcars, even cemeteries. In the 1890s the South became for the first time a fully segregated society by law.

The Supreme Court of the United States soon ratified the South's decision. In the case of *Plessy v. Ferguson* (1896) the Court ruled that segregation was not discriminatory—that is, it did not violate black civil rights under the Fourteenth Amendment—provided that blacks had accommodations equal to those of whites. The "separate but equal" doctrine of course had little regard for the realities of southern life: segregated facilities were rarely if ever "equal" in any material sense, and segregation was itself intended to underscore the inferiority of blacks. With a similar disregard for reality, the Supreme Court in *Williams v. Mississippi* (1898) validated the disfranchising devices of the southern states: so long as race was not a specified criterion for disfranchisement, the Fifteenth Amendment was not being violated even though the practical effect was the virtually total exclusion of blacks from politics in the South.

Race hatred became an accepted part of southern life, manifested in a wave of lynchings and race riots and in the public vilification of blacks. For example, Benjamin R. Tillman, governor of South Carolina and after 1895 a senator, excoriated blacks as "an ignorant

and debased and debauched race." This ugly racism came from several sources, including intensified competition between whites and blacks during the depression of the 1890s and the reaction of whites against a less submissive black generation born after slavery. Recent scholarship also suggests more deep-seated psychological causes for this unreasoning and often murderous racism: the rage against blacks served as a way of reasserting a traditional sense of southern "manhood" that was under assault by rapid social and economic change. Lynching, moreover, occurred most frequently in transitional areas such as the Gulf plain and the new cotton country where the population was thinly spread, community ties were weak, and blacks and whites were strangers to one another.

But what triggered the antiblack offensive was the crisis over Populism. From then on white supremacy propped up the one-party system that the Redeemers had been fighting for ever since Reconstruction. If the southern elite had to share political power with demagogic poor white leaders such as Tom Watson and James K. Vardaman, this sharing would be on terms agreeable to them—the exclusion from the political arena of any serious challenge to the economic status quo.

The Black Response

Where did this leave blacks? In 1890 African-Americans comprised more than half the population of Grimes County, a cotton-growing area in east Texas. They had kept the local Republican party going after Reconstruction and regularly sent black representatives to the Texas legislature during the 1870s and 1880s. More remarkably, the local Populist party that appeared in 1892 among white farmers proved immune to the Democrats' taunts of "black rule." A Populist-Republican coalition swept the county elections in 1896 and 1898, surviving well after the collapse of the national Populist movement.

In 1899 defeated Democratic office seekers and prominent citizens of Grimes County organized the secret White Man's Union. Armed men prevented blacks from voting in town elections that year. The two most important black county leaders were shot down in cold blood. Night riders terrorized both white Populists and black Republicans. When the Populist sheriff proved incapable of enforcing the law, the game was up. The White Man's Union, now out in the open, became the county Democratic party in a new guise. The Democrats won Grimes County by an overwhelming vote in 1900. The day after the election members of the Union laid siege to the Populist sheriff's office. They killed his brother and a friend and drove the sheriff, badly wounded, out of the county forever.

The White Man's Union ruled Grimes County for
the next fifty years. The whole episode was the handiwork of the county's "best citizens," suggesting how respectable the use of terror had become in the service of
white supremacy. The Union intended, as one of its
leaders said, to "force the African to keep his place."
After 1900 blacks could survive in Grimes County only
if they tended to their own business and stayed out of
trouble with whites.

Like the blacks of Grimes County, southern blacks
in many places resisted white oppression as best they
could. When Georgia adopted the first Jim Crow law
applying to streetcars in 1891, Atlanta blacks declared a
boycott, and over the next fifteen years there were boycotts against segregated streetcars in at least twenty-five
cities. "Do not trample on our pride by being 'jim
crowed,'" the Savannah *Tribune* urged its readers:
"Walk!" Ida Wells-Barnett emerged as the most outspoken black crusader against lynching, so enraging the
Memphis white community with the editorials in her
newspaper *Free Speech* that she was forced to leave the
city in 1892. And there were individual blacks, such as
Robert Charles (see American Lives, pages 610–611),
who, driven beyond endurance, struck back, at the inevitable sacrifice of their own lives.

Like Charles, some were drawn to the back-to-
Africa movement. It was a sign of their despair that
Africa was again seen as the place of black salvation.
But emigration was not a real choice, and like the blacks
of Grimes County, African-Americans everywhere had
to bend to the raging forces of racism and find a way to
survive.

The Atlanta Compromise. Booker T. Washington, the
foremost black leader of the South of his day, responded
to that grim reality in a famous speech in Atlanta in
1895. Washington marked out a line of retreat from the
defiant stand of an older generation of black abolitionists exemplified by Frederick Douglass, who died the
same year that the Atlanta speech launched Washington
into national prominence. Washington was conciliatory
toward the South; it was a society that blacks understood and loved. He considered "the agitation of the
question of social equality the extremest folly." Washington accepted segregation, provided that blacks had
equal facilities. He accepted educational and property
qualifications for the vote, provided that they applied
equally to blacks and whites.

Washington's doctrine came to be known as the Atlanta Compromise. His approach was "accommodationist" in the sense that it avoided a direct assault on
white supremacy. Despite the humble face he put on be-

Booker T. Washington

In an age of severe racial oppression, Washington emerged as
the acknowledged leader of black people in the United States.
He was remarkable both for his ability as spokesman to
white Americans and his deep understanding of the aspirations of black Americans. Born a slave, Washington suffered
the indignities experienced by all blacks after Emancipation.
But having been befriended by several whites as he grew to
manhood, he also understood what it took to gain white support—and maneuver around white hostility—in the black
struggle for equality.

fore white audiences, however, Washington did not con-
cede the struggle. Behind the scenes he did his best to resist Jim Crow laws and disfranchisement. More
important, his Atlanta Compromise, while abandoning
the field of political protest, opened up a second front of
economic struggle.

Washington sought to capitalize on a particular
southern dilemma about the economic role of the black
population. Racist dogma dictated that blacks be kept
down and that they conform to their image as lazy,
shiftless workers. But for the South to prosper it needed
an efficient labor force. Washington made this need the
target of his efforts. As founder of the Tuskegee Institute in Alabama in 1881, he advocated *industrial educa-*

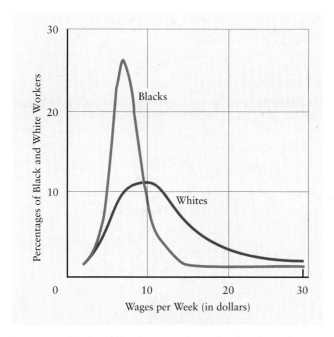

Source: Gavin Wright, *Old South, New South: Revolutions in the Southern Economy since the Civil War* (New York: Basic Books, 1986), p. 184.

FIGURE 19.2

Distributions of Weekly Wages for Black and White Workers in Virginia, 1907
This graph reveals that wages for common labor were nondiscriminatory (otherwise no or few whites would have been bunched at the low end of the wage scale) but that discrimination denied blacks entry into higher-paying southern jobs.

tion—that is, manual and agricultural training. He preached the virtues of thrift, hard work, and property ownership. Washington's industrial education program won generous support from northern philanthropists and businessmen and, following his Atlanta speech, applause from progressive supporters of the New South.

Washington assumed that black economic progress would be the key to winning political and civil rights. He regarded members of the white southern elite as crucial allies, because ultimately only they had the power to act. More important, they could see "the close connection between labor, industry, education, and political institutions." When it was in their economic interest and when they had grown dependent on black labor

and black enterprise, white men of business and property would recognize the justice of black rights. As Washington put it, "There is little race prejudice in the American dollar."

Do the facts suggest that Washington was right? Or, to put the question as an economist might: Was it the impersonal market or race prejudice that most determined the economic treatment of blacks? For southern industry the answer seems mixed. Employers did not discriminate very much in wage rates—that is, they did not pay whites higher wages than they paid blacks for the same work. But racial barriers certainly prevented blacks from moving into better-paid and more highly skilled jobs. This hard truth is made graphically clear in the comparative wage distributions of whites and blacks shown in Figure 19.2. In agriculture, too, the picture was mixed. The opportunity for black farmers to advance themselves clearly did exist. The proportion who became landowners inched slowly upward to roughly 25 percent in 1900. But the racial gap remained very wide, with whites almost three times as likely as blacks to be landowners.

To what extent black self-help—hard work, industrial education, the husbanding of small resources—might counterbalance the barriers of race prejudice was the nub of Booker T. Washington's problem. Where the almighty dollar reigned, there was some hope of progress. Elsewhere, as Washington saw it, there was none.

For twenty years after his Atlanta address Washington dominated organized black life in America. In an age of severe racial oppression no black dealt more skillfully than Washington with the leaders of white America or wielded greater political influence. The black community knew him as a hard taskmaster. Intensely protective of his authority, he did not regard opposition kindly. Black politicians, educators, and editors stood up to him at their peril.

Even so, a crack began to appear after 1900, especially among younger educated blacks, who thought Washington was conceding too much. He instilled black pride, but of a narrowly middle-class and utilitarian kind. What about the special genius of blacks that W. E. B. DuBois celebrated in his collection of essays, *The Souls of Black Folk* (1903)? And what of the "talented tenth" of the black population whose promise could only be stifled and restrained by manual education? Blacks also became increasingly impatient with Washington's silence on segregation and lynching. By the time of his death in 1915 Washington's approach had been superseded by a strategy that relied on the courts and political leverage, not on black self-help and accommodation (see Chapter 21).

Robert Charles:
Black Militant

The trouble began in an ordinary way. Two black men were sitting quietly on the steps of a house on Dryades Street in New Orleans, between Washington and 6th streets. It was Monday evening, July 24, 1900. One was nineteen-year-old Leonard Pierce; the other was an older man named Robert Charles. They were waiting for a friend of Charles's, Virginia Banks, and her roommate to return from a day at Baton Rouge. Around 11 P.M. three policemen approached Pierce and Charles and began to question them roughly. When Charles stood up, Officer Mora grabbed him. A scuffle followed, and Mora began to beat Charles about the head with his billy club. Charles, a big man, broke away. There was an exchange of gunfire, wounding both in the thigh, Officer Mora more seriously. In a hail of bullets, Charles ran off.

"In any law-abiding community Charles would have been justified in delivering himself up immediately to the properly constituted authorities and asking for a trial by a jury of his peers," wrote the antilynching crusader Ida Wells-Barnett in her pamphlet on what followed. "Charles knew that his arrest in New Orleans, even for defending his life, meant nothing short of a long term in the penitentiary, and still more probable death by lynching at the hands of a cowardly mob." Those must have been Charles's thoughts as he made his way back to the room he shared with Pierce on 4th Street, took down his Winchester rifle, and got ready to fight.

In the meantime Pierce had been brought to the police station, where Charles's name and address were soon "sweated" out of him. Captain John T. Day, a local hero who had rescued fourteen people from a hotel fire, led a squad to bring Charles in. The entrance to Charles's room was along an alley. When the police arrived, Charles swung open the door, shot Day through the heart, then turned and fatally wounded a second officer. The other two policemen cowered along the wall and slipped into another house, where they hid in the dark. The officers on the street refused to enter the unlit alley. When reinforcements arrived at 5 A.M.,

Robert Charles
This is the only known picture of Charles, an engraving done for the cover of Ida Wells-Barnett's pamphlet on Charles's slaying.

Charles had slipped away, and the manhunt commenced.

The New Orleans newspapers labeled Charles a "fiend incarnate." No one who had known him would have said so. Robert Charles was one of thousands of rural blacks who had sought to escape from grinding poverty by migrating to southern cities. Robert Charles was born just after the end of slavery, in 1865 or 1866, in Copiah County, Mississippi. His parents were sharecroppers, and he was one of ten children. He worked as a day laborer on the railroads and, after arriving in New Orleans around 1894, at a variety of odd jobs. In July 1900 he was unemployed. Charles was unmarried and rather stylish in his dress, favoring a brown derby hat. Acquaintances remembered him as quiet and intelligent. He had received little education, but his room contained the well-thumbed books and papers of a studious man. One other thing about Charles: he ardently believed that blacks should return to Africa.

The back-to-Africa movement, which enjoyed a revival in those hard years, reflected the despair that poor blacks like Robert Charles felt about life in America. Africa was their only salvation, preached Bishop Henry M. Turner, the combative leader of the movement: "I see no other shelter from the stormy blast, from the red tide of persecution, from the horrors of American prejudice." Charles was a reader of Bishop Turner's fiery paper, *Voice of Missions*, and in 1899 began to sell subscriptions. He also became a local agent for the International Migration Society, working on commission to sign up members who would secure transportation to Liberia by contributing a dollar a month for forty months.

Recent events fortified Charles's conviction that blacks had no hope in America. He was said to have been infuriated by the most infamous lynching of the era, the burning and dismemberment of Sam Hose in Georgia in 1899. In Louisiana, moreover, blacks had been disfranchised in 1898, and a crisis was brewing in state politics. As the elections of 1900 approached, the Democrats vowed that on no account would they allow the Republicans and Populists to emerge as winners. In Charles's pocket was a newspaper clipping about an opposition leader who had called on his supporters to "*oil up their Winchesters* and prepare to fight" if Democrats tried to steal the election. In *Voice of Missions* there was a similarly desperate message: in one editorial Bishop Turner had urged that "Negroes Get Guns" in self-defense.

Charles, in fact, habitually carried a Colt .38 revolver; it was in his belt when Officer Mora accosted him. There is no knowing what went through his mind when he chose not to submit to the policeman's abuse.

But by drawing his gun Charles had stepped across the line. From then until his inevitable death, he was making a political statement.

That was how the whites of New Orleans saw Charles too: he was challenging the white power structure. As a leader of the mob that gathered in the streets on Wednesday put it:

> The only way you can teach these niggers a lesson and put them in their place is to go out and lynch a few of them as an object lesson. String up a few of them, and the others will trouble you no more. . . . On to the Parish Prison and lynch Pierce!

The mob couldn't get at Pierce, but they took their fury out on any other unfortunate black they encountered as they surged through the city. In the next two days at least six people were killed and dozens of others were brutally beaten. Only late on Thursday did the police and militia restore a semblance of law and order to New Orleans. But Charles remained at large. Then, on Friday afternoon, July 27, the police got a tip that he was hiding in a small house on Saratoga Street.

Springing from a back closet, Charles shot down the two police officers who came to investigate and then made his way up to the second story. A crowd soon surrounded the house, peppering it with bullets. Dodging from window to window, Charles returned the fire for nearly two hours. In grudging admiration, one reporter wrote of his "diabolical coolness" and "wonderful marksmanship [that] never failed him for a moment." More than twenty of his attackers were hit, three fatally. As dusk began to fall, the building was set ablaze, and Charles was forced out. Still defiant, he almost made it across the courtyard when he was stopped by a bullet and went down. The crowd was on him in an instant, firing dozens of shots into him, and stomping on his head. His body was carried off in a police wagon, his battered head hanging grotesquely from the back. Later that night the mob broke loose again, burning buildings and murderously attacking six more blacks.

No New Orleans black would have dared say out loud that Robert Charles had done right. But Ida Wells-Barnett, writing from the safety of Chicago, insisted that he had: "The white people of this country may charge that he was a desperado, but to the people of his own race Robert Charles will always be regarded as the hero of New Orleans." Five weeks after Charles's burial in a potter's field, a neighbor of Fred Clark's on South Ramparts Street came up behind Clark, put a gun to his head and shot him dead. Fred Clark was the black man who had given away Charles's hiding place to the police.

Summary

When Reconstruction ended in 1877, national politics became less issue-oriented and, as a formal process, less important in American life. This situation resulted from weaknesses in governmental institutions, the prevailing philosophy of laissez-faire, and the paralysis of evenly matched political parties. Yet politics in the years after 1877 had great vigor, as can be seen in the high levels of popular participation. For one thing, politics was the arena in which the nation's ethnic and religious conflicts were largely fought out. Equally important, the party machines were powerful and performed crucial functions that properly belonged to, but were still beyond the capacity of, governmental institutions. Finally, despite the slow headway made toward woman suffrage, women's organizations carved out for themselves a broadening public sphere of social reform activity.

During the 1890s national politics again became an important arena. Threatened by the rise of Populism, the Democratic party committed itself to free silver and made the election of 1896 a contest over issues of real significance. The Republicans won decisively, ending a paralyzing party stalemate that had lasted for twenty years and assuring themselves of political dominance for the next thirty years. At the same time, the 1890s saw, in the failure of Populism, the last great challenge to the mainstream two-party system. And in the South the Populist failure turned into a grim reaction that disfranchised African-Americans, completed a rigid segregation system, and let loose a terrible cycle of racial hatred and violence. Blacks resisted but had to bend to overwhelming white power. The accommodationist philosophy of Booker T. Washington seemed to be the best strategy for black survival in an age of extreme racism.

TIMELINE

1874	Woman's Christian Temperance Union (WCTU) founded
1877	Rutherford B. Hayes inaugurated; end of Reconstruction
1881	President James A. Garfield assassinated
1883	Pendleton Civil Service Act Supreme Court strikes down Civil Rights Act of 1875
1884	Mugwump reformers bolt the Republican party to support Grover Cleveland, first Democrat elected president since 1856
1887	Interstate Commerce Act creates the Interstate Commerce Commission to regulate railroads Florida adopts first law segregating railroad travel
1888	James Bryce's *The American Commonwealth*
1890	The McKinley Tariff Democrats sweep Congressional elections, inaugurating brief era of Democratic party dominance Mississippi becomes first state to adopt literacy test to disfranchise blacks
1892	People's (Populist) party founded
1893	Panic of 1893 leads to national depression Repeal of Sherman Silver Purchase Act (1890)
1894	Coxey's army
1895	Booker T. Washington sets out Atlanta Compromise
1896	Election of William McKinley; free silver campaign crushed *Plessy v. Ferguson* upholds constitutionality of "separate-but-equal" facilities
1897	Economic depression ends; era of agricultural prosperity begins

BIBLIOGRAPHY

The best introductions to American politics in the late nineteenth century are John A. Garraty, *The New Commonwealth, 1877–1890* (1968), and R. Hal Williams, *Years of Decision: American Politics in the 1890s* (1978). More detailed and comprehensive is Morton Keller, *Affairs of State: Public Life in Late Nineteenth-Century America* (1977).

The Politics of the Status Quo

Various aspects of national politics are discussed in Robert D. Marcus, *Grand Old Party: Political Structure in the Gilded Age* (1971); J. Rogers Hollingsworth, *The Whirligig of Politics: The Democracy of Cleveland and Bryan* (1963); H. Wayne Morgan, *From Hayes to McKinley: National Party Politics, 1877–1896* (1969); and David J. Rothman, *Politics and Power: The Senate, 1869–1901* (1966). On the development of public administration, see Leonard D. White, *The Republican Era, 1869–1901* (1958), and Stephen Skowronek, *Building a New American State: The Expansion of National Administrative Capacities* (1982).

The ideological basis for conservative national politics is fully treated in Sidney Fine, *Laissez Faire and the General Welfare State, 1865–1901* (1956); Robert G. McCloskey, *American Conservatism in the Age of Enterprise* (1951); and the opening section of Morton J. Horwitz, *The Transformation of American Law, 1870–1960* (1992). On the popular sources of political participation, see especially Michael E. McGerr, *The Decline of Popular Politics: The American North, 1865–1928* (1986), and Paul Kleppner, *The Third Electoral Party System, 1853–1892: Parties, Voters, and Political Cultures* (1979). On the Mugwump reformers, see John G. Sproat, *The "Best Men": Liberal Reformers in the Gilded Age* (1965); Gerald W. McFarland, *Mugwumps, Morals and Politics, 1884–1920* (1975); and Ari Hoogenboom, *Outlawing the Spoils: The Civil Service Reform Movement, 1865–1883* (1961). The existence of a women's political culture in the late nineteenth century can be traced in Carl N. Degler, *At Odds: Women and the Family from the Revolution to the Present* (1979). A valuable book setting the stage is Ellen Carol DuBois, *Feminism and Suffrage: The Emergence of an Independent Women's Movement in America, 1848–1869* (1978).

The Crisis of American Politics

The most recent synthesis on Populism is Robert C. McMath, *American Populism* (1993). Richard D. Hofstadter, *The Age of Reform* (1955), stresses the darker side of Populism, in which intolerance and paranoia figure heavily. Hofstadter's thesis, which once dominated debate among historians, has given way to a much more positive assessment. The key book here is Lawrence Goodwyn, *Democratic Promise: The Populist Moment in America* (1976), which argues that Populism was a broadly based radical response to industrial capitalism. Peter H. Argersinger, *The Limits of Agrarian Radicalism: Western Populism and American Politics* (1994), offers a careful assessment of the politics of western Populism. Two stimulating books that follow the history of Populism into the twentieth century are Grant McConnell, *The Decline of Agrarian Democracy* (1953), which focuses on farm organizations, and Michael Kazin, *The Populist Persuasion* (1995), which describes how the language of Populism entered the discourse of mainstream American politics.

The money question is elucidated in Walter Nugent, *Money and American Society, 1865–1880* (1968), and Allan Weinstein, *Prelude to Populism: Origins of the Silver Issue* (1970). On the politics of the 1890s, see especially Robert F. Durden, *Climax of Populism: The Election of 1896* (1965), and Paul W. Glad, *McKinley, Bryan, and the People* (1964).

Race and Politics in the South

On southern politics the seminal book for the post-Reconstruction period is C. Vann Woodward, *Origins of the New South, 1877–1913* (1951), which still defines the terms of discussion among historians. The most far-reaching revision is Edward L. Ayers, *The Promise of the New South* (1992). Complementary books on the social basis of southern politics are Dwight B. Billings, *Planters and the Making of "New South": North Carolina, 1865–1900* (1979), and Paul Escott, *Many Excellent People: Power and Privilege in North Carolina, 1850–1900* (1985).

The classic book on segregation is C. Vann Woodward, *The Strange Career of Jim Crow* (2d ed., 1968), but it should be supplemented by Howard N. Rabinowitz, *Race Relations in the Urban South, 1865–1890* (1978). A powerful analysis of southern racism, stressing its psychosocial roots, is Joel Williamson, *A Rage for Order: Black/White Relations in the American South since Emancipation* (1986). Disfranchisement is treated with great analytic sophistication in J. Morgan Kousser, *The Shaping of Southern Politics: Suffrage Restriction and the Establishment of the One-Party South, 1880–1910* (1974), and as an aspect of progressivism in Jack Temple Kirby, *Darkness at the Dawning: Race and Reform in the Progressive South* (1972). August Meier, *Negro Thought in America, 1880–1915* (1963), is a key analysis of black accommodation and protest. The preeminent exponent of accommodation is the subject of a superb two-volume biography by Louis B. Harlan, *Booker T. Washington: The Making of a Black Leader* (1973) and *Wizard of Tuskegee* (1983); and equally fine on Washington's main critic is David Levering Lewis, *W.E.B. Du Bois: Biography of a Race, 1868–1919* (1993).

Indianapolis in the 1890s

Theodore Groll, a German who had come to America for the
World's Columbian Exposition of 1893, painted this massive
canvas of Indianapolis at dusk. The view is of Washington
Street, with its clanging horsecars, street peddlers, busy
shoppers, and general bustle. In this prosperous medium-
sized city—the novelist Booth Tarkington, a native son, called
it a "typical American" place—urban life seemed less remote
from traditional America than in great metropolises such as
New York or Chicago.

The Rise of the City

★   ★   ★

In 1820, after 200 years of settlement, fewer than 5 percent of Americans lived in cities with a population of 10,000 or more. But after that, decade by decade, the urban population swelled, turning into a flood after midcentury. The same process was happening in Europe, but at a slower pace. During the nineteenth century, the percentage of Europeans living in cities tripled whereas in the United States the increase was sevenfold.

By 1900 one of every five Americans lived in an urban center of 100,000 or more residents. The greatest growth took place in the great metropolitan cities. Nearly a tenth of the nation—6.5 million persons—lived in just three cities: New York, Chicago, and Philadelphia. The late nineteenth century, an economist remarked in 1899, was "not only the age of cities, but the age of great cities."

The growth of the cities had enormous implications for American society. The city was the arena of the nation's vibrant economic life. Here the factories went up, and here the multitudes of working people settled. New immigrants swelled the ranks of the working class. At the turn of the century upwards of 30 percent of the residents of major American cities were foreign-born. Here, too, lived the millionaires and a growing urban middle class of white-collar workers and businessmen. For all these people the city was more than a place to make a living. It provided the setting for an urban culture unlike anything seen before in the United States. City people, although differing vastly among themselves, became distinctively and recognizably urban.

Urbanization

The march to the cities seemed inevitable to nineteenth-century Americans. "The greater part of our population must live in cities—cities much greater than the world has yet known," declared the Congregational minister Josiah Strong in 1898. "In due time we shall be a nation of cities." There was "no resisting the trend," said another writer. Urbanization became inevitable because of its link to another inevitability of American life—industrialization.

The Sources of City Growth

Until the Civil War, cities had been centers of commerce, not industry. Located strategically along transportation routes, they were the places where merchants bought and sold goods for distribution into the interior or shipment out to the world market. Early industrialism, on the other hand, sprang up in the countryside.

Mills and factories needed water power from streams and rivers, access to sources of fuel and raw materials, and workers drawn from the surplus farm population. Only five of the nation's cities in 1860 reported as much as 10 percent of the labor force engaged in manufacturing activity.

After midcentury industry began to abandon the countryside. Once they had access to steam engines, mill operators no longer needed to locate along streams. In the iron industry coal replaced charcoal as the primary fuel, and so iron makers did not have to be near forests. Improved transportation, especially the railroads, gave entrepreneurs a greater choice in selecting the best sites in relation to supplies and markets. The result was a geographical concentration of industry. Iron makers gravitated to Pittsburgh because of its access not only to coal and iron ore but also to markets for iron and steel products. Chicago, ideally located between livestock suppliers and consuming markets, became a great meat-packing center (see Map 20.1).

Many smaller industrial cities depended on a high degree of economic specialization. Youngstown, Ohio,

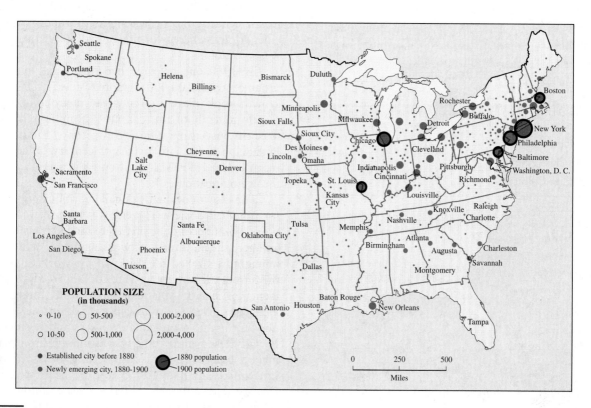

MAP 20.1

The Growth of America's Cities, 1880–1900
The number of Americans living in urban places more than doubled between 1880 and 1900. The most dramatic increases occurred in the largest metropolitan centers. New York grew from 1.2 million to 3.4 million, and Chicago from 500,000 to 1.7 million. Notable among newly emerging cities—places that had been small towns or minor cities in 1880—were Los Angeles, Seattle, Birmingham, Omaha, and Atlanta.

and Johnstown, Pennsylvania, specialized in iron and steel; Brockton and Haverhill, Massachusetts, in boots and shoes; Troy, New York, in collars and cuffs; and East Liverpool, Ohio, in pottery. Other cities processed the raw materials of their regions. Sacramento canned fruits and vegetables, Richmond made cigarettes, Minneapolis milled grain, and Memphis handled lumber and produced cottonseed oil.

This geographical concentration of industry was one source of urban growth in the late nineteenth century. Another was the increasing scale of production that became characteristic of modern industry. A factory that employed thousands of workers instantly created a small city in its vicinity. The result was often a company town—for example, Aliquippa, Pennsylvania, which became body and soul the property of the Jones and Laughlin Steel Company. Many firms set up their plants near a large city so they could draw on its labor supply and transportation facilities. George Pullman located his sleeping-car works and model town southwest of Chicago, and George Westinghouse built his electrical equipment plant just east of Pittsburgh. Sometimes the nearby metropolis spread and absorbed the smaller city, as happened with Pullman, Illinois. Elsewhere, as in northern New Jersey or along the lakeshore south of Chicago, the lines between industrial towns blurred and an extended urban-industrial area emerged. The same process could be seen in Europe, where industrial regions were emerging in northeastern France around Lille and in Germany's Ruhr Valley.

The established commercial cities also grew significantly in this era, benefiting from industry's need for complex marketing and administrative structures. The greatest centers—New York and Chicago—became headquarters for corporations operating across the country. Finance, publishing, distribution, advertising, and fashion were concentrated in the metropolitan centers.

These commercial centers also offered factory sites and economic services that attracted certain kinds of industries. Warehouse districts could readily be converted to small-scale manufacturing; a distribution network and transportation facilities were right at hand. In addition, as gateways for immigrants, port cities offered abundant cheap labor. Boston, Philadelphia, Baltimore, and San Francisco became hives of small-scale, labor-intensive industrial activity. New York's enormous pool of immigrant workers made that city a magnet for the garment trades, cigar making, and diversified light industry. Preeminent as a city of trade and finance, New York also ranked as the nation's largest manufacturing center.

By 1870 a core industrial region had formed from New England down through the Middle Atlantic states to Maryland. In this region the percentage of people living in urban places was twice the national average. Forty years later, in 1910, the original industrial core was nearly three-quarters urbanized. It had also thrust westward to include the Great Lakes states, which became America's industrial heartland. Important new centers for steelmaking, manufacturing, and food processing sprang up in this region. Pittsburgh, Cleveland, Detroit, Milwaukee, Minneapolis—all of them small cities or modest commercial centers in 1870—had by 1910 grown into major industrial cities with 300,000 to well over half a million inhabitants.

TABLE 20.1

Ten Largest Cities by Population, 1870 and 1910

1870		1910	
City	Population	City	Population
1. New York	942,292	New York	4,766,883
2. Philadelphia	674,022	Chicago	2,185,283
3. Brooklyn*	419,921	Philadelphia	1,549,008
4. St. Louis	310,864	St. Louis	687,029
5. Chicago	298,977	Boston	670,585
6. Baltimore	267,354	Cleveland	560,663
7. Boston	250,526	Baltimore	558,485
8. Cincinnati	216,239	Pittsburgh	533,905
9. New Orleans	191,418	Detroit	465,766
10. San Francisco	149,473	Buffalo	423,715

*Brooklyn was consolidated with New York in 1898.
Source: U.S. Census data.

City Building

"The only trouble about this town," wrote Mark Twain on arriving in New York in 1867, "is that it is too large. You cannot accomplish anything in the way of business, you cannot even pay a friendly call, without devoting a whole day to it. . . . The distances are too great." Finding ways of moving nearly a million New Yorkers around was not as hopeless as it might have seemed to Twain, but it did pose a challenge to city builders. The city demanded innovation no less than did industry itself and, in the end, compiled an equally impressive record of technological achievement.

The commercial cities of the early nineteenth century had been compact places, densely settled around a harbor or along a river. As late as 1850, when it had 565,000 people, greater Philadelphia covered only 10 square miles. From the foot of Chestnut Street on the Delaware River a person could walk to almost anywhere in the city within forty-five minutes. Thereafter, however, Philadelphia—and indeed all American cities—tended to spread out as it developed.

A downtown area emerged, usually in what had been the original commercial city. Downtown in turn broke up into shopping, financial, warehousing, manufacturing, hotel and entertainment, and red-light districts. Although somewhat fluid at their edges, all these districts were well-defined areas of specialized activity. Moving out from the center, industrial development tended to follow the arteries of transportation—railroads, canals, and rivers—and, at the city's outskirts, to spread out into complexes of heavy industry. At the same time the middle class moved in large numbers out to new suburban areas.

Urban development was markedly different in continental Europe, where even rapidly growing cities remained physically compact, with boundaries that broke sharply at the surrounding countryside. In America, cities constantly expanded, spilling beyond their formal boundaries and forming what the federal census began to designate in 1910 as metropolitan areas. While American cities were highly congested at the center, their population density was actually much below that of European cities: 22 persons per acre for fifteen American cities in the 1890s, for example, versus 157.6 for a comparable group of German cities. Given this difference, the development of efficient urban transportation had a much higher priority in the United States than in Europe.

Mass Transit. The first innovation, dating back to the 1820s, was the omnibus, an elongated version of the horse-drawn coach. The omnibus was a convenience, but it did not do much to relieve congestion; downtown, people could walk just as fast. Much more effective was the horsecar, which ran on iron tracks. The

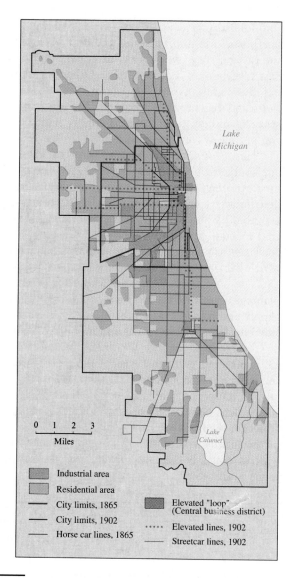

MAP 20.2

The Expansion of Chicago

In 1865 Chicagoans depended on horsecar lines to get around town. By 1900 the city limits had expanded enormously, accompanied by an equally dramatic extension of streetcar service, by then electrified. Elevated trains also helped ease congestion in the urban core. New streetcar lines, some extending beyond the city limits, were important to suburban development in the coming years.

horsecar carried more passengers, moved them at a faster clip through congested city streets, and reached out into residential areas. All this happened because of a modest but crucial refinement in railroad track design in 1852—a grooved rail that was flush with the pavement. For the next forty years horsecars became the mainstay of urban transit across America, accounting for 70 percent of the traffic in 1890.

The horse was less than an ideal source of locomotion. It moved slowly, had limited pulling power, and

Traffic Jam in Downtown Chicago, 1905
The purpose of urban transit systems was to move masses of people rapidly and efficiently through the city. However, better transportation brought more congestion as well, as this scene of gridlock at Randolph and Dearborn streets in Chicago shows.

left piles of manure behind. Among various early improvements was the cable car, which was pulled by an undergound cable set below the tracks and driven by steam engines at a central power house. The first cable cars ran in San Francisco in 1873, and more than twenty other cities used them during the 1880s. But the cable car could run only at a slow, unvarying speed, and systemwide breakdowns occurred frequently.

Then came the electric trolley car. Its development was primarily the work of Frank J. Sprague, an electrical engineer once employed by the inventor Thomas A. Edison. In 1887 Sprague designed an electricity-driven system for Richmond, Virginia: a "trolley" carriage running along an overhead power line was attached by cable to streetcars equipped with an electric motor—hence the name *trolley car*. After Sprague's success, the electric trolley swiftly displaced the horsecar and by 1900 became the primary means of public transportation in most American cities.

In the great metropolitan centers, however, mounting congestion led to demands that public transit be moved off the streets. The railroad had long been used by affluent suburbanites to commute to the city. The problem was how to harness railway technology to serve the needs of ordinary city dwellers. In 1879 the first elevated lines went into operation on Sixth and Ninth avenues in New York City. Powered at first by steam engines, the "els" converted to electricity following Sprague's success with the trolley. Chicago developed elevated transit most fully (see Map 20.2). New York, on the other hand, turned to the subway. Although Boston opened a short underground line in 1897, the completion in 1904 of a subway running the length of Manhattan demonstrated the full potential of underground rapid transit. Thinly settled areas of northern Manhattan and the Bronx, predicted the *New York Times*, would soon boast "a population of ten millions . . . housed comfortably, healthfully and relatively cheaply." The subway would especially delight "all who travel with the sole purpose of 'getting there' in the least time possible." Mass transit had become *rapid* transit.

The Chicago Elevated, 1900
This is Wabash Avenue, looking north from Adams Street. For Americans from farms and small towns, this photograph by William Henry Jackson captured something of the peculiarity of the urban scene. What could be stranger than a railroad suspended above the streets in the midst of people's lives?

Nowhere else in the world was the demand for mass urban transit as acute as it was in U.S. cities. In 1890 the number of passengers carried on American street railways was more than 2 billion per year, over twice that of the rest of the world combined. Berlin, which boasted the best system in Europe, had a per capita usage that was exceeded by twenty-one American cities. In Great Britain the horsecar remained dominant long after it had disappeared from American streets. In Tokyo, the biggest Asian city, the horsecar was not even introduced until 1882, and the electric streetcar appeared for the first time in 1903.

Bridges. Rivers had in earlier times been the city's lifeline of trade; now they became barriers that interrupted rail traffic and hindered urban expansion. Hundreds of iron and steel bridges went up in the second half of the nineteenth century. Some from this great age of bridge construction—among them the Eads Bridge (1873) spanning the Mississippi River at St. Louis and the Brooklyn Bridge (1883) over New York's East River—are still in use. The Brooklyn Bridge, linking Brooklyn and Manhattan, took fifteen years to build. A giant suspension structure, the Brooklyn Bridge was not only an engineering marvel but the symbol of a new kind of functional architecture—"the first product of the age of coal and iron to achieve completeness of expression," wrote the twentieth-century architectural critic Lewis Mumford.

The Skyscraper. If urban transit evolved in response to the geographical expansion of the American city, the need for more space in the downtown business districts drove advances in building construction. New materials made it possible to construct commercial buildings of greater height, interior space, and fire resistance. With the availability by the 1880s of steel girders, mass-produced durable plate glass, and the passenger elevator, a wholly new way of construction developed. A steel skeleton would support the building, and the walls, previously weight-bearing, would serve as curtains enclosing the structure; the sky, so to speak, became the limit.

The first "skyscraper" to be built on this principle was the ten-story Home Insurance Building (1885) in Chicago. Although this pioneering effort was itself conventional in appearance—it looked just like the other commercial buildings in the downtown district—the steel-girdered structure swiftly liberated the aesthetic perceptions of American architects. A Chicago school sprang up, dedicated to the design of buildings whose form expressed, rather than masked, their structure and function. The masterpiece of the Chicago school was Louis Sullivan's Carson, Pirie, Scott and Company department store (1904). Chicago pioneered skyscraper construction, but New York, with its unrelenting need

for prime downtown space, took the lead after the mid-1890s. The climax of New York's construction surge came with the completion in 1913 of the fifty-five-story Woolworth Building. Aptly called the "Cathedral of Commerce," this building towered over its neighbors and marked the beginning of the modern Manhattan skyline.

By contrast, the magnificent rail terminals that graced the great cities tried to mask their function. Reflecting the architectural forms of ages past, the terminals were marvels of structural design in their soaring interiors and use of steel, glass, and stone. New York's Grand Central Station (1913), built in the French baroque style, was completely electrified. It made superb use of underground space and had a loop system that enabled trains to turn around without reversing course. New York's other great terminal, Pennsylvania Station (1910), was modeled after a Roman bath.

The Electric City. For ordinary citizens the electric lights that dispelled the gloom of the city at night probably offered the most dramatic evidence that times had changed. The mainstay of city lighting since the early

Manhattan's First Skyscraper
The Tower Building at 50 Broadway was completed in 1889. To the modern eye, this first New York skyscraper seems modest and old-fashioned. Compared with its squat neighbors, however, it was a revolutionary building based on new principles of slender, soaring architecture.

nineteenth century had been the gaslight—which used illuminating gas produced from coal—but at 12 candle-power, gaslight was too dim to brighten the downtown streets and public spaces of the modern city. When generating technology for electricity became commercially feasible in the 1870s, the first application was for better city lighting. Charles F. Brush's electric arc lamps, installed in the windows of the Wanamaker department store in Philadelphia in 1878, threw a brilliant light and soon replaced gas lamps in stores and hotel lobbies and on city streets across the country. The following year Thomas Edison created the first practical incandescent bulb, which brought electric lighting into American homes. Edison's motto—"Let there be light!"—truly described the experience of the modern city.

Electricity was the source of the quickening tempo of city life. Before it had any significant effect on industry, electricity lifted and lowered elevators and powered streetcars and subway trains. Electric lighting was integral to the designs of the pioneering steel-frame buildings of the Chicago school. Meanwhile, the telephone, patented by Alexander Graham Bell in 1876, speeded up communication beyond anything imagined previously. Twain's complaint of 1867 that it was impossible to carry on business in New York had been answered: all one needed to do was pick up the phone. By 1900, 1.5 million telephones were in use, linking urban activity into a network of instant communication.

The Private City

City building was very much an exercise in private enterprise. The lure of profit spurred the great innovations—the trolley car, electric lighting, the skyscraper, the elevator, the telephone—and drove urban real-estate development. The investment opportunities looked so tempting that new cities sprang up almost overnight from the ruins of the Chicago fire of 1871 and the San Francisco earthquake of 1906. Real-estate interests, eager to develop subdivisions, often were instrumental in pushing streetcar lines outward from the central districts of cities.

Urban transit became big business. In the early 1880s Peter A. B. Widener and William L. Elkins teamed up to unite much of Philadelphia's streetcar system in the Philadelphia Traction Company. They did the same in alliance with Charles T. Yerkes in Chicago and William C. Whitney and Thomas Fortune Ryan in New York. By 1900 their syndicate controlled streetcar systems in more than a hundred cities and had expanded to include utilities supplying gas and electricity to urban customers. The city, like industry, became an arena for enterprise and profit.

Providing city services privately, however, was a matter of choice. Under the law, cities had extensive powers of self-development. In a key decision in 1897, New York state courts authorized New York City to build a municipally owned subway, ruling that cities had to determine their needs and then carry out their responsibilities as they saw fit. Even the use of privately owned land was subject to whatever regulations the city might impose.

But unlike in Europe, American cities generally hesitated to use their broad powers. America produced what the urban historian Sam Bass Warner has called the "private city"—one shaped primarily by the actions of many private individuals. All these persons pursued their own goals and tried to maximize their own profit. The prevailing belief was that the sum of such private activity would far exceed what the community could accomplish through public effort. This meant that the city itself handled only functions that could not be undertaken efficiently or profitably by private enterprise.

Despite that limitation, American cities actually compiled an impressive record of public works in the late nineteenth century. Nowhere in the world were there more massive public projects: water aqueducts, sewage systems, street paving, bridge building, extensive park systems. Though by no means free of the corruption and wastefulness of earlier days, city governments in these years became more centralized, better administered and more professional, and, above all, more expansive in the functions they undertook. How else could they have gathered the resources and built the infrastructure on which the modern industrial city depended?

Massive though it was, however, this public contribution did not undercut the prevailing conception of the city as an arena for private enterprise. The nation paid an enormous price for such unrestricted development. A century later we are still adding up the costs in terms of the quality of American urban life.

The Urban Environment. Some of those costs could be seen right away. In 1879 a British visitor observed the blight that spread along streets on which elevated trains operated:

> The nineteen hours and more of incessant rumbling day and night from the passing trains; the blocking out of a sufficiency of light; the full, close view passengers on the cars can have into rooms on the second and third floors.

Skyscrapers also shut out the light and added to downtown congestion. People regarded such conditions as sad but inevitable costs of progress.

Other consequences were more clearly the result of deliberate choice. Priority was given to projects considered vital to a city's economic development. Thus bridge construction flourished. Grand public buildings, symbols of a city's eminence, enjoyed great popularity. Philadelphia's city hall, said one critic, had been "projected on a scale of magnificence better suited for the capitol of an empire than the municipal building of a debt-burdened city." On the other hand, the condition of the streets, mainly a matter of convenience for the people, often remained scandalously bad. "Three or four days of warm spring weather," remarked a New York journalist, would turn Manhattan's garbage-strewn, snow-clogged streets into "veritable mud rivers."

A visitor to Pittsburgh noted "the heavy pall of smoke which constantly overhangs her . . . until the very sun looks coppery through the sooty haze." As for the lovely hills rising from the rivers, "they have been leveled down, cut into, sliced off, and ruthlessly marred and mutilated, until not a trace of their original outlines remains." Pittsburgh presented "all that is unsightly and forbidding in appearance, the original beauties of nature having been ruthlessly sacrificed to utility."

These failings resulted not only from the low value placed on the quality of urban life. The city's dynamism confounded efforts to provide adequate services. When it was completed in 1842, New York's Croton aqueduct was hailed as "more akin in magnificence to the ancient and Roman aqueducts [than anything] achieved in our times." Yet less than a decade later water consumption was outstripping the capacity of the aqueduct. In 1885 New York started to build a second and larger aqueduct. That one also failed to meet the city's needs, and so New York built still another aqueduct a hundred miles away in the Catskill Mountains. Each new facility and innovation seemed to fall short, not merely outstripped by the rising demand but also contributing to that demand. This occurred with urban transportation, high-rise building, and modern sanitation systems. They attracted more users, created new needs, and caused additional crowding and shortages.

It was not that America lacked an urban vision. On the contrary, an abiding rural ideal had exerted a powerful influence on American cities for many years and inspired many urban planners. Frederick Law Olmsted, who designed New York's Central Park and many other great parks, wanted cities that exposed people to the beauties of nature. One of Olmsted's projects, the Chicago Columbian Exposition of 1893, gave rise to the influential "City Beautiful" movement. The results included larger park systems, broad boulevards and parkways, and, after the turn of the century, zoning laws and planned suburbs.

But cities usually heeded urban planners too little and far too late. "Fifteen or twenty years ago a plan might have been adopted that would have made this one of the most beautiful cities in the world," Kansas City's park commissioners reported in 1893. At that time "such a policy could not be fully appreciated." Nor, even if Kansas City had foreseen its future, would it have shouldered the "heavy burden" of trying to shape its development. The American city had placed its

faith in the dynamics of the marketplace, not the restraints of a planned future.

Housing. Hardest hit by urban growth were the poor. In earlier times low-income city residents had lived in makeshift wooden structures in the alleys and back streets and, increasingly, in the subdivided homes of more prosperous families that had fled to other neighborhoods. When rising land values after the Civil War made this practice unprofitable, speculators began to build housing specifically designed for the urban masses. In New York City, the dreadful result was the "dumbbell" tenement, shaped to utilize nearly all the standard lot of 25 by 100 feet. A five-story building of this type could house twenty families in cramped, airless apartments (see Figure 20.1). In New York's Eleventh Ward an average of 986 persons occupied each acre, a density matched only in Bombay, India. In other cities crowding was not as severe. Chicago, Boston, and St. Louis relied on two- and three-story buildings for low-income housing, whereas Philadelphia and Baltimore made do with dingy row houses.

Civic-minded people everywhere considered these districts to be blights on the city. Here is how one investigator described Chicago's Halsted Street in 1896:

> The filthy and rotten tenements, the dingy courts and tumble-down sheds, the foul stables and dilapidated outhouses, the broken sewer pipes, the piles of garbage fairly alive with diseased odors, and . . . children filling every nook, working and playing in every room, eating and sleeping in every windowsill, pouring in and out of every door, and seeming literally to pave every scrap of "yard."

Reformers recognized the problem but seemed unable to solve it. Some favored model tenements financed by public-spirited citizens willing to accept a limited return on their investment. When private philanthropy failed to make much of a dent in the problem, cities turned to housing codes. The most advanced of these was New York's Tenement House Law of 1901, which required interior courts, indoor toilets, and fire safeguards for new housing but did little to remedy the problems of existing housing stock. Commercial development had pushed up land values in downtown areas. Only high-density, cheaply built housing could earn a sufficient profit for the landlords of the poor. This economic fact defied nineteenth-century solutions.

A Balance Sheet: Chicago and Berlin. In 1902 Chicago and Berlin had virtually equal populations. Their histories were, however, profoundly different. Seventy years earlier, when Chicago was just a muddy frontier outpost, Berlin had 250,000 inhabitants and was the royal seat of the Hohenzollerns of Prussia. With German unification in 1871, the imperial authorities rebuilt Berlin

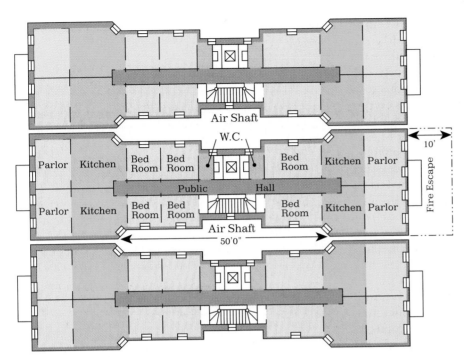

FIGURE 20.1

Floor Plan of a Dumbbell Tenement

In a contest for a design that met an 1879 requirement that every room have a window, the dumbbell tenement won. The interior indentation, which created an airshaft between adjoining buildings, gave the tenement its "dumbbell" shape. What was touted as a "model" tenement demonstrated instead the futility of trying to reconcile maximum land usage with decent housing. Each floor contained four apartments of three or four rooms, the largest only 10 by 11 feet. The two toilets in the hall became filthy or broke down under the daily use of forty or more people. The narrow airshaft provided almost no light for the interior rooms and served mainly as a dumping ground for garbage. So deplorable were these tenements that they became the stimulus for the next wave of New York housing reform.

on a grander scale. "A capital city is essential for the state, to act as a pivot for its culture," proclaimed the Prussian historian Heinrich von Treitschke, and Berlin served that national purpose—"a center where [Germany's] political, intellectual, and material life is concentrated, and its people can feel united." Chicago had no such pretensions. It was strictly a place of business, made great by virtue of its strategic grip on the commerce of America's industrial heartland. Nothing in Chicago evoked the grandeur of Berlin's boulevards or its monumental palaces and public buildings, nor were Chicagoans ever witness to the pomp and ceremony of the imperial parades through the Brandenburg Gate and up broad, tree-lined Unter den Linden to the national cathedral.

Yet as a functioning city Chicago was in many ways superior to Berlin. Chicago's waterworks pumped 500 million gallons of water a day, providing 139 gallons of water per person, whereas Berliners had to make do with 18 gallons. Flush toilets, a rarity in Berlin in 1900, could be found in 60 percent of Chicago's homes. Its streets were lit by electricity whereas Berlin still relied mostly on gaslight. Chicago had a much more extensive streetcar system, twice as much acreage devoted to parks, and a public library containing many more volumes than Berlin's. And Chicago had just completed an amazing sanitation project to protect its water supply in Lake Michigan. By means of the new Sanitary and Ship Canal, the course of the Chicago River had been reversed so that its waters—and the city's sewage—would flow away from the lake and southward down into the Illinois and Mississippi rivers. The giant canal, involv-

ing the excavation of over 30 million cubic yards of dirt, was the greatest earth-moving project in municipal history up to that time.

Giant sanitation projects were one thing; an inspiring urban environment was something else. For well-traveled Americans admiring of things European, the sense of inferiority was palpable. "We are enormously rich," admitted the journalist Edwin L. Godkin, "but . . . what have we got to show? Almost nothing. Ugliness from an artistic point of view is the mark of all our cities." Thus the urban balance sheet: a utilitarian infrastructure that was superb by nineteenth-century standards but "no municipal splendors of any description, nothing but population and hotels."

City People

The city symbolized energy and enterprise with its soaring skyscrapers, rushing subways and jostling traffic, and hum of business activity. When the budding writer Hamlin Garland and his brother arrived in Chicago from rural Iowa in 1881, they knew immediately that they had entered a new world: "Everything interested us. . . . Nothing was commonplace, nothing was ugly to us." In one way or another every city-bound migrant, whether from the American countryside or from a foreign land, experienced something of this exhilaration and wonder.

But with the opportunity and boundless variety came disorder and uncertainty. The urban world was utterly unlike the rural communities that the newcomers had left. In the countryside every person had been known to his or her neighbors. Mark Twain found New York "a splendid desert, where a stranger is lonely in the midst of a million of his race. A man walks his tedious miles through the same interminable streets every day, yet never seeing a familiar face, and never seeing a strange one the second time. . . . Every man rushes, rushes, rushes, and never has time to be companionable—never has any time at his disposal to fool away on matters which do not involve dollars and duty and business." If rural roles and obligations had been well understood, in the city the only predictable relationships were those dictated by the marketplace.

The newcomers could never re-create in the city the worlds they had left behind. But new ways developed to meet the social needs of urban dwellers—to give them a sense of their place in the community, teach them how to function in an impersonal, heterogeneous environment, and make the complex, dynamic city understandable. An urban culture emerged, and through it there developed a new breed of American who was entirely at home in the modern city.

Immigrants

At the turn of the century upwards of 30 percent of the residents of New York, Chicago, Boston, Cleveland, Minneapolis, and San Francisco were foreign-born. Except in the South, America's cities had attracted large numbers of immigrants for many years. In 1900 the dominant groups still represented mainly the earlier mi-

TABLE 20.2

Foreign-Born Population of Philadelphia, 1870 and 1910

	1870	1910
Irish	96,698	83,196
German	50,746	61,480
Austrian	519	19,860
Italian	516	45,308
Russian	94	90,697
Hungarian	52	12,495
Foreign-born population	183,624	384,707
Total population	674,022	1,549,008

Source: Allen F. Davis and Mark Haller, *The Peoples of Philadelphia* (Philadelphia: Temple University Press, 1973), 205.

gration from northern Europe. The biggest ethnic group in Boston was Irish; in Minneapolis, Swedish; in most other northern cities, German. But by 1910 the influx from southern and Eastern Europe had changed the ethnic complexion of many of these cities. The experience of Philadelphia is shown in Table 20.2. In Chicago, Poles and Russians (mostly Jewish) took the lead; in New York, Italians were second to Russians; and in San Francisco, Italians became the largest foreign-born group.

All these immigrants—old and new—carried experiences and customs from the homeland that shaped their lives in the New World. But for the later arrivals from southern and Eastern Europe there was less intermingling with the older populations than had been possible in the earlier "walking cities." Beginning in the 1880s, observers invariably reported that only foreign-born people lived in the poorer downtown areas of the great eastern and midwestern cities. "One may find for the asking an Italian, a German, a French, African, Spanish, Bohemian, Russian, Scandinavian, Jewish, and Chinese colony," remarked the Danish-American journalist Jacob Riis in his study of New York in 1890. "The one thing you shall vainly ask for in the chief city of America is a distinctively American community."

The foreign-born had little choice about where they lived; they needed to be near their jobs and could not afford better housing. Some, such as Maksymilian Markiewicz (see American Voices, page 626), gravitated to the outlying factory districts; others settled in the congested downtown ghettos. The immigrants did not settle randomly in those districts, however. Even where that seemed to happen, as in Philadelphia, closer study revealed that ethnic groups clustered in certain houses and portions of blocks. More commonly, as Riis discov-

Italian Bread Peddlers, New York City
Because of crowded conditions in East Side tenements, immigrant life spilled out onto the streets, which offered a bit of fresh air, a chance to socialize with neighbors, and a place to shop for food, including bread.

The Economy of the Ghetto

Downtown immigrant neighborhoods would not have struck the casual observer as industrial districts, but tucked away in the tenements were commercial lofts and small workshops. An entire ready-made clothing industry flourished within the ghettos of large cities, drawing especially on the young women of the neighborhood to perform the low-paid sewing tasks.

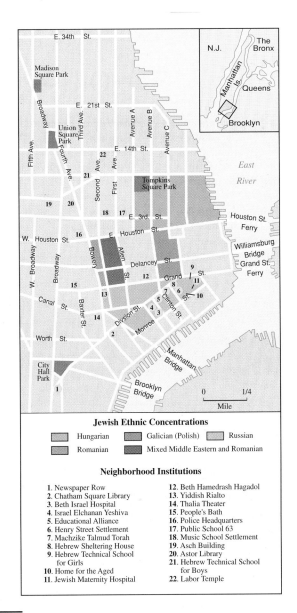

Jewish Ethnic Concentrations

Hungarian   Galician (Polish)   Russian
Romanian   Mixed Middle Eastern and Romanian

Neighborhood Institutions

1. Newspaper Row
2. Chatham Square Library
3. Beth Israel Hospital
4. Israel Elchanan Yeshiva
5. Educational Alliance
6. Henry Street Settlement
7. Machzike Talmud Torah
8. Hebrew Sheltering House
9. Hebrew Technical School for Girls
10. Home for the Aged
11. Jewish Maternity Hospital
12. Beth Hamedrash Hagadol
13. Yiddish Rialto
14. Thalia Theater
15. People's Bath
16. Police Headquarters
17. Public School 63
18. Music School Settlement
19. Asch Building
20. Astor Library
21. Hebrew Technical School for Boys
22. Labor Temple

MAP 20.3

The Lower East Side, New York City

As this map shows, the Jewish immigrants dominating Manhattan's Lower East Side preferred living in neighborhoods populated by those from their home regions of Eastern Europe. It was their sense of a common identity, however, that made for a remarkable flowering of educational, cultural, and social institutions on the Jewish East Side.

ered, an ethnic group took over an entire neighborhood. In New York (see Map 20.3), Italians crowded into the Irish neighborhoods west of Broadway, and Russian and Polish Jews pushed the Germans out of the Lower East Side. A dense colony of Hungarians lived around Houston Street, and Bohemians occupied stretches along the Upper East Side between Fiftieth and Seventy-sixth streets.

Within ethnic groups, one could also spot clusterings of people from the same province or even the same village. Among New York Italians, for example, Neapolitans and Calabrians populated the Mulberry Bend district whereas Genoese lived on Baxter Street. Other northern Italians occupied the Eighth and Fifteenth wards west of Broadway. In 1903, along a short stretch of Elizabeth Street, there lived several hundred families from a single Sicilian fishing town, Sciacca, and as in Sicily, Sciacca's patron saint was celebrated every year.

Capitalizing on the fellow feeling that drew ethnic groups together, a variety of institutions sprang up to meet their needs. Wherever substantial numbers of immigrants lived, newspapers appeared. In 1911 the 20,000 Poles in Buffalo, New York, supported two Polish-language daily papers. Immigrants throughout the country avidly read *Il Progresso Italo-Americano* and the Yiddish-language *Jewish Daily Forward*, both

published in New York City. Conviviality could always be found on street corners, in barbershops and club rooms, and in saloons. A 1905 survey showed that Chicago had as many saloons as grocery stores, meat markets, and dry-goods stores together. Italians marched in saints' day parades, Bohemians gathered in singing societies, and New York Jews patronized a vibrant Yiddish theater. To provide help in times of sick-

AMERICAN VOICES

Maksymilian Markiewicz

The Odyssey of a Polish Immigrant

In these letters to his cousin Waclaw (whom he addresses as "brother"), Maksymilian Markiewicz records the life experience of a typical Polish immigrant to urban America.

South Chicago, August 7, 1906

Dear Brother Waclaw: Fortune arranged it so that unexpectedly we both became pilgrims to America. So I feel my brotherly attachment to you, and that it is so, let it be proved by my letter to you. . . . So I inform you that I came to America, i.e., to New York, on February 13, and then I went to my friends in New Kensington [Pennsylvania] . . . . I worked in a glass factory for 8 hours a day. The work was not heavy, but hot. I earned $12.50 to $14.00 a week; it depended on how much glass was made.

I left because the factory closed. . . . I went to Chicago. There I found my acquaintances and my cousin Leonard Król, my mother's uncle's son, with whom I am living up to the present. Since I came to South Chicago, I am working with Polish carpenters 8 hours a day. I am paid 35 cents an hour. And naturally, while it is summer, I am very busy with this work, but in winter it will surely stop. Then I hope to get into a factory.

Indiana Harbor, April 30, 1908

Dear Brother Waclaw: I inform you that I moved from South Chicago to Indiana Harbor, nearer my work, so that now I can go on foot to the factory and I don't need to pay 15 cents a day for the railway passage. . . .

I got a letter from our country, from mother, father and brother Wiktor. When Wiktor was still in Petersburg I wrote him that I intended to marry in America, and that I would therefore never come back to our country. . . . My mother begs me much, in her first letter to me, to remove these thoughts from my head, to come back to our country. . . . My heart grieves at the words of my beloved mother, and I am ready to satisfy her wish in the future.

As to the question how I look upon religion and socialism, dear brother, I don't bother myself profoundly with either the first or the second. . . . I am not devout, for I have no time to pray, because every Sunday I must work, and—I confess it to you alone—I worked even on Easter from 7 until 2. . . . But nevertheless I desire to remain a Catholic up to my death.

December 14, 1908

Dear Brother: In the factory where I am working very few men have good work—only the engineers and we three carpenters. As to ordinary workers in the mill, may God pity them, so bad is their work. . . . With me everything is good . . . only I am bored here, because in this small town I am as solitary as in a forest. . . . Write me what you think about the Polish National Alliance and the Polish Sokols [gymnastic societies].

October 5, 1909

Dear Brother Waclaw: My old boss told me today that he had much work, so perhaps I knew some carpenters, and if so I should send them to him. . . . I advise you to come, dear brother. . . . We would live in the foreign land together. . . . We could meet in South Chicago and speak about the business while drinking a glass of beer.

Source: William I. Thomas and Florian Znaniecki, *The Polish Peasant in Europe and America* (Urbana: University of Illinois Press, 1984, abridged ed.), 123–133.

---

ness and death, the immigrants organized mutual-aid societies. The Italians in Chicago had sixty-six of these organizations in 1903, composed mainly of people from particular provinces and towns. Immigrants built a rich and functional institutional life in urban America, to an extent unimagined in their native villages.

Urban Blacks. The vast majority of African-Americans— 85 percent in 1880—lived in the rural South. In the ensuing years some of them migrated to the modestly growing southern cities. By 1900 blacks constituted roughly a third of the South's urban population, ranging from 20 percent in Louisville and Dallas to absolute majorities in Memphis and Charleston.

The great African-American migration to northern cities was just beginning. The black population of New York increased by 30,000 between 1900 and 1910, making New York second only to Washington, D.C., as a black urban center, but the 91,000 blacks in New York in 1910 represented fewer than 2 percent of the population, as did Chicago's 45,000 black residents and Cleveland's 6,000.

Despite their relatively small numbers, urban blacks could not escape becoming targets of the fierce racism of the age. In northern cities generally, residential segregation was intensifying, and the scattered black neighborhoods were giving way to concentrated ghettos— Chicago's Black Belt on the south side, for example, or the early outlines of New York's Harlem. Because of race prejudice, job opportunities were likewise narrowing. Whereas 26 percent of Cleveland's blacks had been skilled workers in 1870, only 12 percent were by 1890, and entire occupations, such as barbering (except for a black clientele), disappeared. Two-thirds of Cleveland's blacks in 1910 worked as domestic and day laborers, with little hope of moving up the job ladder.

In the face of segregation and pervasive discrimination, urban blacks built their own communities. They created a flourishing press, fraternal orders, a vast array of women's organizations, and a middle class of doctors, lawyers, and small entrepreneurs. Above all, there were the black churches—twenty-five in Chicago in 1905, mainly Methodist and Baptist. More than any other institution, remarked one scholar in 1913, it was the church "which the Negro may call his own. . . . A new church may be built . . . and . . . all the machinery set in motion without ever consulting any white person. . . . [It] more than anything else represents the real life of the race." Just as it was in the southern countryside, the church was the central institution for city blacks, and the preacher—"a leader, a politician, an orator, a 'boss', an intriguer, an idealist," so W. E. B. Du Bois described him—was the most important local citizen. Manhattan's Union Baptist Church, housed like many others in a storefront, attracted the "very recent residents of this new, disturbing city" and, ringing with spirituals and fervent prayer, made Christianity come "alive Sunday mornings."

Ward Politics

Race and ethnicity tended to divide newcomers to the city and turn them in on themselves. Politics, on the other hand, acted as a powerful instrument for integrating immigrants and blacks into the larger urban society. The basic unit of city governance was the *ward*, each one entitled to its representative on the city council or board of aldermen. Whether realizing it or not, every migrant to an American city automatically belonged to a ward and, by living on a particular street, immediately acquired a spokesman at city hall.

In earlier days the aldermen had been the dominant figures in urban politics, but that was no longer the case in the late nineteenth century. Power had largely passed to the mayor's office and the various citywide administrative agencies. But the city council still represented the parochial interests of the wards, and immigrants learned very quickly that if they needed anything from city hall, the alderman was the person for them. That was how streets got paved, or water mains were extended, or variances were granted—so that, for example, in 1888 Vito Fortounescere could "place and keep a stand for the sale of fruit, inside the stoop-line, in front of the northeast corner of Twenty-eighth Street and Fourth Avenue" in Manhattan, or that the parishioners of Saint Maria of Mount Carmel could set off fireworks at their Fourth of July picnic.

Interlinked with this formal representation was the pervasive presence of party machines in immigrant and black neighborhoods. Machine control of political parties existed at every level of American politics (see Chapter 19). The system flourished most luxuriantly, however, in the big cities. Most famous was Tammany Hall, the political machine that dominated Manhattan's Democratic party; but the major parties of most large cities—Democratic or Republican—had their versions of Tammany.

The power of urban machines depended on a loyal party constituency. This meant organization down to the grass roots. The wards were divided into election districts of a few blocks, each with a district captain who reported to the ward boss (who might also have been the alderman). It was the main job of these functionaries to be accessible and, as best they could, to serve the needs of the party's constituents.

The machine performed a similar function for the business community. Entrepreneurs of many kinds wanted something from the city. Contractors sought city business; gas companies and streetcar lines wanted licenses and privileges; manufacturers needed services and not-too-nosy inspectors; and the liquor trade and numbers racket relied on a tolerant police force. All of them turned to the machine boss and his lieutenants. In addition to these everyday functions, the machine continuously mediated among conflicting interests and oiled the wheels of city government. The machines filled a void in the public life of the nineteenth-century city, doing informally much of what the municipal system left undone. "Nowhere else in the world," remarked the journalist Henry Jones Ford, "has party organization had to cope with such enormous tasks . . . and its efficiency in dealing with them is the true glory of our political system."

Of course, the machine exacted a price for all these services. The tenement dweller gave his vote. The businessman wrote a check. Those who became the machine's beneficiaries enabled it to function. Corruption permeated this informal system. Some of the money that changed hands inevitably ended up in the pockets of machine politicians. This boodle could take the form of outright corruption: kickbacks by contractors; protection money from gamblers, saloonkeepers, and prostitutes; and payoffs from gas and trolley companies. The Tammany ward boss George Washington Plunkitt, however, insisted that he had no need for kickbacks and bribes. He favored what he called "honest graft," the easy profits that came to savvy insiders. Plunkitt himself made most of his money building wharves on Manhattan's waterfront. Big Tim Sullivan (see American Lives, pages 628–629) used his contacts to build a vaudeville empire. One way or another, legally or otherwise, machine politics rewarded its supporters.

For the young and ambitious this was reason enough to favor the machine system. American society

Big Tim Sullivan: Tammany Politician

Timothy D. Sullivan was born on July 23, 1863, near the Hudson River docks in Lower Manhattan. His parents were Irish immigrants, part of the mass migration of potato famine victims that flooded into New York in the 1840s. Four years later Tim's father died, leaving his young widow, Catherine Connelly Sullivan, with four small children. Soon thereafter Catherine married Lawrence Mulligan, an Irish laborer, and the family moved to the notorious Five Points district on the Lower East Side. There the 1870 census found them, a household of ten (including three boarders) living in an overcrowded tenement at 25 Baxter Street (see Map 20.3 for the urban geography of Sullivan's career).

Tim had a harsh childhood. His stepfather drank heavily and regularly beat his wife and children. To make ends meet, Catherine took in washing and Tim went to work at age seven bundling paper for $1.50 a week on Newspaper Row across from City Hall. Tim got through grammar school, but his family needed his earnings too much for him to go on to high school. "Free as it was," he later remarked, "it was not free enough for me to go there." Instead—Horatio Alger style—he made his way up in the newspaper business and by age eighteen was well established as a wholesale newspaper dealer. He soon became the proprietor of two saloons and, in his early twenties, was ready for politics. Sullivan was a big fellow, over six feet tall, handsome, and quick with his fists. He gained a local reputation by thrashing a tough he had encountered on the street beating up a woman. True or not, the story helped him win the Democratic nomination at age twenty-three for the New York State Assembly from the Second District.

In 1889 Sullivan opposed a bill granting Manhattan's police virtually unlimited powers to detain people with jail records. The champion of the bill was Thomas F. Byrnes, chief inspector of the New York Police Department and the most celebrated detective in the country. Byrnes did not take kindly to opposition from small-time politicians. He raided Sullivan's saloons, arrested two barkeepers for excise tax violations, and denounced Sullivan as a consorter with criminals. Against the advice of friends, Sullivan took the Assembly floor to answer the charge. In tearful tones Sullivan cast him-

Big Tim Sullivan

self as an "honest Bowery boy," describing his impoverished childhood, his saintly mother, and his struggle to rise in the world. "When, at the conclusion [so a reporter recorded], he asked if he had any time or money to spend with thieves, there was a 'No' on nearly every member's lips." It was the making of the obscure assemblyman. Although he gained a notoriety with uptown New Yorkers that would dog him throughout his career, he won the hearts of his constituents, who reveled in the success story of one of their own. They thought "Big Tim" a fine fellow, and so did the Tammany leaders.

The Bowery at Night, 1895
This painting by W. Louis Sonntag, Jr., shows Big Tim's stomping ground, the Bowery, crowded with shoppers and pleasure-seekers. It was during this time that the Bowery gained its raffish reputation.

When the Tammany machine swept into power in the 1892 elections, Boss Richard Croker tapped Sullivan to run the new Third Assembly District centering on the Bowery. Sullivan swiftly consolidated his power. His inner circle was all Irish, but for election district captains he appointed Jews, Italians, and Germans who were well connected in the immigrant communities that populated his fiefdom. Sullivan became famous for his summer "chowders," when he transported his constituents by riverboat to the country for a rowdy day of picnicking. At Christmas there was a fine dinner for all who were in need. And in February Sullivan handed out wool socks and shoes—always with the sentimental tale of how a teacher had given him free shoes one cold winter. Big Tim also attended assiduously to the nitty-gritty business of running a political machine. He got jobs for his supporters, visited the jails regularly to offer bail and other aid to the inmates, and on election day made sure his strong-arm crews patrolled the polling places. Sullivan's district became the best organized in the city, and Tammany hailed him as "the most popular man on the East Side."

In the meantime, Sullivan was making his fortune. His particular form of "honest graft" was commercial entertainment. Big Tim knew instinctively how important a good time was to city people. Besides, the main street of his district, the Bowery, was the gaudy center of low-life entertainment for the entire city, lined with burlesque houses, concert saloons, restaurants, and cheap hotels. In the mid-1890s Sullivan formed a partnership with two theatrical producers and began to invest in vaudeville houses. He contributed not only money and a shrewd head but the political contacts that assured lax enforcement of building codes and easy access to liquor licenses. Sullivan also became involved in professional boxing, horse racing, and, more illicitly, the gambling dens that dotted his district.

Sullivan was accused of trafficking in East Side prostitution, but this he indignantly denied. "Nobody who knows me well will believe I would take a penny from any woman, much less from the poor creatures who are more to be pitied than any other human beings on earth. I'd be afraid to take a cent from a poor woman of the streets for fear my old mother would see me. I'd a good deal rather break into a bank and rob the safe. That would be a more manly and decent way of getting money."

When Boss Croker resigned in 1902, Sullivan might have succeeded him, but Big Tim preferred his own district and threw his support to Charles F. Murphy, who ruled Tammany for the next twenty-two years. Sullivan served briefly in Congress, made a lot more money investing in the early movie industry and in vaudeville syndicates across the country, and in the final phase of his career became a champion of progressive social legislation in the New York Senate. In 1912 Sullivan suffered a severe mental breakdown, possibly caused by tertiary syphilis. A year later he died under the wheels of a freight train after running off from his brother's house outside New York. His funeral procession down the Bowery was one of the largest in memory and brought out an immense crowd from every stratum of New York society, from statesmen to prizefighters and scrubwomen.

celebrated personal achievement but denied economic opportunity to poor immigrants. Not only did they lack the means to get started in business, remarked Robert A. Woods about the inhabitants of Boston's South End, "but they have to meet strong prejudices of race and religion. Politics, therefore, is for them apparently the easiest way to success in life." In the mid-1870s over half of Chicago's forty aldermen were foreign-born, sixteen of them Irish immigrants. The first Italian was elected to the board in 1885 and the first Pole in 1888, followed in the 1890s by Czechs and Scandinavians. Blacks did not manage to get on Chicago's board of aldermen until after 1900; but in Baltimore an African-American represented the Eleventh Ward from 1890 onward, and Philadelphia had three black aldermen by 1899. As a ladder for social mobility, machine politics (like professional sports, entertainment, and organized crime) was the most democratic of American institutions.

For most tenement dwellers, however, the machine had a more modest value. It acted as a rough-and-ready social service agency, providing jobs for the jobless, a helping hand for a bereaved family, and intercession with an unfeeling city bureaucracy. As a Boston ward boss remarked, "There's got to be in every ward somebody that any bloke can come to—no matter what he's done—and get help. *Help, you understand; none of your law and justice, but help.*" The Tammany ward boss Plunkitt had a "regular system" when fires broke out in his district. "Any hour of the day or night, I'm usually there . . . as soon as the fire engines. If a family is burned out I don't ask whether they are Republicans or Democrats, and I don't refer them to the Charity Organization Society. . . . I just get quarters for them . . . and fix them up till they get things runnin' again. It's philanthropy, but it's politics, too—mighty good politics. . . . The poor look up to George W. Plunkitt as a father, come to him when they are in trouble—and don't forget him on election day."

Plunkitt was an Irishman, and so were most of the ward politicians controlling Tammany Hall. But by the 1890s Plunkitt's Fifteenth District was filling up with Italians and Eastern European Jews. In general the New York Irish had no love for these newer immigrants, but Plunkitt played no favorites. On any given day (as recorded in a diary) he might attend an Italian funeral in the afternoon and a Jewish wedding in the evening, and at each he probably paid his respects with a few Italian words or a bit of Yiddish.

"Think what New York is and what the people of New York are," remarked Richard Croker, the powerful head of Tammany during the 1890s, and Plunkitt's boss:

One half, more than half, are of foreign birth. . . . They do not speak our language, they do not know our laws, they are the raw material from which we have to build up the state. . . . [Tammany] looks after

them for the sake of their vote, grafts them upon the Republic, makes citizens of them, in short. . . . Who else would do it if we did not? . . . There is not a mugwump in the city who would shake hands with the [immigrant voter].

The Mugwump reformer (see page 594) would doubtless have responded that the nation could do without citizens whose notion of politics was only what was in it for them. But Croker spoke a powerful truth. In an era when so many forces acted to isolate ghetto communities, politics served an *integrating* function, cutting across ethnic lines and giving immigrants and blacks a stake in the larger urban order.

Religion and Ethnicity

Among immigrant groups, religion was an abiding concern and was so intertwined with ethnic identity as to be inseparable from the story of how the newcomers adapted to the American city.

Jewish Immigrants. When Jews from Eastern Europe began their mass migration in the 1880s, about 250,000 Jews, mostly of German origin, were living in America. The German Jews, well established and increasingly prosperous, embraced Reform Judaism, abandoning religious practices "not adapted to the views and habits of modern civilization." Anxious to preserve the traditional piety, Yiddish-speaking immigrants founded their own Orthodox synagogues, often in vacant stores and ramshackle buildings. The number of synagogues in the United States jumped from 270 in 1880 to 1,901 in 1916.

Many Jewish immigrants found it difficult, however, to adhere to the traditional forms of their religion. In the isolated villages of Eastern Europe, Judaism stood for not only worship and belief but an entire way of life. Not even the closely confined urban American ghetto could re-create the communal environment essential for strict religious observance. "The very clothes I wore and the very food I ate had a fatal effect on my religious habits," confessed the hero of Abraham Cahan's novel *The Rise of David Levinsky* (1917). "If you . . . attempt to bend your religion to the spirit of your surroundings, it breaks. It falls to pieces." Levinsky shaved off his beard and plunged into the Manhattan clothing business. Orthodox Judaism survived this shattering of faith, but only by sharply reducing its claims on the lives of the faithful.

Catholic Immigrants. Catholics faced much the same problem. The issue, explicitly defined within the Roman Catholic Church as "Americanism," turned on how far Catholicism should respond to American society. Catholics fought out the question on many fronts. Should

Catholic children attend parochial or public schools? Should they intermarry with non-Catholics? Should the traditional education for the clergy be changed? Bishop John Ireland of St. Paul, Minnesota, felt that "the principles of the Church are in harmony with the interests of the Republic." But traditionalists, led by Archbishop Michael A. Corrigan of New York, denied the possibility of such harmony and argued, in effect, for insulating the Church from a hostile environment.

In 1895 Pope Leo XIII announced his support of the traditionalists. America, with its religious pluralism and sharp separation of church and state, did not afford "the most desirable status of the Church." The pope regretted the absence of the benefits that came from state support and urged Catholics "to prefer to associate with Catholics, a course which will be very conducive to the safeguarding of their faith." Because of its hierarchical structure, Catholicism had a better chance than Judaism to resist American influences.

The Church's traditional wing had the support of immigrant Catholics, who wanted to preserve the religion as they had known it in Europe. But the needs of the immigrants extended beyond religious matters; they wanted the Church also to be an expression of their ethnic identities. Newly arrived Catholics wanted their own parishes where they could celebrate their own customs and holidays, speak their own languages, and educate their children in their own parochial schools. When they became numerous enough, they also demanded their own bishops.

The Church had difficulty responding. The demands of its immigrant congregations seemed to challenge the Catholic hierarchy, which was dominated by Irish Catholics, and even the integrity of the Church itself.

The desire for ethnic parishes did more than divide Catholics; it also led to demands for local control of Church property. In addition, if the Church appointed bishops with jurisdiction over specific ethnic groups, that would mean disrupting the diocesan structure that unified the Church.

The severity of the conflict depended partly on the religious traditions of each ethnic group. Italians, for example, harbored strong anticlerical feelings, much strengthened by the papacy's opposition to the unification of Italy. Italian men also had a tradition of religious apathy. On the other hand, the Church played such an important part in the lives of Polish immigrants that they resented any interference by the Catholic hierarchy. In 1907 fifty parishes formed the Polish National Catholic Church of America, which adhered to Catholic ritual without recognizing the pope's authority.

On the whole, however, the Church reconciled its authority with the ethnic needs of the immigrant faithful. It met the demand for representation in the hierarchy by appointing Polish and other immigrant priests as auxiliary bishops within existing dioceses. Before World War I, American Catholics worshiped in more than 2,000 foreign-language churches and in many others that were bilingual. The Catholic Church thus became a central institution for the expression of ethnic identity in urban America.

Urban Protestantism. For the Protestant churches the city posed different but not easier challenges. With each wave of immigration urban populations became increasingly non-Protestant. At the same time, Protestant congregations were abandoning the older residential neighborhoods. Many formerly prosperous churches

Immaculate Heart of Mary Church, 1908

In crowded immigrant neighborhoods the church rose from undistinguished surroundings to assert the centrality of religious belief in the life of the community. This photograph is a view of Immaculate Heart of Mary Church taken from Polish Hill in Pittsburgh in 1908.

Paddy and Friends

Newsboys of New York

City dwellers encountered poverty every day in the form of ragged newsboys hawking papers on the streets. In 1854 the first Newsboys' Lodging House was opened as a shelter for these mostly homeless youngsters. By trial and error, the Lodging House accommodated itself to the fierce independence of the newsboys, who continued to ply their trade and indeed contributed to the upkeep of the Lodging House. Charles Loring Brace, a major Protestant charity figure who was well known to the boys, brought some friends to hear what the boys had to say: "Whom do you choose for your speaker?"

"Paddy, Paddy!" they shouted. "Come out, Paddy, an' show yerself."

Paddy came forward and mounted a stool; a youngster not more than twelve, with little round eyes, a short nose profusely freckled, and a lithe form full of fun.

"Bummers," he began, "Snoozers and citizens, I've come down here among yer to talk to yer a little. Me an' me friend Brace have come to see how yer gittin' along an' to advise yer. You fellers w'at stands at the shops with yer noses over the railin', a smellin' of the roast beef an' hash,— you fellers who's got no home,—think of it, how are we to encourage yer? [Derisive laughter, and various ironical kinds of applause.] I say bummers, for

ye're all bummers, [in a tone of kind patronage] I was a bummer once meself. [Great laughter.] I hate to see yer spending yer money for penny ice-creams an' bad cigars. Why don't yer save yer money? I have hopes fer yer all. . . . I want yer to grow up to be rich men,—citizens, gover'ment men, lawyers, ginerals, an' inflooence men. Well, boys, I'll tell yer a story. Me dad was a hard un. One beautiful day he went on a spree. . . . He clipped me over the head with an iron pot an' knocked me down, an' me mother drapped in on him an' at it they wint. . . . Ye should have seen 'em, an' whilst they were a fightin' I slipped meself out o' the back dure an' away I wint like a scart dog. . . . I ran away, an' here I am. Now, boys, be good, mind yer manners, copy me, an' see what ye'll become."

One solution much touted by reformers was to send homeless boys to the West to live with farm families. No doubt some of the streetwise newsboys suspected that they were wanted only as cheap farm labor. But this speaker on that Sunday evening had higher hopes:

"Do ye want to be newsboys always, an' shoeblacks, an' timber merchants in a small way sellin' matches? If ye do, ye'll stay in New York; but if ye don't, ye'll go out West an' begin to be farm-

City Newsboys

ers, for the beginnings of a farmer, me boys, is the makin' of a Congressman an' a President. Do ye want to be rowdies an' loafers an' shoulder-hitters? . . . I'm booked for the West in the next company from the Lodging-House. I hear they have big school-houses there, an' a place for me in the winter time. I've made up me mind to be somebody, an' you'll find me on a farm in the West . . . I can't say no more at present, boys. Good bye."

Source: Helen Campbell, *Darkness and Daylight: or, Lights and Shadows of New York Life* (Hartford, 1892) reprinted in Sigmund Diamond, ed., *The Nation Transformed* (New York: George Braziller, 1963), 300–301.

found themselves stranded in squalid ghetto neighborhoods. Seventeen Protestant churches moved out of lower Manhattan during the twenty years after 1868 as the area below Fourteenth Street filled up with immigrants.

Nearly every major city retained great downtown churches where wealthy Protestants worshiped. Some of those churches, richly endowed, took pride in nationally prominent pastors, including Henry Ward Beecher of the Plymouth Congregational Church in Brooklyn

and Phillips Brooks of the Trinity Episcopal Church in Boston. The eminence of those churches, with their fashionable congregations and imposing edifices, emphasized the growing remoteness of Protestantism from much of its urban constituency. "Where is the city in which the Sabbath day is not losing ground?" lamented a minister in 1887. The families of businessmen, lawyers, and doctors could be seen in any church on Sunday morning, he noted, "but the workingmen and their families are not there."

To counter this decline, the Protestant churches responded in two ways. They evangelized among the unchurched and indifferent, for example, through the Sunday-school movement. Protestants also made their churches instruments of social uplift. Starting in the 1880s, many city churches provided facilities such as reading rooms, day nurseries, clubhouses, and vocational classes. Sometimes the churches linked evangelism and social uplift. Protestant reformers did charity work of many kinds in the cities, such as the Newsboys' Lodging Houses (see American Voices, page 632). The Salvation Army, which arrived from Great Britain in 1879, spread the gospel of repentance among the urban poor and built an assistance program that ranged from soup kitchens to homes for former prostitutes. When all else failed, the down-and-outers of American cities knew they could count on the Salvation Army.

The Young Men's and Women's Christian Associations attracted large numbers of the young single people who flocked into the cities. Originating in Britain, the two organizations had arrived in the United States before the Civil War and had flourished. By the mid-1880s virtually all large cities had YMCAs equipped with gymnasiums, auditoriums, and dormitories. Housing for single women was an especially important mission of the YWCAs. No other organizations better met the needs of young adults for physical recreation, education, and companionship, or so effectively combined those services with an evangelizing appeal in the form of Bible classes, nondenominational worship, and a religious atmosphere.

The need of many people to unite religion with social uplift could be seen in the enormous popularity of a book called *In His Steps* (1896). The author, the Congregational minister Charles M. Sheldon, told the story of a congregation that resolved to live by Christ's precepts for one year. "If the church members were all doing as Jesus would do," Sheldon asked, "could it remain true that armies of men would walk the streets for jobs, and hundreds of them curse the church, and thousands of them find in the saloon their best friend?"

Urban Revivalism. The most potent form of urban evangelism—revivalism—said little about social uplift. From its beginnings in the eighteenth century, revivalism had steadfastly focused on the individual and had stressed personal redemption. The defeat of earthly problems would follow the conversion of the people to Christ. Beginning in the mid-1870s, revival meetings swept through the cities.

The pioneering figure was Dwight L. Moody, a former Chicago shoe salesman and YMCA official. After preaching in Britain for two years, Moody returned to America in 1875. With his talented chorister and hymn writer, Ira D. Sankey, Moody staged revival meetings that drew thousands. He preached an optimistic, uncomplicated, nondenominational message. Eternal life could be had for the asking, Moody shouted as he held up his Bible. His listeners needed only "to come forward and take, TAKE!"

Many other preachers followed in Moody's path. The most notable was Billy (William Ashley) Sunday, a hard-drinking former outfielder for the Chicago White Stockings who mended his ways and found religion. Like Moody and other city revivalists, Sunday was a farm boy. His ripsnorting cries against "Charlotte-russe Christians" and the "booze traffic" carried the ring of rustic America. By realizing that many people remained villagers at heart, revivalists found the key to bringing city dwellers back into the church.

In a larger sense, however, revivalism was expressive of a more general fundamentalist movement that sought to preserve old-time religion against the increasing complacency and doctrinal liberalism of mainstream Protestantism. Just as Methodism had arisen against the Church of England in the eighteenth century, so now in the late nineteenth century new churches arose against Methodism. The Holiness evangelical movement was at first nondenominational but then began to spawn new denominations such as the Church of the Nazarene (1908). Out of the Holiness Revival came the more radical Pentecostal movement, which by 1914 had brought together many local bodies into the Assemblies of God.

Leisure in the City

City people divided life's activities into separate units, setting workplace apart from home and working time apart from free time. "Going out" became a necessity, demanded not only as relief from a day of hard work but as proof that life was better in the New World than in the old. "He who can enjoy and does not enjoy commits a sin," a Yiddish-language paper told its readers. And enjoyment now meant buying a ticket and being entertained. A realm of public entertainment had emerged, open to all, created by a new class of entrepreneurs who gave the public what it wanted.

Public Entertainment. Amusement parks—Boston's Paragon Park, Philadelphia's Willow Grove, Atlanta's Ponce de Leon Park, Cleveland's Euclid Beach, San Francisco's the Chutes—went up at the end of trolley lines in cities across the country. Most remarkable was Luna Park at New York's Coney Island, "an enchanted, storybook land of trellises, columns, domes, minarets, lagoons, and lofty aerial flights. . . . It was a world removed—shut away from the sordid clatter and turmoil of the streets." In fact, that escape from everyday urban life explains the appeal of amusement parks. The cre-

Luna Park, Coney Island
Luna Park was the Disneyland of the industrial age, but more unbuttoned and casual, intended to lift city dwellers out of their workaday lives for a few hours. The view is down the main thoroughfare looking toward the entrance.

ators of Luna Park intended it to be "a different world—a dream world . . . where all is bizarre and fantastic . . . gayer and more different from the every-day world."

The theater likewise attracted huge audiences. Chicago had six vaudeville houses in 1896 and twenty-two in 1910. Evolving from cheap variety and minstrel shows, vaudeville moved from boisterous beer halls into grand theaters. Vaudeville cleaned up its routines, making them suitable for the entire family, and turned them into thoroughly professional entertainment handled by national booking agencies. With its standard program of nine acts of singing, dancing, and comedy, vaudeville attained enormous popularity just as the movies arrived. The first primitive films, a minute or so of humor or glimpses of famous people, appeared in 1896 in penny arcades and as filler in vaudeville shows. Within a decade millions of city people were watching dramatic films of increasing length and artistry at nickelodeons (named after the five-cent admission charge) across the country.

For young unmarried workers the cheap amusements of the city created a new social space. "I want a good time," a New York clothing operator told an investigator. "And there is no . . . way a girl can get it on $8 a week. I guess if anyone wants to take me to a dance he won't have to ask me twice." Hence the widespread ritual among the urban working class of "treating." The girls spent what money they had dressing up; their beaus were expected to pay for the fun. Parental control over courtship broke down, and amid the bright lights and lively music of the dance hall and amusement park, working-class youth forged a more easygoing culture of sexual interaction and pleasure-seeking.

The functionally defined geography of the big city carved out ample space for commercialized sex. Prostitution was not new to urban life, but in the late nineteenth century it became less closeted and more intermingled with other forms of public entertainment. In New York the most famous sex district in this period was the Tenderloin, running northward from Twenty-third Street between Fifth and Eighth avenues and eventually up to Times Square and beyond. This was also the locale of the city's fanciest restaurants, the best hotels, and the theater district. On the side streets many of the brownstones, abandoned by their well-to-do owners for the quieter parts of town, were taken over by brothels. The nearby concert saloons—the forerunners of the nightclub—featured not only stage shows and bartenders but also well-dressed prostitutes working the premises.

The Tenderloin and the Bowery were also the sites of a robust gay subculture. The long-held notion that homosexual life was covert, in the closet, in Victorian America appears not to be true, at least not in the country's premier city. Homosexuality was illegal, but as with prostitution, the law was mostly a dead letter. In certain corners of the city a gay world flourished, with a full array of saloons, meeting places, and drag balls, which were widely known and often patronized by uptown "slummers."

Baseball. Of all forms of male diversion none was more specific to the city, nor so spectacularly successful, as professional baseball. The game's promoters decreed that baseball had been created in 1839 by Abner Doubleday in the village of Cooperstown, New York. Actually, baseball was neither of American origin—it developed from the British game of rounders—nor a product of rural life.

Organized play began in the early 1840s in New York City, where a group of gentlemen enthusiasts competed on an empty lot. During the next twenty years the aristocratic tone of baseball disappeared. Clubs sprang up across the country, and intercity competition developed on a scheduled basis. In 1868 baseball became openly professional, following the example of the Cincinnati Red Stockings in signing players to contracts at a negotiated salary for the season.

Big-time commercial baseball came into its own with the launching of the National League in 1876. The team owners were profit-minded businessmen who carefully shaped the sport to please the fans. Wooden grandstands gave way to the concrete and steel stadiums of the early twentieth century, such as Fenway Park in Boston, Forbes Field in Pittsburgh, and Shibe Park in Philadelphia.

The National Pastime
This lithograph celebrates the opening game of the 1889 season, with the Boston Base-Ball Club taking on the New York Base-Ball Club. The National League was then scarcely twelve years old. The fielders played barehanded, but otherwise the game today is much as the artist pictured it a century ago, down to the umpire's characteristic stance.

For the urban multitudes baseball grew into something more than an occasional afternoon at the ballpark. By rooting for the home team, fans found a way of identifying with the city they lived in. Amid the diversity and anonymity of urban life, the common experience and language of baseball acted as a bridge among strangers.

Students of the game have suggested that baseball was peculiarly attuned to city life. It followed strict, precise rules, which indicated an underlying order to the chaotic city. Far from respecting the rules, however, the players tried to get away with whatever they could in order to win. Did this not match the competitive scramble of urban life? The blue-coated umpire, the symbol of authority, was scorned by players and derided by fans. What better substitute for the resentment against the powers-that-be who ruled the lives of city people? Baseball, like many other emerging urban institutions, served as a mechanism for inducting people into the life of the modern city.

Newspapers. The press undertook this task in a clear-eyed, calculated way. Ever since Benjamin H. Day had established the New York *Sun* in 1833, American newspapers had aimed for a broad audience. James Gordon Bennett, founder of the New York *Herald*, wanted "to record the facts . . . for the great masses of the community." Journalism defined the news to be whatever interested city readers. The *Herald* covered crime, scandal, and sensational events. After the Civil War the *Sun's* editor, Charles A. Dana, added the human-interest story, which made news of ordinary, insignificant happenings. Newspapers also targeted specific audiences. A women's

page offered recipes and fashion news, separate sections covered sports and high society, and the Sunday supplement helped fill the weekend hours.

Newspaper wars erupted periodically, as when Joseph Pulitzer, the owner of the St. Louis *Post-*

Joseph Pulitzer
Pulitzer (1847–1911) left Hungary at seventeen because he wanted to be a soldier, and his best chance was with the Union army in America. He was the greatest newspaper publisher of the century, extraordinary for his insight into what an urban reading public wanted from a newspaper and because he came to this task as a foreigner, without English as his mother tongue and without roots in American society.

Dispatch, invaded New York in 1883 by buying the *World*. In 1895 William Randolph Hearst, who owned the San Francisco *Examiner*, bought the New York *Journal* and challenged the *World* (see American Lives, Chapter 22). Hearst developed a sensational style of newspaper reporting and writing that became known as *yellow journalism*. The term, linked to the first comic strip to appear in color, "The Yellow Kid" (1895), referred to a type of reporting that treated accuracy as less important than a good story.

"He who is without a newspaper," said the great showman P. T. Barnum, "is cut off from his species." Barnum was speaking of city people and their hunger for information. By meeting this need, newspapers revealed their sensitivity to the public they served.

Upper Class/Middle Class

Wealth, more than anything else, has determined social class and standing in the United States. By that measure, American society was highly stratified during the nineteenth century. The top 1 percent of Americans held roughly a quarter of the country's wealth, and the richest 12 percent of households owned about 86 percent. This concentration of wealth appeared early in America's Industrial Revolution and remained relatively constant throughout the nineteenth century. Income levels were also sharply unequal. In 1890 industrial workers averaged $439 a year, clerical workers in manufacturing made twice that—$848 a year—whereas middle-class people such as doctors, lawyers, editors, and managers earned between $3,000 and $5,000. In the topmost ranks, of course, earnings derived less from salaries and wages than from investments. The top 10 percent of households had a larger income than the bottom 50 percent.

Wealth, of course, needed to be translated into the visible signs of social position. In the compact city of the early nineteenth century, class distinctions had been expressed by the way men and women dressed, the way they behaved, and the deference they demanded from or granted to others. As the industrial city grew, these interpersonal marks of class began to lose their force. In the anonymity of a large city, recognition and deference no longer served as mechanisms for conferring status. Instead, people began to rely on external signs: conspicuous displays of wealth, exclusive association in clubs and similar social organizations, and, above all, the choice of a neighborhood.

People's places of residence had previously depended primarily on the location of their work. For the poor that continued to be true. But for higher-income urbanites, where to live became a matter of personal means and social preference.

The Urban Elite

As early as the 1840s Boston merchants took advantage of the new railway service to move out of the congested central city. Fine rural estates appeared in Milton, Newton, and other outlying towns. By 1848 roughly 20 percent of Boston's businessmen were making the long trip from the countryside to their downtown offices. They traveled on 118 scheduled trains that served stations within 15 miles of the city center. Ferries that plied the harbor between Manhattan and Brooklyn or New Jersey served the same purpose for New Yorkers.

As commercial development engulfed downtown residential areas and as transportation services improved, the exodus from cities by the well-to-do spread across America. In Cincinnati wealthy families settled on the scenic hills rimming the crowded, humid tableland that ran down to the Ohio River. On those hillsides, a traveler noted in 1883, "the homes of Cincinnati's merchant princes and millionaires are found . . . elegant cottages, tasteful villas, and substantial mansions, surrounded by a paradise of grass, gardens, lawns, and tree-shaded roads." Residents of the area, called Hilltop, founded several country clubs, the Cincinnati Riding Club, the New England Society, five downtown gentlemen's clubs, and many other institutions that assured an exclusive social life for Cincinnati's elite.

Despite the temptations of country life, many of the very richest people preferred the heart of the city. Chicago had its Gold Coast; San Francisco, Nob Hill; Denver, Quality Hill; and Manhattan, Fifth Avenue. The New York novelist Edith Wharton recalled how the comfortable midcentury brownstones—"all so much alike that one could understand how easy it would be for a dinner guest to go to the wrong house"—gave way to the "'new' millionaire houses," which then spread northward beyond Fifty-ninth Street and up Fifth Avenue along Central Park. Great mansions, reminiscent of European aristocratic houses and filled with Old World artifacts, lined Fifth Avenue at the turn of the century.

By carving out fashionable areas in the heart of a city, the rich visibly demonstrated their capacity to assert their will over the larger society. But great fortunes did not automatically confer high social standing. An established elite stood astride the social heights even in relatively raw cities such as San Francisco and Denver. It had taken only a generation—and sometimes less—for money made in commerce or real estate to shed its tarnish and become "old" and genteel. In older cities such as Boston wealth passed intact through several generations. A high degree of intermarriage occurred there among the so-called Brahmin families. By withdrawing from trade, and by asserting a high cultural and moral code, the proper Bostonians kept moneyed newcomers at bay. Elsewhere urban elites tended to be more open, but only to the socially ambitious who were prepared to make visible and energetic use of their money.

New York's Metropolitan Opera was one of the products of this ongoing struggle among the wealthy. The Academy of Music, home to the city's opera since 1854, was controlled by the Livingstons, the Bayards, the Beekmans, and other old New York families. Frustrated in their efforts to purchase boxes at the Academy, the Vanderbilts and their allies decided to sponsor a rival opera house. In 1883, with its glittering opening to the strains of Gounod's *Faust*, the Metropolitan proclaimed its ascendancy in the opera world and in due course won the patronage of even the Beekmans and Bayards. During this battle of the opera houses the Vanderbilt circle achieved social recognition.

"High Society." New York became the home of a national elite as the most successful people gravitated to this preeminent center of American economic and cultural life. Manhattan's extraordinary vitality, in turn, kept the city's high society fluid and relatively open. The tycoon Frank Cowperwood, in Theodore Dreiser's novel *The Titan* (1914), reassured his unhappy wife that if Chicago society would not accept them, "there are other cities. Money will arrange matters in New York— that I know. We can build a real place there, and go in on equal terms, if we have money enough." New York thus came to be a magnet for millionaires. The city attracted them not only because of its importance as a fi-

nancial center, but also through the opportunities it offered for display and social recognition.

From Manhattan an extravagant life of leisure radiated outward to resort centers such as Saratoga Springs, New York; Palm Beach, Florida; and Newport, Rhode Island. Newport featured a grand array of summer "cottages" crowned by the Vanderbilts' Marble House and the Breakers. To these resorts and elsewhere, the affluent traveled in great comfort by private railway car. A style of living emerged that was incredible for its lavish excess, ranging from yachting and horse racing to huge feasts at luxurious restaurants such as Sherry's and Delmonico's. "Our forefathers would have been staggered at the cost of hospitality these days," remarked one New Yorker.

This infusion of wealth shattered the older elite society of New York. Seeking to be assimilated into the upper class, the flood of moneyed newcomers simply overwhelmed it. There followed a curious process of reconstruction, a deliberate effort to define the rules of conduct and identify those who properly "belonged" in New York society.

The key figure in this process was Ward McAllister, a southern-born lawyer who made a quick fortune in gold-rush San Francisco and then devoted himself to a second career as the arbiter of New York society. In 1888 McAllister compiled the first *Social Register*, which announced that it would serve as a "record of society, comprising an accurate and careful list" of all those deemed acceptable to participate in New York so-

The Breakers

The favorite summering place of the New York elite was the historic colonial port of Newport, Rhode Island. The opulent mansions there were known as "cottages." The Breakers was built in 1892 at a cost of $5 million for Cornelius Vanderbilt II. Designed in the style of an Italian palace, the Breakers had seventy-three rooms, thirty-three of them to house the small army of servants. The ornate dining room is shown in this photograph.

ciety. McAllister instructed the socially ambitious on how to select guests, set a proper table, arrange a ball, and launch a young lady into society. McAllister fostered an ordered social round of assemblies, balls, and dinners that defined the boundaries of an elite society. The key lay in the creation of associations sponsored by established social leaders, "organized social powers, capable of giving a passport of society to all worthy of it." To top things off, McAllister got the idea of "the Four Hundred"—the true cream of New York society. His list corresponded to those invited to Mrs. William Astor's great ball of February 1, 1892.

Social registers, coming-out balls for debutantes, and lesser versions of Ward McAllister soon popped up in cities throughout the country. In this fashion, the socially ambitious struggled to master the fluidity at the height of the social order.

Americans were adept at making money, noted the journalist Edwin L. Godkin in 1896, but they lacked the European traditions for spending it. "Great wealth has not yet entered our manners," Godkin remarked. "No rules have yet been drawn to guide wealthy Americans in their manner of life." In their struggle to find rules and establish standards, the moneyed elite made an indelible mark on urban life. If there was magnificence in the American city, it was mainly their handiwork. And if there was conspicuous waste and vulgarity, it was also their doing. In a democratic society wealth finds no easier outlet than through public display.

The Middle Class

The middle class left a smaller imprint on the public and the cultural faces of urban society. Its members, unlike the rich, preferred privacy and retreated into the domesticity of suburban comfort and family life.

The emerging corporate economy spawned a new middle class. Bureaucratic organizations required managers, accountants, and clerks. Advancing technologies called for engineers, chemists, and technicians. The distribution system sought salesmen, advertising executives, and buyers. These salaried ranks increased sevenfold between 1870 and 1910, growing at a much faster rate than any other occupational group. The traditional business class that had emerged in the first stages of industrialization before the Civil War—independent businessmen and professionals—also grew, but only at a third the rate of salaried personnel. Nearly 9 million people held white-collar jobs in 1910, more than a fourth of all employed Americans.

The middle class, particularly its salaried portions, was an urban population. Some lived within the city, in the row houses of Baltimore or Boston or the comfortable apartment houses of New York and other metropolitan centers. But many more preferred to escape the clamor and congestion of the city. They were attracted by a persisting "rural ideal." They agreed with the landscape architect Andrew Jackson Downing, who thought that "nature and domestic life are better than the society and manners of town." With the extension of rapid transit service from the city center, middle-class Americans followed the wealthy into the countryside. All sought what a Chicago developer promised for his North Shore subdivision in 1875: "qualities of which the city is in a large degree bereft, namely, its pure air, peacefulness, quietude, and natural scenery." And advanced building techniques—mass-produced materials and balloon-frame construction—made suburban housing affordable for the American middle class.

No major American city escaped rapid suburbanization during the last third of the nineteenth century. City limits everywhere expanded rapidly. By 1900 more than half of Boston's people lived in "streetcar suburbs" outside the original city. The U.S. Census of 1910 reported that nationwide about 25 percent of the urban population lived in suburbs outside the city limits.

On the European continent, by contrast, cities remained highly concentrated, and insofar as expansion occurred, it was the poor, not the well-to-do, who inhabited the margins. Unlike their American counterparts, the European middle class was not attracted (except in Britain) to the rural ideal and valued urban life for its own sake. In Europe mass transit developed much more slowly, traditional beam-and-post construction techniques persisted, and there was little of the freewheeling real-estate development that encouraged American suburbanization. Nor, finally, did the culturally homogeneous European cities give rise to the impulse felt by middle-class Americans to escape from the racially and ethnically diverse urban masses who occupied the city centers.

American suburbs were middle-class territory, but the middle class was not monolithic. It ranged from prosperous business proprietors and lawyers to clerks and traveling salesmen who earned no more than did foremen and craft workers. Close in to the city, the suburbs increasingly took on a working-class character.

The geography of the suburbs was truly a map of class structure in America, because where a family lived told where it ranked. The farther the distance from the center of the city, the finer the houses and the larger the lots. The affluent had the leisure and flexible schedules to travel the long distance into town. People closer in wanted direct transit lines convenient to home and office. Lower-income suburbanites were more likely to have more than one wage earner in the family, less secure employment, and jobs requiring movement around the city. They needed easy access to crosstown transit lines, which ran closer in to the city center.

Divisions within suburbs, although always a precise measure of economic ranking, never became rigidly tern, while efficient for laying out lots and providing utilities, offered no natural focus for group life. Nor did the stores and services that lay scattered along the trolley-car streets. Not even schools and churches were located where they could become centers of community life. Suburban development conformed to the economics of real estate and transportation, and so did the thinking of middle-class homeseekers entering the suburbs. They wanted a house that gave them good value and convenience to the trolley line.

The need for community had lost some of its force for middle-class Americans. Two other attachments assumed greater importance: work and family.

Middle-Class Families

The family had been the primary productive unit in the preindustrial economy. Farmers, merchants, and artisans had carried on their work within a family setting, and the value of family members could be reckoned by their economic contribution. The family circle included not only blood relatives but all others living and working in the household. As industrialism progressed, production gradually moved out of the household. For the middle class in particular, the family became dissociated from economic activity. The father left the home to earn a living, clothing was bought ready-made, food came increasingly in cans and packages, and children spent more years in school. Middle-class families became smaller, excluding all but nuclear members and consisting in 1900 typically of husband, wife, and three children.

Within this family circle relationships became intense and affectionate. "Home was the most expressive experience in life," recalled the literary critic Henry Seidel Canby of his growing up in the 1890s. "Though the family might quarrel and nag, the home held them all, protecting them against the outside world." In a sense, the family served as a refuge from the competitive, impersonal business world. The suburbs provided a fit setting for such middle-class families. The quiet, tree-lined streets created a domestic world insulated from the hurly-burly of commerce and enterprise.

The Wife's Role. The burdens of this domesticity fell heavily on the wife. It was nearly unheard of for her to seek an outside career; that was her husband's role. She had the job of managing the household. "The woman who could not make a home, like the man who could not support one, was condemned," Canby remembered. But with better household technology, greater reliance on purchased goods, and fewer children, the wife's workload declined. Moreover, servants still played an important part in middle-class households. In 1910 there were about 2 million domestic servants, the largest job category for women.

Cincinnati Suburb
The lives of the people inhabiting these neat homes along this tree-lined street were woven into the dynamic capitalism of a major industrial metropolis, including the children lounging on the corner, who were most certainly being educated for service in the new economic order. Looking at the bucolic setting of this Cincinnati street, no one would have thought so, and that was just the illusion that the suburb was intended to create: that Americans still partook of a rural ideal and could hold at bay the modern industrial order of which they were now a part.

fixed. People in the city center who wanted to better their lives moved to the cheapest suburbs. Those already settled there fled from these newcomers, in turn pushing the next higher group farther out in search of space and greenery.

Suburbanization was the sum of countless individual decisions. Each move represented an advance in living standards—not only more light, air, and quiet but also better housing than the city afforded. Suburban housing had more space and better design as well as indoor toilets, hot water, central heating, and, by the turn of the century, electricity. Even people in the inner suburbs came to regard these amenities as standard comforts. The suburbs also restored a basic opportunity that had seemed sacrificed by rural Americans when they moved to the city: home ownership again became the norm. "A man is not really a true man until he owns his home," propounded the Reverend Russell H. Conwell in his famous sermon on the virtues of making money, "Acres of Diamonds."

The small town of the rural past had fostered community life. Not so with the suburbs. The grid street pat-

Middle-Class Domesticity
For middle-class Americans the home was a place of nurture, a refuge from the world of competitive commerce. Perhaps that explains why their residences were so heavily draped and cluttered with bric-a-brac, every space filled with overstuffed furniture. All of it emphasized privacy and pride of possession. The young woman shown playing the piano symbolizes another theme of American domesticity—wives and daughters as ornaments and as bearers of culture and refinement.

As the physical burdens of household work eased, higher-quality homemaking became the new ideal. This was the message of Catharine Beecher's best-selling book *The American Woman's Home* (1869) and of magazines such as the *Ladies' Home Journal* and *Good Housekeeping*, which first appeared during the 1880s. The wife did more than make sure food was on the table, clothes were washed and mended, and the house was kept clean. She had the higher calling of bringing sensibility, beauty, and love to the household. "We owe to women the charm and beauty of life," wrote one educator. "For the love that rests, strengthens and inspires, we look to women." In this idealized view, the wife made the home a refuge for her husband and a place of nurture for their children.

Womanly virtue, even if a happy marriage depended on it, by no means put wives on equal terms with their husbands. Although the legal status of married women—the right to own property, control separate earnings, make contracts and bring suit, and get a divorce—improved markedly during the nineteenth century, sufficient legal discrimination remained to establish their subordinate role within the family. More important, custom dictated a wife's submission to her husband. She relied on his ability as the family breadwinner and, despite her superior virtues and graces, ranked as his inferior in vigor and intellect. Her mind could be employed "but little and in trivial matters," wrote one prominent physician, and her proper place was as "the companion or ornamental appendage to man."

No wonder that bright, independent-minded women rebelled against marriage. The marriage rate in the United States fell to its lowest point during the last forty years of the nineteenth century. More than 10 percent of women of marriageable age remained single, and the rate was much higher among college graduates and professionals. Only half the Mount Holyoke College class of 1902 married. "I know that something perhaps, humanly speaking, supremely precious has passed me by," remarked the writer Vida Scudder. "But . . . how much it would have excluded!" Married life "looks to me often as I watch it terribly impoverished, for women."

The strains of marriage were manifest in the number of middle-class families that broke up. Most of these domestic failures went unrecorded because of the stigma attached to divorce. In a Chicago suburb in the 1880s, at a time when divorce was virtually unknown there, about 10 percent of households had an absent spouse. The annual divorce rate increased from 1.2 per 1,000 marriages in 1860 to 7.7 in 1900. It was more difficult to document the other ways in which women responded to marriages that denied their autonomy and downplayed their sexuality. Middle-class women became the principal victims of neurasthenia, a disorder whose symptoms included depression and general disability. Some unhappy housewives found "silent friends" in opium and alcohol, which often were dispensed in well-laced patent medicines.

A happier release came through the companionship of other women. In an age that defined separate spheres for men and women, close ties commonly formed between schoolmates, cousins, and mothers and daughters. The intimacy and intensity of such attachments can be sensed in the letters of separated friends. Such enduring female ties yielded an emotional gratification not always found in marriage. Husbands, absorbed in business, frequently played a secondary and remote role in the lives of their wives. Women's own sphere often filled that emotional vacuum.

Changing Views of Sexuality. In earlier times sexuality and reproduction had been more or less in harmony. A large family was considered a good thing, and the heavy toll of repeated pregnancies on the wife was accepted as God's will. In lower-class families this fatalism persisted, but not among middle-class couples, who increasingly wanted to limit the size of their families. Birth control, however, was not an easy matter. From the 1830s onward information about contraception became widely available, as did an array of commercial devices—condoms, diaphrams, sponges, douches. But the knowledge purveyed was imperfect or, as with advice about the rhythm method, absolutely wrong (doctors thought women were most fertile around the menstrual period). And the devices were for the most part not very effective or, as in the case of the condom, were stigmatized by association with the brothel.

Before these barriers could be surmounted, birth control was swept up in the social-purity campaign championed by Anthony Comstock. From the 1870s onward contraceptive devices and birth-control information were legally classified as obscene, barred from the mails, and criminalized in many states. Abortion, which had long been protected by the common law, became illegal except to save the mother's life. Although the practice of abortion probably remained widespread, it was expensive and dangerous, and shameful besides.

A painful tension existed between sexuality and family planning. The most prudent course would have been to delay marriage and then, except when a child was desired, to practice restraint. Sexual discipline was indeed the official wisdom of the day. Many doctors objected to contraception because they believed that by uncoupling sexuality from procreation, the sexual appetites of men would be released, to the detriment of their health and the moral fiber of society. It is this official writing that has given us the notion of a Victorian age of sexual repression. Letters and diaries suggest that in the privacy of their homes husbands and wives acted otherwise. Yet they must have done so in constant fear of unwanted pregnancy and with anxieties that exacted a heavy toll on middle-class marriage. A fulfilling sexual relationship was not easily squared with the desire to limit and space childbearing.

Around 1890 a change set in. Although the birth rate continued to decline, more young people married, and at an earlier age. These developments reflected the beginnings of a sexual revolution in the American middle-class family. Despite the Comstock laws, contraception became more acceptable and reliable. Experts began to abandon the notion, put forth by one popular medical text, that "the majority of women (happily for society)

are not very much troubled by sexual feeling of any kind." In succeeding editions of his book *Plain Home Talk on Love, Marriage, and Parentage*, the physician Edward Bliss Foote began to favor a healthy sexuality that gave pleasure to both women and men.

During the 1890s the artist Charles Dana Gibson created the image of the "new woman" in his drawings for *Life* magazine. The Gibson girl was tall, spirited, athletic, and chastely sexual. Constrictive clothing such as bustles, hoop skirts, and hourglass corsets gave way to shirtwaists and other natural styles that did not hide or disguise the female form. In the city, moreover, women's sphere began to take on a more public character. Among the new urban institutions catering to women, the most important was the department store, which became a temple for their emerging role as consumers.

The New Woman
John Singer Sargent's painting *Mr. and Mrs. Isaac Newton Phelps Stokes* (1897) captures on canvas the essence of the "new woman" of the 1890s. Nothing about Mrs. Stokes, neither how she is dressed nor how she presents herself, suggests physical weakness or demure passivity. She confidently occupies center stage, a fit partner for her husband, who is relegated to the shadows of the picture.

And the Children. The children of the middle class went through their own revolution. In the past, American children everywhere had been regarded as an economic asset—added hands for the family farm, shop, or countinghouse. That no longer held true for the urban middle class. Parents stopped treating their children as working members of the family. In the old days, Ralph Waldo Emerson remarked in 1880, "children had been repressed and kept in the background; now they were considered, cosseted, and pampered." There was such a thing as "the juvenile mind," lectured Jacob Abbott in his book *Gentle Measures in the Management and Training of the Young* (1871). The family was responsible for providing a nurturing environment in which the young personality could grow and mature.

Preparation for adulthood became increasingly linked to formal education. School enrollment went up 150 percent between 1870 and 1900. High school attendance, while still encompassing only a small percentage of teenagers, increased at the fastest rate. The years between childhood and adulthood began to stretch out, and a new stage of life—adolescence—emerged. Rooted in an extended period of family dependency, adolescence at the same time shifted much of the socializing role from parents to peer group. A youth culture—one of the hallmarks of American life in the twentieth century—was starting to take shape.

The Higher Culture

America's metropolitan centers, repositories of the nation's wealth, became the site for new institutions of higher culture. A hunger for the cultivated life did not of course originate in cities. Before the Civil War the lyceum movement had sent lecturers to the remotest towns, bearing messages of culture and learning. The Chautauqua movement, founded in upstate New York in 1874, carried on this work of cultural dissemination in the last decades of the nineteenth century. However, large cultural institutions such as museums, public libraries, opera companies, and symphony orchestras could flourish only in metropolitan centers.

The first major art museum, the Corcoran Gallery of Art, opened in Washington, D.C., in 1869. New York's Metropolitan Museum of Art started in rented quarters two years later. In 1880 that museum moved to its permanent site in Central Park and launched an ambitious program of art acquisition. J. P. Morgan became chairman of the board in 1905, assuring the Metropolitan's preeminence. The Boston Museum of Fine Arts was founded in 1876, and Chicago's Art Institute in 1879. By 1914 virtually every major city and about three-fifths of all cities with more than a 100,000 people had an art museum.

Top-flight orchestras also appeared, first in New York under the conductors Theodore Thomas and Leopold Damrosch in the 1870s. Symphonies started in Boston and Chicago during the next decade. National tours by these leading orchestras planted the seeds for orchestral societies in many other cities. Public libraries grew from modest collections (in 1870 only seven had as many as 50,000 books) into major urban institutions. The greatest library benefactor was Andrew Carnegie, who announced in 1881 that he would build a library in any city that was prepared to maintain it. By 1907 Carnegie had spent more than $32.7 million to establish about a thousand libraries throughout the country.

If the late nineteenth century was the great age of moneymaking, it was also the great age of money *giving*. Surplus private wealth flowed in many directions, particularly to universities. These schools included Vanderbilt, Tulane, and Johns Hopkins universities, all named for their chief benefactors, and the University of Chicago, founded by John D. Rockefeller. Urban cultural institutions also received their share, partly as a matter of civic pride. To some extent patronage of the arts also served the need of the newly rich to establish themselves in society, as in the founding of the Metropolitan Opera in New York. But the higher culture was not only a commodity of civic pride and social display; museums and opera houses received support out of a sense of cultural deprivation.

"In America there is no culture," pronounced the English critic G. Lowes Dickinson in 1909. Science and the practical arts, yes, "every possible application of life to purposes and ends," but "no life for life's sake." Such condescending remarks received a respectful hearing in the United States because of a deep sense of cultural inferiority to the Old World. In 1873 Mark Twain and Charles Dudley Warner published a novel, *The Gilded Age*, satirizing America as a land of moneygrubbers and speculators. This enormously popular book touched a nerve in the American psyche. Its title has in fact been appropriated by historians to characterize the late nineteenth century—America's "Gilded Age"—as an age of materialism and cultural shallowness.

Some members of the upper class, including the novelist Henry James, despaired of the country and moved to Europe. Others spent their lives in the kind of perpetual alienation that Henry Adams described in his ironic memoir *The Education of Henry Adams* (1907).

The more common response was to try to raise the nation's cultural level. The newly rich had a hard time of it. They did not have much opportunity to cultivate a taste for art, and a great deal of what they collected was mediocre and garish. On the other hand, George W. Vanderbilt, grandson of the rough-hewn Cornelius Vanderbilt, became a patron of the Art Students League in New York and an early champion of French Impressionism. And the coal and steel baron Henry Clay Frick built a brilliant art collection that remains housed as a public museum in his mansion in New York City. The enthusiasm of moneyed Americans—not always well directed—largely fueled the great cultural institutions that arose in many cities during the Gilded Age.

A deeply conservative idea of culture sustained this generous patronage. The aim was to embellish urban life, not to probe or reveal its meaning. "Art," says the hero of the Reverend Henry Ward Beecher's sentimental novel *Norwood* (1867), "attempts to work out its end solely by the use of the beautiful, and the artist is to select out only such things as are beautiful."

Culture had also become firmly linked to femininity. In America, remarked one observer, culture was "left entirely to women. . . . It is they, as a general rule, who have opinions about music, or drama, or literature, or philosophy. . . . Husbands or sons rarely share in those interests." Men represented the "force principle," said the clergyman Horace Bushnell, and women represented the "beauty principle."

Literature. The treatment of life, an eminent editor wrote, "must be tinged with sufficient idealism to make it all of a truly uplifting character. We cannot admit stories which deal with false or immoral relations. . . . The finer side of things—the idealistic—is the answer for us." The *genteel tradition*, as this literary school came to be called, dominated American cultural agencies such as universities and publishers from the 1860s on.

Rebellion against the genteel tradition sparked the main creative impulses of late nineteenth-century American literature. *Realism* became the rallying cry of a new generation of writers. Their champion, William Dean Howells, resigned in 1881 as editor of the *Atlantic Monthly*, a stronghold of the genteel tradition. He became the editor of *Harper's Monthly* and called for literature that "wishes to know and to tell the truth" and seeks "to picture the daily life in the most exact terms possible." In a series of realistic novels—*A Modern Instance* (1882), *The Rise of Silas Lapham* (1885), and *A Hazard of New Fortunes* (1890)—Howells captured the world of the urban middle class.

Henry James, a greater writer, also treated the novel as "a direct impression of life" and aimed at achieving "an air of reality." He wrote about the world of leisured Americans, and his central concern was the study of moral decay and regeneration. This concern, often set in motion by the confrontation of American innocence with European corruption, appears in *The American* (1877), *The Portrait of a Lady* (1882), and *The Golden Bowl* (1904).

The nostalgia of urbanized Americans for their agrarian past helped sustain a vigorous literature of local color and regionalism. These writings included the mining camp stories of Bret Harte, the Uncle Remus tales of Joel Chandler Harris, the Indiana poetry of James Whitcomb Riley, and the New England fiction of Sarah Orne Jewett. Such literature fit comfortably within the genteel tradition, for it was generally sentimental, reassuring, and morally uplifting.

Mark Twain, on the other hand, was an entirely different kind of regional writer. Starting his career as a western journalist and humorist (see Chapter 17), Twain avoided the influence of the eastern literary establishment. His greatest novel, *The Adventures of Huckleberry Finn* (1884), violated the custom of keeping "low" characters in their proper place for the amused inspection of the culturally superior reader. Huck, an outcast boy, seizes control of the story. The words are his, and so is the innocence with which he questions right and wrong in America. No other novel so fully engaged the themes of racism, injustice, and brutality in nineteenth-century America.

Although not graced with Twain's genius, other novelists did begin to come to grips with the hard realities of city life. Stephen Crane's *Maggie: A Girl of the Streets* (1893), privately printed because no publisher would touch it, unflinchingly described the destruction of a slum girl. In another urban novel, Henry Blake Fuller's *The Cliff-Dwellers* (1893), the city itself occupied the author's imagination. This story traces the fortunes of the occupants—"cliff-dwellers"—of an immense Chicago office building. In *McTeague* (1899) Frank Norris captured the sights, sounds, and, most acutely, smells of the city. Although the novel was set in San Francisco, Norris insisted that it "could have happened in any big city, anywhere."

These *naturalistic* novels stressed the insignificance of the individual and his or her helplessness in the face of urban life and the inexorable logic of Darwin's survival of the fittest. Frank Norris's character McTeague, more animal than man, is the creature of his instincts and his environment and cannot escape coming to a bad end. In Norris's *The Octopus* (1901) the implacable force is the Southern Pacific Railroad; in *The Pit* (1903) it is the Chicago grain market. The city itself, however, most powerfully influenced the naturalistic writers.

The best of those authors, Theodore Dreiser, surmounted the crude determinism of Frank Norris. But the city people as they exist in his great novels *Sister Carrie* (1900), *Jennie Gerhardt* (1911), *The Financier* (1912), and *The Titan* (1914) are no less hostage to an urban world that they cannot understand or control. Dreiser tried to capture this world in all its spectacular detail, "to talk about life as it is, the facts as they exist, the game as it is played."

Visiting his fiancée's Missouri farm home in 1894, Dreiser had been struck by "the spirit of rural America, its idealism, its dreams." But this was an "American tradition in which I, alas!, could not share." Said Dreiser, "I had seen Pittsburgh. I had seen Lithuanians and Hungarians in their 'courts' and hovels. I had seen the girls of the city—walking the streets at night." The city had irrevocably entered the American imagination. By the early 1900s it had become a main theme of American art and literature and an overriding concern of the Progressive Era.

Summary

America, an agrarian society since its birth, became increasingly urbanized after the Civil War. By 1900 about 20 percent of the population was living in cities with 100,000 or more people. City growth stemmed primarily from industrialization—the concentration of industry at key points, the increasingly large scale of production, and the need for commercial and administrative services that were best located in urban centers. A burst of innovation, including mass transit systems, steel-frame buildings, the telephone, and electric lighting, solved the problems arising from the concentration of an extremely large population in a confined area. Although amply endowed with regulatory powers, American cities left decision making as much as possible in the hands of private interests. The result was dramatic growth but not much attention to the impact of growth on the urban environment.

In the cities geography defined the social order of the population. The poor were found in the city centers and the factory districts, the middle class spread out into the suburbs, and the rich lived insulated in exclusive central sections of the cities or beyond the suburbs. A distinctive urban culture emerged, drawing heavily on ethnic social institutions and new leisure activities, enabling city dwellers to accommodate themselves to the world of the city. For the wealthy, an elite society emerged, stressing an opulent life-style and exclusive social organizations. The middle class, on the other hand, withdrew into the private world of the family. For wives, the cult of domesticity reigned, but its more repressive features began to relax as the idea of the "new woman" took hold in the 1890s. Child nurturance persisted, but as the years of dependent childhood lengthened, a new phase of adolescence began to emerge that would draw teenagers out of the family orbit.

The great cities of the United States became the sites of a higher culture, including art museums, opera companies, symphony orchestras, and libraries. A new literature emerged that took the urban world as its subject. From the late nineteenth century on, American life would increasingly be defined by what happened in the nation's cities.

TIMELINE

1869	Corcoran Art Gallery opens in Washington, D.C.
1871	Chicago fire
1873	Mark Twain and Charles Dudley Warner publish *The Gilded Age*
1875	Dwight L. Moody launches urban revivalist movement
1876	Alexander Graham Bell patents the telephone National Baseball League founded
1878	Electric arc-light system installed in Philadelphia
1879	Thomas Edison's incandescent light bulb Salvation Army arrives from Britain
1881	Carnegie offers to build libraries for every American city
1883	New York City's Metropolitan Opera founded Brooklyn Bridge opens Joseph Pulitzer purchases the *New York World*
1885	William Jenney builds first steel-frame structure, Chicago's Home Insurance Building
1888	First electric trolley line constructed in Richmond, Virginia
1892	Rockefeller founds University of Chicago
1893	Chicago Columbian Exposition "City Beautiful" movement
1895	William Randolph Hearst enters New York journalism The comic strip "The Yellow Kid" appears
1897	Boston builds first American subway
1900	Theodore Dreiser publishes *Sister Carrie*
1901	New York Tenement House Reform Law
1904	New York subway system opens
1906	San Francisco earthquake
1913	Woolworth Building, New York City

★   ★   ★

BIBLIOGRAPHY

Useful introductions to urban history are Charles N. Glaab and A. Theodore Brown, *A History of Urban America* (1967); Arthur M. Schlesinger, *The Rise of the City* (1936), a pioneering study; and Blake McKelvey, *The Urbanization of America, 1860–1915* (1963). A sampling of the innovative scholarship that opened new historical paths can be found in Stephan Thernstrom and Richard Sennett, eds., *Nineteenth-Century Cities: Essays in the New Urban History* (1969).

Urbanization

Allan Pred, *Spatial Dynamics of U.S. Urban Growth, 1800–1914* (1971), traces the patterns in which cities grew. On the revolution in urban transit, see the pioneering book by Sam B. Warner, *Streetcar Suburbs: The Process of Growth in Boston, 1870–1900* (1962). In a subsequent work, *The Private City: Philadelphia in Three Periods* (1968), Warner broadened his analysis to show how private decision-making shaped the character of the American city. Innovations in urban construction are treated in Carl Condit, *American Building Art: Nineteenth Century* (1969) and *Chicago School of Architecture* (1964); Robert C. Twombly, *Louis Sullivan* (1986); Alan Trachtenberg, *The Brooklyn Bridge* (1965); and Harold L. Platt, *The Electric City: Energy and the Growth of the Chicago Area, 1880–1930* (1991). The problems of meeting basic human needs are treated in Jon C. Teaford, *The Unheralded Triumph: City Government in America, 1870–1900* (1984); Eric H. Monkkonen, *Police in Urban America, 1860–1920* (1981); and David B. Tyack, *The One Best System: A History of American Urban Education* (1974). The struggle to reshape the chaotic nineteenth-century city can be explored in John D. Fairchild, *The Mysteries of the Great City: The Politics of Urban Design, 1877–1937* (1993); William H. Wilson, *The City Beautiful Movement in Kansas City* (1964); and David Schuyler, *The New Urban Landscape: The Redefinition of City Form in Nineteenth-Century America* (1986).

City People

Among the leading books on immigrants and the city are Moses Rischin, *The Promised City: New York's Jews, 1870–1914* (1962); Josef Barton, *Peasants and Strangers: Italians, Rumanians, and Slovaks in an American City, 1890–1950* (1975); and Humbert S. Nelli, *The Italians in Chicago, 1860–1920* (1970). On blacks in the city, see Gilbert Osofsky, *Harlem: The Making of a Ghetto, 1890–1930* (1966); Allan H. Spear, *Black Chicago, 1860–1920* (1966); and Kenneth L. Kusmer, *A Ghetto Takes Shape: Black Cleveland, 1870–1930* (1976). David C. Hammack, *Power and Society: Greater New York at the Turn of the Century* (1982), is a sophisticated treatment that places the party machine in the larger context of municipal power politics. Also useful are Zane Miller, *Boss Cox's Cincinnati* (1968), and Bruce M. Stave, ed., *Urban Bosses, Machines, and Progressive Reformers* (1972). The encounter of Protestantism with the city is treated in Henry F. May, *Protestant Churches and Urban America* (1949); Aaron I. Abell, *The Urban Impact on American Protestantism* (1943); and William G. McLoughlin, *Modern Revivalism* (1959). On the Catholic Church see Robert D. Cross, *The Emergence of Liberal Catholicism in America* (1958). Aspects of an emerging city culture are studied in Gunther Barth, *City People: The Rise of Modern City Culture in Nineteenth-Century America* (1982); Susan Porter Benson, *Counter Cultures: Saleswomen, Managers, and Customers in American Department Stores, 1890–1940* (1986); John F. Kasson, *Amusing the Million: Coney Island at the Turn of the Century* (1978); Timothy J. Gilfoyle, *City of Eros: New York City, Prostitution and the Commercialization of Sex, 1790-1920* (1991); Kathy Peiss, *Cheap Amusements: Working Women and Leisure in Turn-of-the-Century New York* (1986); and David Nasaw, *Going Out: The Rise and Fall of Public Amusements* (1993). George Chauncey, *Gay New York: Gender, Urban Culture, and the Making of the Gay New York World, 1890–1940* (1994), reveals a terrain hitherto invisible to the historian.

Upper Class/Middle Class

Urban social mobility is the focus of Stephan Thernstrom, *The Other Bostonians: Poverty and Progress in an American City, 1880–1970* (1973), which also contains a useful summary of mobility research on other cities. On the social elite, see Frederic C. Jaher, *The Urban Establishment: Upper Strata in Boston, New York, Charleston, Chicago, and Los Angeles* (1982). Two recent books greatly advance our understanding of the urban middle class: Stuart S. Blumin, *The Emergence of the Middle Class: Social Experience in the American City, 1760–1900* (1989), and Olivier Zunz, *Making America Corporate, 1870–1920* (1990). Aspects of middle-class life are revealed in Richard Sennett, *Families against the City: Middle-Class Homes of Industrial Chicago, 1872–1890* (1970); Margaret Marsh, *Suburban Lives* (1990); Gwendolyn Wright, *Moralism and the Model Home: Domestic Architecture and Cultural Conflict in Chicago, 1873–1913* (1980); Susan Strasser, *Never Done: A History of American Housework* (1983); John F. Kasson, *Rudeness and Civility: Manners in Nineteenth-Century America* (1990); and, on the entry of immigrants into the middle class, Andrew R. Heinze, *Adapting to Abundance: Jewish Immigrants, Mass Consumption, and the Search for American Identity* (1990). Contemporary notions of sexuality are skillfully captured in John S. Haller and Robin M. Haller, *The Physician and Sexuality in Victorian America* (1980). Whether those views actually applied to the private world of the middle class is strongly questioned in Karen Lystra, *The Searching Heart: Women, Men, and Romantic Love in Nineteenth-Century America* (1989). Control over reproduction is fully explored in Janet Farrell Brodie, *Contraception and Abortion in Nineteenth-Century America* (1994). On the fostering of high culture in the American city, see Daniel M. Fox, *Engines of Culture: Philanthropy and Art Museums* (1963). The best introduction to intellectual currents in the emerging urban society is Alan Trachtenberg, *The Incorporation of America: Culture and Society, 1865–1893* (1983).

The Cliff Dwellers

This 1913 painting by George Bellows shows a poor
tenement neighborhood in New York's Lower East Side.

The Progressive Era

1900–1914

★   ★   ★

On the face of it, the political ferment of the 1890s ended after the election of 1896. The bitter struggle over free silver left the victorious Republicans with no stomach for political crusades. The McKinley administration devoted itself to maintaining business confidence: sound money and high tariffs were the order of the day. The main thing, as party chief Mark Hanna said, was to "stand pat and continue Republican prosperity."

Yet beneath the surface a deep uneasiness was taking hold of the country. The depression of the 1890s had unveiled harsh truths not acknowledged in better days. One such discovery was the power of vested economic interests. In Wisconsin, for example, utility and transit companies had raised prices, reduced services, and received special tax relief—all at the expense of the public. This discovery of corporate arrogance launched movements in Wisconsin for tax reform, municipal ownership of utilities, and an end to boss-run party politics.

The labor unrest of the 1890s taught a similar lesson. The Cleveland administration had broken the great Pullman strike of 1894 by plotting with the railroad operators, issuing injunctions against the strike leaders, and sending in troops to get the trains moving. The architect of that policy, Attorney General Richard Olney, took little satisfaction from his success in suppressing the strike. He asked himself what might be done in the future to avoid the need for such one-sided intervention. Olney began to advocate labor legislation—the Erdman Mediation Act of 1898 marked the first step—that would regulate labor relations on the railroads and prevent crippling strikes. In such ways did the crisis of the 1890s turn the nation's thinking to reform.

The problems themselves, however, were of much older origin. For more than half a century Americans had been absorbed in developing their nation. At the beginning of the twentieth century they paused, looked around, and began to add up the costs. With industrialization had come a frightening concentration of corporate economic power and, equally troubling, a restless working class. The cities had spawned widespread misery and corrupt machine politics. The heritage of an earlier America seemed to be succumbing to the demands of the new industrial order.

With the crisis of the 1890s over, reform became an absorbing concern of many Americans. It was as if social awareness had reached a critical mass around 1900 and set reform activity going as a major, self-sustaining phenomenon. For this reason the years from 1900 to World War I have come to be known as the Progressive Era.

The Course of Reform

Historians have sometimes spoken of a progressive "movement." But progressivism was not a movement in any meaningful sense. There was no single progressive constituency, no agreed-upon agenda, and no unifying organization or leadership. At different times and places, different social groups became active. People who were reformers on one issue might be conservative on another. The term *progressivism* embraces a widespread, many-sided effort after 1900 to build a better society. Progressive reformers shared only this objective, plus an intellectual style that can be called "progressive."

The Intellectual Roots of Progressivism

Intellectual climates change. Why they change is usually hard to explain, but it is not so difficult to tell when new ideas are taking hold. Such a change of ideas clearly seemed about to happen as the twentieth century began.

A Sense of Mastery. The Progressive Era was an age of scientific investigation. The federal government conducted massive statistical studies of immigration, women's and children's labor, and working conditions in many industries. Vice commissions studied prostitution, gambling, and other moral ills of American cities. Among private investigations the classic was the *Pittsburgh Survey* (1911–1914). Financed by Margaret Olivia Sage and other New York City philanthropists, a team of investigators recorded in great detail living and working conditions in Pittsburgh's steel district.

The facts were important because they formed the basis for corrective action. When the young journalist Walter Lippmann wrote *Drift and Mastery* (1914), he asserted the progressive's confidence in people's ability to act purposefully and constructively. This sense of mastery expressed itself in many ways. For example, people had great faith in academic experts. In Wisconsin the state

university became a key resource for Governor Robert M. La Follette's progressive administration. "The close intimacy of the university with public affairs explains the democracy, the thoroughness, and the scientific accuracy of the state in its legislation," boasted one La Follette supporter.

Scientific management exerted a particularly strong attraction on progressives. The original aim of scientific management had been to reorganize and rationalize work in factories (see Chapter 18, page 574). But its founder, Frederick W. Taylor, argued that his basic approach—the "scientific" analysis of human activity—offered solutions to waste and inefficiency in municipal government, schools and hospitals, and even homes and churches. "The fundamental principles of scientific management are applicable to all kinds of human activities," Taylor insisted, and could solve all the social ills that arise "through such of our acts as are blundering, ill-directed, or inefficient."

Attacking Nineteenth-Century Formalism. The essential thing, in the progressive view, was to resist intellectual formulations that denied people this sense of mastery. This denial characterized the Social Darwinian writings of the British philosopher Herbert Spencer and his many disciples among American conservative thinkers (see Chapter 19, page 589). Spencer argued that society develops according to fixed laws that cannot be changed. Spencer's intellectual approach was *formalistic*; that is, its conclusions were based not on factual investigation but on abstract theory.

Critics of Spencer denied that the evolution of society is guided by absolute and unvarying rules. "It is folly," protested the Harvard philosopher William James, "to speak of the 'laws of history,' as of something inevitable, which science only has to discover, and which any one can then foretell and observe, but do nothing to alter or avert." Man could "shape environmental forces to his own advantage," the sociologist Lester F. Ward argued. Society could advance through "rational planning" and "social engineering."

The assault against formalism took place in many academic disciplines. In classical economics, for example, scholars assumed that markets were perfectly competitive and thus perfectly responsive to the laws of supply and demand. Such a system left no room for reform, which would only disrupt what could not be improved. Critics of classical economics—they called themselves "institutional economists"—denied that the market ever operated so perfectly. They conducted field research to determine how institutions and power relationships influenced the operation of the marketplace. In his *Theory of the Leisure Class* (1899) and *The Instinct of Workmanship* (1914) the economist Thorstein Veblen lampooned the classical economists' abstract image of economic man. In the real world, Veblen contended, people acted not out of pure economic calculation but from complex motives ranging from vanity to pride in their work.

In legal thought, too, formalism had dominated the field. The courts treated legal rights as if they were eternal principles that were not rooted in—or to be tested by—social reality. Thus, in the famous *Lochner v. New York* decision (1905) the Supreme Court invalidated a law limiting the long working hours of bakers in New York State. Such regulation, the Court concluded, violated the contractual freedom of *both* employers and workers. Justice Oliver Wendell Holmes, the leading dissenter, objected; in his view, the *Lochner* decision was based on a fictional equality. If the choice was between working and starving, could it really be said that workers freely accepted jobs requiring that they labor fourteen hours a day, or that limiting their working hours violated their liberty of contract?

Holmes had earlier asserted the essence of the progressive legal critique: "The life of the law has not been logic; it has been experience. The felt necessities of the time, even the prejudices which judges share with their fellow-men, have had a good deal more to do than [logic] in determining the rules by which men shall be governed." "Sociological jurisprudence," as Dean Roscoe Pound of the Harvard Law School termed it, called for "the adjustment of principles and doctrines to the human conditions they are to govern rather than assumed first principles." The law, moreover, should not claim a false neutrality; on the contrary, as Pound's student Felix Frankfurter argued, law should be "a vital agency for human betterment."

In philosophy, it was William James who led the assault on formalism as an intellectual system. James denied the existence of absolute truths. In his philosophy of *pragmatism*, ideas were judged by their consequences; ideas served as guides to action that produced desired results. Philosophy should be concerned with solving problems, not with contemplating ultimate ends.

James's most important disciple was John Dewey. Like James, Dewey had a great interest in psychology, whose insights he applied to education. In his Laboratory School at the University of Chicago, Dewey broke from the rigid curriculum of traditional education and instead stressed problem solving and practical activity as the keys to children's personal growth. Children were encouraged to explore and discover for themselves rather than learn lessons by rote. Nowhere could the intellectual bent of progressivism in action be better seen than in Dewey's experiments, which, fittingly, came to be known as progressive education.

Idealism. Progressive reformers prided themselves on being tough-minded. They had confidence in people's capacity to take purposeful action. But there was another side to the progressive mind. It was deeply infused with idealism. Progressives framed their intentions in terms of high principle. The progressive cause, pronounced Theodore Roosevelt, "is based on the eternal principles of righteousness."

Much of this idealism came from the American past. No American hero loomed larger in the minds of progressives than Abraham Lincoln. For many, such as Jane Addams, the Great Emancipator was a lifelong guide. Lincoln's example, in particular, inspired the battle for political reform. "Go back to the first principles of democracy; go back to the people," Robert La Follette told his audience when he launched his attack on the Republican machine in Wisconsin. Political reformers typically described their work as political restoration. They frequently said that they had converted to reform after discovering how far party politics had drifted from the ideals of representative government.

Progressive idealism also derived from American radical traditions. Many progressives traced their conversion to Henry George's *Progress and Poverty* (1879), which asked why, in the midst of fabulous wealth, so many Americans should be condemned to poverty. George's answer—that private control of land siphoned the community's wealth into the hands of nonproductive landlords—led to a Single Tax movement that served as a school for many budding progressives. Others traced their awakening to Edward Bellamy's novel *Looking Backward* (1888), with its utopian vision of an ordered, affluent American socialism, or to the Chicago social democrat Henry Demarest Lloyd's *Wealth against Commonwealth* (1894), with its powerful indictment of the Standard Oil trust. In later years this radical tradition was transmitted mainly through the Socialist party, which flourished after 1900 under the leadership of Eugene V. Debs. Walter Lippmann and many other young reformers passed through socialism on their way to progressivism, whereas others, such as Charlotte Perkins Gilman, never left the socialist camp.

The most important source of progressive idealism, especially among social reformers, was religion. Protestant churches had long been concerned with the plight of the urban poor (see Chapter 20, page 631). Now that concern blossomed into a major doctrine—the Social Gospel. The Baptist cleric Walter Rauschenbusch, its most influential exponent, had been deeply affected by his ministry near the squalid Hell's Kitchen section of New York City. Shocked by the conditions there, Rauschenbusch fought for more playgrounds and better housing in slum neighborhoods. The churches had to reassert the "social aims of Jesus," he argued. The "Kingdom of God on Earth" would be achieved not by striving for personal salvation but by struggling for social justice. To coordinate that effort, reform-minded clerical leaders formed the Federal Council of Churches in 1908. The council aimed at "promoting the application of the law of Christ in every relation to human life."

Progressive leaders characteristically grew up in families imbued with evangelical piety. Many went through a religious crisis, having sought and failed to experience a conversion, and ultimately settled on a career in social work, education, journalism, or politics, where they could translate inherited religious belief into modern secular action. Jane Addams, for example, had taken up settlement-house work with this intention. She believed that by uplifting the poor in tenement districts, settlement workers would themselves be uplifted: they would experience "the joy of finding Christ" by acting "in fellowship" with the needy.

Progressive thought thus contained a pervading Christian undercurrent. The philosopher John Dewey called democracy "a spiritual fact" and the "means by which the revelation of truth is carried on." Theodore Roosevelt launched his Progressive party in 1912 with the battle cry, "We stand at Armageddon and we battle for the Lord." His supporters at the party's national convention marched around the hall singing "Onward Christian Soldiers."

The Muckrakers. The progressive mode of thought—idealistic in intent and tough-minded in approach—nurtured a new kind of reform journalism. A growing urban audience had created a market during the 1890s for a rash of popular magazines, including *Munsey's,*

McClure's, and *Collier's.* Unlike the highbrow *Atlantic Monthly* or *Harper's,* these journals sold for only 10 cents and catered to a broad audience. Almost by accident—Lincoln Steffens's article "Tweed Days in St. Louis" in the October 1902 issue of *McClure's* is credited with getting things started—magazine editors discovered that what most excited readers was the exposure of evildoing and set investigative reporters such as Charles Edward Russell (see American Voices, page 651) on the trail of evildoers.

In a series of powerful articles Lincoln Steffens wrote about "the shame of the cities"—the corrupt ties between business and political machines. Ida M. Tarbell attacked Standard Oil, and David Graham Phillips told how money controlled the Senate. William Hard exposed industrial accidents in "Making Steel and Killing Men" (1907) and child labor in "De Kid Wot Works at Night" (1908). Others described slum conditions, Wall Street abuses, and the adulteration of food. Hardly a sordid corner of American life escaped the scrutiny of these tireless reporters. They were moralists as well, infusing their factual accounts with a powerful spirit of personal indignation. "The sights I saw," wrote the pioneering slum investigator Jacob Riis, "gripped my heart until I felt I must tell of them, or burst, or turn anarchist."

President Roosevelt, among many others, thought these journalists went too far. In a 1906 speech he com-

Ida Tarbell Takes on Rockefeller
A popular biographer of Napoleon and Lincoln in the 1890s, Ida Tarbell turned her journalistic talents to muckraking. Her first installment of "The History of the Standard Oil Company" appeared in *McClure's Magazine* in November 1902. John D. Rockefeller, she wrote, "was willing to strain every nerve to obtain for himself special and illegal privileges from the railroads which were bound to ruin every man in the oil business not sharing them with him." As Tarbell built her case, criticism rained down on Rockefeller. A more sympathetic cartoon in the magazine *Judge* pleads with Rockefeller's critics: "Boys, don't you think you have bothered the old man just about enough?"

Charles Edward Russell

Muckraking

In this autobiographical account Charles Russell, a newspaperman, describes how he got into muckraking journalism and what he thought it was all about. He never did, by the way, get back to writing music.

All America had been accustomed to laud and bepraise the makers of great fortunes. . . . Money had become the touchstone and perfect measure of worth. . . . Now, of a sudden, men began to discover that these great and adored fortunes had been gathered in ways that not only grazed the prison gate but imposed burdens and disadvantages upon the rest of the community; that vast hoards for one man meant much less for others. In the shock of this discovery, a literature of exposition arose and daily the magazine editors looked for new dark, malodorous corners of money-grabbing upon which the spotlight could be turned.

Pure accident cast me, without the least desire, into the pursuit of this

fashion. I had finally withdrawn from the newspaper business, and having enough money to live modestly I was bent upon carrying out a purpose long cherished in quite a different line. [I had concluded] that what we call the separate arts of music and poetry are really but one, and I now conceived that with a piano, my Swinburne, and some sheets of music paper I could demonstrate this priceless fact to a palpitating world. Upon this task I was intent when the whole business was upset with a single telegram.

One day, Mr. J. W. Midgley, who was a famous expert on railroad rates and conditions . . . let loose a flood of startling facts about the impositions practised by the owners and operators of refrigerator cars. My friend, Mr. Erman J. Ridgway . . . of *Everybody's Magazine* wired asking me to see Mr. Midgley and get him to write for *Everybody's* an article along the lines of his testimony. I conferred accordingly and Mr. Midgley positively refused all offers to become an exposé

writer. [So] Ridgway wire[d] asking me to furnish the article *Everybody's* wanted. I had not the least disposition to do so, except only that Ridgway was my friend. . . . The next thing I knew a muck-rake was put into my hand and I was plunged into the midst of the game. . . .

I wrote two or three articles on the refrigerator car scandal and then went on to write a series on the methods of the Beef Trust and was not in the least astonished to find that I was become an unmitigated scoundrel, a hired assassin of character, a libeller of good men, an enemy of society and of the government, and probably an Anarchist in disguise. . . . We were all up and away, full of the pleasures of the chase . . . and all that business about poetry and music sheets forgotten. It was exhilarating sport, hunting the money octopus.

Source: Charles Edward Russell, *Bare Hands and Stone Walls* (New York, Charles Scribner's Sons, 1933), 135–139.

---

pared them to the man with the muckrake in *Pilgrim's Progress* by the seventeenth-century English preacher John Bunyan. That man was too absorbed with raking the filth on the floor to look up and accept a celestial crown. Thus the term *muckraker* became attached to journalists who exposed the underside of American life. Their efforts were in fact health-giving. More than any other group, the muckrakers called the people to arms.

Political Reformers

Progressives acted out of a deep sense of idealism. And they were confident about the human capacity to take purposeful action. This much all progressives had in common but, in pursuit of reform, they were not all drawn to the same targets. Nor, in making their choices, were progressives indifferent to their own self-interests. In politics especially, the battles for reform reflected mixed motives of self-regard and civic betterment.

Municipal Reform. In many cities the demand for better government came from local businessmen. They complained that the economic burdens of old-fashioned party rule had become too heavy. Taxes went up, but needed services always lagged. There had to be an end, as one manufacturer said, to "the inefficiency, the sloth, the carelessness, the injustice and the graft of city administrations." The solution, argued John Patterson of the National Cash Register Company, lay in putting "municipal affairs on a strict business basis." Cities should be run "not by partisans, either Republican or Democratic, but by men who are skilled in business management and social service."

In 1900 a hurricane devastated Galveston, Texas, drowning 5,000 people and destroying the municipal port. Local businessmen took over and, in the course of rebuilding the city, replaced the mayor and board of aldermen with a five-member commission. The Galveston plan, although widely copied, had a serious flaw: it gave too much power to the individual commissioners. Dayton, Ohio, resolved this problem by assigning policy matters to a nonpartisan commission and administrative functions to an appointed city manager. The commission-manager system aimed at running the American city "in exactly the same way as a private business corporation." Municipal political reform was chiefly the work of the business community and overtly a matter of the balance sheet.

It was also a way of grabbing power. Municipal reformers favored citywide elections, nonpartisanship, and professional city administration. All these reforms attacked the ward politics that traditionally had given ethnic and working-class groups access to political power. As a result, municipal control shifted to the urban middle class. In fact, municipal reform contained a decidedly antidemocratic bias. "Ignorance should be excluded from control," said former Mayor Abram Hewitt of New York in 1901. "City business should be carried on by trained experts selected upon some other principle than popular suffrage."

A different kind of urban progressive opposed such elitist reform. Mayor Brand Whitlock of Toledo, Ohio, believed "that the cure for the ills of democracy was not less democracy, as so many people were always preaching, but more democracy." The prototype of this new breed of urban politician was the shoe manufacturer Hazen S. Pingree, who led the Republicans to victory against the Democratic machine in Detroit in 1889. Although drafted by a business coalition, Pingree skillfully appealed for support from trade unions and ethnic groups. His administration not only attacked municipal corruption and inefficiency but also concerned itself with the needs of Detroit's working people. An increasing number of cities came under the leadership of such progressive mayors, including Samuel M. "Golden Rule" Jones in Toledo, Tom Johnson in Cleveland, and Mark Fagan in Jersey City. By combining popular programs and campaign magic, they won over the urban masses and challenged the rule of the machines.

State Politics. The major battles for democratic reform, however, took place at the state level. Preeminent among state progressives was Robert M. La Follette of Wisconsin. La Follette was a seasoned politician. Born in 1855, he had followed a conventional party career as a lawyer, district attorney, and then congressman for three terms before breaking with the Wisconsin Republican machine in 1891, allegedly because of an attempt by the top party boss to bribe him. La Follette became a tireless exponent of political reform. "I was merely expressing a common and widespread, though largely unconscious, spirit of revolt among the people," La Follette said of his fight to unseat the state's Republican old guard. At first it was an uphill battle. But after a decade of unremitting campaigning, La Follette finally

gained the Republican nomination and won the governorship in 1900 on a platform of higher taxes for corporations, stricter utility and railroad regulation, and political reform.

La Follette's key proposal was a direct primary law by which party candidates would be chosen through popular election rather than in machine-run conventions. Pushed through in 1903, this democratic reform both expressed La Follette's political ideals and suited his particular political talents. The party regulars opposing him were insiders, more comfortable in the caucus room than out on the hustings. But that was where La Follette excelled. A brilliant campaigner, he aimed at dramatizing the issues and generating grass-roots support. The direct primary gave La Follette the means to control the Republican party in Wisconsin through good times and bad until his death twenty-five years later.

What was true of La Follette was more or less true of all successful progressive politicians. Albert B. Cummins of Iowa, Harold U'Ren of Oregon, and Hiram Johnson of California all espoused democratic ideals and made skillful use of the direct primary to win polit-

Robert M. La Follette
La Follette was transformed into a political reformer when a Wisconsin Republican boss attempted to bribe him in 1891 to influence a judge in a railway case. As he described it in his *Autobiography*, "Out of this awful ordeal came understanding; and out of understanding came resolution. I determined that the power of this corrupt influence . . . should be broken." This photograph captures La Follette at the top of his form, taking his case in 1897 to the people of Cumberland, Wisconsin.

ical power and push through reform programs. If they were newcomers—as Woodrow Wilson was when he left academic life to enter New Jersey politics in 1910—they showed a quick aptitude for politics and gained a solid mastery of the trade. Once in office, they asserted control over their parties and beat the political bosses at their own game. They practiced a new kind of popular politics. In a reform age, it could be a more effective way to power than were the backroom techniques of the old-fashioned machine politicians.

Not even the most radical progressive reforms—the initiative, the referendum, and the recall—lived up to their billing. All three reforms were put forth as mechanisms for returning political power to the people. Under the *initiative*, ordinary citizens could get issues of interest to them placed on the ballot. The *referendum* enabled voters to decide big legislative issues (including propositions arising from the initiative) by popular vote, whereas the *recall* empowered citizens to remove from office politicians who had lost the public's confidence. It soon became clear, however, that direct democracy did not supplant organized politics. Initiative, referendum, and recall campaigns put a premium on organization, money, and expertise, and those were attributes not of the people at large but of well-organized special interests. As with the direct primary, the initiative, referendum, and recall had as much to do with power relations as with democratic idealism.

The Woman Progressive

Reform movements arise through a process of *recruitment*. Why do people enlist in a great cause? Because they are linked in some personal way to an evil crying out for correction. For middle-class women of the Progressive Era, the link was between their domestic identity as wives and mothers and the responsibility this gave them for the social well-being of their communities.

Middle-class women had long borne the burden of humanitarian work in American cities. Characteristically, they did most of the legwork for the charity organization societies that since the 1870s had sprung up to coordinate citywide private relief. As voluntary investigators, women visited needy families, assessed their problems, and referred them to relief agencies.

After many years of dedicated charity work, Josephine Shaw Lowell of New York City concluded that it was not enough to give assistance to the poor. "If the working people had all they ought to have, we should not have the paupers and criminals," she declared. "It is better to save them before they go under, than to spend your life fishing them out afterward." Lowell founded the New York Consumers' League in 1890. Her goal was to improve the wages and working conditions of female clerks in the city's stores. To bring pressure on reluctant merchants, the league issued a "White List"—a very short one at first—of shops that met its standards for a living wage and decent treatment of clerks.

From these modest beginnings, the league became broadly concerned with exploitation in women's occupations, spread to other cities, and blossomed into the National Consumers' League in 1899. By then the women who ran the league had concluded that voluntary action was insufficient and that only state action could rescue poor urban families. Under the crusading leadership of Florence Kelley, formerly a chief factory inspector in Illinois, the Consumers' League became a powerful lobby for protective legislation for women and children.

Among its achievements, none was more important than the *Muller v. Oregon* decision (1908), which upheld an Oregon law limiting to ten hours the workday of women workers. The Consumers' League had pushed that law through the state legislature and recruited the brilliant Boston lawyer Louis D. Brandeis to defend it before the Supreme Court. In his brief, Brandeis devoted only two pages to legal citations on the narrow constitutional issue—whether, under its police powers, Oregon had the right to regulate women's working hours. Instead Brandeis rested his case on a vast amount of data gathered by the Consumers' League showing how long hours damaged women's health and family roles. The *Muller* decision, which accepted Brandeis's reasoning, was a victory for the new "sociological jurisprudence" (see page 671) and cleared the way for a wave of protective laws across the country.

Women's organizations became a strong voice in state legislatures and in Congress on behalf of women and children (see American Lives, pages 654–655). Their victories included the first law providing public assistance for mothers with dependent children, in Illinois in 1911; the first minimum wage law for women, in Massachusetts in 1912; more effective child labor laws in many states; and, at the federal level, the Children's and Women's bureaus in the Labor Department, in 1912 and 1920, respectively. The welfare state, insofar as it arrived in America in those years, was what women progressives had made of it; they had erected a "maternalist" welfare system.

The Settlement Houses. In addition to public advocacy, women's urban activism sought direct engagement with the underprivileged. This was the aim of the settlement-house movement, which began in 1884 when Oxford University students founded Toynbee Hall in the slums of London. Inspired by that example, two young American women, Jane Addams and Ellen Gates Starr, established Hull House on Chicago's West Side in 1889.

Frances Kellor: Woman Progressive

From the day its doors opened in 1892, the University of Chicago was a major center of American learning. Financed by John D. Rockefeller, the university modeled itself on the great German research universities and, unlike Yale and Harvard, concentrated on graduate education. At Chicago and other American universities modern social science was taking shape, breaking from its nineteenth-century moral foundations and seeking a scientific basis for the study of society. Economics, political science, and sociology demanded a rigorous course of study certified by the granting of the Ph.D. But if the social sciences were becoming professional, their guiding purpose was not yet disinterested research but the improvement of society. The University of Chicago saw the city surrounding it as a great laboratory for social betterment. Its students were being prepared, whether they knew it or not, to be in service to the American progressivism of the next decade. The University of Chicago, moreover, was receptive to the admission of women, and for them in particular, graduate education was a breeding ground for careers as social reformers.

Among the women entering in 1898 was Frances Alice Kellor, a recent graduate of Cornell University. Kellor was born in Columbus, Ohio, in 1873. Her father abandoned the family before she was two, and her mother made a hard living as a domestic and laundress. This was not the kind of privileged background from which most woman progressives sprang, but Kellor's experience came closer to the norm than her threadbare circumstances might have suggested. In 1875 her family moved to Coldwater, Michigan, a former abolitionist center (and station on the underground railroad) and a stronghold of Yankee culture. From the Coldwater community, with its high moral standards and strong educational institutions, Kellor received the reformist values that other budding progressives learned from their families. Kellor, moreover, had a remarkable talent for finding patrons, gaining by her wits the financial means her fellow progressives were born to. Her first patrons were the well-to-do librarians of Coldwater,

Mary and Frances Eddy, who befriended her and took her into their home. Born Alice, Kellor began to call herself "Frances" as a sign that she considered herself adopted by the Eddy sisters. She graduated from high school, became a reporter for the *Coldwater Republican,* and then, with the backing of the Eddys, enrolled at Cornell in 1895. Highly athletic, Kellor made her first mark as a fighter for equal rights on a sports issue: she led the campaign for a women's crew. She got a solid education in the social sciences at Cornell and decided to become a criminologist.

Sociology was an infant discipline when Frances Kellor arrived in Chicago in 1898, with little in the way of systematic theory and an emphasis on high-minded investigations of social problems. Kellor's interest in crime was encouraged by the Chicago faculty. The prevailing theory of the time, advanced by the Italian Cesare Lombroso, was that criminality was an inherited trait. Criminals were born criminal, and this was manifest in their physical features. Skeptical, Kellor conducted a study of the female inmates of five midwestern prisons. Comparing them with a control group of college women, she could find no physical differences. Kellor concluded that it was not heredity, but social environment, economic disadvantage, and poverty, that made for criminality. Kellor also rejected "the prevailing opinion that when women are criminal they are more degraded and more abandoned than men." People thought so only because of "the difference in the standards which we set for the two sexes."

A second project on criminality among southern blacks likewise rejected heredity and stressed environmental factors, but Kellor's conclusions were pessimistic and racially conservative. Centuries of slavery and indolent southern life had left blacks so morally weakened that "the Negro at present has neither the perceptions nor the solidity of character that would enable him to lead his race." She considered the southern restrictions on blacks' legal and politic rights unfortunate but necessary, and she believed that "the free intermingling of the two races is impossible, at least for many generations."

Frances Kellor
This photograph of Kellor was taken in her early twenties, when she was a student at Cornell University.

In drawing these illiberal conclusions, Kellor was echoing the views of her teachers and indeed of most white progressives of her generation.

Despite her precocious record, Kellor left the university in 1902 without a degree. The reasons are not altogether clear but doubtless had something to do with a painful truth of which Kellor must have been aware: the University of Chicago almost never placed its female graduate students in university teaching jobs. To be a professor, it seemed, was still a male prerogative. There was, however, a positive side to Kellor's decision. Like many of her fellow students, she had fallen under the spell of Jane Addams. Kellor lived periodically at Hull House, joined the circle of social reformers that congregated there, and began to see her future out among the disadvantaged rather than in the university. When she left Chicago, it was to do social research for New York's College Settlement Association.

Her first project was a study of unemployment. Kellor rejected the prevailing notion that being jobless was a sign of personal weakness. She was among the first investigators to see that unemployment was an economic problem, the result not primarily of individual shiftlessness or incompetence but the impersonal operations of the labor market. Her book *Out of Work* (1904) was a truly pioneering investigation, paving the way for the modern study of unemployment. Kellor was especially concerned with the plight of jobless women and their exploitation by commercial employment agencies. Representing the Women's Municipal League of New York, Kellor lobbied successfully for state regulation of these agencies. Kellor thus employed her research to bring about social change. The combination of professional investigation and robust political advocacy became the hallmark of Kellor's progressivism. Her next study, on the problems of immigrants in New York, led to the establishment of the New York State Bureau of Industries and Immigration in 1910. Kellor was chosen to be its head, the first woman to hold so high a post in New York's state government.

The high point of Kellor's career came two years later, when Theodore Roosevelt launched the Progressive party. Convinced that social reform required strong government, Kellor was drawn to the New Nationalism. She linked it with her own fervent advocacy of women's political rights. Always a fighter, she was entirely at ease in the rough-and-tumble of partisan politics. After Roosevelt's defeat in 1912, the Progressive party set up the National Progressive Service, a kind of think tank to study social problems and formulate legislative proposals. The idea was mainly Kellor's, and she was tapped to chair the Service. This was truly a pinnacle for a woman in American politics at a time when women in most states could not vote in national elections. Unfortunately, Kellor's emphasis on scientific investigation put her at odds with the practical politicians, and she was forced out in early 1914. Hers was a brief run in national politics, exhilarating while it lasted and unique for a woman of her generation.

Kellor never married. Like many other woman progressives, including Jane Addams, she found personal fulfillment in an enduring relationship with another woman. This was Mary Dreier, one of two wealthy sisters who played leading roles in New York progressivism. From the time Kellor moved into the Dreier home in Brooklyn Heights in 1904 until her death almost fifty years later, she and Mary were constant companions. Kellor's later professional life was devoted to a distinguished career with the American Arbitration Association.

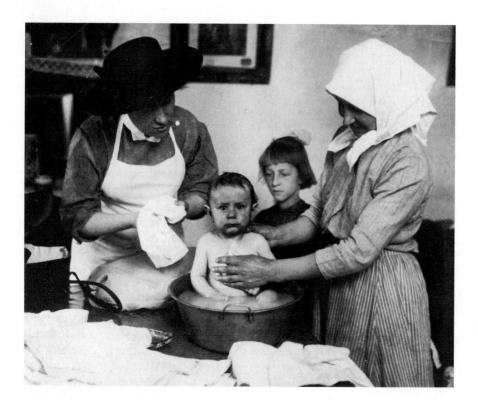

Saving the Children
In the early years at Hull House, Jane Addams recalled, toddlers sometimes arrived for kindergarten tipsy from a breakfast of bread soaked in wine. To settlement-house workers, the answer to such ignorance was in child care education, and so began the program to send visiting nurses into immigrant homes. They taught mothers the proper methods of caring for children—including, as this photograph shows, the daily infant bath, in a dishpan if necessary.

During the next fifteen years scores of settlement houses sprang up in the slum neighborhoods of the nation's cities. The settlement houses served as community centers run by middle-class residents, who acted as amateur social workers for the surrounding immigrant communities. Hull House had meeting rooms, an art gallery, clubs for children and adults, and a kindergarten. Addams herself led battles for garbage removal, playgrounds, better street lighting, and police protection. At the Henry Street Settlement in New York City, Lillian D. Wald made visiting nursing a major service. Mary McDowell, head of the University of Chicago Settlement, installed a bathhouse, a children's playground, and a citizenship school for immigrants.

Beyond the modest good they did in slum neighborhoods, settlement houses served as a breeding ground for social reform. At least half the women residents went on to careers in social service. Settlement houses thus contributed significantly to the emerging profession of social work. To a remarkable degree, the leaders of social reform—both men and women—served apprenticeships in settlement houses.

For the middle-class residents, more deep-seated needs were also being satisfied. In a famous essay Jane Addams spoke of the "subjective necessity" of the settlement house. She meant that it was as much a response to the desire of educated young men and women to serve as it was a response to the needs of slum dwellers. Addams herself was a case in point. She had grown up in a comfortable Illinois family and had graduated from Rockford College. Then she faced an empty future as an ornamental wife if she married or a sheltered spinster if she did not. Hull House became her salvation. The settlement was "a protest against a restricted view of education," against the genteel schooling that never got her beyond "the always getting ready for life." Now, at Hull House, she could "begin with however small a group to accomplish and to live."

The Revival of the Struggle for Women's Rights. Almost imperceptibly, women activists such as Jane Addams and Florence Kelley breathed new life into the suffrage movement. Why should a woman who was capable of running a settlement house or lobbying for a bill be denied the right to vote? Suffrage, moreover, became firmly linked to social reform. If women had the right to vote, they and their male supporters argued, more enlightened legislation and better government would certainly result. Finally, through their activities among working-class women, women progressives helped broaden the social base of the suffrage movement.

Believing that working women should be encouraged to help themselves, social reformers founded the National Women's Trade Union League in 1903. Financed and led by wealthy supporters, the league organized women workers, played a considerable role in their strikes, and, perhaps most important, helped to develop working-class leaders. For example, Rose

Rose Schneiderman, 1913

In their battles for better conditions, women garment workers produced their own leaders, and none was more devoted to their cause or more fiery on the platform than Rose Schneiderman. The daughter of a widowed immigrant woman, Schneiderman went to work at thirteen, quickly got caught up in union activities, and fashioned for herself a lifetime career as a trade unionist, including becoming president of the National Women's Trade Union League.

Schneiderman became a union organizer among garment workers in New York City, and Agnes Nestor led women glove workers in Illinois; both were also lobbyists for protective legislation. Athough often resenting the patronizing ways of their well-to-do sponsors, such trade-union women identified their cause with the broader struggle for women's rights. When New York State held referenda on woman suffrage in 1915 and 1917, strong support came from the Jewish and Italian precincts inhabited by unionized garment workers.

Suffrage activity began to revive nationwide. Women won the right to vote in the state of Washington in 1910, in California in 1911, and in four more western states during the next three years (see Map 21.1). Women also altered their tactics. In Britain, suffragists had begun to picket Parliament, assault politicians, and go on hunger strikes in jail. This disruptive strategy, which gave the cause of the British suffragists new power, impressed their sisters in the United States.

Most important among the American converts was Alice Paul, a young Quaker who had lived in Britain and knew how to apply the confrontational tactics of the British suffragists. Rejecting the slower route of enfranchisement by the states, Paul advocated a constitutional amendment that in one stroke would give women across the country the right to vote. In 1916 Paul organized the militant National Woman's party. The National Ameri-

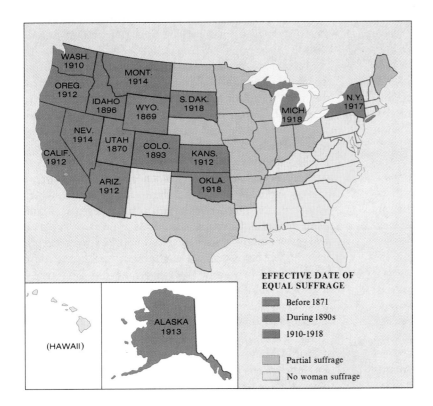

MAP 21.1

Woman Suffrage, 1869–1918

By 1909, after more than sixty years of agitation, only four lightly populated western states had granted women full voting rights. A number of other states offered partial suffrage, limited mostly to voting for school boards and such issues as taxes. Between 1910 and 1918, as the effort shifted to the struggle for a constitutional amendment, eleven states (and Alaska) joined the list granting full suffrage. The most stubborn resistance was in the South.

Suffragists on Parade, 1912
After 1910 the suffrage movement went
into high gear. Suffragist leaders decided
to demand a constitutional amendment
rather than rely on gaining the vote state
by state. In 1912 they served notice on
both parties that they meant business
and, as shown in this suffragist parade
in New York, made their demands a visible part of the presidential campaign.

can Woman Suffrage Association (NAWSA), from which
Paul had split off, was also rejuvenated. Carrie Chap-
man Catt, a skilled political organizer from the New
York movement, took over as national leader in 1915.
Under her guidance, NAWSA brought a broad-based or-
ganization to the campaign for a federal amendment.

Feminism. In the midst of this suffrage struggle something new and more fundamental began to happen. A
new generation of women activists who were college
graduates or experienced trade unionists was arising.
Out in the world and self-supporting, these women
were determined not to be hemmed in by the social constraints of women's "separate sphere." "Breaking into
the Human Race" was the intention they proclaimed at
a mass meeting in New York in 1914. "We intend simply to be ourselves," declared the chair Marie Jenny
Howe, "not just our little female selves, but our whole
big human selves."

The women at this meeting called themselves *feminists,* a term that was just coming into use. In this, its
first incarnation, feminism meant freedom for full personal development. In its specifics this covered many
things—freedom to follow a career, freedom from the
double standard in sexual morality, freedom from social
convention—but in a larger sense it meant freedom from
the stifling stereotypes of women's separate sphere. Thus
did Charlotte Perkins Gilman, famous for her advocacy
of communal kitchens as a means of liberating women
from homemaking, imagine the new woman: "Here she
comes, running, out of prison and off pedestal; chains
off, crown off, halo off, just a live woman."

Feminists were militantly prosuffrage but, unlike
their more traditional suffragist sisters, did not stake
their claim on any presumed uplifting effect of the
women's vote on American politics. Rather, they demanded the right to vote because they considered themselves fully equal to men. At the point that the suffrage
movement was about to triumph, it was overtaken by a
larger revolution that redefined the struggle for women's
rights as a battle against all the constraints that prevented women from achieving their potential as human
beings.

Feminism gave a fresh thrust to social uplift, bringing forth a new and more radical type of woman progressive: Margaret Sanger. As a public health nurse in
New York, Sanger had been repeatedly asked by immigrant women about the "secret" of how to avoid having
more babies. When one of her patients died of a
botched abortion, Sanger decided to devote herself to
teaching poor immigrant women about birth control.
This brought her up against the Comstock laws, which
outlawed contraceptive literature and devices as obscene materials (see Chapter 20, page 641). Whereas it
was easy enough for the educated middle class to evade
those laws, birth control could only reach the poor
through an open campaign of education. Undeterred
by police raids or public disapproval, Sanger gave
speeches, published the pamphlet *Family Limitation,*
and in 1916 opened the first birth control clinic in the
United States. If her ends were not different from those
of Jane Addams—both wanted to uplift the downtrodden—the means used by Sanger posed a more provocative challenge to the status quo.

Urban Liberalism

The evolution of the women's movement—in particular, the recruitment of working-class women to what had been a middle-class struggle—was entirely characteristic of how progressivism evolved more generally.

When Hiram Johnson first ran for governor of California in 1910, he was the candidate of the urban middle class and the farming community. He had made a name as prosecutor of the corrupt San Francisco boss Abe Ruef. Johnson pledged to purify California politics and curb the Southern Pacific Railroad, the dominating power in the state's economic and political life. By his second term Johnson was championing social and labor legislation. His original base in the middle class had eroded and had been replaced by an immigrant working-class vote that kept him in power for years. These events illustrated the most enduring achievement of progressivism: the activation of America's working people as a force in reform politics and the launching of the strain of progressivism that historians have called *urban liberalism*. In New York the starting point for urban liberalism was a tragic fire.

Thirty minutes before quitting time on Saturday afternoon, March 25, 1911, fire broke out at the Triangle Shirtwaist Company in downtown New York City (see American Voices, page 660). The flames trapped the workers, mostly young immigrant women. Forty-seven leapt to their deaths; another ninety-nine never made it to the windows. The tragedy caused a national furor

and led two months later to the creation of the New York State Factory Commission.

In the next four years the commission developed a remarkable program of labor reform: fifty-six laws dealing with fire hazards, unsafe machines, homework, and wages and hours for women and children. The chairman of the commission was Robert F. Wagner; the vice-chairman, Alfred E. Smith. Both were Tammany Hall politicians and Democratic party leaders in the state legislature. Wagner and Smith sponsored the resolution establishing the commission, participated fully in its work, and marshaled the party regulars to pass the proposals into law. All this the two men did with the approval of the Tammany machine. The labor code that resulted was the most advanced in the United States.

Tammany's reform role reflected a trend in American cities. Urban political machines increasingly recognized their limitations as social agencies in the modern industrial age: only the state could prevent future Triangle fires or cope with the evils of factory work and city life. Also, a new generation had entered machine politics. Al Smith and Robert Wagner, men of social vision, absorbed the lessons of the Triangle investigation. They formed durable ties with middle-class progressives such as the social worker Frances Perkins, who sat on the commission as the representative of the New York Consumers' League.

For all their organizational muscle, the urban machines could not ignore popular sentiment. In the successes of reform politicians such as Toledo's Sam Jones

The Triangle Shirtwaist Fire

The doors were the problem. Most were locked (to keep the working girls from leaving early); the few that were open became jammed by bodies as the flames spread. When the fire trucks finally came, the ladders were too short. Compared with those caught inside, the girls who leapt to their deaths were the lucky ones. "As I looked up I saw a love affair in the midst of all the horror," a reporter wrote. A young man was helping girls leap from a window. The fourth "put her arms about him and kiss[ed] him. Then he held her out into space and dropped her." He immediately followed. "Thud—dead, Thud—dead . . . I saw his face before they covered it. . . . He was a real man. He had done his best."

Pauline Newman

Working for the Triangle Shirtwaist Company

Pauline Newman was an organizer and educational director for the International Ladies Garment Workers Union until her death in 1986. As a child she had worked at the notorious Triangle Shirtwaist factory in New York.

A cousin of mine worked for the Triangle Shirtwaist Company and she got me on there in October of 1901. It was probably the largest shirtwaist factory in the city of New York then. They had more than two hundred operators, cutters, examiners, finishers. Altogether more than four hundred people on two floors. . . . We started work at seven-thirty in the morning, and during the busy season we worked until nine in the evening. They didn't pay you any overtime and they didn't give you anything for supper money. . . . What I had to do was not really very difficult. It was just monotonous. When the shirtwaists were finished at the machine there were some threads that were left, and all the youngsters—we had a corner on the floor that resembled a kindergarten—we were given little scissors to cut the threads off. It wasn't heavy work, but it was monotonous, because you did the same thing from seven-thirty in the morning until nine at night.

Well, of course, there were [child labor] laws on the books, but no one bothered to enforce them. The employers were always tipped off if there was going to be an inspection. "Quick," they'd say, "into the boxes!" And we children would climb into the big boxes the finished shirts were stored in. Then some shirts were piled on top of us, and when the inspector came—no children. The factory always got an okay from the inspector, and I suppose someone at City Hall got a little something, too.

The employers didn't recognize anyone working for them as a human being. . . . If you went to the toilet and you were there longer than the floor lady thought you should be, you would be laid off for half a day and sent home. And, of course, that meant no pay. You were not allowed to have your lunch on the fire escape in the summertime. The door was locked to keep us in. That's why so many people were trapped when the fire broke out. . . .

I stopped working at the Triangle Factory during the strike in 1909 and I didn't go back. The union sent me out to raise money for the strikers. I apparently was able to articulate my feelings and opinions about the criminal conditions, and they didn't have any-

one else who could do better so they assigned me. . . .

After the 1909 strike I worked with the union, organizing in Philadelphia and Cleveland and other places, so I wasn't at the Triangle Shirtwaist Factory when the fire broke out, but a lot of my friends were. . . . It's very difficult to describe the feeling because I knew the place and I knew so many of the girls. The thing that bothered me was the employers got a lawyer. . . . One hundred and forty-six people were sacrificed, and the judge fined Blank and Harris seventy-five dollars!

Conditions were dreadful in those days. But . . . even when things were terrible, I always had that faith. . . . Only now, I'm a little discouraged sometimes when I see the workers spending their free hours watching television—trash. We fought so hard for those hours and they waste them. We used to read Tolstoy, Dickens, Shelley, by candlelight, and they watch the "Hollywood Squares." Well, they're free to do what they want. That's what we fought for.

Source: Joan Morrison and Charlotte Fox Zabusky, eds., *American Mosaic: The Immigrant Experience in the Words of Those Who Lived It* (New York: E.P. Dutton, 1980), 9–14. Copyright © 1980 by Joan Morrison and Charlotte Fox Zabusky. Reprinted by permission.

and Cleveland's Tom Johnson, the machines saw the appeal of progressive programs in working-class wards. There was a threat from the left as well. The Socialist party was making headway in the cities, electing Milwaukee's Victor Berger as the nation's first socialist congressman in 1910 and winning municipal elections in towns and cities across the country. The political universe of the urban machines had changed, and they had to pay more attention to opinion in the precincts.

The Labor Movement. Always highly pragmatic, city machines adopted urban liberalism without much of an

ideological struggle. The same could not be said of trade unions, the other institution that represented American working people. During its early years the American Federation of Labor (AFL) had strongly opposed state interference in labor's affairs. Samuel Gompers preached that workers should not seek from government what they could accomplish through their own initiative and activities. Economic power and self-help, not the state, would be the worker's salvation. *Voluntarism*, as trade unionists called this doctrine, did not die out, but it weakened substantially during the progressive years.

Organized labor enlisted in the cause of urban liberalism partly for defensive reasons. In the early twentieth century the labor movement came under severe attack by antiunion employers who had at their disposal powerful legal weapons. For one thing, they could sue unions under the Sherman Antitrust Act. In the Danbury Hatters case (1908), the Supreme Court found a labor boycott—a call by the Hatters' Union for people not to patronize the antiunion D. E. Loewe & Company—to be a conspiracy in restraint of trade and awarded triple damages to the company. Hundreds of union members stood to lose their homes and life savings until the labor movement raised the money to pay the fines. More harmful to the economic power of the unions was the employers' routine use of the labor *injunction*—a court order prohibiting a union from carrying out a strike or boycott. The justification was to prevent "irreparable damage" to an employer while the legality of a union's acts was being adjudicated, but the effect of this "temporary" measure was to immobilize and defeat the union; this had happened, for example, to the American Railway Union in the great Pullman boycott of 1894 (see Chapter 18, pages 579–580).

Only a political response could blunt these assaults on labor's economic weapons. In its "Bill of Grievances" of 1906 the AFL demanded that Congress grant unions immunity from court attack. Rebuffed, the labor movement decided to become more politically active, adopting a strategy of nonpartisan support for candidates who favored its program. The AFL intended to "reward our friends and punish our enemies." The practical effect of this "nonpartisan" strategy was to draw labor closer to the Democratic party, which was more responsive than the Republican party to labor's pleas for a curb on the courts.

Once into politics, the labor movement had difficulty denying the case for social legislation. The AFL, after all, claimed to speak for the entire working class. When muckrakers exposed exploitation of women and children and middle-class progressives came forward with solutions, how could the labor movement fail to respond? Gompers served on the Triangle factory commission, and if—according to Frances Perkins—he was a less eager student than the Tammanyite members, learn he did. In state after state, organized labor joined the battle for progressive legislation and increasingly became its strongest advocate.

Conservative labor leaders offered the excuse that protective laws were for women and children, who could not defend themselves. In practice, however, trade unions became more flexible about legislative protection for men as well, and on the issue of workers' compensation they lobbied vigorously for new legislation.

Accidents took an awful toll in American factories and mines. Two thousand coal miners were killed every year, dying from cave-ins and explosions at a rate 50

percent higher than that in German mines. Liability laws, which were still governed by common-law principles, so heavily favored the employer that victims of industrial accidents rarely got compensation. Nothing cried out more for reform than the plight of maimed workers and penniless widows. In Germany and Britain, state-funded accident insurance guaranteed compensation regardless of fault. Efforts to provide comparable protections for American workers quickly received the backing of the trade unions. Between 1910 and 1917 workers' compensation for industrial accidents went into effect in all the industrial states.

Social Insurance Deferred. But the United States fell far behind European countries on other fronts. Health insurance and unemployment compensation, although widely accepted in Europe, scarcely made it onto the American political agenda. Old-age pensions, which Britain adopted in 1908, got a serious hearing, only to come up against an odd barrier: the United States already had a pension system of a kind. This was for Civil War veterans, 1 million of whom were drawing benefits in 1900. Thus, the constituency for a pension system was already largely satisfied: as many as half of all native-born white men over sixty-four or their survivors were receiving veterans' pensions in the early twentieth century. It did not help, moreover, that pensions had long been a partisan issue shamelessly exploited by the Republican party; that administration of the program was notoriously corrupt and laced with patronage; or, finally, that easy access to veterans' benefits often reinforced fears of state-induced dependency. Clarence J. Hicks, a famous industrial-relations expert, recalled Civil War pensioners idling away the hours around the wood stove in the grocery store in his Wisconsin town. They had decided "that the country owed them a living," lost their initiative, and "retreat[ed] from the battle of life."

It would take another generation and the ravages of the Great Depression before the country would be ready for social insurance. A secure old age, unemployment compensation, health insurance—these human needs of a modern industrial order were beyond the reach of urban liberals in the Progresive Era.

In Defense of Cultural Pluralism. Urban liberalism was driven not only by the plight of the economically downtrodden but also by a sharpening attack on the cultural values and way of life of immigrants. Old-stock evangelical Protestants had long agitated for laws that would impose their moral and cultural norms on American society. After 1900 those activities gained a new lease on life, forming a strand of progressive reform that conflicted with urban liberalism. The Anti-Saloon League, which called itself "the Protestant church in action," became a formidable force for prohibition in many states. Outlawing the sale of liquor was related to other reform targets: the saloon made for dirty politics, poverty, and bad labor conditions. Like progressives on other fronts, prohibitionists pronounced their movement a "Revolt of Decent Citizens."

The moral-reform agenda expanded to include a new goal: restricting the immigration of southern and Eastern Europeans into the United States. "The entrance . . . of such vast masses of peasantry, degraded below our utmost concepts, is a matter which no intelligent patriot can look upon without the gravest apprehension and alarm," warned Francis A. Walker, the president of the Massachusetts Institute of Technology. These concerns were shared by many progressive academics, such as by La Follette's close adviser Edward A. Ross of the University of Wisconsin, who denounced the "pigsty mode of life" of immigrants. The danger, respected social scientists argued, was that the nation's Anglo-Saxon population would be "mongrelized" and its civilization swamped by "inferior" Mediterranean and Slavic cultures. Feeding on this fear, the Immigration Restriction League spearheaded a movement to end America's historic open-door policy. Like prohibition, immigration restriction was considered by its proponents to be a progressive reform.

Urban liberals thought otherwise. They bitterly resented demands for prohibition and immigration restriction as attacks on the personal liberty and worthiness of urban immigrants. Prohibition, protested one Catholic academic, was "despotic and hypocritical domination." The Tammany politician Martin McCue accused the Protestant ministry of "seeking to substitute the policeman's nightstick for the Bible."

Urban liberal leaders championed both the economic needs of city dwellers and their right to follow their religious and cultural preferences. In many ways, certainly until the Great Depression of the 1930s, ethnocultural issues provided the stronger basis for urban liberal politics. And because the northern wing of the party cultivated the immigrant vote, the Democrats became the beneficiaries of the rise of urban liberalism. The rapid growth of this city vote destined the Democrats to become the majority party. The shift from Republican domination, although not completed until the 1930s, began during the Progressive Era.

Racism in an Age of Reform

The direct primary was the flagship of progressive politics—the crucial reform, as La Follette said, for defeating the party bosses and returning politics to "the people." The primary electoral system of nominating party candidates originated not in Wisconsin, however, but in the South, and by the time La Follette got his primary law in 1903, it was already operating in seven southern states. As in the North, the southern primary

was celebrated as a democratizing reform, and its adoption frequently brought reform administrations into power.

In the South, however, it was a *white* primary; black voters were excluded. Since the Democratic nomination was tantamount to election, to be excluded from the primary meant in effect to be disfranchised. The direct primary was a reform *intended*, among other things, to drive blacks out of politics. How could democratic reform and white supremacy be thus wedded together?

The answer is to be found in the racist thinking of the age. "A black skin means membership in a race of men which has never of itself succeeded to reason," pronounced Professor John W. Burgess of Columbia University in a 1902 book on Reconstruction; for Congress to have granted blacks the vote after the Civil War was a "monstrous thing." Burgess was a southern-born historian, but he was confident that his northern audience saw the "vast differences in political capacity" between blacks and whites and approved of black disfranchisement in the South. Even the Republican party, once it reconciled itself to relying on "lily white" organizations in the South midway through Roosevelt's administration, had no quarrel with this view. Indeed, as president-elect in 1908, William Howard Taft applauded the southern laws as necessary to "prevent entirely the possibility of domination by . . . an ignorant electorate" and reassured southerners that "the federal government has nothing to do with social equality."

In the North the Progressive Era was marked by growing racial tensions. Over 200,000 blacks migrated from the South between 1900 and 1910. Their arrival in northern cities invariably sparked white resentment. Attacks on blacks became widespread. The worst episode was a bloody race riot in Springfield, Illinois, in 1908. Even more indicative of racist sentiment was the huge success of D. W. Griffith's epic film *Birth of a Nation* (1915), with its crude depiction of Reconstruction as a moral struggle between rampaging blacks and a chivalrous Ku Klux Klan. Woodrow Wilson found the film's history "all so terribly true." His Democratic administration marked a low point for the federal government as the ultimate guarantor of equal rights: during Wilson's tenure, segregation of the U.S. civil service would have gone into effect had there not been an outcry among black leaders and a handful of influential white progressives.

The Revival of the Civil Rights Struggle. In these bleak years a core of young black professionals, mostly northern-born, began to fight back. The key figure was William Monroe Trotter, the pugnacious editor of the Boston *Guardian* and an outspoken critic of Booker T. Washington (see Chapter 19, page 608). "The policy of compromise has failed," Trotter argued. "The policy of resistance and aggression deserves a trial." In this endeavor, Trotter was joined in 1903 by W. E. B. Du Bois, a Harvard-trained sociologist and preeminent black intellectual of his generation. In 1906 the two of them, having broken with Washington, called a meeting of twenty-nine supporters at Niagara Falls—but in Canada, because no hotel on the U.S. side would admit blacks. The Niagara Movement, which resulted from that meeting, had an impact far beyond the scattering of members and local bodies it organized. The principles it affirmed would define the struggle for the rights of African-Americans: first, encouragement of black pride by all possible means; second, an uncompromising demand for full political and civil equality. Above all, "We refuse to allow the impression to remain that the Negro-American assents to inferiority, is submissive under oppression and apologetic before insults."

The revival of black protest found a small echo within white progressivism. Going against the grain, a handful of reformers were drawn to the plight of African-Americans. Among the most devoted was Mary White Ovington. By upper-class background and social outlook, she very much resembled Jane Addams, except that Ovington came from a family of abolitionists and thought of herself as a socialist. Like Addams, Ovington became a settlement-house worker, but among urban blacks rather than in an immigrant neighborhood. News of the bloody Springfield race riot of 1908 changed her life. Convinced that her duty lay in the struggle for equal rights, Ovington called a meeting of sympathetic white progressives that led to the formation of the National Association for the Advancement of Colored People (NAACP) in 1909.

The Niagara Movement, torn by internal disagreements, was breaking up, and most of the black activists joined the NAACP. Its national leadership was, in the early years, dominated by whites, however. The one exception proved to be of crucial importance. Du Bois became the editor of the NAACP's journal, *The Crisis*. With a passion that only a black voice could provide, Du Bois used that platform to proclaim the demand for black equality.

In the field of social welfare the principal concern during the Progressive Era was to help black migrants arriving in northern cities. In 1911 the National Urban League united the principal organizations that had sprung up for this purpose. Like the NAACP, the Urban League was interracial, including white reformers such as Ovington and black welfare activists such as William Lewis Bulkley, a New York school principal who played the most important role in the founding of the Urban League.

Progressivism was a house of many chambers. Most were infected by the respectable racism of the age, but not all. There was a saving remnant of white progressives who allied themselves with black activists and created, in the NAACP and the Urban League, the national institutions that would dominate the black struggle for a better life over the next half century.

Progressivism and National Politics

The gathering forces of progressivism reached the national scene slowly. Reformers had been activated by immediate concerns—by problems that affected them directly and by evils that were visible to them. Washing-

Editorial Office, The Crisis
In its early years no activity undertaken by the NAACP was more important than the publication of its journal, *The Crisis*, which under the brilliant editorship of W. E. B. Du Bois became the strongest voice for equal rights and black pride in the country. In this photograph of the magazine's editorial office, Du Bois is the balding man at the right rear.

TABLE 21.1

Progressive Legislation and Supreme Court Decisions

State Laws	Federal Laws	Supreme Court Decisions
1903 Wisconsin primary law Oregon ten-hour law for women	1898 Erdman Railway Mediation Act	1895 *U.S. v. E.C. Knight* shelters manufacturing from antitrust law
1910 New York Bureau of Industries and Immigration Washington State adopts women's suffrage	1902 Newlands Reclamation Act 1903 U.S. Bureau of Corporations 1906 Hepburn Railway Act Pure Food and Drug Act	1898 *U.S. v. Trans-Missouri* quashes "rule of reason" in antitrust suits
1911 Illinois law providing aid for mothers with dependent children New York State Factory Commisssion	1909 Payne-Aldrich Tariff Act 1913 Underwood Tariff Act Federal Reserve Act	1904 *U.S. v. Northern Securities* orders dissolution of a company ruled a monopoly under the Sherman Act
1912 Massachusetts minimum wage law for women and children	1914 Federal Trade Commission Act Clayton Antitrust Act 1916 Seamen's Act	1905 *Lochner v. New York* invalidates a state law limiting hours of bakers
		1908 *Muller v. Oregon* approves a state law limiting working hours of women *Loewe v. Lawlor* (Danbury Hatters case) finds a labor boycott to be a conspiracy in restraint of trade
		1911 *U.S. v. Standard Oil* restores rule of reason as guiding principle in antitrust cases

ton seemed remote from the battles that they were waging in their cities and states. But progressivism was bound to come to the capital. In 1906 Robert La Follette moved from the governor's office in Wisconsin to the U.S. Senate. Other seasoned progressives, also ambitious for a wider stage, made the same move. By 1910 a highly vocal progressive bloc was making itself heard in both houses of Congress.

The crucial entry point of progressivism into national politics was not Congress, however, but the presidency. This was partly because the White House was a "bully pulpit," to use Theodore Roosevelt's phrase, for mobilizing opinion and defining national issues. But just as important was the twist of fate that brought Roosevelt—the epitome of the progressive politician—to the White House on September 14, 1901.

The Making of a Progressive President

Except for his aristocratic background, Theodore Roosevelt was cut from much the same cloth as other progressive politicians. Born in 1858, he came from a wealthy old-line New York family, attended Harvard, and might have chosen the life of a leisured literary gentleman. Instead, scarcely out of college, he plunged into

Republican politics, and in 1882 entered the New York state legislature. His reasons matched the high-minded motives of other budding progressives. Like most of them, Roosevelt had received a moralistic, Christian upbringing. A political career would enable him to act constructively on those beliefs. Roosevelt always identified himself—loudly—with the side of righteousness, but he did not scorn power and its uses. He showed contempt for the amateurism of the Mugwumps— "those political and literary hermaphrodites," he called them—and much preferred the professionalism of party politics. Roosevelt rose in the New York party because he skillfully translated his moral fervor into broad popular support and thus forced himself on reluctant state Republican bosses.

After returning from the Spanish-American War as the hero of San Juan Hill (see Chapter 22), Roosevelt won the New York governorship in 1898. During his single term he clearly signaled his reformist inclinations by pushing through civil-service reform and a tax on corporate franchises. He discharged the corrupt superintendent of insurance over the Republican party's objections and asserted his confidence in the government's capacity to improve the life of the people.

Hoping to neutralize him, the party bosses promoted Roosevelt in 1900 to what normally would have been a dead-end job as William McKinley's vice-president. Roosevelt accepted reluctantly. But on September 6, 1901, an anarchist named Leon F. Czolgosz shot the president. When McKinley died eight days later, Roosevelt became president. It was a sure bet, groaned Republican boss Mark Hanna, that "that damn cowboy" would make trouble in the White House.

Roosevelt in fact moved cautiously. In his first official statement he reassured the nation that he would "continue absolutely unbroken" McKinley's policies. The conservative Republican bloc in Congress greatly limited Roosevelt's freedom of action. He treated the Senate leader, Nelson W. Aldrich of Rhode Island, with kid gloves. Much of Roosevelt's energy was devoted to consolidating his position as he skillfully used the patronage powers of the presidency to gain control of the Republican party. But Roosevelt was also restrained by uncertainty about what reform role the federal government ought to play. At first the new president might have been described as a progressive without a cause.

Even so, Roosevelt gave early evidence of his activist bent. An ardent outdoorsman, he devoted part of his first annual message to Congress to conservation. A national movement had begun late in the nineteenth century to protect the country's natural resources and scenic wonders against reckless exploitation. With the establishment of Yellowstone National Park in 1872, the national park system had been launched, and the Forest Reserve Act of 1891 began the process of withdrawing timberland from unregulated commercial use.

Unlike John Muir (see Chapter 17, page 543), Roosevelt was not a preservationist broadly opposed to exploitation of the nation's wilderness. Rather, he wanted to *conserve* the country's resources. He was not against commercial development as long as it was regulated and mindful of the public interest. Roosevelt added more than 125 million acres to the national forest reserve and brought mineral lands and water power sites into the reserve system. In 1902 he backed the Newlands Reclamation Act, which designated the proceeds from public land sales for irrigation in arid regions. His administration upgraded the management of public lands and, to the chagrin of some Republicans, energetically prosecuted violators of federal land laws. In the cause of conservation Roosevelt demonstrated his enthusiasm for exercising executive authority and his disdain for those who sought profit "by betraying the public."

The same inclinations influenced Roosevelt's handling of the anthracite coal strike of 1902. Hard coal was the main fuel for home heating in those days. As cold weather approached with no settlement in sight, the government faced a national emergency. The United Mine Workers, led by John Mitchell, were willing to submit to arbitration, but the coal operators adamantly opposed recognition of the union. Roosevelt's advisers told him there was no legal basis for federal intervention. Nevertheless, the president called both sides to a conference at the White House on October 1, 1902. When the conference failed, Roosevelt threatened the operators with a government takeover of the mines. He also persuaded the financier J. P. Morgan to use his considerable influence with them. At that point the coal operators caved in. The strike ended with the appointment by Roosevelt of an arbitration commission to rule on the issues, another unprecedented step. Roosevelt did not especially support organized labor, but he became infuriated by the "arrogant stupidity" of the mine owners.

"Of all the forms of tyranny the least attractive and the most vulgar is the tyranny of mere wealth," Roosevelt wrote in his autobiography. He was prepared to deploy all his presidential authority against the "tyranny" of irresponsible business.

The Trust Problem. The economic issue that most concerned Roosevelt was a disturbing assault on the competitive market by big business. The drift toward large-scale enterprise had been under way for many years as entrepreneurs sought the efficiencies of nationwide, vertically integrated firms (see Chapter 18, pages 561–562). But larger business units also could be used to limit competition and control markets. The depression of the 1890s, which had intensified competition and caused staggering business losses, led to a scramble to merge rival firms once economic recovery began in 1897. These mergers—*trusts*, as they were called—greatly increased the degree of business concentration in the economy. Of the seventy-three largest industrial companies in 1900, fifty-three had not existed three years earlier. By 1910, 1 percent of the nation's manufacturers accounted for 44 percent of the total industrial output.

The sheer economic power of the new combines was not their only disturbing feature. Most of them were heavily *watered*; that is, the stocks and bonds they issued greatly exceeded the real value of the properties they controlled. For their underwriting services in launching the new trusts, moreover, investment bankers such as J. P. Morgan charged huge fees. Worse yet, financiers did not relinquish control over the combines they had fathered, for they sat on the boards of directors of the new firms and exerted a backroom influence on the operating executives. Almost overnight a "money power"—a cabal of Wall Street bankers—seemed to have gained a stranglehold on the American economy.

Roosevelt's sense of the nation's uneasiness became evident as early as his first annual message, in which he referred to the "real and grave evils" of economic concentration. But what weapons could the president use in response?

The basic legal principles upholding free competition were already firmly established. Under the common law—the body of judge-made legal precedents that

Jack and the Wall Street Giants

In this vivid cartoon from the humor magazine *Puck*, Jack (Theodore Roosevelt) has come to slay the giants of Wall Street. To the country, trust-busting took on the mythic qualities of the fairy tale—with about the same amount of awe for the fearsome Wall Street giants and hope in the prowess of the intrepid Roosevelt. J. P. Morgan is the giant leering at front right.

America had inherited from Britain—it was illegal for anyone to conspire to restrain or monopolize trade; persons who were economically injured by such actions could sue for damages. These common-law rights had been enacted into statute law in many states during the 1880s and then, because the problem went beyond state jurisdictions, had been incorporated into the Sherman Antitrust Act of 1890 and had become part of federal law.

Neither the Cleveland administration nor the McKinley administration had been much inclined to enforce the Sherman Act, except against organized labor.

Of the eighteen federal suits brought before 1901, half were against trade unions. Nor were the courts any more enthusiastic about attacking business. In *U.S. v. E. C. Knight* (1895) the Supreme Court ruled that manufacturing was not covered by the Constitution's commerce clause and thus was beyond the reach of federal antitrust regulation. This ruling crippled the Sherman Act but did not kill it. The potential of the act rested above all on the fact that it incorporated common-law principles of unimpeachable validity. In the right hands, the Sherman Act could be a strong weapon against the abuse of economic power.

Trust-Busting. Roosevelt made his opening move when he strengthened the government's capacity to administer the law. In 1903, despite considerable opposition, Congress accepted Roosevelt's proposal for a Bureau of Corporations within the newly created Department of Commerce and Labor. Empowered to investigate business practices, the bureau provided the factual record on which the Justice Department could mount antitrust suits. The first suit had been filed in 1902 against the Northern Securities Company, a combination of the railroad systems of the Northwest. In a landmark 1904 decision the Supreme Court ordered Northern Securities dissolved. The next year the Court reversed the *Knight* doctrine by ruling that manufacturing fell under the commerce clause and was therefore subject to federal antitrust law.

In 1904 Roosevelt handily defeated a weak conservative Democratic candidate, Judge Alton B. Parker. Now president in his own right, Roosevelt stepped up the attack on the trusts, taking on forty-five of the nation's giant firms, including Standard Oil, American Tobacco, and DuPont. The president accompanied these actions with a rising crescendo of rhetoric. He became the nation's trustbuster, a crusader against "predatory wealth."

Despite his rhetoric, Roosevelt was not antibusiness; he regarded large-scale enterprise as a natural result of modern industrialism. Only firms that abused their power deserved punishment. But how would those companies be identified? Under the common law and under the Sherman Act as originally intended, it had been up to the courts to decide whether an act in restraint of trade was "unreasonable," that is, actually harmed potential competitors or damaged the public interest. This was a highly flexible arrangement that allowed the courts to evaluate the actions of corporations on a case-by-case basis. In 1897, however, the Supreme Court had repudiated this "rule of reason" in the *Trans-Missouri* case. Now, even if the impact on the market was not harmful, actions that restrained or monopolized trade would automatically put a firm in violation of the Sherman Act.

Little noticed when it was first decided, *Trans-Missouri* placed Roosevelt in an awkward position when he began to enforce the Sherman Act. Roosevelt had no desire to hamstring legitimate business activity, but he could not rely on the courts to distinguish between "good" and "bad" trusts. The only solution was for Roosevelt to assume that responsibility. This the president could do because it was up to him—or his attorney general—to decide whether or not to initiate antitrust prosecutions in the first place.

That Roosevelt would use this discretionary power became clear in November 1904, shortly after the Bureau of Corporations began to investigate the United States Steel Corporation. The company's chairman, Elbert H. Gary, asked for a meeting with Roosevelt. Gary proposed an arrangement: cooperation in exchange for preferential treatment. The company would open its books to the Bureau of Corporations; if the bureau found evidence of wrongdoing, the company would be advised privately and given a chance to set matters right. Roosevelt accepted this "gentlemen's agreement," which was followed by one with International Harvester the next year. J. P. Morgan controlled both firms, and from his standpoint the arrangement seemed entirely sensible. Two great powers, one political and the other economic, would meet as equals and settle matters between them. For Roosevelt, the gentlemen's agreements solved a serious dilemma: he could accommodate the realities of the modern industrial order while maintaining his public image as the champion against the trusts.

Railroad Regulation. Abuse of economic power by the railroads posed a different kind of problem for Roosevelt. As quasi-public enterprises, the railroads had always been subject to public regulation. Initially, this had been the responsibility of the states, but with the passage of the Interstate Commerce Act of 1887, the federal government had entered the field, establishing in the Interstate Commerce Commission (ICC) the nation's first federal regulatory agency. As with the Sherman Act, however, railroad regulation remained pretty much a dead letter in its early years. Restrained by a hostile Supreme Court, the ICC lapsed into inactivity. Roosevelt was convinced, however, that the railroads needed firm regulation. The Elkins Act of 1903 empowered the ICC to act against discriminatory rebates, that is, reductions on published rates for preferred or powerful customers. Then, with the 1904 election behind him, Roosevelt made his push for a major expansion of railroad regulation.

The central issue was the setting of rates. Roosevelt considered it essential that the ICC have that power. Senator Nelson Aldrich and his conservative bloc opposed it just as firmly. In 1906, after nearly two years of wrangling, Congress passed the Hepburn Railway Act, which empowered the ICC to set maximum rates upon complaint of a shipper and to prescribe uniform methods of bookkeeping. But as a concession to the conservative bloc the courts retained broad powers to review ICC rate decisions.

The Hepburn Act was a triumph of Roosevelt's skills as a political operator. He had maneuvered brilliantly against determined opposition and had come away with the essentials of what he wanted. Despite grumbling by Senate progressives critical of any compromise, Roosevelt was satisfied. He had achieved a landmark expansion of the government's regulatory powers over business.

Consumer Protection. The regulation of consumer products, another hallmark of progressive reform, was very much the handiwork of muckraking journalists. In 1905 Samuel Hopkins Adams published a series of eye-opening articles on the patent-medicine business in *Collier's*. The first paragraph opened with these riveting words:

J. Pierpont Morgan
J. P. Morgan was a giant among American financiers. He had served an apprenticeship in investment banking under his father, a leading Anglo-American banker in London. A gruff man of few words, Morgan had a genius for instilling trust and the strength of will to persuade others to follow his lead and do his bidding—qualities the great photographer Edward Steichen captured in this portrait.

Gullible America will spend this year some seventy-five millions of dollars in the purchase of patent medicines. In consideration of this sum it will swallow huge quantities of alcohol, an appalling amount of opiates and narcotics, a wide assortment of varied drugs ranging from powerful and dangerous heart depressants to insidious liver stimulants; and, far in excess of all other ingredients, undiluted fraud. For fraud, exploited by the skillfullest of advertising bunco men, is the basis of the trade.

Numerous pure food and drug bills introduced in Congress in 1905 had been stymied by industry lobbies. Then, in 1906, Upton Sinclair's novel *The Jungle* appeared. Sinclair meant to expose labor exploitation in Chicago meat-packing plants, but his graphic descriptions of rotten meat and filthy conditions excited—and sickened—the nation. President Roosevelt, previously not greatly concerned about consumer issues, entered the legislative battle, initiating a federal investigation of conditions in the stockyards and threatening to make public its harsh findings unless Congress took swift action. The Pure Food and Drug Act and the Meat Inspection Act were passed within months, and another administrative agency was added to the federal bureaucratic structure that Roosevelt was building: the Food and Drug Administration.

The Square Deal. During the 1904 presidential campaign Roosevelt had taken to calling his program the Square Deal. This kind of labeling was new to American politics. It introduced a political style that dramatized issues, mobilized public opinion, and asserted leadership. But the Square Deal meant something of substance as well. After many years of passivity and weakness, the federal government was reclaiming the role it had abandoned after the Civil War. Now, however, the target was the new economic order. When companies misused corporate power, the government had the responsibility to intercede and assure ordinary Americans a "square deal." Under Roosevelt's leadership, progressivism had come to national politics.

The Fracturing of Republican Progressivism

During his two terms as president Theodore Roosevelt struggled to bring a modern corporate economy under regulatory control. He was well aware, however, that his Square Deal was built on nineteenth-century foundations; in particular, antitrust doctrine, which was aimed at enforcing competition, seemed inadequate to the demands of a large-scale industrial order. A better approach, Roosevelt felt, would be to give the federal government administrative powers to oversee and regu-

late big business. In his final presidential speeches Roosevelt dwelled on the need for a reform agenda for the twentieth century. When he left office in 1909 he thought he had arranged matters so that there would be steady movement in that direction. He was mistaken. By the time Roosevelt returned from a yearlong safari in Africa, turmoil reigned in Washington.

The Presidency of William Howard Taft. The agents of historical change sometimes take strange forms. A person out of tune with the times can, by the sheer friction he or she generates, serve as the catalyst for great events. Such was the fate of William Howard Taft, Roosevelt's hand-picked successor.

Taft's Democratic opponent in the 1908 campaign was William Jennings Bryan. This was Bryan's third—and last—try for the presidency, and he made the most of it. Eloquent as ever, Bryan showed again why he was known as the Commoner, the voice of the people. He attacked the Republicans as the party of the "plutocrats" and outdid them in urging tougher antitrust legislation, lower tariffs, stricter railway regulation, and labor legislation so favorable to the unions that he gained the support of the officially nonpartisan AFL. Bryan's campaign moved the Democratic party into the

Campaigning for the Square Deal
When William McKinley ran for president in 1896, he sat on his front porch in Canton, Ohio, and received delegations of voters. That was not Theodore Roosevelt's way. He considered the presidency a "bully pulpit" and used the office brilliantly to mobilize public opinion and assert his leadership. The preeminence of the presidency in American public life began with Roosevelt's administration. Here, at the height of his crusading powers, he stumps for the Square Deal in the 1904 election.

mainstream of national progressive politics, but that was not enough to offset Taft's advantages as Roosevelt's candidate.

Taft won comfortably, if by a smaller margin than Roosevelt's smashing 1904 victory, and he entered the White House with a mandate to pick up where Roosevelt had left off.

William Howard Taft was an estimable man in many ways. He had been an able jurist and a superb administrator. He had served Roosevelt loyally and well as governor-general of the Philippines and as secretary of war. He was an avowed Square Dealer. But he was not by nature a progressive politician. Taft was incapable of dramatizing issues or stirring the people. He disliked the give-and-take of politics, distrusted power, and generally deferred to Congress. In fundamental ways, moreover, Taft was deeply conservative. He sanctified property rights, revered the processes of the law, and, unlike Roosevelt, found it hard to trim his means to fit his ends.

By 1909 the ferment of reform had unsettled the Republican party. On the right, the conservatives were girding themselves against further losses. Under Senator Aldrich they were still a force to be reckoned with both on Capitol Hill and within the party. On the left, progressive Republicans were rebellious. They had broad popular support—especially in the Midwest—and, in Robert La Follette, a fiery leader. They felt that Roosevelt had made too many concessions to business interests. With the resourceful Roosevelt gone from the White House, the Congressional progressives were determined to have their way. Reconciling these conflicting forces within the Republican party would have been a daunting task for the most accomplished politician. For Taft, it spelled disaster.

First there was the tariff. Progressives generally considered high tariffs to be a major cause of the decline of competition and the rise of the trusts. Taft had campaigned for a "sizable reduction." During the lengthy drafting process, however, he was won over by the conservative Republican bloc and gave his approval for the protectionist Payne-Aldrich Tariff Act of 1909, which favored eastern industry.

Next came the battle over "Uncle Joe" Cannon, Speaker of the House of Representatives. A dyed-in-the-wool conservative, Cannon controlled the flow of legislation in the House. Progressives were determined to depose him. Taft abandoned them in exchange for Cannon's help on administration legislation. When a House revolt finally broke the Speaker's power in 1910, Cannon's defeat was regarded as a defeat for the president as well.

Equally damaging to Taft was the Ballinger-Pinchot affair. U.S. Chief Forester Gifford Pinchot, an ardent conservationist and a chum of Roosevelt's, accused Sec-

retary of the Interior Richard A. Ballinger of conspiring to transfer public coal lands in Alaska to a private syndicate. When Pinchot made the charges public in January 1910, Taft fired him for insubordination. The fact that Taft was actually a dedicated conservationist somehow did not matter. In the eyes of the progressives the Ballinger-Pinchot affair marked Taft for life as a friend of the "interests" plundering the nation's resources.

Solemnly pledged to carry on in Roosevelt's tradition, Taft found himself propelled into the conservative Republican camp. And largely in reaction to Taft, the reformers in the party turned into a distinct, organized faction. By 1910 they were calling themselves "Progressives" or, in more belligerent moments, "Insurgents." Taft responded by trying to purge them in the Republican primaries that year. This vendetta climaxed Taft's record of clumsy leadership.

The Progressive Insurgency. The Progressives emerged from the 1910 elections stronger and angrier. In January 1911 they formed the National Progressive Republican League and began a drive to take over the Republican party. La Follette was the Progressives' leader and designated presidential candidate, but they knew that their best chance to win lay with Theodore Roosevelt.

Roosevelt, home from Africa, yearned to reenter the political fray. He was not easily reconciled to the absence of power and would have been troublesome for Taft under any circumstances. As it was, the president's handling of the Progressives fed Roosevelt's mounting sense of outrage. But Roosevelt was too loyal a party man to defy the Republican establishment and too astute a politician not to recognize that a party split would benefit the Democrats. He could be spurred into rebellion only by the discovery of a true clash of principles. On the question of the trusts, just such a clash materialized.

From the start Roosevelt had been troubled by the Sherman Antitrust Act. Enforcing competition seemed to him to fly in the face of the inevitable tendency toward economic concentration. By distinguishing between good and bad trusts, Roosevelt had managed to reconcile public policy and economic reality. But this was a makeshift solution that depended on a president who was willing to stretch his powers to the limit. Taft had no such inclination. His legalistic mind rebelled at the notion that he as president should decide which trusts should be prosecuted. The Sherman Act was on the books. "We are going to enforce that law or die in the attempt," Taft promised grimly.

In its *Standard Oil* decision (1911) the Supreme Court eased Taft's problem by reasserting the common-law principle of the "rule of reason" in antitrust actions: once again, it would be up to the courts to distinguish between good and bad trusts. With that burden lifted from the executive branch, Attorney General George W. Wickersham stepped up the pace of antitrust actions.

The United States Steel Corporation immediately became a prime target. Among the charges against the Steel Trust was that it had violated the antimonopoly provision of the Sherman Act by acquiring the Tennessee Coal and Iron Company (TCI). The purchase had been made in 1907 from a banking house that had fallen into trouble and urgently needed to sell its TCI stock to raise capital. Roosevelt had personally approved the acquisition as a necessary step—as U.S. Steel representatives had explained it to him—to prevent a financial collapse on Wall Street. Taft's suit against U.S. Steel thus amounted to an attack on Roosevelt: he had as president entered into a private agreement with U.S. Steel to circumvent the Sherman Act. Nothing was better calculated to propel Roosevelt into action than an issue that was both an affair of personal honor and a question of broad principle.

The New Nationalism. The country did not have to choose between breaking up big business and submitting to corporate rule, Roosevelt argued. There was a third way. The federal government could be empowered to oversee big business to make sure it acted in the public interest. The tool would be a federal trade commission with powers comparable to those exerted by the Interstate Commerce Commission over the railroads. Industrial corporations would be treated in effect as if they were natural monopolies or public utilities and would be placed under direct public oversight.

In a speech in Osawatomie, Kansas, in August 1910 Roosevelt made his case for what he called the New Nationalism. The central issue, he argued, was human welfare versus property rights. In modern society property had to be controlled "to whatever degree the public welfare may require it." The government would become "the steward of the public welfare."

This formulation removed the restraints from Roosevelt's thinking. Ultimately, he did not stop short of advocating government price-fixing for corporate industry. He took up the cause of social justice, adding to his program a federal child labor law, federal workers' compensation, regulation of labor relations, and a national minimum wage for women. Most radical, perhaps, was Roosevelt's attack on the legal system. Insisting that the courts should not be making social policy, Roosevelt proposed sharp curbs on their powers, even raising the possibility of popular recall of court decisions.

Beyond these specifics, the New Nationalism presented a new political philosophy. The key source was a book by the journalist Herbert Croly, *The Promise of American Life* (1909), which called for a uniting of rival strains in the American political tradition. From Hamilton's federalism Croly drew his emphasis on strong national government; from Jefferson's republicanism came Croly's enthusiasm for democracy and the primacy of the interests of the common citizen. The result, however, was a genuine break from America's political past. The New Nationalism offered a *statist* solution—an enormous expansion of the role of the federal government—to the problem of corporate power.

Early in 1912 Roosevelt announced his candidacy for the presidency and immediately swept the Progressive Republicans into his camp. A bitter and divisive party battle ensued in which Taft proved to be a tenacious opponent. Roosevelt won the states that held primary elections, but Taft controlled the party organizations elsewhere. Dominated by the party regulars, the Republican convention chose Taft.

Roosevelt, considering himself cheated out of the nomination, led his followers into a new Progressive party that was soon nicknamed the "Bull Moose" party. In a crusading campaign Roosevelt offered the New Nationalism to the people.

Woodrow Wilson and the New Freedom

While the Republicans battled among themselves, the Democrats were on the move. The scars caused by the free silver campaign of 1896 had faded, and in the 1908 campaign William Jennings Bryan had established the progressive credentials of the rejuvenated party. The Democrats made dramatic gains in 1910, taking over the House of Representatives for the first time since 1892, winning ten Senate seats, and capturing a number of traditionally Republican governorships. After fourteen years as the party's standard-bearer, Bryan reluctantly made way for a new generation of leaders.

The ablest was Woodrow Wilson of New Jersey. Wilson was an academic, a noted political scientist who, as president of Princeton, had brought it into the front rank of American universities. In 1910, without any experience with public office, he left Princeton to accept the Democratic nomination for governor of New Jersey. Wilson compiled a brilliant record: he cleaned up the boss system and passed a direct primary law, workers' compensation, and stronger regulation of railroads and utilities. With those credentials as a reformer, Wilson went on, in a bruising battle, to win the Democratic presidential nomination in 1912.

Wilson possessed, to a fault, the moral certainty that characterized the progressive politician. He almost instinctively assumed the mantle of righteousness and showed little tolerance for the views of his critics. Only gradually, however, did Wilson hammer out, in reaction to Roosevelt's New Nationalism, a coherent reform program, which he called the New Freedom.

HARPER'S WEEKLY
EDITED BY GEORGE HARVEY

July 13 1912   THE NEW RIDER   Price 10 Cents

On to the White House

At the Democratic convention Woodrow Wilson only narrowly defeated the front-runner, Champ Clark of Missouri. *Harper's Weekly* triumphantly depicted Wilson immediately after his nomination—the scholar turned politician riding off on the Democratic donkey, with his running mate, Thomas R. Marshall, hanging on behind. The magazine's editor, George Harvey, had identified Wilson as presidential timber back in 1906, long before the Princeton president had thought of politics, and had worked on his behalf from then on.

It is important to recognize how much ground Wilson shared with Roosevelt. *"The old time of individual competition is probably gone by,"* Wilson stressed. "We will do business henceforth, when we do it on a great and successful scale, by means of corporations." Like Roosevelt, Wilson opposed not bigness but the abuse of economic power. Nor did Wilson think that the abuse of power could be prevented without a strong federal government. He parted company from Roosevelt over *how* the authority of government should be used to restrain private power.

Roosevelt's advocacy of direct public control over corporations was anathema to Wilson. As he warmed to the debate, Wilson cast the issue in the fundamental terms of slavery and freedom. "This is a struggle for emancipation," he proclaimed in October 1912. "If America is not to have free enterprise, then she can have

freedom of no sort whatever." Wilson also scorned Roosevelt's social program. Welfare might be benevolent, he declared, but it also would be paternalistic and contrary to the traditions of a free people. The New Nationalism represented a future of collectivism, Wilson warned, whereas the New Freedom would preserve the political and economic liberties of the individual.

How, then, did Wilson propose to deal with the problem of corporate power? Court enforcement of the Sherman Act was Wilson's basic answer. His task was to figure out how to make that long-established antitrust approach work better. In this effort Wilson relied heavily on a new adviser, Louis D. Brandeis, famous as the "people's lawyer" for his public service in many progressive causes (including the landmark *Muller* case).

An expert on regulatory matters, Brandeis understood that an all-powerful trade commission was likely to end up not as a defender of the public interest but in a cozy relationship with the industries it was supposed to regulate. Nor did Brandeis believe that bigness meant efficiency. On the contrary, he argued that trusts were wasteful compared with firms that vigorously competed in a free market. The main thing was to prevent the trusts from unfairly using their power to curb free competition. It should be the aim of public policy "so [to] restrict the wrong use of competition that the right use of competition will destroy monopoly."

The 1912 election fell short of being a referendum on the New Nationalism versus the New Freedom. The outcome turned on a more humdrum reality: Wilson was elected because he kept the traditional Democratic vote while the Republicans split between Roosevelt and Taft. Although he won by a landslide in the electoral college (see Map 21.2), Wilson received only 42 percent of the popular vote, 115,000 fewer votes than Bryan had amassed against Taft in 1908.

Moreover, turnout fell substantially, from 65.4 percent of eligible voters in 1908 to 58.8 percent in 1912. If there was a beneficiary of the reform ferment sparked by the presidential campaign, it was not Wilson but the Socialist candidate, Eugene V. Debs, who captured 900,000 votes, 6 percent of the total. At best it could be said that the 1912 election signified that the American public was in the mood for reform: only 23 percent, after all, had voted for the one candidate who stood for the status quo, President Taft. Woodrow Wilson's own reform program, however, had not received a mandate from the people.

Yet anticlimactic as it might have seemed, the 1912 election proved to be a decisive event in the history of national reform. The debate between Roosevelt and Wilson had brought forth, in the New Freedom, a program capable of finally resolving the crisis over corporate power that had gripped the nation for a decade. Just as important, the election created a rare opportu-

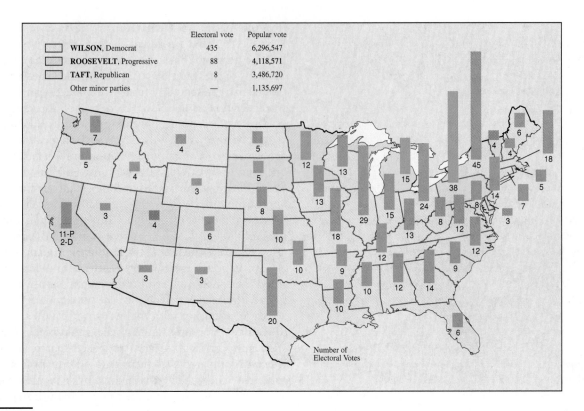

	Electoral vote	Popular vote
WILSON, Democrat	435	6,296,547
ROOSEVELT, Progressive	88	4,118,571
TAFT, Republican	8	3,486,720
Other minor parties	—	1,135,697

Number of Electoral Votes

MAP 21.2

The Election of 1912

The 1912 election reveals why the two-party system is so strongly rooted in American politics. The Democrats, although a minority party, won an electoral landslide because the Republicans divided their vote between Roosevelt and Taft. This result indicates what is at stake when major parties splinter. The Socialists, despite a record vote of 900,000, got no electoral votes. To vote Socialist in 1912 meant in effect to throw away one's vote.

nity for decisive legislative action in Washington. Wilson became president with the Democrats in firm control of both houses of Congress and united in their eagerness to get on with the New Freedom.

The New Freedom in Action. Upon entering the White House, Wilson chose a flanking attack on the problem of economic power. So long out of office, the Democrats were hungry for tariff reform. From the prevailing average of 40 percent, the Underwood Tariff Act of 1913 pared rates down to an average of 25 percent. Targeting especially the trust-dominated industries, Democrats confidently expected the Underwood Tariff to spur competition and reduce prices for consumers by opening protected American markets to foreign products.

The administration then turned to the nation's banking system, whose key weakness was the absence of a central reserve bank. The main functions of a central bank are to regulate private banks and to back them up in case they cannot meet their obligations to depositors. In practice, this role had been assumed by the great New York banks, which handled the accounts of outlying banks and assisted them when they came under pressure. However, if the New York banks weakened, the entire system could collapse. That had nearly happened in 1907, when the Knickerbocker Trust Company failed and panic swept through the nation's financial markets.

The need for a reserve system became widely accepted, but the form it should take was hotly debated.

Wall Street wanted a centralized system controlled by the bankers. Rural Democrats and their spokesman, Senator Carter Glass of Virginia, preferred a decentralized network of reserve banks. Progressives in both parties agreed that the essential feature should be public control over the reserve system. The bankers, whose practices were already under scrutiny by Congress, were on the defensive in this contest.

President Wilson, who was no expert to begin with, learned quickly and reconciled the reformers and bankers. The monumental Federal Reserve Act of 1913 gave the nation a banking system that was resistant to financial panic. The act delegated reserve functions to twelve district reserve banks, which would be controlled by their member banks. The Federal Reserve Board imposed public regulation on this regional structure. In one stroke the act strengthened the banking system and placed a measure of restraint on the "money trust."

The Clayton Act and the FTC. Having dealt with tariff and banking reform, Wilson turned to the question of corporate power. He wanted to rely on the Sherman Act but was not sure how to make its antitrust principles more effective. Brandeis had already formulated two main approaches. One was to define with precision the prohibited practices: interlocking directorates, discriminatory pricing, and exclusive contracts that shut out competitors. The second approach was to create a new federal trade commission that would aid the executive branch in administering the antitrust laws.

Both approaches contained knotty problems. Was it feasible to make strict definitions of illegal practices? Brandeis finally decided that it was not, and Wilson assented. In the Clayton Antitrust Act of 1914, revising the Sherman Act, the definition of illegal practices was modified by these crucial words: "where the effect may be to substantially lessen competition or tend to create a monopoly in any line of commerce." As for the trade commission, the problem was: How much power and what functions should it have? Wilson was understandably sensitive on this matter, given his principled opposition to Roosevelt's conception of a powerful trade commission overseeing American business. Initially Wilson wanted only an advisory, information-gathering agency. But ultimately, under the 1914 law establishing it, the Federal Trade Commission (FTC) received broader powers to investigate companies and issue "cease and desist" orders against unfair trade practices that violated antitrust law. FTC decisions, however, were subject to court review, so that Wilson's entire program was situated within the original conception of antitrust enforcement. As before, it would ultimately be up to the courts to decide which business practices were illegal.

Despite a good deal of commotion, this arduous legislative process was actually an exercise in consensus building. Wilson himself had opened the debate in a conciliatory way. "The antagonism between business and government is over," he said, and the time was ripe for a program representing the "best business judgment in America." Afterward, Wilson felt he had brought the long controversy over corporate power to a successful conclusion, and in fact he had. Steering a course between Taft's conservatism and Roosevelt's radicalism, Wilson carved out a middle way—what the historian Martin J. Sklar has termed "corporate liberalism." This middle way brought to bear the powers of government without threatening the constitutional order and dealt to some degree with abuse of corporate power without threatening the capitalist system.

Wilson's Social Program. On social policy, too, Wilson carved out a middle way. During the 1912 campaign he had denounced the social program of the New Nationalism as paternalistic. Compared with his accommodation to big business, Wilson was resistant to special legislation for workers and farmers. He accepted cosmetic language in the Clayton Act stating that labor and farm organizations were not illegal combinations, but he rejected exempting them from antitrust prosecution.

The labor vote had grown increasingly important to the Democratic party, however. As his second presidential campaign drew nearer, Wilson lost some of his scruples about prolabor legislation. In 1915 and 1916 he championed a host of bills beneficial to American workers: a model federal workers' compensation law, a federal child labor law, the Adamson eight-hour law for railroad workers, and the landmark Seamen's Act, which eliminated age-old abuses of sailors aboard ship and granted them the individual rights held by other workers. Likewise, after stubborn earlier resistance, Wilson approved in 1916 the Federal Farm Loan Act, providing the low-interest rural credit system long demanded by farmers.

Wilson encountered the same dilemma that confronted all successful progressives: the claims of moral principle versus the unyielding realities of political and economic life. Progressives were high-minded but not radical. They saw evils in the system, but they did not consider the system itself evil. Furthermore, they prided themselves on being realists as well as moralists. So it stood to reason that Wilson, like other progressives who achieved power, would find his place at the center.

Summary

A new chapter in American reform began at the start of the twentieth century. For decades the problems resulting from industrialization and urban growth had been mounting. Now, after 1900, reform activity began to dominate the nation's public life. The unifying element in progressive reform was a common intellectual outlook, highly principled and idealistic as to goals and confident of the human capacity to find the means.

Beyond this shared outlook, progressives broke up into diverse and often conflicting groups. Political reformers included business groups concerned chiefly with improving the efficiency of city government, while other progressives, such as Robert La Follette, opposed privilege and wanted to democratize the political process. Both groups worked to enhance their power at the expense of entrenched party machines.

Social welfare became the province of American women, and that effort reinvigorated the struggle for women's rights. In the cities, working people and immigrants also became reform-minded and set in motion a new political force—urban liberalism. While progressivism was infected by the prevailing racism in American life, there was a reform wing that joined with black activists to forge the major institutions of black protest and uplift of the twentieth century: the National Association for the Advancement of Colored People and the Urban League.

At the national level, progressives focused primarily on controlling the economic power of corporate business. This overriding problem led to Theodore Roosevelt's Square Deal, then to his New Nationalism, and finally to Woodrow Wilson's New Freedom. The role of the federal government expanded dramatically, but in service to a cautious and pragmatic approach to the problems of the country.

TIMELINE

1887	Interstate Commerce Commission established
1889	Jane Addams and Ellen Gates Starr found Hull House
1890	Sherman Antitrust Act
1893	Economic depression (until 1897)
1899	National Consumers' League founded
1900	Robert M. La Follette elected Wisconsin governor First commission form of city government in Galveston, Texas
1901	President McKinley assassinated; Theodore Roosevelt succeeds United States Steel Corporation formed
1902	President Roosevelt settles national anthracite strike
1903	National Women's Trade Union League
1904	Supreme Court dissolves the Northern Securities Company
1905	*Lochner v. New York* overturns law restricting length of the workday
1906	Hepburn Railway Act AFL adopts Bill of Grievances Upton Sinclair's *The Jungle*
1908	*Muller v. Oregon* upholds regulation of working hours for women Federal Council of Churches founded William Howard Taft elected president
1909	NAACP formed Herbert Croly's *Promise of American Life*
1910	Roosevelt announces the New Nationalism Woman suffrage movement revives; suffrage victory in Washington State
1911	*Standard Oil* decision restores "rule of reason" Triangle Shirtwaist fire
1912	Progressive party formed Woodrow Wilson elected president
1913	Federal Reserve Act Underwood Tariff
1914	Clayton Antitrust Act

★   ★   ★

BIBLIOGRAPHY

The most recent survey of the Progressive Era is John Milton Cooper, *Pivotal Decades: The United States, 1900–1920* (1990). Two older but still serviceable narrative accounts are George E. Mowry, *The Era of Theodore Roosevelt, 1900–1912* (1958), and Arthur S. Link, *Woodrow Wilson and the Progressive Era, 1910–1917* (1954). A highly influential interpretation of progressive reform that is worth reading despite its disputed central arguments, is Richard Hofstadter, *The Age of Reform* (1955). Robert H. Wiebe, *The Search for Order, 1877–1920* (1967), places progressive reform in a broader context of organizational development. On the debate over progressivism as a movement see Daniel Rodgers, "In Search of Progressivism," *Reviews in American History* 10 (1982).

The Course of Reform

The progressive mind has been studied from many different angles. The religious underpinnings are stressed in Robert M. Crunden, *Ministers of Reform: The Progressives' Achievement in American Civilization, 1889–1920* (1982). In *The New Radicalism in America, 1889–1963* (1965), Christopher Lasch sees progressivism as a form of cultural revolt. Samuel Haber traces the influence of Frederick W. Taylor in *Efficiency and Uplift: Scientific Management in the Progressive Era* (1964). On the intellectual basis for progressivism the key book is Morton G. White, *Social Thought in America: The Revolt against Formalism* (1975). Most useful on political thinkers is Charles Forcey, *The Crossroads of Liberalism: Croly, Weyl, Lippmann, and the Progressive Era* (1961). A provocative study set in an international context is James T. Kloppenberg, *Uncertain Victory: Social Democracy and Progressivism in European and American Thought, 1870–1920* (1986). On the journalists see David M. Chalmers, *The Social and Political Ideas of the Muckrakers* (1964), and Harold S. Wilson, *McClure's Magazine and the Muckrakers* (1970).

Political reform has been the subject of a voluminous literature. Wisconsin progressivism can be studied in David P. Thelen, *The New Citizenship: Origins of Progressivism in Wisconsin, 1885–1900* (1972). Important progressives are discussed in Spencer C. Olin, *California's Prodigal Son: Hiram Johnson and the Progressive Movement* (1968), and Richard Lowitt, *George W. Norris: The Making of a Progressive* (1963). On city reform see Bradley R. Rice, *Progressive Cities: The Commission Government Movement* (1972); Jack Tager, *The Intellectual as Urban Reformer: Brand Whitlock and the Progressive Movement* (1968); and Melvin G. Holli, *Reform in Detroit: Hazen S. Pingree and Urban Politics* (1969).

The best treatment of the settlement-house movement is Allen F. Davis, *Spearheads of Reform* (1967). Allen F. Davis, *American Heroine: Jane Addams* (1973); George Martin, *Madame Secretary: Frances Perkins* (1976); and Kathryn Kish Sklar, *Florence Kelley and the Nation's Work: The Rise of Women's Political Culture* (1995), deal with leading woman progressives. The connection to working women is effectively treated in Nancy S. Dye, *As Equals and Sisters: Feminism, the Labor Movement, and the Women's Trade Union League of New York* (1980). Women garment workers, the key labor constituency for women progressives, are studied with great skill and insight in Susan A. Glenn, *Daughters of the Shtetl:*

Life and Labor in the Immigrant Generation (1990). Two pathbreaking books on the origins of American feminism are Rosalind Rosenberg, *Beyond Separate Spheres: The Intellectual Origins of Modern Feminism* (1982), and Nancy F. Cott, *The Grounding of Modern Feminism* (1987). The leading social reformer to spring from feminism is treated in Ellen Chesler, *Woman of Valor: Margaret Sanger and the Birth Control Movement* (1992).

On urban liberalism the standard book is John D. Buenker, *Urban Liberalism and Progressive Reform* (1973). The relationship to organized labor can be followed in Irwin Yellowitz, *Labor and the Progressive Movement in New York State* (1965). Two important recent books by historical sociologists treat the halting progress toward the welfare state: Theda Skocpol, *Protecting Soldiers and Mothers* (1992), and, in a comparison of the United States with Canada and Britain, Ann Shola Orloff, *The Politics of Pensions* (1993). The most comprehensive survey is Morton Keller, *Regulating a New Society: Public Policy and Social Change In America, 1900–1933* (1994). On the South see Dewey Grantham, *Southern Progressivism* (1983), and on the racial conservatism of social progressives see Elizabeth Lasch-Quinn, *Black Neighbors: Race and the Limits of Reform in the American Settlement-House Movement* (1993). The revival of black protest is vigorously described in Stephen R. Fox, *The Guardian of Boston: William Monroe Trotter* (1971), and David Levering Lewis, *W. E. B. Du Bois: Biography of a Race, 1868–1919* (1993).

Progressivism and National Politics

National progressivism is best approached through its leading figures. John Milton Cooper, *The Warrior and the Priest* (1983), is a provocative joint biography of Roosevelt and Wilson that emphasizes their shared world view. Other good biographies include John Morton Blum, *The Republican Roosevelt* (1954); Donald E. Anderson, *William Howard Taft* (1973); John Morton Blum, *Woodrow Wilson and the Politics of Morality* (1956); and Melvin I. Urofsky, *Louis D. Brandeis and the Progressive Tradition* (1981). Lewis S. Gould, *The Presidency of Theodore Roosevelt* (1991), provides a useful synthesis. Aspects of national progressive politics can be followed in James Penick, *Progressive Politics and Conservation: The Ballinger-Pinchot Affair* (1968); James Holt, *Congressional Insurgents and the Party System* (1969); and David Sarasohn, *The Party of Reform: The Democrats in the Progressive Era* (1989). On the socialists, in addition to the books cited in Chapter 18, see Aileèn S. Kraditor, *The Radical Persuasion, 1890–1917* (1981), and James Weinstein, *The Decline of American Socialism, 1912–1925* (1967). Naomi Lamoreaux, *The Great Merger Movement in American Business, 1895–1904* (1985), offers a sophisticated modern analysis of trust activity, and Thomas K. McCraw, ed., *Regulation in Perspective* (1981), contains valuable interpretative essays on the problems of trust regulation. Albro Martin, *Enterprise Denied: The Origins of the Decline of American Railroads, 1897–1917* (1971), assesses the impact of railway regulation. A comprehensive rethinking of the progressive struggle to fashion a regulatory policy for big business is offered in Martin J. Sklar, *The Corporate Reconstruction of American Capitalism, 1890–1916: The Market, the Law, and Politics* (1988).

Battle of Santiago de Cuba, 1898

James G. Tyler's dramatic painting of the final sea battle of
the Spanish-American War showcased America's newest
weapon of war, the battleship.

An Emerging World Power

1877–1914

★　　　★　　　★

I n 1881 Great Britain sent a new envoy to Washington. He was Sir Lionel Sackville-West, son of an earl, brother-in-law of the Tory leader Lord Denby, but otherwise distinguished only as the steadfast lover of a celebrated Spanish dancer. His well-connected friends wanted to park Sir Lionel somewhere comfortable and out of harm's way, so they made him minister to the United States.

Twenty years later such an appointment would have been unthinkable. All the major European powers had by then elevated their missions in Washington to embassies and routinely staffed them with top-of-the-line ambassadors. And they treated the United States, without question, as a fellow Great Power.

When Sir Lionel arrived in Washington in 1881, the United States scarcely cast a shadow on world affairs. As a military power the United States was puny, even comical. Its army was smaller than Bulgaria's; its navy ranked thirteenth in the world and was a threat mainly to the crews on its unseaworthy ships. Twenty years later, however, the United States was flexing its muscles. It had just made short work of Spain in a brief but decisive war and acquired for itself an empire that stretched from Puerto Rico to the Philippines. America's standing as a rising naval power was manifest, and so was its aggressive assertion of national interest in the Caribbean and the Pacific.

In practice, the United States still acted as a regional power, but Europeans had become keenly aware of its capacity to cut a wider swath whenever it chose to do so. "Are we to be confronted by an American peril . . . before which the Old World is to go down to irretrievable defeat?" wondered a former French foreign minister. The notion of an "American peril" became a lively topic after 1900 among Europeans surveying the industrial and military potential of the United States. No one could be sure what America's role would be, since the

United States retained its traditional policy of nonalignment in European affairs. But in chanceries across the Continent, the importance of the United States was universally acknowledged and its likely response to every event was carefully assessed.

How the United States emerged onto the world stage in the decades before World War I is the subject of this chapter.

The Roots of Expansionism

In 1880 the United States had a population of 50 million and by that measure ranked with the great European powers. It was the world's leading producer of wheat and cotton. In industrial production the United States was second only to Britain and was rapidly closing the gap. Anyone who doubted the military prowess of Americans needed only to recall the ferocity with which they had fought one another in the Civil War. The great campaigns of Lee, Sherman, and Grant entered the military textbooks and were closely studied by army strategists everywhere. In the encounter between the *Monitor* and the *Merrimack* at Hampton Roads on March 9, 1862, the world had seen the first example of modern naval warfare.

Nor, when its vital interests were at stake, had the United States shown itself to be lacking in diplomatic vigor. Both major crises with European powers arising from the Civil War had been settled to America's satisfaction. In 1867 France abandoned its imperial adventure in Mexico and withdrew its forces. And in 1871 Britain expressed regret for belligerent acts against the Union during the war and agreed to the arbitration of the *Alabama* claims (see Chapter 16, page 509).

Diplomacy in the Gilded Age

In the years that followed, the United States lapsed into diplomatic isolation not out of weakness but for lack of any clear national purpose in world affairs. In this industrializing age George Washington's warning against entangling alliances seemed as pertinent as it had when America had been a thinly populated land of farmers. The business of building the nation's industrial economy absorbed Americans and turned their attention inward. And while the new international telegraphic cables provided the country with swift overseas communication after the 1860s, wide oceans still kept the world at a distance and gave Americans a sense of isolation and security. Nor did European power politics, which centered on Franco-German rivalry and on nationalistic conflict in the Balkans, seem to matter very

much. As far as Cleveland's secretary of state, Thomas F. Bayard, was concerned, "we have not the slightest share or interest [in] the small politics and backstage intrigues of Europe . . . upon which we look with impatience and contempt."

As for the empire building in which the European powers were now avidly engaged, this expression of national prowess did not tempt the United States. Even so ardent an American nationalist as the young Theodore Roosevelt saw the folly of overseas expansion. "We want no unwilling citizens to enter our Union," he wrote in 1886. "European nations war for the possession of thickly settled districts which, if conquered, will for centuries remain alien and hostile to the conquerors; we, wiser in our generation, have seized the waste solitudes that lay near us."

In those circumstances, with no external threat to be seen, what was the point of maintaining a big navy? After making certain of the French departure from Mexico in 1867, the American government began to dismantle the Civil War fleet. The ships that remained on duty gradually deteriorated. Of the 125 ships on the navy's active list, only about 25 were seaworthy at any given time. No effort was made to keep up with European advances in weaponry and battleship design; the American fleet consisted mainly of sailing ships and obsolete ironclads.

During the administration of Chester A. Arthur (1881–1885) the navy began a modest upgrading program. New ships were put into service, standards for the officer corps were raised, and the Naval War College was founded. But the fleet remained small, and the squadrons lacked a unified naval command. The mission of the navy remained as before: to maintain coastal defenses and a modest cruising fleet capable of preying on enemy commerce at sea. An expenditure of 1 percent of the gross national product for the entire military establishment seemed entirely adequate in the 1880s.

The conduct of diplomacy was likewise of little account. Appointment to the foreign service was made mostly through the spoils system. American ministers and consular officers were a mixed lot, with many idlers and drunkards among the hardworking and competent. Domestic politics, moreover, made it difficult to develop a coherent program. Although foreign relations was an executive responsibility, the U.S. Senate jealously guarded its right to give "advice and consent" on treaties and diplomatic appointments. Partisan squabbling between Democrats and Republicans left the White House with even less room for maneuver. For its part the State Department tended to be inactive, exerting little control over policy or its missions abroad. It was remarkable how many actions (some of them later repudiated or simply ignored by the State Department) were taken independently by consuls and naval officers out in the field. In remote parts of the world, the American presence was often primarily religious: the intrepid missionaries bent on Christianizing the native populations of Asia, Africa, and the Pacific islands.

Latin American Diplomacy. In the Caribbean the United States remained the dominant power, but the expansionist enthusiasms of the Civil War era subsided. Nothing came of the grandiose plans of Secretary of State William H. Seward or of President Grant's efforts to purchase Santo Domingo in 1870, and the Senate regularly blocked later moves to acquire bases in Haiti, Cuba, and Venezuela. The long-cherished interest in an interoceanic canal across Central America also faded. Despite pronouncing that no one else should build such a canal, the United States stood by when a French company headed by the builder of the Suez Canal, Ferdinand de Lesseps, started to dig across the Panama isthmus in 1880. That project failed after a decade, but the reason was bankruptcy, not American opposition.

On becoming secretary of state in 1881, James G. Blaine engaged in a flurry of diplomatic activity in Latin America. He got involved in a border dispute between Mexico and Guatemala, tried to settle a war Chile was waging against Peru and Bolivia, and called the first Pan-American conference. Blaine's interventions in Latin American disputes went badly, however, and his successor canceled the Pan-American conference after Blaine left office in late 1881. This was a characteristic instance of Gilded Age diplomacy, driven partly by partisan politics and carried out without any clear sense of national purpose.

Pan-Americanism—the notion of a community of American states—took root, however, and in 1888 Congress asked President Cleveland to call a conference of American states to promote trade and peace in the Western Hemisphere. Blaine, returning in 1889 for a second stint at the State Department under the new Republican administration of Benjamin Harrison, took up the plans that had already been made for a new Pan-American conference. An impressive agenda called for a customs union, improved communications, and arbitration treaties. But the only result was the creation of an agency in Washington that was later named the Pan-American Union. Any Latin American goodwill won by Blaine's efforts was soon blasted by the humiliation the United States visited upon Chile because of a riot against American sailors in the port of Valparaiso in 1891. Threatened with war, Chile was forced to apologize to the United States and pay an indemnity of $75,000.

Pacific Episodes. In the Pacific, American interest centered on Hawaii. American missionaries had long been active among the islanders. With a climate ideal for rais-

Sugar Cane Plantation, Hawaii
Over 300,000 Asians from China, Japan, Korea, and the Philippines came to work in the Hawaiian cane fields between 1850 and 1920. The hardships they endured are reflected in plantation work songs, such as this one by Japanese laborers:

> *Hawaii, Hawaii*
> *But when I came what I saw was Hell*
> *The boss was Satan*
> *The lunas [overseers] his helpers.*

ing sugarcane, Hawaii also attracted American planters and investors. Nominally an independent nation with its own monarchy, Hawaii came increasingly within the American orbit. An 1875 treaty granted Hawaiian sugar duty-free entry to the American market and declared the islands off limits to other powers. A second treaty in 1887 gave the United States naval rights at Pearl Harbor.

Having encouraged the sugar economy in Hawaii, the United States abruptly withdrew Hawaii's trading advantages in the McKinley Tariff of 1890 by removing the duty on all foreign sugar while granting domestic producers a special subsidy to compensate for the drop in sugar prices. Anxious to gain the same benefit, American planters in Hawaii began to plot for annexation to the United States. Aided by the U.S. minister to Hawaii and with American sailors conspicuously present, they revolted in January 1893 against Queen Liliuokalani. Within a month the provisional government that they installed negotiated a treaty of annexation with the Harrison administration. Before annexation could be approved by the Senate, however, Grover Cleveland returned to the presidency and, after an investigation of the Hawaiian episode, withdrew the treaty. To annex Hawaii, he declared, would violate both America's "honor and morality" and its "unbroken tradition" against acquiring territory far from the nation's shores.

The American presence elsewhere in the Pacific had meanwhile grown stronger. In the northern Pacific this was the result of the 1867 purchase of Alaska from imperial Russia, which gave the United States not only a huge territory with vast natural resources but an unlooked-for presence stretching across the northern Pacific.

Far to the south, with even less forethought, the United States had become involved in the remote Samoan islands. In 1878 the United States secured the right to a coaling station in Pago Pago harbor—a key link on the route to Australia—and in exchange promised local Polynesian leaders to use its good offices in Samoa's relations with other foreign powers. An informal protectorate resulted. In the mid-1880s Germany began to press its claims to the islands, and the United States, stung by German arrogance, responded with equal fervor. In 1889 naval warfare might have broken out but for a fierce hurricane that wrecked the German and American fleets. At that point, agreement on a tripartite protectorate (the third European power was Britain) averted further strife and preserved American rights in Pago Pago.

American diplomacy in these years has been characterized as a series of incidents, not the pursuit of a foreign *policy*. Many things happened, but intermittently and without a plan, driven by individuals and pressure groups, not by any well-founded and coherent conception of national objectives. This was possible because, as the Englishman James Bryce remarked in 1888, America still sailed "upon a summer sea." In the stormier waters that lay ahead, a different kind of American diplomacy would be required.

Economic Sources of Expansionism

"A policy of isolation did well enough when we were an embryo nation," remarked Senator Orville Platt of Connecticut in 1893. "But today things are different. . . . We are 65 million people, the most advanced and powerful on earth, and regard to our future welfare demands an abandonment of the doctrines of isolation."

America's gross national product quadrupled between 1870 and 1900, and industrial output quintupled. But were there sufficient markets to absorb the staggering volume of goods flowing from America's farms and factories? It was true that America itself constituted an enormous market. Over 90 percent of American output in the late nineteenth century was consumed at home. Even so, foreign markets were important. Roughly a fifth of the nation's agricultural output was exported, and for the major staple crops—cotton, wheat, tobacco—the proportion was much higher, up to 80 percent, for example, in the case of cotton.

As the industrial economy expanded, so did factory exports. Between 1880 and 1900, the industrial share of total exports jumped from 15 percent to over 30 percent. Although only 9 percent of manufactured output went overseas in 1900, the export share in key industries was much larger: 57 percent for petroleum products, 50 percent for copper, 25 percent for sewing machines, and 15 percent for iron and steel.

The importance of foreign sales was evident in the efforts of major firms to develop overseas production and marketing facilities. As early as 1868 the pioneering Singer Sewing Machine Company established its first foreign plant in Glasgow, Scotland. The most prominent American firm doing business abroad was Standard Oil. Beginning with the Anglo-American Oil Company in 1888, Rockefeller's firm created affiliates across Europe to operate its tankers, establish bulk stations, and distribute its kerosene to foreign retailers. In Asia, Standard Oil's kerosene cans, converted into utensils and roofing tin, became an infallible index of American market penetration. Brand names such as Kodak

The Singer Sewing Machine
The sewing machine was an American invention that swiftly found markets abroad. The Singer Company, the dominant firm, not only exported large quantities but produced 200,000 machines annually at a Scottish plant that employed 6,000 workers. Singer's advertising rightly boasted of its prowess as an international company and of a product that was "The Universal Machine."

(cameras), McCormick (agricultural equipment), and later Ford (the Model T) became household words around the world.

Foreign trade was important partly for reasons of international finance. As a developing economy, the United States attracted a lot of foreign capital but sent relatively little abroad—scarcely 1 percent of all the money Americans invested in the late nineteenth century. The result was a heavy outflow of dollars from the United States in the form of interest and dividend payments to foreign investors. To balance this account, the United States needed to export more goods than it imported. In fact, a favorable import-export balance was achieved in 1876 (see Figure 22.1). But because of its status as a net importer of capital, America would have to be constantly vigilant about the health of its foreign trade.

Even more important, however, was the relationship that many Americans perceived between foreign markets and the nation's social stability. In hard times, as we have seen, farmers took up radical politics and workers became militant strikers. The problem, many thought, was that the nation's capacity to produce was outrunning its capacity to consume. And when the economy slowed and domestic demand fell, the impact on farmers and workers was devastating, driving down farm prices and wages and causing layoffs and farm foreclosures across the country. The answer was to make sure that there would always be enough buyers for America's surplus products, and this meant, more than anything else, access to foreign markets.

Overseas Trade and Foreign Policy. The nub of the question was how these concerns about foreign markets linked up to America's foreign policy. The bulk of American exports in the late nineteenth century—over 80 percent—went to Europe and Canada (Table 22.1). In those countries the normal instruments of diplomacy

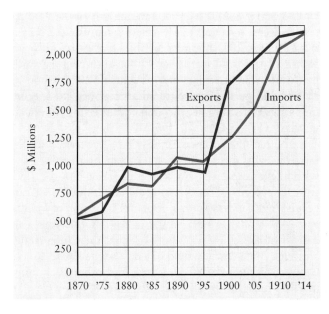

FIGURE 22.1

Balance of U.S. Imports and Exports, 1870–1914
By 1876 the United States had become a net exporting nation. The brief reversal after 1888 aroused fears that the United States was losing its foreign markets and helped fuel the expansionist drive of the 1890s.

sufficed. In Europe, for example, a major issue during the 1880s was the restrictions placed on imports of American pork, allegedly on health grounds. The United States protested vigorously, threatened to embargo the imports of countries that discriminated against American meat products, and in 1891 negotiated a satisfactory settlement.

But other foreign markets—Asia, Latin America, and other "backward" regions—seemed to demand a more vigorous kind of American intervention. Here the

TABLE 22.1

Exports to Canada and Europe Compared with Exports to Asia and Latin America

Year	Exports to Canada and Europe ($)	Percentage of Total	Exports to Asia and Latin America ($)	Percentage of Total
1875	494,000,000	86.1	72,000,000	12.5
1885	637,000,000	85.8	87,000,000	11.7
1895	681,000,000	84.3	108,000,000	13.4
1900	1,135,000,000	81.4	200,000,000	14.3

Source: Compiled from information in *Historical Statistics of the United States,* 1960; U.S. Department of Commerce, *Long Term Growth, 1860–1965,* 1966; National Bureau of Economic Research, *Trends in the American Economy in the Nineteenth Century,* 1960.

United States found itself competing with other industrial powers. Asia and Latin America represented only a modest part of America's export trade—roughly an eighth of the total in the late nineteenth century. Still, this trade was growing—it was worth $200 million in 1900—and parts of it mattered a great deal to specific industries, for example, the China market for American textiles.

The real importance of these non-Western markets, however, was not so much the extent of current trade with them as it was the fact that they, not Europe, were expected to be the future market for American goods. With its enormous population of potential customers, China exerted a powerful hold on the American mercantile imagination. Many felt that the China trade, although quite small, would one day be the key to American prosperity. Therefore, China and other beckoning markets must not be closed to the United States.

From the mid-1880s onward, with the surge of European imperialism, the fear of being excluded became more real. In a burst of modernizing energy Japan transformed itself into a major power and began to challenge China's claims over Korea. In the Sino-Japanese War of 1894–1895, Japan won an easy victory and started a scramble among the Great Powers, including Russia, to carve China up into spheres of influence. In Latin America, United States interests began to be challenged more aggressively by Britain, France, and Germany. On the European continent, moreover, the free-trade liberalism of earlier years gave way after the 1870s to protectionism, threatening established European markets for American goods just as empire building was closing off new markets elsewhere.

On top of all this came the Panic of 1893, setting in motion labor strikes and agrarian protests that many Americans, such as Cleveland's secretary of state, Walter Q. Gresham, took to be "symptoms of revolution." With the nation's social stability seemingly at stake, securing the markets of Latin America and Asia became an urgent necessity that inspired the expansionist diplomacy of the 1890s.

The Making of an Expansionist Foreign Policy

"Whether they will or no, Americans must now begin to look outward. The growing production of the country requires it." So wrote Captain Alfred T. Mahan, America's leading naval strategist, in his book *The Influence of Seapower upon History* (1890). An obscure naval officer posted to a rickety ship cruising Latin America, Mahan had spent his spare time reading history. In a library in Lima, Peru, he hit upon the idea that great empires—first Rome and, in modern times, Great Britain—had derived their power from control of the

Alfred T. Mahan
Mahan's theory about the influence of sea power on history came to him while he was killing time on a tour of naval duty reading Roman history in a library in Lima, Peru, in 1885. His insight was personal as well as intellectual: embarrassed by the decrepit ships on which he served, Mahan thought the United States should have a modern fleet in which officers like himself could serve with pride (and with some hope of professional advancement).

seas. From this insight Mahan developed a naval analysis that became the cornerstone of American strategic thinking.

The United States should no longer regard the oceans as barriers, Mahan argued, but as "a great highway . . . over which men pass in all directions." Traversing that highway required a robust merchant marine (America's had fallen on hard times since its heyday in the 1850s) and a powerful navy to protect American commerce. "When a question arises of control over distant regions . . . it must ultimately be decided by naval power," Mahan advised. To sustain its navy and its commerce, the United States needed strategic overseas bases. Here technology played a role because, having converted to steam, navies required coaling stations far from home. Without such stations, Mahan warned, warships were "like land birds, unable to fly far from their own shores."

Mahan called for a canal across Central America to connect the Atlantic and Pacific oceans. Such a canal would enable the eastern United States to "compete with Europe, on equal terms as to distance, for the markets of East Asia." The canal's approaches would need to be guarded by bases in the Caribbean Sea. And Hawaii would have to be annexed to extend American power into the Pacific, a step that Mahan considered "natural, necessary, irrepressible." This, it should be noted, was a distinctive and limited form of colonialism—not the rule over large territories and native populations to which European empire builders aspired, but control over strategic bases from which American power could be asserted in areas where Americans wanted to trade.

Mahan was offering the United States a *coherent* foreign policy: first, foreign markets secured for the nation's surplus products; second, of equal importance, the nation's development as a naval power; and third, sustaining both of those goals, an expansionist strategy anchored on an interoceanic canal and bases in the Caribbean and the Pacific.

Mahan's reasoning was eagerly taken up by other exponents of a powerful America, including Whitelaw Reid of the New York *Tribune* and young politicians such as Theodore Roosevelt and Henry Cabot Lodge. The influence of those men, few in number but strategically placed, increased during the 1890s. They pushed steadily for what Lodge called a "large policy." But mainstream politicians also accepted Mahan's underlying logic, and from the inauguration of Benjamin Harrison in 1889 onward, a surprising consistency began to emerge in the conduct of American foreign policy.

Rebuilding the Navy. This consensus was most evident in the rethinking of naval strategy. The crucial thing, Mahan argued, was to drop the reliance on shore defense and lightly armed cruising ships and create instead a battleship fleet capable of roaming the far seas and striking a decisive first blow against an enemy. This was the line that Benjamin F. Tracy, Harrison's secretary of the navy, took in his first annual report. Battleships might be expensive, but they were "the premium paid by the United States for the insurance of its acquired wealth and its growing industries." In 1890 Congress appropriated funds for the first three battleships in the two-ocean

fleet envisioned by Secretary Tracy. The battleship took on a special aura for those, such as the young Roosevelt, who wanted to see the United States flexing its muscles: "Oh, Lord! if only the people who are ignorant about our Navy could see those great warships in all their majesty and beauty, and could realize how [well fitted they are] to uphold the honor of America!"

The incoming Cleveland administration was less spread-eagled and, by canceling Harrison's scheme for annexing Hawaii, established its antiexpansionist credentials. But after a brief period of hesitation the Democrat Cleveland picked up the naval program of his Republican predecessor, pressing Congress just as forcefully for more battleships (five were authorized) and making the same basic argument. The nation's commercial vitality—"free access to all markets," in the words of Cleveland's second secretary of state, Richard Olney—depended on its naval power.

While rejecting the colonialist aspects of Mahan's thinking, Cleveland absorbed the underlying strategic arguments about where America's vital interests lay. This explains the remarkable crisis that suddenly blew up in 1895 with Great Britain over Venezuela.

The Venezuela Crisis. For years a border dispute had simmered between Venezuela and British Guiana. In the past the United States had urged arbitration, only to be told by the haughty British that they did not submit their interests to the judgments of third parties. Now that answer could no longer be accepted. Britain's claims seemed to be part of a larger pattern of European aggressiveness in Latin America, including ominous moves against Nicaragua, Brazil, Trinidad, and Santo Domingo. European empire building was carving up Africa and Asia in this period. How could the United States be sure that Europe did not have similar designs

The Battleship Oregon

The battleship was the centerpiece of naval strategy in the industrial age and the key marker in the naval arms race among the Great Powers. Building a battleship fleet was America's ticket of entry to that race.

on Latin America? Indeed, prompted by President Cleveland, Secretary of State Olney made that point in a bristling note to London on July 25, 1895, demanding that Britain accept arbitration or face the consequences.

Invoking the Monroe Doctrine, Olney warned that the United States could not tolerate any European attempt to intimidate or overthrow nations in the Western Hemisphere. "Today the United States is practically sovereign upon this continent, and its fiat is law upon the subjects to which it confines its interposition," Olney asserted. Olney's words sound bombastic, but they were intended to convey a clear message to Britain and the European powers that the United States would brook no challenge to its vital interests in the Caribbean. (Note that these were America's vital interests, not those of Venezuela, which was not consulted during the entire dispute.)

Because the Venezuela crisis blew up so suddenly, because it seemed so out of proportion to the boundary issue itself, and because it created war hysteria in the United States—for these reasons historians have found it difficult to recognize that the pugnacious stand of the Cleveland administration was not an aberration but a logical step in the new American foreign policy. Once the British realized that Cleveland meant business, they backed off and agreed to arbitration of the boundary dispute. Afterward, Secretary of State Olney remarked with satisfaction that, as a great industrial nation, the United States needed "to accept [its] commanding position" and take its place "among the Powers of the earth." And those countries would have to accommodate the American need for access to "more markets and larger markets for the consumption and products of the industry and inventive genius of the American people."

The Ideology of Expansionism. As policy makers hammered out a new foreign policy, a sustaining body of ideology took shape. One source of expansionist dogma was the Social Darwinist theory that dominated the political thought of this era (see Chapter 19, page 589). If animals and plants evolved through the survival of the fittest, so did nations. "Nothing under the sun is stationary," warned the American social theorist Brooks Adams in *The Law of Civilization and Decay* (1895). "Not to advance is to recede." By this criterion, the United States had no choice; if it wanted to survive, it had to expand.

Linked to Social Darwinism was a spreading belief in the inherent superiority of the Anglo-Saxon "race." On both sides of the Atlantic, Anglo-Saxonism was in vogue. John Fiske, an American philosopher and historian, popularized Social Darwinism and Anglo-Saxonism by lecturing the nation on its future responsibilities. "The work which the English race began when it colonized North America," Fiske declared, "is destined to go on until every land on the earth's surface that is not al-

ready the seat of an old civilization shall become English in its language, in its religion, in its political habits, and to a predominant extent in the blood of its people."

Fiske entitled his lecture "Manifest Destiny." This term had been used half a century earlier to convey the sense of national mission—America's "manifest destiny"—to sweep aside the native American peoples and occupy the continent. In his widely read book *The Winning of the West* (1896) Theodore Roosevelt drew a parallel between expansionism in his own time and the suppression of the Indians. It mattered little what happened to "backward peoples" because their conquest was "for the benefit of civilization and in the interests of mankind. It is indeed a warped, perverse and silly morality which would forbid a course of conquest that has turned whole continents into the seats of mighty and flourishing civilized nations." More than historical parallels, however, linked Manifest Destiny of the past and present.

In 1890 the U.S. Census reported the end of the westward movement: there was no longer a frontier line beyond which land remained to be conquered. The psychological impact of that news on Americans was profound, spawning among other things a new historical interpretation that stressed the importance of the frontier in shaping the nation's character. In his landmark essay setting out this thesis—"The Significance of the Frontier in American History" (1893)—the young historian Frederick Jackson Turner suggested a linkage between the closing of the frontier and overseas expansion. "He would be a rash prophet who should assert that the expansive character of American life has now entirely ceased," Turner wrote. "Movement has been its dominant fact, and, unless this training has no effect upon a people, the American energy will continually demand a wider field for its exercise." As Turner predicted, Manifest Destiny did turn outward.

Thus a strong current of ideas, deeply rooted in American experience and ideology, justified the new diplomacy of expansionism. The United States was eager to step onto the world stage. All it needed was the right occasion.

An American Empire

Ever since Spain had lost its vast empire in South America in the early nineteenth century, Cubans had yearned to join their mainland brothers and sisters in freedom. Movements for independence had sprung up repeatedly, most recently in a rebellion that had lasted from 1868 to 1878. In February 1895, inspired by the poet Jose Martí, Cuban patriots again rebelled against Spanish rule. Although Martí died in an early skirmish and no mass uprising occurred, the rebels built up substantial fighting forces and mounted a guerrilla war against the Spaniards. A standoff developed; the Spaniards controlled the towns, while insurgents held much of the countryside. In early 1896 the newly appointed Spanish captain general, Valeriano Weyler, adopted a harsh policy of *reconcentration*. The Spaniards forced entire populations into armed camps and treated any Cuban on the outside as a rebel. Because it was not followed by aggressive pursuit, reconcentration only inconvenienced the guerrilla fighters. The toll on civilians, however, was extremely brutal. Out of a population of 1.6 million, as many as 200,000 died of starvation, exposure, or dysentery.

The Cuban Crisis

The rebel leaders shrewdly saw that their best hope was not military but political: they had to draw the United States into their struggle. Some Cubans lived in the country, mostly in Florida, where Cuban cigar makers taxed themselves heavily for the cause of independence. But the nerve center of the United States was New York City, and it was there that a key group of exiles—the *junta*—set up shop to make the case for *Cuba Libre*. By itself, their cause would not have stirred much interest. The Spaniards were not behaving more dishonorably than any other colonial power in similar circumstances; nor were atrocities in short supply elsewhere in the world if Americans cared to know. The Cuban exiles, however, came on the scene at a critical juncture in American sensationalist journalism. William Randolph Hearst had just purchased the nearly moribund *New York Journal* and was in a hurry to build circulation (see American Lives, pages 686–687). Cuba was ideal for his purposes. Locked in a furious circulation war, Hearst's *Journal* and Joseph Pulitzer's *New York World* elevated Cuba's agony into flaming front-page headlines.

Across the country powerful sentiments began to be stirred, mixing humanitarian concern for the Cubans, a superpatriotism that was tagged *jingoism*, and increasing demands that the Cubans be freed. Responding to public opinion, Congress passed resolutions for limited Cuban self-government in 1896 and for complete independence early the next year.

The White House took a cooler view of the situation. Cleveland was still in office when the rebellion broke out. As with Venezuela, his concern was with America's vital interests, which, he told Congress, were "by no means of a wholly sentimental or philanthropic character." First, economic interests were at stake. The rebellion was disrupting the sizable trade between the two countries and destroying profitable American investments, especially in Cuban sugar plantations. Of course, it was the rebels who were burning the crops, but Spain was accountable for not maintaining security.

Then there were strategic considerations. The United States could no longer tolerate instability in the Caribbean and worried that Spain's troubles might draw other European powers into the situation. A chronically unstable Cuba was not compatible with America's increasing strategic interests in the region, especially its plans for an interoceanic canal whose approaches would have to be safeguarded.

If Spain could put down the rebellion, that was fine with Cleveland. But as Spain's impotence became clear, he urged the Spanish government to make reforms and warned that the United States would have to intervene unless there was a speedy resolution of the crisis.

On that central matter there was continuity between Cleveland and the McKinley administration that took office in March 1897. Both were guided by the conception of the United States as the dominant Caribbean power, with vital interests that had to be defended. McKinley, however, was inclined to take a tougher line with the Spaniards. For one thing, he was more appalled by Spain's "uncivilized and inhumane conduct" in Cuba and was not as indifferent as Cleveland to the aspirations of the rebels. In addition, McKinley had to contend with rising jingoism in the Republican party. At the 1896 national convention the Republicans had adopted a bristling platform calling for Cuban independence and proclaiming a new American imperialism. But the notion, long held by historians, that McKinley was swept along against his better judgment by popular opinion and by a Republican war faction led by Theodore Roosevelt, Henry Cabot Lodge, and other aggressive advocates of a "large policy" is not true. McKinley was very much his own man. He was a skilled politician and a canny, if undramatic, president. He would not proceed until he sensed a broad national consensus for war. In particular, he was sensitive to business interests fearful of disruption to an economy that was just recovering from a depression.

The Road to War. On September 18, 1897, the American minister in Madrid asked the Spanish government "whether the time has not arrived when Spain . . . will put a stop to this destructive war." If Spain could not assure an "early and certain peace," the United States would take whatever steps it "should deem necessary to procure this result." At first the Spanish response sparked some hope. The conservative regime fell, and a liberal government, upon taking office in October 1897, moderated its Cuban policy. Spain recalled Weyler, limited reconcentration, and adopted an autonomy plan that would grant Cuba a degree of self-rule but not independence. Madrid's incapacity soon became clear, however. In January 1898, Spanish loyalists in Havana rioted against the offer of autonomy. The Cuban rebels, encouraged by the prospect of American intervention, demanded full independence.

William Randolph Hearst: Jingo

William Randolph Hearst, born in San Francisco on April 29, 1863, was no Horatio Alger hero. His father, George Hearst, had struck it rich in Nevada's Comstock lode, and Willie grew up in the lap of luxury: grand houses, trips to Europe, private tutors, Harvard (class of 1886). His mother, Phoebe, doted on him, at once indulging and smothering her only child. From these unpromising beginnings sprang a strappingly handsome young man of remarkable contradictions, beginning with his voice, which was incongruously thin and high-pitched. Hearst was painfully shy but simultaneously hell-bent on mischief; his pranks at Harvard (which finally got him expelled) were legendary. He was outwardly diffident but had to dominate everyone around him. He was sentimental and generous but also without scruples. When he wanted something, he really wanted it, and he was known late into his life to throw tantrums when he was denied. All this would be of no historical moment—doubtless there were others like him among the progeny of the new millionaires—except for one thing: Hearst did not end up a dissipated alcoholic or, as it was known to happen, even a quietly exemplary citizen. No, Hearst became a great newspaperman and, driven by his inner demons, cut a swath through American history.

His father happened to own the *San Francisco Examiner*, a money-loser that served as the elder Hearst's political organ. At Harvard the son took to reading the *Examiner* and decided that he wanted to run it. His inspiration was Joseph Pulitzer, who had a few years earlier taken over the moribund *New York World* and transformed it into a hugely successful daily. While still a junior, Hearst wrote a remarkable letter to his father outlining his plans for the paper, which would be, like the *World*, "of that class which appeals to the people and which depends for its success upon enterprise, energy and a certain startling originality and not upon the wisdom of its political opinions or the lofty style of its editorials." The elder Hearst was unimpressed. He was thinking about unloading the paper, not pouring more money into it. Supposing it became a great success, he asked the business manager, how much might it make? Maybe $100,000 a year, came the answer. "Hell!" snorted Hearst. "That ain't no money." But the son wasn't interested in the money; he was interested in the *circulation* and the delight he would take from orchestrating the emotions—and maybe even the actions—of thousands upon thousands of readers.

In early 1887 the young Hearst, not yet twenty-four, finally got his wish and, on taking command, immediately pronounced the sleepy *Examiner* "Monarch of the Dailies." It would be "THE LARGEST, BRIGHTEST AND BEST NEWSPAPER ON THE PACIFIC COAST," providing readers with the best news and "THE LATEST AND MOST ORIGINAL SENSATIONS." Sensation was what Hearst was after, copy that would arouse, in his editor's words, "the gee-whiz emotion." For example: Were any grizzly bears left in California? Hearst dispatched an intrepid newsman to the Tehachapi Mountains, where after three months of arduous trapping he caught a grizzly. The beast was chained in a beer wagon, paraded with great fanfare around San Francisco, and given a home in Golden Gate Park. Naturally, it was named Monarch. All this the *Examiner* reported in exhaustive detail, building suspense as the search progressed and ending triumphantly with the carnival display of the unfortunate bear. There was much more of the same: rescues, murders, scandal, sob stories, anything that might give readers the "gee-whiz emotion." The other string in Hearst's bow was that he became a champion of "the people." The *Examiner* embarked on a series of noisy crusades—against the water trust, and got rates cut by 15 percent; against a city charter crafted by venal politicos and their business cronies, and got it defeated; and, on many fronts, against the rapacious Southern Pacific Railroad.

By the early 1890s the *Examiner's* circulation was soaring and Hearst was making money. Looking around for greener fields, his eye fixed on New York City. The *Journal* was for sale, and Hearst got it cheaply. It was an anemic paper, close to folding, but Hearst didn't care. He intended to transform it, pouring money in as he had with the *Examiner* and applying everything he had learned in San Francisco. He was going to war against Pulitzer's *New York World*.

When Hearst took over the *Journal* in October 1895, the Cuban insurrection had already begun. Until then Hearst had shown no interest in foreign affairs,

William Randolph Hearst

but he genuinely felt for the underdog Cubans and, more to the point, saw in their cause just what he needed to drive his circulation war against Pulitzer. Not much actual news could be gotten out of Cuba, for the sporadic fighting took place in the remote interior, beyond the reach of Hearst's correspondents in Havana. It did not matter. Rebel claims were good enough for Hearst, and a drumbeat of superheated articles began to appear about mostly nonexistent battles and about Spanish atrocities. When General Valeriano Weyler took command, the *Journal* immediately dubbed him the "Butcher":

Weyler the brute, the devastator of haciendas, the destroyer of families and the outrager of women. . . . Pitiless, cold, an exterminator of men . . . inventing tortures and infamies of bloody debauchery. . . .

Weyler's reconcentration program soon put meat into the *Journal's* wild charges and American public opinion began to harden against the Spanish.

The *Journal* was stridently for war. Hearst's jingoism sounded very much like his old crusade again the San Francisco water trust: it was the people versus the interests all over again, the freedom-loving masses against the peace-at-any-price plutocrats. President McKinley was Wall Street's puppet, with the nefarious Senator Hanna pulling the strings. When the *Maine* went down, the *Journal* was ablaze with fiery headlines charging Spanish treachery. That week circulation

passed a million. Impatient for action, Hearst found ammunition even in the suicide of poor Mrs. Mary Wayt:

GRIEVED OVER OUR DELAY

"The Government May Live in
Dishonor," Said She,
"I Cannot."

The next day, April 19, the Senate passed the war resolution, and hostilities commenced. The news from Manila Bay got this screaming headline: "VICTORY . . . Complete! . . . Glorious! . . . THE MAINE IS AVENGED." A few days later, the front page asked readers: "HOW DO YOU LIKE THE JOURNAL'S WAR?"

Was it true? Had Hearst caused the war? For many years historians thought so. Now, with a better understanding of McKinley's administration, they are more inclined to stress the country's endangered strategic interests. Yet there is no denying Hearst's contribution. The war hysteria he nurtured was like a ticking bomb, forcing the president's hand because, as New York's Senator Platt noted, McKinley knew "that the people of the United States will not tolerate much longer the war in Cuba." There were also longer-term consequences. For one, public opinion became a weightier factor in the conduct of American foreign policy: whether democracy and diplomacy are compatible has been debated ever since Hearst's time. Second, Hearst introduced and never let go of a superpatriotism—"Americanism," he called it—that became a permanent, if volatile, element of the nation's political debate.

As for the war with Spain, Hearst had a grand time of it. He hired a boat, took a crew of newsmen down to Cuba, came under fire at El Caney, wrote some creditable dispatches when his star reporter was wounded, rounded up Spanish survivors of the Santiago naval battle, and returned to New York feeling that the world was his oyster.

At that time Hearst was thirty-five, with another fifty-three years to live. The news business, ultimately a huge empire, remained the core of his being. But he also entered New York politics in a quixotic quest for the presidency. He plunged into Hollywood moviemaking and formed a permanent liason with one of his creations, the movie star Marion Davies. He built a castle at San Simeon and entertained extravagantly the rich and famous. All the while he became more enigmatic, more dictatorial, more alone.

In the end Hearst gained immortality in an utterly modern way: he became the inspiration for Orson Welles's great movie *Citizen Kane* (1941). Ordinarily, we do not look to the movies for historical insight, but Welles captured something in Hearst. The plot turns on Kane's dying word, *rosebud*, which proves to be just the name of a sled remembered from his childhood.

On February 9, 1898, the *New York Journal* published a private letter of Dupuy de Lôme, the Spanish minister to the United States. De Lôme called President McKinley "weak" and "a bidder for the admiration of the crowd." Worse, he suggested that the Spanish government was not taking the American demands for reform seriously. De Lôme immediately resigned, but the damage had been done.

A week later the U.S. battleship *Maine* blew up and sank in Havana harbor, with the loss of 260 seamen. "Whole Country Thrills with the War Fever," proclaimed Hearst's *New York Journal*. From that moment onward popular passions against Spain became a major factor in the march toward war.

But McKinley kept his head. He assumed that the sinking had been accidental: What motive could the Spanish have had for attacking the *Maine*? A naval board of inquiry, however, submitted a more damaging report. Disagreeing with a separate Spanish inquiry, the American board concluded that the sinking had been caused by a mine, not, as seems more likely, by an accidental explosion inside the *Maine*. No evidence linked the Spanish to the sinking, but they had failed to protect the American vessel from attack.

This was damning evidence that Spanish control over Cuba had broken down, and it was reinforced by a memorable speech by Senator Redfield Proctor of Vermont after a visit to Cuba. This anti-imperialist senior Republican's account of the devastation in the Cuban countryside made a deep impression and led even the skeptical to conclude that Spain had lost the right to rule Cuba.

McKinley had no stomach for the martial spirit engulfing the country. He was not swept along by the calls for blood to avenge the sinking of the *Maine*. But he did have to attend to an aroused public opinion. Hesitant business leaders also became impatient for the dispute to end. War was preferable to the unresolved Cuban crisis. On March 27, McKinley cabled to Madrid what was in effect an ultimatum: an immediate armistice for six months, abandonment of the practice of reconcentration, and, with the United States as mediator, peace negotiations with the rebels. A telegram the next day added that only Cuban independence would be regarded as a satisfactory outcome to the negotiations.

In response, Spain made a series of desperate concessions, climaxed on April 9 by a unilateral declaration of an armistice whose duration would be at the discretion of the Spanish military. But it rejected American mediation as well as the demand for an independent Cuba. There had never been any chance that the proud Spanish would accept that final humiliation.

On April 11, McKinley sent a message to Congress asking for authority to intervene to end the fighting in Cuba. His motives were as he described them: "In the name of humanity, in the name of civilization, in behalf of endangered American interests which give us the right and the duty to speak and to act, the war in Cuba must stop." The war hawks in Congress—a mixture of Republican jingoists and western Democrats who sympathized with the cause of Cuban independence—were impatient with McKinley's cautious progress. But the president did not lose control of things. On the one crucial difference he had with the war hawks, McKinley prevailed. He beat back their effort to recognize the rebel republican government, which would have greatly reduced the administration's freedom of action in dealing with Spain.

"Remember the Maine!*"*

In late January 1898 the *Maine* entered Havana harbor on a courtesy call. On the evening of February 15 a mysterious blast sent the U.S. battleship to the bottom. This dramatic lithograph conveys something of the impact of that event on American public opinion. Although no evidence ever linked the Spanish authorities to the explosion, the sinking of the *Maine* fed the emotional fires that prepared the nation for war with Spain.

Added to the resolutions empowering the president to employ American forces in Cuba was an amendment by Senator Henry M. Teller of Colorado disclaiming any intention by the United States to use intervention as a pretext for taking possession of Cuba. Teller wanted to make it impossible for European governments to say that "when we go out to make battle for the liberty and freedom of Cuban patriots, that we are doing it for the purpose of aggrandizement for ourselves or the increasing of our territorial holdings." This had to be made clear with regard to Cuba, "whatever," Senator Teller added, "we may do as to some other islands."

Did McKinley have in mind "some other islands"? Was this really a war of aggression secretly motivated by a desire to seize strategic territory from Spain? In a strict sense, almost certainly no. It was not *because* of expansionist ambitions that McKinley forced Spain into a corner. On the other hand, once war came, he saw it as an opportunity to be exploited. As he wrote privately after hostilities began: "While we are conducting war and until its conclusion, we must keep all we get; when the war is over we must keep what we want." Precisely what would be forthcoming, of course, would depend on the fortunes of battle.

The Spoils of War

Hostilities formally began when Spain declared war on April 24, 1898. The day before, President McKinley had called for 125,000 volunteers. Across the country regiments began to form up. Theodore Roosevelt immediately resigned as assistant secretary of the navy, ordered a fancy uniform, and was commissioned lieutenant colonel in a volunteer cavalry regiment that became famous as the Rough Riders. Raw recruits poured into makeshift bases around Tampa, Florida. Confusion reigned. Tropical uniforms did not arrive; the food was bad, the sanitation worse; and rifles were in short supply. No provision had been made for getting the troops to Cuba; the government hastily began to collect a miscellaneous fleet of yachts, lake steamers, and commercial boats. Fortunately, the small regular army was a disciplined, highly professional force, and its seasoned 28,000 troops provided a nucleus for the 200,000 civilians who had to be turned into soldiers inside of a few weeks.

The navy was in better shape and was, as it turned out, the key to the outcome of the war. So outclassed were the Spanish that the Atlantic fleet admiral, Pascual Cervera, expected that his navy would "like Don

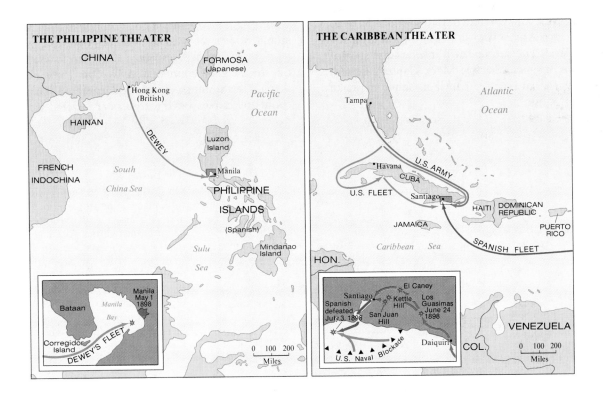

MAP 22.1

The Spanish-American War
The swift American victory in the Spanish-American War resulted from overwhelming naval superiority. Dewey's destruction of the Spanish fleet in Manila harbor doomed the Spaniards in the Philippines. In Cuba, American ground forces won a hard victory on San Juan Hill, for they were ill equipped and poorly supplied. With the United States in control of the seas, the Spaniards saw no choice but to give up the battle for Cuba.

Quixote go out to fight windmills and come back with a broken head." Cervera had nothing to match the U.S. Navy's seven battleships and armored cruisers, and the ships he had were undermanned and ill prepared for battle.

On April 23, acting on plans already drawn up, Commodore George Dewey's small Pacific fleet set sail from Hong Kong for the Philippines. Here, at this Spanish possession in the far Pacific, not in Cuba, the decisive engagement of the war took place. On May 1 the American ships cornered the Spanish fleet in Manila Bay and destroyed it (see Map 22.1). The victory produced euphoria in the United States. Immediately, part of the army being trained for the Cuban campaign was diverted to the Philippines. Manila, the Philippine capital, fell on August 13, 1898.

With Dewey's naval victory, American strategic thinking clicked into place. "We hold the other side of the Pacific and the value to this country is almost beyond imagination," declared Senator Lodge. "We must on no account let the [Philippine] Islands go." President McKinley agreed, and so did his key advisers. An anchor in the western Pacific had long been coveted by naval strategists. At this time, too, the Great Powers were carving up China into spheres of influence. If American commerce wanted a place in that glittering market, the power of the United States would have to be projected into Asia. "With a strong foothold in the Philippine Islands, we can and will take a large slice of the commerce of Asia," Senator Mark Hanna asserted. "That is what we want . . . and it is better to strike while the iron is hot."

Once the decision for a Philippine base had been made, other decisions followed almost automatically. The question of Hawaii was quickly resolved. In 1897 McKinley had reintroduced an annexation proposal in Congress, but it had stalled. In July 1898 Congress pushed Hawaiian annexation through by joint resolution. Hawaii had suddenly acquired a crucial strategic value: it was a halfway station on the way to the Philippines. The navy pressed for a coaling base in the central Pacific; that meant Guam, a Spanish island in the Marianas. There was also a need for a strategically located base in the Caribbean; that meant Puerto Rico. By July, before the assault on Cuba, the full scope of McKinley's war aims had crystallized. There was no question that he had the people behind him. In the wake of Dewey's victory, enthusiasm for colonial annexations swept the country and, as one close reader of the nation's press reported, was "getting so strong it will mean the political death of any man to oppose it pretty soon."

The campaign in Cuba (see Map 22.1) was something of an anticlimax. The Spanish fleet was bottled up in Santiago harbor, and the city itself became the strategic key to the military campaign. Half trained and ill equipped, the American forces moving on Santiago might have been checked by a determined opponent, but the Spaniards lacked the heart for battle. They would fight to maintain their honor, but they had no stomach for a real war against the Americans.

The main battle, on July 1, occurred near Santiago on the heights commanded by San Juan Hill. Roosevelt's dismounted Rough Riders (there had been no room for horses on the transports) seized Kettle Hill.

The Battle of San Juan Hill

On July 1, 1898, the key battle for Cuba took place on heights overlooking Santiago. African-American troops bore the brunt of the fighting. Although generally overlooked, the black role in the San Juan battle is done justice in this contemporary lithograph, without the demeaning stereotypes by which blacks were normally depicted in an age of intensifying racism. Even so, the racial hierarchy is maintained. The blacks are the foot soldiers; their officers are white.

George W. Prioleau

Black Soldiers in a White Man's War

The chaplain of the Ninth Cavalry regiment expresses his bitterness toward the racism experienced by black troopers in the South on their way to battle in Cuba.

Hon. H. C. Smith
Editor, Gazette

Dear Sir:
The Ninth Cavalry left Chickamauga on the 30th of April for Tampa, Fla. We arrived here (nine miles from Tampa) on May 3. From this port the army will sail for Cuba. We have in this camp here and at Tampa between 7,000 and 8,000 soldiers, artillery, one regiment of cavalry (the famous fighting Ninth) and the Twenty-fourth and Twenty-fifth infantries. The Ninth Cavalry's bravery and their skillfulness with weapons of war . . . is well known by all who have read the history of the last Indian war. . . .

Yesterday, May 12, the Ninth was ordered to be ready to embark at a moment's notice for Cuba. . . . These men are anxious to go. The country will then hear and know of the bravery of these sable sons of Ham.

The American Negro is always ready and willing to take up arms, to fight and to lay down his life in defense of his country's flag and honor. All the way from northwest Nebraska this regiment was greeted with cheers and hurrahs. At places where we stopped the people assembled by the thousands. While the Ninth Cavalry band would play some national air the people would raise their hats, men, women and children would wave their handkerchiefs, and the heavens would resound with their hearty cheers. The white hand shaking the black hand. The hearty "goodbyes," "God bless you," and other expressions aroused the patriotism of our boys. . . . These demonstrations, so enthusiastically given, greeted us all the way until we reached Nashville. At this point we arrived about 12:30 A.M. There were about 6,000 colored people there to greet us (very few white people) but not a man was allowed by the railroad officials to approach the cars. From there until we reached Chattanooga there was not a cheer given us, the people living in gross ignorance, rags and dirt. Both white and colored seemed amazed; they looked at us in wonder. Don't think they have intelligence enough to know that Andrew Jackson is dead. . . .

The prejudice against the Negro soldier and the Negro was great, but it was of heavenly origin to what it is in this part of Florida, and I suppose that what is true here is true in other parts of the state. Here, the Negro is not allowed to purchase over the same counter in some stores that the white man purchases over. The southerners have made their laws and the Negroes know and obey them. They never stop to ask a white man a question. He (Negro) never thinks of disobeying. You talk about freedom, liberty, etc. Why sir, the Negro of this country is a freeman and yet a slave. Talk about fighting and freeing poor Cuba and of Spain's brutality; of Cuba's murdered thousands, and starving reconcentradoes. Is America any better than Spain? Has she not subjects in her very midst who are murdered daily without a trial of judge or jury? Has she not subjects in her own borders whose children are half-fed and half-clothed, because their father's skin is black. . . . Yet the Negro is loyal to his country's flag. . . .

The four Negro regiments are going to help free Cuba, and they will return to their homes, some then mustered out and begin again to fight the battle of American prejudice. . . .

Yours truly,
Geo. W. Prioleau
Chaplain, Ninth Cavalry

Source: Cleveland *Gazette* (May 13, 1898), reprinted in Willard B. Gatewood, *"Smoked Yankees" and the Struggle for Empire, 1898–1902* (Urbana: University of Illinois Press, 1971), 27–29.

Then the frontal assault against the San Juan heights began. Four black regiments took the brunt of the fighting (see American Voices, above). White observers grudgingly credited much of the victory to the "superb gallantry" of the black soldiers. In fact, it was not quite a victory. The Spaniards, driven from their forward positions, retreated to a well-fortified second line. The Americans had suffered heavy casualties and were exhausted by heat and illness. It was questionable whether they could have mounted a second assault. They were spared that test, however, by the Spanish. On July 3, in a last futile gesture, Cervera's fleet in Santiago harbor made a suicidal daylight attempt to run the American blockade and was destroyed. A few days later, convinced that Santiago could not be saved, the Spanish forces agreed to surrender.

Three weeks later, Spain sued for peace. The two nations signed an armistice in which Spain agreed to give up Cuba and cede Puerto Rico and Guam to the United States. American forces would occupy Manila pending a peace treaty that would decide the fate of the Philippines.

The Imperial Experiment

The big question was the Philippines. This was an arch-ipelago of over 7,000 islands populated—as William R. Day, McKinley's secretary of state, put it with the char-acteristic racism of that era—by "eight or nine millions of absolutely ignorant and many degraded people." Not even the most avid American expansionists had advo-cated colonial rule over such a population: that was European-style imperialism, not what Mahan and his followers had in mind. Both Mahan and Lodge initially advocated keeping only Manila as a western Pacific base. It gradually became clear, however, that Manila was not defensible without controlling the whole of Luzon, the large island on which the city is located.

McKinley and his advisers surveyed the options. One possibility was to return most of the islands to Spain, but the reputed evils of Spanish rule made that a "cowardly and dishonorable" solution. Another possi-bility was to partition the Philippines with one or more of the Great Powers. There would have been no dearth of takers, particularly Germany, whose ships were prowling the nearby waters. But as McKinley observed, to turn over valuable territory to "our commercial ri-vals in the Orient—that would have been bad business and discreditable."

Most plausible was the option of granting the Philip-pines independence. As in Cuba, Spanish rule had al-ready stirred up a rebellion, led by the fiery patriot Emilio Aguinaldo. It would have been feasible to make an arrangement like the one being negotiated with the Cubans over Guantanamo Bay: the lease of a naval base to the Americans as the price for freedom. But after some hesitation McKinley was persuaded that "we could not leave [the Filipinos] to themselves—they were unfit for self-rule—and they would soon have anarchy and mis-rule over there worse than Spain's was."

In October 1898, while the peace negotiations were in progress, McKinley made a two-week speaking tour of the Midwest to get a reading on public opinion. What he heard from the crowds confirmed his own be-lief that the United States would have to take the entire archipelago. On October 26 he cabled instructions to that effect to the American delegation in Paris. He had concluded that the United States "cannot let go."

As for the Spaniards, they had little choice against what they considered "the immoderate demands of a conquerer." In the Treaty of Paris they ceded the Philip-pines to the United States for a payment of $20 million. The treaty encountered harder going at home and was ratified by the Senate (requiring a two-thirds majority) on February 6, 1899, with only a single vote to spare.

The Anti-Imperialists. The narrowness of the adminis-tration's victory signaled the revival of an antiexpan-sionist tradition that had been mostly silenced by the patriotic passions of a nation at war. In the Senate op-ponents of the treaty invoked the country's republican principles. Imperial expansion, argued the conservative Republican George F. Hoar, meant accepting "the fun-damental idea [of the European imperial powers] that the people of immense areas of territory can be held as subjects, never to become citizens." Under the Constitu-tion, "no power is given to the Federal Government to acquire territory to be held and governed permanently as colonies" or "to conquer alien people and hold them in subjugation." And making 8 million Filipinos eligible for citizenship—be it noted, only the prospect of an an-nexed Philippines had fired real opposition to the treaty—was equally unpalatable to the anti-imperialists, who were no more champions of "these savage people" than were the expansionists who denigrated the self-governing capacity of the Filipinos.

Leading citizens enlisted in the anti-imperialist cause, including the steelmaker Andrew Carnegie, who offered a check for $20 million to purchase the indepen-dence of the Philippines; the labor leader Samuel Gom-pers, who feared the competition of cheap Filipino labor; and Jane Addams, who believed that women should stand for peace. The key group, however, was a social elite of old-line Mugwump reformers such as Carl Schurz, Charles Eliot Norton, and Charles Francis Adams. In November 1899 Boston Mugwumps formed the first Anti-Imperialist League, from which blossomed a national movement over the next year, with chapters in major cities across the country, 30,000 members, and, so they claimed, half a million contributors.

Skillful as they were at publicizing their cause, the anti-imperialists never managed to build a truly popular movement. They were an ill-assorted lot, divided in many ways and, within the Mugwump core, lacking the common touch needed to attract mass support. Nor was it easy to translate anti-imperialism into a viable politi-cal cause because the Democrats, once the treaty had been adopted, waffled over the issue. The Democratic standard-bearer, William Jennings Bryan, although an outspoken anti-imperialist, provided confused leader-ship—he had confounded his friends by favoring ratifi-cation of the treaty—and afterward hesitated to stake his party's future on a crusade against a national policy he privately believed to be irreversible. Still, if it was an accomplished fact, Philippine annexation lost the moral high ground because of the remonstrations of the anti-imperialists and the awful events that began to unfold in the Philippines.

War in the Philippines. Two days before the Senate rat-ified the treaty, on February 4, 1899, fighting broke out between American and Filipino patrols on the edge of Manila. Confronted by the prospect of American an-nexation, Aguinaldo asserted his nation's independence and turned his guns on the occupying American forces.

The ensuing conflict far exceeded in ferocity the war that had just been concluded with Spain. Fighting tenacious guerrillas, the U.S. Army resorted to the same tactics of reconcentration used by the Spaniards in Cuba, which included moving people into towns, carrying out indiscriminate attacks beyond the perimeters, and burning crops and villages (see American Voices, pages 694 and 695).

Atrocities became commonplace on both sides. The American forces specialized in the "water cure"—forcing water into a person's stomach and then pounding it out—to make captured guerrillas talk. In more than three years of warfare 4,200 Americans and many thousands of Filipinos died. The fighting ended in 1902, and Judge William Howard Taft, who had been appointed governor in 1901, set up a civilian government. He intended to make the Philippines a model of American road building and sanitary engineering.

McKinley's convincing victory over William Jennings Bryan in the 1900 election, although by no means a referendum on American expansionism, at least suggested popular satisfaction with America's overseas adventure. Yet a strong undercurrent of misgivings was evident. Americans had not anticipated the brutal methods needed to subdue the Filipino guerrillas. "We are destroying these islanders by the thousands, their villages and cities," protested the philosopher William James. "No life shall you have, we say, except as a gift from our philanthropy after your unconditional surrender to our will. . . . Could there be any more damning indictment of that whole bloated ideal termed 'modern civilization'?" And when the fighting ended, it was not apparent just what the United States had achieved. The

Emilio Aguinaldo

At the start of the war with Spain, U.S. military leaders brought the Filipino patriot Aguinaldo back from Singapore because they thought he would stir up a popular uprising that would help defeat the Spaniards. Aguinaldo came because he thought the Americans favored an independent Philippines. These differing intentions—it has remained a matter of dispute what assurances Aguinaldo received—were the root cause of the Filipino insurrection that proved far costlier in American and Filipino lives than the war with Spain that had preceded it.

Fighting the Filipinos

The United States went to war against Spain in 1898 partly out of sympathy with the Cuban struggle for independence. Yet the United States found it necessary to use the same brutal tactics to put down the Filipino struggle for independence that the Spaniards had used against the Cubans. Here the Twentieth Kansas Volunteers march through the burning village of Caloocan.

Major General Arthur MacArthur

Subduing the Filipinos—the Ideal

In 1902 MacArthur, the commanding general of U.S. forces in the Philippines, appeared before a Senate committee investigating conditions there. In his presentation he expressed a widely held view of the necessity—and desirability—of American rule.

At the time I returned to Manila [May 1900] to assume the supreme command it seemed to me that we had been committed to a position by process of spontaneous evolution. . . . [O]ur permanent occupation of the islands was simply one of the necessary consequences in logical sequence of our great prosperity. . . . Our conception of right, justice, freedom, and personal liberty was the precious fruit of centuries of strife; that we had inherited much in these respects from our ancestors, and in our own behalf have added much to the happiness of the world, and as beneficiaries of the past and as the instruments of future progressive social development we must regard ourselves simply as the custodians of imperishable ideas held in trust for the general benefit of mankind. In other words, I felt that we had attained a moral and intellectual height from which we were bound to proclaim to all as the occasion arose the true message of humanity as embodied in the principles of our own institutions. . . .

To my mind the archipelago is a fertile soil upon which to plant republicanism. . . . We are planting the best traditions, the best characteristics of Americanism in such a way that they never can be removed from that soil. That in itself seems to me a most inspiring thought. It encouraged me during all my efforts in those islands, even when conditions seemed most disappointing, when the people themselves, not appreciating precisely what the remote consequences of our efforts were going to be, mistrusted us; but that fact was always before me—that going down deep into that fertile soil were the imperishable ideas of Americanism.

Second Thoughts about American Empire
After the shouting was over and the United States had its empire, doubts began to creep in, as is evident in this *Puck* cover in celebration of July 4, 1904. There is the American eagle in all its glory, but with wings spreading far out to the Philippines in one direction and to Puerto Rico in the other, grumbling: "Gee, but this is an awful stretch!"

adventure, wrote Roosevelt's attorney general, "has cost us a great deal of money; and any benefits which have resulted from it to this country are, as yet, imperceptible to the naked eye."

There were, moreover, disturbing constitutional issues that needed to be resolved. Did the Constitution extend to the acquired territories? Did their inhabitants automatically become citizens? In 1901 the Supreme Court ruled negatively on both questions; these were matters for Congress to decide. The special commission appointed by McKinley recommended ultimate independence after an indefinite period of U.S. rule, during which time the Filipinos would be prepared for self-government. In 1916 the passage of the Jones Act formally committed the United States to granting Philippine independence but set no date.

The ugly business in the Philippines rubbed off some of the moralizing gloss but left undeflected the global aspirations driving the United States. In a few years the United States had acquired the makings of a strategic overseas empire: Hawaii, Puerto Rico, Guam, the Philippines, and finally, in 1900, several of the Samoan islands that had been jointly administered with Germany and Britain. The United States, the legal scholar John Bassett Moore remarked in 1899, had moved "from a position of comparative freedom from entanglements into a position of what is commonly called a world power."

Robert P. Hughes and Richard T. O'Brien

Subduing the Filipinos—the Realities

Brigadier General Hughes offered the Senate Committee on the Philippines a different picture of the implanting of American ideals in Filipino soil.

Sen. Rawlins . . . [In] burning towns, what would you do? Would the entire town be destroyed by fire or would only offending portions of the town be burned?

Gen. Hughes: I do not know that we have ever had a case of burning what you would call a town in this country, but probably a barrio or a sitio; probably half a dozen houses, native shacks, where the insurrectos would go in and be concealed, and if they caught a detachment passing they would kill some of them.

Sen. Rawlins: What did I understand you to say would be the consequences of that?

Gen. Hughes: They usually burned the village.

Sen. Rawlins: All the houses in the village?

Gen. Hughes: Yes, every one of them.

Sen. Rawlins: What would become of the inhabitants?

Gen. Hughes: That was their lookout. . . .

Sen. Rawlins: If these shacks were of no consequence what was the utility of their destruction?

Gen. Hughes: The destruction was as a punishment. They permitted these people to come in there and conceal themselves and they gave no sign. It is always—

Sen. Rawlins: The punishment in that case would fall, not upon the men, who could go elsewhere, but mainly upon the women and little children.

Gen. Hughes: The women and children are part of the family, and where you wish to inflict punishment you can punish the man probably worse in that way than in any other.

Sen. Rawlins: But is that within the ordinary rules of civilized warfare? . . .

Gen. Hughes: These people are not civilized.

Richard T. O'Brien, of M Company, 26th Infantry Volunteers, U.S. Army, gave this account to the Senate Committee.

[How] the order started and who gave it I don't know, but the town was fired on. I saw an old fellow come to the door, and he looked out: he got a shot in the abdomen and fell to his knees and turned around and died. . . .

After that two old men came out, hand in hand. I should think they were over 50 years old, probably between 50 and 70 years old. They had a white flag. They were shot down. At the other end of the town we heard screams, and there was a woman there; she was burned up, and in her arms was a baby, and on the floor was another child. The baby was at her breast, the one in her arms, and this child on the floor was, I should judge, about 3 years of age. They were burned. Whether she was demoralized or driven insane I don't know. She stayed in the house.

Source: U.S. Senate, Committee on the Philippines, *Hearings*, 57th Congress, 1st Session (1902).

Onto the World Stage

From the standpoint of Europeans, the flexing of America's muscles against Spain caused a certain amount of consternation. The assault on an ancient, if decayed, European state seemed to many government leaders the work of a country that was, in the words of the French envoy to Washington, "ignorant, brutal, and quite capable of destroying the complicated European structure." At the instigation of Kaiser Wilhelm II of Germany, the major powers of Europe had tried before war broke out to intercede on Spain's behalf—but only tentatively, because no one was looking for trou-

ble with the Americans. President McKinley had listened politely to the representations of their envoys on April 6, 1898, and had then, dismissively, proceeded with his war.

The decisive outcome confirmed what the Europeans already suspected. After Dewey's naval victory the semiofficial French paper *Le Temps* observed that "what passes before our eyes is the appearance of a new power of the first order." And in a long editorial the London *Times* concluded: "This war must . . . effect a profound change in the whole attitude and policy of the United States. In the future America will play a part in the general affairs of the world such as she has never played before."

A Power among Powers

The politician who most ardently agreed with the London *Times*'s vision of America's future was the man who, with the assassination of William McKinley, became president on September 14, 1901, Theodore Roosevelt. As we have seen, Roosevelt had needed to feel his way on the domestic front, only gradually formulating his progressive program. Roosevelt harbored no such uncertainty about foreign affairs. He was an avid student of the subject, widely traveled abroad and acquainted with many of the European leaders. He had no doubt about how the United States should act now that it was a Great Power.

It was important, first of all, to uphold the country's honor in the community of nations. "I am not hostile to any European power in the abstract," Roosevelt once wrote. "I am simply American first and last, and therefore hostile to any power which wrongs us." Nor should the country ever shrink from righteous battle. "All the great masterful races have been fighting races," Roosevelt declared. Nothing would be worse for the United States, already too commercial for his aristocratic taste, than "slothful and ignoble peace." But when he spoke of war, Roosevelt had in mind actions by the "civilized" nations against "backward peoples" (such as the Filipinos, whose struggle for freedom was being subdued when he entered the White House). Roosevelt felt "it incumbent on all civilized and orderly powers to insist on the proper policing of the world." That was why he sympathized with European imperialism and how he justified American dominance over the Caribbean states.

As for the "civilized and orderly" policemen of the world, however, the worst thing that could happen was for them to fall to fighting among themselves. Roosevelt had an acute sense of the fragility of the world balance of power and was prescient about the chances—in this he was truly exceptional among Americans—of a catastrophic world war. He believed in an American responsibility for helping to maintain the balance of power and recognized that conducting foreign policy to that end would be his most demanding task.

Anglo-American Amity. After the Spanish-American War the European powers had been uncertain about how to deal with the victor. Germany toyed briefly with the notion of an American alliance, but only Great Britain had a clear view of what it wanted from the United States. In the late nineteenth century Britain's position in Europe had steadily worsened. It was being challenged industrially and militarily by a unified Germany. Clashing expansionist ambitions in North Africa and across Asia soured Britain's relations with France

and Russia. And there was general European hostility toward British imperial policy in South Africa, a policy that resulted in the Boer War against the independent-minded Dutch settlers at the end of the 1890s. In its growing isolation Britain turned to the United States. This explains why Britain had bowed to American demands in the Venezuela dispute of 1895. From that time onward, after a century of cool relations (or worse) with its former colonies, Britain strove consistently for a *rapprochement* (literally, a "coming together") with the United States.

In the Hay-Pauncefote Agreement of 1901 Britain gave up its treaty rights to joint participation in any Central American canal project, clearing the way for a canal exclusively under U.S. control. And two years later the last of the vexing U.S.–Canadian border disputes, this one involving British Columbia and Alaska, was settled, again to American satisfaction. The lone British member of the U.S.–Canadian tribunal cast the deciding vote awarding to the United States the Pacific inlets and ports that provided the only convenient access to the Klondike goldfields of the Canadian Yukon.

No formal alliance was forthcoming, but Anglo-American friendship had been placed on such a firm basis that, beginning in 1901, the British admiralty designed its war plans on the assumption of a friendly U.S. Navy. The assumption was that America was "a kindred state with whom we shall never have a parricidal war." Roosevelt heartily agreed: "England and the United States, beyond any other two powers, should be friendly." In his unflagging efforts to maintain a global balance of power, the cornerstone of Roosevelt's policy was the British relationship.

The Big Stick. Among nations, however, what counted was strength, not merely goodwill. Roosevelt wanted "to make all foreign powers understand that when we have adopted a line of policy we have adopted it definitely, and with the intention of backing it up with deeds as well as words." In Roosevelt's famous words: "Speak softly and carry a big stick." By a "big stick" he meant above all naval power.

Under Roosevelt, the battleship program went on apace. By 1904 the U.S. Navy stood fifth in the world, and by 1907 it was second. Roosevelt was a friend of Captain Mahan and a close student of his geopolitical writings. Mahan's program called for a big navy and strategic bases and, as a final step, a canal across Central America. Indeed, the Spanish-American War had demonstrated that strategic need in the most graphic way: the entire country had waited breathlessly as the battleship *Oregon* had sped for sixty days from the Pacific around the tip of South America to join the final action against the Spanish fleet in Cuba.

The Panama Canal. A canal was at the top of Roosevelt's agenda. With the surrender by Britain of its treaty right to a joint canal enterprise in 1901, Roosevelt proceeded to more troublesome matters. For $40 million, the United States purchased from the New Panama Canal Company the assets of de Lesseps's earlier project. Panama was a province of Colombia, so the Roosevelt administration entered into negotiations with Colombia to lease the strip of land through which the canal would run. The Colombian legislature voted down the proposed treaty, partly because the company's rights would soon expire and the sale to the United States could then be negotiated on terms more favorable to Colombia. Furious over what seemed to him a breach of faith, Roosevelt contemplated outright seizure of Panama but settled on a more devious solution.

The key intermediary in the sale of the de Lesseps assets, an engineer named Philippe Bunau-Varilla, let Roosevelt know that an independence movement was brewing in Panama. The United States in turn informed Bunau-Varilla that American ships were steaming toward Panama. The idea was that the Americans would provide cover for the expected uprising. There was a mix-up when the cruiser *Nashville* arrived at Colon, however, and the American commander failed to prevent 400 Colombian troops from disembarking at that small Atlantic port on November 3. Using their wits, the conspirators managed to keep those troops from proceeding to Panama City, and the bloodless revolution against Colombian rule went off on schedule. On November 7 the United States recognized Panama. Less than two weeks later, with Bunau-Varilla serving as the representative of the new republic, Panama signed a treaty that granted the United States a perpetually re-

The Panama Canal

The Canal Zone was acquired through devious means from which Americans could take little pride (and which led in 1978 to the Senate's decision to restore the property to Panama). But the building of the Panama Canal itself was a triumph of American ingenuity and drive. Dr. William C. Gorgas cleaned out the malarial mosquitoes that had earlier stymied the French. Under Colonel George W. Goethals, the U.S. Army overcame formidable obstacles in a mighty feat of engineering. This photograph shows the massive effort under way in December 1904 to excavate the Culebra Cut so that oceangoing ships would be able to pass through.

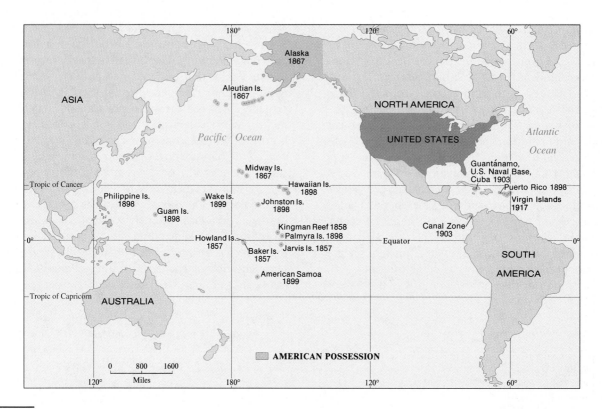

MAP 22.2

The American Empire

In 1890 Alfred T. Mahan wrote that the United States should regard the oceans as "a great highway" across which America would carry on world trade. That was precisely what resulted from the empire the United States acquired after the Spanish-American War. The Caribbean possessions, the strategically located Pacific islands, and, in 1903, the Panama Canal Zone gave the United States commercial and naval access to a wider world.

newable lease on a canal zone. These machinations were a dirty business, but they got Roosevelt what he wanted.

Roosevelt never regretted the victimization of Colombia, although the United States, as a kind of conscience money, paid Colombia $25 million in 1922. Building the canal was one of the heroic engineering feats of the century, involving a swamp-clearing project to rid the area of malaria and yellow fever, the construction of a series of great locks, and the excavation of 240 million cubic yards of earth. It took the U.S. Army Corps of Engineers eight years to finish the huge project. When it opened in 1914, the Panama Canal gave the United States a commanding commercial and strategic position in the Western Hemisphere (see Map 22.2).

Policeman of the Caribbean. Next came the task of making the Caribbean basin secure. The countries there, said Secretary of State Elihu Root, had been placed "in the front yard of the United States" by the

Panama Canal. Therefore, as Roosevelt put it, they had to "behave themselves."

In the case of Cuba, this was readily managed in the settlement that followed the Spanish-American War. Before the United States withdrew from Cuba in 1902, it reorganized Cuban finances and concluded a swamp-clearing program that eliminated yellow fever, a disease that had ravaged Cuba for many years (and had killed probably 4,000 of the occupying U.S. troops). As a condition for gaining independence, Cuba was required to include in its constitution a proviso called the Platt amendment, which gave the United States the right to intervene if Cuban independence was threatened or if Cuba failed to maintain internal order. Cuba also granted the United States a lease on Guantanamo Bay, where the U.S. Navy built a large base.

Roosevelt believed that instability in the Caribbean invited the intervention of European powers. For example, Britain and Germany blockaded Venezuela in 1902–1903 for failing to meet its debt payments. In

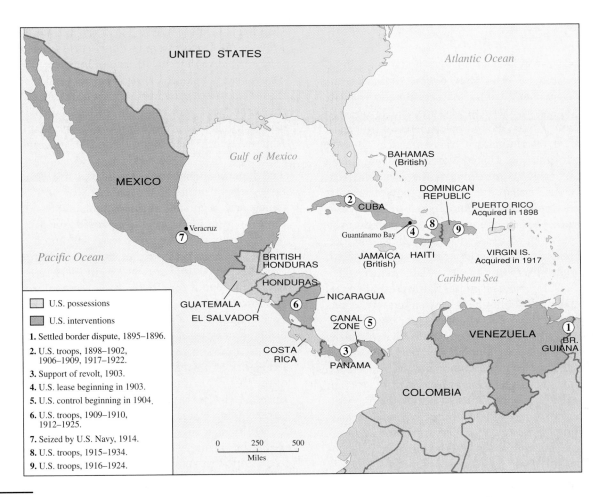

MAP 22.3

Policeman of the Caribbean
After the Spanish-American War the United States vigorously asserted its interest in
the affairs of its neighbors to the south. As the record of interventions shows, the
United States truly became the "policeman" of the Caribbean.

1904 Roosevelt announced that the United States would act as "policeman" of the region, stepping in "however reluctantly, in flagrant cases . . . of wrong doing or impotence."

This policy became known as the Roosevelt Corollary to the Monroe Doctrine. It transformed what had been a broad principle of opposition to European expansionist ambitions in Latin America into an unrestricted American right to regulate Caribbean affairs. The Roosevelt Corollary was not a treaty with other states; it was a unilateral declaration sanctioned only by American power and national interest.

Under the Roosevelt Corollary the United States intervened regularly in the internal affairs of Caribbean states. In 1905 American authorities took over the customs and debt management of the Dominican Republic; similar financial supervision was imposed on Nicaragua

in 1911 and Haiti in 1916. When internal order broke down, the United States did not hesitate to send in the Marines. Cuba was occupied in 1906, Nicaragua in 1909, and Haiti and the Dominican Republic in later years (see Map. 22.3).

Roosevelt's thinking was primarily strategic; his successor, William Howard Taft, took a more commercial view. American investments in the Caribbean region had grown dramatically after 1900. The United Fruit Company owned about 160,000 acres in Central America by 1913, and U.S. investments in Cuban sugar plantations quadrupled in fifteen years. Taft quickly intervened when disorder threatened American property. But he also regarded business investment as a force for stability in underdeveloped areas. Taft spoke for Dollar Diplomacy—the aggressive coupling of American diplomatic and economic interests abroad.

The Open Door

In the Far East, commercial interests had always stood at the forefront of American policy, especially the prospect of the huge China market. But by the late 1890s Japan, Russia, Germany, France, and Britain had all moved into China, carved out spheres of influence, and instituted discriminatory trade practices in their zones. Fearful that the United States was being frozen out of China, in 1899 Secretary of State John Hay sent an "Open Door" note to the occupying powers: he was attempting to establish the right of equal trade access— an Open Door—for all nations that wanted to do business in China. Even with its control over the Philippines, the United States was in a weak position compared with the occupying powers on the scene. The best that Hay was able to achieve were responses that were ambiguous and highly conditional, but he chose to interpret them as an acceptance of the American Open Door position.

When a secret society of Chinese nationalists launched the Boxer Rebellion in 1900, the United States sent 5,000 troops from the Philippines and joined the multinational campaign to raise the siege of the foreign legations in Peking (Beijing). America took the opportunity to assert a second principle of the Open Door: that China would be preserved as a "territorial and administrative entity." As long as the legal fiction of an independent China survived, so would American claims to equal access to the China market.

With a network of bases stretching across the Pacific, American power could now be projected into Asia. But here the United States faced formidable rivals. The European powers had acceded to American claims to preeminence in the Caribbean, including the Roosevelt Corollary. In the Far East, however, Britain, Germany, France, and Russia were strongly entrenched and were not inclined to defer to American interests. The United States also confronted a strategically placed Asian nation—Japan—that had its own vital interests. Although the Open Door was important to Roosevelt, he quickly saw in the Pacific a more intricate game that called on America to help maintain a balance of power.

The Japanese Challenge. Japan had unveiled its military strength in the Sino-Japanese War of 1894–1895, which had begun the dismemberment of China. With the formation of the Anglo-Japanese Alliance in 1902, the strategic advantage in East Asia shifted to Japan, emboldening it to confront Russia over their rival claims in Manchuria and Korea. In 1904, provoked by Russian demands for a military withdrawal from northern Korea, Japan suddenly attacked the tsar's fleet at Port Arthur, Russia's leased port in China. In a series of brilliant victories the Japanese demolished the Russian military forces in Asia. Roosevelt, eager to restore some semblance of a balance of power, mediated a settlement of the Russo-Japanese War at Portsmouth, New Hampshire, in 1905. Japan emerged as the predominant power in East Asia.

Dismissive of other Asian nations, Roosevelt admired the Japanese—"a wonderful and civilized people . . . entitled to stand in absolute equality with all the other peoples of the civilized world." He conceded that Japan had "a paramount interest in what surrounds the Yellow Sea, just as the United States has a paramount interest in what surrounds the Caribbean." But American strategic and commercial interests in the Pacific had to be accommodated. In exchange for Japanese accep-

The Japanese in California

The Japanese who flocked into California from 1890 onward made a mighty contribution to the state's agriculture, and through tireless labor many of them became independent and highly productive farmers. But the prejudice against them was unrelenting, and when San Francisco's school board sought to segregate Japanese children in 1906, an international incident occurred. President Roosevelt got the segregation order rescinded, and Japan voluntarily agreed to limit emigration to the United States. Despite this so-called gentlemen's agreement, a festering wound had been opened in the relations between the two countries.

tance of American sovereignty over the Philippines, the United States approved of Japan's protectorate over Korea in 1905 and raised no objection when that became full sovereignty six years later. However, a surge of anti-Asian feeling in California complicated Roosevelt's efforts. In 1906 San Francisco's school board placed all Asian students in a segregated school, infuriating Japan. The "gentlemen's agreement" of 1907, in which Japan agreed to restrict immigration to the United States, smoothed matters over, but the periodic resurgence of racism in California led to continuing tensions with the Japanese.

Roosevelt meanwhile moved to balance Japan's military power by increasing American naval strength in the Pacific. American battleships visited Japan in 1908 and then made a global tour in an impressive display of sea power. Late that year, near the end of his administration, Roosevelt achieved a formal accommodation with Japan. The Root-Takahira Agreement confirmed the status quo in the Pacific as well as the principles of free oceanic commerce and equal trade opportunity in China.

However, William Howard Taft entered the White House in 1909 convinced that the United States had been shortchanged. An exponent of Dollar Diplomacy, Taft pressed for a larger role for American bankers and investors in the Far East, especially in railroad construction going on in China. Taft hoped that American capital would counterbalance Japanese power and pave the way for increased commercial opportunities. When the Chinese Revolution of 1911 toppled the ruling Manchu dynasty, Taft supported the Chinese Nationalists as a counterforce to the Japanese. The United States thus entered a long-term rivalry with Japan that would end in war thirty years later.

The triumphant thrust across the Pacific lost some of its luster. The United States had become embroiled in a distant struggle that promised many future liabilities but little of the fabulous profits that had lured Americans to Asia. It was a chastening experience for an emerging world power.

Woodrow Wilson and Mexico

When Woodrow Wilson became president in 1913, he was bent on reform in American foreign policy no less than in domestic politics. Taft's Dollar Diplomacy seemed to Wilson to be an extension abroad of the arrogant business practices that he and other progressives were trying to curb at home. Wilson did not really differ with his predecessors on the importance of economic development overseas. He applauded the "tides of commerce" that would arise from the Panama Canal. But he opposed a commercial diplomacy that bullied weaker

countries into inequitable financial relationships and gave undue advantage to American business. It seemed to Wilson "a very perilous thing to determine the foreign policy of a nation in terms of material interest."

Within two weeks of taking office Wilson demonstrated what he had in mind. American banks had joined an international consortium to provide a loan to China. When the investment banker J. P. Morgan sought his approval, Wilson refused on the grounds that the terms of the loan threatened the independence of the Chinese government. The plan "was obnoxious to the principles upon which the government of our people rests."

The United States, Wilson insisted, should conduct its foreign policy in conformity with its democratic principles. He intended to foster the "development of constitutional liberty in the world" and above all to extend it to the nation's neighbors in Latin America. In a major policy speech in October 1913 he promised those nations that the United States would "never again seek one additional foot of territory by conquest." The president said he would strive to advance "human rights, national integrity, and opportunity" in Latin America. To do otherwise would make "ourselves untrue to our own traditions." Guided by such a moral policy, future generations would arrive at "those great heights where there shines unobstructed the light of the justice of God."

The Mexican Intervention. Mexico became the primary object of Wilson's ministrations. A cycle of revolutions had begun there in 1910. The long dictatorship of Porfirio Diaz was overthrown by Francisco Madero, who spoke much as Wilson did about liberty and constitutionalism. But before Madero could get very far with his reforms, he was deposed and murdered in February 1913 by one of his generals, Victoriano Huerta. Other powers quickly recognized Huerta's provisional government, but the United States had not acted when Wilson entered the White House the next month.

Wilson abhorred Huerta; he called his coup a "usurpation" and Huerta a murderer. Wilson pledged "to force him out." The United States denied recognition to Huerta's government, although that act contradicted America's long-standing tradition of granting quick recognition to new governments. Wilson also subjected Mexico to other pressures, including the threatened use of force. By intervening in this way, Wilson insisted, "we act in the interest of Mexico alone. . . . We are seeking to counsel Mexico for its own good." Wilson meant that he intended to put the Mexican Revolution back on the constitutional path started by Madero. Wilson was not deterred by the fact that American business interests, with enormous investments in Mexico, favored Huerta. On the contrary, that seemed to make him more determined to get Huerta out.

Carranza

Venustiano Carranza (1859–1920), the son of a landowner, was a provincial political figure who turned revolutionary when the dictator Diaz intervened in his election for the governorship of his native state of Coahuila in 1910. Carranza was crucial in bringing the Mexican Revolution to fruition, but he proved to be only a transitional figure because, as an old-fashioned liberal, he opposed the statist direction the revolution took. Before his term as first elected president ended in 1920, he was overthrown and killed in an ambush.

The emergence of armed opposition to Huerta in northern Mexico under Venustiano Carranza strengthened Wilson's hand. Carranza's Constitutionalist movement, as it became known, gave Wilson some grounds for denying recognition to Huerta, whose government did not fully control the country. More important, Carranza signified to Wilson the vitality of the reformist politics that he wanted to foster in Mexico.

But the Constitutionalists were ardent nationalists. They had no desire for American intervention in Mexican affairs. Carranza angrily rebuffed Wilson's efforts to bring about elections through a compromise between the rebels and the Mexican government. He also vowed to resist by force any intrusion of U.S. troops in his country. All he wanted from Wilson, Carranza asserted, was recognition of the Constitutionalists' belligerent status so that they could purchase arms in the United States. In exchange for vague promises to respect property rights and "fair" foreign concessions, Carranza finally got his way in 1914. American weapons began to flow to his troops.

The American contribution to the Constitutionalists' cause went well beyond selling them arms. For one thing, Wilson isolated Huerta diplomatically. Huerta's crucial support came from the British, who wanted to ensure a steady flow of Mexican oil for their fleet. Under intense pressure from Washington, the British withdrew recognition from Huerta in late 1913. In return, the United States became the guarantor of British property interests in Mexico.

When it became clear that neither the loss of British support nor the supplying of Carranza would turn the tide against Huerta, the United States threw its own forces into the game. Using the pretext of a minor insult to the U.S. Navy at Tampico, Wilson ordered the occupation of the major port of Veracruz on April 21, 1914. This action cost 19 American and 126 Mexican lives. At that point the Huerta regime began to crumble. Carranza nevertheless condemned the United States for intervening, and his forces came close to engaging the Americans. When he entered Mexico City in triumph in August 1914, Carranza had some cause to thank the Yankees. But if any sense of gratitude existed, it was overshadowed by the anti-Americanism inspired by Wilson's insensitivity to Mexican pride and revolutionary zeal.

This sad chapter in Mexican-American relations had a chastening effect on Wilson. It revealed to him the difficulties of acting on, or even living up to, well-meant ideals amid the confusion of war, revolution, and clashing national interests. Indeed, there were even more egregious examples on which he might have drawn: despite his anti-imperialist pronouncements, Wilson acted just as his predecessors had by sending in the U.S. Marines when law and order broke down in Haiti in 1915 and in the Dominican Republic in 1916.

The Gathering Storm in Europe

In the meantime, Europe had begun to drift toward a great world war. There were two main sources of tension. One derived from the deadly rivalry between Germany, the new military and economic superpower of Europe, and the European states threatened by its might—above all France, which had been humiliated in the Franco-Prussian War of 1870 and forced to cede the Alsace-Lorraine provinces to Germany. The second danger zone was the Balkans, where the Ottoman Empire was disintegrating and where, in the midst of explosive ethnic rivalries, Austria-Hungary and Russia were maneuvering for dominance. On the basis of these conflicts an alliance system had emerged, with Germany, Austria-Hungary, and Italy (the Triple Alliance) on one side and France and Russia (the Dual Alliance) on the other.

The tensions in Europe were, to some degree, released by European imperial adventures, especially by France in Africa and by Russia in Asia. These activities placed France and Russia in opposition to imperial Britain, effectively excluding Britain from the European alliance system. Fearful of Germany, however, Britain in 1904 composed its differences with France, and the two countries reached a friendly understanding, or *entente*. When Britain came to a similar understanding with Russia in 1907, the basis was laid for the Triple Entente. A deadly confrontation between two great European power blocs became possible.

In these European quarrels Americans had no obvious stake or any inclination, in the words of a cautionary Senate resolution, "to depart from the traditional American foreign policy which forbids participation . . . [in] political questions which are entirely European in scope." But on becoming president, Theodore Roosevelt had taken a lively interest in European affairs, and he was eager, as the head of a Great Power, to make a contribution to the cause of peace there. In 1905 he got his chance.

The Anglo-French entente of the previous year had been based partly on an agreement arranging spheres of influence in North Africa: the Sudan was conceded to Britain, and Morocco to France. Now Germany suddenly challenged France over Morocco. It was a disastrous move, contravening Germany's self-interest in keeping France's attention diverted from Europe by its colonial involvements overseas. Instead, the Morocco issue brought France into conflict with Germany and produced a great European crisis. Kaiser Wilhelm turned to Roosevelt for help. Finding in an obscure commercial treaty with Morocco the basis for American involvement, Roosevelt persuaded France to participate in an international conference, which was held in January 1906 at Algeciras, Spain. With U.S. diplomats playing a key role, the crisis was defused: Germany got a few token concessions, but France's dominance over Morocco was sustained.

Algeciras marked, in actuality, an ominous turning point in which the power blocs that would become locked in battle in 1914 first squared off against one another. But at the time it looked like a diplomatic triumph, and Roosevelt's secretary of state, Elihu Root, boasted of America's success in "preserv[ing] world peace because of the power of our detachment."

Root's words prefigured how the United States would define its role among the Great Powers: it would be the apostle of peace, distinguished by its "detachment," its lack of selfish interests in European affairs. But opposing this internationalist impulse was the tenacious grip of America's traditional isolationism.

The Peace Movement. Enthusiasm ran high in America for the international peace movement that had been launched by the Hague Peace Conference of 1899. The Permanent Court of Arbitration that had been created by the Hague conference offered new hope for the peaceful settlement of international disputes. Both the Roosevelt and the Taft administrations negotiated arbitration treaties with other countries that pledged to submit their disputes to the Hague Court, only to see the treaties emasculated by a Senate unwilling to permit the nation's sovereignty to be compromised in any significant way. Nor was there any sequel to Roosevelt's initiative at Algeciras. It had been coolly received in the Senate and by the nation's press. Roosevelt's successor, William Howard Taft, was not inclined to transgress the doctrine of nonentanglement.

When Woodrow Wilson became president, he chose William Jennings Bryan to be his secretary of state. Bryan was a great apostle of world peace and devoted himself to negotiating a series of "cooling off" treaties with other countries—so called because the parties agreed to wait for one year while the disputed issues were submitted to a conciliation process. These bilateral agreements were admirable, but they were irrelevant to the explosive power politics of Europe. As tensions there reached the breaking point in 1914, the United States remained effectively on the sidelines.

Yet at Algeciras Roosevelt had rightly seen what the future would demand of America. So did the French writer Andre Tardieu, who remarked in 1908:

> The United States is . . . a world power. . . . Its power creates for it . . . a duty—to pronounce upon all those questions that hitherto have been arranged by agreement only among European powers. These powers themselves, at critical times, turn toward the United States, anxious to know its opinion. . . . The United States intervenes thus in the affairs of the universe. . . . It is seated at the table where the great game is played, and it cannot leave it.

Summary

In 1877 the United States was, by any economic or population measure, already a great power. But America's orientation was inward-looking. The lax conduct of its foreign policy—and the neglect of its naval power—reflected the absence of significant overseas concerns. America's rapid economic development, however, began to force the country to look outward, in particular because of the felt need for outlets for its surplus products. By the early 1890s a new strategic outlook had taken hold, best expressed in the writings of Alfred T. Mahan, that called for a battleship navy, an interoceanic canal, and overseas bases from which American naval power could be projected to ensure access to markets in Latin America and Asia. Accompanying this new expansionism were legitimating ideas drawn from Social Darwinism, Anglo-Saxon racism, and America's earlier tradition of Manifest Destiny.

With the Spanish-American War, an opportunity for acting on these imperialist impulses presented itself. On the one hand, America's traditional antiexpansionism was briefly silenced; on the other hand, swift victory enabled the United States to seize from Spain the key possessions it wanted. In taking the Philippines, however, the United States overstepped the bounds of the kind of colonialism palatable to the country—overseas bases, not the rule of alien populations. The result was a resurgence of anti-imperialist sentiment that was deepened by Filipino resistance to annexation. Even so, the McKinley administration realized the strategic goals it had set, and the United States entered the twentieth century poised to fulfill its destiny as a Great Power.

In Europe the immediate consequences were few. Only in its *rapprochement* with Britain and in Roosevelt's involvement in the Moroccan crisis did the United States begin to depart from its traditional policy of avoiding European entanglements. Regarding its regional interests in the Caribbean and Asia, however, the United States moved much more decisively, building the Panama Canal, asserting its dominance over the nearby states, and pressing for the Open Door in China. When Woodrow Wilson became president, he tried to bring the conduct of America's foreign policy into closer conformity with the nation's political ideals, only to have the limitations of that departure driven home by his intervention in the Mexican Revolution. That lesson, however, did not stay Wilson's hand when a great world war engulfed Europe in 1914.

TIMELINE

1875	Treaty brings Hawaii within U.S. orbit
1876	United States achieves favorable balance of trade
1881	Secretary of State James G. Blaine inaugurates Pan-Americanism
1889	Conflict with Germany in Samoa President Harrison begins rebuilding U.S. Navy
1890	Alfred Thayer Mahan publishes *The Influence of Seapower upon History*
1893	Annexation of Hawaii fails Frederick Jackson Turner's "The Significance of the Frontier in American History" Panic of 1893 ushers in economic depression (until 1897)
1894	Sino-Japanese War begins breakup of China into spheres of influence
1895	Venezuela crisis Cuban civil war
1898	Outbreak of Spanish-American War Hawaii annexed Anti-imperialist movement launched
1899	Treaty of Paris Guerrilla war in the Philippines Open Door policy in China
1901	Theodore Roosevelt becomes president; diplomacy of the "big stick" Hay-Pauncefote Agreement
1902	U.S. withdraws from Cuba; Platt amendment gives U.S. right of intervention
1903	U.S. recognizes Panama and receives grant of Canal Zone
1904	Roosevelt Corollary
1905	U.S. mediates Franco-German crisis over Morocco at Algeciras
1907	Gentlemen's Agreement with Japan
1908	Root-Takahira Agreement
1909	Taft becomes president; Dollar Diplomacy
1913	Wilson asserts new principles for American diplomacy Intervention in the Mexican Revolution
1914	Panama Canal opens World War I begins

★   ★   ★

BIBLIOGRAPHY

Two useful surveys of late nineteenth-century diplomatic history are Foster R. Dulles, *Prelude to World Power, 1865–1900* (1965), and Charles S. Campbell, *The Transformation of American Foreign Relations, 1865–1900* (1976). Invaluable as an historiographical guide is Robert L. Beisner, *From the Old Diplomacy to the New, 1865–1900* (2d ed., 1986).

The Roots of Expansionism

Standard works on the preexpansionist era are David M. Pletcher, *The Awkward Years: American Foreign Relations under Garfield and Arthur* (1963), and Milton Plesur, *America's Outward Thrust: Approaches to American Foreign Affairs, 1865–1890* (1971). Walter LaFeber's highly influential *The New Empire, 1860–1898* (1963) places economic interest—especially the need for overseas markets—at the center of scholarly debate over the sources of American expansionism. On American business overseas the definitive work is Myra Wilkins, *The Emergence of the Multinational Enterprise: American Business Abroad from the Colonial Era to 1914* (1970). Other important books dealing with aspects of American expansionism are David Healy, *U.S. Expansionism: The Imperialist Urge in the 1890s* (1970); Robert Seager, *Alfred Thayer Mahan* (1977); Michael Hunt, *Ideology and U.S. Foreign Policy* ((1987); and Kenneth J. Hagan, *This People's Navy: The Making of American Seapower* (1991).

An American Empire

On the war with Spain, see John Offner, *An Unwanted War: The Diplomacy of the United States and Spain over Cuba, 1895–1898* (1988); David S. Trask, *The War with Spain in 1898* (1981); Frank Freidel, *A Splendid Little War* (1958); and Lewis Gould, *The Spanish-American War and President McKinley* (1982), which emphasizes McKinley's strong leadership. Ernest R. May, *Imperial Democracy: The Emergence of America as a Great Power* (1961), exemplifies the earlier view that McKinley was a weak figure who was driven to war by jingoistic pressures. On the Philippines, see Richard E.

Welch, *Response to Imperialism: The United States and the Philippine-American War, 1898–1903* (1979), and, for the subsequent history, Peter Stanley, *A Nation in the Making: The Philippines and the United States, 1899–1921* (1974). Robert L. Beisner, *Twelve against Empire: The Anti-Imperialists, 1898–1900* (1968) remains the best book on that subject.

Onto the World Stage

On the European context a useful introduction can be found in the early chapters of Felix Gilbert, *The End of the European Era, 1890 to the Present* (4th ed., 1991). For a stimulating interpretation see L. C. B. Seaman, *From Vienna to Versailles* (1955). On American relations with Britain the standard work is Bradford Perkins, *The Great Rapprochement: England and the United States, 1895–1914* (1968). On Roosevelt's diplomacy the starting point remains Howard K. Beale, *Theodore Roosevelt and the Rise of America to World Power (1956)*. There are keen insights into the diplomatic views of both Roosevelt and Wilson in John Milton Cooper, *The Warrior and the Priest* (1983). On the thrust into the Caribbean, see Walter LaFeber, *The Panama Canal* (1979); Richard Lael, *Arrogant Diplomacy: U.S. Policy toward Colombia, 1903–1922* (1987); David Healy, *Drive to Hegemony: The United States in the Caribbean, 1898–1917* (1888); and Thomas D. Schoonover, *The United States in Central America, 1860–1911* (1991). America's Asian involvements are treated in Thomas J. McCormick, *China Market: America's Quest for Informal Empire, 1893–1901* (1967); Michael H. Hunt, *The Making of a Special Relationship: The United States and China to 1914* (1983); and Akira Iriye, *Pacific Estrangement: Japanese and American Expansion, 1897–1911* (1972). On the Mexican involvement see John S. D. Eisenhower, *Intervention! The United States and the Mexican Revolution* (1993). There is a lively and critical analysis of Wilson's misguided policies in Robert E. Quirk, *An Affair of Honor: Woodrow Wilson and the Occupation of Veracruz* (1962). The revolution as experienced by the Mexicans is brilliantly depicted in John Womack, *Zapata and the Mexican Revolution* (1968).

P A R T **5**

The Modern State and Society

1914–1945

THEMATIC TIMELINE

	Government	Diplomacy	Economy	Society	Culture
	The Rise of the State	**From Isolation to World Leadership**	**Prosperity, Depression, and War**	**Nativism, Migration, and Social Change**	**The Emergence of a Mass National Culture**
1914	Wartime agencies expand power of the federal government	U.S. enters World War I, 1917 Wilson's Fourteen Points, 1918	Shift from debtor to creditor nation Agricultural glut	Southern blacks begin migration to northern cities	Silent screen; Hollywood becomes movie capital of the world
1920	Republican ascendancy Prohibition, 1920–33 Business-government partnership	Treaty of Versailles rejected by U.S. Senate, 1920 Washington Conference sets naval limits, 1922	Economic recession, 1920–21 Booming prosperity, 1922–29 Welfare capitalism	Rise of nativism National Origins Act (1924) Mexican-American immigration increases	Jazz Age Advertising promotes consumer culture, supports radio and new magazines
1930	Franklin D. Roosevelt becomes president, 1933 The New Deal: unprecedented government intervention in economy, social welfare, arts	Roosevelt's Good Neighbor Policy toward Latin America, 1933 Abraham Lincoln Brigade fights in Spanish Civil War U.S. neutrality proclaimed, 1939	Great Depression, 1929–41 Rise of labor movement	Farming families migrate from Dust Bowl states to California and the West Indian New Deal	Documentary impulse Federal patronage of the arts
1940	Government mobilizes industry for war production and rationing	U.S. enters World War II, 1941 Allies defeat Axis powers; bombing of Hiroshima, 1945	War moblization ends depression	Rural whites and blacks migrate to war jobs in cities Civil rights movement revitalized	Film industry enlisted to aid war effort

By 1914 industrialization, economic expansion abroad, and the growth of a vibrant urban culture had laid the foundations for a distinctly *modern* American society. By 1945, after having fought two world wars and weathering a dozen years of economic depression, the edifice of the new society was largely complete.

First, an essential building block of modern American society was a strong national state. This state came late and haltingly to America compared with the industrialized countries in Western Europe. Wary of a permanent concentration of government power in Washington, policy makers quickly dismantled the centralized wartime bureaucracies in 1919. During the 1920s the Harding and Coolidge administrations embraced a philosophy of business-government partnership, believing that unrestricted corporate capitalism would provide for the welfare of the American people. It took the Great Depression, with its uncounted business failures and unprecedented levels of unemployment, to overthrow that long-cherished idea. Franklin D. Roosevelt's New Deal dramatically expanded federal responsibility for the economy and the welfare of ordinary citizens. An even greater expansion of the state resulted from the massive mobilization necessitated by America's entry into World War II. Unlike the experience after World War I, the new state apparatus remained in place when the war ended.

The second defining feature of modern American society was established when the United States was slowly and somewhat reluctantly drawn into the position of world leadership that it still occupies. In 1918 American troops helped provide the margin of victory for the Allies in World War I, and President Wilson helped shape the treaties that ended the war. The United States was not prepared to embrace Wilson's internationalist vision and refused to join the League of Nations, but America's dominant economic position guaranteed an active role in world affairs in the 1920s and 1930s. The globalization of America accelerated in 1941, when the nation threw all its energies into defeating Germany and Japan. The United States became the leader of the alliance that fought those nations and emerged as the dominant world power.

The third characteristic of modern America was the strength of its domestic economy. In the period between the two world wars the American industrial economy was the most productive in the world. American businesses successfully competed in world markets, and American financial institutions played the leading role in international economic affairs. Large-scale corporate organizations replaced smaller family-run businesses. The automobile industry symbolized the ascendancy of mass-production techniques. Many workers shared in the general prosperity but also bore the brunt of economic downturns. These economic uncertainties fueled the dramatic growth of the labor movement in the 1930s.

The fourth step toward modernity was taken when American society was transformed by the great wave of European immigration and the movement from farms to cities. The growth of metropolitan areas gave the nation an increasingly urban tone, and geographical mobility broke down regional differences. Many old-stock white Americans viewed these processes with alarm; in 1924 nativists succeeded in all but eliminating immigration except from within the Western Hemisphere. But internal migration continued to change the face of America as African-Americans moved north to take factory jobs and Dust Bowl farmers moved to the Far West to find better lives.

The fifth defining feature of modern America was the emergence of a mass culture. Americans were drawn into a web of interlocking cultural experiences. Advertising and the new entertainment media—the movies, radio, and magazines—disseminated the values of consumerism. Not even the Great Depression could divert Americans from their desire for leisure, self-fulfillment, and consumer goods. The emphasis on consumption and a quest for a rising standard of living would define the American experience for the rest of the twentieth century.

Despite the forces combining to centralize power and nationalize American culture, modern America has been marked by diversity. The lives of ordinary Americans have been shaped by whether they live in cities or rural areas and whether they are white or nonwhite, male or female, rich or poor, young or old. Describing the centralizing tendencies in modern American life while connecting them to the ongoing diversity of social experience offers clues to the complexity of America's history in the 1914–1945 period and beyond.

America and the War Effort

Irving Berlin's 1918 sheet music captured the ambivalence surrounding American participation in World War I: soldiers were proud to serve, but it was still hard to get up in the morning.

War and the American State

1914–1920

★ ★ ★

"It would be the irony of fate if my administration had to deal chiefly with foreign affairs," Woodrow Wilson told a friend early in his first term. But the United States was no longer just a regional power—it was seated at the table of the "great game" of international politics. When war broke out in Europe in August 1914, Wilson had to play his hand. For more than two years he tried to be an honest broker for the two sides. Only when Germany's resumption of unrestricted submarine attacks threatened American lives and shipping did he reluctantly ask Congress for a declaration of war.

The American decision to enter the conflict in 1917 confirmed one of the most important shifts of power in the twentieth century. The pre–World War I world had been dominated by Europe; the postwar world was increasingly dominated by the United States. America would have emerged as the principal world power eventually because of its economic strength, but World War I hastened the process. The historian Akira Iriye calls this broad transformation the "globalization" of America— how the United States increasingly became "involved in security, economic, and cultural affairs in all parts of the world." This process, which is usually thought to begin with World War II and its aftermath, actually started in 1917.

Once the war was under way, Wilson led the country with the same idealism he had brought to domestic concerns during the Progressive Era (see Chapter 21). In the first major U.S. intervention in Great Power politics, Wilson aimed for a new international order based on democratic ideals.

Despite Wilson's rhetoric, the United States was not ready to wage a modern war in 1917. New federal bureaucracies had to be created to coordinate the efforts of business, labor, and agriculture, a process that hastened the emergence of a national administrative state. War meant new opportunities for women and for blacks and other ethnic minorities. It also meant new divisions among Americans and new hatreds, first of Germans and Austrians and then of "Bolshevik" Reds. When the war ended, the United States was forced to confront the deep class, racial, and ethnic divisions that had surfaced during wartime mobilization.

The Great War, 1914–1918

When war erupted in August 1914, most Americans saw no reason to get involved in a struggle among Europe's imperialistic powers. No vital American interests were at stake; indeed the United States had good relationships with both sides. But a combination of factors—economic interests, violations of neutral rights, cultural ties with Great Britain and France, and German miscalculations—drew the United States into the war on the Allied side in 1917.

War in Europe

Almost from the moment France, Russia, and Britain formed the Triple Entente in 1907 to counter the Triple Alliance of Germany, Austria-Hungary, and Italy (see Chapter 22), European leaders began to prepare for what they saw as an inevitable conflict. The spark that ignited war came in Europe's perennial tinderbox, the Balkans. Most of the Balkans, including Bosnia, Herze-

govina, and Serbia, had been part of the Turkish Ottoman Empire since the sixteenth century. As the Ottoman Empire slowly disintegrated during the nineteenth century, Austria-Hungary and Russia competed for power and influence in the Balkans. Austria's seizure of the provinces of Bosnia and Herzegovina in 1908 enraged Russia and its client, the independent state of Serbia, which had hoped to form a greater South Slavic state. Serbian terrorists recruited Bosnians to agitate against Austrian rule, and on June 28, 1914, one of them assassinated Franz Ferdinand, the heir to the Austro-Hungarian throne, and his wife in the Bosnian town of Sarajevo.

After the assassination the complex European system of alliances that had for years maintained a fragile peace pulled all the major powers into war. Austria-Hungary blamed Serbia for the assassination and demanded concessions. The Serbs did meet most of the demands and asked for arbitration of the rest. However, this was not enough for Austria, which, assured of support from Germany, declared war on Serbia on July 28. Russia, which had a secret treaty with Serbia, began preparations for war. Germany in turn declared war on Russia and Russia's ally, France. Acting on its Schlieffen Plan, which was designed to eliminate one enemy at a time (that is, overrun France before Russia could mobilize), Germany invaded neutral Belgium as a prelude to conquering France. The brutality of the invasion and Britain's commitment to Belgian neutrality prompted Great Britain to declare war on Germany on August 4. Two days later Russia and Austria-Hungary formally entered the conflict.

The Landscape of War
World War I devastated the countryside: this was the battleground at Ypres in 1915. The carnage of trench warfare also scarred the soldiers who served in these surreal settings, causing the "gas neurosis," "burial-alive neurosis," and "soldiers' heart"—all symptoms of shell shock.

MAP 23.1

Europe at the Start of World War I
In early August 1914 a complex set of interlocking alliances drew the major European powers into war. At first the United States avoided the conflict. Not until April 1917 did America enter the war on the Allied side.

The combatants were thus divided into two rival blocs. The Allied Powers consisted of Great Britain, France, Japan, Russia, and in 1915 Italy. They were pitted against the Central Powers: Germany, Austria-Hungary, and Turkey, joined by Bulgaria in 1915 (see Map 23.1). Because of the alliance system, the conflict spread to parts of the world far beyond Europe, making this a truly global war. The Austrians and Germans faced the Russians on the Eastern Front; Turkey squared off against Russian and British troops in the Middle East and Mesopotamia; and the British, French, and Japanese seized German territories in Africa, China, and the South Pacific. The worldwide scope of the conflict and the huge casualties resulting from campaigns such as Gallipoli in the Dardanelles caused it to be known as the Great War, or later, World War I. It was also the first modern war in which extensive harm was done to civilian populations.

Military Technology. Since the American Civil War and the Franco-Prussian War in 1870, massive industrialization and an escalating arms race among the Great Powers had transformed the technology of war. Every soldier in World War I carried a long-range, high-velocity rifle that could hit a target at 1,000 yards, a vast improvement over the 300-yard range of the rifle-musket used in the American Civil War. Significantly, the mass production of rifles in Europe relied on the adoption of technology developed in Connecticut factories. Another innovation, the machine gun, also had American roots. Its Maine-born inventor, Hiram Maxim, had moved to

Great Britain in the 1880s, heeding a friend's advice: "If you want to make your fortune, invent something which will allow those fool Europeans to kill each other more quickly."

The concentrated fire of rifles and machine guns gave a tremendous advantage to troops in defensive positions. For four bloody years, between 1914 and 1918, the Allies and the Central Powers faced each other on the Western Front, a narrow swath of territory in Belgium and northern France crisscrossed by 25,000 miles of heavily fortified trenches, enough to circle the globe. (Barbed wire, invented to fence the western range, became a devastating weapon of war when coiled above the trenches.) Trench warfare produced unprecedented numbers of casualties. If one side tried to break the stalemate by venturing into the "no-man's-land" between the trenches, its soldiers were mowed down by artillery fire or poison gas, first used by the Germans at Ypres in April 1915. Between February and December 1916 the French suffered 550,000 casualties and the Germans 450,000 as Germany tried to break through the French lines at Verdun. The front did not move.

Military strategists struggled to find ways to break the stalemate on the Western Front. Tanks, first used in the Battle of the Somme in the fall of 1916, proved effective against the machine gun and could crash through the barbed wire protecting enemy trenches, but they did not play the decisive military role that they would in World War II. Neither did airplanes, despite the dramatic advances in aviation since the Wright brothers' 12-second, 120-foot flight at Kitty Hawk,

North Carolina, in 1903. The technology of aerial bombardment was still primitive, so airplanes mainly flew photographic reconnaissance missions.

The Perils of Neutrality

Two weeks after the outbreak of war in Europe President Wilson made the American position clear. In a message widely printed in the newspapers the president called on Americans to be "neutral in fact as well as in name, impartial in thought as well as in action." Wilson wanted to keep out of war partly in order to play a larger, not a smaller, role in world affairs. The child of a Presbyterian minister, Wilson approached foreign affairs with missionary zeal. He never doubted the superiority of the Christian values he had learned as a boy or questioned the chauvinistic belief that the United States was better than the rest of the world. Only if he kept America aloof from the European quarrel, Wilson reasoned, could he impartially arbitrate—and influence—its ultimate settlement.

The nation's divided loyalties also influenced Wilson's policy. Many Americans, including Wilson, felt deep cultural ties to the Allies, especially Britain and France, yet most Catholic Irish-Americans resented the centuries-long British occupation of their home country and the cancellation of Home Rule in 1914. Also 10 million immigrants had come from Germany and Austria-Hungary, and German-Americans made up one of the largest and best established ethnic groups in the United States. Many aspects of German culture, including classical music and Germany's university system, were widely admired. It would not have been easy for Wilson to rally Americans to the Allied side in 1914.

Many Americans had no sympathy for either side. Pacifist sentiment was diffuse but broad, rooted in isolationism as well as disillusionment with America's experience in the Spanish-American War. Progressive Republicans such as Senators Robert La Follette of Wisconsin and George Norris of Nebraska vehemently opposed American participation in the European conflict. Progressive Democrats, including Secretary of State Williams Jennings Bryan, and many western and southern progressives, felt the same. Practically the entire political left, led principally by Eugene Debs and the Socialist party, condemned the war as imperialism, whereas African-American leaders such as A. Philip Randolph identified it as a conflict of the white race only. Newly formed antiwar groups, among them the American Union against Militarism and the Women's Peace Party, both founded in 1915, also mobilized popular opposition. The feminists Jane Addams and Crystal Eastman spoke out against war as an instrument of national policy. Prominent industrialists, notably Andrew Carnegie and Henry Ford, bankrolled antiwar activi-

ties. Ford spent almost half a million dollars in December 1915 to send more than a hundred men and women to Europe on a "peace ship" to negotiate an end to the war.

Conflict on the High Seas. With no stake in the territorial struggles among the European powers, the United States might well have remained neutral if the conflict had not spread to a new theater—the high seas. Here the United States initially had as many arguments with Britain as with Germany. The most troublesome issue concerned freedom of the seas and neutrality rights—the freedom to trade with nations on both sides of a conflict.

By the end of August 1914 the British had imposed a naval blockade on the Central Powers. The Allies were hoping to cut off military supplies and starve the German people into submission, but their actions also prevented neutral nations such as the United States from trading with Germany and its allies. The United States chafed at this infringement of its neutrality rights but chose to do little besides complain, largely because the spectacular increase in trade with the Allies more than made up for the lost trade with the Central Powers. American trade with Britain and France grew from $824 million in 1914 to $3.2 billion in 1916, and by 1917 U.S. bankers had lent the Allies $2.5 billion. In contrast, American trade with and loans to Germany in 1917 totaled only $29 million and $27 million, respectively.

To challenge British control of the seas, the German navy launched a devastating new weapon, the U-boat, short for *Unterseeboot* (undersea boat, or submarine). In February 1915, Germany announced a naval blockade of Great Britain: German submarines would attack any ship transporting military supplies to the British Isles. Traditional rules of naval warfare required submarine commanders to warn and search a ship before sinking it. If a submarine surfaced to do this, however, it would lose its greatest advantage—surprise—and leave itself vulnerable to attack.

Although the Germans sank an American merchant ship without warning on May 1, 1915, it was the sinking of a British luxury liner, the *Lusitania*, off the Irish coast six days later that brought the United States to the brink of war. When the *Lusitania* went down, 1,198 people died, including 128 Americans. The passenger ship, although unarmed, was carrying thousands of cases of ammunition, and an advertisement in a New York newspaper had warned passengers about the risk of attack. Newspapers called the loss of innocent civilian lives "mass murder," and the former president Theodore Roosevelt characterized the attack as "an act of piracy." The National Security League, one of the leading voices in the "preparedness" campaign, intensified its calls for increased appropriations for the armed forces and a system of universal military training.

Wilson sent a series of strongly worded notes to Germany to protest this assault on the freedom of non-belligerents to travel on the high seas, although he did not ban Americans from traveling on the ships of Germany's enemies. The *Lusitania* crisis divided Wilson's government into pro- and anti-British factions. Secretary of State William Jennings Bryan resigned in protest, unable to support Wilson's harsh criticism of Germany's violation of neutrality rights while the president remained silent about Britain's violation of American rights with its blockade.

After the sinking of the *Lusitania*, Wilson had confided to a cabinet member, "I wish with all my heart I saw a way to carry out the double wish of our people, to maintain a firm front in respect of what we demand of Germany and yet do nothing that might by any possibility involved us in war." The crisis continued until September 1915, when Germany announced that submarine commanders would not attack passenger ships without warning. (Eight months later the Germans halted, at least temporarily, attacks on merchant shipping.) For the Germans the danger of drawing the United States into the war far offset the benefits of attacking British ships. A temporary lull set into the naval war.

Throughout 1915 and 1916, Wilson tried at several points to mediate an end to the European conflict through his aide, Colonel Edward House. But House concluded that neither side was interested in serious peace negotiations. Worsening tensions with Germany in turn caused Wilson to rethink his earlier opposition to preparedness. In the fall of 1915 he decided that a half-billion dollar buildup of the army and navy was prudent and desirable, and by 1916 rearmament was well under way.

The 1916 Election. The election of 1916 did not serve as a referendum on the American stance toward the war. The Republican party passed over the prowar belligerence represented by Theodore Roosevelt in favor of Supreme Court Justice Charles Evans Hughes, a former governor of New York. The Democrats renominated Woodrow Wilson, whose campaign emphasized the progressive reform record he had accomplished during his first term (see Chapter 21). The Democrats also picked up votes with their widely circulated campaign slogan, "He kept us out of war." They won a narrow victory over a Republican party reunited after its 1912 split. Despite getting 3 million more votes than he had in 1912, Wilson defeated Hughes by only about 600,000 votes and by 277 to 254 in the electoral college. That slender margin limited Wilson's options in mobilizing the nation for war and planning the postwar peace.

Toward War. The events of early 1917 diminished Wilson's hopes of staying out of the conflict. On January 31 Germany announced the resumption of unrestricted submarine attacks, a decision dictated by the impasse of the land war. Although the Germans knew that this would almost certainly bring the United States into the war, the German general staff assured the government that its submarines could paralyze Allied shipping before the Americans joined the fighting. In response, Wilson broke off diplomatic relations with Germany on February 3.

The release of the "Zimmermann telegram" in late February 1917 also moved the country closer to war. Newspapers published an intercepted communication from Germany's foreign secretary, Arthur Zimmermann, to the German minister in Mexico City, which contained conclusive evidence of German interference in Mexican affairs. In a direct challenge to the Monroe Doctrine, Zimmermann urged Mexico to join the Central Powers in the war. In return, Germany promised to help Mexico recover "the lost territory of Texas, New

The 1916 Campaign
This campaign van sponsored by the Women's Bureau of the Democratic National Committee linked Woodrow Wilson to the themes of progressivism, prosperity, and preparedness. Note the variation on the popular slogan, "Who keeps us out of war?"

Mexico, and Arizona." When the telegram was made public on February 27, this threat to the territorial integrity of the United States jolted both Congressional and public opinion, especially in the West, where support for the war had lagged. Combined with the resumption of unrestricted submarine warfare, the telegram further inflamed anti-German sentiment.

Although the likelihood of Mexico reconquering the border states was slim, the highly volatile situation there (see Chapter 22) continued to concern American policy makers. In the final stages of the Mexican Revolution, the Constitutionalist movement led by Venustiano Carranza consolidated its power against the rebel Pancho Villa. When the United States stopped giving aid to Villa to concentrate its support behind Carranza, Villa orchestrated retaliatory raids along the border, killing sixteen U.S. citizens in January 1916 and razing the town of Columbus, New Mexico, in March. As the Mexican civil war threatened to spill over the Rio Grande into the United States, Wilson sent troops led by General John J. Pershing into Mexico to capture the elusive Villa; soon Pershing's forces resembled an army of occupation rather than troops on a punitive expedition. Strongly supported by Mexican public opinion, Carranza demanded that Pershing withdraw immediately. The two governments backed off, and U.S. troops began to leave early in 1917. The Carranza government received official recognition from Washington on March 13, 1917, less than a month before the United States entered World War I.

Declaring War. Throughout March, U-boats attacked American shipping without warning, sinking three ships on March 18 alone. On April 2, 1917, after consulting his cabinet, Wilson appeared before a special session of Congress to ask for a declaration of war. "It is a fearful thing to lead this great peaceful people into war," Wilson declared. He shared the fears of many Americans who dreaded entering a conflict that had already proved so costly—millions of Europeans killed, their landscapes and social structures destroyed. America had no selfish aims: "We desire no conquest, no dominion. We seek no indemnities for ourselves, no material compensation for the sacrifices we shall freely make. We are but one of the champions of the rights of mankind." In a memorable phrase that was intended to ennoble America's role, he decided that "the world must be made safe for democracy."

Four days later, on April 6, 1917, the United States declared war on Germany. Reflecting the divided feelings of the country as a whole, the vote was far from unanimous. Six senators and fifty members of the House voted against the action, including Representative Jeannette Rankin of Montana, the first woman elected to Congress. "I want to stand by my country," she declared, "but I cannot vote for war."

The First Woman in Congress
In 1916, Jeannette Rankin, a former suffrage organizer, became the first woman elected to Congress. Her vote against U.S. entry into World War I cost her a chance for election to the Senate in 1918. In 1940 Rankin again won election to Congress from Montana. True to her lifelong pacifism, she cast the only vote against American entry into World War II.

Over There

To native-born Americans, Europe seemed a great distance away, literally "over there," as the lyrics of George M. Cohan's popular song described it. After the declaration of war many citizens were surprised to learn that the United States planned to send troops to Europe; they had assumed that the nation's participation could be limited to military and economic aid.

In May 1917 General John J. Pershing, recently returned from the unsuccessful pursuit of Pancho Villa in Mexico, traveled to London and Paris to determine how America could best support the war effort. The answer was clear: as Marshal Joseph Joffre of France put it, "Men, men, and more men." The problem was that the United States had never maintained a large standing army in peacetime. Only about 200,000 soldiers, mostly lifetime volunteers, were on active duty in early 1917. To field a large enough fighting force to enter a global war, the government turned to conscription.

Conscription. The passage of the Selective Service Act in May 1917 demonstrated the increasing impact of the state on ordinary citizens. Unlike the resistance to the draft during the Civil War, no major riots occurred. The selective service system worked in part because it combined central direction from Washington with local administration and civilian control and thus did not tread on the tradition of individual freedom and local autonomy. Draft registration also demonstrated the potential bureaucratic capacity of the American state. On a single day, June 5, 1917, more than 9.5 million men between the ages of twenty-one and thirty were processed for military service in their local voting precincts.

Although compliance was not universal, most male citizens went along with the draft's premise of service (a key progressive word) as a responsibility of modern citizenship. By the end of the war almost 4 million men, plus a few thousand female navy clerks and army nurses, were in uniform. Nearly 3 million men were inducted through a draft lottery; the rest volunteered. Over 300,000 men evaded the draft (they were called "slackers"), and another 4,000 were classified as conscientious objectors.

Wilson chose General Pershing to head the American Expeditionary Force (AEF), but the newly raised

Call to Arms
To build popular support for the war effort, the government called on artists such as Howard Chandler Christy, Charles Dana Gibson, and James Montgomery Flagg. This 1917 recruiting poster by Flagg was adapted from a June 1916 cover of *Leslie's Illustrated Weekly Newspaper*. The model was the artist.

army did not have an immediate impact on the fighting. The new recruits had to be trained and outfitted and then wait for one of the few available transport ships to take them across the submarine-infested Atlantic. By June 1917 only 15,000 AEF troops had arrived in France.

At first the main American contribution was to secure the safety of the seas. When the United States entered the war, German submarines were sinking Allied ships at a rate of about 900,000 tons a month. The U-boats had hampered America's ability to send supplies and munitions to the Allies and threatened the transport of American troops to the European front. Adopting a plan that aimed for safety in numbers, the government began sending armed convoys across the Atlantic. The plan worked: no American soldiers were killed on the way to Europe. Allied shipping losses were cut to 400,000 tons a month by late 1917 and to 200,000 tons by April 1918.

Meanwhile, trench warfare continued its deadly grind on the Western Front. Allied commanders pleaded for American reinforcements for their units, but Pershing was reluctant to put his independent fighting unit under foreign commanders. Because the AEF was not ready as a fighting force until May 1918, the brunt of the fighting continued to fall on the French and British.

The Russian Revolution and the Collapse of the Eastern Front. On the Eastern Front the strain of fighting the Germans had exposed the weaknesses of the Russian government of Tsar Nicholas II, and a general mutiny of the troops led to the overthrow of the monarchy in March 1917. The new provisional government headed by Prince George Lvov and the socialist Alexander Kerensky, which Woodrow Wilson supported, promised democratic reforms but insisted on continuing the war. Russian workers and peasants were sick of the seemingly endless food shortages at home, sick of the horrendous casualties at the front. Conditions were ripe for a second, more sweeping, revolution.

The communist theorist and political activist Vladimir Ilych Lenin, who had been living in exile in Switzerland when the March revolution took place, saw his chance. Lenin was a follower of German political philosopher Karl Marx and anticipated that a period of "dictatorship of the proletariat" (workers) would be necessary to root out capitalism before an ideal, classless society could emerge. The Germans, hoping to promote internal strife in Russia, cannily arranged Lenin's safe passage home in a sealed railroad car. Lenin and a group of Bolshevik revolutionaries arrived in Petrograd (later renamed Leningrad and now St. Petersburg) in April 1917 and began to agitate against the provisional government. On November 6 Lenin directed a Bolshevik-led coup and quickly consolidated his control by promising "peace, land, and bread" to the long-suffering masses.

The new Bolshevik government kept the first part of its promise: Russia agreed to a cease-fire with Germany and Austria-Hungary on December 15, 1917, and signed the Treaty of Brest-Litovsk on March 3, 1918. In return for an end to hostilities, the Bolsheviks surrendered about one-third of Russia's territories, including Russian Poland, Ukraine, the Baltic provinces, and Finland. Yet instead of peace the Russian people got three more years of a devastating civil war.

Allied Victory in the West. The civil war in the new Soviet state would command the Allies' attention only after the armistice. Once hostilities with Russia ended, Germany used its full fighting force to break the stalemate on the Western Front. On March 21, 1918, the Germans launched a major offensive. By May the German army had advanced to the Marne River, within 50 miles of Paris, and attempted to subdue the city by bombardments. Allied leaders intensified their calls for American troops, and Pershing, who was under orders to keep the AEF a separate fighting unit, relented a bit to help the Allies bolster their defenses. About 60,000 American soldiers helped the French repel the Germans in the battles of Château-Thierry and Belleau Wood in May and June. During the fighting, the AEF encountered firsthand the terrible effects of poison gas (see American Voices, page 717).

American reinforcements soon began to arrive in large numbers. Fresh troops flooded the ports of Liverpool in Britain and Brest and Saint Nazaire in France—245,000 in May 1918, 278,000 more in June, and an additional 306,000 in July. From there they worked their way slowly to the front along the clogged French transportation system. The Allied force, augmented by 85,000 American troops, brought the German offensive to a halt in mid-July. At that point a million American troops were in France, and the counteroffensive began. On July 18 the Allies, with 270,000 American troops, began a successful campaign to drive the Germans back from the Marne. Approximately 100,000 American soldiers helped the British push the Germans north of the Somme River (see Map 23.2).

In mid-September 1918 General Pershing, leading 500,000 American and 100,000 French soldiers, launched an offensive to close a hole in the Allied lines at Saint-Mihiel. After four days of heavy shelling of their positions, the Germans, who had already been preparing to evacuate the area, retreated. On September 26 Pershing launched the last major assault of the war, which pitted over a million American soldiers against vastly outnumbered and exhausted German troops. The Meuse-Argonne campaign, the main American military contribution to the fighting, allowed Pershing to confront the Germans frontally, rather than getting locked in a defensive war of attrition. This successful maneuver pushed the enemy back across the Selle River near Verdun and broke the German defenses at a cost of over 26,000 American lives.

The flood of American troops and supplies during the last six months of the war helped provide the Allied margin of victory. In many ways this contribution was emblematic of the shift in international power as Euro-

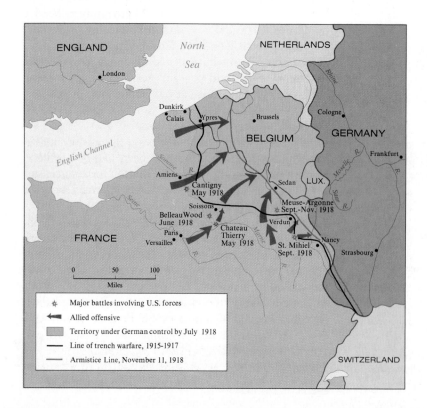

MAP 23.2

U.S. Participation on the Western Front, 1918

When American troops reached the European front in significant numbers in 1918, the Allied and Central powers had been grinding each other down in a war of attrition for almost four years. The influx of American troops and supplies broke the stalemate. Successful offensive maneuvers by the American Expeditionary Force included Belleau Wood, Château-Thierry, and the Meuse-Argonne campaign.

Frederick Pottle

Mustard Gas

Frederick Pottle volunteered for service as an enlisted man in the Medical Corps. He describes here the effects of mustard gas during the battles of Belleau Wood and Château-Thierry in June 1918.

Indeed, those dreadful mustard-gas cases were probably the most painful we had to witness in all our service. As a matter of fact, the majority were in much less serious plight than the wounded men. Mustard gas (it has nothing to with mustard) is a heavy liquid, which, though fairly volatile, will remain for some time clinging to grass and undergrowth, and will burn any flesh with which it comes in contact. It is especially adapted for use by a retreating army. By soaking down with mustard gas the area through which the pursuing American troops had to advance, the Germans made sure that a large number of the advancing force would be incapacitated. The soldier's clothing soon becomes im-

pregnated with the stuff as he brushes through the undergrowth, and the burns develop through the help of moisture. Those parts of the body subject to excessive perspiration are especially affected. The burns are extremely painful, but in general not fatal unless the gas has been inhaled, or (as with other surface burns) a third or more of the total skin area has been affected. A bad feature of mustard gas, however, is that it almost invariably produces temporary, but complete, blindness. Nothing demoralizes a man so much as the fear of losing his sight, and telling him that he will see again in a day or two generally fails to reassure him. The gas cases began to arrive at Juilly as early as June 12. Since most of them were immediately evacuable, we made temporary wards for them in the great cloisters which ran around two sides of the court in front of Wards F and G— the children's dormitories. By the sixteenth there were nearly seven hundred gassed men there, just out of the glare

of the sunny court, lying fully dressed on blanket-covered cots, some of them badly gassed in the lungs and fighting horribly for breath, which could be a little prolonged by giving them oxygen; nearly all blinded, many delirious, all crying, moaning, tossing about. For most of the patients there was nothing to do but renew frequently the wet dressings which relieved somewhat the smart of the burns, and to try to restore their lost morale. For those who had been gassed worst, nothing effectual could be done. They were spared much by being in general delirious, but it required the constant attention of several orderlies to keep some of them in bed. Later on, the hospital service was so organized that the gas cases were handled by special gas hospitals. After we left Juilly we almost never received gas victims unless they were also wounded.

Source: Frederick A. Pottle, *Stretchers: The Story of a Hospital Unit on the Western Front* (New Haven: Yale University Press, 1929), 117–118.

pean diplomatic and economic dominance declined and the United States emerged as a world leader. World War I ended on November 11, 1918, when German and Allied representatives signed an armistice in the railway car of Marshal Ferdinand Foch of France.

The American Fighting Force

About 2 million American soldiers were in France when the war ended. Two-thirds of them had seen at least brief action on the Western Front, but most American "doughboys" had escaped the horrors of sustained trench warfare that had sapped the morale of Allied and German troops. (The origin of the nickname "doughboy" is unclear, but may involve the buttons on the uniforms of American infantrymen, which resembled dumplings made of dough.) During the eighteen months in which the United States fought, 50,585 American servicemen were killed in action. Another 60,000 died from other causes, mainly the influenza epidemic that

swept the world in 1918–1919. These casualties were minimal compared with the 8 million soldiers lost by the Allies and the Central Powers. The French lost far more soldiers in the siege of Verdun than the United States did in the entire war.

Although individual bravery was increasingly anachronistic in modern warfare, the war generated its share of American heroes. Sergeant Alvin York single-handedly killed 25 Germans and took 132 prisoners at the battle of Châtel-Chéhéry in the Meuse-Argonne campaign. Although air power played only a minor role in the conduct of the war, it captivated the popular imagination. One of America's best known aces was the former professional race car driver Eddie Rickenbacker (see American Lives, pages 718–719). The aerial exploits of daredevil pilots, often fighting in single combat like medieval knights, provided a thrill that contrasted with the monotony of trench warfare. The popular fascination with York and Rickenbacker suggests a deep-seated need to anoint heroes in what had become an increasingly depersonalized and mechanized pursuit of war.

Edward Vernon Rickenbacker:
Fighter Pilot

He was born Edward Rickenbacher in Columbus, Ohio, on October 8, 1890. Note the slight but significant difference in the spelling: he adopted a less Germanic version of his last name and added an English middle name at the beginning of World War I. Even before his designation as the "American Ace of Aces" for shooting down more enemy aircraft than any other pilot, Eddie Rickenbacker was front-page news as a celebrity race car driver. He began racing at the age of sixteen, and in 1911 competed in the first Indianapolis 500 road race. The holder of the world speed record of 134 miles per hour, he earned the fabulous sum of $60,000 at the height of his racing career in 1916.

When the United States entered the war in 1917, Rickenbacker enlisted immediately. He was sent to France as a member of General John J. ("Black Jack") Pershing's motor car staff, although he was not Pershing's personal chauffeur, as legend has it. But his skills as a mechanic and a driver brought him to the attention of Colonel Billy Mitchell, one of the members of Pershing's senior air staff, who helped arrange Rickenbacker's transfer to the Air Service. At that point Rickenbacker had never flown a plane. He was originally told that at age twenty-eight he was too old to fly in combat, but he proved the doubters wrong: the quick reflexes and competitive instincts honed by his racing career made him a superb pilot. Rickenbacker dutifully informed his mother about his change in assignment, telling her that flying was safer than race car driving because there was lots of room in the sky. She in turn cautioned him to fly slow and close to the ground.

In March 1918 Rickenbacker was posted to the 94th Aero Pursuit Squadron, the first all-American air squadron on the Western Front. The 94th was known as the "hat in the ring" squadron for the American custom of throwing a hat into the ring as an invitation to fight, and the pilots adopted that image as the insignia for their planes. But at first the American pilots did not have much of an impact on the fighting, hampered by antiquated French planes that did not have machine guns. Only in August 1918 did the 94th get new planes, French made SPADs, fast and reliable single seat pursuit fighters equipped with machine guns.

When the war broke out, airplanes were used mainly for reconnaissance and artillery spotting, but the addition of machine guns transformed planes into offensive weapons. With guns mounted in front, combat pilots zoomed in on the tail of an enemy craft; to aim the machine gun, they pointed the plane at the intended target and poured bullets into both the plane and the pilot before beating a hasty retreat. The French inventor Roland Garros made aerial combat possible by synchronizing the firing of bullets with the rotation of the propeller.

Although German squadrons often hunted in packs (the so called flying circus under the direction of Baron Manfred von Richthofen, the German ace known as the "Red Baron"), American pilots preferred to sneak up on their targets one at a time. Pilots of both nations had great respect for each other's skills, often jousting in the air for position until one of them ran low on fuel and headed home. Eddie Rickenbacker remembered no personal animosity toward his German foes and was always delighted to learn that a downed pilot had escaped with his life. (This rarely happened, since few aircraft were equipped with parachutes.) But once locked in a dogfight, Rickenbacker remembered, "I had no regrets over killing a fellow human being. I do not believe that at that moment I even considered the matter. Like nearly all air fighters, I was an automaton behind the gun barrels of my plane. I never thought of killing an individual but of shooting down an enemy plane." He fought in 134 air battles and narrowly escaped death on several occasions.

In September 1918 Rickenbacker was named commander of the 94th Squadron, and most of his victories came in the last two months of the war. In one encounter, for which he was later awarded the Congres-

Flying Aces
One of America's best known aces was former professional race car driver Eddie
Rickenbacker (middle). Note the "hat-in-the-ring" insignia on the plane.

sional Medal of Honor, he single-handedly took on seven German planes and downed two of them. He shot down fourteen enemy aircraft in October alone, bringing his total to twenty-six confirmed victories and clinching his status as the American Ace of Aces. Under his leadership, the 94th Squadron became the most victorious American air unit of the war. Rickenbacker returned to the United States a national hero, publishing a book about his war experiences, *Fighting the Flying Circus*, in 1919.

World War I dramatically accelerated the growth of aviation in both its commercial and its military applications. After the war Rickenbacker dabbled in racing and automobile production before joining Eastern Airlines as its general manager in 1935; in 1938 he became its president. As head of Eastern, then one of the flagships of modern aviation, Rickenbacker served as a spokesperson for commercial aviation until his retirement in 1963. Over the course of his lifetime (he died in 1973) this new industry grew up. Rickenbacker symbolized the fascination of early flight, even in the unlikely arena of war, and its possibilities for individual heroism. Just as significantly, he stood for the development of commercial aviation, which in the years after World War II would revolutionize world travel. But perhaps most of all his career suggests the symbiotic relationship between technology and modern warfare, one of the twentieth century's defining characteristics.

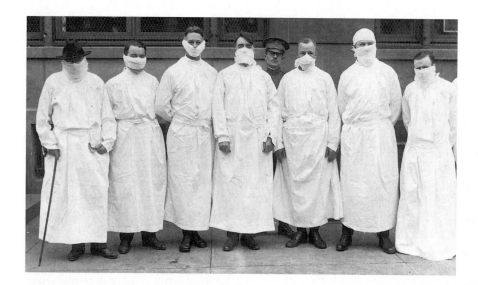

Fighting the Flu
The influenza epidemic of 1918–1919 strained the resources of a public health system already fully mobilized for the war effort. Here doctors, army officers, and reporters don surgical masks and gowns before touring hospitals that treat influenza patients.

Military Morality. The high ideals of progressivism set the tone for military service. Reformers urged the adoption of progressive solutions to the "vices" of alcohol and sex, and government and military officials agreed. Reflecting the antiliquor fever taking hold in America, Secretary of the Navy Josephus Daniels declared navy ships dry. The army banned drinking by soldiers in uniform and prohibited liquor on army bases and the surrounding localities.

The army also mounted an ambitious program of sex education. In an era when people rarely discussed sex in public, the army brought the subject into the open. Concerned that venereal disease (VD) might sap the strength of the fighting men (antibiotics had not yet been developed), the army launched an anti-VD campaign. As soldiers ate in the mess hall, they looked up at posters that proclaimed "A German Bullet Is Cleaner Than a Whore" and "How could you look the flag in the face if you were dirty with gonorrhea?" In France the army continued its campaign for moral purity, although it could not stop American soldiers from patronizing French prostitutes. Army-issue condoms and safety razors, a novelty that changed the shaving habits of future generations of men, were two of the souvenirs that American soldiers brought home from France.

World War I also marked the first time that homosexuality emerged as a major social issue. Urban reformers were concerned that military recruits would fall prey to the "urban degeneracy" of "male perversion" while passing through embarkation points such as New York City. As they cracked down on prostitution, they also attempted to curb the city's thriving gay subculture. The military also targeted male homosexuality as part of its campaign against vice. At the Newport (Rhode Island) Naval Training Station in 1919, the navy undertook an extensive undercover operation against the

"immoral conditions" associated with suspected "sexual perverts," which led to more than twenty arrests.

Intelligence Testing. Intelligence testing linked the progressive belief in social science to wartime needs. To sort its conscripts, the army used the newly developed Stanford-Binet intelligence test. Army psychologists, who administered the test to all recruits, expressed shock at the level of illiteracy among draftees—as high as 25 percent. Racial and ethnic variations in the test scores reinforced stereotypes about the supposed intellectual inferiority of blacks and immigrants, although their lower scores stemmed from the cultural and environmental biases of the tests rather than from innate differences in intelligence. How many recent immigrants or rural blacks knew whether the Knight engine powered the Packard, Stearns, Lozier, or Pierce Arrow automobile or knew the importance of the French painter Rosa Bonheur? The army dropped the test in 1919, but revised versions of intelligence tests soon became a standard part of the American educational system.

Reformers expressed high hopes for democratization and education in the military services. Theodore Roosevelt, whose offer to raise an independent regiment was politely but firmly refused by President Wilson, hoped that army duty would foster class unity. "The military tent where they all sleep side by side will rank next to the public school among the great agents of democratization," Roosevelt predicted. Yet the army reflected the divisions in American society. About a fifth of the American soldiers had been born in another country, leading some people to call the AEF the American Foreign Legion. Army censors had to be able to read forty-nine languages to check letters written home by American doughboys. The "Americanization" of the army remained imperfect at best.

Racism in the Armed Forces. African-American soldiers received the worst treatment. White southerners especially became alarmed at the idea of training blacks to bear arms, and few whites from any part of the country would have consented to serve under a black officer. As a result, blacks were organized into rigidly segregated units, almost always under the control of white officers. In addition, blacks were assigned to the most menial tasks, working as laborers, stevedores, and messboys. Although the policy of segregation minimized contact between black and white recruits, racial violence erupted at several camps. The worst incident occurred in Houston in August 1917, when black members of the Twenty-fourth Infantry's Third Battalion killed fifteen white soldiers and police officers in retaliation for a string of racial incidents, including the beating of a black woman by a white police officer. Sixty-four soldiers were tried in military courts, and nineteen were hanged. The army quickly disbanded the battalion, but the legacy of racial mistrust lingered for the rest of the war.

Racial equality had never been part of the progressive agenda, and the black experience in World War I reflected the persistent gap between democratic rhetoric and reality. Over 400,000 black men served in the military, accounting for 13 percent of the armed forces; 92 percent were draftees, a far higher rate than for whites. Black soldiers found that the French were more willing to socialize with them on an equal basis than were many white American soldiers. Despite documented cases of extreme heroism, no black received the Congressional Medal of Honor, the nation's highest military award, even though they had been so honored in the Civil War and the Spanish-American War. The French, however, had no qualms about awarding the Croix de Guerre (Legion of Honor) to several hundred African-American soldiers.

Demobilization. Just as it had taken months to get troops to Europe to join the fighting, similar delays slowed demobilization at the war's end. June 1919 was the peak month for returns, with 368,000 men—plus a few thousand women who had served in France as telephone operators, canteen workers, and nurses—coming home to begin the process of readjusting to civilian life. When their ships sailed into New York harbor, many mouthed the old vaudeville saying: "If the Statue of Liberty wants to see my face again, she'll have to turn around."

After the armistice the war lived on in the minds of the men and women who had gone "over there." Spared the horror of sustained battle, many members of the AEF had experienced the war more as tourists than as soldiers. Before joining the army, most recruits had barely traveled beyond their hometowns, and for them the journey across the ocean to Europe was a monumental, once-in-a-lifetime event. In 1919 a group of former AEF officers formed the American Legion "to preserve the memories and incidents of our association in the great war." The word *legion* perfectly captured the romantic, almost chivalric memories that many veterans held of their wartime service. Only later did disillusionment over the contested legacy of World War I set in.

A Black Veteran Returns Home
Black soldiers received segregated and unequal treatment at every stage of military service. When the war ended, black veterans faced hostility from many whites alarmed that blacks no longer "knew their place."

Mobilizing the Home Front

Fighting World War I required extraordinary economic mobilization on the home front in which business, the work force, and the public all cooperated. At the height of mobilization a fourth of the gross national product went for war production. Business and government proved especially congenial partners, a collaboration that typified the pattern of state building in America. Similarly, the rapid dismantling of that apparatus when the war ended reflected the unease that Americans felt about a strong bureaucratic state.

Financial and Economic Mobilization

Even before the formal declaration of war the United States had geared up as the arsenal for Allied supplies and the source of financing. As hundreds of tons of American grain and military supplies crossed the Atlantic, the United States reversed its historical position as a debtor and became a leading creditor nation when the Allies paid for their purchases in gold. In addition, U.S. financial institutions increasingly provided capital for investment in the world market now that British financial reserves were being diverted to the war effort. This shift from debtor to creditor status, which would last until the 1980s, guaranteed the nation a major role in international financial affairs after the war and confirmed the new role of the United States as a world power.

Paying for the War. The monetary cost to the United States of World War I reached $33 billion, a huge sum for a government unaccustomed to large expenditures. The disruption in international trade after the outbreak of war in 1914 had reduced the money raised by tariffs, ordinarily a major source of federal revenues. Wilson's treasury secretary, William McAdoo, had two options: to impose a national sales tax or increase income taxes. (The Sixteenth Amendment to the Constitution, which instituted a federal income tax, had been approved in 1913.) Wilson and McAdoo, in conjunction with progressive Democratic leaders in Congress, chose the second option. The resulting War Revenue bills of 1917 and 1918 transformed the limited income tax into the foremost instrument of federal taxation, one of the lasting legacies of World War I. And the Wilson administration did this along lines influenced by progressivism: following the lead of the steeply graduated Revenue Act of 1916, it rejected a tax on all wages and salaries in favor of placing the burden on corporations and wealthy individuals. The corporate excess-profits tax contained in the 1917 law signaled a direct and unprecedented intrusion of the state into the workings of corporate capitalism. By 1918 U.S. corporations were paying over $2.5 billion in excess-profits taxes per year, more than half of all federal taxes.

In all, the United States raised about a third of the cost of the war through taxes; the rest of the financing came from loans, especially the popular Liberty bonds, which encouraged public support for the war effort. The government also paid for the war by using the Federal Reserve System to expand the money supply, making it easier to borrow money. Even so, the federal debt increased from $1 billion in 1915 to $20 billion in 1920. Federal expenditures never again dropped to their prewar levels, but by 1920 the federal budget was posting a surplus.

Wartime Economic Regulation. In addition to financing the war, mobilization required the coordination of economic production. The government never seriously considered exercising total control over the economy, but the war sped up the creation of a centralized national administrative structure that would match the consolidated power of the business and banking communities. The government also created an added incentive for business cooperation by suspending antitrust laws. For economic expertise the government turned primarily to those who knew the capacities of the economy best—the nation's business leaders. Executives flocked to Washington, regarding war work as both a duty and an opportunity for professional advancement.

A series of boards and agencies tried to rationalize and coordinate the economy. The Overman Act of 1918 granted the president control over these agencies, a signficant milestone in the growth of presidential power. A network of industrial committees linked war agencies to organizations in private industry, and government leaders used a combination of public and private power to enforce their decisions. This semivoluntarist approach represented an attempt to find a middle ground between total state control of the economy and letting business operate without direction. Like most compromises, it had mixed results.

The Fuel Administration, directed by Harry Garfield, the president of Williams College, allocated the coal needed for operation of the nation's railroads and factories. Its task became more difficult during the severe winter of 1917–1918, when there were coal shortages in major northeastern cities and industries. At one point Garfield ordered all factories east of the Mississippi River to shut down for four days. By raising the price of coal to artificially high levels, the Fuel Administration stimulated the production of coal from previously unprofitable mines to meet the nation's energy needs.

The Railroad War Board, under Secretary of the Treasury McAdoo, coordinated the nation's sprawling transportation system by taking over the railroads in December 1917. (The army needed trains to move its troops.) The board guaranteed railroad owners a "standard return" equal to their average earnings between 1915 and 1917 and promised that the carriers would be returned to private control no later than twenty-one months after the war. Although reformers had hoped to continue the experient, the government fulfilled that pledge after the armistice.

Perhaps the most successful government agency was the Food Administration, created in August 1917 and led by the future president Herbert Hoover, a Stanford-trained engineer. Using the slogan "Food will win the war," Hoover encouraged the expansion of domestic production of wheat and other grains from 45 million acres in 1917 to 75 million in 1919. The increased output not only fed the large domestic market but also allowed a threefold rise in food exports to war-torn Europe. At no time did the government contemplate domestic food rationing. "Wheatless" Mondays, "meatless" Tuesdays, and "porkless" Thursdays and Saturdays resulted in substantial voluntary conservation of food resources. Most consumers patriotically followed the government's advice to "Serve Just Enough" and "Use All Left-Overs," and Hoover emerged from the war as one of the nation's most admired public figures.

The War Industries Board. The central agency for mobilizing wartime industry was the War Industries Board (WIB), which was established in July 1917. After a fumbling start that showed the limits of voluntarism in a national emergency, in March 1918 the Wilson administration reorganized the board under the centralized control of Bernard Baruch, a Wall Street financier. Baruch's financial experience and ability to cajole business into cooperating with the government contributed significantly to the success of the WIB.

The WIB reflected the ambivalent attitude of Americans toward government intervention in the economy. While Wilson recognized the need for central authority in wartime, he always saw the WIB as a temporary expedient. Baruch organized the WIB around specific commodities and industries, whose administrators then negotiated issues such as market allocation with their equivalents in private industry. This frequent consultation blurred the lines between the needs of business and those of the government and often left patterns of private power undisturbed.

The WIB produced an unparalleled expansion of the economic powers of the federal government: it allocated scarce resources, gathered economic data and statistics, controlled the flow of raw materials, ordered the conversion of factories to war production, set prices, imposed efficiency and standardization procedures, and coordinated purchasing. The board had the authority to compel compliance, but Baruch preferred to win voluntary acceptance from industry, often through personal intervention. Business generally supported this governmental expansion because federal growth coincided with its interests so well. Despite higher taxes, corporate profits soared, aided by the suspension of antitrust laws and guaranteed prices for war work. War profits produced an economic boom that continued without interruption until 1920.

With the signing of the armistice in November 1918, the United States scrambled to dismantle wartime controls. Wilson disbanded the WIB effective January 1, 1919, resisting suggestions that keeping the board in place would help stabilize the economy during demobilization. Wilson was determined to take "the harness off." Like most Americans, he could tolerate putting planning power in the hands of the government during an emergency but not as a permanent feature of the economy.

Although U.S. participation in the war lasted only eighteen months, it left an important legacy for the modern bureaucratic state. Entire industries had been organized as never before, linked to a maze of government agencies and executive departments. The contours of the modern system of graduated income taxation took shape. The collaboration between business and government had been mutually beneficial, a lesson that both partners would put to use in the state building that occurred in the 1920s and afterward.

Mobilizing American Workers

Wars are never won solely by armies and business and government leaders. Farmers, factory workers, and civilians have crucial roles to play. However, World War I produced fewer rewards for workers than it did for owners and managers.

Organized Labor. Labor's position improved during the war, although it remained a junior partner to business and government. Samuel Gompers, leader of the American Federation of Labor (AFL), traded labor's support of the war for a voice in government policy, specifically a spot on the National Defense Advisory Commission. That bargain proved acceptable to government and business leaders concerned with averting crippling strikes. Also, the War Labor Policies Board headed by Felix Frankfurter, a Harvard law professor, coordinated labor and welfare programs in government and industry, while the United States Employment Service placed 4 million workers in war jobs.

The National War Labor Board. Far more important to workers was the National War Labor Board (NWLB), established in April 1918, which arbitrated labor disputes. Composed of representatives of labor, management, and the public, the NWLB was chaired by former president William Howard Taft, representing management, and Frank P. Walsh, a labor lawyer. In some ways the NWLB functioned more as a judicial than an administrative body; labor leaders often called it "labor's Supreme Court."

The board's decisions favored labor more often than management, giving important federal support to the goals of the labor movement. During the eighteen months of the NWLB's existence it arbitrated about 1,250 cases. The board established an eight-hour day for war workers, with time and a half for overtime, and endorsed equal pay for women workers. Workers were not allowed to disrupt war production through strikes or other disturbances; in return, the NWLB supported their right to organize unions and required employers to deal with shop committees. The NWLB had ample power to enforce its decisions and intervene in disputes. For example, when the Smith and Wesson arms plant in Springfield, Massachusetts, flouted NWLB rules by discriminating against union employees, the federal government took over the firm.

After years of federal hostility toward labor, the actions of the NWLB improved labor's status and power. From 1916 to 1919 AFL membership grew by almost a million workers, reaching over 3 million at the end of the war. Few of the wartime gains lasted, however. Wartime inflation ate up most of the wage hikes, and a virulent postwar antiunion movement caused a rapid decline in union membership that lasted into the 1930s. The labor movement did not yet have enough power to bargain on an equal basis with business and government.

Black and Mexican-American Workers. When soldiers go to war, jobs open up for workers who normally are excluded from them. Black men, for example, found jobs in northern defense industries that would not have hired them in peacetime. The magnet of industrial jobs and escape from the southern agricultural system lured between 400,000 and 450,000 blacks to northern and midwestern cities such as St. Louis, Chicago, Cleveland, and Detroit during the war. Henry Ford sent agents to the South to recruit black workers for his automobile plants and provided special trains to bring them north. In Detroit black men shared in the unprecedented daily wage of $5 that Ford had instituted in 1914. The migration of blacks from the South, which began around 1910 and continued until the 1970s, was one of the largest population shifts of the twentieth century.

Mexican-Americans in California, Texas, New Mexico, and Arizona also found new opportunities during the war. Continued political instability in Mexico encouraged many to relocate, temporarily or permanently, across the border, a process facilitated by newly opened railroad lines. The disruption of immigration from abroad opened up industrial opportunities, as did the conscription of U.S. citizens. Urban growth in the Southwest created a labor shortage, and many Mexican-Americans left farm labor for new industrial opportunities. They often settled in segregated neighborhoods (*barrios*) in urban areas, meeting discrimination similar to that experienced by African-Americans.

Other Mexican-Americans, however, feared being drafted into the army and returned to Mexico. The exodus of so many workers increased the labor shortage in agriculture. The government quickly exempted agricultural workers from the draft, and at least 100,000 Mexican-Americans entered the United States between 1917 and 1920.

Women and the War Effort

Women were the largest group that took advantage of new opportunities in wartime. White women and, to a lesser degree, black and Mexican-American women found that jobs in factories and war industries had been opened to them. About 1 million women joined the labor force for the first time. In addition, many of the nation's 8 million women who already held jobs switched from low-paying fields such as domestic service to higher-paying industrial work. Americans soon got used to the sight of female streetcar conductors, train engineers, and defense workers. But everyone—including the working women—believed that those jobs would return to men after the war.

Professional women also found opportunities in government service. Mary Van Kleeck, an industrial sociologist and an expert on the problems of woman workers, joined the Department of Labor to lobby for

Wartime Opportunities
Women took on new jobs during the war, working as mail carriers, police officers, drill-press operators, and farm laborers attached to the Women's Land Army. These three women clearly enjoyed the camaraderie of working in a railroad yard in 1918. When the war ended, women usually lost such employment.

equal pay and better working conditions for woman workers. Pauline Goldmark, a social reformer from the National Consumers' League, acted as a women's rights advocate at the Railroad Administration. Mary Anderson, a trade unionist who had been Van Kleeck's assistant, became the first director of the Women's Bureau established by the Labor Department in 1920. Women's groups failed, however, to get a woman named to the National War Labor Board.

World War I proved especially liberating for middle-class women outside the work force. Women's clubs and groups had grown steadily since the nineteenth century, and they turned much of their organizational energy to the war effort. Suffragist leaders such as Carrie Chapman Catt and Anna Howard Shaw mobilized women's support for the war through the Women's Committee of

the Council of National Defense. Housewives played a crucial role in the success of Herbert Hoover's Food Administration. Other groups, including the American Red Cross and the Young Women's Christian Association (YWCA), sent volunteers to France to organize relief work and recreational activities in conjunction with the AEF.

Suffrage Victory. The war had an important impact on the battle for woman suffrage. The main suffrage organization, the National American Woman Suffrage Association (NAWSA), threw the support of its 2 million members behind the Wilson administration. Carrie Chapman Catt, president of the organization, argued that women had to prove their patriotism to avoid jeopardizing the suffrage movement. But NAWSA continued

Votes for Women
Mass suffrage parades, introduced in the final stages of the campaign, provided an effective and eye-catching way to build popular support. Many of the banners and posters carried in the parades, such as this one by B. M. Boye, were in the suffrage colors of green, purple, or gold.

Rose Winslow

An Imprisoned Suffrage Militant

The suffragist Rose Winslow smuggled out descriptions of the treatment she and Alice Paul, founder of the National Woman's Party, endured in Occuquan prison. The process of forcible feeding that she mentions, which involved inserting a 20-inch-long tube through the nostril to the stomach while the patient was restrained, was excruciatingly painful as well as demeaning.

The women are all so magnificent, so beautiful. Alice Paul is as thin as ever, pale and large-eyed. We have been in solitary for five weeks. There is nothing to tell but that the days go by somehow. I have felt quite feeble the last few days—faint, so that I could hardly get my hair brushed, my arms ached so. But today I am well again. Alice Paul and I talk back and forth though we are at opposite ends of the building and a hall door also shuts us apart. But occasionally—thrills—we escape from behind our iron-barred doors and visit. Great laughter and rejoicing! . . .

Alice Paul is in the psychopathic ward. She dreaded forcible feeding frightfully, and I hate to think how she must be feeling. I had a nervous time of it, gasping a long time afterward, and my stomach rejecting during the process. I spent a bad, restless night, but otherwise I am all right. The poor soul who fed me got liberally besprinkled during the process. I heard myself making the most hideous sounds. . . . One feels so forsaken when one lies prone and people shove a pipe down one's stomach. . . .

We still get no mail; we are "insubordinate." It's strange, isn't it; if you ask for food fit to eat, as we did, you are "insubordinate"; and if you refuse food you are "insubordinate." Amusing. I am really all right. If this continues very long I perhaps won't be. I am interested to see how long our so-called "splendid American men" will stand for this form of discipline.

All news cheers one marvelously because it is hard to feel anything but a bit desolate and forgotten here in this place.

All the officers here know we are making this hunger strike that women fighting for liberty may be considered political prisoners; we have told them. God knows we don't want other women ever to have to do this over again.

Source: Doris Stevens, *Jailed for Freedom* (1920; rpt. New York: Schocken Books, 1976), 188–91.

its suffrage organizing too, concentrating on lobbying for support for the proposed woman suffrage amendment to the Constitution.

Alice Paul and the National Woman's Party took a more militant and confrontational tack, widening the split in the suffrage movement that had occurred after 1914 (see Chapter 21). To the dismay of NAWSA leaders, suffrage militants led by the NWP began picketing in front of the White House in July 1917 to protest their lack of the vote. The Washington, D.C., police quickly arrested the suffragists on charges of obstructing traffic and blocking sidewalks; after hasty trials, the protesters were sentenced to seven months in jail, an unusually harsh sentence. To gain recognition as political prisoners, Alice Paul and other women prisoners went on a hunger strike, which prison authorities met with forced feeding (see American Voices, above). Public shock at their treatment made them matryrs.

In the end it took both suffrage militancy and the NAWSA's policy of patient persuasion to break the logjam. Woodrow Wilson, who had accepted the Democratic platform's endorsement of woman suffrage in 1916 but preferred to leave the matter to the states, withdrew his opposition to a federal woman suffrage amendment in January 1918. The constitutional amendment quickly passed the House but took eighteen months to get through the Senate. Then came another year of hard work for ratification by the states. Finally, on August 26, 1920, Tennessee gave the Nineteenth Amendment the last vote it needed. The goal that had first been declared at the Seneca Falls convention in 1848 was finally achieved seventy-two years later, in large part because of women's contributions to the war effort. Especially effective was a simple moral challenge: How could the United States fight to make the world safe for democracy while denying half its citizens the right to vote?

Promoting National Unity

The course of American participation in World War I was fundamentally shaped by the progressive period that preceded the war. Reformers eagerly embraced American involvement as an opportunity to put progressive ideals into practice. The educator and philosopher John Dewey, a staunch supporter of the war, argued that wars represented a "plastic juncture" in which societies became more open to reason and new ideas. In the collective effort of fighting and winning a war, society could be improved. Dewey's optimistic view matched the spirit of the times. Unfortunately, a dissenting observation by Randolph Bourne, an outspoken pacifist and intellectual who had once been a pupil of Dewey's, came closer to reality. "If the war is too strong for you to prevent," Bourne asked, "how is it going to be weak enough for you to control and mould to your liberal purposes?"

Although the enactment of woman suffrage confirmed Dewey's prediction that social progress could occur in a war context, the excesses committed in the name of building national unity corroborated Bourne's warning that passions could get out of control during wartime. Wilson had shared Bourne's foreboding: "Once lead this people into war, and they'll forget there ever was such a thing as tolerance." But the president also realized the need to manufacture support for the war: "It is not an army we must shape and train for war, it is a nation."

Wartime Propaganda. In April 1917 Wilson designated the Committee on Public Information (CPI) to promote public backing for the war, which was never a foregone conclusion. This government propaganda agency, headed by the journalist George Creel, acted as a magnet for progressive reformers and muckraking journalists such as Ida Tarbell and Ray Stannard Baker. The CPI professed high-sounding goals such as educating citizens about democracy, promoting national unity, Americanizing immigrants, and breaking down the isolation of rural life. Indirectly, it acted as a nationalizing force by promoting the development of a common ideology.

The CPI touched the lives of practically every American during World War I. It distributed 75 million pieces of patriotic literature. At local movie theaters before the feature presentation (which might be a CPI-supported film such as *The Hun Within* or *The Kaiser, Beast of Berlin*) a volunteer called a "four-minute man" made a short speech supporting the war. (The name, a reference to Revolutionary War heroes, also reassured audiences and theater owners that the featured entertainment would be delayed only briefly.) Those speeches reached an audience estimated at more than 300 million, three times the population of the United States at the time. But the CPI sometimes went too far. In early 1918, for example, it encouraged speakers to use inflammatory stories of alleged German atrocities to build support for the war effort.

A Climate of Suspicion. As a spirit of conformity pervaded the home front, many Americans found themselves targets of suspicion. Local businesses paid for newspaper and magazine ads that asked citizens to report to the Justice Department "the man who spreads pessimistic stories, cries for peace, or belittles our ef-

A Human Statue of Liberty
Patriotic gestures knew no bounds, as shown by the 18,000 soldiers at Camp Dodge in Iowa, who formed a human replica of the Statue of Liberty. One wonders if the conscripts shared the photographer's enthusiasm for the project after what must have been a long afternoon in the sun.

forts to win the war." Posters encouraged Americans to be on the lookout for German spies. One of the most popular posters, called "Spies and Lies," warned that "German agents are everywhere." An unintended by-product of this propaganda was the stimulation of the advertising industry, which became a major force in shaping patterns of consumption in the 1920s.

The CPI also urged ethnic groups to give up their Old World customs and become "Unhyphenated Americans" in the spirit of "One Hundred Percent Americanism." German-Americans bore the brunt of the Americanization campaign. In an orgy of hostility generated by propaganda about German militarism and atrocities, everything German became suspect. German music, especially opera, was banished from concert halls. Publishers removed pro-German references from textbooks, and many communities banned the teaching of the German language. Sauerkraut was renamed "liberty cabbage," and hamburgers were transformed into "liberty sandwiches." Even the German measles got a new name—"liberty measles." Anti-German hysteria

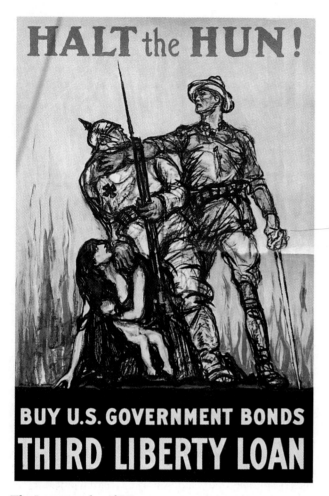

HALT the HUN!

BUY U.S. GOVERNMENT BONDS
THIRD LIBERTY LOAN

The Iconography of War

This poster made clear who the enemy was and the proper patriotic American response. The iconography builds on traditional gender definitions, with the male American soldier pushing back a German Hun who is about to ravish a woman and her child, who stand for European civilization.

mainly dissipated when the war ended, although vestiges survived into the 1920s.

Quasi-vigilante groups such as the American Protective League mobilized about 250,000 self-appointed "agents" to spy on neighbors and co-workers. The American Protective League (whose members were furnished with badges issued by the Justice Department) and other groups including the Sedition Slammers and the Boy Spies of America staged violent raids against draft evaders and other war opponents in 1918.

Curbing Dissent. Law enforcement officials tolerated little criticism of established values and institutions in wartime, as the militant suffragists picketing the White House had found out. The main legal tools for curbing dissent were the Espionage Act of 1917 and the Sedition Act of 1918. The espionage law imposed stiff penalties for antiwar activities and allowed the federal government to ban treasonous material from the mails. The

definition of treason was left to the postmaster general. The sedition law went further, punishing anyone who might "utter, print, write, or publish any disloyal, profane, scurrilous, or abusive language about the form of government of the United States, . . . or the uniform of the Army or the Navy. . . . " More than a thousand people were convicted under these broad restrictions on freedom of speech.

The Justice Department also targeted the Industrial Workers of the World (IWW), or Wobblies (see Chapter 18). IWW organizers spoke out against militarism and threatened to disrupt war production in the western lumber and copper industries. In September 1917 the Justice Department arrested 113 IWW leaders for interfering with the war effort. Vigilante groups contributed their own reprisals: a mob in Butte, Montana, dragged IWW organizer Frank Little through the streets and hanged him from a railroad trestle. By the end of the war the Wobblies had been decimated.

Socialists encountered similar attacks for criticizing the war and the draft. The postmaster general revoked their mailing privileges, which virtually shut down their publications. Party leader Eugene Debs was sentenced to ten years in jail for stating that the master classes declared wars while the subject classes fought the battles. (He was pardoned by President Warren G. Harding in 1921.) Victor Berger, a Milwaukee socialist, was twice prevented from taking his seat in the U.S. House of Representatives. Berger had served in the House from 1911 to 1913 and was reelected in 1918 and 1919, but the House refused to seat him because he had been jailed under the Espionage Act for his antiwar views. The Supreme Court reversed Berger's conviction in 1921, and he served in the House again from 1923 to 1929.

The reversal in the Berger case was an exception, however. The Supreme Court rarely overturned these wartime excesses. In *Schenck v. United States* (1919) Justice Oliver Wendell Holmes ruled in a unanimous decision that if an act of speech was uttered in circumstances that would "create a clear and present danger to the safety of the country," Congress could constitutionally restrict it. The defendant, the general secretary of the Socialist party, Charles T. Schenck, had been convicted of mailing pamphlets that urged draftees to resist induction. In *Abrams v. United States* (1919) the Court upheld the conviction for sedition of Jacob Abrams, a Russian anarchist and recent immigrant. Abrams had dumped Yiddish and English pamphlets denouncing American military intervention in Russia from tenement windows in New York. Holmes dissented in this case, seeing no clear threat to the conduct of the war. He and Justice Louis Brandeis made up the minority in the 7-to-2 decision. Because of the national war emergency the Court upheld limits on freedom of speech that would not have been acceptable in peacetime.

An Unsettled Peace, 1919–1920

In January 1917 Woodrow Wilson had proposed a "peace without victory," since only a "peace among equals" could last. His goal was "not a balance of power, but a community of power; not organized rivalries, but an organized common peace." The keystone of his postwar plans was a permanent league of nations. With victory achieved, Wilson confronted the task of constructing the new moral international order. But he would first have to win over a Senate openly hostile to the treaty he had brought home. At the same time, ethnic and racial tensions that had smoldered during the war erupted in controversy and strife, and fears of domestic radicalism boiled over in the Red Scare.

The Treaty of Versailles

Wilson scored an early victory when the Allies accepted his Fourteen Points as the basis for the peace negotiations that began in January 1919. First put forward in a speech to Congress in early 1918, the Fourteen Points represented Wilson's clearest articulation of his blueprint for the postwar world. The president called for open diplomacy, "absolute freedom of navigation upon the seas," removal of barriers to trade, an international commitment to territorial integrity, and arms reduction. The fifth point reaffirmed Wilson's long-standing commitment to national self-determination. He proposed redrawing national boundaries after the breakup of the Austro-Hungarian, Russian, Ottoman, and German empires, including the restoration of an independent Polish state. Essential to Wilson's vision was the creation of a multinational organization "for the purpose of affording mutual guarantees of political independence and territorial integrity to great and small States alike." The League of Nations became Wilson's obsession.

The Fourteen Points matched the spirit of progressivism. Widely distributed as propaganda during the final months of the war, Wilson's declaration proposed to extend the benefits of the American way of life—democracy, freedom, and peaceful economic expansion—to the rest of the world. The League of Nations, acting as a kind of Federal Trade Commission for the world, would serve as a mediator of international disputes so that future wars could be avoided. It would supervise disarmament, provide for arbitration of disputes, and—according to the crucial Article X of its covenant—curb unilateralism by allowing League-organized collective military action. By pegging American involvement to such lofty goals, however, Wilson guaranteed disappointment. Even though the Allies won the war, his ideals for world reformation were too far-reaching to be practical or attainable.

Many factors limited Wilson's ability to enforce his view of a just peace. Despite the president's plea to make the 1918 Congressional elections a referendum for his peace plan, American voters returned a Republican majority to Congress. Wilson shortsightedly failed to appoint even one Republican senator to the American delegation to the peace conference, a political gaffe that later helped doom the treaty's chances for approval in the Senate.

The peace delegation sailed for Europe in December 1918. Wilson toured the major European capitals and received a tumultuous welcome. To European citizens the American president represented the hope for national self-determination that had become a major justification for the war. In Paris 2 million people lined the Champs-Élysées to pay tribute to "Wilson the Just." This reception encouraged Wilson to press ahead with his plan to dominate the peace conference.

Intervention in the U.S.S.R. The Allies deliberately excluded representatives of the new Bolshevik state from the peace conference. Wilson was deeply disturbed by Lenin's calls for a proletarian revolution to liberate the world from capitalism and imperialism, a direct challenge to the Wilsonian international order and American economic interests. Not only did Wilson refuse to recognize Lenin's legitimacy, but the Allies also took steps to topple the Bolshevik regime. Using the excuse of helping 60,000 trapped Czechoslovakians return west to fight the Germans, Wilson deployed 2,000 American troops to Vladivostok in eastern Russia in June 1918 and sent an additional 3,000 troops to northwestern Russia in July. Britain and Japan also sent troops. The unstated purpose of this military maneuver was to support anti-Bolshevik forces within Russia. American troops remained on Soviet soil until the spring of 1920, leaving a bitter legacy for American-Soviet relations.

Negotiating the Treaties. Twenty-seven countries sent representatives to the peace conference in Versailles, near Paris; like the Soviet Union, Germany was not invited. The Big Four—Wilson, Prime Minister David Lloyd George of Great Britain, Premier Georges Clemenceau of France, and Prime Minister Vittorio Orlando of Italy—did most of the negotiating. The three European leaders sought a peace that differed radically from Wilson's plan. They wanted to punish Germany through heavy reparations and treat themselves to the spoils of war. In fact, Britain, France, and Italy had already made secret treaties to divide up the German colonies before the war ended.

Territorial Settlements. It is a tribute to Wilson that he managed to influence the peace agreement as much as he did. His presence at Versailles softened some of the harshest demands for reprisals against Germany. National self-determination, a fundamental principle enunciated in Wilson's Fourteen Points, bore fruit in the creation of the independent states of Austria, Hungary, Poland, Yugoslavia, and Czechoslovakia from the defeated empires of the Central Powers. The establishment of a *cordon sanitaire* ("safety zone") consisting of the new nations of Finland, Estonia, Lithuania, and Latvia further served Wilson's (and the Allies') determination to isolate the Soviet Union from the rest of Europe. Although Lenin did not attend the peace conference, Allied leaders realized that the new Soviet state was changing the complexion of power in Eastern Europe—and the world.

The president won only limited concessions regarding the colonial empires of the defeated powers. The old Central and Eastern European empires were dismantled, but the overseas empires of the victorious allies were enlarged by the addition of the colonies of the defeated nations. Those colonies were placed under a mandate system of protectorates and were assigned to various nations to administer as trustees. France and Britain received parts of the old Turkish and German empires in the Middle East and Africa, and Japan assumed responsibility for the German colonies in the Far East. Germany's loss of all its colonies and their transfer to imperialist powers such as Britain and Japan hardly constituted national self-determination.

Wilson failed to prevail on many other issues as well. The secret negotiating sessions held by the Big Four at Versailles mocked Wilson's call for "open covenants of peace openly arrived at." Certain topics, such as freedom of the seas and free trade, never made the agenda because of Allied resistance. More troubling, economic issues were not faced as squarely as were territorial ones. Wilson yielded to French and British demands for a "war guilt" clause, which provided the justification for the restitution demanded from Germany. France was especially adamant about reparations, since the war on the Western Front had been fought primarily on French soil. The final figure, set in 1921, was $33 billion.

In the face of his many disappointments, Wilson consoled himself with the peace conference's commitment to his proposed League of Nations. He acknowledged that the treaty had defects but expressed confidence that they could be resolved by a permanent international organization that brought nations together for the peaceful resolution of disputes.

The Fate of the Treaty

German leaders reacted with dismay to the severity of the treaty, but with that nation reduced almost to starvation by the Allied blockade, they had to accept it. On June 28, 1919, representatives of the participating nations and Germany gathered in the Hall of Mirrors in the Palace of Versailles to sign the treaty. Wilson sailed home immediately after the ceremony and presented the treaty to the Senate on July 10. The treaty was already in trouble, however, with support in the Senate far short of the two-thirds vote necessary for ratification. Would Wilson compromise? "I shall consent to nothing," he told the French ambassador. "The Senate must take its medicine."

The Peace at Versailles
This painting by Sir William Orpen of the signing of the peace treaty in the Hall of Mirrors at Versailles in June 1919 captures the solemnity of the occasion and the grandeur of the surroundings. Wilson was justifiably proud of his role in the peace negotiations, but he faced strong opposition in the Senate.

Congressional Opposition. Opposition to the treaty came from several sources. One group, called the "irreconcilables," consisted of western progressive senators such as William E. Borah of Idaho, Hiram W. Johnson of California, and Robert M. La Follette of Wisconsin. They disagreed fundamentally with the premise of permanent U.S. participation in European affairs represented by the League of Nations. Moreover, they were horrified at the harshnesss of the treaty toward Germany and gravely concerned that League membership would require the United States to uphold it.

Less dogmatic but more influential was a group of Republicans led by Senator Henry Cabot Lodge of Massachusetts. They too expressed strong reservations about the implications of American membership in the League of Nations. Lodge's Republicans proposed a list of amendments centered around Article X, the section of the covenant that called for collective security measures when a member nation was attacked. Lodge correctly argued that this provision restricted Congress's constitutional authority to declare war. More important, Lodge and many other senators felt that the treaty imposed unacceptable restrictions on the freedom of the United States to pursue a unilateral foreign policy.

Wilson refused to budge, especially to placate Lodge, his hated political rival. Hoping to mobilize support for the treaty, in September 1919 the president launched an extensive speaking tour in a last great effort to take his case directly to the American people. In three weeks he traveled 10,000 miles by train and gave forty speeches, sometimes to tens of thousands of people, without the aid of a public address system. He brought large audiences to tears with his impassioned defense of the treaty, but the strain proved too much for the ailing sixty-two-year-old president, who collapsed in Pueblo, Colorado, in late September. The tour had to be cut short. One week later in Washington, Wilson suffered a severe stroke that left one side of his body paralyzed.

Defeat. We will never know whether a healthy Wilson could have mobilized public support for the League of Nations and gained Senate ratification. If he had allowed the Democrats to compromise, the treaty might have been saved. From his sickbed, however, Wilson ordered Democratic senators to vote against all Republican amendments. The treaty came up for a vote in November 1919 and was not ratified. Another attempt in March 1920 fell seven votes short of approval, and the issue was dead.

While the president's wife, Edith Bolling Galt Wilson, his physician, and the various cabinet heads oversaw the routine business of government, Wilson slowly recovered, but he was never the same again. He had delusions of making the 1920 election campaign "a great and solemn referendum" on the League of Nations

and even briefly hoped to run for a third term. Neither dream was a serious possibility. Wilson died in 1924, "as much a victim of the war," David Lloyd George noted, "as any soldier who died in the trenches."

The United States never ratified the Versailles treaty or joined the League of Nations. Many wartime issues remained only partially resolved, notably the future of Germany, the fate of colonial empires, and rising nationalist demands for self-determination. These unsolved problems played a major role in the coming of World War II; some, like competing nationalisms in the Balkans, remain unresolved today.

Racial Strife

Wilson spent only ten days in the United States between December 1918 and June 1919. This fact illustrates his total preoccupation with the peacemaking process at Versailles. For more than six months Wilson was practically an absentee president. Unfortunately, many urgent domestic problems demanded his attention.

The immediate postwar period brought a severe decline in race relations throughout the country. The volatile mix of black migration, intensified segregation in the South, and raised black expectations as a result of service in World War I combined to exacerbate white hostility to blacks. In the South the number of lynchings rose from forty-eight in 1917 to seventy-eight in 1919, and several African-American men were lynched while wearing military uniforms. Northern blacks also faced hostility. Serious racial violence broke out in more than twenty-five cities, and the death toll for the summer of 1919 reached 120.

The riots were precipated in part by the increased northward migration set in motion by World War I: between 1916 and 1919 approximately 500,000 black southerners moved to northern cities. Superficially at least, the North promised new freedoms, but the black migrants faced a difficult adjustment to the diverse urban environment after the South's traditional patterns of deference to whites. In turn, white northerners reacted with hostility to this perceived onslaught of unwelcome newcomers, especially when competition for jobs was added to racism. Violence between blacks and whites erupted as early as 1917 in Houston and Philadelphia. In East St. Louis, Illinois, nine whites and more than forty blacks died in a riot sparked by competition over jobs at a defense plant.

Riots in Chicago. One of the worst race riots in American history took place in Chicago in July 1919. It began at a Lake Michigan beach when a black teenager named Eugene Williams swam into an area of the lake customarily reserved for whites. Someone threw a rock that hit

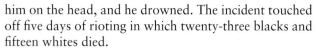

Racial Violence in Chicago
Much of the violence against blacks during the 1919 race riot was perpetrated by young white men, many of Irish descent, who belonged to gangs such as the "Dirty Dozen" and "Our Flag." A city commission later concluded that without the gang activities, "it is doubtful if the riot would have gone beyond the first clash."

him on the head, and he drowned. The incident touched off five days of rioting in which twenty-three blacks and fifteen whites died.

Chicago on the eve of the riot was a tinderbox waiting to ignite. The arrival of 50,000 black newcomers during the war years had strained the city's social fabric. In politics black voters often determined the winners of close elections. (Unlike in the South, northern blacks generally were not prevented from voting.) Blacks and whites competed for jobs, and the more heavily unionized white population deeply resented blacks who became strikebreakers; white stockyard workers considered the words *Negro* and *scab* to be synonymous. Blacks and whites competed for scarce housing as well, and blacks soon overflowed the racially segregated South Side and moved into Chicago's other intensely ethnic neighborhoods. Even before that sultry July afternoon at the beach, tensions had led to the bombing of black homes and other forms of harassment.

Chicago blacks did not sit meekly by as whites destroyed their neighborhoods. They fought back both in self-defense and for their rights as citizens. World War I had an indirect effect on their actions, since many blacks had served in the armed forces. The rhetoric about democracy and self-determination raised their expectations, too.

Labor Unrest

Workers had similar hopes after the war. The war years had provided important breakthroughs for many industrial employees, including higher pay, shorter hours, and better working conditions. Soon after the armistice, however, many employers resumed their attacks on union activity. Many consumers blamed workers for the rising cost of living, and many native-born Americans continued to identify unions with radicalism and foreigners. Nevertheless, workers hoped to keep, perhaps even expand, their wartime gains. The worst problem was rapidly rising inflation, which threatened to wipe out their wage increases. In 1919 the cost of living was 77 percent higher than its prewar level.

1919—A Year of Strikes. More than 4 million workers—one in every five—went on strike in 1919, a proportion never since equaled. The year began with a walkout by shipyard workers in Seattle, a strong union town. Their action spread into a general strike that crippled the city. In the fall the Boston police force went on strike. The idea of public employees trying to unionize shocked many Americans. Governor Calvin Coolidge of Massachusetts propelled himself into the political spotlight by declaring, "There is no right to strike against the public safety by anybody, anywhere, any time." Coolidge fired the entire police force, and the strike failed. The public supported this harsh reprisal, and Coolidge was rewarded with the Republican vice-presidential nomination in 1920.

The most extensive labor disruption in 1919 was the great steel strike in which more than 350,000 steelworkers across the country walked off the job in late September. The main issue was union recognition, but the strikers were also protesting twelve-hour shifts and seven-day workweeks. Elbert H. Gary, chair of the United States Steel Corporation, refused even to meet with representatives of the steelworkers' union to discuss their demands. The company hired Mexicans and blacks to break the strike and maintained steel production at about 60 percent of the normal level.

This high production rate doomed the strike. Striker solidarity began to slacken as winter approached, and in January the strike collapsed. The union charged that U.S. Steel's "arbitrary and ruthless misuse of power" had crushed the strike. Just as important to the union's defeat, though, was the lack of public support for the goals of organized labor. Unions had made important gains during the war, but they were unable to hold on to them.

The Eighteenth Amendment

Another issue demanding national attention as the war ended was the century-old campaign for Prohibition. On the eve of World War I, nineteen states had passed Prohibition laws and many more allowed communities to regulate liquor sales and consumption. Generally, only highly industrialized states with large immigrant populations, such as New York, Massachusetts, Rhode Island, Illinois, and California, had resisted the trend toward alcohol restriction (see Map 23.3).

In early twentieth-century America, Prohibition was viewed as a progressive reform, not a denial of individual freedom. Urban reformers who were concerned about good government, urban poverty, and public morality supported a nationwide ban on drinking. Among the Progressive Era leaders who supported Prohibition were William Jennings Bryan, the Supreme Court Justice Louis Brandeis, the former presidents William Howard Taft and Theodore Roosevelt, and the settlement-house leader Jane Addams.

The drive for Prohibition also had substantial backing in rural communities. Many people equated liquor with all the sins of the city: prostitution, crime, machine politics, and public disorder. In addition, the churches with the greatest strength in rural areas, such as the Methodists, Baptists, and Mormons, strongly condemned drinking. Protestants from rural areas dominated the membership of the Anti-Saloon League, which in the 1910s supplanted the Woman's Christian Temperance Union as the leading proponent of Prohibition.

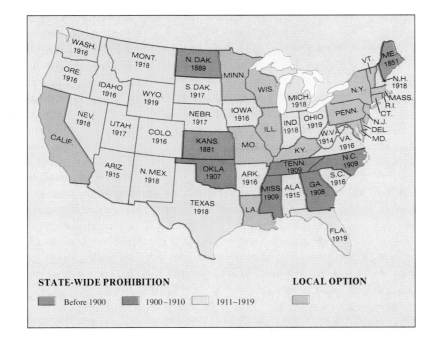

MAP 23.3

Prohibition on the Eve of the Eighteenth Amendment

Prohibition had already made headway in the states before the adoption of the Eighteenth Amendment in 1919. States such as Maine, North Dakota, and Kansas had been dry since the nineteenth century; by 1919 two-thirds of the states had passed laws banning liquor. Most states that resisted the trend were industrial centers or had large immigrant populations.

STATE-WIDE PROHIBITION　　　　**LOCAL OPTION**

Before 1900　　1900–1910　　1911–1919

Support for the right to drink existed primarily in the nation's heavily urbanized areas, places where immigrants had settled. Alcoholic beverages, especially beer and whiskey, played an important role in the social life of certain ethnic cultures, especially those of German-Americans and Irish-Americans. Most saloons were in working-class neighborhoods and were gathering places for workers at the end of the day. Machine politicians conducted much of their business in bars.

During World War I those who supported a constitutional amendment to prohibit drinking had the political momentum. One spur to action was the intense anti-German hysteria of the war years. Because several major breweries (Pabst and Busch, for example) had German names, beer drinking became unpatriotic in many people's minds. As part of the drive to conserve food, Congress prohibited the use of foodstuffs such as hops and barley to make distilled beverages. In December 1917 Congress passed the proposed Eighteenth Amendment prohibiting the manufacture, transport, and sale of intoxicating liquors. Every state, with the exceptions of Connecticut and Rhode Island, ratified it by 1919, and it went into effect on January 16, 1920. Among its few exemptions were alcohol prescribed for medicinal reasons and wine consumed for sacramental purposes.

The passage of the Eighteenth Amendent was another example of how "progressive" solutions to issues of purity, poverty, and public safety were adopted in the climate of war. It also demonstrated the widening influence of the state on matters of personal behavior. Yet the ethnic and urban-rural clashes over Prohibition also foreshadowed the ethnocultural debates after the war. Unlike woman suffrage, the other constitutional amendment that won passage at this time, Prohibition would never gain general acceptance.

The Red Scare

Underlying many of the social tensions in the aftermath of World War I was the fear of radicalism. Wartime hatred of the German Hun was quickly replaced by postwar hostility toward the Bolshevik Red. The Russian Revolution of 1917 set those fears in motion. The founding of the Third International (or Comintern) in 1919 to export revolution throughout the world threatened the Wilsonian vision of an international order based on democracy, capitalism, and harmony. As labor unrest increased, Americans began to see radicals everywhere.

Ironically, as the public became increasingly concerned about domestic Bolshevism, American radical-

ism rapidly lost members and political power. No more than 70,000 Americans belonged to the fledgling U.S. Communist party or the Communist Labor party in 1919, and the IWW and the Socialist party had been weakened by wartime repression and internal dissension. Yet the public and the press continued to blame almost every disturbance, especially labor conflicts, on radicals. "REDS DIRECTING SEATTLE STRIKE—TO TEST CHANCE FOR REVOLUTION," warned a typical newspaper headline.

Then a series of bombings shocked the nation in the early spring. "The word 'radical' in 1919," the historian Robert Murray observed, "automatically carried with it the implication of dynamite." Thirty-four mail bombs addressed to prominent government officials were discovered by postal workers before they exploded. Many people suspected that the intended bombings had been timed to coincide with the communist celebration of International Labor Day on May 1. In June a bomb exploded outside the Washington town house of the recently appointed attorney general, A. Mitchell Palmer. His family escaped unharmed, but the bomber was blown to bits. Despite intensive efforts, law enforcement agencies never traced the origin of a single bomb.

As hysteria mounted in the fall of 1919, the federal government became involved. One aspect of the expansion of state power was increased surveillance of citizens and repression of dissent. President Wilson's debilitating stroke prevented him from providing decisive leadership, but Attorney General Palmer seized the moment. Angling for the presidential nomination, Palmer rode the crest of public fears about domestic radicalism into 1920.

The Palmer Raids. Palmer set up an antiradicalism division in the Justice Department, appointing as its director a young government attorney named J. Edgar Hoover. Hoover's division soon became the Federal Bureau of Intelligence. In November 1919, on the second anniversary of the Russian Revolution, the attorney general staged the first of what became known as "Palmer raids." Federal agents stormed the headquarters of radical organizations and captured such supposedly revolutionary booty as a set of drawings that turned out to be blueprints for an improved phonograph, not sketches for a bomb. The dragnet pulled in thousands of aliens who had committed no crime but were suspect because of their anarchist or revolutionary beliefs or their immigrant background. Lacking the protection of U.S. citizenship, they faced deportation without formal trial or indictment. In December 1919 the U.S.S. *Buford*, nicknamed the "Soviet Ark," embarked

Awaiting Their Fate
As the executions of Nicola Sacco and Bartolomeo Vanzetti approached in 1927, they sparked protests from around the world. This painting by Ben Shahn shows the two handcuffed together as they wait to hear whether their verdicts will be overturned. The judicial system declined to reopen the case. (Ben Shahn, *Bartolomeo Vanzetti and Nicola Sacco*, 1931–1932. © 1997 Estate of Ben Shahn/ Licensed by VAGA, New York, NY)

for Finland and the Soviet state with a cargo of 294 deported radicals. Its passengers included two famous anarchists, Emma Goldman and Alexander Berkman.

The peak of Palmer's power came with his New Year's raids in January 1920. In one night, with the greatest possible newspaper publicity, Palmer rounded up 6,000 radicals. Agents invaded private homes, union headquarters, and meeting halls. The government held both citizens and aliens without specific charges and denied them legal counsel, a violation of their civil liberties. Some prisoners were forced to march through the streets handcuffed to one another. The height of absurdity came when "patriotic" prisoners in a Chicago jail rioted when ordered to share cells with arrested radicals. "There are some things at which even a Chicago crook draws the line," a newspaper reported.

Palmer was riding high in his ambitions for the presidency, but then he overstepped himself. Palmer predicted that on May Day 1920 an unnamed conspiracy would attempt to overthrow the U.S. government. State militia units and police went on twenty-four-hour alert to guard the nation against the threat of revolutionary violence, but not a single incident occurred. The hysteria of the Red Scare began to abate as the summer of 1920 passed without major labor strikes or renewed bombings.

The Sacco-Vanzetti Case. One dramatic episode kept the wartime legacy of antiradicalism alive well into the next decade. In May 1920, at the height of the Red

Scare, Nicola Sacco, a shoemaker, and Bartolomeo Vanzetti, a fish peddler, were arrested for the robbery and murder of a shoe company's paymaster in South Braintree, Massachusetts. Sacco and Vanzetti were self-proclaimed anarchists and Italian aliens who had evaded the draft; both were armed at the time of their arrest.

Sacco and Vanzetti were convicted in 1921 and sat on death row for six years while supporters appealed their verdicts. Regardless of their guilt or innocence, it is clear that they did not receive a fair trial. Shortly before his execution in the electric chair on August 23, 1927, Vanzetti claimed triumph:

> If it had not been for these thing, I might have live out my life among scorning men. I might have die, unmarked, unknown, a failure. Now we are not a failure. This is our career and our triumph. Never in our full life can we hope to do such work for tolerance, for justice, for man's understanding of man, as now we do by an accident.
>
> Our words—our lives—our pains—nothing! The taking of our lives—lives of a good shoemaker and a poor fish-peddlar—all! That last moment belongs to us— that agony is our triumph.

This often-quoted elegy captures the eloquence and tolerance of a victim caught in the last spasm of antiradicalism and fear that capped America's participation in World War I.

Summary

The outbreak of the Great War in 1914 posed a great challenge to American diplomacy. For more than two years President Wilson kept the nation out of war, attempting to use American power and prestige to mediate between the two sides. The United States finally entered the war in 1917 because of violations of its neutral rights at sea but, more broadly, because the country's foreign policy reflected the same moral concerns that animated the domestic reform movement. On April 6, 1917, Congress declared war on Germany.

American participation in the war was brief but decisive. Two million freshly recruited "doughboys" helped to turn the tide for the Allies on the Western Front in 1918. Flush with victory, Wilson sought to bring about a peace that would reflect his vision of a new world order. Yet the Versailles treaty only partially reflected the president's hopes for freedom of the seas, peaceful economic expansion, and national self-determination. His postwar plans suffered a worse blow when the Senate refused to ratify the treaty, which included American participation in the League of Nations.

As the Wilson administration put the nation on a war footing, progressive reform energies were largely diverted to the war effort. An army had to be created almost from scratch, American agriculture and manufacturing had to be federally coordinated to produce for the Allies as well as the home market, and American workers had to be recruited for war work and kept on the job. All this absorbed the energies of a new group of professional experts turned government bureaucrats. World War I thus helped create the tools of the modern bureaucratic state, which (though laid aside temporarily at the war's end) would be taken up again during the nation's worst peacetime crisis, the Great Depression.

The government tried to mobilize the minds of the American people as well but succeeded mainly in inflaming passions. Certain groups, such as woman suffragists, found success during the war. But others became targets of repression, including blacks who migrated to northern cities, labor activists, and socialists and other radicals who criticized the government. Domestic tensions erupted in race riots in many northern cities, widespread labor strikes in 1919, and in the Red Scare of 1919–1920.

TIMELINE

1914	Outbreak of war in Europe United States declares neutrality
1915	German submarine sinks *Lusitania*
1916	Wilson reelected Pershing's expedition to Mexico
1917	U.S. enters World War I Revenue Act passed Selective Service Act passed War Industries Board established Suffrage militancy East St. Louis race riot Espionage Act Bolshevik Revolution Committee on Public Information
1918	Wilson proposes Fourteen Points Meuse-Argonne campaign Eugene Debs imprisoned under Sedition Act Armistice ends war U.S. troops intervene in Soviet Union
1919	Treaty of Versailles Chicago race riot Steel strike Red Scare and Palmer raids; *Schenck v. United States* American Legion founded League of Nations defeated in Senate Eighteenth Amendment (Prohibition) War Industries Board disbanded
1920	Nineteenth Amendment (woman suffrage) "Soviet Ark" sails
1924	Woodrow Wilson dies

★   ★   ★

BIBLIOGRAPHY

Ronald Schaffer, *America in the Great War: The Rise of the War Welfare State* (1991), and David M. Kennedy, *Over Here: The First World War and American Society* (1980), provide comprehensive overviews of the period. On the links between the Progressive Era and the war, see Neil A. Wynn, *From Progressivism to Prosperity: World War I and American Society* (1986); John A. Thompson, *Reformers and War* (1987); and Robert M. Crunden, *Ministers of Reform: The Progressives' Achievement in American Civilization, 1889–1920* (1982). Ellis W. Hawley, *The Great War and the Search for a Modern Order, 1917–1933* (1979), stresses the continuities between the war years and the 1920s.

The Great War

On America's entry into World War I, see John Coogan, *The End to Neutrality* (1981); Ross Gregory, *The Origins of American Intervention in the First World War* (1971); and Thomas A. Bailey and Paul Ryan, *The Lusitania Disaster* (1975). Recent studies of Wilson include August Hecksher, *Woodrow Wilson* (1991); Kendrick Clements, *The Presidency of Woodrow Wilson* (1992); Robert Ferrell, *Woodrow Wilson and World War I* (1985); John Milton Cooper, Jr., *The Warrior and the Priest: Woodrow Wilson and Theodore Roosevelt* (1983); and Edwin Weinstein, *Woodrow Wilson: A Medical and Psychological Biography* (1981).

For American participation in the war, Russell Weigley, *The American Way of War* (1973), and Edward M. Coffman, *The War to End All Wars* (1968), provide useful introductions. They can be supplemented by Laurence Stallings, *The Doughboys: The Story of the AEF, 1917–1918* (1963), and A. E. Barbeau and Florette Henri, *The Unknown Soldiers: Black Troops in World War I* (1974). John Whiteclay Chambers II, *To Raise an Army* (1987), covers the draft. Allan Brandt, *No Magic Bullet* (1985), discusses anti–venereal disease campaigns. Paul Chapman, *Schools as Sorters* (1988), describes the intelligence-testing movement. Material on Eddie Rickenbacker and other wartime aces can be found in his *Fighting the Flying Circus* (1919) and his autobiography, *Edward Rickenbacker* (1967).

Mobilizing the Home Front

Robert D. Cuff, *The War Industries Board: Business-Government Relations during World War I* (1973), provides an excellent case study of mobilization for war. See also Stephen Skowronek, *Building a New American State: The Expansion of National Administrative Capacities, 1877–1920* (1982), and W. Elliot Brownlee, *Federal Taxation in America* (1996). Valerie Jean Conner, *The National War Labor Board* (1983), covers federal policies toward labor. Jordan Schwarz, *The Speculator* (1981), is a biography of Bernard Baruch.

Maurine Greenwald, *Women, War, and Work* (1980), and Barbara Steinson, *American Women's Activism in World War I* (1982), provide good overviews of women's wartime experiences. Anne F. Scott and Andrew Scott, *One Half the People* (1975); Eleanor Flexner, *Century of Struggle* (1959); and Christine A. Lunardini, *From Equal Suffrage to Equal Rights: Alice Paul and the National Woman's Party, 1910–1928* (1986), cover the final stages of the woman suffrage campaign. On the peace movement, see C. Roland Marchand, *The American Peace Movement and Social Reform, 1898–1918* (1973); Charles Chatfield, *For Peace and Justice: Pacifism in America, 1914–1941* (1971); and Charles DeBenedetti, *Origins of the Modern Peace Movement* (1978). Allen F. Davis, *American Heroine* (1974), is a biography of Jane Addams.

Efforts to promote national unity are covered in Stephen Vaughan, *Holding Fast the Inner Lines: Democracy, Nationalism, and the CPI* (1980); William J. Breen, *Uncle Sam at Home* (1984); and Paul L. Murphy, *World War I and the Origins of Civil Liberties* (1979). On free speech, see Richard Polenberg, *Fighting Faiths: The Abrams Case, the Supreme Court, and Free Speech* (1987), as well as Zechariah Chaffee, Jr., *Free Speech in the United States* (1941). For the experiences of Mexican-Americans, see Rodolfo Acuna, *Occupied America* (1980), and Wayne Cornelius, *Building the Cactus Curtain: Mexican Migration and U.S. Responses from Wilson to Carter* (1980).

An Unsettled Peace

On Wilson's diplomacy, see Thomas Knock, *To End All Wars: Woodrow Wilson and the Quest for a New World Order* (1992); Lloyd Ambrosius, *Woodrow Wilson and the American Diplomatic Tradition* (1987); Arthur Walworth, *Wilson and the Peacemakers* (1986); and N. Gordon Levin, Jr., *Woodrow Wilson and World Politics* (1968). For more on Versailles and the League of Nations, see Thomas Bailey, *Woodrow Wilson and the Great Betrayal* (1945); Ralph A. Stone, *The Irreconcilables: The Fight against the League of Nations* (1970); and Arno J. Mayer, *Politics and Diplomacy of Peacemaking: Containment and Counter Revolution at Versailles* (1967). See also William Widenor, *Henry Cabot Lodge and the Search for an American Foreign Policy* (1980). Anglo-American responses to revolution between 1913 and 1923 are covered in Lloyd C. Gardner, *Safe for Democracy* (1984). On American intervention in Russia, see George F. Kennan, *The Decision to Intervene* (1958); John L. Gaddis, *Russia, The Soviet Union, and the United States* (1978); and Peter Filene, *Americans and the Soviet Experiment, 1917–1933* (1967). Ronald Steel's fine biography, *Walter Lippmann and the American Century* (1980), offers another view of the Versailles conference.

Robert K. Murray, *The Red Scare* (1955), summarizes the antiradicalism of the postwar period. See also John Higham, *Strangers in the Land* (1955); Burl Noggle, *Into the Twenties* (1974); and William D. Miller, *Pretty Bubbles in the Air: America in 1919* (1991). David Brody, *Labor in Crisis* (1965), describes the steel strike of 1919; for a more general overview, see David Montgomery, *The Fall of the House of Labor: The Workplace, the State, and American Labor Activism, 1865–1925* (1987). On race relations, see Joe William Trotter, Jr., ed., *The Great Migration in Historical Perspective* (1991); James R. Grossman, *Land of Hope: Chicago, Black Southerners, and the Great Migration* (1989); William M. Tuttle, Jr., *Race Riot: Chicago in the Red Summer of 1919* (1970); Robert V. Haynes, *A Night of Violence: The Houston Riot of 1917* (1976); and Elliot M. Rudwick, *Race Riot at East St. Louis, July 2, 1917* (1964). For an introduction to the Sacco and Vanzetti case, see Louis Joughin and Edmund Morgan, *The Legacy of Sacco and Vanzetti* (1948), and Roberta Strauss Feuerlicht, *Justice Crucified* (1977).

Advertising Modernity

Artist Maxfield Parrish's calendars for General Electric,
such as this 1920 "Prometheus" for Mazda lamps, gave him
widespread visibility and indicate the power of modern
advertising.

CHAPTER 24

Modern Times

The 1920s

★ ★ ★

In 1924 the sociologists Robert Lynd and Helen Merrell Lynd arrived in Muncie, Indiana, to study the life of a small American city. They observed how the citizens of Middletown (the fictional name they gave the city, which they chose for its middle-of-the-road quality) made a living, maintained a home, educated their young, practiced religion, organized community activities, and spent their leisure time. As the Lynds' fieldwork proceeded, they were struck by how much had changed over the past thirty-five years—the actual lifetime of a middle-aged Middletown resident—and decided to contrast the Muncie of the 1890s with the Muncie of the 1920s. When *Middletown* was published in 1929, this "study in modern American culture" became an unexpected best seller.

Many of the characteristics of modern America were in place by the end of World War I. Participation in the war had made the United States a major player in the world economy; the foundations of large-scale corporate enterprise and a modern state were firmly established. The 1920s, however, rather than World War I, were the watershed in the development of a mass national culture. The Protestant work ethic and the old values of self-denial and frugality began to give way to a fascination with consumption, leisure, and self-realization that is the essence of modern times. In economic organization, political outlook, and cultural values, the 1920s have more in common with the United States today than with the industrializing America of the late nineteenth century.

The prosperity and economic innovations of the 1920s gave the United States the highest standard of living in the world, although not every American benefited from the new way of life. Most farmers, urban blacks, and recent immigrants could not afford many of the new mass-produced consumer goods; instead, they sampled them selectively, adapting them to their traditional life-styles. Other Americans found that the convenience of consumer goods and the new emphasis on materialism conflicted with religious and cultural mandates to work hard and live frugally. But despite ambivalence toward these changes, the patterns of consumption and leisure that appeared during the "new era" of the 1920s quickly became part of American life.

The Business-Government Partnership of the 1920s

The business-government partnership accelerated by World War I continued to expand on an informal basis throughout the 1920s. The success of the economy from 1922 to 1929 seemed to confirm its ability to regulate itself with minimal government intervention. Gone, or at least submerged, was the reform impulse of the Progressive Era. Business leaders were no longer villains but respected public figures. President Warren Harding captured the prevailing political mood when he offered the American public "not heroics but healing, not nostrums but normalcy."

The Economy

America's transition from a wartime to a peacetime economy was not smooth. In the immediate postwar years the worst problem was runaway inflation. Prices jumped by a third in 1919, accompanied by feverish economic activity. The postwar boom was less an indication of solid economic growth than a reflection of consumers' desire to buy before prices went higher. In an attempt to decrease the postwar federal debt ($20 billion in 1920), the Wilson administration sharply reduced federal expenditures to stop the inflationary spiral. The Federal Reserve System tightened credit because its expansive money policies had encouraged people to borrow and spend and thus had pushed prices even higher. The new policy resulted in a recession, demonstrating that the government had much to learn about achieving economic stability.

The recession of 1920–1921 was the sharpest short-term downturn the United States had ever faced. Unemployment reached 10 percent. Foreign trade dropped by almost half, from $13.5 billion in 1920 to less than $7 billion in 1921, as European nations resumed production after the disruptions of war. Prices fell so dramatically—more than 20 percent—that much of the inflation of World War I was wiped out. The recession lasted only a short time. By 1922 the economy had started to recover, and the recovery continued, interrupted only by brief, mild downturns, until 1929. Unemployment hovered around 3 or 4 percent, and inflation was negligible. Between 1922 and 1929 the gross national product grew from $74.1 billion to $103.1 billion, approximately 40 percent. Per capita income rose from $641 in 1921 to $847 in 1929. Soon the federal government was recording a budget surplus. This economic expansion provided the backdrop for the partnership between business and government that flourished in the 1920s.

An abundance of new consumer products, particularly the automobile, stimulated recovery and prosperity in the 1920s. Manufacturing output expanded 64 percent, with industries churning out automobiles, appliances, chemicals, electricity, radios, aircraft, and movies. Behind the growth lay new management and

The Assembly Line
The success of the automobile industry contributed significantly to the prosperity of the 1920s, and mass production made automobiles affordable for ordinary citizens, not just the well-to-do. This photograph suggests the aptness of the phrase "rolling off the assembly line." By 1929 there were more than 23 million cars on the road.

mass-production techniques, which resulted in a 40 percent increase in workers' productivity. The value of new construction increased from $6 billion in 1921 to $12 billion in 1927. The demand for goods and services kept unemployment low in most industries throughout the 1920s, but the expanded demand was not strong enough to produce inflation.

One sector of the economy that never fully recovered from the 1920 recession was agriculture. During the inflationary period 1914–1920 farmers had borrowed heavily to finance mortgages and buy farm equipment as they expanded wartime production in response to government incentives, increased demand, and rising prices. When the war ended and European countries resumed agricultural production, the world market was glutted. The price of wheat dropped 40 percent as the government withdrew wartime price supports. Corn prices fell 32 percent and hog prices 50 percent, causing farm income to plunge.

Since American farmers produced mainly for the world market, one key to agricultural recovery was to prevent worldwide surpluses from further depressing domestic prices. Farmers turned to the political system for help. The McNary-Haugen bill, a far-reaching attempt to create permanent federal price supports for agricultural products, used the idea of a "fair exchange value" to guarantee that farmers would recover their production costs no matter what the price was on the world market. A 1924 bill restricting that principle to grain failed in Congress, where the eastern business wing of the Republican party and President Coolidge opposed it as special-interest legislation for agriculture. When midwestern supporters of the bill added cotton, rice, and tobacco to win southern farm support, the measure passed, only to be vetoed by Coolidge in 1927 and again in 1928. The farmers' share of the national income plummeted from 16 percent in 1919 to 8.8 percent at the end of the 1920s.

Besides agriculture, certain "sick industries," such as coal and textiles, missed out on the prosperity of the 1920s. These industries had expanded in response to World War I demands only to face overcapacity or unprofitability and grew sluggishly, if at all, in the 1920s. This underside of economic life foreshadowed the depression of the 1930s.

The Republican Ascendancy

Except for two terms under Woodrow Wilson, the national government had been controlled by the Republican party since 1896. With Wilson's progressive coalition floundering in 1918, the Republicans were in a position to regain the presidency in the upcoming election. In 1920 the Democrats passed over the ailing Wilson in favor of Governor James M. Cox of Ohio, with Assistant Secre-

tary of the Navy Franklin D. Roosevelt as the candidate for vice-president. The Democratic platform called for ratification of U.S. participation in the League of Nations and a continuation of Wilsonian progressivism whereas the Republicans, led by Warren G. Harding and Calvin Coolidge, promised a return to "normalcy," which meant a strong probusiness stance and conservative cultural values. Harding and Coolidge won in a landslide, marking the beginning of a new Republican era that would last until 1932.

Hardly a towering national figure, Harding had built an uninspiring record in Ohio politics before winning election to the U.S. Senate in 1914. With a Republican victory almost a certainty in 1920, party leaders wanted a candidate they could dominate. Genial, loyal, and mediocre, "Uncle Warren" filled the bill.

Harding knew his limitations and tried to assemble a strong cabinet to help him guide the government. Charles Evans Hughes, a former presidential candidate and Supreme Court justice, headed the State Department. As secretary of agriculture, Henry C. Wallace set up conferences between farmers and government agencies such as the Bureau of Agricultural Economics. The financier Andrew W. Mellon ran the Treasury Department, engineering a massive tax cut to reduce the federal surplus. Most of the benefits went to the wealthy, fulfilling Mellon's goal of freeing money for private investment and undercutting the progressive Revenue Acts of 1916, 1917, and 1918.

By far the most active member of the Harding administration was Secretary of Commerce Herbert Hoover, who had successfully headed the Food Administration during the war. Hoover embodied the business-government cooperation of the 1920s, continuing the pattern of state building that had begun during World War I. Unlike Mellon, who wanted to minimize government intervention, Hoover supported expansion of the federal government in what he called the spirit of "associationalism." Voluntary cooperation in the public interest, Hoover maintained, would stabilize prices and assure economic stability in volatile sectors of the economy such as agriculture, construction, and mining. He used persuasion, educational conferences, and fact-finding commissions to accomplish his goals.

Hoover actively promoted trade associations as the key to "associated individualism." There were about 2,000 of these instruments of voluntary cooperation, representing almost every major industry and commodity. Trade associations were supposed to give stability to the economy through conferences, conventions, publicity, lobbying, and trade practice controls. Trade associations used statistics gathered by the Commerce Department and by private groups such as the National Bureau of Economic Research in corporate planning, allocating investments, and controlling markets. Trade conferences organized by the Commerce Department provided a forum for the exchange of information. The Republican-dominated Federal Trade Commission ignored antitrust laws that forbade such anticompetitive practices. In this it followed the lead of the Supreme Court, which in 1920 had dismissed the long-pending antitrust case against the United States Steel Corporation, ruling that largeness in business was not against the law as long as some competition remained.

Unfortunately, not all of Harding's appointees were as capable as Hoover. Harding was an honest man, but some of his political associates had low ethical standards. When Harding died suddenly in San Francisco in August 1923, evidence of widespread fraud and corruption in his administration had just started to come to light. Charles Forbes, the director of the newly established (1921) Veterans Administration, appeared to be an efficient administrator, until evidence surfaced that he had stolen or squandered $250 million in federal funds. An even more damaging scandal concerned the government's secret leasing of oil reserves in Teapot Dome, Wyoming, and Elk Hills, California, to private companies without competitive bidding. Secretary of the Interior Albert Fall eventually was convicted of taking $300,000 in bribes and became the first cabinet officer in American history to serve a prison sentence.

After Harding's death Vice-President Calvin Coolidge moved into the White House. In contrast to Harding's political cronyism and outgoing style, Coolidge personified Vermont rectitude. As vice-president "Silent Cal" often sat through official functions without uttering a word. A dinner partner once challenged him by saying, "Mr. Coolidge, I've made a rather sizable bet with my friends that I can get you to speak three words this evening." Responded Coolidge icily, "You lose." Like Harding, Coolidge backed business and believed in limited government; he was said to perform all his presidential duties in four hours a day. Coolidge's image of unimpeachable morality reassured voters in the wake of the Harding scandals, and he soon announced that he would run for president in 1924.

The 1924 Election. The Democratic party found it difficult to mount an effective challenge to its more popular and better-financed rival, whose strength came chiefly from the native-born Protestant middle class, augmented by small businesspeople, skilled workers, farmers, northern black voters, and wealthy industrialists. Democrats drew their support mainly from the South and from northern urban political machines such as Tammany Hall in New York, but the interests of those two constituencies often collided. Until the Democrats could build an effective national organization to rival that of the Republicans, they would remain a minority party.

When the Democrats gathered that year in the sweltering July heat of New York City, they were more di-

vided than usual. Their convention, the first to be broadcast live on national radio, lasted seventeen days, prompting the humorist Will Rogers to say, "This thing has got to come to an end. New York invited you people here as guests, not to live." The convention became hopelessly deadlocked between Governor Alfred E. Smith of New York, who had the support of northern urban politicians, and William G. McAdoo of California, Wilson's secretary of the treasury (and son-in-law), the western and southern choice. After 103 ballots the delegates compromised on John W. Davis, a Wall Street lawyer who had served as a West Virginia congressman and an ambassador to Great Britain. To attract rural voters the Democrats chose as their vice-presidential candidate Governor Charles W. Bryan of Nebraska, the brother of William Jennings Bryan.

The 1924 campaign also featured a third-party challenge by Senator Robert M. La Follette of Wisconsin, who ran on the Progressive party ticket. His candidacy mobilized reformers and labor leaders as well as disgruntled farmers. The Progressive party platform called for nationalization of railroads, public ownership of utilities, and the right of Congress to overrule Supreme Court decisions. It also favored the election of the president directly by the voters rather than by the electoral college.

The Republicans won an impressive victory, with Coolidge receiving 15.7 million popular votes to 8.4 million for Davis and winning decisively in the electoral college. Despite La Follette's vigorous campaign, he could not draw many midwestern farm leaders away from the Republican party; his labor support also proved soft. La Follette got almost 5 million popular votes, but carried only Wisconsin in the electoral college.

Perhaps the most significant aspect of the 1924 election was the low voter turnout. Only 52 percent of the electorate voted, compared with the more than 70

Leisure and Politics
Calvin Coolidge was from Vermont but that did not keep Wisconsin boosters from using his campaign slogan to promote tourism in their state.

Women Write the Children's Bureau

The Children's Bureau in the Department of Labor was in charge of administering the Sheppard-Towner Act from 1921 to 1929. In addition to setting up clinics and providing prenatal care, the staff answered letters from anxious mothers, such as the two excerpted here.

Dear Doctor Sherbon:
You can not imagine how much I have enjoyed the Course. As soon as I received it I lay down and never stopped until I read it through. It is splendid, and if every woman could follow each lesson to the letter there would be less suffering. But how are we going to convince our families that such care is necessary? Of course the children can be taught these things, but the husbands and our mothers think it is foolishness to take such care of ourselves.

Do you think it proper to explain to children where they come from and the science of life? I have told my stepson, age 18, all of these things and how he should take care of himself, and also how he should treat girls and how much suffering there was to childbirth, and I was very much criticized by some of the family.

I must close. I am taking up your valuable time and am losing much time of my own. Thank you for all the help and the good you are doing, not only for myself but others.

Dear Madam:
I took your correspondence course last winter and enjoyed it very much although I have been a mother three times and expect to be again as [I] am pregnant three months now. Maybe you have something for me or that might help me in some way, so [I] thot that I would drop you a line.

We are a poor family and live in western Kansas and [are] heavily in debt, so this ordeal is hard for me at present. But what I would like to ask you is if a poor mother can get any county or state aid. My teeth are badly in need of dental work, and [I have] no money to pay the bill and the doctor bill worries me too. The doctor we have gone to is so high I don't see how we can afford it. We owe $125 in doctor bills in another county . . . and I dread any more until back ones are paid.

Isn't there a law in Kansas that unless a confinement case is obstetrical the limit charge is $15 and if obstetrical the limit is $25? He says he charges $25 for a confinement case and $1.00 mileage which would make a total of $37 for us for doctor bill, besides a nurse or lady to nurse and do the work

too. But if you know anything about such things you know that mother and babe are sadly neglected if the nurse has all the house work to do too. . . .

Does the county doctor tend to such cases and look to the community for his money? It looks like we ought to be able to do and care for such things without asking for help, but you know there are just lots and lots of mothers in my fix that just drag along and worry because they have no way of buying the most needy things at such a time and are too proud to find out if there is any way to get help. My husband thinks it's awful to get help in any way besides paying for it, but when I know he is not financially able to help, I don't see why I should suffer if there is any way to help me, as any mother or doctor knows at that time a mother needs the best of care in every way. And it's because I have always had to work too soon after childbirth that I am broken down now.

I will see what I hear from you before going into details any more. Hoping you will not think it too trifling a matter to interest you and will answer me as soon as possible. Yours truly.

Source: Molly Ladd-Taylor, *Raising a Baby the Government Way: Mothers' Letters to the Children's Bureau, 1915–1932* (New Brunswick: Rutgers University Press, 1986), 131–132, 136–138.

percent who had voted in presidential elections in the late nineteenth century. The nation's newly enfranchised women were not to blame, however: the long-term drop in voting by men, not apathy among women, was responsible for the decline.

Women in Politics. Instead of resting after their suffrage victory, women increased their political activism in the 1920s. Partisan women tried to break into party politics, but the Democrats and Republicans granted them only token positions on party committees. For women, political officeholding remained a "widow's game": about two-thirds of the women in Congress had been appointed to finish their late husbands' terms.

Women were more influential as lobbyists. The

Women's Joint Congressional Committee, a Washington-based coalition of ten major women's organizations including the newly formed League of Women Voters and the National Consumers' League, lobbied for reform legislation. Its major accomplishment was the passage in 1921 of the Sheppard-Towner Federal Maternity and Infancy Act, the nation's first federally funded health care program. In an attempt to reduce the high rate of death associated with childbirth, Congress appropriated $1.25 million for well-baby clinics, educational programs, and visiting-nurse projects. Isolated rural women were especially grateful for this government aid, and eagerly sought information from government agencies like the Children's Bureau, which administered the program (see American Voices, above).

The Sheppard-Towner bill passed because politicians feared that if it didn't, women would vote them out of office. As one supporter noted, "If the members could have voted in the cloak room, it would have been killed." However, by the late 1920s politicians realized that women did not vote as a bloc. And other powerful lobbying groups, such as the American Medical Association, strenuously objected to the state being involved in health care at all. In 1929, Congress cut off appropriations for the program.

At mid-decade the Republicans were in an enviable position. The scandals of the Harding years were behind them, and the economy continued to be strong, supporting their policy of placing the responsibility for the national well-being in the hands of corporate capitalism. The informal business-government partnership worked—or so it seemed—until the depression.

Corporate Capitalism

The 1920s saw the triumph of the management revolution that had been reshaping American business since the late nineteenth century (see Chapter 19). Large-scale

River Rouge
Industrial photographers in the 1920s celebrated the power and raw beauty of industrial technology. Charles Sheeler's 1927 photograph shows Ford's River Rouge plant outside Detroit. But where are the workers?

corporate organizations with bureaucratic structures of authority replaced family-run businesses. Ownership was divorced from the control of daily operations, and what the eighteenth-century economist Adam Smith had called the "invisible hand" of market forces gave way to the visible hand of management. But business leaders, indeed most American citizens, remained leery of direct state intervention into the economy.

There were more mergers in the 1920s—368 in 1924 and 1,245 in 1929—than at any time since the heyday of combinations in the 1880s and 1890s. The largest number occurred in rapidly growing industries such as chemicals, electrical appliances and machinery, and automobiles. By 1930 the 200 largest corporations controlled almost half the nonbanking corporate wealth in the United States. It was rare for one corporation to monopolize an entire industry; instead, oligopolies, in which a few large producers controlled an industry, became the norm, such as in auto manufacturing, oil refining, and steelmaking.

By 1920 many industries, especially in manufacturing, had modern organizational structures. The multiunit enterprise coordinated production and distribution through divisions organized by functions, such as sales, operations, and investment. Alfred P. Sloan, Jr., an engineer and midlevel manager at General Motors in the 1920s, refined this structure by relieving top management of the day-to-day control of production. This shift in responsibility freed management to concentrate on long-range planning while autonomous, integrated divisions met short-range production goals. General Motors' innovative structure set the pattern for large companies in the 1920s and 1930s.

Corporations greatly increased their commitment to research and development, using current earnings to create future profits. Corporate mergers were a major source of capital for this purpose. By 1927 more than a thousand corporations had set up independent research programs, among them Bell Laboratories, the research arm of the American Telephone and Telegraph Company, which was formally incorporated in 1925.

These huge modern corporate structures called for a new breed of man: the professional manager. (Women found few opportunities in the corporate hierarchy until the 1970s.) Increasingly, corporations relied on graduate schools of business, such as Wharton and Harvard, to produce managers, consultants, and executives, many of whom had engineering training. In the 1920s the chief executives at General Motors, General Electric, Singer, Du Pont, and Goodyear had all been engineering classmates at the Massachusetts Institute of Technology.

The nation's financial institutions expanded and consolidated along with its corporations. Total bank assets rose from almost $48 billion in 1919 to $72 billion in 1929, largely because of rising deposits in savings institutions and business and loan associations, along with life insurance policies and annuities. Mergers between Wall Street banks enhanced the role of New York as the financial center of the United States and the world. In 1929 almost half the nation's banking resources were controlled by 1 percent, or 250, of American banks.

Business leaders enjoyed enormous popularity and respect in the 1920s, their reputations often surpassing those of the era's lackluster politicians. Many politicians and commentators drew parallels between religious activity and business leadership. President Coolidge solemnly declared, "The man who builds a factory builds a temple. The man who works there worships there." The secularization of religion and the glorification of business reached a new height in a book called *The Man Nobody Knows* (1924) by the advertising executive Bruce Barton. The man of the title was Jesus Christ, whom Barton portrayed as the founder of modern business, writing that Christ "picked up twelve men from the bottom ranks of business and forged them into an organization that conquered the world." Barton's parable was an instant best seller.

The most respected businessman of the decade was Henry Ford, whose rise from poor farm boy to corporate giant symbolized the values of rural society and American individualism in a rapidly changing world. Ford's factories, especially the River Rouge plant in suburban Detroit, represented the triumph of mass production. Ironically, this American capitalist hero achieved great popularity in the Soviet Union. At a time when the United States and the Soviet Union had no formal diplomatic relations, Ford sold the Russians 25,000 tractors between 1920 and 1926.

Labor and Welfare Capitalism

Workers shared in the prosperity of the 1920s, although labor lagged behind business in reaping the benefits of technology. Business supported higher wages as a way to increase workers' buying power. With a shorter workweek (five full days and a half day on Saturday), many workers had more leisure time; large firms such as International Harvester offered employees two weeks of paid vacation a year. But scientific management techniques, first put forth in 1895 by Frederick W. Taylor but only widely implemented in the 1920s, reduced labor's control over the work environment.

Decisions from an extremely probusiness Supreme Court led by Chief Justice William Howard Taft also affected workers adversely. For example, in the 1925 *Coronado Coal Company v. United Mine Workers* the Court ruled that a striking union could be prosecuted for restraint of trade. It also struck down federal legislation regulating child labor in *Bailey v. Drexel Furniture Company* (1922) and the minimum wage for women workers in the District of Columbia in *Adkins v. Children's Hospital* (1923).

The 1920s was also the heyday of "welfare capitalism," a system of labor relations that stressed management's responsibility for the well-being of its employees. Though tinged with paternalism, this system provided benefits to workers at a time when unemployment compensation and old-age pensions did not exist. Employee security was not, however, the primary concern of those corporate programs, which were established mainly to deter the formation of unions.

Welfare capitalism took several forms. Workers could increase their stake in the company by buying stock below the market price, though only a small minority could actually afford to do so. Some firms subsidized mortgages or contributed to employees' savings funds; others set up insurance and pension plans. Many adopted programs for consultation between management and elected representatives of the workers. These employee representation schemes, another device to avert unionization, were called the American Plan in order to establish the idea that unions were un-American. Management's long-term goals included control over the workplace, an open (nonunion) shop, and worker loyalty.

However, the system had serious disadvantages for workers, including a lack of protection against unemployment. Furthermore, welfare capitalism appeared primarily in the largest, most prosperous firms, such as General Electric and U.S. Steel, and reached only a minority of workers. Corporate profits often dictated the nature of the programs. The Proctor & Gamble Company guaranteed forty-eight weeks of employment a year to its soap-manufacturing workers because of the steady demand for soap, but workers in another division who processed vegetable oils, which were subject to sales fluctuations, received no such guarantee.

Welfare capitalism represented a form of labor relations that was squarely in keeping with the values of the 1920s. It placed the responsibility for economic welfare in the private sector rather than the public sector, avoiding the possibility of government interference in the workplace on the side of labor. It also satisfied management's desire to reverse the tide of unionization: union membership dropped from 5.1 million in 1920 to 3.6 million in 1929, about 10 percent of the nonagricultural work force. The number of strikes also fell dramatically from the level in 1919. Welfare capitalism seemed to represent the wave of the future in industrial relations.

Economic Expansion Abroad

As the domestic economy expanded, so did the nation's international position. During the 1920s the United States was the most productive country in the world, with an enormous capacity to compete in foreign markets. Underlying this increase in international activity was a growing demand from abroad for American consumer products such as radios, telephones, automobiles, and sewing machines. The demand for U.S. capital was just as important. America's emergence as the world's largest creditor nation, a reversal of its pre–World War I status as a debtor nation, represented a dramatic shift of power in world capital markets. American investment abroad more than doubled between 1919 and 1930: by the end of the 1920s American corporations had invested $15.2 billion in foreign countries. This American capital sustained the international economic system in the 1920s.

Manufacturers led the way in foreign investment. Electric companies, including General Electric, built new plants in Latin America, China, Japan, and Australia. Ford had major facilities throughout the British Empire, and General Motors took over established automakers such as Vauxhall in England and Opel in Germany. The International Telephone and Telegraph Corporation, founded in 1920, employed 95,000 workers outside the country, more than did any other U.S. company.

Other American companies invested internationally during the 1920s to take advantage of lower production costs or procure raw materials and supplies, concentrating mainly on Latin America. The three major American meat packers—Swift, Armour, and Wilson—built plants in Argentina to capitalize on its low livestock prices. Fruit growers such as the United Fruit Company established plantations in Costa Rica, Honduras, and Guatemala. American capital ran sugar plantations in Cuba and rubber plantations in the Philippines, Sumatra, and Malaya.

American companies also invested heavily in mining and oil, especially in South America and Canada. The Anaconda Copper Corporation owned Chile's largest copper mine. Standard Oil of New Jersey led American oil companies in acquiring oil reserves in Mexico and Venezuela. (American involvement in the oil-rich Persian Gulf became significant only after World War II.)

American banks supported U.S. enterprises abroad, especially in Europe. European countries, particularly Germany, needed private American capital to finance economic recovery after World War I. Germany had to rebuild its economy and pay reparations to the Allies; Britain and France had to repay wartime loans. As late as 1930 the Allies still owed the United States $4.3 billion. American political leaders, responding to voters' disenchantment with the cost of the nation's participation in the war, rigidly demanded payment. Referring to the European nations, President Coolidge scoffed, "They hired the money, didn't they?"

European countries had trouble repaying their debts because the United States maintained high protective tariffs to keep foreign-made goods out. The Fordney-McCumber Tariff of 1922 followed the long-standing Republican policy of protectionism, and the Hawley-Smoot Tariff of 1930 took economic nationalism even further. American manufacturers favored those high tariffs because they feared that foreign competition would reduce their profits. But the difficulty of selling goods in the United States made it harder for European nations to pay off their debts in dollars.

Concerned about debt repayment, the American banking community and many U.S. corporations with European investments opposed excessively high tariffs and urged modification of the debt structure. They recognized that a rapidly recovering Europe and a freer trade environment would help American business, whereas a weak European economy might undermine long-term loans and investments.

In 1924, at the prodding of the United States, France, Great Britain, and Germany joined with the United States in a plan to improve and promote European financial stability. The Dawes Plan, named for Charles G. Dawes, a Chicago banker who negotiated the agreement, offered substantial loans to Germany and a reduction in the amount of reparations owed to the Allies. But the Dawes Plan did not provide a permanent solution. The international economic system, which depended on the flow of American capital to Germany, reparations payments from Germany to the Allies, and the repayment of debts to the United States, was inherently unstable. If the flow of capital from the United States slowed or stopped, the world financial structure could collapse.

Foreign Policy in the 1920s

Foreign affairs in the interwar period are often viewed through the lens of isolationism, the view that the United States, disillusioned after World War I, willfully retreated from involvement in world affairs. But the term *isolationism* masks the active role that the United States played in world affairs both before and after the Great War. *Globalization* is a more accurate term. Economic expansion into new markets was a major component of the prosperity of the 1920s, and the United States ardently sought a peaceful and stable world order to facilitate American investments in Latin American, European, and Pacific Rim markets. This expansion abroad, which was a continuation of Taft's policy of Dollar Diplomacy (see Chapter 22), was warmly abetted by the appropriate branches of the federal government, such as the State and Commerce departments.

In the 1920s the United States continued its quest for peaceful ways to dominate the Western Hemisphere economically and diplomatically but retreated slightly from military intervention in Latin America. The United States withdrew troops from the Dominican Republic in 1924 but maintained military forces in Nicaragua almost continuously from 1912 to 1933. American troops also occupied Haiti from 1915 to 1934. Relations with Mexico remained tense as a legacy of U.S. intervention during the Mexican Revolution.

There was little popular or political support, however, for entangling diplomatic commitments to allies, European or otherwise. The United States never joined the League of Nations or the Court of International Justice (the World Court). International cooperation had to come through other forums.

The Washington Conference and the Kellogg-Briand Pact. The 1921 Washington Naval Arms Conference represented a milestone in the history of disarmament and the fulfillment of one of Woodrow Wilson's goals. By placing limits on naval expansion, policy makers hoped to encourage stability in areas such as the Far East and protect the fragile postwar world economy from excessive spending on arms. A hidden agenda was to contain Japan, whose expansionist tendencies were already seen as threatening two decades before the outbreak of World War II.

Led by Secretary of State Charles Evans Hughes, the three leading naval powers—Britain, the United States, and Japan—joined other countries in agreeing to halt construction of large battleships for ten years and maintain current tonnage among Britain, the United States, Japan, Italy, and France at a ratio of 5:5:3:1.75:1.75. (This maintained parity among the big three, since the Japanese fleet operated only in the Pacific.) The conferees even agreed to scrap some existing warships, leading one commentator to exclaim that in a thirty-five-minute speech the secretary of state had sunk "more ships than all the admirals of the world have sunk in a cycle of centuries." Not until the 1980s would the world see another such concerted effort to disarm.

In a similar spirit of international cooperation, the 1928 Kellogg-Briand Peace Pact condemned militarism as a tool for advancing national interests. In 1927 the French foreign minister, Aristide Briand, had asked the United States to sign an agreement guaranteeing France's territorial integrity and outlawing war between France and the United States. Instead, Coolidge's secretary of state, Frank Kellogg, proposed a broader treaty in which participating countries would agree to "condemn recourse to war for the solution of international controversies, and renounce it as an instrument of national policy." Fifteen nations signed the pact in Paris in 1928, with forty-eight more approving it later. The Kellogg-Briand Pact was enthusiastically supported by U.S. peace groups such as the Women's International League for Peace and Freedom and the Conference on the Cause and Cure of War, and the U.S. Senate ratified it 85 to 1. Yet critics claimed that it was nothing more than an "international kiss": lacking enforcement machinery, it was only as effective as its signers made it. For many who abhorred war, however, the pact's broad moral statement was an important contribution to the maintenance of peace.

In the end, fervent hopes and pious declarations were no cure for the massive economic, political, and territorial problems that World War I had left behind. The United States vacillated, as it would in the 1930s, between wanting to play a larger role in world events and fearing that treaties and responsibilities would limit its ability to act unilaterally. Rather than criticize the diplomatic efforts of the 1920s as naive or misguided, it is better to see them as honest but ultimately inadequate efforts to find a will to peace.

A New National Culture

The 1920s represented an important watershed in the development of a mass national culture. A new emphasis on leisure, consumption, and amusement characterized the modern era, although its benefits were more accessible to the white middle class than to minorities and other disadvantaged groups. Automobiles, paved roads, the parcel post service, movies, radios, telephones, mass-circulation magazines, brand names, and chain stores linked Americans in mill towns in the southern Piedmont, rural outposts on the Oklahoma plains, western mining settlements, and ethnic enclaves on the coasts in an expanding web of national experience. In fact, with the exportation of automobiles, radios, and movies to consumers throughout the world, one can even begin to speak of the globalization of the American experience.

Consumption and Advertising

In homes across the country in the 1920s Americans sat down to a breakfast of Kellogg's corn flakes with toast prepared in a General Electric toaster. They got into a Ford Model T to go about their business, perhaps shopping at one of the chain stores, such as Safeway and A & P, which had sprung up across the country. In the evening the family gathered to listen to radio programs such as "Great Moments in History" and "True Story" or read the latest issue of the *Saturday Evening Post*, *Reader's Digest*, or *Collier's*. On weekends they might hop in the car to see the latest Charlie Chaplin film at the local movie theater. Millions of Americans now shared the same daily experiences.

The 1920s was a critical decade in the development of the American consumer society. Although not every family participated in the new life-style, consumption became a cultural ideal for most of the middle class, often providing the criterion for judging self-worth that was once supplied by character, religion, and social standing. Spending money on more and better possessions became a form of self-fulfillment, a gratification of personal needs.

Yet participation in commercial mass culture did not necessarily mean a total conversion to American middle-class values. Buying a Victrola or a radio on credit and listening to the opera singer Enrico Caruso could have been a way for Italian immigrants to keep their culture alive. Nor was owning a car simply a symbol of consumption. "I had bought a jalopy in 1924, and it didn't change me," remembered one Communist party activist. "It just made it easier for me to function." The historian Lizabeth Cohen concluded that "Chicago's ethnic workers were not transformed into more Americanized, middle-class people by the objects they consumed. Buying an electric vacuum cleaner did not turn Josef Dobrowolski into *True Story's* Jim Smith."

The unequal distribution of income limited some consumers' ability to buy the enticing new products. At the height of prosperity in the 1920s, about 65 percent of America's families had an income less than $2,000 a year, which barely supported a decent living standard. The average family income in the bottom 40 percent of the population was $725. Of that amount, a family spent about $290 a year for food, $190 for housing, and $110 for clothing, leaving only $135 for everything else, including medical expenses and emergencies.

Retailers and automobile manufacturers addressed this situation by selling on the installment plan. In those days "buy now, pay later" was a revolutionary concept. Before World War I most urban families paid cash for everything except a house, but in the 1920s the automobile became such an object of desire that consumers put aside their fears of buying on time. In 1927 two-thirds of the cars in the United States were being paid off on the installment plan. Once people saw how easy it was to finance a car, they bought radios, refrigerators, and sewing machines on credit. "A dollar down and a dollar forever," a cynic remarked. But by 1929, banks, finance companies, credit unions, and other institutions were lending consumers over $7 billion a year and consumer lending was the tenth largest business in the United States.

Many of the new products were electric appliances, for which consumers spent about $667 million in 1927. By 1930, 85 percent of American nonfarm households had electricity to run their favorite gadgets. Irons and vacuum cleaners were the most popular appliances, followed by phonographs, sewing machines, and washing machines. Radios, whose production increased twenty-five-fold in the 1920s, sold for around $75. One of the most expensive items was a refrigerator, which cost $900 at the beginning of the decade. Improvements in the technology quickly brought the price down to $180, but many families still had to make do with an old-fashioned icebox.

Because much of the new technology was concentrated in the home, it had a dramatic impact on women's lives. Domestic chores became less arduous: it was far easier to plug in an electric iron than to heat an iron on the stove, and it was quicker and easier to use a vacuum cleaner than a broom and a rug beater. Paradoxically, however, the time women spent on housework did not decline. More middle-class women began to do their own housework and laundry as electric servants replaced human ones. Technology also raised standards of cleanliness so that a man could wear a clean shirt every day instead of just on Sunday, and a house could be vacuumed daily rather than swept weekly.

Advertising became a big business in the 1920s. In 1929 advertisers spent an average of $15 annually on every man, woman, and child in the United States—a total of $2.6 billion—to entice them to buy automobiles, cigarettes, radios, and refrigerators. That year the advertising industry, which the historian Roland Marchand called the "town criers" of modernity, accounted for 3 percent of the gross national product, comparable to its share after World War II.

The Flapper
The flapper phenomenon was not limited to Anglos. This 1921 photograph of a young Mexican-American woman shows how American fads and fashions reached into Hispanic communities across the country.

Portrait of Ettie
This 1923 painting by New York artist Florine Stettheimer of her sister Ettie suggests the personal flamboyance and languid style associated with modern women in the 1920s. No wonder their mothers and grandmothers were shocked. (Columbia University in the City of New York)

wore makeup (previously assumed to be a sign of sexual availability in lower-class women) and lit up cigarettes in public, a shocking affront to ladylike decency. Like so many cultural icons, the flapper represented only a tiny minority of women. Yet the image mass-marketed the belief in women's postsuffrage emancipation.

The Automobile Culture

As the predominant symbol of the 1920s, the automobile typified the new consumer-based economy. "Why on earth do you need to study what's changing this country?" a Muncie, Indiana, resident asked the sociologists Robert and Helen Lynd, who were studying American culture and values. "I can tell you what's happening in just four letters: A-U-T-O!" Another Middletowner volunteered, "We'd rather do without clothes than give up the car."

The showpiece of modern capitalism and the ultimate consumer toy, the automobile revolutionized the ways Americans spent their money and leisure time. The isolation of rural life broke down in the wake of the automobile. New phrases such as "filling station" (or, as they were known west of the Rockies, "service stations") entered the nation's vocabulary. The automobile even affected crime, providing gangsters with a "getaway car" and the possibility of "taking someone for a ride." Cars touched so many aspects of American life that the word *automobility* was coined to describe their impact on production methods, the landscape, and American values.

The automobile stimulated the prosperity of the 1920s. Before the introduction of the moving assembly line in 1913, it took Ford workers twelve and a half hours to assemble an auto; it took only ninety-three minutes on an assembly line. In 1927 Ford produced a car every twenty-four seconds. Car sales climbed from 1.5 million in 1921 to 5 million in 1929, when Americans spent $2.58 billion on new and used cars. By the late 1920s a new Ford Model T, which cost $1,000 in 1908, sold for only $295 (at a time when an industrial worker earned about $5 a day). Lower cost and installment buying increased yearly car registrations from 8.5 million in 1920 to 23 million in 1929. By the end of the decade Americans owned about 80 percent of the world's automobiles, an average of one car for every five people.

The growth of the auto industry had a ripple effect on the American economy. In 1929, 3.7 million workers directly or indirectly owed their jobs to the automobile. Auto production stimulated the steel, petroleum, chemical, rubber, and glass industries. Total U.S. demand for oil, mainly in the form of gasoline, multiplied two and a half times between 1919 and 1929, and domestic oil production expanded to meet the need. (The United

Few of the new consumer products could be considered necessities, so advertisements appealed to people's social aspirations by projecting images of successful, elegant, sophisticated people who smoked a certain brand of cigarettes or drove a recognizable make of car. Ad writers also sold products by preying on people's insecurities, coming up with a variety of socially unacceptable diseases, including "sneaker smell," "paralyzed pores," "office hips," "ashtray breath," and the dreaded "BO" (body odor). After the term *halitosis* was discovered in a British medical journal, many consumers rushed out to buy Listerine mouthwash. Yet American consumers were not passive victims of advertisers who manipulated their every whim. America gloried in its role as the world's first mass-consumption economy.

Many of these cultural images came together in the flapper, the media version of the emancipated woman of the 1920s. With her slim, boyish figure, bobbed hair, short skirt, and rolled-down silk stockings, the flapper symbolized the personal freedom trumpeted by movies, advertisements, and other elements of the emerging mass culture. Neither maternal nor wifely, the flapper

States was the world's chief supplier of oil in the 1920s.) The advertising industry grew along with the automobile; cars and cigarettes were two of the most heavily marketed products of the decade. Highway construction became a billion-dollar-a-year enterprise financed by federal subsidies and state gasoline taxes. Car ownership also spurred the growth of suburbs and contributed to real-estate speculation. It spawned the first shopping center, Country Club Plaza, in Kansas City in 1924. Not even the deaths of 25,000 people a year in traffic accidents, 70 percent of them pedestrians, could dampen America's passion for the automobile.

Nowhere was this most obvious than in the way Americans spent their leisure time. They took to the roads, becoming a nation of tourists. The American Automobile Association, founded in 1902, reported that in 1929 about 45 million people—almost a third of the population—took vacations by automobile. Of the $10 billion spent on recreation in 1930, two-thirds went for cars and related expenses. People preferred the freedom of automobiles to the rigid timetables and predetermined routes of trains. With improved roads, motorists could average more than 45 miles an hour on their way to the "autocamps" and tourist cabins that were the forerunners of motels.

Like movies and other products of the new mass culture, cars changed the dating patterns of young Americans. Contrary to many parents' views, sex was not invented in the backseat of a Ford, but a Model T offered more privacy and comfort than did the family living room or the front porch. City elders in Muncie overreacted by calling automobiles "prostitution on wheels."

The most popular car of the decade was the Model T. The Ford Motor Company manufactured over 15 million Model T's between 1908 and 1927. A "Tin Lizzie," as these dependable cars were called, required a mechanically inclined driver. The motorist had to hand crank the car to start it and keep one hand on the accelerator and the other on the wheel while driving. There was no gas gauge—one had to remove the front seat and peer into the tank to see how much gas there was. As late as 1919 only about 10 percent of cars had roofs. As for color, Henry Ford intoned, "The customer can have a Ford any color he wants—so long as it's black."

Consumers eventually became discontented with the plain Model T, and Ford faced stiff competition from General Motors (GM). GM's five automobile divisions turned out cars for specialized markets and introduced the concept of "trading up." The luxury Cadillac cost the most and had the lowest volume of sales; the Chevrolet had the cheapest price tag and the highest volume of sales; Oldsmobile, Pontiac, and Buick were geared to incomes in between. GM cars also featured self-starters and foot accelerators. Henry Ford finally bowed to consumer demands when he introduced the Model A in 1927. More than a million New Yorkers visited the Ford showroom during the five days after the new model was unveiled. At prices ranging from $495 to $570, the Model A fulfilled consumers' demands for different styles, more colors, and greater comfort and helped make the automobile a permanent part of American culture.

The Movies and Mass Culture

The movie industry probably did more than anything else to disseminate common values and attitudes throughout the United States. Its growth coincided with America's transformation into a predominantly urban, industrial society. In contrast to Europe, where cinema developed as an avant-garde, highbrow art form, American movies were part of popular culture almost from the start, a mass-entertainment industry that was both democratic and highly lucrative.

The Silent Era. Movies began around the turn of the century in nickelodeons, where for a nickel the mostly working-class audience could see a one-reel silent film such as *What Demoralized the Barbershop* (1901), *The Girl at the Window* (1903), and the spectacularly successful *The Great Train Robbery* (1903). Because the films, mostly comedies and melodramas, were silent, they could be understood by immigrants who did not speak English. The new medium grew in popularity and profitability.

During the first years of the twentieth century most films were made in New York City or Fort Lee, New Jersey. After 1910 moviemakers such as D. W. Griffith and Cecil B. DeMille flocked to southern California, which had cheap land, plenty of sunshine, and varied scenery—mountains, deserts, cities, and the Pacific Ocean—within easy reach. Another attraction was Los Angeles's reputation as an antiunion town. Actors also flocked to California, especially to Hollywood, a fast-growing suburb of Los Angeles. The early movie stars—the comedians Buster Keaton, Charlie Chaplin, and

The Tramp
Charlie Chaplin did not invent the tragicomic figure of the tramp, but it soon became his screen persona. Chaplin grew up poor in the London slums, but the movies brought him wealth and fame. In 1919 he joined Douglas Fairbanks, Mary Pickford, and D. W. Griffith to form United Artists.

Harold Lloyd; Mary Pickford (though born in Canada, "America's Sweetheart"); and dashing leading men Douglas Fairbanks, Wallace Reid, and John Gilbert—became national idols. So did Clara Bow, one of the biggest stars, male or female, from the decade (see American Lives, pages 752–753).

Movies quickly outgrew their working-class origins and reached middle-class audiences. D. W. Griffith's racist epic *Birth of a Nation* (1915) helped establish the feature film as popular entertainment. Griffith used many technical and artistic innovations in this film, which glorified the Reconstruction-era Ku Klux Klan. The outbreak of World War I in Europe eliminated competition from Italian and French moviemakers. (The chemicals used to produce celluloid for film were needed for the manufacture of gunpowder.) By the war's end the United States was making 90 percent of the world's films, and Hollywood reigned as the world movie capital for the next several decades. Foreign distribution of Hollywood films stimulated the market for the American material culture so lavishly displayed on the screen.

Movies fed the desires of a mass-consumption economy and set national trends in clothing and hairstyles. They also served as a form of sex education. Rudolph Valentino, best known as the romantic hero of *The Sheik* (1921), epitomized sexual passion on the screen, and the message was not wasted on the nation's youth. "It was directly through the movies that I learned to kiss a girl on her ears, neck, and cheeks, as well as on the mouth," confessed one boy. Many girls noticed that actresses kissed with their eyes closed, and so they followed suit. The sociologist Edward Alsworth Ross concluded that movies made young people more "sex-wise, sex-excited, and sex-absorbed" than any previous generation. The impact of the movies on sexual attitudes and morality has remained strong ever since.

The Coming of Sound. Movies were a big business. Power was concentrated in large studios such as United Artists, Paramount, and Metro-Goldwyn-Mayer, which were controlled mainly by Eastern European Jewish immigrants such as Adolph Zukor and Samuel Goldfish (later Goldwyn). Those studios operated for maximum profitability, not for artistic expression or creativity. In 1926 they grossed $1.5 billion a year. The studios controlled distribution as tightly as they did production by establishing chains of theaters, thereby achieving complete vertical integration of the movie industry.

Though most movies were made in Hollywood, the studios were financed by eastern banks. Those financial connections were strained in the late 1920s, when all the major studios borrowed huge sums to convert from silent production to "talkies." The cost of conversion reached $300 million, but the overwhelming success of the new films quickly paid back the investment.

Clara Bow:
The "It" Girl

When Clara Bow, the "It" Girl of the 1920s, was asked to define what "it" meant, she replied, "I ain't real sure." To most fans, "it" was synonymous with sex appeal, but Elinor Glyn, the British writer who coined the phrase, had a more convoluted definition: "To have 'It' the fortunate possessor must have that strange magnetism which attracts both sexes. 'It' is purely virile quality belonging to a strong character. . . . There must be physical attraction, but beauty is unnecessary. Conceit or selfconsciousness destroys 'It' immediately." Whatever "it" was, when Paramount released a movie in 1927 based on the Elinor Glyn novella of the same name and starring Clara Bow, the film grossed $1 million. Soon Bow was receiving almost 35,000 fan letters a month, many addressed simply to "The 'It' Girl, Hollywood U.S.A." In 1927 she was all of twenty-two years old.

The thin plot of the film hardly seems capable of launching a national obsession. Bow played a department store clerk named Betty Lou Spense who is out to catch her rich, handsome boss. He too is smitten, and when he calls on her in her modest home, he finds her minding a friend's baby. However, he jumps to the mistaken conclusion that she is an unmarried mother and propositions her. She is indignant at the insult, but after several plot twists they resolve their differences. In the final scene they kiss on the store owner's yacht, *Itola*, with the embrace obscuring all but the first two letters of the yacht's name. That's right—IT!

"It" was typical of Hollywood's fascination with flapper themes in the 1920s. (The term *flapper* originated with women's fad of leaving galoshes unbuckled, which made them flap.) On screen and off the flapper was emancipated, urban, and young, befitting the worship of youth characteristic of the 1920s. She was a working girl with money to spend, time on her hands, and a wardrobe of mass-produced fashions, especially short skirts suitable for dancing and dating. On screen she was sensual but not promiscuous, often marrying the male lead at the end. The Hollywood stars Colleen Moore and Louise Brooks also played flapper roles.

Clara Bow—the Twenties' Sex Symbol
In this photograph Bow appears as the typical flapper—young and liberated but amenable to marriage.

Before Bow became indelibly known as the "It" girl, her studio had tried to promote her as the "Brooklyn Bonfire." The name never stuck, but it revealed her background. Clara Bow was born on July 29, 1905, to an extremely poor family in Brooklyn, New York; her mother was mentally unstable, and her father was often unemployed. She dropped out of school during the eighth grade. The only place she found refuge from her grim family life was at the movies. Like many other young girls, Bow decided that she wanted to be an actress.

Her break came when she won a 1921 "Fame and Fortune" beauty contest sponsored by three movie magazines, which helped her land a bit part in *Beyond the Rainbow* (1922). Unfortunately her scenes ended up on the cutting room floor, but they were restored after she became a star. In 1923 Bow won a Hollywood contract, and by 1924 she had made thirteen films, none memorable. Her roles improved when she signed with Paramount in 1925; it was her performances in *Dancing Mothers* (1926) and *Mantrap* (1926), two movies with Jazz Age themes, that led Elinor Glyn to pronounce that Bow had "it" on the screen.

Clara Bow had an amazing screen presence. On screen she never seemed to stay still. Studio executive B. P. Schulberg called her "the hottest jazz baby in films." Observed a young man who first saw her at age seventeen, "I've never taken dope, but it was like a shot of dope when you looked at this girl." The New York *Times* wrote of her performance in *Mantrap*, "She could flirt with a grizzly bear." She had a boyish figure, and what one reviewer called "flirts eyes." She was especially known for her shock of red hair. In the 1920s redheads were thought to be highly sexed. Just as the vamp of the 1910s had dark hair and the the typical star of the 1930s was a platinum blonde, the 1920s were the decade of the redhead.

Yet Bow's career lasted less than five years after the success of *It*. Somewhat unstable emotionally, she had several nervous breakdowns. As she once said, "A sex symbol is a heavy load to carry when one is tired, hurt, and bewildered." She was also hurt by scandals in her personal life, including widely publicized affairs with Gary Cooper and the director Victor Fleming and a legal dispute with a former secretary. Furthermore, like many silent stars, she found the transition to talkies difficult. It was not only her Brooklyn accent—voice lessons could have smoothed that out. But her whole style of acting, which was very emotional and involved constant movement around the set, was not suited to the early days of sound recording, when an actor had to stay close to a stationary microphone to speak dialogue.

In 1931 Bow announced that she was leaving Hollywood to live with Rex Bell, a Nevada rancher whom she married later that year. She returned briefly to make two films before declaring "I've had enough" in 1933. She devoted her time to marriage and the two sons she and Bell had in 1934 and 1938, but her emotional instability made it hard for her to find happiness, and she

"Rough-House Rosie"
A hand-painted poster was created for this 1927 film.

and Bell eventually separated. She died in Los Angeles in 1965, long before her films had become cult classics. On seeing *It* for the first time in 1987, sixty years after its release, her son said, "If I ever saw Mother, I saw her in that movie. The tremendous facial expression. . . . It brought back so vividly what she was like." But it also reinforced the huge gulf between the on-screen charisma of the "It" Girl and Bow's fragile off-screen persona.

Toward the end of her life Bow reflected on the differences between Hollywood in the 1920s and the 1960s in a way that makes clear where her sympathies lay: "We had individuality. We did as we pleased. We stayed up late. We dressed the way we wanted. Today, stars are sensible and end up with better health. But *we* had more fun."

All That Jazz
George E. Lee's Singing Novelty Orchestra was a popular Kansas City act. Part of the novelty was his sister Julia Lee, who was both pianist and singer.

Warner Brothers's *The Jazz Singer* (1927), starring Al Jolson, was the first feature-length film to offer sound. By 1929 all the major studios had completed the changeover to talkies. Although no one had thought of movies as silent until talkies took their place, silent films soon became obsolete. By the end of the 1920s the nation had almost 23,000 movie theaters, including elaborate palaces built by the studios in major cities. Movie attendance rose from 60 million in 1927 to 90 million in 1930. By then movies were thoroughly entrenched as the most popular—and probably the most influential—form of the new urban-based mass media.

Jazz. It is perhaps no coincidence that the first talkie was *The Jazz Singer*. Jazz was such a popular part of the new mass culture that the 1920s are often called "the Jazz Age." This style of music remains one of the most distinctive American art forms. An improvisational style whose notes were (and are) rarely written down, jazz originated in the dance halls and bordellos of New Orleans's Storyville quarter around the turn of the century. The origin of the word is obscure, but many link it to a vulgar term for sexual intercourse. Arising in the cosmopolitan atmosphere of New Orleans, jazz was a synthesis of earlier African-American music, such as ragtime and the blues, but also drew on African and European styles. With roots in urban culture, jazz gave black people an outlet for expression of dissent and opposition to white values. Its popularity also suggested the symbiotic relationship between African-American and American culture in the 1920s and beyond.

Most of the early jazz musicians were black. As they left the South, they took jazz to Chicago, New York, Kansas City, Los Angeles, and other cities. Some of the best known were the composer-pianist Ferdinand "Jelly Roll" Morton, who wrote "Dead Man Blues" and "Black Bottom Stomp"; the trumpeter Louis Armstrong, who got his start with Joseph "King" Oliver's Creole Jazz Band in Chicago in the early 1920s; and the singer Bessie Smith, the "empress of the Blues." One of the most creative jazz innovators, Edward "Duke" Ellington, traveled to New York with his band in 1927 and performed at the Cotton Club in Harlem. Phonograph records, especially those made by Louis Armstrong in the late 1920s, increased the appeal of jazz by capturing its spontaneity; in turn, jazz boosted the infant recording industry. Soon this uniquely American art form had caught on in Europe, especially in France.

Journalism and Radio. Besides movies and sound recordings, other forms of mass media helped establish national standards of taste and behavior. In 1922, ten magazines claimed a circulation of at least 2.5 million and twelve others sold a million copies of each issue. The *Saturday Evening Post*, the *Ladies' Home Journal*, *Collier's Weekly*, and *Good Housekeeping* could be found in homes throughout the country. *Reader's Digest*, *Time*, and *The New Yorker* all started in the 1920s. Thanks to syndicated columns and features in newspapers, people could read the same articles across the United States. They also could read the same books, preselected by a board of expert judges for the Book of the Month Club, which was founded in 1926.

Tabloid newspapers—sometimes called jazz journalism—also became part of the national scene. In 1919, just two days before the signing of the Versailles treaty, publisher Joseph Medill Patterson introduced *The New York Illustrated Daily News*. Half the size of a regular newspaper, with bold headlines, large photographs, and short, sensational stories, tabloids were meant to be read quickly, for instance, while riding the subway to work. All the major cities had at least one tabloid competing with more sedate dailies by 1932.

The newest instrument of mass culture was truly a child of the 1920s. On November 2, 1920, professional radio broadcasting began when station KDKA in Pittsburgh carried the presidential election returns. By 1929 about 40 percent of the nation's households had a radio. There were more than 800 stations, most affiliated with the Columbia Broadcasting Service (CBS), formed in 1928, or the National Broadcasting Company (NBC), started in 1926, which had two networks, Red and Blue. (These corporations would dominate the next leap forward in mass communication: television.) Unlike European networks, which were government monopolies, American radio stations operated for profit. The federal government licensed the stations, but their revenue came primarily from advertisers and corporate sponsors.

Americans loved radio. They listened avidly to the World Series and other sports events and to variety entertainment shows featuring performers such as the Lucky Strike Orchestra and the A & P Gypsies, sponsored (not surprisingly) by advertisers of those major brand-name products. One of the most popular radio shows of all time, "Amos 'n' Andy," premiered on NBC in 1928, featuring two white actors playing stereotypical black characters. Soon fractured phrases from "Amos 'n' Andy," such as "check and double check," became part of everyday speech. So many people "tuned in" (another new phrase of the 1920s) that the country seemed to come to a halt during popular programs.

New Patterns of Leisure

One of the most significant developments in modern life has been the growing freedom of workers from constant physical toil. As the workweek shrank and some workers won the right to paid vacations, Americans had more time—and energy—to spend on leisure. Like so much else in the 1920s, leisure became increasingly tied to consumption and mass culture.

Sports and Recreation. Public recreation flourished in the 1920s as cities and suburbs built baseball diamonds, tennis courts, swimming pools, and golf courses. In the New York metropolitan area the city planner Robert Moses masterminded a vast system of parks, playgrounds, and picnic areas. His greatest achievement was Jones Beach on Long Island. Moses not only created the state park but built limited-access highways to it. Any New Yorker with a car—an important limit on freedom of consumption—could escape to a public beach in less than forty minutes.

People not only played sports but had the time and money to watch them. Professional sports became increasingly commercialized. As they had previously, people could watch a game in a comfortable stadium, but now they could also listen to the contest on the radio or see highlights of it in a newsreel at a movie theater. One of the most widely followed sports was boxing; Jack Dempsey was one of the decade's celebrity athletes. Baseball drew between 9 million and 10 million fans a year. Tarnished in 1919 by the "Black Sox" scandal when gamblers bribed Chicago White Sox players to throw the World Series, baseball bounced back with the

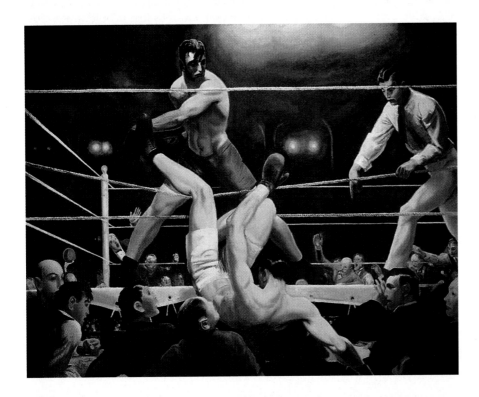

Boxing Heroes
George Bellows (1882–1925) often painted boxing scenes. *Dempsey and Firpo* (1924) depicts a heavyweight fight between Jack Dempsey, the "Manassa Mauler," and challenger Luis Firpo, the "Wild Bull of the Pampas." Dempsey is the one being unceremoniously knocked out of the ring. Boxing was one of the most popular sports in the sports-crazy 1920s. (Whitney Museum of American Art)

rise of heroes such as Babe Ruth of the New York Yankees. Nicknamed the "Sultan of Swat," Ruth electrified crowds by hitting more home runs—and hitting them farther—than any player up to that time. Yankee Stadium became known as the "house that Ruth built." Sports reflected the racism of society as a whole: black athletes played in the Negro Leagues, which were formed in the 1920s.

Newspapers, especially the tabloids, capitalized on popular interest in sports. Sports coverage, especially the latest scores and fight results, sold papers. College football games such as the annual Harvard-Yale game and the Rose Bowl received national coverage. Football fans followed the fortunes of the Four Horsemen of Notre Dame, the most famous backfield in college football history. In 1924 Red Grange of the University of Illinois became nationally known for scoring five touchdowns against the University of Michigan the first five times he carried the ball.

Other sports gave the public more heroes. Bobby Jones ranked as the decade's best golfer. Bill Tilden dominated men's tennis, and Helen Wills and Suzanne Lenglen reigned in the women's game. The decade's best-known swimmer, male or female, was Gertrude Ederle, who swam the English Channel in 1926 in just over fourteen hours. Thanks to the attention of the media, the popularity of sports figures rivaled that of movie stars.

Without a doubt the decade's most popular hero was the aviator Charles Lindbergh, a former stunt flyer and airmail pilot from Minnesota. On May 20, 1927, Lindbergh made the first successful solo nonstop flight between New York and Paris. For the 3,610-mile, 33½-hour flight in *The Spirit of St. Louis* Lindbergh took only five sandwiches and one day's worth of tinned rations, saying, "If I get to Paris, I won't need any more, and if I don't get to Paris, I won't need any more either." Lindbergh captivated the nation because he combined the mastery of new technology (the airplane) with the traditional American virtues of individualism, self-reliance, and hard work. His charm and boyish good looks didn't hurt, either. He was twenty-five years old at the time of his record-breaking flight, and in 1928 *Time* magazine chose him as its first Man of the Year.

Dissenting Values and Cultural Conflict

Many Americans were deeply disturbed by the secular values of the 1920s. To rural Americans the new values were an affront to a more traditional way of life rooted in small towns and farming communities. Cultural and political conflict broke out over issues such as immigration

restriction, Prohibition, and race relations. Tension between city and country played a part in all those conflicts but was not the sole cause. Many city dwellers had been born and raised in the country, and their memories were strong. Fear of and resistance to change and ambivalence about modernity—feelings that transcended the urban-rural polarity—probably had a greater influence.

Urban Majority, Rural Minority

"The United States was born in the country and has moved to the city," the historian Richard Hofstadter observed. When the 1920 census revealed that for the first time city people outnumbered rural ones, Americans realized that a dramatic change had taken place, rivaling the closing of the frontier in 1890. In 1920, 52 percent of the population lived in urban areas, compared with 28 percent in 1870.

The 1920 census exaggerated the extent of urbanization because its guidelines classified cities as towns with as few as 2,500 people (see Map 24.1). By 1929, ninety-three cities had a population over 100,000. During the 1920s New York City exceeded 7 million, Chicago had close to 3 million, and the population of Los Angeles doubled to more than 1.2 million. Outside the major cities growth was even more impressive. As a result of the availability of cheap land and better transportation—notably the automobile—expanded metropolitan areas and suburbs sprang up. This trend started long before the post–World War II suburban boom.

The conflict over values that had been building since the late nineteenth century intensified in the 1920s. After the recession of 1920–1921, farmers continued to struggle, and rural communities lost people to the cities at an alarming rate. During the 1920s about 6 million Americans left the farms for the cities, including many blacks who abandoned the South for the seemingly greater freedom of the North. Political districts did not reflect this population shift, however, and rural areas still controlled most state legislatures. Battles over the equitable use of tax dollars, especially for city services, intensified the rural-urban political conflict.

Yet it would be wrong to describe this conflict as a last-ditch effort by rural America to maintain political and cultural dominance. The lives of rural people had been affected by the same forces that influenced urban life. Much of the new technology—especially electricity and automobiles—enhanced rural life. Rural people were tempted by the new materialistic values proclaimed by radio programs, magazines, and movies. Even though they tried to resist, many found more to attract than to repel them in the new ways. The cultural conflicts of the 1920s might have been so heated precisely because both rural and urban dwellers realized how far they had already strayed from older values.

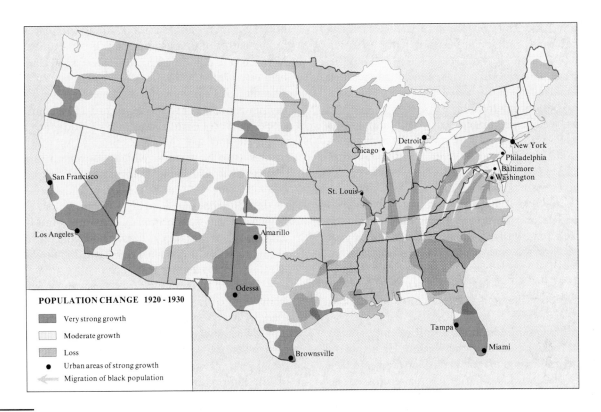

POPULATION CHANGE 1920 - 1930

- Very strong growth
- Moderate growth
- Loss
- Urban areas of strong growth
- Migration of black population

MAP 24.1

The Shift From Rural to Urban Population, 1920–1930
Despite the increasingly urban tone of modern America after 1920, regional patterns
of population growth and decline were far from uniform. Cities in the South and
West grew most dramatically as southern farmers moved to more promising areas
with familiar climates. An important factor in the growth of northern cities, such as
New York and Chicago, was the migration of southern blacks set in motion by World
War I.

The Rise of Nativism

When native-born white Protestant Americans looked
at their communities in 1920, they saw a nation that
had changed vastly in only forty years. During that time
more than 23 million immigrants had come to America.
Most of them had peasant backgrounds, and many
were Catholics or Jews. Senator William Bruce of
Maryland called them "indigestible lumps" in the "national stomach," implying that the nation would be unable to absorb their large numbers and different
customs. As President Coolidge said in 1924, "America
must be kept American." Such sentiments, which were
widely shared, came to be known as *nativism.*

These feelings were the basis of a successful drive
against immigration in the 1920s. The original targets of
immigration restriction had been Asians. In 1882 the
Chinese were totally excluded, and in 1908 Theodore
Roosevelt negotiated a "gentlemen's agreement" to limit
Japanese immigration. But nativists demanded broader
measures aimed at European immigrants. In 1917 the
United States required all immigrants to pass a literacy
test, but that proved to be only a slight deterrent. If immigrants were determined to find a new life in America,
they were willing to learn enough English to pass a simple test.

World War I and its aftermath had a direct impact
on the immigration question. Nativists played up the
popular association of immigrants with radicalism and
labor unrest, a legacy of the Red Scare. When the end of
the war made it possible to cross the Atlantic in safety
again, many native-born Americans feared that a new
wave of immigrants would cause social unrest and take
jobs away from Americans. In 1921 Congress passed an
emergency bill limiting the number of immigrants to 3
percent of each national group as counted in the 1910
census. President Wilson refused to sign it, but the bill
was reintroduced and passed under Warren Harding.
The new law produced immediate results. In the twelve-
month period ending in June 1921, 805,228 immigrants
had entered the United States; in the next twelve
months, the number dropped to 309,556.

For many Americans this quota system was still a sieve with too many holes. The National Origins Act of 1924 cut immigration back to 2 percent of each nationality as reflected in the 1890 census, which had included relatively small numbers of people from the "undesirable" areas of southeastern Europe and Russia. The legislation was specifically intended to limit immigrants from those regions. In 1924 this cut the total immigration to 164,000 persons, mostly from Great Britain, Ireland, and Germany. Japanese and Chinese immigrants continued to be excluded entirely.

In 1929 an even more restrictive quota went into effect by which only 150,000 immigrants would be admitted each year, with national origins to be apportioned in accordance with the 1920 census. President Herbert Hoover lowered the quota still further in 1931. The next year, during the depths of the Great Depression, more foreigners left the United States than entered.

The last remaining loophole permitted unrestricted immigration from countries in the Western Hemisphere. This became increasingly significant over the years (see Figure 24.1) as Central and Latin Americans crossed the border in increasing numbers, filling the places vacated by the cutoff of immigrants from Europe and the Pacific Rim. Over 1 million Mexicans entered the United States between 1900 and 1930.

Puerto Ricans provided another growing source of immigration. After the Jones Act of 1917 conferred U.S. citizenship on Puerto Ricans, they could go to and from the mainland without restriction. Most of the movement was to New York, which was only a four-day sea voyage away. Thriving Puerto Rican communities, or *colonias*, sprang up in East Harlem and the Greenpoint section of Brooklyn. As with other migrants, the lure of New York City was primarily economic, and Puerto Ricans took jobs that previously had gone to European immigrants. But once hard times hit, the flow of Puerto Ricans stopped temporarily.

Nativism took a number of forms during the 1920s. Many elite colleges instituted quotas to limit the enrollment of Jewish students, and many law firms refused to hire Jewish lawyers. Henry Ford spoke for many Americans when he warned of the menace of the "International Jew," referring to the supposed Jewish domination of international finance. Ford became so closely identi-

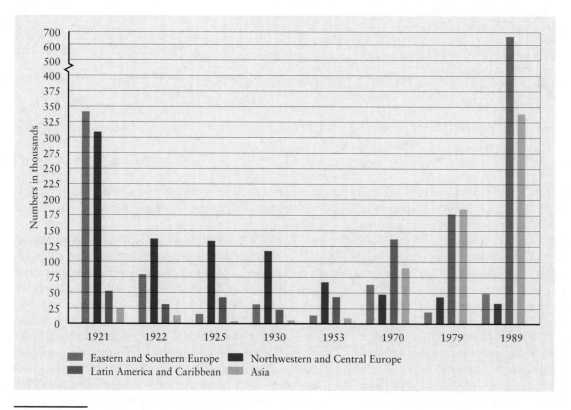

FIGURE 24.1

American Immigration after World War I

Nativism slowed the influx of immigrants after 1920, as did the dislocations brought on by depression and war in the 1930s and 1940s. Note the higher rate of non-European immigration since the 1970s.

Robert Coughlan

The Klan Comes to Kokomo

Robert Coughlan grew up in Kokomo, Indiana, and as a young boy witnessed a Ku Klux Klan Konklave, or gathering. As Catholics living in a pro-Klan neighborhood, Coughlan's family had reason to feel uncomfortable on the hot July day in 1923 when the Klan came to central Indiana.

The Konklave was an important day in my life. I was nine years old, with a small boy's interest in masquerades and brass bands. But I was also a Catholic, the son of a Catholic who taught in the public schools and who consequently was the object of a good deal of Klan agitation. If anything worse was to come, the Konklave probably would bring it. Every week or so the papers had been reporting Klan atrocities in other parts of the country—whippings, lynchings, tar-and-feather parties—and my father and my family were logical game in our locality. . . .

As we sat on our front porch after watching the parade, we could see the Klansmen of our neighborhood trickling home. Some still wore their regalia, too tired to bother with taking it off before they came into sight. Others

carried little bundles of white; they were the ones who still made some pretense of secrecy about being members. One of the last to come down the street was old Mrs. Crousore, who lived a few doors away. Her white robe clung damply, and her hood was pushed back. As she climbed her steps and sank solidly into a rocking chair on her porch, we could hear her groan, "Oh, my God, my feet hurt!"

Mrs. Crousore spoke with such feeling that her words seemed to summarize the whole day. My parents adopted her comment as a family joke. July 4, 1923, became for us the day when Mrs. Crousore's feet hurt. But it was clear to me when I grew a little older that my parents needed that joke as much as Mrs. Crousore needed her rocking chair. There were wild rumors in the town in the months that followed: Father Pratt, the pastor at St. Patrick's Church, was on the list for tar-and-feathering; the church was going to be burned; the Klan was going to "call" on the Jewish merchants; it was going to "get" my father and Miss Kinney, another Catholic who taught in the public schools. Considering all the violent acts committed by the Klan

elsewhere in the country, it seemed quite possible that any or all of these notions might mature into action.

As it turned out none of them did. . . . Perhaps the answer lay in the dead level typicalness of the town; a population overwhelmingly white Protestant, with small, well-assimilated numbers of Catholics, Jews, foreigners, and Negroes, and an economy nicely balanced between farming and industry. There were few genuine tensions in Kokomo in 1923, and hence little occasion for misdirected hate to flame into personal violence.

It may be asked why, then, did the town take so wholeheartedly to the Klan, which made a program of misdirected hate? And the answer to that may be, paradoxically enough, that the Klan supplied artificial tensions. Though artificial, and perhaps never quite really believed in, they were satisfying. They filled a need—a need for Kokomo and all the big and little towns that resembled it during the early 1920s.

Source: Robert Coughlan, "Konklave in Kokomo," in Isabel Leighton, ed., *The Aspirin Age, 1919–1941* (New York: Simon & Schuster, 1976) 107, 110–111.

fied with anti-Semitism that decades passed before some Jewish families could bring themselves to buy his company's cars.

The New Klan. The most striking example of nativism in the 1920s was the revival of the Ku Klux Klan (KKK). Shortly after the 1915 premiere of *Birth of a Nation*, a group of southerners gathered on Stone Mountain outside Atlanta to revive the KKK. Klan leaders chose as their motto "Native, white, Protestant supremacy." The modern Klan appealed to both urban and rural people, but it was mainly an urban phenomenon. Spreading out from its southern base and encouraged by the superpatriotism of the war years, it found significant support in the Far West, the Southwest, and the Midwest, especially Indiana, Oklahoma, and Oregon. Unlike its earlier

incarnation after the Civil War, the Klan of the 1920s did not limit its harassment to blacks; its targets were just as likely to be Catholics and Jewish immigrants (see American Voices, above). Its tactics, however, remained very much the same: arson, physical intimidation, and economic boycotts directed at Klan targets. At the height of its power in 1925 the Klan had over 3 million members, including a strong contingent of women who pursued their own distinctive political agenda, combining racism, nativism, and a commitment to equal rights for white Protestant women.

After 1925 the Klan declined rapidly. Battles between rival factions and disclosures of rampant corruption hurt its image. Especially damaging was the revelation that Grand Dragon David Stephenson, the Klan's national leader, had kidnapped and sexually as-

Women of the Klan

The Ku Klux Klan was so well integrated into the daily life of white Protestants that one woman from rural Indiana remembered her time in the KKK in the 1920s as "just a celebration . . . a way of growing up." Perhaps as many as 500,000 women joined the Women of the Ku Klux Klan (WKKK) in the 1920s, including these Indiana Klanswomen in August 1924.

saulted his former secretary, driving her to suicide. Along with the passage of the 1924 immigration act, the decline in the nativist fervor that was a legacy of World War I robbed the Klan of its most potent issue.

Religious Fundamentalism

The religious debate between modernist and fundamentalist Protestants that had been simmering since the 1890s (see Chapter 20) came to a boil in the 1920s. Modernists, or liberal Protestants, tried to reconcile religion with scientific discoveries such as Darwin's theory of evolution whereas fundamentalists favored a literal interpretation of the Bible. Most major Protestant denominations underwent heated internal conflicts in the 1920s, especially the Baptists and the Presbyterians, with the losers frequently splitting off to form their own churches. The most conspicuous evangelical figures were outside the established denominations, however. Popular preachers such as Billy Sunday and Aimee Semple McPherson used revivals, storefront churches, and open-air preaching to popularize their own brands of charismatic fundamentalism.

The modernist-fundamentalist controversy soon entered the political arena. The scientific theories in Charles Darwin's *On the Origin of Species* (1859) conflicted with the account of creation in the book of Genesis. Some states enacted legislation to prevent the teaching of evolution in schools. In 1925 Tennessee passed a law declaring that "it shall be unlawful . . . to teach any theory that denies the story of the Divine creation of man as taught in the Bible, and to teach instead that man has descended from a lower order of animals." The recently formed American Civil Liberties

Union (ACLU) challenged the constitutionality of that law in a test case involving John T. Scopes, a high school biology teacher in Dayton, Tennessee, who had taught evolution to his class. The famous criminal lawyer Clarence Darrow defended Scopes. The prosecuting attorney was William Jennings Bryan, three-time presidential candidate, a spellbinding orator, and a fundamentalist.

The Scopes trial in July 1925 came to be known as the "monkey trial," referring both to Darwin's theory that human beings and other primates share a common ancestor and to the circus atmosphere in the courtroom. More than a hundred journalists crowded the sweltering courthouse, and the Chicago radio station WGN broadcast the proceedings live.

The trial quickly turned to volatile questions of faith and scientific theory. The judge rebuffed defense efforts to call expert scientific witnesses on evolution, dismissing such testimony as hearsay because the scientists had not been present when lower forms of life had evolved. Darrow countered by calling Bryan to the stand as an expert on the Bible. Under oath, Bryan asserted his belief that a "big fish" had swallowed Jonah, that Eve had been created from Adam's rib, and that God had created the world in six days. He hedged, however, about whether the "days" were literally twenty-four hours long, an inconsistency that Darrow ruthlessly exploited.

Even so, the jury took only eight minutes to find Scopes guilty. The Tennessee Supreme Court overturned the conviction on a technicality, but the reversal prevented further appeal of the case, and the controversial law remained on the books for more than thirty years. As the 1920s ended, science and religion faced each other in an uneasy standoff.

Prohibition

The most notorious cultural debate of the 1920s was the battle over Prohibition. The Eighteenth Amendment, which took effect on January 20, 1920 (see Chapter 23), did make Americans drink less; beer consumption declined the most, because beer was more difficult to manufacture and distribute illegally than hard liquor. But once people showed their willingness to flout the law, this effort to legislate private morality was doomed.

More than any other issue, Prohibition gave the decade its reputation as the Roaring Twenties. In major cities, whose ethnic populations had always opposed Prohibition, noncompliance was widespread. Illegal saloons called speakeasies sprang up—more than 30,000 in New York City alone. People who preferred to drink at home imitated rural moonshiners by learning to distill "bathtub gin." Liquor smugglers operated with ease along borders and coastlines. Organized crime, already a factor in major cities, supplied a ready-made distribution network for bootleg liquor, and gangsters used the "noble experiment" to entrench themselves more deeply in city politics. Said the decade's most notorious gangster, Al Capone, "Everybody calls me a racketeer. I call myself a businessman. When I sell liquor, it's bootlegging. When my patrons serve it on a silver tray on Lake Shore Drive, it's hospitality."

By the middle of the decade Prohibition was clearly failing. Government appropriations for its enforcement were woefully inadequate, and the few highly publicized raids hardly made a dent in the liquor trade. In 1929 Attorney General William D. Mitchell conceded that liquor could be bought "at almost any hour of the day or night, either in rural districts, the smaller towns, or the cities." A committee appointed by President Hoover in 1931 to study Prohibition only weakly recommended that it be retained.

But Prohibition was not just the law, it was in the Constitution. So the forces for repeal—the "wets," as opposed to the "drys," who continued to support the Eighteenth Amendment—began the long process of gaining the necessary majorities in Congress and state legislatures to amend the Constitution again. The Women's Organization for National Prohibition Repeal, headed by Pauline Sabin, a wealthy New York Republican, lobbied Congress and mobilized support from other national organizations.

The onset of the Great Depression hastened repeal. People argued that liquor production would provide jobs and prop up the faltering economy. On December 5, 1933, the Eighteenth Amendment was repealed. Ironically, drinking became more socially acceptable, although not necessarily more widespread, than it had been before the Prohibition experiment began its rocky course.

Intellectual Currents and Crosscurrents

The Lost Generation. The most articulate and embittered dissenters from American life in the 1920s were writers and intellectuals who were disillusioned by the horrors of World War I and the crass materialism of the new American consumer culture. Some artists felt so at odds with what they saw as the complacent, anti-intellectual, moralistic tone of American life that they

The Speakeasy
There aren't many photographs of speakeasies; after all, they were supposed to be private clubs tucked away beyond the reach of the law. Fancy hotels were unable to compete with speakeasies once their bars were shut down, and many went out of business in the 1920s. But John Sloan's 1928 painting shows the rich enjoying themselves at New York's posh Lafayette Hotel. It is likely that these gentlemen and ladies had a flask concealed somewhere in their evening finery. (The Metropolitan Museum of Art)

settled in Europe—some temporarily, such as the novelists Ernest Hemingway and F. Scott Fitzgerald, and others permanently, such as the writer Gertrude Stein. (The strong dollar, another legacy of World War I, made this a cheap and attractive way to leave American materialism behind.) African-Americans such as the dancer Josephine Baker, the writer Langston Hughes, and the painter Henry O. Tanner sought a temporary escape from racism by moving to France. The poet T. S. Eliot, who left the United States before the war, became a British citizen. His despairing poem *The Waste Land* (1922), with its images of a fragmented civilization in ruins after the war, influenced a generation of writers. Other writers also made powerful antiwar statements, including John Dos Passos, whose first novel, *The Three Soldiers* (1921), was inspired by the war; the novelist Edith Wharton; and above all Ernest Hemingway. Hemingway described the dehumanizing consequences and futility of the war in *In Our Time* (1924), *The Sun Also Rises* (1926), and *A Farewell to Arms* (1929), which drew on his experience as an ambulance driver in Italy.

But the artists and writers who migrated to Europe, particularly to Paris, were not just a "Lost Generation" fleeing America; they were also drawn to Paris as the cultural and artistic capital of the world. Paris, as Gertrude Stein put it, was "where the twentieth century was happening." The *modernist* movement in literature, art, and music, which was marked by skepticism and technical experimentation, invigorated American writing abroad and at home. Whether they settled in Paris or remained in their home country, as did the poets Wallace Stevens and Marianne Moore and the novelists Willa Cather and William Faulkner, American writers entered the modernist movement.

This movement had begun before the war as intellectuals reacted with excitement to the cultural and social changes that science, industrialization, and urbanization had brought to America. In the 1920s the business culture and corruption of the Harding years caused intellectuals to cast a more critical eye on American society. One of the sharpest critics was H. L. Mencken, a Baltimore journalist and literary critic who founded the *American Mercury* in 1922. Mencken directed his mordant wit against small-town America and its guardians of public morals, American mass culture, and the "booboisie," his contemptuous term for the middle class. In the *American Mercury* Mencken championed writers such as Sherwood Anderson, Sinclair Lewis, and Theodore Dreiser, who satirized the provincialism of American society.

In *Main Street* (1920) Lewis scathingly depicted the narrow-mindedness of a midwestern farming town; in *Babbitt* (1922) he satirized the stifling conformity of a middle-class businessman. In 1925 Dreiser wrote his naturalistic masterpiece *An American Tragedy*, which was an indictment of the American myth of success and materialism, as was John Dos Passos's *Manhattan Transfer*. In the same year Fitzgerald wrote *The Great Gatsby*, which showed the consequences of the mindless pursuit of wealth.

The literature of the 1920s was varied and rich as writers responded to the intellectual excitement of the decade and produced a large number of classics. Poetry enjoyed a renaissance in the works of Robert Frost, Wallace Stevens, Marianne Moore, and William Carlos Williams. Edith Wharton's novels described the changing social relationships in a society where a new class of wealth was being created. Wharton won a Pulitzer Prize for *The Age of Innocence* (1920), the first woman so honored. Influenced by Freudian psychology, the novelist William Faulkner began his exploration of the mind of the South. Faulkner's first critical success, *The Sound and the Fury* (1929), is set in the fictional Mississippi county of Yoknapatawpha, whose inhabitants cling to the old values of the agrarian South as they try to adjust to modern industrial capitalism. The dramatist Eugene O'Neill also employed Freudian psychology in his experimental plays, which had aspects of Greek tragedy. O'Neill was a prolific playwright, producing thirteen plays between 1920 and 1933, including *The Hairy Ape* (1922) and *Desire under the Elms* (1924).

Although Faulkner and O'Neill went on to produce major works in the 1930s, the creative energy of the literary renaissance of the 1920s did not sustain itself into the 1930s. The Great Depression, social and ideological unrest, and the rise of totalitarianism reshaped the intellectual landscape.

Harlem Renaissance. A different kind of cultural affirmation took place in the black community of Harlem in the 1920s. In the words of the Reverend Adam Clayton Powell, Sr., pastor of the influential Abyssinian Baptist Church, Harlem loomed as "the symbol of liberty and the Promised Land to Negroes everywhere." In literature its writers championed racial pride and cultural identity in the midst of white society. The intent of the movement was artistic, not political. The poet Langston Hughes, who became a leading exponent of the Harlem Renaissance, captured its affirmative spirit when he asserted, "I am a Negro—and beautiful."

The Harlem Renaissance was led by a creative group of young writers and artists who broke with the older genteel traditions of black literature to reclaim a cultural identity with African roots. The critic and teacher Alain Locke, editor of *The New Negro* (1926), an anthology that gave the Harlem writers national exposure, summed up the character of the movement when he stated that through art, "Negro life is seizing its first

The Harlem Renaissance
The Crisis, edited by W.E.B. DuBois, was the magazine of the National Association for the Advancement of Colored People (NAACP). This 1929 cover suggests the cultural and political awakenings associated with the Harlem Renaissance.

essays. Zora Neale Hurston, born in Florida to a family of poor tenant farmers, attended Howard University and won a scholarship to study anthropology at Barnard College. She spent a decade collecting folklore in the South and the Carribbean and incorporated that material into her short stories and novels. Her genius for storytelling and the tension between her rural folk education and her formal education, which she drew on in her writing, won her acclaim.

The vitality of the Harlem Renaissance was short-lived. Although the NAACP's magazine *The Crisis* was a forum for the Harlem writers, the black middle class and the intellectual elite in Harlem were relatively small and could not support the group's efforts. The movement was thus dependent on white patronage for support and access to publication. Many writers were ambivalent about this dependency as they struggled to attain an authentic voice in their fiction. Langston Hughes became disillusioned with his white patron when she withdrew support as he began to write about common black people in Kansas and New York rather than using African themes. Claude McKay expressed the dilemma of black intellectuals in the novel *Home to Harlem*: how to be an intellectual and not lose the vitality and energy of the black heritage.

During the Jazz Age, when Harlem was in vogue, the publishing industry courted its writers, but the stock market crash of 1929 brought that interest to a sudden end. The movement waned in the 1930s as the depression continued. The writers of the Harlem Renaissance influenced a future generation of black writers when their works were rediscovered by black intellectuals during the civil rights movement of the 1960s.

Marcus Garvey and the UNIA. Although the cultural developments of the Harlem Renaissance had little impact on the African-American masses, other movements built racial pride and challenged white political and cultural hegemony. The most successful was the Universal Negro Improvement Association (UNIA), which championed black separatism under the leadership of the Jamaican-born Marcus Garvey. Based in Harlem, the UNIA was the black working class's first mass movement. At its height it claimed 4 million followers, many of whom were recent migrants to northern cities. Like several nineteenth-century reformers, Marcus Garvey urged blacks to return to Africa because, he said, blacks would never be treated justly in countries ruled by whites. His wife, Amy Jacques Garvey, appealed to black women by combining black nationalism with an emphasis on women's contributions to culture and politics.

The UNIA grew rapidly in the early 1920s. It published a newspaper called *Negro World* and opened "liberty halls" in New York, Chicago, Detroit, New Or-

chances for group expression and self-determination." Authors such as Claude McKay, Jean Toomer, Jessie Fauset, and Zora Neale Hurston explored the black experience and represented the "New Negro" in fiction. Countee Cullen and Langston Hughes turned to poetry, and Augusta Savage used sculpture to draw attention to black accomplishments. The outpouring of literary work showed the ongoing African-American struggle to find a way, as W. E. B. DuBois put it, "to be both a Negro and an American."

Jean Toomer, a writer passionately committed to black self-expression, wrote the influential novel *Cane* in 1923. With its poems, sketches, and stories about a northern black's discovery of the rural black South, it inspired other African-American artists and writers. Langston Hughes drew on the black artistic forms of blues and jazz in *The Weary Blues* (1926), a groundbreaking collection of poems. Considered the most original black poet and the most representative African-American writer, Hughes also wrote novels, plays, and leans, Mobile, Jacksonville, and other cities. The UNIA also undertook extensive business ventures to support black capitalism. Its most ambitious project was the Black Star Line, a steamship company that would ferry cargo between the West Indies and the United States and take American blacks to Africa. The Black Star Line caused the downfall of the UNIA. Irregularities in fund-raising led to Garvey's conviction for mail fraud in 1925, and he was sentenced to five years in prison. President Coolidge paroled him in 1927, and Garvey was deported to Jamaica. Without his charismatic leadership, the movement collapsed.

The 1928 Election

The concerns of the Lost Generation and the Harlem Renaissance touched only a small minority of Americans in the 1920s, but emotionally charged issues such as Prohibition, religious fundamentalism, and nativism eventually spilled over into national politics. The Democratic party, which drew on Protestant rural supporters in the South and West as well as ethnic voters in northern cities, was especially vulnerable to the urban-rural conflicts of the 1920s. Four years earlier the 1924 Democratic national convention had revealed intense polarization between the party's urban forces and its rural wing.

Alfred E. Smith. The Democrats approached the 1928 campaign in somewhat better shape. The death of Senator Robert La Follette in 1925 ended the threat of another challenge by the Progressive party. William Jennings Bryan died the same year, just a week after his impassioned defense of fundamentalism in the Scopes trial, removing another potential spoiler from the field. Former contender William McAdoo was well into his sixties and was considered too old for the nomination. As a result, Al Smith, who had just been elected to his fourth term as governor of New York, stood in a commanding position to win the Democratic nomination. In 1924 the Democrats had needed more than a hundred ballots to select a candidate, but in 1928 they nominated Smith on the first vote.

Alfred E. Smith was the first presidential candidate to reflect the aspirations of the urban working classes. The grandson of Irish immigrants and a Catholic, Smith had worked his way up in politics from Tammany Hall to the governor's mansion in Albany. He was proud of his urban background and adopted "The Sidewalks of New York" as his campaign song. Democrats hoped Smith would attract recent immigrants and workers

who traditionally voted Republican. Belle Moskowitz, a New York social worker who served as Smith's political adviser, made him more attractive to women and liberal urban Jews.

But Smith had liabilities. He spoke in a heavy New York accent, sprinkling his speeches with "ain't" and "he don't," which did not play well on the radio. His early career in Tammany Hall troubled many voters, suggesting incorrectly that he was little more than a cog in a political machine. Smith's stand on Prohibition alienated even more voters. Although he promised to enforce Prohibition, he made no secret of his support for repeal. Smith chose John J. Raskob, a wealthy entrepreneur and one of the nation's most ardent "wets," as head of the Democratic National Committee.

By far the most damaging handicap to Smith's campaign was his Catholicism. Many Protestant Americans were not ready for a Roman Catholic president in 1928. Although Smith insisted that his religion would not interfere with his duties as president, being Catholic cost him support from Democrats and Republicans alike. Protestant clergymen, who already opposed Smith because he supported the repeal of Prohibition, led the drive against him. "No Governor can kiss the papal ring and get within gunshot of the White House," declared a Methodist bishop from Buffalo. A Baptist minister warned, "If you vote for Al Smith, you're voting against Christ and you'll all be damned."

Herbert Hoover. Just as Smith marked a new kind of presidential candidate for the Democrats, so did Herbert Hoover for the Republicans. Coolidge's unexpected decision not to run for reelection in 1928 opened the field, and Hoover led from the start. His popularity and power as head of the Food Administration during the war and more recently as secretary of commerce under Harding and Coolidge left no room for the other main contenders, Vice-President Charles G. Dawes and Frank O. Lowden, former governor of Illinois.

As a professional administrator and engineer, Hoover embodied the new managerial and technological elite that was restructuring the economic order. He had never been elected to political office. During his campaign, in which he gave only seven speeches, Hoover promised that his vision of individualism and cooperative endeavor would banish poverty from the United States. Many voters considered him to be more progressive than Smith.

Hoover won a stunning victory (see Map 24.2), receiving 58 percent of the popular vote to Smith's 41 percent, and 444 electoral votes to 87 for Smith. For the first time since Reconstruction a Republican candidate

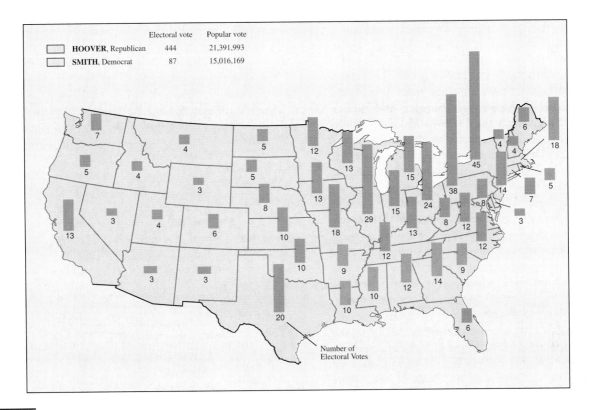

Electoral vote   Popular vote

HOOVER, Republican   444   21,391,993

SMITH, Democrat   87   15,016,169

Number of
Electoral Votes

MAP 24.2

The Election of 1928

Historians still debate the extent to which 1928 was a critical election—that is, one that produced a significant realignment in voting behavior. Although the Republican Herbert Hoover swept the electoral college, Democrats were heartened by the fact that Alfred E. Smith won the heavily industrialized states of Rhode Island and Massachusetts. For the first time, the Democratic ticket carried the nation's twelve largest cities, garnering strong support from immigrants and urban dwellers.

carried Virginia, Texas, and North Carolina, largely because many Democrats refused to vote for a Catholic. The voter turnout rose from 52 percent in 1924 to 56.9 percent in 1928, partly as a result of extensive education campaigns undertaken by the League of Women Voters. Also, the transfer of polling places to schools and churches from their former locations in saloons made women feel more comfortable with their new role as voters. Many Catholic and immigrant women voted for Smith, but even more native-born Republican women supported Herbert Hoover.

The 1928 election reflected important underlying political changes. The Democratic turnout, despite the party's overwhelming loss, increased substantially in urban areas. Smith won the industrialized states of Massachusetts and Rhode Island and carried the na-

tion's twelve largest cities. The Democrats were on their way to forging a new identity as the party of the urban masses, including ethnic voters, a reorientation that the New Deal completed in the 1930s.

It is unlikely that any Democratic candidate, let alone a Catholic, could have won the presidency in 1928. With a seemingly prosperous economy, a national consensus on foreign policy, and strong support from the business community, the Republicans were unbeatable. Ironically, Herbert Hoover's victory put him in the unenviable position of leading the United States when the Great Depression struck in 1929. Having claimed credit for the prosperity of the 1920s, the Republicans found it difficult to escape blame for the depression. Twenty-four years would pass before a Republican won the presidency again.

Summary

By the 1920s modern America had arrived. The Republican party controlled the national government and cemented the partnership between business and government that had been accelerated by World War I. In foreign policy the United States promoted disarmament and the reduction of German war reparations but otherwise generally steered clear of European political affairs. The chief U.S. interest was to ensure a stable environment for economic expansion abroad, especially in the Western Hemisphere. With the exception of the 1920–1921 recession, the economy performed well, although agriculture never recovered from the postwar slump and some industries remained overextended after their wartime expansion. The automobile industry typified the new mass-production techniques that dominated economic life in the United States and revolutionized American society.

During the 1920s a national culture began to develop. It was characterized by new ways of spending leisure time, a heightened emphasis on consumption and advertising, and the wide diffusion of new, more secular ideas and values through movies, radio, and other mass media. The new life-styles of the decade, often called the "Roaring Twenties" or the "Jazz Age," captured the popular imagination but were limited to a minority of the population. Families needed a middle-class income to buy cars, radios, vacuum cleaners, and toasters. Those left outside the circle of prosperity included farmers, coal miners, textile workers, and minority groups such as blacks and Mexican-Americans.

Not everyone welcomed the new secular values of the 1920s. Conflicts arose over Prohibition, religion, race, and immigration. Those cultural disputes spilled over into politics, disrupting the already fractured Democratic party. The 1928 election showed that the nation could not yet accept a Catholic as president. The Republican ascendancy continued under Herbert Hoover, who looked forward to a term filled with even greater prosperity and progress.

TIMELINE

1920-1921	Recession
1920	First commercial radio broadcast Warren G. Harding elected president Census reveals shift from farms to cities Sinclair Lewis, *Main Street*
1921	Sheppard-Towner Act Immigration Act passed Washington Conference on Naval Disarmament Edith Wharton, *The Age of Innocence*
1922	Fordney-McCumber Tariff T. S. Eliot, *The Waste Land*
1923	Calvin Coolidge succeeds Harding as president *Time* magazine founded Jean Toomer, *Cain*
1924	Dawes Plan reduces German reparations payments Bruce Barton, *The Man Nobody Knows* Teapot Dome scandal U.S. troops withdrawn from Dominican Republic National Origins Act passed
1925	F. Scott Fitzgerald, *The Great Gatsby* *Coronado Coal Company v. United Mine Workers* Height of Ku Klux Klan Scopes ("monkey") trial
1926	Alain Locke, *The New Negro* anthology
1927	First "talkies" Charles Lindbergh's solo flight Ford's Model A Kellogg-Briand Pact
1928	Herbert Hoover elected president
1929	*Middletown* published Ernest Hemingway, *A Farewell to Arms* William Faulkner, *The Sound and the Fury*

BIBLIOGRAPHY

General overviews of the 1920s are provided by Lynn Dumenil, *Modern Temper* (1995); Ellis Hawley, *The Great War and the Search for a Modern Order, 1917–1933* (1979); William Leuchtenburg, *The Perils of Prosperity* (1958); and Frederick Lewis Allen, *Only Yesterday* (1931). Ann Douglas, *Terrible Honesty: Mongrel Manhattan in the 1920s* (1995), uses New York City to look broadly at culture in the 1920s. Robert S. Lynd and Helen Merrell Lynd, *Middletown: A Study in Modern American Culture* (1929), remains a superb study of American life in the 1920s.

The Business-Government Partnership

Alfred Chandler provides a stimulating introduction to business life in *The Visible Hand* (1977). See also Robert Himmelberg, *The Origins of the National Recovery Administration: Business, Government, and the Trade Association Ideal, 1921–1933* (1976), and James Gilbert, *Designing the Industrial State* (1972). Irving Bernstein, *The Lean Years* (1960); David Brody, *Workers in Industrial America* (1980); and David Montgomery, *The Fall of the House of Labor* (1987), cover labor developments. See also Dana Frank, *Purchasing Power: Consumer Organizing, Gender, and the Seattle Labor Movement, 1919–1929* (1994).

The domestic and international aspects of the economy are treated in Jim Potter, *The American Economy between the Wars* (1974); and Emily Rosenberg, *Spreading the American Dream* (1982). Interpretations of foreign policy include Akira Iriye, *The Globalizing of America, 1913–1945* (1993); Warren Cohen, *Empire without Tears* (1987); and William Appleman Williams, *The Tragedy of American Diplomacy* (1962). Walter LaFeber, *Inevitable Revolutions* (1983), covers the American involvement in Central America.

General introductions to politics in the 1920s can be found in David Burner, *The Politics of Provincialism* (1967), and Robert Murray, *The Politics of Normalcy* (1973). Biographies of the decade's major political figures include Donald McCoy, *Calvin Coolidge* (1967); David Burner, *Herbert Hoover* (1979); and Paula Elder, *Governor Alfred E. Smith: The Politician as Reformer* (1983). On women in politics see J. Stanley Lemons, *The Woman Citizen* (1973); Nancy Cott, *The Grounding of Modern Feminism* (1987); and Elisabeth Israels Perry, *Belle Moskowitz* (1987).

A New National Culture

Daniel Boorstin, *The Americans: The Democratic Experience* (1973), and David Nasaw, *Going Out: The Rise and Fall of Public Amusements* (1993), introduce the emerging mass culture. On movies, see Robert Sklar, *Movie-Made America* (1975); Larry May, *Screening Out the Past* (1980); and Lewis A. Erenberg, *Steppin' Out* (1981). Material on Clara Bow can be found in David Stenn, *Clara Bow, Runnin' Wild* (1988). Erik Barnouw, *A Tower in Babel* (1966), and Susan Douglas, *Inventing American Broadcasting* (1987) discuss radio. See also Melvin Patrick Ely, *The Adventures of Amos 'n' Andy: A Social History of an American Phenomenon* (1991). Stewart Ewen, *Captains of Consciousness* (1976); Daniel Pope, *The Making of Modern Advertising* (1983); Roland Marchand,

Advertising the American Dream (1985); and T. J. Jackson Lears, *Fables of Abundance* (1994), cover advertising. Paula Fass, *The Damned and the Beautiful* (1977), and Beth L. Bailey, *From Front Porch to Back Seat* (1988), cover youth, whereas Susan Strasser, *Never Done* (1982), and Ruth Schwartz Cowan, *More Work for Mother* (1983), discuss the lives of white middle-class women. Lizabeth Cohen, *Making a New Deal: Industrial Workers in Chicago, 1919–1939* (1990), suggests how working-class communities adapted mass culture for their purposes. Joan Shelley Rubin describes the middle class in *The Making of Middlebrow Culture* (1992).

The impact of the automobile on modern American life is amply documented by James Flink, *The Automobile Age* (1988), and Clay McShane, *Down the Asphalt Path: The Automobile and the American City* (1994); on women and the automobile, see Virginia Scharff, *Taking the Wheel* (1991). For sports, see Allen Guttmann, *A Whole New Ball Game* (1988); Harvey Green, *Fit for America* (1986); and Susan Cahn, *Coming on Strong: Gender and Sexuality in 20th Century Women's Sport* (1994). The Negro Leagues are covered in Robert W. Peterson, *Only the Ball Was White* (1970), and Donn Rogosin, *Invisible Men* (1985).

Dissenting Values and Cultural Conflict

Paul Carter, *Another Part of the Twenties* (1977), and Isabel Leighton, *The Aspirin Age, 1919–1941* (1949), outline the decade's deeply felt cultural controversies. Background on rural and urban life is provided by Don Kirschner, *City and Country: Rural Responses to Urbanization in the 1920s* (1970); Zane Miller, *The Urbanization of America* (1973); and Jon Teaford, *The Twentieth-Century American City* (1986). John Higham, *Strangers in the Land* (1955), describes immigration restriction and nativism. Richard K. Tucker, *The Dragon and the Cross* (1991), and Nancy MacLean, *Behind the Mask of Chivalry* (1994), cover the Klan's rise and fall, whereas Kathleen M. Blee, *Women of the Klan* (1991), offers a provocative discussion of racism and gender in the 1920s. See also Kenneth Jackson, *The Ku Klux Klan in the City, 1915–1930* (1965). George M. Marsden, *Fundamentalism and American Culture* (1980), and William G. McLoughlin, *Fundamentalism in American Culture* (1983), cover religion. Robert Crunden, *From Self to Society, 1919–1941* (1972); Roderick Nash, *The Nervous Generation: American Thought, 1917–1930* (1969); and Daniel Singal, ed., *Modernist Culture in America* (1991), cover intellectual developments. Virginia Sanchez Korrol, *From Colonia to Community* (1983), covers the history of Puerto Ricans in New York City. On the Harlem Renaissance, see Jervis Anderson, *This Was Harlem, 1900–1950* (1982); Nathan Huggins, *Harlem Renaissance* (1971); and Gloria T. Hull, *Color, Sex, and Poetry: Three Women Writers of the Harlem Renaissance* (1987); see also Burton Peretti, *The Creation of Jazz* (1992). Judith Stein, *The World of Marcus Garvey* (1985), describes Marcus Garvey. On Prohibition, see Andrew Sinclair, *Prohibition: The Era of Excess* (1962), and Norman Clark, *Deliver Us from Evil* (1976). The 1928 election is covered in Oscar Handlin, *Al Smith and His America* (1958); Kristi Andersen, *The Creation of a Democratic Majority, 1928–1936* (1979); and Allan J. Lichtman's quantitative study, *Prejudice and the Old Politics* (1979).

The Dust Bowl

Sand and dust everywhere, and not a drop of water—that
was how many midwesterners experienced the worst drought
in U.S. climatological history. This 1934 painting by
Alexandre Hogue captures the bleakness of the drought-
stricken landscape. (Alexandre Hogue. *Drought-Stricken
Area* 1939. Oil on canvas. 30″ × 42¼″. Dallas Museum of
Art, Dallas Art Association Purchase, 1945)

CHAPTER 25

The Great Depression

★   ★   ★

Flappers and movie stars in the 1920s, breadlines and hoboes in the 1930s: were the 1920s just "one long party" after which "everyone had a hangover—known as the depression—in the morning"? Did the country really go from unprecedented prosperity to the poorhouse overnight?

Obviously, the contrast between the flush times of the 1920s and the hard times of the 1930s has been too starkly drawn. The vaunted prosperity of the 1920s was never as widespread or as deeply rooted as many believed at the time. Although America's mass-consumption economy was the envy of the world, many people lived on its margins. Nor was every American devastated by the depression. Those with a secure job or a fixed income survived the economic downturn in relatively good shape, and some people even managed to get rich. But few could escape contact with the depression's wide-ranging effects on social, political, and cultural developments.

Almost all our impressions of the 1930s are black and white, in part because widely distributed photographs taken by Farm Security Administration photographers etched this stark visual image of depression America on the popular consciousness. Not every event of the 1930s should be viewed through the lens of the depression, but more than any other factor, it provides the unifying theme for the decade.

The Coming of the Great Depression

Booms and busts are a permanent feature of the business cycle in capitalist economies. Since the beginning of the Industrial Revolution early in the nineteenth century the United States had experienced recessions or panics at least every twenty years. The most recent downturn had been the postwar recession of 1920–1921. But no slump was as severe or lasted as long as the Great Depression.

The Causes of the Depression

The Great Depression began slowly and almost imperceptibly. After 1927, consumer spending declined and housing construction slowed. Inventories piled up, and in 1928 and 1929 manufacturers began to cut back production and lay off workers. Reduced incomes and buying power reinforced the downturn. By the summer of 1929 the economy was clearly in a recession, although not as severe a downturn as the one that had begun in 1920.

Stock Market Speculation and the Great Crash. Among the causes of the Great Depression, a flawed stock market was an important but not the dominant influence. By 1929 the market had become the symbol of the nation's prosperity and an icon of American business culture. The financier John J. Raskob captured this attitude in a *Ladies' Home Journal* article, "Everyone Ought to Be Rich." Invest $15 a month in sound common stocks, Raskob advised, and in twenty years the investment will grow to $80,000. Not everyone was playing the stock market, however. About 4 million Americans owned stock in 1929, representing about 10 percent of the nation's households. Only 1.5 million had portfolios large enough to require the services of a stockbroker.

Stock prices had been rising steadily since 1921, but in 1928 and 1929 they surged forward, with the average price of stocks rising over 40 percent. All this economic activity was essentially unregulated. Margin buying in particular proceeded at a feverish pace as stockbrokers permitted many of their customers to borrow up to 75

percent of the purchase price of stocks. That easy credit lured more speculators and less creditworthy investors into the market. The Federal Reserve Board warned member banks not to lend money for stock speculation—if prices dropped, many investors would not be able to pay their debts—but no one listened. As long as prices continued to soar, everyone felt like a winner. A noted economist proclaimed in mid-October 1929 that "stock prices have reached what looks like a permanently high plateau."

The stock market had been sliding since early September, but people ignored the warning. On "Black Tuesday"—October 29, 1929—the bubble burst. More than 16 million shares changed hands in frantic trading. Overextended investors, suddenly finding themselves heavily in debt, began to sell their stocks, leading others to follow suit to protect their investments. That set off waves of panic selling, and many stocks found no buyers. Practically overnight, stock values fell from a peak of $87 billion (at least on paper) to $55 billion. The precipitate decline of stock prices became known as the Great Crash.

The impact of Black Tuesday was felt far beyond the trading floors of Wall Street. Speculators who had borrowed from banks to buy their stocks could not repay the loans because they could not sell the stock. These defaults in turn caused bank failures. Since bank deposits were uninsured before the 1930s, a bank failure meant that all the depositors' money was lost. This was a tremendous shock to the middle class, many of whom lost their life savings and had no other resources to cope with the crisis.

The stock market crash intensified the course of the Great Depression in several ways. Besides wiping out the savings of thousands of Americans, it hurt commercial banks that had invested heavily in corporate stocks. Less tangibly, it destroyed the optimism of people who

Wall Street, October 1929
When the stock market collapsed, Julius Rosenwald, the chairman of Sears, Roebuck and Company, offered to guarantee the accounts of Sears employees who had bought stock on margin. The comedian Eddie Cantor jokingly asked for a job as a Sears office boy.

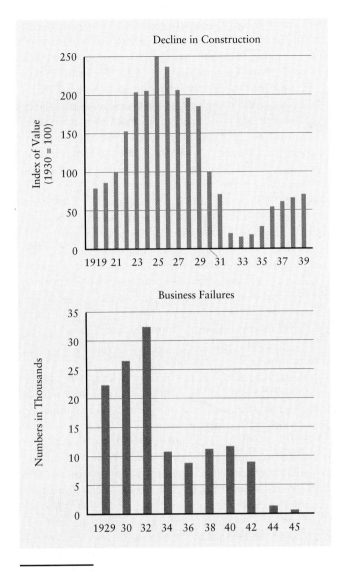

FIGURE 25.1

Statistics of the Depression

The top graph shows the decline in construction, as reflected in the value of new building permits; the bottom graph gives the numbers of business failures.

Source: Historical Statistics of the United States, Colonial Times to 1970 (Washington, D.C.: U.S. Government Printing Office, 1975), 626, 912.

had regarded the stock market as the crowning symbol of American prosperity, causing a crisis of confidence that prolonged the depression.

However, the stock market crash and its immediate consequences cannot account for the severity and the length of the Great Depression, especially the deep plunge between 1931 and 1933. The drag of "sick" industries, the growing inequality of wealth, the unstable international financial situation, and the flawed monetary policies of the Federal Reserve System all contributed to the prolonged decline (see Figure 25.1).

Structural Weaknesses. The crash exposed long-standing weaknesses in the American economy. Agriculture was in the worst shape; farmers had never recovered from the recession of 1920–1921. They faced high fixed costs for equipment and mortgages incurred during the inflationary war years. At the same time, prices fell because of overproduction and the resulting surpluses, forcing farmers to default on mortgage payments and risk foreclosure. In 1929 the yearly income of a farmer averaged only $273, compared with $750 in other occupations. Because farmers accounted for about a fourth of the nation's gainfully employed workers in 1929, their difficulties weakened the general economic structure.

Certain basic industries also had economic troubles during the prosperous 1920s, many of them dating back to World War I or the depression of 1920–1921. The textile industry, for example, had steadily declined after the war. Textile firms abandoned New England for cheaper labor markets in the South but continued to suffer from decreased demand and excess capacity. The railroad industry was hit by shrinking passenger revenues, stagnant freight levels, and inefficient management. In addition, the railroads faced stiff competition from truck transportation on publicly subsidized roads.

Mining and lumbering, which had expanded in response to wartime demands, produced too much during peacetime. Coal mining especially was battered by overexpansion, technological obsolescence, and a legacy of bitter labor struggles. New energy sources, including hydroelectric power, fuel oil, and natural gas, were competing with coal. As secretary of commerce, Herbert Hoover had plans to help those ailing industries, but the trade associations that he promoted were ineffectual.

Unequal Distribution of Wealth. The country's unequal distribution of wealth also contributed to the severity of the depression. During the 1920s the share of national income going to families in the upper- and middle-income brackets increased. The tax policies of Secretary of the Treasury Andrew Mellon contributed to that concentration of wealth by lowering personal income tax rates, eliminating the wartime excess-profits tax, and increasing deductions that favored affluent individuals and corporations. In 1929, the lowest 40 percent of the population received only 12.5 percent of aggregate family personal income whereas the top 5 percent received 30 percent. Once the depression began, not enough people could afford to spend the amounts of money necessary to revive the economy.

The Worldwide Depression. The economic problems of the United States had an impact on the rest of the world, and vice versa. The international economic system had been out of kilter since World War I. It could function only as long as American banks exported enough capital to allow European countries to repay their debts and continue to buy American manufactured goods and agricultural products. By the late 1920s European economies were staggering under the weight of large debts and trade imbalances with the United States, which undercut the recovery that had looked possible earlier in the decade. By 1931 most European economies had collapsed.

In an interdependent world the downturn of the American economy had enormous repercussions. In 1929 the United States had produced over 40 percent of the world's manufactured goods, twice as much as Great Britain and Germany combined; it held 50 percent of the world's gold reserve and accounted for 16 percent of international trade. When American companies cut back production, they also cut back their purchases of raw materials and supplies abroad, and this devastated many foreign economies. American financiers sharply reduced foreign investment and consumers bought fewer European goods, making debt repayment even more difficult and straining the gold standard, the foundation of interwar multilateralism. As economic conditions worsened on the Continent, European demand for American exports fell drastically. When the Hawley-Smoot Tariff of 1930 raised rates to all-time highs, foreign governments retaliated by imposing their own trade restrictions. That further limited the market for American goods, especially agricultural products, and deepened the worldwide depression.

The Deepening Economic Crisis

The Great Depression became self-perpetuating. The more the American economy contracted, the longer people expected the depression to last, and the longer they expected it to last, the more afraid they were to spend or invest their money (if they had any), which was exactly what was needed to stimulate economic recovery. The economy showed some improvement in the summer of 1931 when low prices encouraged consumption, but plunged again late in the fall.

At that point the chronically depressed agricultural sector put pressure on the commercial banking system, worsening the economic contraction. The nation's banks had already been weakened by the stock market crash. When agricultural prices and incomes fell more steeply than usual in 1930, many farmers went into bankruptcy. Rural banks failed in alarming numbers—particularly in the cotton belt—after the harvest of 1930. By November and December so many rural banks had defaulted on their obligations that urban banks also began to fail. The wave of bank failures frightened depositors into withdrawing their savings, further deepening the crisis.

Flawed Monetary Policy. A change in the nation's monetary policy in 1931 added to the banking problems. In the first phase of the depression the Federal Reserve Sys-

tem had reacted cautiously, but in October 1931 the system's managers took several gravely incorrect steps. The New York Reserve Bank significantly increased the discount rate—the interest rate it charged on loans to member banks—and cut back the amount of money it placed in circulation through its purchase of government securities. Those actions hampered the ability of the banking system to meet the domestic demand for currency and credit. By March 1933, when the economy reached its lowest point, the money supply had fallen by about a third from its August 1929 level.

The inadequate money supply forced prices down and deprived businesses of funds for investment. In the face of that money shortage, the American people could have pulled the country out of the depression only by spending faster. But because of falling prices, rising unemployment, and a troubled banking system, Americans preferred to keep their dollars, stashing them under the mattress rather than depositing them in the bank, further limiting the amount of money in circulation.

International Repercussions. Adherence to the gold standard had long been the most sacrosanct principle in the international business community because gold provided a fixed standard against which the value of currencies could be pegged. Great Britain unilaterally decided to abandon the gold standard in 1931, striking another blow against the already shaky international economic system. Currencies no longer had a definite value in relation to gold—and thus to each other—but "floated" in accordance with supply and demand, depriving the world market of a system for the orderly adjustment of the values of currencies. By 1932 forty-one countries had followed Britain's example, and fear spread in Europe that despite Herbert Hoover's unwavering support for the gold standard the United States would follow suit. Consequently, holders of dollars abroad began to demand gold, and gold flowed out of the United States. The Federal Reserve's decision in October 1931 to drive up short-term interest rates successfully attracted gold holders to U.S. investments, temporarily saving the gold standard.

President Hoover later blamed the severity of the depression in the United States on the international economic situation. No other major trading nation was hit as hard as the United States. Although domestic factors far outweighed international ones in causing America's protracted decline, Hoover had a point. During the depression no country stepped forward to provide leadership and stability in the world market as Britain had done before World War I. Instead, nations raised tariff barriers and imposed exchange controls to hoard precious gold, dollars, and pounds sterling in a fit of economic nationalism that prolonged the depression. By 1933 the world economy was showing signs of recovery, although progress remained uneven.

The Downward Spiral. Herbert Hoover personally chose the term *depression* to describe America's post-1929 economic downturn, feeling that that term sounded less ominous than *panic* or *crisis*. Whatever one calls the condition of the American economy from 1929 to 1932, the statistics paint a stark picture. From the height of the prosperity before the stock market crash in 1929 to the depths of the depression in 1932–1933 the gross national product was cut almost in half, declining from $103.1 billion to $58 billion in 1932. Consumption expenditures dropped by 18 percent, construction fell by 78 percent, private investment plummeted by 88 percent, and farm income, already low, was more than cut in half. In this period, 9,000 banks went bankrupt or closed their doors, and 100,000 businesses failed. The consumer price index declined by 25 percent, and corporate profits fell from $10 billion to $1 billion.

Most tellingly, unemployment rose from 3.2 percent to 24.9 percent, affecting approximately 12 million workers (see Figure 25.2). Statistical measures at that time were fairly crude, and unemployment was probably even higher. At least one in four workers was out of a job. Even those who had jobs faced wage cutbacks or the possibility of being laid off. Their stories put a human face on the almost incomprehensible dimensions of this economic downturn.

Employment Agency (detail)
Isaac Soyer's 1937 painting captures the resignation and despair of Americans searching for a job, any job, in the midst of the Great Depression. (Whitney Museum of American Art)

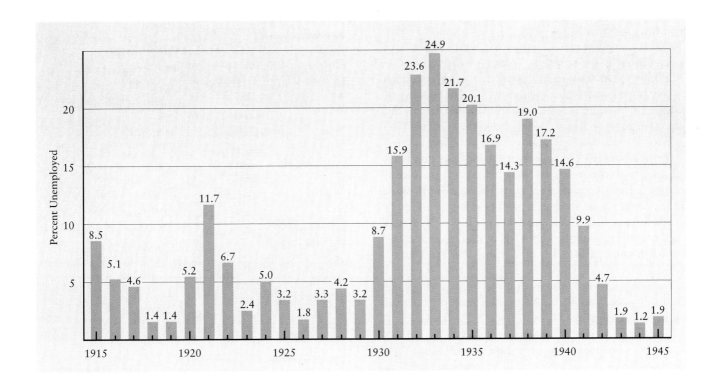

FIGURE 25.2

Unemployment, 1915–1945
As this graph shows, the historically low unemployment levels of the 1920s began to rise in 1930. By 1933 one in four American workers was out of a job.

Hard Times

"We didn't go hungry, but we lived lean." That statement sums up the experiences of many American families during the Great Depression. The vast majority were neither very rich nor very poor. For most the depression did not mean losing thousands of dollars in the stock market or pulling children out of boarding school; nor did it mean going on relief or living in a shanty-town. In a typical family in the 1930s, the husband still had a job and the wife was still a homemaker. Life was not easy, but it usually consisted of "making do" rather than suffering stark deprivation.

The Invisible Scar

"You could feel the depression deepen," recalled the writer Caroline Bird, "but you could not look out the window and see it." Many people never saw a breadline or a man selling apples on the corner. The depression caused a private kind of despair that often simmered behind closed doors. "I've lived in cities for many months broke, without help, too timid to get in breadlines," the writer Meridel LeSueur remembered. "I've known many women to live like this until they simply faint on the street from privations, without saying a word to anyone. A woman will shut herself up in a room until it is taken away from her, and eat a cracker a day and be as quiet as a mouse."

"Mass unemployment is both a statistic and an empty feeling in the stomach," observed the writer Cabell Phillips. "To fully comprehend it, you have to both see the figures and feel the emptiness." The victims of the depression were a varied group. The depression did not create poverty; it merely publicized the conditions of the poor. People who had always been poor were joined by the newly poor. Those formerly solid working-class and middle-class families strongly believed in the Horatio Alger ethic of upward mobility through hard work but suddenly found themselves floundering in a society that no longer had a place for them. They were proud people who felt humiliated by their plight, and many blamed themselves for their misfortune. "What is going to become of us?" asked an Arizona man. "I've lost twelve and a half pounds this last month, just thinking. You can't sleep, you know. You wake up at 2 A.M. and you lie and think."

Hard times were distressing for old people, who faced total destitution in their final years. Some lost their savings in bank failures. In a cartoon from the 1930s a squirrel asks a man on a park bench why he did not save for a rainy day. "I did," the man replies listlessly. Children, by contrast, often escaped the sense of bitterness and failure that gripped their elders; some

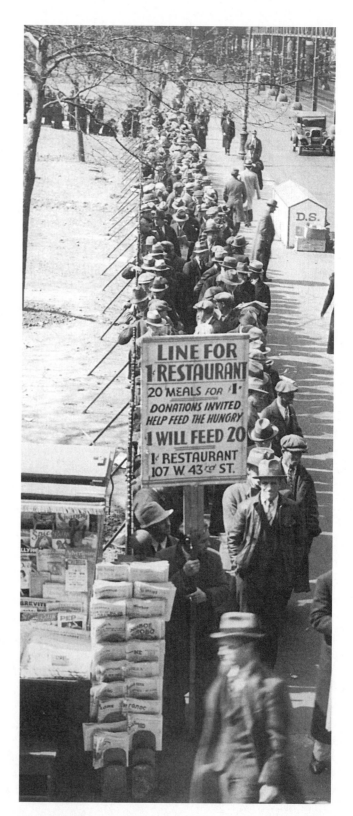

The Breadline
Some of the most vivid images from the depression were breadlines and men selling apples on street corners. Note that all the people in this breadline are men. Women rarely appeared in breadlines, often preferring to endure private deprivation rather than violate standards of respectable behavior.

youngsters thought it was fun to stand in a soup line. Yet hard times made children grow up fast.

Downward mobility was especially hard for middle-class Americans. An unemployed man in Pittsburgh told the journalist Lorena Hickok, "Lady, you just can't know what it's like to have to move your family out of the nice house you had in the suburbs, part paid for, down into an apartment, down into another apartment, smaller and in a worse neighborhood, down, down, down, until finally you end up in the slums." Before a laid-off chauffeur started a relief construction job, he spent the day watching how the other men handled their picks and shovels so he could "get the hang of it and not feel so awkward." A wife broke into tears when her husband, a white-collar worker, put on his first pair of overalls to go to work.

The key to surviving the depression was to maintain one's self-respect. One man spent two years painting his father's house (in fact, he painted it twice). Keeping up appearances, keeping life as close to normal as possible, was an essential strategy. Camaraderie and cooperation helped many families and communities survive as people found that they were all in the same boat. When a driver "accidentally" dumped a load of oranges or coal off the back of his truck, he was contributing to the welfare of the neighborhood. Hoboes developed an elaborate system of sidewalk chalk marks to tell one another at which back doors they could get a meal, an old coat, or some spare change.

After their savings and credit had been exhausted, many families faced the humiliation of going on relief. Seeking aid from state or local governments hurt people's pride and disrupted the traditional pattern of turning to relatives, neighbors, churches, and mutual-aid societies in times of need. A young caseworker tearfully remembered her embarrassment when investigating the homes of these proud people:

> The father was a railroad man who had lost his job. I was told by my supervisor that I really had to see the poverty. If the family needed clothing, I was to investigate how much clothing they had at hand. So I looked into this man's closet . . . he was a tall, gray-haired man, though not terribly old. He let me look into the closet—he was so insulted. . . . He said, "Why are you doing this?" I remember his feeling of humiliation . . . this terrible humiliation. He said, "I really haven't anything to hide, but if you really must look into it. . . ." I could see he was very proud. He was so deeply humiliated. And I was, too.

Even if families survived the demeaning process of being certified for state or local relief, the amount was a pittance. In New York State, for example, where benefits were among the highest in the nation, a family received only $2.39 a week.

Such hardships left deep wounds—the "invisible scar" described by Caroline Bird. One elderly civil servant bought a plot of land outside Washington so that if the depression recurred, she would have the means to live. The labor organizer Larry Van Dusen described another common reaction: "The depression left a legacy of fear, but also a desire for acquisition—property, security. I now have twenty times more shirts than I need, because all during that time, shirts were something I never had." Virginia Durr, a white civil rights activist from Alabama, concurred: "The great majority reacted by thinking money is the most important thing in the world. Get yours. And get it for your children. Nothing else matters. Not having that stark terror come at you again." For many Americans that was the Great Depression: "that stark terror" of losing control over their lives.

Families Face the Great Depression

Sociologists who studied family life during the 1930s found that the depression usually intensified existing behavior. For example, if a family had been stable and cohesive before the depression, it pulled together to overcome the new obstacles. However, if a family had shown signs of disintegration, the depression made the situation worse. On the whole, researchers thought that far more families hung together than broke apart.

In many ways the depression disrupted women's lives less than men's. Millions of men lost their jobs, but few of the nation's 28 million homemakers lost that position in the home. In fact, women's domestic role took on greater importance.

Men and women experienced the Great Depression differently, partly because of the traditional gender roles that governed male and female behavior in the 1930s. Men had been trained from childhood to be breadwinners and considered themselves failures if they could no longer support their families. Women, however, felt their self-importance increase as they struggled to keep their families afloat. The sociologists Robert and Helen Lynd noticed this phenomenon in their follow-up study of Middletown (Muncie, Indiana), published in 1937:

> The men, cut adrift from their usual routine, lost much of their sense of time and dawdled helplessly and dully about the streets; while in the homes the women's world remained largely intact and the round of cooking, housecleaning, and mending became if anything more absorbing.

Even if a wife took a job when her husband lost his, she retained almost total responsibility for housework and child care.

Women made many contributions to family survival during the depression years. With the national median annual income at $1,160, a typical married woman had $20 to $25 a week to feed, clothe, and provide shelter for her family. Deflation had lowered the cost of living so that milk sold for 10 cents a quart, bread for 7 cents a loaf, and butter for 23 cents a pound. Yet housewives still had to watch every penny. Two friends who often bought hamburger together split 2 pounds for 25 cents and took turns keeping the extra penny. Eleanor Roosevelt described the effects of the depression on these women's lives: "It means endless little economies and constant anxiety for fear of some catastrophe such as accident or illness which may completely swamp the family budget." The line between making do and doing without was often thin.

Despite the hard times, Americans maintained a fairly high level of consumption. Continuing the pattern of the 1920s, households in the middle-income range, the 50.2 percent of American families with an income of $500 to $1,500 in 1935, did much of the buying. Several factors enabled those families more or less to maintain their former standard of living despite pay cuts or unemployment. Deflation lowered the cost of living almost 20 percent between 1929 and 1935, and families spent their reduced income differently. For example, telephone use and clothing sales dropped sharply, but people had a harder time giving up cigarettes, movies, radio, and newspapers, once considered luxuries but now regarded as necessities. The automobile proved to be one of the most depression-proof items in the family budget. Sales of new cars dropped, but gasoline sales were stable, suggesting that people bought used cars or kept their old models running longer.

Some families maintained their life-styles in the 1930s through "deficit living"—that is, using installment payments and credit to stretch their income. This strategy added about 10 percent to a family income under $500 and 2 to 5 percent to a family income in the range of $500 to $1,500. By 1936 consumer credit in the United States had increased by 20 percent over 1929 levels. A Middletown resident summed up the prevailing attitude toward installment buying: "Most of the families I know are after the same things today that they were after before the Depression, and they'll get them in the same way—on credit."

To maintain their families' life-styles, housewives substituted their own labor for goods and services they had formerly purchased. Women sewed their own clothes and canned fruits and vegetables. They practiced small economies such as buying day-old bread and heating several dishes in the oven at once to save fuel. Women who had employed servants did their own housework. Those economies helped pay for cars and movies, which could not be manufactured at home. Women generally accepted their new work stoically. "We had no choice," remembered one housewife. "We just did what had to be done one day at a time."

Demographic Trends

The depression directly affected demographic trends in the 1930s. The marriage rate fell from 10.14 per thousand persons in 1929 to 7.87 in 1932. The divorce rate dropped as well because people could not afford the legal expenses of dissolving failed unions. Although marriage and divorce rates rebounded after 1933, postponement of marriage sometimes became permanent. Elsa Ponselle, a Chicago schoolteacher who later became the principal of one of that city's largest elementary schools, recalled her experience:

> Do you realize how many people in my generation are not married? . . . It wasn't that we didn't have a chance. I was going with someone when the Depression hit. We probably would have gotten married. He was a commercial artist and had been doing very well. . . . Suddenly he was laid off. It hit him like a ton of bricks. And he just disappeared.

The birth rate was the demographic factor most affected by the depression. The birth rate had fallen steadily since 1800, but from 1930 to 1933 it dropped from 21.3 live births per thousand population to 18.4, a 14 percent decrease. The 1933 level, if maintained, would have led to a population decline. The overriding concern was whether a couple could afford to raise a child. The birth rate rose slightly after 1934, but by the end of the decade it had reached only 18.8. In contrast, at the height of the baby boom following World War II, the birth rate was 25 per thousand population.

Birth Control. The extensive limitation of births during the Great Depression would not have been possible without access to effective contraception. The production of diaphragms and condoms was one business that thrived in the 1930s. Abortion remained illegal, but the number of women who had the procedure increased. Because many abortionists operated under unsafe or unsanitary conditions, between 8,000 and 10,000 women died each year from those illegal operations.

The 1930s marked a significant stage in the long history of the birth control movement in America. In 1936 a federal court decision in the case of *United States v. One Package of Japanese Pessaries* struck down all federal restrictions on the dissemination of contraceptive information. Doctors now had wide discretion in prescribing birth control for married couples, which became legal in all states except Massachusetts and Connecticut. Public support for contraception also increased: in a 1936 Gallup poll 63 percent of those interviewed favored making birth control information more widely available.

Margaret Sanger played a major role in encouraging popular acceptance of birth control. She had started her career as a public health nurse in the slums of New York in the 1910s. Anxious immigrant women continually asked Sanger to tell them the "secret" of how to avoid having more babies. When a patient who had been referred to her died after a botched abortion, Sanger dedicated her life to expanding access to birth control. At first she joined forces with socialist movements aimed at the working class. In the 1920s and 1930s, however, she appealed to the middle class for support, identifying this segment of the population as the key to the movement's success. Sanger also courted the medical profession, pioneering the establishment of birth control clinics staffed by doctors and winning the American Medical Association's endorsement of contraception in 1937. Birth control became less a feminist demand and more a medical issue.

Contraception had long been a private decision between individuals. Its public acceptance increased greatly during the 1930s because of the widespread desire to limit family size for economic reasons. In 1942 the American Birth Control League, which Sanger had founded in 1921, became Planned Parenthood, an organization that remains active today.

Women on the Job

One way for families to make ends meet in the 1930s was to send an additional member of the household to work. At the turn of the century that additional family worker probably would have been a child or a young unmarried adult; in the 1930s it was increasingly a married woman. Instead of expelling women from the work force, the depression solidified their position in it: the 1940 census reported almost 11 million women in the work force, approximately a fourth of the nation's workers and a small increase over 1930. The number of married women employed outside the home rose 50 percent.

Working women, especially married ones, encountered sharp resentment and outright discrimination when they entered the depression workplace. After calculating that the number of employed women roughly equaled the 1939 unemployment total, the editor Norman Cousins suggested this tongue-in-cheek remedy: "Simply fire the women, who shouldn't be working anyway, and hire the men. Presto! No unemployment. No relief rolls. No depression." A 1936 Gallup poll asked whether wives should work when their husbands had jobs, and 82 percent of the people interviewed said no. From 1932 to 1937 the federal government would not allow a husband and wife to hold government jobs at the same time. Many states adopted laws that prohibited married women from working. Such laws were especially widespread in the field of education, yet the proportion of married female schoolteachers rose from 17.9 percent in 1930 to 24.6 percent in 1940.

The attempt to make women scapegoats for the depression rested on shaky moral and economic grounds. Most women worked because they had to. A sizable minority were the sole support of their families, because their husbands had left home or lost their jobs. Single, divorced, deserted, or widowed women had no husbands to support them. Moreover, women rarely took jobs away from men. "Few of the people who oppose married women's employment," observed one feminist in 1940, "seem to realize that a coal miner or steel worker cannot very well fill the jobs of nursemaids, cleaning women, or the factory and clerical jobs now filled by women." Custom, rather than law or economics, made crossovers rare.

The division of the work force by gender gave women a small edge during the depression. Many fields with large numbers of female employees, including clerical, sales, and service and trade occupations, suffered less from economic contraction than did the steel industry, mining, and manufacturing, which employed men almost exclusively. As a result, unemployment rates for women, although extremely high, were somewhat lower than those for men. This small bonus came at a high price, however. The jobs women held reinforced the traditional stereotypes of female work. When the depression ended, women found themselves even more concentrated in low-paying dead-end jobs than when it began.

This gender advantage also benefited white women at the expense of minority group women. To make ends meet, white women willingly took jobs usually held by blacks or minority workers—entering domestic service, for example—and employers were quick to act on their preference for a white work force. White men also took jobs previously held by minority group males.

During the Great Depression there were few feminist demands for equal rights at home or on the job. On an individual basis, women's self-esteem probably rose because of their importance to family survival. Most men and women, however, continued to believe that the two sexes should have fundamentally different roles and responsibilities and that a woman's life cycle should be shaped by marriage and her husband's career. The substantial contributions made by women in the 1930s actually reinforced their overall identification with the home, laying the foundation for the so-called feminine mystique of the 1950s.

Hard Times for Youth

The depression hit the nation's 21 million young people especially hard. Although children only dimly glimpsed the sacrifices made in the 1930s, adolescents knew that making do usually meant doing without. The writer Maxine Davis, who traveled 10,000 miles in 1936 to interview the nation's youth, described them as "runners, delayed at the gun." She added, "The depression years have left us with a generation robbed of time and opportunity just as the Great War left the world its heritage of a lost generation." Studies of social mobility confirm that the young men who entered their twenties during the depression era had less successful careers than did those before or since. About 250,000 young people became so demoralized that they took to the road as hoboes and "sisters of the road," as female tramps were called.

Because job prospects were so dim, some young people chose to stay in school longer. Public schools were free and were warm in the winter. In 1930 less than half the nation's youth attended high school, compared with three-fourths in 1940, at the end of the depression. This was partly due to increased attendance by boys, who had traditionally dropped out of school to work at an earlier age than did girls.

College, however, remained the privilege of a distinct minority. About 1.2 million young people, or 7.5 percent of the population between eighteen and twenty-four, attended college in the 1930s, 40 percent of them women. After 1935 college became a little more affordable because of the National Youth Administration (NYA), which gave part-time employment to more than 2 million college and high school students. This government agency also provided work for 2.6 million out-of-school youths.

College students worked hard in the 1930s; financial sacrifices encouraged seriousness of purpose. The influence of fraternities and sororities declined during the depression, and many students became involved in political movements. Fueled by disillusionment with World War I, thousands took the "Oxford Pledge" never to support a war in which the United States might be involved. In 1936 the Student Strike against War drew support from several hundred thousand students across the country.

Because young people spent more time in school, participating in organized athletics and extracurricular activities, adolescence became increasingly institutionalized in the 1930s, and teenagers developed their own values and patterns of behavior. Peers, rather than parents, influenced their values and tastes. Magazines and movies promoted a youth culture that was closely tied to an ethos of consumption. Teenagers throughout the country read the same comics, wore the same style clothes, and saw the same movies. They also experimented with necking, petting, and dating rituals that shocked their elders. The youth culture became a distinct feature of modern times.

Popular Culture

Popular culture played an important role in pulling the United States through the trauma of the depression. As the novelist Josephine Herbst observed, there was "an almost universal liveliness that countervailed universal suffering." The mass culture that grew so dramatically in the 1920s flourished in the decade that followed.

Movies. The most popular form of entertainment in the 1930s was the movies. More than 60 percent of Americans saw at least one movie a week, with weekly attendance ranging from 60 million to 75 million. In the 5,000 films made during the depression decade, movie-goers were transported to a world where hard times were practically unknown. Yet movies offered more than escapism. Hollywood in the 1930s, observed the film historian Robert Sklar, "directed its enormous powers of persuasion to preserving the basic moral, social and economic tenets of traditional American culture."

World Premiere
Margaret Mitchell's 1936 novel, *Gone with the Wind*, broke all sales records in the 1930s. When it was made into a 1939 movie starring Clark Gable and Vivien Leigh, more than 12,000 fans gathered in Atlanta for the film's premiere at Loew's Grand Theater, which had been transformed into a southern mansion for the event.

Movies remained a big business in the 1930s, but the industry was not depression-proof. Although theaters lowered admission prices from 30 cents to 20, attendance dropped in the early 1930s, and by 1933 one-third of the nation's movie theaters were dark. Many of the major studios, dependent on Wall Street financing, were hurting. Not until 1934 did the industry begin to revive.

In many ways films in the 1930s reflected the progress of the depression. In the grim early years gangster films were especially popular. Two of the most successful were *Little Caesar* (1930), starring Edward G. Robinson, and *The Public Enemy* (1931), in which James Cagney shoved a grapefruit in Mae Clark's face. Those movies were replaced by extravagant Busby Berkeley musicals such as *Gold Diggers of 1933*, suggesting an upswing in the public mood. The Marx brothers kept people laughing with irreverent classics such as *Animal Crackers* (1930) and *Duck Soup* (1933).

The Grapes of Wrath
John Steinbeck's best-selling 1939 novel became one of 1940's top movies, one of the few Hollywood films that tackled contemporary social problems. Ma Joad, played by Jane Darwell, expressed the central message: "We're the people that live. They ain't gonna wipe us out. Why, we're the people—we go on."

Dancing Cheek to Cheek
During the Great Depression, Americans turned to inexpensive recreational activities such as listening to the radio and going to the movies. One of the most popular attractions in Hollywood movies was the dance team of Fred Astaire and Ginger Rogers, who starred together in ten movies.

Mae West titillated audiences with lines such as "It's not the men in my life, but the life in my men that counts" and "I used to be Snow White, but I drifted."

For some moviegoers Mae West's sexual innuendos went too far. To win back customers Hollywood made a highly publicized commitment to upholding ideals of decency and good taste. The Production Code Administration, headed by Joseph Breen, represented Hollywood's effort at self-censorship, an attempt to correct the perceived excesses of early talkies. Fearing a boycott from religious groups such as the Catholic Legion of Decency, studios in 1934 agreed to banish explicit sex, immorality, and violence from the screen. The new standards were so strict that censors barely permitted Rhett Butler to utter the famous last line of *Gone with the Wind*: "Frankly, my dear, I don't give a damn." Critics charged that movies were cutting themselves off from reality, but the repressive standards held sway until the 1950s.

In part because of the Production Code, movies made after 1934 had a different feel compared with those made before that year. Sophisticated, fast-paced "screwball comedies" such as *It Happened One Night*, which swept the Oscars in 1934, epitomized Hollywood's new direction. Walt Disney emerged as a cultural mythmaker during the depression, producing 198 cartoons and classics such as *Snow White and the Seven Dwarfs* (1937), the first feature-length animated film. The 1940 Hollywood adaptation of John Steinbeck's novel *The Grapes of Wrath* was one of the few popular films to depict the depression in a serious, realistic manner. Even the newsreels downplayed the depression in favor of heroes and heroines from the worlds of sports, entertainment, and popular culture.

At the height of the depression, movies continued to influence consumers. One of the decade's top box-office stars was a curly-headed little girl named Shirley Temple, who made twenty-one films by 1941. Shirley Temple dolls, books, and clothes flooded the market. Similarly, because of the popularity of glamorous blondes such as Jean Harlow, Carole Lombard, and Mae West, sales of peroxide hair rinse skyrocketed. Undershirt sales fell drastically after Clark Gable, a leading sex symbol of the 1930s, took off his shirt in *It Happened One Night* and revealed his bare chest.

Headline History. People relied on newspapers and newsreels for quick coverage of world events. The kidnapping of the twenty-month-old son of Charles and Anne Morrow Lindbergh in 1932 instantly became a national news story. Seventy-five days later the child's body was found in the woods near the Lindbergh home in New Jersey. "BABY DEAD" ran the headlines, and

everyone knew what the two words meant. Other leading news events of the depression years included the birth of the Dionne quintuplets in Canada in 1934; the gunning down of John Dillinger, "Public Enemy Number One," by the FBI in 1934; Jesse Owens's four gold medals at the 1936 Berlin Olympics; the abdication in 1936 of King Edward VIII of Great Britain to marry "the woman I love," an American divorcée named Wallis Warfield Simpson; the disappearance of the aviator Amelia Earhart on a round-the-world flight in 1937; and the fiery crash of the *Hindenburg*, a German dirigible, at Lakehurst, New Jersey, in 1937.

Radio Days. Radio occupied an increasingly large place in popular culture during the 1930s (see Map 25.1). At the beginning of the decade about 13 million households had a radio set; by the end, 27.5 million owned one. Listeners tuned in to daytime serials such as "Ma Perkins" or picked up useful household hints on the "The Betty Crocker Hour." Variety shows featured Jack Benny, George Burns and Gracie Allen, and the ventriloquist Edgar Bergen and his impudent dummy Charlie McCarthy. Millions of listeners followed the adventures

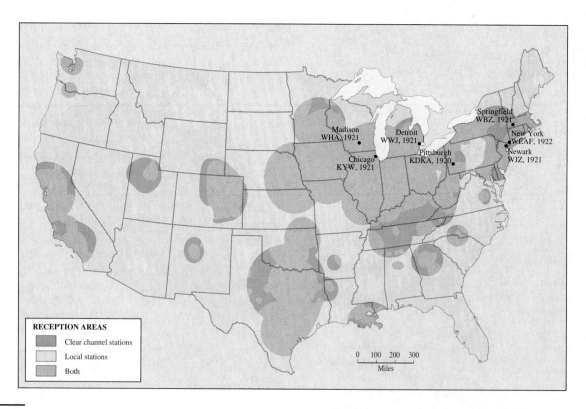

MAP 25.1

The Spread of Radio

In 1938 more than 26 million American households, or about three-quarters of the population, had a radio. Four national networks dominated the field, broadcasting news and entertainment across the country. Powerful clear-channel stations reached listeners hundreds of miles distant. By 1939 only a few sparsely populated areas were beyond radio's reach.

of the Lone Ranger ("Hi-Ho Silver"), Superman, the Shadow, and Dick Tracy.

Radio also brought music to depression-era audiences. Classical music devotees could listen to live Saturday afternoon performances of New York's Metropolitan Opera (begun in 1931 and still being broadcast) or the NBC Symphony Orchestra under the baton of Arturo Toscanini. On the lighter side people loved the new Big Band "swing" music of Benny Goodman, Duke Ellington, and Tommy Dorsey, an outgrowth of the jazz craze of the 1920s, and Cole Porter songs such as "Begin the Beguine" and "Night and Day" from Broadway shows. Radio increased the consumer market for 78-r.p.m. phonograph records of classical music, swing, and Broadway show tunes.

The depression also encouraged a return to traditional values. Attendance at religious services rose. The home once again became a center of leisure activity, with an evening by the radio providing a cheap form of family entertainment. Reading aloud from books borrowed from the public library was another affordable diversion. "Talking was the Great Depression pastime," recalled the columnist Russell Baker. "Unlike the movies, talk was free."

The Social Fabric of Depression America

Much writing about the 1930s has focused on white working-class or middle-class families that were caught in a spiral of downward social mobility. For such groups as African-Americans, farmers, and Mexican-Americans, times had always been hard and during the 1930s they got much harder. As the poet Langston Hughes noted, "The depression brought everybody down a peg or two. And the Negroes had but few pegs to fall."

Blacks and the Depression

Discrimination and limited opportunities had always been part of the lives of African-Americans, who thus viewed the depression differently than most whites did. Black people did not blame themselves for their misfortunes. "It didn't mean too much to him, the Great American Depression, as you call it," one man remarked. "There was no such thing. The best he could be is a janitor or a porter or shoeshine boy. It only became official when it hit the white man." The novelist and poet Maya Angelou, who grew up in Stamps, Arkansas, recalled, "The country had been in the throes of the Depression for two years before the Negroes in Stamps knew it. I think that everyone thought the Depression, like everything else, was for the white folks."

Despite the black migration to northern cities that had begun before World War I, as late as 1940 more than 75 percent of African-Americans still lived in the South. Nearly all the farmers who were black lived in the South, their condition scarcely better than it had been at the end of Reconstruction. Only 20 percent of black farmers owned their own land; the rest toiled at the bottom of the exploitative southern agricultural system, working as tenant farmers, farmhands, and sharecroppers. African-Americans rarely earned more than $200 a year. The earnings of black women cotton pickers in one Louisiana parish averaged only $41.67 a year.

Throughout the 1920s southern agriculture had suffered from falling prices and overproduction. During the depression an already desperate situation got worse. Some black farmers tried to protect themselves by joining the Southern Tenant Farmers Union (STFU), which was founded in 1934. The STFU was one of the few southern groups that welcomed both blacks and whites. "The same chain that holds you holds my people, too," an elderly black farmer reminded whites on the organizing committee. "If we're chained together on the outside we ought to stay chained together in the union." Landowners, however, had a stake in keeping black and white sharecroppers from organizing, and they countered the union's efforts with repression and harassment. In the end the STFU could do little to reform an agricultural system dependent on a single crop—cotton.

The Scottsboro Case. The Scottsboro case epitomized the harsh social and political discrimination that almost all blacks faced in the South in the 1930s. On March 25, 1931, a freight train pulled into Scottsboro, Alabama, carrying a number of hoboes and transients who had caught a free ride. Acting on a tip from the conductor, sheriff's deputies arrested nine black men for fighting with some of the white hoboes.

Suddenly, two white women wearing men's clothing stepped off the boxcar and claimed they had been raped by the nine blacks. The officers accepted without question the accusations of the women, Victoria Price and Ruby Bates, and barely restrained an angry white mob from lynching the accused men on the spot. Two weeks later juries composed entirely of white men found the nine defendants guilty of rape and sentenced eight of them to death. (One defendant escaped the death penalty because he was a minor.) The U.S. Supreme Court overturned the sentences in 1932 and ordered new trials because the defendants had been denied adequate legal counsel.

The youth of the Scottsboro defendants, their hasty trials, and the harsh sentences stirred public protest. The International Labor Defense (ILD), a labor organization closely tied to the Communist party, took over the defense of the so-called Scottsboro boys. The Communist party had targeted the struggle against racism as

The Lynch Mob and Silent Witness
The threat of lynching remained a terrifying part of life for
African-Americans in the 1930s, and not just in the South.
The photograph on the top shows two young blacks who
were lynched by an Indiana mob in 1930. Each day that a
person was lynched, the NAACP hung a banner (bottom)
outside the window of its New York office. NAACP appeals
for federal antilynching legislation received little support
from politicians, however.

a priority in the early 1930s but was making little headway. "It's bad enough being black, why be red?" was a
common reaction. White southerners resented the interference of those radicals as well as the fact that almost
all those involved in the Scottsboro defense were northerners and Jews. In the words of a local solicitor, "Alabama justice cannot be bought and sold with Jew
money from New York."

The case was complicated by the southern myth of
the inviolate honor and chastity of white womanhood.
The stories of the two women contained many inconsistencies, and Ruby Bates later recanted. However, in the
South, when a white woman claimed to have been
raped by a black man, she was taken at her word. As a
court observer remarked, Victoria Price "might be a
fallen woman, but by God she is a white woman."

The case dragged on through the courts for the next
decade. In new trials held in 1936 and 1937 five of the
defendants were convicted and sentenced to long prison
terms. The charges against the other four were dropped
in 1937. Four of the convicted men were paroled in
1944. The fifth escaped to Michigan, whose governor
refused to return him to Alabama.

The Scottsboro case received wide coverage in black
communities across the country. Along with the increase
in lynching in the early 1930s (twenty blacks were
lynched in 1930, twenty-four in 1933), it provided
black Americans with a strong incentive to head for
northern and midwestern cities. However, the lure of the
North was offset by the lack of economic opportunities
caused by the depression. About 400,000 black men
and women left the South during the 1930s, only about
half the number that had departed in the 1920s. Nevertheless, by 1935 eleven cities had more than 100,000
African-Americans. Two of the most popular destinations were the South Side of Chicago and Harlem in
New York City.

Harlem in the 1930s In the late nineteenth century
Harlem had been a neighborhood of wealthy white
families—New York's first suburb—and as late as 1900,
blacks made up only a small minority of its population.
Then around 1910 the great migration from the South
began, a process accelerated by World War I. As blacks
moved into Harlem, second-generation Italians and
Jews began to move out.

Harlem reached the height of its fame in the 1920s,
when it became a mecca for both whites and blacks (see
Chapter 24). Adventurous New Yorkers associated
Harlem with the Cotton Club and other glittering jazz
palaces that catered to white audiences. (Although the
clubs featured black performers, they were white-only
establishments from which black patrons were excluded.) During the 1920s the black population of New
York City increased by about 115 percent, straining
Harlem's housing facilities and community services.

The Cotton Club

The Cotton Club, "the aristocrat of Harlem" at Lenox Avenue and 142nd Street, was home to performers such as Duke Ellington, Ethel Waters, and Cab Calloway. Even though blacks provided the floor show and were hired as waiters and busboys at this swinging nightclub, they were not admitted as customers unless they were light-skinned enough to pass for white.

This once-prosperous middle-class community was on the way to becoming a slum.

The depression aggravated the situation. Residential segregation kept blacks from moving elsewhere. African-Americans paid excessive rents to unscrupulous owners who allowed their buildings to deteriorate. Crowded living conditions caused disease and death rates to climb; tuberculosis became a leading cause of death in Harlem. At the height of the depression shelters and soup kitchens staffed by the Divine Peace Mission, under the leadership of the charismatic black religious leader Father Divine, provided 3,000 meals a day for Harlem's destitute. Unemployment rose to 50 percent—twice the national rate—as whites clamored for jobs traditionally held by blacks—waiters, domestic servants, elevator operators, and garbage collectors.

In March 1935 Harlem exploded in the nation's only major race riot of the decade. Its residents were angry about the lack of jobs, a slowdown in relief, and the economic exploitation of the black community. Although entirely dependent on black trade, white-owned stores would not employ blacks. The arrest of a teenage black shoplifter, followed by rumors that he had been severely beaten by white police officers, triggered the riot. False reports of his death fueled the panic, and the city mobilized 500 police officers. Four blacks were killed, and property damage totaled $2 million.

However, the picture was not totally bleak for African-Americans in the 1930s. The New Deal would channel significant amounts of relief money toward blacks outside the South, partly in response to the 1935 riot but mainly in return for growing black allegiance to the Democratic party (see Chapter 26). The National Association for the Advancement of Colored People continued to publicly challenge the status quo of race relations. Although calls for racial justice went largely unheeded during the depression, World War II and its aftermath would provide better opportunities for the struggle for black equality.

Dust Bowl Migrations

Distressed conditions in agriculture had been one of the causes of the Great Depression. In the 1930s things only got worse, especially for farmers on the Great Plains. The decade became known as the "Dirty Thirties" because of the dust storms that blighted the land. The worst drought in the country's history began in 1930 and lasted until 1941. Throughout the decade the three words most often uttered by farmers were "if it rains."

Farmers who moved onto the semiarid Great Plains after the 1870s had always risked the ravages of drought (see Chapter 17). Even in wet years the average rainfall was 20 inches or less—barely enough to raise grain crops. But low rainfall alone did not create the Dust Bowl. National and international market forces, such as the demand for wheat during World War I, caused farmers to push the farming frontier beyond its natural limits by working increasingly marginal land to capture a profit. After that land had been stripped of its natural vegetation, the delicate ecological balance of the plains was destroyed. Nothing remained to hold the soil when the rains dried up and the winds came.

Dust became a plague of everyday life throughout the Great Plains but especially in Oklahoma, Texas, New Mexico, Colorado, Arkansas, and Kansas (see Map 25.2). When the clouds of dust rolled in, streetlights blinked on as if night had fallen. Dust seeped into houses and "blackened the pillow around one's head, the dinner plates on the table, the bread dough on the back of the stove" (see American Voices, page 785). The dust storms were not confined to the plains. In May 1934 the wind took dust clouds to Chicago, where filth fell like snow, dumping the equivalent of 4 pounds of debris per person on the city. Several days later the same clouds blackened the skies and dirtied the streets of Buffalo, Boston, New York, and Washington. That winter red snow fell on New England.

This ecological disaster caused a mass exodus from the land. Their crops ruined, their lands barren and dry, their homes foreclosed for debts they could not pay, thousands of farm families loaded their belongings into

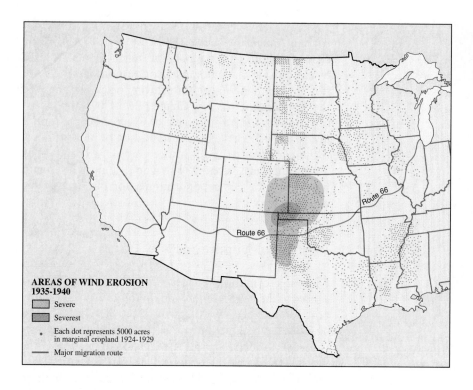

MAP 25.2

The Dust Bowl

A U.S. Weather Bureau scientist called the drought of the 1930s "the worst in the climatological history of the country." Conditions were especially severe in the southern plains, where the dramatic increases in farming on marginal land had strained production before the drought struck. Many farm families saw no choice but to follow Route 66, the highway that went west through Missouri, Oklahoma, and north Texas to California, the promised land.

AREAS OF WIND EROSION 1935-1940

Severe

Severest

• Each dot represents 5000 acres in marginal cropland 1924-1929

— Major migration route

beat-up Fords and headed west along Route 66 to the promised land of California. The migrants were called "Okies" whether or not they were from Oklahoma. John Steinbeck's novel *The Grapes of Wrath* (1939) immortalized their journey. In the novel the Joads abandon their land not only because of drought but also as a result of the economic forces changing American agriculture. Large-scale commercialized farming had spread to the plains, where family farmers still used draft animals. After the bank forecloses on the Joads' farm, a gasoline-engine tractor, the symbol of mechanized farming, plows under their crops and demolishes their house.

Although a powerful work of fiction, the story of the Joads' struggle does not convey the diversity of the westward migration, which was both a response to hard times and part of the larger migration out of the nation's agricultural heartland that had begun around World War I and continued through the 1970s. Not all Okies were destitute dirt farmers; perhaps one in six was a professional, a business proprietor, or a white-collar worker. Many were participating in chain migrations, that is, following family members or friends to a specific place. For most the drive west was fairly easy: Route 66 was a paved two-lane road, and in a decent car it took three to four days to make it from Oklahoma or Texas to California.

Before the 1930s, California had already undergone changes that had created a type of agriculture different from that practiced by southwestern and midwestern farmers. Agriculture in California was large-scale, intensive, and diversified. The state's wealth came primarily from specialty crops whose staggered harvests

required a great deal of transient labor for short picking seasons. The steady supply of cheap migrant labor provided by Chinese, Mexicans, Okies, and, briefly, East Indians made such farming economically feasible. Carey McWilliams, whose nonfiction *Factories in the Field* (1939) focused national attention on migrant workers, noted that California agriculture was basically industrial in nature:

> Ownership is represented not by physical possession of the land, but by ownership of corporate stock; farm labor, no longer pastoral in character, punches a time clock, works at piece or hourly wage rates, and lives in a shack or company barracks, and lacks all contact with the real owners of the farm factory on which it is employed.

Encouraged by handbills promising good jobs in California, at least 350,000 southwesterners headed west in the 1930s. Some went to metropolitan areas, but about half settled in rural areas. White, native-born Americans had made up about 20 percent of the migratory farm labor force before the depression, but their proportion increased to more than 85 percent in the late 1930s. Since growers needed only 175,000 workers at the peak of the picking season, this surplus assured them a cheap supply of labor, usually docile and willing to work at any price. That price was incredibly low in the 1930s. The average yearly family income of migrant farm workers in California ranged from $350 to $450, less than a third of the subsistence level. Yet what they earned in California was more than what they had left behind.

Ann Marie Low

A Dust Bowl Diary

Born in 1912, Ann Marie Low kept diaries from 1927 to 1937, which describe the devastation wracked by drought and the depression on her family's farm in the Badlands of southeastern North Dakota. They record both a young woman's coming of age and the harshness of life on the farm in the Dust Bowl.

April 25, 1934, Wednesday
Last weekend was the worst dust storm we ever had. We've been having quite a bit of blowing dirt every year since the drouth started, not only here, but all over the Great Plains. Many days this spring the air is just full of dirt coming, literally, for hundreds of miles. It sifts into everything. After we wash the dishes and put then away, so much dust sifts into the cupboards we must wash them again before the next meal. Clothes in the closet are covered with dust.

Last weekend no one was taking an automobile out for fear of ruining the motor. I rode Roany to Frank's place to return a gear. To find my way I had to ride right beside the fence, scarcely able to see from one fence post to the next.

Newspapers say the deaths of many babies and old people are attributed to breathing in so much dirt.

May 21, 1934, Monday
Ethel has been having stomach trouble. Dad has been taking her to doctors though suspecting her trouble is the fact that she often goes on a diet that may affect her health. The local doctor said he thought it might be chronic appendicitis, so Mama took Ethel by train to Valley City last week to have a surgeon there remove her appendix.

Saturday Dad, Bud, and I planted an acre of potatoes. There was so much dirt in the air I couldn't see Bud only a few feet in front of me. Even the air in the house was just a haze. In the evening the wind died down, and Cap came to take me to the movie. We joked about how hard it is to get cleaned up enough to go anywhere. . . .

May 30, 1934, Wednesday
Ethel got along fine, so Mama left her at the hospital and came to Jamestown by train Friday. Dad took us both home.

The mess was incredible! Dirt had blown into the house all week and lay inches deep on everything. Every towel and curtain was just black. There wasn't a clean dish or cooking utensil. . . . It took until 10 o'clock to wash all the dirty dishes. That's not wiping them—just washing them. The cupboards had to be washed out to have a clean place to put them.

Saturday was a busy day. Before starting breakfast I had to sweep and wash all the dirt off the kitchen and dining room floors, wash the stove, pancake griddle, and dining room table and chairs. There was cooking, baking, and churning to be done for those hungry men. Dad is 6 feet 4 inches tall, with a big frame. Bud is 6 feet 3 inches and almost as big-boned as Dad. We say feeding them is like filling a silo.

Mama couldn't make bread until I carried water to wash the bread mixer. I couldn't churn until the churn was washed and scalded. We just couldn't do anything until something was washed first. Every room had to have dirt almost shoveled out of it before we could wash floors and furniture.

We had no time to wash clothes, but it was necessary. I had to wash out the boiler, wash tubs, and the washing machine before we could use them. Then every towel, curtain, piece of bedding, and garment had to be taken outdoors to have as much dust as possible shaken out before washing. The cistern is dry, so I had to carry all the water we needed from the well.

That evening Cap came to take me to the movie, as usual. Ixnay. I'm sorry I snapped at Cap. It isn't his fault, or anyone's fault, but I was tired and cross. Life in what the newspapers call "the Dust Bowl" is becoming a gritty nightmare.

Source: Ann Marie Low, *Dust Bowl Diary* (Lincoln: University of Nebraska Press, 1984), 95, 96–98.

Those migrants had a lasting impact on California culture. At first they met outright hostility from old-time Californians, a demoralizing experience for white, native-born Protestants who were ashamed of the negative "Okie" stereotype. But they stayed, filling important roles in the expanding California economy. Soon communities in the San Joaquin Valley—Bakersfield, Fresno, Merced, Modesto, Stockton—took on a distinctly Okie cast, identifiable by southern-influenced evangelical religion and the growing popularity of country music.

Mexican-American Communities

The Mexican-American experience in the West differed from that of Dust Bowl refugees. In the depths of the depression, with American fears about competition from foreign workers at a peak, perhaps a third of the Mexican-American population, primarily immigrants, returned to Mexico. A formal deportation policy instituted by the U.S. government was partly responsible for the exodus, but many more Mexicans left "voluntarily" when work ran out and local relief agencies refused to extend assistance to them. Pervasive racism and the proximity of Mexico made Mexicans the only immigrants targeted for deportation during the depression.

The deportation of Mexican-Americans was not a response to the arrival of migrants from the Dust Bowl. The largest number of deportations occurred during the Hoover administration, well before the Dust Bowl exodus reached its peak. Most occurred in California and Texas, but Indiana, Illinois, Michigan, and Colorado also repatriated unwanted workers. In 1932, a one-way train ticket cost the equivalent of a week's relief allotment, and officials in many southwestern communities realized that it was cheaper to send migrant workers back to Mexico than to support them during the winter, when there were no crops to pick.

In 1930 Los Angeles was home to 150,000 Mexican-Americans, making it the largest Mexican city outside Mexico. Mexican-Americans spilled out of the downtown area known as "Sonoratown" into neighborhoods or *colonias* in Belvedere and East Los Angeles, where mutual-aid societies, Spanish-language newspapers, and the Catholic Church fostered a sense of community. But Los Angeles lost approximately one-third of its Mexican population during the repatriation drives of the 1930s, which caused profound social dislocations. Although the free trip home at government expense was the source of some *chistes* (jokes), it also caused family separations, disruptions of education for children who were pulled out of school, and extreme financial hardships during the worst years of the depression. And for those who remained in America, repatriation was an unmistakable reminder of the fragility of their status in the United States.

Mexican migration to the United States—legal and illegal—increased steadily throughout the twentieth century, except during the Great Depression and for short periods after the two world wars. The first *bracero* (day laborer) program promoting Mexican immigration had been established during World War I to meet labor shortages. (*Bracero* comes from *brazo*, which means "arm" in Spanish; *braceros* are hired hands, those who work with their arms.) The importation of cheap Mexican labor continued throughout the 1920s. After being deported during the depression, Mexican workers were coaxed back again when World War II caused another labor shortage. The influx of Spanish-speaking migrants with their own culture helped shape the patterns of life and work in the Southwest and the West.

The experiences of his family members as migrant workers during the 1930s influenced a Mexican-American named César Chávez to become one of the twentieth century's most influential labor organizers. Chávez was a child of ten in 1934, when his father lost the family farm, located near Yuma, Arizona. The Chávez family joined the army of migrant workers that followed the crops in California. They experienced continual discrimination, even in restaurants, where signs proclaimed "White Trade Only." César's father became involved in several bitter labor struggles in the Imperial Valley in the mid-1930s. In 1933 thirty-seven major agricultural strikes occurred in California, including one in the San Joaquin Valley that mobilized 18,000 cotton pickers, the largest agricultural strike to date. All the strikes failed, but they gave the young Chávez a background in labor organizing, which he used to found a national farm workers' union in 1962.

Not all Mexican-Americans were migrant farm workers. A significant number lived in urban areas and held industrial jobs, especially in steel mills, meat-packing plants, and refineries, where they established a vibrant tradition of labor activism. Mexican-American smelter and refinery workers joined the International Union of Mine, Mill and Smelter Workers (known colloquially as "Mine-Mill") in large numbers and became key leaders. Bert Corona launched his career as a labor organizer with the International Longshoremen's and Warehousemen's Union in Los Angeles (see American Lives, pages 788–789). Labor activism was not limited to men. Mexican-American women made up 75 percent of the dressmakers who toiled in Los Angeles's sweatshops, many for less than $5 a week. In 1933 Rose Pesotta, a Polish immigrant labor organizer for the International Ladies' Garment Workers Union (ILGWU), used bilingual appeals to lead a four-week strike of the garment workers in which Mexican-American women were the most active participants.

Migrant Labor in California
Mexican-American workers had faced deportation in the early years of the depression, but their cheap agricultural labor was too essential to growers to make the exile permanent. Here a Chicano worker hauls peppers.

Mexican-American Poverty in Texas
In 1937 Antonia and Pablo Martinez lived in a one-room house in San Antonio, Texas, with his parents and older brother. If either Pablo or Antonia was employed in 1937, it was probably in San Antonio's pecan-shelling industry, which depended heavily on the cheap labor of Mexican-Americans.

In California, Mexican-Americans also found employment in fruit and vegetable processing plants, especially young single women who preferred the higher wages of cannery work to domestic service, needlework, and farm labor. Corporate giants such as Del Monte (California Packing Corporation, or Cal Pak) and Libby, McNeill, and Libby dominated California's food-processing industry. In those plants Mexican-American women earned around $2.50 a day, while their male counterparts earned $3.50 to $4.50. So pervasive was the "cannery culture" that workers could say, "We met in spinach, fell in love in peaches, and married in tomatoes," and their friends would know they were referring to the harvests of March, August, and October. In 1939 labor unions came to the canneries in the form of the United Cannery, Agricultural, Packing, and Allied Workers of America (UCAPAWA), an unusually democratic union in which women, who formed a majority of the rank-and-file workers, played a leading role.

This activism of the 1930s, in the fields and in the factories, demonstrated how the second generation of Mexican immigrants, born in the United States, increasing turned its orientation toward issues of political and economic justice in the United States, rather than retaining primary allegiance to Mexico. According to historian George Sanchez, they were creating "their own version of Americanism without abandoning Mexican culture." Joining American labor unions and becoming more involved in American politics were important steps in creating a Mexican-American ethnic identity.

Herbert Hoover and the Great Depression

During the presidential campaign of 1928 Herbert Hoover predicted that "the poorhouse is vanishing from among us" and stated that America was "nearer to the final triumph over poverty than ever before in the history of any land." Once elected, Hoover planned to preside over an era of Republican prosperity and governmental restraint. Even after the stock market crash in 1929, he stubbornly insisted that the downturn was only temporary. He greeted a business delegation in June 1930 with these words: "Gentlemen, you have come sixty days too late. The Depression is over." In 1931 and 1932, as the country hit rock bottom, Hoover finally acted, but by then it was too little, too late.

The Republican Response

In 1932 the journalist William Allen White wrote an article about the outgoing president entitled "Herbert Hoover—The Last of the Old Presidents, or the First of the New?" White concluded that Hoover had been a little of both, as have historians ever since. Hoover's early efforts to fight the depression are now seen as predecessors of many New Deal programs, and his reputation among historians has risen steadily over the years. Hoover, who lived until 1964, offered a simple explanation for the improvement in his historical stature, telling Chief Justice Earl Warren of the Supreme Court that he had simply managed "to outlive the bastards."

Hoover's approach to the Great Depression was shaped by his priorities as secretary of commerce: he turned to the business community for leadership in overcoming the economic downturn. Hoover asked business to maintain wages voluntarily, keep up production, and work with the government to build confidence in the system.

Fiscal Policy. Hoover did not rely solely on public pronouncements, but also used public funds and federal action to encourage recovery. Soon after the stock market crash he cut federal taxes and called on state and local governments to increase capital spending in the "energetic yet prudent pursuit" of public construction. The 1929 Agricultural Marketing Act gave the federal government its largest role to date in a program of agricultural stabilization and farm relief. In 1930 and the first half of 1931 Hoover raised the federal public-works budget to $423 million, a dramatic increase in an area not traditionally seen as the federal government's responsibility. Hoover also eased the international crisis by declaring, early in the summer of 1931, a moratorium on the payment of Allied debts and reparations.

Bert Corona and the Mexican-American Generation

Bert Corona always considered himself a child of the revolution—the Mexican Revolution. His father, Noe Corona, had crossed the border from Mexico to the United States around 1915 or 1916, seeking safety after being wounded while fighting in Pancho Villa's army. Settling temporarily in El Paso, he married Margarita Escápite Salayandia, and they had four children, including Humberto (his Anglo teachers later Americanized his name to Bert), who was born in 1918.

The border is an apt metaphor for Mexican-American life, capturing the fluidity of crossing back and forth between two countries and two cultures. Bert's family returned to Mexico in 1922, where two years later Noe Corona was assassinated by unknown assailants, presumably political enemies. This loss had a profound effect on Noe's six-year-old son: "The Revolution, my father's role in it, and his martyrdom symbolized the struggle for social justice. This would be the same struggle I would later pursue."

The Corona family resettled in El Paso, where Bert's mother secured a job at the Mexican customs house on the El Paso–Ciudad Juarez border and his grandmother, a doctor, pursued her practice of medicine and midwifery. Being raised by these two women provided Bert with strong female role models. The El Paso school system provided a searing introduction to the discrimination against and unequal treatment of Mexican immigrants in the Southwest. Corona's segregated "Mexican" school in the barrio, geared primarily toward vocational education, was far inferior to white schools. Although he attended an integrated high school with a good academic reputation, racism and discrimination remained very much part of his education, both in daily encounters with his Anglo teachers and classmates and in the general lack of respect for Mexican history and culture in the curriculum. His grandmother said tartly, "Well, you have to understand that the United States writes its history to its own convenience. It always has, and these people always will."

When Bert graduated from high school in 1934 at age sixteen, it was the height of the Great Depression, and El Paso was hard hit. Fortunately, his mother kept her job at the Juarez customs house, but hard times forced many Mexicans to leave. El Paso was a major border crossing for *los repatriados* as they fled the depression and the threat of deportation, but Mexicans were not the only group on the move. The Corona backyard faced the train tracks, and Bert vividly remembered the thousands of Dust Bowl migrants traveling through El Paso on their way west. A hundred-car freight train could carry a thousand Dust Bowlers, and there were three trains in the morning and three in the evening: "It was like the population of a small town coming in every day."

After working for two years in El Paso, Bert headed to the University of Southern California, where he hoped to play basketball and continue his education on an athletic scholarship. But an injury cut short his sports career, and he soon found new interests that took him away from his studies, although he later regretted not getting a college degree. What could possibly have taken precedence over his family's strong belief in education? Participating in the revitalized labor movement and fostering Mexican-American political consciousness, the two causes that shaped the rest of Corona's life.

The Congress of Industrial Organization, or CIO (see Chapter 26), became his vehicle for labor activism: "I had a sense of the historical importance of the CIO, and I viewed the CIO as a movement whose time had come. Nothing could stop it, and—for a time—nothing did." In the 1930s many labor activists focused on organizing Mexican-American migrant workers in the fields, but Corona concentrated on recruiting Los Angeles industrial workers into the newly constituted International Longshoremen's and Warehousemen's Union (ILWU). His organizing was not restricted to Mexican workers, however. Like the CIO, he wanted the entire

Bert Corona addresses a press conference at the National Chicano Political Caucus in 1972.

working class to join unions to work for social change in the workplace and in society as a whole. While organizing at an aviation plant in 1941 he met his future wife, Blanche Taff. The daughter of Polish Jewish immigrants, she shared his commitment to progressive social change. Their marriage fit right into the interracial and interethnic culture of the CIO. So great was their commitment to organized labor that they gave up their honeymoon to participate in a major CIO organizing drive.

In addition to labor organizing, Bert Corona felt a deep commitment to the political mobilization of Spanish-speaking peoples throughout the United States. In 1939 he joined El Congreso Nacional del Pueblo de Habla Español (the National Congress of Spanish-Speaking Peoples), a militant organization founded to fight for the rights of Mexican-Americans and other Latinos as part of the larger struggle against racial and class oppression. There he worked with noted activists such as Luisa Moreno, a Guatemalan-born CIO organizer who had been active in the cannery industry, and

Josefina Fierro, a radical young Mexican-American married to the screenwriter John Bright, who was part of Hollywood's leftist community. Their activist agenda was far to the left of organizations such as the League of United Latin American Citizens (LULAC), founded in 1929, which focused on discrimination and civil rights from a distinctly middle-class perspective.

After serving in the armed forces during World War II, Corona continued to be a labor and community activist. In the 1960s he became involved in the Mexican-American Political Association, or MAPA (see Chapter 30), which mobilized Latino political power to force the Kennedy and Johnson administrations to do more for those constituencies. Since then he has been involved in community organizing, especially of undocumented Mexican workers entering the United States.

Bert Corona exemplifies what the historian Mario Garcia has called the "Mexican-American Generation." These men and women, who were born and raised in the United States, came of political age between the 1930s and the 1950s. They filled the leadership vacuum created when *los repatriados*, mainly older and Mexican-born, returned permanently to that country in the 1930s. Even before terms such as *Mexican-American*, *Hispanic*, and *Latino* were widely used, this generation had the "double consciousness" that W. E. B. DuBois described in African-Americans: a sense of being both *mexicanos* and American citizens. Many members of the Mexican-American Generation shared Corona's commitment to organizing for social change—in their communities, on the job, and in the wider political arena. Tracing their political activism over the years provides a window on the changing character of Mexican-American communities in the United States.

Since the 1930s Bert Corona has seen a dramatic expansion of Latino empowerment, but he remains modest about his role in this story. "It's hard for me to think how I would like to be remembered by history," he told Mario Garcia as they collaborated on a book about his life. "I never planned my life. It just happened the way it did. . . . If my life has meant anything, I would say that it shows that you can organize workers and poor people if you work hard, are persistent, remain optimistic, and reach out to involve as many people as possible. . . . But my life is not over yet, and I continue *la lucha*, the struggle." For Bert Corona that commitment to *la lucha* had its roots in his Mexican heritage, but it first began to flower during the turbulent 1930s.

The federal government's efforts to stimulate business activity were moderately effective, but the depression continued.

By 1931 more drastic action was required, but Hoover faced a cruel dilemma that had been created by the Federal Reserve's contraction of the money supply. If he embraced deficit financing and encouraged recovery through increased government spending, interest rates would remain high, since the federal government would be competing for borrowed capital with corporations and private investors. Hoover decided that significantly higher interest rates posed the greater danger to recovery, so in December 1931 he asked Congress for a 33 percent tax increase to balance the budget. The Revenue Act of 1932 represented the largest peacetime tax increase in the nation's history. Like monetary restriction, higher taxes choked both consumption and investment and contributed significantly to the severity of the Great Depression.

Not all the steps taken by the Hoover administration were so ill conceived. The president pushed Congress to create a system of government home-loan banks in 1932. He also supported the Glass-Steagall Banking Act of 1932, which made government securities available to guarantee Federal Reserve notes and thus counter credit contractions caused by withdrawals of gold. This step temporarily propped up the ailing banking system. The federal government under Hoover also spent $700 million—an unprecedented sum for the time—on public works.

However, Hoover remained adamant in his refusal to consider any plan for direct federal relief for unemployed Americans. Throughout his career he had believed that private organized charities were sufficient to meet social welfare needs. During World War I Hoover had headed the Commission for Relief of Belgium, a private group that distributed 5 million tons of food to relieve the suffering of Europe's civilian population. In 1927 he coordinated a rescue and cleanup operation after a devastating Mississippi River flood left 16.5 million acres of land under water in seven states. This effort involved private charities, including the Red Cross and the Rockefeller Foundation, as well as government agencies such as the U.S. Public Health Service and the National Guard. The success of these and other predominantly voluntary responses to public emergencies confirmed Hoover's belief that private charity, not federal aid, was the "American way." But charities and state and local relief agencies were unable to meet the growing needs of the unemployed.

The Reconstruction Finance Corporation. The centerpiece of Hoover's new initiative to combat the depression was the Reconstruction Finance Corporation (RFC), which Congress approved in January 1932. Modeled on the War Finance Corporation of World War I and developed in collaboration with the business and banking communities, the RFC was the first federal institution created to intervene directly in the economy during peacetime. It was designed to alleviate the credit crunch for business by providing federal loans to railroads, financial institutions, banks, and insurance companies in a strategy that has been called *pump priming.* Money lent at the top of the economic structure stimulates production, which in turn creates new jobs and increases consumer spending. Benefits thus "trickle down" to the rest of the economy.

Congress allocated $500 million for the RFC, but the agency's cautiousness in lending money limited its influence. In July 1932 Congress doubled that amount and authorized loans to the states for relief and public works. Once again the RFC acted far too cautiously, lending only $30 million by the end of 1932. It allocated and spent only 20 percent of the $1.5 billion appropriated for public works projects.

The RFC was a watershed in American political history and the rise of the state. When voluntary cooperation failed, the president turned to federal action to stimulate the economy. Yet Hoover's break with the past had clear limits. In many ways his support of the RFC was just another attempt to encourage business confidence. Compared with previous presidents, Hoover responded to the national emergency on an unprecedented scale. But the nation's needs during the Great Depression were also unprecedented, and federal programs failed to meet them.

Rising Discontent

As the depression deepened, many citizens came to hate Herbert Hoover. Once the symbol of business prosperity, he became the scapegoat for the depression. His declarations that nobody was starving and that hoboes were better fed than ever before seemed cruel and insensitive. His apparent willingness to bail out business and banks while leaving individuals to fend for themselves added to his reputation for coldheartedness (see American Voices, page 791). New terms entered the vocabulary: *Hoovervilles* (shantytowns where people lived in packing crates and other makeshift shelters), *Hoover flags* (empty pockets turned inside out), and *Hoover blankets* (newspapers). The columnist Russell Baker remembered his aunt's exaggerated recital of Hoover's offenses:

> People were starving because of Herbert Hoover. My mother was out of work because of Herbert Hoover. Men were killing themselves because of Herbert Hoover, and their fatherless children were being packed away to orphanages . . . because of Herbert Hoover.

Signs of rising discontent and rebellion began to emerge

The Despair of the Unemployed

In 1931 an unemployed tool and dye designer wrote to the director of the President's Organization for Unemployment Relief (POUR), but his letter drew only this penciled response: "no use answering."

Detroit, Mich.
September 29, 1931

Mr. Walter Gifford
Dear Sir:

You and Pres. Hoover shows at times about the same degree of intelligence as Andy [of the "Amos & Andy" radio show] does. The other night Andy was going to send a fellow a letter to find out his address.

You have told us to spend to end the slump, but you did not tell us what to use for money, after being out of work for two years you tell us this, Pres. Hoover on the other hand tells the working man to build homes, and in face of the fact nearly every working man has had his home taken off him, "some more intelligence." This is a radical letter but the time is here to be radical. when an average of two a day has to take their own life right in the City of Detroit because they can not see their way out. right in the city where one of the worlds riches men lives who made last year 259 000 000 dollars. where hundreds of peoples are starving to death. . . . Mr. Gifford why not come clean . . . remember you have the all seeing eye of God over you. Tell us the reason of the depression is the greed of Bankers and Industrialist who are taking too great of amount of profits . . . . The other day our Pres. Hoover came to Detroit and kidded the soldier boys out of their bonus. Pres Hoover a millionaire worth about 12 000 000 dollars drawing a salary of 75 000 per year from the government asking some boys to forgo their bonus some of them have not 12 dollars of their own "Some more nerve."

Am I right when I say you and he shows the same degree of intelligence as Andy.

J. B.

Source: Quoted in Robert S. McElvaine, *Down & Out in the Great Depression* (Chapel Hill: University of North Carolina Press, 1983), 46–47.

as the country entered the fourth year of the depression. Farmers were among the most vocal groups, banding together to harass the bank agents and government officers who enforced evictions and farm foreclosures and to protest the low prices they received for their crops. Midwestern farmers had watched the price of wheat fall from $3 a bushel in 1920 to barely 30 cents in 1932. Now they formed the Farm Holiday Association under the charismatic leadership of Milo Reno, the sixty-four-year-old former president of the Iowa Farmers' Union. Farmers barricaded local roads and dumped milk, vegetables, and other farm produce because the prices they would fetch on the market would not cover the farmers' costs. Nothing better captured the cruel irony of underconsumption and maldistribution than farmers dumping food at a time when thousands of people were hungry.

Hoovervilles

By 1930 shantytowns had sprung up in most of the nation's cities. In New York City squatters camped out along the Hudson River railroad tracks, built makeshift homes in Central Park, or lived in the city dump. This scene from the old reservoir in Central Park looks east toward the fancy apartment buildings of Fifth Avenue and the Metropolitan Museum of Art, at left.

Protest was not confined to rural America. Bitter labor strikes occurred in the depths of the depression despite the threat that strikers would lose their jobs. In Harlan County, Kentucky, miners struck in 1931 over a 10 percent wage cut, only to see their union crushed by the mine owners and the National Guard. At Ford's River Rouge factory outside Detroit in 1932 a demonstration provoked violence from police and Ford security forces; three demonstrators were killed, and fifty were seriously injured. Some 40,000 people viewed the coffins under a banner charging that "Ford Gave Bullets for Bread."

In 1931 and 1932 violence broke out in the nation's cities. Groups of unemployed citizens battled local authorities over inadequate relief; people staged rent riots and hunger marches. Fearing the consequences of trying to stop this civil disorder, Mayor Anton J. Cermak of Chicago challenged a Congressional committee to send relief or troops.

Some of these urban actions were organized by the Communist party as a challenge to the American capitalist system. For example, the Communist party helped organize "unemployment councils" that agitated for jobs and food and coordinated a hunger march on Washington, D.C., in 1931. The marches were well attended and often got results from local and federal authorities, but they did not necessarily win converts to communism. In the early 1930s the Communist party was still a tiny organization with only 12,000 members.

It was not radicals but veterans who staged the most publicized—and tragic—protest. In the summer of 1932 the "Bonus Army," a ragtag group of about 15,000 unemployed World War I veterans, hitchhiked to Washing-

ton to demand that their bonuses, originally scheduled for distribution in 1945, be paid immediately. While they unsuccessfully lobbied Congress, members of the "Bonus Expeditionary Force" (parodying the wartime American Expeditionary Force) camped out in the capital, a visible reminder of the plight of the unemployed. "We were heroes in 1917, but we're bums now," one veteran remarked bitterly. When the marchers refused to leave their Anacostia Flats camp, Hoover called out riot troops led by General Douglas MacArthur, assisted by Majors Dwight D. Eisenhower and George S. Patton, to clear the area. MacArthur's forces burned the encampment to the ground, and in the fight that followed more than a hundred marchers were injured. Newsreel footage captured the deeply disturbing spectacle of the U.S. Army firing on American citizens, and Hoover's popularity plunged even further.

The 1932 Election

Despite evidence of discontent, the nation was not in a revolutionary mood as it approached the 1932 election. Despair and apathy, not anger, characterized the feelings of most citizens. The Republicans, who could find no credible way to dump an incumbent president, unenthusiastically renominated Hoover. The Democrats turned to Governor Franklin Delano Roosevelt of New York, who capitalized on that state's innovative relief and unemployment programs to win the nomination.

Roosevelt's route to the presidential nomination began on a Hudson River estate north of New York City. Born into a wealthy family in 1882, he attended the Groton School, Harvard, and Columbia Law School. Roosevelt gave up his law career in 1910 for a seat in New York's state legislature. He served as assistant secretary of the navy in the Wilson administration, and that earned him the vice-presidential nomination on the losing Democratic ticket in 1920. Except for his allegiance to Democratic rather than Republican party ideology, he consciously modeled his career on that of his distant cousin Theodore Roosevelt, whose niece Eleanor he married in 1905.

Franklin Roosevelt was sidetracked from his path to the White House in 1921 by an attack of polio that left both his legs paralyzed for the rest of his life. Roosevelt fought back from his infirmity, emerging from the ordeal a stronger, more resilient man. "If you had spent two years in bed trying to wiggle your toe, after that anything would seem easy," he said. Eleanor Roosevelt strongly supported her husband's return to public life, serving as his stand-in during the 1920s. She and Louis Howe, Roosevelt's devoted political aide, masterminded his reentry into Democratic politics. Roosevelt won the New York governorship in 1928 and the Democratic presidential nomination in 1932.

The Bonus Army
These children were camped out in the summer of 1932 on the Anacostia Flats of Washington, D.C., while their fathers lobbied Congress for early payment of World War I bonuses. Congress said no, and the U.S. Army violently disbanded the veterans' encampment.

The 1932 campaign foreshadowed little of the New Deal. Roosevelt hinted at new approaches to the depression but stated his goals in vague terms: "The country needs and, unless I mistake its temper, the country demands bold, persistent experimentation." Roosevelt won easily, receiving 22.8 million votes to Hoover's 15.7 million. Despite the economic collapse, Americans remained firmly committed to the two-party system. The Socialist party candidate, Norman Thomas, got fewer than a million votes. The Communist party drew only 100,000 votes for its candidate, party leader William Z. Foster (see Map 25.3).

The 1932 election marked a turning point in American politics: the emergence of a Democratic coalition that would dominate political life for the next four decades. In 1932 Roosevelt won with the support of the Solid South, which returned to the Democratic fold after defecting in 1928 because of Al Smith's religion and views on Prohibition. Roosevelt also drew substantial support in the West. An increasingly large urban vote continued a trend that was first noticed in the 1928 election, when the Democrats successfully appealed to recent immigrants and ethnic groups in the cities. However, Roosevelt's election was hardly a mandate to reshape American political and economic institutions. Many people voted as much against Hoover as for Roosevelt.

The Interregnum. Having spoken, the voters had to wait until March 1933 before Roosevelt could put his ideas into action. (The interval between election and inauguration was shortened so that it ended on January 20 by the Twentieth Amendment in 1933.) In the worst winter of the depression Americans could do little but hope that things would get better. According to the most conservative estimates, unemployment stood at 20 to 25 percent. The rate was as high as 50 percent in Cleveland, 60 percent in Akron, and 80 percent in Toledo—cities dependent on manufacturing jobs in industries that had basically shut down. The nation's banking system was so close to collapse that many state governors temporarily closed banks to avoid further panic.

By the winter of 1932–1933 the depression had totally overwhelmed public welfare institutions. Private charity and local public relief, whose expenditures had risen dramatically, still reached only a fraction of the needy. Hunger haunted cities and rural areas alike. When a teacher tried to send a coal miner's daughter home from school because she was weak from hunger, the girl replied, "It won't do any good . . . because this is sister's day to eat." In New York City, hospitals reported ninety-five deaths from starvation. This was the America that Roosevelt inherited when he took the oath of office on March 4, 1933.

MAP 25.3

The Election of 1932

Franklin Roosevelt's convincing electoral victory over Herbert Hoover in 1932 resulted from a political realignment and dissatisfaction with the incumbent president. Even in the midst of the gravest crisis capitalism had ever faced, candidates of the Communist and Socialist parties received fewer than 1 million votes out of almost 40 million cast.

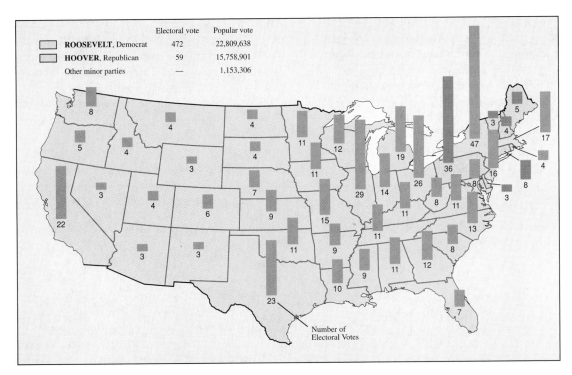

	Electoral vote	Popular vote
ROOSEVELT, Democrat	472	22,809,638
HOOVER, Republican	59	15,758,901
Other minor parties	—	1,153,306

Number of Electoral Votes

Summary

The economic prosperity of the 1920s rested on shaky ground. After the stock market crash of 1929 the economy entered a downward spiral that did not bottom out until 1932–1933. In addition to the collapse of the stock market, the main causes of the depression were underconsumption, an unstable international financial situation, a legacy of "sick industries" and agricultural distress from the 1920s, and the flawed monetary policies of the Federal Reserve System. At first Hoover did not want to intervene in the economy because of his reliance on private charities and his adamant stance on maintaining a balanced budget. Then in 1932 the Hoover administration authorized the first direct federal intervention in the economy during peacetime, the Reconstruction Finance Corporation, to win business and public confidence. Though unprecedented, such measures did not end the Great Depression.

The Great Depression left an "invisible scar" on many people who lived through the 1930s, especially white middle-class Americans. Those who wanted to work blamed themselves if they could not find a job. The impact of the depression was especially catastrophic for African-Americans, Mexican-Americans, and other minorities, for whom times had always been hard. And for farmers in the Midwest things got even worse than they had been in the 1920s. Misguided agricultural practices and drought created the Dust Bowl, forcing many farmers off their land.

Despite the devastating impact of the depression, many aspects of American life and culture continued to conform to traditional patterns. Families pulled together, with women taking on expanded roles—and often new jobs—to help support their households. Young people stayed in school longer. Families sought relief in popular culture, especially movies and radio programs. In 1932 the nation turned to Franklin D. Roosevelt and the Democrats.

TIMELINE

1929	Stock market crash Agricultural Marketing Act
1930	Midwestern drought begins Hawley-Smoot Tariff
1931	Scottsboro case Great Britain abandons gold standard Hoover declares moratorium on Allied war debts Miners strike in Harlan County, Kentucky
1932	Reconstruction Finance Corporation Bonus Army Lindbergh kidnapping Revenue Act of 1933 Height of deportation of Mexican migrant workers Farm Holiday Association founded Strike at Ford's River Rouge plant in Michigan Communist-led hunger marches
1933	Unemployment rises to highest level Franklin Delano Roosevelt becomes president Birth rate drops to lowest level
1934	Southern Tenant Farmers Union founded *It Happened One Night* sweeps Oscars
1935	National Youth Administration Harlem race riot
1936	Student Strike against War Margaret Mitchell's *Gone with the Wind* Jesse Owens wins four gold medals at Berlin Olympics Birth control legalized
1937	*Hindenburg* crash Amelia Earhart disappears
1939	John Steinbeck's *Grapes of Wrath*

BIBLIOGRAPHY

Useful overviews of the Great Depression are T. H. Watkins, *The Great Depression: America in the 1930s* (1993); John A. Garraty, *The Great Depression* (1987); and Robert S. McElvaine, *The Great Depression, 1929–1941* (1984).

The Coming of the Great Depression

Historians and economists continue to debate the causes of the Great Depression. See John Kenneth Galbraith, *The Great Crash* (1954); Milton Friedman and Anna Schwartz, *The Great Contraction, 1929–1933* (1965); Charles Kindelberger, *The World in Depression* (1974); Peter Temin, *Did Monetary Forces Cause the Great Depression?* (1976); and Michael Bernstein, *The Great Depression: Delayed Recovery and Economic Change in America, 1929–1939* (1988). Irving Bernstein, *The Lean Years* (1960), offers a compelling portrait of hard times during the Hoover years.

Hard Times

A wealth of material brings the voices of the 1930s to life. The Federal Writers' Project, *These Are Our Lives* (1939); Tom Terrill and Jerrold Hirsch, eds., *Such as Us: Southern Voices of the Thirties* (1978); and Ann Banks, ed., *First-Person America* (1980), all draw on oral histories collected by the Works Progress Administration during the 1930s. See also Richard Lowitt and Maurine Beasley, eds., *One-Third of a Nation: Lorena Hickock Reports the Great Depression* (1981), and Robert S. McElvaine, ed., *Down & Out in the Great Depression* (1983), for firsthand accounts. Evocative secondary sources include Studs Terkel, *Hard Times: An Oral History of the Great Depression* (1970), and Caroline Bird, *The Invisible Scar* (1966).

Descriptions of family life in the 1930s include Robert and Helen Lynd, *Middletown in Transition* (1937); Mirra Komarovsky, *The Unemployed Man and His Family* (1940); and Roger Angell, *The Family Encounters the Depression* (1936). Russell Baker's autobiography, *Growing Up* (1982), provides an often humorous description of family life in the 1930s. Glen H. Elder, Jr., *Children of the Great Depression* (1974), and John A. Clausen, *American Lives: Looking Back at the Children of the Great Depression* (1993), look at the long-term effects. For more on youth, see Maxine Davis, *The Lost Generation* (1936); Eileen Eagan, *Class, Culture, and the Classroom* (1981); Beth L. Bailey, *From Front Porch to Back Seat* (1988); and John Modell, *Into One's Own: From Youth to Adulthood, 1920–1975* (1989).

Frederick Lewis Allen, *Since Yesterday* (1939), provides an impressionistic overview of popular culture in the 1930s. Specific studies of movies and Hollywood include Robert Sklar, *Movie-Made America* (2d ed., 1987); Andrew Bergman, *We're in the Money* (1971); Molly Haskell, *From Reverence to Rape: The Treatment of Women in the Movies* (2d ed., 1987); and Thomas Schatz, *The Genius of the System: Hollywood Film Making in the Studio Era* (1988).

Material on women in the 1930s can be found in Susan Ware, *Holding Their Own* (1982); Winifred Wandersee, *Women's Work and Family Values, 1920–1940* (1981); and Lois Scharf, *To Work and to Wed* (1981). For the special dimensions of white rural women's lives, see Margaret Hagood, *Mothers of the South* (1939). Jeane Westin, *Making Do: How Women Survived the '30s* (1976), is a lively account drawn from interviews. The birth control movement is surveyed in Linda Gordon, *Woman's Body, Woman's Right* (2d ed., 1990); James Reed, *From Private Vice to Public Virtue* (1978); Estelle Freedman and John D'Emilio, *Intimate Matters: A History of Sexuality in America* (1988); and Ellen Chesler, *Woman of Valor: Margaret Sanger and the Birth Control Movement in America* (1992).

The Social Fabric of Depression America

Developments in the black community during the 1930s are covered in Cheryl Lyn Greenberg, *"Or Does It Explode?": Harlem in the Great Depression* (1991); Gilbert Osofsky, *Harlem: The Making of a Ghetto* (1966); Gunnar Myrdal, *An American Dilemma* (1944); David Lewis, *When Harlem Was in Vogue* (1981); Jervis Anderson, *This Was Harlem, 1900–1950* (1982); and Robert Weisbrot, *Father Divine and the Struggle for Racial Equality* (1983). James Goodman, *Stories of Scottsboro* (1994), and Dan T. Carter, *Scottsboro* (1969), cover that case. Donald Grubbs, *Cry from Cotton* (1971), tells the story of the Southern Tenant Farmers Union. Robin D. G. Kelley, *Hammer and Hoe* (1990), is an excellent account of Alabama communists during the Great Depression. Donald Worster, *Dust Bowl* (1979), evokes the plains during the "Dirty Thirties," as does Ann Marie Low's memoir, *Dust Bowl Diary* (1984). James N. Gregory, *American Exodus: The Dust Bowl Migration and Okie Culture in California* (1989), treats the experiences of migrants and their impact on California culture and the economy.

On the experiences of Mexican-Americans during the 1930s, see Mario T. Garcia, *Mexican Americans: Leadership, Ideology, and Identity, 1930–1960* (1989) and *Memories of Chicano History: The Life and Narrative of Bert Corona* (1994). George J. Sanchez, *Becoming Mexican American* (1993), examines Chicano Los Angeles from 1900 to 1945. See also Carey McWilliams, *North from Mexico: The Spanish-Speaking People of the United States* (1948), and Richard A. Garcia, *The Rise of the Mexican-American Middle Class* (1990). For Mexican-American women's lives, see Vicki Ruiz, *Cannery Women, Cannery Lives: Mexican Women, Unionization, and the California Food Processing Industry, 1930–1950* (1987), and Patricia Zavella, *Women's Work and Chicano Families* (1987).

Herbert Hoover and the Great Depression

Hoover's response to the depression is chronicled in Alfred Romasco, *The Poverty of Abundance* (1965), and Jordan Schwartz, *The Interregnum of Despair* (1970). See also David Burner, *Herbert Hoover* (1978); Joan Hoff Wilson, *Herbert Hoover: Forgotten Progressive* (1975); and William Barber, *Herbert Hoover, the Economists, and American Economic Policy, 1921–1933* (1986). Eliot Rosen, *Hoover, Roosevelt, and the Brain Trust* (1977), treats the transition between the two administrations, as does Frank Freidel, *Launching the New Deal* (1973). On the 1932 election and the beginnings of the New Deal coalition, see David Burner, *The Politics of Provincialism* (1967); Samuel Lubell, *The Future of American Politics* (1952); and John Allswang, *The New Deal in American Politics* (1978).

New Deal Art

This 1937 poster designed by Lester Beall for the Rural Electrification Administration celebrated the power of radio, one of the most potent cultural forces of the 1930s.

The New Deal
1933–1939

★   ★   ★

In his bold inaugural address on March 4, 1933, President Franklin Delano Roosevelt declared, "The only thing we have to fear is fear itself." That memorable phrase rallied a nation that had already endured almost four years of the worst economic contraction in its history, with no end in sight.

With his demeanor grim and purposeful, Roosevelt preached his first inaugural address like a sermon. He spoke of the economic and social problems that the nation faced and their possible solutions only in the most general terms. Promising "a leadership of frankness and vigor," Roosevelt issued ringing declarations of his vision of governmental activism: "This Nation asks for action, and action now." Roosevelt repeatedly compared combating the depression to fighting a war. The most explicit parallel was his willingness to ask Congress for "broad Executive power to wage a war against the emergency, as great as the power that would be given to me if we were in fact invaded by a foreign foe." This conception of presidential leadership was well suited to Roosevelt's self-confident personality and pragmatic political style.

In the end, however, Roosevelt intended not to scare the American people but to reassure them. The democratic system was basically sound, he told them, and hard times could be overcome, but only if a dispirited nation chose not to wallow in lethargy. On that cold March day in 1933 Roosevelt urged his fellow citizens to return to the values of hard work, cooperation, and sacrifice that had made the country great. Roosevelt's restoration of hope and confidence was perhaps his greatest contribution to American life during the Great Depression.

The New Deal Takes Over, 1933–1935

When Roosevelt first used the term *New Deal* in his acceptance speech at the Democratic National Convention in 1932, he did not realize that he had named his era. Plucked from deep in the speech by the newspaper cartoonist Rollin Kirby, the term came to stand for the Roosevelt administration's response to the depression. The federal government dominated political and economic life so thoroughly during the 1930s that the term *New Deal* is often used as a synonym for that decade.

The Roosevelt Style of Leadership

Every president since the 1930s has lived in the shadow of FDR. Few of his successors have matched his raw political talent; none have had to face and surmount the twin crises of depression and war. "I have no expectation of making a hit every time I come to bat," Roosevelt disarmingly told his critics. "What I seek is the highest possible batting average." Roosevelt parlayed

FDR
President Franklin Delano Roosevelt was a consummate politician who loved the adulation of a crowd. He consciously adopted a cheerful mien to keep people from feeling sorry for him because of his infirmity, knowing that he could not be a successful politician if the public pitied him.

that experimental tone into a highly effective political and governmental style.

The New Deal represented many things to many people, but one unifying factor was the personality of its master architect, Franklin Delano Roosevelt. The New Deal was "a very personal enterprise." Roosevelt, a superb and pragmatic politician, crafted his administration's program in response to shifting political and economic conditions instead of following a set ideology or plan. He experimented with an idea, and if it did not work, he tried another. Roosevelt juggled advice in the same way. Senator Huey Long of Louisiana complained, "When I talk to him, he says 'Fine! Fine! Fine!' But Joe Robinson [the Senate majority leader] goes to see him the next day and again he says 'Fine! Fine! Fine!' Maybe he says 'Fine!' to everybody."

President Roosevelt established an unusually close rapport with the American people. "Mr. Roosevelt is the only man we ever had in the White House who would understand that my boss is a son of a bitch," remarked one worker. Many ordinary citizens credited him with the positive changes in their lives, saying, "He gave me a job" or "He saved my home." Roosevelt's masterful use of the new medium of radio, typified by the sixteen "fireside chats" he broadcast during his first two terms, fostered this personal identification. More than 450,000 letters poured into the White House in the week after the inauguration, and an average of 5,000 to 8,000 arrived weekly for the rest of the decade. One person had handled public correspondence during the Hoover administration, but it took a staff of fifty under Roosevelt. Roosevelt also became the first president to hire a press secretary.

Franklin Roosevelt continued the expansion of presidential power begun in the administrations of Theodore Roosevelt and Woodrow Wilson. From the beginning Roosevelt centralized decision making in the White House and dramatically expanded the role of the executive branch in initiating policy. For policy formulation he turned to his talented cabinet, which included Interior Secretary Harold Ickes, Frances Perkins at Labor, Henry A. Wallace at Agriculture, and an old friend, Henry Morgenthau, Jr., as secretary of the treasury. During the interregnum he relied so heavily on the advice of the Columbia University professors Raymond Moley, Rexford Tugwell, and Adolph A. Berle, Jr., that the press dubbed them the "Brains Trust."

When searching for new ideas and fresh faces, Roosevelt was just as likely to turn to advisers and administrators scattered throughout the New Deal bureaucracy. Eager young people flocked to Washington to join the New Deal—"men with long hair and women with short hair," wags quipped. Lawyers in their mid-twenties fresh out of Harvard found themselves drafting legislation or being called to the White House for strategy sessions with the president. Paul Freund, a Harvard Law

School professor who worked in the Reconstruction Finance Corporation and the Department of Justice, remembered, "It was a glorious time for obscure people." Many young New Dealers who went on to distinguished careers in government or public service later recalled that nothing could match the excitement of the early New Deal.

The Hundred Days

The first problem that the new president confronted was the banking crisis. Since the stock market crash about 9 million people had lost their savings, a total of $2.5 billion. On the eve of his inauguration thirty-eight states had closed their banks, and banks operated on a restricted basis in the rest. The collapse of the banking system, far more than the stock market crash, brought the depression home to the middle class.

On March 5, the day after his inauguration, the president declared a national "bank holiday" (a euphemism for closing all the banks) and called Congress into special session. On March 9 Congress passed Roosevelt's proposed emergency banking bill, which permitted banks to reopen beginning on March 13, but only if a Treasury Department inspection showed that they had sufficient cash reserves. The House approved the plan after only thirty-eight minutes of debate.

Emergency Banking Act. The Emergency Banking Act, which Roosevelt developed in consultation with banking leaders, was a conservative document that could have been proposed by Herbert Hoover. The difference was the public's reaction. On the Sunday evening before the banks reopened Roosevelt made his first "fireside chat" to a radio audience estimated at 60 million. In

The CCC

The Civilian Conservation Corps (CCC) was one of the most popular New Deal programs. Over ten years, it enrolled 2.75 million young Americans who worked for $1 a day on projects such as soil conservation, disaster relief, reforestation, and flood control. The CCC was limited to men, although a few camps employed out-of-work young women.

simple terms he reassured the people that the banks were now safe, and Americans believed him. When the banks reopened on Monday morning, deposits exceeded withdrawals. "Capitalism was saved in eight days," observed Raymond Moley, who had served as Roosevelt's speechwriter in the 1932 campaign. The banking bill did its job: more than 4,000 banks failed in 1933 (the vast majority in the months before the law took effect), but only 61 closed their doors in 1934 (see Table 26.1).

The Banking Act was the first of fifteen pieces of major legislation enacted by Congress in the opening months of the Roosevelt administration. This legislative session, which came to be called the "Hundred Days," remains one of the most productive ever. Congress created the Home Owners Loan Corporation to refinance home mortgages threatened by foreclosure; fully 20 percent of the nation's homeowners took advantage of it. A second banking law, the Glass-Steagall Act, curbed speculation by separating investment banking from commercial banking. The Glass-Steagall Act also created the Federal Deposit Insurance Corporation (FDIC), which insured bank deposits up to $2,500. The Civilian Conservation Corps (CCC) sent 250,000 young men to live in camps where they did reforestation and conservation work. The Tennessee Valley Authority (TVA) received legislative approval for its innovative plan of govern-

TABLE 26.1

American Banks and Bank Failures, 1920–1940

Year	Total Number of Banks	Total Assets ($ billion)	Bank Failures
1920	30,909	53.1	168
1929	25,568	72.3	659
1931	22,242	70.1	2,294
1933	14,771	51.4	4,004
1934	15,913	55.9	61
1940	15,076	79.7	48

Source: Historical Statistics of the United States: Colonial Times to 1970 (Washington, D.C.: U.S. Government Printing Office, 1975), 1019, 1038–1039.

ment-sponsored regional development and public energy. The price of electricity in the seven-state Tennessee Valley area soon dropped from 10 cents a kilowatt-hour to 3 cents. And in a move that lifted public spirits immeasurably, Roosevelt legalized beer in April. Full repeal of Prohibition came eight months later, in December 1933.

The Agricultural Adjustment Act. The Roosevelt administration targeted three pressing problems: agricultural overproduction, business failures, and unemployment. Roosevelt considered a farm bill "the key to recovery." The Agricultural Adjustment Act (AAA) was developed by Secretary of Agriculture Henry A. Wallace, Assistant Secretary Rexford Tugwell, and the agricultural economist M. L. Wilson in close collaboration with the leaders of major farmers' organizations. A domestic allotment system for seven major commodities (wheat, cotton, corn, hogs, rice, tobacco, and dairy products) gave cash subsidies to farmers who cut production; those benefits were financed by a tax on processing (such as the milling of wheat), which was passed on to consumers. New Deal planners hoped prices would rise in response to the federally subsidized scarcity and thus spur a more general recovery. The AAA firmly established the practice of paying federal subsidies to farmers, a tradition that continues to the present day.

The AAA stabilized the agricultural situation, but its benefits were distributed unevenly. The subsidies for reducing production went primarily to the owners of large and medium-size farms, who often cut production by reducing the acreage of their renters and sharecroppers but continuing to farm their own land. In the South that strategy had a racial component, because many sharecroppers were black whereas the landowners and government administrators were white. As many as 200,000 black tenant farmers were displaced from their land by the AAA. Thus New Deal agricultural policies fostered the migration of marginal farmers in the South and Midwest to northern cities and California and consolidated the economic and political clout of larger landholders.

NRA. The New Deal attacked the problem of economic recovery with the National Industrial Recovery Act, which created the National Recovery Administration (NRA). This agency drew on the World War I experience of Bernard Baruch's War Industries Board and continued the reliance on trade associations of the Coolidge and Hoover administrations. The NRA set up a system of industrial self-government to handle the problems of overproduction, cutthroat competition, and price instability. To achieve its objectives, it established codes of fair competition tailored to prevent the specific practices in each industry that had forced prices downward. The codes set prices and established maximum production quotas, sim-

ilar to what the AAA did for farm products. In effect, those legally enforceable agreements suspended the antitrust laws. Each code also contained provisions covering working conditions. For example, the codes established minimum wages and maximum hours and outlawed child labor completely. One of the most far-reaching provisions, Section 7(a), guaranteed workers the right to organize and bargain collectively "through representatives of their own choosing," and this dramatically spurred the growth of the labor movement.

General Hugh Johnson, a colorful if erratic administrator, headed the NRA. He supervised negotiations for more than 600 NRA codes, ranging from large industries such as coal, cotton, and steel to dog food, costume jewelry, and even burlesque theaters. The negotiating process theoretically took into account equal input from management, labor, and consumers, but business trade associations basically set the terms. Because large companies dominated the trade associations, the code-drafting process further solidified the power of large businesses at the expense of smaller enterprises. Labor had little input, and consumer interests had almost none. An extensive public relations campaign, complete with plugs in Hollywood films such as *Gold Diggers of 1933* and stickers with the NRA slogan, "We Do Our Part," was used to sell the program to skeptical consumers and businesspeople.

Unemployment. The early New Deal also addressed the critical problem of unemployment. The total exhaustion of private and local sources of charity made some form of federal relief essential in the fourth year of the depression, and Roosevelt moved reluctantly toward federal responsibility for the unemployed. The Federal Emergency Relief Administration (FERA), set up in May 1933 under the direction of Harry Hopkins, a New York social worker, offered federal money to the states for relief programs. It was designed to keep people from starving until other recovery measures took hold. Hopkins distributed $5 million in his first two hours in office. When told that some of the projects he had authorized might not be sound in the long run, Hopkins replied, "People don't eat in the long run—they eat every day." During its two-year existence FERA spent $1 billion.

Roosevelt always maintained a strong distaste for the dole. Wherever possible, his administration promoted work relief over cash subsidies; it also consistently favored relief jobs that did not compete directly with the private sector. The Public Works Administration (PWA), under Secretary of the Interior Harold L. Ickes, received a $3.3 billion appropriation in 1933 for a major public-works program. However, Ickes's cautiousness in starting up projects limited the PWA's effectiveness in spurring recovery and providing jobs. In November 1933 Roosevelt assigned $400 million in

PWA funds to a new agency, the Civil Works Administration (CWA), headed by Harry Hopkins. Within thirty days the CWA put 2.6 million men and women to work; at its peak in January 1934 it employed 4 million. CWA workers received $15 a week for jobs such as repairing bridges, building highways, constructing public buildings, and setting up community projects. The CWA, regarded as a stopgap measure to get the country through the winter of 1933–1934, lapsed the next spring after spending all its funds.

Many of these early emergency measures were deliberately inflationary; that is, they were designed to trigger price rises that were thought necessary to stimulate recovery and halt the steep deflation. Another element of this strategy was Roosevelt's executive order on April 18, 1933, to abandon the gold standard and let gold rise in value like any other commodity. As the price of gold rose, so too would agricultural prices, a key to general recovery. The budget director, Lew Douglas, warned that abandoning the gold standard would lead to "the end of Western civilization." That did not happen, but neither did this action have much of an impact on the domestic economy. Its main significance lay in the adoption of a flexible currency system. The Federal Reserve System could now manipulate the value of the dollar in accordance to economic conditions rather than tying the value of the dollar to a fixed standard. This represented an important shift in control over the economy to the public sector.

"Gulliver's Travels"
So many new agencies flooded out of Washington in the 1930s that one almost needed a scorecard to keep them straight. Here a July 1935 *Vanity Fair* cartoon by William Gropper substitutes Uncle Sam for Captain Lemuel Gulliver, tied to the ground by Lilliputians in a parody of Jonathan Swift's *Gulliver's Travels*.

When an exhausted Congress recessed in June 1933, much had been accomplished. Rarely had a president so dominated a legislative session. A mass of "alphabet agencies," as the New Deal programs came to be known, flowed from Washington. They gave the impression of action, but despite a slight economic upturn, they had not turned the economy around.

Nevertheless, Americans saw a ray of hope. In April 1933, at the height of the excitement over the Hundred Days, Walt Disney released a cartoon film called *The Three Little Pigs*. Echoing FDR's assertion that they had nothing to fear but fear itself, many people hummed the film's theme song, "Who's Afraid of the Big Bad Wolf?" as they started down the road toward renewed confidence.

Consolidating the Hundred Days

If the measures taken during the Hundred Days had cured the Great Depression, the rest of the New Deal probably would not have occurred. When the depression stubbornly persisted, FDR and Congress turned to more far-reaching structural reform to replace the emergency recovery measures of 1933. Reforming business practices would be one way to prevent future depressions.

Reforming Wall Street. One obvious target was Wall Street, where insider trading, fraud, and other abuses had contributed to the 1929 crash. In 1934 Congress established the Securities and Exchange Commission (SEC) to regulate the stock market. The commission had the power to regulate the purchase of stocks on credit, or margin buying, and to restrict speculation by those with inside information on corporate plans. The Public Utilities Holding Company Act of 1935 limited the widespread practice of pyramiding holding companies on top of utilities for the sole purpose of issuing stock and inflating profits.

The banking system also came under scrutiny. The Banking Act of 1935 represented a significant consolidation of federal control over the nation's banks. The law authorized the president to appoint a new Board of Governors of the Federal Reserve System. This reorganization placed control of interest rates and other money market policies at the federal level rather than with regional banks. By requiring all large state banks to join the Federal Reserve System by 1942 as a condition for using the federal deposit insurance system, the law further encouraged centralization of the nation's banking system.

Roosevelt was not hostile toward business. He heartily accepted the capitalist system but realized that modern industrial life required more direct federal control to limit some of capitalism's excesses. "To preserve we had to reform," Roosevelt commented succinctly.

Even though he styled himself as the savior of capitalism, he provoked strong hostility from many well-to-do Americans. To the wealthy, Roosevelt became simply "That Man," a traitor to his class. Business leaders and conservative Democrats formed the Liberty League in 1934 to lobby against the New Deal and its "reckless spending" and "socialist" reforms.

The conservative majority on the Supreme Court also disagreed with the direction of the New Deal. On "Black Monday," May 27, 1935, the Supreme Court struck down the NRA, Roosevelt's business recovery plan. In the case of *Schechter v. United States*, the court unanimously ruled that the National Industrial Recovery Act represented an unconstitutional delegation of legislative power to the executive. The so-called sick-chicken case concerned a Brooklyn, New York, firm convicted of violating NRA codes by selling diseased poultry. In its decision the Court also ruled that the NRA was regulating commerce *within* an individual state and that the Constitution limited federal regulation to *interstate* commerce. Roosevelt publicly protested that the Court's narrow interpretation would return the Constitution "to the horse-and-buggy definition of interstate commerce" but could only watch helplessly as the Court threatened to invalidate the entire New Deal.

Challenges from the Left

Other citizens thought the New Deal had not gone far enough. Francis Townsend, a Long Beach, California, doctor, spoke for the nation's elderly. Many Americans feared poverty in old age because few had pension plans and many had lost their life savings in bank failures. In 1933 Townsend proposed an Old Age Revolving Pension Plan, which would give $200 a month (a considerable sum at the time) to citizens over the age of sixty. To receive payments, people would have to retire from their jobs, thereby opening their positions to others, and agree to spend the money within a month. Townsend Clubs soon sprang up across the country, particularly in the Far West.

Father Charles Coughlin also challenged Roosevelt's leadership and attracted a large following, especially in the Midwest. Coughlin, a parish priest in the Detroit suburb of Royal Oak, had turned to the radio in the mid-1920s to enlarge his pastorate. In 1933 about 40 million Americans listened regularly to the "Radio Priest." In many Roman Catholic neighborhoods Coughlin's sermons could be heard blaring from open windows during the summer. At first Coughlin supported the New Deal, but he soon broke with Roosevelt over the president's refusal to support nationalization of the banking system and expansion of the money supply. In 1935 Coughlin

organized the National Union for Social Justice to promote his views as an alternative to "Franklin Double-Crossing Roosevelt." Being both Canadian-born and a Catholic priest, Coughlin could not run for president, but his rapidly growing constituency threatened to become a factor in the 1936 election.

The most direct threat to Roosevelt came from Senator Huey Long. In a single term as governor of Louisiana the flamboyant Long had achieved stunning popularity. Voters applauded his attacks on big business as he lowered their utility bills and increased the share of taxes paid by corporations. And Long's ambitious program of public works, which included the construction of new highways, bridges, hospitals, and schools, benefited all Louisianans and created many jobs. But Long's accomplishments came at a price: to push through his reforms he seized almost dictatorial control of the state government. He maintained control over Louisiana's political machine even after his election to the U.S. Senate in 1930. Long supported Roosevelt in 1932 but made no secret of his own presidential ambitions.

In 1934 Senator Long broke with the New Deal, arguing that its programs did not go far enough. Like Coughlin, he established his own national movement, the Share Our Wealth Society, which had over 4 million

The Kingfish
Huey Long, the Louisiana governor and senator, was one of the most controversial figures in American political history. He took his nickname "Kingfish" from a character in the popular radio show "Amos 'n' Andy." Long inspired one of the most powerful political novels of all time, Robert Penn Warren's *All the King's Men*, which won a Pulitzer Prize in 1946.

followers in 1935. Long argued that the unequal distribution of wealth in the United States was the fundamental cause of the depression. Long's solution was to tax 100 percent of all incomes over $1 million and all inheritances over $5 million and distribute the money to the rest of the population. Every family would be guaranteed about $2,000 annually, he predicted. Long's rapid rise in popularity suggested the potential depth of public dissatisfaction with the Roosevelt administration. The president's strategists feared that Long might join forces with Coughlin and Townsend to form a third party, enabling the Republicans to win the 1936 election.

The Second New Deal, 1935–1938

By 1935 Roosevelt had abandoned his hope of building a classless coalition of rich and poor, workers and farmers, and rural and urban dwellers. Pushed from the left to do more and bitterly criticized by the right for what he had already done, the president had no choice but to abandon the middle ground. For both political and ideological reasons, and with an eye fixed firmly on the 1936 election, Roosevelt moved dramatically to the left. Historians use the term *Second New Deal* to describe the outpouring of legislation that followed.

Legislative Accomplishments

The first beneficiary of Roosevelt's change of direction was the labor movement. The rising number of strikes in 1934, about 1,800 involving a total of 1.5 million workers, reflected the dramatic growth of rank-and-file militancy. After the Supreme Court declared the NRA unconstitutional in 1935, labor demanded legislation that would protect its rights to organize and bargain collectively. Senator Robert F. Wagner of New York, one of labor's staunchest supporters in Congress, had introduced legislation to strengthen and make permanent the protections guaranteed by Section 7(a) of the NIRA even before the Supreme Court decision. Only when Congress was on the verge of passing Wagner's bill did Roosevelt reluctantly support the legislation, signing the National Labor Relations Act, also known as the Wagner Act, on July 5, 1935.

The Wagner Act placed the weight of the federal government on labor's side in the struggle to organize. Most important, it upheld the right of industrial workers to join a union. (The Wagner Act did not cover farm workers' unions.) The law also outlawed many unfair labor practices employers used to squelch unions, such

General Strike, San Francisco, 1934
San Francisco's general strike began with the longshoremen and soon spread to almost every union member (and some middle-class supporters as well) in the city. This striker has been shot in the head during an altercation with police. On July 19, union leaders voted to accept government arbitration, and the strike ended.

as spying on workers, requiring yellow-dog contracts (in which workers had to agree not to join a union in order to be hired), and firing or blacklisting workers because of their union activities. The act established the nonpartisan National Labor Relations Board (NLRB) to protect workers from employer coercion, supervise representation elections, and enforce the guarantee of collective bargaining. If a union won a majority of the votes in a secret election, usually conducted by the NLRB, it was entitled to recognition as the sole bargaining agent for all the employees in a factory or other appropriate bargaining unit. The NLRB had the authority to force employers to comply.

Social Security. The Social Security Act signed by Roosevelt on August 14, 1935, was the second major piece of legislation in this phase of the New Deal. The law was a response to the political mobilization of the nation's elderly through the Townsend and Long movements. It also reflected the prodding of social reformers such as Grace Abbott, head of the Children's Bureau, and Secretary of Labor Frances Perkins. The Social Security Act provided pensions for most workers in the private sector, although agricultural workers and domestics were not initially covered. The pensions were paid out of a federal-state pension fund to which both employers and employees contributed. Roosevelt's advisers decided to fund the program with payroll deductions rather than general tax revenues to insulate it from political attack. The act also established a joint federal-state system of unemployment compensation funded by an unemployment tax on employers and employees.

The Social Security Act was a milestone in the creation of the modern welfare state. With this law, the United States joined industrialized countries such as Great Britain and Germany in providing old-age pensions and unemployment compensation to its citizens. (The Roosevelt administration chose not to push for national health insurance even though most other industrialized nations offered such protection.) The law also mandated categorical assistance, such as aid to the blind, deaf, and disabled and to dependent children. Those recipients were the so-called deserving poor, people who could not support themselves through no fault of their own. The categorical assistance programs, which formed a small part of the New Deal, gradually expanded over the years until they were integral parts of the American welfare system.

The WPA. Roosevelt was never enthusiastic about large expenditures for social welfare programs. As he said in January 1935, the government "must and shall quit this business of relief." But 10 million Americans were still out of work in the sixth year of the depression, a pressing political and moral issue for FDR and the Democrats. The Works Progress Administration (WPA), the main federal relief agency for the rest of the depression, addressed the needs of the unemployed. Harry Hopkins, who had run the Federal Emergency Relief Administration from 1933 to 1935, took command of the new agency. Whereas the FERA had supplied grants to the states for relief programs, the WPA put relief workers on the federal payroll. Between 1935 and 1943 the WPA employed 8.5 million Americans and spent $10.5 billion. The agency constructed 651,087 miles of roads, 125,110 public buildings, 8,192 parks, and 853 airports and built or repaired 124,087 bridges.

The WPA, although an extravagant operation by the standards of the 1930s (it inspired nicknames such as "We Putter Around" and "We Poke Along"), never reached more than a third of the nation's unemployed. Its average wage of $55 a month, well below the gov-

Posters of the WPA
During its eight-year existence the WPA produced 2 million posters from 35,000 designs. WPA posters such as this one designed for the National Park Service to support wildlife conservation show the vitality of American graphic design in the 1930s.

ernment-defined subsistence level of $100 a month, enabled workers to eke out a bare living. The government cut back the program severely in 1941 and ended it in 1943, when the WPA was no longer needed in the full-employment economy resulting from World War II.

The Revenue Act of 1935 showed Roosevelt's willingness to push for reforms that were considered too controversial earlier in his presidency. Much of the business community had already turned violently against Roosevelt in reaction to the NRA, the Social Security Act, the Wagner Act, and the Public Utilities Holding Companies Act. In 1935 he further antagonized the wealthy by proposing a tax reform bill that included federal inheritance and gift taxes, higher personal income tax rates in the top brackets, and increased corporate taxes. Conservatives quickly labeled this an attempt to "soak the rich." Roosevelt, seeking to defuse the popularity of Huey Long's Share Our Wealth plan, was just as interested in the political mileage of the tax bill as in its actual results. The final version of the bill increased federal revenues by only $250 million a year (Table 26.2).

TABLE 26.2

Major New Deal Legislation

Agriculture

1933 Agricultural Adjustment Act (AAA)
1935 Resettlement Administration (RA)
      Rural Electrification Administration
1937 Farm Security Administration (FSA)
1938 Second Agricultural Adjustment Act

Business and Industry

1933 Emergency Banking Act
      Glass-Steagall Act
        (FDIC)
      National Industrial Recovery Act (NIRA)
1934 Securities and Exchange Commission (SEC)
      Public Utilities Holding Company Act
1935 Banking Act of 1935
      Revenue Act (wealth tax)

Conservation and the Environment

1933 Tennessee Valley Authority (TVA)
      Civilian Conservation Corps (CCC)
1936 Soil Conservation and Domestic Allotment Act

Labor and Social Welfare

1933 Section 7(a) of NIRA
1935 Wagner Act
      National Labor Relations Board (NLRB)
      Social Security Act
1937 National Housing Act
1938 Fair Labor Standards Act (FLSA)

Relief

1933 Federal Emergency Relief Administration (FERA)
      Civil Works Administration (CWA)
      Public Works Administration (PWA)
1935 Works Progress Administration (WPA)
      National Youth Administration (NYA)

The 1936 Election

As the 1936 election approached, the broad range of New Deal programs brought new voters into the Democratic coalition. Many had been personally helped by federal programs; others benefited because their interests had found new support in the expanded functions of the government. Roosevelt could count on a potent urban-based coalition of workers, organized labor, northern blacks, white ethnic groups, Catholics, Jews, liberals, intellectuals, progressive Republicans, and middle-class families concerned about old-age dependence and unemployment. The Democrats also held on, though with some difficulty, to their traditional strength among white southerners.

The Republicans realized that they could not compete directly with Roosevelt's popularity and the potent New Deal coalition. To run against Roosevelt, they chose the progressive governor of Kansas, Alfred M. Landon, who accepted the general precepts of the New Deal. But Landon and the Republicans stridently criticized the inefficiency and expense of many New Deal programs and accused FDR of harboring dictatorial ambitions.

Roosevelt's victory in 1936 was one of the biggest landslides in American history. The assassination of Huey Long in September 1935 had deflated the threat of a serious third party challenge; the candidate of the combined Long-Townsend-Coughlin camp, Congressman William Lemke of North Dakota, garnered fewer than 900,000 votes (1.9 percent) for the Union party ticket. Roosevelt received 60.8 percent of the popular vote and carried every state except Maine and Vermont; Landon received 36.5 percent. Landon fought such an uphill battle that the columnist Dorothy Thompson quipped, "If Landon had given one more speech, Roosevelt would have carried Canada." The New Deal was at high tide.

Stalemate

"I see one-third of a nation ill-housed, ill-clad, ill-nourished," the president declared in his second inaugural address in January 1937. Roosevelt's appraisal suggested that he was considering further expansion of the welfare state that had begun to form late in his first term. However, retrenchment, controversy, and stalemate, not further reform, marked the second term.

The Supreme Court Fight. Only two weeks after his inauguration Roosevelt stunned Congress and the nation by asking for fundamental changes in the structure of the Supreme Court, believing that a grave constitutional crisis called for drastic judicial reorganization. After the Supreme Court found the NRA unconstitutional in the *Schechter* decision, in the early months of 1936 it struck down the Agricultural Adjustment Act, the Guffey-Snyder Coal Conservation Act, and New York State's minimum wage law. With the Wagner Act, the TVA, and Social Security coming up on appeal, the future of New Deal reform legislation appeared in doubt.

In response, Roosevelt proposed adding one new justice to the Court for each currently sitting justice over the age of seventy. That scheme, which Roosevelt tried

to pass off as a way to reduce the workload of the elderly justices, would have increased the number of justices from nine to fifteen. Roosevelt's opponents quickly
accused him of trying to "pack" the Court with justices
favorable to the New Deal. The president's proposal was
also regarded as an assault on the principle of separation
of powers. The issue became moot when the Supreme
Court, in what journalists tagged "a switch in time that
saved nine," upheld several key pieces of New Deal legislation, including the Social Security Act, Washington
State's minimum wage law, and the Wagner Act.

Charitably, one could say that Roosevelt had lost a
skirmish but won the war. In the spring of 1937 one
conservative justice, Willis Van Devanter, resigned.
Other resignations soon followed. Within four years
Roosevelt reshaped the Supreme Court to suit his liberal
philosophy with seven new appointments, including
Hugo Black, Felix Frankfurter, Stanley F. Reed, and
William O. Douglas. Yet his handling of this issue was a
costly blunder at a time when he was vulnerable to the
lame-duck syndrome that often afflicts second-term administrations. No one yet suspected that FDR would
break with tradition by seeking a third term.

Congressional conservatives had long opposed the
direction of the New Deal, but the Court-packing episode galvanized the conservatives by demonstrating that
Roosevelt was no longer politically invincible. Throughout Roosevelt's second term a conservative coalition in
Congress, composed mainly of southern Democrats and
Republicans from rural areas, blocked or impeded social legislation. Two pieces of reform legislation that did
win passage were the National Housing Act of 1937,
which mandated the construction of low-cost public
housing, and the Fair Labor Standards Act of 1938,
which made permanent the minimum wage, maximum
hours, and anti–child labor provisions in the NRA
codes.

Roosevelt's attempts to reorganize the executive
branch met a different fate. In both 1937 and 1938
Congress refused to consider a plan that would have
consolidated all independent agencies into cabinet-rank
departments, extended the civil service system, and created the new position of auditor general. Conservatives
effectively played on lawmakers' fears that centralized
executive management would dramatically reduce Congressional power. Opponents also linked Roosevelt's attempt to reorganize the executive branch to popular
fears of fascism and dictatorship abroad, fears fanned
especially by Hitler's rise to power in Germany. Roosevelt settled for a weak bill in 1939 that allowed him to
create the Executive Office of the President and name
six administrative assistants to the White House staff.
The White House also took control of the all-important
budget process by moving the Bureau of the Budget to
the Executive Office from its old home in the Treasury
Department.

The Roosevelt Recession. The "Roosevelt recession" of
1937–1938 dealt the most devastating blow to the president's political standing in the second term. Until that
point the economy had made steady progress. From
1933 to 1937 the gross national product grew at a
yearly rate of about 10 percent, and industrial output finally reached 1929 levels in 1937, as did real income.
Unemployment declined from 25 percent to 14 percent,
which meant that almost half the people without a job
in 1933 had found one by 1937. Many Americans
agreed with Senator James F. Byrnes of South Carolina
that "the emergency has passed."

The steady improvement cheered Roosevelt. Basically a fiscal conservative, he had never overcome his
dislike of large federal expenditures for relief. Accordingly, Roosevelt slashed the federal budget in 1937.
Congress cut the WPA's funding in half between January and August, causing layoffs for about 1.5 million
workers. Moreover, the $2 billion withheld from work-
ers' paychecks to initiate the new Social Security System
further reduced purchasing power. Finally, the Federal
Reserve, fearing inflation, tightened credit. The stock
market promptly collapsed, and unemployment soared
to 19 percent, which translated into more than 10 million workers without jobs. Roosevelt found himself in
the same situation that had confounded Hoover. Having taken credit for the recovery between 1933 and
1937, he had to take the blame for the recession.

Roosevelt shifted gears and spent his way out of the
downturn. Large WPA appropriations and a resumption of public-works projects poured enough money
into the economy to lift it out of the recession by early
1938. Roosevelt and his economic advisers were grop-
ing toward the general theories advanced by John May-
nard Keynes, a British economist. Keynes proposed that
governments use deficit spending to stimulate the economy when private spending proved insufficient. But
Keynes's theories would not be conclusively proved
until a dramatic increase in federal defense spending for
World War II finally ended the Great Depression.

As the 1938 election approached, Roosevelt decided
to "purge" some of his most conservative opponents
from the Democratic party. In the spring primaries he
campaigned against members of his own party who had
blocked legislation in Congress and who had generally
been hostile or unsympathetic to New Deal initiatives.
The purge failed abysmally and widened the liberal-
conservative rift in the Democratic party. In the general
election Republicans capitalized on the "Roosevelt recession" and the Court-packing backlash to pick up 8
seats in the Senate and 81 in the House. The Republicans also gained 13 governorships.

By 1938 the New Deal had basically run out of
steam. For six years Roosevelt had inspired confidence
that hard times could be overcome. He showed himself
to be a superb politician, successfully balancing de-

mands for more government programs with his own assessment of what was politically feasible. Throughout the New Deal, however, the president always demonstrated clear limits on how far he was willing to go. His instincts were basically conservative, not revolutionary; he saved the capitalist economic system by reforming it. This new activism was a major step beyond the informal and one-sided business-government partnership of the previous decade, but only because the emergency of the depression pushed Roosevelt in that direction. Under normal circumstances, he would have served out his second term, and a new president would have been elected in 1940. Roosevelt won a third term (and eventually a fourth) primarily because the outbreak of World War II in Europe in 1939 made Americans reluctant to risk a change in leadership during such perilous times.

The New Deal's Impact on Society

The New Deal was "somehow more than the sum of its parts." To understand its impact on society, one must look beyond the federal programs that came out of Washington and consider broader changes in political and social life. The New Deal set in motion dramatic growth in the federal bureaucracy. The Roosevelt administration opened unprecedented opportunities for women, blacks, and labor in public life. Its programs and priorities had an enormous impact on the public landscape, and it laid the groundwork for the welfare system that lasted until the 1990s.

Bureaucratic Growth

The New Deal accelerated the expansion of the federal bureaucracy that had been under way since the turn of the century. The number of civilian government employees increased 80 percent in a decade, exceeding a million in 1940. The number of federal employees who worked in Washington grew at an even faster rate, doubling between 1929 and 1940. Power was increasingly centered in the nation's capital, not in the states. In 1939 a British observer summed up the new orientation: "Just as in 1929 the whole country was 'Wall Street conscious,' now it is 'Washington conscious.'"

The new bureaucrats administered federal budgets of unprecedented size. In 1930 the Hoover administration had spent $3.1 billion and had run a surplus of almost $1 billion. With the increase in federal programs to fight the depression, federal expenditures grew steadily to $4.8 billion in 1932, $6.5 billion in 1934, and $7.6 billion in 1936. In 1939, the last year before war mobilization affected the federal budget, expenditures reached $9.4 billion. Government spending outstripped

receipts throughout this period, producing yearly deficits of about $3 billion. Roosevelt had come close to balancing the budget in 1938 but had triggered a major recession. The deficit climbed toward $3 billion again the following year.

The beginnings of big government and bureaucracy are often associated with the Roosevelt years, but many of the problems commonly ascribed to the New Deal belong to later eras. The real step toward expanded government spending came during World War II, not the depression. Federal outlays routinely surpassed $95 billion in the 1940s, and deficits grew to $50 billion. Although the deficit declined in the postwar era, government expenditures never returned to pre–World War II levels.

Women and the New Deal

In the experimental climate of the New Deal unprecedented numbers of women were offered positions in the Roosevelt administration, both as policy makers and as middle-level bureaucrats. Frances Perkins served as secretary of labor throughout all four terms, the first woman named to a cabinet post (see American Lives, pages 808–809). Molly Dewson, a social reformer turned politician, headed the Women's Division of the Democratic National Committee, where she pushed an issue-oriented program that supported New Deal reforms. Roosevelt's appointments of women included the first female director of the mint, the head of a major WPA division, and a judge on the circuit court of appeals. Many of those women were close friends as well as professional colleagues and cooperated in an informal network to advance feminist and reform causes.

Eleanor Roosevelt exemplified the growing prominence of women in public life. In the 1920s she had worked closely with other reformers to increase women's power in political parties, labor unions, and education, an invaluable apprenticeship for her White House years. Franklin and Eleanor's marriage represented one of the most successful political partnerships of all time. He was the pragmatic politician, always aware of what could be done; she was the idealist, the gadfly, always pushing him—and the New Deal—to do more. Eleanor Roosevelt observed in her autobiography,

> He might have been happier with a wife who was completely uncritical. That I was never able to be, and he had to find it in other people. Nevertheless, I think I sometimes acted as a spur, even though the spurring was not always wanted or welcome. I was one of those who served his purposes.

Eleanor Roosevelt underestimated her influence. She served as the conscience of the New Deal.

Frances Perkins:
New Deal Reformer

How should the first woman to serve in the cabinet be addressed? the press wanted to know. "Miss Perkins," came her no-nonsense reply. But the press said "Mr. Secretary" to the secretary of state; how was it to address a woman who was the secretary of labor? After consultation with Speaker of the House Henry Rainey and *Robert's Rules of Order*, the verdict came down: Frances Perkins was to be addressed as "Madam Secretary." As usual, the first woman in the cabinet took the attention to her sex in stride. She kept a deliberately low profile, wearing conservative black dresses, always accessorized with a distinctive tricorne hat. When asked later if being a woman had ever been a handicap, she replied matter-of-factly, "Only in climbing trees."

Frances Perkins's career shows the continuity between Progressive Era activism and New Deal reform. Born in 1880 in Massachusetts, Perkins took advantage of the new opportunities for higher education for women to graduate from Mount Holyoke College in 1902. She then worked in the settlement house movement, in the woman suffrage campaign, and with reform groups trying to pass a bill establishing a fifty-four-hour workweek for New York women and children. Her service on the commission set up to investigate New York factory conditions in the wake of the 1911 Triangle Shirtwaist fire, which killed 146 female garment workers, confirmed her commitment to legislative solutions for social problems. "I'd much rather get a law passed than organize a union," she later said. That orientation shaped her priorities as secretary of labor.

In 1913, at the age of thirty-three, Perkins married Paul C. Wilson, an economist and reformer. She kept her given name and continued to work after her daughter, Susanna, was born in 1916. As she later recalled, "I suppose I had been somewhat touched by feminist ideas and that was one of the reasons I kept my maiden name. My whole generation was, I suppose, the first generation that openly and actively asserted—at least some of us did—the separateness of women and their personal independence in the family relationship." In 1918 her husband became seriously ill and then spent the rest of

his life in and out of mental institutions. Out of necessity, Perkins became the family breadwinner.

Perkins moved into government service in 1918 when the newly elected governor, Alfred E. Smith, whom she had met during the Triangle investigation, appointed her to the New York State Industrial Commission. Smith appointed Perkins to the State Industrial Board in 1922 and made her its chairperson in 1926. In 1928 she became New York's industrial commissioner under Smith and then Franklin D. Roosevelt, who replaced Smith as governor that year. Those positions made Perkins one of the highest-ranked women in state government in the immediate postsuffrage period.

When Franklin Roosevelt ran for president in 1932, talk began to circulate that Perkins might be offered a spot in the cabinet, a rumor that she dismissed as a "pipe dream." But to politicians such as Molly Dewson, whose background in social welfare paralleled that of Perkins, Roosevelt's election offered an unprecedented opportunity for women to serve at the national level. Dewson set about convincing Roosevelt of the wisdom of choosing Perkins and overcoming Perkins's own doubts. Perkins was reluctant to leave New York and a job she loved and feared the effect of unwanted publicity on her husband and teenage daughter; the job also would cause financial hardship. Molly Dewson blithely dismissed all those objections, emphasizing the importance of the appointment to the nation's women. "After all, you owe it to the women," Dewson argued repeatedly. "You probably will have this chance and you must step forward to do it." At other times Dewson's pressure was less subtle: "Don't be such a baby. Frances, you do the right thing. I'll murder you if you don't!"

Duty to her sex finally carried the day. As Perkins later explained to the suffrage leader Carrie Chapman Catt, "The overwhelming argument and thought which made me do it in the end in spite of personal difficulties was the realization that the door might not be opened to a woman again for a long, long time, and that I had a kind of duty to other women to walk in and sit down on the chair that was offered, and so establish the right of others long hence and far-distant in geography to sit in the high seats." Franklin Roosevelt announced Perkins's appointment on February 28, and she was sworn in five days later. Among the members of Roosevelt's original cabinet, only Perkins and Secretary of the Interior Harold Ickes served for all four terms.

As secretary of labor, Perkins took as her mandate the promotion of the general welfare of American workers rather than specific advocacy of the interests of organized labor. She built the Department of Labor into a smoothly functioning bureaucracy and attracted many talented men and women to Washington. She played an especially important role in drafting the 1935 Social Security Act and the 1938 Fair Labor Standards Act. She did not ignore the labor movement, however, and after a period of initial doubt labor leaders realized that Madam Secretary was an important ally in the turbulent era of union mobilization in the 1930s.

An important key to Perkins's success was her personal rapport with Franklin Roosevelt, who, unlike many male politicians, felt comfortable working with strong-minded women. (He, of course, was married to one and met many of the talented women he brought into the New Deal administration through Eleanor.) Perkins called Roosevelt the most complicated human being she had ever met but emphatically asserted that he had never let her down. In 1946 she published *The Roosevelt I Knew*, an autobiographical account of her participation in the New Deal that many believe offers the most perceptive account of the elusive Roosevelt personality.

After Roosevelt's death, Perkins served on the Civil Service Commission under President Harry Truman. When the Republicans regained power in 1952, she left government service for a fulfilling career as a lecturer, maintaining an affiliation with the Cornell School of Industrial and Labor Relations. Perkins died in 1965. Her role in laying the foundation of the modern welfare state was her greatest legacy, but just as important was her demonstration of the contributions that public-spirited women could make to politics and government.

Secretary of Labor
Frances Perkins being greeted by workers at the Carnegie Steel Company in Pittsburgh.

Although Franklin Roosevelt's expansion of the personalized presidency had roots in the administrations of Theodore Roosevelt and Woodrow Wilson, the nation had never seen a first lady like Eleanor Roosevelt. She held press conferences for women journalists, wrote a popular syndicated column called "My Day," and traveled extensively throughout the country. Some people wondered why the first lady did not stay home at the White House like a good wife, but in a Gallup poll in January 1939, 67 percent approved of her conduct, a higher approval rating than the president's at that time. In 1938 *Life* magazine hailed her as the greatest American woman alive.

Without the vocal support of prominent women such as Eleanor Roosevelt, Molly Dewson, and the rest of the female political network, women's needs during the depression might have been overlooked. Grave flaws still marred the treatment of women in New Deal programs. For example, a fourth of the NRA codes set a lower minimum wage for women than for men performing the same jobs. New Deal agencies such as the Civil Works Administration and the Public Works Administration gave jobs almost exclusively to men, mainly because construction work was considered unsuitable for women; only 7 percent of CWA workers were female. The Social Security and Fair Labor Standards acts did not cover major areas of customarily female employment, such as domestic service. The CCC excluded women entirely, leaving critics to ask, Where is the "she-she-she"?

Eleanor Roosevelt and Civil Rights
One of Eleanor Roosevelt's greatest legacies was her commitment to civil rights. For example, she publicly resigned from the Daughters of the American Revolution (DAR) in 1939 when the group refused to let the black operatic singer Marian Anderson perform at Constitution Hall. Roosevelt developed an especially close working relationship with Mary McLeod Bethune of the National Youth Administration, shown here at a conference on black youth in 1939.

Women fared somewhat better under the Works Progress Administration. At the WPA's peak, 405,000 women were on its rolls. The Women's and Professional Projects Division of the WPA, headed by Ellen Sullivan Woodward, a Mississippi social worker, created hundreds of programs to put women to work. Still, at a time when women accounted for about 23 percent of the labor force, they constituted only 14 to 19 percent of WPA workers. For the most part, progress for women did not come from specific attempts to single them out as a group but occurred as part of a broader effort to improve the economic security of all Americans.

Blacks and the New Deal

There were striking parallels between the situation of blacks and women. African-Americans benefited more from the general social and economic programs of the New Deal than from any concerted commitment to civil rights. For black women, race proved more important than gender in determining treatment from the New Deal.

Mary McLeod Bethune, an educator who ran the Office of Minority Affairs of the National Youth Administration, headed the "black cabinet." This informal network worked for fairer treatment of blacks by New Deal agencies in the same way that the women's network advocated feminist causes. Both groups benefited greatly from the support of Eleanor Roosevelt. The first lady's promotion of equal treatment for blacks in the New Deal ranks as one of her greatest legacies.

The vast majority of the American people did not regard civil rights as a legitimate area for federal intervention in the 1930s. The New Deal provided little specific aid for blacks, for whom hard times were a permanent feature that the depression only made worse. Many New Deal programs reflected prevailing racist attitudes. CCC camps segregated blacks, and many NRA codes did not protect black workers. Most tellingly, Franklin Roosevelt repeatedly refused to support legislation making lynching a federal crime, claiming that it would antagonize southern members of Congress whose support he needed to pass New Deal measures.

Nevertheless blacks did receive enormous benefits from New Deal relief programs directed toward poor Americans, regardless of race or ethnic background. Public works projects channeled funds into black communities. Blacks made up about 18 percent of the WPA's recipients although they constituted only 10 percent of the population (see American Voices, page 811). The Resettlement Administration, established in 1935 to help small farmers buy land and aid in the resettlement of sharecroppers and tenant farmers onto more productive land, fought for the rights of black tenant farmers in the South—that is, until angry southerners in Congress cut its appropriations drastically. Still, many

Nora Mair

The Great Depression in Harlem

Nora Mair and her husband, Jack, both Jamaican immigrants, lived in Harlem throughout the 1930s. She worked in a linen shop on Madison Avenue, and he struggled to find employment of any kind. Like many other Americans, black and white, the WPA was their salvation.

We were poor. We didn't pretend. But our gas bill was always paid. Our rent bill was always paid. And we always knew where our next meal was coming from. We shopped on Eighth Avenue. We had everything there. We moved out of West Harlem to 100th Street and Madison Avenue in 1933 because the rent was less than half of what we were paying in West Harlem. We were paying thirty-two dollars a month for a five-room apartment. In Harlem, we would have paid sixty-five dollars, and we had a lovely landlord who painted our house every year. It was a lovely neighborhood—a pot-pourri of many nationalities. . . .

My husband worked in the day and went to school nights. He graduated from Mechanical Institute in 1928,

and right after that the Depression came, and he couldn't get work in his profession. In the meantime he drove a cab. It was no living at all as a taxi driver. I've known him to work around the clock and only make a dollar and a half.

He would come in in the morning and eat his dinner for his breakfast and then go to bed. I've known him to be so cold, because in those days the cabs only had three doors, that he'd come in and all he would take off was his hat, his shoes, and his overcoat and then into the bed until he was warm. Those things I did resent, because he had more to offer. He met so many people on the cab line—people he knew from Jamaica. He met professors who were driving cabs and couldn't get a job. First it was color. Then it was color and Depression.

There was nothing my husband did not do to make a living. He did not want welfare, and he wanted to be independent. But he couldn't get work as a draftsman. Once, while he was driving a cab, he saw an ad in the paper for a draftsman. He went downtown to

this office, and there was the reception-ist. She didn't even look up. She waved him around the back, so he thought to himself, "She didn't ask what I wanted. She just motioned me to the back of the building. What kind of office could be back there?"

When he got back there, a white man with a pail and a mop said to him, "There is the pail and the mop."

"Pail and the mop for what?"

And said Mr. White Man, "Well, that's what you're here for, isn't it? A porter's job?"

Well, I won't tell you what my husband said when he came home, because he came home frothing at the mouth, and told me what he told him.

When the WPA came in, that was the first time he got to work in his profession. He worked on theaters, schools. They did everything, and it meant a lot that he was finally able to work in his field.

Source: Jeff Kisseloff, *You Must Remember This: An Oral History of Manhattan from the 1890s to World War II* (New York: Schocken, 1989), 326–327, 328.

---

blacks reasoned that the tangible aid coming from Washington outweighed the discrimination that marred many federal programs.

Help from the WPA and other New Deal programs and a belief that the White House—at least Eleanor Roosevelt—cared about their plight caused a dramatic change in blacks' voting behavior. Since the Civil War blacks had voted Republican, a loyalty resulting from Abraham Lincoln's freeing of the slaves. As late as 1932 black voters in northern cities overwhelmingly supported Republican candidates.

Then, in less than four years, blacks turned Lincoln's portrait to the wall and substituted that of Franklin Roosevelt. Because of the harshness of the depression, national politics assumed a new relevance for black Americans outside the South, who gave Roosevelt 71 percent of their votes in 1936. In Harlem, where relief dollars increased dramatically in the wake of the

1935 riot (see Chapter 25), the support was an extraordinary 81.3 percent. Black voters have remained overwhelmingly Democratic ever since.

The Rise of Organized Labor

During the 1930s, labor relations became a legitimate arena for federal action and intervention, and organized labor claimed a place in national political life. Labor's dramatic growth in the 1930s was one of the most important social and economic changes of the decade, an enormous contrast to its demoralized state at the end of the 1920s.

Several factors encouraged the growth of the labor movement: the inadequacy of welfare capitalism in the face of the depression, New Deal legislation such as the Wagner Act, the rise of the Congress of Industrial Organizations (CIO), and the growing militancy of rank-and-file workers. By the end of the decade the number of unionized workers had tripled to almost 9 million, covering 23 percent of the nonfarm work force. Union strength grew rapidly in manufacturing, transportation, and mining. Organized labor not only won the battle for union recognition but also for higher wages, seniority systems, and grievance procedures. Labor greatly expanded its political involvement as well.

The CIO served as the cutting edge of the union movement by promoting industrial unionism, that is, organizing all the workers in an industry, both skilled and unskilled, into one union. John L. Lewis, the leader of the United Mine Workers and a founder of the CIO, was the leading exponent of industrial unionism. His philosophy put him at odds with the American Federation of Labor (AFL), which favored organizing workers on a craft-by-craft basis. Lewis began to detach himself from the AFL in 1935, and the break was complete by 1938. Although the CIO generated much of the excitement on the labor front in the 1930s, the AFL gained more than a million new members between 1935 and 1940.

Organize

The Steelworkers' Organizing Committee was one of the most vital labor organizations contributing to the rise of the CIO. Note that the artist Ben Shahn chose a male figure to represent the American labor movement in this poster from the late 1930s. Such iconography reinforced the notion that the typical worker was male, despite the large number of women who joined the CIO.

The CIO scored its first major victory in the automobile industry. On December 31, 1936, General Motors workers in Flint, Michigan, staged a sit-down strike, vowing to stay at their machines until management agreed to bargain collectively. The workers lived in the factories and machine shops for forty-four days before General Motors recognized the United Automobile Workers (UAW). The CIO soon won another major victory at the U.S. Steel Corporation. Despite a long history of bitter opposition to unionization (as demonstrated in the 1919 steel strike), "Big Steel" capitulated without a fight and recognized the Steel Workers Organizing Committee (SWOC) on March 2, 1937.

The victory in the steel industry was not complete, however. A group of companies known as "Little Steel" chose not to follow the lead of U.S. Steel in making peace with the CIO, and steelworkers struck the Republic Steel Corporation plant in South Chicago. On Memorial Day, May 31, 1937, strikers and their families gathered for a holiday picnic and rally outside the plant's gates. Tension mounted, rocks were thrown, and the police fired on the crowd, killing ten protesters. All were shot in the back. A newsreel photographer recorded the scene, but Paramount Pictures considered the film of the "Memorial Day Massacre" too inflammatory for distribution. The road to recognition for labor, even with New Deal protections, was still long and violent. Workers in Little Steel did not win union recognition until 1941.

The 1930s were one of the most active periods of labor solidarity in American history. The sit-down tactic spread rapidly. In March 1937, 167,210 workers staged 170 sit-down strikes. Labor unions called for nearly 5,000 strikes that year and won favorable terms in 80 percent of them. Yet large numbers of middle-class Americans felt alienated by sit-down strikes, which they considered attacks on private property. The Supreme Court agreed and in 1939 upheld a law that banned the practice.

The CIO attracted new groups to the union movement. Mexican-Americans and blacks, for example, found the CIO's commitment to racial justice a strong contrast to the AFL's long-established patterns of exclusion and segregation. About 800,000 women workers also found a limited welcome in the CIO. Women participated in major CIO strikes and served as union organizers, especially in textile organizing drives in the South. Few blacks, Mexican-Americans, or women held leadership positions, however.

Women found other ways to participate in the labor movement. During the Flint sit-down strike in 1937 the Women's Emergency Brigade, a group of wives, sisters, and girlfriends of striking workers, supplied food and first aid. Wearing distinctive red berets and armbands, they picketed, demonstrated, and occasionally resorted to tactics such as breaking windows to dissipate the tear

The Sit-Down Strike
These members of the United Auto Workers helped pioneer the sit-down tactic at a General Motors plant in Flint, Michigan, in 1937. In their forty-four-day siege, the workers made use of the car seats awaiting final assembly in GM cars while they passed the time. To avoid any taint of immorality, union leaders asked all women workers in the Flint plant to leave once the sit-down strike began, and the women complied.

gas used against the strikers (see American Voices, page 814). After the strike, however, UAW leaders politely but firmly told the women to go back home where they supposedly belonged.

Labor's new vitality spilled over into political action. The AFL had always stood aloof from partisan politics, but the CIO quickly allied itself with the Democratic party. Through Labor's Nonpartisan League, the CIO gave $770,000 to Democratic campaigns in 1936. Labor also provided one of the few solid lobbies behind Roosevelt's plan to reorganize the Supreme Court. In the 1940s the CIO's Political Action Committee became a major contributor to the Democratic war chest.

Despite the breakthroughs of the New Deal, the labor movement never developed into as dominant a force in American life as had seemed possible in the heyday of the late 1930s. Roosevelt never made the growth of the labor movement a high priority, and many workers remained indifferent or even hostile to unionization.

Although the Wagner Act guaranteed unions a permanent place in American industrial relations, it did not revolutionize working conditions. The important gain of collective bargaining did not redistribute power in American industry; it merely granted labor a measure of legitimacy. Management even found that unions could be a useful buffer against rank-and-file militancy. New Deal social welfare programs also diffused some of the pre-1937 radical spirit by channeling economic benefits to workers whether they belonged to unions or not. In the 1940s the labor movement entered a period of consolidation and then stagnation that continued for several decades.

New Deal Murals
The social realist painter William Gropper portrayed the contributions of labor to modern industry in the heroic, dynamic style that was typical of public art during the depression. This mural, *Construction of a Dam*, was commissioned in 1937 for the Department of the Interior Building in Washington, D.C.

Genora Johnson Dollinger

Labor Militancy

During the Flint, Michigan, sit-down strike Genora Johnson Dollinger, the wife of a General Motors striker and the mother of two small children, organized the Women's Emergency Brigade. Women like Dollinger played a major role in the Flint victory.

I was twenty-three years old on December 30, 1936, when the strike started. It lasted forty-four days, a very dramatic forty-four days, until February 11, 1937.

It was New Year's Eve when I realized women had to organize and join in the fight. I was on the picket lines when the men's wives came down. They didn't know why their husbands were sitting inside the plant. Living in a company town, you see, they got only company propaganda through the press and radio. So when they came down on New Year's Eve, many were threatening to divorce their striking husbands if they didn't quit and get back to work to bring home a paycheck.

I knew then that union women must organize on their own in order to talk with these wives. . . .

This was an independent move. It was not under the direction of the union or its administrators—I just talked it over with a few women—the active ones—and told them this is what we had to do.

Women might, after all, be called upon to give their lives. That was exactly the appeal I made while we were forming the brigade—I told the women, "Don't sign up for this unless you are prepared. If you are prone to hysteria or anything like that you'd only be in our way." I told them they'd be linking arms and withstanding the onslaughts of the police and if one of our sisters went down shot in cold blood there'd be no time for hysteria.

Around 500 women answered that call. We bought red berets and made arm bands with the white letters "EB" for Emergency Brigade. It was a kind of military uniform, yes, but it was mainly identification. We wore them all the time so we'd know who to call on to give help in an emergency. I had five lieutenants—three were factory women. I chose them because they could be called out of bed at any hour, if necessary, or sleep on a cot at the union hall. Mothers with children couldn't answer calls like that—although they did sign up for the brigade. Even a few grandmothers became brigadiers and, I remember, one young girl only sixteen.

We had no communication system to speak of. Very few people had telephones so we had to call one woman who was responsible for getting the messages through to many others.

We organized a first aid station and child care center—the women who had small children to tend and couldn't join the EB took care of these jobs.

Listen, I met some of the finest women I have ever come across in my life. When the occasion demands it of a woman and once she understands that she's standing in defense of her family—well, God, *don't fool around with that woman then.* . . .

It's a measure of the strength of those women of the Red Berets that they could perform so courageously in an atmosphere that was often hostile to them. We organized on our own without the benefit of professional leadership, and yet, we played a role, second to none, in the birth of a union and in changing working families' lives forever.

Source: Genora Johnson Dollinger, quoted in Jeane Westin, *Making Do* (Chicago: Follett Publishing, 1976), 223, 225–226, 229.

Other New Deal Constituencies

The growth of the federal government in the 1930s increased the potential impact of its decisions (and spending) on various constituencies. The New Deal considered a broader spectrum of the population worthy of inclusion in the political process, especially if people organized themselves into pressure groups. Politicians recognized the importance of satisfying the concerns of certain blocs of voters to cement their allegiance to the Democratic party. As a result, women, blacks, and labor received more attention from the federal government and gained greater visibility in public life than ever before.

The same was true of Mexican-Americans. The election of Franklin Roosevelt had an immediate effect on Mexican-American communities demoralized by the depression and the deportations of the Hoover years. Mexican-Americans in cities such as Los Angeles and El Paso found it easier to qualify for relief under New Deal guidelines, plus there was more relief to go around. Even though New Deal guidelines prohibited discrimination based on legal status, the new climate encouraged a marked rise in requests for naturalization papers, the first step toward citizenship. Inspired by New Deal rhetoric about economic recovery and social progress through cooperation, Mexican-Americans increasingly identified their future with the United States, not Mexico. This shift was especially evident among members of Bert Corona's "Mexican-American generation"—the American-born children of Mexican immigrants who filled the leadership vacuum created by the deportations in the early 1930s (see Chapter 25).

Many Mexican-Americans felt a personal connection to President Roosevelt. They warmly applauded his Good Neighbor Policy towards Latin America, whose emphasis on economic cooperation instead of military intervention was seen as a great step forward in hemispheric relations. Mexican-Americans also supported and benefited from the New Deal's labor policies, such as Section 7(a) of the NIRA and the Wagner Labor Relations Act, which fostered an upsurge in labor organizing. For many Mexican-Americans, joining the CIO was an important step in becoming an American.

Participating in the political system increasingly became a part of Mexican-American life. Los Angeles activist Beatrice Griffith noted, "Franklin D. Roosevelt's name was the spark that started thousands of Spanish-speaking persons to the polls." The CIO urged its members to support the Democratic party and the New Deal in local and national elections. In 1939 El Congreso Nacional del Pueblo de Habla Español, the first national civil rights conference for Spanish-speaking peoples, called on its members to become American citizens and vote. The New Deal made it clear that it welcomed the votes of Mexican-Americans and considered them to be an important part of the New Deal coalition. This politicalization was well under way before World War II, and it provided additional spurs to political activism.

But what about groups that were not politically mobilized or that were not recognized as key components of the New Deal coalition? The New Deal's impact on those groups and communities often depended on whether they had sympathetic government administrators in Washington to promote their interests.

Native Americans were one of the nation's most disadvantaged and powerless minorities. Annual individual income in 1934 was only $48, and the unemployment rate was three times the national average. Concerned New Deal administrators such as Secretary of the Interior Harold Ickes and Commissioner of the Bureau of Indian Affairs John Collier tried to correct some of those inequities. The Indian Section of the Civilian Conservation Corps brought needed money and projects to reservations throughout the West, and Indians also received benefits from FERA and CWA work relief projects.

Of far greater significance was the Indian Reorganization Act of 1934, sometimes called the "Indian New Deal." That law reversed the Dawes Severalty Act of 1887 by promoting more extensive self-government through tribal councils and constitutions. The government also reversed the direction of federal Indian policy by abandoning attempts to force native Americans to assimilate into American society in favor of a commitment to cultural pluralism. The New Deal pledged to help preserve Indian languages, arts, and traditions and other aspects of the tribal heritage. The problems of native Americans were so severe, however, that these changes in federal policy produced only marginal results.

The New Deal and the Land

Concern with the land was one of the dominant motifs of the New Deal, and the shaping of the public landscape is among its most visible legacies. Roosevelt brought to the presidency a love of forestry and a conservation ethic nurtured from childhood on his Hudson River estate. New Deal administrators such as Interior Secretary Harold Ickes were avid conservationists. The expansion of federal responsibilities in the 1930s, especially the need to put the unemployed to work on public projects, created a climate conducive to action, as did public concern that was heightened by dramatic images of the drought and devastation of the Dust Bowl. The resulting national resources policy stressed scientific management of the land, conservation instead of commercial development, and the aggressive use of public authority to safeguard both privately and publicly held land.

The most extensive New Deal environmental undertaking was the Tennessee Valley Authority (see Map 26.1). The need for dams to control flooding and erosion in the Tennessee River Basin, a seven-state area with some of the country's heaviest rainfall, had been recognized since World War I. During the 1920s progressives led by Senator George Norris of Nebraska pushed for a public corporation to control flooding and to create a cheap source of electric power on the Tennessee River, but utility companies blocked the project. In 1933 the Tennessee Valley Authority won approval to develop the region's resources under public control. The TVA was the ultimate watershed demonstration area, with its integrated plans for flood control, reforestation, and agricultural and industrial development, including a chemical fertilizer plant. Its hydroelectric grid provided cheap electric power for the valley's residents. The TVA was admired worldwide, becoming one of the most popular destinations for visitors to the United States.

The Dust Bowl helped focus attention on land management and ecological balance. Agents from the Soil Conservation Service in the Department of Agriculture taught farmers the proper technique for tilling hillsides. (Quipped the journalist Alistair Cooke, the New Deal's conception of the common man was someone who could "take up contour plowing late in life.") Government agronomists also tried to remove marginal land from cultivation and prevent soil erosion through better agricultural practices. One of their most widely publicized programs was the creation of the Shelterbelts, which involved planting a line of 220 million trees running roughly along the 99th meridian from Abilene,

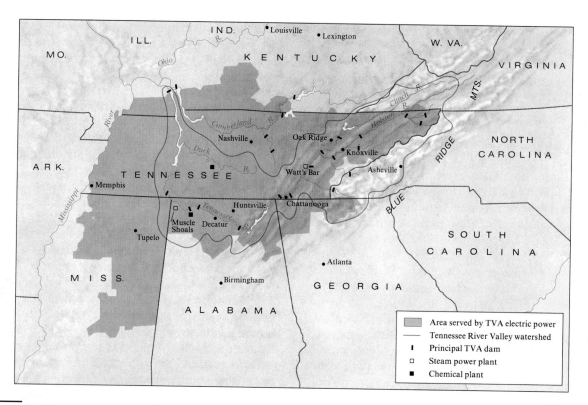

MAP 26.1

The Tennessee Valley Authority

The Tennessee Valley Authority was one of the New Deal's most far-reaching environmental projects. Between 1933 and 1952 the TVA built twenty dams and improved five others. The cheap hydroelectic power generated by the dams brought electricity to hundreds of thousands of local residents.

Texas, to the Canadian border. Planted as a windbreak, the trees also prevented soil erosion. The Shelterbelt program was a personal favorite of Franklin Roosevelt's.

Sometimes political reality dictated specific legislation affecting the environment, such as the Soil Conservation and Domestic Allotment Act of 1936. This legislation filled the void created when the Supreme Court ruled the Agricultural Adjustment Act unconstitutional in January of that year. Under the new act, farmers received payments for cutting the commercial production of crops such as wheat and cotton, which depleted the soil, and planting instead soil-building grasses and legumes such as clover and soybeans. Wheat and cotton were in fact major surplus commodities, and the law provided a way to cut production as well as encourage soil conservation. The Agricultural Adjustment Act of 1938 continued the policy of price supports and payments to farmers to limit production and established soil conservation as a permanent program.

Another priority of the Roosevelt administration was helping rural Americans stay on the land. The Rural Electrification Administration, established in 1935, which brought power to farms, was part of this attempt to im-

prove the quality of rural life (see New Technology, page 817). The New Deal also encouraged urban dwellers to return to rural areas. This "back to the land" motif animated many New Deal projects, especially those planned by the Resettlement Administration under the direction of Rexford Tugwell. Some of the best known examples were planned cooperative communities in rural areas, such as Arthurdale in West Virginia, and the "Greenbelt" residential towns outside Washington, D.C., Cincinnati, and Milwaukee.

Although the TVA, Shelterbelts, and Greenbelt towns were primarily environmental programs, they also put large numbers of the unemployed to work. The Civilian Conservation Corps, the so-called Tree Army, planted some 2 billion trees by 1941, a dozen for every American citizen at the time. Not only was this sound conservation, but it gave the 2.5 million CCC workers a job to do. Similarly, many WPA projects helped achieve conservation and recreational goals.

New Deal construction projects affecting the natural environment are all around us, artifacts from the depression era. CCC and WPA workers built the Blue Ridge Highway, the consummate parkway of the 1930s, con-

Rural Electrification

In 1935 fewer than one-tenth of the nation's 6.8 million farms had electricity. For millions of farm families that stark fact meant a life of unremitting toil made even harsher by the lack of simple conveniences. Farm families used an average of 200 gallons of water a day. Any chore requiring water—and most did—meant pumping the water from a distant well and carrying it to the house or barn in a pair of buckets that weighed as much as 60 pounds. Water had to be heated on a woodstove that required constant tending. Meeting a family's yearly water needs took sixty-three eight-hour days and involved carrying water a distance of 1,750 miles.

Rural women suffered especially from the lack of electricity. Canning, a necessity before refrigeration, kept women standing over steaming vats of fruit or vegetables, often in the worst summer heat, before the freshly harvested produce spoiled. Wash day, traditionally Monday, called for three large zinc washtubs for washing, rinsing, and bleaching. A week's wash consisted of four to eight loads, each requiring three washtubs of clean water hauled from the well. Few rural households could afford commercial soap, so women used lye, which barely got ground-in dirt out of soiled clothes and was very harsh on hands.

If farm women dreaded Monday, they hated Tuesday even more. Tuesday meant ironing, another all-day job. The iron, a 6- or 7-pound wedge of metal, had to be heated on the stove, and because it did not retain heat for more than a few minutes, it took several irons to do a shirt. The women in Texas's hill country called them "sad irons."

A day that began in darkness and was given over to twelve hours of backbreaking toil brought few comforts in the evening. Reading by kerosene lamps strained the eyes. Children's eyes might be strong enough to read in the semidarkness, but few older people could read without squinting. The absence of electricity also meant no radios, which meant no contact with the outside world, no amusement to brighten the darkness.

Studies showed that farmers would find many uses for electricity and would make good customers, but power companies balked at the prospect of electrifying the countryside, claiming that it was not economically feasible to run lines to individual farms. In 1935 the federal government made a commitment to bring power to rural America. The Rural Electrification Administration, an independent agency, promoted the formation of nonprofit farm cooperatives to bring electricity to their regions. For a $5 down payment local farmers could join an association and become eligible for low-interest federal loans covering the cost of installing

"Blue Monday"
Laundry was one of women's hardest household chores. Although this woman did not have to haul water from an outdoor well, she still had to pump it by hand in order to do the wash because her home lacked electricity. She also had to wring out the wet clothes manually, another arduous task.

power lines. Each household was committed to a monthly minimum usage, usually about $3, but as usage increased, the rates came down. By 1940, 40 percent of the nation's farms had electricity; in 1950, the rate reached 90 percent.

Electricity brought relief from the drudgery and isolation of farm life. An electric milking machine saved hours of manual labor, most of it previously done before dawn by the faint glow of a kerosene lamp, so farmers could devote the daylight hours to outdoor chores. An electric water pump lightened many chores, especially hauling water. Electric irons, vacuum cleaners, and washing machines eased women's burdens.

People's responses to rural electrification were poignant. A small child told his mother, "I didn't realize how dark our house was until we got electric lights." One farm woman remembered, "I just turned on the light and kept looking at Paw. It was the first time I'd ever really seen him after dark." Another family, caught unaware by the timing of the hookup, saw its house from a distance and thought it must be on fire. Schoolteachers noticed that children did better at school when they had light to do homework by. Along with the automobile, electricity probably did more than any other technological innovation to break down the barriers between urban and rural life in twentieth-century America.

necting the Shenandoah National Park in Virginia with the Great Smoky Mountain National Park in North Carolina. Government workers built the San Francisco Zoo, Berkeley's Tilden Park, and the canals of San Antonio; the CCC helped complete the East Coast's Appalachian Trail and the West Coast's Pacific Crest Trail through the Sierras. In state parks across the country, cabins, shelters, picnic areas, lodges, and observation towers were built in a style that has been called "government rustic." All those projects shared the New Deal ethos of leisure and recreation coexisting with nature.

What was the long-term impact of the New Deal on land use and conservation? On the Great Plains, probably not very much. Without proper care, many of the Shelterbelts deteriorated, and dust storms struck again in the 1950s. When the CCC and WPA lost their funding in the early 1940s, maintenance work lapsed. But many of the facilities they built still exist today, relics of the conservation ethic and the need to put citizens to work.

Although the New Deal was ahead of its time in its attention to conservation, its legacy to later environmental movements is mixed. Many of the tactics of New Deal projects—damming rivers, blasting fire roads, altering the natural landscape with buildings and shelters—would now be considered too intrusive. The TVA came under attack in the 1970s for its long-standing practice of strip mining and the pollution caused by its power plants and chemical factories. Because of environmental concerns, a project as massive as the TVA probably could never be built today, an ironic conclusion to what was hailed at the time as an enlightened use of government power for the public good.

The Legacies of the New Deal

The New Deal set in motion far-reaching changes, notably the growth of a modern state of significant size. For the first time people experienced the federal government as a concrete part of everyday life. During the 1930s more than a third of the population received direct government assistance from new federal programs such as Social Security, farm loans, relief, and mortgage guarantees. Furthermore, the government made a commitment to intervene in the economy when private instruments of power could not guarantee economic stability. New legislation regulated the stock market, reformed the Federal Reserve System by placing more power in the hands of Washington policy makers, and brought many practices of modern corporate life under federal regulation. The New Deal thus continued and accelerated the pattern begun during the Progressive Era of using federal regulation to bring order and regularity to economic life.

The New Deal also laid the foundations of America's welfare state, that is, the federal government's ac-

The New York World's Fair
The theme of the 1939 World's Fair was "Building the World of Tomorrow." After grimly struggling for a decade to overcome hard times, many Americans were ready to embrace a rosy future of social harmony, interdependence, and material progress. Joseph Binder's prize-winning poster featured the Trylon and the Perisphere, the fair's instantly recognizable symbols.

ceptance of primary responsibility for the individual and collective welfare of the people. Although the New Deal offered more benefits to American citizens than they had ever received before, its safety net had many holes, especially in comparison with the far more extensive welfare systems in Western Europe. The greatest defect of the emerging welfare system was its failure to reach a significant minority of American workers. For example, the Social Security program excluded domestic workers and farm workers for many years. And since state governments administered the programs, benefits varied widely, with southern states consistently providing the lowest amounts. Not until the Great Society programs of President Lyndon Johnson in the 1960s did social welfare programs reach significant numbers of America's poor.

To its credit, the New Deal recognized that poverty was a structural economic problem, not a matter of personal failure. New Deal reformers assumed that once the depression was over, full employment and an active economy would take care of welfare needs, and poverty would wither away. It did not. When later administrations confronted the persistence of inequality and unemployment, they grafted welfare programs onto the jerry-built system left over from the New Deal. Thus the American welfare system would always be marked by its birth during the crisis atmosphere of the Great Depression.

New Deal Coalition. Even if the early welfare system had some serious flaws, it was brilliant politics. The Democratic party courted the allegiance of citizens who benefited from New Deal programs. Organized labor aligned itself with the administration that had made it a legitimate force in modern industrial life. Blacks voted Democratic in direct relation to the economic benefits that poured into their communities. The Women's Division of the Democratic National Committee mobilized 80,000 women at the grass-roots level who supported what the New Deal had done for their communities. The unemployed also looked kindly on the Roosevelt administration. According to one of the earliest Gallup polls, 84 percent of those on relief voted the Democratic ticket in 1936.

The Democratic party did not attract only the down-and-out. Roosevelt's magnetic personality and the dispersal of New Deal benefits to families throughout the social structure brought middle-class voters, many of them first- or second-generation immigrants, into the Democratic fold. The New Deal thus completed the transformation that had begun in the 1920s toward a Democratic party that reflected the interests of ethnic groups, city dwellers, organized labor, blacks, and a broad cross-section of the middle class. Those voters provided the backbone of the Democratic coalition for decades to come.

Yet even in the 1930s the New Deal coalition contained potentially fatal contradictions, mainly involving the issue of race. Because Roosevelt depended on the support of southern white Democrats to pass New Deal legislation, he was unwilling to challenge the economic and political marginalization of blacks in the South. At the same time, New Deal programs were changing the face of southern agriculture by undermining the sharecropping tenant system and encouraging the migration of southern blacks to northern and western cities. Outside the South blacks were not prevented from voting, thus guaranteeing that civil rights would enter the national agenda. The resulting fissures would eventually weaken the coalition that had seemed so invincible at the height of Roosevelt's power.

Culture and Commitment

Many American artists redefined their relationship to society in response to the depression. Never had there been a decade, noted the critic Malcolm Cowley in 1939, "when literary events followed so closely on the flying coat-tails of social events." Political engagement replaced the personal alienation of the 1920s as world events such as the rise of fascism demanded intellectuals' energy. For the first time American culture was considered a valid subject for serious artistic creativity—previously, artists had felt compelled to draw on European models and themes. Although not all art in the decade was federally funded, the New Deal helped foster creative expression through its wide-ranging and controversial experiment in federal patronage of the arts.

New Deal Culture

The depression had dried up traditional sources of private patronage, and creative artists, like most Americans, had nowhere to turn except Washington. The WPA project known as "Federal One" put unemployed artists, actors, and writers to work. Federal One's spirit and purpose extended far beyond relief. New Deal administrators wanted to redefine the relationship between artists and the community so that art would no longer be the province only of the elite. "Art for the millions" became a popular New Deal slogan.

The Federal Art Project (FAP) gave work to many of the twentieth century's leading painters, muralists, and sculptors at a point in their careers when the lack of private patronage might have prevented them from continuing their artistic production. Jackson Pollock, Alice Neel, Willem de Kooning, and Louise Nevelson all received support. Under the direction of Holger Cahill, an expert on American folk art, the FAP commissioned murals for public buildings and post offices across the country. Huge WPA murals covered the walls and ceilings of terminals at the newly constructed La Guardia Airport in New York. As artistic tastes changed in the 1940s and 1950s, most of La Guardia's murals were painted over, but those at its Marine Air Terminal have been restored to their original splendor.

Under the direction of Nicholas Sokoloff, the conductor of the Cleveland Symphony Orchestra, the Federal Music Project employed 15,000 musicians. Government-sponsored orchestras toured the country, presenting free concerts of classical and popular music. Like many New Deal programs, the Music Project emphasized American themes. The composer Aaron Copland wrote his *Billy the Kid* (1938) and *Rodeo* (1942) ballets for the WPA, compositions he based on western folk motifs. The distinctive "American" sound and ath-

Relief Blues
Between 1934 and 1939 an Italian immigrant, O. Louis Guglielmi, found work on the Federal Art Project of the WPA, to which he submitted this painting in 1938. Entitled *Relief Blues*, it represents the social concern and urban realism prominent in American painting during the 1930s. The starkness of the room and its occupants is intensified by the bright red slippers, the pink rose on the floor, and the red lipstick and nail polish of the woman on the left.

letic dance style of these works made them immensely appealing to audiences. The musicologist Charles Seeger and his wife, the composer Ruth Crawford Seeger, cataloged hundreds of American folk songs.

The former journalist Henry Alsberg headed the Federal Writers' Project (FWP), which employed about 5,000 writers at its height (see American Voices, page 821). Young FWP writers who later achieved fame include Saul Bellow, Ralph Ellison, Tillie Olsen, and John Cheever. The black folklorist and novelist Zora Neale Hurston finished three novels while on the Florida FWP, among them *Their Eyes Were Watching God* (1937). Richard Wright won the 1938 *Story* magazine prize for the best tale by a WPA writer and used his spare time to complete *Native Son* (1940).

The FWP produced more than a thousand publications. It collected oral histories of Americans in many walks of life, including a set of 2,000 narratives of former slaves. Its most ambitious project was a set of state guidebooks. Fifty-one state and territorial guides, city guides, and twenty regional guides, including *U.S. One: Maine to Florida*, were published, mostly by commercial presses. Combining tourism, folklore, and history, the guides reflected the resurgence of interest in everything American. They became widely popular, but the choice of subjects sometimes annoyed politicians and state boosters. For example, the 675-page guide to Massachusetts devoted only fourteen lines to the Boston Tea Party and five to the Boston Massacre but allotted thirty-one to the Sacco-Vanzetti case.

Of all the federal creative programs the Federal Theatre Project (FTP) was the most ambitious. American drama thrived in the 1930s, the only time that the United States has had a federally supported national theater. Under the gifted direction of Hallie Flanagan, former head of Vassar College's Experimental Theater, the Theatre Project reached an audience of 25 million to 30 million in the four years of its existence. Talented directors, playwrights, and actors, including Orson Welles, John Huston, and Arthur Miller, offered their talents and services.

The Theatre Project's most successful productions included T. S. Eliot's *Murder in the Cathedral*, Mark Blitzstein's *The Cradle Will Rock*, Shakespeare's *Macbeth* with an all-black cast in a Haitian voodoo setting, and the *Swing Mikado*, a jazz rendition of the Gilbert and Sullivan operetta. Sinclair Lewis's antifascist *It Can't Happen Here* opened simultaneously in eighteen cities across the country, including productions in Spanish and Yiddish. Also popular were miniplays called "Living Newspapers," among them *Triple A Plowed Under*, about farm problems, and *Power*, which dealt with public ownership of utilities.

The theater was one of the most politically committed fields of American creative life in the 1930s. However, Congress was unwilling to appropriate federal funds for what it saw as left-leaning productions, and the FTP was terminated in 1939. Federal One limped along under federal-state sponsorship until 1943, when wartime priorities dealt it a final blow.

Anzia Yezierska

Artists on Relief

Anzia Yezierska's powerful descriptions of immigrant life, particularly *Hungry Hearts* (1920) and *Bread Givers* (1925), brought her fame and a Hollywood movie contract in the 1920s, but she found herself penniless once the depression hit. The Federal Writers' Project was her salvation.

FOUR BILLION DOLLARS FOR JOBS . . . One after another picked up the newspaper, disbelieving. Perhaps because they had fought so hard for it they were stunned. It was too good to be true. And when they were finally convinced that their dream was about to be realized, the discussion became a joyous shouting celebration.

A new world was being born. A world where artists were no longer outcasts, hangers-on of the rich, but backed by the government, encouraged to produce their best work.

The President said so.

People who no longer hoped or believed in anything but the end of the world began to hope and believe again.

In the weeks that followed, radios boomed with it. Everywhere—at grocers, cigar stores, lunch counters, in

the streets—people were discussing the President's plan to end unemployment. Every day we read announcements in the newspapers of the prominent men and women appointed by the President to direct the various departments of W.P.A.

One morning as I was in the kitchen of my rooming house fixing breakfast, the radio broadcast a special news item about W.P.A.: a headquarters had just been set up for the new Writers' Project. I hurried to the address, eager to work. Ever since I had marched with the unemployed I was full of ideas for stories. All I needed to begin writing again was the security of a W.P.A. wage to get my typewriter out of the pawnshop. . . .

Each morning I walked to the Project as lighthearted as if I were going to a party. The huge, barracks-like Writers' Hall roared with laughter and greetings of hundreds of voices. As we signed in, we stopped to smoke, make dates for lunch and exchange gossip. Our grapevine buzzed with budding love affairs, tales of salary raises, whispers of favoritism, the political maneuvers of the big shots, and the way Barnes told off Somervell over the

phone. There was a hectic camaraderie among us, although we were as ill-assorted as a crowd on a subway express—spinster poetesses, pulp specialists, youngsters with school-magazine experience, veteran newspaper men, art-for-art's-sake literati, and the clerks and typists who worked with us—people of all ages, all nationalities, all degrees of education, tossed together in a strange fellowship of necessity. . . .

"Thank God for the depression!" a tall, gaunt man spouted. "The depression fathered W.P.A.!" His tattered coat hung loose on his shrunken body. A safety pin fastened the frayed collar of his shirt. Unaware of his rags, his ghastly appearance, he fixed his eyes on me. "Roosevelt will go down to posterity as the savior of art in America."

"The savior of art!" I laughed. "At the bargain price of $23.86 per artist."

Source: Anzia Yezierska, *Red Ribbon on a White Horse* (New York: Charles Scribner's Sons, 1950; reprint, New York: Persea Books, 1981), 150, 156, 165.

The Documentary Impulse

The WPA arts projects were influenced by a broad artistic trend called the *documentary impulse.* Combining social relevance with distinctively American themes, this approach characterized artistic expression in the 1930s. The documentary, probably the decade's most distinctive genre, influenced practically every aspect of American culture: literature, photography, art, music, film, dance, theater, and radio.

The documentary impulse involved the communication of real life, the presentation of actual facts and events in a way that aroused the interest and emotions of the audience. Emphasizing observation and narration without relying on overembellished prose for impact, this technique exalted the ordinary, finding beauty and

emotion in subjects not usually considered the province of art. It tried to make you, the audience, experience the subject as if you were actually on the scene.

The documentary impulse is evident in John Steinbeck's fiction (see Chapter 25) and John Dos Passos's *U.S.A.* trilogy, which used actual newspaper clippings, dispatches, and headlines in its fictional story. The *March of Time* newsreels, which movie audiences saw before the feature film, presented the news of the world for the pretelevision age, as did the standard opening of radio news broadcasts, "We now take you to. . . ." The filmmaker Pare Lorentz commissioned the composer Virgil Thompson to create music that set the mood for documentary movies such as *The Plow That Broke the Plains* (1936) and *The River* (1936). The new photojournalism magazines, including *Life* and *Look*, founded in 1936 and 1937, respectively, reflected this documentary approach. So did many creative works of the New Deal, from the "Living Newspapers" of the Federal Theatre Project to the American Guide series and oral history interviews prepared by the FWP. The New Deal actually institutionalized the documentary impulse by sending investigators such as the journalist Lorena Hickok and the writer Martha Gellhorn into the field to report on the conditions of people on relief.

The camera was the prime instrument of the documentary impulse. The use of cameras to document social conditions dated back to the probing work of Jacob Riis and Lewis Hine at the turn of the century. When the nation entered another period of intense social and economic questioning in the 1930s, photographers revived and updated this technique. With their haunting images of sharecroppers, Dust Bowl migrants, and the urban homeless, the photographers Dorothea Lange, Walker Evans, and Margaret Bourke-White permanently shaped the image of the Great Depression.

Life
Margaret Bourke-White's photograph of the Fort Peck Dam, with the two human figures in the foreground establishing its scale, graced the inaugural cover of *Life* magazine in 1936. Fort Peck was part of a series of dams the WPA was constructing in the Columbia River Basin for flood control. *Life*'s first issue also contained a photo essay about the town nearest to the Fort Peck Dam, which was named, appropriately, New Deal, Montana.

The federal government played a leading role in compiling the photographic record of the 1930s. In 1935 Roy Stryker, a Columbia economics instructor who had been a teaching assistant under Brains Trust member Rexford Tugwell, took charge of the Historical Section of the Resettlement Administration, with a mandate to document and photograph the American scene for the government. Stryker gathered a talented group of photographers for this massive task, including Evans, Lange, Ben Shahn, Arthur Rothstein, and Marion Post Wolcott. The government hired those photographers solely for their professional skills, not to provide relief, as was done with Federal One's projects. The photographs collected by the Historical Section, which in 1937 became part of the newly created Farm Security Administration (FSA), rank as the best visual representation of life in the United States during the depression decade.

Intellectuals and the Popular Front

In the mid-1930s the rise of fascism in Europe and the Far East called for new forms of political engagement by writers and other intellectuals. Many literary figures participated in a broad leftist movement dedicated to stopping the spread of fascism. The Communist party played a leading role in rallying intellectuals against the fascist threat.

The period from 1935 to 1939 marked the Communist party's greatest appeal in America. Marxism, having predicted the collapse of capitalism, provided an alternative vision of social and economic organization. Communists were scattered throughout all walks of life in the 1930s: working-class activists, intellectuals, housewives, union organizers, farmers, blacks, and even a few New Deal administrators. No longer a small sectarian group, party membership peaked at about a hundred thousand.

The Communist party exerted an especially powerful influence on American writers in the 1930s. Some intellectuals joined the party; many more did not join, but considered themselves "fellow travelers." They sympathized with the party's objectives, wrote for the *Daily Worker* and other party newspapers, and associated with organizations sponsored by the party. The author Mary McCarthy recalled the fascination the party held for her and other intellectuals: "For me, the Communist Party was *the* party, and even though I did not join it, I prided myself on knowing that it was the pinnacle."

The Rise of Fascism in Europe. The courting of intellectuals was part of an important shift in the Communist party's tactics in response to the rise of fascism. Benito Mussolini had established the first fascist regime in Italy in 1922, but fascism did not become a worldwide threat until Adolf Hitler and the National Socialist party took power in Germany in 1933 and began a program of massive rearmament and expansion of the German state (see Chapter 27).

Fearful of a world war set in motion by fascist aggression, the Soviet Union attempted to mobilize support in democratic countries. In Europe and the United States communist parties called for a "popular front" and welcomed the cooperation of any group concerned about the threat of fascism to civil rights, organized labor, and world peace. As part of the popular front, the American Communist party adopted the slogan "Communism is 20th Century Americanism" and worked for Roosevelt's reelection in 1936; Eleanor Roosevelt, whom communists once depicted as a slave of the ruling class, was now lauded for her humanitarianism. This alliance with American liberal groups at mid-decade represented the height of the party's influence in the United States.

The Spanish Civil War. The popular-front strategy became even more urgent with the outbreak of the Spanish Civil War in 1936. Army forces led by Generalissimo Francisco Franco led a rebellion against the elected republican coalition government. Franco received strong support from the fascist regimes in Germany and Italy, while only the Soviet Union and Mexico backed the Spanish government forces, called the Loyalists. The governments of the United States, Great Britain, and France sympathized with the Loyalists but stayed neutral. In the United States strict neutrality legislation in 1935, 1936, and 1937 forbade arms shipments to either side. Because Franco was receiving substantial military aid from Germany and Italy, the neutrality policy doomed the Loyalists.

Most American activists and intellectuals, overcoming their distaste for war, expressed shock at the policy of nonintervention. The Spanish Civil War became the most vital issue of their generation. "People of my sort," observed the writer Malcolm Cowley, "were more deeply stirred by the Spanish Civil War than by any other international event since the World War and the Russian Revolution." Ernest Hemingway immortalized the conflict in his novel *For Whom the Bell Tolls* (1940).

Approximately 3,200 American men and women volunteered to fight on the Loyalist side. Calling themselves the Abraham Lincoln Brigade, they formed part of an international force of soldiers, ambulance drivers, and support personnel. Years later survivors recalled the struggle as the "good fight." Despite assistance from the Soviet Union, the Loyalists were outnumbered and inadequately supplied. In March 1939 the Spanish republic fell to Franco's forces. More than half the American volunteers died in the carnage, which claimed over 700,000 lives altogether.

Although American intellectuals applauded the Soviet Union's active support of the Spanish Loyalists, many literary figures began to feel uncomfortable in leftist circles. The communists remained suspicious of intellectuals, many of whom were too independent to submit to party discipline. A number of writers found it increasingly difficult to satisfy both their artistic urges and the party's demand for fiction that reflected working-class concerns. They were also deeply distressed by mounting evidence of the Soviet leader Joseph Stalin's widespread political repression.

The Nazi-Soviet Pact. The final blow to the popular front came in August 1939, when the Soviet Union, eager to avoid war, signed a nonaggression pact with Nazi Germany. Stalin's willingness to deal with Hitler devastated many supporters of the popular front. Diehard party members loyally accepted Stalin's about-face, but others left the party in disgust. The heyday of American communism ended abruptly.

With the signing of the Nazi-Soviet pact, the world again stood on the brink of war. Although many Americans considered themselves isolationists and hoped the United States would remain aloof from the coming European conflict, they began to realize that the nation faced a greater enemy than the economic problems that had gripped it for the past decade. Barely twenty years after the "war to end all wars," the United States prepared once again to enter a worldwide struggle for the survival of democracy.

The Spanish Civil War
American volunteers who fought on the Loyalist side against Franco in the Spanish Civil War associated their fight against fascism with the figure of Abraham Lincoln, symbol of democracy and human rights. In a similar spirit, the American machine gun detachment of the Abraham Lincoln Brigade called itself the Tom Mooney Company in honor of the World War I labor activist imprisoned for his alleged role in planting a bomb during a preparedness parade in 1916.

Summary

The New Deal offered a broad-based program of political and economic reform, but its programs were hardly revolutionary. President Hoover had taken the first steps toward involving the federal government more actively in economic life, a trend that Roosevelt continued and expanded. The New Deal never cured the depression, but it restored confidence that Americans could overcome hard times. And it provided a measure of economic security against the worst depression in American history by relieving many of its tragic effects.

The New Deal dramatically expanded the size and power of the federal government, continuing a trend that had begun in the late nineteenth and early twentieth centuries. Decisions made in Washington touched millions of individual lives. The New Deal provided new opportunities and a larger role in public life for blacks, women, and the labor movement. In politics the Democratic coalition of white southerners and the urban working class that had begun to emerge in the 1920s reached a climax in the landslide victory of 1936. By 1938, however, the New Deal had run out of steam and hard times were far from over.

The collapse of the economy encouraged a reassertion of American values in literature and the arts. This artistic flowering was partly supported by a unique experiment in government patronage of the arts through the WPA. Many writers blended artistic concerns with intense political commitment. This activism culminated in the popular front, an alliance of liberals and Communists who joined together to oppose the spread of fascism, especially in the Spanish Civil War. This brief period of cooperation ended in 1939 when the Soviet Union signed an agreement with Nazi Germany, bringing the world to the brink of war again.

TIMELINE

1933	Banking crisis
	FDR's first fireside chat
	Emergency Banking Act
	Glass-Steagall Act establishes FDIC
	Agricultural Adjustment Act
	National Industrial Recovery Act
	Tennessee Valley Authority
	United States abandons gold standard
	Townsend Clubs
1934	Securities and Exchange Commission
	Indian Reorganization Act
1935	Supreme Court finds NRA unconstitutional
	National Union for Social Justice (Father Charles Coughlin)
	Resettlement Administration
	National Labor Relations (Wagner) Act
	Social Security Act
	Works Progress Administration
	Huey Long assassinated
	CIO formed
1935–1939	Communist party at height of influence
1936	Supreme Court finds Agricultural Adjustment Act unconstitutional
	Black cabinet
	Roosevelt reelected
	The Plow That Broke the Plains and *The River*
	Life magazine founded
1936–1939	Spanish Civil War
1937	Sit-down strikes
	Memorial Day Massacre
	Supreme Court reorganization fails
	National Housing Act
1937–1938	"Roosevelt recession"
1938	Aaron Copland, *Billy the Kid*
	Fair Labor Standards Act
1939	Federal Theatre Project terminated
	Nazi-Soviet pact

BIBLIOGRAPHY

Comprehensive introductions to the New Deal include Robert S. McElvaine, *The Great Depression* (1984); William E. Leuchtenburg, *Franklin D. Roosevelt and the New Deal* (1963); Barry Karl, *The Uneasy State* (1983); John A. Garraty, *The Great Depression* (1987); Roger Biles, *A New Deal for the American People* (1991); and Harvard Sitkoff, ed., *Fifty Years Later: The New Deal Evaluated* (1985).

The New Deal Takes Over

The New Deal has inspired a voluminous bibliography. Frank Freidel, *Launching the New Deal* (1973), covers the first hundred days in detail. Monographs include Bernard Bellush, *The Failure of the NRA* (1975); Thomas K. McCraw, *TVA and the Power Fight* (1970); John Salmond, *The Civilian Conservation Corps* (1967); Roy Lubove, *The Struggle for Social Security* (1968); Susan Kennedy, *The Banking Crisis of 1933* (1973); Michael Parrish, *Securities Regulation and the New Deal* (1970); Mark Leff, *The Limits of Symbolic Reform: The New Deal and Taxation, 1933–1939* (1984); James Olson, *Saving Capitalism: The Reconstruction Finance Corporation and the New Deal, 1933–1940* (1988); and Bonnie Fox Schwartz, *The Civilian Works Administration, 1933–1934* (1984). Ellis Hawley, *The New Deal and the Problem of Monopoly* (1966), provides a stimulating account of economic policy. Agricultural developments are covered in Theodore Saloutos, *The American Farmer and the New Deal* (1982); Paul Mertz, *The New Deal and Southern Rural Poverty* (1978); and Sidney Baldwin, *Poverty and Politics: The Rise and Decline of the Farm Security Administration* (1968). Greg Mitchell, *The Campaign of the Century* (1992), describes Upton Sinclair's campaign for the California governorship, and Alan Brinkley, *Voices of Protest* (1982), covers the Coughlin and Long movements. See also Leo Ribuffo, *The Old Christian Right: The Protestant Far Right from the Great Depression to the Cold War* (1983).

Roosevelt's second term has drawn far less attention than has the 1933–1936 period. James MacGregor Burns, *Roosevelt: The Lion and the Fox* (1956), provides an overview, as does Barry Karl, *The Uneasy State* (1983). Alan Brinkley, *The End of Reform* (1995), discusses the New Deal and liberalism between 1937 and 1945. The growing opposition to the New Deal is treated in James T. Patterson, *Congressional Conservatism and the New Deal* (1967); Richard Polenberg, *Reorganizing Roosevelt's Government* (1966); and Barry Karl, *Executive Reorganization and Reform in the New Deal* (1963).

The New Deal's Impact on Society

Katie Louchheim, ed., *The Making of the New Deal: The Insiders Speak* (1983), provides an engaging introduction to some of the men and women who shaped the New Deal. See also Peter Irons, *New Deal Lawyers* (1982). On women in the New Deal, see Susan Ware, *Beyond Suffrage* (1981). Blanche Cook, *Eleanor Roosevelt* (1991), takes the story to 1933; see also Lois Scharf, *Eleanor Roosevelt* (1987). George Martin, *Madam Secretary* (1976), covers the career of Frances Perkins. Also of interest is Perkins's memoir, *The Roosevelt I Knew* (1946).

On minorities and the New Deal, see Harvard Sitkoff, *A New Deal for Blacks* (1978); John B. Kirby, *Black Americans in the Roosevelt Era: Liberalism and Race* (1980); Robert Zangrando, *The NAACP Crusade against Lynching, 1909–1950* (1980); and Nancy J. Weiss, *Farewell to the Party of Lincoln* (1983). George J. Sanchez, *Becoming Mexican American: Ethnicity, Culture and Identity in Chicano Los Angeles, 1900–1945* (1993), describes the politicization of Mexican Americans in the 1930s.

Irving Bernstein, *The Turbulent Years* (1970) and *A Caring Society: The New Deal, the Worker, and the Great Depression* (1985), chronicle the story of the labor movement through 1941 in compelling detail. Additional studies include Peter Friedlander, *The Emergence of a UAW Local* (1975); Sidney Fine, *Sit-Down: The General Motors Strike of 1936–1937* (1969); David Brody, *Workers in Industrializing America* (1980); Ronald Schatz, *The Electrical Workers* (1983); Bruce Nelson, *Workers on the Waterfront* (1988); and Lizabeth Cohen, *Making a New Deal: Industrial Workers in Chicago, 1919–1939* (1990). Steven Fraser, *Labor Will Rule* (1991), is a fine biography of Sidney Hillman.

On Indian policy, see Donald Parman, *Navajoes and the New Deal* (1976); Laurence Hauptman, *The Iroquois and the New Deal* (1981); and Laurence C. Kelly, *The Assault on Assimilation: John Collier and the Origins of Indian Policy Reform* (1983). For material on rural electrification, see D. Clayton Brown, *Electricity for Rural America* (1980), and Marquis Childs, *The Farmer Takes a Hand* (1952).

The creation of the New Deal's welfare system is treated in James T. Patterson, *America's Struggle against Poverty* (1981), which carries the story through 1980. Linda Gordon, *Pitied but Not Entitled* (1994), looks at single mothers and the history of welfare. See also Michael Katz, *In the Shadow of the Poorhouse: A Social History of Welfare in America* (1986). For the enduring impact of Franklin Roosevelt on the political system, see William Leuchtenburg, *In the Shadow of FDR* (1983).

Culture and Commitment

The various New Deal programs have found historians in Jerry Mangione, *The Dream and the Deal: The Federal Writers' Project, 1935–1943* (1972); Monty Penkower, *The Federal Writers' Project* (1977); Richard McKinzie, *The New Deal for Artists* (1973); and Jane DeHart Mathews, *The Federal Theater, 1935–1939* (1967). Marlene Park and Gerald Markowitz, *Democratic Vistas* (1984), surveys New Deal murals and art. General studies of cultural expression include William Stott, *Documentary Expression and Thirties America* (1973), and Richard Pells, *Radical Visions and American Dreams* (1973). See also Karen Becker Ohrn, *Dorothea Lange and the Documentary Tradition* (1980), and F. Jack Hurley, *Portrait of a Decade: Roy Stryker and the Development of Documentary Photography in the Thirties* (1972).

Daniel Aaron, *Writers on the Left* (1961), provides an overview of literary currents in the decade. Material on the relationship between intellectuals and the Communist party can be found in Harvey Klehr, *The Heyday of American Communism* (1984). Warren Susman provides a provocative analysis of culture and commitment in the 1930s in *Culture as History* (1984). Peter Carroll, *The Odyssey of the Abraham Lincoln Brigade* (1994), tells the story of Americans in the Spanish Civil War.

Don't Let That Shadow Touch Them

Buy WAR BONDS

Mobilizing the Hearts and Minds of America

This poster used the sinister threat of fascism to American
family life to whip up support for the war effort. (Courtesy of
the War Memorial Museum of Virginia)

CHAPTER 27

The World at War

1939–1945

★ ★ ★

On a Sunday night in October 1938 the actor Orson Welles's "Mercury Theater of the Air" broadcast a modern version of *The War of the Worlds* (1898) by the British writer H. G. Wells. The fictional news bulletins, interspersed with simulated on-the-spot reports, convinced many people that Martians had landed near Princeton, New Jersey, and were invading the countryside. Even though the broadcast included four announcements that the radio program was a dramatization, some people fled their homes. No one doubted the power of radio anymore.

The reason that so many people believed in that fictional invasion might have been that in September of 1938 radio programs had been interrupted repeatedly by ominous news bulletins about a possible European war. Even the September 30 reports of the Munich agreement among Britain, France, and Germany, which put off the threat of immediate war, did not ease people's fears.

In the late 1930s popular culture reflected America's involvement in international events. The coming of World War II would intensify that involvement. When radios announced on December 7, 1941, that the Japanese had attacked Pearl Harbor, Americans realized that this news flash was not a hoax.

World War II ranks with the New Deal as a crucial period of political and economic change in America. Mobilization pumped money and confidence into the economy, ending the Great Depression. The task of fighting a global war increased the government's influence on people's lives and caused dramatic social changes on the home front. But the most far-reaching impact was international as the United States accepted a leading, and continuing, role in world affairs. However, within wartime strategies lay the seeds of the Cold War that would follow.

The Road to War

The rise of fascism in Europe and Asia in the 1930s threatened the fragile peace that had prevailed since the end of World War I. Established by the Versailles treaty, the League of Nations, which the United States never joined, proved too weak to deal with threats to world peace. Roosevelt foresaw the possibility of America's participation in another European war but bowed to the isolationist sentiment that was predominant in the country. By 1939, however, he was leading the nation toward war.

Depression Diplomacy

During the early years of the New Deal, America's involvement in international affairs, especially in Europe, remained limited. Roosevelt put the national interest first, reasoning that only when the United States regained a stable economy could it be an effective international leader. His message to the 1933 London Economic Conference stated that the United States would not participate in plans to stabilize world currencies and effectively killed any hope of common action. One of Roosevelt's few diplomatic initiatives in the early days of the New Deal was formal recognition of the Soviet Union in November 1933.

The Good Neighbor Policy. During his first term Roosevelt and Secretary of State Cordell Hull worked to consolidate American influence in the Western Hemisphere through a network of trade, economic, and cultural agreements with the Latin American countries. That diplomatic strategy, which combined political and economic goals, became known as the Good Neighbor Policy. At its core was Roosevelt and Hull's recognition that the friendship of Latin American countries was essential to the security of the United States and that to win that trust the United States had to develop more equal partnerships with its neighbors.

To that end, the United States voluntarily renounced the use of military force and armed intervention in the Western Hemisphere. At the Pan-American Conference in Montevideo, Uruguay, in December 1933 Hull proclaimed that "no state has the right to intervene in the internal or external affairs of another." In 1934 Congress repealed the Platt Amendment, a relic of the Spanish-American War, which had asserted the United States's right to intervene in Cuba's internal affairs. The U.S. Navy kept (and still keeps) a major base at Cuba's Guantanamo Bay, a symbol of the American presence.

Debates over Isolationism. Although most Americans wanted to avoid foreign entanglements in the early to mid-1930s, Roosevelt disagreed. An internationalist at heart, he wanted the United States to play a prominent role in an international economic and political system that would foster the long-term prosperity necessary for a lasting peace. But FDR was hampered in that wish by isolationism in both Congress and the nation.

Isolationism had been building throughout the 1920s, a product of disillusionment with American participation in World War I. In 1934 Gerald P. Nye, a Republican senator from North Dakota, began a Congressional investigation into the profits of munitions makers during World War I and then widened the investigation to determine the influence of economic interests on America's decision to declare war. Nye's committee concluded that war profiteers, whom it called "merchants of death," had maneuvered the nation into the war for financial gain.

Most of the committee's charges were dubious or simplistic, but they gave momentum to the isolationist movement. In late 1934 Roosevelt revived a proposal that had been supported by the Republican administrations of the 1920s for the United States to join the World Court, a mild internationalist gesture of symbolic rather than real importance. The Senate rejected it.

The Neutrality Act of 1935 pushed the United States farther along an isolationist course. Explicitly designed to prevent a recurrence of the events that had pulled the United States into World War I, the act imposed an embargo on trading arms with countries at war and declared that American citizens traveled on the ships of belligerent nations at their own risk.

In 1936 Congress expanded the Neutrality Act to ban loans to belligerents, and in 1937 it adopted a "cash and carry" provision: if a country at war wanted to purchase nonmilitary goods from the United States, it had to pay for them in cash and pick them up in its own ships. The goal was to protect American commercial ships from attack. Roosevelt did not like that system because it gave him no discretion to decide whether some belligerents, such as the Spanish Loyalists, deserved American support. But he realized how strong the isolationist spirit was and accepted the verdict of Congress. The neutrality policy would soon be put to the test.

Aggression and Appeasement

World War II had its roots in the settlement of World War I (see Chapter 23). Germany deeply resented the international order laid down by the Treaty of Versailles, while other nations, notably Japan and Italy, revived their dreams of an overseas empire. The League of Nations, the collective security system established at Versailles, proved unable to stop aggression. After 1931 force was used by those who wanted to upset the status quo but never by those who wanted to maintain it.

The first challenge came from Japan. In 1930 that country was controlled by an aggressive and militaristic regime with designs on dominating the Pacific Basin in what would later be known as the Greater East Asia Co-Prosperity Sphere. To become an imperial and industrial power, Japan needed raw materials and markets for its goods. In 1931, desiring a buffer against its enemy, the Soviet Union, Japan occupied Manchuria, the northernmost province of China. China appealed to the League of Nations, which ruled against Japan, but imposed no sanctions and took no action. Japan simply served the required one-year notice of withdrawal from the League. In 1937 Japan launched a full-scale invasion of China, and the League was again helpless to stop the aggression.

Japan's defiance of the League encouraged a dictator half a world away: Italy's Benito Mussolini, who had come to power in 1922 and introduced a fascist system. Fascism in Italy and, later, in Germany rested on an ideology of state control of economic affairs, the subordination of individual rights to the "collectivity," and suppression of the labor movement and the left. Above all, it called for a strong dictatorial leader. Parliamentary government and democratic guarantees were superseded by what Mussolini called, far too benevolently, a "dictatorship of the State over many classes cooperating."

Mussolini had long been unhappy with the Versailles treaty, which had not awarded Italy any former German or Turkish colonies. Also, the Italians had never forgotten their stinging defeat by Abyssinia (modern Ethiopia) in 1896, the first time Africans had successfully defended themselves against white imperialists. In 1935 Italy invaded Ethiopia, one of the few independent countries left in Africa. The Ethiopian emperor, Haile Selassie, appealed to the League of Nations, which condemned the invasion as aggression and this time imposed sanctions. However, the member nations could not agree to impose an oil embargo, so the League's actions had little effect. By 1936 Italian subjugation of Ethiopia was complete.

Not Italy but Germany presented the gravest threat to the world order in the 1930s. The Weimar Republic of the 1920s was fundamentally unstable, saddled with huge reparations payments and a guilt clause for World War I that inflamed nationalist passions. Runaway inflation, fear of communism, labor unrest, and rising unemployment were conditions that Adolf Hitler and his National Socialist (Nazi) party skillfully exploited. On January 20, 1933, Hitler became chancellor of Germany, and the *Reichstag* (legislature) soon gave him dictatorial powers. Hitler took the title of *Führer* ("leader"), proclaimed the Third Reich, and outlawed other political parties.

Hitler's goal was nothing short of world domination, as he made clear in his book *Mein Kampf (My*

Hitler
Adolf Hitler seized power in Germany in 1933 and embarked on a plan for world domination. Here he delivers an impassioned address to followers at a 1939 rally. Note the swastika—the Nazi symbol—prominently displayed on the *Führer*'s sleeve and pocket.

Struggle). He would seek to overturn the territorial settlements of the Versailles treaty, "restore" all the Germans of Central and Eastern Europe to a single greater German fatherland, and annex large areas of Eastern Europe to provide *Lebensraum*, or "living space," for Germans. "Inferior races" such as Jews, Gypsies, and Slavs and "undesirables" such as homosexuals and the mentally impaired would have to make way for the "master race." Hitler opened a campaign of persecution against the Jews, including the racial laws of 1933, which forbade marriages between Jews and non-Jews. The first concentration camp was established at Dachau in that year.

Hitler's strategy for gaining territory was to provoke a series of crises that gave Britain and France no alternative but to let him have his way. Germany withdrew from the League of Nations in 1933, and two years later Hitler announced that he planned to rearm Germany in violation of the Versailles treaty. No one stopped him. In 1936 Germany reoccupied the Rhineland, which had been declared a demilitarized zone under the treaty; once again France and Britain took no action. Later that year Hitler and Mussolini joined forces in the Rome-Berlin Axis, a political and military alliance. After the Spanish Civil War broke out in 1936, Germany and Italy armed the Spanish fascists (see Chapter 26).

To fulfill his global strategy, Hitler needed an Asian ally. The obvious choice was Japan. On November 26, 1936, Japan entered into the Anti-Comintern Pact with Germany. The announced purpose was to oppose communism, but the pact was really a military alliance between Japan and the Axis, which was formalized in 1940.

The Failure of Appeasement. Persecution of the Jews and other minorities escalated in Germany, and Hitler's ambitions grew. In 1938 he sent troops to annex Austria, proclaiming an *Anschluss* (union) between Germany and Austria. France and Britain hoped he would go no further, but the German dictator was scheming to seize part of Czechoslovakia, the keystone of Central Europe. Because Czechoslovakia had an alliance with France, war seemed imminent. At the Munich Conference in September 1938 Prime Minister Neville Chamberlain of Britain and Prime Minister Edouard Daladier of France capitulated, agreeing to let Germany annex the Sudetenland, the German-speaking border areas of Czechoslovakia, in return for Hitler's pledge to seek no more territory.

Within six months Hitler's forces overran the rest of Czechoslovakia and threatened to march into Poland, exposing the folly of Chamberlain's pronouncement that the Munich agreement had guaranteed "peace with honor . . . peace for our time." Britain and France realized that their policy of appeasement had been disastrous, and they prepared to take a stand, each relying on its own defenses—Britain on its island isolation and France on the massive fortification of the Maginot Line on its eastern borders. In August 1939 Hitler shocked the world by signing a nonaggression pact with the Soviet Union, allowing Germany to avoid waging war on two fronts. German troops attacked Poland on September 1, 1939, and two days later Britain and France declared war on Germany. World War II had begun.

American Neutrality, 1939–1941

Because it had become a major world power, whatever the United States did would affect the course of the European conflict. Two days after the war started the United States officially declared neutrality. Roosevelt made no secret of his sympathies, however. He pointedly rephrased Woodrow Wilson's declaration of 1914: "This nation will remain a neutral nation, but I cannot ask that every American remain neutral in thought as well." The overwhelming majority of Americans supported the Allies (Britain and France) over the Nazis—84 percent to 2 percent, with 14 percent neutral, according to a 1939 poll—but most Americans did not want to be drawn into another world war.

So began what *Time* magazine would later call America's "thousand-step road to war." After a bitter battle in Congress Roosevelt won a modification of the neutrality laws in November 1939. The Allies could now buy weapons from the United States, but only on the same cash and carry basis established for nonmilitary goods by the 1937 Neutrality Act. To avoid a repetition of the conflicts that drew the United States into World War I, Congress authorized the president to restrict American citizens and ships from entering combat zones and to prevent American merchant ships from carrying cargo to combatants' ports.

After the German conquest of Poland in September 1939, a false calm settled over Europe. This "phony war" lulled many Americans into believing that arming the Allies would be enough to defeat Germany. Hitler soon shattered their complacency. In a few hours on April 9, 1940, Nazi tanks overran Denmark. Norway fell to the Nazi *Blitzkrieg* ("lightning war") next, and the Netherlands, Belgium, and Luxembourg soon followed. Then the Germans stormed into France from the north, bypassing the Maginot Line and making short work of the combined British and French troops. On June 22,

America First
In rallies, radio broadcasts, newspaper advertisements, and even bumper stickers (such as the one pictured here), the America First Committee expressed its opposition to U.S. entry into World War II. This bumper sticker was more likely to have been seen in the Midwest, where the movement was strongest, than in the South. And it would likely have been removed after Pearl Harbor, when the America First Committee pledged full support to the war effort.

1940, France fell. Only Britain stood between the United States and Hitler's plans for world domination.

Intervention Gains. During the summer and fall of 1940 German planes bombarded Britain mercilessly in the Battle of Britain, destroying the myth of its island invincibility. In America the debate between interventionists and isolationists continued. The journalist William Allen White and his Committee to Defend America by Aiding the Allies led the interventionists. Isolationists, including the aviator Charles Lindbergh, Senator Gerald Nye, and the former National Recovery Administrator Hugh Johnson, formed the America First Committee in 1940 to keep the nation out of the war. The Chicago *Tribune*, the Hearst newspapers, and other conservative publications, especially in the Midwest, supported the isolationist cause.

Despite the efforts of the America Firsters, in 1940 the United States moved closer to involvement. Roosevelt began putting the economy and the government on a defense footing by creating the National Defense Advisory Commission and the Council of National Defense in May 1940. In June of that election year he brought two prominent Republicans, Henry Stimson and Frank Knox, into his cabinet as secretaries of war and the navy, respectively, to give a bipartisan character to the war preparations. During the summer the president traded fifty World War I destroyers to Great Britain for the right to build military bases on British possessions in the Atlantic, circumventing the 1939 neutrality legislation through an executive order. In October a bipartisan majority in Congress approved a large increase in defense spending and instituted the first peacetime draft registration and conscription in American history. Another draft law, which came up in August 1941, lengthening draftees' service from one year to two and a half years, passed by a single vote.

The 1940 Election. While the Nazi *Blitzkrieg* raged in Europe, the United States prepared for the 1940 election. Would Roosevelt seek an unprecedented third term? He had not designated a successor, and the war in Europe convinced him that he should run. He submitted to a "draft" at the Democratic National Convention. Although the delegates acclaimed Roosevelt's renomination, they balked at his choice for vice-president, liberal Secretary of Agriculture Henry A. Wallace, to replace John Nance Garner of Texas, a conservative who had long since broken with the New Deal. Wallace's nomination went through only after Eleanor Roosevelt flew to the convention in Chicago and asked the delegates to put politics aside in a national crisis.

The Republicans nominated a political newcomer, Wendell Willkie of Indiana, a lawyer and the president of the Commonwealth and Southern Electric Utilities Company. Willkie, a former Democrat, supported many of the New Deal's domestic and international policies, including Roosevelt's trade of destroyers for military bases. Trying to compete against the charismatic Roosevelt, Willkie portrayed himself as a man of the people, provoking crusty Secretary of the Interior Harold Ickes to call him "a simple barefoot Wall Street lawyer." The platforms of the two parties differed only slightly. Both pledged aid to the Allies but stopped short of calling for American participation in the war.

Initially Willkie conducted his campaign in a bipartisan spirit, but as the election approached, Republican leaders pressured him to go on the offensive. Charging that Roosevelt was leading the country into war, Willkie promised that he would not send "one American boy into the shambles of another war." Roosevelt's reply on October 28, 1940, probably clinched his victory: "I have said this before, but I shall say it again and again and again: Your boys are not going to be sent into foreign wars." (Of course, if the United States was attacked, it would no longer be a foreign war.) Willkie's spirited campaign resulted in a closer election than those of 1932 and 1936, but Roosevelt and the vital Democratic coalition won 55 percent of the popular vote and a more lopsided victory in the electoral college.

Lend-Lease. With the election behind him Roosevelt was in a better position to persuade the American people to increase aid to Britain, which had been at war for eighteen months. In Roosevelt's view the survival of Britain was the key to American security, so anything that helped that country's defense was crucial to the United States. American sympathy for the British was on the rise as scenes of destruction from the nightly German bombings appeared in the newspapers, on the radio, and in newsreels. German submarines were sinking British ships faster than they could be replaced. When Britain could no longer afford to pay cash for arms, Roosevelt decided to "eliminate the dollar sign."

At a press conference in early December 1940 Roosevelt used the analogy of lending a neighbor a garden hose to put out a fire to explain what later became known as lend-lease: "I don't say to him, . . . 'Neighbor, my garden hose cost me $15; you have to pay me $15 for it.' . . . I don't want $15—I want my garden hose back after the fire is over." In a fireside chat at the end of that month Roosevelt reinforced the idea that supplying arms to Britain would not bring the United States closer to war but would enable the nation to serve as "the great arsenal of democracy." In his State of the Union address to Congress in January 1941 Roosevelt connected lend-lease to the defense of democracy at home as well as in Europe. He presented what he called "four essential human freedoms . . . everywhere in the world," his counterparts to Wilson's Fourteen Points of 1918, as reasons for American intervention and as goals for an international postwar society (see Chapter 23). The

Four Freedoms were freedom of speech and expression, freedom of worship, freedom from want, and freedom from fear. Although Roosevelt avoided stating explicitly that America had to enter the war to protect those freedoms, he intended them to be justifications for exactly that occurrence, which he regarded as inevitable.

The United States virtually entered the war when Congress passed the Lend-Lease Act in March 1941. To administer the program, Roosevelt turned to the former relief administrator Harry Hopkins, who became one of his most trusted advisers during the war years. The legislation authorized the president to "lease, lend, or otherwise dispose of" arms and other equipment to any country whose defense was considered vital to the security of the United States. After Germany invaded the Soviet Union in June 1941 (an abandonment of the Nazi-Soviet pact of two years earlier), the United States extended lend-lease to the Soviet Union, which became part of the Allied coalition.

The Atlantic Charter. Roosevelt's determination to aid Britain was reinforced by the rapport he was developing with the British prime minister, Winston Churchill. The two leaders had formed a friendly working relationship while corresponding over aid to Britain but had not met. In August 1941 Roosevelt and Churchill conferred secretly aboard a battleship off the Newfoundland coast to discuss goals and military strategy. Their joint press release, which became known as the Atlantic Charter, provided the ideological foundation of the western cause and of the peace to follow, even before the Japanese attack on Pearl Harbor. The Charter was not an official document, but like Roosevelt's Four Freedoms, it had many similarities to Wilson's Fourteen Points. It called for postwar economic collaboration and guarantees of political stability to ensure that "all men in all the lands may live out their lives in freedom from fear and want." The Charter also supported free trade and the principle of collective security and condemned territorial gains achieved as the spoils of victory.

As in World War I, when Americans started supplying the Allies, Germany attacked American and Allied ships. By September 1941 Nazi submarines and American vessels were fighting an undeclared naval war in the Atlantic, unknown to the American public. In October, Congress authorized the arming of merchant vessels. However, without an actual enemy attack, Roosevelt still hesitated to ask Congress for a declaration of war.

The Attack on Pearl Harbor

The final provocation came not from Germany but from Japan. Tensions between Japan and the United States had been building throughout the 1930s. Japanese military advances in China had upset the balance of

political and economic power in the Pacific, where the United States had long enjoyed the economic benefits of the Open Door policy, especially access to the raw materials and large markets of China (see Chapter 22). After the Japanese invasion of China in 1937, Roosevelt denounced "the present reign of terror and international lawlessness," suggesting that aggressors such as Japan be "quarantined" by peace-loving nations. But he deliberately left the meaning of *quarantine* vague, a political necessity because isolationism was still strong in the land. Despite this, initial public reaction to the speech was strongly favorable, even among some isolationists, though the Hearst newspapers denounced it vigorously.

Even when directly provoked, the United States avoided taking a stand. During the brutal sack of Nanking in 1937 the Japanese sank an American gunboat, the *Panay*, in the Yangtze River. The United States allowed Japan to apologize and accepted more than $2 million in damages, and the incident was quickly smoothed over.

Japan's intentions soon became more expansionist. In 1940 Japan signed the Tri-Partite Pact with Germany and Italy. In the fall of 1941 Japanese troops occupied the northern part of French Indochina. The United States retaliated by effectively cutting off trade with Japan, including vital oil shipments that accounted for almost 80 percent of Japanese consumption. (At that time the United States was producing two-thirds of the world's oil.) Before its supplies ran down, Japan had to decide whether to go to war or accept American demands that it cease its expansionism in Asia. In July 1941 Japanese troops occupied the rest of Indochina; Roosevelt froze Japanese assets in the United States and instituted an embargo on trade with Japan.

In September 1941 the government of Prime Minister Hideki Tojo began secret preparations for war against the United States. Talks between the two nations continued without progress. By November American military intelligence knew that Japan was planning an attack but did not know where it would come. In fact, Japan had decided to mount simultaneous surprise attacks on all the principal British and U.S. naval bases in the western Pacific. Early on Sunday morning, December 7, 1941, Japanese bombers attacked Pearl Harbor, killing more than 2,400 Americans. Eight battleships, three cruisers, three destroyers, and almost two hundred airplanes were destroyed or heavily damaged. Luckily there were no aircraft carriers in port at the time—those vessels would be far more important in the war to come. The Japanese also failed to destroy Pearl Harbor's ship repair facilities and oil reserves, which would have stranded the navy in Hawaii until oil shipments arrived from the West Coast, thousands of miles away. From a military standpoint the Japanese attack was something of a failure.

Pearl Harbor
The U.S. destroyer *Shaw* exploded into flames after receiving a direct hit during the surprise Japanese attack on Pearl Harbor on December 7, 1941. It was early Sunday morning, and many of the servicemen were still asleep. More than 2,400 Americans were killed; the Japanese suffered only light losses.

The attack also failed in its aim to demoralize the United States. Instead, Pearl Harbor united the American people in anger and a determination to fight. Pearl Harbor Day is etched in the memories of millions of Americans who remember precisely what they were doing when they heard about the attack. The next day Roosevelt went before Congress and, calling December 7 "a date which will live in infamy," asked for a declaration of war against Japan. The Senate unanimously voted for war, and the House concurred by a vote of 388 to 1. The lone dissenter was Jeannette Rankin of Montana, who had also opposed American entry into World War I. Three days later Germany and Italy declared war on the United States, and the United States in turn declared war on those nations.

Mobilizing for Victory

The task of fighting a global war accelerated the growing influence of the state on all aspects of American life. Coordinating the changeover from civilian to war production, raising an army, and assembling the necessary work force taxed government agencies to the limit. Mobilization on such a scale demanded cooperation between business executives and political leaders in Washington, solidifying a partnership that had been growing since World War I. But the most dramatic expansion of power occurred at the presidential level when Congress passed the War Powers Act of December 18, 1941, giving Roosevelt unprecedented authority over all aspects of the conduct of the war.

Defense Mobilization

Defense mobilization did more than just end the Great Depression: it caused the economy to more than double. In 1940 the gross national product was at $99.7 billion; it reached $211 billion by the end of the war (see Figure 27.1). After-tax profits of American business companies rose from $6.4 billion in 1940 to $10.8 billion in 1944. Agricultural output grew by a third.

During the war the federal government spent $186 billion on war production, sometimes as much as $250 million a day. The peak of mobilization occurred in late 1943, when two-thirds of the economy was directly involved in the war effort, as opposed to only one-quarter in World War I. By 1945 the United States had turned out 86,000 tanks, 296,000 airplanes, 15 million rifles and machine guns, 64,000 landing craft, and 6,500 ships. Mobilization on this gigantic scale gave a tremendous boost to the economy and, after years of depression, restored faith in the capitalist system.

In this period the federal bureaucracy grew far more than it had during the eight years of the New Deal. The number of civilians employed by the government increased almost fourfold, to 3.8 million. The government gave the civil service exam two or three times a day at the height of wartime hiring. The federal budget of $95.2 billion in 1945 was ten times that of 1939. The national debt grew sixfold, topping out at $258.6 billion in 1945. Along with huge federal budgets came greater acceptance of Keynesian economics, that is, the use of fiscal policy to stimulate economic growth.

Financing the War. Taxes paid about half the cost of the war, compared with 30 percent of the cost of World War

FIGURE 27.1

Government Spending as Percent of GNP

Government defense spending was a minuscule percent of the gross national product in the 1930s, but ballooned during World War II and rose again during the Korean War. Nondefense government spending did not display as wild fluctuations, just a steady, upward trend.

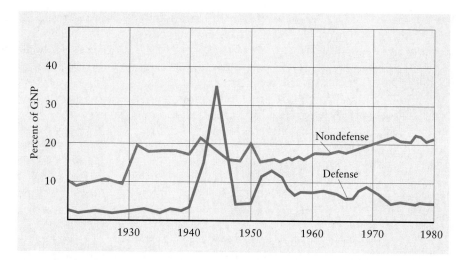

I. The Revenue Act of 1942 continued the income tax reform that had begun during World War I by reaching beyond wealthy individuals and corporations to average citizens. The number of people paying income tax increased from 3.9 million in 1939 to 42.6 million in 1945; tax collections rose from $2.2 billion to $35.1 billion, facilitated by the payroll deductions and tax withholding instituted in 1943. This mass-based tax system, a revolutionary change in the financing of the modern state, was sold to the taxpayers as a way to express their patriotism. War bond drives gave people an opportunity to put their savings at the disposal of the government by buying long-term Treasury bonds, which financed the remaining cost of the war. War bonds had the additional benefit of withdrawing money from circulation, which helped hold down inflation.

Like Woodrow Wilson during World War I, Roosevelt turned to business leaders to run the war economy. Defense preparations had been under way since 1940; 25 percent of the economy was already devoted to war production before Pearl Harbor. In January 1941 Roosevelt established the Office of Production Management under William Knudsen, the president of General Motors. After the Japanese attack Roosevelt disbanded that agency and replaced it with the War Production Board (WPB), headed by Donald Nelson, a former Sears, Roebuck executive.

The WPB awarded defense contracts, evaluated military and civilian requests for scarce resources, and oversaw the conversion of industries to military production. The last Ford rolled off the assembly line in 1942 as automobile plants were converted to bomber production. Business leaders, who had opposed the New Deal and still had the depression on their minds, were reluctant to invest in plant expansion or new production. As a spur, the government granted generous tax write-offs for plant construction. It also approved contracts with cost-plus provisions that guaranteed profits and promised that industries could keep the new factories after the war.

In the interest of efficiency and maximum production, the WPB found it easier to deal with major corporations than with small businesses. The fifty-six largest corporations got three-fourths of the war contracts, with a third going to the top ten. This system of allocating contracts, along with the suspension of antitrust prosecution during the war, hastened the trend toward large corporate structures. In 1940 the hundred largest companies manufactured 30 percent of the nation's industrial output; in 1945 their share was 70 percent. Those corporations formed the core of the military-industrial complex of the postwar years (see Chapters 28 and 29).

The Office of Price Administration and Civilian Supply (OPA) supervised the domestic economy, allocating resources and trying to keep inflation down. By February 1942 retail prices were rising 2 percent a month. In April the OPA froze most prices and rents at their March 1942 levels. When loopholes, especially regarding food prices, undermined that effort, Congress passed the Anti-Inflation Act, which stabilized prices, wages, and salaries. The consumer price index rose 28.3 percent between 1940 and 1945, but most of the inflation occurred before 1943.

Roosevelt remained unsatisfied with the mobilization effort; there were too many government agencies, and their actions often overlapped. In October 1942 he persuaded Justice James F. Byrnes to resign from the Supreme Court to head the Office of Economic Stabilization and, after 1943, the Office of War Mobilization. Byrnes soon became the second most powerful person in the administration and finally brought order to production goals for civilian and military needs. The results were remarkable.

Shipbuilding showed that American productive capacity was at full strength. By 1941 the German navy had crippled transatlantic transport, sinking about 12 million tons of mostly U.S.-built Allied shipping in the North Atlantic. Producing replacement vessels became a high priority. By turning out clunky but easy-to-build

Liberty ships, the United States produced 19 million tons of merchant shipping by 1943, up from 1 million tons two years earlier.

Henry J. Kaiser, a West Coast shipbuilder, performed shipyard production miracles. Using the mass-production techniques of the automobile industry, Kaiser cut the time needed to build a transport ship from 300 days to 17. He motivated workers through high pay and fringe benefits, including one of the country's first prepaid medical programs (see American Lives, pages 836–837). Kaiser's name became synonymous with getting things done fast. Although not all industries could boast of freedom from snafus (an acronym coined during the war from the expression "situation *n*ormal, *a*ll *f*ouled *up*"), business and government compiled an impressive record. As in World War I, industry played a significant role in the military victory.

Mobilizing the American Fighting Force

Going to war meant mobilizing human resources on both the battlefield and the home front. Under the chief of staff, George C. Marshall, the army grew from 200,000 soldiers in 1939 to over 8 million in 1945. By the end of World War II the U.S. armed forces numbered more than 15 million men and women. The army, including those who served in the Army Air Force, enlisted the most, but almost 4 million served in the navy, 600,000 in the marines, and 240,000 in the coast guard.

Draft boards registered about 31 million men between the ages of eighteen and forty-four and ordered physical examinations for about a sixth of the male population. More than half the men failed to meet the physical standards, with defective teeth and poor vision causing the greatest number of rejections.

The military also tried to screen out homosexuals, but its attempts were ineffectual. Once in the services, homosexuals found opportunities to participate in a gay subculture more extensive than that in civilian life.

Class distinctions and racial discrimination prevailed in the armed forces, mainly directed against the approximately 700,000 blacks in uniform. African-Americans served in all branches of the armed forces but were assigned the most menial duties; a great number served as messmen on navy ships, for example. The army even segregated black and white blood banks, a practice without scientific merit. The National Association for the Advancement of Colored People (NAACP) and other civil rights groups chided the government with reminders such as "A Jim Crow army cannot fight for a free world," but the military continued to segregate African-Americans. In contrast, Mexican-Americans were never officially segregated. Unlike blacks, they were welcomed into combat units, and seventeen Mexican-Americans won the Congressional Medal of Honor.

Women in Military Service. About 350,000 American women, both black and white, enlisted in the armed services and achieved a permanent status in the military. There were about 140,000 WAC (Women's Army Corps), 100,000 naval WAVES (Women Appointed for Volunteer Emergency Service), 23,000 members of the Marine Corps Women's Reserve, and 13,000 SPARs (for *Semper Paratus*, or *Always Ready*, the coast guard's motto) in the coast guard. In addition, about 1,000 WASPs (Women's Airforce Service Pilots) ferried planes and supplies in noncombat areas. A third of the nation's registered nurses volunteered for military duty: about 60,000 served in the army and 14,000 in the navy.

The armed forces limited the types of duty assigned to women, as it did with blacks. Women were barred from combat, although nurses and medical personnel sometimes served close to the front lines, risking capture or death. Most jobs reflected stereotypes of women's roles in civilian life—clerical work, communications, and health care. The widely distributed pinups of Betty Grable in a bathing suit, Rita Hayworth in a flimsy nightgown, and, for the black soldiers, the singer Lena Horne were probably closer to the average GI's view of women than a WAC or a WAVE was.

Join the Marines
Government ads pitched patriotic appeals to join the military, and women quickly enlisted. As this poster makes clear, however, one of women's main functions was to free up men so that they could go to the front. (Courtesy of the War Memorial Museum of Virginia)

Henry J. Kaiser:
World War II's "Miracle Man"

Henry Kaiser was a workaholic. He hated being alone and hated taking vacations. He worked twenty-hour days and expected his top managers to do the same. If ordinary mortals were trying to sleep in California, he made a long-distance call to an associate in another time zone. "Whenever he had a new idea—and he commonly had a score or so daily—he reached for the telephone," noted his biographer, Mark Foster. As early as 1942 his company was running up then-extravagant phone bills of $250,000 a year.

Kaiser was one of the most widely known figures of the 1940s, a genuine folk hero to many for his ability to get things done but an example of an entrepreneur totally dependent on costly federal boondoggles to his critics. After shipyard triumphs such as building an entire Liberty ship in four days, fifteen hours, and twenty-six minutes in November 1942, the press dubbed him the "Miracle Man." Franklin Roosevelt seriously considered the industrialist for the vice-presidential slot on the 1944 Democratic ticket.

Kaiser's career and the rise of the modern American West went hand in hand. Born in upstate New York in 1882 to German immigrant parents, he left school at thirteen to make his way in the world. In 1906 he headed west to Spokane, Washington, to try to establish himself in business so that he could marry his fiancée; in 1921 he and his family settled permanently in Oakland, California. From 1914 to 1931 Kaiser's contracting business built roads, trying to keep up with the West's insatiable demand for highways for the new automobiles rolling off the assembly lines in Detroit. In the 1930s Kaiser was part of a six-company partnership that successfully bid for massive engineering projects such as building the Hoover and Grand Coulee dams, federally funded public-works projects that permanently changed the western landscape. In the 1930s he also lobbied extensively in Washington, developing contacts with New Deal bureaucrats that would prove invaluable during the war years.

Moved largely by wartime opportunities, Kaiser left construction to launch a career as an industrialist. He made his first big splash—literally—building Liberty ships faster and better than anyone else. But before he could build ships he had to build shipyards. Drawing on the availability of vacant tracts of waterfront unavailable to older shipyards in the East, he constructed work spaces large enough to accommodate the assembly of prefabricated ship components. Kaiser's Richmond, California, shipyards were designed like a city grid, complete with numbered and lettered streets. "It was a city without houses," remembered one worker, "but the traffic was heavy. Cranes, trucks, trains noised by." Recalled a recent migrant from a small Iowa town, "It was such a huge place, something I had never been in. People from all walks of life, all coming and going and working, and the noise. The whole atmosphere was overwhelming to me."

Although Kaiser did not invent the subassembly technique, he was the most successful at applying mass production to shipbuilding. Previously, most jobs in shipbuilding had been skilled or semiskilled, requiring apprenticeship and training far too lengthy for the wartime emergency. To train new workers more quickly, the work process was broken down into small, specialized tasks, in effect deskilling what had previously been a craft. As Kaiser put it, "production is not labor anymore, but a process."

The Kaiser shipyards were known as much for their corporate welfare programs as for their bureaucratized work climate. Kaiser offered his workers innovations such as day care, financial and job counseling, subsidized housing, and especially health care, his most significant long-term contribution. The Kaiser Permanente Medical Care Program was founded in 1942, an outgrowth of prepaid health care plans first tried on remote federal construction projects in the 1930s. This health care system, what is now called a health maintenance organization (HMO), was available to Kaiser workers for the nominal paycheck deduction of 50 cents a week. Almost 90 percent of his workers exercised that option. Kaiser provided health care for both philanthropic and business reasons. The initial investment was quickly repaid in the form of healthier workers, lower absenteeism, and greater productivity. As a Permanente executive explained, "To the private physician, a sick person is an asset. To Permanente, a sick person is a liability. We'd go bankrupt if we didn't keep most of our members and their families well most of the time."

Whereas many business executives faced the postwar period with cautious trepidation, Kaiser looked forward to peacetime reconversion with the boundless optimism of a farsighted entrepreneur. He was especially excited about opportunities for industrial expansion in the West. Between 1944 and 1946 he identified opportunities in areas such as steel, magnesium, and aluminum as well as foreseeing a demand for mass-produced suburban tract housing. In the 1950s he headed a multinational corpo-

rate empire that included dozens of companies with assets close to $1 billion.

To many Americans Henry Kaiser was a twentieth-century incarnation of Horatio Alger, even though he was a portly sixty years old in 1942, when he launched the Richmond shipyards. In terms of managerial style, he was more an old-style "seat-of-the-pants" entrepreneur than a modern corporate bureaucrat. He was a maverick, challenging traditional ways of doing business at every stage of his career. He was a visionary in the role that he saw for an industrial West, a dream which was amply fulfilled in the postwar era. But he was also lucky, his success being the product of a highly favorable set of economic conditions both in the West and globally during World War II and its aftermath. After his death in 1967 his industrial empire largely disappeared, but Kaiser Permanente lives on, one of the country's largest and most successful health maintenance organizations.

The Miracle Man
In November 1942, Henry Kaiser uses an 81-piece, 14-foot-long model of the 10,400-ton Liberty freighter to show shipowners and navy representatives how it was built in the amazing time of 4 days, 15 hours, and 25 minutes.

The WACS Overseas
Not all military women were relegated to stateside duty.
These eager WACS, members of the first Women's Army
Corps unit to go overseas, have just arrived in North Africa
in 1943 to begin their assignments.

Women and the War Effort

When millions of citizens entered military service, a
huge hole opened in the American work force. The
backlog of depression-era unemployment quickly disappeared, and the United States faced a critical labor
shortage. The nation's defense industries provided jobs
for about 7 million new workers, including great numbers of women and blacks who were given employment
opportunities for the first time.

Government planners "discovered" women while
looking for workers to fill the jobs vacated by departing
servicemen. The recruiting campaign drew on patriotism. One poster urged, "Longing won't bring him back
sooner . . . GET A WAR JOB!" Recruiters promised
that women would take to riveting machines and drill
presses "as easily as to electric cake-mixers and vacuum
cleaners." The artist Norman Rockwell supported the
campaign by creating his famous "Rosie the Riveter"
cover for the *Saturday Evening Post.*

Although the government directed its propaganda
at housewives, women who were already employed
gladly abandoned low-paying "women's" jobs as domestic servants or file clerks for higher-paying jobs in
defense factories. Suddenly the nation's factories were
full of women working as riveters, welders, blast furnace cleaners, and drill press operators (see American
Voices, page 839). Women made up 36 percent of the
labor force in 1945 compared with 24 percent at the beginning of the war.

Government planners and employers regarded
women as just filling in while the men were away. Employers rarely offered day care or flexible hours, and
government child care programs set up by the 1940 Lan-
ham Act reached only 10 percent of those who needed
them. Because women were responsible for home care as
well as their jobs, they had a higher absentee rate than
did men. Often, the only way to get shopping done or
take a child to the doctor was to skip work. Women war
workers also faced discrimination on the job. In shipyards women with the most seniority and responsibility
earned $6.95 a day, whereas the top men made as much
as $22.

When the men came home from war and the plants
returned to peacetime operations, Rosie the Riveter was
out of a job. However, many women refused to put on
an apron and stay home. Women's participation in the
labor force dropped temporarily when the war ended
but rebounded steadily for the rest of the 1940s, especially among married women.

Wartime Workers
The photographer Dorothea Lange captured these shipyard
construction workers coming off their shift at a factory in
Richmond, California, in 1942. Note the large number of
women workers and the presence of minority workers. Sev-
eral of the workers prominently display their union buttons.
(Courtesy of the Dorothea Lange Collection. The City of
Oakland. The Oakland Museum, 1982)

Fanny Christina Hill

"Rosie the Riveter"

Like many black women, Fanny Christina Hill had been trapped in domestic service until she got a job at North American Aircraft. After quitting near war's end to have a child, she returned to North American Aircraft, where she worked from 1946 until her retirement in 1980—one of the few wartime women who got their jobs back.

I don't remember what day of the week it was, but I guess I must have started out pretty early that morning. When I went there, the man didn't hire me. They had a school down here on Figueroa and he told me to go to the school. I went down and it was almost four o'clock and they told me they'd hire me. You had to fill out a form. They didn't bother too much about your experience because they knew you didn't have any experience in aircraft. Then they give you some kind of little test where you put the pegs in the right hole.

There were other people in there, kinda mixed. I assume it was more women than men. Most of the men was gone, and they weren't hiring too many men unless they had a good excuse. Most of the women was in my bracket, five or six years younger or

older. I was twenty-four. There was a black girl that hired in with me. I went to work the next day, sixty cents an hour. . . .

I was a good student, if I do say so myself. But I have found out through life, sometimes even if you're good, you just don't get the breaks if the color's not right. I could see where they made a difference in placing you in certain jobs. They had fifteen or twenty departments, but all the Negroes went to Department 17 because there was nothing but shooting and bucking rivets. You stood on one side of the panel and your partner stood on this side, and he would shoot the rivets with a gun and you'd buck them with the bar. That was about the size of it. I just didn't like it. I didn't think I could stay there with all this shooting and a'bucking and a'jumping and a'bumping. I stayed in it about two or three weeks and then I just decided I did *not* like that. I went and told my foreman and he didn't do anything about it, so I decided I'd leave.

While I was standing out on the railroad track, I ran into somebody else out there fussing also. I went over to the union and they told me what to do. I went back inside and they sent me to another department where you did bench work and I liked that much bet-

ter. You had a little small jig that you would work on and you just drilled out holes. Sometimes you would rout them or you would scribe them and then you'd cut them with a cutters.

I must have stayed there nearly a year, and then they put me over in another department, "Plastics." It was the tail section of the B-Bomber, the Billy Mitchell Bomber. I put a little part in the gun sight. You had a little ratchet set and you would screw it in there. Then I cleaned the top of the glass off and put a piece of paper over it to seal it off to go to the next section. I worked over there until the end of the war. Well, not quite the end, because I got pregnant, and while I was off having the baby the war was over. . . .

It made me live better. I really did. We always say that Lincoln took the bale off of the Negroes. I think there is a statue up there in Washington, D.C., where he's lifting something off the Negro. Well, my sister always said—that's why you can't interview her because she's so radical—"Hitler was the one that got us out of the white folks' kitchen."

Source: Sherna Berger Gluck, *Rosie the Riveter Revisited: Women, the War, and Social Change* (Boston: Twayne, 1987), 37–38, 42.

Organized Labor

The labor movement also seized opportunities during the wartime mobilization effort. No dramatic changes occurred, but the war confirmed the industrial breakthroughs of the 1930s. By the end of the war almost 15 million workers—a third of the nonagricultural labor force, up from 9 million at the end of the previous decade—belonged to unions.

Organized labor responded to the war with an initial burst of patriotic unity. On December 23, 1941, representatives of major unions made a "no strike" pledge—although nonbinding—for the duration of the war. In January 1942 Roosevelt set up the National War

Labor Board (NWLB), composed of representatives of labor, management, and the public. The board established wages, hours, and working conditions and had the authority to order government seizure of plants that did not comply. Forty plants were seized during the war.

During its tenure the NWLB handled 17,650 disputes affecting 12 million workers. It faced two controversial issues: union membership and wage increases. Union organizers favored either the union shop or the closed shop, but management preferred the open shop. (In a union shop the employees must belong to a certain union or join it within a specified period. In a closed shop the employer may hire only workers who are already members of a union. In an open shop the company usually employs only nonunion workers.) As a compromise, the NWLB imposed the principle of maintenance of membership. Workers did not have to join a union, but those already in a union had to maintain their membership during the life of the contract.

Agitation for wage increases caused a more serious disagreement. In contrast to the deflation of the depression, inflation pushed prices up throughout the war. Because management wanted to keep production (and profits) running smoothly, it was willing to pay higher wages. However, such raises would conflict with the OPA policy of keeping inflation as low as possible. In 1942 the NWLB established the "Little Steel Formula," which granted a 15 percent wage increase to match the increase in the cost of living since January 1, 1941. Although the NWLB froze hourly wages in principle, it allowed them to rise another 24 percent by 1945. Actually, incomes rose as much as 70 percent because workers earned overtime pay, which was not covered by wage ceilings. The tremendous increase in output during World War II occurred largely because people worked overtime.

Although incomes were higher than anyone could have dreamed of during the depression, many union members felt cheated as they watched corporate profits soar while their wages remained frozen. The high point of dissatisfaction came in 1943. First a nationwide railroad strike was narrowly averted, and then John L. Lewis led more than half a million United Mine Workers out on strike, demanding wages higher than the Little Steel Formula allowed. Lewis won concessions but alienated Congress and, because he had defied the government, became one of the most disliked public figures of the 1940s.

Congress countered Lewis's action by overriding Roosevelt's veto of the Smith-Connally Labor Act of 1943, which required a thirty-day cooling-off period before a strike and prohibited strikes in defense industries entirely. Nevertheless, about 15,000 strikes occurred during the war. Less than one-tenth of a percent of working hours were lost to strikes, but the public perceived the disruptions as far more extensive. Labor unions won acceptance during the war years but also provoked hostility.

Rising Winds of Change for African-Americans

A new mood of militancy appeared among the nation's minorities during wartime. World War II disrupted a number of traditional patterns, and many barriers to racial equality tottered or fell. "A wind is rising throughout the world of free men everywhere," Eleanor Roosevelt wrote during the war, "and they will not be kept in bondage." Black leaders pointed out parallels between anti-Semitism in Germany and racial discrimination in America. Civil rights leaders pledged themselves to a "Double V" campaign: victory over Nazism abroad and over racism and inequality at home.

Even before Pearl Harbor there was evidence that the war might encourage greater black activism. In 1940 only 240 of the nation's 100,000 aircraft workers were black, and most of them were janitors. Black leaders demanded that the government require defense contractors to integrate their work forces. When the government took no action, A. Philip Randolph, head of the Brotherhood of Sleeping Car Porters, a black union, announced plans for a "March on Washington" in the summer of 1941. Roosevelt was not a strong supporter of civil rights, but he feared the embarrassment of a massive public protest. Even more, he worried about a disruption of war preparations. The president agreed to take action, and Randolph canceled the march.

In June 1941 Roosevelt issued Executive Order 8802, declaring it to be the policy of the United States "that there shall be no discrimination in the employment of workers in defense industries or government because of race, creed, color, or national origin." To oversee the policy, he established the Fair Employment Practices Committee (FEPC) in the Office of Production Management.

This federal commitment to minority employment rights was unprecedented but limited in scope. For instance, it did not affect segregation in the armed forces. Moreover, the FEPC, which could not require compliance with its orders, often found that the needs of defense production took precedence over fair employment practices. The FEPC received more than 8,000 complaints, of which it resolved about a third. Blacks made up 8 percent of defense workers in 1944, probably due more to the labor shortage than to FEPC prodding. Another beneficial federal action was the National War Labor Board's decision to ban racial wage differentials, the first time that they had been prohibited by federal law.

Encouraged by the ideological climate of the war years, civil rights organizations increased their membership. The NAACP grew ninefold to 450,000 in 1945. In 1942 James Farmer helped found the Congress of Racial Equality (CORE). Unlike the NAACP, which favored lobbying and legal strategies, CORE used tactics such as demonstrations and sit-ins. In 1944 CORE forced several restaurants in Washington, D.C., to serve blacks after picketing them with signs that read "Are You for Hitler's Way or the American Way? Make Up Your Mind."

An awareness of civil rights was heightened in other ways as well. The Swedish sociologist Gunnar Myrdal wrote a monumental study of race relations, *An American Dilemma: The Negro Problem and Modern Democracy* (1944), focusing many white Americans' attention on the issue for the first time. In 1944 the Supreme

Court ruled in *Smith v. Allwright* that Texas's all-white primary election, a device commonly used to disfranchise blacks in southern states, was unconstitutional. After the Court's decision Congressman Wright Patman of Texas vowed that blacks in his district would vote "over my dead body." Soon, however, in his reelection campaigns Patman was courting black voters at church picnics and other social events. These wartime developments laid the groundwork for the civil rights revolution of the 1950s and 1960s.

Politics in Wartime

At a press conference late in 1943 Roosevelt playfully announced that "Dr. Win the War" had replaced "Dr. New Deal." During the 1940s Roosevelt rarely pressed for social and economic change, thus placating the conservative members of Congress whose bipartisan support he needed to conduct the war. With little protest, he agreed to drop several popular New Deal programs, which were less necessary once war mobilization brought full employment. In 1942 the Civilian Conservation Corps was dismantled, followed in 1943 by the National Youth Administration and the Works Progress Administration. Severe budget cuts crippled the Farm Security Administration, which had represented the interests of poor farmers. The speed with which the government terminated those agencies suggested that they had been more a response to the crisis of the depression than a commitment to promoting the general welfare through federal programs. Programs such as Social Security were left untouched, however.

The war years brought a significant decline in the reform spirit that had flourished in Washington during the 1930s. Few public figures talked about using the war to bring about social change, as they had in World War I. (One exception was reform of the tax system.) Business executives replaced the reformers and social activists who had staffed New Deal relief agencies in the 1930s. Those executives became known as "dollar-a-year men" because they volunteered for government service while remaining on the corporate payroll.

Roosevelt had hoped politics could be shelved for the duration of the war, but that proved unreasonable. The Republicans picked up seats in both houses of Congress and increased their share of state governorships in the 1942 election. Those gains reflected the tendency of the party out of power to improve its position in off-year elections. The Republicans also benefited from a low voter turnout. Relocations caused by enlistment and residency requirements, which temporarily disfranchised newcomers, contributed to the low turnout.

Roosevelt himself did not give up politics. After concluding that continuation of the war made a fourth term necessary, he went on a mild offensive to attract

Democratic voters. In his State of the Union address in 1944, the president called for a second Bill of Rights. As the basis of postwar prosperity, he pledged rights such as jobs, adequate food and clothing, a decent home, medical care, and education.

The president's sweeping commitment remained largely rhetorical. Congressional support for this vast extension of the welfare state did not exist in 1944. It was possible, however, to win some of those rights for a special group of American citizens: veterans. The Servicemen's Readjustment Act, known as the GI Bill of Rights, passed in 1944, provided education, job training, medical care, pensions, and mortgage loans for men and women who had served in the armed forces during the war.

The Election of 1944. "I am an old campaigner and I love a good fight," Roosevelt had said during the 1940 election. He approached the 1944 campaign with the same verve, but the years had taken their toll. Concern about Roosevelt's health and the need for a successor prompted the Democrats to drop Vice-President Henry Wallace, whose outspoken support for labor, civil rights, and domestic reform was too extreme for many party leaders. In Wallace's place they chose Senator Harry S. Truman of Missouri.

Truman, a World War I veteran and Kansas City haberdasher whose business had failed in the 1920–1921 recession, found success in politics. Sponsored by Thomas Pendergast, the Democratic boss in Kansas City, he was elected to the Senate in 1934 and again in 1940. Truman became known for heading a Senate investigation of gov-

Labor and Politics
The CIO's Political Action Committee was formed to harness the political power of new recruits for labor's postwar agenda, especially full employment. Ben Shahn's vivid 1944 poster reinforced the CIO's commitment to racial equality. (Ben Shahn, "For Full Employment after the War Register Vote," 1944, Collection of the Museum of Modern Art)

ernment waste and inefficiency in defense contracts during the war.

The Republicans nominated Governor Thomas E. Dewey of New York. Only forty-two years old, Dewey had won fame fighting organized crime as a U.S. attorney. He accepted the broad outlines of the welfare state and belonged to the internationalist wing of the Republican party. The 1944 election was the closest since 1916 as Roosevelt received 53.5 percent of the popular vote. The Democrats lost ground among farmers, but most ethnic groups remained solidly Democratic. Roosevelt got his customary support from the South, augmented by the overwhelming allegiance of members of the armed forces, who voted by absentee ballot. His margin of victory came from the cities. In urban areas with more than 100,000 people the president drew 60 percent of the vote.

Roosevelt also received strong support from organized labor. Under the prodding of CIO leaders Sidney Hillman and Philip Murray, labor contributed more than $1.5 million, or about 30 percent of the Democratic party's election funds. The CIO's Political Action Committee canvassed door to door and conducted voter registration campaigns. Organized labor continued to play a significant role in the Democratic party after the war.

Life on the Home Front

In contrast to World War I, once Congress declared war, there was almost no domestic opposition to the nation's role in World War II. Americans fought for their way of life and to preserve democracy against Nazi and Japanese totalitarianism. Because the enemies seemed so evil and America's will to win was so strong, many remember it as the "good war." By the spring of 1945 soldiers who had finished their military duty, which averaged sixteen months, were beginning to return home. Fighting had been a dirty, bloody job, a far cry from their visions of saving democracy and stopping fascism. Dreams of marriage, a house in the suburbs, and a new car sustained many soldiers through the horror and tedium of the war. In 1947 veterans and their families made up a fourth of the American population.

"For the Duration"

Although the United States did not suffer the physical devastation that ravaged much of Europe and the Pacific, the war affected the lives of those who stayed behind. Every time relatives of a loved one overseas saw the Western Union boy on his bicycle, they were afraid it meant a telegram from the War Department telling them that their son, husband, or father would not be

coming home. Other Americans tolerated small deprivations daily. "Don't you know there's a war on?" became the standard reply to any request that could not be fulfilled. People accepted the fact that their lives would be different "for the duration."

Just like the soldiers in uniform, people on the home front had a job to do. They worked on civilian defense committees, donated blood, collected old newspapers and scrap material, and served on local rationing and draft boards. About 20 million home "Victory gardens" produced 40 percent of the vegetables grown in the United States. Advertising campaigns displaying the popular "V for Victory" slogan stressed patriotism. All seven war bond drives were oversubscribed.

However, many Americans remember the war years as a time of returning prosperity. Unemployment disappeared, and per capita income rose from $691 in 1939 to $1,515 in 1945. Despite geographical dislocations and shortages of many items, about 70 percent of Americans admitted midway through the war that they had personally experienced "no real sacrifices." A Red Cross worker put it bluntly: "The war was fun for America. I'm not talking about the poor souls who lost sons and daughters. But for the rest of us, the war was a hell of a good time."

During the war years demographic patterns rebounded from their depression-induced declines. Young

Wartime Prosperity
War mobilization brought prosperity to many American households. This photograph, taken in 1942, shows the Hall family of Sheffield, Alabama, in their comfortable home, part of a defense housing project connected with the TVA. The picture looks posed, but the new levels of consumption and affluence it represented were true for many Americans like the Halls.

people could afford to marry, and the imminent departure of men for military service induced many couples to take that step sooner rather than later. Not all those marriages survived the strain of separation or wartime relocation, and the divorce rate also rose. The birth rate went up, with many babies being conceived before their fathers went off to war. In effect, the wartime birth patterns marked the beginning of the "baby boom" that characterized American culture in the postwar period.

Popular Culture. Popular culture, especially the movies, reinforced the connections between the home front and the troops serving overseas. Hollywood escaped the restrictions and cutbacks that affected other industries, in part because studio heads argued that movies built morale. Many Hollywood directors lent their services to the military. Director Frank Capra's "Why We Fight" films, a documentary series produced for the War Department, explained war aims to new soldiers and sailors. John Huston provided an intense portrayal of men in combat in his documentary *The Battle of San Pietro* (1944).

Average weekly movie attendance soared to over 100 million during the war. Demand was so high that many theaters operated around the clock to accommodate defense workers on the swing and night shifts. Many movies had patriotic themes, and films such as *Wake Island* (1942) and *Thirty Seconds over Tokyo* (1945) portrayed life in the armed services. Other movies, such as Frank Capra's *Meet John Doe* (1943) and Alfred Hitchcock's *Lifeboat* (1944), depicted the danger of fascism at home and abroad. Dramas about the struggle on the home front were also popular. In the box-office hit *Since You Went Away* (1943) Claudette Colbert took a war job after her husband left to fight, and the Oscar-winning Greer Garson played a courageous British housewife in *Mrs. Miniver* (1942). Newsreels accompanying feature films kept the public up to date on the war, as did on-the-spot radio broadcasts by commentators such as Edward R. Murrow. Thus popular culture reflected America's new international responsibilities at the same time that it built up morale on the home front.

War correspondents such as John Hersey and Ernie Pyle (who was killed in a foxhole on Ie Shima by a Japanese bullet) reported on the GIs (short for "government issue") for readers back home. Reporters often portrayed the GIs as ordinary boys doing their patriotic duty. "When you looked into the eyes of those boys, you did not feel sorry for the Japs: you felt sorry for the boys," John Hersey wrote of the marines in Guadalcanal in 1944. Another marine who fought at Guadalcanal remembered it as a matter of simple survival: "The only way you could get it over with was to kill them off before they killed you. The war I knew was totally savage."

Entertaining the Troops
The original Stage Door Canteen opened in the basement of a Broadway theater in 1942. It provided servicemen with coffee, doughnuts, and big-time entertainment volunteered by Broadway and Hollywood stars. The canteen's popular weekly radio show was the inspiration for the 1943 movie *Stage Door Canteen*.

Throughout the war the Japanese were hated far more than the Germans were. Whereas Americans often differentiated between evil Nazi leaders and ordinary "good Germans" forced to go along with Nazi excesses, they lumped all Japanese together. Racial epithets like "slant eyes" and "yellow monkeys" were widely used in conversation, and even respected magazines such as *Time*, *Life*, and *Newsweek* routinely referred to the enemy as "Japs." Between American attitudes toward Japan and Nazi atrocities against Jews, racism was a constant undercurrent of World War II.

Rationing. During the war almost anything that Americans ate, wore, or used was subject to rationing or regulation. Rubber became the first scarce item. The Japanese conquest of Malaya and the Netherlands East Indies cut off 97 percent of America's imports of natural rubber, an essential raw material for war production. An entire new industry in synthetic rubber was born, and by late 1944 the United States was producing 762,000 tons of it a year, mostly for the war effort.

Meanwhile, to conserve rubber, the government restricted the sale of tires, a hard sacrifice for the nation's 30 million car owners, many of whom put their autos up on blocks for the duration. If people walked instead of drove, they wore out their shoes. In 1944 shoes were rationed to two pairs per person a year, barely half the average number that people bought before the war.

The government also rationed gasoline and fuel oil. Shortages of fuel oil forced schools and restaurants to shorten their hours, and home thermostats were lowered to 65 degrees. Gasoline rationing, introduced in December 1942, represented both a response to depleted domestic gasoline supplies and an attempt to save wear on precious rubber tires. To further discourage gasoline consumption, Congress imposed a nationwide speed limit of 35 miles per hour; highway death rates dropped dramatically.

People found it harder to cut back on sugar. When sugar disappeared from grocery shelves, the government rationed it at a rate of 8 to 12 ounces per person a week. However, the manufacturers of products such as Coca-Cola and Wrigley's chewing gum received unlimited quantities of sugar by convincing the government that their products helped the morale of the men and women in the armed forces.

By 1943 the amount of meat, butter, and other foods Americans could buy was regulated by a complicated system of rationing points and coupons. Most people cooperated with the restrictions, but almost a fourth occasionally bought items on the black market, especially meat, gasoline, and cigarettes.

Shortages of other consumer products also hit the home front. People finally had enough money to buy refrigerators, cars, and radios, but the components of those items—including rubber, copper, and steel—were earmarked for war production. To placate consumers, many companies ran advertisements promising delayed gratification. After the war, they told the public, you can buy that new house and fill it with all the appliances you want.

But some purchases could not wait. Among the most sought-after items on the black market were women's stockings. In the 1930s women had worn silk stockings, but when the war with Japan cut off imports of silk, they switched to nylon. Unfortunately, nylon was essential to war production: thirty-six pairs of nylons equaled one parachute. In a dramatic fashion change (and one associated with the image of Rosie the Riveter) many women began wearing slacks in public. The strict rationing of food and other items eased in the summer of 1944, when victory appeared on the horizon.

Migration and Family Life. The war not only affected what people ate, drank, and wore, it affected where they lived. People moved from one part of the country to another in unprecedented numbers. When men volunteered for or were drafted into the armed services, their families often followed them to training bases or points of debarkation. The lure of high-paying defense jobs encouraged others to move. About 15 million Americans changed residence during the war years, half of them by moving to another state. The pace of urbanization increased, but this movement was not simply an exodus from rural to urban areas. About 5.4 million people left farms, but 2.5 million moved onto them. The greatest number of people went west.

The federal government supported the growth of industry in the West. The western states not only served as staging areas for the war in the Pacific, they also had room for the new ship- and airplane-building industries. Their remote regions (for instance, Hanford, Washington, and Los Alamos, New Mexico) were ideal places to conduct top-secret research.

As a center of defense production California was affected by wartime migration more than any other state was. "The Second Gold Rush Hits the West," headlined the *San Francisco Chronicle* in 1943. During the war one-tenth of all federal dollars went to California, and the state turned out one-sixth of total war production. California welcomed nearly 3 million new residents during the war, a 53 percent growth in population. They went where the defense jobs were—to Los Angeles, San Diego, and the San Francisco Bay Area. Some towns grew practically overnight. Just two years after the Kaiser Corporation opened a shipyard in Richmond, the population quadrupled.

Migration and relocation often caused strains. Many towns with defense industries had scarce housing and inadequate public transportation; conflicts over public space and recreation erupted between old-timers and newcomers. Of special concern were the young people the war had set adrift from traditional community restraints. Newspapers were filled with stories of "latchkey" children who stayed home alone while their mothers worked in defense plants. Adolescents were even more of a problem. Teenage girls who hung around army bases looking for a good time were known as "victory girls." In 1942 and 1943 juvenile delinquency seemed to be reaching epidemic proportions.

Spurred by the new economic opportunities in defense and factory work, blacks migrated from the South in increasing numbers after the temporary slowdown of the depression. More than a million African-Americans moved to defense centers in California, Illinois, Michigan, Ohio, and Pennsylvania. Their need for jobs and housing led to racial conflict in several cities.

Some of the worst racial violence took place in Detroit, the new home of a large number of southern migrants, both black and white. Competition for scarce housing caused many of the disputes. Early in 1942 black families encountered resistance and intimidation when they tried to move into the Sojourner Truth housing project in the Polish community of Hamtramck. Similar tensions erupted into violence in June 1943, when a major race riot in Detroit left thirty-four people dead, including twenty-five blacks. Racial conflicts broke out in forty-seven cities across the country during 1943.

Racial violence was not confined to African-Americans. In Los Angeles male Latino teenagers organized *pachuco* (youth) gangs, dressing in broad-brimmed felt hats, pegged trousers, and clunky shoes; wearing long slicked-down hair; and carrying pocket knives on gold chains. The young women that they hung out with favored long coats, *huarache* sandals, and pompadour hairdos. Although "zoot suits" were most popular among Latinos, that style was also taken up by blacks and by a few white working-class teenagers in Los Angeles, Detroit, New York, and Philadelphia as a symbol of alienation and self-assertion. To adults and many Anglos, however, the zoot suit came to symbolize wartime juvenile delinquency.

In Los Angeles white hostility toward Mexican-Americans had been smoldering for some time, and zoot suiters became the targets. In July 1943 rumors that a *pachuco* gang had beaten a white sailor set off a four-day riot, during which white servicemen entered Mexican-American neighborhoods and attacked zoot suiters, tak-

Zoot Suits

Zoot suits gained wide popularity among young Americans during the war. In 1943 this well-dressed teenager greased his hair in a ducktail and wore a loosely cut coat with padded shoulders ("fingertips") that reached midthigh, baggy pleated pants cut tight ("pegged") around the ankles, and a long gold watch chain.

ing special pleasure in slashing the pegged pants of their victims. The attacks occurred in full view of white police officers, who did nothing to stop the violence.

Japanese Relocation

Although racial confrontations and zoot suit riots recalled the widespread racial tensions of World War I, the mood on the home front was generally calm in the 1940s. German culture and German-Americans did not come under suspicion, nor did Italian-Americans. Leftists and communists faced little domestic repression, mainly because after Pearl Harbor the Soviet Union became an ally of the United States. There was one glaring exception to this record of tolerance: the internment of Japanese-Americans on the West Coast. The prejudice and hysteria directed at Japanese-Americans are a reminder of the fragility of civil liberties in wartime.

Immediately after Pearl Harbor the West Coast remained calm. Then, partly as a reflection of the region's vulnerability to attack but also because of inflammatory rhetoric in the Hearst newspapers, coastal residents began to demand protection against supposed Japanese spies. California had a long history of antagonism toward both Japanese and Chinese immigrants (see Chapters 17 and 22). The Japanese-Americans, who clustered together in highly visible communities, were a small, politically impotent minority, numbering only about 112,100 in the three coastal states. Unlike German- and Italian-Americans, the Japanese stood out. "A Jap's a Jap," General John DeWitt stated. "It makes no difference whether he is an American citizen or not."

Mounting fears on the West Coast brought a far-reaching decision from Washington in early 1942, when Roosevelt approved a War Department plan to intern Japanese-Americans in relocation camps for the rest of the war. In March 1942 Milton Eisenhower, a career civil servant and the brother of General Dwight D. Eisenhower, took over the War Relocation Authority, a civilian agency created to carry out that policy. Despite the lack of evidence of disloyalty or sedition—no Japanese-American was ever charged with espionage—few public leaders opposed the plan. The Supreme Court upheld its constitutionality as a legitimate exercise of power during wartime in *Hirabayashi v. United States* (1943) and *Korematsu v. United States* (1944).

The relocation announcement shocked Japanese-Americans, more than two-thirds of whom were native-born American citizens. (They were the *Niseis*, the children of the foreign-born *Isseis*.) The government gave families only a few days to dispose of their belongings and prepare for relocation. Businesses that took a lifetime to build were liquidated overnight, and speculators snapped up Japanese real estate for a fraction of its value. A Japanese-American music teacher got only $30 for her

Japanese Internment
A Japanese-American family arrives at its new "home" in Heart Mountain, Wyoming, after being relocated from the West Coast military zone. The average internee spent 900 days—more than two and a half years—confined behind the barbed wire, which is not visible in this picture.

treasured piano. Another woman, rather than accept $17.50 from a secondhand dealer for her family's heirloom porcelain, broke every piece of it. The government later estimated that the total financial loss to Japanese-Americans was $400 million, but Congress appropriated only $38 million in compensation after the war. Partial restitution came decades later, in 1988, when Congress voted to issue a public apology and give $20,000 in cash to each of the 60,000 surviving internees.

Relocation took place in two stages. First the government sent Japanese-Americans to temporary assembly centers such as the Santa Anita racetrack in Los Angeles, where they lived in stables that horses had occupied a few days earlier. Then they were moved to ten permanent camps away from the coast. Those internment camps in California, Arizona, Utah, Colorado, Wyoming, Idaho, and Arkansas "were in places where nobody had lived before and no one has lived since," a historian commented (see Map 27.1). Milton Eisenhower had hoped the relocation camps would resemble the CCC youth camps of the New Deal, but the barbed wire and enforced communal living mocked his hopes. Although sometimes compared to Nazi concentration camps, the relocation centers more closely resembled Indian reservations (see American Voices, page 847).

All ten camps were in hot, dusty places, and their communal bathroom and dining facilities made family life nearly impossible. Eight people often lived in a space measuring 25 by 20 feet. No one had any privacy; boredom was a major problem. Generational differences between the Issei, with an average age of fifty-five, and the Nisei, with an average age of seventeen, added to the tensions.

Almost every Japanese-American in California, Oregon, and Washington was involuntarily detained for some period during World War II. Ironically, the Japanese-Americans who made up one-third of the population of Hawaii and presumably posed a greater threat because of their numbers and proximity to Japan were not affected.

They were less vulnerable to detention because of the islands' multiracial heritage. The Japanese also provided much of the unskilled labor on the islands, and the Hawaiian economy could not function without them.

Cracks soon appeared in the relocation policy. Japanese-Americans had played an important role in California agriculture, and even with stepped-up recruitment of Mexican-Americans through the *bracero* program, the labor shortage in farming led the government to furlough seasonal Japanese-American agricultural workers from the camps as early as 1942. In addition, about 4,300 young people who had been in college when the relocation order came through were allowed to stay in school if they transferred out of the

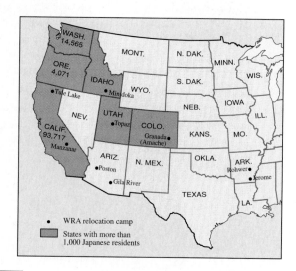

MAP 27.1

WRA Relocation Camps

In 1942 the government ordered 112,000 Japanese-Americans living on the West Coast into internment camps in the nation's interior because of their supposed threat to public safety. Some of the camps were as far away as Arkansas.

AMERICAN VOICES

Peter Ota

The Insult and Injury of Internment

Peter Ota's father had come from Okinawa in 1904 and had built up a successful fruit and vegetable business in the Los Angeles area. Here the son, a Nisei, remembers his family's internment during World War II. When Peter reached draft age, he was inducted into the army, even though his father and sister remained in the relocation camp for the rest of the war.

It was just my sister and myself. I was fifteen, she was twelve. In April, 1942, we were evacuated to Santa Anita. At the time we didn't know where we were going, how long we'd be gone. We didn't know what to take. A toothbrush, toilet supplies, some clothes. Only what you could carry. We left with a caravan.

Santa Anita is a race track. The horse stables were converted into living quarters. My sister and I were fortunate enough to stay in a barracks. The people in the stables had to live with the stench. Everything was communal. We had absolutely no privacy. When you went to the toilet, it was communal. It was very embarrassing for women, especially. . . .

We had orders to leave Santa Anita in September of 1942. We had no idea where we were going. Just before we left, my father joined us. . . . I can still picture it to this day; to come in like cattle or sheep being herded in the back of a pickup truck bed. We were near the gate and saw him come in. He saw us. It was a sad, happy moment, because we'd been separated for a year.

He never really expressed what his true inner feelings were. It just amazes me. He was never vindictive about it, never showed any anger. I can't understand that. A man who had worked so hard for what he had and lost it overnight. There is a very strong word in Japanese, *gaman*. It means to persevere. Old people instilled this into the second generation: you persevere. Take what's coming, don't react.

He had been a very outgoing person. Enthusiastic. I was very, very impressed with how he ran things and worked with people. When I saw him at Santa Anita, he was a different person.

We were out on a train, three of us and many trains of others. It was crowded. The shades were drawn. During the ride we were wondering, what are they going to do to us? We Niseis [first-generation Japanese-Americans] had enough confidence in our government that it wouldn't do anything drastic. My father had put all his faith in this country. This was his land.

Oh, it took days. We arrived in Amache, Colorado. That was an experience in itself. We were right near the Kansas border. It's a desolate, flat, barren area. The barracks was all there was. There were no trees, no kind of landscaping. It was like a prison camp. Coming from our environment, it was just devastating. . . .

When I think back to my mother and father, what they went through quietly, it's hard to explain. [Cries.] I think of my father without ever coming up with an angry word. After all those years, having worked his whole life to build a dream—an American dream, mind you—having it all taken away, and not one vindictive word. His business was worth more than a hundred thousand. He sold it for five. When he came out of camp, with what little money he had, he put a down payment on an apartment building. It was right in the middle of skid row, an old rooming house. . . . He died a very broken man.

Source: Studs Terkel, *"The Good War": An Oral History of World War Two* (New York: Pantheon, 1984), 29–30, 32–33.

West Coast military zone. Another route out of the camps was enlistment in the armed services. The 442d Infantry Combat Team, a segregated unit serving in Europe and composed entirely of Nisei volunteers, was the most decorated unit in the armed forces.

Most Japanese-Americans accepted relocation stoically. "*Shikata gu nai*," they said—it can't be helped, hardship must be borne. Many Japanese-Americans of the third generation, called the *Sansei*, some of whom were born in the internment camps, and the fourth generation, the *Yonsei*, think their elders should have protested more strongly. With each generation the memory of internment grows dimmer, but this shameful episode has been burned into the national conscience.

Fighting and Winning the War

World War II, noted the military historian John Keegan, was "the largest single event in human history." Fought on six continents at a cost of 50 million lives, it was far more global than World War I. At least 405,000 Americans were killed and 671,000 were wounded in the fighting, representing less than half of 1 percent of the U.S. population. In contrast, the Soviets counted as many as 21 million military and civilian dead during the war, about 8 percent of their people. Dropping the atomic bomb on Hiroshima and Nagasaki in 1945 was the final stage in this most destructive of human conflicts.

Wartime Aims and Strategies

The Allied coalition was composed of Great Britain, the United States, and the Soviet Union, with other nations, notably China and France, playing lesser roles. Franklin Roosevelt, Britain's Winston Churchill, and Joseph Stalin, the premier of the Soviet Union, took the lead in setting overall strategy. The Atlantic Charter, drafted aboard ship during the Churchill-Roosevelt rendezvous off the Newfoundland coast in August 1941, formed the basis of the Allies' vision of the postwar international order. However, Stalin was not part of that agreement, and that would cause later disagreements over its goals.

As far back as the lend-lease negotiations of early 1941, Churchill and Roosevelt had agreed that defeating Germany would be the first military priority because of that country's huge armies, massive industrial capacity, and mastery of technology. Roosevelt's unswerving commitment to Britain's survival provided the basis for a strong, if not always smooth, relationship with Churchill. (Roosevelt's aide Harry Hopkins described his role as that of a "catalytic agent between two prima donnas.") Stalin, however, was something of a mystery. He and Roosevelt did not meet until late in 1943. Although the United States and Great Britain disagreed on issues such as the postwar fate of colonial empires, the potential for conflict with the Soviet Union was far greater.

One way to wear down the Germans was to open a second front on the European continent, preferably in France. The Russians strongly argued for this strategy because it would draw German troops away from Russian soil. The issue came up so many times that the Soviet foreign minister, Vyacheslav Molotov, was said to know only four English words: *yes, no,* and *second front*.

Roosevelt assured Stalin informally that such a front would be opened in 1942. However, the time needed to raise American war production to full capacity and British opposition caused a two-year delay. As a result, for most of the war the Soviet Union bore the brunt of the land battle against Germany. Roosevelt and Churchill's unfulfilled pledges angered Stalin, who was already suspicious about American and British intentions. That mistrust and bitterness carried over into the postwar world in the Cold War that followed.

At various points during the war the three leaders of the Grand Alliance held a series of meetings to discuss military strategy and plan the postwar peace. In January 1943 Roosevelt and Churchill met in Casablanca, Morocco; Stalin did not attend because the Battle of Stalingrad had reached a crucial point. The main outcome of the conference was the Allied demand for unconditional surrender of the Axis powers as a condition for peace. In November 1943 Roosevelt, Churchill, and the Chinese leader Jiang Jeishi (Chiang Kai-Shek) met in Cairo to discuss military operations in the Pacific theater, a conference designed to keep China in the war. To Roosevelt's dismay, Jiang seemed more interested in fighting the communist revolution in his country (see Chapter 28) than in mobilizing the Chinese people to expel the Japanese invaders.

Traveling directly from Cairo to Teheran, Iran, Roosevelt finally met Stalin late in November 1943. At the Teheran Conference Roosevelt and Churchill agreed to Stalin's demand for a second front within six months. In return, Stalin promised to join the fight against Japan after the war in Europe ended, a promise he kept. The three leaders also issued the Teheran Declaration, in which they welcomed the cooperation of all nations in the war and invited them to join the Big Three in a "world family of democratic nations."

At Teheran Churchill and Roosevelt also agreed tacitly to Stalin's demand that Poland's borders be redrawn to give the Soviet Union more territory. But the three leaders disagreed sharply about who should control the rest of Poland and the other Eastern European states. Roosevelt expressed confidence that the personal rapport he had developed with Stalin would aid postwar relations among the superpowers, but Stalin's territorial ambitions in Eastern Europe foreshadowed later divisions.

The War in Europe

During the first six months of 1942 the military news was so bad that it threatened to swamp the Grand Alliance. The Allies suffered severe defeats throughout Europe and on the Atlantic. German armies pushed deeper into Soviet territory, reaching the outskirts of Moscow and Leningrad, and simultaneously started an offensive in North Africa aimed at seizing the Suez Canal. At sea German submarines were crippling American convoys carrying supplies to Europe. Since the United States was the main supplier of oil to the Allies, those attacks struck at the heart of the war effort, which was increasingly dependent on petroleum-based military equipment such as tanks and airplanes.

The major turning point of the war in Europe occurred in the winter of 1942–1943, when the Soviets halted the German advance in the Battle of Stalingrad. The Germans had taken most of the city in over 140 days of sometimes house-to-house fighting, when the Soviets counterattacked. The Germans lost 330,000 soldiers and twenty-two divisions; Russian casualties were also huge. Now came the task of pushing the Germans all the way back through Eastern Europe. By October 1943 Soviet armies stood on the east bank of the Dnieper River, ready to push through the Ukraine into Romania. By mid-1944 those forces had driven the German army out of the Soviet Union.

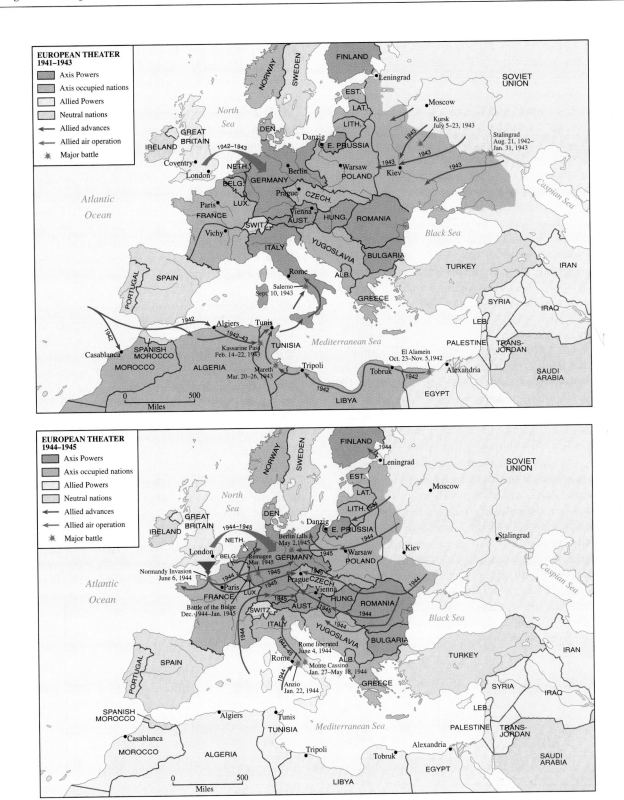

MAP 27.2

War in Europe

a. 1941–1943 Hitler's Germany reached its greatest extent in 1942, when Nazi forces stalled at Leningrad and Stalingrad. The tide of battle turned in the fall, when the Soviet army launched a massive counterattack at Stalingrad and Allied forces began to drive the Germans from North Africa. In 1943 the Allies invaded Sicily and the Italian mainland.

b. 1944–1945 On June 6, 1944 (D-Day), the Allies finally invaded France. It would take almost a year for the Allied forces to close in on Berlin—the Soviets from the east and the Americans, British, and French from the west. Germany surrendered on May 8, 1945.

At the same time, the Allies launched a major offensive in North Africa, Churchill's substitute for a second front in France. Between November 1942 and May 1943 Allied troops under the leadership of Generals Dwight D. Eisenhower and George S. Patton (both protégés of George C. Marshall) defeated Germany's crack Afrika Korps led by General Erwin Rommel.

From Africa the Allied command followed Churchill's strategy of attacking the Axis through what he called its "soft underbelly": Sicily and the Italian peninsula. In July 1943 the fascist regime of Benito Mussolini fell, and the new government joined the Allies. The Allies invaded Italy the following fall. Despite help from Italian partisans, the mountainous terrain and heavy resistance from German troops kept them from entering Rome until June 1944 (see Map 27.2). The last German forces in Italy did not surrender until May 1945.

D-Day. The long-awaited invasion of France came on D-Day, June 6, 1944. That morning, after an agonizing delay caused by bad weather, the largest armada ever assembled moved across the English Channel. The beaches of Normandy where the Allies landed—Utah, Omaha, Juno, Gold, and Sword—soon became household words in the United States. Under the command of General Dwight Eisenhower, more than 1.5 million American, British, and Canadian soldiers crossed the Channel over the next few days. In August Allied troops helped liberate Paris, and by September they had driven the Germans out of most of France and Belgium.

In the autumn of 1944 the German military situation looked hopeless. All that year, long-range Allied bombers had made daring daylight raids, damaging Nazi military and industrial installations and pulverizing cities such as Cologne, Dresden, and Berlin, the German capital. The air campaign killed 305,000 people and wounded 780,000, both soldiers and civilians. No one was safe from attack.

Victory in Europe. The Germans were not ready to give up. In December 1944 German forces in Belgium mounted an attack that began the Battle of the Bulge, so called because it made a dent in the Allied defenses. After ten days of heavy fighting in what was to be the final German offensive of the war, the Allies regained their momentum and pushed the Germans back across the Rhine River. Their goal was to take Berlin, the German capital. American and British troops led the drive from the west, and Soviet troops advanced from the east through Poland, getting their first. On April 30, with much of Berlin in rubble from Allied bombing, Hitler committed suicide in his bunker. Germany surrendered on May 8, 1945, which became known as V-E (Victory in Europe) Day.

The Holocaust. When Allied troops advanced into Germany in the spring of 1945, they came face to face with Hitler's "final solution of the Jewish question": the extermination camps where 6 million Jews had been put to death along with another 6 million Poles, Slavs, Gypsies, homosexuals, and other "undesirables." Photographs from Nazi death camps at Buchenwald, Dachau, and Auschwitz, of bodies stacked like cordwood and survivors so emaciated that they were barely alive, horrified the American public and the rest of the world. But it is inaccurate to claim that no one knew about the camps before the German surrender. The Roosevelt administration had reliable information about the death camps as early as November 1942.

The lack of response by the U.S. government to the systematic near annihilation of European Jewry ranks as one of the gravest failures of the Roosevelt administration. So few Jews got out because the United States and the rest of the world would not take them in. State Department policies allowed only 21,000 refugees to enter this country during the war. The War Refugee Board, established in 1944 with little support from the

Hitting the Beach at Normandy
These American reinforcements landed on the beach at Normandy two weeks after D-Day, June 6, 1944. More than a million Allied troops came ashore during the next month. The Allies liberated Paris in August and pushed the retreating Nazi forces behind the German border by September.

The Living Dead
When Allied troops advanced into Germany in the spring
of 1945, they came face to face with what had long been ru-
mored—concentration camps, Adolf Hitler's "final solution
of the Jewish question." Margaret Bourke-White was one of
the first photographers on the scene. This haunting image
from the Buchenwald death camp appeared in *Life* magazine.

Roosevelt administration, eventually helped save about
200,000 Jews. Several factors combined to inhibit U.S.
action: anti-Semitism; fear of economic competition
from a flood of refugees in a country just recovering
from the depression; the failure of the media to grasp
the magnitude of the story and publicize it accordingly;
and the failure of religious leaders, Jews and non-Jews
alike, to speak out.

In justifying the American course of action, Roosevelt claimed that winning the war would be the
strongest contribution America could make to liberating the camps. But it is hard to escape the conclusion
that the United States could have done much more to
lessen the Holocaust's terrible human toll.

The War in the Pacific

After the victory in Europe the Allies still had to defeat
Japan. American forces bore the brunt of the fighting in
the Pacific, just as the Russians had done in the land
war in Europe.

At the beginning of 1942 the news from the Pacific
was uniformly grim. In the wake of Pearl Harbor, Japan
had scored quickly with seaborne invasions of Hong
Kong, Wake Island, and Guam. Japanese forces conquered much of Burma, Malaya, and the Philippines as
well as the Solomon Islands and threatened Australia
and India (see American Voices, page 852). Japan

achieved this huge territorial expansion in only three
months. One of the few boosts for American morale
came on April 18, 1942, when Colonel James H. Doolit-
tle led sixteen American bombers on the first air raid on
Tokyo, but the attack had little military value.

The more significant battles were far to the south.
On May 7–8, 1942, in the Battle of the Coral Sea near
southern New Guinea, American naval forces halted the
Japanese offensive against Australia. Then, in June, at
the island of Midway, the Americans inflicted crucial
damage on the Japanese fleet. For the first time a major
sea battle was waged—and decided—primarily by planes
launched from aircraft carriers that never came within
sight of each other. Submarines also played an important
role in the naval battles, but the human cost was high: 22
percent of American submariners lost their lives during
the war, the highest death rate in any branch of the
armed services.

After the Battle of Midway the American military
command, under General Douglas MacArthur and Admiral Chester W. Nimitz, took the offensive in the Pacific. For the next eighteen months American forces
advanced arduously from one island to the next, win-

A New Type of Naval Warfare
The battles of Coral Sea and Midway in 1942 marked a revolution in naval warfare. For the first time, major sea battles
were waged—and decided—primarily by planes launched
from aircraft carriers. This panorama shows the vastness of
these naval encounters.

AMERICAN VOICES

Anton Bilek

The War in the Pacific

Anton Bilek was taken prisoner when the Japanese overran the Bataan peninsula of the Philippines in April 1942. He describes the infamous "Bataan Death March" and its aftermath.

The next morning, we got orders to get rid of all our arms and wait for the Japanese to come. General King had surrendered Bataan. They came in. First thing they did, they lined us up and started searchin' us. Anybody that had a ring or a wristwatch or a pair of gold-rimmed spectacles, they took 'em. Glasses they'd throw on the floor and break 'em and put the gold rims in their pockets. If you had a ring, you handed it over. If you couldn't get it off, the guy'd put the bayonet right up against your neck. Fortunately I never wore a ring. I couldn't afford one.

They moved us about on the road. Here was a big stream of Americans and Filipinos marchin' by. They told us to get in the back of this column. This was the start of the Death March. (A long, deep sigh.) That was a sixty-mile walk. Here we were, three, four months on half-rations, less. The men were already thin, in shock. Undernourished, full of malaria. Dysentery is beginning to spread. This is even before the surrender. We had two hospitals chuck-full

of men. Bataan peninsula was the worst malaria-infected province of the Philippines.

The Japanese emptied out the hospitals. Anybody that could walk, they forced 'em into line. You found all kinda bodies along the road. Some of 'em bloated, some had just been killed. If you fell out to the side, you were either shot by the guards or you were bayoneted and left there. We lost somewhere between six hundred and seven hundred Americans in the four days of the march. The Filipinos lost close to ten thousand. At San Fernando, we were stuffed into boxcars and taken about thirty-five miles further north. The cars were closed, you couldn't get air. In the hot sun, the temperature got up there. You couldn't fall down because you were held up by the guys stacked around you. You had a lot of guys blow their top, start screamin'. From there, they marched us another seven, eight miles to Camp O'Donnell, which was built hurriedly for the Philippine army. It was built like the huts were built, of native bamboo and *nipa* and grass. There must've been about nine thousand of us and about fifty thousand Filipinos. Americans in one camp, Filipinos in the other. We had to leave after a month and a half.

The monsoon season was starting. A hurricane blew down two of the barracks. Eighty men were killed. Just crushed.

I went blind, momentarily. It scared the hell out of me. I was at the hospital for about two weeks, and the doctor, an American, said, "There's nothing I can do with you. Rest is the only thing. Eat all the rice you can get. That's your only medicine." That's the one thing that pulled me through. He said, "You won't have to go on details." The Japanese were comin' in and they'd take two, three hundred and start 'em repairing a bridge that was blown up. We were losin' a lot of men there. They couldn't work any more. They were dyin'. . . .

I'm back home. It's all over with. I'd like to forget it. I had nothin' against the Japanese. But I don't drive a Toyota or own a Sony. . . . A lotta friends I lost. We had 185 men in our squadron when the war started. Three and a half years later, when we were liberated from a prison camp in Japan, we were 39 left. It's them I think about. Men I played ball with, men I worked with, men I associated with. I miss 'em.

Source: Studs Terkel, *"The Good War": An Oral History of World War Two* (New York: Pantheon, 1984), 85, 90–91, 95–96.

---

ning major victories at Tulagi and Guadalcanal in the Solomon Islands and at Tarawa and Makin in the Gilberts. They reached the Marshall Islands in early 1944. In October 1944 the reconquest of the Philippines began with a victory in the Battle of Leyte Gulf, a massive naval encounter in which the Japanese lost practically their entire fleet while the Americans suffered only minimal losses (see Map 27.3).

By early 1945 victory over Japan was in sight. The campaign in the Pacific moved slowly toward an anticipated massive and costly invasion of Japan. For a successful assault on the main Japanese island, the Americans needed to capture Iwo Jima and Okinawa. Airstrips there would put U.S. planes within striking distance of Tokyo. American marines won the battles for Iwo Jima (Febru-

ary 1–March 20, 1945) and Okinawa (April 1–June 10) in some of the fiercest fighting of the war. At Iwo Jima the marines sustained more than 20,000 casualties, including 6,000 dead; at Okinawa the toll reached 7,600 dead and 32,000 wounded. The closer U.S. forces got to the Japanese home islands, the more fiercely the Japanese fought. Almost all of the 21,000 Japanese on Iwo Jima died.

By mid-1945 Japan's army, navy, and air force had suffered devastating losses. American bombing of the mainland had killed about 330,000 civilians and crippled the Japanese economy, which had difficulty functioning once oil imports were cut off and in any case could not match American war production. In a last-ditch effort to stem the tide, Japanese pilots began suicidal *kamikaze* missions, crashing their planes and boats

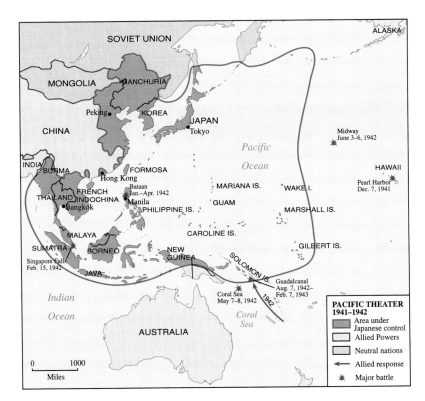

MAP 27.3

War in the Pacific

a. 1941–1942 After the attack on Pearl Harbor in December 1941 the Japanese rapidly extended their domination in the Pacific. The Japanese flag soon flew as far east as the Marshall and Gilbert islands and as far south as the Solomon Islands and parts of New Guinea. Japan also controlled the Philippines, much of Southeast Asia, and parts of China, including Hong Kong. American naval victories at the Coral Sea and Midway stopped further Japanese expansion.

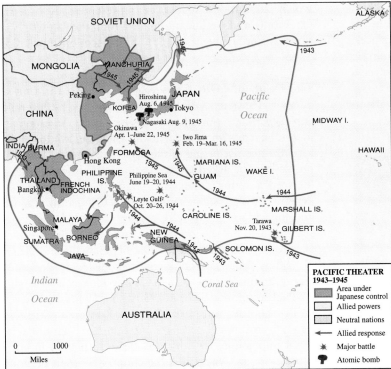

b. 1943–1945 Allied forces retook the islands in the Central Pacific in 1943 and 1944 and the Philippines early in 1945. The capture of Iwo Jima and Okinawa put U.S. bombers in position to attack Japan itself. The Japanese offered to surrender on August 10, after the United States dropped atomic bombs on Hiroshima and Nagasaki.

into American ships. This desperate action, combined with the Japanese military leadership's refusal to surrender, suggested that Japan would keep up the fight despite overwhelming losses. American military commanders grimly predicted millions of casualties in the upcoming invasion.

Planning the Postwar World

In February 1945 Roosevelt, Churchill, and Stalin held what would be their last conference at Yalta, a Black Sea resort. Victory in Europe and the Pacific was in sight, but no agreement had been reached on the peace to come. Roosevelt remained focused on maintaining Allied unity, the key to postwar peace and stability.

The commitment of the Allies to national self-determination as expressed in the Atlantic Charter presented the three leaders with their thorniest problems during the war and afterward. The fate of British colonies such as India, where an independence movement had already begun, caused friction between Roosevelt and Churchill. A more serious source of conflict was Stalin's desire for a band of Soviet-controlled satellite states to protect his western border.

Stalin had become increasingly inflexible on the issue of Eastern Europe, insisting that he needed friendly (that is, Soviet-dominated) governments there to provide a buffer for Soviet national security. Roosevelt acknowledged the legitimacy of that demand but hoped for democratically elected governments in Poland and the neighboring countries. Unfortunately, the two goals proved mutually exclusive.

At Yalta, Roosevelt and Churchill agreed in principle to the idea of a Soviet sphere of influence in Eastern Europe but left its dimensions deliberately vague. Furthermore, Roosevelt failed to inform the American public of the concessions he had made to maintain the increasingly fragile wartime alliance. In return, Stalin pledged to hold "free and unfettered elections" at an unspecified time. (Those elections never took place.) The compromise reached at Yalta was open to multiple interpretations. Admiral William D. Leahy, Roosevelt's chief military aide, described the agreement as "so elastic that the Russians can stretch it all the way from Yalta to Washington without technically breaking it."

The Yalta conference also proceeded with plans to divide Germany into four zones to be controlled by the United States, Great Britain, France, and the Soviet Union. Berlin, which lay in the middle of the Soviet zone, would also be partitioned among the four powers. The issue of German reparations remained unsettled.

At Yalta the Big Three made further progress toward a postwar international organization in the form of the United Nations. Roosevelt, determined to avoid Woodrow Wilson's mistakes, had already cultivated Congressional support; realizing that such an organization would be impotent without the Soviets' participation, he cultivated their support as well. British, American, and Soviet representatives had already met at Dumbarton Oaks, an estate in Washington, D.C., in September 1944 to begin planning the structure of the organization. At Yalta the Big Three agreed that the Security Council of the United Nations would consist of the five major Allied powers—the United States, Britain, France, China, and the Soviet Union—plus six nations elected on a rotating basis. They also decided that the permanent members of the Security Council should have veto power over decisions of the General Assembly, in which all nations would be represented. Roosevelt, Churchill, and Stalin announced that the United Nations would convene in San Francisco on April 25, 1945.

The Death of FDR. Roosevelt returned to the United States in February, visibly exhausted by his 14,000-mile trip. When he reported to Congress on the Yalta agreements, he made an unusual acknowledgment of his physical infirmity. Referring to the heavy steel braces he wore on his legs, he asked Congress to excuse him if he gave his speech sitting down. The sixty-three-year-old president was a very sick man, suffering from heart failure and high blood pressure. On April 12, 1945, during a short visit to his vacation home in Warm Springs, Georgia, Roosevelt suffered a cerebral hemorrhage and died.

Many Americans could not imagine any leader other than Franklin Roosevelt in the White House. Those who reached adulthood in the 1930s and 1940s had never known another president. Perhaps Roosevelt's greatest legacy was a model of leadership that has been difficult, if not impossible, for later presidents to match. In both depression and war he led the country through perilous times. As a global strategist he grasped America's predominant role and helped educate the country to accept its new international responsibilities.

V-E Day came less than a month after Roosevelt died and Harry Truman succeeded to the presidency. The war in the Pacific ended after Truman ordered the dropping of atomic bombs on two Japanese cities, Hiroshima on August 6 and Nagasaki on August 9. Many later questioned why the United States did not warn

The Big Three at Yalta
With victory in Europe at hand, Roosevelt journeyed to Yalta, on the Black Sea, in 1945, to meet one last time with Churchill and Stalin. It was here that they discussed the problems of peace settlements. The Yalta agreement mirrored a new balance of power and set the stage for the Cold War.

Hiroshima
This was all that remained of Hiroshima's Museum of Science and Industry on August 6, 1945. The shell of the building later became the center of a memorial to those who died in the atomic blast.

Japan about the attack or choose a noncivilian target; the rationale for dropping the second bomb was even less clear. At the time, however, the belief that Japan's military leaders would never surrender unless their country was utterly devastated convinced policy makers that they had to deploy the new weapon. The atomic bombs killed 100,000 people at Hiroshima and 60,000 at Nagasaki. Tens of thousands more died slowly of radiation poisoning. Japan offered to surrender on August 10 and signed a formal treaty of surrender on September 2, 1945. World War II had ended, but a new atomic age of insecurity had begun.

The Onset of the Atomic Age

The development of the atomic bomb was closely linked to wartime military strategy. In December 1938 German scientists had discovered that the nuclei of atoms could be split into smaller particles, a process called fission. With materials prepared from uranium, a chain reaction of nuclear fission would release tremendous amounts of energy. American scientists, including Enrico Fermi and Leo Szilard, many of them refugees from fascist Italy and Nazi Germany, produced the first controlled chain reaction on December 2, 1942, at the University of Chicago.

Scientists soon began working frantically to harness nuclear reactions for military purposes. Their goal was the development of an atomic bomb for use against Germany or, later, Japan. The secret research, called the Manhattan Project, cost $2 billion, employed 120,000 people, and involved the construction of thirty-seven

installations in nineteen states under the direction of General Leslie R. Groves of the U.S. Army Corps of Engineers. In the final stages a team consisting of most of the country's top physicists assembled the bomb at an isolated desert site in Los Alamos, New Mexico. All this was hidden from Congress, the American people, and even Vice-President Truman. The secrecy and scope of this alliance between science and government constitute a dramatic example of how much the power of the state grew during wartime.

Roosevelt had followed the bomb's progress closely. He and his advisers had planned to deploy the bomb to end the war without the dreadful number of American casualties that would have resulted from an invasion of Japan. At the same time, policy makers hoped that the possession of such a powerful weapon—the "master card," in the words of Secretary of War Henry Stimson—might enhance American power in the postwar world. Instead, the new weapon became the first step in a deadly arms race between the United States and the Soviet Union.

Until the last moment the scientists did not know if the atomic bomb would work. On July 16, 1945, near Alamogordo, New Mexico, they watched in wonder as the test bomb exploded in a huge mushroom cloud. President Truman received news of the successful detonation in Potsdam, near Berlin, where he was about to meet with Churchill and Stalin in the final wartime conference about the shape of postwar Europe (see Chapter 28). Truman, who had not known about the bomb before he became president, was ecstatic about its potential. After the bombing of Hiroshima he told aides, "This is the greatest thing in history." Others were not so sure. J. Robert Oppenheimer, one of the leading scientists on the Manhattan Project, watched the test early on that July morning in the New Mexico desert. Overwhelmed by its frightening power, he recalled the words from the *Bhagavad Gita*, a Hindu sacred text: "I am become Death, Destroyer of Worlds."

Franklin Roosevelt's death and the dropping of the atomic bomb came at a critical juncture in world affairs. Many issues had been left deliberately unresolved in the hopes of keeping the wartime alliance intact to guide the transition to peace. But as the war ended, issues such as the fate of Poland and Germany demanded action. The resulting compromises, not all of which were fully reported to the American people, tended to promote spheres of influence as the new basis of international power instead of the ideals of national self-determination and economic cooperation laid out in the Atlantic Charter. Once the common enemies had been defeated, the wartime alliance became strained and then began to split apart in ways so fundamental that it is unlikely that Roosevelt could have kept it together if he had lived. Perhaps the greatest legacy of World War II was the Cold War that followed.

Summary

With the rise of fascism and totalitarianism in Germany, Italy, and Japan, the international situation deteriorated rapidly throughout the 1930s, and the world was at war by 1939. Although most Americans clung to strong isolationist sentiment, President Roosevelt began mobilizing public opinion for intervention and converting the economy to war production. The Japanese attack on Pearl Harbor on December 7, 1941, brought the nation into World War II.

Defense mobilization ended the Great Depression and caused the economy to more than double. As with World War I, mobilization led to a dramatic expansion of the state. On the home front, the war resulted in rationing and shortages of many items but no serious hardships. Geographical mobility increased as labor shortages opened job opportunities for women, blacks, and Mexican-Americans. The labor movement surged, and the ideological climate of fighting Nazism aided the cause of civil rights. However, Japanese-Americans on the West Coast suffered a devastating denial of civil liberties when the government moved them into internment camps.

World War II was a global war, consisting of massive military campaigns in both Europe and the Pacific. The war news was bleak at first, but by 1943 the Allies had started to move toward victory, first in Europe and then in the Pacific. Soviet forces bore the brunt of the fighting in the European theater, while American forces primarily orchestrated the war effort in the Pacific. More than 15 million American men and women served in the armed forces, and at least 405,000 lost their lives.

While the Allied forces mobilized to defeat Germany and Japan, Roosevelt attempted to maintain harmony among the United States, Great Britain, and the Soviet Union. Many of the disagreements over wartime diplomacy would become major problems in the postwar world, especially the fate of Eastern Europe and the intentions of the Soviet Union. Of all the major powers that fought in World War II, only the United States emerged physically unharmed. And at the end of the war, only the United States had a powerful new weapon, the atomic bomb.

TIMELINE

1934	Platt Amendment repealed
1935	Italy invades Ethiopia
1935–1937	Neutrality Acts
1936	Rome-Berlin Axis established Japan joins Anti-Comintern Pact
1937	Japan invades China
1938	Munich agreement *War of the Worlds* broadcast
1939	Nazi-Soviet pact World War II breaks out in Europe
1940	Conscription reinstated America First movement
1941	Roosevelt's third term begins Roosevelt promulgates Four Freedoms Hitler invades Soviet Union Lend-Lease Act passed Fair Employment Practices Commission Atlantic Charter Japanese attack Pearl Harbor
1942	Battles of Coral Sea and Midway halt Japanese advance in the Pacific Women recruited for war industries Japanese relocation Revenue Act of 1942
1942–1945	Rationing
1943	Race riots in Detroit and Los Angeles Fascism falls in Italy Teheran Conference
1944	Gunnar Myrdal, *An American Dilemma* D-Day Reconquest of Philippines GI Bill of Rights
1945	Roosevelt's fourth term begins Germany surrenders Battles of Iwo Jima and Okinawa Yalta Conference Harry S. Truman becomes president after Roosevelt's death United Nations convenes Atomic bombs dropped on Hiroshima and Nagasaki Japan surrenders

★   ★   ★

BIBLIOGRAPHY

John Morton Blum, *V Was for Victory* (1976), and William O'Neill, *A Democracy at War* (1993), offer good introductions to American politics and culture during the war years. A provocative oral history of the war is Studs Terkel, *"The Good War": An Oral History of World War Two* (1984). John Keegan, *The Second World War* (1990), offers the best one-volume account of the battlefront aspects.

The Road to War

Depression and wartime diplomacy are covered in Robert Dallek, *Franklin D. Roosevelt and American Foreign Policy, 1932–1945* (1979), and Akira Iriye, *The Globalizing of America, 1913–1945* (1993). On American isolationism see Wayne Cole, *Roosevelt and the Isolationists, 1932–1945* (1983). Warren T. Kimball, *The Most Unsordid Act* (1969), describes the lend-lease controversy of 1939–1941, whereas *The Juggler: Franklin Roosevelt as Wartime Statesman* (1991), provides an overview of Roosevelt's leadership. Roberta Wohlstetter, *Pearl Harbor* (1962); Herbert Feis, *The Road to Pearl Harbor* (1950); and Gordon W. Prange, *At Dawn We Slept* (1981), describe the events that led to American entry.

Mobilizing for Victory

George Flynn, *The Mess in Washington* (1979), and Harold G. Vatter, *The U.S. Economy in World War II* (1985), discuss America's economic mobilization. David Brinkley, *Washington Goes to War* (1988), offers an engaging journalistic perspective. Mark S. Foster, *Henry J. Kaiser: Builder in the Modern American West* (1989), is a comprehensive biography. Alan Winkler, *The Politics of Propaganda* (1978), covers the Office of War Information. On labor's role during war, see George Lipsitz, *Rainbow at Midnight: Labor and Culture in the 1940s* (1994); Nelson Lichtenstein, *Labor's War at Home: The CIO in World War II* (1982); and Paul Koistinen, *The Hammer and the Sword: Labor, the Military, and Industrial Mobilization, 1920–1945* (1979). For more on politics in wartime, see James McGregor Burns, *Roosevelt: The Soldier of Freedom* (1970), and Alan Brinkley, *The End of Reform* (1995).

Women's roles in wartime are covered by Susan Hartmann, *The Home Front and Beyond* (1982); Karen Anderson, *Wartime Women* (1980); D'Ann Campbell, *Women at War with America* (1984); Ruth Milkman, *Gender at Work* (1987); and Sherna B. Gluck, *Rosie the Riveter Revisited: Women, the War, and Social Change* (1987). Judy Barrett Litoff and David C. Smith, *We're in This War, Too* (1994), includes letters from American women in uniform.

Life on the Home Front

William M. Tuttle, Jr., *"Daddy's Gone to War"* (1993), describes World War II from the perspective of the nation's children. Alan Clive, *State of War* (1979), provides a case study of Michigan during the war; Marilynn S. Johnson, *The Second Gold Rush* (1993), describes Oakland and the East Bay. See also Gerald D. Nash, *The American West Transformed: The Impact of the Second World War* (1985), and Marc Scott Miller, *The Irony of Victory: World War II and Lowell, Massachusetts* (1988). Clayton R. Koppes and Gregory D. Black, *Hollywood Goes to War* (1987), covers the film industry. The experience of black Americans is treated in Albert Russell Buchanan, *Black Americans in World War II* (1977), and Neil Wynn, *The Afro-American and the Second World War* (1975). On racial tensions, see Dominic Capeci, Jr., *Race Relations in Wartime Detroit* (1984), and Mauricio Mazan, *The Zoot Suit Riots* (1984). August Meier and Elliott Rudwick, *CORE* (1973), describes the founding of an important civil rights organization. Richard Dalfiume, *Desegregation of the U.S. Armed Forces* (1969), covers black soldiers in the military. Alan Berube, *Coming Out under Fire* (1990), is an oral history of gay men and lesbians in the military; see also John D'Emilio, *Sexual Politics, Sexual Communities* (1983), for the impact of the war on gay Americans. Maurice Isserman, *Which Side Were You On?* (1982), analyzes the American Communist party during the war. Two compelling accounts of Japanese relocation are Audre Girdner and Anne Loftus, *The Great Betrayal* (1969), and Roger Daniels, *Prisoners without Trial: Japanese-Americans in World War II* (1993). See also Peter Irons, *Justice at War: The Story of the Japanese-American Internment Cases* (1983). Valerie Matsumoto, *Farming the Home Place* (1993), describes a Japanese-American community in California from 1919 to 1982.

Fighting and Winning the War

Extensive material chronicles the American military experience during World War II. Albert Russell Buchanan, *The United States and World War II* (1962), and Russell F. Weigley, *The American Way of War* (1973), provide overviews; Ronald Schaffer, *Wings of Judgement: American Bombing in World War II* (1985), and Bradley F. Smith, *The Shadow Warriors: OSS and the Origins of the CIA* (1983), are more specialized. Cornelius Ryan, *The Last Battle* (1966); John Toland, *The Last Hundred Days* (1966); and Stephen Ambrose, *D-Day, June 6, 1944* (1994) describe the end of the fighting in Europe. David S. Wyman, *The Abandonment of the Jews* (1984), devastatingly describes the lack of American response to the Holocaust from 1941 to 1945. On the Far East, see John W. Dower, *War without Mercy: Race and Power in the Pacific War* (1986); Ronald H. Spector, *Eagle against the Sun: The American War with Japan* (1984); and John Toland, *Rising Sun: The Decline and Fall of the Japanese Empire* (1970).

American diplomacy and the strategy of the Grand Alliance are surveyed in Robert Dallek, *Franklin D. Roosevelt and American Foreign Policy, 1932–1945* (1979), and Lloyd Gardner, *Spheres of Influence* (1993). The relationship between the wartime conferences and the onset of the Cold War are treated in Walter LaFeber, *America, Russia, and the Cold War* (7th ed., 1993), and Stephen Ambrose, *Rise to Globalism* (7th ed., 1993). Richard Rhodes, *The Making of the Atomic Bomb* (1987); McGeorge Bundy, *Danger and Survival* (1988); and Martin Sherwin, *A World Destroyed* (1975), provide compelling accounts of the development of the bomb. See also Gar Alperowitz, *The Decision to Use the Atomic Bomb* (1995); Ronald Takaki, *Hiroshima: Why America Dropped the Atomic Bomb* (1995); and Gregg Herken, *The Winning Weapon* (1980). John Hersey, *Hiroshima* (2d ed., 1985), on the aftermath of the bombing, retains its power fifty years after its original publication.

P A R T 6

America and the World
1945 to the Present

In 1945 the United States entered an era of unprecedented international power and influence. Unlike the period after World War I, American leaders did not avoid international commitments; instead they aggressively pursued U.S. interests abroad, vowing to contain communism around the globe. The consequences of that struggle profoundly influenced the nation's domestic economy, political affairs, and social and cultural trends for the next half century.

First, and most important, the United States took a leading, or hegemonic, role in global diplomatic and military affairs. When the Soviet Union challenged America's vision of postwar Europe, the Truman administration responded by crafting the policies and alliances that came to define the Cold War. That bipolar struggle lasted for more than forty years, spawned two long "hot" wars in Korea and Vietnam, and fueled a terrifying and debilitating nuclear arms race. Although the policy of détente pursued by Richard Nixon and later presidents helped ease tensions, the cold war mentality prevailed until the final collapse and disintegration of the Soviet Union in 1991.

Second, the nation's global commitments had dramatic consequences for American government. Until the national consensus fractured over the Vietnam War, liberals and conservatives agreed on keeping the country in a state of permanent mobilization and maintaining a large and well-equipped military establishment. And all administrations, Republican and Democratic, were willing to intervene in the economy when private initiatives could not maintain steady growth. But liberals also pushed for a larger role for the federal government in the area of social welfare. Under Truman, John F. Kennedy, and especially Lyndon Johnson, the government went beyond the New Deal to erect an extensive structure of federal social programs. In recent years, especially during the presidency of Ronald Reagan in the 1980s and the Republican control of Congress in the mid-1990s, conservatives began to cut back on many of the major programs and tried to delegate federal powers to the states.

Third, thanks to the growth of a military-industrial complex of enormous size and the expansion of consumer culture, the quarter century after 1945 represented the heyday of American capitalism. Economic dominance abroad translated into unparalleled affluence at home. In the early 1970s competition from other countries began to challenge America's economic supremacy. Today, the United States remains the world's largest economy, but increased foreign competition and slow productivity growth since the 1970s have meant declining real wages and stagnant family incomes for most American workers.

Fourth, the victory over fascism in World War II led to renewed calls for America to make good on its promise of liberty and equality for all. In great waves of protests in the 1950s and 1960s African-Americans and then women, Latinos, and other groups challenged the political domination of elite white men. The resulting reforms brought concrete gains for many Americans, but since the late 1970s, conservatives have challenged these initiatives, slowing the progress toward social equality.

Fifth, American economic power in the postwar era accelerated the development of a consumer society. As millions of Americans migrated to new suburban developments after World War II, growing baby-boom families provided an expanded market for household products of all types. Among the most significant were new technological devices—television, video recorders, personal computers—that helped break down the isolation of suburban and rural living. Beginning in the 1960s, however, some people began to question the American obsession with material consumption and the environmental degradation that it caused.

Americans today are living in an increasingly interwoven network of national and international forces. Outside events shape ordinary lives in ways that were inconceivable a century ago. As the cold war era fades into history, the United States remains the sole military superpower, but it shares economic leadership in the new interdependent global system. Will international cooperation replace cold war patterns of confrontation, or will the United States pull back from its global commitments? In tackling domestic problems, will policy makers continue to roll back federal involvement in social and environmental concerns, or will they ultimately seek new solutions? The next chapter of America's history remains to be written.

Danger and Survival

With its first successful test of a hydrogen bomb in 1952,
the United States entered the nuclear age.

Cold War America

1945–1960

★   ★   ★

When Harry Truman arrived at the White House on April 12, 1945, after learning of Roosevelt's death, he asked the president's widow, "Is there anything I can do for you?" Eleanor Roosevelt responded with another question, "Is there anything we can do for you? For you are the one in trouble now."

Truman inherited the presidency at one of the most perilous times in modern American history. World War II had catapulted the United States into a position of international leadership, and America emerged from the war as the most powerful country in the world. Of all the former combatants, only the Soviet Union represented an obstacle to American hegemony, or dominance, in global affairs. As the Truman administration set out to create conditions that would maintain American supremacy, Soviet leaders sought to protect their country's interests. Soon the two superpowers were locked in a Cold War that took economic, political, and military forms but did not entail a direct Soviet-American confrontation on the battlefield. The Cold War continued in the 1950s under the Republican presidency of Dwight Eisenhower, who modified some of Truman's initiatives but did little to ease overall tensions. For better or worse, the United States had become a permanent and preeminent force in the international arena.

The Soviet-American conflict of the postwar years had important domestic repercussions. The Cold War boosted military expenditures and fueled a growing arms race with damaging physical and psychological consequences. Moreover, the Cold War fostered a climate of fear and suspicion about internal subversion and a hunt for "subversives" in government, education, and the media. But the economic benefits of internationalism also gave rise to a period of unprecedented affluence and prosperity. That affluence gave the United States the highest standard of living in the world (see

Chapter 29) and helped underwrite a continuation and in some cases an expansion of federal power, perpetuating the New Deal state in the postwar era.

The Early Cold War

The defeat of Germany and Japan did not bring stability to the world. Six years of war had unsettled the international system by creating power vacuums in those nations, devastating Western Europe, and helping to dissolve colonial empires. Even before the war ended the United States and the Soviet Union were struggling for advantage in those unstable areas, and after the war they engaged in a protracted global conflict. Hailed as a battle between communism and capitalism, the Cold War was in reality a more complex power struggle over a broad range of economic, strategic, and ideological issues. As each side tried to protect its own national security and way of life, its actions aroused fear in the other, contributing to a cycle of distrust and animosity that shaped U.S.–Soviet relations for the next four decades.

Sources of Conflict

When World War II ended, much of the world lay in ruins. Fifty million people had perished in the conflict, and tens of millions were left homeless. Berlin, Warsaw, Leningrad, Tokyo, and dozens of other cities had been reduced to rubble. The European and Asian countryside was devastated; the war had destroyed railroad lines, dams, crops, and livestock. Famine and disease plagued parts of China and the Soviet Union. In Europe, food production in 1945–1946 fell to less than two-thirds of its prewar level.

Despite 400,000 American casualties, the United States emerged from the war as the world's strongest, wealthiest nation. Unscathed by bombing, U.S. industry and agriculture had grown rapidly during the war, making America the world's leading manufacturer and exporter. The nation's gross national product soared, growing to three times that of the Soviet Union, its nearest competitor. The United States also wielded enormous military power. American air and naval forces were the world's best, and the United States alone possessed the atomic bomb. As the historian Melvyn Leffler has argued, the United States held "preponderant power" in 1945; in the postwar era U.S. policy makers tried to maintain that hegemony and rebuild the world in America's image.

The Soviet Union, by contrast, was relatively weak. With 20 million casualties and extensive physical devastation, the U.S.S.R.'s military and economic sectors were exhausted and in disarray. The Soviet Union's greatest asset was its army, including a vast force of troops occupying Eastern Europe and parts of Germany at the end of the war. A victim of German aggression in both world wars, the Soviet Union relied on its military power in those areas to build a security zone along its western flank. Soviet dominance, however, did not extend beyond Eastern Europe. While the Soviets might have sought to export communist revolution throughout the world, as their leaders sometimes proclaimed, they were in no position to do so in 1945. American policy makers agreed that the U.S.S.R. presented no immediate military threat; its power was regional, not global.

The Soviet presence in Eastern Europe, however, raised concerns among U.S. policy makers who feared Russian expansion in the long term. If the Soviet Union could someday capture the industrial resources of Western Europe, they reasoned, American security would be in danger. With the defeat and dismantling of the Nazi

Postwar Devastation, 1947
Munich, Germany, was one of many European cities reduced to rubble during the war. U.S. policy makers worried that physical devastation and economic disorder would make many areas of Europe vulnerable to communist influence.

government, American leaders worried that Soviet influence would spread across postwar Germany. Elsewhere in Europe economic chaos threatened to disrupt the political status quo. The growing popularity of left-wing parties in many European countries exacerbated those fears. During the war, when Communists played key roles in antifascist movements, membership in Communist parties showed rapid gains, particularly in Czechoslovakia, France, Greece, and Italy. In Britain and Sweden labor-led socialist governments came to power after 1945 by promising social and economic reforms to ease postwar deprivation. Although those parties generally remained independent of Moscow, American policy makers viewed them as tools of the Kremlin, which would be sympathetic to Soviet initiatives. American security, those leaders argued, required a strong, noncommunist Europe that could serve as a military and economic partner of the United States.

Political instability also characterized the Third World, where the war hastened the disintegration of colonial empires. Rising nationalist movements in developing regions and financial pressures on war-torn European countries after 1945 led to a severing of colonial ties and client-state relationships. In Turkey, Vietnam, Iran, and other countries, European nations solicited U.S. help in regaining their colonies or supporting governments favorable to Western interests; the Soviet Union also cultivated local leaders sympathetic to its interests. American-Soviet rivalry for these areas was keen since they provided essential markets for finished goods and had vital resources such as oil, tin, zinc, and manganese. In an air-age world where national defense stretched far beyond domestic borders, Third World nations also offered strategic sites for U.S. and Soviet military bases. The struggle for these economic and strategic benefits sparked a series of conflicts in Asia, the Middle East, and other parts of the world.

Finally, the end of World War II marked the beginning of the nuclear age and the rise of atomic diplomacy. In 1945 the United States had sole possession of the atomic bomb and held it, as Secretary of War Henry Stimson explained, "rather ostentatiously on our hip." Emboldened by that monopoly, President Harry Truman decided to "get tough" with the Russians, a stance that provoked equally stubborn resistance on the part of the Soviet leader, Joseph Stalin. Both sides were inflexible in their demands and remained suspicious of the other's motives and actions. While the Americans accused the Soviets of "communist aggression," the Soviets feared "capitalist encirclement." Stalin and Truman came to dislike one another so much that they refused to meet after the war. From 1945 to 1955, some of the tensest years of the Cold War, there were no summit meetings between Soviet and American heads of state. This climate of mutual distrust and suspicion was not conducive to negotiation or compromise.

Descent into Cold War, 1945–1946

Franklin Roosevelt had worked effectively with Stalin during the war and was determined to continue good relations with the Soviet Union in peacetime. In particular, he hoped that the United Nations would provide a forum for resolving postwar conflicts. Avoiding the disagreements that had doomed American membership in the League of Nations after World War I, the Senate approved America's participation in the United Nations in December 1945. Coming eight months after Roosevelt's death, the vote was in part a memorial to the late president's hopes for postwar peace.

Shortly before his death, however, Roosevelt had been disturbed by Soviet actions in Eastern Europe. As the Soviet army drove the Germans out of Russia and back through Eastern Europe, the U.S.S.R. sponsored provisional governments in those occupied countries. At the Yalta Conference in February both American and British diplomats, including President Roosevelt, had in effect agreed to recognize this Soviet "sphere of influence" with the proviso that "free and unfettered elections" would be held as soon as possible. But in the coming months the Soviets made no move to hold elections and rebuffed Western attempts to reorganize Soviet-installed governments. When Truman assumed the presidency after Roosevelt's death, he immediately questioned whether the United States could cooperate with its former wartime ally. "We must stand up to the Russians," he stated privately.

Over the next few months Truman backed away from the Yalta pledges and took an increasingly belligerent stance toward the Soviet Union. At a meeting shortly after he took office, the new president berated the Soviet foreign minister, V. M. Molotov, for not honoring agreements on Poland. Molotov had never "been talked to like that in my life," he told Truman, and stormed out of the room. Truman used what he called "tough methods" again that July at the Potsdam Conference of the United States, Britain, and the Soviet Union. After learning of the successful test of America's atom bomb, Truman "told the Russians just where they got off and generally bossed the whole meeting," recalled British Prime Minister Winston Churchill. Negotiations on critical postwar issues deadlocked, revealing serious cracks in the Grand Alliance.

The one issue that was tentatively resolved at Potsdam was the fate of occupied Germany. At Yalta the defeated German state had been divided into four occupation zones controlled by the United States, France, Britain, and the Soviet Union. At Potsdam the Allies agreed to disarm the country, dismantle its military production facilities, terminate Nazi laws and institutions, and permit the occupying powers to extract reparations from their respective zones. By 1946 the United States was encouraging the gradual rebuilding of the German industrial heartland in its zone as part of the larger goal of reviving the European economy. The Soviet Union also began to develop the industrial capacities of its zone. Plans to reunify the country stalled as the United States and the Soviet Union worried that a reunified German state would fall into the other's sphere. The economic base was thus laid for what eventually became the political division into East and West Germany.

In both Germany and Eastern Europe the Americans and Soviets based their actions on different understandings of the past. Stalin was determined to prevent the rebuilding and rearming of Russia's traditional foe, Germany, and for further protection insisted on a security zone of friendly governments in Eastern Europe. Accordingly, between 1945 and 1947 the Soviets repressed democratic parties and installed puppet governments in Poland, Hungary, Rumania, and Bulgaria. Truman, recalling Britain's disastrous appeasement of Hitler in 1938, decided that the United States had to take a hard line against Soviet expansion and stand up to the Soviet dictator. "There isn't any difference in totalitarian states," he said, "Nazi, Communist, or Fascist." Increasingly, Truman and his advisers used the phrase *Red Fascism* to describe the Soviet threat.

The former British prime minister Winston Churchill articulated the deepening pessimism about the Soviet Union shared by American diplomats in 1946. Out of power and eager to establish a platform for his views, Churchill accepted an invitation from President Truman to deliver a major policy address in March 1946 in Fulton, Missouri. Churchill had gone along with plans for a Soviet sphere of influence in Eastern Europe at Yalta but had developed second thoughts, warning ominously about the "expansive tendencies" of the Soviet Union: "From Stettin in the Baltic to Trieste in the Adriatic, an Iron Curtain has descended across the Continent." If the West hoped to preserve peace and freedom in the face of the Soviet challenge, Churchill declared, it must remember that "there is nothing they [the Soviets] admire so much as strength, and there is nothing for which they have less respect than for weakness, especially military weakness."

Churchill's widely publicized Iron Curtain speech helped convince many Americans that the Soviet Union posed a serious threat to national security. That shift represented a return to the American hostility toward Bolshevism first articulated by Woodrow Wilson after the 1917 revolution, a distrust that had delayed diplomatic recognition of the Soviet Union until 1933. The wartime collaboration necessitated by the common fight against fascism receded quickly from memory.

Hopes of international cooperation in the control of atomic weapons also faded. Although U.S. leaders were willing to consider international control in the long run, they did not want to give up their advantage. In the Baruch Plan submitted to the United Nations in 1946, the United States proposed a system of international control that relied on mandatory inspection and supervision but preserved the American nuclear monopoly. The Soviets rejected the plan categorically and worked assiduously to complete their own bomb. The Truman administration pursued its own plans to develop nuclear energy and weapons further. The failure of the Baruch Plan thus signaled the beginning of a frenzied nuclear arms race between the two superpowers.

From the Truman Doctrine to NATO, 1947–1949

By 1947 a new American policy—*containment*—was taking shape. Although its precepts were agreed on in Washington policy-making circles, containment is usually associated with George F. Kennan, an intense, scholarly diplomat who had devoted his career to studying the Soviet Union (see American Lives, pages 866–867). Kennan first articulated containment's basic premises in February 1946 in an 8,000-word cable from his post at the U.S. Embassy in Moscow to his superiors in Washington, where it was widely circulated. He expanded on those ideas in an influential article in the journal *Foreign Affairs* in July 1947. According to Kennan, who was identified only as "X," the Soviets were moving "inexorably along the prescribed path, like a persistent toy automobile wound up and headed in a given direction, stopping only when it meets unanswerable force." To stop this expansionism, Kennan argued, it was necessary to pursue a policy of "firm containment, designed to confront the Russians with unalterable counterforce at every point where they show signs of encroaching upon the interests of a peaceful and stable world."

Kennan's initial formulation recommended economic and diplomatic means to enforce containment, but the policy soon took on a military cast. In one version or another containment defined the foreign policy of every subsequent administration, both Democratic and Republican, well into the 1980s. It ultimately served at least three purposes. By identifying an evil, expansionist enemy, the containment doctrine provided a rallying cry for Americans to unite behind the president in fighting the Soviet threat; it justified the creation of a vast peacetime military machine; and it obscured other objectives of American foreign policy in the economic arena and the Third World. Kennan later denounced the militarization of containment and the vilification of the Soviet Union, charging that such policies and beliefs had undercut attempts at diplomacy.

The emerging containment policy crystallized in 1947 over the situation in Greece. Local communist-inspired guerrillas, whom American advisers mistakenly believed were controlled by Moscow, had fought for control of Greece since the end of 1944. After elections installed the royalist Popular party in the spring of 1946, several thousand communist guerrillas launched a full-scale civil war against the government and the British occupation authorities. In February 1947 the British informed Truman that they could no longer afford to assist the Greek anticommunists. Fearing a communist takeover in Greece, U.S. policy makers worried that growing Soviet influence there would pose a threat to American and European interests in the eastern Mediterranean and the Middle East, especially in strategically located Turkey and the oil-rich state of Iran.

To counter those threats the president announced what became known as the Truman Doctrine. In a speech to Congress on March 12 he requested large-scale military and economic assistance to Greece and Turkey and called for all Americans "to support free peoples who are resisting attempted subjugation by armed minorities or by outside pressures." To win popular support for the global fight against communism, and to squeeze money out of a stingy Congress, the president followed the advice of Republican Senator Arthur Vandenberg to "scare hell" out of the country. If Greece fell to communism, Truman warned, "the effect upon its neighbor, Turkey, would be immediate and serious. Confusion and disorder might well spread throughout the entire Middle East." This notion of communist contagion was an early version of what Dwight Eisenhower would later call the "domino theory." Not just Greece but freedom itself was at issue, Truman declared: "If we falter in our leadership, we may endanger the peace of the world—and we shall surely endanger the welfare of our own nation."

Despite the open-endedness of this military commitment, Congress quickly approved Truman's request for $300 million in aid to Greece and $100 million for Turkey. The appropriation reversed the postwar policy of sharp cuts in foreign spending and marked a new level of commitment to the emerging Cold War. Truman's skillful manipulation of public opinion helped build a base of bipartisan support in Congress that gave him a greater role in determining future foreign policy.

The Truman administration also worked with Congress to pass the National Security Act, which was designed to streamline defense operations. Signed in July 1947, the act created three new bodies: a single Department of Defense to replace the previous Departments of War and the Navy; the National Security Council, an advisory body charged with helping the president set defense and military priorities; and the Central Intelligence Agency, a national intelligence-gathering operation that replaced the wartime Office of Strategic Services. The Atomic Energy Commission, established in 1946 under the executive branch, worked with the new agencies in the development of atomic energy and weapons. The establishment of these new bureaucratic structures marked the emergence of the *national security state*, a collection of powerful and highly secretive operations in the executive branch. Such structures accelerated the shift of policy-making initiative to the White House.

The Marshall Plan. During this period Secretary of State George Marshall, who had been army chief of staff under Roosevelt, proposed a plan to provide economic as well as military aid to Europe. European economies had been devastated by the war, and conditions worsened in the terrible winter of 1947. Only with a massive influx of outside capital could Europeans begin the process of rebuilding and revitalization. Speaking at Harvard University's commencement in June 1947, Marshall urged the nations of Europe to work out a comprehensive recovery program and then ask the United States for aid. "Any government that is willing to assist in the task of recovery," he promised, "will find full cooperation . . . on the part of the United States government." In Truman's words, the Marshall Plan was "the other half of the walnut" (the first half being the aggressive containment policy of the Truman Doctrine). By bolstering European economies devastated by the war, Marshall and Truman believed, the United States could forestall economic dislocation that would give rise to communism.

The Marshall Plan in Action
Between 1948 and 1951 the European Recovery Program, popularly known as the Marshall Plan after Secretary of State George C. Marshall, contributed over $13 billion toward its objective of "restoring the confidence of the European people in the economic future of their own countries and of Europe as a whole." Here a sign prominently announces that Berlin is being rebuilt with help from the Marshall Plan.

The Wise Men: Architects of Containment

They were, as their biographers Walter Isaacson and Evan Thomas tallied it up, two bankers (W. Averell Harriman, Robert Lovett), two lawyers (Dean Acheson, John McCloy), and two diplomats (Charles Bohlen, George Kennan). Those six friends were among the main architects of the containment policy that dominated American foreign relations from the 1940s through at least the 1960s. Individually their names are not that well known, but collectively they had an enormous impact on postwar developments. In 1965, the presidential aide McGeorge Bundy dubbed these senior statesmen "the wise men," and the name stuck.

At first glance the social profile of the six men, all born between 1893 and 1904, suggests that the foreign policy elite was synonymous with the rich and the powerful in the United States. W. Averell Harriman was the son of the founder of the Union Pacific Railroad, and Robert Lovett's father was the elder Harriman's second in command. Dean Acheson was the son of the Episcopal bishop of Connecticut, and Charles Bohlen was descended from the first American ambassador to France. But the establishment was more of a meritocracy than a closed club: John McCloy came from a poor family in Philadelphia, and George Kennan was an outsider from Milwaukee. Access to education at the elite eastern institutions that trained generations of leaders—prep schools such as Groton and St. Paul's and universities such as Harvard, Yale, and Princeton—was crucial to membership. Averell Harriman taught Dean Acheson to row crew at Groton, they went to Yale together, and their lives remained linked until they died.

After graduation from college, these privileged young men embarked on careers, mainly on Wall Street or in Washington. Charles Bohlen went into the foreign service and became a specialist on Soviet affairs; he was assigned to the first U.S. mission to that country in 1934. George Kennan was also a foreign service officer in Moscow in the 1930s. Dean Acheson spent most of the 1920s and 1930s in private legal practice, as did John McCloy; W. Averell Harriman devoted his attention to business, and Robert Lovett worked with the

banking firm of Brown Brothers, which merged with the Harriman empire in 1931.

A common thread among the six lives in the 1920s and 1930s was extensive contact with European affairs, including familiarity with the Soviet Union. The result was a collective internationalism that stood in stark contrast to the isolationism of the 1930s. Not surprisingly, all six ended up in Washington during World War II, a period when their personal and professional relationships coalesced. McCloy and Lovett served as assistant secretaries of war, where they were known as "the Heavenly Twins"; Harriman was ambassador to the Soviet Union, where one of his advisors was George Kennan; Acheson became assistant secretary of state for economic affairs; and Bohlen served as the State Department's chief translator and expert on Soviet affairs, accompanying Roosevelt to Teheran and Yalta.

When the war ended, the six men all joined the Truman administration and embarked on seven years of extraordinary power and influence at one of the most critical moments in modern American history: the onset of the Cold War and the formulation of the policy of containment of the Soviet Union through diplomacy and force. Although containment is associated with George Kennan, its underlying assumptions were shared by all six. They fervently believed that the United States had a moral destiny to provide world leadership in the struggle against communism. The Truman Doctrine and the Marshall Plan epitomized the sweeping commitments they were willing to undertake to promote that world view.

The policy-making process in the Truman administration was fairly intimate and decentralized and hence was amenable to the kind of behind-the-scenes power these members of the establishment thrived on. Acheson was the most influential member of the group, serving as undersecretary of state from 1945 to 1947 and then secretary of state from 1949 to 1953. Charles Bohlen was his special assistant until Bohlen was named minister to France in 1949. George Kennan also served in various capacities in the State Department before being named ambassador to the Soviet Union in 1951. Harriman joined the cabinet as secretary of commerce and then became a special assistant to the president, where he played a key role in setting the strategy for the conduct of the Korean War. McCloy served as president of the World Bank and became a vigorous proponent of the Marshall Plan; in 1949 Truman named him U.S. high commissioner for Germany.

These six men wielded power individually, but their impact was enhanced by how they functioned as a group. They had much in common, especially their belief in the cold war ideology of containment. Just as important was their commitment to public service: remarkably free of personal ambition, they saw themselves as public servants who stood above the fray of partisan politics. However, their pattern of alternating between government service and lucrative positions on Wall Street suggests that they had no trouble reconciling public service with private gain.

Dwight Eisenhower's election sent most of the wise men into temporary retirement from public service, but the election of John Kennedy in 1960 called them in from what their biographers called "the wilderness years." Now generally in their fifties and sixties, this older generation served the young president in a variety of capacities: Bohlen and Kennan as ambassadors to France and Yugoslavia, respectively; Harriman as assistant secretary of state for Far Eastern affairs; amd McCloy, Lovett, and Acheson as advisers. Their service demonstrates the continuity of the postwar foreign policy elite from World War II through the 1960s.

After Kennedy's assassination Lyndon Johnson continued to seek their counsel, especially as the Vietnam War escalated. But these six men, who had so forcefully supported standing up to communism in the 1940s and 1950s, began to doubt the American commitment in Southeast Asia. One by one they dropped their support for the war, and some, such as Kennan, who had become a professor at Princeton's Institute for Advanced Study, criticized it publicly. At a March 1968 meeting of the wise men, even Dean Acheson, the epitome of the establishment, told Johnson that the United States had to get out of Vietnam. The defection of the foreign policy elite, those who had framed the Cold War, played a major role in Johnson's decision to begin negotiations to end the war.

The wise men proved to be a hardy bunch, with Harriman, Lovett, and McCloy living into their nineties. They shared the experience of shaping America's cold war policy and overseeing the dramatic expansion of American power and influence in the 1950s and 1960s. But of those who had been "present at the creation" (the title of Acheson's memoirs), only George Kennan was still alive to see the end of the Cold War and the dissolution of the Soviet Union. These events would no doubt have astounded and pleased the "wise men" who had so tirelessly served their country in the postwar years.

President Truman (far left) confers with Secretary of State Robert Lovett and State Department aides George Kennan and Charles Bohlen (from left to right). In the photo on the right Averell Harriman (left) and President Harry Truman (right) greet Secretary of State Dean Acheson on his return from a NATO conference in 1952. McCloy is not shown.

American economic self-interest was also a contributing factor—the legislation required that foreign aid dollars be spent on U.S. goods and services. Moreover, a revitalized Europe centered on a strong West German economy would provide a better market for U.S. goods, and a European common market could serve as a model for economic cooperation.

Within Congress, however, there was significant opposition to Truman's pledge of economic aid to European economies. Republicans called the Marshall Plan a huge "international W.P.A.," a "European T.V.A.," and a "bold Socialist blue-print," none of which was meant as a compliment. As the bill came up for a vote in 1948, an election year, Republicans were reluctant to give the Democratic president a major foreign policy triumph. But not all Republicans were opposed. Senator Arthur Vandenberg, the Republican isolationist turned internationalist who chaired the Senate Foreign Relations Committee, supported the Marshall Plan, just as he had favored the appropriations for Greece and Turkey under the Truman Doctrine.

In the midst of this Congressional stalemate came the communist coup in Czechoslovakia. Czechoslovakia had been one of the few Eastern European countries to hold free elections after the war. The Communists won 38 percent of the vote in May 1946, necessitating a coalition government; neither President Eduard Beneš nor Foreign Minister Jan Masaryk, both greatly admired in the West, were Communists. By early 1948 the fragile coalition had faltered, and the Communists took control in a coup on February 25, 1948. Two weeks later the Communist leadership assassinated Masaryk, an event that Truman said "sent a shock throughout the civilized world." A stark reminder of the menace of Soviet expansion in Europe, the coup served to rally Congressional support for the Marshall Plan. Congress voted overwhelmingly to approve funds for the program in March 1948. Like most other foreign policy initiatives of the 1940s and 1950s, the Marshall Plan won bipartisan support despite the opposition of an isolationist wing of the Republican party.

The historian Thomas J. McCormick calls the Marshall Plan "arguably the most innovative piece of foreign policy in American history." Over the next four years the United States contributed nearly $13 billion to a highly successful recovery effort. Western European economies revived and industrial production increased 64 percent, opening new areas for international trade. The Marshall Plan did not specifically exclude Eastern Europe or the Soviet Union, but it required that all participating nations exchange economic information and work toward the elimination of tariffs and other trade barriers. Soviet leaders denounced those conditions as attempts to draw Eastern Europe into the American orbit and forbade their satellite states of Czechoslovakia, Poland, and Hungary to participate.

The Berlin Airlift. The Marshall Plan accelerated American and European efforts to rebuild and reunify the West German economy. After agreeing to fuse their zones of occupation, the United States, France, and Britain initiated a currency reform program in West Berlin in June

The Berlin Airlift

For 321 days American planes like this DC-6 flew 272,000 missions to bring food and other supplies to Berlin after the Soviet Union had blocked all surface routes into the former German capital. The blockade was finally lifted on May 12, 1949, after the Soviets conceded that it had been a failure.

MAP 28.1

Cold War Europe, 1955

In 1949 the United States sponsored the creation of the North Atlantic Treaty Organization, an alliance of ten European nations, the United States, and Canada. West Germany was formally admitted to NATO in May 1955. A few days later the Soviet Union and seven other communist nations established a rival alliance, the Warsaw Pact.

1948. The economic revitalization of Berlin, located deep within the Soviet zone of occupation, alarmed Soviet policy makers, who feared a resurgent Germany aligned with the West. To forestall that development, the Soviet Union imposed a blockade on all highway, rail, and river traffic to West Berlin that June. In that tense situation Truman responded with an airlift. For nearly a year American and British pilots, who had been dropping bombs on Berlin only four years earlier, flew in 2.5 million tons of food and fuel, nearly a ton for each Berlin resident. On May 12, 1949, Stalin lifted the blockade, which by then had made West Berlin a symbol of resistance to communism.

NATO. The coup in Czechoslovakia and the Berlin crisis convinced U.S. policy makers of the need for a collective security pact. In April 1949, for the first time since the American Revolution, the United States entered into a peacetime military alliance, joining with Western Europe and Canada to create the North Atlantic Treaty Organization (NATO). To back up America's new stance Truman asked Congress for $1.3 billion in military assistance to NATO and authorized the basing of four U.S. army divisions in Western Europe. Under the NATO pact the United States, Britain, France, Italy, Belgium, the Netherlands, Luxembourg, Denmark, Norway, Portugal, Iceland, and Canada agreed that "an armed attack against one or more of them in Europe or North America shall be considered an attack against them all." In May 1949 those nations also agreed to the creation of the Federal Republic of Germany (West Ger-

many). All assumed that it would join NATO, which it did in 1955 (see Map 28.1).

Distressed by the aggressive American effort to promote a new European economic and political order and the deployment of substantial numbers of American troops in Western Europe, the Soviet Union tightened its grip on Eastern Europe in October 1949 by creating a separate government for East Germany, which became the German Democratic Republic. The Soviets also sponsored an economic association, the Council for Mutual Economic Assistance, or COMECON (1949), and a military alliance for Eastern Europe, the Warsaw Pact (1955). The postwar division of Europe was nearly complete.

The "Fall" of China

As mutual suspicion between the United States and the Soviet Union deepened, cold war doctrines influenced the American stance toward Asia as well. American policy there was based on Asia's importance in the world economy as much as on the desire to contain communism. Initially American postwar economic plans for the region centered on a revitalized China, but political instability there prompted the Truman administration to focus instead on developing the Japanese economy. After dismantling Japan's military forces and weaponry, American occupation forces under General Douglas MacArthur supervised the country's reconstruction as a bulwark of Asian capitalism. MacArthur drafted a democratic constitution, directed the rebuilding of the economy, and paved the way for the restoration of Japanese sovereignty in 1951.

In China the situation was more precarious. A civil war had been raging in that populous country since the 1930s. Communist forces led by Mao Zedong (Mao Tse-tung) and Zhou Enlai (Chou En-lai) contended for power with conservative Nationalist forces under Jiang Jieshi (Chiang Kai-shek). Jiang had strong connections with the Chinese business community and the West. His wealthy wife had been educated at Wellesley College in Massachusetts and had influential American friends. In contrast, Mao was the son of struggling peasants, a tough, uncompromising leader who inspired loyalty in his associates. Mao won the devotion of China's over-taxed, land-hungry peasants, whom Jiang had alienated with the widespread corruption of his regime and his suppression of agrarian reform. The communists also won support for their resistance against the Japanese forces occupying their country. By 1944 Mao's forces were gaining the upper hand.

Although dissatisfied with the Jiang regime, the Truman administration saw no good alternative to Mao and resigned itself to working with the Nationalists. Between 1945 and 1949 the United States provided more than $2 billion to Jiang's forces, but to no avail. In 1947 General Albert Wedemeyer, who had tried to work with Jiang, reported to President Truman that "until drastic political and economic reforms" were undertaken by the "corrupt, reactionary, and inefficient Chinese National government, United States aid cannot accomplish its purpose." When those reforms did not occur, the Truman administration cut off aid to the Nationalists in August 1949, sealing their fate. The People's Republic of China was formally established on October 1, 1949, and what was left of Jiang's government fled to the island of Formosa (Taiwan).

Many Americans viewed Mao's success as a defeat for the United States. The Republican statesman John Foster Dulles, who would become secretary of state under Eisenhower, called the communist victory in China "the worst defeat the United States has suffered in its history." A pro-Nationalist "China lobby" supported by Senators Karl Mundt of South Dakota, William S. Knowland of California, and other Republicans protested that the State Department under the leadership of Truman's newly appointed secretary of state, Dean Acheson, was responsible for the "loss of China." The publisher Henry R. Luce, born in China to missionary parents, spread those accusations through his magazines, including *Time* and *Life*.

As a result of pressure from the China lobby, most of the State Department's experts on the Far East were forced to resign for supposedly having been too sympathetic to the Chinese communists. The loss of those experts created a critical knowledge gap that would handicap the United States for decades in dealing with Vietnam and other Asian trouble spots. The United States refused to recognize what it called "Red China," instead giving diplomatic recognition to the Nationalists in Taiwan. The United States also used its influence to block China's admission to the United Nations. For almost twenty years afterward, U.S. administrations treated mainland China, the world's most populous country, as a diplomatic nonentity.

Containment Militarized: NSC-68

September 1949 brought another shock: American military intelligence detected a rise in radioactivity in the atmosphere, proof that the Soviet Union had set off an atomic bomb. The American atomic monopoly, which some military and political advisers had argued would last for decades, had ended in just four years. In combination with the communist takeover in China, Russian possession of the bomb made the world look even more threatening.

The end of the American atomic monopoly forced a major reassessment of the nation's foreign policy. To devise a new diplomatic and military blueprint, Truman turned to the National Security Council (NSC). In April 1950 the NSC delivered its report, known as NSC-68, to the president. Using alarmist rhetoric and exaggerated assessments of Soviet capabilities, the document reflected the bleak assumptions that American policy makers held about the Soviet Union: "It is quite clear from Soviet theory and practice that the Kremlin seeks to bring the free world under its dominion by the methods of the cold war." Because the Soviet Union had the military power to "back up infiltration with intimidation," policy makers predicted an "indefinite period of tension and danger." In the immediate postwar period, Kennan's formulation of containment emphasized economic aid and diplomatic pressure to counter Soviet expansionism, but policy makers became increasingly dependent on military force. The new stance thus pointed to far greater militarization of the Cold War.

NSC-68 made several specific recommendations. It favored the development of a hydrogen bomb, an advanced weapon that was a thousand times more destructive than the atomic bombs that had destroyed Hiroshima and Nagasaki. (The United States exploded its first hydrogen bomb in November 1952; the Soviet Union followed suit in 1953.) It supported increases in U.S. conventional forces and a strong system of alliances. Most important, it called for an increase in taxes to finance "a bold and massive program of rebuilding the West's defensive potential to surpass that of the Soviet world." NSC-68 envisioned defense budgets totaling up to 20 percent of the gross national product, four times their level at that time (see Figures 29.1 and

29.2). The United States would function in a state of permanent mobilization, whether or not the country was officially at war.

The call for increased defense spending in NSC-68 was a response to America's loss of atomic supremacy. The United States had been relying heavily on atomic deterrence at the expense of its conventional military forces. Now that the atomic monopoly had been broken, Truman's advisers also looked to build up conventional forces to maintain American superiority. Truman was reluctant to make a commitment to a major defense buildup, fearing that it would overburden the budget. But the Korean War, which began just two months after NSC-68 was completed, provided an opportunity to sell the new policy to the president, Congress, and the American public. As a state department aide recalled, "thank God Korea came along." In early 1950 the military budget stood at $13 billion. In just six months Truman more than tripled it to nearly $50 billion.

The Korean War

Although Truman acknowledged that communist success in China raised urgent questions for American foreign policy, he recognized the limits of American power in Asia. In December 1949 Secretary of State Dean Acheson clarified American policy. The United States, he said, would help Asian nations realize their aspirations but would consider itself bound to protect only a "defensive perimeter" that ran from the Aleutian Islands in Alaska to Japan, the Ryukyus (a chain of small islands stretching from Japan to Taiwan), and the Philippines (a former American protectorate that had won its independence from the United States in 1946). If an attack occurred outside that perimeter—in Korea, Taiwan, or Southeast Asia, for example—"the initial reliance must be on the people attacked to resolve it and then upon . . . the United Nations."

A test of the new policy came quickly in Korea, a country whose artificial division after World War II contained the seeds for later conflict. Both the United States and the Soviet Union had troops in Korea at the end of the fighting in 1945, and neither side was willing to abandon its occupied territories. Soon those two countries divided Korea at the 38th parallel, creating competing spheres of influence. Both occupying forces remained until 1948, when a communist government led by Kim Il Sung took power in North Korea, while Syngman Rhee, a longtime Korean nationalist backed by the United States, took over in South Korea. Soon sporadic fighting between North and South Koreans broke out along the 38th parallel, and a civil war began.

In 1950 the North Koreans attempted to reunify the country, launching a surprise attack across the 38th parallel on June 25 (see Map 28.2). The impetus for Ko-

rean reunification came from the North Korean leader Kim Il Sung, but Stalin approved of and supported the mission (although the extent of Soviet involvement was unknown at the time). Soviet and North Korean leaders may have expected Truman to ignore this armed challenge, but the president immediately asked the United Nations Security Council to authorize a "police action" against the invaders. Because the Soviet Union was temporarily boycotting the Security Council to protest the exclusion of the People's Republic of China from the U.N., it could not veto Truman's request, and the Security Council voted to send a peacekeeping force. Three days later Truman ordered General Douglas MacArthur, the head of the American occupation forces in Japan, to send U.S. troops to help Rhee.

The American intervention in Korea revealed the extent to which foreign policy formulation had been

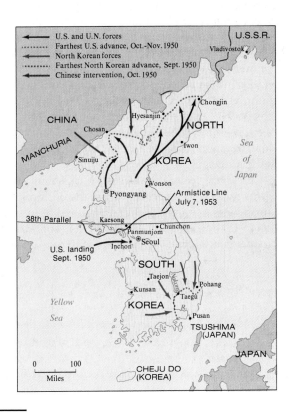

MAP 28.2

The Korean War, 1950–1953

The first months of the Korean War featured dramatic shifts in control up and down the 600-mile peninsula. From June to September 1950 North Korean troops overran most of the territory south of the 38th parallel. On September 15, U.N. forces under General Douglas MacArthur counterattacked behind enemy lines at Inchon and pushed north almost to the Chinese border. Massive Chinese intervention forced the U.N. troops to retreat to the 38th parallel in January 1951, and the war was a stalemate for the next two years.

transferred from Congress to the president. When the isolationist Republican Senator Robert A. Taft of Ohio argued that the president should have obtained Congressional approval before committing American troops to Korea, Truman boldly insisted that he already had the power he needed as commander in chief of the armed forces and executor of the treaty binding the United States to the United Nations. The Truman administration enjoyed widespread popular support for this action: in a July 1950 poll 77 percent of the respondents approved of U.S. intervention. The Korean conflict thus became the first major American war undertaken without a formal declaration of war by Congress.

Fighting the War. The rapidly assembled United Nations army in Korea remained overwhelmingly American, even though fourteen other noncommunist members sent troops, including Australia, Canada, and Great Britain. At the request of the Security Council, President Truman named General MacArthur to head the U.N. forces. At first the North Koreans held an overwhelming advantage, controlling practically the entire peninsula except the area around Pusan. Then, on September 15, 1950, MacArthur launched a surprise amphibious attack at Inchon, far behind the lines of the North Korean invasion, while U.N. forces staged a breakout from Pusan. Within two weeks the U.N. forces controlled Seoul, the South Korean capital, and almost all the territory up to the 38th parallel.

Encouraged by this success, MacArthur sought the authority to lead his forces across the 38th parallel into North Korea. Truman's initial plan had been to restore the 1945 border; now he won U.N. support for the broader goal of creating "a unified, independent and dem-ocratic Korea." The Chinese government in Beijing warned repeatedly that such a move would provoke its retaliation, but American officials did not take the warnings seriously. MacArthur's troops crossed the 38th parallel on October 9, reaching the Chinese border at the Yalu River by the end of the month. Just after Thanksgiving, however, a massive Chinese counterattack of almost 300,000 troops forced a retreat to the 38th parallel. On January 4, 1951, communist troops reoccupied Seoul. "They really fooled us when it comes right down to it, didn't they?" a senator later asked Secretary of State Acheson. "Yes, sir," he replied.

Two months later the American forces and their allies counterattacked, regained Seoul, and pushed back to the 38th parallel. Then stalemate set in. Public support in the United States dropped after Chinese intervention increased the likelihood of a long war. As a poll revealed in early January 1951, 66 percent of Americans thought the United States should withdraw, and 49 percent felt that it was a mistake to have intervened in the first place.

Given those domestic and international constraints, Truman and his advisers decided to work for a negotiated peace. They did not want to tie down large numbers of U.S. troops in Asia, far from what they considered more strategically important trouble spots in Europe and the Middle East. As Dean Acheson had said just before the Korean War broke out, "We cannot scatter our shots equally all over the world. We just haven't got enough shots to do that." If the Korean War had become a larger war with China, General Omar N. Bradley, chairman of the Joint Chiefs of Staff, reasoned, it would have been "the wrong war, at the wrong place, at the wrong time, and with the wrong enemy."

The Korean War
The American GIs who fought in Korea were often the younger brothers of men who had served in World War II. Unlike their older brothers, Korean War soldiers served in integrated units. Here members of a U.S. Combat Engineers battalion sweep a mountain trail for mines and booby traps.

The Fate of MacArthur. MacArthur disagreed. Headstrong, arrogant, and brilliant, he fervently believed that the nation's future opportunities lay in Asia, not in Europe. Disregarding Truman's instructions, MacArthur traveled to Taiwan and urged the Nationalists to join in an attack on mainland China. He pleaded for American use of the atomic bomb against targets in China. In an inflammatory letter to the House minority leader, the Republican Joseph J. Martin of Massachusetts, he denounced the Korean stalemate. "We must win," MacArthur declared. "There is no substitute for victory."

Martin released MacArthur's letter on April 6, 1951, as part of a concerted Republican campaign to challenge Truman's conduct of the war. The strategy backfired. On April 11 Truman relieved MacArthur of his command in Korea and Japan, accusing him of insubordination. "MacArthur left me no choice," Truman later insisted. "Even the Joint Chiefs of Staff came to the conclusion that civilian control of the military was at stake. . . . I didn't let it stay at stake very long." Truman named General Matthew B. Ridgway to replace MacArthur.

Truman's decision was highly unpopular. According to a Gallup poll, 69 percent of the American people supported MacArthur. The allure of decisive victory under a charismatic military leader temporarily pushed aside doubts about the war. The general returned to tumultuous receptions in San Francisco, Chicago, and New York. He delivered an impassioned address to a joint session of Congress that ended with a line from an old West Point ballad, "Old soldiers never die, they just fade away." But when the shouting died down, Truman had the last word. After failing to get the Republican presidential nomination in 1952, MacArthur faded from public view.

The war dragged on for more than two years after MacArthur's dismissal. Truce talks began in Korea in July 1951, but a final armistice was not signed until July 1953. Approximately 45 percent of American casualties were sustained in this period. The final settlement left Korea divided very near the original border at the 38th parallel, with a demilitarized zone between the two countries. North Korea remained firmly allied with the Soviet Union; South Korea signed a mutual defense treaty with the United States in 1954, associating itself with the American sphere of influence in the Pacific.

The Impact of the Korean War. The three-year conflict was costly for the United States: 54,200 American soldiers died, 103,000 were wounded, and military expenditures totaled $54 billion. Much of the money was channeled into military facilities in Japan, where it helped revitalize that nation's economy. At home limited mobilization stimulated the economy and reduced unemployment, contributing to the prosperity of the 1950s. But few American soldiers felt the patriotic fer-

MacArthur's Return from Korea
General Douglas MacArthur received a tumultuous welcome in San Francisco in 1951, the first time the popular general had set foot on the American mainland in fourteen years. The public outcry over President Truman's dismissal of MacArthur for insubordination reflected frustration with the stalemated Korean War.

vor that had characterized service during World War II. Struggling against heavy snow and subzero cold, the men grew to hate the endless fighting that characterized the stalemate. "I'll fight for my country," a corporal from Chicago complained, "but I'm damned if I see why I'm fighting for this hell-hole." When the armistice was signed, there were few public celebrations.

The Korean War had a lasting impact on the conduct of American foreign policy. Truman's decision to commit troops to Korea without Congressional approval signaled an expansion of executive power and set a precedent for future undeclared wars. The war also expanded American involvement in Asia, transforming containment into a truly global policy. During and after the war the United States stationed large numbers of troops in South Korea, increased military aid to Nationalist Chinese forces in Taiwan and French forces fighting communist insurgents in Indochina (see Chapter 31), and signed a mutual defense pact with Australia and New Zealand. Such commitments were costly. Overall defense expenditures grew from $13 billion in 1950, roughly one-third of the federal budget, to $50 billion in 1953, nearly two-thirds of the budget. Although military expenditures dropped briefly after the Korean War, defense spending remained at over $35 billion annually throughout the 1950s. American foreign policy had become more global, more militarized, and more costly.

Harry Truman and the Fair Deal

Harry S. Truman brought a complex personality to the presidency. Alternately humble and cocky, he had none of Roosevelt's patrician ease and was a distinctly unpopular president. Yet he handled affairs with an assurance and crisp dispatch that have endeared him to later generations. "If you can't stand the heat, stay out of the kitchen," he liked to say of presidential responsibility. The major domestic issues that he faced were reconversion to a peacetime economy and fears of communist infiltration and subversion, fears that his administration played a part in fanning. Truman kept the New Deal coalition alive by proposing new federal programs to advance the interests of its constituencies, and his "Fair Deal" would influence the Democratic party's agenda for the next twenty years.

The Challenge of Reconversion

Truman never intended to be merely a caretaker president for the balance of Roosevelt's fourth term. On September 16, 1945, just fourteen days after Japan formally surrendered, Truman staked his claim to domestic leadership by presenting to Congress a twenty-one-point plan for expanded federal responsibilities. Anticipating a period of affluence rather than the austerity that had shaped the New Deal, Truman phrased his proposals in terms of the rights of individual citizens—the right to a "useful and remunerative" job, protection from monopoly, good housing, "adequate medical care," "protection from the economic fears of old age," and a "good education." Later Truman added support for civil rights and called his program the Fair Deal.

When Truman became president, Americans welcomed him with an initial approval rating of 87 percent, according to Gallup polls. Within a year his popularity had dropped to 32 percent, and new phrases such as "To err is Truman" entered the political language. What had happened? New to the presidency, Truman had to oversee the complex conversion of a war economy to a peacetime one. In part because govern-

ment planners had not known about the atomic bomb, they had assumed that reconversion could be phased in while the country went through the process of winning a land war in Japan that was expected to last through 1946. Instead it ended before adequate reconversion plans were in place.

The main fear on the public's mind in 1945 was that the depression would return once war production ended. The specter of mass unemployment was very real to those who had lived through the grim sacrifices of the 1930s and to older Americans who remembered the recession that had followed World War I. To their relief, the economy escaped that fate. Despite a drop in government spending after the war, consumer spending increased because workers had amassed substantial wartime savings that they were eager to spend. The Servicemen's Readjustment Act of 1944, popularly known as the GI Bill, also put money into the economy by providing educational and economic assistance to returning veterans. Despite some temporary dislocations as war production shifted back to civilian uses and veterans were reabsorbed into the work force, unemployment did not soar. The most visible layoffs involved the "Rosie the Riveters" who had taken high-paying defense jobs during the war and were now forced to find jobs in traditional areas of women's employment at much lower pay.

Helen Gahagan Douglas
Representative Helen Gahagan Douglas of California, a former Broadway and film star, illustrated a 1947 speech supporting the reestablishment of price controls by bringing a shopping basket of food to a press conference. Douglas served in Congress from 1944 until 1950, when she was defeated in a bid for the Senate by Representative Richard M. Nixon. In their bitterly fought campaign Nixon linked her with communism by calling her pink.

Postwar Strikes
As American corporations earned record profits after the war, most workers saw their real wages decline due to inflation and reduced hours. Like many unions, the United Autoworkers, shown here picketing General Motors headquarters in Detroit in 1945, went on strike to protest these developments.

But the transition was hardly trouble-free. The main domestic problem was inflation. Consumers wanted to end wartime restrictions and price rationing, but Truman feared economic chaos if he lifted all controls immediately. In the summer of 1945 he eased industrial controls but retained the wartime Office of Price Administration (OPA). When the OPA was disbanded and almost all controls were lifted in November 1946, prices soared. That year saw an annual inflation rate of 18.2 percent. The persistent shortages of food and products also irritated consumers.

In consultation with Leon Keyserling and other economic advisers, Truman tried to develop a more coherent economic policy. The result was the Employment Act of 1946, which proposed federal fiscal planning on a permanent basis—not just in times of economic crisis—to achieve full employment. Besides supporting the Keynsian notion of government spending to spur economic growth, the act promoted the use of tax policy as a tool for managing the economy by cutting taxes to spur economic growth or raising taxes to slow inflation. Yet the legislation was weak. It merely supported rather than mandated such planning measures and failed to establish clear economic priorities, such as the proper relationship between the commitment to full employment and the need for a balanced budget. And the new three-member Council of Economic Advisers, appointed by the president and directly responsible to the White House, could only make recommendations. Nevertheless, the Employment Act of 1946 was an important milestone in establishing federal responsibility for the performance of the economy.

Postwar Strikes. The rapidly rising cost of living prompted demands for higher wages by the nation's workers. By 1945 the number of union members had swelled to more than 14 million—two-thirds of all workers in the mining, manufacturing, construction, and transportation industries. Under government-sanctioned agreements the labor movement had held the line on wages during the war, but afterward unions expressed frustration as corporate profits doubled while real wages declined as a result of the loss of wartime overtime pay and a burst of postwar inflation. Determined to make up for their war-induced sacrifices, workers mounted strikes in major sectors of the economy, crippling the automobile, steel, and coal industries. General strikes effectively closed down business in more than a half dozen cities in 1946. By the end of that year 5 million workers had idled factories and mines for a total of 107,476,000 workdays.

Truman never doubted his course of action. Even if it meant alienating organized labor, an important component of the Democratic coalition, Truman felt that it was the president's job to ensure economic stability. "If you think I'm going to sit here and let you tie up this whole country, you're crazy as hell," he told the leaders of a nationwide railroad strike in the spring of 1946. Truman used his executive authority to place the nation's railroad system under federal control and asked Congress for the power to draft striking workers into the army, a move that infuriated labor but pressured strikers to go back to work. Three days later he seized control of the nation's coal mines to end a strike by the United Mine Workers. Such actions won Truman support from Americans fed up with labor disruptions but incurred the enmity of organized labor.

These domestic upheavals did not bode well for the Democrats at the polls. In the 1946 elections Republicans capitalized on popular dissatisfaction with the myriad reconversion problems with the simple slogan "Had enough?" (The original version was "Have You Had Enough of the Alphabet?"—a reference to the "alphabet soup" of New Deal agencies. Less was definitely more.) The Republicans gained control of both houses of Congress for the first time since the elections of 1928. Truman and the Democrats seemed to have been thoroughly repudiated.

The Taft-Hartley Act. The Republican Congress elected in 1946 was determined to undo the New Deal's social welfare measures, and it singled out labor legislation as a special target. In 1947 Congress passed the Taft-Hartley Act, a rollback of several provisions of the 1935 National Labor Relations Act. Unions especially disliked Section 14b, which allowed states to pass "right to work" laws that outlawed the closed shop. The act also restricted the political power of unions by prohibiting the use of their dues for political activity and allowed the president to declare an eighty-day cooling-off period in strikes with a national impact. Truman issued a ringing veto of the Taft-Hartley bill in June 1947, calling it "bad for labor, bad for management, and bad for the country." Congress easily overrode the veto, but Truman's action brought labor back into the Democratic fold.

The 1948 Election

Most observers believed that Truman faced an impossible task in the presidential campaign of 1948. The Republicans were united and well led. They maintained the loyal support of most middle- and upper-income Protestants outside the South and that of many farmers and skilled workers. Eager to attract votes from traditional Democratic constituencies, they renominated Thomas E. Dewey, the politically moderate governor of New York. Dewey had demonstrated his attractiveness as a national candidate by garnering 46 percent of the popular vote in his 1944 campaign against Roosevelt (see Chapter 27). To increase their appeal in the West the Republicans nominated Earl Warren, governor of California, for vice-president. Their brief platform promised to continue most New Deal reforms and supported a bipartisan foreign policy.

Truman, in contrast, led a party in disarray. Both the left and right wings of the Democratic party split off and nominated their own candidates. Henry A. Wallace, a former New Deal liberal whom Truman had fired as secretary of commerce in 1946 because he was perceived as too "soft" on communism, ran as the candi-

date of the new Progressive party. Wallace advocated increased government intervention in the economy, more power for labor unions, and cooperation with the Soviet Union.

Southern Democrats bolted the party over the issue of civil rights. At the Democratic national convention, northern liberals such as Mayor Hubert H. Humphrey of Minneapolis and gubernatorial candidate Adlai E. Stevenson of Illinois had pushed through a platform calling for the repeal of Taft-Hartley, the establishment of a permanent Fair Employment Practices Commission, and federal antilynching and anti–poll tax legislation. The civil rights planks went well beyond Truman's original platform and precipitated a breakaway of southern Democrats who would not tolerate federal interference in race relations. Three days after the convention 6,000 southern Democrats met in Birmingham, Alabama, to set up the States' Rights party, popularly known as the Dixiecrats. They nominated Governor J. Strom Thurmond of South Carolina for president.

Truman responded to these challenges with one of the most effective presidential campaigns ever waged. He dramatically called Congress back into summer session to give the Republicans a chance to enact their platform into law. When they failed to do so, he launched a strenuous cross-country speaking tour, blasting the "do-nothing Republican Congress." He also hammered away at the Republicans' support for the antilabor Taft-Hartley Act and their opposition to legislation on hous-

Truman Triumphant
In one of the most famous photographs in American political history, Harry S. Truman gloats over an inaccurate headline in the *Chicago Tribune*. Pollsters had predicted an overwhelming victory for Thomas E. Dewey. Their primitive techniques, however, did not reflect the dramatic surge in support for Truman during the last days of the campaign.

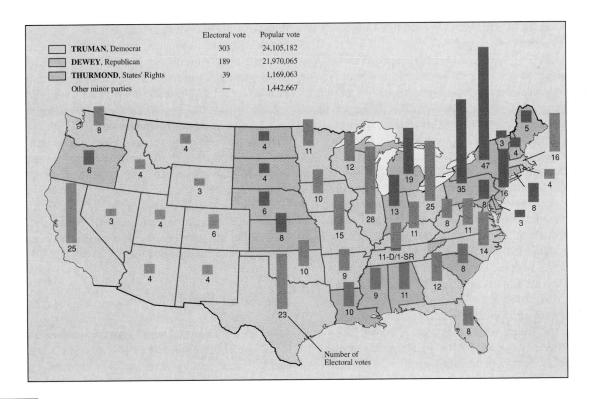

	Electoral vote	Popular vote
TRUMAN, Democrat	303	24,105,182
DEWEY, Republican	189	21,970,065
THURMOND, States' Rights	39	1,169,063
Other minor parties	—	1,442,667

MAP 28.3

The Election of 1948

Political advisor Clark Clifford planned Truman's electoral strategy in 1948, arguing that the president should concentrate his campaign in urban areas where the Democrats had their greatest strength. In an election with a low turnout Truman held onto enough support from the Roosevelt coalition of blacks, union members, and farmers to defeat Dewey by more than 2 million votes.

ing, medical insurance, and civil rights. By combining these domestic themes with attacks on the Soviet menace abroad, Truman began to salvage his troubled campaign. At his rallies enthusiastic listeners took up the cry "Give 'em hell, Harry!"

Truman won a remarkable victory, receiving 49.6 percent of the vote to Dewey's 45.1 percent (see Map 28.3). Strom Thurmond carried only four southern states, and Henry Wallace failed to win any electoral votes. The Democrats also regained control of both houses of Congress. As a commentator in *The New Republic* observed, "Harry Truman won this election because Franklin Roosevelt had worked so well." Truman retained the support of organized labor and Jewish and Catholic voters in the big cities, and the loyalty of northern black voters to the Democratic party offset southern losses to the Dixiecrats. (The discovery that the Democrats could capture the presidency without the Solid South made the passage of future civil rights legislation politically feasible.) Most important, Truman appealed effectively to people like himself who hailed from the farms, towns, and small cities in the nation's heartland. He had grasped something the pollsters had missed: "Everybody's against me but the people."

Fair Deal Liberalism

Truman's Fair Deal represented the essential aspects of postwar liberalism. Liberals believed in an activist federal government that would use its powers to stimulate economic growth, redress imbalances, and encourage social progress. With a stated commitment to civil rights and economic abundance for all, liberalism called for the modern state to extend the benefits of capitalism to ever greater numbers of citizens. But the Fair Deal was not a radical program. By expanding the welfare state at home while fighting communism abroad, Truman sought to steer a middle course between socialism on the left and fascism on the right. The historian Arthur Schlesinger, Jr., dubbed this brand of liberalism "the Vital Center."

Truman's agenda ran up against a generally hostile Congress. Despite its Democratic majority, the Senate and the House contained a fair number of conservatives of both parties. The same conservative coalition had blocked Roosevelt in his second term and had dismantled or cut popular New Deal programs during wartime. Only parts of the Fair Deal won adoption: the minimum wage went up from 40 cents an hour to 75, the Social Security system was extended to cover 10 million new workers, and benefits were raised by 75 percent. The National Housing Act of 1949 called for the construction of 810,000 units of low-income housing, although only half that number was actually built under the program.

Truman's record on civil rights illustrates the opportunities and obstacles facing proponents of the Fair Deal. Although civil rights issues had long preoccupied the country, they took on a new urgency in the 1940s. The callous treatment of black soldiers during World War II and the lynching of more than forty black men after the war—many of them veterans—sparked widespread black anger. At the same time, black expectations had been raised by wartime opportunities and by symbolic victories such as Jackie Robinson's joining the Brooklyn Dodgers in 1947, breaking the color line in major league baseball. Truman's sympathies for civil rights were reinforced by the realization that black voters were playing an increasingly large role in the Democratic party as they migrated from the South, where they were effectively disfranchised, to northern cities. Finally, Truman was sensitive to the world's view of America's treatment of blacks, especially since the Soviet Union often compared segregation of southern blacks with the Nazis' treatment of Jews.

Lacking a popular mandate on the civil rights issue, Truman resorted to a variety of means to advance the cause. In 1946 he appointed a National Civil Rights Commission; its 1947 report, *To Secure These Rights*, called for an expanded federal role in civil rights that foreshadowed much of the legislation of the 1960s. He ordered the Justice Department to prepare an *amicus curiae* ("friend of the court") brief in the Supreme Court case of *Shelley v. Kraemer* (1948), which struck down as unconstitutional restrictive covenants that enforced residential segregation by barring home buyers on the basis of race or religion. In the same year, Truman signed an executive order desegregating the armed forces. With the outbreak of the Korean War, conditions for black soldiers improved compared with the discrimination that they had faced in World War II. During the rapid mobilization, demands for quick processing of draftees outweighed customary practices such as keeping black and white draftees separate, thus speeding up integration. The Truman administration also proposed a federal antilynching law, federal protection of voting rights (such as an end to poll taxes), and a permanent federal agency to guarantee equal employment opportunities. A filibuster by southern conservatives, however, blocked such legislation in Congress.

Interest groups successfully opposed other key items on the Fair Deal agenda. The American Medical Association quashed a labor-backed movement for national health insurance by denouncing it as the first step toward "socialized medicine." Catholics successfully opposed legislation for aid to education because it did not include subsidies for parochial schools. Farmers refused to join labor in supporting the repeal of Taft-Hartley. In general, the Truman administration failed to mobilize popular and Congressional support for dramatically enlarged federal responsibilities in the economic and social spheres.

Two other factors further limited the Fair Deal's chances for legislative success. One was the outbreak of the Korean War in 1950, which diverted national attention to foreign affairs. The other was the nation's growing fear of internal subversion. The anticommunist crusade was only one manifestation of the way the Cold War was increasingly permeating all facets of American life. Truman's administration played a major role in heightening those domestic tensions.

The Great Fear

As American relations with the Soviet Union deteriorated in the late 1940s and early 1950s, fear of communism fueled a widespread campaign of domestic repression. Americans often call this phenomenon "McCarthyism," after Senator Joseph R. McCarthy of Wisconsin, the decade's most vocal anticommunist. But this "Great Fear" involved more than the work of just one man. It built on the distrust of radicals and foreigners that had manifested itself in the 1850s and in the Red Scare after World War I. Worsening cold war tensions intersected with those deep-seated anxieties and partisan politics to spawn an obsessive concern with internal subversion. Republicans used accusations of communist subversion to discredit the Truman administration, while Truman responded with a government loyalty crusade to protect himself against charges that he was "soft on communism." Ultimately, few Communists were found in positions of power; far more Americans became innocent victims of false accusations and innuendos. The postwar red scare was particularly devastating to the political left, where accusations of guilt by association affected progressives of all stripes.

HUAC. The roots of postwar anticommunism date back to the late 1930s, when liberals and Communists had cooperated in a "popular front" against fascism and often joined together to support New Deal social programs. In 1938 Congressman Martin Dies of Texas and other conservatives launched the House Committee on Un-American Activities (HUAC) to investigate alleged fascist and communist subversion. In the early 1940s HUAC focused almost exclusively on the latter, probing left-wing activity in labor unions and New Deal agencies. During America's wartime alliance with the Soviet Union, HUAC's visibility declined, but it reemerged after the war as Americans grew concerned over Russian expansionism in Eastern Europe. Revelations in

Mark Goodson

Red Hunting on the Quiz Shows, or What's My Party Line?

Active in the television industry from its earliest days, Mark Goodson is a highly successful producer whose game shows have included "What's My Line?" "To Tell the Truth," "Password," and "Family Feud." In this interview Goodson recalls his experience in the industry in the early 1950s, when rampant anticommunism plagued the entertainment business.

I'm not sure when it began, but I believe it was early 1950. At that point I had no connection with the blacklisting that was going on, although I heard about it in the motion picture business and heard rumors about things that had happened on other shows, like *The Aldrich Family*. . . .

Soon afterwards, CBS installed a clearance division. There wasn't any discussion. We would just get the word—"drop that person"—and that was supposed to be it. Whenever I booked a guest or a panelist on *What's My Line?* or *I've Got a Secret*, one of our assistants would phone up and say, "We're going to use so-and-so." We'd either get the okay, or they'd call back and say, "Not clear," or "Sorry, we can't use them." Even advertising agencies—big ones, like Young & Ru-

bicam and BBD&O—had their own clearance departments. They would never come out and say it. They would just write off somebody by saying, "He's a bad actor." You were never supposed to tell the person what it was about; you'd just unbook them. They never admitted there was a blacklist. It just wasn't done. . . .

Anna Lee was an English actress on a later show of ours called *It's News to Me*. The sponsor was Sanka Coffee, a product of General Foods. The advertising agency was Young & Rubicam. One day, I received a call telling me we had to drop one of our panelists, Anna Lee, immediately. They said she was a radical, that she wrote a column for the *Daily Worker*. They couldn't allow that kind of stuff on the air. They claimed they were getting all kinds of mail. It seemed incongruous to me that this little English girl, someone who seemed very conservative, would be writing for a Communist newspaper. It just didn't sound right.

I took her out to lunch. After a little social conversation, I asked her about her politics. She told me that she wasn't political, except she voted Conservative in England. Her husband was a Republican from Texas.

I went back to the agency and said, "You guys are really off your rocker. Anna Lee is nothing close to a liberal." They told me, "Oh, you're right. We checked on that. It's a different Anna Lee who writes for the *Daily Worker*." I remember being relieved and saying, "Well, that's good. You just made a mistake. Now we can forget this." But that wasn't the case. They told me, "We've still got to get rid of her, because the illusion is just as good as the reality. If our client continues to get the mail, no one is going to believe him when he says there's a second Anna Lee." At that point I lost it. I told them their demand was outrageous. They could cancel the show if they wanted to, but I would not drop somebody whose only crime was sharing a name. When I got back to my office, there was a phone call waiting for me. It was from a friend of mine at the agency. He said, "If I were you, I would not lose my temper like that. If you want to argue, do it quietly. After you left, somebody said, 'Is Goodson a pinko?'"

Source: Griffin Fariello, *Red Scare* (New York: Norton, 1995), 320–324.

1946 of a Soviet spy ring operating in Canada and the United States accentuated American fears of Soviet subversion.

In 1947 HUAC helped launch the postwar red scare by holding widely publicized hearings on communist infiltration of the film industry. A group of writers and directors, soon dubbed the "Hollywood Ten," went to jail for contempt of Congress when they cited the Fifth Amendment in refusing to testify about their past associations. Soon afterward ex-FBI agents in Hollywood circulated a list of actors, directors, and writers whose names had been mentioned in the HUAC investigation or whose associates and friends had been described as

politically dubious. Industry executives denied the existence of a blacklist, but for ten years hundreds of people were shut out of work in the entertainment industry (see American Voices, above). The Weavers, a popular folk-singing group, were blacklisted, and politically active actors such as Zero Mostel and John Garfield had difficulty finding work. One day the actress Jean Muir headlined the popular radio show "The Aldrich Family"; the next she was out of a job—fired, the network said, not because she was a Communist but because gossip about her had made her too "controversial."

Anticommunism also emerged as a divisive force in the labor movement. In the 1930s Communists had been

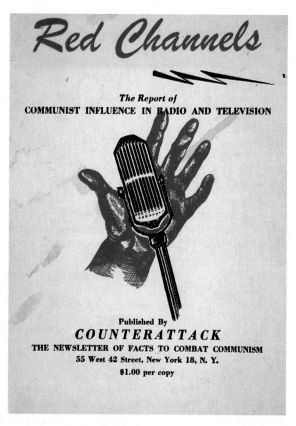

The Red Scare and the Media

After HUAC's 1947 investigation of the film industry, television and radio sponsors became wary of possible communist subversion on the airwaves. In 1950 three ex-FBI agents employed by a private consulting firm produced *Red Channels*, a booklet identifying 151 allegedly subversive entertainers. It was widely circulated among producers and was one of the key tools of the cultural Cold War.

very active in labor organizing, and their contributions had been welcomed, if not openly acknowledged. But as conservatives charged that Soviet-led Communists were taking over American unions, the labor movement reversed itself and purged Communists in the late 1940s. The Taft-Hartley Act fueled this campaign by requiring labor leaders to take oaths swearing they were not Communists before their unions could participate in federally supervised elections. The CIO's president, Phillip Murray, subsequently denounced Communist sympathizers as "skulking cowards . . . apostles of hate." Eleven unions that refused to oust their communist or communist-sympathizing leaders were expelled from the CIO.

The Truman administration inflamed the hysteria by issuing an executive order in March 1947 initiating a comprehensive investigation into the loyalty of all federal employees. More than 6 million individuals were subjected to security checks, 14,000 underwent inten-

sive FBI investigation, and 2,000 were dismissed. The case of Dorothy Bailey, a forty-one-year-old graduate of Bryn Mawr College and the University of Minnesota, was typical. Bailey lost her job with the U.S. Employment Service, where she had worked for fourteen years, because an unidentified informer claimed she was a Communist and associated with known Communists. Denying the charge, she was brought before the District of Columbia regional loyalty board, which introduced no evidence against her and called no witnesses to support its case. She was fired anyway.

Following Washington's lead, many state and local governments, universities, political organizations, churches, and businesses undertook their own antisubversion campaigns. All 11,000 faculty members at the University of California were required to take a loyalty oath; UCLA alone fired 157 who refused to do so. Many Catholic organizations became hotbeds of anticommunism, urging their members to combat "enemies" within the church. Because of the Communist party's historic defense of racial equality, civil rights organizations such as the NAACP and the National Urban League were attacked as communist-front groups; they subsequently purged their left-wing members. Some postwar liberals, such as Henry Wallace and his followers in the Progressive party, continued to seek cooperation with the Soviet Union and defended the participation of Communists in their organizations. But many other liberals, most notably those in Americans for Democratic Action, founded in 1947, shunned potential left-wing allies and embraced a strident anticommunism.

The anticommunist crusade intensified in 1948 when HUAC began an investigation of Alger Hiss, a former New Deal State Department official who had accompanied Franklin Roosevelt to Yalta. The case against Hiss rested on the testimony of the former Communist Whittaker Chambers, a senior editor at *Time*. Chambers claimed that Hiss was a member of a secret communist cell in the government and had passed him classified documents in the 1930s. Hiss categorically denied the allegations and denied even knowing Chambers. Republican Congressman Richard M. Nixon of California orchestrated the HUAC investigation, an event that brought him national recognition and boosted his political career. The Hiss investigation culminated in the dramatic release of the so-called Pumpkin Papers, microfilm that Chambers had hidden in a pumpkin patch on his Maryland farm. (When this supposedly incriminating cache was declassified, it was found to contain only Navy Department documents on life rafts and fire extinguishers.) Because the statute of limitations on espionage had expired by 1949, Hiss was charged instead with perjury for lying about his communist affiliations and acquaintance with Chambers. The first trial resulted in a hung jury; the second, in early 1950, found Hiss guilty and sentenced him to five years in federal prison. The conviction of Hiss increased paranoia about a communist conspiracy in the federal government, but after 1950 HUAC's role would be overshadowed by a new investigating committee led by Joseph McCarthy in the Senate.

The Rise and Fall of McCarthy.

In February 1950 Senator Joseph McCarthy of Wisconsin delivered a bombshell during a speech in Wheeling, West Virginia: "I have here in my hand a list of the names of 205 men that were known to the Secretary of State as being members of the Communist Party and who nevertheless are still working and shaping the policy of the State Department." McCarthy never revealed the names on his list and later lowered the number to 81 and then to 57. The public was so responsive to his charges that those inconsistencies failed to dent his credibility. For the next four years McCarthy became the central figure in the virulent campaign of anticommunism that consumed the country.

A Marine Air Corps veteran who had won a Senate seat in the 1946 Republican landslide, McCarthy soon discovered that anticommunist rhetoric could boost his political fortunes. Like other Republicans in the late 1940s, he leveled accusations of communist subversion in the government to embarrass Truman and the Democrats. McCarthy's political genius lay in his ability to make his name synonymous with the cause of uncovering subversives in government. Politicians who attacked him exposed themselves to charges of being "soft" on communism, the kiss of death in the postwar political climate. And McCarthy did not hesitate to charge that his critics were themselves part of "this conspiracy so immense." At first his supporters were more visible than his detractors; for example, Democratic Congressman John F. Kennedy of Massachusetts thought "McCarthy may have something." But President Truman called McCarthy's charges "slander, lies, character assassination," although he could do nothing to curb them. When Republican Dwight D. Eisenhower was elected president in 1952, he did not publicly challenge his party's most outspoken senator.

A series of national and international events allowed McCarthy to retain credibility despite his failure to identify a single Communist in the government. The trial and conviction of Alger Hiss in 1950 set the stage for McCarthy's allegations. The Korean War broke out soon afterward, embroiling the United States in a frustrating fight against communism in a faraway land. And in a sensational case in 1951 Julius and Ethel Rosenberg were convicted of passing atomic secrets to the Soviet Union. After a highly controversial trial they were executed in 1953. (Recently released documents from Project Verona, a top-secret intelligence mission during World War II, provide strong evidence of the Rosenbergs' guilt.) Throughout this period McCarthy lashed out against alleged Communists in the State Department and other branches of the government, allegations that he aired before the Senate Permanent Investigating Committee in 1953–1954.

McCarthy overreached himself in early 1954 by launching an investigation into possible subversion in the U.S. Army. The lengthy televised hearings brought McCarthy's smear tactics and leering innuendos into the nation's living rooms, and support for him declined. The passing of the Korean War and the death of Stalin in 1953 also undercut public interest in McCarthy's red-hunting campaign. In December 1954 the Senate voted 67 to 22 to censure McCarthy for unbecoming conduct. He died three years later at the age of forty-eight, his name forever attached to a period of political repression of which he was only the most flagrant manifestation.

The Army-McCarthy Hearings
These 1954 hearings contributed to the downfall of Senator Joseph McCarthy by showing his reckless accusations, bullying tactics, and snearing innuendos to the huge television audience that tuned in each day. Some of the most heated exchanges took place between McCarthy (right) and Joseph Welch (seated, left), the lawyer representing the army. When an exasperated Welch asked, "Have you no decency left, sir?" McCarthy merely shrugged. But the audience broke into applause because someone had finally had the courage to stand up to the senator from Wisconsin.

"Modern Republicanism"

The 1952 election occurred in the middle of the Korean stalemate and at the height of the Great Fear. The newly elected president, Dwight D. Eisenhower, worked quickly to end the Korean War, but the grip of McCarthyism lasted longer. Eisenhower set the tone for what historians call "modern Republicanism," an updated GOP approach that emphasized a slowdown, but not a dismantling, of federal responsibilities. Compared with their predecessors in the 1920s and their successors in the 1980s and 1990s, Eisenhower and other modern Republicans were more tolerant of government intervention in social and economic affairs, though they sought to limit the scope of federal action. Eisenhower's low-key style of governing was well suited to those seemingly prosperous and confident times. In foreign policy the Republicans continued to see the world in cold war terms while expanding the defense buildup that had begun during the Korean War.

The Soldier Becomes President

The Republican party's greatest strength lay in the largely Protestant and rural states of the Midwest. Since only a third of the nation's registered voters were Republicans, however, the party had to find a candidate who could attract Democrats and independents. Republican leaders quickly realized that General Dwight D. Eisenhower would be just such a candidate.

Eisenhower's status as a war hero was his greatest political asset. Born in 1890 and raised in Abilene,

Kansas, he had graduated from the United States Military Academy at West Point in 1915. General Douglas MacArthur chose him as his aide in the early 1930s, and Eisenhower rose quickly through the ranks. After Pearl Harbor he came to Washington under the sponsorship of a second mentor, General George C. Marshall. Eisenhower oversaw the Allied invasion of North Africa in 1942, and in 1944 became Supreme Commander of Allied Forces in Europe, where he had the mammoth task of coordinating the D-Day invasion of France. To hundreds of thousands of soldiers and to the millions who followed the war on newsreels, he was simply "Ike," the best known and best liked of the nation's military leaders. His appeal was captured in the popular campaign slogan "I Like Ike."

Eisenhower was in a superb position for a presidential campaign. After serving as president of Columbia University from 1948 to 1950, he returned to active duty as the commander of NATO forces in Europe at Truman's request. As a professional military man he claimed to stand "above politics." While in the army he had never voted, insisting that such political activity represented an intrusion of the military into civilian affairs. Many Democrats had hoped to make him their candidate for president in 1948 and again in 1952. Eisenhower wanted the office, but as a Republican.

When the conservative Senator Robert A. Taft of Ohio did well in the early primaries of 1952, Eisenhower resigned his military position to campaign. He quickly proved to be an effective politician, winning several primaries and taking delegates away from Taft in a tough fight at the Republican National Convention. Eisenhower then asked Senator Richard M. Nixon of California to be his running mate. Young, tirelessly par-

They Liked Ike
Eisenhower's immense personal popularity, captured in the campaign slogan "I Like Ike," propelled him to the largest victory of any candidate to date in the 1952 election. Here delegates show their enthusiasm at the Republican National Convention that year.

tisan, and with a strong anticommunist record from his crusade against Alger Hiss, Nixon brought an aggressive campaign style as well as regional balance to the ticket.

The Democrats never seriously considered renominating Harry Truman, who by 1952 was a thoroughly discredited leader. During the last two years of his presidency, Truman's public approval rating had never risen above 32 percent and at one point had plunged to 23 percent. Lack of popular enthusiasm for the Korean War dealt the most severe blow to Truman's support, but a series of widely publicized scandals involving federal officials in bribery, kickback, and influence-peddling schemes caused voters to complain about the "mess in Washington." With a certain relief the Democrats turned to Governor Adlai E. Stevenson of Illinois, who enjoyed the support of respected liberals such as Eleanor Roosevelt and that of organized labor. To appease southern voters who feared Stevenson's liberal agenda, the Democrats nominated Senator John A. Sparkman of Alabama for vice-president.

Throughout the 1952 campaign Stevenson advocated New Deal–Fair Deal policies with an almost literary eloquence, but Eisenhower's artfully unpretentious speeches were more effective with the voters. Eager to get maximum support from a broad electorate, Eisenhower played down specific questions of policy. Instead, he attacked the Democrats with the "K_1C_2" formula— "Korea, Communism, and Corruption." In a campaign pledge that clinched the election he vowed to go to Korea and end the stalemated war if elected. Stevenson lamely quipped, "If elected, I shall go to the White House."

The only problem in the Republican campaign was the revelation that wealthy Californians had set up a secret "slush fund" for Richard Nixon. While Eisenhower contemplated dropping him from the ticket, Nixon adroitly used a televised speech to appeal directly for voters' sympathy, asserting that he had not misused campaign funds. Whereas Truman appointees had accepted mink coats from contractors—a reference to a widely reported case involving a loan examiner for the Reconstruction Finance Corporation—his wife wore only a "respectable Republican cloth coat." Nixon did admit accepting one gift, a puppy his young daughters had named Checkers. That gift he would not give back, he declared earnestly. Nixon's televised pathos turned an embarrassing incident into an advantage as sympathetic viewers flooded Republican headquarters with telegrams and phone calls in his support. Outmaneuvered, Republican leaders had no choice but to keep him on the ticket. The "Checkers" speech showed how politicians could use the powerful medium of television to their advantage.

Eisenhower won 55 percent of the popular vote, carrying all the northern and western states and four southern states. Republican candidates for Congress did not fare quite as well. They regained the Senate but won control of the House of Representatives by only a slen-

The "Checkers" Speech
Illustrating the power of the new medium of television, vice-presidential candidate Richard Nixon's "Checkers" speech kept him on the 1952 ticket despite allegations of an illegal campaign slush fund. Today the half-hour speech seems stilted and amateurish, but viewers in 1952 were so impressed by Nixon's earnest delivery that they flooded Republican headquarters with telegrams demanding that he stay on the ticket.

der margin of 4 seats. In 1954 the Democrats would regain control of both houses, an advantage that they held even when the enormously popular Eisenhower won easy reelection over Adlai Stevenson in 1956.

The Hidden-Hand Presidency

Seeking a middle ground between liberalism and conservatism, Eisenhower offered modern Republicanism as an alternative to the Democrats' liberal agenda. He did his best to set a quieter national mood, hoping to decrease the need for federal intervention in social and economic issues. Eisenhower deliberately avoided confrontation. He refused to speak out publicly against Senator McCarthy and displayed little leadership in the emerging area of civil rights. As the columnist Richard L. Strout observed in *The New Republic*, "The less he does the more they love him. Here is a man who doesn't rock the boat."

Yet Eisenhower was no stooge as president. The political scientist Fred Greenstein has characterized his style of leadership as the "hidden-hand presidency," pointing out that Eisenhower maneuvered deftly behind the scenes while not concerning himself publicly with partisan questions. Others cite the president's skillful handling of the press. When his press secretary, James Hagerty, asked what he would say about a tricky foreign policy issue at a press conference, Eisenhower replied, "Don't worry, Jim. If that question comes up, I'll just confuse them." He proved just as adept in personnel situations. In a characteristic move, Eisenhower recognized the outspoken anticommunism of Clare Booth Luce, an author, playwright, and former Republican member of Congress from Connecticut, by making her the nation's second woman ambassador. At the same time, by sending Luce to Italy, he removed her strident opinions from the Washington scene.

Unlike Truman, Eisenhower showed little commitment to civil rights. He proposed no major initiatives in this area and dealt a major blow to native American rights by backing a Congressional measure terminating federal involvement in Indian affairs (see Chapter 29). Inadvertently, though, he contributed to the advancement of the black cause by naming Governor Earl Warren of California as chief justice of the Supreme Court in September 1953. Warren's quiet persuasion convinced the Court to rule unanimously in *Brown v. Board of Education of Topeka* (1954) that racial segregation in the public schools was unconstitutional (see Chapter 29). Eisenhower was disturbed by the decision, asserting, "I don't believe you can change the hearts of men with laws or decisions." Nonetheless, in 1957 he sent federal troops to enforce the integration of Central High School in Little Rock, Arkansas. He also signed the Civil Rights Act of 1957, a Democratic bill that created the U.S. Commission on Civil Rights to study federal laws and policies dealing with equal protection. Though admittedly weak, the act was the first national civil rights legislation passed since Reconstruction.

Eisenhower presided over other cautious increases in federal activity. When the Soviet Union launched the first satellite, *Sputnik*, in 1957, Eisenhower supported a U.S. space program to catch up with the Russians. The National Aeronautics and Space Administration (NASA) was founded the following year. Arguing that the Cold War required more scientists and experts on foreign affairs, he persuaded Congress to appropriate additional money for college scholarships and to increase its support for research and development in universities and industry. He also yielded to the demands of interest groups to increase federal outlays for veterans' benefits, unemployment compensation, housing, and Social Security. The minimum wage was raised from 75 cents an hour to a dollar. The creation of the new Department of Health, Education and Welfare (HEW) in 1953 consolidated government control of social welfare programs, confirming federal commitments in that area.

Some of the most extensive federal activity was in the realm of transportation. The Eisenhower administration oversaw a massive expansion of the nation's water and highway routes. It cosponsored with Canada the construction of the St. Lawrence Seaway to link the Great Lakes with the Atlantic Ocean, a project that had been discussed since the 1930s. In a move that drastically altered the American landscape and favored the trend toward privately owned automobiles, the Interstate Highway Act of 1956 authorized $26 billion over a ten-year period for the construction of a nationally integrated highway system. The St. Lawrence Seaway and interstate highway projects were the largest public works programs to date, surpassing anything the New Deal had undertaken. They highlighted the vital role of federal spending in American life, even under a Republican administration.

Eisenhower realized that the vast federal budget, which reached almost 23 percent of the gross national product in the late 1950s, gave the government a major responsibility for the overall health of the nation's economy. The president made the fight against inflation, not full employment, his top economic priority. Eisenhower believed that a balanced budget and stable prices would encourage business confidence and lead to prosperity. His policies pleased investors: the economy grew 2.9 percent per year between 1953 and 1961, while inflation averaged only 1.5 percent annually. Nevertheless, periodic bouts of unemployment and recession (1953–1954, 1957–1958, and 1960–1961) continued. The unemployment rate fluctuated from a low of 2.9 percent in 1953 to a high of 6.8 percent in 1958.

Modern Republicanism, it turned out, resisted the unchecked expansion of the state but did not generally cut back federal power. Only in the area of natural resource development did the Eisenhower administration move to reduce federal activity through the relinquishing of federal offshore oil contracting to the states in 1953 and the authorization of privately financed hydroelectric dams on the Snake River in 1955. In most other

The Sputnik *Crisis*
The Soviet launching of the *Sputnik* space satellite in 1957 precipitated a crisis of confidence in American science and education. That sense of crisis was reflected in a 1950s "Space Race" card game, in which those dealt the Sputnik card would lose two turns.

areas the responsibilities that the federal government had accepted—social welfare programs inherited from the New Deal, Keynesian intervention in the economy, and increased defense expenditures necessitated by the nation's growing role abroad—signaled an abandonment of the Republican style of limited government that had prevailed in the 1920s. When Eisenhower retired from public life in 1961, the federal government had become an even greater presence in everyday life than it had been when he took office.

Alliances and Arms

Eisenhower had earned a reputation for excellent judgment in military and diplomatic affairs during his years in the armed forces. One of his first acts as president was to put that skill to use in negotiating an end to the Korean War. As he had pledged in the campaign, he visited Korea in December 1952. The final settlement was signed in July 1953 at Panmunjom after the parties reached a compromise on the tricky issue of prisoner exchange.

Once the Korean War was settled, Eisenhower turned his attention to Europe. Secretary of State John Foster Dulles played an important role in defining the administration's foreign policy. Dulles, an experienced international lawyer and diplomat, was an outspoken critic of "atheistic communism." Rather than just limiting Soviet expansion, he argued, the United States ought to promote the "liberation" of the "captive nations" of Eastern Europe. This aggressive approach, known as *rollback*, went well beyond the containment policy and proved to be an unworkable strategy in the perilous climate of the Cold War.

The Soviet Union under Khrushchev. At the beginning of the Eisenhower administration the Soviet Union briefly appeared to be interested in better relations. After Stalin's death in March 1953, Georgi Malenkov assumed temporary leadership and adopted a more conciliatory tone toward the West. After an intraparty struggle that lasted until 1956, Nikita S. Khrushchev emerged as Stalin's successor. He soon startled Communists throughout the world by denouncing Stalin as "a distrustful man, sickly and suspicious" and detailing publicly Stalin's crimes and use of torture in the 1930s and 1940s. Khrushchev also surprised Westerners by calling for "peaceful coexistence" between communist and capitalist societies. He also seemed willing to tolerate the different approaches to communism developed by Yugoslavia's Marshal Josip Tito and Poland's Wladislaw Gomulka. When Gomulka, who had once been jailed in a Stalinist purge, insisted that his nation's Communists be allowed to work out Poland's problems in their own way, Khrushchev agreed.

However, Khrushchev made certain that Russia's Eastern European satellites did not deviate too far from the Soviet path. When nationalists revolted in Hungary in 1956 and moved to take the country out of the Warsaw Pact, Soviet tanks rapidly moved into Budapest. At that time the United States was preoccupied by an international crisis in the Suez (see pages 887–888) that temporarily weakened the unity of the NATO alliance. Taking advantage of the chaotic conditions in the Middle East, the Soviets crushed the Hungarian revolt and installed a puppet regime. Despite Dulles's aggressive rhetoric, there was little the United States could do beyond loosening immigration quotas for Hungarian refugees. The Soviet repression of the Hungarian revolt showed that American policy makers had few, if any, options for rolling back Soviet power in Eastern Europe short of going to war with the U.S.S.R.

The "New Look" in Foreign Policy. Although Eisenhower strongly opposed communism, he hoped to keep the cost of containment at a manageable level. As a fiscal conservative, he rejected the tenets of NSC-68, which called for ever larger defense expenditures. Under his "New Look" defense policy Eisenhower sought to enhance American nuclear capabilities and encourage U.S. allies to bear greater military responsibility through increased foreign aid and an extensive system of defense alliances. One by-product of the New Look was a larger role for the CIA, an agency that was relatively cheap as a foreign policy tool and could work covertly, removed from public scrutiny.

As part of the New Look, Eisenhower and Dulles embraced the policy of *massive retaliation*. They believed that the United States could economize by developing an effective nuclear deterrent rather than relying on expensive conventional forces. Nuclear weapons delivered "more bang for the buck," in the words of Defense Secretary Charles E. Wilson. Since Eisenhower and Dulles believed that the nation's major foreign enemy was a worldwide communist movement led by Moscow, they reasoned that the United States did not need to keep a large number of soldiers under arms. Atomic weapons could threaten the Soviet Union directly and force it to back down. To that end, the Eisenhower administration expanded its commitment to the hydrogen bomb, including extensive atmospheric testing in the South Pacific and in western states such as Nevada, Colorado, and Utah. To improve U.S. defenses against an air attack from the Soviet Union, the administration supported research to develop the long-range bombing capabilities of the Strategic Air Command and installed the Distant Early Warning line of radar stations in Alaska and Canada in 1958.

Those efforts did little to improve the nation's security as the Soviets matched the United States weapon for weapon in an escalating arms race. The Soviet Union carried out its own atmospheric tests of hydrogen bombs between 1953 and 1958 and developed a fleet of long-range bombers. It briefly won the race to build an inter-

Testing an Atomic Bomb

Throughout the 1950s the Atomic Energy Commission conducted aboveground tests of atomic and hydrogen bombs. Thousands of soldiers were exposed to fallout during the tests, such as this one at Yucca Flats, Nevada, in April 1952. The AEC, ignoring or suppressing medical evidence to the contrary, mounted an extensive public relations campaign to convince local residents that the tests did not endanger their health.

continental ballistic missile (ICBM), but the United States launched its own ICBM in 1958. In 1960 an American nuclear submarine was the first to launch an atomic-tipped Polaris missile, and Soviet leaders raced to produce an equivalent weapon. While boosting the military-industrial sectors of the United States and the Soviet Union, the arms race debilitated both countries by funneling immense resources into soon-to-be obsolete weapon systems.

A Web of Alliances. The New Look policy also sought to extend collective security agreements between the United States and its allies. To complement the NATO alliance in Europe, Dulles negotiated bilateral defense treaties with South Korea and the nationalist Chinese regime in Taiwan in 1954. In the same year, he orchestrated the creation of the Southeast Asia Treaty Organization (SEATO), linking America and its major European allies with Australia, Pakistan, Thailand, New Zealand, and the Philippines. In 1955 the United States sponsored but did not join the Baghdad Pact, a defensive alliance between Turkey and Iraq that was important to U.S. national security because of those countries' strategic location on the borders of the Soviet Union. This "pactomania," as some called it, required that the United States to come to the defense of more than forty other countries.

U.S. policy makers also tended to support stable governments, no matter how repressive, as long as they were overtly anticommunist. Some of America's staunchest allies—the Philippines, Iran, Cuba, Nicaragua, and the Dominican Republic—had military dictatorships or repressive right-wing civilian governments that lacked broad-based popular support. The secretary of state regarded the establishment of these alliances as an imperative. "Neutrality," Dulles maintained, was not only "obsolete" but "immoral."

CIA Activities. Convinced of the righteousness of his cause, Dulles did not shrink from covert interventions against governments that were, in his opinion, too closely aligned with communism. For such tasks he used the Central Intelligence Agency, which was headed by his brother, Allen Dulles. During the Eisenhower administration the CIA moved beyond its original mandate of intelligence gathering to active, if secret, involvement in the internal affairs of foreign countries when such covert action suited American objectives. By the late 1950s the CIA was devoting the majority of its budget and personnel to covert actions such as toppling foreign governments, bribing public officials, and financing pro-American insurgents.

In the 1950s the CIA successfully directed the overthrow of several foreign governments. When Iran's nationalist premier, Muhammad Mossadegh, seized British oil properties in 1953, CIA agents helped the young shah, Muhammad Reza Pahlavi, depose him. Using both economic leverage and a repressive secret police, the shah soon solidified his power. In 1954 the CIA supported a coup in Guatemala against the popularly elected Jacobo Arbenz Guzman, who had expropriated 250,000 uncultivated acres held by the American-owned United Fruit Company and accepted arms from the communist government of Czechoslovakia. The CIA also tried, unsuccessfully, to overthrow Achmed Sukarno of Indonesia in 1958 and Fidel Castro of Cuba in 1961. Eisenhower specifically approved those efforts. "Our traditional ideas of international sportsmanship," he wrote privately in 1955, "are scarcely applicable in the morass in which the world now flounders."

The Emerging Third World

American leaders had devised the containment policy in response to Soviet expansion in Eastern Europe, but they soon extended it to the new nations that were emerging from disintegrating European empires in Africa, Asia, and the Middle East. Seeking to integrate those countries into an American-led world system, U.S. policy makers encouraged the development of stable market economies in those areas. Also important was the commitment to national self-determination that had shaped American participation in both world wars. Third World political problems generally had a low priority, however, unless a short-term crisis demanded U.S. attention. And in certain areas, such as Latin America, traditional patterns of American penetration and dominance played a more significant role in determining U.S. policies than did global politics. But in all dealings with the Third World the imperatives of the Cold War affected U.S. policy.

Nationalism, socialism, and religion had inspired powerful anticolonial movements before World War II; those forces intensified and spread, especially in the Middle East, Africa, and the Far East, in the 1940s and 1950s. Between 1947 and 1962 the British, French, Dutch, and Belgian empires all but disappeared. The British withdrawal from India in 1947 and the subsequent creation of the states of India (predominantly Hindu) and Pakistan (predominantly Muslim) represented an especially important milestone.

The end of colonial empires fulfilled a goal that the United States had sought in vain after World War I, and the nation in general welcomed the independence of the new states. At the same time, both the Truman and Eisenhower administrations were so caught up in the polarities of the Cold War that they often failed to recognize that indigenous nationalist or socialist movements in emerging nations had their own goals and were not necessarily under the control of either local Communists or the Soviet Union. This failure to appreciate the complexity of local conditions limited the effectiveness of American policy toward the emerging Third World.

The Middle East. The Middle East, an oil-rich area that was playing an increasingly central role in strategic planning, presented one of the most complicated challenges. Zionism, the Jewish nationalist movement, had long encouraged Jews to return to their ancient homeland. After World War II many of the Jews who had survived the Nazi extermination camps resettled in Palestine, which was still controlled by Britain under a World War I mandate. On November 29, 1947, the U.N. General Assembly voted for the partition of Palestine into Jewish and Arab states. On May 14, 1948, the British mandate ended and Zionist leaders proclaimed the state of Israel. Egypt, Jordan, and other Arab League states rejected the partition and invaded Israel. Israel survived, but the land destined for the planned Palestinian state was informally divided among Jordan, Israel, and Egypt, creating a large number of Palestinian refugees who had no homeland. President Truman quickly recognized Israel, alienating the Arabs but winning crucial support from Jewish voters in the 1948 election.

Britain had been the dominant foreign power in the Persian Gulf since the nineteenth century, and its withdrawal from Palestine in 1947 created a power vacuum in an already unstable area. When Gamal Abdel Nasser came to power in Egypt in 1954, two years after independence from Britain, he pledged to lead not just his country but the entire Middle East out of its dependent, colonial relationship through a form of pan-Arab socialism. Nasser obtained arms and promises of economic assistance from the Soviet Union in return for Egyptian cotton. When the Soviets offered to finance a dam on the Nile River at Aswan, Secretary of State Dulles countered with an offer of American assistance. But Nasser refused to distance himself from the Russians, declaring Egypt's neutrality in the Cold War. Unwilling to accept this nonaligned stance, Dulles abruptly withdrew the U.S. offer in July 1956.

A week later Nasser retaliated against the withdrawal of western financial aid by nationalizing the Suez Canal, over which Britain had retained administrative authority and through which three-quarters of Western Europe's oil was transported. Nasser said he would use

The Birth of Israel, 1948
Prime Minister David Ben-Gurion reads Israel's Declaration of Independence to the new country's assembled officials. The photograph on the wall is of Theodor Herzl, the founder of the modern Zionist movement.

the tolls from the canal to build the dam himself. After several months of fruitless negotiation Britain and France, in alliance with Israel, attacked Egypt and retook the canal. The seizure of the canal by America's European allies occurred at the same time as the Soviet repression of the Hungarian revolt, placing the United States in the potentially awkward position of denouncing Soviet aggression while tolerating a similar action by its own allies. Eisenhower and the United Nations condemned the European actions in Egypt, forcing France and Britain to pull back. Egypt took possession of the Suez Canal and built the Aswan Dam with Soviet support. In the end the Suez crisis increased Soviet influence in the Third World, intensified anti-Western sentiment in Arab countries, and produced dissension among leading members of the NATO alliance.

The Eisenhower Doctrine. In the aftermath of the Suez crisis the president persuaded Congress early in 1957 to approve the Eisenhower Doctrine. Addressing concerns over declining British influence in the Middle East, the policy stated that American forces would assist any nation in the region "requiring such aid, against overt armed aggression from any nation controlled by International Communism." Eisenhower invoked the doctrine when he sent the U.S. Sixth Fleet to the Mediterranean Sea to aid King Hussein of Jordan in 1957. A year later Eisenhower landed 8,000 troops to back up a pro–United States government in Lebanon.

The attention that the Eisenhower administration paid to developments in the Middle East in the 1950s demonstrated how the desire for access to steady supplies of oil increasingly affected foreign policy. Indeed, by the late 1950s the Middle East contained about 65 percent of the world's known reserves. More broadly, attention to the Middle East confirmed the global scope of American interests. Just as the Korean War had stretched the application of containment from Europe to Asia, the Eisenhower Doctrine revealed U.S. intentions to bring the Middle East into its sphere as well.

The Impact of the Cold War

The Cold War extended to the most distant corners of the globe, but it also had a devastating impact on the health of American citizens at home who became unwitting guinea pigs in the nation's nuclear weapons program. In the late 1950s a small but growing number of citizens became concerned about the effects of radioactive fallout from aboveground bomb tests. In later years federal investigators documented a host of illnesses, deaths, and birth defects among families of veterans who had worked on weapons tests (see American Voices, page 889) and among "downwinders"—residents near nuclear test sites and weapons facilities. The most shocking revelations, however, came to light in 1993 when the Department of

Energy released millions of previously classified documents on human radiation experiments conducted under the auspices of the Atomic Energy Commission (AEC) and other federal agencies in the late 1940s and 1950s. The documents described over 16,000 cases involving the deliberate irradiation of human subjects, often without their consent or understanding. Whereas some of the tests involved research for legitimate medical procedures, others simply measured human tolerance of radioactive substances, some of which were known at the time to be extremely dangerous.

Fred Sours, a businessman from Gates, New York, was one of the unlucky subjects. Entering a Rochester hospital to get treatment for a skin disorder in 1946, Sours was injected with plutonium 239—now known to be a lethal radioactive substance—as part of a program to test human radiation tolerance. He subsequently developed an assortment of ailments and died of pneumonia in July 1947. Thirty years later, when the AEC exhumed his body for a secret follow-up investigation, it found traces of plutonium throughout his system. There is no evidence that he was ever informed about the experiment. As it turned out, Sours was among the more educated and affluent test subjects. Many others, most of whom later died, were indigent hospital patients, retarded children, prisoners, low-income pregnant women, and other relatively powerless members of society.

Nuclear Proliferation. The nuclear arms race affected all Americans by fostering a climate of fear and uncertainty. Bomb shelters, civil defense drills, and other preparations for postbomb survival provided a daily reminder of the threat of nuclear war. Even Eisenhower, whose policies accelerated the arms race, had second thoughts about a nuclear policy that was based on the premise of annihilating the enemy, even if one's own country was destroyed—the aptly named acronym MAD (Mutual Assured Destruction). He also found spiraling arms expenditures a serious hindrance to balancing the federal budget, one of his chief fiscal goals. Consequently, Eisenhower tried to negotiate an arms limitation agreement with the Soviet Union. Laying the diplomatic groundwork for a possible arms treaty, Eisenhower and Khrushchev held a summit meeting in Geneva, Switzerland, in 1955—the first such meeting since the Potsdam Conference ten years before—and followed up with further disarmament talks over the next two years.

Although those meetings did not yield the "open skies" mutual arms inspection treaty Eisenhower wanted, they did produce plans for another summit meeting with Khrushchev in May 1960. Then, on May 5, the Soviets shot down an American U-2 spy plane over their territory and captured its pilot, Francis Gary Powers. Eisenhower initially denied that the plane was engaged in espionage but later admitted that he had authorized this and other secret flights over the U.S.S.R. by high-flying

George Mace

An Atomic Bomb Veterans Remembers

George Mace's life was changed by his participation in atomic testing in the Pacific in the 1950s. He blames his on-going health problems on the thirty-five atomic and hydrogen bomb blasts that he witnessed there. He became in-volved in the National Association of Atomic Veterans, founded in 1979 to pressure the government to release in-formation on the human impact of atomic testing in the 1940s and 1950s. Much of the story remained secret until the early 1990s, when President Bill Clinton ordered the declassifica-tion of thousands of documents held by the Department of Energy.

I graduated from high school in 1953 and enlisted in the Air Force in 1955 to gain a trade. . . . In 1957, orders came down assigning me to Joint Task Force 7 on the Enewetak atoll in the Mar-shall Islands of the South Pacific. . . . I was twenty-two. . . .

Immediately we were briefed on the island's facilities and its very tight security. I remember being told that we couldn't write home about anything we saw or did and that our mail would be checked and edited. . . .

We were never told that a shot was going to occur until the day of the event. And every day there was a shot, they'd march us out to the beach and make us sit there with our backs to the lagoon. At the time, I always asked

how far we were away from it, and I was always told about fifty miles. But in 1979, when I got the declassified documents, I found out that I was only five to fifteen miles from the bombs—never more than fifteen miles! So there was a clear deception on the part of the government.

Watching the shots got to be kind of pointless after a while; there was no follow-up study of us at all. They were just preparing the troops for the age of atomic war. We were never told about any effects of radiation, and being young and ignorant, I had no fear of it. But I *did* fear the tremendous strength of each blast. . . . We'd cover our eyes until the fireball passed. A few seconds after the explosion went off you would see this tremendous flash, and then a tremendous wave of heat you could feel like the sun coming up on your back. The biggest one I ever saw—code named Oak—got to the point of being uncomfortable.

The Oak explosion was nine mega-tons. I will never forget it; we sand-bagged the island beforehand, because it was only seven feet above sea level. When it went off there was this wink of light that I sensed through my closed eyes and hands, just like a flashbulb be-hind me. And when I turned to see the column of water rising out of the la-goon, it was so tremendous that no one spoke. You could hear the sound waves

bouncing off the island—Boom! Boom! And when the sound wave hit Enewe-tak, the whole island shook and a hot wind blew our baseball caps off.

The column was surrounded by ragged haloes of white shock waves which produced an electrical field. I actually experienced an electrical field passing through me; my hair stood up and there was a cracking sensation all through me that was as much felt as heard.

And that thing just continued to build and grow until it had risen about sixty or seventy thousand feet. The mushroom covered the entire island chain. Fifteen miles of islands were all shadowed by this terrifying, magnifi-cent thing. I remember talk of an evac-uation, but it never occurred. . . .

After that shot the water was off limits for swimming for three days. but the ironic part of it was that the ocean was the source of our drinking water after it went through the de-salinization plant. I didn't have any knowledge of radiation, so I wasn't afraid of it. . . . I wasn't worried—I trusted my country. In 1958, I really did. To be truthful with you, I was proud to be there.

Source: Sam Totten and Martha Wescoat Totten, *Facing the Danger: Interviews with 20 Anti-Nuclear Activists* (Trumansburg, N.Y.: The Crossing Press, 1984), 52–56.

---

reconnaissance aircraft. In the midst of the dispute the summit meeting was canceled, and Eisenhower's last chance to negotiate an arms agreement evaporated.

The Military-Industrial Complex. When Eisenhower left office in January 1961, he warned against the power of what he termed the "military-industrial complex," which by then employed 3.5 million Americans. Its per-vasive influence, he said, "is felt in every city, every state-house, every office of the Federal Government." Even though his administration had fostered this growth in the defense establishment, Eisenhower was gravely con-cerned about its implications for a democratic people:

In the councils of Government, we must guard against the acquisition of unwarranted influence, whether sought or unsought, by the military-industrial com-plex. . . . We must never let the weight of this combi-nation endanger our liberties or democratic processes. We should take nothing for granted. Only an alert and knowledgeable citizenry can compel the proper mesh-ing of the huge industrial and military machinery of defense with our peaceful methods and goals, so that security and liberty may prosper together.

With those words Dwight Eisenhower showed how well he understood the major transformations that the Cold War had brought to American life.

Summary

Emerging from World War II as the world's powerful nation, the United States took the leading role in international affairs and tried to shape the world system to further its own interests. A resurgent Soviet Union with its own agenda stymied American goals, and the resulting clash between the two powers brought about the Cold War. Containment originally emerged in response to Soviet pressure on Eastern Europe, but that doctrine was soon expanded to include resistance to communism and left-wing revolution wherever they appeared. The Truman administration used economic aid abroad to ensure the political and economic stability of its allies while building up America's military arsenal, particularly its conventional forces. Eisenhower's New Look policy stressed a strong nuclear arsenal, collective security arrangements, and increased military aid abroad.

Tension over communism abroad fostered domestic repression and fear at home. Government, unions, schools, and other organizations instituted loyalty oaths as a requirement for employment; media organizations blacklisted suspected Communists; and Congressional committees conducted highly prejudicial and sensationalized public investigations of alleged communist subversion. Red-hunting activities peaked during the anticommunist crusade of Senator Joseph McCarthy in the early 1950s, shattering the lives and careers of many.

The Cold War also enhanced the power of the president and the national security state. With bipartisan support, the president gained greater latitude in foreign policy making and increasingly relied on covert operations of the Central Intelligence Agency to maintain friendly governments in the Third World. The national security state also required increased defense expenditures that took up an ever larger part of the gross national product. Besides paying for defense through taxes and growing deficits, Americans now lived in a world where small foreign wars were a constant possibility and fear of a nuclear attack was part of daily life.

The Democratic party set much of the legislative agenda for the postwar period, expanding the reforms introduced by Franklin Roosevelt in the 1930s. Harry Truman's Fair Deal won only limited legislative victories; a generally hostile Republican Congress blocked his initiatives on educational aid, health care, and civil rights. But by integrating the armed forces and establishing a federal civil rights commission, Truman placed the issue of racial equality back on the national political agenda. The Republican administration of Dwight Eisenhower did not seek to roll back the New Deal and in fact presided over cautious increases in federal power in the areas of scientific research and interstate transportation.

TIMELINE

1945	Yalta and Potsdam conferences Harry S. Truman succeeds Roosevelt as president End of World War II
1946	Kennan sends "long telegram" outlining containment policy Churchill's Iron Curtain speech Baruch Plan for international control of atomic weapons fails Employment Act
1947	Taft-Hartley Act Jackie Robinson breaks color line in major league baseball Truman Doctrine National Security Act Marshall Plan
1948	Desegregation of armed forces State of Israel created Berlin airlift
1949	North Atlantic Treaty Organization (NATO) founded People's Republic of China established National Housing Act Soviet Union detonates atomic bomb; U.S. atomic monopoly ends
1950–1953	Korean War
1950	Alger Hiss convicted of perjury McCarthy presents list of alleged Communists in government NSC-68 calls for permanent mobilization
1952	Dwight D. Eisenhower elected president U.S. detonates hydrogen bomb
1953	Stalin dies
1954	Army-McCarthy hearings *Brown v. Board of Education of Topeka*
1956	Suez crisis Interstate Highway Act
1957	Eisenhower Doctrine U.S.S.R. launches *Sputnik* Eisenhower sends U.S. troops to Little Rock to ensure school integration
1958	NASA established
1959	St. Lawrence Seaway completed
1960	U-2 spy plane shot down over Soviet Union

★   ★   ★

BIBLIOGRAPHY

General works on the politics and diplomacy of the cold war era include William Chafe, *The Unfinished Journey* (3d ed., 1995); Paul Boyer, *Promises to Keep* (1995); and Eric F. Goldman, *The Crucial Decade and After: America, 1945–1960* (1961).

The Early Cold War

The best overviews of the Cold War are Walter LaFeber, *America, Russia, and the Cold War, 1945–1990* (7th ed., 1992); Thomas G. Paterson, *On Every Front: The Making and Unmaking of the Cold War* (rev. ed., 1992); and Stephen Ambrose, *Rise to Globalism* (7th ed., 1993). Melvyn P. Leffler presents a masterful and exhaustive synthesis of Truman's foreign policy in *A Preponderance of Power* (1992). For critical views of American aims, see H. W. Brands, *The Devil We Knew* (1993); Richard Ned Lebow and Janice Gross Stein, *We All Lost the Cold War* (1994); and Joyce Kolko and Gabriel Kolko, *The Limits of Power* (1970). John Lewis Gaddis, *Strategies of Containment* (1982), blames the Cold War on both the United States and the Soviet Union, although his more recent works, *The Long Peace* (1987) and *The United States and the End of the Cold War* (1992), are more sympathetic to American policy making. Specialized studies include Ernest R. May, ed., *American Cold War Strategy: Interpreting NSC-68* (1993); Laurence S. Kaplan, *The United States and NATO* (1984); Michael Hogan, *The Marshall Plan* (1987); and Richard Freeland, *The Truman Doctrine and the Origins of McCarthyism* (1972).

The descent into the Cold War can also be viewed through the works of individual policy makers. Indispensable are George F. Kennan, *American Diplomacy, 1900–1950* (1952), and *Memoirs, 1925–1950* (1967), and Dean Acheson's modestly titled *Present at the Creation* (1970). Walter Isaacson and Evan Thomas, *The Wise Men* (1986), trace the impact of Dean Acheson, Charles Bohlen, Averell Harriman, George Kennan, Robert Lovett, and John McCloy on postwar foreign policy. Walter Lippmann, *The Cold War* (1947), offers a thoughtful critique of American foreign policy by a contemporary.

McGeorge Bundy, *Danger and Survival* (1989); Martin J. Sherwin, *A World Destroyed* (1975); and Gar Alperovitz, *Atomic Diplomacy* (2d ed., 1994), cover the impact of atomic weapons on American policy. David Holloway, *Stalin and the Bomb* (1994), examines Soviet nuclear weapons development and its impact on the Cold War.

For developments in Asia, Akira Iriye, *The Cold War in Asia* (1974), is a good starting point. See also William Borden, *The Pacific Alliance* (1984); Warren I. Cohen, *America's Response to China* (2d ed., 1980); Kenneth Shewmaker, *Americans and the Chinese Communists* (1971); and Michael Schaller, *The United States and China in the Twentieth Century* (1979) and *The American Occupation of Japan* (1985).

There is an abundance of scholarship on the Korean War, including Clay Blair, *The Forgotten War* (1988); Max Hastings, *The Korean War* (1987); Callum McDonald, *Korea: The War before Vietnam* (1987); Burton Kaufman, *The Korean War* (1986); and Rosemary Foot, *The Wrong War* (1985) and *A Substitute for Victory* (1990). Especially influential are the two volumes of *The Origins of the Korean War* by Bruce Cumings: *Liberation and the Emergence of Separate Regions, 1945–1947* (1981) and *The Roaring of the Cataract, 1947–1950* (1990). Sergei N. Goncharov et al., *Uncertain Partners* (1994), uses newly released Soviet and Chinese documents to analyze the role of those countries in the war. William Manchester, *American Caesar* (1979), and Michael Schaller, *Douglas MacArthur* (1989), offer stimulating biographies of a leading figure of the war.

Harry Truman and the Fair Deal

Harry Truman, *Memoirs* (1952–1962), tells Truman's story in characteristically pointed language; see also Merle Miller's oral history, *Plain Speaking* (1980), and David McCullough's generally sympathetic biography, *Truman* (1992). General accounts of the Truman presidency can be found in Robert J. Donovan, *Tumultuous Years: The Presidency of Harry S. Truman, 1949–1953* (1982) and his earlier *Conflict and Crisis* (1977); Alonzo Hamby, *Beyond the New Deal: Harry S. Truman and American Liberalism* (1973); Donald R. McCoy, *The Presidency of Harry S. Truman* (1984); and William Pemberton, *Harry S. Truman* (1989). Critical perspectives are presented in Barton J. Bernstein, ed., *Politics and Policies of the Truman Administration* (1970). Arthur M. Schlesinger, Jr., states the case for Fair Deal liberalism in *The Vital Center* (1949).

The literature on McCarthyism is voluminous. Recent works include Richard Gid Powers, *Not without Honor* (1996); Richard Fried, *Nightmare in Red: The McCarthy Era in Perspective* (1990); and Stephen J. Whitfield, *The Culture of the Cold War* (1991). David Caute, *The Great Fear* (1978), provides another introduction, which can be supplemented by Victor Navasky, *Naming Names* (1980), and Athan Theoharis, *Spying on Americans* (1978). Two biographies are Thomas C. Reeves, *The Life and Times of Joe McCarthy* (1982), and David Oshinsky, *A Conspiracy so Immense* (1983), but Richard Rovere, *Senator Joseph McCarthy* (1959), still commands attention.

"Modern Republicanism"

Two standard overviews of the Eisenhower administration, Herbert S. Parmet, *Eisenhower and the American Crusades* (1972), and Charles C. Alexander, *Holding the Line* (1975), can be supplemented by Fred I. Greenstein, *The Hidden-Hand Presidency* (1982), and Stephen Ambrose, *Eisenhower the President* (1984). Blanche Wiesen Cook, *The Declassified Eisenhower* (1981), contrasts the covert activities of the administration with its public image.

For the complex foreign policy of the 1950s, consult LaFeber, *America, Russia, and the Cold War*; Ambrose, *Rise to Globalism*; and Thomas McCormick, *America's Half-Century* (1989). Gabriel Kolko, *Confronting the Third World, 1945–1980* (1988), offers a highly critical view of U.S. policy. On American involvement in the Middle East, see Bruce Kuniholm, *The Origins of the Cold War in the Near East* (1980), and Michael Stoff, *Oil, War, and American Security* (1980). On Latin America, see Stephen Rabe, *Eisenhower and Latin America: The Foreign Policy of Anticommunism* (1988).

The Saturday Evening

POST

June 4, 1955 · 15¢

America's Mighty Mile:
THE SOO

LOOK, MOM—NO WHEELS!
The Vehicle That Floats
on Land

Sargent

Life in the Suburbs

In the 1950s the *Saturday Evening Post* celebrated the suburban ideal: family, leisure, and a nurturing wife and mother.

CHAPTER 29

Affluence and Its Contradictions

1945–1965

★   ★   ★

In 1959 Vice-President Richard M. Nixon traveled to Moscow to open the American National Exhibit. It was the height of the Cold War and the postwar baby boom. After sipping Pepsi-Cola, Nixon and Soviet Premier Nikita Khrushchev got into a heated debate about the relative merits of Soviet and American societies. But instead of debating rockets, submarines, and missiles, they talked about dishwashers, toasters, and televisions. Both the subject of the animated conversation and its site (the kitchen of a American model home) led to its popular designation as the "kitchen debate."

The Moscow exhibition was designed to showcase American consumer and leisure goods. Its main attraction was a full-scale replica of a six-room ranch-style house, filled with appliances and labor-saving devices that supposedly were typical of an American home. Over the next three weeks more than 3 million Russians toured the exhibition, no doubt awed by the gadgets and consumer appliances unavailable in Soviet society.

What was so striking about the Moscow exhibition was the way that its American planners enlisted affluence and mass consumption in the service of cold war politics. The suburban life-style trumpeted in the exhibition symbolized the superiority of capitalism over communism. For more than a quarter century after World War II American citizens enjoyed the highest standard of living in the world. The strong performance of the American economy was based on the explosion of consumer demand after years of depression and war, a burgeoning military-industrial complex, the development of new technologies, and an abundant supply of petroleum. But also important was the relative weakness of America's competitors, whose economies had been physically and financially devastated by the war. The much-touted American affluence of the "fifties"—a period that really stretched from 1945 through the early 1960s—was an extraordinary phenomenon that was never as widespread as the Moscow exhibition implied.

Technology and Economic Change

At the end of 1945 war-induced prosperity had made the United States the richest country in the world. Over the next two decades the gross national product more than tripled, benefiting a wider segment of society than anyone would have dreamed possible in the dark days of the depression. Industrial workers in the largest manufacturing industries won acceptance of their unions, and this translated into rising wages, expanding benefits, and a growing rate of suburban home ownership. Successful white-collar workers—New York accountants, Georgia factory managers, Chicago engineers, San Francisco advertising executives, Dallas office managers—also moved their families into new homes in the suburbs as they climbed the corporate ladder. At the heart of this postwar prosperity lay the involvement of the federal government in national economic life. Federal outlays for defense and domestic programs, combined with galloping consumer spending, seemed to promise a continuously rising standard of living.

The Economic Record

The United States enjoyed overwhelming political and economic advantages at the end of World War II. Unlike the Soviet Union, Western Europe, and Japan, America emerged physically unscathed from the war because the impact of wartime mobilization had laid the foundations for postwar economic success. With new housing construction curtailed and many consumer goods rationed, consumers had accumulated wartime savings of $140 billion, which they were eager to spend. Business quickly applied the scientific and technological innovations developed for military purposes, such as plastics and synthetic fibers, to the production of consumer goods. The federal government eased the conversion to a peacetime economy by allowing businesses to buy factories built for the war effort at a fraction of their cost.

Bretton Woods System. The period from World War II through the late 1960s and early 1970s was the heyday of modern American capitalism. U.S. corporations and banking institutions so dominated the world economy that the period has been called the *Pax Americana.* American global supremacy rested in part on institutions created at a United Nations economic conference held in Bretton Woods, New Hampshire, in July 1944: the International Bank for Reconstruction and Development (known commonly as the World Bank) and the International Monetary Fund (IMF). The World Bank provided private loans for the reconstruction of war-torn Europe as well as for the development of Third World countries.

The IMF was set up to stabilize the value of currencies, providing a secure and predictable monetary environment for trade. It did this by encouraging fixed exchange rates, which facilitated the free convertibility of currencies to gold or the currencies of other trading nations; the strong U.S. dollar served as the benchmark. In 1947 multinational trade negotiations resulted in the first General Agreement on Tariffs and Trade (GATT), which led to the establishment of an international body to oversee trade rules and practices.

The World Bank, the IMF, and GATT were the cornerstones of the so-called Bretton Woods system that guided the world economy after the war. The United States dominated the World Bank and the IMF because it contributed the most capital to them and because of the pivotal role of the dollar in international currency exchange. Thus, these independent international organizations worked along lines that favored American-style internationalism and opposed the economic nationalism that was traditional in most other countries. The World Bank, the IMF, and GATT encouraged stable prices, the liberalization of trade barriers and the reduction of tariffs, flexible domestic markets, and free trade based on fixed exchange rates. As long as the dollar remained the strongest currency, the Bretton Woods system effectively served America's global economic interests.

The Fruits of American Hegemony. American economic leadership abroad translated into affluence at home. The country's gross national product (GNP) grew from $213 billion in 1945 to more than $500 billion in 1960; in 1970 the GNP approached $1 trillion (see Figure 29.1). To working Americans, this steady economic growth meant a 25 percent rise in real income between 1946 and 1959. Most Americans rightly felt that they had more money to spend than ever before. In 1940, 43 percent of American families owned their homes; by 1960, 62 percent did.

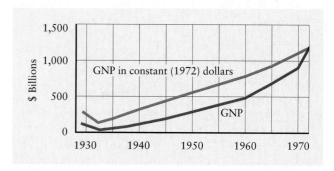

FIGURE 29.1

Gross National Product (GNP), 1929–1972
After a sharp dip during the Great Depression, the gross national product rose steadily in both real and constant dollars in the postwar period.

Consumer Culture

This 1962 painting by Tom Wesselmann mocks the consumer culture that it so lavishly illustrates with a table well stocked with brand-name goods. Realistic painting in the 1960s took on an air of cynicism, especially in the works of artists such as Andy Warhol. Wesselman's *Still Life #24* treats the most ordinary objects of American life as icons, hinting at the new power of consumerism in popular culture. (Nelson Atkins Museum of Art)

The Military-Industrial Complex

One of the most important forces driving postwar prosperity was defense spending (see Figure 29.2). The military-industrial complex that President Eisenhower identified in his 1961 farewell address had its roots in the business-government partnerships of both world wars. But the massive commitment of government dollars to the defense industry in the postwar era was unprecedented, a concrete reminder of how much the state had grown since the 1930s. Even though the country was at peace (with the exception of the Korean War), the economy and the government operated practically on a war footing—in a state of permanent mobilization.

With its headquarters at the sprawling Pentagon in Arlington, Virginia, the Defense Department evolved into a massive bureaucracy that profoundly influenced the postwar economy. Some companies did so much of their business with the government that they became dependent on Defense Department orders. By the mid-1960s Boeing and General Dynamics were receiving 65 percent of their income from military contracts, Raytheon 60 percent, Lockheed 81 percent, and Republic Aviation 100 percent. The Pentagon reinforced the concentration of economic power at the top by awarding contracts to the largest firms.

The impact of permanent mobilization was felt far beyond the defense industry: science, corporate capital-

Another feature of the postwar prosperity was low inflation. After the immediate postwar reconversion period, inflation slowed to 2 to 3 percent annually during the 1950s, and it stayed low until 1965 and the escalation of the Vietnam War. Low inflation meant stable and predictable prices, providing a sense of security for those on fixed incomes and ever-growing prosperity for working Americans.

Despite a high rate of economic growth, a rise in real income, and low inflation, there was an unevenness to the postwar economy that limited the rosy picture of economic success and affluence. The rising standard of living was not accompanied by a redistribution of income; the top 10 percent of Americans still earned more than did the bottom 50 percent. Moreover, the economy was plagued by periodic recessions accompanied by high unemployment in which the permanently unemployed, the aged subsisting on Social Security, female heads of households, and most nonwhites were at a greater disadvantage. In *The Affluent Society* (1958) the economist John Kenneth Galbraith argued that the poor were only an "afterthought" in the minds of economists and politicians, who assumed that poverty was on the way to extinction. Yet in 1957 nearly one in four Americans lived below the official poverty line.

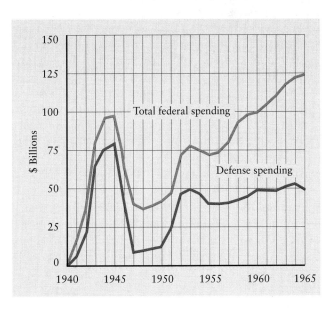

FIGURE 29.2

National Defense Spending, 1940–1965

In 1950 the defense budget was $13 billion, less than a third of total federal outlays. In 1961 defense spending reached $47 billion, fully half the federal budget and almost 10 percent of the gross national product.

The Military-Industrial Complex
This nuclear reactor in Hanford, Washington, was one of dozens of new weapons-related facilities that had sprung up in the southern and western regions of the United States in the 1940s and 1950s. Even though local residents profited from new employment opportunities generated by the plants, the environmental and health dangers posed by the nuclear industry became a growing source of concern.

ism, and the federal government became increasingly intertwined in the postwar period. According to the National Science Foundation, federal money underwrote 90 percent of the cost of research on aviation and space, 65 percent of that on electricity and electronics, 42 percent of that on scientific instruments, and 24 percent of that on automobiles. With the government footing part of the bill, corporations transformed new ideas into useful products with unprecedented speed. After the Pentagon backed IBM's investment in integrated circuits in the 1960s, those new devices, which were crucial to the computer revolution, were in commercial production within three years (see New Technology, page 898).

The growth of this military-industrial establishment reflected a dramatic shift in national priorities. Military spending took up a greater percentage of national income as measured by the GNP. Between 1900 and 1930, except for the two years that the United States fought in World War I, the country spent less than 1 percent of GNP for military purposes. In the early 1960s the figure was close to 10 percent.

The defense buildup created jobs, and lots of them (see Map 29.1). Taking into account the multiplier effect, which measures the indirect benefits of such employment (the additional jobs created to serve and support defense workers), perhaps one worker in seven nationally owed his or her job to the military-industrial complex in the 1960s. In the South and West, where much of the new military activity was concentrated, dependence on federal defense spending was even greater.

That increased spending put money in the pockets of the millions of people working in defense-related industries but also limited the resources available for domestic social needs. Critics of military spending calculated the trade-offs: the cost of a nuclear aircraft carrier and support ships equaled that of a subway system for Washington, D.C.; and the money spent on one Huey helicopter matched that required for sixty-six units of low-income housing.

Military mobilization also affected Americans in a personal way—for the first time in the nation's history there was a peacetime draft. In the past the armed forces had shrunk to a skeleton volunteer force at the end of each war or foreign engagement. But when World War II ended, the draft was kept in place to meet the military commitments associated with the Cold War: occupation forces in defeated Axis countries, missile deployment operations in Europe, and counterinsurgency forces in the Third World. Suddenly every neighborhood seemed to have a boy in the armed forces; many people made military service a career.

Corporate Strategies

The Cold War and the growth of the state brought major changes to American life, hastening the concentration of power in ever larger economic and political structures. Successful corporate managers adopted flexible strategies to take advantage of the postwar economic climate. They tapped federal money for research and development, diversified their range of products, expanded their multinational operations, and improved their ability to plan.

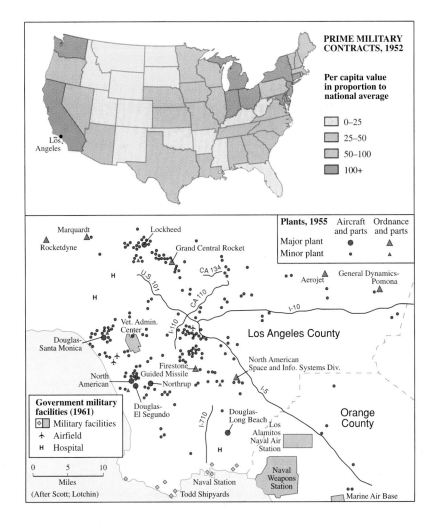

PRIME MILITARY CONTRACTS, 1952

Per capita value in proportion to national average

- 0–25
- 25–50
- 50–100
- 100+

Los Angeles

MAP 29.1

The Military-Industrial Complex in Los Angeles

The development and expansion of military facilities and defense contracting during the Cold War helped boost the populations and economies of Los Angeles and other Sun Belt cities and made the economies of some states highly dependent on defense expenditures.

Plants, 1955

	Aircraft and parts	Ordnance and parts
Major plant	●	▲
Minor plant	·	▴

Marquardt · Lockheed
Rocketdyne · Grand Central Rocket
CA 134
Aerojet · General Dynamics-Pomona
U.S. 101 · H
CA 110
Vet. Admin. Center
I-110
Douglas-Santa Monica
Los Angeles County
North American Space and Info. Systems Div.
Firestone · Guided Missile
North American · Northrup
Douglas-El Segundo
I-5
Douglas-Long Beach
Los Alamitos Naval Air Station
Orange County
I-710
H
Naval Station
Todd Shipyards
Naval Weapons Station
Marine Air Base

Government military facilities (1961)
- Military facilities
- ✈ Airfield
- H Hospital

0   5   10
Miles

(After Scott; Lotchin)

The predominant thrust of modern corporate life after 1945 continued to be consolidation of economic and financial resources by oligopolies, a few large producers who controlled the national and, increasingly, the world market. In 1970 the top four U.S. firms produced 91 percent of the motor vehicles sold in the domestic market; the top four in tires produced 72 percent, in cigarettes 84 percent, and in detergents 70 percent. Despite laws restricting branch banking to a single state, in 1970 the four largest banks held 16 percent of the nation's banking assets; the top fifty banks held 48 percent.

Diversification was the most important corporate strategy in the postwar era. The classic corporation of the early twentieth century had produced a single line of products; its growth had depended on the vertical integration of related firms (see Chapter 18). After World War II the most successful firms invested heavily in research and development, produced new product lines, and moved into new markets. Because the largest corporations could afford research laboratories, they diversified more easily. CBS, for example, hired the Hungarian inventor Peter Goldmark, who perfected

color television during the 1940s, long-playing records in the 1950s, and a video recording system in the 1960s. As the head of CBS Laboratories, Goldmark patented more than a hundred new devices.

Postwar managers also diversified through mergers and acquisitions, creating larger firms called *conglomerates*. By combining companies in unrelated industries, conglomerates offered protection from instability in any single market, making them more effective international competitors. International Telephone and Telegraph became a diversified conglomerate by acquiring Continental Baking, Sheraton Hotels, Avis Rent-a-Car, Levitt and Sons home builders, and Hartford Fire Insurance. Ling-Temco-Vought, another conglomerate, simultaneously produced steel, built ships, developed real estate, and brought cattle to market. These and other corporate acquisitions resulted in the nation's third great merger wave (the first two had taken place in the 1890s and the 1920s), which reached its peak in the 1960s. In 1947 the largest 200 corporations accounted for 30 percent of all value added by manufacturing, but in 1972 the largest 200, by then heavily diversified, accounted for 43 percent of the value added.

The Computer Revolution

The first modern computers—information-processing machines capable of storing and manipulating data according to specified programs—appeared in the 1940s. During World War II engineers and mathematicians at the University of Pennsylvania developed a general-purpose, programmable electronic calculator called ENIAC (Electronic Numerical Integrator and Computer), which could add 5,000 ten-digit decimal numbers in one second. It stood 8 feet tall, measured 80 feet long, and weighed 30 tons; it used 18,000 vacuum tubes for computations. When it performed complex mathematical computations, one scientist noted, ENIAC sounded "like a roomful of ladies knitting." Although ENIAC lacked a central memory and could not store a program, it was the bridge to the modern computer revolution.

Six computers were under construction by 1947, including UNIVAC (Universal Automatic Computer), the first commercial computer system. To the general public in the 1950 the word *UNIVAC* was synonymous with computers. UNIVAC was basically a data-processing system that could be tailored to an individual customer's needs. In 1951 the U.S. Census Bureau bought the first UNIVAC. Soon CBS-TV signed on, using a UNIVAC to predict the outcome of the 1952 presidential election. At 9 P.M., after only the East Coast polls had closed and with only 7 percent of the votes counted, UNIVAC predicted that Dwight D. Eisenhower would sweep the election with 438 electoral votes. CBS programmers and network executives, who had expected a closer election, got jittery and altered the program to give Eisenhower a far narrower margin. When the final tally gave him 442 electoral votes, only 4 votes off the original projection, the commentator Edward R. Murrow observed, "The trouble with machines is people."

Computers are essentially collections of switches, and programs tell the machine which switches to turn on and off. The puzzle that early computer scientists had to solve was how to increase the speed of this basic operation while lowering the cost. The first generation of computers needed vacuum tubes for computation power and used punched cards for writing programs and analyzing data. Computers such as ENIAC were room-sized machines, and programming them could take several days because the programmers had to manually set thousands of switches in the on or off position. The vacuum tubes were the weakest part of early computers; a burnout of

This early computer–data-processing center featured an IBM 704 computer.

just a few tubes could shut down the entire system. Furthermore, the tubes gave off enormous amounts of heat, necessitating noisy and cumbersome air-conditioning units wherever computers operated. After a critical signal relay stopped one early program, scientists finally located the problem—a dead moth trapped in the apparatus, the origin of the term *debugging*.

The 1948 invention of the transistor, a development that revolutionized computers and the whole field of electronics, made the second generation of computers possible. Transistors, like vacuum tubes, served as on-off switches but did not generate heat, burn out, or consume vast quantities of energy. They also were inexpensive to manufacture. The invention of integrated circuits (IC) in 1959 ushered in the third computer generation, characterized by greater sophistication in miniaturization, which meant that the number of transistors that could be installed on a silicon chip increased dramatically, with a corresponding increase in computational power. The fourth computer generation arrived in 1971 with the development of the microprocessor, which placed the entire central processing unit (CPU) of a computer on a single silicon chip (about the size of the letter "O" on this page).

Miniaturization progressed so rapidly that by the mid-1970s a $1 chip provided as much processing power as had the ENIAC of 30 years earlier. Computers and computer technology have become so much a part of modern life that it is hard to remember how recent the origins of this technological revolution are.

The development of giant corporations was also based on the penetration of foreign markets. American products were considered the best in the world and were widely sought after abroad. International strategies enabled American business to enter new regions when domestic markets became saturated or when American recessions cut into sales. During the 1950s U.S. exports nearly doubled, giving the nation a trade surplus of close to $5 billion in 1960.

In their effort to direct large organizations through the uncertainties of the postwar economy, managers placed more emphasis on planning. Increasingly, companies recruited top executives who had business-school training, the ability to manage information, and skills in corporate planning, marketing, and investment. To plan and coordinate effectively, corporate managers had to work more closely with their counterparts in other corporations, large banks, investment firms, law firms, economic research organizations, the federal government, and even the World Bank and the IMF.

The Changing World of Work

Since the late nineteenth century the proportion of Americans employed in the service sector—as professionals, clerical workers, civil servants, and other service workers—had grown steadily. Industrial mobilization during World War II temporarily halted this trend, but it resumed with a vengeance in the postwar era. By 1960 employees in the service sector accounted for more than 60 percent of the labor force. Soon the panelists on the quiz show "What's My Line?" learned to ask mystery guests, "Do you deal in services?"

The New Managerial Class. One of the fastest-growing groups consisted of salaried office workers. From 1947 to 1957 that occupational group increased by 61 percent, whereas the number of factory workers decreased by 4 percent. Growing corporate bureaucracies and increased access to a college education through the GI Bill helped expand the white-collar ranks. Young, predominantly male college graduates used their skills to advance more quickly and at an earlier age than was the case in previous generations.

Such advancement usually led them through the giant bureaucratic structures—big business, government agencies, universities, and the military—that have dominated life in the second half of the twentieth century. As young managers and professionals advanced in their careers, they changed jobs frequently. In the 1950s Atlas Van Lines estimated that corporate managers moved an average of fourteen times—once every two and a half years—during their careers. Perpetually mobile IBM managers joked that the company's initials stood for "I've Been Moved."

Climbing the corporate ladder rewarded men who could get along in a variety of situations. Corporate managers worked hard, sometimes with the assistance of the resident corporate psychologist, to be "well adjusted." Their philosophy was "Evade, don't confront." In *The Lonely Crowd* (1950) the sociologist David Reisman contrasted the stern, formal small business and professional types of earlier years with the corporate managers of the postwar world. He concluded that the new professionals were "other-directed," more concerned about their relations with associates than about adherence to fundamental principles. Critics worried that the conformity of marching off each day in gray flannel suits to work at interchangeable middle-management jobs in huge corporations was stifling men's creativity. The sociologist William Whyte painted a somber picture of "organization men" who left the home "spiritually as well as physically to take the vows of organization life."

Organization Men (and a Few Women)
What happened when the 5:57 discharged commuters in Park Forest, Illinois, a suburb of Chicago? This was the subject of William H. Whyte's *The Organization Man* (1956). Were these hordes of commuters thinking about their stressful day at the office or the martini waiting for them when they walked in the door of their suburban home?

But the popular obsession with the middle-class organization man obscured other significant changes in the postwar work force. Many of the new white-collar employees were clerical workers whose jobs were not too different from factory work—narrow and repetitive tasks that did not allow for control and autonomy. In most cases their salaries were lower than the hourly wages of unionized blue-collar workers. Millions of other service workers were blue collar, performing manual labor for hourly wages under factory-like conditions in laundries, restaurants, warehouses, and other businesses.

Women and Work. Many of the new service workers were female: there were twice as many women working outside the home in 1960 as there were in 1940. Because of the expanding postwar population and economy, there was a demand for workers in fields traditionally filled by women, such as clerical work, teaching, and nursing. For nonwhite and working-class women, a low-paying "pink-collar" ghetto offered jobs in restaurants, hotels, hospitals, and beauty salons.

Occupational segmentation remained characteristic of women's work in the postwar period. Until 1964 the classified sections of most newspapers separated employment ads into columns headed "Help Wanted Male" and "Help Wanted Female." More than 80 percent of all working women did stereotypical "women's work" as salespersons, health care technicians, waitresses, stewardesses, domestic servants, receptionists, telephone operators, and secretaries. In 1960 women represented only 3.5 percent of all lawyers (many top law schools did not admit women at all) and 6.1 percent of all physicians, but 97 percent of all nurses, 85 percent of all librarians, and 57 percent of all social workers. Along with women's jobs went women's pay, which averaged 60 percent of men's pay in 1963.

Challenges for the Labor Movement

The postwar era was the heyday of organized labor, but it also marked the beginning of its decline. Labor unions reached the peak of their strength around the end of World War II, representing over 35 percent of the nonfarm work force, and remained strong and politically influential through the 1960s. But the changing composition of the work force and the shifting nature of work posed difficult challenges for the labor movement, foreshadowing a rocky and uncertain future (see Figure 29.3).

The strength and influence of organized labor in this period were in part a by-product of its organizational unity. With the purge of Communists and communist-influenced unions in the late 1940s, the Congress of Industrial Organizations enjoyed more cordial relations with its old adversary, the American Fed-

eration of Labor. In 1955 Walter P. Reuther of the United Auto Workers led the CIO back into a formal alliance with the AFL. That merger created a single organization, the AFL-CIO, which represented more than 90 percent of the nation's 17.5 million union members. George Meany, a New York building-trades unionist, headed this organization for the next 24 years.

New priorities shaped labor-management relations after the war. Concerns about inflation and increased levels of consumption led unions to demand higher wages. Management agreed to contracts that gave many workers secure, predictable, and steadily rising incomes. In exchange, union leaders promised labor peace and stability, that is, fewer strikes. In 1950 General Motors (GM) and the United Automobile Workers signed a contract containing two novel provisions: an escalator clause providing that wages would be adjusted to reflect changes in the cost of living, and a productivity clause guaranteeing that wages would rise as productivity in the industry increased. Autoworkers won a guaranteed annual wage in 1955.

The GM contracts were typical in addressing union members' needs as consumers rather than workers. George Meany's goal was to ensure that labor got its share of the postwar prosperity. In return for higher wages and fringe benefits, workers put aside their traditional demands for control over the pace and duration of work and allowed technologically minded managers

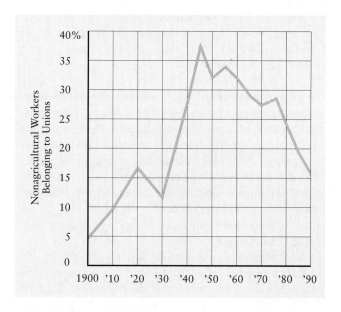

FIGURE 29.3

Labor Union Strength, 1900–1990
Labor unions reached their peak strength immediately after World War II. For the next thirty years they consistently represented more than a quarter of the nonfarm work force. But the influence of labor unions declined dramatically after 1975. (*Source:* AFL-CIO Information Bureau, Washington, D.C.)

to exert increasing control over their lives on the job.

But labor still had to fight for legitimacy in postwar society. The 1947 Taft-Hartley Act, which chipped away at some of the protections guaranteed by the 1935 National Labor Relations Act, represented the most virulent attack (see Chapter 28). Taft-Hartley showed that the New Deal labor reforms remained controversial a decade after their passage.

The Impact of Automation. Mechanization had long threatened skilled workers, but in the 1950s new technology also affected the jobs of unskilled and semiskilled factory workers, many of whom were union members. Thousands of workers lost their jobs in steel manufacturing, coal mining, automobile assembly, and other industries that were rapidly automating. The Ford Motor Company introduced automatic drilling machines at a Cleveland engine plant in 1952, requiring only 41 workers to do a job that formerly took 117. When the labor leader Walter Reuther inspected one of those automated engine plants, a Ford manager kidded him: "Well, you won't be able to collect dues from all these automated machines." Reuther replied, "What is bothering me is, how are you going to sell cars to all of these machines?" Reuther's reply was right on the mark. Unless workers earned enough income to continue buying consumer goods, the postwar economic boom would eventually come to an end.

New Recruits. With the reduction in the number of manufacturing jobs—organized labor's traditional constituency—the labor movement had to look elsewhere for new recruits. Large sectors of the work force remained unorganized in the postwar era, including many less skilled, often black or Latino, workers in the lower-paying service and agricultural sectors and the millions of secretaries and file clerks in the nation's offices, who were predominantly women. To maintain its strength, the union movement had to expand its industrial midwestern base into the southern and western states, areas of rapid economic growth that were traditionally antiunion. Organized labor also had to woo younger workers who now saw unions as part of management rather than as advocates of the rank and file. Finally, it had to branch out to organize white-collar employees in previously untapped professions such as teaching, nursing, and municipal services.

Organized labor met some, but not all, of these new challenges. Union organizing was most effective among workers in large bureaucratic organizations such as government, health care, and education. But labor made few gains in the smaller, scattered service operations where many of the lowest-paid workers toiled, and it could not break the hold of antiunion forces in the South. By the mid-1950s the labor movement had stalled, and union membership declined steadily afterward.

The Agricultural Sector

The agricultural sector also experienced a marked decline in the postwar period. In 1945 the nation's farm population numbered around 24 million, or 17.5 percent of the total population. Over the next twenty-five years, however, that figure dropped to under 10 million, or less than 5 percent of the population (see Table 29.1). The farm-to-city migration of some 14 million people during those years was the culmination of a long-term trend away from family farming and toward large-scale agribusiness.

Mechanization and corporate organization had become increasingly prevalent in American agriculture since the late nineteenth century. In the 1930s and 1940s there was a sharp decline in the supply of farm labor as New Deal agricultural programs accelerated the mechanization of farming and as defense mobilization for World War II lured rural dwellers to the cities. The continuing shortage of agricultural labor in the postwar era spurred American manufacturers to introduce new tractors, harvesters, and other farm machinery onto the market. New technology contributed to an astonishing increase in agricultural productivity after 1945, but it also required major capital investments. Between 1940 and 1955, the cost of fuel, fertilizer, and repairs for farm machines quadrupled, and total operating costs tripled. Family farms often lacked the capital

TABLE 29.1

Trends in American Farming, 1935–1992

	Number of Farms (thousands)	Farm Population (thousands)	Percent of Total Population
1935	6,814	32,161	25.3
1940	6,350	30,547	23.1
1945	5,967	24,420	17.5
1950	5,648	23,048	15.2
1956	4,514	18,712	11.1
1960	3,963	15,635	8.7
1965	3,356	12,363	6.4
1970	2,949	9,712	4.7
1975	2,521	8,864	4.2
1980	2,428	6,051	2.7
1985	2,293	5,355	2.4
1990	2,143	4,801	2.1
1992	2,093	4,665	1.8

Source: Gilbert Fite, *American Farmers* (Bloomington: Indiana University Press, 1981), 101 used by permission; *U.S. Statistical Abstract* (1993); and *Agricultural Statistics* (1994).

to compete with the large, technologically advanced farm units, and many families left the land.

Technological innovations transformed the lives of many of the farmers who remained on the land. They now managed specialized organizations—small factories that poured industrial materials into the land and extracted raw products for immediate sale. They relied on outside industrial sources for fertilizer, feed, seed, and pesticides and for the fuel they needed to run the expanding array of gasoline-powered equipment. These ties made farmers, like other businesspeople, increasingly dependent on national and international market conditions, scientific and technological developments, and federal farm policies such as prices supports, loans, and subsidies. The fuller integration of farmers into the national economy and the diminishing number of Americans who farmed greatly reduced the differences between rural and urban life.

A Suburban Society

Americans had been gravitating toward urban areas in large numbers throughout the twentieth century. In the postwar period the urbanization process was characterized by two new patterns: a shift away from older cities in the Northeast and Midwest toward newer urban centers in the South and West, and a mass defection from the cities to the suburbs.

In the 1950s all but one of the nation's twelve most populous cities lost population. The exception was Los Angeles, where vast tracts of undeveloped land allowed for suburban-style development. In the other eleven cities, the population of the metropolitan areas (suburbs and cities combined) showed a net gain. These same trends continued and intensified in the 1960s, draining population, jobs, and tax dollars away from older northern cities and toward newer suburbs and the emerging "Sun Belt."

The South and West

The growth of new metropolitan areas was most striking in the South and West, where a large proportion of the population had traditionally been rural and impoverished. Some of the most explosive urban and suburban growth occurred in Florida, Texas, and California (see Map 29.2). Between 1940 and 1970, Miami's metropolitan population increased by 79 percent with the addition of more than a million new residents, many of them older or retired. Texas cities grew as the petrochemical industry expanded rapidly after 1945. The oil and gas industries, together with the banks and law

firms that served them, were concentrated in Houston and Dallas, boosting their metropolitan populations by 76 and 66 percent, respectively. Other expanding cities included Atlanta, Baton Rouge, Long Beach (California), Mobile, and Phoenix. Overall, the South and West grew twice as fast as the Northeast did between 1940 and 1970.

California provides the most dramatic example of this growth, adding 2.6 million people in the 1940s and 3.1 million more in the 1950s. Much of the growth was spurred by the expansion of defense industries in the Los Angeles, San Francisco, and San Diego metropolitan areas (see Map 29.1). In 1970 California had about a tenth of the U.S. population, and in 1972 it replaced New York as the state with the largest number of electoral votes.

Boosters in California and other emerging Sun Belt states worked tirelessly to promote regional development. Local leaders lobbied for new defense installations and contracts, wooed scientific and artistic talent from the Northeast, and even purchased professional sports teams. In 1958, for example, investors moved the Brooklyn Dodgers to Los Angeles and the New York Giants to San Francisco. Boosters thus promoted their towns as "big-league" cities and touted the region's sunny climate, attractive landscapes, and relaxed lifestyles to attract new residents.

In subsequent decades, however, the success of Sun Belt cities raised new problems and challenges. Booming urban populations brought higher crime and poverty rates, making southern and western cities more like those in the Northeast. By the 1970s, in fact, Atlanta and Houston had homicide rates double those of New York. The sprawling suburban pattern of Sun Belt cities sometimes encroached on surrounding scenic areas, threatening the natural amenities that had attracted new residents.

In the West increasing demands for water and energy resulted in environmental and health problems. As arid southwestern cities competed for scarce water resources, they depleted underground aquifers and dammed scenic rivers. The proliferation of coal-burning power plants increased air pollution and scarred rural landscapes through strip mining. The nuclear industry, which brought jobs and income to the West, also brought radiation contamination to residents near atomic test sites, nuclear waste facilities, and uranium mines. In the West, as elsewhere, postwar economic development often carried a significant social cost.

The Growth of Suburbia

One postwar trend that all regions shared was the decisive shift in population from the central cities to the suburbs. At the end of World War II many cities had

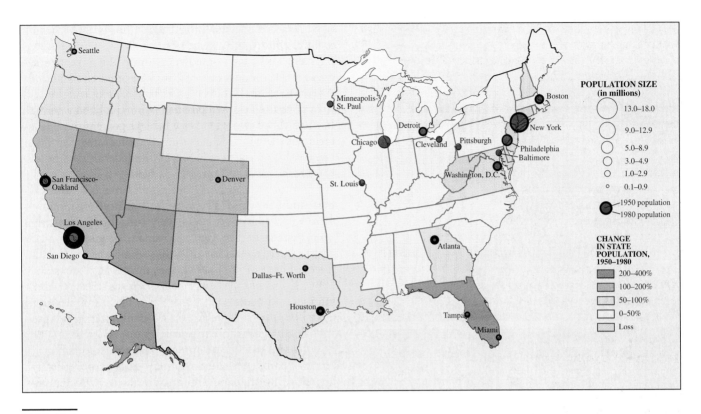

MAP 29.2

Metropolitan Growth, 1950–1980

A metropolitan area generally is defined as a central city that, in combination with its surrounding territory, forms an integrated economic and social unit. The U.S. Census Bureau introduced the "Standard Metropolitan Statistical Area" (SMSA) in 1950, but later changes in the definition of an SMSA make it difficult to generalize from the 1950 figures. This map compares the population of central cities in 1950 with population figures for the more broadly defined metropolitan areas in 1980 to illustrate the extent and geographical distribution of metropolitan growth in the postwar period.

pastures and working farms on their outskirts. Just five or ten years later those cities were surrounded by tract housing, factories, and shopping centers. By 1960 more Americans—particularly whites—lived in suburbs than in cities.

The Housing Boom. People flocked to the suburbs in part because they followed the available housing. Very little new housing had been built during the depression or war years, and the returning veterans and their families faced a critical housing shortage. There was a dramatic surge in construction in the late 1940s and 1950s. A fourth of all the housing in the country in 1960 had been built during the preceding decade, most of it single-family, owner-occupied homes.

The suburban housing market was revolutionized by a Long Island building contractor named Arthur Levitt, who applied mass production techniques to home construction. His company could build 150 homes per

week, a rate of one every sixteen minutes. Levitt's basic four-room house, complete with kitchen appliances and an attic that could be converted by a handy homeowner into two additional bedrooms, was priced at less than $10,000 in 1947. Levitt did not need to advertise; word of mouth brought more customers than his firm could handle.

Levitt built planned communities in New York, New Jersey, and Pennsylvania (all named, not surprisingly, Levittown). The developments attracted few old people and even fewer unmarried adults. Even the trees were young. Owners had to agree to cut their lawns once a week between April and November and not to hang out the laundry on weekends. When residents complained that the streets and houses were so similar that they could not find their way home, Levitt added variety in styles and site placements.

Soon other developers were snapping up the cheap farmland surrounding urban areas. On the West Coast,

The Trappings of Suburbia
With a ranch house, three cars in the driveway, and a rotary
lawn mower, this homeowner in Baton Rouge, Louisiana,
embodied the middle-class suburban life-style.

the former shipbuilding magnate Henry Kaiser moved
into housing construction in the postwar era, building
subdivisions in and around Los Angeles and San Francisco. Dozens of other developers followed suit, hastening the exodus from the farm and the central city.

Many families financed their homes with mortgages
from the Federal Housing Administration and the Veterans Administration. Before World War II, banks, primarily the savings and loan industry that served this
fairly stable market, usually demanded a 50 percent
down payment and granted no more than ten years to

pay back the balance. After the war the Federal Housing
Administration required only a 5 to 10 percent down
payment and gave homeowners up to thirty-year mortgages at the modest rate of 2 to 3 percent. The Veterans
Administration was even more lenient, requiring only a
token one dollar down payment from qualified veterans.
In 1955 those two agencies wrote 41 percent of all nonfarm mortgages. Such lending demonstrated the quiet
yet revolutionary way in which the federal government
was entering and influencing daily life.

The new suburban homes—and much of the savings and loan and Veterans Administration money—
were reserved almost exclusively for whites. Levittown
homeowners had to sign a covenant prohibiting occupation "by members of other than the Caucasian
Race"; Levitt did not sell houses directly to blacks until
1960. Even then the company carefully screened black
families and made sure that no two black families lived
next door to each other. Other communities adopted
similar covenants to exclude Jews or Asians. In *Shelley
v. Kraemer* (1948) the Supreme Court ruled that restrictive covenants were illegal, but the custom prevailed informally until the civil rights laws of the 1960s banned
private discrimination.

Even though suburbia was often portrayed as a homogeneous, even bland, environment, there were strong
cultural and class variations between suburbs. Older,
wealthy suburbs already occupied the most pleasant locations, including the hills north and west of Los Angeles, Chicago's North Shore, and the heights well to the
east of Cleveland's industrial Cuyahoga Flats. When
less affluent firefighters, plasterers, machine-tool makers, and sales clerks moved to the suburbs, they were far
more likely to move to a modest Levittown than to an
upper-middle-class suburb such as Winnetka, Illinois, or

The Suburban Boom
Hundreds of thousands of World War II
veterans took advantage of low-interest
loans under the G.I. Bill to purchase
new homes in suburban subdivisions
like this one in Los Angeles's San Fernando Valley. (Huntington Library, San
Marino, California, Whittington Collection)

Shaker Heights, Ohio. Blacks shut out of white suburbs established their own communities, such as Lincoln Heights outside Cincinnati, Robbins on the edge of Chicago, and Kinloch near St. Louis. In well-equipped living quarters at bargain prices, working-class and black families could share in the ultimate postwar suburban dream of giving "every kid an opportunity to grow up with grass stains on his pants."

Cars and Highways. Automobiles and highways were essential to this dramatic suburban growth. Suburbanites needed cars to get to work and to take their children to school and piano lessons. About 90 percent of suburban families owned cars, and 20 percent had more than one. In 1945 Americans owned 25 million cars; by 1965 the number had tripled to 75 million.

The car culture that emerged in the 1920s expanded dramatically during the 1950s, with cars becoming symbols of status and success. With gas plentiful and cheap at 15 cents a gallon, no one cared about fuel efficiency (8 miles to the gallon for the biggest gas guzzlers!). American cars became heavier and bigger, creating a disparity in size compared with Japanese or European models that still remains, despite the downsizing of American vehicles since the 1970s.

More cars required more highways, which were funded largely by the federal government. In 1947 Congress authorized the construction of 37,000 miles of highways; the National Interstate and Defense Highway Act of 1956 increased this commitment by another 42,500 miles. One of the largest civil engineering projects in world history, the new roads would be at least four lanes wide and would link the entire country in an integrated interstate system. Gas taxes and user fees for commercial vehicles provided the funding. Congressional supporters justified highway building on the grounds of civil defense at a time of growing anxiety about the Soviet nuclear threat (highways ostensibly would be used as evacuation routes). But its real purpose was to provide a transportation infrastructure for the diffuse pattern of urban and suburban development that characterized the postwar era.

The interstate system changed both the cities and the countryside. It rerouted traffic through rural areas, by-passing old main roads such as Route 1 on the eastern seaboard and the cross-country Route 66, and created new communities of gas stations, fast-food outlets, and motels at anonymous cloverleaf exchanges. In urban areas new highways cut wide swaths through old neighborhoods. Cities were soon plagued by the problems that cars brought to modern life: air pollution and traffic jams. Critics now complained about "autosclerosis," a hardening of the urban arteries.

The federally constructed highways also siphoned funding away from mass transit. Los Angeles, a city now largely dependent on freeways, had a viable mass transit system as late as the 1940s. The Highway Trust Fund set up in 1956 specifically prohibited the use of the fees it collected to promote urban mass transit. By 1960 two-thirds of Americans drove to work each day. The percentage was even higher—between 80 and 95 percent—in Los Angeles, Albuquerque, and Phoenix.

Highway construction had far-reaching effects on patterns of consumption and shopping. Instead of taking a train into the city or walking to a corner grocery store, people hopped into their cars and drove to suburban shopping malls and supermarkets. Although the first mall had appeared in the 1920s, there were only 8 in 1945; by 1960 the number had mushroomed to almost 4,000. When a 110-store complex at Roosevelt Field on suburban Long Island opened in 1956, it was conveniently situated at an expressway exit and had parking for 11,000 cars. Downtown retail areas and department stores soon declined.

Highways and suburbs also lured corporate business and manufacturing away from the cities. In the early 1950s Stanford University in Palo Alto, California, built one of the nation's first *industrial parks*, a suburban, campuslike facility for light manufacturing. Exploiting its ties with university researchers, Stanford Industrial Park attracted cold war defense contractors such as General Electric, Lockheed, and Hewlett-Packard. Those firms soon formed the nucleus of an electronic and high-tech region known as Silicon Valley. On the East Coast, a similar high-tech boom occurred outside Boston along Route 128, led by firms such as Polaroid and the Digital Equipment and Wang computer manufacturers. In the Midwest the number of factories in suburban Chicago doubled between 1947 and 1954, and suburban Detroit had a 220 percent increase.

The U.S. government's financing of highways and home building after World War II helped fuel a suburban explosion that was unique to North America. In war-ravaged European cities postwar housing construction was centered in high-density city neighborhoods or along mass transit lines. Not until the 1960s and 1970s would Europeans experiment with low-density suburban housing, and their central cities never declined as precipitously as American cities did.

State and Local Government. The burgeoning populations of metropolitan areas posed new challenges for state and local governments. Those government bureaucracies experienced rapid growth in the postwar period, requiring ever larger budgets (see Figure 29.4). State and local expenditures totaled $14 billion in 1946; in 1970 they rose to almost $150 billion. Employment climbed correspondingly. In 1970 roughly one in seven Americans in the labor force worked for a government bureaucracy, another example of the growth of the state.

FIGURE 29.4

*Federal, State, and Local
Government Employees, 1946–1970*
Although every level of government
added employees in this period, the
most dramatic growth took place in
local government—counties, cities, and
towns.

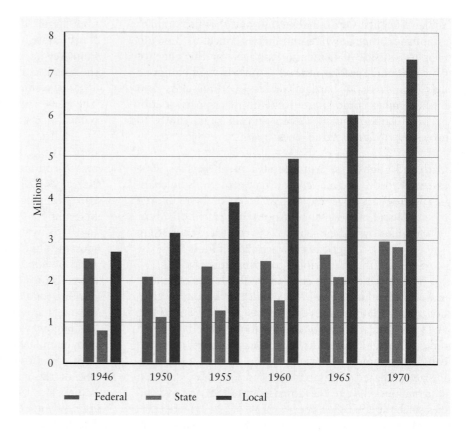

State and local revenues came from a variety of taxes. During the 1950s those governments relied on property and sales taxes for almost half their revenues; income taxes and federal aid were much less significant sources. State and local governments spent more money on education than on any other item, with expenditures for education taking up approximately one-third of most budgets in 1965. The rest went to welfare and social services (the second largest category), highways, health and hospitals, and other services.

Central cities and their surrounding suburban areas often had grossly unequal resources to meet local needs. Since the property tax provided a sizable part of local budgets, a wealthy community such as Grosse Pointe in the suburbs of Detroit could far more easily provide funds for first-rate schools and police departments than could the city of Detroit, whose tax base shrank as businesses and middle-class residents relocated to the suburbs. The disparity was greatest in older northeastern and midwestern cities, where decaying urban infrastructures (streets, sewers, and school buildings) required large-scale funding to repair or replace.

Although cities and their surrounding areas shared many of the same problems of urban life—sewage, traffic, pollution, crime, and fire hazards—existing forms of government did not readily allow for cooperation. Political fragmentation was the rule. There were more than 1,000 governmental units in the Chicago area and

1,400 in the New York City region. Suburban communities were reluctant to surrender their fiscal independence and tradition of local self-rule to huge cities with myriad social and economic problems. This political fragmentation reinforced the growing social and economic gap between city dwellers and their suburban neighbors.

The Other America

As middle-class whites flocked to the suburbs, a diverse group of poor and working-class migrants, many of them nonwhite, moved into the central cities. With jobs and financial resources flowing to the suburbs, urban newcomers inherited a declining economy and a decaying environment. This "other America" remained largely invisible to affluent white suburbanites. Only in the South, where African-Americans organized to combat legal segregation, did the problem of social injustice come to public attention.

Postwar Immigration

Newly arrived immigrants were one of several groups moving into the nation's cities in the postwar era. Until

1965 U.S. immigration policy followed the restrictive national origins quota system set up in 1924 (see Chapter 24). Such restrictions, for example, had limited the entry of Jews fleeing Nazi Germany. But World War II and its cold war aftermath led to a slight loosening of the law. The Chinese Exclusion Act was repealed in 1943 in a bow to America's wartime alliance with China, reflecting the growing realization that explicit racism was no longer tenable. The 1952 McCarran-Walter Act ended the exclusion of Japanese, Koreans, and southeast Asians from immigration and naturalization. At the height of the Cold War, Congress passed the measure to demonstrate to the world America's commitment to democracy. (The act, however, also banned the entry of Communists and other radicals.)

Foreign policy shaped immigration priorities in other ways. In 1945 Congress passed the War Brides Act, which allowed the entrance and naturalization of the wives and children of Americans, mainly servicemen, abroad. As a result of the Korean War, approximately 17,000 Koreans entered the United States between 1950 and 1965, the vast majority war brides. In recognition of the freeing of the Philippines from American control on July 4, 1946, Filipinos received their own quota. A major increase in immigration from Asian countries, however, would not occur until after 1965.

Changes in the immigration laws had a stabilizing impact on Asian immigrant communities. On the eve of World War II the Chinatowns in major cities were populated primarily by Chinese men. Though many of those men were married, their wives had remained in China. The repeal of the Chinese Exclusion Act, coupled with the granting of the right of naturalization to Chinese already here, encouraged those men to bring their wives to America. The result was a more balanced sex ratio, a pattern also seen in the Filipino-American and Japanese-American communities. Approximately 135,000 men and 100,000 women of Chinese origin were living in the United States in 1960, the majority of them in New York State and California.

Proposals to admit displaced persons and refugees from Europe were more controversial. Many Americans feared being swamped with immigrants from devastated Europe, including displaced Jews who could not or would not return to their former homelands. (In fact, most Jews headed to the newly established state of Israel, one of the few alternatives open to them.) Approximately 415,000 Europeans were admitted under the 1948 Displaced Persons Act, including a sizable number of former Nazis such as Wernher von Braun, whose expertise in rocket science was deemed essential to national security. The act was allowed to expire in 1952.

Latino Immigration. One of the largest groups of postwar migrants came from Mexico. Nearly 275,000 Mexi-cans came in the 1950s, and almost 444,000 in the 1960s. They moved primarily to western and southwestern cities such as Los Angeles, Long Beach, El Paso, and Phoenix, where they found jobs as migrant workers or in the expanding service sector. Large numbers of Mexican-Americans also settled in Chicago, Detroit, Kansas City, and Denver. Whereas most Mexican-Americans had lived in rural areas and engaged in agricultural work before World War II, by 1960 a majority were living in urban areas where they joined more settled communities of service and manufacturing workers.

The U.S. government had actively sought Mexican labor under the *bracero* program to ease labor shortages during World War II (see Chapter 27). The initiative was renewed in 1951, when the Korean War created new labor shortages. At its peak in 1959, 450,000 *braceros* entered the United States, accounting for one-quarter of the nation's seasonal workers. The *bracero* program was discontinued in 1964, but an estimated 350,000 postwar *braceros* settled permanently in the United States.

Even as the federal government invited Mexicans to enter the country as *braceros*, it deported those who stayed on illegally. In response to the recession of 1953–1954 and high unemployment throughout the nation, federal authorities deported nearly 4 million Mexicans under a program called "Operation Wetback." The level of illegal immigration was reduced for a few years before rising again after 1965.

Another major group of Spanish-speaking migrants came from the American-controlled territory of Puerto Rico. Residents of that island had been American citizens since 1917, and in 1952 Puerto Rico was granted commonwealth status. Thus, their migration was not affected by immigration laws. Migration increased dramatically after World War II, when the mechanization of the island's sugarcane industry pushed many rural Puerto Ricans off the land. When airlines began to offer cheap direct flights between San Juan and New York City (in the 1940s the fare was about $50, or two weeks' wages), Puerto Ricans became this country's first group to immigrate by air, not by sea.

Most Puerto Ricans went to New York, where they settled first in East ("Spanish") Harlem and then in other areas throughout the city's five boroughs. This massive migration, which grew from 70,000 in 1940 to 613,000 just twenty years later, transformed the ethnic composition of the city. More Puerto Ricans now lived in New York City than in San Juan. They faced conditions common to all recent immigrants: crowded and deteriorating housing, segregation, unemployment or restriction to menial jobs, poor schools, and the problems of a bilingual existence.

Cuban refugees constituted the third large group of Spanish-speaking immigrants. In the six years after Fidel Castro's seizure of power in 1959 an estimated 180,000 people fled Cuba for the United States. More refugees

West Side Story
In 1961 United Artists released the movie version of Leonard Bernstein's 1957 Broadway hit, *West Side Story*. The plot recast Shakespeare's *Romeo and Juliet* in a Puerto Rican neighborhood on New York's West Side in the 1950s. Confrontations between members of youth gangs and adult figures of authority, as pictured here in a still from the movie, were set to highly stylized song and dance routines.

came after 1965 with the establishment of a Havana-to-Miami airlift under an agreement between the Johnson administration and the Castro regime. The Cuban refugee community grew so quickly that it turned Miami into a cosmopolitan, bilingual city almost overnight. Unlike most new migrants to urban America, Miami's Cubans quickly prospered, in large part because they had arrived with more resources. They differed from most other Latino immigrants in that they were predominantly middle class and politically conservative.

Internal Migration. Internal migration also brought large numbers of people to the cities, especially African-Americans, continuing a trend that had begun during World War I (see Chapter 23). Black migration was hastened by the transformation of southern agriculture. New Deal agricultural policies and the development of synthetic fibers such as rayon and Dacron after World War II caused cotton acreage in the South to decline from 43 million acres in 1929 to less than 15 million in 1959. In addition, the ongoing mechanization of agriculture reduced the demand for farm labor. The mechanical cotton picker, introduced in 1944, further eroded the sharecropper system; it could pick 1,000 pounds an hour compared with the 20 pounds picked by an experienced hand. As a result of these changes, the southern farm population fell from 16.2 million in 1930 to 5.9 million in 1960. Although both whites and blacks left the land, the starkest decline was among black farmers. By 1990 there would be only 69,000 black farmers in the entire nation, just 1.5 percent of the country's farmers.

Where did they go? Some of the migrants settled in southern cities, where they obtained industrial jobs. White southerners from Appalachia moved north to "hillbilly" ghettos such as Cincinnati's Over the Rhine neighborhood and Chicago's Uptown. In the most dramatic population shift as many as 3 million blacks headed to Chicago, New York, Washington, Detroit, Los Angeles, and other cities between 1940 and 1960. Certain sections of Chicago seemed like the Mississippi Delta transplanted, so pervasive were the migrants. By 1960 about half the nation's black population was living outside the South, compared with only 23 percent before World War II.

Indian Relocation. In western cities, an influx of native Americans also contributed to the rise in the nonwhite urban population. Seeking to end federal involvement in Indian affairs, Congress passed a resolution in 1953 authorizing a program to terminate the legal standing of native tribes and move their members off reservations. The program reflected a cold war preoccupation with conformity and assimilation and enjoyed strong support from mining, timber, and agricultual interests that wanted to open those lands for private development. The Bureau of Indian Affairs encouraged voluntary migration to urban areas by subsidizing moving costs and establishing relocation centers in San Francisco, Denver, Chicago, and other cities. The relocation program proved problematic, as many Indians found it difficult to adjust to an urban environment and culture. Although the policy of forced termination was halted in 1958, some 60,000 Indians had moved to the cities by 1960. Despite the program's stated goal of assimilation, most native American migrants settled together in poor urban neighborhoods alongside other nonwhite groups.

American cities thus saw their nonwhite populations swell at the same time that whites were flocking to the suburbs. From 1950 to 1960 the nation's twelve

Claude Brown

Harlem: Dream and Reality

Claude Brown's *Manchild in the Promised Land* (1965) graphically described the conditions that awaited blacks when they journeyed to the "promised land" of Harlem in the postwar period. Brown dedicated the book to Eleanor Roosevelt, a benefactor of the Wiltwyck School for Boys, which helped troubled youths like Claude Brown break out of the ghetto.

Everybody I knew in Harlem seemed to have some kind of dream. I didn't have any dreams, not really. I didn't have any dreams for hitting the number. I didn't have any dreams for getting a big car or a fine wardrobe. I bought expensive clothes because it was a fad. It was the thing to do, just to show that you had money. I wanted to be a part of what was going on, and this was what was going on.

I didn't have any dreams of becoming anything. All I knew for certain was that I had my fears. I suppose just about everybody else knew the same thing. They had their dreams, though, and I guess that's what they had over me. As time went by, I was sorry for the people whose dreams were never realized.

When Butch was alive, sometimes I would go uptown to see him. He'd be sick. He'd be really messed up. I'd give him some drugs, and then he'd be more messed up than before. He wouldn't be sick, but I couldn't talk to him, I couldn't reach him. He'd be just sitting on a stoop nodding. Sometimes he'd be slobbering over himself.

I used to remember Butch's dream. Around 1950, he used to dream of becoming the best thief in Harlem. It wasn't a big dream. To him, it was a big dream, but I don't suppose too many people would have seen it as that. Still, I felt sorry for him because it was his dream. I suppose the first time he put the spike in his arm every dream he'd ever had was thrown out the window. Sometimes I wanted to shout at him or snatch him by the throat and say, "Butch, what about your dream?" But there were so many dreams that were lost for a little bit of duji [heroin]. . . .

I used to feel that I belonged on the Harlem streets and that, regardless of what I did, nobody had any business to take me off the streets.

I remember when I ran away from shelters, places that they sent me to, here in the city. I never ran away with the thought in mind of coming home. I always ran away to get back to the streets. I always thought of Harlem as home, but I never thought of Harlem as being in the house. To me, home was the streets. I suppose there were many people who felt that. If home was so miserable, the street was the place to be. I wonder if mine was really so miserable, or if it was that there was so much happening out in the street that it made home seem such a dull and dismal place.

When I was very young—about five years old, maybe younger—I would always be sitting out on the stoop. I remember Mama telling me and Carole to sit on the stoop and not to move away from in front of the door. Even when it was time to go up and Carole would be pulling on me to come upstairs and eat, I never wanted to go, because there was so much out there in that street.

You might see somebody get cut or killed. I could go out in the street for an afternoon, and I would see so much that, when I came in the house, I'd be talking and talking for what seemed like hours. Dad would say, "Boy, why don't you stop that lyin'? You know you didn't see all that. You know you didn't see nobody do that." But I knew I had.

Source: Claude Brown, *Manchild in the Promised Land* (New York: Macmillan, 1965), 427–429.

---

largest cities lost 3.6 million whites while gaining 4.5 million nonwhites. This trend continued in the 1960s as urban decay and racial fears accelerated white flight to the suburbs.

Urban Neighborhoods, Urban Poverty

By the time that blacks, native Americans, and Latinos moved into the inner cities, urban America was in poor shape. Housing continued to be a crucial problem. City planners, politicians, and real-estate developers responded to that dilemma with *urban renewal* programs, razing blighted city neighborhoods to make way for modern construction projects. Local residents were rarely consulted about whether they wanted their neighborhoods "renewed." Urban renewal often produced grim high-rise housing projects that destroyed feelings of neighborhood pride and created anonymous open areas that were vulnerable to crime. Between 1949 and 1967 urban renewal demolished almost 400,000 buildings and displaced 1.4 million people.

Urban renewal projects often benefited the wealthy at the expense of the poor. Many downtown "revitalization" projects replaced established racial-ethnic neighborhoods with expensive rental housing or office buildings where suburban commuters worked. Boston's West End, a poor but flourishing Italian community, was

The Dreary Deadlock of Public Housing

As federal funding for public housing dwindled in the early 1950s, some local housing authorities economized by building acres of grim high-rise housing projects that destroyed old neighborhoods and created vacant spaces that proved vulnerable to street crime.

razed by a private developer between 1958 and 1960 to build Charles River Park, an apartment complex whose rents were far too steep for the old residents. In San Francisco some 4,000 residents of the Western Addition, a predominantly black neighborhood, were displaced under an urban renewal program that built luxury housing, a shopping center, and an express boulevard. In both cities residents were forced into less desirable parts of the city, cut off from the vitality of their former neighborhoods. The 575,000 units of public housing built nationwide by 1964 came nowhere close to satisfying the need for affordable urban housing.

Postwar cities were increasingly becoming a place of last resort for the nation's poor. Unlike earlier immigrants, for whom cities were gateways to social and economic betterment, inner-city residents in the postwar period faced diminishing hopes for improvement (see American Voices, page 909). Lured by the promise of plentiful jobs, migrants found that many of those opportunities had relocated to the suburban fringe. Steady employment was out of reach for those who needed it most.

The poor were also trapped in the cities because of racism. Migrants to the city, especially blacks, faced racial hostility and institutional barriers to mobility. Two separate Americas were emerging: a white society in suburbs and peripheral areas, and an inner city populated by blacks, Latinos, and other disadvantaged groups.

Black Activism in the South

In the South black Americans faced not only urban poverty but legal segregation as well. In most southern states in the 1950s it was illegal for whites and blacks to eat in the same rooms in restaurants and luncheonettes,

use the same waiting rooms and toilet facilities at bus and train stations, or ride in the same taxis. All forms of public transportation were rigidly segregated by custom or by law. Even drinking fountains were labeled "White" and "Colored."

Beginning with World War II, the National Association for the Advancement of Colored People (NAACP) redoubled its efforts to combat segregation (see Chapter 27). Throughout the 1940s NAACP lawyers Thurgood Marshall and William Hastie litigated a series of test cases challenging segregation in housing, transportation, and other areas.

Brown v. Board of Education. In 1954 the Supreme Court handed down one of its most far-reaching decisions in a group of challenges to school segregation, consolidated as *Brown v. Board of Education of Topeka, Kansas*. The NAACP had filed the Topeka case on behalf of Linda Brown, a black student who attended a segregated school several miles from her home rather than the nearby white elementary school. The NAACP's chief counsel, Thurgood Marshall, argued that the legal segregation mandated by the Topeka Board of Education was inherently unconstitutional because it stigmatized an entire race and thereby denied it the "equal protection of the laws" guaranteed by the Fourteenth Amendment. In a unanimous decision announced on May 17, 1954, the Supreme Court agreed, overturning the "separate but equal" doctrine of *Plessy v. Ferguson* (see Chapter 19). Speaking for the Court, Chief Justice Earl Warren ruled:

> To separate Negro children . . . solely because of their race generates a feeling of inferiority as to their status in the community that may affect their hearts and minds in a way unlikely ever to be undone. . . . We

conclude that in the field of public education the doctrine of "separate but equal" has no place. Separate educational facilities are inherently unequal. . . . Any language in *Plessy v. Ferguson* contrary to these findings is rejected.

In response to NAACP suits over the next several years, the Supreme Court used the *Brown* precedent to overturn segregation in city parks, public beaches and golf courses, all forms of interstate and intrastate transportation, and public housing. Meanwhile, progress in desegregating schools was frustratingly slow. In a 1955 decision implementing the Topeka decision known as *Brown II*, the Court declared simply that integration should proceed "with all deliberate speed." Many critics would later note that the deliberation was far more evident than the speed.

When it became clear that the Court was not going to back down on civil rights, white resistance solidified. In 1956, 101 members of Congress signed a Southern Manifesto denouncing the *Brown* decision as "a clear abuse of judicial power" and encouraging their constituents to defy it. In that year 500,000 southerners joined White Citizens' Councils dedicated to blocking school integration and other civil rights measures. Some whites revived the old tactics of violence and intimidation, swelling the ranks of the Ku Klux Klan to levels not seen since the 1920s.

So far Eisenhower had accepted the *Brown* decision as the law of the land but had not committed federal power to enforcing it. A crisis in Little Rock, Arkansas, finally forced him to intervene, although reluctantly, on the side of desegregation. In September 1957 nine black students attempted to enroll at the all-white Central High School after the local school board won a court order to implement a desegregation plan. Governor Orval Faubus called out the National Guard to bar them, despite the court order. Then the mob took over. Every day a white crowd taunted the poised but obviously terrified black students with chants such as "Go back to the jungle." As the vicious scenes were replayed on television night after night, Eisenhower reluctantly decided to act. He sent 1,000 federal troops to Little Rock and nationalized 10,000 members of the Arkansas National Guard, ordering them to protect the students. Eisenhower thus became the first president since Reconstruction to use federal troops to enforce the rights of blacks.

The *Brown* decision had shown that the NAACP's strategy of judicial challenge could bring fundamental change, but the magnitude of white resistance to integration had also made it clear that winning in court was not enough. A new strategy was needed to challenge the pervasive racism and segregation that persisted in practice if not in law. Sparked by one tiny but monumental act of defiance, southern black leaders embraced nonviolent protest.

Integration at Little Rock
Angry crowds taunted the nine black students who tried to register in 1957 at the previously all-white Central High School in Little Rock, Arkansas, with chants such as "Two-four-six-eight, we ain't gonna integrate." The court-ordered integration proceeded only after President Eisenhower reluctantly nationalized the Arkansas National Guard.

The Montgomery Bus Boycott. On December 1, 1955, Rosa Parks, a seamstress and a member of the NAACP in Montgomery, Alabama, refused to give up her seat on a city bus to a white man. She was promptly arrested and charged with violating a local segregation ordinance. "I felt it was just something I had to do," Parks stated. Although Parks was hardly the first black southerner to challenge Jim Crow laws, her upstanding social reputation and political connections soon made her case a cause célèbre in the black community.

As the local black community met to discuss the proper response, it turned to the Reverend Martin Luther King, Jr., who had become the pastor at Montgomery's Dexter Street Baptist Church the year before. The son of a prominent black minister in Atlanta, King had received a B.A. from Morehouse College and a Ph.D. in theology from Boston University. King later embraced the teachings of Mahatma Gandhi, who had organized the brilliant campaigns of passive resistance that had led to India's independence from Britain in 1947. After Parks's arrest, King endorsed a plan by a local black women's organization to boycott Montgomery's bus system until it was integrated.

For the next 381 days a united black community formed car pools or walked to work. The bus company neared bankruptcy, and downtown stores complained about the loss of business. But not until the Supreme Court ruled in November 1956 that bus segregation was unconstitutional did the city of Montgomery finally comply. "My feets is tired, but my soul is rested," said one woman boycotter.

The Montgomery bus boycott catapulted King to national prominence. In 1957, with the Reverend Ralph Abernathy and other southern black clergy, he founded the Southern Christian Leadership Conference (SCLC), based in Atlanta. The black church had long been the center of African-American social and cultural life. Now it lent its moral and organizational strength, as well as the voices of its most inspirational preachers, to the civil rights movement. Black churchwomen were one of the movement's strongest constituencies, transferring the skills that they had honed through years of church work to the fight for racial change. The SCLC joined the NAACP as one of the main advocacy groups for racial justice. Even though these groups achieved only limited victories in the 1950s, they laid the organizational groundwork for the dynamic civil rights movement that would emerge in the 1960s.

American Society during the Baby Boom

While black southerners confronted racial prejudice and violence, the lives of most white Americans during those years were more sedate. For much of the white middle class, the postwar era was a period of tranquillity as Americans turned inward to home and family. Couples flocked to the new suburban developments, where they had more children per family than at any time since 1920. They raised their families in a climate of affluence that spawned a pervasive culture of consumption and conformity.

Consumer Culture

As we have seen, prosperity and affluence were a reality for many Americans in the postwar years. In some respects the consumer culture of the 1950s seemed like a return to the 1920s—an overabundance of new gadgets and appliances, the expansion of consumer credit and advertising, more leisure time, the growing importance of the automobile, and the development of new types of mass media—yet there was a significant difference. The postwar economy was far better balanced than that of the 1920s; there was no depressed agricultural sector to detract from the general prosperity. By the 1950s consumption had become a hallmark of middle-class culture. Because of rising incomes, even blue-collar families had discretionary income to spend on consumer goods.

As in the 1920s, though, prosperity was helped along by a dramatic increase in consumer credit, which enabled families to stretch their incomes. Between 1946 and 1958 short-term consumer credit rose from $8.4

billion to almost $45 billion, much of it in the form of car loans. The Diners Club credit card, introduced in 1950 and followed by the American Express card and Bank Americard in 1959, was initially geared toward the business traveler. But by the 1970s the ubiquitous plastic credit cards had revolutionized personal and family finances.

Advertising. With the greater availability of credit, product makers sought to stimulate consumer demand through more aggressive advertising. In 1951 businesses spent more on advertising ($6.5 billion) than taxpayers did on primary and secondary education ($5 billion); advertising expenditures topped $10 billion in 1960. The 1950s gave Americans the Marlboro man; M&M's that melt in your mouth, not in your hand; the Hathaway eye patch; Wonder Bread to build strong bodies in twelve ways; and the "does she or doesn't she?" Clairol woman. Motivational research delved into the subconscious to suggest how the messages should be pitched.

Landmark for Hungry Americans
Conveniently located on major highways and in shopping centers, Howard Johnson's Motor Lodges and Restaurants (colloquially referred to as HoJos) were instantly recognizable by their bright orange roofs. Like the McDonald's Golden Arches, those roofs became familiar roadside beacons for travelers and suburbanites alike.

The ads of the period reflected an uncritical view of American life that suggested falsely that all Americans were white and middle class, all women were homemakers, and all families were nuclear and intact.

Automobiles continued to be the most heavily advertised item in the 1950s, but advertising also promoted a variety of new consumer appliances to fill the suburban home. Many appliances had been unavailable during the war; others were new to the postwar market. In 1946 automatic washing machines replaced the old machines with hand-cranked wringers, and electric dryers also came on the market that year. In 1955, 1.2 million dryers were sold, twice the 1953 total, and commercial laundries across the country struggled to stay in business. Another new item on the market was the home freezer, which enabled families to eat seasonal foods, such as fruits and vegetables, all year and encouraged the dramatic growth of the frozen-food industry. Partly because of the purchase of electrical gadgets for the home, consumer use of electricity doubled during the 1950s.

Leisure Time. Consumers had more free time in which to spend their money than ever before. In 1960 the average worker put in a five-day week, with eight paid holidays a year (double the 1946 standard) plus a paid two-week vacation. The travel industry grew rapidly during the 1950s, with Americans devoting a seventh of the GNP to spending on leisure and entertainment. Americans took to the interstate highway system by the millions, encouraging the dramatic growth of motel chains, roadside restaurants, and fast-food eateries. (The first McDonald's restaurant opened in 1954 in San Bernardino, California; the Holiday Inn motel chain started in Memphis in 1952.) Among the most popular destinations were national and state parks and Disneyland, which opened in Anaheim, California, in 1955. Aided by the strong U.S. dollar and the introduction of jet air travel in 1958, families flooded Europe each summer, earning the unflattering epithet of "ugly Americans" because they expected things to be just like home.

Television

Americans also engaged in new leisure activities at home, television watching being the most popular. TV's leap to cultural prominence was swift and overpowering. There were only ten broadcasting stations in the country and a meager 7,000 sets in American homes in 1947. But in 1948 the CBS and NBC radio networks began offering regular programming on television. Just two years later Americans had purchased 7.3 million TV sets. By 1960, 87 percent of American families had at least one television set.

Television developed as a government-controlled or subsidized service in other countries, but in the United States it emerged as private enterprise geared toward entertainment. Although stations were licensed by the Federal Communications Commission after 1941, television, like radio, depended entirely on advertising and corporate sponsorship for profits. Soon television supplanted radio as the chief diffuser of popular culture. Movies, too, lost the cultural predominance they had enjoyed from the 1920s through the 1940s. Movie attendance shrank throughout the postwar period, and studios increasingly relied on overseas distribution of American films to earn a profit.

At first television brought people together at a neighbor's home or perhaps in a local tavern to watch the World Series or a political convention, but soon it had the opposite effect, isolating and atomizing leisure in the private home. Television fostered a mass national culture far more completely than radio had in the 1920s. Its national network programming promoted homogeneity and reduced regional and ethnic differences (the first live nationwide broadcast, the signing of the peace treaty ending the American military occupation of Japan, occurred in 1951). Viewers had only three or four channels to choose from; public television did not begin until 1967, and cable was a phenomenon of the 1980s.

Television encouraged the consumerism and advertising that have characterized mass culture since the 1920s. As in the golden era of radio in the 1920s and 1930s, corporations produced and sponsored major television shows such as the "Texaco Star Theater" with Milton Berle, the "Camel News Caravan" with John Cameron Swayze, and the "General Electric Theater" hosted by Ronald Reagan. New items entered the home, such as frozen TV dinners of turkey, peas, and mashed potatoes, first introduced in 1954. Now a family could eat a meal in front of the television without having to talk. *TV Guide*, founded in television's breakthrough year of 1948, became the most successful new periodical of the 1950s. Television even affected city services. In 1954 the Toledo water commissioner wondered why water consumption rose dramatically during certain three-minute periods. The answer? All across Toledo, TV watchers flushed their toilets during commercials.

What Americans saw on television, besides the omnipresent commercials, was an overwhelmingly white, Anglo-Saxon world of nuclear families, suburban homes, and middle-class life. A typical show was "Father Knows Best," starring Robert Young and Jane Wyatt. Father left home each morning wearing a suit and carrying a briefcase. Mother was a full-time housewife, always available to and actively interested in her three children but also prone to stereotypical feminine behavior such as bad driving and bursting into tears. The children engaged in amusing antics and harmless rebellion, but family conflicts were invariably resolved. Shows such as "The Honeymooners," starring Jackie Gleason as a Brooklyn bus

"The Honeymooners"
Sewer worker Ed Norton (left, played by Art Carney) and bus driver Ralph Kramden (Jackie Gleason) joust in an episode from the popular television series "The Honeymooners." When Alice Kramden (played by Audrey Meadows) tried to get a word in edgewise, Ralph's reply was likely to be, "One of these days, Alice, one of these days, pow! Right in the kisser!"

driver, and "Life of Reilly," a situation comedy featuring a California aircraft worker, were rare in their treatment of working-class lives. Nonwhite characters appeared mainly as servants, such as Jack Benny's Rochester.

Probably the most popular situation comedy of the 1950s was "I Love Lucy," which revolved around the adventures of a wacky housewife and her Cuban-born bandleader husband, portrayed by Lucille Ball and Desi Arnaz. Because they were married in real life as well as on television, the show even incorporated Lucy's pregnancy into the story line. Twice as many Americans—44 million, the figure courtesy of the new sampling firm of A. C. Nielsen—watched the 1956 show where Lucy had her baby as watched the inauguration of President Dwight Eisenhower the next day. The couple later divorced, but off screen.

The types of television programs developed in the 1950s built on older entertainment genres but also pioneered new ones. Taking over a popular radio and movie category, television offered some thirty westerns by 1959, including "Gunsmoke," "Wagon Train," and "Bonanza," the first color show. National television coverage made professional sports big-time entertainment and big business—far exceeding the potential of radio. Programming geared to children, such as Walt Disney's "Mickey Mouse Club," "Howdy Doody," and "Captain Kanga-

roo," created the first generation of children to grow up glued to the tube. The appeal of popular quiz shows such as "Twenty-One" and "The $64,000 Question" was not diminished even when it was revealed in 1959 that contestants had received the questions in advance. Although the new medium did offer some serious programming, notably live theater and documentaries, Federal Communications Commissioner Newton Minow concluded in 1963 that television was "a vast wasteland." Its reassuring images of family life and postwar society, however, dovetailed with the social expectations of many American families.

The Baby Boom

The dislocations of the depression and war years made both men and women yearn for material and psychological security and a return to traditional values. A popular 1945 song was called "Gotta Make Up for Lost Time," and Americans did just that. The postwar generation approached life with an optimism and confidence notably absent from the depression generation of the 1930s. The GI Bill and other federal programs aided their quest for unprecedented levels of material security, as did the general prosperity of the postwar era. As usual, those options were far more available to the white middle class than to minorities.

Such individual life choices were taking place against the backdrop of the Cold War. The historian Elaine Tyler May used the formulation "cold war, warm hearth" to capture how home and family seemed to offer a secure, private retreat from the Cold War and the atomic age. As Richard Nixon argued in the kitchen debate with Nikita Khrushchev, stable suburban families would provide a bulwark against the Soviet threat.

Two things were noteworthy about the men and women who formed families between 1940 and 1960. First, their marriages were remarkably stable. Not until the mid-1960s did the divorce rate begin to rise sharply. Second, they were intent on having children. Everyone expected to have two or more children—it was part of adulthood, almost a citizen's responsibility. After a century and a half of declining family size, the birth rate shot up: more babies were born between 1948 and 1953 than were born in the previous thirty years (see Figure 29.5). As a result, the American population rose dramatically from 140 million in 1945 to 179 million in 1960 and to 203 million in 1970.

There are several reasons for this twenty-year upsurge that demographers call the *baby boom*. Because a sustained rise in the birth rate did not occur in all the countries affected by World War II, it was not simply a response to the losses of war. More important was the drop in the marriage age, a trend that had begun during the war. The average age at marriage fell to twenty-two

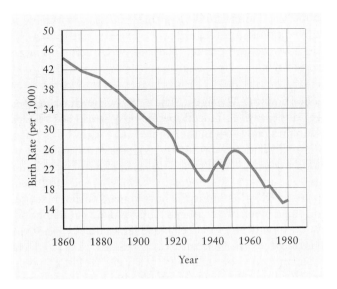

FIGURE 29.5

The Declining American Birth Rate, 1860–1980
When birth rates are viewed over more than a century, the postwar baby boom was clearly an aberration.

for men and twenty for women; in 1951 a third of all women were married by age nineteen. The drop in the marriage age resulted in a surge of young married couples who produced a bumper crop of children.

Even though younger couples were having babies earlier, they were not necessarily having huge numbers of children. Women who came of age in the 1930s had an average of 2.4 children; their counterparts in the 1950s averaged 3.2 children. What made the baby boom happen was that everyone was having children at the same time. This explosion in fertility peaked in 1957 and remained at a high level until the early 1960s. Since the 1960s the birth rate has generally declined, returning to earlier long-term patterns. The postwar baby boom was thus a departure from the norm.

Increased Life Expectancy. A declining death rate also contributed to population growth. Life expectancy at birth had improved steadily over the first half of the twentieth century, from forty-seven years in 1900 to sixty-three years in 1940. Continued improvements in diet, public health, and medical practices further lengthened the life span to seventy-one years in 1970. So did "miracle drugs" such as penicillin (introduced in 1943), streptomycin (1945), and cortisone (1946). When Dr. Jonas Salk perfected a polio vaccine in 1954, he became a national hero. The free distribution of Salk's vaccine in the nation's schools, followed in 1961 by Dr. Albert Sabin's oral polio vaccine, demonstrated the potential of government-sponsored public health programs. The conquest of polio made the children of the 1950s one of the healthiest generations ever.

"Scientific" Child-Rearing. To rear all those baby-boom children and keep them healthy, middle-class parents increasingly relied on the advice of experts. Dr. Benjamin Spock's best-selling *Baby and Child Care* sold a million copies a year after its publication in 1946. Spock urged mothers to abandon the rigid feeding and baby care schedules of an earlier generation. New mothers found Spock's commonsense approach liberating, but it did not totally soothe their insecurities. If mothers were too protective of their children, Spock and others argued, they might hamper their adjustment to a normal adult life. Mothers who wanted to work outside the home felt guilty because Spock recommended that they be constantly available to respond to their children's needs.

The baby boom had a broad and immediate impact on American society. The consumer needs of all those babies fueled the economy as families bought food, diapers, toys, and clothing for their expanding broods. Family spending on consumer goods joined federal expenditures on national security in fueling the unparalleled prosperity and economic growth of the 1950s and 1960s.

The baby boom also prompted a major expansion of the nation's educational system. The new middle class, America's first college-educated generation, placed a high value on education. Suburban parents approved 90 percent of proposed school bond issues during the 1950s. By 1970 school expenditures accounted for 7.2 percent of the gross national product, double the 1950 level.

Polio Pioneers
These Provo, Utah, children each received a "Polio Pioneer" souvenir button for participating in the trial of the Salk vaccine in 1954. Dr. Jonas Salk's announcement the next year that the vaccine was safe and effective made him a national hero.

The postwar baby boom would have a continuing impact on America for many decades. In the 1960s the baby-boom generation swelled college enrollments and, not coincidentally, the ranks of student protesters. By the 1970s, when the baby-boom generation entered the workplace, it had to compete for a limited number of jobs in what had become a stagnant economy. The delayed marriages and later childbearing of the career-oriented baby boomers temporarily caused the birth rate to rise again in the 1980s. And in the 1990s the aging of that group prompted widespread concerns about the future viability of old-age assistance programs such as Social Security and Medicare. The decisions made by many couples in the immediate postwar period to have large families will continue to affect American life well into the twenty-first century.

Contradictions in Women's Lives

"The suburban housewife was the dream image of the young American woman," the feminist Betty Friedan has said of the 1950s. "She was healthy, beautiful, educated, concerned only about her husband, her children, and her home." Friedan gave up a psychology fellowship and a career as a journalist to marry, move to the suburbs, and raise three children. "Determined that I

Home Life: One Reality
This young mother in New Rochelle, a suburb of New York City, was photographed in 1955. Her frenzied situation hints at why 24,000 American women responded to a 1960 *Redbook* magazine article entitled "Why Young Mothers Feel Trapped."

find the feminine fulfillment that eluded my mother . . . I lived the life of a suburban housewife that was everyone's dream at the time," she said (see American Voices, page 917).

The Feminine Mystique. The 1950s were characterized by a pervasive, indeed pernicious, insistence that a woman's place was in the home. There was nothing new about this idea. What Betty Friedan called the "feminine mystique" of the 1950s—that "the highest value and the only commitment for women is the fulfillment of their own femininity"—bore remarkable similarities to the nineteenth-century's cult of true womanhood. But women's lives had changed dramatically since the nineteenth century because of increased access to education and jobs, a declining birth rate, and the greater availability of consumer goods and services. It was much harder to persuade women to stay at home in the 1950s than it had been in the 1850s. In fact, the shrillness with which the message of domesticity was proclaimed represented a reaction to how far women had already strayed from total identification with the home.

The updated version of the cult of domesticity drew on new elements of twentieth-century science and culture, even Freudian psychology, to give it more force. Psychologists equated motherhood with "normal" female sex role identification and berated mothers who worked outside the home. Television, popular music, films, and advertising reinforced that notion by depicting career women as social and sexual misfits. The postwar consumer culture also emphasized women's domestic role as purchasing agent for home and family. "Love is said in many ways," ran an ad for toilet paper. Another asked, "Can a woman ever feel right cooking on a dirty range?"

Although the feminine mystique held cultural sway in the postwar period, not all housewives were as unhappy or as neurotic as Friedan later implied in her 1963 best seller, *The Feminine Mystique.* Many working-class women embraced their new roles as housewives; unlike their mothers and unmarried sisters, they were not compelled to take low-paid employment outside the home. Middle-class wives found constructive outlets for their energy in groups such as the League of Women Voters, the PTA, and the Junior League. As in earlier periods, some women used the rhetoric of domesticity and maternalism to justify political activism, which in this period involved issues of community improvement, racial integration, and nuclear disarmament.

More fundamentally, not all American families could, or did, live by the norms of suburban domesticity. Such ideals were out of reach or totally irrelevant to many racial minorities, inner-city residents, recent immigrants, rural Americans, and homosexuals. Once again there was a significant gap between popular culture and the reality of American lives.

Joy Wilner

A Fifties Housewife

Like millions of middle-class women in the 1950s, Joy Wilner married an ambitious young professional and had children in quick succession. In this passage she recounts the joys and frustrations of her early years of marriage and motherhood and her struggle to accommodate herself to what Betty Friedan has termed the *feminine mystique*.

I felt totally fulfilled, totally happy. We were the perfect couple—Ted was supportive of me and I was supportive of him and we never argued. Well, we didn't know how. We'd had no experience with conflict. Everything was fine. I had my next child sixteen months after the first. The second child was neither exactly planned nor unplanned. I didn't really intend to get pregnant again, but on the other hand, we weren't using birth control because, after all, we already had *one*. . . .

After the second baby, that was the first time I can remember conflict, feelings of being trapped, wondering what I was doing with my life. These weren't very distinct feelings, not like I wonder if this is the right man for me. Just uncomfortable feelings. At some point I expressed some of these feelings, in a very tentative way, to Ted and he said, "Well, if you feel that way, maybe we should get a divorce." I was terrified. The idea of divorce was inconceivable. I never mentioned the subject again.

At the same time, I got such pleasure, real physiological pleasure, from my children—from playing with them, feeding them, watching them develop. Then we moved and Ted went into general practice, and at about the same time I had another child. I became his secretary, his nurse, and I was also handling the children, keeping them out of

his hair. And of course, we were also establishing our identity as the doctor and his wife, so there was a lot of socializing. It was a busy time.

What amazes me now is that it never occurred to me not to do this. His career was just my life. There came a time when I felt I didn't have the strength for all this and I started breaking down. I can remember going into the shower and screaming—in the shower so that no one could hear me. Even then I didn't have conscious thoughts of "I hate this life"—I didn't think there was anything objectively wrong with the way I was living, just that I couldn't take it any more.

Source: Brett Harvey, ed., *The Fifties: An Oral History* (New York: HarperCollins, 1993), 103–104.

Women at Work. Another contradictory aspect of postwar culture was that at the height of the feminine mystique more than one-third of American women held jobs outside the home. As the service sector expanded, there was a steady demand for workers in fields traditionally filled by women. The economist Eli Ginzberg called the dramatic rise in the number and kind of women who worked for pay outside the home "the single most outstanding phenomenon of our century."

The increase in the number of working women coincided with another change of equal significance—the dramatic rise in the number of older, married middle-class women who took jobs. At the turn of the century the typical female worker was a young recent immigrant who worked only until she married. By mid-century the typical woman worker was in her forties, married, and had children in school. In 1940 only 15 percent of wives worked; that proportion had doubled by 1960 and reached 40 percent by 1970.

Many women entered the paid labor force to supplement the family income and keep pace with rising standards of living. The wages that many men earned even in the prosperous 1950s and 1960s could not pay

for all the necessities of middle-class life: cars, houses, vacations, and a college education for the children. Poorer households needed more than one wage earner just to get by.

How could the society of the 1950s so steadfastly uphold the domestic ideal while an increasing number of wives and mothers took jobs? In many ways the dramatic increase was kept invisible by the women themselves. Fearing public disapproval of their decisions, such women usually justified their work in individual or family-oriented terms: "Of course I believe a woman's place is at home, but I took this job to save for college for our children." Moreover, when women took jobs outside the home, they still bore full responsibility for child care and household management, and this allowed families and society to avoid facing the implications of women's new roles. As one overburdened woman noted, she now had "two full-time jobs instead of just one—underpaid clerical worker and unpaid housekeeper."

Women unionists, particularly those in the female-dominated service occupations, sought to ease this double burden by pushing for part-time schedules, employer-sponsored child care, and paid maternity leave. They were partly successful in securing their demands in fields such as nursing, where women's labor was in heavy demand. They did not, however, challenge the sexual division of the work force or question the belief that women should shoulder the bulk of domestic responsibilities. The absence of an active feminist movement in the 1940s and 1950s left most women to cope on their own.

Youth Culture

In 1956, only partly in jest, the CBS radio commentator Eric Sevareid questioned "whether the teenagers will take over the United States lock, stock, living room, and garage." Sevareid captured the sense of shock and anxiety felt by many Americans whose children were rebelling against the safe and insulated suburban world that their parents had worked so hard to create. The centrality of youth culture to modern times, a trend first noticed in the 1920s, had its roots in the democratization of education, the growth of peer culture, and the growing consumer independence of teenagers in an age of affluence. Like so much else in the 1950s, the youth culture came down to having money.

Market research convinced advertisers of the existence of a distinct teen market in the 1950s. A 1951 *Newsweek* story noted with awe that the $3 weekly spending money of the average teen was enough to buy 190 million candy bars, 130 million soft drinks, and 230 million sticks of gum. In 1956 advertisers projected an adolescent market of $9 billion for items such as transistor radios (first introduced in 1952), 45-rpm records, clothing, and fads such as Silly Putty (1950) and Hula Hoops (1958). Increasingly, advertisers targeted the young, both to capture their spending money and to exploit their influence on family spending patterns. Note the changing slogans for Pepsi-Cola: "Twice as much for a nickel" (1935), "Be sociable—have a Pepsi" (1948), "Now it's Pepsi for those who think young" (1960), and finally "the Pepsi Generation" (1965).

Hollywood movies played a large role in fostering and legitimizing a separate teenage culture. At a time when general movie attendance was declining because of competition from television, young people made up the largest audience for motion pictures. Soon Hollywood studios catered to this market with films such as *The Wild One* (1951), starring Marlon Brando, and *Rebel without a Cause* (1955), starring James Dean, Natalie Wood, and Sal Mineo. "What are you rebelling against?" a waitress asks Brando in *The Wild One*. "Whattaya got?" he replies.

What really defined this generation, however, was its music. Rejecting the rigid boundaries of earlier American popular music, teenagers in the 1950s discovered rock 'n' roll, an amalgam of white country and western music and the black urban music known as

rhythm and blues. The Cleveland disc jockey Alan Freed played a major role in introducing white America to the new African-American sound by playing rhythm and blues records on white radio stations beginning in 1954. Young white performers such as Bill Haley, Elvis Presley, and Buddy Holly incorporated this sound into their own music and capitalized on the new market (see American Lives, pages 920–921). Between 1953 and 1959 record sales increased from $213 million to $603 million, with rock 'n' roll as the driving force.

Many white adults were appalled. They saw in rock 'n' roll music, teen movies, and magazines such as *Mad* (introduced in 1952) an invitation to race mixing, rebellion, and disorder. The media featured hundreds of stories on problem teens, and in 1955 a Senate subcommittee headed by Estes Kefauver conducted a high-profile investigation of juvenile delinquency and its origins in the popular media. Denunciations of the new youth culture, however, only increased its popularity.

Cultural Dissenters

The youth rebellion was only one aspect of a broader undercurrent of discontent with the conformist culture of the 1950s. Postwar artists, jazz musicians, and writers also expressed their alienation from mainstream society through intensely personal, introspective art forms. In New York, Jackson Pollock and other painters rejected the social realism of the 1930s for an unconventional style that became known as abstract expressionism. Swirling and splattering paint onto giant canvases, Pollock emphasized self-expression in the act of painting and captured the chaotic atmosphere of the nuclear age.

A similar trend characterized jazz, where black musicians developed a hard-driving improvisational style known as bebop. Whether the "hot" bebop of saxophonist Charlie Parker in the 1940s or the more subdued "cool" West Coast sound of the trumpeter Miles Davis in the 1950s, postwar jazz was cerebral, intimate, and individualistic. As such, it stood in stark contrast to the commercialized, dance-oriented "swing" bands of the 1930s and 1940s.

Black jazz musicians found eager fans not only in the African-American community but among young white *beats*. Centered in New York and San Francisco, the beats were a group of writers and poets who disdained the middle-class conformity and suburban materialism of the 1950s. In his poem "Howl" (1956), which became a manifesto of the beat generation, Allen Ginsberg lamented: "I saw the best minds of my generation destroyed by madness, starving hysterical naked, dragging themselves through the angry streets at dawn looking for an angry fix. . . ." In works such as Jack Kerouac's novel *On the Road* (1957) the beats glorified spontaneity, sexual adventurism, drug use, and spirituality. Like other

members of the postwar generation, the beats were apolitical; their rebellion was strictly cultural. In the 1960s, however, the beats would inspire a new generation of young rebels who championed both political and cultural change.

The Fifties: The Way We Were?

Like the 1920s, the 1950s are defined almost entirely in cultural terms. But once again an emphasis on affluence, popular culture, and consumption is too superficial to describe such a complex period of economic and social transformation. The popularized view of the "happy days" of the 1950s reflects only a tenuous rendering of reality.

For many Americans the 1950s represent the norm of American society. Families were portrayed as close-knit and intact; children were happy; the economy was growing; and despite the fear of nuclear annihilation, Americans were confident that theirs was the strongest country, both economically and morally, in the world. Changes in American family, political, and social life since 1960 are often seen as declines from this ideal.

But perhaps the fifties were an aberration, not the norm—the result of a unique combination of circumstances that could not be sustained on a permanent basis. The postwar baby boom was certainly an aberration in a 200-year trend toward smaller families. The stability of marriages in the 1940s and 1950s was also atypical in light of the liberalization of social mores in the 1920s and 1930s and the increasing divorce rates after the mid-1960s. Scarred by memories of depression and World War II–era dislocations and scared by the ambiguities of living in the atomic age, the postwar generation embraced family life with a vengeance. Their children, growing up in a more economically and psychologically secure environment, rebelled against this traditional orientation. When social conditions changed in the 1960s, the profamily orientation gave way to a more individualistic ethos that characterized the rest of the century.

Perhaps the greatest aberration, and the reason why our view of the 1950s as the norm is so misleading, is that the postwar affluence was based on international economic conditions that could not continue indefinitely. When the war-devastated economies of Japan and West Germany were rebuilt, those countries took advantage of new technology to compete with and eventually challenge American economic supremacy in one industry after another: steel, rubber, automobiles, electronics, footwear, and textiles. So too did emerging industrial centers in the Pacific Rim such as South Korea, Hong Kong, and Singapore. If we regard the economic dominance of the 1950s as the norm, any decline will appear to be a disturbing loss of American power and economic strength rather than a return to a more balanced state of economic affairs.

The stereotypes of the 1950s are misleading, if not downright false, in other ways too. The picture painted in popular culture of boundless affluence hides, indeed makes invisible, those who did not share equally in the postwar American dream. Many people—displaced factory workers, destitute old people, female heads of households, blacks, and Latinos—watched the affluent society from the outside and wondered why they were not permitted to share in its bounty. Not until the publication of Michael Harrington's *The Other America* in 1962 did Americans begin to realize that in the richest country in the world more than a quarter of the population was poor.

The contrast between suburban affluence and the "other America," between the lure of the city for the poor and minorities and the grim reality of its segregated existence, and between a heightened emphasis on domesticity and widening opportunities for women, would spawn protest and change in the turbulent 1960s. Amid the booming prosperity of the late 1940s and 1950s, however, these fundamental social and economic contradictions were barely noticed.

Elvis Presley: Teen Idol of the 1950s

When Elvis Presley performed on the "Ed Sullivan Show" in 1956, the television cameras zoomed in on his head and shoulders. The close-ups were inspired not by the young singer's good looks but by a deliberate attempt to conceal his lower body. After several scandalous TV appearances earlier that season, CBS decided that Presley's sexually suggestive bumping and grinding were unsuitable for family viewing.

Despite the censorship, Presley's performance was an unprecedented success, claiming over 80 percent of the television audience. His records sold 10 million copies that year alone and would account for a quarter of RCA's record sales over the next decade. More than any other recording artist of the 1950s Presley popularized the new hybrid music known as rock 'n' roll.

Born in East Tupelo, Mississippi, in 1935, Elvis Aron Presley grew up in a white working-class family that keenly felt the hardships of the depression. Like many poor southerners, the Presleys moved frequently in search of work as laborers and mill hands. When Elvis was thirteen, his father found a job at a paint factory in Memphis, and the Presleys settled in one of that city's new public housing projects.

Elvis's earliest exposure to music came through gospel singing at the Pentecostal First Assembly of God church, where his uncle was pastor. Later, when his family lived in or adjacent to the black districts of Tupelo and Memphis (as the South's poorest whites often did), Elvis gravitated toward local churches, bars, and clubs where he gained a lifelong love of blues, gospel, and other black music.

Local radio was an equally powerful force in his musical education. In the late 1940s, commercial radio offered a diverse selection of musical programming, catering to the growing audience of rural migrants who had been moving to southern cities since World War II. Although there had always been significant cross-fertilization between black and white musical styles, industry promoters maintained artificially distinct genres of "hillbilly" and "race" music. After World War II those derogatory labels gave way to the more respectable terms *country and western* and *rhythm and blues*, but the programming remained rigidly segregated.

Young white southerners such as Presley, however, listened to both types of programs. They admired the traditional vocal styles and guitar picking that they heard on the "Grand Ole Opry" and other country shows but also developed a keen appreciation for the blues progressions and driving rhythms of black music. White youngsters' growing fascination with rhythm and blues was not generally acknowledged and was considered somewhat scandalous. But a small group of disc jockeys and record promoters realized the potential of the new market. As the Memphis record producer Sam Phillips once said, "If I could find a white man who had the Negro sound and the Negro feel, I could make a billion dollars."

Phillips found that man in Elvis Presley. In 1953 the nineteen-year-old Presley was working as a truck driver and occasionally stopped by Phillips's Sun Studios to make sample recordings for his friends and family. Phillips remembered his unusual vocal style and later asked him to cut a record with a local band. The result was an eclectic mix of musical styles: a white version of a black blues song, "That's All Right," on one side and a black-influenced interpretation of a bluegrass number, "Blue Moon of Kentucky," on the other. The record was an overnight local sensation and launched Presley into a national recording career the following year. Over the next decade he produced dozens of hits for RCA, including "Hound Dog," "Heartbreak Hotel," "Jailhouse Rock," and "Blue Suede Shoes."

Presley's success was based not only on his music but on his stage presence and his relationship with the audience. With his slicked-back hair, long sideburns, and tight pants, Presley cultivated a lower-class "greaser" look that proved immensely popular with teenage fans. His quivering legs, gyrating pelvis, and playful sneer drove young female fans wild; they frequently mobbed the stage, grabbing at his clothes for souvenirs. Many

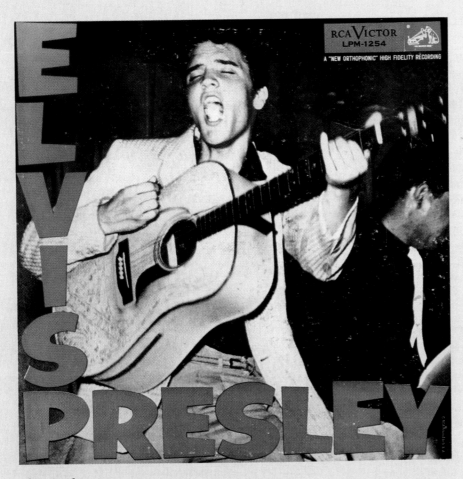

Elvis Presley
The young Elvis Presley (shown here on the cover of his first album in 1956) embodied cultural rebellion against the conservatism and triviality of adult life in the 1950s.

adults, however, condemned such antics, associating them with juvenile delinquency, sexual immorality, and "race mixing." After his first television appearance, a critic described Presley's performance as "suggestive and vulgar, tinged with the kind of animalism that should be confined to dives and bordellos," and another called it "a strip-tease with clothes on." For many adults rock 'n' roll was an invitation to rebellion.

African-Americans found Presley's success and notoriety somewhat ironic. Black musicians such as Chuck Berry had been performing such music for years but with little commercial success among white audiences. To many, the appropriation of black rhythm and blues by white artists was out-and-out theft. In the long run, however, the popularity of rock 'n' roll introduced

black performers such as Little Richard, Fats Domino, and James Brown to white as well as black audiences.

Presley's musical popularity declined with his induction into the army in 1958 (the long arm of the state reached even the most popular stars). Afterward he headed for Hollywood, acting and singing in dozens of mostly mediocre teen-oriented movies. He enjoyed a comeback starting in 1968, but his career was hampered by personal problems. In 1977 he died of an accidental drug overdose. Since then he has become a cult figure, spawning hundreds of books and articles and a spate of Elvis impersonators. Graceland, his garish home in Memphis, attracts more visitors per year than does George Washington's estate at Mount Vernon.

Summary

Postwar affluence rested on several foundations, especially the global hegemony of the United States in the immediate postwar period. Federal intervention in the economy, especially in the form of defense spending, fueled prosperity, as did spending for consumer goods. Consumer spending played an especially important role in the reconversion to a peacetime economy. New corporate investment strategies helped expand U.S. influence abroad, and technological change stimulated productivity in both agriculture and industry. These developments influenced the workplace, eliminating jobs in manufacturing and accelerating the growth of the service sector. Organized labor benefited from the postwar economic boom in the form of rising wages and benefits but could not maintain its earlier organizing momentum.

Much of the new economic activity in the postwar period was concentrated in the southern and western states and in the suburban periphery. Cold war defense spending boosted the economies and populations of California, Texas, Florida, and other emerging Sun Belt states. Federal home loan programs and highway construction spurred rapid suburban development, siphoning jobs and white middle-class residents out of the central cities. Blacks, Latinos, native Americans, and other low-income groups largely remained trapped in declining inner-city areas amid growing unemployment, rising crime, and deteriorating housing and education. In the South early civil rights campaigns challenged racial inequality and laid the organizational groundwork for the larger movement that followed in the 1960s. But elsewhere Americans remained mostly quiescent during those years.

After years of depression and war-induced insecurity, Americans turned inward toward home and family. Postwar couples married young, had several children, and—if they were white and middle class—raised them in a climate of suburban affluence. The profamily orientation of the 1950s celebrated social conformity and traditional gender roles, even though millions of women entered the work force. Their children also departed from traditional roles as they embraced a rebellious youth culture of rock 'n' roll music, teen movies, and other consumer phenomena aimed at a youth market.

Jazz musicians, abstract expressionist painters, and beat poets and writers also rebelled against conformity, but their dissent was cultural, not political, in nature. Many of the smoldering contradictions of the postwar period—an unequally shared affluence, institutionalized racism that limited opportunities for nonwhite Americans, and tensions in women's lives—soon surfaced in the social protest movements of the 1960s.

TIMELINE

1944	Bretton Woods economic conference World Bank and International Monetary Fund (IMF) founded Mechanical cotton picker introduced
1946	Dr. Benjamin Spock, *Baby and Child Care*
1947	Levittown, New York, built General Agreement on Tariffs and Trade (GATT) UNIVAC computer developed
1948	CBS and NBC begin regular television programming
1953–1958	Operation Wetback and Indian termination programs
1954	Polio vaccine developed by Dr. Jonas Salk *Brown v. Board of Education of Topeka, Kansas* First McDonald's opens
1955	AFL and CIO reunited Montgomery bus boycott Disneyland opens in Anaheim, California
1956	Interstate Highway Act Elvis Presley popularizes rock 'n' roll via television
1957	Peak of postwar baby boom Eisenhower sends federal troops to protect black students during school desegregation battle in Little Rock, Arkansas Southern Christian Leadership Conference (SCLC) founded
1958	Brooklyn Dodgers move to Los Angeles
1959	Nixon and Khrushchev's "kitchen debate"
1963	California replaces New York as most populous state
1965	Immigration Act abolishes national quota system

BIBLIOGRAPHY

General introductions to postwar society include Paul Boyer, *Promises to Keep* (1995); William Chafe, *The Unfinished Journey* (3d ed., 1995); John Diggins, *The Proud Decades* (1988); and David Halberstam, *The Fifties* (1993).

Technology and Economic Change

For overviews on the economic changes of the postwar period, see W. Elliot Brownlee, *Dynamics of Ascent* (1979); David P. Calleo, *The Imperious Economy* (1982); and Harold G. Vatter, *The U.S. Economy in the 1950s* (1963). Robert Kuttner, *The End of Laissez-Faire* (1991), provides ample background on the Bretton Woods system. Herman P. Miller, *Rich Man, Poor Man* (1971), and Gabriel Kolko, *Wealth and Power in America* (1962), discuss inequality in income distribution. Michael Harrington, *The Other America* (1962), documents the persistence of poverty in the postwar era, as does Harry M. Caudill, *Night Comes to the Cumberlands* (1963).

John L. Shover, *First Majority—Last Minority* (1976), analyzes the transformation of rural life in America. David Brody, *Workers in Industrial America* (1980); James R. Green, *The World of the Worker* (1980); and Robert Zeiger, *American Workers, American Unions, 1920–1985* (1986), provide overviews of labor in the twentieth century. On the impact of technology and automation, see Elting E. Morison, *From Know-How to Nowhere* (1974), and David F. Noble, *Forces of Production* (1984). The most influential study of the new middle class remains David Reisman et al., *The Lonely Crowd* (1950). William H. Whyte, *The Organization Man* (1956), provides a similar perspective. See also the work of C. Wright Mills, especially *White Collar* (1951) and *The Power Elite* (1956).

Alfred D. Chandler, *The Visible Hand* (1977), is the definitive history of American corporate structure and strategy. Myra Wilkin, *The Maturing of Multinational Enterprise* (1974), and Richard J. Barnet and Ronald E. Muller, *Global Reach* (1974), describe American business abroad. See also Robert Sobel, *The Age of Giant Corporations* (1972), and the early sections of Barry Bluestein and Bennett Harrison, *The Deindustrialization of America* (1982).

A Suburban Society

The best overviews of urbanization in the South and West are Carl Abbott, *The New Urban America* (1981), and Richard Bernard and Bradley Rice, eds., *Sunbelt Cities* (1983). Kenneth Jackson, *Crabgrass Frontier* (1985), provides an overview of suburban development, which can be supplemented by Jon C. Teaford, *City and Suburb* (1979); Robert Fishman, *Bourgeois Utopias* (1987); and Zane Miller, *Suburb* (1981). Herbert Gans, *The Levittowners* (1967), and Bennett M. Berger, *Working-Class Suburb* (1960), are sociological studies of suburbia written by contemporaries.

The Other America

Reed Ueda, *Postwar Immigrant America* (1994), and David Reimers, *Still the Open Door* (1985), examine new trends in immigration since 1945. Nicholas Lemann examines postwar black migration in *The Promised Land* (1991), and Jacqueline Jones compares black and white urban migrants in *The Dispossessed* (1992). Donald Fixico, *Termination and Relocation* (1986), looks at federal Indian policy from 1945 to 1970.

Jon C. Teaford, *Rough Road to Renaissance* (1990); John Mollenkopf, *The Contested City* (1983); and Kenneth Fox, *Metropolitan America* (1985), offer the most complete accounts of postwar urban development. Herbert Gans, *The Urban Villagers* (1962), tells the story of a Boston Italian community displaced by urban renewal.

Richard Kluger, *Simple Justice* (1975), and Mark Tushnet, *The NAACP's Legal Strategy against Segregated Education* (1987), analyze the *Brown* decision and its context, whereas Anthony Lewis, *Portrait of a Decade* (1964), covers southern reaction to the decision. Martin Luther King, Jr., recounts his experience in the Montgomery bus boycott in *Stride toward Freedom* (1958); and Taylor Branch, *Parting the Waters: America in the King Years, 1954–1963* (1988), provides a good account of King's early years.

American Society during the Baby Boom

Books that highlight the social and cultural history of the 1950s include Elaine Tyler May, *Homeward Bound* (1988); Lary May, ed., *Recasting America* (1989); Douglas T. Miller and Marion Nowak, *The Fifties* (1977); and Stephen Whitfield, *The Culture of the Cold War* (1991).

On popular culture, George Lipsitz, *Time Passages* (1991), surveys postwar television, music, film, and popular culture, and his *Rainbow at Midnight* (2d ed., 1994) looks at working-class culture and rock 'n' roll. Eric Barnouw, *Tube of Plenty* (2d. ed., 1982), chronicles the impact of television. Other treatments of the mass media include James L. Baughman, *The Republic of Mass Culture* (1992); Peter Biskind, *Seeing Is Believing* (1983); and Nora Sayre, *Running Time* (1982). Vance Packard's influential unmasking of the advertising industry, *The Hidden Persuaders* (1957), can be supplemented by Stephen Fox, *The Mirror Makers* (1984).

Richard Easterlin, *American Baby Boom in Historical Perspective* (1962) and *Birth and Future* (1980), analyze the demographic changes. Jane S. Smith, *Patenting the Sun* (1990), looks at Salk's development of the polio vaccine. Diane Ravitch describes education from 1945 to 1980 in *The Troubled Crusade* (1983).

Elaine May's *Homeward Bound* is the classic introduction to postwar family life, providing a historical corollary to Betty Friedan's *Feminine Mystique* (1963). Recent revisionist work challenging this view can be found in Joanne Meyerowitz, ed., *Not June Cleaver* (1994). William H. Chafe, *The American Woman* (1972), and Alice Kessler-Harris, *Out to Work* (1982), survey women's role in the work force.

Youth culture is the subject of William Graeber's *Coming of Age in Buffalo* (1990). James Gilbert, *A Cycle of Outrage* (1986), looks at juvenile delinquency in the 1950s. Peter Guralnick, *Last Train to Memphis* (1994), is the definitive biography of Elvis Presley's early years. Discussions of cultural dissent in the 1950s can be found in Serge Guibaut, *How New York Stole the Idea of Modern Art* (1983); Bruce Cook, *The Beat Generation* (1971); and Dan Wakefield, *New York in the Fifties* (1992).

La Huelga

Long live the cause, long live the strike, proclaimed Paul
Davis's poster for a 1968 Carnegie Hall benefit for César
Chávez's farm workers' union.

The Ascent of Liberalism

1960–1970

★ ★ ★

In his 1961 inaugural address President John Fitzgerald Kennedy challenged a "new generation of Americans" to take responsibility for the future: "Ask not what your country can do for you, ask what you can do for your country." Over the next decade many young Americans responded to that sense of mission. As a civil rights volunteer explained in 1964, "I want to do my part. There's a moral wave building among today's youth, and I intend to catch it."

Ironically, the roots of 1960s activism lay in the tranquil America of the 1950s. The postwar affluence of the middle class produced a self-assured generation of young whites who were optimistic about their ability to cure the nation's social ills. For young African-Americans the affluence of the white middle class was a stark reminder of racial inequality. In the 1960s that same baby-boom generation swelled college enrollments, providing recruits for the civil rights campaign and other student movements. Among women, increased access to education and greater participation in the work force in the postwar era sparked a revival of feminism. Finally, the lofty cold war rhetoric of international freedom and democracy prompted many to press for economic and racial justice at home.

The civil rights movement was the earliest and most influential protest movement in this period. The antisegregation campaign waged by black southerners in the 1950s grew into a nationwide civil rights movement, taking on controversial issues such as voting rights, economic inequality, and community control. The tactics it pioneered—legislative and judicial challenges, nonviolent direct action, and mobilization of public opinion—were soon adopted by women, Mexican-Americans, native Americans, and other groups to press their demands.

The sense of optimism and activism that characterized the social movements of the 1960s also pervaded politics. Drawing on a new generation of academic and corporate leaders, the administrations of John F. Kennedy and—to a much greater extent—Lyndon B. Johnson acted on an abiding faith in the positive influence of government and tried to use federal power to ensure the public welfare at home and protect American interests abroad. This political orientation—known as liberalism—was a continuation of Franklin Roosevelt's New Deal but went beyond it. Under the Great Society, a burst of social legislation in 1964–1965, which marked the high tide of postwar liberalism, the Johnson administration expanded federal activism in areas such as health care, education, and civil rights. Through those programs and other social welfare measures, liberals sought to spread the abundance of a consumer society to greater numbers of people. In essence, they attempted to use the fiscal powers of the state to redress the imbalances of the private economy without directly challenging capitalism.

Liberals also pursued an activist stance abroad. The Kennedy and Johnson administrations sought to protect American political and economic interests in the international arena and took aggressive action against communist influence in Europe, the Caribbean, Vietnam (see Chapter 31), and elsewhere. The growing financial and political costs of that ambitious agenda, however, hampered the further progress of domestic programs and revealed ominous cracks in the postwar liberal consensus.

The Kennedy Magnetism
John Kennedy, the Democratic candidate for president in 1960, used his youth and personality to attract voters. Here the Massachusetts senator draws an enthusiastic crowd on a campaign stop in Elgin, Illinois.

John Kennedy and the Politics of Expectation

Franklin Roosevelt's activist administration had heightened expectations for presidential leadership, and the expansion of presidential power had continued under Truman and Eisenhower. In the 1960s, when American power and resources seemed limitless, many citizens looked to Washington for solutions to international, national, and local problems. Few presidents came to Washington more primed for action than John Kennedy. His "New Frontier" promised to get America moving again through vigorous governmental activism at home and abroad. The British journalist Henry Fairlie referred to this activist impulse as the "politics of expectation." But the legislative achievements of Kennedy's New Frontier, particularly in domestic affairs, were modest.

The New Politics and the 1960 Campaign

The Republicans would have been happy to renominate Dwight D. Eisenhower for president in 1960 but were prevented from doing so by the Twenty-second Amendment. Passed in 1951 by a Republican-controlled Congress to prevent a repetition of Franklin Roosevelt's four-term presidency, the amendment limited future presidents to two full terms.

The Republicans turned to Vice-President Richard M. Nixon, who, like a good 1950s junior executive, had patiently waited for his turn at the top. Nixon campaigned for an updated version of Eisenhower's policies but was hampered by lukewarm support from Eisenhower. Asked whether Nixon had helped make any major policy decisions in his administration, Eisenhower replied, "If you give me a week I might think of one."

In the Democratic primaries, which took on new importance in the television era, Senator John Fitzgerald Kennedy of Massachusetts defeated Senator Hubert Horatio Humphrey of Minnesota. The Senate majority leader, Lyndon Johnson of Texas, who also sought the nomination but did not participate in the primary race, joined the ticket as the vice-presidential nominee. Kennedy, an alumnus of Harvard and a World War II hero, had inherited his love of politics from his grandfathers, both of whom had been colorful Irish-Catholic politicians in Boston. His wealthy father, Joseph P. Kennedy, had headed the Securities and Exchange Commission and served as ambassador to Great Britain under Roosevelt. First elected to Congress in 1946, John Kennedy moved to the Senate in 1952. Ambitious and hard-driven, Kennedy launched his New Frontier campaign in 1960 with a platform calling for civil rights legislation, health care for the elderly, aid to education, urban renewal, expanded military and space programs, and containment of communism abroad. With the country in the middle of a recession that had pushed unemployment to a postwar high, Kennedy vowed to "get America moving again."

Kennedy's main liabilities were his Catholicism and his youth. At forty-three he was poised to become the youngest man ever elected to the presidency and the nation's first Catholic chief executive. The first Catholic nominee since Al Smith in 1928, Kennedy dealt with the issue of religion directly. In a September address to a group of Protestant ministers in Houston he affirmed his belief in the separation of church and state and declared his political independence from the Vatican. He also handled the youth question skillfully.

Turning his youth into a powerful campaign asset, Kennedy practiced what came to be called the "new politics"—an approach that emphasized youthful charisma, style, and personality rather than issues and platforms. Using the power of the media (particularly television) to reach voters directly, practitioners of the new politics relied on professional media consultants, political pollsters, and mass fund-raising. Kennedy's youth, attractiveness, and charm made for a superb television image. His family's wealth and the contributions he raised from

sources outside traditional party networks paid for his expensive campaign. His mastery of the media enabled him to appeal to voters directly rather than only through the Democratic party.

A series of four televised debates between the two principal candidates, a major innovation of the 1960 campaign, showed how important that medium was becoming to political life. Nixon, far less photogenic than Kennedy and recovering from a minor illness, looked sallow and unshaven under the intense studio lights. Kennedy, in contrast, looked vigorous, cool, and self-confident on screen and dispelled voters' fears that he was not as well prepared for the presidency as the current vice-president was. Polls showed that television did sway political perceptions: voters who listened to the first debate on the radio concluded that Nixon had won, whereas TV viewers judged in Kennedy's favor.

Despite the ground Kennedy picked up in the debates, he won only the narrowest of victories, receiving 49.7 percent of the popular vote to Nixon's 49.5 percent (see Map 30.1). Kennedy had successfully appealed to the diverse elements of the Democratic coalition, attracting large numbers of Catholic and black voters and a sig-

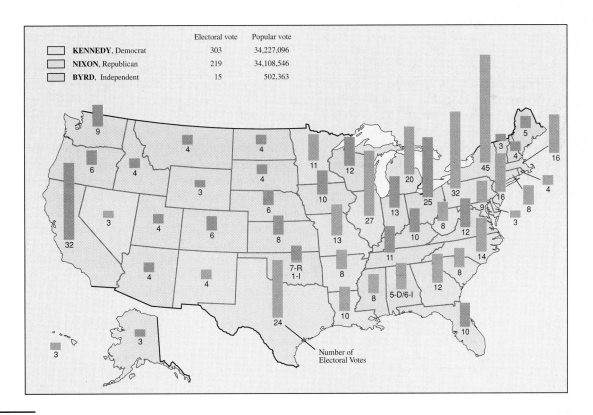

	Electoral vote	Popular vote
KENNEDY, Democrat	303	34,227,096
NIXON, Republican	219	34,108,546
BYRD, Independent	15	502,363

Number of Electoral Votes

MAP 30.1

The Election of 1960

The Kennedy-Nixon contest was the closest since 1884. Kennedy won twelve states, including Illinois, by less than 2 percent of the two-party vote tally; he lost six others, including California, by a similarly small margin. Fifteen electors cast their votes for the Independent Democrat, Harry F. Byrd. Despite his razor-thin margin of victory, Kennedy won 303 electoral votes, the same number Truman had won in 1948, showing that the electoral college vote can be a misleading indicator of popular support.

nificant sector of the middle class; the vice-presidential nominee, Lyndon Johnson, brought in southern white Democrats. Yet only 120,000 votes separated the two candidates, and the shift of a few thousand votes in key states such as Illinois (where there were confirmed cases of voting fraud) would have reversed the outcome. The electoral results hardly gave Kennedy a mandate for sweeping change, and the Republicans, though still in the minority in Congress, gained 21 seats in the House.

Kennedy's activist bent attracted unusually talented and ambitious people—"the best and the brightest" as the journalist David Halberstam called them. A host of corporate and academic leaders flocked to join the new administration, which was christened "Camelot" by the admiring media after the recently opened Broadway musical about King Arthur. Robert S. McNamara, the former president of the Ford Motor Company, came on board as secretary of defense and introduced modern management techniques to that department. The Republican banker C. Douglas Dillon brought a corporate manager's desire for expanded markets and stable economic growth to the Department of the Treasury. The national security adviser McGeorge Bundy, the State Department planner Walt Rostow, and other trusted advisers came from Harvard, MIT, and other leading universities to join the Kennedy foreign policy team.

Reflecting the all-male Ivy League world in which Kennedy traveled, the administration was overwhelmingly male. He appointed fewer women to federal positions than had Eisenhower or Truman and made only a token attempt to address women's issues with the establishment of the Presidential Commission on the Status of Women in 1961. Subsequent allegations of Kennedy's womanizing and philandering also hurt his reputation in this area.

Activism Abroad

Kennedy's inaugural address was devoted almost entirely to foreign affairs, reflecting the priorities of his presidency: "Let every nation know, whether it wishes us well or ill, that we shall pay any price, bear any burden, meet any hardship, support any friend, oppose any foe to assure the survival and success of liberty." A resolute cold warrior whose family had supported the red-hunting campaign of Senator Joseph McCarthy, Kennedy took a hard line against communist expansionism. He therefore set out to reverse the fiscal conservatism that had limited military growth under the Eisenhower administration, bringing defense spending to its highest level (as a percentage of total federal expenditures) in the cold war era.

The Military Buildup. During the 1960 presidential campaign Kennedy charged that the Eisenhower administration had permitted the Soviet Union to develop superior nuclear capabilities. Once in office, however, he found that no "missile gap" existed. In fact, Eisenhower had built up the American nuclear arsenal at the expense of conventional weapons. In his first national security message to Congress, Kennedy proposed a new policy of *flexible response*, stating that the nation must be prepared "to deter all wars, general or limited, nuclear or conventional, large or small." Congress quickly granted Kennedy's military requests, boosting the number of combat-ready army divisions from eleven to sixteen and authorizing the construction of ten Polaris nuclear submarines and other warships. The result was a major expansion of the military-industrial complex as thousands of workers were recruited to build more weapons systems and military equipment.

Those measures were designed to deter nuclear or conventional attacks by the Soviet Union. But what about the new kind of warfare, the wars of national liberation that had broken out in many Third World countries when their inhabitants sought to overthrow colonial rulers or unpopular dictatorships? In early 1961 the Soviet premier, Nikita Khrushchev, proclaimed that conflicts in Vietnam, Cuba, and other countries were "wars of national liberation," worthy of Soviet support. To counter that threat, Kennedy adopted the new military doctrine of *counterinsurgency*. U.S. Army Special Forces, called the Green Berets for their distinctive headgear, received intensive training in repelling the random, small-scale attacks typical of guerrilla warfare. Vietnam soon provided a testing ground for counterinsurgency techniques (see Chapter 31).

The Peace Corps and Foreign Aid. The idealism and commitment to public service that characterized the New Frontier were perhaps most evident in the newly established Peace Corps, headed by Kennedy's brother-in-law, Sargent Shriver. The idea, Kennedy explained on March 1, 1961, was to create "a pool of trained American men and women" to be sent "overseas by the United States government or through private organizations and institutions to help foreign countries meet their urgent needs for skilled manpower." Thousands of young Americans, many of them recent college graduates, responded to the call, agreeing to devote two or more years to teaching English to Filipino schoolchildren or helping African villagers obtain adequate supplies of water. Embodying the idealism of the early 1960s, the Peace Corps was also a cold war weapon designed to bring Third World countries into the American orbit and away from communist influence.

Kennedy also tried to reinforce American ties to developing countries through programs of economic aid. The State Department's Agency for International Development coordinated foreign aid for the Third World, and its Food for Peace program distributed surplus agricultural products to developing nations. In March 1961 the

The Peace Corps
The Peace Corps, a New Frontier program initiated in 1961, attracted thousands of idealistic young Americans, including this New York woman who volunteered at a hospital in Rio de Janeiro, Brazil.

president proposed "a ten-year plan for the Americas" called the Alliance for Progress, a $20 billion partnership between the United States and the republics of Latin America. Designed to reduce the appeal of communism, the Alliance provided funds for food, education, medicine, and other services but did little to enhance economic growth or improve social conditions in Latin America during the 1960s.

Kennedy often turned to a small circle of personal aides for foreign policy advice rather than relying on the Pentagon and the State Department. Taking the institutional changes of the 1947 National Security Act a step further, he enhanced the authority of the National Security Council by moving its chief into the White House. That shift further concentrated foreign policy initiative in the executive office.

The Bay of Pigs Invasion. The nation's strengthened military arsenal and streamlined security apparatus failed to bring Kennedy the diplomatic success that he had anticipated. In April 1961 Kennedy undertook his first major foreign policy initiative—an effort to overthrow the new Soviet-supported regime in Cuba.

Although the United States had renounced its right to intervene in Cuba's internal affairs in 1934 (see Chapter 27), it retained a base at Guantánamo Bay and nearly total economic and political dominance of the island. In

1956 American companies owned 80 percent of Cuba's utilities, 90 percent of its mining operations, and 40 percent of its sugar plantations. On New Year's Day in 1959 Fidel Castro overthrew the corrupt and unpopular dictatorship of Fulgencio Batista and called for a revolution to reshape Cuban society. At first Castro was willing to deal with the United States on friendly terms, but as he instituted agrarian reforms that affected American interests and nationalized American-owned banks and industries, relations with Washington deteriorated. By early 1961 the United States had declared an embargo on all exports to Cuba, cut back on imports of Cuban sugar, and broken off diplomatic relations with Castro's regime. Isolated by the United States, Cuba turned increasingly toward the Soviet Union for economic and military support.

Concerned about Castro's growing friendliness with the Soviets, in early 1961 Kennedy used plans originally drawn up by the Eisenhower administration to dispatch Cuban exiles to foment an anti-Castro uprising. The invaders had been trained by the Central Intelligence Agency (CIA) but were ill prepared for their task and had little popular support on the island. After landing at Cuba's Bay of Pigs on April 17, the tiny force of 1,400 men was crushed by Castro's troops. Symptomatic of the inept CIA planning, pilots taking off from Nicaragua to provide air cover for the landing forces forgot to set their watches ahead to Cuban time and arrived at the beach an hour late. The anticipated rebellion never occurred.

The Bay of Pigs invasion was an embarrassing failure and cast doubts on Kennedy's activist approach to international affairs. It also adversely affected U.S.-Soviet relations. Khrushchev interpreted the invasion as evidence that American troops would launch an offensive against Cuba in the future and responded by stepping up military aid to Castro.

The Berlin Wall. The growing mistrust between Kennedy and Khrushchev intensified during a June 1961 summit meeting of the United States and the Soviet Union. Weakened by the botched Cuban invasion, Kennedy met with Khrushchev to discuss a nuclear test ban treaty, the civil war in Laos, and the status of Berlin. At the meeting both men were combative, especially about Berlin, which was located squarely in the middle of East Germany but had remained divided into eastern and western sectors. Khrushchev wanted it declared a "free city," which would mean the withdrawal of both Soviet and western occupation forces, but he did not get his way.

Just days after the meeting, Khrushchev heightened international tensions by deploying soldiers to sever East Berlin from the western sector of the city. Determined to confront the Soviets publicly, Kennedy declared in a televised speech on July 25 that Berlin was the "great testing

The Berlin Wall
A West Berlin resident walks alongside a section of the Berlin wall in 1962, a year after its construction. Note the numerous loudspeakers, which the East Germans used to broadcast propaganda over the barricade that divided the city.

place of Western courage and will." He announced that he would ask Congress for large increases in military spending, a massive fallout shelter program, and the authority to mobilize the National Guard, call up the reserves, and extend military enlistments in response to the crisis. With Congressional approval, Kennedy added 300,000 troops to the armed forces and dispatched 40,000 of them to Europe. Undeterred, the Soviets supervised East German construction of the Berlin wall in mid-August to stop the exodus of East Germans to the West; East German guards then began policing the border, with instructions to shoot to kill those trying to escape. Transforming the Berlin wall into a propaganda weapon, Kennedy later visited the city and—standing beside the wall—invoked the solidarity of the free world by declaring "*Ich bin ein Berliner*" ("I am a Berliner"). Until it was dismantled in 1989, the Berlin wall was the supreme symbol of the Cold War.

The Cuban Missile Crisis. The climactic confrontation of the Cold War came in October 1962. After the failed Bay of Pigs invasion, the Kennedy administration increased economic pressure against Cuba and resumed its covert efforts to overthrow the Castro regime (see Map 30.2). Under the code name Operation Mongoose, the CIA attempted to disrupt Cuban trade, supported raids against the island from Florida, and plotted to assassinate Castro. In response to those hostile actions and fearing another U.S. invasion, the Soviets stepped up military aid to Cuba, including the installation of defensive missiles. In early October, American U-2 reconnaissance aircraft photographed Soviet-built bases for intermediate-range ballistic missiles (IRBMs), which could reach U.S. targets as far as 2,200 miles away. At

least some of those nuclear weapons had already been installed, and more were on the way from the Soviet Union. Moreover, the Soviet military commanders in Cuba might have been authorized to use them in the event of an American invasion.

Rather than work through State Department or diplomatic channels, Kennedy confronted the Soviet Union publicly in a somber televised address on Monday, October 22. Displaying the reconnaissance photos as evidence, he announced that the United States would use its newly enlarged navy to impose a "quarantine on all offensive military equipment" intended for Cuba. As the United States and the Soviet Union went on full military alert, people around the world believed that this long-dreaded direct confrontation between the two superpowers would end in nuclear war. Americans living in cities within range of the missiles restocked their bomb shelters and calculated the fastest routes out of town. When Khrushchev denounced the quarantine, tensions mounted higher.

While the world held its breath, the Russian ships halted their voyage. Khrushchev wrote to Kennedy that if the United States agreed not to invade Cuba, the Soviets would remove the missiles. In a second letter Khrushchev demanded the removal of American missiles in Turkey as a condition for resolving the crisis. On his brother Robert's advice, the president publicly agreed to the terms of the first letter but ignored the second one. (He later secretly agreed to remove the missiles from Turkey.) On the following Sunday, after the most harrowing week of the nuclear age, Kennedy and Khrushchev both announced concessions: Kennedy pledged not to invade Cuba, and Khrushchev promised to dismantle the missile bases. "We're eyeball to eyeball," Secretary of State Rusk observed, "and I think the other fellow just blinked."

Although the risk of nuclear war was greater during the Cuban missile crisis than it was at any other time in the postwar period, it led to a slight thaw in U.S.-Soviet relations. In the words of the national security adviser McGeorge Bundy, "having come so close to the edge, the leaders of the two governments have since taken care to keep away from the cliff." Sobered by the Cuban missile crisis and the close brush with nuclear war, Kennedy began to seek ways to reduce international tensions. He turned away from the cold war rhetoric that had characterized his campaign and the first two years of his presidency and began to strive for peaceful coexistence. In a notable speech at American University in June 1963, he stressed the need to "make the world safe for diversity." Russians and Americans alike, he observed, "inhabit this small planet. We all breathe the same air. We all cherish our children's future. And we are all mortal." Soviet leaders, also chastened by the confrontation over Cuba, were willing to talk. In August 1963 the three nuclear powers—the United States, the Soviet Union, and Great Britain—agreed to ban the testing of nuclear weapons in the atmosphere, in space, and underwater. Underground

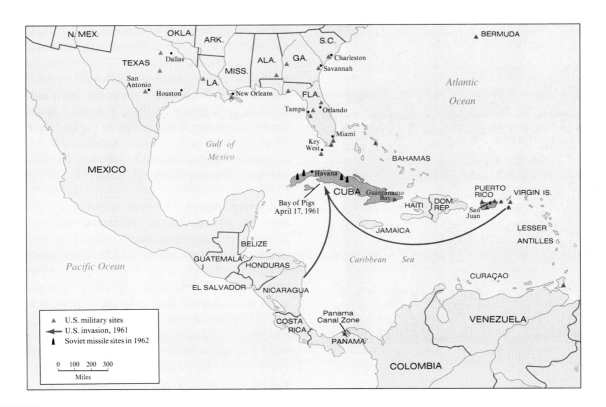

MAP 30.2

The United States and Cuba, 1961–1962

Fidel Castro's takeover in Cuba in 1959 brought cold war tensions to the Caribbean. In 1961 the United States tried unsuccessfully to overthrow Castro's regime by supporting the invasion of Cuban exiles launched from Nicaragua. In 1962 a major confrontation with the Soviet Union occurred over Soviet missile sites in Cuba. The Soviets removed the missiles after President Kennedy ordered a naval blockade of the island, which lies just 90 miles south of Florida.

testing, however, was allowed to continue. The partial test ban treaty was approved by the Senate in the fall of 1963. The new emphasis on peaceful coexistence and mutual accommodation also led to the establishment of a Washington-Moscow telecommunications "hot line" in 1963 so that leaders could contact each other quickly during potential crises.

But no matter how often American leaders talked about opening channels of communication with the Soviets, the obsession with the Soviet military threat to American security remained a cornerstone of U.S. policy. Nor did Soviet leaders moderate their concern over the threat that they believed the United States posed to the survival of the U.S.S.R. The Cold War—and the escalating arms race that accompanied it—would continue for another twenty-five years.

Kennedy's Thousand Days

The expansive vision of presidential leadership that Kennedy and his advisers brought to the White House worked less well at home than it did abroad. Kennedy, hampered by the lack of a popular mandate in the 1960 election, could not mobilize public support for the domestic agenda of the New Frontier. A conservative coalition of southern Democrats and western and midwestern Republicans effectively stalled most liberal initiatives. More important, Kennedy was not nearly as impassioned about domestic reform as he was about foreign policy.

One domestic program that won both popular and Congressional support was increased funding for space exploration. In response to the Soviet launching of *Sputnik* in 1957, the United States had established the National Aeronautics and Space Administration (NASA), which began the Mercury space program in 1958. On May 5, 1961, just three months after Kennedy took office, Alan Shepard became the first American in space; on February 2, 1962, John Glenn became the first American to orbit the earth. (The Soviet cosmonaut Yuri Gagarin earned the distinction of being the first person in space when he made a 108-hour flight in April 1961.) At the height of American fascination with space, Kennedy proposed in 1961 that "this nation should commit

Project Mercury
Astronaut John Glenn was the first American to orbit the
earth as part of the Mercury space program in 1962.

itself to achieving the goal, before this decade is out, of
landing a man on the moon and returning him safely to
earth." To support this mission (accomplished in 1969),
he greatly increased NASA's budget.

Economic Policy. Kennedy's most striking domestic
achievement was his use of modern economics to shape
fiscal policy. Initially Kennedy had shared the belief of
Eisenhower and many business leaders that the federal
government could best contribute to economic growth
by reducing the national debt and balancing the budget.
However, at the urging of Walter Heller, chairman of the
Council of Economic Advisers, Kennedy decided on a
different course. Rather than increase federal spending
to stimulate the economy, he proposed a reduction in the
income tax paid by businesses and the public. A tax cut,
he argued, would leave more money in the hands of taxpayers, who would then buy more, thus creating more
jobs. For a time federal expenditures would exceed federal income, but after a year or two the expanding economy would raise American incomes and generate higher
tax revenues.

Congress predictably balked at this unorthodox
proposal. Although the federal government had practiced Keynesian economics during the depression of the
1930s, the purposeful use of deficits in a relatively
healthy economy was highly controversial. The measure
initially died in Congress, but Lyndon Johnson pressed
for it after Kennedy's assassination and signed it into law

in February 1964. The Kennedy-Johnson tax cut marked
a milestone in the use of fiscal policy to encourage economic growth. Although economic expansion started
before the effects of the tax cut could be felt, Kennedy
and his economic advisers got credit for it anyway. The
gross national product grew at a rate of 5 percent during
the 1960s, nearly twice the rate of the Eisenhower years.
Much of the growth, however, was fueled by massive defense expenditures, especially spending for the escalating
Vietnam War.

A Limited Agenda. Kennedy's interest in stimulating
economic growth did not include a corresponding commitment to spending for domestic social needs, although
he did not entirely ignore the liberal legislative agenda
of Franklin Roosevelt and Harry Truman. Kennedy did
manage to push through legislation raising the minimum wage and expanding Social Security benefits, and
in 1961 he signed into law the Area Redevelopment Act,
which provided economic aid for depressed industrial
and rural areas. But on some of his most important issues—federal aid to education, wilderness preservation,
federal investment in mass transportation, and medical
insurance for the elderly—he ran into determined Congressional opposition from both Republicans and dissenters in his own party.

Discord within the Democratic coalition was particularly evident in the case of aid to education. Most
northern Democrats favored such aid but disagreed
about important details. Civil rights advocates insisted
that federal school aid go only to desegregated schools,
while Catholics insisted that federal assistance be extended to parochial systems. Kennedy persuaded most
black leaders to accept a school aid plan that ignored
existing segregation, but he told southern whites that
federal aid would not be guaranteed to segregated
schools in the future. Because he was a Catholic, however, Kennedy feared angering non-Catholics by proposing a bill that permitted aid to parochial schools. In
the absence of a bill acceptable to all those groups, the
education proposal died in committee.

The Warren Court. Some of the most controversial policies of the early 1960s came not from the Kennedy administration but from the Supreme Court. Unlike the
New Deal years, when the Court played an obstruction-
ist role, in the postwar period it often acted as a catalyst
for sweeping social change. Much of this judicial activism was linked to Earl Warren, the chief justice from
1953 to 1969.

The decisions of the Warren Court arguably had a
greater impact on American society than did anything
proposed by the president or Congress. The most important decision of the Court, *Brown v. Board of Education*, requiring the desegregation of public schools,
had been handed down in 1954 during the Eisenhower

administration (see Chapter 29). In the 1960s the Court made landmark decisions in the area of defendants' rights. In *Gideon v. Wainwright* (1963), *Escobedo v. Illinois* (1964), and *Miranda v. Arizona* (1966) the Supreme Court greatly expanded the rights of people accused of crimes. Tackling the issue of the reapportionment of state legislatures in *Baker v. Carr* (1962) and *Reynolds v. Sims* (1964), the Court put forth the doctrine of "one person, one vote," which substantially increased the representation of both suburban and urban areas, with their concentrations of black and Spanish-speaking residents, at the expense of rural regions. Perhaps the most controversial decision was *Engel v. Vitale* (1962), which banned organized prayer in public schools as a violation of the First Amendment's injunction that "Congress shall make no law respecting an establishment of religion."

President Kennedy, like President Eisenhower before him, pledged to uphold these decisions even when he disagreed with their scope or content. But in allowing the Court to take the lead on such issues, Kennedy surrendered critical opportunities to exercise presidential leadership.

The Kennedy Assassination. Although the first two years of Kennedy's presidency had been plagued by foreign policy crises and domestic inaction, many political observers believed the tide was turning in 1963. But just as Kennedy was maturing as a national leader, tragedy struck. On November 22, 1963, Kennedy went to Texas, a state he needed to win for reelection in 1964, to heal divisions in the party organization there. As he and his wife, Jacqueline, rode in an open car past the Texas School Book Depository in Dallas, he was shot. Kennedy died a half hour later. (Whether the accused killer Lee Harvey Oswald, a twenty-four-year-old loner who had spent three years in the Soviet Union, was the sole gunman became a matter of considerable controversy.) Before *Air Force One* left Dallas to take the president's body back to Washington, a grim-faced Lyndon Johnson was sworn in as president. Kennedy's stunned widow, still wearing her bloodstained pink suit, looked on.

By 1 P.M. Dallas time, just thirty minutes after the shooting, 68 percent of adults in the United States, about 75 million people, knew that Kennedy had been shot. By late afternoon, the proportion had risen to 99.8 percent, showing how the mass media could reach virtually every person in the nation within a few hours. As on Pearl Harbor Day in 1941, people never forgot what they were doing when they heard that Kennedy had been shot. Many ordinary Americans were deeply shocked by the assassination, reflecting their personal identification with the occupants of the White House.

The Kennedy assassination set off a national wave of self-examination. Americans debated whether the murder of the president had been an isolated act or an expression of a tragic flaw in the democratic system. The argument

Burying a President
A grief-stricken Jacqueline Kennedy walked behind her slain husband's casket at his 1963 funeral. To her left is brother-in-law Robert Kennedy, who would be assassinated five years later.

that there was something wrong with the nation gained credence two days after the assassination, when Jack Ruby, a nightclub owner, gunned down Lee Harvey Oswald in the basement of Dallas's police headquarters. Since the television networks were covering Oswald's transfer to another jail, the shooting was broadcast live across the nation. Chief Justice Earl Warren warned ominously about the "forces of hatred and malevolence" that made such acts possible, and newspapers and magazines asked, "What sort of nation are we?"

Kennedy's image of buoyant youth, the trauma of his assassination, and the collective sense that Americans had been robbed of a promising leader contributed to a powerful mystique. Only forty-six at the time of his death, he was the first president born in the twentieth century. The Kennedy mythologizing process had begun even before his tragic death. In June 1963 about 59 percent of the people surveyed claimed to have voted for Kennedy, a big jump over the 49.7 percent who actually had; after the assassination, that figure rose to 65 percent. A British journalist called it "a posthumous landslide."

The Kennedy mystique has overshadowed what most historians agree was at best a mixed record. Kennedy exercised bold presidential leadership in foreign policy, but his flexible response program and his initiatives in Cuba and Berlin marked the height of superpower confrontation during the Cold War. His enthusiasm for fighting communism abroad, however, had no domestic equivalent. Kennedy's proposals for educational aid, medical insurance, and other liberal reforms stalled, and his tax cut bill languished in Congress until after his death. But perhaps his greatest failing was his reluctance to act on civil rights, which would become the most important domestic issue of the 1960s.

The Civil Rights Movement

Encouraged by *Brown v. Board of Education* and other favorable civil rights decisions, black southerners had stepped up their efforts to dismantle legal segregation in the late 1950s. The Montgomery bus boycotters, Martin Luther King, Jr., and the Southern Christian Leadership Conference (SCLC) developed a strategy of nonviolent direct action that was adopted and expanded by a younger generation of activists in the early 1960s. Those young people, primarily black college students, successfully challenged segregation through more assertive tactics such as sit-ins, freedom rides, and voter registration campaigns.

Sit-Ins and Freedom Rides

A new phase of the movement began in Greensboro, North Carolina, on February 1, 1960, when four black students from North Carolina Agricultural and Technical College—Ezell Blair, Jr., Franklin McCain, Joseph McNeill, and David Richmond—took seats at the "whites only" lunch counter of a local Woolworth's, determined to "sit in" until they were served. When Blair ordered something to eat, "The waitress looked at me as if I were from outer space." The target of their protest demonstrated the capricious nature of southern segregation laws. Blacks could buy toothpaste, underwear, and magazines alongside whites at Woolworth's, but not a sandwich or a cup of coffee.

Although Blair and his fellow protesters were arrested, the sit-in tactic worked and quickly spread to other southern cities. A few months later Ella Baker, an SCLC administrator and a lifelong activist, helped organize the Student Non-Violent Coordinating Committee (SNCC, pronounced "snick") to facilitate the student sit-ins (see American Lives, pages 936–937). By the end of the year, about 50,000 people had participated in sit-ins or other demonstrations, and 3,600 of them had been jailed, usually for disturbing the peace. White store owners quickly realized that they would lose business if the disruptions continued. Black activists and a number of white supporters were thus able to desegregate lunch counters in 126 cities throughout the South.

The success of SNCC's unorthodox tactics encouraged the Congress of Racial Equality (CORE), an interracial group founded in 1942, to adopt a more confrontational strategy. In 1961 CORE's executive director, James Farmer, organized a series of *freedom rides* on interstate bus lines throughout the South. Farmer targeted buses, waiting rooms, toilets, and terminal restaurants to call attention to the continuing segregation of public transportation despite the Supreme Court rulings. Activists, mostly young, both black and white, signed on for the potentially dangerous trips. In Anniston, Alabama,

Racial Violence in Montgomery
The lunch counter sit-ins organized by black students often provoked violence among hostile whites. Here a man swings a baseball bat at a black shopper on a Montgomery, Alabama, street corner the day after an unsuccessful sit-in in 1960.

Racial Violence in Birmingham
When thousands of blacks marched to downtown Birmingham, Alabama, to protest racial segregation in April 1963, they were met with fire hoses and attack dogs unleashed by Police Chief "Bull" Connor. The violence, which was televised on the national evening news, shocked many Americans and helped build sympathy for the civil rights movement among northern whites.

club-wielding Ku Klux Klansmen attacked one of the buses with stones and set it on fire. The freedom riders escaped only moments before the bus exploded. Other riders were brutally beaten in Montgomery and Birmingham, but Alabama's governor, John Patterson, refused to intervene, saying, "I cannot guarantee protection for this bunch of rabble rousers."

Although the Kennedy administration generally opposed the freedom riders' activities, scenes of the beatings and the bus burning on the nightly news prompted Attorney General Robert Kennedy to send in federal marshals to restore order. He also prodded the Interstate Commerce Commission to tighten regulations against segregation on interstate vehicles and in terminal facilities. Faced with potential Justice Department intervention against those who defied the Interstate Commerce Commission rules, most southern communities quietly acceded to the changes. CORE meanwhile learned the lesson that nonviolent protest could succeed if it provoked vicious white resistance and generated publicity. Only when forced to, it appeared, would the federal authorities act.

White southerners also staged violent attacks against blacks who registered to vote. In 1962–1963, when SNCC and CORE began conducting voter registration drives in the South, blacks who tried to register faced pressure, economic intimidation, and physical violence. For example, when Fannie Lou Hamer participated in a SNCC voter registration campaign in 1962, she was evicted from the farm where she had sharecropped for eighteen years. The FBI agents sent to the South, supposedly to protect the voting rights activists, usually sided with the white authorities and occasionally the Ku Klux Klan or did nothing.

JFK and Civil Rights

With the exception of protecting the freedom riders, the Kennedy administration lent little support to the growing civil rights movement. Behind the scenes Kennedy even authorized clandestine FBI surveillance of Martin Luther King, Jr., and a subsequent smear campaign against him. Kennedy seemed to view civil rights protests as irritating political embarrassments that distracted him from more important domestic and international issues.

Political realities, especially tensions within the Democratic coalition, also dampened Kennedy's enthusiasm for civil rights. On the one hand, Kennedy needed the votes of southern Democrats to get his programs through Congress and did not want to alienate them by embracing civil rights. For the same reason, he appointed a number of white supremacist judges to southern benches. On the other hand, blacks had given him strong support in the 1960 election, and Kennedy needed to keep them in the coalition. Thus he reached out to black constituencies with actions such as appointing former National Association for the Advancement of Colored People (NAACP) lawyer Thurgood Marshall to the U.S. Circuit Court of Appeals. But as the civil rights movement became more active and confrontational, Kennedy could not maintain that delicate balancing act.

Events came to a head in 1963 in Birmingham, Alabama, when Martin Luther King, Jr., and the Reverend Fred Shuttlesworth called for a protest against conditions in what King called "the most segregated city in the United States." In April thousands of black demonstrators marched downtown to picket Birmingham's department stores. They were met by Eugene ("Bull") Connor, the city's commissioner of public safety, who used

Ella Baker:
Civil Rights Mentor

"Who the hell is this old lady here?" asked more than one impudent and unknowing newcomer to the offices of the Student Non-Violent Coordinating Committee (SNCC) in Atlanta. Regal, matronly, conservatively dressed in a business suit, and always referred to as "Miss Baker," fifty-seven-year-old Ella Baker stood out from the black and white college students who flocked to SNCC in the early 1960s. But once activists watched her in action, few doubted that she belonged. As the veteran SNCC activist John Lewis recalled, "She was much older in terms of age, but I think in terms of ideas and philosophy and commitment she was one of the youngest persons in the movement."

When Baker used her position as the executive secretary of the Southern Christian Leadership Conference (SCLC) to act as the midwife for the birth of SNCC in 1960, she already had years of experience as an organizer and facilitator of social change, almost all of it be-

hind the scenes. As she recalled, "You didn't see me on television, you didn't see news stories about me. The kind of role that I tried to play was to pick up pieces or put together pieces out of which I hoped organization might come. My theory is, strong people don't need strong leaders." Ella Baker recognized the large and often unheralded roles that women played in the emergence of the civil rights movement: "the movement of the Fifties and the Sixties was carried largely by women, since it came out of church groups. . . . The number of women who carried the movement is much larger than that of the men." Her life is a prime example.

Ella Baker was born in Norfolk, Virginia, in 1903 and grew up in rural North Carolina on land that her grandparents had originally farmed as slaves. She drew enormous strength from her family, with her mother's community and church work providing a model for her own later activism. Reflecting the importance placed on

Ella Baker
Baker was a woman of action with a lifelong commitment to social change.

education by black families, especially for daughters who would have to work even if they married, Baker was sent to Shaw College in Raleigh, North Carolina. Soon after graduating in 1927, she headed north to Harlem, arriving just as the Great Depression was drying up opportunities in the promised land of the North. Instead of going to graduate school in sociology as she had hoped, she worked as a journalist, did some political organizing, and was involved in Works Progress Administration consumer projects. She also was married briefly, and unhappily, to a black minister. In the 1940s she traveled around the country as a field organizer for the National Association for the Advancement of Colored People (NAACP) but quit that job when she took on the responsibility of raising a seven-year-old niece. Throughout her career, Baker rarely held a regular job. "How did I make a living? I haven't. I have eked out existence."

When the SCLC was established in 1957 in the wake of the successful Montgomery bus boycott, Baker was recruited "temporarily" to be its executive secretary. She ended up staying two and a half years. Her organizational skills were very important to the developing movement, but she found herself increasingly restive under King's cautious leadership. In addition, she realized, not for the first time, that her lack of deference to male leadership, outspoken manner, and willingness to talk back made black men uncomfortable. She had an especially hard time working with King, who held very traditional ideas about gender roles.

When the student sit-ins erupted spontaneously in early 1960, Baker watched that development with interest and excitement. She persuaded the SCLC to put up $800 toward a conference of student leaders to be held on the campus of her alma mater in Raleigh in April 1960. More than 300 young people attended, a huge outpouring. At the convention Baker encouraged student leaders to chart an independent role, not just to become the "youth wings" of established groups such as the SCLC, the NAACP, and CORE. She did not come right out and say "Don't let Martin Luther King tell you what to do," Julian Bond remembered, but that was clearly what she meant. The students followed her advice, and SNCC remained independent from existing civil rights organizations. Baker's faith in the students was totally in keeping with her lifelong commitment to grass-roots, "group-centered leadership." Probably her greatest dissatisfaction with the SCLC was the way that it revolved so completely around Martin Luther King's leadership.

During the turbulent 1960s Baker offered her organizational skills and material support to SNCC. She never intervened directly in the internal struggles and endless discussions that characterized the group, choosing instead to serve as a facilitator for group consensus and action. She provided not just a bridge across generations but a powerful role model of political engagement and activism. This model was especially important to women, both black and white, who drew the lesson that women could be just as effective as men in the roles of organizer and participant. The nonhierarchical structure of SNCC, with its emphasis on local leadership and individual initiative, provided an egalitarian climate far more conducive to the utilization of female talent than was American society at large. For some women, especially the white volunteers, their experience in SNCC laid the groundwork for the emergence of the women's movement later in the decade.

Voter registration had always been a top priority for SNCC, and in 1964 Baker got involved in an attempt to wrest political power from the regular Democratic party, which remained rigidly all white in the South. Denied access to the right to vote, SNCC organized an alternative political party—the Mississippi Freedom Democratic party (MFDP). Fannie Lou Hamer became the movement's most visible public orator, but Baker played a crucial behind-the-scenes role. Testifying before the credentials committee at the Democratic convention in Atlantic City that summer, Hamer and Baker led the unsuccessful effort to unseat the all-white Mississippi delegation in favor of the MFDP. When President Johnson and the Democratic leadership offered the MFDP token representation in the delegation, the MFDP rejected that compromise as an insult. Baker was not bitter or discouraged by this outcome or the many other setbacks she faced in her career: "I keep going because I don't see the productive value of being bitter. What else *do* you do?"

Ella Baker continued her lifelong commitment to participatory democracy and social change long after SNCC had lost its place on the cutting edge on the civil rights movement. She died in 1986 on her eighty-third birthday. At her memorial service, the civil rights activist Bernice Johnson Reagon, the founder of the singing group Sweet Honey in the Rock, led the assembled friends in a favorite song that captured the determination and spirituality that shaped Ella Baker's lifelong activism: "Guide my feet while I run this race . . . for I don't want to run this race in vain."

snarling dogs, electric cattle prods, and high-pressure fire hoses to break up the crowd; the hoses were so powerful that they ripped bark from trees and tore bricks from buildings. Television cameras captured the entire scene. "The civil rights movement should thank God for Bull Connor," President Kennedy noted. "He's helped it as much as Abraham Lincoln."

Realizing that he could no longer straddle the issue, Kennedy decided to step up the federal role in civil rights. On June 11, 1963, he went on television to promise major civil rights legislation banning discrimination in public accommodations and empowering the Justice Department to seek desegregation on its own authority. Black leaders hailed the speech as a "Second Emancipation Proclamation," but for one person Kennedy's speech came too late. That night, Medgar Evers, the president of the Mississippi NAACP, was shot in the back and killed in his driveway in Jackson. The martyrdom of Evers became a spur to further action.

The March on Washington

To rouse the conscience of the country at large and then to marshal support for Kennedy's bill, civil rights leaders turned to a tactic that A. Phillip Randolph had first suggested in 1941: a massive march on Washington. Martin Luther King, Jr., of the SCLC, Roy Wilkins of the NAACP, Whitney Young of the National Urban League, and the black socialist Bayard Rustin were the principal organizers. They drew support from a broad coalition, including the National Council of Churches, the National Conference of Catholics for Interracial Justice, the American Jewish Congress, and the AFL–CIO's Industrial Union Department.

On August 28, 1963, about 250,000 black and white demonstrators—the largest demonstration up to that time—gathered at the Lincoln Memorial. Speakers and performers alternately uplifted, challenged, and entertained the crowd. The march culminated in a memorable speech that Martin Luther King delivered, indeed preached, in the evangelical style of the black church:

> I have a dream that one day on the red hills of Georgia the sons of former slaves and the sons of former slave-owners will be able to sit down together at the table of brotherhood. I have a dream that one day even the state of Mississippi, a desert state sweltering with the heat of injustice and oppression, will be transformed into an oasis of freedom and justice. I have a dream that my four little children will one day live in a nation where they will not be judged by the color of their skin but by the content of their character.

He ended with an invocation from an old Negro spiritual: "Free at last! Free at last! Thank God almighty, we are free at last!"

Martin Luther King, Jr.
The Reverend Martin Luther King, Jr. (1929–1968), was one of the most eloquent advocates of the black cause in the 1950s and 1960s. For many people, his speech at the 1963 March on Washington was the high point of the event.

King's eloquence and the sight of blacks and whites marching solemnly together did more than any other event to make the civil rights movement acceptable to white Americans. The March on Washington seemed to justify the liberal faith that blacks and whites could work together to promote racial harmony, and it marked the climax of the nonviolent phase of the civil rights movement. It also confirmed King's position, especially in the white liberal community, as the leading speaker for the black cause. Winning the Nobel Peace Prize in 1964 enhanced his stature.

Despite the impact of the march on public opinion, few Congressional votes were changed by the event. Southern senators continued to block Kennedy's legislation by threatening a filibuster. Even more troubling was a new outbreak of violence by white extremists, determined to oppose equality for blacks at all costs. In September a Baptist church in Birmingham was bombed, and four black girls attending Sunday school were killed. Only two months after the Birmingham bombing, President Kennedy was assassinated in Dallas.

Fannie Lou Hamer

Registering to Vote in Mississippi

Fannie Lou Hamer was the youngest of twenty children born to a sharecropping family in Montgomery County, Mississippi. When she tried to register to vote in 1962, she lost her job as a timekeeper on a cotton plantation. In 1964 she led the challenge of the Mississippi Freedom Democratic party to the all-white party regulars in that state.

So then that was in 1962 when the civil rights workers came into this county. Now I didn't know anything about voter registration or nothin' like that, 'cause people had never been told that they could register to vote. . . . So they had a rally. I had gone to church that Sunday, and the minister announced that they were gon' have a mass meeting that Monday night. Well, I didn't know what a mass meeting was, and I was just curious to go to a mass meeting. So I did . . . and they was talkin' about how blacks had a right to register and how they had a right to vote. . . . Just listenin' at 'em, I could just see myself

votin' people outa office that I know was wrong and didn't do nothin' to help the poor. I said, you know, that's sumpin' I really wanna be involved in, and finally at the end of that rally, I had made up my mind that I was gonna come out here when they said you could go down that Friday [August 31, 1962] to try to register. . . .

He [the registrar] brought a big old book out there, and he gave me the sixteenth section of the Constitution of Mississippi, and that was dealing with de facto laws, and I didn't know nothin' about no de facto laws, didn't know nothin' about any of 'em. I could copy it like it was in the book . . . but after I got through copying it, he told me to give a reasonable interpretation and tell the meaning of that section that I had copied. Well, I flunked out. . . .

Monday, the fourth of December, I went back to Indianola to the circuit clerk's office and I told him who I was and I was there to take that literacy test again.

I said, "Now, you cain't have me fired 'cause I'm already fired, and I won't have to move now, because I'm not livin' in no white man's house." I said, "I'll be here every thirty days until I become a registered voter."

I passed that second test, but it made us become like criminals. We would have to have our lights out before dark. It was cars passing that house all times of the night, driving real slow with guns, and pickups with white mens in it, and they'd pass that house just as slow as they could pass it . . . three guns lined up in the back. . . . Pap couldn't get nothin' to do. . . .

So I started teachin' citizenship class, and I became the supervisor of the citizenship class in this county. So I moved around the county to do citizenship education and later on I become a field secretary for SNCC.

Source: Howell Raines, *My Soul Is Rested* (New York: Putnam, 1977), 249–250, 252.

Landmark Legislation

Lyndon Johnson promptly turned the passage of civil rights legislation into a memorial to his slain predecessor, a slightly ironic twist in light of Kennedy's lukewarm support for the cause. As a southerner, Johnson was eager to prove to the nation and to Kennedy's skeptical staff that he was a true liberal and a champion of racial equality. The Civil Rights Act, passed in June 1964 after a two-and-a-half-month filibuster by southern senators, was a landmark in the history of American race relations and one of the greatest achievements of the 1960s. Its keystone, Title VII, outlawed discrimination in employment on the basis of race, religion, national origin, or sex. Another section barred discrimination in public accommodations. The law gave integrationists two powerful new weapons: they could ask the U.S. attorney general to withhold federal funds from any government-run program that was not desegregated, and they could appeal

discrimination in public accommodations and employment to the Equal Employment Opportunity Commission, which Kennedy had established soon after taking office. The Civil Rights Act resulted in the desegregation of public facilities throughout the South, including many public schools, but obstacles to black voting rights persisted.

Freedom Summer. In 1964, with the Civil Rights Act on the brink of passage, black organizations and churches mounted a major civil rights campaign in Mississippi known as Freedom Summer. Drawing on several thousand volunteers from across the country, including many idealistic white college students, Freedom Summer workers established freedom schools for black children, conducted a major voter registration drive, and organized the Mississippi Freedom Democratic party, a political alternative to the all-white Mississippi Democratic organization (see American Voices, above). White

Andy Warhol on Race Relations

The artist Andy Warhol (1928–1987) is usually associated with pop-art spoofs of consumer culture, such as paintings of Campbell's soup cans and Brillo pads, along with magnetic images of popular icons such as Marilyn Monroe and Elizabeth Taylor. Yet he also treated political subjects, as in this provocative 1963 painting, *Red Race Riot*, depicting violence at a civil rights demonstration.

southerners reacted swiftly and violently to those efforts. In June, James Chaney, a CORE volunteer from Mississippi; Andrew Goodman, a student from New York; and Michael Schwerner, a New York social worker, disappeared from Philadelphia, Mississippi, and were presumed murdered. As public demand for an investigation grew, Rita Schwerner, Michael's wife, noted, "We all know that this search . . . is because Andrew Goodman and my husband are white. If only Chaney was involved, nothing would have been done." Six weeks later the FBI discovered the three bodies inside a newly constructed dam five miles away. Goodman and Schwerner had been killed by a single bullet each,

whereas Chaney had been brutally beaten with a chain and shot several times. An investigation later determined that members of the Ku Klux Klan had committed the crime. During Freedom Summer, fifteen civil rights workers were murdered; only about 1,200 black voters were registered.

The Voting Rights Act of 1965. The need for federal action to support voting rights became even clearer in 1965. In February sheriff's deputies in Marion, Alabama, killed Jimmy Lee Jackson, a black voting rights advocate, during a voter registration march. In protest, Martin Luther King and other black leaders called for a massive march on Sunday, March 7, from nearby Selma to the state capital, Montgomery, 54 miles away. Governor George Wallace banned the march, disingenuously citing concern for public safety. As soon as the marchers left Selma, mounted state troopers attacked them in broad daylight with tear gas and clubs. The scene was shown on national television later that night; ironically, ABC broke into *Judgment at Nuremberg*, a film about the Nazi war crimes trials, to show police officers attacking American citizens on the Pettus Bridge.

Lyndon Johnson called Bloody Sunday "an American tragedy" and redoubled his efforts to get Congress to pass his pending voting rights legislation. In a televised speech to a joint session of Congress on March 15 Johnson asserted, "It is wrong—deadly wrong, to deny any of your fellow Americans the right to vote in this country." Then, dramatically and repeatedly, Johnson invoked the best-known slogan of the civil rights movement, "We shall overcome." Watching the speech on television, Martin Luther King was moved to tears.

On August 6 Congress passed the Voting Rights Act of 1965, the second legislative landmark of the civil rights movement. The act suspended the literacy tests and other measures that most southern states had used to prevent blacks from registering to vote. It also authorized the attorney general to send federal examiners to register voters in any county where less than 50 percent of the voting-age population was registered, placing the entire registration and voting process under federal control. Together with the adoption in 1964 of the Twenty-fourth Amendment to the Constitution, which outlawed the federal poll tax, and successful legal challenges to state and local poll taxes, the Voting Rights Act allowed millions of blacks to register and vote for the first time. Congress reauthorized the Voting Rights Act in 1970, 1975, and 1982.

The results in the South were stunning. In 1960 only 20 percent of eligible blacks were registered; in 1964 the figure had risen to 39 percent, and in 1971 to 62 percent (see Map 30.3). As Hartman Turnbow, a Mississippi farmer who had risked his life to register in 1964, later declared, "It won't never go back where it was."

Registering to Vote

Once black citizens could register to vote, they changed the nature of southern politics, opening new channels of political participation and electoral success. In 1989 there were over 4,440 elected black officials in the South, including 578 in Mississippi alone, a dramatic change in the twenty-five years since the passage of the Voting Rights Act of 1965.

Lyndon Johnson and the Great Society

After building a reputation as a crusader for civil rights and an activist in the Kennedy tradition, Johnson went on to win the 1964 presidential election less than a year after assuming office. His landslide victory far exceeded Kennedy's meager mandate in 1960. Johnson then used his astonishing energy and genius for compromise to bring to fruition many of Kennedy's stalled programs and more than a few of his own. Those legislative accomplishments are referred to as the Great Society, Johnson's own phrase to describe his commitment to ending poverty and racial injustice. It was the Great Society, not the much less ambitious New Frontier, that fulfilled and in some cases surpassed the New Deal liberal agenda of the 1930s.

The Great Coalition Builder

Lyndon Baines Johnson brought to the presidency far more legislative experience than had any other modern president, and he used his talent to great effect. Born in the central Texas hill country in 1908, Johnson had served in government since 1932 as a Congressional aide, New Deal administrator, congressman, senator, Senate majority leader, and finally vice-president.

A man of singular force, he often got his way by using what the journalists Rowland Evans and Robert Novak called the "Johnson treatment." Approaching an unsuspecting colleague, he moved "in close, his face

MAP 30.3

Black Voter Registration in the South

After passage of the Voting Rights Act of 1965, black registration in the South increased dramatically. The bars show the number of blacks registered in 1964, before the act was passed, and 1975, after it had been in effect for ten years. States in the Deep South, such as Mississippi, Alabama, and Georgia, had the biggest rises.

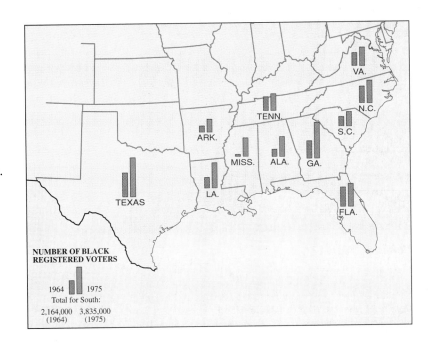

a scant millimeter from his target, his eyes widening and narrowing, his eyebrows rising and falling. From his pockets poured clippings, memos, statistics. Mimicry, humor, and the genius of analogy made the Treatment an almost hypnotic experience." Johnson invariably left his targets overwhelmed and bruised—and willing to go along with his requests. In his first year as president he used his powers of persuasion to push through the Civil Rights Act and the Kennedy-Johnson tax cut. His major legislative achievements, however, came after his election in 1964.

If 1964 was a year of liberal triumph in Congress, it was a year of conservative retrenchment in the Republican party. The Republican nominee for president in 1964 was Senator Barry Goldwater of Arizona. Goldwater, who was determined to offer "a choice, not an echo," campaigned against the expansion of federal power in areas such as the economy and civil rights. Goldwater's crisp speeches rejected Republican efforts to build a moderate coalition. "Extremism in the defense of liberty is no vice," he stated in his acceptance speech at the Republican convention. "Moderation in the pursuit of justice is no virtue." On foreign affairs Goldwater was an aggressive anticommunist who once joked about "lobbing [a nuclear bomb] into the men's room of the Kremlin."

The 1964 Campaign
Barry Goldwater's 1964 Republican campaign produced some very creative political memorabilia, such as bumper stickers that proclaimed "AuH_2O" (the symbols for gold and water) and this gold elephant wearing glasses like the candidate's.

President Johnson easily won the Democratic nomination. Reaffirming his commitment to the party's liberal agenda, but putting some distance between himself and the Kennedy clan, Johnson passed over Robert F. Kennedy for vice-president in favor of Senator Hubert H. Humphrey of Minnesota, who in 1948 had introduced a controversial civil rights plank that had split the party (see Chapter 28). An attempt by the avowed segregationist George C. Wallace, governor of Alabama, to exploit a white backlash against civil rights showed early strength but then fizzled. Ironically, given his later ordeal in Vietnam, Johnson presented himself as the peace candidate. Using a frightening TV commercial showing a billowing mushroom cloud, Johnson forces exploited public fears about Goldwater's bellicose foreign policy. (The ad was pulled two days later in response to public outcries against fear mongering.)

The Johnson-Humphrey ticket won by one of the largest margins in history, receiving 61.1 percent of the popular vote. This surpassed even the 1936 landslide of that great coalition builder Franklin D. Roosevelt, Johnson's political idol and mentor. And Johnson's coattails were long; his sweeping victory brought Democratic gains in both Congress and the state legislatures.

The "Johnson Treatment"
Lyndon B. Johnson, a shrewd and adroit politician, learned many of his legislative skills while serving as majority leader of the Senate from 1953 to 1960. Here he zeroes in on Senator Theodore Francis Green of Rhode Island. After assuming the presidency Johnson remarked, "They say Jack Kennedy had style, but I'm the one who's got the bills passed."

Enacting the Liberal Agenda

Like most New Deal liberals, Johnson held an expansive view of presidential leadership and the positive role of government. The 1964 election gave him the popular

TABLE 30.1

Major Great Society Legislation

Civil Rights

1964	Twenty-fourth Amendment	Outlawed poll tax in federal elections
	Civil Rights Act	Banned discrimination in employment and public accommodations on the basis of race, religion, sex, or national origin
1965	Voting Rights Act	Outlawed literacy tests for voting; provided federal supervision of registration in historically low-registration areas

Social Welfare

1964	Economic Opportunity Act	Created Office of Economic Opportunity (OEO) to administer War on Poverty programs such as Head Start, Job Corps, and Volunteers in Service to America (VISTA)
1965	Medical Care Act	Provided medical care for poor (Medicaid) and elderly (Medicare)
1966	Minimum Wage Act	Raised hourly minimum wage from $1.25 to $1.40 and expanded coverage to new groups

Education

1965	Elementary and Secondary Education Act	Granted federal aid for education of poor children
	National Endowment for the Arts and Humanities	Provided federal funding and support for artists and scholars
	Higher Education Act	Provided federal scholarships for post-secondary education

Housing and Urban Development

1964	Urban Mass Transportation Act	Provided federal aid to urban mass transit
	Omnibus Housing Act	Provided federal funds for public housing and rent subsidies for low-income families
1965	Housing and Urban Development Act	Created Department of Housing and Urban Development (HUD)
1966	Metropolitan Area Redevelopment and Demonstration Cities acts	Designated 150 "model cities" for combined programs of public housing, social services, and job training

Environment

| 1964 | Wilderness Preservation Act | Designated 9.1 million acres of federal lands as "wilderness areas," barring future roads, buildings, or commercial use |
| 1965 | Air and Water Quality acts | Set tougher air quality standards; required states to enforce water quality standards for interstate waters |

Miscellaneous

1964	Tax Reduction Act	Reduced personal and corporate income tax rates
1965	Immigration Act	Abandoned national quotas of 1924 law, allowing more non-European immigration
	Appalachian Regional Development Act	Provided federal funding for roads, health clinics, and other public works projects in economically depressed regions

mandate and, more important, the filibuster-proof Senate majority that he needed to push his programs forward. "Hurry boys, hurry," he urged his staff. "Get that legislation up to the Hill and out. Eighteen months from now ol' Landslide Lyndon will be Lame-Duck Lyndon." Under Johnson's Great Society, including a multifaceted War on Poverty program, the Eighty-ninth Congress en-

acted more social reform measures than any session had since Roosevelt's first term, offering legislation for every important element of the Democratic coalition (see Table 30.1).

One of Johnson's first big successes was breaking the Congressional deadlock on aid to education. Passed in April 1965, the Elementary and Secondary Education

Act authorized $1 billion in federal funds to benefit impoverished children. By dispensing aid to schools on the basis of the number of needy children in attendance, the act sidestepped the religious issue by granting funds to public and parochial schools alike. In practice, the compromise measure spread funding to a broad spectrum of schools, and the results did not necessarily benefit poor children. Undeterred by such flaws, Johnson pressed for further educational subsidies. Six months later he signed the Higher Education Act, providing the first federal scholarships for college students.

The Eighty-ninth Congress also gave Johnson enough votes to enact the federal health insurance legislation first proposed by Truman. Realizing that it could no longer block some form of federal health insurance, the American Medical Association proposed that federal funds be used to pay doctors as well as hospitals. The result was two new programs: Medicare, a health plan for the elderly funded by a surcharge on Social Security payroll taxes, and Medicaid, a plan for the poor paid for by general tax revenues. Because Congress did not impose a cap on medical expenses, which the medical industry opposed, federal expenditures for the two programs quickly escalated. Once again, by seeking legislative compromises that pleased multiple constituencies, the Johnson administration created expansive and economically unwieldy programs.

Administration programs did not aid only the poor—the middle class benefited, too. Federal urban renewal and home mortgage assistance helped those who could afford to live in single-family homes or modern apartments. Medicare assistance went to every elderly person covered by Social Security, regardless of need. Much of the federal aid to education benefited the children of the middle class. In addition, Johnson successfully pressed for environmental measures that benefited American society as a whole: the expansion of the national park system, improvement of air and water quality, increased land-use planning, and, at the insistence of his wife, Lady Bird Johnson, the Highway Beautification Act of 1965. That year also saw the creation of the National Endowment for the Arts, which supported the performing and creative arts, and the National Endowment for the Humanities, which funded efforts to understand and interpret the nation's cultural and historical heritage. Reaching out to new ethnic constituencies, Johnson signed the Immigration Act of 1965, which abandoned the quota system of the 1920s that had favored European immigrants (see Chapter 24), and replaced it with more uniform hemispheric restrictions. This combination of legislative initiatives helped unite a diverse array of Democratic constituencies and reflected the liberal belief that federal activism could ensure the public welfare and promote fairness. But it involved legislative compromises as well, compromises that ultimately limited the effectiveness of certain programs.

The War on Poverty

Johnson always insisted that the top priority of his Great Society was to put "an end to poverty in our time." The problem of poverty was very real. Poor people made up about a fourth of the American population; three-fourths of the poor were white. The poor in the United States consisted of isolated farmers and miners in Appalachia, blacks and Puerto Ricans in urban ghettos, Mexican-Americans in migrant labor camps and urban barrios, native Americans on reservations, women raising families on their own, and the abandoned and destitute elderly. As Michael Harrington had pointed out in his influential 1962 book, *The Other America*, the poor were everywhere, but their poverty was curiously invisible in an affluent suburban society. Modern technology had "made a longer, healthier, better life possible," Harrington observed, yet it left the poor "on the margin": "They watch the movies and read the magazines of affluent America, and these teach them that they are internal exiles."

New Deal social welfare programs had failed to reach these people. Because unemployment insurance ran out after a few months, it did not provide protection against extended joblessness. Social Security and other social insurance programs provided benefits to workers who paid for them through special taxes, but not all workers were covered. Social welfare programs such as Old Age Assistance, Aid to Dependent Children, and Aid to the Blind had strict restrictions regarding eligibility.

Responding to Harrington and other advocates for the poor, the Johnson administration tried to reduce poverty by expanding long-established social insurance, welfare, and public works programs. It broadened Social Security to include waiters and waitresses, domestic servants, farm workers, and hospital employees. Social welfare expenditures increased rapidly, especially for Aid to Families with Dependent Children (AFDC), as did public housing and rent subsidy programs. Food Stamps, begun in 1964 largely to stabilize farm prices, grew into a major program of assistance to low-income families. The Appalachian Regional Development Act of 1965 provided federal funding for local roads, health clinics, and other public works projects in that poverty-stricken region. As in the New Deal, the social welfare system continued to develop in a piecemeal fashion, with no overall coordination.

The Office of Economic Opportunity (OEO), established by the omnibus Economic Opportunity Act of 1964, became the Great Society's showcase in the War on Poverty. Built around the twin strategies of equal opportunity and community action, OEO programs were so numerous and diverse that they recalled the alphabet agencies of the New Deal. Officials at the OEO quickly realized that identifying poverty was one thing; drafting and implementing programs to address it was quite an-

ons, urging black inmates to take charge of their lives by adopting a strict code of personal behavior, including the Muslim ban on the use of drugs, alcohol, and tobacco. The Nation of Islam's ideology was extremely hostile to whites, whom its leader Elijah Muhammad called "blue-eyed devils." Forcefully promoting black nationalism, the group stressed black pride, unity, and self-help.

The Black Muslims' most charismatic figure was Malcolm X. Born Malcolm Little in 1925, he converted to the Nation of Islam while serving time in prison for attempted burglary. Taking the name Malcolm X, he portrayed his transformation from street hustler to minister of Islam as evidence of the redemptive powers of the Black Muslim faith. A brilliant debater and a spellbinding speaker, Malcolm X preached a philosophy quite different from Martin Luther King's. Malcolm advocated militant protest and separatism, although he condoned the use of violence only for self-defense and self-assertion. He was hostile to the traditional civil rights organizations, caustically referring to the 1963 march as the "Farce on Washington" and mocking the "angry revolutionists all harmonizing 'We Shall Overcome . . . Suum Day' while tripping and swinging along arm-in-arm with the very people they were supposed to be angrily revolting against."

In 1964, after a power struggle with Elijah Muhammed, Malcolm X broke with the Nation of Islam. He then made a pilgrimage to Mecca, the holiest site of traditional Islam, and toured Africa, where he embraced the liberation struggles of all colonized peoples. After his return to the United States, he founded the Organization of Afro-American Unity to promote this internationalist vision and moved away from antiwhite rhetoric. On February 21, 1965, Malcolm X was assassinated while giving a speech at the Audubon Ballroom in Harlem. Three Black Muslims were later convicted for the murder. His autobiography, ghostwritten by Alex Haley and published soon after Malcolm's death, became one of the decade's most influential books.

Black Power. Malcolm X's call for black cultural and political independence appealed to young black activists in SNCC and CORE, but many balked at the idea of converting to Islam, preferring a secular black nationalist movement. Soon many of these activists were embracing *black power*, a more aggressive call for black self-reliance and racial pride. As a result of this growing militancy, most civil rights organizations went through a major identity crisis. CORE's decision to bar whites from leadership positions in 1965 was a clear indication of those tensions. The next year, the SNCC leader Stokely Carmichael christened a new era in the black struggle: "The only way we gonna stop them white men from whoopin' us is to take over. We been saying freedom for

Malcolm X (1925–1965)
Charismatic, controversial, and caustic, Malcolm X rarely minced words. "Yes, I'm an extremist," he told the writer Alex Haley. "The black race here in North America is in extremely bad condition. You show me a black man who isn't an extremist and I'll show you one who needs psychiatric attention!" Director Spike Lee's 1992 film, *Malcolm X*, reignited old controversies and started some of its own.

six years and we ain't got nothin'. What we gonna start saying is Black Power!" Carmichael's words marked a public avowal of black power, but his pronouncement merely confirmed the militant forces already present in SNCC and other civil rights groups. In fact, by 1966 most whites had been effectively ejected from the civil rights movement. Focusing on community control and black self-determination, SNCC and other groups admonished whites to go home and work against racism in their own backyards.

In the same year Huey Newton and Bobby Seale, two college students in Oakland, California, founded the Black Panthers as a militant self-defense organization to protect local blacks from police violence. The Panthers' influence quickly spread to other cities, where they undertook a wide range of community organizing projects, including a number of interracial efforts. But the Panthers' affinity for Third World revolutionary movements and armed struggle became their most publicized attribute.

Only three years after Martin Luther King's "I Have a Dream" speech, radical black power activists proposed a new agenda: not nonviolence but armed self-defense, not integration but separatism, not working within the system but preparing for revolution. Among the most significant legacies of black power was the assertion of racial pride. Many young blacks insisted on the term *Afro-American* rather than *Negro*, a term they found demeaning because of its historical association with slavery and racism. Rejecting white tastes and standards, blacks wore African clothing and Afro hairstyles and helped awaken interest in black history, art, and literature. By the 1970s many colleges and universities were offering programs in black studies.

The new black assertiveness alarmed many white Americans. They had been willing to go along with the moderate reforms of the 1950s and early 1960s but became wary when blacks started demanding immediate access to higher-paying jobs, housing in white neighborhoods, integrated schools, and increased political power. In 1966, 84 percent of all whites thought blacks were demanding too much change, up from 34 percent five years earlier.

Summer in the City

A major reason for the erosion of white support was a wave of riots that struck the nation's cities. Every summer from 1964 to 1968 images of defiant black youths and burning buildings filled the nightly news. The rapid growth of de facto segregation in metropolitan areas provided the backdrop for the riots. Without the education

Watts in Flames
The nation's worst racial disturbance since the Detroit race riot of 1943 began in the Watts section of Los Angeles on August 11, 1965. An altercation broke out when white police officers stopped two blacks for a minor traffic violation. Thirty-four persons died in the Watts riot.

and skills needed for most city jobs, successive generations of blacks moving out of the rural South were unable to find employment that paid an adequate wage. Many were unemployed. Moreover, they were angry with white landlords who owned the substandard housing that they were forced to live in, white shopkeepers who earned money from black trade but would not hire black clerks or salespeople, and all-white unions—especially in the construction industry—that controlled access to skilled jobs. Most critically, many blacks came to resent the police, whose violent presence in black neighborhoods made them seem like "an occupying army." Stimulated by the successes of southern blacks who had challenged whites and gotten results, young urban blacks expressed their grievances through their own brand of "direct action."

The first "long hot summer" began in July 1964 in New York City, when police shot a young black criminal suspect in Harlem. Angry youths looted and rioted for a week. The volatile issue of police brutality would set off riots in a number of cities over the next four years. In August 1965 the arrest of a young black motorist in the Watts section of Los Angeles sparked six days of rioting that left thirty-four blacks dead. Ironically, Watts erupted only five days after President Johnson hailed the passage of the Voting Rights Act of 1965 as the next great step toward racial equality. For many young urban blacks the legal gains of the civil rights movement were irrelevant to their daily experience of poverty and economic exploitation. Instead of singing "We shall overcome," Watts rioters shouted "Burn, baby, burn."

The riots of 1967 were the most serious of all (see Map 30.4). Rioting began in several southern cities in the spring, spread to other cities in June, and engulfed twenty-two cities in July and August. The most devastating outbreaks occurred in Newark and Detroit. Forty-three people were killed in Detroit alone, nearly all of them black, and $50 million of property was destroyed. Federal paratroopers, some just back from service in Vietnam, were sent in to restore order, and Mayor Jerome Cavanaugh compared the city to war-ravaged Berlin in 1945. As in most of the riots, the arson and looting were directed at white-owned stores and property, but there was little physical violence against white people. Almost all the reported sniping turned out to involve wild shooting by the police.

The riots finally provoked a response from the federal government. On July 29, 1967, President Johnson appointed a special commission under Governor Otto Kerner of Illinois to investigate the reasons for the rioting. The final report of the National Advisory Commission on Civil Disorders, released in March 1968, detailed the continuing inequality and racism of urban life. It also issued a warning: "Our nation is moving toward two societies, one black, one white—separate and unequal. . . .

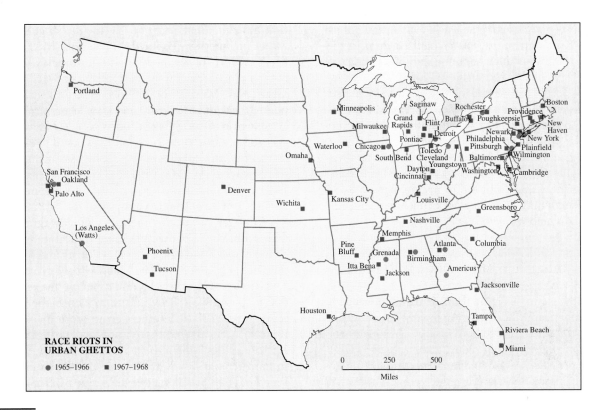

RACE RIOTS IN URBAN GHETTOS

● 1965–1966   ■ 1967–1968

0   250   500
Miles

MAP 30.4

Racial Unrest in America's Cities, 1965–1968
American cities suffered through four "long hot summers" of rioting in the mid-1960s. In 1967, the worst year, riots broke out across the United States, including the South and West. Major riots usually did not occur in the same city two years in a row.

What white Americans have never fully understood—but what the Negro can never forget—is that white society is deeply implicated in the ghetto. White institutions created it, white institutions maintain it, and white society condones it."

The Assassination of Martin Luther King, Jr. Barely a month after the Commission on Civil Disorders released its report, Martin Luther King was assassinated in Memphis, Tennessee, where he had gone to support a strike by predominantly black sanitation workers. On April 4, 1968, he was shot by James Earl Ray, a white ex-convict whose motive was unknown. King's death set off an explosion of urban rioting. Major violence broke out in more than a hundred cities. As violence and looting engulfed most of Chicago's West Side, Mayor Richard J. Daley ordered police to "shoot to kill" suspected arsonists. In Washington, National Guard troops with machine guns protected the Capitol; on television, it was framed by the fires from neighboring ghettos.

With King's assassination the civil rights movement lost the black leader best able to stir the conscience of white America. At the time of his death, King was only

thirty-nine years old. During the last years of his life he had moved toward a more comprehensive view of the structural problems of poverty and racism faced by blacks in contemporary America. In 1966 he had confronted the issue of residential segregation in a losing campaign for open housing in Chicago. He also spoke out eloquently against the Vietnam War. In 1968 he was planning a poor people's campaign to raise issues of economic injustice and inequality. How successful King would have been in those endeavors will never be known, but his death marked the passing of an important national leader and was symptomatic of the troubled course of the civil rights movement.

The Legacy of the Civil Rights Movement. The 1950s and 1960s brought permanent, indeed revolutionary, changes in American race relations. Jim Crow segregation was overturned in less than a decade, and federal legislation ensured protection of black Americans' basic civil rights. The enfranchisement of blacks in southern states ended political control there by a lily-white Democratic party and allowed black candidates to enter the political arena. White candidates who had once been ardent segregationists now courted the black vote. In time Martin Luther King's greatness was recognized even in the South; in 1986 his birthday became a national holiday.

However, much remained undone. The more entrenched forms of segregation and discrimination persisted despite the legal reforms of the 1960s. African-Americans, particularly those in the central cities, continued to make up a disproportionate number of the poor, unemployed, and undereducated. As the civil rights movement gradually disintegrated, its agenda remained unfinished. Nevertheless, it continued to inspire many outside the black community, including Mexican-Americans, native Americans, and women.

The Spreading Demand for Equal Rights

Following the example set by the civil rights movement, Mexican-Americans and native Americans organized to press their claims. Although both groups had long histories of organizing for equal rights, the black civil rights movement provided a fresh and innovative model for social change, particularly among the young. As a civil rights worker observed, "What started out as an identify crisis for Negroes turned out to be an identity crisis for the nation."

Mexican-American Activism. Although Mexican-Americans had been actively working for civil rights since the 1930s (see Chapter 25), the emphasis had been on labor organizing, veterans' rights, and community affairs. Until 1960 few Spanish-speaking Americans had participated in electoral politics. Poverty, an uncertain legal status, and language barriers made political mobiliza-

tion difficult. That situation began to change when the Mexican-American Political Association (MAPA) mobilized support for Kennedy in 1960, probably providing his margin of victory in the closely contested states of Texas, New Mexico, and Illinois. In return, Kennedy appointed several Mexican-American leaders to posts in Washington. Over the next four years, MAPA and other political organizations successfully worked to elect Mexican-American candidates to Congress, including Edward Roybal of California and Henry González and Elizo de la Garza of Texas in the House, and Joseph Montoya of New Mexico in the Senate.

Younger Mexican-Americans quickly grew impatient with MAPA, however. More radical and more inclined to celebrate cultural achievements and traditions, the younger leaders pursued increasingly diverse goals. The barrios of Los Angeles and other western cities produced the militant Brown Berets, who modeled themselves on the Black Panthers (who wore black berets). Rejecting the assimilationist approach of their elders, 1,500 Mexican-American students met in Denver in 1969 to hammer out a new nationalist political and cultural agenda. They proclaimed a new term, *Chicano*, to replace *Mexican-American* and subsequently organized a political party, La Raza Unida ("The United Race"), to promote Mexican-American interests and candidates. Chicano students in California and other southwestern states also staged demonstrations and boycotts to press for bilingual education, the hiring of more Chicano teachers, and the creation of programs in Chicano studies. By the 1970s there were dozens of those programs in universities throughout the region.

Chicano strategists also pursued economic objectives. Working in the fields around Delano, California,

César Chávez

Mexican-American labor leader César Chávez addresses a rally in Guadalupe, California. Chávez won national attention in 1965 during a strike of migrant farm workers, most of them Mexican-Americans, against California grape growers. Drawing on tactics from the civil rights movement, Chávez called for nonviolent action and effectively mobilized support by persuading white liberals to boycott nonunion table grapes.

the labor leader César Chávez organized the United Farm Workers (UFW), the first union to represent migrant workers successfully. A 1965 grape pickers' strike and a nationwide boycott of table grapes brought Chávez and his union national publicity. They won the support of the AFL–CIO and Senator Robert F. Kennedy of New York, and Chávez was soon receiving almost as much media attention as was Martin Luther King, Jr. Protesting employer harassment of the UFW and subsequent outbreaks of violence in the fields, Chávez undertook a twenty-five-day fast in 1968. Victory came in 1970, when California grape growers signed contracts recognizing the UFW.

Asserting Rights for Native Americans. American Indians also found a model in the civil rights movement. Native Americans, who numbered nearly 800,000 in the 1960s, were an exceedingly diverse group, divided by language, tribal history, region, and degree of integration into mainstream American life. Moreover, the termination policy that had begun in the 1950s (see Chapter 29) had accelerated the breakdown of tribal life and the dispersal of native American populations. But native Americans also shared certain things, such as an unemployment rate ten times the national average, the worst poverty, the most inadequate housing, the highest disease rates, and the least access to education of any group in the United States.

As early as World War II, the National Council of American Indians had lobbied for the improvement of those conditions, but now some Indian groups became more assertive. In 1961 representatives of sixty-seven tribes issued a Declaration of Indian Purpose that foreshadowed much of the later civil rights activism. During the War on Poverty, Indian groups successfully lobbied the Johnson administration to channel antipoverty funds into their communities. Paralleling the growing militancy in the black civil rights movement, younger native Amer-

icans challenged the accommodationist approach of their elders. Like blacks and Mexican-Americans, they proposed a new name for themselves—*native Americans*—and organized protests and demonstrations to build support for their cause. In 1968 several Chipewyan from Minnesota organized the militant American Indian Movement (AIM), which drew its strength from the third of the native American population that lived in "red ghettos" in cities throughout the West.

AIM consciously modeled itself on the black power movement, and for a few years its tactics attracted considerable public attention. In November 1969 AIM seized the deserted federal penitentiary on Alcatraz Island in San Francisco Bay, offering the government $24 worth of trinkets to pay for it. (This was supposedly what the Dutch had paid the native inhabitants for Manhattan Island in 1626.) The occupation of Alcatraz lasted until the summer of 1971. In November 1972 a thousand protesters occupied the headquarters of the Federal Bureau of Indian Affairs in Washington, D.C., which was to many native Americans a hated symbol of the inconsistent federal policy on tribal welfare (see American Voices, page 952).

In February 1973, 200 Sioux organized by AIM leaders began an occupation of the tiny village of Wounded Knee, South Dakota, the site of the army massacre of the Sioux in 1890 (see Chapter 17). They were protesting the light sentences given to a group of white men convicted of killing a Sioux in 1972. The protesters took eleven hostages and occupied several buildings to dramatize their cause. But when a gun battle with the FBI left one protester dead and another wounded, the seventy-one-day siege collapsed. These militant confrontations captured media attention but alienated many white onlookers. In general, however, the new native American activism helped spur government action on tribal issues (see Chapter 32).

Wounded Knee Revisited
In 1973 members of the American Indian Movement staged a seventy-one-day protest at Wounded Knee, South Dakota, the site of the 1890 massacre of 200 Sioux by U.S. soldiers. The takeover was sparked by the murder of a local Sioux by a group of whites but quickly expanded to include demands for basic reforms in federal Indian policy and tribal governance.

Mary Crow Dog

The Trail of Broken Treaties

In November 1972 nineteen-year-old Mary Crow Dog and several hundred other Sioux from the Rosebud and Pine Ridge reservations in South Dakota traveled to Washington, D.C. Their group was one of several caravans participating in a protest known as the Trail of Broken Treaties, which ended in a six-day occupation of the Bureau of Indian Affairs headquarters.

When we arrived in Washington we got lost. We had been promised food and accommodation, but due to government pressure many church groups which had offered to put us up and feed us got scared and backed off. . . .

Somebody suggested, "Let's all go to the BIA." It seemed the natural thing to do, to go to the Bureau of Indian Affairs building on Constitution Avenue. They would have to put us up. It was "our" building after all. Besides, that was what we had come for, to complain about the treatment the bureau was dishing out to us. . . . Next thing I knew we were in it. We spilled into the build-

ing like a great avalanche. Some people put up a tipi on the front lawn. . . . The building finally belonged to us and we lost no time turning it into a tribal village. . . .

We pushed the police and guards out of the building. Some did not wait to be pushed but jumped out of the ground-floor windows like so many frogs. We had formulated twenty Indian demands. These were all rejected by the few bureaucrats sent to negotiate with us. . . . Soon we listened to other voices as the occupation turned into a siege. I heard somebody yelling, "The pigs are here." I could see from the window that it was true. The whole building was surrounded by helmeted police armed with all kinds of guns. A fight broke out between the police and our security. Some of our young men got hit over the head with police clubs and we saw the blood streaming down their faces. . . .

We barricaded all doors and the lowest windows with document boxes, Xerox machines, tables, file cabinets,

anything we could lay our hands on. . . .

From then on, every morning we were given a court order to get out by six P.M. Come six o'clock and we would be standing there ready to join battle. I think many brothers and sisters were prepared to die right on the steps of the BIA building. . . .

In the end a compromise was reached. The government said. . . they would appoint two high administration officials to seriously consider our twenty demands. Our expenses to get home would be paid. Nobody would be prosecuted. Of course, our twenty points were never gone into afterward. From the practical point of view, nothing had been achieved. . . . But morally it had been a great victory. We had faced White America collectively, not as individual tribes. We had stood up to the government and gone through our baptism of fire. We had not run.

Source: Mary Crow Dog, *Lakota Woman* (New York: Grove Weidenfeld, 1990), 84–85,88–91.

Identity Politics. Civil rights, once seen as a movement exclusively for the rights of black people, also sparked a new awareness among some predominantly white groups. Americans of Polish, Italian, Greek, and Slavic descent, most of them working-class and Catholic, proudly embraced a new ethnic identity modeled on black pride. George Wiley organized poor people, mostly women on welfare, into the National Welfare Rights Organization. Calling welfare a right, not a privilege, activists staged sit-ins at government offices to demand better treatment and higher benefits.

Homosexual men and women also banded together to protest legal and social oppression based on sexual orientation. Moving beyond an older legalistic approach to homosexual rights, the gay liberation movement was born in 1969 with the "Stonewall riot" in New York City, in which patrons of a gay bar in Greenwich Village fought back against police harassment. The assertion of

gay pride that followed the Stonewall incident drew heavily on the language and tactics of the civil rights movement. Activists took the new name of *gay* rather than homosexual; founded advocacy groups, newspapers, and political organizations to challenge discrimination and prejudice; and provided emotional support for those who "came out" by publicly affirming their homosexual identity. Models for increased political activism based on heightened group identity represented one of the most significant legacies of the African-American struggle to the rest of American society.

The Revival of Feminism

The black civil rights movement also helped reactivate feminism, a movement that had been languishing since the 1920s. Just as the abolition movement had been the training ground for an earlier generation of women's rights advocates in the nineteenth century, young feminists in the 1960s were inspired and influenced by the black struggle. But the revival of feminism also grew out of postwar social and demographic changes that affected younger and older women alike.

Women's Changing Lives. In the 1960s more women were attending college and working outside the home than ever before. At the same time, married women were having fewer children and were more likely to get a divorce. The most sweeping change was the dramatic rise in women's participation in the work force. In 1950 almost one-third of women were employed, and one-quarter of those workers were married. By 1970, 42.6 percent of women were working, and four out of ten working women were married (see Figure 30.2). Especially significant was the growth in the number of working women with preschool children—up from 12 percent in 1950 to 30 percent in 1970. In the postwar consumer society working mothers were becoming both socially accepted and economically necessary.

Women also benefited from increased access to education. Immediately after World War II the percentage of women college students declined: the GI Bill gave men a temporary advantage in access to higher education, and many college women dropped out to marry and raise families at the height of the baby boom. By 1960, however, the percentage of women students had climbed to 35 percent, and in 1970 it reached 41 percent.

The meaning of marriage was changing, too. The baby boom turned out to be only a temporary interruption of the century-long decline in the birth rate. The introduction of the birth control pill, first marketed in 1960, and the intrauterine device (IUD) helped women control their fertility. Women had fewer children and, because of increased life expectancy (75 years in 1970, up from 54 years in 1920), devoted fewer years to raising children. At the same time, the divorce rate, which

had risen slowly throughout the twentieth century, grew precipitously as the states liberalized divorce laws. It doubled from 15 per thousand marriages in 1960 to 32 per thousand in 1975. Women could no longer assume that their marriages would last until "death do us part."

As a result of these changes, traditional gender expectations were dramatically undercut. American women's lives now usually included work and marriage, often child-rearing and a career, and possibly bringing up children as a single parent after a divorce. Those changing social realities created a major constituency for the emerging women's movement of the 1960s.

Paths to Feminism. Two distinct movements helped stimulate the revival of feminism during those years. The women's rights branch, led by the National Organization for Women (NOW), consisted of older, politically active professional women who sought change by working through the political system. The women's liberation branch, by contrast, attracted primarily younger women, especially recent college graduates who had been active in civil rights and the protests against the Vietnam War. Their vision of feminism was more radical and confrontational. Mirroring the separatism of black power advocates, they were initially somewhat hostile to men.

In 1961 John Kennedy established a Presidential Commission on the Status of Women, an attempt to counter criticism of his administration's poor record on women's issues. Eleanor Roosevelt served as honorary head of the commission. The group's 1963 report documented the employment and educational discrimination faced by women, but its impact extended beyond its rather conservative recommendations. Most important, the presidential commission and the state commissions that were its offshoots set up a rudimentary nationwide network of women in public life who were concerned about feminist issues.

Another spark that ignited the revival of feminism was Betty Friedan's best-selling book, *The Feminine Mys-*

FIGURE 30.2

Women in the Labor Force, 1800–1994

Over the past two centuries women have steadily increased their participation in the labor force. Paid employment outside the home has become part of the life cycle of most women.

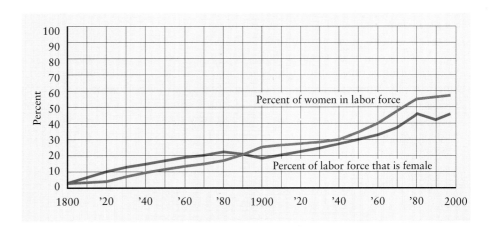

tique, published in 1963. That book, a pointed indictment of women's suburban domesticity, grew out of Friedan's experiences as a housewife in the 1950s. Friedan called it "the problem that has no name":

> As she made the beds, shopped for groceries, matched slipcover material, ate peanut butter sandwiches with her children, chauffeured Cub Scouts and Brownies, lay beside her husband at night—she was afraid to ask even of herself the silent question—"Is this all?"

Women responded enthusiastically to Friedan's story, especially white, college-educated, middle-class women whose backgrounds resembled the author's. Friedan's book sold 3 million copies, and many more women read excerpts in major women's magazines. *The Feminine Mystique* gave women a vocabulary for their dissatisfaction and introduced many of them to the powerful ideas of modern feminism—women's self-realization through employment, continuing education, and other activities outside the home.

Legislating Women's Rights. Like so many constituencies in postwar America, women's rights activists looked to the federal government for action. In 1963, as recommended by the Presidential Commission on the Status of Women, Congress passed the Equal Pay Act, which directed that men and women be paid the same wages for doing the same job. Even more important was the Civil Rights Act of 1964, which had as great an impact on women as it did on blacks and other minorities. The key provision, Title VII, barred discrimination in employment on the basis of race, color, religion, national origin, or sex. The category of sex was added by a conservative representative who hoped to make the bill so controversial that it would be killed. His strategy backfired. Title VII eventually became a powerful tool in the fight against sex discrimination. Initially, however, the Equal Employment Opportunity Commission avoided implementing it.

Dissatisfied with the commission's reluctance to defend women's rights, Friedan and others founded the National Organization for Women in 1966. NOW, modeling itself on groups such as the NAACP, aimed to be a civil rights organization for women. "The purpose of NOW," its statement of purpose declared, "is to take action to bring women into full participation in the mainstream of American society now, exercising all the privileges and responsibilities thereof in truly equal partnership with men." Friedan served as NOW's first president, and its membership grew from 1,000 in 1967 to 15,000 in 1971. Men made up a fourth of NOW's early membership. It is still the largest feminist organization in the United States.

Women's Liberation. Women's liberationists came to feminism by a different path. White women had made up about half the students who went south with SNCC in the 1964 Freedom Summer project. While in Mississippi, they received conflicting messages. College women developed self-confidence and organizational skills and found role models in the black women and older southern white women who were prominent in the civil rights movement, such as Ella Baker, Anne Braden, and Virginia Foster Durr. Yet women volunteers also found that they were expected to do all the cleaning and cooking at the Freedom Houses where SNCC volunteers lived. "We didn't come down here to work as a maid this summer," one complained.

Intensely committed to black civil rights and lacking a feminist vocabulary to express their concerns, Freedom Summer volunteers raised their objections only tentatively. When they did, they compared women's position to that of blacks. "Assumptions of male superiority are as widespread and deeply rooted and every bit as crippling to the woman as the assumptions of white superiority are to the Negro," they argued. Both black and white men in the movement laughed off those attempts to raise feminist issues. Stokely Carmichael made one of the most notorious retorts: "The only position for women in SNCC is prone."

After 1965 black power militancy made white women unwelcome in the civil rights movement. But when they transferred their energies to the student and antiwar groups that were emerging in that period (see Chapter 31), they found that New Left groups were equally male-dominated and unsupportive. Once again women were expected to take notes or serve coffee while men monopolized the leadership roles. As the antiwar movement adopted draft resistance as its central strategy, women found themselves treated primarily as sex objects. "Girls say yes to guys who say no" was a popular slogan. Women who tried to raise feminist issues at conventions were shouted off the platform with jeers such as "Move on, little girl, we have more important issues to talk about here than women's liberation." The "little girl" who received that taunt was Shulamith Firestone, whose subsequent book, *The Dialectic of Sex* (1971), became an early text of the women's movement.

Around 1967 groups of radical women realized that they needed their own movement. The contradiction between the New Left's commitment to egalitarianism and women's actual treatment by male leaders had become so striking that women felt that they had no other choice. This process occurred independently in five or six cities, including Chicago, San Francisco, and New York. In contrast to women's rights groups such as NOW, which had traditional organizational structures

Feminism on the March
The visibility of the feminist movement reached a new peak in 1970 when thousands of women in New York and other cities around the country marched to celebrate the fiftieth anniversary of women's suffrage. (© Bettye Lane)

and dues-paying members, radical women participated in loose collectives with shifting memberships that often lacked any coordinating structure.

The women's liberation movement (or "women's lib," as it was dubbed by the somewhat hostile media) went public when it staged a protest at the 1968 Miss America pageant. The demonstration included a "freedom trash can" into which women were encouraged to throw false eyelashes, hair curlers, brassieres, and girdles—all considered symbols of female oppression. The media quickly labeled the radical feminists "bra burners." The derisive name stuck, although no brassieres were actually burned.

A technique with a more lasting impact was *consciousness raising*—group sessions in which women shared their experiences of being female. Swapping stories about being passed over for promotion, needing a husband's signature on a credit card application, and enduring the humiliation of whistles and leers while walking down the street helped participants realize that their individual problems were part of a wider pattern of oppression. The slogan "The personal is political" became a rallying cry of the early radical feminists.

The High Tide of Feminism. Before 1969 most women learned about the feminist movement through word of mouth. After that time, media attention brought women's issues to a much broader audience than could have been reached by NOW or the women's liberation collectives. A flood of new converts broke down the barriers between the two branches of the movement. Feminism's

potential as a mass movement was demonstrated on August 26, 1970, when thousands of women throughout the country marched to celebrate the fiftieth anniversary of the Nineteenth Amendment. The feminist movement as a whole, however, remained largely white and middle-class.

The distinction between women's rights and women's liberation also began to blur because of a growing convergence of interests. Radical women learned that key feminist goals—child care, equal pay, abortion rights—could best be achieved in the political arena. At the same time, more traditional political activists developed a broader view of women's oppression, including tentative support for divisive issues such as abortion and lesbian rights. Feminists were beginning to think of themselves as part of a broad, growing, and increasingly influential social movement.

The rebirth of feminism in the 1960s laid the foundation for more vigorous activism among women in the 1970s (see Chapter 32). Not until then would the movement grapple with the fact that perhaps as many issues divided women—race, class, age, sexual preference—as unified them.

Summary

The contradictions of postwar affluence gave rise to new social and political activism in the early 1960s. As Americans looked to Washington for solutions to the nation's social and economic ills, the Democrats offered a diverse array of federal programs designed to appeal to a broad range of constituencies. John F. Kennedy first set the agenda for this politics of expectation in his 1960 presidential bid, but the domestic accomplishments of his New Frontier were limited. Kennedy's activism was more evident in foreign policy, where he remained a resolute cold warrior. A potential nuclear confrontation during the Cuban missile crisis, however, resulted in a more accommodating approach toward the Soviet Union after 1962. As Kennedy worked to remake the New Frontier for a second term, an assassin's bullet ended his life in November 1963.

On the social front, the most significant expression of 1960s activism was the civil rights movement. Led by established religious figures such as Martin Luther King, Jr., and energized by a younger generation of black college students, the movement won major legislative victories, including the passage of the Civil Rights and Voting Rights acts of 1964–1965. Through those measures the nation ended legal segregation, outlawed racial discrimination, and expanded black voting rights and political power.

On the national level, Lyndon Johnson played a critical role in pushing civil rights legislation through Congress. Moreover, Johnson used his formidable political skills to usher in the most ambitious legislative reform program since the New Deal. Under his Great Society, Congress funded an array of new programs in education, medical care, social welfare, housing, transportation, and environmental protection. But even though the Great Society raised hopes, it could not always deliver on its promises. Increasing military expenditures for the escalating Vietnam conflict limited federal funds for domestic programs. And as federal functions and responsibilities grew, it became increasingly difficult to accommodate the diverse and often competing constituencies in the Democratic coalition. By the late 1960s the liberal consensus had broken down.

The civil rights movement also began to disintegrate during this period. Rising militancy and racial strife divided the movement and fueled white opposition to change. At the same time, however, the new black power movement encouraged racial pride and assertiveness, serving as a model for other minority groups and women in their struggles for equality.

TIMELINE

1960	Greensboro, North Carolina, sit-ins Birth control pill becomes available John F. Kennedy elected president
1961	Presidential Commission on the Status of Women established Peace Corps established Freedom rides Bay of Pigs invasion Berlin wall erected
1962	Michael Harrington, *The Other America*, describes the persistence of poverty John Glenn orbits the earth Cuban missile crisis
1963	Betty Friedan, *The Feminine Mystique* Civil rights protest in Birmingham, Alabama Equal Pay Act March on Washington Test ban treaty John F. Kennedy assassinated; Lyndon B. Johnson assumes presidency
1964	Tax Reduction Act Freedom Summer Civil Rights Act Economic Opportunity Act inaugurates War on Poverty Johnson elected president Wilderness Preservation Act
1965	Malcolm X assassinated Civil rights march from Selma to Montgomery, Alabama Voting Rights Act Medicare and Medicaid Elementary and Secondary Education Act Immigration Act Air and Water Quality acts
1966	National Organization for Women (NOW) founded Stokely Carmichael proclaims black power
1967	Height of race riots in northern cities
1968	Martin Luther King, Jr., assassinated Women's liberation movement emerges
1969	American Indian Movement seizes Alcatraz Stonewall riot leads to gay liberation movement United States lands first astronauts on the moon

BIBLIOGRAPHY

There are a growing number of survey works on the 1960s; among the best are David Steigerwald, *The Sixties and the End of Modern America* (1995); David Farber, *The Age of Great Dreams: America in the 1960s* (1994); and Allen J. Matusow, *The Unraveling of America* (1984).

The Politics of Expectation

The literature on the Kennedy years is voluminous. Among the best general accounts are Richard Reeves, *President Kennedy: Profile of Power* (1993); James Giglio, *The Presidency of JFK* (1991); David Burner, *JFK and a New Generation* (1988); and Jim F. Heath, *Decade of Disillusionment: The Kennedy-Johnson Years* (1975). Critical views appear in David Halberstam, *The Best and the Brightest* (1972); Henry Fairlie, *The Kennedy Promise: The Politics of Expectation* (1973); and Garry Wills, *The Kennedy Imprisonment* (1980).

On foreign policy in the Kennedy years, see Michael Beschloss, *The Crisis Years: Kennedy and Khrushchev, 1960–1963* (1990); Thomas Paterson, *Kennedy's Quest for Victory* (1989); and Richard Walton, *Cold War and Counterrevolution* (1972). Robert Kennedy, *Thirteen Days* (1969), provides a participant's account of the Cuban missile crisis, which can be supplemented by James Nathan, *The Cuban Missile Crisis Revisited* (1992); Raymond Garthoff, *Reflections on the Cuban Missile Crisis* (1989); and Thomas Paterson, *Contesting Castro* (1994). On the Warren Court, see Bernard Schwartz, *Super Chief: Earl Warren and the Supreme Court* (1983). Earl Warren was the chief author of the Warren Report (1964) investigating the Kennedy assassination. More recently, Gerald Posner, *Case Closed* (1993), provides the most definitive treatment of that event.

The Civil Rights Movement

Robert Weisbrot, *Freedom Bound* (1990); Harvard Sitkoff, *The Struggle for Black Equality* (2nd ed., 1993); and Clayborne Carson, et al., *The Eyes on the Prize Civil Rights Reader* (1991), offer comprehensive overviews. Histories of the major civil rights organizations include Carson's study of SNCC, *In Struggle* (1981), and August Meier and Elliot Rudwick, *CORE* (1973). Mary Aickin Rothschild, *A Case of Black and White* (1982), and Doug McAdam, *Freedom Summer* (1988), describe the experiences of northern volunteers during Freedom Summer. Two fine oral histories of the civil rights movement are Howell Raines, *My Soul Is Rested* (1977), and Henry Hampton and Steve Fayer, *Voices of Freedom* (1990).

Local accounts of grass-roots organizing include William H. Chafe's superb study of Greensboro, North Carolina, *Civilities and Civil Rights* (1980), and two recent studies of Mississippi, John Dittmer, *Local People* (1994), and Charles M. Payne, *I've Got the Light of Freedom* (1995). The role of women in the civil rights movement is examined in Vicki L. Crawford et al., *Women in the Civil Rights Movement: Trailblazers and Torchbearers, 1941–1965* (1990).

The material on Martin Luther King, Jr., is extensive and continues to grow. King told his own story in *Why We Can't Wait* (1964). His biographers include David Garrow, *Bearing the Cross* (1986); Taylor Branch, *Parting the Waters* (1988); Stephen Oates, *Let the Trumpet Sound* (1982); and David Lewis, *King* (1970).

Lyndon Johnson and the Great Society

Lyndon Johnson's account of his presidency can be found in *The Vantage Point* (1971). Doris Kearns, *Lyndon Johnson and the American Dream* (1976), and Merle Miller, *Lyndon: An Oral Biography* (1980), are based on extensive conversations with LBJ. Rowland Evans and Robert D. Novak offer a vigorous portrait in *Lyndon B. Johnson: The Exercise of Power* (1966). Robert A. Caro focuses on Johnson's early career in *The Path to Power* (1982) and *Means of Ascent* (1989), as does Robert Dallek in *Lone Star Rising* (1991).

Michael Harrington called attention to poverty in *The Other America* (1962) and later critiqued the War on Poverty in *The New American Poverty* (1984). Charles Murray's conservative viewpoint in *Losing Ground: American Social Policy, 1950–1980* (1983) can be balanced by Michael Katz's liberal perspective in *The Undeserving Poor* (1989).

The Continuing Struggle for Civil Rights

Major texts of the black power movement include Stokely Carmichael and Charles Hamilton, *Black Power* (1967); James Baldwin, *The Fire Next Time* (1963); and Eldridge Cleaver, *Soul on Ice* (1968). *The Autobiography of Malcolm X* (cowritten with Alex Haley) has become a black literary classic. Hugh Pearson, *The Shadow of the Panther* (1994), looks at Huey Newton and the Black Panthers, as does the former Black Panther Elaine Brown, *A Taste of Power* (1992).

Report of the National Advisory Commission on Civil Disorders (1968) analyzes the decade's major race riots. See also Joe R. Feagin and Harlan Hahn, *Ghetto Revolts* (1973), and Robert Fogelson, *Violence as Protest* (1971). Sidney Fine's book on the Detroit riot, *Violence in the Model City* (1989), provides the most thorough historical treatment of race rioting in this period.

Carlos Muñoz, Jr., *Youth, Identity and Power: The Chicano Movement* (1989), and Juan Gomez-Quiñones, *Chicano Politics* (1990), examine the rise of the Chicano movement in the 1960s. Peter Matthiessen, *In the Spirit of Crazy Horse* (1983), chronicles the American Indian Movement's ongoing conflict with the FBI and the federal government. See also Stan Steiner, *The New Indians* (1968); Helen Hertzberg, *The Search for an American Indian Movement* (1971); and Wilcomb Washburn, *Red Man's Land, White Man's Law* (1971). John D'Emilio, *Sexual Politics, Sexual Communities* (1983), describes the emergence of gay identity between 1940 and 1970, while Martin Duberman, *Stonewall* (1993), looks at the birth of the gay movement in the late 1960s.

Jo Freeman, *The Politics of Women's Liberation* (1975); Barbara Deckard, *The Women's Movement* (1975); and Judith Hole and Ellen Levine, *The Rebirth of Feminism* (1971), chronicle the revival of feminism in the 1960s and 1970s. Sara Evans, *Personal Politics* (1979), traces the roots of feminism in the civil rights movement and the New Left, and Alice Echols, *Daring to Be Bad* (1989), examines radical feminism from 1967 to 1975. General histories of women's activism in the 1960s include Cynthia Harrison, *On Account of Sex: The Politics of Women's Issues, 1945–1968* (1988); Leila J. Rupp and Verta Taylor, *Survival in the Doldrums: The American Women's Rights Movement* (1987); and Susan M. Hartmann, *From Margin to Mainstream: American Women and Politics since 1960* (1989).

Jungle Warfare

Guerrilla warfare in Vietnam was characterized by frequent
skirmishes and casualties, but large battles were rare. Enemy
lines were unclear in the heavy jungle underbrush, and
territory conquered one day was often lost the next. For
many soldiers, waging war under such conditions was
frustrating and demoralizing.

The Vietnam Experience
1961–1975

★　　　★　　　★

Just as the civil rights movement revealed the short-comings of American domestic life in the 1960s, the Vietnam War challenged the fundamental assumptions of the nation's foreign policy. Since the late 1940s American policy makers—Democratic and Republican alike—had agreed on the need to maintain American military and economic superiority and contain communism around the globe. This cold war policy led to numerous military and diplomatic conflicts between the United States and the Soviet Union, including a three-year war in Korea. Whereas some Americans questioned the policy of global containment, most U.S. policy makers were convinced that aggressive action against communism was imperative, particularly in the developing nations of the Third World. The future of democracy and the credibility of American power in the postwar world appeared to be at stake.

The struggle over Vietnam called those assumptions into question. Like many new nations in the postcolonial world, Vietnam was characterized by a volatile mix of nationalist sentiments, religious and cultural conflicts, economic needs, and political turmoil. The rise of communism in Vietnam was only one phase of that nation's larger struggle against colonialism, which eventually resulted in a bloody civil war. But American policy makers viewed these events through the lens of the Cold War, interpreting them as communist-inspired moves toward global domination. Their failure to understand the complexity of Vietnam's internal conflicts led to a long and ultimately disastrous war.

Spanning nearly thirty years, the Vietnam conflict occupied American administrations from Truman to Ford. U.S. troops fought in Vietnam for more than eleven years—from 1961 to 1973—making it the nation's longest war. Moreover, as the country's first major military defeat, the war shook American confidence and damaged the international credibility it was supposed to uphold. The war also took its toll at home. While defense spending temporarily boosted the economy, it fueled inflation and diverted resources from domestic uses. As the war dragged on, a growing number of citizens came to oppose U.S. involvement as antiwar sentiments spread across college campuses to the nation's streets, living rooms, and halls of state. Not since the Civil War had the nation been so deeply and bitterly divided. Debates about the meaning and lessons of the war still resonate in American life.

Into the Quagmire, 1945–1968

Although most Americans first learned about the Vietnam War in the mid-1960s, the roots of U.S. involvement date back to the Truman administration. At the end of World War II the political instability produced by the decolonization of Southeast Asia became a source of concern for policy makers wary of communist infiltration. The Eisenhower and Kennedy administrations gradually increased economic and military aid to South Vietnam, laying the groundwork for a major escalation of U.S. involvement under Lyndon Johnson.

The Roots of American Involvement

Vietnam had been part of the French colony of Indochina (along with Laos and Cambodia) since the late nineteenth century but was occupied by Japan during World War II. Native resistance to the Japanese was led by Ho Chi Minh and the Vietnam Independence League, the Vietminh. A former schoolteacher and maritime worker, Ho Chi Minh had embraced communism in 1920 and later lived in Moscow. First and foremost, however, Ho and the Vietminh were nationalists who wanted to end foreign rule in Vietnam. During World War II the Vietminh resisted the Japanese occupation, working with the U.S. Office of Strategic Services to conduct espionage missions and rescue downed American pilots.

The Japanese surrender in 1945 created a political vacuum and an opportunity for Vietnamese independence. With words drawn from the American Declaration of Independence, Ho proclaimed an independent republic of Vietnam that September. Hoping to maintain its overseas empire, France rejected his claim and reasserted control over the country, granting it only a token measure of freedom. Tensions between the French and the Vietminh escalated, and in December 1946 a French warship bombarded Haiphong, killing 6,000 Vietnamese civilians. Ho and the military strategist Vo Nguyen Giap then launched counterattacks to drive out the French. Thus began the first phase of the conflict, an eight-year struggle that the Vietminh called the Anti-French War of Resistance. Appealing to American anticolonial sentiment, Ho called on President Truman to support the struggle for Vietnamese independence. Truman, however, ignored those appeals and offered covert support to the French in hopes of stabilizing a politically chaotic region and rebuilding the French economy. While proclaiming official neutrality in the conflict, the United States made $160 million available to the French for use in Indochina in 1946 and subsequently allowed them to use Marshall Plan funds for military operations there.

By the end of the decade cold war developments and objectives prompted the United States to take a stronger and more public stand on behalf of the French. After the Chinese revolution of 1949, the United States was concerned that China—along with the Soviet Union—might actively support Asian anticolonial struggles and that newly independent countries would align themselves with the communists. At the same time, Republican charges that the Democrats had "lost China" influenced Truman to take a firmer stand against perceived communist aggression in both Korea and Vietnam. Truman also wanted to maintain good relations with France, whose support was crucial to the success of the new NATO alliance. Finally, Indochina played a strategic role in Secretary of State Dean Acheson's plans for an integrated Pacific Rim regional economy centered on a reindustrialized Japan. Envisioning Indochina as a supplier of cheap raw materials and a profitable market for Japanese goods and services, American policy makers insisted that it remain a part of the capitalist free-market system.

For all these reasons, when the Soviet Union and the new Chinese leaders recognized Ho's government early in 1950, the United States—along with Great Britain—recognized the noncommunist government of Bao Dai that had been installed by the French the previous year. After the outbreak of the Korean War, Truman also decided to send supplies to French troops stationed in Vietnam to deter a possible communist invasion there. Military support continued under the Eisenhower administration. By mid-1954 the United States had sent more than $2 billion worth of military supplies to the French in Vietnam, plus another $703 million in technical and economic assistance, shouldering nearly 80 percent of the cost of the war. President Eisenhower argued that such aid was essential in preventing what he called the domino effect: "You have a row of dominoes set up, you knock over the first one, and what will happen to the last one is the certainty that it will go over very quickly." The loss of South Vietnam, Eisenhower asserted in April 1954, "would have grave consequences for us and for freedom."

Dienbienphu and the Geneva Accords. Despite these joint French-American efforts, the Vietminh forces gained strength in northern Vietnam. In the spring of 1954 the

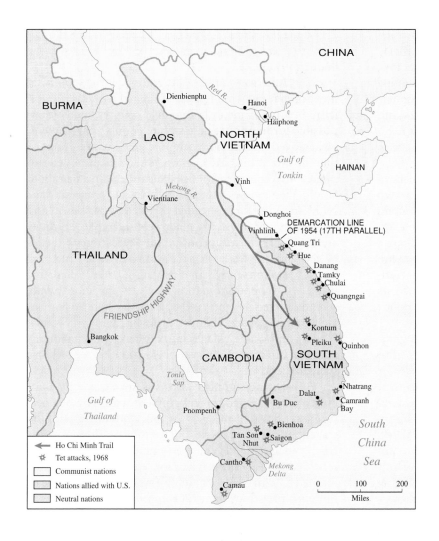

MAP 31.1

The Vietnam War, 1954–1975
The Vietnam War was a guerrilla war, fought in skirmishes and inconclusive encounters rather than decisive battles. Supporters of the National Liberation Front filtered into South Vietnam along the Ho Chi Minh Trail, which wound through Laos and Cambodia. In January 1968 Vietcong forces launched the Tet offensive, a surprise attack on several South Vietnamese cities and provincial centers shown at left. American vulnerability to these attacks served to undermine U.S. credibility and fueled opposition to the war.

French made a last stand at the isolated administrative fortress of Dienbienphu, where the Vietminh surrounded them. France asked the United States to launch air strikes from nearby carriers to break the siege. Several members of the Joint Chiefs of Staff urged Eisenhower to take action (including the possible use of nuclear weapons), but Congressional opposition at home and Britain's refusal to join a pro-French coalition convinced him to abstain from direct military intervention. Dienbienphu fell in May after a fifty-six-day siege.

The dramatic turn of events at Dienbienphu enhanced the negotiating position of the Vietminh at a conference in Geneva sponsored by Britain and the Soviet Union to discuss problems in the Far East. The resulting 1954 Geneva Accords temporarily partitioned Vietnam at the 17th parallel (see Map 31.1), committed France to withdraw its forces north of that line within ten months, and forbade both North and South Vietnam to enter into a military alliance with an outside power. A final declaration provided that the two partitioned sectors would hold free elections within two years to choose a unified government for the entire nation. Eight of the nine national delegations in atten-

dance signed the agreements, including China and the Vietminh, both of which were confident that Ho would win the elections of 1956. The United States refused to sign the Geneva Accords but issued a separate protocol acknowledging the agreements and promising to "refrain from the threat or use of force to disturb them."

The Creation of South Vietnam. Eisenhower had no intention of allowing a communist electoral victory in Vietnam and wanted to establish a permanent South Vietnamese state. With the help of CIA military operatives, the Eisenhower administration had made sure that a pro-American government took power in South Vietnam in June 1954, just before the accords were signed. Ngo Dinh Diem, an anticommunist Roman Catholic who had spent the previous eight years in the United States, returned to Vietnam and was installed as the premier of the French-backed South Vietnamese government under Emperor Bao Dai. The next year Diem disposed of Bao Dai through a national referendum establishing Diem as the president of an independent South Vietnam. In a rigged election—in which his ballots were printed on red paper, a Vietnamese symbol of good luck, whereas Bao Dai's were green, which stood for misfortune—Diem won an unlikely 98.2 percent of the vote. With the support of the United States, he then called off the reunification elections scheduled for 1956, mainly because he realized that the popular Ho Chi Minh would win easily in both the north and the south. Diem's was just one in a long line of U.S.-backed governments that failed to win the allegiance of the Vietnamese population.

From the perspective of the Vietnamese, the Geneva Accords marked only a brief interlude between two wars, one to end French colonial control and a second to reunify Vietnam. In March 1956 the last French soldiers left Saigon, and the United States replaced France as the dominant foreign power in South Vietnam. American policy makers now asserted that a noncommunist South Vietnam was vital to the security interests of the United States, and they charted American policy accordingly.

In reality, Vietnam was too small to play a significant role in the international balance of power; its communism was regional and intensely nationalistic, not expansionist. Nevertheless, Eisenhower and subsequent U.S. presidents continued to see South Vietnam as vital to American security. Between 1955 and 1961 the Eisenhower administration sent Diem an average of $200 million a year in aid, mostly military. In addition, approximately 675 American military advisers were stationed in Saigon, the capital of South Vietnam. Having stepped up U.S. involvement considerably, Eisenhower left office, passing the Vietnam situation to his successor, John F. Kennedy.

The Kennedy Years

President Kennedy saw Vietnam as an ideal laboratory to try out the counterinsurgency techniques that were the centerpiece of his military policy (see Chapter 30). But he first had to prop up the faltering regime of Ngo Dinh Diem, who remained highly unpopular because of his administration's corruption and ruthless brutality, aloofness from the peasantry, and greedy land policy. The Diem regime also faced a growing military threat after December 1960, when the North Vietnamese Communist party organized most of Diem's opponents in South Vietnam into a revolutionary movement known as the National Liberation Front (NLF). To shore up Diem's administration, Kennedy increased the number of American military "advisers" (an elastic term that included helicopter units, special forces, minesweeping details, and reconnaissance pilots) to more than 16,000 by November 1963. As part of the counterinsurgency strategy he also sent economic development specialists to win the "hearts and minds" of Vietnamese peasants away from the insurgents while at the same time in-

creasing agricultural production. Kennedy refused, however, to send American combat troops to assist the South Vietnamese.

The American aid did little good. Diem's political inexperience and corruption, combined with his Catholicism in a predominantly Buddhist country, made it impossible for him to create a stable, popular government. He enjoyed much more support in faraway America than he did in his native land. As the situation deteriorated, Diem consistently misled his American allies about South Vietnamese military and social progress. The NLF's guerrilla forces—called the Vietcong by Diem and his American advisers—made considerable headway against the Diem regime, using the revolutionary tactics of the Chinese leader Mao Zedong to blend into the South Vietnamese civilian population "like fish in the water." But opposition to Diem was far more widespread. Large segments of the peasantry had been alienated by his strategic hamlet program, which uprooted families and whole villages into barbed wire compounds in a vain attempt to separate them from Ho Chi Minh's sympathizers.

Anti-Diem sentiment also was strong among Buddhists, who charged the government with religious persecution. Starting in May 1963, militant Buddhists staged a dramatic series of demonstrations against Diem, including several self-immolations that were recorded by American television crews. Diem's regime retaliated with raids on temples and mass arrests of Buddhist priests in August, prompting more antigovernment demonstrations.

Kennedy decided that Diem had to be removed. Ambassador Henry Cabot Lodge, Jr., let it be known in Saigon that the United States would support a military coup that had "a good chance of succeeding." On November 1, 1963, Diem was driven from office and assassinated by a faction of the South Vietnamese army. America's role in the coup reinforced the links between the United States and the new regime in South Vietnam, making the prospect of withdrawal from the region less acceptable to U.S. policy makers.

Less than a month later Kennedy himself was assassinated. Although historians continue to debate whether Kennedy would have withdrawn American forces from Vietnam if he had lived, the actions of his administration clearly accelerated U.S. involvement. When Lyndon Johnson took his place as president, he retained many of Kennedy's foreign policy advisers and quickly declared his intention to maintain support for South Vietnam. "I am not going to be the President who saw Southeast Asia go the way China went," Johnson asserted weeks after taking office. A new phase in the Americanization of the war was about to begin. When Johnson assumed the presidency, there were 16,000 American troops in Vietnam; when he left office in January 1969, there were more than 500,000.

Escalation

The removal of Diem did not lead to improvements in the efficiency or popularity of the Saigon government. Various military governments, most notably a coalition headed by General Nguyen Khanh, tried to build popular support, but with little success. American policy makers realized that the Eisenhower-Kennedy policy of sending military advisers and supplies could no longer save the situation. But Johnson would need at least tacit Congressional support, perhaps even a declaration of war, to commit U.S. forces to an offensive strategy. Originally Johnson had wanted to wait until after the 1964 election to place this controversial request before Congress, but events gave him an opportunity to win authorization sooner.

The Gulf of Tonkin Resolution. During the summer of 1964 American naval forces conducted surveillance missions off the North Vietnamese coast to aid South Vietnamese amphibious attacks on the area. The North Vietnamese resisted the attacks, and President Johnson told the nation that on August 2 and 4 North Vietnamese torpedo boats had fired on American destroyers in international waters in the Gulf of Tonkin. At Johnson's request, Congress authorized him to "take all necessary measures to repel any armed attack against the forces of the United States and to prevent further aggression." On August 7 the Gulf of Tonkin resolution passed 88 to 2 in the Senate and 416 to 0 in the House. Only Senators Wayne Morse of Oregon and Ernest Gruening of Alaska opposed it as a "predated declaration of war" that further increased the president's ability to carry out foreign policy without consulting Congress (both subsequently lost their bids for reelection).

Many questions were later raised about the resolution. A draft had been ready for several months, awaiting just such an incident. The evidence of a North Vietnamese attack was particularly sketchy in the case of the second incident. In the middle of heavy wind, rain, and fog, the U.S.S. *Maddox* and *C. Turner Joy* had reported that they were under attack by torpedoes and had begun firing at targets that they saw on their radar screens. Naval aircraft called in to support the destroyers saw no enemy boats but fired missiles as instructed. Soon afterward Captain John J. Herrick, commander of the *Maddox*, contacted Washington and expressed doubt that an attack had occurred, attributing the phenomenon to faulty radar caused by bad weather. As the president admitted soon afterward, "For all I know, our navy was shooting at whales out there." But this unverified attack got Johnson what he wanted—a sweeping mandate to conduct Vietnam operations as he saw fit. It was the only formal approval of American intervention in Vietnam ever granted by Congress. Johnson's outspokenness on the Gulf of Tonkin incident also served to undercut claims by the Republican presidential contender, Barry Goldwater, that Johnson was unwilling to take a firm stand against communist aggression in Vietnam.

During the 1964 presidential campaign (see Chapter 30) Johnson declared, "We are not going to send American boys nine or ten thousand miles away from home to do what Asian boys ought to be doing for themselves." Yet plans were already being drawn up for a possible escalation of American efforts. Johnson's secretary of defense, Robert McNamara, and other top advisers argued that only a rapid, full-scale deployment of U.S. forces could prevent the imminent defeat of the South Vietnamese government and lay the groundwork for an eventual victory over the communists. With Congressional support assured and the 1964 election safely over, the Johnson administration began the fateful move toward the total Americanization of the war. The escalation, which was accomplished during the first several months of 1965, took two forms: the initiation of direct bombing campaigns against North Vietnam and the deployment of ground troops.

Operation Rolling Thunder. The first phase of escalation was Operation Rolling Thunder, a protracted campaign of bombing attacks against North Vietnam that was launched on March 2, 1965. Retaliatory air strikes against North Vietnamese targets had already been undertaken in February; what was significant about the new plans was that the bombing was not linked to a specific act of provocation but was an open-ended policy. Such bombing raids, the national security adviser McGeorge Bundy reasoned, would cripple the North Vietnamese economy and force the communists to the bargaining table. A special target was the Ho Chi Minh Trail, an elaborate network of paths, bridges, and shelters that stretched from North Vietnam through Cambodia and Laos into South Vietnam (see Map 31.1). By 1967 some 20,000 Vietnamese soldiers moved southward along that route each month, along with the military hardware and other resources necessary to supply them.

Between 1965 and 1968 Operation Rolling Thunder (named for a Protestant hymn) dropped a million tons of bombs on North Vietnam, 800 tons a day for three and a half years. Each B-52 bombing sortie cost $30,000; by early 1966 the direct costs of the air war exceeded $1.7 billion. From 1965 to 1973 the United States dropped three times as many bombs on North Vietnam, a country roughly the size of Texas, as had fallen on Europe, Asia, and Africa during World War II. The several hundred captured pilots downed in the raids then became pawns in negotiations with the North Vietnamese over the fate of prisoners of war.

To the amazement of American advisers, the bombing had little effect on the ability of the Vietnamese to wage war. The flow of troops and supplies to the south continued unabated as the North Vietnamese quickly

...

Aerial Bombing in Vietnam
The bombs dropped by U.S. forces in an attempt to root out Vietcong sympathizers inflicted heavy damage on the countryside and caused many civilian deaths. B-52s dropped most of the bombs.

rebuilt roads and bridges, moved munitions plants underground, and constructed a network of tunnels and shelters. Instead of destroying enemy morale and bringing the North Vietnamese to the bargaining table, Operation Rolling Thunder intensified their nationalism and will to fight. The bombing continued nevertheless.

The Arrival of U.S. Ground Troops. A week after the launching of Operation Rolling Thunder, the United States made its first official assignment of ground troops to combat duty in South Vietnam. On March 8 the first U.S. Marines waded ashore at Danang, South Vietnam's second largest city, to protect the nearby American air base—the launching site for Operation Rolling Thunder sorties. Soon they were patrolling the countryside and skirmishing with the enemy. Beginning in the summer of 1965, combat operations shifted from a defensive stance to a search-and-destroy mission designed to uncover

and kill Vietcong forces. Fearing Congressional opposition to this expanded military commitment, the Johnson administration did not reveal that a major change in policy had occurred.

Over the next three years the number of American troops in Vietnam grew dramatically. Although in 1965 U.S. troops were accompanied by military forces from Australia, New Zealand, and South Korea, the war increasingly became an American struggle, fought for American aims. More than 75,000 soldiers were fighting there in June 1965, and 189,000 by the end of that year. In 1966 more than 380,000 American soldiers were stationed in Vietnam; there were 485,000 in 1967; and 536,000 in 1968 (see Figure 31.1). The increasing demands of General William Westmoreland, commander of the U.S. forces in Vietnam, confirmed a prediction made by the presidential adviser George Ball in 1961. Ball had warned President Kennedy that if Amer-

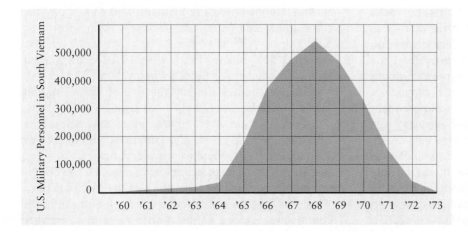

FIGURE 31.1

U.S. Troops in Vietnam, 1960–1973
When Lyndon Johnson escalated the Vietnam War, troop levels rose from 23,300 in December 1964 to 184,300 a year later. Troop levels eventually peaked to more than 543,000 personnel. Under Richard Nixon's Vietnamization program, beginning in the summer of 1969 levels drastically declined; the last U.S. military forces left South Vietnam on March 29, 1973.

ican ground troops were committed to Vietnam, there would be 300,000 on the ground within five years. Kennedy had laughed and said, "George, you're crazier than hell." But as Kennedy observed before his death, requests for troops were like having a drink: "The effect wears off, and you have to take another."

The massive commitment of troops and air power after 1965 threatened to destroy Vietnam's countryside and fragile resources. Taking to the extreme Johnson's call "to leave the footprints of America in Vietnam," the campaign of extensive defoliation and military bombardment made it difficult for peasants to practice the agriculture that provided the economic and cultural base of Vietnamese society. After one devastating but not unusual engagement the commanding U.S. officer claimed, using the logic of the time, "It became necessary to destroy the town in order to save it." Graffiti on a plane that dropped defoliants read, "Only you can prevent forests." (In later years chemicals such as Agent Orange were found to have highly toxic effects on humans and the environment.) The devastation was not limited to North Vietnam. South Vietnam, America's ally, suffered major damage and absorbed more than twice the total bomb tonnage dropped on the north. In Saigon and other South Vietnamese cities the influx of American soldiers and dollars distorted the local economy, leading to corruption and prostitution and setting off uncontrollable inflation and black market activities.

Why did the dramatically increased American presence in Vietnam from 1965 on fail to turn the tide of the war? Certain advisers, such as former Lieutenant Colonel John Paul Vann, argued that military intervention would do little unless it was accompanied by reform of the Saigon government and increased efforts at building popular support in the countryside. Throughout the war, however, most South Vietnamese remained distrustful of and disaffected from the brutal and corrupt Saigon government. Other critics claimed that the war was lost because the United States never committed its full military might to total victory, although what total victory would have entailed remains in dispute. It is true, however, that military strategy was inextricably tied to political considerations. For domestic reasons, policy makers often searched for the elusive "middle ground" between an all-out invasion (and the possibility of sparking a nuclear exchange between the superpowers) and the politically unacceptable alternative of disengagement. Hoping to win a war of attrition, the Johnson administration assumed that American superiority in personnel and weaponry would ultimately triumph. But this limited commitment was never enough to ensure victory, however defined.

The determination of the Vietnamese was also a major factor. In the 1940s Ho Chi Minh had told his French imperialist foes, "You can kill ten of my men for every one I kill of yours, but even at those odds, you will lose and I will win." That same statement held true twenty years later against the Americans. The Vietcong were prepared to accept limitless casualties and to fight for as many years as necessary. North Vietnamese strategists astutely realized that the war did not have to be won on the battlefield, accurately predicting that American public opinion would not tolerate an extended war of attrition. Time was on the Vietcong's side, although at an enormous cost to both Vietnam and the United States.

Vietnam from the Perspective of Americans Who Fought the War

Volunteers and Recruits. Approximately 2.8 million Americans served in Vietnam. With an average age of only nineteen, this was one of the youngest fighting forces in U.S. history. Whereas most of those servicemen and -women were too young to vote or drink (the voting age was twenty-one until the passage of the Twenty-sixth Amendment in 1971), they were old enough to fight . . . and die. They served for a variety of reasons. Some were volunteers, including some 7,000 women enlistees who joined out of a sense of patriotic duty or because they had few options at home and wanted to "see the world."

But many others served because they were drafted. Until the country shifted to an all-volunteer force in 1973, the draft stood as a concrete reminder of the government's impact on the lives of ordinary Americans. As troop needs increased, the draft reached deeper into the male population. The casualty figures reflected the increasing role of draftees in Vietnam. In 1965 draftees accounted for 16 percent of total battle deaths; that figure rose to 34 percent in 1967. By 1969, 62 percent of army deaths involved draftees. Blacks were drafted and died roughly in the same proportion to their share of the draft-age population (about 12 to 13 percent), although black casualty rates were significantly higher in the early 1960s. Even more than in other recent wars, sons of the poor and the working class shouldered a disproportionate amount of the fighting, forming an estimated 80 percent of the enlisted ranks. Young men from more affluent backgrounds were more likely to avoid combat through student deferments, medical exemptions, and appointments to National Guard and reserve units—alternatives that made Johnson's Vietnam policy more palatable to the middle class.

Life in "Nam." Many draftees and enlistees initially shared cold war assumptions about the need to fight communism and believed in the superiority of the American military. However, the Vietnam experience quickly challenged simple notions of patriotism and the inevitability

Ron Kovic

A Vietnam Veteran Remembers

Born on the Fourth of July in 1946, Ron Kovic wanted to be an American hero. He enlisted in the marines and was sent to Vietnam. Kovic came home in a wheelchair and, after a long period of recovery, joined the antiwar movement.

Ron Kovic

I had been shot. The war had finally caught up with my body. I felt good inside. Finally the war was with me and I had been shot by the enemy. I was getting out of the war and I was going to be a hero. I kept firing my rifle into the tree line and boldly, with my new wound, moved closer to the village, daring them to hit me again. For a moment I felt like running back to the rear with my new million-dollar wound but I decided to keep fighting in the open. A great surge of strength went through me as I yelled for the other men to come out from the trees and join me. I was limping now and the foot was beginning to hurt so much, I finally lay down in almost a kneeling position, still firing into the village, still unable to see anyone. I seemed to be the only one left firing a rifle. Someone came up from behind me, took off my boot and began to bandage my foot. The whole thing was incredibly stupid, we were sitting ducks, but he bandaged my foot and then he took off back into the tree line.

For a few seconds it was silent. I lay down prone and waited for the next bullet to hit me. It was only a matter of time, I thought. I wasn't retreating, I wasn't going back, I was lying right there and blasting everything I had into the pagoda. The rifle was full of sand and it was jamming. I had to pull the bolt back now each time trying to get a round into the chamber. It was impossible and I started to get up and a loud crack went off next to my right ear as a thirty-caliber slug tore through my right shoulder, blasted through my lung, and smashed my spinal cord to pieces.

I felt that everything from my chest down was completely gone. I waited to die. I threw my hand back and felt my legs still there. I couldn't feel them but they were still there. I was still alive. And for some reason I started believing, I started believing I might not die, I might make it out of there and live and feel and go back home again. I could hardly breathe and was taking short little sucks with the one lung I had left. The blood was rolling off my flak jacket from the hole in my shoulder and I couldn't feel the pain in my foot anymore, I couldn't even feel my body. I was frightened to death. I didn't think about praying, all I could feel was cheated.

All I could feel was the worthlessness of dying right here in this place at this moment for nothing.

Source: Ron Kovic, *Born on the Fourth of July* (New York: McGraw-Hill, 1976), 221–222.

of American victory (see American Voices, above). The first thing new soldiers noticed when they got off the plane was the stench of death, napalm, and human waste in this torrid jungle country. Sometimes they had to sprint from the plane to the safety of the base buildings because of mortar attacks, a sign of the boldness with which enemy forces operated throughout the country.

Unlike World War II soldiers, who served "for the duration," Vietnam soldiers had a one-year tour of duty. For many it was simply a matter of getting through 365 days. For the first ninety days or so they were "cherries," slang for virgins. Once they neared the end of the tour, soldiers might carry a "short-timer's stick" notched for the remaining days left; as each day passed, they would cut off another notch until only a small stub remained. Some soldiers even longed for "million-dollar wounds"—

serious but nonfatal injuries that would result in permanent removal from the battlefield. "Grunts" (ordinary infantrymen) and "bloods" (the name that black draftees called themselves) were a superstitious lot and were always afraid of being "wasted" (killed) with only a few days to go. Some soldiers deliberately avoided making close friends in case their buddies caught a grenade or triggered a booby trap on a routine patrol.

In "Nam" (soldiers' shorthand for Vietnam) days passed in boring menial work punctuated by flashes of intense fighting. "Most of the time, nothing happened," a soldier recalled, "but when something did, it happened instantaneously and without warning." The pressure of waging war in those conditions drove many soldiers to seek escape in alcohol or cheap and readily available drugs.

The fighting had a surreal quality. Combat often intensified at night, with incoming and outgoing firepower lighting up the sky while soldiers huddled sleeplessly on watch. There were rarely large-scale battles, only skirmishes; no front lines or conquering of territory, just operations during the day in areas that reverted to Vietcong control at night. Although whole units might be ambushed, casualties typically came in twos and threes. A former marine captain recalled:

> You never knew who was the enemy and who was the friend. They all looked alike. They all dressed alike. They were all Vietnamese. Some of them were Vietcong. Here's a woman of twenty-two or twenty-three. She is pregnant, and she tells an interrogator that her husband works in Danang and isn't a Vietcong. But she watches your men walk down a trail and get killed or wounded by a booby trap. She knows the booby trap is there, but she doesn't warn them. Maybe she planted it herself.

He concluded graphically, "It wasn't like the San Francisco Forty-Niners on one side of the field and the Cincinnati Bengals on the other. The enemy was all around you."

Because territorial gains were often temporary and illusory, American success was measured in gruesome "body counts"—the number of enemy soldiers killed—and "kill ratios"—the ratio between enemy losses and U.S. casualties. "If it's dead and Vietnamese, it's VC [Vietcong]" was the rule of thumb in the bush. Casualty figures were often deliberately inflated. As a twenty-four-year-old army captain recalled, "I went out and killed one VC and liberated a prisoner. Next day the major called me in and told me that I'd killed fourteen VC and liberated six prisoners. You want to see the medal?"

Racism was a fact of everyday life in Vietnam. It was difficult to differentiate between friendly South Vietnamese and Vietcong sympathizers, and many soldiers lumped them together as "gooks." A draftee noted of his indoctrination, "The only thing they told us about the Vietcong was they were gooks. They were to be killed. Nobody sits around and gives you their historical and cultural background. They're the enemy. Kill, kill, kill."

Fighting and surviving in such conditions took its toll. "War is not killing," one soldier recalled. "Killing is the easiest part of the whole thing. Sweating twenty-four hours a day, seeing guys drop all around you of heatstroke, not having food, not having water, sleeping only three hours a night for weeks at a time, that's what war is. Survival." Another veteran echoed that sentiment: "The hardest thing to come to grips with was the fact that making it through Vietnam—surviving—is probably the only worthwhile part of the experience. It wasn't going over there and saving the world from communism or defending the country." Such cynicism and bitterness were common.

Women who served in Vietnam shared many of these experiences. As WACs, nurses, and civilian service workers with organizations such as the USO, women volunteers witnessed massive doses of death and mutilation, mainly inflicted on soldiers barely out of their teens. They tried not to get caught up in it emotionally, but as a navy nurse recalled, "It's pretty damn hard not getting involved when you see a nineteen- or twenty-year-old blond kid from the Midwest or California or the East Coast screaming and dying. A piece of my heart would go with each."

The Consensus Begins to Unravel

During the Kennedy and early Johnson years there was a broad consensus for the administration's conduct of foreign affairs, as there had been generally throughout the cold war period. Both Democrats and Republicans supported Johnson's escalation of the war, and public opinion polls showed strong popular support for his policies in 1965–1966. But in the late 1960s public opinion began to turn against the war. In July 1967 a Gallup poll revealed that for the first time, a majority of Americans disapproved of Johnson's Vietnam policy and believed that the war had reached a stalemate.

The Television War. Television had much to do with shaping American attitudes toward the war. Vietnam was the first war in which television brought the fight-

A Televised War
This harrowing scene from Saigon during the Tet offensive in 1968 was broadcast on U.S. network news. The NBC bureau chief described the film in a terse telex message: "A VC OFFICER WAS CAPTURED. THE TROOPS BEAT HIM. THEY BRING HIM TO [Brigadier General Nguyen Ngoc] LOAN WHO IS HEAD OF SOUTH VIETNAMESE NATIONAL POLICE. LOAN PULLS OUT HIS PISTOL, FIRES AT THE HEAD OF THE VC, THE VC FALLS, ZOOM ON HIS HEAD, BLOOD SPRAYING OUT. IF HE HAS IT ALL ITS STARTLING STUFF."

ing directly into the nation's living rooms. The escalation in Vietnam came just two years after the expansion of the nightly network news broadcast from fifteen minutes to half an hour in 1963. By 1967 CBS and NBC were spending $5 million a year to cover the war from their expanded Saigon bureaus. This investment guaranteed that Vietnam appeared on the news every night. Reporters soon learned that combat footage—what they called "shooting bloody"—had a better chance of airing than did reports about social reform or political developments. Every night Americans saw U.S. soldiers advancing steadily in the countryside and heard about staggering Vietcong losses and minimal U.S. casualties.

Growing Doubts. Despite the glowing reports that were fed to the American public about the progress of the war, by 1967 many administration officials had privately reached more pessimistic conclusions. Secretary of Defense Robert McNamara, one of the architects of the war, expressed opposition to the expansion of the air war and sent a memo to the president in November arguing that continued escalation "would be dangerous, costly in lives, and unsatisfactory to the American people." A few weeks later McNamara left the Defense Department for the World Bank. "I do not know," he later wrote, "whether I quit or was fired." McNamara's doubts were confirmed by Pentagon analysts who estimated that the Vietcong, with only minimal assistance from other communist powers, could marshal 200,000 guerrillas a year indefinitely.

Despite that prognosis, President Johnson continued to insist that victory in Vietnam was vital to U.S. national security and prestige. Journalists, especially those who had spent time in Vietnam, soon commented that the Johnson administration suffered from a "credibility gap." The administration, they charged, was concealing important and discouraging information about the progress of the war. Television coverage of hearings by the Senate Foreign Relations Committee in February 1966 (chaired by J. William Fulbright, an outspoken critic of the war) also raised questions about the administration's Vietnam policies.

Economic events also put Johnson and his advisers on the defensive. In 1966 the federal deficit was $9.8 billion. It jumped to $23 billion in 1967, with the Vietnam War costing the taxpayers $27 billion that year. Although the war was consuming only 3 percent of the gross national product, compared with 42 percent at the height of World War II and 12 percent during the Korean War, its costs became more evident as the growing federal deficit nudged the inflation rate upward. But only in the summer of 1967 did Johnson ask for a 10 percent surcharge on individual and corporate income, which Congress delayed approving until 1968. By then the inflationary spiral that would plague the American economy throughout the 1970s was already well under way.

The Early Antiwar Movement. Another major problem facing the Johnson administration was the growing strength and visibility of the antiwar movement. As in every American military conflict, a small group of dissenters opposed the war from the beginning, including pacifist organizations such as the War Resisters League and the Women's International League for Peace and Freedom and religious groups such as the Fellowship for Reconciliation and the Quakers. Those groups were joined by a new generation of peace activists that had emerged in the 1950s to protest atmospheric nuclear testing. Concern over fallout and traces of radioactive strontium 90 in milk led to the founding of groups such as SANE (the National Committee for a Sane Nuclear Policy), Physicians for Social Responsibility, and Women Strike for Peace. Those activists opposed the escalating arms race in general and atmospheric testing in particular and lobbied successfully for the 1963 nuclear test ban treaty between the United States and the Soviet Union.

Between 1963 and 1965, as the American presence in Vietnam grew, peace activists in both older and newer organizations staged periodic protests, vigils, and petitioning and letter-writing campaigns against U.S. involvement in the war. After the escalation of combat in the spring of 1965, various antiwar coalitions organized several mass demonstrations in Washington that brought out 20,000

Women March for Peace, 1962
Members of the Women's Strike for Peace set up picket lines at the Capitol in December 1962 to urge an end to atmospheric testing of nuclear weapons by the United States and the Soviet Union. Such protest groups were forerunners of the broader movement that opposed the Vietnam War after 1965.

to 30,000 people. Pacifist and religious groups were joined by growing numbers of students, housewives, politicians, artists, and other Americans opposed to the war. Although they were a diverse lot, the participants shared a common skepticism about the means and aims of U.S. policy. Critics of intervention argued that the war was morally wrong and antithetical to American ideals; that the goal of an independent, anticommunist South Vietnam was unattainable; and that American military involvement would not help the Vietnamese people.

Norman Morrison provides an example of how strongly some Americans felt about Vietnam. In November 1965 Morrison, a thirty-two-year-old Quaker activist, married and the father of an eighteen-month-old daughter, set himself on fire and burned to death near the gates of the Pentagon, 40 yards from Defense Secretary McNamara's office. He undertook this protest against the immorality of the war after reading an account by a French priest who had despaired at seeing his Vietnamese parishioners burned by napalm (a lethal incendiary substance) during a bombing attack. Like the priest, Morrison was anguished about his inability to stop the carnage. To his wife of ten years he left this note: "Know that I love thee but must act for the children of the priest's village."

Morrison's suicide shocked the nation. Even McNamara later admitted that he was horrified by this "outcry against the killing that was destroying the lives of so many Vietnamese and American youth." Three weeks later an estimated 30,000 antiwar protesters converged on the White House, including a large contingent of college students. Over the next few years student protesters flocked to the antiwar movement in great numbers, increasing its visibility and political clout. The fervor of this new generation drove not only the antiwar movement but a youthful rebellion that challenged authority on nearly every front.

The Challenge of Youth, 1962–1970

"There is everywhere protest, reevaluation, attack on the Establishment," the social critic Paul Goodman asserted at the end of the 1960s. The novelist Norman Mailer agreed: "We're in a time that's divorced from the past. . . . There's utterly no tradition anymore." The sources of this youthful rebellion lay in the political and social developments of the postwar era, particularly the early 1960s. The idealism of Kennedy's New Frontier raised students' expectations of what they and their society could accomplish. The civil rights movement ignited the challenge to established institutions, teaching college students protest tactics such as marches, sit-ins, and mass confrontations.

Finally, the escalation of the Vietnam War in 1965 offered a compelling political cause to rally around, especially as the draft affected more college-age men. Vietnam would become the defining political issue of their generation.

Student Activism

The 1960s witnessed the first active student movement since the 1930s. But whereas most of that depression-scarred generation had been unable to afford higher education, its children—the baby boomers—flocked to colleges and universities in the postwar period. In addition, many soldiers who had served in World War II and the Korean War used the benefits of the GI Bill to finance higher education that otherwise would have been out of their reach. Those veterans, many of them from working-class backgrounds, later sent their children to college as well. In 1940 only 15 percent of all youth between the ages of eighteen and twenty-one attended college; in 1963 the proportion had reached almost 50 percent.

In the 1950s most students accepted the practical career-oriented values of their society. Engineering and business administration (for men) and home economics and teaching (for women) were the most popular courses of study, and students took little part in politics. Some critics suggested that students, responding to the repressive atmosphere of McCarthyism, had become a "silent generation." Even so, many young people felt dissatisfied in the 1950s. The youthful rebellion evident in rock 'n' roll and portrayed in Hollywood films such as *Rebel without a Cause* (see Chapter 29) was one expression of this dissatisfaction. J. D. Salinger's best-selling novel *The Catcher in the Rye* (1951) offered a more explicit critique of the materialism of postwar American society. With a dawning awareness of the existence of poverty and the ever present threat of nuclear war, the novel's teenage protagonist gradually sheds his naiveté and quietly rejects the middle-class pretensions of his family, neighbors, and schoolmates. The book is a withering attack on the hypocrisy of a society that insists that all is well because the economy is booming—a notion that found wide acceptance among youths in the 1960s.

Early Stirrings. Youth rebellion took a distinctly political form in the early 1960s. In June 1962 forty students from Big Ten and Ivy League universities met at a United Auto Workers conference center in Port Huron, Michigan, to found Students for a Democratic Society (SDS). Their manifesto, written by Tom Hayden, a University of Michigan student, drew heavily on the writings of the radical Columbia University sociologist C. Wright Mills. The Port Huron Statement expressed hostility toward bureaucracy, rejected cold war ideology (including but not limited to the Vietnam conflict), emphasized participatory politics, and designated students as the major force for change in society. SDSers referred to their movement as the "New Left" to distinguish themselves from the "Old Left"—communists, socialists, and other left-wing sectarians of the 1930s and 1940s. Consciously adopting the activist tactics pioneered by the civil rights movement, SDS devoted much of its early attention to grass-roots organizing in cities and on college campuses.

The first student protests broke out at the University of California at Berkeley. In the fall of 1964 the university administration banned political activity near the Telegraph Avenue entrance to the campus, where student groups had traditionally distributed leaflets and recruited volunteers. In response, all the major student organizations, from SDS to the conservative Youth for Goldwater, formed a coalition to protest what they considered to be an abridgment of free speech. The Free Speech Movement organized a sit-in at the main administration building and persuaded the university to drop the ban.

The Free Speech Movement owed a strong debt to the civil rights movement. Berkeley had sent more volunteers to Freedom Summer in Mississippi in 1964 than had any other campus, and the students had been radi-

Free Speech at Berkeley, 1964
Students at the University of California's Berkeley campus protested the administration's decision to ban political activity in the school plaza. Free speech demonstrators, many of them active in the civil rights movement, relied on the tactics and arguments that they learned in that struggle.

calized by the experience. The student leader Mario Savio spoke for many of them:

> Last summer I went to Mississippi to join the struggle there for civil rights. This fall I am engaged in another phase of the same struggle, this time in Berkeley. The two battlefields may seem quite different to some observers, but this is not the case. The same rights are at stake in both places—the right to participate as citizens in a democratic society and to struggle against the same enemy. In Mississippi an autocratic and powerful minority rules, through organized violence, to suppress the vast, virtually powerless majority. In California, the privileged minority manipulates the university bureaucracy to suppress the students' political expression.

On a deeper level Berkeley students were challenging the university because it had grown too big, too impersonal, and too insulated from the major social issues of the day. The largest universities, like the largest corporations, had grown the fastest in the postwar era. In 1940 only two campuses had as many as 20,000 students; in 1969 thirty-nine were at least that large. Many students felt that they were treated brusquely and impersonally in those "multiversities." Emboldened by the Berkeley experience, students at institutions across the country were soon protesting everything from dress codes to course requirements, tenure decisions, and academic grading systems.

Students also protested the universities' complicity in the problems of the ghettos that surrounded many urban campuses. Columbia, for example, was a major property owner in Harlem, which borders its campus. In 1968 Columbia announced plans to build a new gymnasium, displacing local stores and housing. Chanting "Gym Crow must go," students tore down the fence at the construction site and took over several university buildings, including the office of the president, Grayson Kirk. (Photographs of protesters sampling Kirk's cigars and sherry did little to build public support.) At Berkeley, students and administrators clashed in 1969 over a parcel of vacant land near the campus that a coalition of students and residents had turned into a "People's Park." When the university asserted its right to the land, a violent confrontation broke out and an onlooker was killed. At both Columbia and Berkeley the administration decided to use city police officers to break up the demonstrations; the brutality of the police radicalized many more students than had originally supported the protests. As campus disturbances spread, more and more university buildings were blocked, occupied, or picketed, and classes were frequently dismissed or canceled.

Although black students participated in many of the protests, student movements increasingly split along racial lines, reflecting the separatism that characterized the civil rights movement in the mid-1960s. Whereas white students focused increasingly on the antiwar movement, black students inspired by the black power movement demanded courses in African-American history and culture. University administrators were open to such demands as a way to ease campus unrest, and many universities established Afro-American or black studies departments in the late 1960s and early 1970s. By including the study of black society and culture in the curriculum and acknowledging race as a key factor in American life, those new courses and programs had an enduring impact on the way American history was taught and written. Black protesters also won university support for separate dormitories and cultural centers to provide a sense of community for blacks on predominantly white campuses.

The Antiwar Movement. But no issue provoked more impassioned and sustained protest than the Vietnam War. When President Johnson dramatically escalated the war in March 1965, faculty members and student activists at the University of Michigan organized a teach-in against the war. In marathon sessions they debated the political, diplomatic, and moral aspects of U.S. involvement in Vietnam. Teach-ins quickly spread to other universities as students turned their attention to antiwar protests.

A strong spur to activism was a change in the Selective Service System. In the past, young men could use deferments for college, graduate school, teaching, and parenthood to avoid the draft until they reached the cutoff age of twenty-six. Over the course of the war the government issued more than 8 million deferments, a disproportionate number of which went to wealthy whites. In response to criticism of the class and racial bias inherent in the system, the Selective Service gradually phased out deferments. In January 1966 automatic student deferments were abolished.

Young men's options were limited. Some enlisted in the National Guard or the reserves to avoid being sent to Vietnam. Some reluctant draftees sought sympathetic doctors to give them medical or psychiatric excuses or to help them fail the induction physical. Others filed for conscientious objector status, fulfilling their military commitment through alternative service in the United States or noncombatant duty in Vietnam. Several thousand ignored the induction notice entirely, risking prosecution for draft evasion, while others left the country (Canada and Sweden were the most popular destinations). The Resistance, started at Berkeley and Stanford and widely recognized by its omega symbol, provided support to draft resisters. Opponents of the war burned their draft cards in public acts of civil disobedience, closed down induction centers with mass protests, and on a few occasions broke into Selective Service offices to destroy or mutilate files.

As antiwar and draft protests multiplied, students realized that their universities were deeply implicated in the war effort. In some cases as much as 60 percent of a university's research budget came from government contracts, especially from the Defense Department. Protesters blocked campus recruitment by the Dow Chemical Company because it produced napalm and Agent Orange. Arguing that universities should not train students for war, protesters demanded that the Reserve Officer Training Corps (ROTC) be removed from campus. The ROTC was one of the main targets of student protests at Columbia in 1968 and Harvard in 1969.

Mass demonstrations against the war consumed much of the energy of the student movement in the late 1960s as students became part of the much larger antiwar movement of peace activists, housewives, religious leaders, and a few elected officials. Nationwide student strikes, mass demonstrations in Washington, D.C., and other organized protests became commonplace after 1967. More than 100,000 antiwar demonstrators marched on Washington in October 1967 as part of "Stop the Draft Week." The event culminated in a "siege of the Pentagon" in which protesters clashed with police and federal marshals, resulting in hundreds of arrests and several beatings of demonstrators. Lyndon Johnson, who had earlier dismissed antiwar protesters as "nervous Nellies," rebellious children, or communist dupes, now faced large-scale public opposition to his policies. The administration thus waged a two-front offensive: a military operation in Vietnam and a war for public opinion at home.

The Rise of the Counterculture

Antiwar sentiment and protest accelerated the erosion of confidence in established American institutions and values. But while the New Left took to the streets in protest, a growing number of young Americans chose to undertake their own revolution against the "respectable" standards of middle-class society. Building on the sense of personal alienation and cultural rebellion articulated by the beat generation in the 1950s, youths in the 1960s pioneered new forms of cultural expression. Dubbed the *counterculture* because it challenged so many established values, the movement encouraged personal liberation through new musical and clothing styles, spiritual exploration, and experimentation with sex and drugs.

The impact of the counterculture was readily evident even to the uninitiated. In an amazingly short period of time young people's clothing and hairstyles changed radically. At Berkeley's free speech demonstrations in 1964, young men wore coats and ties and women wore skirts and sweaters. At antiwar protests just three or four years later, youths defiantly dressed in unisex ragged blue jeans, tie-dyed T-shirts, beads, and army fatigues. Unorthodox clothes and long, unkempt hair identified a new phenomenon of American youth culture, the *hippie*.

Flower Children
Yale law professor Charles A. Reich celebrated the new freedom of youth in his best-selling book *The Greening of America* (1970). Reich described a new consciousness that had "emerged out of the wasteland of the Corporate State, like flowers pushing up through the concrete pavement." Counterculture hippies were also called flower children.

The uncomprehending older generation often had a simple response: "Get a haircut."

Popular Music. Throughout the 1960s popular music mirrored changing political moods. The folksinger Pete Seeger set the tone for the era's political idealism with songs such as the antiwar ballad "Where Have All the Flowers Gone?" Another folksinger, Joan Baez, gained national prominence for "We Shall Overcome" and other folk and political anthems that she performed at protest rallies in the mid-1960s. In 1963, the year of the Birmingham demonstrations and President Kennedy's assassination, Bob Dylan's "Blowin' in the Wind" reflected the impatience of people whose faith in liberalism was wearing thin.

Early in 1964 the Beatles, four working-class youths from Liverpool, England, burst onto the American scene. As Elvis Presley had eight years earlier, they thrust their way into the national consciousness through a series of television appearances on "The Ed Sullivan Show." The Beatles' music, by turns lyrical and driving, was phenomenally successful, spawning a commercial and cultural phenomenon called Beatlemania. The more rebellious, angrier music of other British groups, notably the Rolling Stones, found a broad American audience shortly afterward.

The Drug Culture. Drugs were almost as important as rock music in the youth culture of the 1960s. Drugs were hardly new to the American scene: many jazz musicians from the 1920s on had used heroin and cocaine, and the beats had experimented with mind-altering drugs in San Francisco and New York. Now widespread recreational use of drugs extended beyond artistic and jazz circles.

Marijuana was the preferred drug among college students, but stronger drugs also gained popularity. The hallucinogen lysergic acid diethylamide, popularly known as LSD or "acid," was one of the most potent. It was popularized in California by the writer Ken Kesey and his eccentric followers, the Merry Pranksters, who conducted "acid tests" (public "happenings" where tabs of LSD were distributed) in 1965 and 1966. San Francisco bands such as the Grateful Dead and the Jefferson Airplane, the Seattle-born guitarist Jimi Hendrix, and Britain's Pink Floyd developed a style of music known as "acid rock," characterized by long, heavily amplified guitar solos and psychedelic effects. The Beatles, whose early songs had simply stated "I Want to Hold Your Hand" and "Please, Please Me," later recorded tunes such as "Lucy in the Sky with Diamonds" (1967), whose "tangerine trees and marmalade skies" celebrated the new drug-induced consciousness.

For a brief time adherents of the counterculture believed that a new age was dawning. "The closest Western Civilization has come to uniting since the Congress of Vienna in 1815 was the week the *Sgt. Pepper* album was released," gushed a rock critic about the Beatles' 1967 release. Others pointed to the "age of Aquarius"

Sgt. Pepper's Lonely Hearts Club Band
The colorful collage on the cover of this 1967 Beatles album allowed fans to debate (occasionally under the influence of marijuana or LSD) the symbolism of those depicted. Can you identify Mae West, Karl Marx, Bob Dylan, Albert Einstein, Lenny Bruce, and Marilyn Monroe, as well as the "Fab Four" in their various disguises? (©Apple Corps Ltd.)

proclaimed in the 1968 Broadway rock musical *Hair*. In 1967 the "world's first Human Be-In" drew 20,000 people to Golden Gate Park in San Francisco. The beat poet Allen Ginsberg "purified" the site with a Buddhist ritual, political activists embraced "drug freaks," and the LSD advocate Timothy Leary, a former Harvard psychology instructor, urged the gathering to "turn on to the scene, tune in to what is happening, and drop out." In the summer of 1967—dubbed the "Summer of Love"—San Francisco's Haight-Ashbury, New York's East Village, and Chicago's Uptown neighborhoods were crowded with young people as well as swarms of reporters and busloads of tourists who gawked at the so-called flower children. Faith in instant love and peace quickly turned sour, however, as dropouts, drifters, and teenage runaways tried to cope with bad drug trips, venereal disease, loneliness, and violence. In 1967 seventeen murders and more than a hundred rapes were reported in Haight-Ashbury alone.

Meanwhile, the appeal of rock music and drugs continued to spread. In August 1969 400,000 young people journeyed to Bethel, New York, to attend the three-day Woodstock Music and Art Fair. Despite torrential rain and numerous drug overdoses, the festival was heralded as the birth of the "Woodstock nation" as participants "got high" on music, drugs, and sex. A few months later, however, an outdoor concert by the Rolling Stones at Altamont Speedway near San Francisco degenerated into a near riot, leaving four dead and hundreds injured.

Rejecting both the mainstream culture and the growing anarchy of the counterculture, some young people headed for rural communes. Communes were located in isolated areas such as the mountains between Santa Cruz and San Francisco, the wide-open spaces of New Mexico, and the pastoral solitude of Vermont, away from the watchful eye of mainstream America (and local drug enforcement agents). Following in the tradition of earlier American utopian communities, communes provided economic and sexual alternatives to nuclear families. They also promised a return to the land as members banded together to grow their own food, bake their own bread, and reject the materialism and commercialism of American life in an attempt at self-sufficiency. But the communes of the 1960s did not just look backward. Their advocacy of organic farming—growing food without chemicals or pesticides—anticipated and influenced the environmental concerns that would emerge in the 1970s and 1980s (see Chapter 32).

Although the counterculture and the New Left were different movements, the distinction was sometimes blurred. Many antiwar protesters adopted hippie clothing, experimented with drugs, and embraced the more politically oriented rock music. While most flower children professed to be politically apathetic, their antiauthoritarianism seemed threatening to many adults. Furthermore, groups such as the Youth International Party, or "Yippies," led by Abbie Hoffman and Jerry Rubin, combined political and cultural rebellion to attract media attention. During the October 1967 March on Washington the Yippies dressed like witches and attempted to levitate the Pentagon as a way to end the war. To many adult observers the antiwar movement and the counterculture had become indistinguishable.

The Long Road Home, 1968–1975

In 1968, as Lyndon Johnson planned his reelection campaign, Vietnam had become the central domestic and foreign policy issue, eclipsing the struggle for civil rights. Antiwar protests and America's vulnerability on the battlefield—as evidenced by the Tet offensive of January–February 1968—had begun to erode public support for the war. Vietnam also cast a shadow over domestic events as antiwar protests divided and disrupted the Democratic National Convention in Chicago that summer. The Chicago riot, along with two major political assassinations that year, shocked the nation and ushered in a new conservatism represented by the Republican presidency of Richard Nixon. But like his predecessors, Nixon found it difficult to extricate the United States from Vietnam, and American troops fought for nearly five more years.

While the Johnson administration insisted that there was "light at the end of the tunnel" in late 1967, the reality was otherwise. American casualty rates continued to rise, North Vietnamese and Vietcong forces fought on, and the South Vietnamese government enjoyed little popular support. Since the assassination of Diem in 1963 South Vietnam had undergone a confusing series of coups and countercoups by various factions of the military. In June 1965 Generals Nguyen Van Thieu and Nguyen Cao Ky took power in a military coup. After widespread Buddhist uprisings against the new regime in the spring of 1966, the Johnson administration pressured the South Vietnamese government to adopt democratic reforms, including a new constitution and popular elections. With American help Thieu was elected president of South Vietnam in September 1967. Thieu's regime, the Johnson administration hoped, would broaden its support at home, legitimize the South Vietnamese government in the eyes of the American public, and advance the military struggle against the communists.

1968: A Year of Shocks

The Tet Offensive. Those hopes were quickly shattered on January 30, 1968, when the Vietcong unleashed a massive, well-coordinated assault on major urban areas in the south. Known as the Tet offensive, the assault was timed to coincide with the festive Vietnamese holiday of Tet, the lunar new year. Vietcong forces struck thirty-six of the forty-four provincial capitals and five of the six major cities, including a raid on the supposedly impregnable U.S. embassy in Saigon (see Map 31.1). The United States and the South Vietnamese forces were caught off guard, once again having seriously underestimated the capabilities of their foes, who had been planning the attack since the previous fall. "Even had I known exactly what was to take place," an intelligence officer explained, "it was so preposterous that I probably would have been unable to sell it to anybody."

American forces quickly recovered and launched a counterattack. In strictly military terms the Tet offensive was a defeat for the Vietcong since it failed to bring about the collapse of the South Vietnamese government. But its long-term effect was quite different. As one historian observed, Tet was "probably unique in that the side that lost completely in the tactical sense came away with an overwhelming psychological and hence political victory." In the United States, Tet marked the beginning of a new phase of the war.

Television again played a major role in shaping American attitudes. The success of the Vietcong made a mockery of official pronouncements that the United States was winning the war. Suddenly television brought home more disturbing images—the American embassy in Saigon under siege, with a pistol-wielding staff member peering warily from a window, and the Saigon police chief placing a pistol to the head of a Vietcong suspect and executing him on the street. About 20 million television viewers watched the latter scene, which brought home the brutality of the war and the corruption and injustice of the Thieu regime.

The Tet offensive swung American public opinion more clearly against the war. Just before Tet a Gallup poll found that 56 percent of Americans considered themselves "hawks" (supporters of the war) whereas only 28 percent identified themselves as "doves" (opponents). Women and blacks consistently opposed the war more than white men did, and younger people more than older. In April 1968, three months after the Tet offense, doves outnumbered hawks by 42 to 41 percent. This turnaround did not mean that a majority supported the peace movement. Many who called themselves doves had simply concluded that the war was unwinnable and that America ought to cut its losses and withdraw its forces. They opposed the war on pragmatic, rather than moral, grounds. As a housewife told a pollster, "I want to get out, but I don't want to give up."

The growing opposition to the war prompted the administration to end its policy of incremental escalation. President Johnson turned down General Westmoreland's request for 206,000 additional troops, a deployment that would have required the politically explosive course of calling up the reserves. Congressional support was slipping, and many of Johnson's advisers had concluded that the war was unwinnable, including the members of the foreign policy establishment dubbed "the wise men" (see Chapter 28). With the 1968 presidential election only months away, Johnson faced growing resistance to his Vietnam policies within his own party.

At the urging of the antiwar activist Allard Lowenstein, Senator Eugene J. McCarthy of Minnesota had already entered the Democratic primaries as a dovish liberal alternative to Lyndon Johnson. (Lowenstein had first approached Senator Robert Kennedy of New York, whose instincts told him to run but whose advisers said he should wait until 1972.) A core of student activists went "clean for Gene" by cutting their hair and putting away their blue jeans to avoid alienating voters. When the Tet offensive revealed how badly things were going in Vietnam, support for the war eroded further. Although President Johnson won the New Hampshire primary in early March, McCarthy received a stunning 42.2 percent of the vote. McCarthy's share of the vote reflected profound dissatisfaction with the course of the war—even among those who believed Johnson was not hawkish enough. Sensing the president's vulnerability, Robert Kennedy changed his mind and entered the race.

Johnson realized that his political support was evaporating, and at the end of an otherwise mundane televised address on March 31 he stunned the nation by announcing that he would not seek reelection. Johnson also called a partial bombing halt and vowed to devote his remaining months in office to the search for peace in Vietnam. On May 10, 1968, preliminary peace talks between the United States and North Vietnam began in Paris. Johnson's decision to remove himself from the presidential race was a direct result of the lack of consensus at home.

The first months of 1968 thus marked an important turning point in the long history of American involvement in Vietnam. The policy of incremental escalation that had been in force since the 1950s came to an end, and the evaporating domestic consensus for the war meant that future leaders would have to find a way of disengaging from the conflict. But even though a corner had been turned in 1968, no one could see "light at the end of the tunnel."

Political Turmoil. Just four days after Johnson's withdrawal from the presidential race, Martin Luther King, Jr., was assassinated in Memphis, provoking urban riots across the country that left forty-three people dead. Soon afterward, a major student confrontation erupted at Columbia University, ending only when police forcibly removed protesters from the administration buildings that they had occupied, beating and injuring dozens of demonstrators in the process. Student unrest seemed likely to become a worldwide phenomenon in May, when a massive strike by students and labor unions (traditional allies in Europe) toppled the French government.

Then came the final and, for many, the most painful tragedy of the year. As Robert Kennedy celebrated his California primary victory over Eugene McCarthy on June 5, 1968, he was shot dead by Sirhan Sirhan, a young Palestinian who was thought to oppose Kennedy's pro-Israel stance. Once again the nation went through the ritual of burying a Kennedy. In two strokes—the assassinations of Martin Luther King and Robert Kennedy—liberalism had been, as the student leader Tom Hayden put it, "decapitated."

Robert Kennedy's assassination shattered the dreams of many who hoped that social change could be achieved through the political system. His death also had major

RFK
Bobby Kennedy inspired strong passions during his 1968 campaign. Followers often tore off his cuff links as they tried to touch him or shake his hand.

implications for the Democratic party, because only he had seemed able to mobilize a constituency broader than the antiwar movement. In his brief but dramatic campaign Robert Kennedy had excited, indeed energized, the traditional components of the New Deal coalition, including blue-collar workers and black voters, in a way that the more cerebral Eugene McCarthy never did. So widespread was Kennedy's appeal that election-day exit polls in Indiana found that many voters who had supported him in the primary later voted for the conservative candidate George Wallace in November.

The Democratic party, which was still reeling from Johnson's withdrawal when Kennedy was assassinated, never fully recovered. McCarthy proceeded listlessly through the rest of his campaign. Senator George S. McGovern of South Dakota entered the Democratic race in an effort to keep the Kennedy forces together. Meanwhile, Vice-President Hubert H. Humphrey lined up pledges from the traditional Democratic constituencies—unions, city machines, and state political organizations. The Democrats thus found themselves on the verge of nominating not an antiwar candidate but a public figure closely associated with Johnson's war policies. The stage was set for the Democratic National Convention in Chicago in August.

The Democratic National Convention. With Vietnam emerging as the central campaign issue in the 1968 elections, the political divisions generated by the war consumed the Democratic party. The Democrats had experienced disastrous conventions in the past, such as the 103-ballot contest of 1924, but the 1968 convention hit a new low. Most of the drama occurred not in the convention hall but outside, on the streets of Chicago. Led by the Yippie activists Jerry Rubin and Abbie Hoffman, around 10,000 protesters descended on Chicago. With theatrics geared toward maximum media exposure, they announced a platform calling for an end to the war, the legalization of marijuana, and the abolition of money. To mock the "pigs" who ruled America, they nominated a live pig for president, which was promptly confiscated by Chicago's humane society. Their stunts diverted attention from the more serious, and far more numerous, antiwar activists who had come to Chicago as convention delegates or volunteers.

The old-line Democratic mayor, Richard J. Daley, grew increasingly angry at the way protesters were mocking his city and disrupting his convention. He called out the police and gave them broad discretion to break up the demonstrations. Several nights of skirmishes between protesters and police culminated on the evening when the names of candidates were put in nomination. In what an official report later described as a "police riot," the police dispersed protesters with Mace, tear gas, and clubs (see American Voices, page 976). The tear gas was so strong that it wafted into the air-conditioning ducts of the

Steve Lerner

The Siege of Chicago

Steve Lerner published this account of the altercation between protesters and the Chicago police during the Democratic National Convention in August 1968 in the *Village Voice*. The scene is Lincoln Park on Chicago's North Side, where many of the protesters congregated.

Around midnight on Tuesday some four hundred clergy, concerned local citizens, and other respectable gentry joined the Yippies, members of Students for a Democratic Society, and the National Mobilization Committee to fight for the privilege of remaining in the park. Sporting armbands decorated with a black cross and chanting pacifist hymns, the men of God exhorted their radical congregation to lay down their bricks and join in a nonviolent vigil. . . .

During the half-hour interlude between the arrival of the clergy and the police attack, a fascinating debate over the relative merits of strict nonviolence versus armed self-defense raged between the clergy and the militants. While the clergy was reminded that their members were "over thirty, the opiate of the people, and totally irrelevant," the younger generation was warned that "by calling the police pigs and fighting with them you become as bad as they are." Although the conflict was never resolved, everyone more or less decided to do his own thing. By then the demonstrators, some eight hundred strong, began to feel the phalanx of police which encircled the park moving in; even the most militant forgot his quibbles with "the liberal-religious sellout" and began to huddle together around the cross.

When the police announced that the demonstrators had five minutes to move out before the park was cleared, everyone went into his individual kind of panic. One boy sitting near me unwrapped a cheese sandwich and began to stuff it into his face without bothering to chew. A girl standing at the periphery of the circle who had been alone all evening walked up to a helmeted boy with a mustache and ground herself into him. People all over the park were shyly introducing themselves to each other as if they didn't want to die alone. "My name is Mike Stevenson from Detroit; what got you into this?" I heard someone asking behind me. Others became increasingly involved in the details of survival: rubbing Vaseline on their face to keep the Mace from burning their skin, buttoning their jackets, wetting their handkerchief and tying it over their nose and mouth. "If it's gas, remember, breathe through your mouth, don't run, don't pant, and . . . don't rub your eyes," someone thoughtfully announced over the speaker. A boy in the center of the circle got up, stepped over his seated friends, and made his way toward the woods. "Don't leave now," several voices called in panic. The boy explained that he was just going to take a leak.

It happened all in an instant. The night which had been filled with darkness and whispers exploded in a fiery scream. Huge tear-gas canisters came crashing through the branches, snapping them, and bursting in the center of the gathering. From where I lay, groveling in the grass, I could see ministers retreating with the cross, carrying it like a fallen comrade. Another volley shook me to my feet. Gas was everywhere. People were running, screaming, tearing through the trees. Something hit the tree next to me, I was on the ground again, someone was pulling me to my feet, two boys were lifting a big branch off a girl who lay squirming hysterically. I couldn't see. Someone grabbed onto me and asked me to lead them out of the park. We walked along, hands outstretched, bumping into people and trees, tears streaming from our eyes and mucus smeared across our faces. I flashed First World War doughboys caught in no-man's-land during a mustard gas attack. I felt sure I was going to die. I heard others choking around me. And then everything cleared.

Source: Steve Lerner account from the *Village Voice*, excerpted in Norman Mailer, *Miami and the Siege of Chicago: An Informal History of the Republican and Democratic Conventions of 1968* (New York: New American Library, 1968), 151–152.

Hilton Hotel where most of the delegates were staying.

While protesters chanted "The whole world is watching!" the television networks ran film of the riot during the nominating speeches. In one memorable moment, Senator Abraham Ribicoff of Connecticut interrupted his nominating speech for Senator McGovern to interject, "With George McGovern we wouldn't have Gestapo tactics on the streets of Chicago." The cameras panned to Mayor Daley, livid with rage and clearly mouthing obscenities.

Television coverage of the riots was hardly excessive—about 32 minutes on CBS and less than 14 minutes on NBC—but it cemented an impression of the Democrats as the party of disorder. The Democrats dispiritedly gave the nomination to Hubert H. Humphrey, who chose Senator Edmund S. Muskie of Maine as his running mate. The convention approved a middle-of-the-road platform that endorsed Johnson's policy of continuing the fighting in Vietnam while exploring diplomatic means to end the conflict.

Chicago, 1968
On August 28 thousands of antiwar demonstrators gathered outside the Conrad Hilton Hotel in downtown Chicago, site of the Democratic National Convention. When Mayor Richard Daley ordered the Chicago police to disperse the crowd, a violent melee ensued in which hundreds were injured.

Political Backlash

An enduring result of the Democratic convention was the beginning of a backlash against protest. The general public did not differentiate between the antics of the small group of Yippies and the more serious actions of a far greater number of antiwar activists who were trying to work within the system. Polls showed overwhelming support for Mayor Daley and the police.

A Changing Mood. The New Left began to falter after 1968. Discredited by the events in Chicago, SDS members found themselves unable to agree on basic goals and tactics. Moreover, SDS and other antiwar groups fell victim to police harassment and FBI and CIA counterintelligence campaigns that infiltrated and disrupted radical political organizations. After 1968 the New Left splintered into factions, its energy spent. One radical faction broke off from SDS to form the Weathermen (taking the name from a Bob Dylan song). A tiny band of self-styled revolutionaries, the Weathermen and their imitators embraced violence and conducted dozens of terrorist bombings, including the destruction of the Army Math building at the University of Wisconsin at Madison in August 1970. The FBI quickly targeted those groups, and many of their members were forced to go underground to avoid arrest. The violent activities of the Weathermen and other extremist groups alienated many young people from the New Left, but broad-based antiwar protests continued until 1971.

Among the general public, the turmoil surrounding the New Left and the antiwar movement strengthened support for proponents of "law and order," which became the conservative catchphrase of the next several years. Many Americans, though opposed to the war, were fed up with protest and dissent. Governor George C. Wallace of Alabama, a third-party candidate, skillfully exploited the public's growing hostility by making student protests and urban riots his chief campaign issues. Articulating the resentments of many working-class whites, he delivered a populist message that combined attacks on liberal intellectuals and government elites with

Hard Hats
Many construction workers (and the unions they belonged to) were vocal supporters of the Vietnam War. Sometimes hard hats clashed with long-haired protesters during antiwar marches and sidewalk demonstrations.

strident denunciations of school desegregation and forced busing.

Richard Nixon, even more than George Wallace, tapped the growing conservative mood of the electorate. After his unsuccessful presidential campaign in 1960 and his loss in the California gubernatorial race in 1962, Nixon engineered an amazing political comeback. In 1968 the "new" Nixon easily beat back primary challenges by three governors—Ronald Reagan of California, George Romney of Michigan, and Nelson Rockefeller of New York—to win the Republican nomination. He chose Maryland's governor, Spiro Agnew, as his running mate to attract southern voters who opposed Democratic civil rights legislation, especially potential Wallace supporters. In what his campaign adviser Kevin Phillips called the "southern strategy," Nixon hoped to make impressive inroads in the once solidly Democratic South. He also used traditional populist appeals, pledging to represent the "quiet voice" of the "great majority of Americans, the forgotten Americans, the nonshouters, the nondemonstrators." He em-

phatically declared, "The first civil right of every American is to be free from domestic violence."

Despite the Democratic debacle in Chicago, the election was close. Humphrey rallied in the last weeks of the campaign by gingerly disassociating himself from Johnson's war policies. Furthermore, in a televised address on October 31 President Johnson announced a complete halt of the bombing of North Vietnam. Nixon countered by intimating that he had his own plan for ending the war (although in reality no such plan existed). Nixon received 43.4 percent of the vote to Humphrey's 42.7 percent, defeating him by a scant 510,000 votes out of the 73 million cast (see Map 31.2). Wallace finished with 13.5 percent of the popular vote, becoming the most successful third-party candidate since the Progressive party's Robert M. La Follette in 1924. Nixon owed his election largely to the split in the Democratic coalition, but the success of the southern strategy hinted at the future emergence of a new Republican majority. In the meantime, however, the Democrats retained a majority in both houses of Congress.

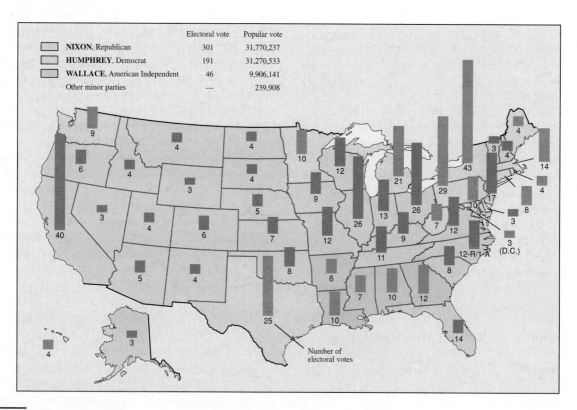

MAP 31.2

The Election of 1968

As late as mid-September the third-party candidate George C. Wallace of Alabama had the support of 21 percent of the voters. But in November he received only 13.5 percent of the vote, winning five states and showing that the South was no longer solidly Democratic. The Republican Richard M. Nixon defeated Hubert H. Humphrey with only 43.4 percent of the popular vote.

The "Silent Majority." The closeness of the 1968 election suggested how polarized American society had become over the Vietnam War and other events of the 1960s. Nixon appealed to what came to be known as the *silent majority*—the average, hardworking, non-protesting (and generally white) American. According to the social scientists Ben J. Wattenberg and Richard Scammon in their influential book *The Real Majority* (1970), the typical American was a white forty-seven-year-old machinist's wife from Dayton, Ohio, and this was what she was concerned about:

> To know that the lady in Dayton is afraid to walk the streets alone at night, to know that she has a mixed view about blacks and civil rights because before moving to the suburbs she lived in a neighborhood that became all black, to know that her brother-in-law is a policeman, to know that she does not have the money to move if her new neighborhood deteriorates, to know that she is deeply distressed that her son is going to a community junior college where LSD was found on campus—to know all this is the beginning of contemporary political wisdom.

Although political appeals after 1968 suggested a growing consensus among voters who were (in the words of Wattenberg and Scammon) "unblack, unpoor, and unyoung," protest and controversy would remain part of the political process until the divisive issue of the Vietnam War was resolved.

Nixon's War

Vietnam, long Lyndon Johnson's war, now became Richard Nixon's; 15,000 Americans would lose their lives in that conflict during Nixon's presidency. Yet Nixon operated in a political climate that differed fundamentally from that of Johnson (see Chapter 32 for Nixon's domestic agenda). Initially Nixon sought to end the war by expanding its scope as a means of pressuring the North Vietnamese to negotiate. But Nixon and his national security adviser, Henry Kissinger, soon realized that the public would not support major sacrifices to win the war and searched for another way out. A new plan to reduce American troop involvement called Vietnamization delegated most of the ground fighting to South Vietnamese troops, but it would take six more years to end U.S. involvement.

Shortly after Nixon took office, he sent a letter to Hanoi proposing mutual withdrawals of American and North Vietnamese forces. In March 1969, to convince Hanoi that the United States meant business, Nixon ordered secret bombing raids on neutral Cambodia, through which the North Vietnamese transported supplies and reinforcements. To keep Congress and the public ignorant about those sorties, the air force officials in charge of the bombings fed accurate information about the raids into one Defense Department computer while placing data omitting the Cambodian targets into another. The faulty projections from the second computer were the ones given to Congress. The secret war culminated in an April 30, 1970, "incursion" by American ground forces into Cambodia to destroy enemy troop havens there. Over the next three months the Americans captured 2,000 enemy troops and destroyed 8,000 bunkers, temporarily disrupting North Vietnamese supply lines. But the invasion proved to be only a short-term setback for North Vietnam and produced a diplomatic stalemate as the North Vietnamese and the Vietcong continued to boycott the Paris peace talks. Most critically, the American invasion of Cambodia—along with the ongoing North Vietnamese intervention there—served to destabilize that country, allowing for a takeover by the ruthless Khmer Rouge in the late 1970s.

The administration's failure to end the war through intensified bombing campaigns persuaded Nixon and Kissinger to pursue Vietnamization. On June 8, 1969, Nixon announced that 25,000 American troops would be withdrawn by August and replaced by South Vietnamese forces. The troop withdrawals helped persuade the North Vietnamese to begin secret negotiations with Kissinger that August, but the diplomatic stalemate continued. Nixon, meanwhile, stepped up attacks against North Vietnamese and Vietcong targets, hoping to pressure Hanoi to negotiate while strengthening Thieu's faltering South Vietnamese government as Vietnamization went into effect. When Nixon took office, more than 543,000 American soldiers were serving in Vietnam; by the end of 1970 there were 334,000, and two years later there were 24,200. American casualties and the political liabilities that they generated fell correspondingly. But the slaughter in Vietnam continued. As the U.S. ambassador to Vietnam, Ellsworth Bunker, noted cynically, it was just a matter of changing "the color of the bodies."

The War at Home. As with Lyndon Johnson, who by 1968 had become so unpopular that his appearance caused protests everywhere except on military bases, antiwar demonstrators denounced Richard Nixon and his Vietnamization policy. On October 15, 1969, millions of people in cities across the country joined a one-day "moratorium" to protest the war. A month later, more than a quarter of a million people mobilized in Washington to call for an end to the fighting, the largest antiwar demonstration to date.

To discredit his critics Nixon denounced student demonstrators as "bums" and stated that "North Vietnam cannot defeat or humiliate the United States. Only Americans can do that." Vice-President Spiro Agnew attacked dissenters as "ideological eunuchs" and "natter-

Kent State

The shootings by National Guardsmen of four students at Kent State University in Ohio on May 4, 1970, set off campus demonstrations and protests across the country. The protester shown here holds a placard memorializing the slain students as well as the two black students killed soon afterward at Jackson State College in Mississippi. The president of Columbia University called May 1970 "the most disastrous month . . . in the history of American higher education."

ing nabobs of negativism." Nixon staunchly insisted that he would not be swayed by the mounting protests against the war. During the November 1969 march on Washington the president barricaded himself in the White House and watched football on television.

The most extensive outbreak of student unrest came in the spring of 1970, after the invasion of Cambodia, when antiwar leaders organized a national student strike. At Kent State University outside Cleveland, panicky National Guardsmen fired into a crowd of students at a noontime antiwar rally on May 4. Four people were killed, and eleven were wounded. Only two of those killed, Jeffrey Miller and Alison Krause, had been at the demonstration; William Shroeder and Sandra Scheur were passing by on their way to class. Soon afterward National Guardsmen shot and killed two black women students while storming a dormitory at Jackson State College in Mississippi. More than 450 colleges closed down on strike, and 80 percent of all American college campuses experienced some kind of protest. In June 1970, immediately after the Kent State slayings, a Gallup poll reported that campus unrest was the main issue troubling Americans.

At the same time, however, dissatisfaction with the war continued to spread. Congressional opposition, which had been growing since Fulbright's Foreign Relations Committee hearings in 1966, intensified with the invasion of Cambodia. In June 1970 the Senate expressed its disapproval by voting to repeal the Gulf of Tonkin resolution authorizing U.S. military action and by passing the Church-Cooper amendment, which cut off all funding for operations in Cambodia by the end of the month. Even American troops in Vietnam showed mounting opposition to their mission. From 1969 to 1971 the number of troops refusing combat orders steadily increased, and thousands of U.S. soldiers deserted. The majority fought on, but many sewed peace symbols onto their uniforms. A number of overbearing junior officers were "fragged," that is, killed or wounded by fragmentation grenades thrown by their own soldiers. At home a group called Vietnam Veterans against the War turned in their combat medals at mass demonstrations at the U.S. Capitol.

My Lai. In 1971 Americans were again confronted with the sheer brutality of the Vietnamese conflict when Lieutenant William L. Calley was court-martialed for atrocities committed in the Vietnamese village of My Lai. In March 1968 Calley had commanded a platoon on a routine search-and-destroy mission. Retaliating for casualties sustained by their buddies in an earlier engagement, the soldiers apparently murdered 350 Vietnamese villagers. The incident came to light because one member of the platoon refused to go along with a military cover-up; the investigative reporter Seymour Hersh of the *New York Times* broke the story. In the court-martial proceedings, a jury of six soldiers who had served in Vietnam sentenced Calley to life imprisonment for his part in the massacre. Yet George Wallace and some Congressional conservatives called Calley a hero rather than a villain, and after President Nixon's intervention, his sentence was reduced, and he was paroled in 1974.

Despite the controversy surrounding the Kent State shootings and the My Lai massacre, antiwar activism declined in the early 1970s. After a final outbreak of protest and violence following Kent State, the universities stayed relatively calm. Student strikes in the spring of 1971 and 1972, while large in numbers, never approached the emotional intensity of earlier demonstrations. Nixon's promises to continue troop withdrawals, end the draft, and institute an all-volunteer army by 1973 deprived the antiwar movement of important organizing issues, particularly on college campuses. In the early 1970s many student activists refocused their energies on causes such as feminism and environmentalism whereas others simply "burned out."

Détente. At the same time that Nixon was prosecuting the war in Vietnam, ostensibly to halt the spread of communism, he was formulating a new policy toward the Soviet Union and China. Known as *détente* (the French word for a relaxation of tensions), Nixon's policy called for peaceful coexistence with those two communist powers and sought to link those overtures of friendship with his own plan to end the Vietnam War. In befriending China and the Soviet Union, Nixon encouraged them to reduce military aid to the North Vietnamese, thus pressuring them to the negotiating table. As a lifelong anticommunist crusader, Nixon had greater political maneuverability to reach out to the two communist superpowers than a Democratic president would have had. After all, no one could accuse Richard Nixon of being soft on communism. Henry Kissinger influenced the president's thinking in this direction.

Since the Chinese revolution of 1949 the United States had refused to recognize the government of the People's Republic of China, instead giving unconditional support to the Nationalist Chinese government in Taiwan. Nixon moved away from that policy, reasoning that the United States could exploit the growing rift between the People's Republic of China and the Soviet Union. He sent Kissinger on a secret mission to Beijing in the summer of 1971 and in July told a startled world that he would visit the People's Republic in the near future. He did so in February 1972, walking along the Great Wall and toasting Chinese leaders in Beijing. Nixon's visit set the stage for the formal establishment of diplomatic relations, which took place in 1979.

In a similar spirit of détente Nixon journeyed to Moscow in May 1972 to sign SALT I, a treaty resulting from Strategic Arms Limitations Talks between the United States and the Soviet Union. Although Nixon boasted that the SALT agreement was a dramatic step toward stopping the arms race, the accords only limited the production and deployment of intercontinental ballistic missiles (ICBMs) and antiballistic missile systems (ABMs). They left untouched newer and equally destructive weapons systems such as multiple independently targetable reentry vehicles (MIRVs), which enabled a single missile to carry up to fourteen separate warheads. Yet the treaty was also an acknowledgment that the United States could no longer afford the massive military spending that would have been necessary to regain the nuclear and military superiority of the immediate postwar years. By the early 1970s factors such as inflation, the decline in American hegemony over the world system, and domestic dissent were limiting and reshaping American options in international relations. Most critically, Nixon hoped that a rapprochement with the Soviets would help resolve the prolonged crisis in Vietnam.

American Withdrawal from Vietnam. The Paris peace talks had been in a stalemate since 1968, hamstrung by the conflicting demands of North Vietnam, South Vietnam, and the United States. In the meantime, Vietnamization continued and American casualties decreased, but the South Vietnamese military was unable to fill the vacuum. In March 1971 the South Vietnamese suffered a major defeat after launching an attack against North Vietnamese supply routes along the Ho Chi Minh Trail in Laos. The South Vietnamese forces were quickly repelled and sustained heavy casualties. Later that year, as American troops withdrew from the region, communist forces stepped up their attacks on Laos, Cambodia, and South Vietnam. The next spring North Vietnamese forces launched a major new offensive, attacking South Vietnamese targets south of the demilitarized zone, in Binh Long province and in the Central Highlands (see American Lives, pages 982–983). As the fighting intensified, Nixon ordered B-52 bombing raids against North Vietnam in April and the mining of all North Vietnamese ports a month later.

Increased combat activity in the spring of 1972 and growing political pressure on the Nixon administration helped revive the Paris peace negotiations. With the fall presidential elections looming, Nixon hoped to undercut his antiwar critics by making concessions to the North Vietnamese. That October Henry Kissinger and the North Vietnamese negotiator Le Duc Tho reached a cease-fire agreement calling for the withdrawal of the remaining U.S. troops, the return of all American prisoners of war, and the continued presence of North Vietnamese troops in South Vietnam (a major sticking point in earlier negotiations). Nixon and Kissinger also promised the North Vietnamese substantial aid for postwar reconstruction. On the eve of the 1972 presidential election Kissinger announced that "peace is at hand," and Nixon returned to the White House with a resounding electoral victory (see Chapter 32).

The peace initiative, however, soon stalled when the South Vietnamese rejected the provision concerning North Vietnamese troop positions. With negotiations deadlocked, Nixon stepped up military action again. For the benefit of President Thieu, home-front hawks, and the Third World in general, he initiated the "Christmas bombings," a final destructive demonstration of American military strength. From December 17 to December 30, 1972, American planes subjected North Vietnamese civilian and military targets in Hanoi and Haiphong to the most devastating bombing of the war. Finally, on January 27, 1973, a cease-fire was signed in Paris by representatives of the United States, North and South Vietnam, and the Vietcong; it differed little from the proposal of the previous October. The Paris Peace Accords

John Paul Vann: Dissident Patriot

The divisions caused by the Vietnam War haunted Arlington National Cemetery on June 16, 1972, when 300 mourners assembled for the funeral of John Paul Vann. "The soldier of the war in Vietnam," Vann had been killed in a helicopter crash in the Central Highlands the week before. Politicians and military leaders closely associated with the war effort were very much in evidence—General William Westmoreland, CIA Director William Colby, the conservative journalist Joseph Alsop, and Secretary of State William Rogers. But so were Daniel Ellsberg, a former Pentagon official who had publicly turned against the war, and Senator Edward Kennedy, another war opponent who had shared Vann's concern about the plight of Vietnamese refugees. In a time of intense polarization over a war that was still going on, this assemblage of "hawks" and "doves" was highly unusual.

Vann's family also showed the rifts over Vietnam that day. His wife of twenty-six years, Mary Jane, had requested two pieces of music: the upbeat "Colonel Bogie March" from the film *The Bridge on the River Kwai*, one of her husband's favorites, and the haunting antiwar ballad "Where Have All the Flowers Gone?" to express her opposition to the war. One of Vann's sons, twenty-one-year-old Jesse, hated the war so profoundly that he tore his draft card in two at the funeral, placing half of it on his father's casket. He planned to give the other half to President Richard Nixon at the White House ceremony after the funeral, where his father would be presented posthumously with the Presidential Medal of Freedom. Only at the last moment was Jesse talked out of his act of defiance, agreeing that this was, after all, his father's day, and that his father had believed in the war in Vietnam.

Also at the funeral was *New York Times* reporter Neil Sheehan, who decided at that moment to write a biography of Vann, which he published sixteen years later, *A Bright and Shining Lie*. Sheehan, along with David Halberstam and other reporters, had fallen under Vann's spell during his first tour of duty in Vietnam in 1963, when Vann seemed to be the only American official who was willing to admit that the war was not going well. Sheehan had continued to rely on Vann's outspoken assessments for the rest of the war. "In this war without heroes, this man had been the one compelling figure," Sheehan concluded. "By an obsession, by an unyielding dedication to the war, he had come to personify the American endeavor in Vietnam."

John Paul Vann was an enormously complicated person—a born leader, a visionary, a man who knew no physical fear, but most of all a true believer in America's mission to share democracy with countries "less fortunate" than ours. His early years were shaped by poverty and lack of opportunity. Born in 1924 to a working-class family in Norfolk, Virginia, he grew up poor during the Great Depression. A colleague later remembered him as a "cocky little red-necked guy with a rural Virginia twang." World War II offered a ticket out; when Vann turned eighteen in 1943, he enlisted and made the army his career. He served with distinction in the Korean War and then took assignments in West Germany and the United States. But in 1959 his service record was stained by accusations of the statutory rape of a fifteen-year-old girl. Even though the army eventually dropped the charges, the scandal effectively prevented him from moving up in the military bureaucracy. Neil Sheehan later concluded that Vann's "moral heroism" in speaking out against the conduct of the war to the seeming detriment of his career was rooted in his awareness that he had nothing to lose, although reporters did not know the full story at the time.

In 1963 the thirty-nine-year-old Lieutenant Colonel Vann was sent to Vietnam, where he served as a senior adviser to a South Vietnamese infantry division in the Mekong Delta. At the battle of Ap Bac he watched his South Vietnamese counterpart purposely refuse to fight the battle the way it had been planned and let the enemy escape. In a moment of epiphany Vann realized that the rosy reports being fed to Saigon and Washington were false, that Saigon suffered from "an institutionalized unwillingness to fight." After unsuccessful attempts to enlighten his superiors, he leaked his meticulously docu-

Planning Strategy
Lieutenant Colonel John P. Vann (left) shown during his tour of duty in Vietnam in 1963 discussing a tactical decision.

mented assessments to reporters such as Halberstam and Sheehan. His candor won him few friends in the military, and at the end of his tour of duty he was reassigned to the Pentagon. He tried to alert the Joint Chiefs of Staff that the war was not being won, but at the last moment the scheduled briefing was canceled, in large part because the Joint Chiefs did not want to hear his version of the problem. Vann resigned from the army soon afterward.

Less than two years later, in 1965, Vann was back in Vietnam just as the major escalation of the war was getting under way. Except for brief trips home, he stayed there until his death. His first position was as a civilian pacification representative for the Agency for International Development, working to win over the peasants to the South Vietnamese side rather than the National Liberation Front. His honesty and unmatched familiarity with conditions in the countryside led him to conclude that the communists were doing a far better job at appealing to the local population than was the corrupt Saigon government: as he wrote to a friend in 1965, "If I were a lad of eighteen faced with the same choice—whether to support the GVN [Government of Vietnam] or the NLF—and a member of a rural community, I would surely choose the NLF." His concern for winning over the local peasantry made him an outspoken opponent of the heavy bombing inflicted on the Vietnamese countryside to roust Vietcong sympathizers. He also strongly criticized General Westmoreland's strategy of sending in more American troops to wear down the Vietcong in a war of attrition, arguing that this would be useless without major reforms in the Saigon government.

Despite his role as a gadfly and even though he was now a civilian, Vann assumed more and more responsibility in the day-to-day conduct of the war. In 1971 he was given authority over all the U.S. military forces in the Central Highlands, the equivalent of the position of major general. But by then, according to Sheehan, Vann had "lost his compass." He was no longer able to assess realistically the ability or will of the South Vietnamese to fight without American aid. He continued to insist that the war could be won through pacification and reform in Saigon despite evidence of growing Vietcong strength. When his helicopter went down at Kontum in 1972, he had almost single-handedly saved the Central Highlands from a North Vietnamese offensive. Within six months the United States formally ended its involvement. Two years later Vietnam was reunited under communist rule.

John Paul Vann never wavered in his belief that in Vietnam America's cause was just and its intentions good. He had no quarrel with the war itself, just with the way it was fought. Vann thought he knew the answers, but Saigon and Washington chose not to listen. His life and death serve as a reminder of the complexities of the Vietnam experience: Could it ever really have been "won," and what would "winning" have meant? Neil Sheehan is convinced that Vann "died believing he had won his war."

Hanoi Devastated
The North Vietnamese capital, Hanoi, sustained heavy damage from bombing raids by American B-52s. The most devastating raids occurred during the "Christmas bombings" in December 1972, just weeks before the Paris Peace Accords were signed.

failed to deliver Nixon's often-repeated promise of "peace with honor." Basically, they mandated the unilateral withdrawal of American troops in exchange for the return of American prisoners of war held in North Vietnam. For most Americans that amount of face-saving was enough.

But the 1973 accords did not resolve Vietnam's civil war. Without massive U.S. military and economic aid and with North Vietnamese guerrillas operating freely throughout the countryside, it was only a matter of time before the South Vietnamese government of General Nguyen Van Thieu fell to the more disciplined and popular communist forces. In March 1975 North Vietnamese forces launched a final offensive. Horrified American viewers watched on television as South Vietnamese officials and soldiers struggled with American embassy personnel for space on the last helicopters that flew out of Saigon before North Vietnamese troops entered the city. On April 29, 1975, Vietnam was reunited; Saigon was renamed Ho Chi Minh City in honor of the communist leader, who had died in 1969.

The Legacy of Vietnam

The Vietnam War exacted an enormous cost from America in human terms. Some 58,000 U.S. troops died, and another 300,000 were wounded. Even those who came back unharmed returned to a sometimes hostile or indifferent reception. Coming home alone, with no deprogramming or counseling, most Vietnam veterans found the transition abrupt and disorienting. Once back, they felt embarrassed when they dove under a table at the sound of firecrackers on the Fourth of July or froze when a plane flew overhead. Mainly the Vietnam experience was ignored. As one vet recalled, "Bringing up the Nam was like farting at the dinner table. Everybody looks away embarrassed and acts like nothing happened. Well, pardon me." The psychological tensions of serving in Vietnam and the abrupt transition back to America sowed the seeds of what is now recognized as posttraumatic stress disorder—recurring physical and psychological problems, often leading to higher than average rates of divorce, unemployment, and suicide. Only in the 1980s did America begin to make its peace with those who had served in the nation's most unpopular war.

In Southeast Asia the damage was far greater. The war claimed an estimated 1.5 million Vietnamese lives and devastated the country's physical and economic infrastructure. Neighboring Laos and Cambodia also suffered, particularly Cambodia, where chaotic conditions led to a political takeover by the deadly Khmer Rouge. From 1975 to 1979 the Khmer Rouge Communists killed an estimated 2 million Cambodians (25 percent of the population) in a brutal "relocation" campaign. All told, the war produced nearly 10 million Southeast Asian refugees, many of whom immigrated to the United States. Among the refugees were thousands of Amerasians, the offspring of American soldiers and Vietnamese women. Spurned by their fathers and most Vietnamese, more than 30,000 Amerasians immigrated to the United States in the 1990s.

The defeat in Vietnam prompted Americans to think differently about foreign affairs and acknowledge the limits of U.S. power abroad. The United States became less willing to plunge into overseas military commitments, a controversial development that conservatives dubbed the "Vietnam syndrome." In 1973 Congress declared its hostility to undeclared wars like those in Vietnam and Korea by passing the War Powers Act, which required the president to report any use of military force within forty-eight hours and directed that hostilities cease within sixty days unless Congress declared war. When

Congress did agree to foreign intervention, as in the Persian Gulf War of 1990–1991, American leaders would insist on obtainable military objectives and careful handling of the media—elements that had often been lacking in Vietnam. Any future foreign entanglement would be evaluated in terms of its potential for becoming "another Vietnam."

The Vietnam War also affected American economic and social affairs. At a total price of over $150 billion, the war siphoned economic resources from domestic needs, added to the deficit, and fueled inflation (see Chapter 32). Lyndon Johnson's Great Society programs had been pared down accordingly, and domestic reform efforts slowed thereafter. Moreover, the war critically shattered the liberal consensus that had supported the Democratic coalition. The discrediting of liberalism, increased cynicism about government, and the growing social turmoil that accompanied the war paved the way for a resurgence of the Republican party.

The Vietnam Veterans' Memorial
Conceived and funded by a small group of veterans, the Vietnam Veterans' Memorial was dedicated in Washington, D.C., in November 1982. The memorial, designed by a Yale architecture student, Maya Ling Lin, consists of two walls of black granite inscribed with the names of 58,183 men and women who died in the war. The wall of names has tremendous emotional impact on viewers and has become one of the most popular tourist destinations in the nation's capital.

Summary

America's involvement in Vietnam lasted nearly thirty years, growing incrementally from one administration to the next. Under Truman and Eisenhower the United States threw its support behind the French and, later, the South Vietnamese government in an effort to contain the communist threat in Asia. Kennedy continued that commitment and increased the number of U.S. military advisers in South Vietnam. But it was under Lyndon Johnson that the war escalated from an ostensibly defensive action to an offensive combat mission. Between 1965 and 1968 sustained bombing attacks on North Vietnam were accompanied by ever larger infusions of U.S. ground troops. But the Tet offensive of January 1968 shook American confidence and marked the beginning of U.S. efforts to disengage from the conflict. Richard Nixon spent another five years trying to end the war, promising Americans "peace with honor." Under his program of Vietnamization, Nixon gradually withdrew U.S. troops while secretly bombing and later invading Cambodia. The final withdrawal of American troops took place in 1973 under the terms of the Paris Peace Accords. The war marked a turning point in U.S. foreign relations, revealing the limitations of American military power in a complex postwar world.

The war also had serious consequences at home as Americans turned against each other in bitter conflict. Beginning with a small number of pacifist, religious, and antinuclear protesters in the early 1960s, the antiwar movement burgeoned after the escalation of the conflict in 1965. The military draft in particular sparked a broad-based antiwar movement among college students and other young people, who staged a series of mass protests between 1967 and 1971. The spirit of rebellion was not limited to the antiwar movement. The New Left challenged university policies and corporate dominance of society, while the more apolitical counterculture preached personal liberation through sex, drugs, music, and spirituality.

The domestic struggle over the war and other issues divided the Democratic party, resulting in a riotous Democratic National Convention in the summer of 1968. The assassinations of Martin Luther King, Jr., and Robert Kennedy and a series of urban riots that year further shocked the nation and fueled a growing public desire for law and order. Even though antiwar protests continued into the early 1970s, a new mood of conservatism took hold in the country, contributing to the resurgence of the Republican party.

TIMELINE

1946	War begins between French and Vietminh
1950	China and Soviet Union recognize Ho Chi Minh's government U.S. recognizes French-backed government of Bao Dai and begins sending military aid to Vietnam
1954	French defeat at Dienbienphu Ngo Dinh Diem takes power in South Vietnam Geneva Accords
1960	Founding of National Liberation Front in South Vietnam
1962	Students for a Democratic Society (SDS) founded
1963	Coup ousts Ngo Dinh Diem in Vietnam
1964	Free Speech Movement at Berkeley Gulf of Tonkin resolution
1965	First U.S. combat troops arrive in Vietnam Operation Rolling Thunder
1967	Hippie counterculture's Summer of Love
1968	Tet offensive Martin Luther King, Jr., assassinated Peace talks open in Paris Robert F. Kennedy assassinated Riot at Democratic National Convention in Chicago
1969	Vietnam moratorium Woodstock festival
1970	Nixon orders invasion of Cambodia; renewed antiwar protests Kent State and Jackson State killings Gulf of Tonkin resolution repealed
1972	Nixon visits People's Republic of China SALT I Treaty with Soviet Union Christmas bombings
1973	Paris Peace Accords War Powers Act
1975	Fall of Saigon

BIBLIOGRAPHY

Among the best general accounts of the Vietnam War are George Herring, *America's Longest War* (2d ed., 1986); Stanley Karnow, *Vietnam: A History* (rev. ed., 1991); and Marilyn Young, *The Vietnam Wars, 1945–1990* (1991). Guenter Lewy offers a controversial defense of American involvement in *America in Vietnam* (1978).

Into the Quagmire

The origins of American involvement in Vietnam are covered in Loren Baritz, *Backfire: A History of How American Culture Led Us into Vietnam* (1985); Larry Berman, *Planning a Tragedy* (1982) and *Lyndon Johnson's War* (1989); Lloyd Gardner, *Approaching Vietnam* (1988); Conrad Gibbons, *The U.S. Government and the Vietnam War* (1986–1989); David Halberstam, *The Best and the Brightest* (1972) and *The Making of a Quagmire* (rev. ed., 1987); Gary Hess, *The United States' Emergence as a Southeast Asian Power, 1940–1950* (1987); and Brian Van-DeMark, *Into the Quagmire* (1991). A fascinating insight into Vietnam policy making in the 1960s can be found in Neil Sheehan, *The Pentagon Papers* (1971). Secretary of Defense Robert McNamara offers an insider's view and belated apologia in *In Retrospect* (1995). James C. Thompson, *Rolling Thunder* (1980), and John Galloway, *The Gulf of Tonkin Resolution* (1970), cover specific topics. Eric Bergerud, *Dynamics of Defeat* (1991), examines the military aspects of the war, and Daniel Hallin, *The Uncensored War* (1986), and Clarence R. Wyatt, *Paper Soldiers* (1993), look at the role of the media. Frances FitzGerald, *Fire in the Lake* (1972), discusses the war in the context of South Vietnamese society.

For a sense of what the war felt like to the soldiers who fought it, see Mark Baker, *Nam* (1982); Philip Caputo, *Rumor of War* (1977); Gloria Emerson, *Winners and Losers* (1976); Michael Herr, *Dispatches* (1977); Tim O'Brien, *If I Die in a Combat Zone* (1973); and Ron Kovic, *Born on the Fourth of July* (1976). Wallace Terry, *Bloods* (1984), surveys the experiences of black veterans, and Keith Walker, *A Piece of My Heart* (1985), introduces the often forgotten stories of the women who served in Vietnam. Lawrence Baskir and William A. Strauss, *Chance and Circumstance: The Draft, the War, and the Vietnam Generation* (1978), explains who was drafted and why. Christian G. Appy offers a class analysis of the Vietnam experience in *Working-Class War* (1993). Neil Sheehan surveys the entire Vietnam experience through the life of the career soldier John Paul Vann in *A Bright and Shining Lie* (1988).

The Challenge of Youth

The student activism of the 1960s has drawn its share of scholarly chroniclers. See Kenneth Keniston, *The Uncommitted* (1965) and *Young Radicals* (1969); Daniel Bell and Irving Kristol, *Confrontation* (1969); Nathan Glazer, *Remembering the Answers* (1970); and Philip Slater, *The Pursuit of Loneliness* (1970). On student revolt, see W. J. Rorabaugh, *Berkeley at War* (1989); Seymour Lipset and Sheldon Wolin, eds., *The Berkeley Student Revolt* (1965); Jerry Avorn, *Up against the Ivy Wall* (1968); Kirkpatrick Sale, *SDS* (1973); Wini Breines, *Community and Organization in the New Left, 1962–1968*

(1982); and James Miller, *Democracy Is in the Streets* (1987). Terry Anderson, *The Movement and the Sixties* (1994), and Irwin Unger, *The Movement: A History of the American New Left* (1974), provide general accounts of 1960s activism. Todd Gitlin, *The Whole World Is Watching* (1980), discusses the impact of the mass media on the New Left.

The definitive book on the antiwar movement is Charles DeBenedetti, with Charles Chatfield, *An American Ordeal* (1990). Nancy Zaroulis and Gerald Sullivan, *Who Spoke Up: American Protest against the War in Vietnam, 1963–1975* (1984), examines the role of the New Left in the antiwar movement, while Melvin Small and William D. Hoover, eds., *Give Peace a Chance: Exploring the Vietnam Antiwar Movement* (1992), is an anthology of recent work.

Morris Dickstein, *Gates of Eden* (1977), is an excellent account of cultural developments in the 1960s. Todd Gitlin, *The Sixties: Years of Hope, Days of Rage* (1987), also treats the counterculture extensively. Other sources include Theodore Roszak, *The Making of a Counter-Culture* (1969), and Charles Reich, *The Greening of America* (1970). Gerald Howard, ed., *The Sixties* (1982), is a good anthology of the decade's art, politics, and culture. Philip Norman, *Shout! The Beatles in Their Generation* (1981), and Jon Weiner, *Come Together: John Lennon in His Times* (1984), cover developments in popular music. Tom Wolfe, *Electric Kool-Aid Acid Test* (1965), describes the antics of Ken Kesey and his Merry Pranksters. Joan Didion, *Slouching toward Bethlehem* (1968) and *The White Album* (1979), explores the darker side of the hippie phenomenon.

The Long Road Home

The Tet offensive is the subject of Don Oberdoffer, *Tet! The Turning Point in the Vietnam War* (1971), whereas the domestic events of 1968 are covered in David Caute, *The Year of the Barricades* (1968); David Farber, *Chicago '68* (1988); and Lewis Chester, Godfrey Hodgson, and Bruce Page, *An American Melodrama* (1970). Norman Mailer provides a contemporary view of the conventions in *Miami and the Siege of Chicago* (1968). Dan Carter, *The Politics of Rage* (1996), examines the political career of George Wallace, while Kevin Phillips, *The Emerging Republican Majority* (1969), and Richard Scammon and Ben J. Wattenberg, *The Real Majority* (1970), describe the voters Richard Nixon tried to reach. Theodore H. White, *The Making of the President—1968* (1969), covers the divisive election of 1968.

Robert S. Litwak, *Détente and the Nixon Doctrine* (1984); Seymour Hersh, *The Price of Power* (1983); and Tad Szulc, *The Illusion of Peace* (1978), are overviews of Nixon's foreign policy. On his Vietnam policy see the general works on Vietnam listed above as well as the highly critical study by William Shawcross, *Sideshow: Kissinger, Nixon, and the Destruction of Cambodia* (1979). An account of the My Lai massacre can be found in Seymour Hersh, *Cover-Up* (1972). Frank Snepp, *Decent Interval* (1977), examines the Paris peace process. Robert Jay Lifton, *Home from the War* (1973); Paul Starr, *The Discarded Army* (1973); and Lawrence Baskir and William A. Strauss, *Chance and Circumstance*, discuss the problems of returning Vietnam veterans.

Our Fragile Environment

NASA photographs from space captured both the beauty and
the fragility of the earth.

The Lean Years

1969–1980

★　　　★　　　★

As the Vietnam War ended, Americans turned inward to attend to their own needs and interests, just as they had done in the years after World Wars I and II. But the 1970s, unlike the 1920s and 1950s, were not a time of post-war prosperity and optimism. To many Americans the withdrawal from Vietnam represented an ignominious defeat that underscored the diminished role of U.S. power in the international arena. Growing economic problems in the early 1970s—rising oil prices, runaway inflation, declining productivity, and stagnating incomes—compounded that sense of disillusionment. In the mid-1970s industrial competition abroad, together with the newly asserted independence of the oil-producing Arab nations, produced a severe economic crisis at home. As the dollar plummeted on the world market and the trade deficit soared, the overwhelming economic superiority of the United States came to an end.

Americans also grew disenchanted with political leadership in the 1970s as one public official after another resigned for misconduct, including President Richard Nixon. The Watergate scandal became the defining experience of the decade, a symbol of the growing cynicism and waning confidence that pervaded the nation in the 1970s. In the wake of Watergate, the lackluster administrations of Gerald Ford and Jimmy Carter failed to provide the leadership necessary to cope with the economic and international insecurities that beset the nation. This failure of political leadership contributed to Americans' growing skepticism about government and its capacity to improve people's lives.

But the 1970s was a paradoxical decade: in the midst of growing disaffection and conservatism there was also an ongoing commitment to social change. Some of the social movements of the 1960s, such as feminism and environmentalism, had their greatest impact in the 1970s. As former student radicals moved into the political mainstream, they took their struggles from the streets and campuses into the courts, schools, work-places, and communities where they settled. But like the civil rights and antiwar movements of the 1960s, social activism in the 1970s stirred fears and uncertainty among some blue-collar and middle-class Americans. Furthermore, the darkening economic climate undercut the sense of social generosity that had characterized the 1960s and fueled a "politics of resentment" promoted by conservatives. Building on the backlash led by George Wallace and Richard Nixon in 1968, this new conservatism became a potent political force in the late 1970s.

The Nixon Years

During his five years in office Richard Nixon set the stage for a conservative political resurgence that would influence the nation for the next several decades. His new federalism heralded a long-term Republican effort to trim back the Great Society, shifting a number of federal responsibilities back to the states. Nixon's courting

Richard Nixon
One of the most resilient political figures in American history, Richard Nixon won the presidential election of 1968 after losing campaigns for president in 1960 and governor of California in 1962. Even after his resignation in 1974, Nixon reemerged as an elder statesman, frequently consulted for his opinions on foreign affairs.

of "the silent majority" and his pledge to achieve "peace with honor" in Vietnam helped him win reelection in 1972 and cemented a new Republican coalition on which future GOP candidates would rely. But unlike his successors in the Republican party, Nixon actively embraced the use of federal power to uphold government responsibility for social welfare, environmental protection, and economic stability. While maintaining a strong federal government, he hoped to reduce governmental inefficiency through better management. Ultimately, however, Nixon's suspicion of his political opponents and ruthless efforts in the 1972 campaign led to his downfall in the Watergate scandal, a political drama that consumed the nation from 1972 to 1974.

Domestic Agendas

Carrying out his 1968 campaign pledge to "the average American," Nixon proclaimed his commitment to a new federalism, vowing to "reverse the flow of power and resources from the states and communities to Washington and start power and resources flowing back . . . to the people." One important innovation was the 1972 program of *revenue sharing*, by which a portion of federal tax revenues was given to the states as block grants to be spent as they saw fit. Nixon's new federalism marked a retreat from the long-term consolidation of federal power that had characterized American political life since the New Deal. In subsequent years revenue sharing would become a key Republican strategy for reducing federal social programs and bureaucracy.

Social Programs. Nixon also worked to scale down certain government programs that had grown dramatically during the two previous Democratic administrations. Many War on Poverty programs received reduced funding, and the Office of Economic Opportunity was dismantled altogether in 1971. During his years in the White House Nixon also *impounded* (refused to spend) billions of dollars appropriated by Congress for urban renewal, pollution control, and other environmental initiatives. The administration claimed to support civil rights but was embarrassed by a leaked 1970 memo by the presidential adviser Daniel Patrick Moynihan, a Democrat who had joined the Nixon White House, which suggested that "the issue of race could benefit from a period of benign neglect." In a decision that would have far-reaching consequences in the decades to follow, Nixon also vetoed a 1971 bill to establish a comprehensive national child care system because it would have committed "the vast moral authority of the national government to communal approaches to child rearing, over against the family centered approach."

As an alternative to Democratic social legislation, the administration put forward its own antipoverty program in an ambitious attempt to overhaul the jerry-built social welfare system. In 1969, following the advice of Moynihan, Nixon proposed a Family Assistance Plan that would guarantee a family of four an income of $1,600 a year, plus $860 in Food Stamps. The appeal of a guaranteed annual income lay in its simplicity: it would eliminate the multiple layers of bureaucrats (caseworkers, local and state officials, and federal employees) who administered the burgeoning Aid to Families with Dependent Children (AFDC) program, the nation's largest welfare program. But the bill floundered in the Senate: conservatives attacked it for putting the federal government too deeply into the welfare business, whereas liberals and social welfare activists opposed it for not going far enough. Although the Family Assistance Plan failed to win approval, welfare reform would remain a contentious political issue for the next twenty-five years.

Although Nixon sought to streamline or scale back certain antipoverty programs, he actively expanded federal entitlement programs and the regulatory apparatus. Facing Democratic majorities in both houses of Congress, Nixon proved to be flexible in legislative matters, agreeing to the growth of major entitlement programs such as Medicare, Medicaid, and Social Security. In 1970, he signed a bill establishing the Environmental Protection Agency (EPA) to coordinate the growing federal responsibilities for environmental action. In 1972, to monitor the health and safety of workers and consumers, Nixon approved legislation creating the Occupational Safety and Health Administration (OSHA) and the Consumer Products Safety Commission. As inflation spiraled upward in 1971, he also made use of the federal powers granted under the Economic Stabilization Act of 1970 to institute wage and price controls, the first such measures since World War II. Although Nixon offered only tepid support for much of this legislation, his administration generally continued the expansion of federal power that had been under way since the New Deal.

The Supreme Court. In an effort to woo southern white voters, Nixon demonstrated his commitment to conservative social values with his appointments to the Supreme Court. One of his first acts was to nominate the conservative Warren Burger to replace retired Chief Justice Earl Warren in the spring of 1969. When another vacancy occurred later that year, Nixon nominated a conservative southern judge as a way to cement his political support in that region. But two nominees in a row, Clement F. Haynsworth and G. Harrold Carswell, failed to win Senate confirmation. Haynsworth, a federal circuit court judge from South Carolina, was turned down after revelations that he had presided over a case in which he had a financial interest. Carswell failed, in part, because he had participated in a white segregationists' scheme in Tallahassee, Florida, to buy a federally financed public

golf course to prevent its integration. Eventually Nixon would name three more Supreme Court justices: Harry Blackmun, Lewis F. Powell, Jr., and William Rehnquist.

Conservative judges did not always give Nixon the decisions he wanted. Despite attempts by the Justice Department to halt further desegregation in the face of determined white opposition, the Court ordered busing to achieve racial balance in the case of *Swann v. Charlotte-Mecklenburg Board of Education* (1971). In *Furman v. Georgia* (1972) the Supreme Court issued strict guidelines restricting the implementation of capital punishment, although it did not rule the death penalty unconstitutional. And in the controversial 1973 case of *Roe v. Wade*, Nixon's nominee Blackmun wrote the decision striking down Texas and Georgia laws prohibiting abortion.

The 1972 Election

Nixon's reelection in 1972 was by no means assured, but his prospects improved as the campaign proceeded. Senator Edmund Muskie of Maine, who had been Humphrey's running mate in 1968, emerged as a strong Democratic front-runner but quickly fell victim to Nixon's campaign attacks. Then, in May, the threat of a conservative third-party challenge from Alabama's governor, George Wallace, ended abruptly when an assailant in a suburban Maryland shopping mall shot Wallace, paralyzing him from the waist down.

Already divided over Vietnam and civil rights, the Democratic party soon found itself in greater disarray. After the 1968 national convention the party had changed its way of selecting delegates and candidates, pledging to include "minority groups, young people and women in reasonable relationship to their presence in the population." The ratification of the Twenty-sixth Amendment in 1971, lowering the national voting age to eighteen, reinforced the power of the youth vote. The widespread belief that the electorate was moving to the left increased the influence of those more liberal constituencies on the Democratic party. Tensions soon arose between those groups and the old-line Democratic officeholders and labor union leaders who had formerly dominated the party.

Senator George McGovern of South Dakota, a noted liberal and an outspoken opponent of the Vietnam War, reaped the greatest benefit from the new Democratic guidelines. By 1972 he was supported by an army of antiwar activists who blitzed precinct caucuses and won delegate commitments far beyond his support among voters. In the past, an alliance of party bosses and union leaders almost certainly would have rejected an upstart candidate such as McGovern, but few old-line leaders qualified as delegates to the nominating convention under the changed rules. Typical of the new Democratic look, the black minister and civil rights veteran Jesse Jackson replaced Mayor Richard Daley of Chicago as head of the Illinois delegation.

McGovern's campaign against Nixon was an unrelieved disaster. Surprised to learn that his running mate, Senator Thomas F. Eagleton of Missouri, had undergone electroshock therapy for depression some years earlier, McGovern first supported him "1,000 percent" and then abruptly insisted that he quit the ticket. Sargent Shriver, the former head of the Peace Corps and the Office of Economic Opportunity, joined the ticket, but McGovern's waffling over Eagleton made him appear weak and indecisive. Moreover, he was far too liberal for many traditional Democrats, who rejected his ill-defined proposals for welfare reform, did not rally around his calls for unilateral withdrawal from Vietnam, and ignored his charges that the Nixon administration had corruptly abused its power.

Nixon's campaign took full advantage of McGovern's weaknesses. Although the president had failed to end the war, his Vietnamization policy had reduced weekly American combat deaths from 300 in 1968 to almost none in 1972. Henry Kissinger's premature declaration that "peace is at hand" raised hopes for a negotiated settlement (see Chapter 31). Those initiatives robbed the Democrats of their greatest appeal—their antiwar stance. In addition, the improving economy helped the Republicans.

Nixon won handily, receiving nearly 61 percent of the popular vote and carrying every state except Massachusetts and the District of Columbia. McGovern's showing pointed to a significant erosion of the traditional Democratic coalition: he received only 18 percent of the southern white Protestant vote and 38 percent of the big-city Catholic vote. Only blacks, Jews, and low-income voters remained loyal. Yet Nixon failed to kindle strong Republican loyalty in the electorate. Only 55.7 percent of eligible voters bothered to go to the polls, and the Democrats maintained control of both houses of Congress.

Watergate

Watergate, the great constitutional crisis of the early 1970s, was a direct result of Nixon's ruthless political tactics, his secretive style of governing (as in the bombing of Cambodia), and his obsession with the anti–Vietnam War movement. Many Americans saw Watergate as consisting of only the evil deeds of one person (Richard Nixon) and one unlawful act (the obstruction of justice after the break-in). But Watergate was not an isolated incident; it was part of a broad pattern of illegality and misuse of power that flourished in the crisis atmosphere of the Vietnam War.

The new administration began to stretch the boundaries of the law under the guise of national security just four months into Nixon's first term. In the spring of 1969, after the *New York Times* reported the secret bombing of Cambodia, the White House asked the FBI to find out who had leaked the story. Without seeking a warrant, the FBI illegally tapped the phone conversations of several journalists and low-level staffers on the National Security Council. The source of the leak was never found, but the precedent for warrantless surveillance had been set.

Over the next several years the Nixon administration would repeatedly invoke supposed domestic threats to national security to justify its actions. In 1970 the White House asked Tom Huston, a former army intelligence officer, to draw up an extensive plan for secret domestic counterintelligence—opening mail, tapping phones, and arranging break-ins—to discredit the antiwar movement. President Nixon approved the scheme, which involved coordinated efforts by the FBI, CIA, and Justice Department. The FBI's director, J. Edgar Hoover, however, refused to cooperate with other government agencies in activities that he interpreted as being exclusively within the domain of the FBI.

The Pentagon Papers. Nixon's obsession with the antiwar movement grew in June 1971, when Daniel Ellsberg, a former Defense Department analyst who had become disillusioned with the war, leaked the so-called Pentagon Papers to the *New York Times*. The Pentagon Papers was a classified study (with accompanying documents) commissioned by Secretary of Defense Robert McNamara in 1967 and completed eighteen months later. The report detailed so many American blunders and misjudgments that McNamara had commented on first reading it, "You know, they could hang people for what is in there." In a subsequent court challenge the Nixon administration attempted to block publication of the Pentagon Papers. In an effort to discredit Ellsberg, White House underlings broke into his psychiatrist's office to look for damaging information. The burglars failed to turn up anything embarrassing on Ellsberg, and the judge dismissed the pending case against him when the break-in was revealed.

In preparation for the 1972 campaign, the White House had established a clandestine intelligence group led by the former CIA agents G. Gordon Liddy and Howard Hunt. Known as the "plumbers" because they were supposed to plug leaks of government information, they relied on tactics such as using the Internal Revenue Service and other agencies to harass opponents of the administration named on an "enemies list" drawn up by the presidential counsel John Dean. A major target of the plumbers was the Democratic party, whose front-runner, Senator Edmund Muskie of Maine, was the object of several "dirty tricks" during the primaries. For example, New Hampshire voters were awakened in the middle of the night by callers from the "Harlem for Muskie" committee, and posters appeared in Florida saying "Help Muskie in Busing More Children Now." Most damaging was a letter to a New Hampshire newspaper forged by one of Nixon's campaign aides accusing Muskie of ethnic insensitivity. Together those "dirty tricks" derailed Muskie's primary campaign.

These secret and highly questionable activities were financed by massive illegal fund-raising efforts by the Committee to Re-Elect the President (known as CREEP), which was headed by Attorney General John Mitchell. In soliciting funds from major corporations, Nixon fundraisers used high-pressure tactics that included implied threats of federal tax audits and other punitive measures for companies that failed to contribute. CREEP subsequently raised over $20 million, a portion of which was used to finance various dirty tricks, including the breakin that led to the Watergate scandal.

The Break-in. Early in the morning of June 17, 1972, an alert security guard noticed something amiss at the door to the headquarters of the Democratic National Committee at the Watergate apartment complex in Washington. Five men carrying cameras, wiretapping equipment, and a large amount of cash were arrested; two accomplices were apprehended soon afterward. Two of the accused men had worked as security consultants in the White House, and a third had held a responsible position in CREEP; the remaining four, all from Miami, had been involved in CIA-linked anti-Castro activities. Nixon's press secretary, Ronald Ziegler, promptly dismissed the breakin as a "third-rate burglary attempt." Nixon claimed that the White House counsel John Dean had conducted a full investigation of the incident (no such investigation ever took place) and stated categorically that "no one on the White House staff, no one in this administration, presently employed, was involved in this very bizarre incident." The cover-up had begun.

Subsequent investigations revealed that six days after the break-in the president had ordered his chief of staff, H. R. Haldeman, to instruct the CIA to tell the FBI not to probe too deeply into connections between the White House and the burglars. That action constituted obstruction of justice. Nixon apparently feared that the Watergate burglary would lead to an investigation of the dubious fund-raising methods and political sabotage practiced by his reelection committee.

Trial and Investigations. The Watergate burglars were convicted in January 1973. With Nixon's approval, John Dean tried to buy their continued silence with $400,000 in hush money and hints of presidential pardons. However, prodded by the presiding judge, John Sirica, one of the convicted burglars began to talk. Two tenacious investigative reporters at the *Washington Post*, Carl Bernstein and Bob Woodward, kept the story alive, exposing the attempted cover-up and tracing it

back to the White House. In February the Senate voted 77 to 0 to establish a select committee to investigate the scandal. Dean started to get nervous, and in March 1973 he warned Nixon, referring to the cover-up, that "there is a cancer within, close to the presidency, that is growing." In April Nixon accepted the resignations of Haldeman, Assistant Secretary of Commerce Jeb Stuart Magruder, and chief domestic adviser John Ehrlichman, all of whom had been implicated in the cover-up. He also fired Dean, who had agreed to testify in the case in exchange for immunity from prosecution.

In May the Senate Watergate committee, chaired by Senator Sam Ervin of North Carolina, began a summer of nationally televised hearings. On June 14 Magruder testified before the committee, confessing his guilt and implicating Attorney General John Mitchell, Dean, and others in the Watergate affair (see American Voices, page 994). In five days of riveting testimony in late June, Dean implicated Nixon in the cover-up. Even more startling testimony from the aide Alexander Butterfield revealed that Nixon had a secret taping system in the Oval Office. "I was hoping you fellows wouldn't ask me about that," Butterfield sheepishly told the committee. Until the existence of the tapes was disclosed, it had been Dean's word against Nixon's; now it appeared possible to find out what had actually been said.

The president steadfastly "stonewalled," citing executive privilege and national security as his reasons for

Watergate Hearings
Some of the most damaging testimony against President Richard Nixon came from the former White House counsel John Dean, shown testifying before the Senate Watergate Committee in June 1973. Revelations from a secret taping system in the Oval Office later confirmed Dean's nearly total recall of conversations he had had with the president.

Jeb Stuart Magruder

The Watergate Hearings

Jeb Stuart Magruder was assistant secretary of commerce in the Nixon administration and a key member of the Committee to Re-Elect the President. After his role in the Watergate scandal came to light in April 1973, he was forced to resign. On June 14, 1973, he testified before the Senate investigating committee on Watergate about his role in the cover-up.

Senator Howard Baker: Was there any question in your mind that the plan [to break in to the Democratic National Committee headquarters in Miami] was agreed to by Mr. Mitchell?

Jeb Stuart Magruder: No, sir, there was no doubt. But it was a reluctant decision. . . . We knew it was illegal, probably inappropriate. We didn't think that much would come of it. . . .

Q. I still can't quite come to grips with why you all had an expressed reservation about this and you still went ahead with it.

A. . . . I had worked for some two years, three years, really in the White House and at that time, I was mainly engaged in the activities trying to generate some support for the President. During that time, we had worked primarily relating to the war situation and worked with antiwar groups.

Now I had gone to college, as an example, under—and had a course in ethics as an example under William Sloane Coffin, whom I respect greatly. I have great regard for him. He was quoted the other day as saying, well, I guess Mr. Magruder failed my course in ethics. And I think he is correct.

During this whole time . . . we saw continuing violations of the law done by men like William Sloane Coffin. He tells me my ethics are bad. Yet he was indicted for criminal charges. He recommended on the Washington Monument grounds that students burn their draft cards and that we have mass demonstrations, shut down the city of Washington.

Now, here are ethical, legitimate people whom I respected. I respect Mr. Coffin tremendously. He was a very close friend of mine. I saw people I was very close to breaking the law without any regard for any other person's pattern of behavior or belief.

So consequently, when these subjects came up although I was aware they were illegal we had become somewhat inured to using some activities that would help us in accomplishing what we thought was a cause, a legitimate cause. . . . that is basically, I think, the reason why that decision was made, because of that atmosphere that had occurred and to all of us who had worked in the White House, there was that feeling of resentment and of frustration at being unable to deal with issues on a legal basis.

Source: Gerald Gold and the staff of the *New York Times*, eds., *The Watergate Hearings: Break-in and Cover-up* (New York: Bantam Books, 1974), 257–259.

refusing to release the tapes. Archibald Cox, a special prosecutor appointed by Nixon to investigate the Watergate case, petitioned a lower federal court to order the president to hand over the tapes. The court issued the order in October, but Nixon again refused to comply. When Cox continued to insist that the president hand over the original tapes, Nixon ordered Attorney General Elliott Richardson to fire Cox. Richardson refused and resigned, as did Assistant Attorney General William Ruckelshaus. Solicitor General Robert Bork, third in command in the Justice Department, carried out the orders, but this "Saturday Night Massacre" sparked public outrage and renewed demands for release of the tapes.

After additional federal subpoenas the following spring, Nixon released heavily edited transcripts of the tapes, whose most frequent words seemed to be *expletive deleted*, a phrase necessitated by the extensive profanity on the tapes. Senate Republican leader Hugh Scott called the edited transcripts "deplorable, disgusting, shabby,

immoral." Most suspicious was an eighteen-minute gap in the tape of a crucial meeting of Nixon, Haldeman, and Ehrlichman on June 20, 1972, three days after the break-in.

The Final Days. The Watergate affair moved into its final phase in the summer of 1974, when a committee of the House of Representatives convened impeachment hearings. On July 30 seven Republicans joined the Democratic majority to vote three articles of impeachment against Richard Nixon: obstruction of justice, abuse of power, and acting in a way that subverted the Constitution. Two days later the Supreme Court ruled unanimously that Nixon had no right to claim executive privilege as a justification for refusing to turn over the additional tapes requested by the second special prosecutor. Under duress, on August 5 Nixon released the unexpurgated tapes, which contained shocking evidence (the so-called smoking gun) that he had ordered the cover-up as early as six days after the break-in. In effect,

Nixon Resigns
On August 9, 1974, Richard M. Nixon became the first American president to resign. He is shown here minutes after turning over the presidency to Gerald R. Ford. Nixon retired to his home in San Clemente, California, refusing to admit guilt for what had happened.

the president had been lying to the American people since that time. A delegation of the most senior members of Congress, led by Senator Barry Goldwater, informed the president that no more than fifteen senators still supported him. Facing certain conviction in a Senate trial, on August 9, 1974, Nixon became the first U.S. president to resign.

The next day Vice-President Gerald Ford was sworn in as president. In 1973 Ford, a former Michigan congressman and house minority leader, had replaced Spiro Agnew, who had been forced to resign after being indicted for accepting kickbacks on construction contracts while serving as governor of Maryland and vice-president. The transfer of power from Nixon to Ford went remarkably smoothly. A month later, however, Ford stunned the nation by granting a "full, free, and absolute" pardon of Nixon "for all offenses he had committed or might have committed during his presidency." Ford took that action, he said, to spare the country the agony of rehashing Watergate.

The Aftermath. In the aftermath of Watergate twenty-five members of the Nixon administration went to prison, including Nixon's closest advisers, H. R. Haldeman, John Ehrlichman, and John Mitchell. Nixon retired to his estate in San Clemente, California. Although named as an "unindicted co-conspirator," he refused to admit guilt for what had happened, conceding only that Watergate represented an error of judgment.

In response to the abuses of the Nixon administration, Congress adopted several reforms to contain the power of what the historian Arthur M. Schlesinger, Jr., called "the imperial presidency." The 1974 Congressional Budget and Impoundment Control Act restricted the president's authority to impound federal funds (that is, refuse to spend money appropriated by Congress for programs opposed by the White House). A strengthened Freedom of Information Act in 1974 gave citizens greater access to files that federal government agencies had amassed on them. Finally, the Fair Campaign Practices Act of 1974 limited campaign contributions and provided for stricter accountability and public financing of presidential campaigns. Ironically, while the campaign law curbed some abuses, it created new ones. Because it allowed an unlimited number of political action committees (PACs) to donate up to $5,000 per candidate, corporations and lobbying groups found that they could increase their influence through multiple donations. By the end of the decade there were close to 3,000 PACs, which together played an increasingly pivotal—and some would argue unethical—role in national elections.

Perhaps the most significant legacy of Watergate was the wave of cynicism that swept the country in its wake. Beginning with Lyndon Johnson's "credibility gap" in the Vietnam War, public distrust of government had accelerated with the disclosure of Nixon's secret bombing of Cambodia and the illegal surveillance and harassment of antiwar protesters and other political opponents. The saga of Watergate seemed to confirm the suspicions of many Americans that politicians were hopelessly corrupt and that the federal government was out of control. Tragically, that cynicism would pervade Americans' thinking about politics for the foreseeable future.

Lowered Expectations and New Challenges

The political disillusionment of Americans was compounded by economic difficulties. After twenty-five years of world leadership, the economic dominance of the United States had begun to fade. Growing international demands for natural resources, particularly oil, and unstable access to foreign supplies wreaked havoc with the domestic economy. At the same time, foreign competitors were successfully expanding their share of the world market, edging out American-made products. The result was a sharp downturn in the economy that marked the end of America's overwhelming economic superiority in the postwar era.

The Hydrocarbon Age

"Without oil," Interior Secretary Harold Ickes had noted back in 1933, "American civilization as we know it could not exist." That continues to be true today, when not only the United States but the entire modern world lives in a hydrocarbon age, dependent on petroleum and its by-products. In the twentieth century oil supplanted coal as the main energy source for the industrial world because it was cheaper, cleaner, and more abundant (see Figure 32.1). Between 1949 and 1972, world energy consumption more than tripled, and the demand for oil increased more than five and a half times. Access to oil, especially at the low prices that prevailed in the 1950s and 1960s, fostered rapid economic growth and rising standards of living in most of the world, especially in the United States.

Until well into the twentieth century the United States was the world's leading producer and consumer of oil. During World War II America still produced two-thirds of the world's oil, but its share fell to only 22 percent in 1972, even though domestic production continued to rise. By the late 1960s the United States was buying more and more oil on the world market to keep up with shrinking domestic reserves and growing de-

mand. Daily imports rose from 3.2 million barrels in 1970 to 6.2 million by the summer of 1973.

America imported oil primarily from the Middle East, where production increased a stupendous 1,500 percent in the twenty-five years after World War II. For decades European and American oil companies had dominated petroleum exploration and production in that region, reaping enormous profits. But with the rise of nationalism and the decline of colonialism in the postwar era, Persian Gulf nations sought to increase their control of the industry. In 1960 oil-producing countries in the Third World formed OPEC (the Organization of Petroleum Exporting Countries) in an attempt to exercise more control over the world oil market. Five of the founding countries—the Middle Eastern states of Saudi Arabia, Kuwait, Iran, and Iraq, plus Venezuela—were the source of more than 80 percent of the world's crude oil exports. In 1960 the oil industry was in the middle of a twenty-year period of surplus capacity, and prices stayed low. In the early 1970s, however, the balance shifted. Several trends—a sharp increase in worldwide demand, the end of excess capacity, political instability in the Middle East, the shift of the United States from a net exporter to a net importer of oil—came together to set the stage for what would soon be OPEC's "golden age."

The year 1973 was the turning point. Between 1973 and 1975 OPEC deliberately raised the price of a barrel of oil from $3 to $12. At the end of the decade the price peaked at $34 a barrel. Because the United States depended heavily on Middle Eastern oil, the price rise set off furious inflation.

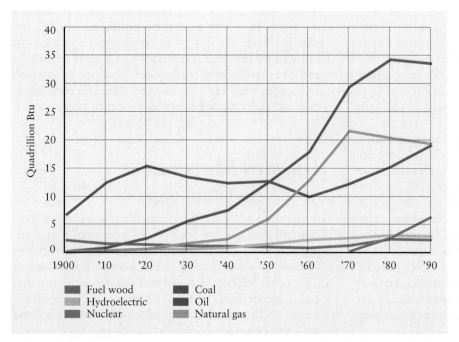

FIGURE 32.1

U.S. Energy Consumption, 1900–1990

Coal was the nation's primary source of energy until the 1950s, when oil and natural gas became the dominant fuels. The use of nuclear and hydroelectric power also rose substantially in the postwar era. Since the late 1970s fuel-efficient automobiles and conservation measures have reduced total energy use.

The United States scrambled to meet its domestic energy needs. Americans were forced to curtail their driving or spend long hours in line at the pumps; gas prices climbed 40 percent in a matter of months. A national speed limit of 55 miles per hour was instituted to conserve fuel. Drivers wanted to buy more fuel-efficient cars, but the U.S. automobile industry had little to offer except "gas-guzzlers" that had been built to run on cheap gasoline. Soon the domestic auto industry was in a slump as Americans bought cheaper, more fuel-efficient foreign cars, primarily those manufactured in Japan and West Germany. Since the United States owed much of its twentieth-century prosperity to the automobile (one in six jobs was tied directly or indirectly to that industry in the 1970s), this downturn had profound implications for the American economy.

The energy crisis was an enormous shock to the American psyche. Suddenly Americans felt like hostages to economic forces beyond their control. As OPEC's oil ministers set higher oil prices at their annual meetings, they seemed to be able to determine whether western economies grew or stagnated. Despite extensive public education about energy conservation and a second gas shortage in 1979 caused by the Iranian revolution, Americans could not wean themselves from foreign oil. In 1970 the United States imported $4 billion of foreign oil; the figure would grow to $90 billion by 1980. Inflation caused only part of the rise. Americans used even more foreign oil after the energy crisis than they had before, a testimony to the enormous thirst of modern industrial and consumer societies for petroleum.

Economic Troubles

While the energy crisis dealt a swift blow to the U.S. economy, other long-term economic developments were equally troubling. The high cost of the Vietnam War and the Great Society, coupled with relatively low tax increases, resulted in a steadily growing federal deficit. In the industrial sector growing competition from the reviving economies of West Germany and Japan reduced demand for American goods worldwide. In 1955 American-made goods accounted for 32 percent of all imports by major capitalist countries; by 1970 U.S. products accounted for only 18 percent of the total, and that proportion continued to decline in the 1970s. In 1971 the dollar fell to its lowest level on the world market since 1949, and the United States posted its first trade deficit in almost a century.

That year Nixon took several bold steps to stem the decline in currency and trade—and to avoid a recession before the 1972 election. Most important, he suspended the Bretton Woods system that had been set up at the United Nations monetary conference in 1944 (see Chapter 29). The dollar now fluctuated in relation to the

No Gas
During the energy crisis of 1973–1974 American motorists faced widespread gasoline shortages for the first time since World War II. Although gas was not rationed, gas stations were closed on Sundays, air travel was cut by 10 percent, and a national speed limit of 55 miles per hour was imposed.

Also in 1973 OPEC instituted an oil embargo, demonstrating that oil could be used as a weapon in global politics. The embargo was a reponse to international actions surrounding a surprise invasion of Israel by Egyptian and Syrian forces on October 6, 1973 (which was Yom Kippur, the holiest day in Judaism). At first American policy makers held back on supporting Israel for fear of jeopardizing relations with the oil-producing countries, which favored the invaders. But the initial attack was so devastating that the United States reversed its stand and quickly sent supplies and military equipment that enabled the Israelis to regain most of their lost territory in a few weeks. A cease-fire soon ended the fighting, but the international repercussions were just beginning. In retaliation against the United States, Western Europe, and Japan, all of which had aided Israel in the Yom Kippur War, OPEC halted all exports to those countries. The embargo lasted until 1974.

price of an ounce of gold, which increased from its former set price of $35 to as much as $800 on the international market during the 1970s. The abandonment of Bretton Woods, one of the pillars of the postwar economic order, was designed to encourage foreign trade by effectively devaluing the dollar, and it represented a frank acknowledgment that America's currency was no longer the world's strongest. Nixon also instituted wage and price controls to curb inflation and offered a "full employment" budget for 1972, including $11 billion in deficit spending to boost the sluggish economy.

Such measures temporarily improved the economic picture, but the general decline persisted. Overall economic growth as measured by the gross national product (GNP) averaged 4.1 percent per year in the 1960s but only 2.9 percent in the 1970s. Tellingly, all the real growth occurred before 1973, the year the OPEC oil embargo began. By 1980 nine Western European countries had surpassed the United States in per capita GNP. Since 1973 most American workers have seen their real incomes drop and have maintained their family income levels only by working longer hours or having additional family members join the paid work force.

These economic changes produced a noticeable decline in most Americans' standard of living. Discretionary income per worker dropped 18 percent between 1973 and the early 1980s. At the same time, galloping inflation forced consumer prices upward, reaching "double-digit" peaks of around 10 percent in 1974 and over 13 percent in 1980 (see Figure 32.2). Housing prices rose even more rapidly; the average cost of a single-family home more than doubled in the 1970s. To combat inflation, the Federal Reserve Board raised interest rates to as much as 20 percent in the late 1970s, making home loans and home ownership inaccessible to wider segments of the working class and middle class, including many baby boomers who were entering adulthood.

Those young adults also faced a constricted job market in the late 1970s as a record number of baby-boom job seekers competed for a limited number of positions. Unemployment peaked at around 9 percent in 1975, declined briefly, and then edged upward again, hovering at around 6 to 7 percent in the late 1970s. The devastating combination of inflation and unemployment—known as *stagflation*—was resistant to traditional government remedies such as deficit spending and tax reduction and bedeviled presidential administrations from Nixon to Reagan.

Deindustrialization. American economic woes were most acute in the industrial sector, which entered a prolonged period of decline. The economists Barry Bluestone and Bennett Harrison estimate that the United States lost between 32 million and 38 million jobs in the 1970s as a direct result of *deindustrialization*, "the widespread, systematic disinvestment in the nation's productive capacity." Investors who had formerly bought stock in basic U.S. industries now speculated on the stock market, or put their money into mergers and acquisitions, or invested in foreign companies. U.S. firms relocated overseas partly to take advantage of cheaper labor and production costs and partly because federal tax law permitted corporations to deduct foreign expenses from their domestic profits. By the end of the 1970s the hundred largest multinational corporations and banks were earning more than a third of their overall profits abroad. For some corporations the proportion was much higher: in 1979, 94 percent of Ford's profits came from overseas operations, as did 83 percent of the profits earned by the banking giant Citicorp in 1977.

The most dramatic consequences of deindustrialization occurred in the older northeastern and midwestern industrial regions that came to be known as the Rust Belt. Nightly newscasts were full of stories of the clos-

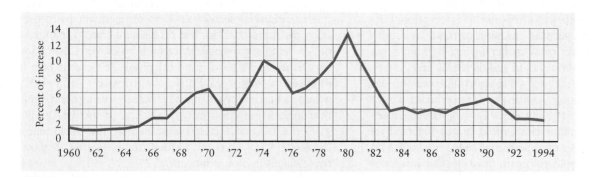

FIGURE 32.2

The Consumer Price Index, 1960–1994
The annual inflation rate peaked in 1980, the last year of Carter's presidency.

Source: U.S. Statistical Abstract, 1995.

ings of unprofitable plants. The dominant images of American industry in the mid-twentieth century—huge factories such as Ford's River Rouge outside Detroit; the General Electric plant in Lynn, Massachusetts; and the U.S. Steel compound in Gary, Indiana—were becoming relics of a past stage of industrial development. In some cases, such as the steel industry, older plants became unprofitable because U.S. firms had failed to invest sufficiently in research and development and were outflanked by foreign competitors.

When a community's major employer closed up shop and left town, the effect was devastating. In 1977 the Lykes Corporation shut down the Campbell Works of the Youngstown Sheet and Tube Company, laying off 4,100 Ohio steelworkers. Two years later the community was still reeling. A third of the displaced workers, too old to retrain for new positions, had been forced to take early retirement at half their previous salaries. Ten percent had moved, many of them to nonunion jobs in the Sun Belt. Another 15 percent were still looking for work, their unemployment compensation long since exhausted. Among the 40 percent who were the "success stories" (those who had found other jobs), many had taken huge wage cuts. A former rigger, for instance, was selling women's shoes for $2.37 an hour. *Fortune* magazine tried to make Youngstown's story upbeat, titling it "Youngstown Bounces Back," but the economic reality belied its cheerful conclusions. The caption of a photograph of an unemployed steelworker sitting at a piano read, "Crane operator Ozie Williams, thirty-two, has a lot of time to practice his music." The impact of such plant closings rippled through communities across America's heartland. Very few have "bounced back," and the number of industrial ghost towns has continued to grow.

Challenges for Labor. The changing economic conditions that fostered foreign investment and plant closings posed critical problems for the labor movement. In labor's heyday during the 1940s and 1950s American managers had often cooperated with unions; with profits high, there was room for accommodation. But as foreign competition cut into American corporate profits in the 1970s, industry was less willing to treat labor as a partner in making economic decisions. Union leaders might learn about a plant closing on the news at the same time that ordinary workers and the general public did. Union leaders shifted their priorities to holding on to gains they had already won.

Under such conditions, the power of organized labor declined. In the 1970s union membership dropped from 28 percent to 23 percent of the work firce. Labor's bargaining position was increasingly vulnerable in the face of multinational conglomerates with vast international resources and mobility. Some employers facing strikes or labor problems simply closed down their

domestic operations and turned to a cheaper, more compliant work force abroad. In a competitive global environment labor's prospects for regaining its earlier strength were dim.

Social Gridlock: Reform and Reaction in the 1970s

The journalist Tom Wolfe labeled the 1970s the "Me Decade" because of its widespread obsession with lifestyles and personal well-being. The historian Christopher Lasch referred derisively to its "culture of narcissism." Yet those labels hardly do justice to a decade in which environmentalism, feminism, lesbian and gay rights, and other social movements blossomed. Furthermore, such characterizations neglect the growing social conservatism that was in part a response to such movements. In fact, all these trends coexisted in a pattern of shifting crosscurrents that made the 1970s a complex and transitional decade.

Turning Inward

The youth culture of the 1960s had revolutionized lifestyles and cultural expression, but after 1970 its spirit was absorbed and marketed by the larger consumer culture. The crowds at Woodstock and other rock festivals had revealed the size of the youth market, and corporate entrepreneurs rushed to cash in. Symbols of cultural defiance were thus co-opted and homogenized by the mass culture. The ragged bell-bottoms of the 1960s became the expensive designer jeans of the 1970s. The unkempt hair and beards of male hippies emboldened some middle-aged executives to sport mustaches or allow their hair to cover their ears. The "Afro" hairstyle, once worn only by radical black activists, influenced blacks and whites of both sexes to let their hair go natural. Health foods soon became a multi-million-dollar business, packaged and sold in the consumer marketplace. Once paragons of the underground press, the *Village Voice* and *Rolling Stone* became respected voices of American journalism. The alternative styles of the 1960s thus filtered into the dominant culture.

As the baby-boom generation moved off college campuses and into the work force, public attention focused on the "selling out" of 1960s radicals. The media reveled in stories about the former Yippie leader Jerry Rubin, who became a Wall Street stockbroker, and the former Black Panther Eldridge Cleaver, who became a clothing designer and a born-again Christian. Leaving the counterculture behind, baby boomers settled down to pursue careers and material wealth.

But the young adults of the 1970s were different from the stereotypical suburbanites of the 1950s. The boomers sought personal fulfillment not only in material goods but in a quest for physical and spiritual well-being. One manifestation was the fitness craze. Millions of Americans, with the health-conscious baby boomers leading the way, began jogging, riding bicycles, and working out on Nautilus machines. The nation's emphasis on health and fitness coincided with heightened environmental awareness to spur demands for pesticide-free foods and vegetarian cookbooks. Some young people embraced the spiritual and self-help techniques of the human potential, or New Age, movement, while others turned to religious cults such as the Hare Krishna, the Church of Scientology, and the Unification Church of the Reverend Sun Myung Moon. The 1960s counterculture thus continued to influence American society.

Whereas many baby boomers focused on self-improvement, others tried to advance the unfinished social and political agendas of the 1960s. Moving into law, education, social work, medicine, and other fields, former radicals practiced their activism on a grass-roots level. Some moved into the left wing of the Democratic party, while others helped establish a host of community-based organizations such as health clinics, food co-ops, and day care centers. On the local level, at least, the progressive spirit of the 1960s lived on.

The Environmental Movement

The environmental movement was one of the most dynamic sources of activism in the 1970s. With the energy crisis and the prospect of global despoliation, Americans flocked to the environmental cause as never before. Interest in the environment and ecology did not originate in the postwar period, of course. John Muir and the Sierra Club had led the fight for the creation of a national park system in the late nineteenth century (see Chapter 17). Those early conservationists had advocated resource management and balancing open space and recreation against development. The post-1945 environmental movement operated in a different social and political context. Protecting nature in its pristine state became the goal: activists talked about the "rights of nature" just as they talked about the rights of women and blacks. Furthermore, Americans became aware of the possible exhaustion of the earth's resources. Since the United States had long consumed vast quantities of natural resources and had built a vigorous economy based on resource exploitation, the idea that there were limits to growth was revolutionary and difficult to accept. In a time of rising unemployment and deindustrialization, the environmental movement also clashed head-on with concerns about economic development, employment, and global competitiveness.

In some ways the environmental movement built on the activism of the 1960s. Many 1960s radicals evolved into 1970s environmental activists, bringing radical political sensibilities to environmental issues. For example, the search for alternative technologies (especially solar power) could be construed as a political statement against a corporate structure that seemed increasingly inhospitable to human-scale technology—and to humans as well. Activists used sit-ins and other protest tactics developed in the civil rights and antiwar movements to mobilize mass support for specific issues or pieces of legislation. Also like those movements, environmentalism was characterized by its decentralized nature and local orientation.

In other ways environmental activism represented something new—the mobilization of a broad mainstream constituency of people concerned about the air that they breathed, the food that they ate, and the ability to find recreation in undeveloped wilderness. Concern about environmental quality and ecological values can be seen as an offshoot of the advanced consumer economy that defined the postwar period. Now that most Americans had bought the basic necessities and then some, they wanted an even higher standard of living that included a healthy environment and corresponding life-styles. That desire led to new demands on the state; citizens expected the federal government to take responsibility for environmental issues.

The birth of the modern environmental movement is often dated to the 1962 publication of Rachel Carson's *Silent Spring*, a powerful analysis of the impact of pesticides, especially DDT, on the food chain. Other issues that galvanized public opinion included a huge oil spill in January 1969 off the coast of Santa Barbara, California; the environmental impact of projects such as the Alaska pipeline and a proposed airport in the Florida Everglades; and the harmful effects to the ozone layer of the earth's atmosphere caused by chlorofluorocarbons and increased levels of carbon dioxide. Environmentalism became a mass movement on the first Earth Day, April 22, 1970, when 20 million citizens gathered across the country to show their support for their endangered planet.

The environmental movement also raised public awareness of the dangers resulting from the careless dumping of toxic wastes. In 1978, outside Niagara Falls, New York, the Love Canal housing development made headlines when local residents discovered that it had been built over an underground chemical waste-disposal site. Lois Gibbs and other residents became aware of abnormally high rates of illness, miscarriages, and birth defects among Love Canal families. In 1980 a state of emergency was declared, and the New York State government paid homeowners to relocate (see American Lives, pages 1002–1003). Soon horror stories appeared about other poorly maintained waste-disposal sites

Chemical Waste at Love Canal
In 1978 residents of Love Canal became painfully aware of the chemical contamination of their neighborhood as rusted metal drums surfaced in backyards, poisonous sludge seeped into basements, and residents noticed abnormally high rates of illness and birth defects in their families.

across the country. "We just don't know how many potential Love Canals there are," a federal official admitted. "There are ticking time bombs all over."

One of the worst offenders was the federal government itself. In the cold war rush to produce bombs and weapons for national security, nuclear weapons plants carelessly released or dumped billions of gallons of radioactive waste into the environment. For example, the uranium-processing plant built in 1954 at Fernald, Ohio, dumped liquid wastes into open-air waste-storage pits, which then leaked into regional waterways. At the Hanford Nuclear Reservation near Richland, Washington, plutonium waste and toxic chemicals contaminated the soil and seeped into the Columbia River. Outside Denver, the Rocky Flats Plant and the Rocky Mountain Arsenal stored dangerous concentrations of plutonium, pesticides, and nerve gas wastes. Environmentalists called on the federal government to clean up this chemical legacy of the Cold War, but with only limited success.

Nuclear Energy. Nuclear energy also became a subject of citizen action in the 1970s, pitting environmental concerns against the need for alternative energy sources.

To reduce dependence on foreign oil, some politicians and utility companies promoted the expansion of nuclear power. Forty-two nuclear power plants were in operation by January 1974, and more than a hundred others were planned. The construction of nuclear power plants and reactors had gone largely unchallenged in the 1950s and 1960s; now community activists protested plans for new reactors, citing inadequate disaster evacuation plans and the unresolved problem of disposing of radioactive waste. Reminiscent of the antiwar demonstrations of the previous decade, the mass protests of the Clamshell Alliance and other antinuclear groups influenced the decisions to delay or prevent the start-up of reactors in Seabrook, New Hamshire, and Shoreham, New York.

Long-standing public fears about nuclear safety seemed to be confirmed in March 1979. At Three Mile Island near Harrisburg, Pennsylvania, a nuclear plant came critically close to a meltdown of its central core reactor. A hundred thousand residents were evacuated as a precaution. A prompt shutdown brought the problem under control before any radioactive material was released into the environment. As a member of the panel investigating the accident admitted, "We were damn lucky." Ultimately, Three Mile Island made Americans reassess the future of nuclear power. Cost overruns, faulty construction, and waste-disposal problems raised doubts that nuclear power could be a viable solution to the nation's energy needs. Grass-roots activism, combined with public fears about the potential dangers of nuclear energy, led many utility companies to abandon their commitment to nuclear power, despite its short-term economic advantages.

Three Mile Island
On March 30, 1979, the Three Mile Island nuclear power plant near Harrisburg, Pennsylvania, came close to sustaining a dangerous meltdown of its central core reactor. The accident, caused by the failure of safety systems and by human error, helped undermine American faith in nuclear technology.

Lois Marie Gibbs:
Environmental Activist

In 1978 Lois Gibbs was a twenty-seven-year-old housewife in Niagara Falls, New York. A chemical worker's wife and the mother of two children, Gibbs spent her days cooking, shopping, and cleaning the family's modest three-bedroom home. Two years later Gibbs was a nationally known figure. As the leader of the fight against toxic waste at the Love Canal, she organized hundreds of local families, squared off with the governor of New York State, testified before Congress, appeared on national television, and was recognized by President Jimmy Carter for her efforts. She was, as she liked to put it, "the housewife who went to Washington."

Born in Grand Island, New York, in 1951, Lois Conn was one of six children in a typical blue-collar family in the industrial region surrounding Buffalo. After graduating from high school in 1969, she worked as a nurse's aide at a convalescent home and married Harry Gibbs, a worker at a local chemical plant. After the birth of their first child they purchased a home in a quiet, tree-lined neighborhood. Lois quit her job to stay at home and gave birth to a daughter in 1975. With no inkling of what lay beneath them, the Gibbses finished their basement, tended their garden, and enjoyed a peaceful suburban existence.

The first sign of trouble came in 1977, when the Gibbses' son, Michael, entered kindergarten at the neighborhood school. Within three months, he developed epilepsy and soon contracted asthma and chronic urinary and ear infections. The following spring Gibbs read newspaper reports about toxic chemicals buried beneath the school and tried to have her son transferred. When school officials rejected her request, insisting that the school was safe, Gibbs launched a petition drive to have the school closed.

At first Gibbs was reticent about approaching her neighbors, afraid of having doors slammed in her face. But what she found surprised her; not only were people interested and concerned about the dangers of chemicals, many of them had health problems of their own, including respiratory ailments, cancer, miscarriages, and birth defects. "The more I heard, the more frightened I became," said Gibbs. "The entire community seemed to be sick."

Gibbs set out to educate herself about the area's history. Consulting local newspaper files, she learned about Love Canal, a six-mile-long canal project developed by William T. Love in the 1890s to connect the upper and lower branches of the Niagara River. Construction had been under way when the depression of 1893 doomed the project, leaving a partially dug trench. The land later became a dump site used mainly by the Hooker Chemical Corporation, which disposed of 22,000 tons of chemical wastes there between 1942 and 1953. (Health officials eventually identified over 200 different compounds at the site, including highly toxic substances such as dioxin—used in the herbicide Agent Orange—toluene, and benzene.) After filling and covering over the site in 1953, Hooker sold the land to the Board of Education for one dollar, stipulating that the company not be held responsible for any future injury or death. Housing subdivisions soon sprung up around the site, and a new elementary school near the corner of the canal opened in 1955.

By the time Gibbs began meeting with her neighbors in 1978, rusted metal drums were surfacing in backyards, chemical sludge was seeping into basements, and residents were complaining about dead trees, burned feet, and a recurring stench. In June of that year the New York State Health Department began collecting air, soil, and blood samples from households closest to the canal. After finding abnormally high rates of birth defects and miscarriages, the health department issued an order on August 2 for reconstruction of the canal site and recommended the evacuation of all pregnant women and children under age two. Soon afterward concerned residents established the Love Canal Homeowners Association (LCHA) to fight for permanent relocation of Love Canal families and elected Lois Gibbs as its president. Under pressure from Gibbs and the LCHA, New York's governor, Hugh Carey, agreed a few days later to relocate the 239 families closest to the canal, purchasing their homes at the replacement value.

While Gibbs and the LCHA applauded Carey's action, they worried about the other 810 families remaining in the neighborhood, many of whose homes also

Lois Gibbs

A 27-year-old housewife in Niagara Falls, New York, Lois Gibbs became leader of a campaign against toxic waste in her neighborhood in 1978. As president of the Love Canal Homeowners Association, Gibbs fought successfully for the permanent relocation of more than 1,000 Love Canal families.

showed dangerous levels of chemicals. Gibbs appealed to federal and local officials for further action but encountered repeated delays, denials, and rebuffs. The mayor of Niagara Falls denounced Gibbs's efforts, claiming that the adverse publicity would destroy the city's tourist industry. Meanwhile, the state health department refused to relocate more families until it could complete further studies. At one point in 1979 the department claimed to have lost the residents' health records and instructed them to start the lengthy documentation process all over again.

Faced with bureaucratic inertia, Gibbs sought out sympathetic scientists to help the residents conduct their own studies. Their most important finding came from a neighborhood survey showing that health problems clustered around swales—underground drainage ditches that led away from the canal—thus suggesting more widespread contamination. The LCHA promptly released the findings to the media. Gibbs got publicity in other ways as well: she appeared on talk shows, organized picketing at the canal construction site, and was arrested for blocking truck traffic. When state officials

still failed to take action, Gibbs led a group of citizens to the state capital, in Albany, bearing cardboard coffins symbolizing Love Canal victims. Throughout the Love Canal crisis Gibbs made frequent trips to Albany and Washington to negotiate with state officials, the governor's office, Senator Daniel Patrick Moynihan, and other federal representatives.

Gibbs's new activities caused tension in her marriage. "My husband was getting upset with me," she recalled, "I was never home . . . dinner was never on time." Like other housewives involved in the crisis, Gibbs gained a new independence through her activities outside the home. She and her husband divorced in 1980.

In May of that year events at Love Canal came to a head when the U.S. Environmental Protection Agency (EPA) released a study showing abnormally high levels of chromosome breakage in Love Canal residents (suggesting increased risks of cancer, miscarriage, and birth defects). In an act of desperation Gibbs and two other housewives took two EPA officials hostage in the LCHA office while hundreds of angry residents surrounded the building, demanding federal relocation of Love Canal families. Coming in the middle of the Iranian hostage crisis, the women's ploy brought national media coverage but also a threat of reprisal from the FBI. To avoid violence Gibbs released the officials, but she also demanded a response from President Jimmy Carter within forty-eight hours. Two days later, on May 21, Carter declared a health emergency at Love Canal, authorizing the temporary relocation of the remaining 810 families. Later that year he signed a bill permitting the permanent relocation of those families and the purchase of their homes; he also signed a bill establishing a "Superfund" to clean up Love Canal and thousands of other toxic waste sites identified by the EPA.

Using part of the $30,000 that the state paid for her home, Gibbs and her children moved to Washington, D.C., in 1981. There she founded the Citizens Clearinghouse for Hazardous Waste, a consulting group for grass-roots organizations working on problems related to pesticides, solid waste, asbestos, and other toxic substances. She married a toxicologist, gave birth to two more children, and has continued to work as the director of the Citizens Clearinghouse to the present day.

One of the communities the Citizens Clearinghouse will be watching is Love Canal. In 1990 the EPA declared Love Canal habitable again after a 12-year, $250 million cleanup. The elementary school and the 239 houses closest to the canal were demolished, but 236 other homes were rehabilitated and sold at discount prices to eager buyers. Public officials insist that the new containment system has safely and permanently sealed off the dump. Lois Gibbs is not so sure.

Environmental Legislation. Citizens' concerns over nuclear power, chemical contamination, pesticide poisoning, and other environmental issues created bipartisan support for a spate of federal legislation in the late 1960s and 1970s. In 1969 Congress passed the National Environmental Policy Act, requiring the developers of public projects to file an environmental impact statement (EIS) to assess the consequences of changing use patterns on a particular ecosystem. The EIS soon became a useful tool for citizens' groups trying to block unwanted development by private industry or government. The next year Nixon established the Environmental Protection Agency and signed the Clean Air Act, which toughened standards for auto emissions to reduce smog and air pollution. Following the lead of several state governments, Congress banned the use of DDT in 1972. Wildlife protection provided by the Endangered Animals Act of 1964 was expanded under the Endangered Species Act (1973), granting species such as snail darters and spotted owls protected status, which had to be balanced against human concerns regarding employment, development, and recreation. In 1980 Jimmy Carter signed a bill creating a $1.6 billion "Superfund" to clean up chemical pollution sites and, through an executive order in 1978, set aside 56 million acres in Alaska as national park and forest lands. Environmental protection thus joined social welfare, defense, and national security as areas for federal intervention in the postwar era.

The Consumer Movement

Paralleling the rise of environmentalism was a growing consumer protection movement that sought to eliminate harmful products and curb dangerous practices by American corporations. The consumer movement had its origins in the Progressive Era with the founding of government agencies such as the Food and Drug Administration (see Chapter 21). After decades of inertia the consumer movement reemerged in the 1960s under the leadership of Ralph Nader, a young Harvard-educated lawyer who took on U.S. automakers over unsafe and wasteful design practices. In his book *Unsafe at Any Speed* (1965) Nader attacked General Motors for putting flashy style ahead of safe handling and fuel economy in its design of the Chevrolet Corvair.

Nader later won a lawsuit against General Motors and used the proceeds to launch a Washington-based consumer protection organization in 1969. Staffed by a handful of lawyers and hundreds of student volunteers known as "Nader's raiders," the organization gave rise to the Public Interest Research Group, a national network of consumer groups that focused on issues ranging from product safety to consumer fraud and environmental pollution. Nader's organization pioneered legal tactics such as the class-action suit (which allowed people with common grievances to sue as a group) and became a model for dozens of other groups that emerged in the 1970s and afterward to combat the health hazards of smoking, unethical insurance and credit practices, and other consumer problems. The establishment of the federal Consumer Products Safety Commission in 1972 reflected the growing importance of consumer protection in American life.

The Women's Movement

Along with environmentalism, feminism proved to be the most enduring movement of the 1960s. In the early 1970s, the women's movement scored significant victories, including increased educational opportunities, a growing network of women-oriented services and organizations, and increased access to abortion.

Women's opportunities expanded dramatically in the area of higher education. Formerly all-male bastions, including Yale, Princeton, and the U.S. Military Academy, admitted women undergraduates for the first time; women's colleges such as Vassar and Sarah Lawrence admitted men. Under pressure from female students and faculty members, hundreds of colleges started women's studies programs, and the proportion of women in most graduate and professional schools rose markedly. With the passage of Title IX of the Educational Amendments Act of 1972, Congress broadened the 1964 Civil Rights Act to include educational institutions, prohibiting colleges and universities that received federal funds from discriminating on the basis of sex. By requiring schools to fund sports programs for women at a level comparable to that for men, Title IX increased women's access to sports and athletic competition.

The women's movement grew more sophisticated, generating an array of women-oriented services and organizations. Rape crisis centers, battered women's shelters, and feminist health collectives proliferated in cities across the country. *Our Bodies Ourselves*, a women's health manual published by a group of Boston women in 1973, quickly became a best seller. Women's bookstores catered to a feminist clientele with an assortment of new women's newspapers, books, and academic journals. In 1972 Gloria Steinem and other journalists founded *Ms.* magazine, the first consumer magazine aimed at a feminist audience. Several new national women's organizations emerged in the early 1970s, and many of the established groups continued to grow. By 1977 the National Organization for Women (NOW) had 65,000 members.

Women and Politics. Women were also increasingly visible in politics and public life. The National Women's Political Caucus, founded in 1971, actively promoted the election of women to public office. Bella Abzug, Elizabeth

Holtzman, Shirley Chisholm, Patricia Schroeder, and Geraldine Ferraro served in Congress; Ella Grasso won election as Connecticut's governor in 1974, and Dixie Lee Ray as Washington's in 1976. Twenty thousand women came to Houston in November 1977 for the first National Women's Conference, part of the observance of the United Nations' International Women's Year. Their "National Plan of Action" represented a hard-won consensus on topics ranging from violence against women to homemakers' rights, the needs of older women, health, and, most controversially, abortion rights and other reproductive issues.

Women's political mobilization resulted in significant legislative and administrative gains. In addition to Title IX, Congress passed the Equal Credit Opportunity Act of 1974, which made it possible for women to get credit, including charge cards and mortgages, in their own names and on the basis of their own (not their husbands') incomes. Congress also authorized child care deductions for working parents and employment benefits for married female federal employees. Under the Carter administration women received a record number of federal appointments, including three cabinet-level positions.

The Expanding Women's Movement
By the late 1970s the feminist movement had broadened its base, attracting women of all ages and backgrounds, such as this delegate to the 1977 National Women's Conference in Houston, Texas. As the slogan on her hat implies, though, the women's movement was already on the defensive against right-wing claims that the feminist movement was undermining traditional values. (© Bettye Lane)

Abortion Rights. The Supreme Court also advanced the cause of women's rights, although not always along the lines favored by the women's movement. In several rulings the Court read a right of privacy into the Ninth and Fourteenth amendments' concept of personal liberty to give women more control over their reproductive lives. In 1965 the case of *Griswold v. Connecticut* had overturned state laws against the sale of contraceptive devices to married adults; in 1972 *Baird v. Eisenstadt* extended this protection to single persons. In 1973 *Roe v. Wade* struck down Texas and Georgia statutes that allowed abortions only if the mother's life was in danger. According to this 7–2 decision, states could no longer outlaw abortions performed during the first trimester, or three months, of pregnancy. Rather than addressing the issue in feminist terms, such as women's right to control their own bodies, the justices interpreted abortion as a medical issue, basing their decision on the confidentiality of the doctor-patient relationship as well as the individual's right to privacy.

Roe v. Wade nationalized the liberalization of state abortion laws that had begun in New York in 1970 but also fueled the development of a powerful antiabortion movement. Believing that the rights of a fetus take precedence over a woman's right to choose whether to terminate a pregnancy, abortion opponents attempted to circumvent and overturn the *Roe v. Wade* decision. In 1976 Representative Henry Hyde of Illinois sponsored an amendment to deny Medicaid funds for abortions for poor women. Passed over a presidential veto, the amendment was upheld by the Supreme Court in 1980. The Hyde Amendment was one of the opening rounds in a protracted legislative and judicial campaign to chip away at the *Roe* decision.

The Equal Rights Amendment. In the 1970s the women's movement increasingly united around the proposed Equal Rights Amendment (ERA) to the Constitution, which stated in its entirety, "Equality of rights under the law shall not be denied or abridged by the United States or any State on the basis of sex." The ERA, first introduced in Congress in 1923 by the National Woman's Party, was dusted off by modern feminists. In 1970 the measure passed the House but died in the Senate. In the 1971–1972 session it passed both houses and was submitted to the states for ratification. Thirty-four states quickly passed the ERA between 1972 and the end of 1974, but then the momentum stopped (see Map 32.1). Only Indiana ratified after that point, leaving the amendment three states short of the necessary three-fourths majority. Most of the nonratifying states were in the South and the West; Illinois also held out despite spirited campaigns there by ERA supporters. Congress extended the deadline for ratification until June 30, 1982, but the Equal Rights Amendment still fell short.

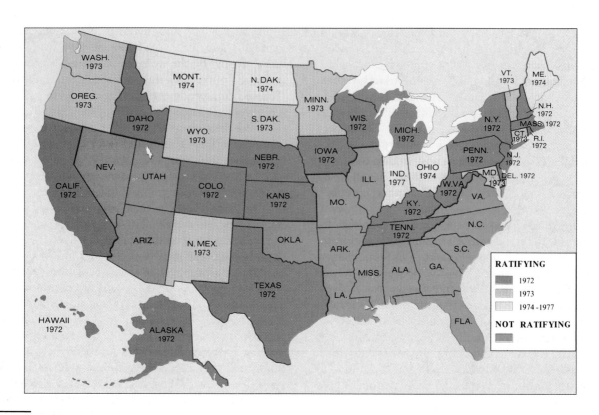

MAP 32.1

States Ratifying the Equal Rights Amendment
The Equal Rights Amendment quickly won support in 1972 and 1973 but then
stalled. ERAmerica, a coalition of women's groups formed in 1976, lobbied extensively, particularly in Florida, North Carolina, and Illinois, but failed to sway the
conservative legislatures in those states. Efforts to revive the ERA in the 1980s were
unsuccessful.

Stalemate. The fate of the ERA and the battle over
abortion rights show that by the mid-1970s the momentum of the women's movement was beginning to slow.
The feminist movement was becoming increasingly divided over issues of race, class, age, and sexual orientation. For many nonwhite and working-class women
the movement seemed to represent the interests of self-
seeking white career women. The ERA, for example,
promised to open certain high-paying occupations to individual women but also would eliminate protective
legislation considered essential by many women workers. At the same time the women's movement faced
growing social conservatism among Americans generally. Although 63 percent of the women polled in 1975
said that they favored "efforts to strengthen and change
women's status in society," a growing minority of men
and women expressed concern over what seemed to be
revolutionary changes in women's traditional roles. Especially disturbing to many conservatives were attitudes
that seemed to denigrate women who chose to be full-
time housewives.

Phyllis Schlafly, long active in conservative causes—
she had written *A Choice, Not an Echo*, a best seller ex-
tolling Barry Goldwater, in 1963—led the antifeminist
backlash. Despite her law degree and active career while
raising five children, Schlafly advocated traditional roles
for women. As she told audiences, "A man's first significant purchase is a diamond for his bride, and the major
financial investment of his life is a home for her to live
in." She baited feminists by opening her speeches with
"I'd like to thank my husband for letting me be here
tonight."

Schlafly's STOP ERA organization claimed that the
amendment would create an unnatural "unisex society,"
permit women to be drafted, legalize homosexual marriages, and prohibit separate toilets for men and women.
(Feminists argued that those charges were groundless.)
Grass-roots networks mobilized conservative women,
who then showed up at statehouses with home-baked
bread and apple pies, symbols of their traditional domestic roles. The message that women would lose more
than they would gain if the ERA passed found favor

among many men and women, especially those troubled by the rapid pace of social change.

Although the feminist movement was on the defensive by the mid-1970s, women's lives showed no signs of returning to the patterns of the 1950s. Pervasive changes in women's employment and family lives that had begun in earlier decades accelerated in the 1970s. Because of increasing economic pressures, the proportion of women in the paid work force continued to rise, from 44 percent in 1970 to 51 percent in 1980. With easier access to birth control, many women enjoyed greater sexual freedom before, during, and after marriage (although they also became more vulnerable to male sexual pressures). With a growing number of career options available to women, particularly educated white women, many stayed single or delayed marriage and child-rearing. The birth rate thus continued its postwar decline, reaching an all-time low in the mid-1970s (see Figure 29.5). At the same time, the divorce rate rose 82 percent in the 1970s as more men and women elected to leave unhappy marriages.

Although such changes brought increased autonomy for many women, they also caused new hardships, particularly in poor and working-class families. Divorce left many women with low-paying jobs and inadequate child care. More tolerant attitudes toward premarital sex, along with other social and economic factors, contributed to rising teenage pregnancy rates. In the 1970s teenage mothers—most of them poor and ill educated—gave birth to one of every six children. Rising divorce and adolescent pregnancy rates produced a sharp rise in the number of female-headed families, which in turn resulted in a "feminization" of poverty. In 1980 women accounted for 66 percent of the nation's adults living below the poverty line. Such developments made many Americans uneasy and fueled a growing wave of social reaction.

Gays and Lesbians

Like the women's movement, the gay liberation movement of the 1960s achieved greater visibility in the 1970s. Thousands of gay men and lesbians "came out" in those years, publicly proclaiming their sexual orientation. Growing gay communities in New York's Greenwich Village, San Francisco's Castro, and other urban enclaves gave rise to hundreds of new gay and lesbian clubs, churches, businesses, and political organizations. In 1973 the National Gay Task Force launched a campaign to have gay men and lesbians included as a protected group under civil rights laws covering employment and housing. Such efforts were most successful on the local level; during the 1970s Detroit, Boston, Los Angeles, Miami, San Francisco, and other cities passed laws barring discrimination on the basis of sexual preference.

Like abortion, the ERA, and other controversial social issues, gay rights came under attack from conservatives who believed that such protection would encourage immoral behavior. When the Miami city council passed a measure banning discrimination against gay men and lesbians in 1977, the singer Anita Bryant led a campaign to repeal the law by popular referendum. Later that year voters overturned the measure by a two-to-one majority, prompting similar anti–gay rights campaigns around the country.

Racial Minorities

Although the civil rights movement was in disarray by the late 1960s, minority group protests produced new policies that led to limited social and economic gains for those groups in the 1970s. Native Americans saw some of the most significant changes as their protests resulted in federal action under the Nixon administration. In 1971 the Alaska Native Land Claims Act restored 40 million acres and paid $960 million in compensation to Eskimos, Aleuts, and other native peoples. Smaller settlements were made with tribes in Maine, New Mexico, South Dakota, and Washington State. Most important, the federal government abandoned the tribal termination program that it had begun in the 1950s (see Chapter 29). Under the Indian Self-Determination Act of 1974, Congress restored the legal status of tribes as governing entities and gave them authority over federal programs on reservations (see Map 32.2).

Busing. The court-mandated busing of children to achieve school integration proved to be the most disruptive social issue of the 1970s. After its 1954 ruling in *Brown v. Board of Education of Topeka*, the Supreme Court had called for desegregation "with all deliberate speed" (see Chapter 29), but progress was limited before 1970. In the 1970s, however, the courts and the Justice Department pushed for more action, beginning in the South, which grudgingly complied, and then in the rest of the country. In 1971 the Supreme Court upheld a federal judge's order requiring the Charlotte-Mecklenberg, North Carolina, school system to transport students from their neighborhoods to more distant schools to integrate the citywide school system. The following year the Supreme Court upheld a lower court decision in Colorado that mandated the use of busing in northern and western states as well. In *Milliken v. Bradley* (1974) the Court narrowly rejected a proposal to combine the schools of a city and its suburbs to achieve racial balance but specified that cities, with their deeply ingrained patterns of residential segregation, had to use busing within municipal boundaries to integrate their classrooms. The decision sparked both class- and race-based resentments; many white working-class city dwellers objected to busing not

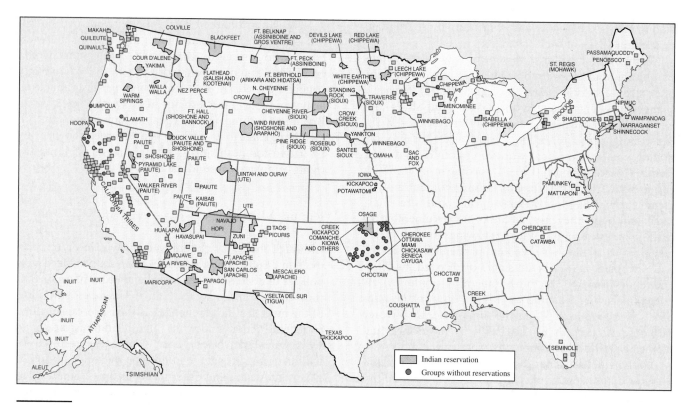

MAP 32.2

American Indian Reservations

Although native Americans have been able to preserve small enclaves in the northeastern states, most Indian reservations are in the West. Beginning in the 1970s, various nations filed land claims against federal and state governments.

only because they opposed racial integration but because such schemes had been devised by affluent suburbanites whose school districts were unaffected by the plans.

The most violent opposition occurred in Boston in 1974–1975. The strongly Irish-Catholic working-class neighborhood of South Boston responded to the arrival of black students from the Roxbury section with mob

scenes reminiscent of Little Rock in 1957 (see American Voices, page 1009). Armed riot police were needed to keep South Boston High School open. Many white parents in Boston and other cities threatened by court-ordered busing transferred their children to private schools; the resulting "white flight" increased the racial imbalance that busing was intended to solve. Some black

An Antibusing Confrontation in Boston

Tensions over court-ordered busing ran high in Boston in 1976. When a black lawyer tried to cross the city hall plaza during an antibusing demonstration, he became another victim of Boston's climate of racial hatred and violence. This photograph by Stanley Forman for the *Boston Herald American*, showing protesters trying to impale the man with a flagstaff, won a Pulitzer Prize.

Phyllis Ellison

Busing in Boston

Nowhere in the North was busing more divisive than in Boston in 1974–1975. Phyllis Ellison was one of fifty-six black students from the predominantly black neighborhoods of Columbia Point and Roxbury assigned to South Boston High School. Here she describes incidents from her sophomore year, including the day that a white student was stabbed by a black student during a melee at the school. The student's wound was not fatal, but the incident led to heightened resistance and recriminations.

I remember my first day going on the bus to South Boston High School. I wasn't afraid because I felt important. I didn't know what to expect, what was waiting for me up the hill. We had police escorts. I think there was three motorcycle cops and then two police cruisers in front of the bus, and so I felt really important at that time, not knowing what was on the other side of the hill.

Well, when we started up the hill you could hear people saying, "Niggers go home." There were signs, they had made a sign saying, "Black people stay out. We don't want any niggers in our

school." And there were people on the corners holding bananas like we were apes, monkeys. "Monkeys get out, get them out of our neighborhood. We don't want you in our schools.". . .

You can't imagine how tense it was inside the classroom. A teacher was almost afraid to say the wrong thing, because they knew that that would excite the whole class, a disturbance in the classroom. The black students sat on one side of the classes. The white students sat on the other side of the classes. . . . In the lunchrooms . . . [it] was the same thing. . . . So really, it was separate, I mean, we attended the same school, but we really never did anything together. . . .

I remember the day Michael Faith got stabbed vividly, because I was in the principal's office and all of a sudden you heard a lot of commotion and you heard kids screaming and yelling and saying, "He's dead, he's dead. That black nigger killed him. He's dead, he's dead." And then the principal running out of the office. There was a lot of commotion and screaming, yelling, hollering, "Get the niggers at Southie." I was really afraid. And the principal came back into the office and said, Call

the ambulance and tell all the black students that were in the office to stay there. A police officer was in there and they were trying to get the white students out of the building, because they had just gone on a rampage and they were just going to hurt the first black student that they saw. . . . The black students were locked in their rooms and all the white students were let go out of their classrooms. I remember us going into a room, and outside you just saw a crowd of people, I mean, just so many people, I can't even count. . . . I remember the police cars coming up the street, attempting to, and people turning over the police cars, and I was just amazed that they could do something like that. The police tried to get horses up. They wouldn't let the horses get up. They stoned the horses. They stoned the cars. And I thought that day that we would never get out of South Boston High School. . . .

Source: Henry Hampton and Steve Fayer, Voices of Freedom: An Oral History of the Civil Rights Movement from the 1950s through the 1980s (New York: Bantam, 1990), 600, 610, 612–613.

parents also came to oppose busing, calling instead for more funding and greater efforts to improve schools in predominantly black neighborhoods. By the late 1970s federal courts were backing away from their earlier insistence on busing to achieve racial balance.

Affirmative Action. Almost as divisive as busing was the implementation of *affirmative action*—procedures designed to redress historical patterns of race and sex discrimination in employment and education. First put forward by Lyndon Johnson's Department of Labor in 1968, affirmative action was refined by a series of Supreme Court and lower court rulings that identified acceptable procedures, including hiring and enrollment goals, special recruitment and training programs, and *set-asides* (specially reserved slots) for women and minority

students, employees, and contractors on government-subsidized construction projects.

Affirmative action programs helped expand opportunities for blacks and Latinos during those years. Among black Americans, access to higher education increased significantly; the number of black students enrolled in colleges and universities doubled between 1970 and 1977 to 1.1 million, or 9.3 percent of the total student enrollment. A small but growing number of black graduates moved into white-collar professions in corporations, banks, universities, and law firms. Others found new opportunities in civil service occupations such as law enforcement and firefighting or entered apprenticeships in the skilled construction trades. Latinos experienced similar gains in education and "token" advances in the professions and skilled trades. On the whole, however, both groups experienced only marginal economic improvement as poor and working-class non-whites bore the brunt of job loss and unemployment in the 1970s.

Nevertheless, many whites, who were also feeling the economic pinch, came to resent affirmative action programs as infringements on their rights. A growing number of white men soon raised the cry of "reverse discrimination," claiming that they had been passed over in favor of less qualified minority group members or women. In 1978 a white man named Allan Bakke sued the University of California Medical School at Davis for rejecting him while admitting minority candidates with lesser qualifications. The Supreme Court ruling in *Bakke v. University of California* was inconclusive: by a 5 to 4 margin the Court proclaimed that the medical school's strict quota—setting aside 16 out of 100 places for "disadvantaged students"—was illegal and ordered Bakke admitted. At the same time, also by a 5 to 4 margin, it ruled that racial factors could properly be considered in making hiring and admission decisions, thus upholding the principle of affirmative action. But the *Bakke* decision was clearly a setback for the proponents of affirmative action, and it set the stage for subsequent efforts to eliminate those programs in the 1990s.

The Politics of Resentment

The often vociferous public opposition to busing, affirmative action, gay rights ordinances, and the Equal Rights Amendment, along with the rapidly growing antiabortion movement, constituted a broad backlash against the social changes of the previous decade. More important, the new conservatism was a product of economic changes in the 1970s that left many working-class and middle-class Americans with lower incomes, rising prices, and higher taxes. Richard Nixon had successfully appealed to those "ordinary Americans" back in 1968; the political power of this appeal grew even stronger with the economic crises of the early 1970s. Such pressures fueled what the conservative writer Alan Crawford has termed the "politics of resentment"—a grass-roots revolt against "special-interest groups" (women, minorities, gays, and so on) and growing expenditures on social welfare. Such groups and programs, conservatives believed, robbed other Americans of educational and employment opportunities and created a fiscal burden on the working and middle classes.

Although the politics of resentment most often centered on socioeconomic issues, it also took the form of local taxpayers' revolts. In 1978 California voters passed Proposition 13, a measure that reduced property taxes and eventually undercut local governments' ability to maintain schools and other public services. Promising tax relief to middle-class homeowners and reduced funding for busing and other programs benefiting the urban

poor, Proposition 13 became the model for similar tax-cutting measures around the country in the late 1970s and 1980s.

Evangelical Religion. The rising popularity of evangelical religion also fueled the conservative resurgence of the 1970s. Fundamentalist, holiness, and Pentecostal sects that fostered a "born-again" experience had been growing steadily since World War II under the leadership of charismatic preachers such as Billy Graham, who used the media, especially television, to spread the gospel. Soon evangelical groups set up their own school systems, newspapers, and broadcasting networks. A new breed of *televangelists*, such as Jerry Falwell, built vast electronic ministries through religious programs aired on the new Christian Broadcasting Network founded by the Virginia preacher Pat Robertson.

In the 1970s, when membership in the liberal mainstream Protestant churches declined, evangelical denominations showed energetic growth. According to a Gallup poll conducted in 1976, some 50 million Americans, about a quarter of the population, were affiliated with evangelical churches. President Jimmy Carter proudly proclaimed the influence of Jesus Christ in his life, as did the singers Pat Boone and Johnny Cash, the former Watergate convicts Jeb Magruder and Charles Colson, and the black power activist Eldridge Cleaver.

The New Right. During the 1970s evangelicals spoke out on a broad range of social and cultural issues, denouncing abortion, busing, sex education, pornography, feminism, and gay rights. Concerned with the same economic issues that engaged other conservatives, the Christian right added a strong dimension of moral indignation, particularly over issues of family life and sexuality. In 1979 Jerry Falwell founded the Moral Majority, a Christian political organization that promoted "family values"—traditional gender roles, heterosexuality, family cohesion—and staunch anticommunism. The extensive media and fund-raising networks of the Christian right became the organizational base for the larger conservative movement known as the New Right. Using computerized mass mailing campaigns that targeted evangelical constituencies, New Right political groups such as the National Conservative Political Action Committee and the American Conservative Union mobilized thousands of followers and millions of dollars to support conservative candidates and causes.

During the 1970s conservatives were most active at the local level, building a national movement from the ground up that would help to elect Ronald Reagan in 1980. Environmentalists and other liberal activists shared this grass-roots approach but were less effective in using modern technological tools to sustain a mass following. Among both liberals and conservatives the dynamism of local organizing developed in the absence of effective political leadership on the national level.

Post-Watergate Politics: Failed Leadership

In the wake of Watergate many citizens became cynical about the federal government and politicians in general. "Don't vote. It only encourages them" read one bumper sticker for the 1976 presidential campaign. "The lesser of two evils is still evil" proclaimed another. Political leaders proved unable to deal with the rising inflation, stagnant growth, and declining productivity that plagued the U.S. economy in the 1970s. The fall of Saigon in 1975 reminded Americans of the failure of the nation's Vietnam policy. The world was changing, and Americans had to grapple with the unsettling idea that perhaps the United States was no longer the all-powerful country it had been for much of the postwar era. As Americans approached the 1980 election, this growing sense of impotence erupted in fury over the Iranian hostage crisis.

Ford's Caretaker Presidency

Gerald Ford, who had become vice-president after Spiro Agnew's resignation, was unable to establish his legitimacy as president during the two years he held the office. His pardon of Nixon a month after becoming president hurt his credibility as a political leader. Moreover, Ford was a less activist executive than Nixon, preferring a more conservative laissez-faire approach that emphasized voluntary action by the private sector. Ford's hostility to federal initiatives often put him at odds with the Democrats, who, in the wake of Watergate, increased their majorities in both houses of Congress in the 1974 elections.

Ford's biggest problem as president was the economy, which was reeling from inflation set in motion by the Vietnam War and worsened by rising OPEC prices and the growing trade deficit. The 1974 inflation rate soared to almost 12 percent. In an attempt to curtail prices, the Federal Reserve Board tightened the money supply and drove up interest rates. Ford's voluntary program to "Whip Inflation Now," complete with much-mocked "WIN" buttons, was ineffective. The following year the economy entered its deepest downturn since the Great Depression. Production declined more than 10 percent, and nearly 9 percent of the work force was unemployed. The 1975 recession temporarily reduced inflation to less than 5 percent, but the rate soon rose again. Many of these economic problems were beyond the president's control, but Ford's failure to take more vigorous action made him appear timid and ineffective.

In foreign policy Ford was equally lacking in presidential leadership. He maintained Nixon's initiatives toward détente by asking Henry Kissinger to stay on as secretary of state, a position he had held since 1973. Ford met with Soviet leaders at Vladivostok to begin hammer-

ing out the details of a hoped-for SALT II (Strategic Arms Limitation Talks) agreement, but there was little concrete progress made on arms control. Ford and Kissinger also continued Nixon's policy of increasing American support for the shah of Iran, failing to notice that the shah's policy of rapid modernization was provoking bitter opposition and antiwestern sentiment among Iran's growing Muslim fundamentalist population.

After the abuses of the Nixon era, Ford's personal style and candor were refreshing, but he failed to convey the assurance and competence needed in a time of mounting economic and international problems. "Gerald Ford is an awfully nice man who isn't up to the presidency," *The New Republic* concluded, and the voters agreed.

Jimmy Carter: The Outsider as President

Only in the skewed political atmosphere of post-Watergate America could the Democrats have chosen their 1976 nominee, James E. Carter, Jr. "Jimmy Who?" the media scoffed at first about this engineer and former entrepreneur in agricultural commodities from Plains, Georgia, popularly portrayed as a peanut farmer. But they soon changed their tune as Carter won key primaries, giving his candidacy momentum and credibility. Carter played up his role as a Washington outsider (his previous political experience had been as governor of Georgia and before that as a state senator) and pledged to restore morality to government. "I will never lie to you," he piously told voters.

The 1976 presidential campaign was one of the blandest in years. On the Republican side President Ford staved off a conservative challenge from Governor Ronald Reagan of California; then he dumped his moderate vice-president, Nelson Rockefeller, in favor of the more conservative Senator Robert J. Dole of Kansas. Carter chose as his running mate Senator Walter F. Mondale of Minnesota, who had ties to the traditional Democratic constituencies of labor, liberals, blacks, and big-city machines. Avoiding issues and controversy, Carter won the election with 50 percent of the popular vote to Ford's 48 percent.

Carter immediately tried to set a different tone for his administration. On Inauguration Day he renounced formal wear in favor of a business suit; instead of riding in a limousine, he and his wife, Rosalynn, walked from the Capitol to the White House. Throughout his term he relied heavily on symbolic gestures—dressing in an informal cardigan sweater for fireside chats to the nation, carrying his own luggage on and off planes, holding town meetings, and staying in the homes of ordinary citizens. Carter's homespun approach soon wore thin as people looked for substance behind the symbols. "If the Carter administration were a television show," the columnist Russell Baker quipped, "it would have been canceled months ago."

Domestic Leadership. Part preacher, part technocrat (he had served on a nuclear submarine in the early 1950s), Carter failed to develop an effective style of domestic leadership, a task made more difficult by the post-Watergate climate of skepticism and apathy. His campaign as an outsider had distanced him from traditional sources of power in Washington, and he did little to heal the breach. Well into the term Carter's chief domestic aide, Hamilton Jordan, had never introduced himself to Thomas ("Tip") O'Neill, the Speaker of the House of Representatives and the most powerful Democrat on Capitol Hill. Shying away from established Democratic leaders, Carter turned to advisers and friends who had worked with him in Georgia, none of whom had national experience. When his budget director, Bert Lance, was questioned about financial irregularities at his Atlanta bank, the case undercut Carter's pledges to restore integrity and morality to the government.

Inflation was Carter's major domestic challenge. When he took office, the nation was still recovering from the severe 1975–1976 recession. To speed the recovery Carter called for increased government spending and lower taxes. When those actions provoked renewed inflation, he reversed himself, calling for spending cuts and a delay in the tax reductions. This zigzag fiscal policy eroded both business and consumer confidence. Unemployment hovered between 6 and 7 percent, and inflation rose from 6.5 percent in 1977 to 13.4 percent in 1980. As the Federal Reserve Board raised rates to counter inflation, interest rates briefly topped 20 percent in 1980, a historic high. A deep recession finally broke the inflationary spiral in 1982, a year after Carter left office.

The domestic initiatives of the Carter administration expanded the federal bureaucracy in some cases while limiting its reach in others. Carter created the separate cabinet-level departments of energy and education and approved new environmental protection measures such as the Superfund and new park and forest lands in Alaska. But continuing a trend begun by President Nixon, Carter also tried to reduce the scope of federal activities. He reformed the civil service system to streamline the federal bureaucracy and presided over the deregulation of the airline, trucking, and railroad industries. With deregulation, federal price controls on passenger fares and freight charges were eliminated in the belief that free market competition would encourage lower prices. Prices often did drop, but the resulting cutthroat competition drove many firms out of business and encouraged corporate consolidation. Carter also unsuccessfully supported gradual decontrol of oil and natural gas prices as a spur to domestic production and conservation.

Overall, however, Carter's attempt to provide leadership during the energy crisis failed. He called efforts for energy conservation "the moral equivalent of war" (borrowing a phrase from the nineteenth-century philosopher William James). The media, unable to find the specifics, reduced the phrase to "MEOW." In early 1979 a revolution in Iran spurred higher oil prices, and gas lines again reminded Americans of their dependence on foreign oil. That summer Carter's approval rating dropped to 26 percent, lower than Richard Nixon's at the height of the Watergate scandal.

Foreign Policy and Diplomacy. Jimmy Carter's commitment to human rights was the centerpiece of his new direction in foreign affairs. He criticized the suppression of dissent in the Soviet Union—especially as it affected the right of Jewish citizens to emigrate—and withdrew economic and military aid from Argentina, Uruguay, Ethiopia, and other noncommunist countries that violated human rights. He also established an Office of Human Rights within the State Department. But he could not change the internal policies of longtime U.S. allies and serious human rights violators such as the Philippines, South Korea, and South Africa. He did, however, raise the profile of human rights as a moral issue, one that future administrations would have to address.

In Latin America, Carter's most important contribution was the resolution of the lingering dispute over control of the Panama Canal. In a treaty signed on September 7, 1977, the United States agreed to turn over control of the canal to Panama on December 31, 1999. In return, the United States retained the right to send its ships through the canal in case of war, even though the canal itself would be declared neutral territory. Despite conservatives' outcry that the United States was giving away more than it got, the Senate narrowly approved the treaty.

President Carter achieved his most stunning success in the Middle East. Relations between Egypt and Israel had remained tense since the 1973 Yom Kippur War. In November 1975 Israel's prime minister, Menachem Begin, moved to break the ice by inviting the Egyptian president, Anwar Sadat, to Israel to discuss the possibility of peace. Sadat came in 1977, but the talks stalled. President Carter broke the stalemate in 1978 by inviting Begin and Sadat to Camp David, the presidential retreat in the Maryland mountains. Two weeks of discussions and Carter's promise of significant additional foreign aid to Egypt persuaded Sadat and Begin to agree on a "framework for peace." The framework included Israel's return of the Sinai peninsula, which it had occupied since 1967; the transfer of Sinai territory took place from 1979 to 1982.

Carter had campaigned to free the United States from its "inordinate fear of Communism," but relations with the Soviet Union soon became tense, largely because of problems surrounding the SALT II arms limitation talks. By the time Carter met the Soviet leader Leonid Brezhnev in Vienna in July 1979 to sign the accords, the president had ordered the construction of a new category of ballistic missiles (Pershing II) and the Soviets had gone ahead with new SS-20 missiles. The SALT II treaty of 1979, which did not cover the new

A Framework for Peace
President Jimmy Carter's greatest foreign policy achievement was the personal diplomacy that he exerted to persuade President Anwar Sadat of Egypt (left) and Prime Minister Menachem Begin of Israel (right) to sign a peace treaty in 1978.

systems, was therefore behind the current technology and could do little to stop the escalating arms race.

In December 1979 hopes for Senate ratification of the arms control treaty were dashed by the Soviet Union's invasion of Afghanistan. Carter called this the most serious threat to world peace since World War II, largely because he feared that the Soviet move was a strategic step toward the rich Middle Eastern oil supplies. In retaliation, the United States curtailed grain sales to the U.S.S.R. and boycotted the 1980 summer Olympic games in Moscow. (The Soviets returned the gesture by boycotting the 1984 summer games in Los Angeles.) When Carter left office in 1981, relations with the Soviet Union were worse than they had been when he came in.

The Iranian Hostage Crisis. The most serious foreign policy problem of the Carter administration occurred in Iran. Ever since the CIA had helped install Muhammad Reza Pahlavi on the throne in 1953, the United States had counted on his regime to be a faithful ally in the troubled Middle East. The shah was a major customer for American arms, using "petrodollars" from the sale of oil to the United States to purchase close to $20 billion worth of weapons between 1972 and 1979. President Carter had visited Iran in late 1977 and declared it "an island of stability in one of the more troubled areas of the world." With this personal endorsement, the human rights advocate Carter overlooked the repressive

tactics of Iran's CIA-trained secret police, SAVAK. For the Carter administration, as it was for the previous cold war policy makers, access to oil reserves and support for the shah's consistently anticommunist stance outweighed all other considerations.

Early in 1979 a revolution led by a fundamentalist Muslim leader, the Ayatollah Ruhollah Khomeini, overthrew the shah's government and drove him into exile. The United States had ignored warning signals that the shah's efforts to westernize Iran had offended fundamentalist Islamic leaders; the CIA had also downplayed the extent to which hatred of the United States had helped coalesce opposition to the shah. Once the mullahs (religious leaders) were in power, the United States was unsure how to deal with the new Iranian officials, who denounced the Soviet Union and the United States with equal ferocity.

In late October 1979 the Carter administration made a controversial decision to admit the deposed shah, who was suffering from incurable cancer, into the United States for medical treatment. Iran's new leaders had warned that such an action would provoke retaliation, but Henry Kissinger and other foreign policy leaders argued that the United States owed it to the shah both for humanitarian reasons and in return for his years of support for American policy. In response, on November 4, 1979, fundamentalist Muslim students under Khomeini's direction seized the U.S. embassy in Teheran, taking American hostages in a flagrant violation of the principle of diplomatic immunity. After the release of nineteen hostages, primarily women, black marines, and those

American Hostages in Iran
Images of blindfolded, handcuffed American hostages seized by Iranian militants at the American embassy in Teheran in November 1979 shocked the nation and created a foreign policy crisis that eventually cost Jimmy Carter the presidency.

with serious illnesses, fifty-two remained in captivity. The hostage takers demanded that the shah be returned to Iran for trial and punishment, but the United States refused. President Carter suspended arms sales to Iran, froze Iranian assets in American banks, and threatened to deport Iranian students in the United States, but no more hostages were released.

For the next fourteen months the Iranian hostage crisis paralyzed the presidency of Jimmy Carter. Night after night humiliating pictures of blindfolded hostages appeared on television newscasts. (Media-conscious Iranian students printed their anti-American placards in English.) The late-night television news program "Nightline," featuring the journalist Ted Koppel, originated as "America Held Hostage," a nightly update on the news from Iran that provided an unexpected way for ABC to compete with Johnny Carson's "Tonight Show."

The extensive media coverage and Carter's insistence that the safe return of the hostages was his top priority enhanced their value to their captors. But amid mounting calls for strong American action Carter could do little to win their release until the Iranian government was willing to negotiate. An attempt to mount a military rescue of the hostages failed miserably in April 1980, six months into the crisis, because of helicopter equipment failures in the desert. Secretary of State Cyrus Vance, who had not been informed about the rescue attempt, resigned in protest, claiming that it had further endangered the lives of the hostages. The abortive rescue mission reinforced the view of Carter as bumbling and ineffective.

The White House took on an embattled tone. President Carter decided not to campaign in the presidential primary elections that were under way in 1980, claiming that he wanted to devote all his energy to the safe return of the hostages. This "above politics" stance helped Carter beat back a challenge from Senator Edward Kennedy of Massachusetts for the Democratic nomination but worked against him during the general presidential campaign.

The Election of 1980

With Carter embroiled in the hostage crisis, the Republicans gained momentum and nominated a former California governor, Ronald Reagan. Born in Tampico, Illinois, Reagan won a modest reputation as a Hollywood actor in the late 1930s and early 1940s. After World War II he served as president of the Screen Actors Guild and was deeply affected by the anticommunist crusade in Hollywood. He testified before the House Un-American Activities Committee in 1947 and cooperated with studio owners and the FBI in blacklisting alleged Communists from the film industry. His political philosophy shifted from New Deal Democrat to conservative Republican, and in 1954 he began to work as a

corporate spokesman on television for General Electric. After endorsing Barry Goldwater in 1964, Reagan decided to enter politics. Following his two terms as governor of California from 1967 to 1975, Reagan made a bid for the presidency but lost the nomination to Gerald Ford. During the 1980 primaries he handily dispatched his opponents, including former U.N. ambassador and CIA director George Bush, whom he then chose as his running mate.

In the final months of the campaign, Carter took on an embattled and defensive tone while Reagan remained upbeat and decisive. Reagan continually harped on the hostage stalemate, calling the Iranians "barbarians" and "common criminals" and hinting that he would take strong action to win the hostages' return. More important, Reagan effectively appealed to the politics of resentment that flourished during the lean years of the 1970s. In a televised debate between the candidates, Reagan emphasized the economic plight of working- and middle-class Americans when he posed the rhetorical question, "Are you better off today than you were four years ago?" Battered by inflation, unemployment, and income stagnation, many viewers answered no.

In the general election in November, Reagan and Bush won handily with 51 percent of the popular vote to Carter's 41 percent (see Map 32.3). The Republican landslide also gave that party control of the Senate for the first time since 1954, although the Democrats maintained their hold on the House. Voter turnout, however, was at its lowest level since the 1920s; only 53 percent of those eligible went to the polls, and many poor and working-class voters stayed away. Nevertheless, the election confirmed the growing power of the Republican party since Richard Nixon's victory in 1968, and Reagan's more hard-line conservatism helped push the party to the right.

One key to the Republican resurgence of the 1970s was money. As the party of the wealthy and the business community, Republicans had access to financial resources that far exceeded those available to the Democrats, whose main support had traditionally come from organized labor. The political action committees that had proliferated under the Fair Campaign Practices Act of 1974 collected large sums for both parties, but particularly for the Republicans. The GOP's financial superiority enabled it to make sophisticated and effective use of television and direct mail to reach voters directly.

Another key was a realignment of the electorate. The core of the Republican party that elected Ronald Reagan remained the upper-middle-class white Protestant voters who supported balanced budgets, disliked government activism, feared crime and communism, and believed in a strong national defense. Those values had been the essence of postwar conservatism. Now new groups gravitated toward the Republican vision, often for reasons of economic self-interest: southern whites disaffected by big government and black civil

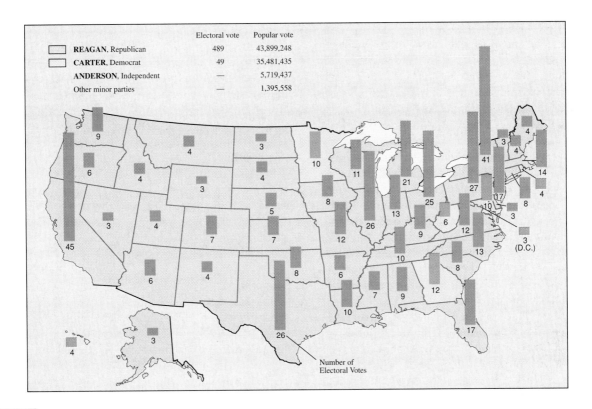

MAP 32.3

The Election of 1980
Ronald Reagan defeated the Democratic incumbent, Jimmy Carter, winning all but five states and the District of Columbia. Winning 51 percent of the popular vote, Reagan cut deeply into the traditional Democratic coalition by wooing many southern whites, urban ethnics, and blue-collar workers. Republicans also won control of the Senate for the first time since 1954.

rights gains; urban ethnics who had moved to the suburbs; blue-collar workers, especially Catholics; young voters who identified themselves as conservatives; and voters in the West, a region traditionally more conservative than the East and the Midwest. With the wooing of these "Reagan Democrats," the Republican party made deep inroads into Democratic territory, eroding that party's traditional coalition of southerners, blacks, laborers, and urban ethnics.

Perhaps the most significant constituency energizing the Republican party was the New Right, whose emphasis on traditional values and fundamentalist Christian morality dovetailed well with conservative Republican ideology. In 1980 its concerns formed the basis for the party's platform, which called for a constitutional ban on abortion, voluntary prayer in the public schools, and a mandatory death penalty for certain crimes. The Republican party also demanded an end to court-mandated busing and, for the first time in forty years, opposed the Equal Rights Amendment. A key factor in the 1980 election, the emergence of the New Right contributed to the conservative rebirth of the Republican party under Ronald Reagan.

At the exact moment when Carter turned over the presidency to Reagan on January 20, 1981, the Iranian government released the American hostages after 444 days of captivity. The hostages returned home to an ecstatic patriotic welcome, a reflection of American frustration over their long ordeal. While most Americans continued to maintain that "We're Number One," the hostage crisis in Iran came to symbolize the loss of America's power to control world affairs. Its psychological impact was magnified because it came at the end of the decade that had witnessed Watergate, the American defeat in Vietnam, and the OPEC embargo. To a great extent this decline in influence was magnified by the unusual predominance the United States had enjoyed after World War II, an advantage that could not realistically have been expected to last forever. The return to economic and political power of Japan and Western Europe, the control of vital oil resources by Middle Eastern countries, and the industrialization of some Third World nations had widened the cast of international actors. Still, many Americans were unable to accept anything less than the economic and political supremacy of the postwar years. Ronald Reagan rode their frustrations to victory in 1980.

Summary

With his election to the presidency in 1968, Richard Nixon became a harbinger of a more conservative period in American social and political life. During his five years in the White House, Nixon sought to trim back the welfare state through federal revenue sharing, cutbacks in Great Society programs, and a weaker commitment to civil rights. But Nixon did not shrink from the use of executive power; he implemented wage and price controls to fight inflation, periodically impounded federal funds, and expanded the role of the federal government in environmental and consumer affairs. Nixon's plans, however, were cut short after his administration took part in a series of illegal acts during his campaign for reelection in 1972. The resulting Watergate scandal led to Nixon's resignation in 1974.

For much of the decade the United States struggled with economic problems, including high inflation, skyrocketing energy costs, stagnation of income, and a diminished position in world trade. A series of gas shortages during the Arab oil embargo of 1973–1974 and the Iranian revolution in 1979 had a devastating impact on American society and caused many people to question the country's voracious pattern of energy consumption.

Although many Americans became cynical about politics after Watergate and Vietnam, some continued to pursue the unfinished social agenda of the 1960s. Most notably, the environmental and women's movements showed dynamic growth and activism at the grass-roots level. Movements for consumer protection, gay and lesbian rights, and racial equality also continued to make modest gains. By the late 1970s, however, a new, more conservative social mood—based in part on the resurgence of evangelical Christianity—limited further progress on issues such as abortion, the Equal Rights Amendment, busing, gay and lesbian rights, and affirmative action.

On the national level, ineffective political leadership under Gerald Ford led to his defeat in 1976 by Jimmy Carter of Georgia, who campaigned as an outsider. Taking a high moral tone, Carter made human rights a priority of his administration and helped negotiate the Camp David peace accords between Egypt and Israel in 1978. But Carter's inexperience, mounting economic problems, and growing troubles abroad plagued his administration. The end of the decade was dominated by the Iranian hostage crisis as Islamic fundamentalists held fifty-two hostages at the U.S. embassy in Teheran for 444 days. The hostage crisis virtually paralyzed Carter's presidency, helping Ronald Reagan win election in 1980.

TIMELINE

1968	Richard Nixon elected president
1970	Earth Day first observed Environmental Protection Agency established
1971	Pentagon Papers published Nixon suspends Bretton Woods system *Swann v. Charlotte-Mecklenberg* institutes busing
1972	Revenue sharing begins Watergate break-in; Nixon reelected Congress passes Equal Rights Amendment
1973	Spiro Agnew resigns; Gerald Ford appointed vice-president *Roe v. Wade* legalizes abortion
1973–1974	Arab oil embargo; gas shortages
1974	Nixon resigns; Ford becomes president and pardons Nixon
1974–1975	Busing controversy in Boston Recession
1976	Jimmy Carter elected president
1978	Carter brokers Camp David accords *Bakke v. University of California* limits affirmative action Love Canal crisis begins
1979	Hostages seized at American embassy in Teheran, Iran Second oil crisis Three Mile Island nuclear accident Formal recognition of People's Republic of China U.S.S.R. invades Afghanistan
1980	Superfund created to clean up chemical pollution Ronald Reagan elected president

BIBLIOGRAPHY

A definitive scholarly history of the 1970s has yet to be written. Peter N. Carroll's popular history, *It Seemed Like Nothing Happened* (1982), provides a general overview of the period, as do Paul Boyer's chapters on the 1970s in *Promises to Keep* (1995).

The Nixon Years

Jonathan Schell, *The Time of Illusion* (1976), offers an insightful discussion of the Nixon administration. Herbert Parmet, *Richard Nixon and His America* (1990), and Stephen Ambrose's three-volume *Nixon* (1987, 1991), are two of many biographies of a complex political leader. Kim McQuaid, *The Anxious Years: America in the Vietnam-Watergate Era* (1989), is an overview of the Nixon era. See also Garry Wills, *Nixon Agonistes* (rev. ed., 1990), and Nixon's own recollections in *RN: The Memoirs of Richard Nixon* (1978).

Stanley Kutler, *The Wars of Watergate* (1990); J. Anthony Lukas, *Nightmare: The Underside of the Nixon Years* (1976); and Theodore H. White, *Breach of Faith* (1975), are comprehensive accounts of the Watergate scandal. Also of interest are the books by the *Washington Post* journalists who broke the story, Carl Bernstein and Bob Woodward: *All the President's Men* (1974) and *The Final Days* (1976).

Lowered Expectations and New Challenges

Barry Commoner, *The Closing Circle* (1971) and *The Poverty of Power* (1976), and Robert Heilbroner, *An Inquiry into the Human Prospect* (1974), cogently assess the origins of the energy crisis and the prospects for the future. See also Lester C. Thurow, *The Zero-Sum Society* (1980); Daniel Yergin, *The Prize* (1991); and J. C. Hurewitz, ed., *Oil, the Arab-Israeli Dispute, and the Industrial World* (1976).

General introductions to the economic developments of the decade are Barry Bluestone and Bennett Harrison, *The Deindustrialization of America* (1982); Richard J. Barnet, *The Lean Years* (1980); John P. Hoerr, *And the Wolf Finally Came: The Decline of the Steel Industry* (1988); Robert Calleo, *The Imperious Economy* (1982); and Gardner Means et al., *The Roots of Inflation* (1975).

Social Gridlock

Tom Wolfe gave the decade its name in "The Me Decade and the Third Great Awakening," *New York Magazine* (August 23, 1976). Influential books include Christopher Lasch, *The Culture of Narcissism* (1978), and Gail Sheehy, *Passages* (1976).

For a general overview of the environmental movement, see Samuel P. Hays, *Beauty, Health, and Permanence: Environmental Politics in the United States, 1955–1985* (1987). Roderick Nash provides a history of environmental ethics in *The Rights of Nature* (1989). Books that were influential in shaping public awareness of ecological issues include Rachel Carson, *Silent Spring* (1962); Paul R. Ehrlich, *The Population Bomb* (1968); and Philip Slater, *Earthwalk* (1974). Lois Marie Gibbs describes her experience with the Love Canal crisis in *Love Canal: My Story* (1982). Charles McCarry chronicles Ralph Nader's crusade for consumer protection in *Citizen Nader* (1972).

On women and feminism in the 1970s, see Alice Echols, *Daring to Be Bad* (1989); Susan M. Hartmann, *From Margin to Mainstream: American Women and Politics since 1960* (1989); and Winifred D. Wandersee, *On the Move: American Women in the 1970s* (1988). Donald G. Mathews and Jane S. De Hart analyze the struggle over the ERA in *Sex, Gender, and the Politics of ERA* (1990). David Garrow, *Liberty and Sexuality: The Right to Privacy and the Making of* Roe v. Wade (1994), is an in-depth examination of the 1973 abortion decision. On the public abortion debate see Faye Ginsberg, *Contested Lives* (1989), and Kristen Luker, *Abortion and the Politics of Motherhood* (1984).

Leigh W. Rutledge surveys the gay and lesbian movement in *The Gay Decades: From Stonewall to the Present* (1992). Thomas Byrne Edsall with Mary D. Edsall, *Chain Reaction: The Impact of Race, Rights and Taxes on American Politics* (1991), examines some of the divisive social issues of the 1970s. J. Anthony Lukas, *Common Ground* (1985), tells the story of the Boston busing crisis in the biographies of three families. Nathan Glazer, *Affirmative Discrimination* (1975); Thomas Sowell, *Race and Economics* (1975); and Allan P. Sindler, *Bakke, DeFunis, and Minority Admissions* (1978), treat the controversial topic of affirmative action.

Alan Crawford, *Thunder on the Right* (1980), and Peter Steinfels, *The Neo-Conservatives* (1979), survey the new conservatism. John Woodridge, *The Evangelicals* (1975), analyzes the rise of evangelical religion, while Quentin J. Schultze looks at evangelicals' use of the media in *Televangelism and American Culture* (1991). On the political role of the Christian right see Michael Liensch, *Redeeming America: Piety and Politics in the New Christian Right* (1993).

Post-Watergate Politics

Much of the material on post-Watergate politics has been provided by journalists rather than historians. James Cannon, *Time and Chance: Gerald Ford's Appointment with History* (1993); Richard Reeves, *A Ford, Not a Lincoln* (1975); and John Osborne, *White House Watch: The Ford Years* (1977), cover the Ford presidency. See also A. James Reichley, *Conservatives in an Age of Change: The Nixon and Ford Administrations* (1981).

Generally unfavorable portraits of the Carter presidency are found in Burton Kaufman, *The Presidency of James Earl Carter, Jr.* (1993); Robert Shogan, *Promises to Keep* (1977); Haynes Johnson, *In the Absence of Power* (1980); and Clark Mollenhoff, *The President Who Failed* (1980). See also Erwin Hargrove, *Jimmy Carter as President* (1989), and Charles Jones, *The Trusteeship Presidency* (1988). See also Jimmy Carter's presidential memoirs, *Keeping Faith* (rev. ed., 1995). James Fallows, *National Defense* (1981), provides an incisive overview of defense developments. See also A. Glenn Mower, Jr., *Human Rights and American Foreign Policy: The Carter and Reagan Experiences* (1987). Gary Sick, *All Fall Down: America's Tragic Encounter with Iran* (1986), provides an account of the Iranian hostage crisis, and Jack Germond, *Blue Smoke and Mirrors* (1981), examines the presidential election of 1980.

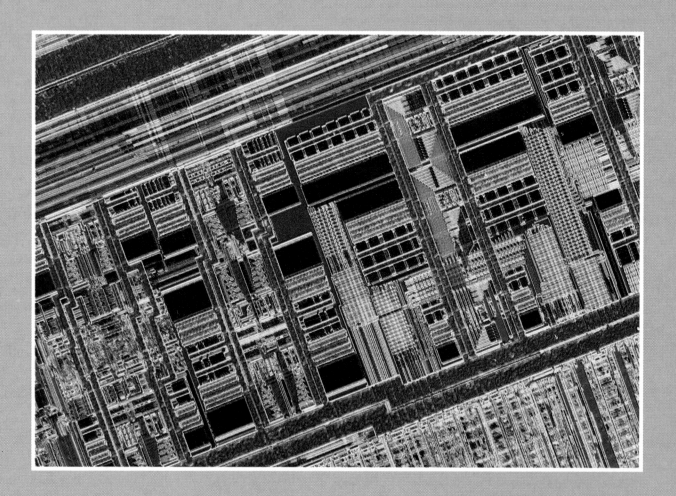

The Soul of the Machine

This magnification of a Pentium computer chip could almost be mistaken for an aerial view of a small town surrounded by well-tended parks and gardens.

A New Domestic and World Order

1981 to the Present

★ ★ ★

I n the 1920s Americans were drawn into a national web of shared experience. In the 1980s and 1990s globalization linked Americans with the rest of the world. Political choices made in Washington had international economic implications. But decisions made in Tokyo, Beijing, Bonn, and Brussels were becoming just as important, affecting the kinds of consumer products Americans could buy, interest rates, and even whether American workers kept their jobs. As the "old world order"—U.S. economic dominance and cold war rivalry—came to an end in the 1980s and 1990s, America began to share power and influence with other nations in an interconnected global economy.

Paradoxically, with the collapse of the Soviet Union in 1991, the United States achieved military dominance as the world's only remaining superpower. For forty-five years the Cold War had shaped American foreign and domestic policy. The "new world order" that would replace the old political relationships among nations was still emerging, but it was clear that the international community continued to seek American leadership on issues of peace and war.

As the United States struggled to redefine its role in the world, a crucial debate raged at home over the role of the state. The rise of the state, one of the most important developments in twentieth-century American history, was slowed and even partially reversed by Ronald Reagan's election in 1980 and the election of a Republican Congress in 1994. New Deal liberalism and an activist federal government were in retreat. In his 1996 State of the Union address, President Clinton acknowledged this new domestic order by declaring, "The era of big government is over." As the United States approached a new century in which the economic challenges of global competition would replace the military challenges of the Cold War, Americans were asking basic questions about the role of government in national life.

The Reagan Presidency, 1981–1989

Ronald Reagan's overwhelming victory in the 1980 election reflected the new electoral clout of the Sun Belt, a region traditionally more conservative than the Northeast or Midwest (see Map 33.1). Reagan seized the chance to redefine the nation's priorities. Since the New Deal programs of the 1930s, Americans had generally assumed that the nation's social and economic problems could best be solved by federal action. The election of Ronald Reagan called into question almost half a century of activism. "Government is not the solution to our problem," he declared. "Government is the problem." During his tenure in office only the defense budget continued to grow dramatically as part of a massive military buildup.

The Reagan Style

When the sixty-nine-year-old Ronald Wilson Reagan took office in January 1981, he was the oldest man ever to serve as president. (He was actually six years older than John F. Kennedy would have been if Kennedy had lived.) He showed his remarkable physical stamina just months into office when he survived an assassination attempt outside a Washington, D.C., hotel. Just as robust was his personal popularity, which remained comparatively high throughout his two terms. He became known as the "Great Communicator" because of his ability to establish a rapport with the American people through the medium of television.

During his long acting career and eight years as governor of California, Reagan had developed a somewhat removed leadership style. Once, when asked what kind of governor he would be, he replied, "I don't know, I've never played a governor." Many observers found him better at generalizations and encouragement than at details: "We have a great task ahead of us," Reagan would say, but he would never state what that task was. Recalled Donald Regan, who was named secretary of the Treasury after one brief phone conversation, "From the first day to the last at Treasury, I was flying by the seat of my pants. The President never told me . . . what he wanted to accomplish in the field of economics."

To maintain his hands-off style of governing, Reagan depended on the support and advice of his ap-

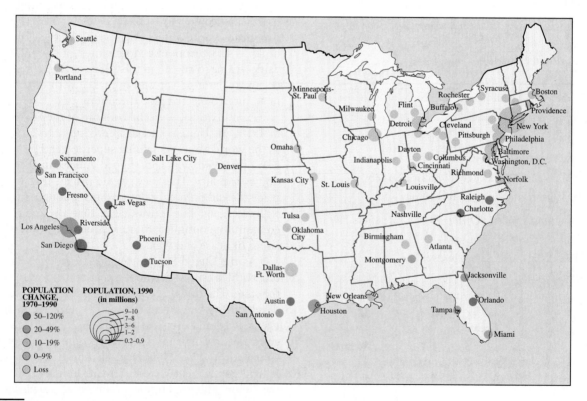

MAP 33.1

The Growth of the Sun Belt, 1970–1990
The Sun Belt states of the South and the West were key to the Republican resurgence in the 1980s. Whereas older industrial cities such as New York, Chicago, Philadelphia, and Detroit lost population, newer metropolises—Phoenix, Houston, and San Diego—grew spectacularly.

The Great Communicator
Ronald Reagan felt totally at home in front of the camera, trading stories and one-liners with audiences and the press. Commentator Gary Wills observed, "Reagan runs continuously in everyone's home movies of the mind. . . . He is, in the strictest sense, what Hollywood promoters used to call 'fabulous'."

pointees. Among his closest advisers were Chief of Staff James Baker, presidential counselors Edwin Meese and Michael Deaver, and Regan, who became chief of staff in 1985 when Baker moved to the Treasury. Reagan also relied heavily on his wife, Nancy, who was fiercely protective of both his image and his schedule, even to the point of consulting an astrologer before planning major White House events.

Reaganomics

Reagan and his economic team's first priority was to reshape the nation's fiscal and tax policies. The term *Reaganomics* came to stand for the tax cuts and domestic budget reductions enacted in 1981 and 1982 and the controversial *supply-side* economic theory that lay behind them. According to this theory, high taxes siphoned capital that would otherwise be invested to stimulate economic growth. Tax cuts would give businesses and individuals more money to invest, investments would cause the economy to expand, and total

tax revenues would be greater—despite the lower tax rates. Government expenditures would be trimmed by shrinking government benefits, especially entitlement programs such as welfare that had begun during the New Deal. And the federal budget deficit would go down. That, at least, was the theory. Critics charged that conservative Republicans deliberately cut taxes to force reductions in federal funding for the social programs that they abhorred.

The first part of this economic policy—tax cuts—was enacted in the Economic Recovery Tax Act of 1981, arguably the most significant legislation of the Reagan years. Based on a proposal by Senator William Roth of Delaware and Representative Jack Kemp of New York, this across-the-board tax cut reduced basic personal income tax rates 25 percent over three years. It also introduced the indexation of tax brackets, which kept tax rates constant when incomes rose solely because of inflation. According to the budget director, David Stockman, the tax cut was supposed to be linked with large cutbacks in expenditures, especially in human services. Congressional resistance kept programs such as Social Security and Medicare intact, but more than half of Reagan's proposed cuts were enacted, including cuts in Food Stamps, unemployment compensation, and welfare programs such as Aid to Families with Dependent Children (AFDC).

All the money saved—and far more—was plowed into a $1.2 trillion, five-year defense buildup orchestrated by the president and Defense Secretary Caspar Weinberger. This huge increase fulfilled Reagan's campaign pledge to "make America Number One again" militarily. The B-1 bomber, which Carter had canceled, was resurrected, and the development of a new missile system, the MX, was begun. Reagan's most ambitious, and controversial, weapons plan was the 1983 Strategic Defense Initiative (SDI), popularly known as "Star Wars" from the movie of that name. SDI would be a satellite and laser shield to detect and intercept incoming missiles. Reagan supporters claimed that SDI would render nuclear war obsolete, but scientists doubted its feasibility.

Another basic tenet of Reaganomics was that many federal regulations were unnecessary and impeded productivity because of the high cost of compliance. Thus, the administration moved to abolish or reduce federal regulations affecting the workplace, health care, consumer protection, and the environment. Much of the responsibility, and the cost, of those activities was transferred to the states.

Meanwhile, the Federal Reserve Board used monetary policy to combat inflation, which had been high since the mid–1970s. By raising the interest rate for corporate borrowers, the Federal Reserve reduced inflation from 12.4 percent in 1980 to 4 percent in 1982. But tightening the money supply in that way also reduced business investment, contributing to a relatively brief but severe recession in 1981–1982. The economy began growing again early in 1983. For the rest of the decade inflation stayed low, aided by a worldwide drop in energy costs, and the Reagan administration presided over the longest peacetime economic expansion in American history. But this economic growth in the 1980s was unexceptional, with the gross national product growing at about 2.5 percent a year (below the average of 2.8 percent in the 1970s) and productivity growth averaging only a little over 1 percent a year.

If all had gone according to the administration's plan, the budget should have been balanced by 1984, but that did not happen. Supply-side economics did not work as advertised, and the promised increased revenue from economic growth fell far short of expectations. Furthermore, despite what seemed like wrenching cuts in federal programs, the drop in revenues from the tax cuts was far steeper than the amount pruned from the budget, mainly because of the military buildup. Federal deficits began to balloon alarmingly.

Foreign Relations

Détente had collapsed late in the Carter administration after the Soviet Union's invasion of Afghanistan. Reagan entered the presidency with a confrontational approach toward the Soviet Union, including a strong commitment to stopping communist expansion in developing nations. Giving voice to the beliefs of Republican hard-liners, Reagan articulated some of the harshest anti-Soviet rhetoric since the 1950s, calling the Soviet Union an "evil empire."

The administration reserved its most concerted attention for Central America. Halting what was seen as the spread of communism in that region became practically an obsession. In El Salvador it supported a repressive right-wing regime that was fighting against leftists. In 1983 Reagan ordered U.S. Marines to invade the tiny Caribbean island of Grenada, claiming that its Cuban-supported communist regime posed a threat to other states in the region.

Reagan's top priority, however, was to overthrow the Sandinista government in Nicaragua. The Sandinistas were former guerrillas who had overthrown the right-wing regime of President Anastasio Somoza in 1979. They were leftists but not communists, although they were friendly with Marxist leaders such as Cuba's Fidel Castro. In 1981 the United States suspended aid to Nicaragua, charging that the Sandinista government, along with Cuba and the Soviet Union, was supplying arms to the rebels in El Salvador, a charge that the Sandinistas denied. At the same time, the CIA began to provide extensive covert support to Nicaragua's opposition forces, known as the "Contras," or counterrevolutionaries. Reagan called the Contras "freedom fighters," but Congress was not convinced. In 1984 it passed the Boland Amendment, banning the CIA or any other intelligence agency from providing military support to the Contras. Thus began a tug of war between Congress and the Reagan administration that would produce the greatest crisis of Reagan's presidency.

Reagan's Second Term

The 1984 Election. In 1984 the Democrats nominated Walter Mondale, Carter's vice-president and a former Minnesota senator, to run against Ronald Reagan. A protégé of Hubert Humphrey with strong ties to labor unions, minority groups, and party leaders, Mondale epitomized the New Deal coalition. He appealed to many women voters by selecting Representative Geraldine Ferraro of New York as his running mate, the first woman on a major party ticket. Reagan campaigned on the theme "It's Morning in America," suggesting that a new day of prosperity and pride was dawning. Voters gave him a landslide victory in which he carried the entire country except Minnesota and the District of Columbia. He did especially well among young (eighteen-to twenty-one-year-old) voters, receiving 62 percent of their support.

After a string of administrations that had ended in discord (Johnson and Vietnam), disgrace (Nixon and Watergate), or frustration (Carter and Iran), many Americans responded warmly to Reagan's confident leadership. Reagan was a convincing performer, and voters believed him when he said he could solve the nation's problems. Reagan's enormous personal popularity recalled that of Dwight Eisenhower in the 1950s. Also like Eisenhower,

A First for the Nation
Geraldine Ferraro, Walter Mondale's running mate in 1984, was the first woman nominated by a major party to its national ticket. Despite her presence, a majority of women voted for Reagan in the 1984 Republican landslide.

his coattails were short: Democrats maintained control of the House and picked up two seats in the Senate; they would regain control of the Senate in 1986.

The Iran-Contra Affair. Reagan's second term was marred by a major scandal in 1986. A Beirut, Lebanon, newspaper broke the story that the administration had negotiated an arms-for-hostages deal with the revolutionary government of Iran, the same government Reagan had denounced during the 1980 hostage crisis. At the instigation of the CIA's director, William Casey, and the national security adviser, Robert McFarlane, the United States had secretly sold arms to Iran, which was locked in a costly and lengthy war with neighboring Iraq. The intent was to gain Iran's help in freeing American hostages held by pro-Iranian forces in Lebanon. (Only one hostage was released.) These arm sales generated large profits, some of which, in the most controversial aspect of what became known as the Iran-Contra affair, were diverted as military aid for the Contras in Nicaragua. The diversion was both illegal (contravening the Boland Amendment) and unconstitutional (bypassing the sole right of Congress to appropriate funds).

The arms-for-hostages deal had been discussed at the highest levels of government, but the diversion of funds to the Contras seems to have been the brainstorm of Marine Lieutenant Colonel Oliver North, who was on assignment to the National Security Council. After the American press picked up the story, North shredded hundreds of documents but missed a key memo that linked the White House to the plan. Congress investigated the mounting scandal in 1986 and 1987, but White House officials testifed that the president knew nothing about the diversion. Ronald Reagan's defense remained simple and consistent: "I don't remember."

The full story of the illegal arms operation may never be known. The scandal bore many similarities to Watergate, including the possibility that the president had acted illegally, but this time there were no significant calls for impeachment. Early in Reagan's administration, Representative Patricia Schroeder of Colorado, one of his harshest critics in Congress, had coined the phrase "Teflon presidency" to describe Reagan—bad news didn't stick; it just rolled off. Reagan weathered "Iran-Contragate," but the scandal did weaken his presidency.

The Return of Détente. His authority diminished by scandal and facing a Congress once again controlled by Democrats, Reagan proposed no bold initiatives in domestic policy in his last two years in office. Surprisingly for a man who had instigated a massive arms buildup to halt the spread of communism and had refused to meet with Soviet leaders, the greatest success of Reagan's second term was a reduction in tensions with the Soviet Union.

This shift was facilitated by the ascent to power in 1985 of Mikhail Gorbachev. In that year, Gorbachev and Reagan met in Geneva at the first superpower summit meeting since 1979. They met again the following year in Reykjavik, Iceland. In December 1987 Reagan and Gorbachev agreed at a Washington summit to eliminate all intermediate-range missiles based in Europe, the first time an existing category of weapons had been scrapped, and the most significant postwar disarmament decision since the 1972 SALT I agreement. Although a fourth summit in Moscow in April 1988 produced no further cuts in nuclear arms, the sight of the two first families attending the Bolshoi Ballet together and strolling amiably in Red Square demonstrated the new cordial relationship between the former rivals. (The incongruity of consummate cold warrior Ronald Reagan in Red Square was on a par with the sight of Richard Nixon strolling along the Great Wall of China in 1972.) When the Soviets announced soon afterward that they were withdrawing from Afghanistan, prospects for cooperation appeared to be even brighter.

Reagan Legacies

Reagan came into the presidency promising to dismantle an intrusive federal bureaucracy, reduce federal entitlement programs, give free-market forces greater scope in the economy, and stand up to the Soviet menace. Whereas he made significant progress toward some of his goals, overall the so-called Reagan Revolution proved to be more of a "Reagan revision." Reagan reordered the priorities of the national government but failed to reduce its size or scope. When he left office, government functions remained much as he had found them. Although spending for most poverty programs had been cut, Social Security and other entitlement programs remained untouched. But the spending cuts and Reagan's antigovernment rhetoric had changed the terms of political debate and laid the foundation for the Republican landslide in 1994.

One of Reagan's most significant legacies was his conservative judicial appointments, the area where the New Right had the greatest impact on his administration. In 1981 Reagan nominated Sandra Day O'Connor to the Supreme Court, the first woman ever to serve; he later appointed two other justices, Antonin Scalia and Anthony Kennedy, who were far more conservative than the moderate O'Connor. Justice William Rehnquist, a noted conservative who had been appointed by Nixon, was elevated to chief justice in 1986. The former Supreme Court justice William Brennan used to tell his clerks, "Five votes can do anything around here," and under Rehnquist's leadership the Court, often by a 5–4 margin, chipped away at the Warren Court's legacy in areas such as individual liberties, affirmative action, and the rights of criminal defendants.

Another Barrier Falls

In 1981 Sandra Day O'Connor (shown here with Chief Justice Warren Burger) became the first woman appointed to the Supreme Court. In 1993 she was joined by Ruth Bader Ginsburg.

Ironically, for a president who had promised to balance the budget by 1984, Reagan's most enduring legacy was the national debt, which tripled during his two terms from the combined effects of vastly increased military spending, substantial tax reductions for high-income taxpayers, and Congress's refusal to approve the deep cuts in domestic programs that Reagan requested (see Figure 33.1). There had been federal deficits before, but never on this scale. In 1989 the national debt stood at $2.8 trillion, more than $11,000 for every American citizen. Interest payments on the borrowed money, $216 billion per year by 1988, were the fastest-growing item in the federal budget.

Trade with other nations was also running at an annual deficit that reached $171 billion in 1987. Exports had been falling since the 1970s as American products encountered increasing competition in world markets. The high exchange rate for dollars in the early 1980s made U.S. goods more expensive for foreign buyers whereas imports became more affordable for Americans. The budget and trade deficits contributed to a major shift in 1985: for the first time since 1915 the United States was a debtor, not a creditor, nation. Since then, with phenomenal speed, the United States has accumulated the world's largest foreign debt.

It was difficult for the political system to address the annual budget deficits and their ramifications. Members of Congress were unwilling to cut programs that their

FIGURE 33.1

The Escalating Federal Debt, 1939–1994

The federal debt, which soared during World War II, remained fairly stable until the huge annual deficits of the 1980s. Deficits still remained high in the 1990s but political pressure to balance the budget promised reductions in the national debt.

Source: U.S. Statistical Abstract, 1995.

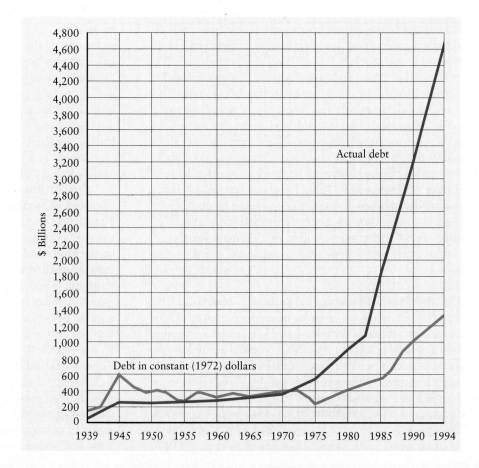

constituents depended on for services or jobs, and few were willing to recommend new taxes. In 1985 Congress passed the Gramm-Rudman Balanced Budget and Emergency Deficit Reduction Control Act, which was intended to achieve a balanced budget by 1991 by mandating specific cuts that would be instituted automatically if deficit reduction targets were not met. (The cuts were never implemented.) The annual deficit peaked at $221 billion in 1986 and then dropped slightly before leveling off, but the damage had been done. The national debt, along with the interest needed to service it, will continue to be a drag on the nation's economy and social fabric well into the twenty-first century.

The Bush Presidency and the End of the Cold War, 1989–1993

George Herbert Walker Bush had been a loyal vice-president, but he did not share all of Reagan's conservative views. In fact, many Americans wondered if he had any ideology at all. The debt inherited from the Reagan years, along with Bush's preference for foreign affairs, kept him from articulating a clear domestic agenda. The end of the Cold War removed the Soviet Union as a credible threat, but new post–cold war challenges quickly appeared. During the Persian Gulf crisis in 1990 Bush called for a "new world order . . . in which nations recognize the shared responsibility for freedom and injustice." As events abroad progressed dramatically, especially the collapse of the Soviet Union in 1991, the United States grappled with the implications of this new world order.

The Bush Administration

The 1988 Election. Bush won the Republican nomination by beating back challenges from the Senate minority leader Robert Dole, the television evangelist Pat Robertson, and the tax-cutting representative Jack Kemp. He chose a young conservative Indiana senator, Dan Quayle, for vice-president. Even many Republicans questioned Quayle's qualifications to assume the duties of the president, while Democrats, noting his hawkish views on defense, charged him with hypocrisy for having avoided service in Vietnam by joining the Indiana National Guard.

The Democratic primaries became a contest between Governor Michael Dukakis of Massachusetts and the charismatic civil rights leader Jesse Jackson, whose populist Rainbow Coalition embraced the diversity of Democratic constituencies. Dukakis, a somewhat bland figure known for a technocratic approach to state government, won the nomination. For his vice-president, he passed over Jackson in favor of Senator Lloyd Bentsen of Texas.

The 1988 campaign had a harsh cast to it, with negative commercials and brief televised *sound bites* replacing discussion of the issues. The sound bite "Read My Lips: No New Taxes" from Bush's acceptance speech at the Republican convention became that party's campaign mantra. A television ad criticizing Massachusetts' prison furlough program pandered to racist fears by including a mug shot of Willie Horton, a black convicted murderer who had committed another murder while on parole. Forced on the defensive, Dukakis failed to mount an effective campaign. Bush carried thirty-eight states, winning the popular vote 53.4 percent to 45.6 percent. Only 50 percent of eligible voters went to the polls.

Domestic and Economic Policy. In his campaign Bush had promised to preside over a "kinder, gentler administration" and, without giving specifics, announced his intention to go down in history as the education and environment president. He made good on the first part by convening the meeting of state governors that launched the Goals 2000 initiative to write national standards for public schools. His environmental policy was less substantial. Bush's appointments to the Environmental Protection Agency, such as William Ruckelshaus as its head, were more moderate than the conservative ideologues named by Reagan, but Bush only reluctantly attended the 1992 Earth Summit in Rio de Janeiro to sign the treaty on global warming.

For the most part Bush's domestic policy was devoted to coping with the failures and the shortcomings of his predecessor's economic policies, especially the budget deficit. In his 1990 message to Congress, the budget director, Richard Darman, compared the federal budget to the Cookie Monster on "Sesame Street" because of its "excessive tendencies towards consumption." The 1985 Gramm-Rudman Act had mandated automatic cuts if budget targets were not met in 1991. Facing the prospect of a halt to nonessential government services and layoffs of thousands of government employees, Congress struggled to produce a deficit-reduction plan. The resulting bipartisan compromise combined cuts in spending with increased taxes and fees in recognition of the fact that the supply-side theory that lower taxes would produce higher revenues had not worked. Bush had been forced by inevitable circumstances to break his "no new taxes" campaign promise. Bush's acceptance of the quantitatively largest tax increase in history earned him the undying emnity of Republican conservatives, who saw it as a betrayal of Reaganomics, and would dramatically hurt his chances for reelection in 1992.

The federal government can run up deficits, but state and local governments cannot. Under Reagan's new federalism, states and localities had been forced to take over some federal programs entirely and cope with cuts in federal grants for many other programs, including housing, education, transportation, public works, and social services. Federal-state programs such as Medicaid, whose costs soared in the 1970s and 1980s as a result of inflation and higher demand, accounted for increasingly large parts of state budgets, as did spending for welfare, education, and prisons. State and local governments could balance their budgets only by finding new sources of revenue (thus risking taxpayer revolts) or by reducing spending and services. Fiscal conditions were especially bad in the Northeast, but California and several midwestern states also faced severe shortfalls.

A recession that began in 1990 further eroded state and local tax revenues. Poverty increased sharply, and incomes declined. In 1991 unemployment approached 7 percent nationwide; state and local governments laid off workers to save money even as they faced greater demands for social services and unemployment compensation. Industrial and white-collar layoffs spread, and in many American families someone had already lost a job or feared that it might happen soon. Recovery was slowed by the massive federal debt, overburdened state and local governments, and decreasing consumer confidence.

The Savings and Loan Crisis. Yet another drag on the economy was the collapse of the savings and loan industry. The scandal had its roots in decisions made during the Reagan administration, but its full impact was felt only after Bush took office.

Savings and loan associations (S & L's), also called "thrifts," invested depositors' savings in home mortgages. Since 1934 deposits in S & L's had been insured by the Federal Savings and Loan Insurance Corporation (FSLIC). After S & L's complained in 1982 that high inflation and soaring interest rates were reducing their profits, Reagan's deregulation program permitted them to invest in commercial real estate and businesses. Such investments were more risky than home mortgages, and lack of supervision from Washington encouraged many speculative deals and some fraudulent ones.

The real-estate market had boomed for most of the 1980s, and so the loans and investments were profitable. But when construction and the oil boom in the Southwest slowed and the stock market tumbled sharply in 1987, savings and loan associations' losses mounted, and the value of their assets plummeted. Some S & L's were taken over by commercial banks, but many simply went bankrupt, forcing the federal government to make good its guarantee to depositors. To recoup some of the massive losses, the Bush administration set up a temporary agency in 1989 to sell the remaining assets, primarily defaulted real estate. It took the Resolution Trust Corporation six years to clear up the mess, at a total cost to American taxpayers of $150 billion.

Supreme Court Conservatism. During the Bush administration the Supreme Court continued to move away from liberal activism toward a more conservative stance. The shift was felt especially in regard to the issue of abortion. The 1989 *Webster v. Reproductive Health Services* decision permitted states to restrict abortion, and the next year, in *Rust v. Sullivan*, the Court upheld a federal regulation that barred personnel at federally funded health clinics from discussing abortion with their clients. In 1992, in *Planned Parenthood v. Casey*, a 5–4 decision upheld a Pennsylvania law mandating a twenty-four-hour waiting period and informed consent before an abortion could be performed. Yet the Court also reaffirmed what it called the "essential holding" of *Roe v. Wade*: women have a constitutional right to abortion.

In 1990 David Souter, a little known federal judge from New Hampshire who appealed to Bush because he had not taken a stand on abortion, easily won confirmation to the Supreme Court. But the next year a major controversy erupted over Bush's nomination of Clarence Thomas, a black conservative with little judicial experi-

A Woman of Conscience
Accusations by University of Oklahoma professor Anita Hill that Supreme Court nominee Clarence Thomas had sexually harassed her sparked fierce political debate. Many felt that if there had been more women in the Senate, Professor Hill's charges would have been treated more seriously. In fact, women's representation did increase after the 1992 election to six women in the Senate and forty-seven in the House of Representatives.

ence. Just as Thomas's confirmation hearings were drawing to a close, his former colleague Anita Hill testified publicly to what she had earlier told Senate investigators: Thomas had sexually harassed her at the Department of Education and the Equal Employment Opportunity Commission in the early 1980s. After widely watched (and widely debated) televised testimony by both Thomas and Hill before the all-male Senate Judiciary Committee, the Senate confirmed Thomas by a narrow margin. In the wake of the hearings, national polls confirmed the pervasiveness of sexual harassment on the job: four out of ten women said that they had been the object of unwanted sexual advances from men at work. Politically minded women vowed to increase their representation in Congress in the 1992 election.

The Collapse of Communism

For years American policy makers had warned about the "domino" effect of countries falling to communism. Now the domino effect was unexpectedly working in the opposite direction. In 1989 the grip of communism on Eastern Europe loosened and then let go completely in a series of mostly nonviolent "velvet revolutions." Soon the Soviet Union itself succumbed to the forces of change.

The background for those dramatic upheavals lay in the changes set in motion by the Soviet president Mikhail Gorbachev after 1985. His policies of *glasnost* (openness) and *perestroika* (economic restructuring) signaled a willingness to tolerate significant changes in the Soviet bloc and in Soviet relationships with the rest of the world. Gorbachev established a strong personal rapport with both Reagan and Bush and raised enormous expectations worldwide about the possibilities of change in the U.S.S.R. But the Soviet leader, who was always more popular outside his country than at home, found it was easier to call for the dismantling of the old system than to build something new. In addition, the desire of a number of Soviet republics to apply the lessons of Eastern Europe and gain independence threatened the very existence of the country.

On August 19, 1991, while Gorbachev was vacationing at his summer home in the Crimea, officials in his own government tried to oust him. The precipitating factor was the imminent signing of the Union Treaty, which would have given limited autonomy to the fifteen Soviet republics and increased power to the republics' recently elected leaders. The plotters—officials of the Communist party, bureaucrats and overlords of the central economy, and leaders of the internal police force and KGB—stood to lose the most from decentralization. But by August 21, the coup had failed and the grip of the Communist party over the Soviet Union was bro-

Gorbachev and Bush
The leaders of the two superpowers, shown here at a press conference during the Malta summit in December 1989, developed a warm personal relationship. Some critics later felt that Bush delayed reacting to changes in the Soviet Union out of loyalty to his friend.

ken. The Baltic republics of Latvia, Estonia, and Lithuania declared their independence and soon gained diplomatic recognition from the United States and the rest of the world. In December the Union of Soviet Socialist Republics formally dissolved itself to make way for the eleven-member Commonwealth of Independent States (CIS). The charismatic reform leader Boris Yeltsin remained as president of the largest and most populous republic, Russia; Gorbachev was out of a job.

In 1956 Nikita Khruschev had told the United States, "We will bury you," but now the tombstone read, "The Soviet Union, 1917–1991." For more than forty years the United States had been locked in an ideological battle with its archenemy, the Soviet Union. American citizens had endured secret radiation experiments, fear of nuclear annihilation, and anticommunist witch-hunts. During the Cold War the United States spent some *$4 trillion* on nuclear weapons alone. Republicans claimed that Reagan's military buildup had caused the Soviet Union to collapse, but George Kennan—the only original architect of containment still alive—disagreed, dismissing such claims as "intrinsically silly": "Nobody—no country, no party, no person—'won' the cold war. . . . That the conflict should now be formally ended is a fit occasion for satisfaction but also for sober re-examination of the part we took in its origin and long continuation." As Kennan concluded, both sides paid a heavy price.

The director of the Central Intelligence Agency summed up the dilemma of forging a post–cold war policy: "We have slain a large dragon, but we live now in a jungle filled with a bewildering variety of poisonous snakes. And in many ways, the dragon was easier to keep track of." Instead of superpower confrontations, violence often arose from regional conflicts over ethnicity, religion, and nationalism, such as in Bosnia after 1991. As the only military superpower, the United States would often be asked to wield its still enormous influence in the void left by the collapse of communism. Far from receding as the Cold War ended, American military and political leadership seemed even more necessary in the new world order.

War in the Persian Gulf, 1990–1991

The first new challenge arose in the Middle East. On August 2, 1990, Iraq invaded Kuwait. Saddam Hussein's brutal conquest of his oil-rich neighbor took American policy makers by surprise. President Bush orchestrated broad international support for a series of United Nations Security Council resolutions condemning Iraq, calling for its withdrawal, and imposing an embargo and trade sanctions. The United Nations was finally working the way its Dumbarton Oaks planners had hoped, in large part because superpower tensions had abated with the end of the Cold War.

When Saddam Hussein showed no signs of complying with the resolutions, Bush prodded the United Nations to create a legal framework for an international military offensive against the man he repeatedly called "the butcher of Baghdad." In November the Security Council voted to use force if Iraq did not withdraw by January 15. In early January, Congress debated whether to give sanctions more time to work, and then, in a close 52–48 vote, the Senate authorized military action. On January 16, President Bush announced to the nation that "the liberation of Kuwait has begun."

The American commitment of 540,000 troops matched the number at the height of the Vietnam War in 1968. But this was a new, all-volunteer military that included thousands of reservists called up from civilian jobs. Blacks and members of other minorities, many attracted to military service by benefits such as education and health care, made up a third of the force. Women, accounting for approximately 10 percent of the troops, were a far greater presence than in Vietnam, although they served in support, not direct combat, positions.

The forty-two-day war was a resounding success for the coalition forces, which, as in the Korean War, were predominantly American. In a series of well-orchestrated briefings, General Colin Powell, Chairman of the Joint Chiefs of Staff, and the commanding general, H. Norman Schwarzkopf, projected a confident new image for the post-Vietnam military. The air-land strategy of Operation Desert Storm began with a month of air strikes to crush communications, destroy armaments, and pum-

mel the morale of the Iraqi troops, followed by a ground offensive against Iraqi troops in Kuwait and southern Iraq. The ground phase of the war was launched on February 23; within days thousands of Iraqi troops fled or surrendered, and the fighting quickly ended. Saddam Hussein remained in power, however (see Map 33.2).

The rapid success of the ground war and relief at the amazingly low number of U.S. casualties (145 Americans killed in action, a stark contrast to the high Iraqi civilian and military casualties) produced a euphoric reaction at home. For many, the stellar performance of American troops had banished the ghost of Vietnam, the antimilitary malaise resulting from that prolonged, inconclusive, and divisive war. "By God, we've kicked the Vietnam Syndrome once and for all," gloated George Bush. One of the biggest winners was the president, whose approval rating approached 90 percent.

Once the cheering stopped, doubts surfaced. Why wasn't George Bush providing the leadership on domestic issues that he had brought to the coalition against Saddam Hussein? If America could apply itself so purposefully to war, why couldn't it do the same for the problems of its inner cities, unemployment, the environment, and AIDS? Would the war help end the recession? One consumer observed, "The country is feeling good about the war, I'm feeling good about it, but I still can't afford a new car."

Women at War
Women played key and visible roles in the Persian Gulf War, comprising approximately 10 percent of the American troops. Increasing numbers of women are choosing to make a career out of the military, despite widespread reports of sexual harassment and other forms of discrimination.

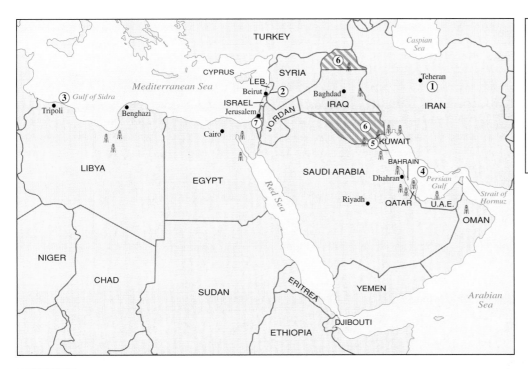

MAP 33.2

U.S. Involvement in the Middle East, 1980–1994

The United States has long played an active role in the Middle East, pursuing the twin goals of protecting Israel's security and assuring a reliable supply of low-cost oil from the Persian Gulf states. By far the largest intervention came in 1991, when, under United Nations auspices, President Bush sent 540,000 American troops to liberate Kuwait from Iraq. The United States also played a major role in the 1994 agreement allowing for Palestinian self-rule in the Gaza Strip and parts of the West Bank.

The 1992 Election

With the end of the Cold War, domestic affairs returned to their normal place at the center of American politics. As the election campaign got under way, the economy was the overriding issue, since the recession that had begun in 1990 showed no signs of abating. Bush easily won renomination, overwhelming his lone opponent, the conservative columnist Pat Buchanan. To solidify the support of the New Right, Vice-President Dan Quayle spoke out strongly for "family values" and other conservative social agendas. Bush responded to criticism that he lacked a vision for domestic affairs by blaming the Democratic Congress for thwarting his initiatives.

Bill Clinton, the longtime governor of Arkansas, one of the nation's poorest states, emerged as the Democratic front-runner. He survived charges of marital infidelity and draft dodging and questions about a dubious Arkansas real estate deal called Whitewater to win the Democratic nomination. For his running mate he chose Al Gore, a second-term senator from Tennessee widely known for his environmental best seller, *Earth in the Balance*. At age forty-four, Gore was a year and a half younger than Clinton, making them the first baby-boom national ticket.

In the middle of the primary season, the Texas billionaire H. Ross Perot announced on CNN's "Larry King Live" that he would run as an independent candidate. Perot capitalized on voters' desire for change in politics as usual, denouncing the power of lobbyists and telling voters that they "owed it to their grandchildren" to rein in the deficit. Although Perot dropped out of the race on the last day of the Democratic convention, he reentered it less than five weeks before the election, adding a well-financed wild card to that most unusual election year.

The Democrats mounted an aggressive, effective campaign that focused on Clinton's plans to solve domestic problems, especially education, health care, and the economy; Gore added expertise on defense and environmental issues. Bush was hurt by the weak economy, his continued focus on foreign policy even though the Cold War was over, and especially his reneging on the "no new taxes" pledge. On election day Clinton received 43 percent of the popular vote to Bush's 38 percent and Perot's 19 percent (see Map 33.3). Although Perot did not win a single state, his popular vote was the

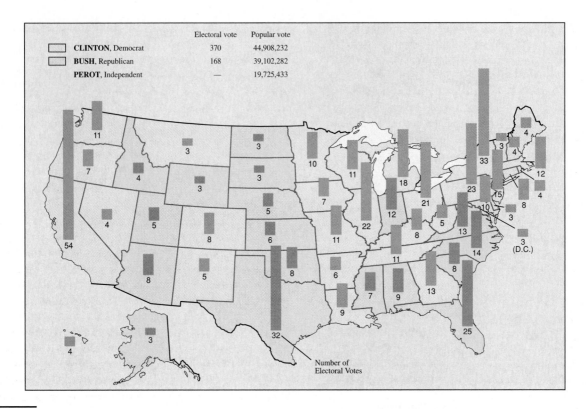

	Electoral vote	Popular vote
CLINTON, Democrat	370	44,908,232
BUSH, Republican	168	39,102,282
PEROT, Independent	—	19,725,433

MAP 33.3

The Election of 1992

The first national election since the end of the Cold War was dominated by concern over the economy. The first-ever all-southerner Democratic ticket of Bill Clinton and Al Gore won broad support across the country, cutting into Republican strongholds in the South and West. The independent candidate, H. Ross Perot, won no electoral votes but polled an impressive 19 percent of the popular vote.

highest for an independent candidate since Theodore Roosevelt in 1912. The Democrats retained control of both houses of Congress, ending twelve years of divided government. But the narrowness of Clinton's victory and the public's perception that he did not really stand for anything did not augur well for his ability to lead the country.

An Age of Anxiety

Opinion polls in the early 1990s showed that Americans were deeply worried about the future—their own and their childrens'. Concerns about the economy topped the list; the economist Paul Krugman called the 1980s and 1990s "the age of diminished expectations." But the uncertainties involved more than the economy. Just as in the 1970s, Americans turned inward toward their own needs and interests, despite the globalization of so many aspects of modern American life.

The New Economic Order

The slow growth in productivity and the growing inequality in income distribution have been the two most salient economic trends of the past two decades. From the late nineteenth century through World War II productivity grew at an average of about 1.8 percent per year, enough to double living standards every forty years. From 1945 until 1973 productivity grew 2.8 percent annually, allowing the standard of living to double in one generation. Since 1973, however, productivity has increased less than 1 percent annually, barely enough to double the standard of living in eighty years. (Productivity began to rise a little more sharply around 1992, but it is too early to tell if this represents a long-term trend.)

Along with slowed productivity went stagnating real income (see Figure 33.2). Adjusted for inflation, the wages of the typical, or median, family basically stayed the same. In 1991 the typical family's real income was only 5 percent higher than it had been in 1973, and that increase was achieved mainly because Americans were working more hours and because multiple members of a household were employed.

At the same time that wage stagnation was squeezing the middle class, economic inequality increased—the rich got richer, the poor got poorer, and the middle class shrank. Instead of the broadly based prosperity of the postwar years, statistics from the Congressional Budget Office showed that the richest *1 percent* of American families reaped most of the gains of Reaganomics in the 1980s. Economists debated the causes for the shift, with some stressing reduced tax rates for the wealthy and others pointing to factors such as higher returns on capital gains and the explosion of executive pay. But the trend was clear—the first significant widening of the gap since the 1920s—and it accelerated in the 1990s. In 1996 the United States was the most economically stratified industrial nation in the world.

In contrast to earlier generations, who had aspired to doing better financially than their parents, many young adults wondered if they would ever achieve even a modest middle-class life-style. This opportunity gap of potential downward mobility seemed especially acute for the 75 million Americans born between 1961 and 1981. Said an insurance administrator from Alabama born in 1965, "I think the next generation will have smaller houses, smaller cars. I cannot outdo my parents and I

don't think I'll ever be able to. We struggle to make ends meet and we're a two-income household. It shouldn't be like that."

These diminished expectations were related in part to the jobs that were available in the 1990s. Lifetime careers with a single employer were increasingly rare. More typically, the average worker could expect to make several job or career shifts over the course of her or his working life. Confirming a long-term pattern, the number of minimum wage service jobs continued to grow, while the number of union-protected manufacturing jobs kept shrinking. The discount retailer Wal-Mart is now the second largest employer in the country after General Motors.

Much of the job growth has occurred in the *contingent* work force, which includes temporary and part-time workers as well as consultants and freelancers. In 1994 more than one-fifth of the work force, almost 25 million workers, had part-time or temporary jobs. (These positions are sometimes referred to as "McJobs," a reference to jobs at fast-food outlets like McDonalds.) Contingent workers are paid far less than are full-time employees, rarely belong to unions, and often do not get job-related benefits such as health insurance, sick leave, and a paid vacation.

The farming out of work to contingent workers was related to another major employment trend of the 1980s and 1990s: *downsizing*, in which companies deliberately shed permanent workers to cut wage costs and increase profits. In the 1970s most layoffs had involved industrial and manufacturing jobs, especially in the Rust Belt (see Chapter 32), but in the 1980s and 1990s downsizing spread to middle management. For example, from 1980 to 1995 IBM shrank its work force from 400,000 to 220,000, a 45 percent decrease. Governments also scaled back, eliminating 454,000 public service jobs between 1979 and 1993. Unlike jobs lost during recessions, those jobs did not come back when the economy picked up after 1992.

The human costs of downsizing were often devastating. When John Thomas, a fifty-nine-year-old AT&T employee who had spent forty years with the company was told that his job was "not going forward," he reacted this way: "I've had to downsize people myself, and now it's happening to me. It's not pleasant. I tried to accept it with class, but I went through a lot of emotions— sadness, worry, concern. Now I have a headache." When a fifteen-person department at Chemical Bank was downsized to one worker, she sobbed for her missing co-workers and wondered why she had been spared. Since the economy continues to generate new jobs, most laid-off workers eventually find work, but often at a large pay cut in addition to their emotional scars. The few federal job retraining programs reach only a minority of displaced workers.

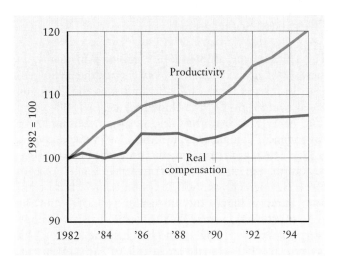

FIGURE 33.2

Productivity and Wages, 1982–1995

Usually as productivity increases, so does labor's share of national income. In the 1990s, however, workers failed to reap the rewards of the increased productivity shown here. Labor's relative loss in real compensation in turn contributed to a rise in corporate profits.

Source: New York Times, January 2, 1996, C20. Copyright © 1996 by The New York Times Co. Reprinted by permission.

Women, Work, and Families. These economic trends put even more pressure on women to seek paid employment outside the home. In 1994, 58.8 percent of women were in the labor force (up from 38 percent in 1962), compared with 75.1 percent of men. The traditional nuclear family of employed father, homemaker wife, and children was found in less than 15 percent of U.S. households. Married working women and single or divorced working women with children continued to bear the major share of household and child care responsibilities. For working parents with children, family schedules were often as intricate as time-motion studies.

While the media often focused on the breakthroughs made by women near the top of the corporate ladder, one of every five working women still held a clerical or secretarial job, the same proportion as in 1950. Women's pay lagged behind men's, with the gap even wider for black and Latino women. Yet women continued to make inroads in male-dominated fields. Among all workers under age thirty-five, women accounted for one in three doctors, four in ten mail carriers, and a majority of purchasing agents.

Other Corporate Strategies. Another major cause of diminished economic expectations in the 1980s and 1990s was the widespread fear that American corporations were no longer competitive in the global marketplace. Americans viewed with increasing alarm the economic success of Germany and Japan, the growing U.S. trade deficit, and the infusion of foreign investment money into the United States.

In an increasingly global economy American corporations tried to respond to rapidly changing market conditions by offering innovative products and services at competitive prices. Using a term popularized by Michael Hammer and James Champy, management consultants advised businesses to "reengineer the corporation," that is, rethink their work processes. Very often the models were corporations in Japan and Germany.

Some American companies did manage to reinvent themselves. In 1980–1981 the Ford Motor Company had lost $2.5 billion despite laying off 150,000 workers. This desperate situation led management to rethink its corporate vision. Instead of the old "us versus them" mentality, Ford tried to implement more of a partnership between management and the rank and file. It also shifted its focus away from maximum output to quality and consumer satisfaction, in effect making assembly-line workers more involved in the company and its products by giving them more responsibility. The popular Ford Taurus, introduced in 1986, typified the new focus on quality.

Labor Movement Responses. At first United Auto Workers (UAW) leaders were dubious about Ford's plans, especially when the company would not rule out future layoffs. But afraid that Ford might go bankrupt, in 1982 the UAW agreed to freeze wages and benefits, delay cost-of-living increases, and stop local strikes. Said the president of the UAW local at Ford's South Chicago plant, "I think we both realized over a period of time that we were in the same boat. When the boat sinks, we all drown. . . . It's a survival thing."

In the 1980s and 1990s the labor movement remained on the defensive, hurt by job losses to other countries, downsizing, fears of further layoffs, government hostility, worker indifference, and its inability to unionize unskilled and low-paid workers. Although union membership was now one-third female and one-fifth black, union leadership remained overwhelmingly white and male. The number of union members declined from 20 million in 1978 to 16.6 million in 1993, representing only 15.8 percent of the labor force. The Reagan administration took a tough antiunion stance from the start, breaking a nationwide strike by air traffic controllers in 1981 and destroying their union. Reagan's action signaled to the business community that it was acceptable to be antiunion, and there were sharp labor confrontations at Eastern Airlines, Greyhound, Phelps Dodge, Ravenswood Aluminum, Caterpillar, and Pittston Coal. In the mid-1990s new union leadership, a wave of union mergers, and an increased emphasis on reaching new members raised hopes that organized labor would reverse its decline.

The Strains of an Increasingly Pluralistic Society

The 1990 census counted 246.9 million Americans, an increase of over 22 million people since the 1980 census. By far the most dramatic shift was the changing racial composition of the United States. In 1990 one in four Americans claimed African, Asian, Hispanic, or American Indian ancestry, up from one in five ten years earlier. The main reason for the shift was increased immigration, especially from Latin America and Asia. In 1994, 8.7 percent of the U.S. population was foreign-born, almost double the 4.8 percent of 1970 and the highest proportion since World War II. This level, however, was still far below its modern historic high of 14.7 percent in 1910 after the great tide of early twentieth-century immigration.

In the 1980s over 7 million immigrants entered the country, accounting for more than a third of the population growth in that decade. LAX and JFK, the Los Angeles and New York international airports, were the main points of entry, replacing Ellis Island, which, after decades of abandonment and decay, was turned into a museum and tourist attraction. The first major immigration legislation since 1965, the 1986 Immigration Reform and Control Act (Simpson-Mazzoli Act), attempted to establish a fair entry process. It also granted legal status to some illegal aliens, primarily Mexicans and other Latinos, who had entered the United States before 1982. Revisions to the law in 1990 expanded the quota of immigrants to 700,000 per year and gave priority to skilled workers and relatives of current residents.

Hispanic Immigration. Much of the new immigration came from Latin America and the Caribbean. In 1950 there were 4 million Hispanics in this country; in 1990 the number was 22.4 million. The terms *Hispanic* and *Latino*, which include Spanish-speaking people from Mexico, Cuba, Puerto Rico, El Salvador, and other Latin American countries, represent a variety of distinctive heritages. Hispanics are the second largest minority group after blacks and the second fastest growing after Asians. Western states such as California, Texas, and New Mexico, which border on Mexico, originally contained the most immigrants, but in the postwar period new arrivals from Puerto Rico and Central and South America increasingly settled on the East Coast. Latinos now live in urban areas throughout the country, making up one-tenth of the populations of Florida and New York, for example (see Map 33.4).

Asian-Americans. Asia was the other major source of immigrants. This migration, which increased almost 108 percent from 1980 to 1990, consisted mainly of Chinese, Filipinos, Vietnamese, Laotians, Cambodians, Koreans, Pakistanis, and Asian Indians. California had more Asian-Americans, almost 10 percent of the population, than did any other state. Chinese-Americans are still the dominant Asian group in the United States, followed by Filipinos (see Map 33.5).

Some of this immigration was traceable to upheavals in Southeast Asia. More than 700,000 Indochinese refugees entered the country in the decade after American involvement in Vietnam ended in 1975. The first arrivals were highly educated people, who, after a few years, generally achieved economic success. Many of the later refugees came with less education and fewer skills and struggled for a foothold in new Indochinese neighborhoods that developed in Arlington, Virginia; Lowell, Massachusetts; and elsewhere. When the Cambodian population in that former textile town of Lowell increased from 3,500 in 1985 to 20,000 just three years later, local resources were strained, and the school system struggled to find bilingual teachers fluent in Khmer, the Cambodian language.

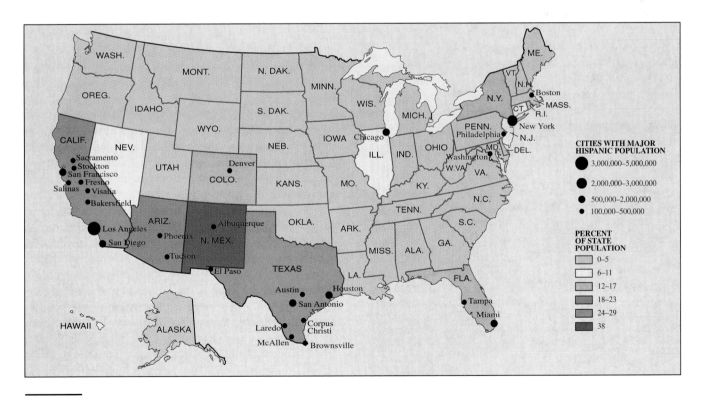

MAP 33.4

Hispanic-American Population, 1990

The Hispanic population of the United States is concentrated in California, New York, Texas, Florida, and Illinois, mainly in their urban areas. Demographers predict that Hispanic-Americans will overtake African-Americans as the largest minority group early in the twenty-first century and that by the year 2050 only about half the U.S. population will be comprised of non-Hispanic whites.

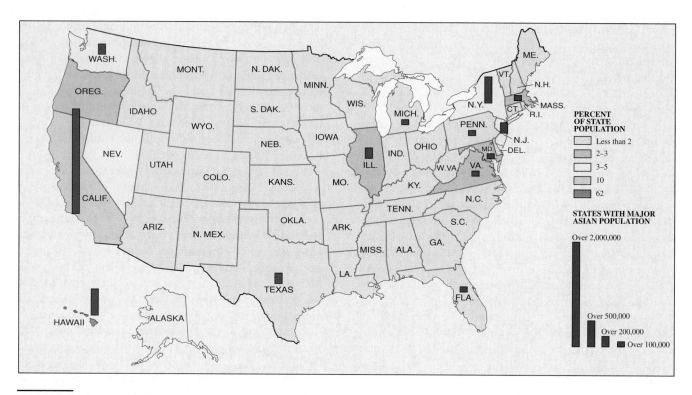

MAP 33.5

Asian-American Population, 1990

In 1990 Asian-Americans made up just under 3 percent of the total U.S. population. Asian population is concentrated on the East and West coasts, especially in California, and in major cities.

New Immigrants

In the 1980s many Korean immigrants got their start by opening small grocery stores in urban neighborhoods. Their success sometimes led to conflict with other racial groups, such as blacks and Hispanics, who were often their customers as well as competitors.

Asian-Americans were often referred to as a "model minority" because of their educational and professional success. Yet this label, which most Asian-Americans see as an unwelcome ethnic stereotype, masked their enormous diversity. Koreans, Laotians, and Chinese did not share a common language or customs, but they were all subjected to racial slurs and blatant discrimination. Informal quotas, especially in college admissions, recalled similar expressions of anti-Semitism as late as the 1950s.

Ethnic Diversity. The new immigration affected the social, economic, and cultural landscape of the country. Thriving ethnic enclaves were one example: Little Saigon in Orange County, California; Little Havana in Miami; Koreatown in Los Angeles. Tens of thousands of Soviet Jews fleeing religious and political persecution in the 1980s created Little Odessa in Brooklyn, New York. At least 300 periodicals served immigrant readers: *Nguoi Viet* in California, *La Voz de Houston* in Texas, and *Korea Times* in Queens, New York. Koreans purchased and revitalized corner grocery stores in New York City, Los Angeles, and Washington, D.C. People from the Indian subcontinent managed small hotel chains in California, and Vietnamese dominated the shrimp industry in

Texas. But demographers noted another pattern in major metropolitan areas with heavy immigration: for every immigrant who moved in, a native-born (usually white) person left.

Anti-Immigrant Sentiment. Immigrants have been the focus of hostility at many points in America's history. In the 1840s fears of Catholic Irish and German immigrants sparked violence and urban riots. At the turn of the century nativists decried the impact of immigrants from southern and Eastern Europe on Anglo-Saxon culture and in 1925 secured the passage of legislation severely restricting immigration from those areas. Anti-immigrant sentiment has always surged in times of unsettling economic or cultural change. Similar patterns were at play in the 1980s and 1990s, when increased immigration caused an agitated debate over access to jobs, education, and social services.

Economists generally believe that immigrants give more than they take, providing a fresh source of predominantly youthful and highly motivated workers who take jobs that are not wanted by other people or move into new jobs in the growing service sector. But many American-born workers still feared that immigrants would adversely affect their job prospects in a time of diminished economic opportunity. Immigrants, both legal and illegal, provided inviting targets when budgetary crises on the state and local levels mandated cutbacks. Polls showed strong public support for denying government assistance to all immigrants, regardless of their legal status, on the unfounded assumption that immigrants were lured here by generous public services.

These tensions came to a head in California, which had absorbed far more immigrants in the 1980s than any other state had. That state grew by 6.1 million, with more than a third of the growth coming from foreign immigration. Although California's overall growth has slowed since 1990, immigration has not. In 1994 California voters overwhelmingly approved a ballot initiative provocatively called "Save Our State," also known as Proposition 187. This initiative barred undocumented aliens from public schools, nonemergency care at public health clinics, and all other state social services. It also required law enforcement officers, school administrators, and social workers to report suspected illegal immigrants to the federal Immigration and Naturalization Service. While the constitutionality of the ballot referendum was immediately challenged, anti-immigrant feeling spread to other parts of the country and would be a hotly debated issue in the 1996 election.

The Plight of Urban America. One by-product of this increased immigration was that black Americans constituted a comparatively smaller percentage of the minority population in 1990 than they had earlier in the century. (Black immigration from the Caribbean and Africa has been too small to affect this trend.) Demographers predict that Latinos will outnumber blacks early in the twenty-first century. Blacks and recent immigrants sometimes found themselves competing for the same jobs. Both African-Americans and new immigrants often lived in urban areas, but rarely in the same neighborhoods as a result of prevailing patterns of ethnic and racial segregation.

The cities where most new immigrants settled in the 1990s were often in dire shape. Urban renewal projects had demolished dilapidated but still livable housing and replaced it with civic complexes and shiny office projects. Government inaction also contributed to the deterioration of the inner cities. Federal attention to urban areas peaked between 1964 and 1972; since then, inner-city problems have largely been left to the cash-strapped cities to solve.

Joblessness became a way of life for inner-city residents, two-parent households were scarce, and social contacts outside the neighborhood were rare. At the heart of the problem was the inability to find productive work. Urban unemployment rates rose as high as 60 percent, in part for demographic reasons: inner cities had a far larger proportion of young people than did the general population as a result of a higher birth rate and a younger age of childbearing. Cities had too few entry-level jobs, and most of the inner cities' unemployed lacked the training necessary for better-paying jobs.

In the 1980s the historical tide of black migration to the cities that had begun before World War I started to recede. Southern blacks who learned about the poor job prospects were less likely to seek new lives in urban areas; quite the contrary, anyone who could was leaving the inner cities, usually for a more stable neighborhood or the suburbs. In Los Angeles, as Asians and Latinos moved in, blacks moved out, usually to neighboring counties such as Riverside, San Bernardino, and Ventura. Some blacks even made a reverse migration back to the South. Compared with the crime-ridden and dilapidated housing projects in Chicago or South-Central Los Angeles, the post–civil rights South seemed attractive. Atlanta was one of the most popular destinations.

In April 1992 the frustration and anger of impoverished urban Americans erupted in five days of riots in Los Angeles, the worst civil disorders since the 1960s. The violence took sixty lives and caused $850 million in damage. The rioting was set off by the acquittal on all but one charge of four white Los Angeles police officers accused of using excessive force while arresting a black motorist, Rodney King, on March 3, 1991. The predominantly white Simi Valley jury was not swayed by a graphic eighty-one-second amateur video of the arrest that showed the officers kicking, clubbing, and beating King. The video, which was shown repeatedly on television, brought renewed attention to the issue of police brutality and the harassment of minorities. Three of the officers were later convicted on federal charges of violating King's civil rights.

To Live and Die in L.A.
The images from South-Central Los Angeles in the wake of the 1992 riots looked eerily similar to those from Watts in 1965. The underlying causes were similar as well—police brutality, racism, and frustration about lack of jobs and opportunity.

The Los Angeles riots exposed the cleavages in urban neighborhoods. Many blacks trapped in the nation's inner cities resented recent immigrants who were struggling to get ahead and often succeeding. As a result some blacks targeted Korean-owned stores for arson and looting. Latinos also felt frustrated about high unemployment and crowded housing conditions. According to the Los Angeles Police Department, Latinos accounted for more than half of those arrested and a third of those killed during the rioting. The riots were not just a case of black rage at white injustice; they also contained a strong class element as people reacted against the failure of the American system to address the needs of all poor people, not just blacks (see American Voices, page 1037).

Affirmative Action. From the beginning of affirmative action in 1965 many white men had protested that it was unfair and discriminatory. Some, like Allen Bakke, even took their cases to court (see Chapter 32). But affirmative action remained official government policy until the 1990s, when arguments over minority and immigrant rights as well as the shrinking economy and white resentment fueled a renewed debate on the issue. Affirmative action had become more than a black-white or women's issue, pitting racial and ethnic groups against each other in a kind of three-dimensional game of chess in which, for example, gains for blacks and Hispanics came at the expense of Asian-Americans.

The impact of affirmative action was most evident in college admissions. The University of California system had undertaken one of the most far-reaching plans. As late as 1984 whites had made up about two-thirds of the undergraduate student body. In 1994, as a result of the implementation of affirmative action, students at the Berkeley campus were 39 percent Asian, 32 percent white, 14 percent Latino, 6 percent black, and 1 percent native American, with 8 percent of students not identifying their race. In 1995, under pressure from the Republican governor, Pete Wilson, the Regents of the University of California reexamined their preference-based system. Despite opposition from the university's president and many faculty members, who warned that repeal would lead to precipitous drops in the numbers of black and Latino freshmen, the Regents narrowly voted to scrap the twenty-year-old policy.

Criticism of affirmative action came from many sources. Some conservative blacks felt it merely reinforced white prejudices that the only way minorities could get ahead was through preferential treatment. Others argued that affirmative action did little to help the truly disadvantaged, offering opportunities instead to those who would probably have been able to get ahead without it. In a time of anxiety about jobs and the economy in general, affirmative action became a scapegoat for many who were not succeeding economically, especially the white men who had borne the brunt of layoffs in the 1980s and 1990s. The 1994 elections transformed the goal of abolishing affirmative action into a mainstream political issue, and a 1995 Supreme Court decision casting doubts on federal programs that gave preference based on race will probably increase the momentum of the opponents of affirmative action.

Culture Wars. One reason affirmative action became a political issue in the 1990s was that many people saw it as part of an ideology that threatened core American values. Lumping affirmative action together with *multiculturalism*—the attempt to represent the diversity of American society and its peoples—critics feared that all this counting by race, gender, sexual preference, and age would lead to a "balkanization" of American society. Attempts to revise American history textbooks along multicultural lines were especially contentious, as were efforts by universities such as Stanford to revise college curricula to include the study of non-European cultures.

Culture wars broke out on other fronts as well. Conservatives in Congress led an effort to eliminate federal funding for the arts, humanities, and public television, arguing that the federal government should not be in the business of supporting works that many found offensive or antithetical to traditional American values. The National Endowments for the Arts and the Humanities survived, but with drastically reduced budgets. Conservatives found another tempting target in the

Rubén Martínez

L.A. Journal

Rubén Martínez, born to Mexican and Salvadoran parents and raised in Los Angeles, describes himself as a member of the generation "that arrived too late for Che Guevara and too early for the fall of the Berlin Wall." In this excerpt he compares daily life in Los Angeles with San Salvador's state of siege.

June 1991

Was that a shotgun? In answer, a series of pops . . . a small automatic? I crouch by the window, look into the hazy balmy night. Mute buildings. Now, from afar, another sound begins, like the whine of a mosquito in the darkness of a stifling room in the tropics. The whine becomes a roar that rattles the windows. A shaft of light pours down from the sky. Sirens shriek in the distance. They come closer . . . closer: patrol cars race up the avenue.

I am not in San Salvador, I tell myself. Those are not soldiers down there, bursting through doors to ransack the apartments of high school kids who participated in a protest march . . . Y is okay, she works for a human rights organization in Los Angeles, she's not FMLN in San Salvador anymore, this is Los Angeles, not San Salvador, this is 1991, not 1979, this is gang strife, not civil war. I don't believe myself. Images past and present merge: It is 1979 and

1991 and San Salvador and Los Angeles and gang strife and civil war all at once.

When the helicopters thud-thud-thud-thud fades away, I light a cigarette. Did the bullets find their mark in a rival gangster, a three-year-old's skull? I wait for the ambulance's siren, but the neighborhood remains quiet. The bullets found nothing but the night, as though the night itself were both target and victim of the desperate rage that led the finger to pull on the trigger.

I return to my post next to the computer, in my Echo Park apartment (my latest stop in search of a home) whose living room holds my altar. Amidst votive candles and before a crucifix, I've gathered together objects from the living and the dead: a wallet-sized photo of Y, her stare questioning me across the distance of our latest— and final?—separation; on a cassette sleeve, a photo of Mexico City kids who look like a cross between Irish idealists U2 and the street toughs of *Los Olvidados*; a black-and-white snapshot of a graffiti artist cradling his brutally scarred arm, result of an evening when the bullets did find their mark; a brittle, yellowed leaf from Palm Sunday at La Placita, where Father Luis Olivares showered the thousands of Mexicanos and Centro-americanos surrounding

him with holy water; the embossed card that says that one Fidel Castro Ruz, *Presidente del Consejo de Estado y del Gobierno de la República de Cuba*, requests my presence at a reception; a rather ugly postcard entitled "La Frontera, Tijuana, BC," that shows an antiseptic-clean highway on one side and a labyrinth of dusty paths on the other . . . shards of my identity. . . .

This jumble of objects is as close as I get to "home." As close as I get, because my home is L.A. and L.A. is an anti-home; that's why I've left it so many times, and returned just as many. . . .

I turn off the overhead light so that the candle flame transforms the shadow of the crucifix on the wall into a pair of wavering, reaching arms. I gaze upon the photos of my late grandparents. This is my history, I tell myself. "This is my home," I whisper, looking out through the window again at the avenues of Echo Park, which are now as deserted and tense as any in San Salvador during a state of siege. . . .

Source: Rubén Martínez, The Other Side: Fault Lines, Guerrilla Saints, and the True Heart of Rock 'n' Roll (Verso: London and New York, 1992), 165–166.

---

speech codes adopted by some colleges to ban racist or sexist comments from everyday language. Whether someone's words were "p.c." (politically correct) became a red flag, with the implication that somehow it had become impossible to say anything without offending someone.

Backlash against Feminism. The women's movement also became a target of conservative critics, who charged that feminist demands had gone too far. In the widely read *Backlash: The Undeclared War on American Women* (1991), the journalist Susan Faludi described a powerful backlash against the gains American women had won in the 1960s and 1970s. Spearheaded by New Right leaders and organizations such as Concerned

Women for America, the backlash was aided by television, newspapers, and even women's magazines. The media held the women's movement responsible for every ill afflicting modern women—from infertility to eating disorders to rising divorce rates to the "man shortage." Too much freedom had caused women unhappiness was the antifeminist message of the 1980s and 1990s. Feminists such as Faludi replied that women were unhappy precisely because they had not yet achieved equality. And despite the conservative attacks, polls showed strong support for many items on the feminist agenda, such as pay equity, increased access to jobs, reproductive rights, and more equitable sharing of household and child care responsibilities.

Backlash

The 1987 movie *Fatal Attraction* typified Hollywood's negative portrayal of independent women in that decade. The plot centers on a homicidal single career woman (played by Glenn Close) who nearly destroys a happily married man (Michael Douglas) after a casual affair. The original screenplay had Close's character slit her throat over her unrequited love, but in the final version she is killed by Douglas's wife. According to the journalist Susan Faludi, the message is clear: "The best single woman is a dead one."

Feminism also exhibited racial and generational fault lines. Despite the attempts of prominent feminist organizations such as the National Organization for Women (NOW) to focus on differences among women, African-Americans and other women of color often resented being tokens in a predominantly white movement. Many young women felt that the movement had become too obsessed with women as passive victims (of date rape, discrimination, sexual harrassment, the media's beauty myth, and so forth) rather than offering women models of empowerment. But other young women, influenced by women's studies programs and the explosion of feminist scholarship, forged a third wave of feminism in the 1990s (see American Voices, page 1039).

The deep national divide over abortion showed how one of the main issues associated with feminism continued to polarize the country. The increase in harassment and violence by abortion opponents was one of the most chilling manifestations of the antifeminism of the 1980s and 1990s. In 1994 four workers were killed, including two receptionists at Boston clinics. Although only a fraction of antiabortion activists supported such extreme acts, disruptive confrontational tactics made it more dangerous to receive what was still a woman's legal right to an abortion. In May 1994 Congress passed the Freedom of Access to Clinic Entrances Act (FACE), which provided federal fines and prison terms for those who used physical obstruction or intimidation to interfere with access to reproductive health services.

Gay Rights. The issue of sexual preference, especially the introduction of educational programs teaching tolerance for gays, also became part of the fractured national debate about multiculturalism. As more gays "came out of the closet," activists gained more political clout in their campaign for gay rights. In more than a hundred communities across the country, civil rights legislation protected gays from discrimination in public housing, education, real estate, public accommodations, and employment. Certain cities, including New York City, Washington, D.C., and San Francisco, allowed same-sex couples to register as domestic partners.

To conservatives, especially the Christian Right and its sympathizers in Congress, a gay life-style was an affront to traditional family values. Pat Robertson, Jesse Helms, and others denounced civil rights protections for gays as undeserved "special rights." Such tactics helped antigay forces win a 1992 Colorado referendum to add a state constitutional amendment barring local jurisdictions from passing laws protecting gays and lesbians from discrimination. The Colorado provision was overturned by the U.S. Supreme Court in 1996, but this had no effect on the rising incidence of antigay harassment and violence. Twenty-five years after Stonewall gay people were more visible in American society but were not universally accepted.

The AIDS Epidemic. One of the largest challenges that the gay community has faced is AIDS, although it is grossly inaccurate to see this solely as a gay issue. Acquired immune deficiency syndrome (AIDS) was first recognized in 1981, and its cause was soon identified as the human immunodeficiency virus (HIV). (HIV is transmitted through the exchange of infected body fluids such as semen and blood.) Initially, little organized action or government funding was directed toward AIDS research or treatment, and critics charged that this reflected society's antipathy toward gay men, who were the disease's earliest victims. AIDS began to gain public attention only when it became clear that heterosexuals, such as hemophiliacs who received the virus through blood transfusions, were affected as well. The 1985 death from AIDS of the film star Rock Hudson, who had hidden his sexual orientation to maintain his Hollywood career, finally broke through the barrier of public apathy. Another galvanizing moment was the 1991 announcement by the basketball great Earvin ("Magic") Johnson that he was HIV-positive.

As early as the mid-1980s AIDS cases began to increase among heterosexuals, especially intravenous drug addicts and their sexual partners, as well as bisexuals. Women now constitute the group with the fastest growing incidence of HIV infection. The new female faces of the AIDS epidemic were represented at the 1992 national party conventions by Elizabeth Glaser and Mary Fisher. Glaser told the assembled Democrats how she

Laurie Ouellette

A Third-Wave Feminist

Laurie Ouellette, born in 1966 and educated at the University of Minnesota, represents the generation of women who benefited from the changes set in motion by the revival of feminism but are confused about what feminism means. She calls on the movement to broaden its vision.

As a member of the first generation of women to benefit from the gains of the '70s women's movement without participating in its struggles, I grew up on the sidelines of feminism—too young to take part in those moments, debates, and events that would define the women's movement but old enough to experience firsthand the societal changes it had wrought.

Ironically, it is due to the modest success of feminism that many young women like myself were raised with an illusion of equality. Like most women my age, I never really thought much about feminism while I was growing up. Looking back, though, I believe it has always influenced me. Growing up with divorced parents, especially a father who was ambivalent about parental responsibilities, probably has much to do with this fact. I was only five when my parents separated in 1971, and I couldn't possibly have imagined or understood the ERA marches or the triumphal result of *Roe v. Wade* that would make history in just a few short years. Certainly I couldn't have defined the word *feminism*. Still, watching my mother struggle emotionally and financially as a single parent made the concept of gender injustice painfully clear. . . .

It was at the University of Minnesota that I first took an interest in feminist classics like *The Feminine Mystique, Sisterhood Is Powerful*, and *Sexual Politics*. They expressed the anger of an earlier generation that simultaneously captivated me and excluded me. Reading them so long after the excitement of their publication made my own consciousness-raising seem anticlimactic. Like many of my white middle-class friends, I believed that we wouldn't have to worry about issues like discrimination, oppression, and getting stuck in the housewife role. We wondered why we should join forces with a battle for women's equality that the media repeatedly declared was already "won."

My experiences after college made me think again about feminism. A public television internship where I was expected to perform menial secretarial tasks while my male (and, I might add, less experienced) co-interns worked on interesting and challenging projects shocked me into realizing the difficulties facing women in the workplace. Likewise, living in an inner-city neighborhood and being involved in community issues there showed me the dire need for feminism in the lives of the poor women, elderly women, and women of color who were my neighbors. Watching these women, many of them single mothers, struggle daily to find shelter, child care, and food made me realize that they had not been touched at all by the women's movement gains of the '70s. . . .

My 24-year-old sister stands out as an example of other routes that feminism must move toward. Whereas I have focused my energies on attending graduate school and working toward a professional career, she has chosen to forfeit similar plans, for now, in favor of marrying young, moving to the country, and raising a family. Does she signify a regression into the homemaker role of the 1950s? On the contrary. For her, issues such as getting midwifery legalized and insured, providing information about breast-feeding to rural mothers, countering the male-dominated medical establishment by using and recommending natural and alternative healing methods, and raising her own daughter with positive gender esteem are central to a feminist agenda.

Only by recognizing and helping to provide choices—both lifestyle and reproductive—for women of all races, economic levels, and ages, as well as supporting all women in their struggles to make those choices, will the women of my generation, the first to be raised in the shadow of feminism and witness its successes and failures, be able to build a successful third wave of the feminist movement.

Source: Laurie Ouellette, "Our Turn Now: Reflections of a 26-Year-Old Feminist," *Utne Reader* (July-August, 1992), 118–120.

had contracted the virus through a tainted blood transfusion and then unknowingly passed it on to her nursing infant and a later child. Mary Fisher, the daughter of a prominent conservative fund-raiser, told the Republicans how she learned from a blood test that she had contracted the virus from her former husband. "If you believe you are safe, you are at risk," said Fisher.

Some people have lived for years symptom-free while being HIV-positive, but no cure or vaccine is in sight. The barriers to further research and effective prevention are as much political and bureaucratic as medical. Many nonurban Americans see the AIDS epidemic as another expression of big-city decay. Federal red tape and prohibitive expense have limited the distribution of drugs such as AZT that delay the onset and reduce the severity of the symptoms despite the dramatic protests of the advocacy group ACT-UP (AIDS Coalition to Unleash Power). More Americans have died of AIDS than

ACT UP

This poster *Untitled* (1989) by artist Keith Haring for the group ACT UP (AIDS Coalition to Unleash Power) was used to mobilize public action against the deadly disease, which would later claim Haring's life.

were killed in the Korean and Vietnam wars combined, and in 1995 AIDS was the leading cause of death among all Americans aged twenty-five to forty-four. The toll, in the United States and throughout the world, continues to rise.

Popular Culture and Popular Technology

Image was everything in the 1980s and 1990s, or so commentators said, pointing to the rock stars Michael Jackson and Madonna and even to President Reagan. One strong influence was MTV, which premiered in 1981. With its creative choreography, flashy colors, and rapid cuts, it seemed a perfect fit to the short attention span of a TV generation raised on shows such as "Sesame Street." The MTV style soon showed up in mainstream advertising, network television shows such as "Miami Vice," and even political campaigns. The national newspaper *USA Today*, which debuted in 1982, adapted the style, featuring eye-catching graphics, color photographs, and short, easy-to-read articles. Soon more staid newspapers followed suit.

New technology, especially satellite transmission and live "minicam" broadcasting, reshaped the television industry. Also new was the increased availability of cable channels. In the 1950s Americans had only three networks to choose from; public television did not debut until 1967. By the end of the 1980s upstarts such as Ted Turner's all-news CNN (Cable News Network), ESPN's all-sports channel, and the Fox network were challenging the major networks for viewers and profits. Media, communications, and entertainment were big business, increasingly drawn into global financial networks, markets, and mergers.

Technology also entered and reshaped the home. The 1980s saw the introduction of videocassette recorders

(VCRs), compact disc players, cellular phones, and inexpensive fax (facsimile) machines. In 1993 more than three-quarters of American households had a VCR. At first Hollywood feared decreasing box office admissions, but it soon found that VCRs created a large new market for recent films, as well as for vintage movies. Video was everywhere—stores, elevators, airplanes, tennis courts, operating rooms. With the introduction of camcorders, the family photo album could be supplemented by a video of a high school graduation, a marriage, or a birth.

But it was the personal computer that truly revolutionized the home and the office. The big breakthrough came from the upstart Apple Computer Company. Two young hobbyists, Steve Jobs and Steve Wozniak, operating from a bedroom and garage in Palo Alto, California, built the first easy-to-use, small, inexpensive computer. In 1977 they offered their Apple II personal computer for only $1,195, and it was a runaway success. Belatedly, other companies scrambled to get into the market. IBM, a leader in producing tabulating machines and mainframe computers for business and government, offered its first personal computer in the summer of 1981. Software companies such as Microsoft and Lotus grew rapidly by providing operating systems and other software for this expanding market (see American Lives, pages 1042–1043). In January 1983 *Time* magazine broke with fifty-five years of tradition by naming the personal computer its "machine of the year." In 1995, 37 percent of American households had at least one personal computer.

The impact of the personal computer on business was nearly universal. More than any other technological advance, the computer created the modern electronic office. Even the smallest business could keep all its records, do all its correspondence and billing, and run its own direct-mail advertising campaigns on a single desktop machine. The very concept of the office was changing as a new class of *telecommuters* were able to work at home via computer, electronic mail, and fax machine.

Over the next decades the world's telecommunications systems will be rebuilt with hair-thin fiber-optic strands with a far greater *bandwidth* (information-carrying capacity) than copper wire. Fiber-optic cables, microwave relays, and satellites can transmit massive quantities of information to and from almost any place on earth and even from space. The term *information superhighway* refers to this vast expansion of communications technology.

The Internet is the aspect of the information superhighway that has reached the most people so far—an estimated 35 million in 160 countries in 1995. The Internet had cold war roots, originating in a 1969 effort by the Pentagon to create a communications network that could survive a nuclear war. The Pentagon gave up control of the Internet in 1984, and the subsequent rapid spread of personal computers, modems, and networked computing made the Internet attractive (some would say addictive) to average citizens and commercial enterprises. Welcome to *cyberspace*, that place behind the computer screen you can't see, but you know is there.

At first the Internet was used mainly by scientists and other professionals to communicate with their peers through electronic mail (*E-mail*), but the arrival of the World Wide Web in 1991 enhanced its commercial possibilities. The Web allowed companies, organizations, political campaigns, and even the White House to create their own "home pages" of visual and textual information for consumers to click on to at their discretion. Businesses and entrepreneurs began to use home pages to sell their products and services, leading critics to fear that the Net would turn into one big shopping mall. But many people think that cyberspace will be one of the driving forces for economic growth in the twenty-first century.

The implications of this almost instantaneous access to information are staggering. On January 5, 1995, the Library of Congress unveiled "Thomas" (named for Thomas Jefferson), an on-line service providing access to legislation, committee reports, and other Congressional documents. During the first four days of its operation 28,000 individuals and 2,500 organizations used Thomas to download more than 175,000 documents. More citizens had accessed Thomas in a day than normally used the Library of Congress in a week.

Whereas this access was touted as making information democratically available to all American citizens, it really was available only to those who had access to the current technology or who could pay the monthly fees to be wired. In many ways, who is going to get on the information superhighway and who is going to be left by the wayside is one of the most troubling issues for the next century. It has been called "information apartheid" or "electronic redlining," a term derived from the banking practice of refusing loans to people in low-income areas.

The gap between information haves and have-nots is wide and getting wider. In 1995 only 10 percent of American households (generally those with incomes above $50,000) had the computers, modems, telephone connections, and gateway software necessary to participate in this revolution. According to a 1993 Census Bureau study, the gap was racial as well as economic: 37.5 percent of whites had computers at home, work, or school, compared with 25 percent of blacks and 22 percent of Hispanics.

The futurists Alvin and Heidi Toffler use the term Third Wave to describe how these new computing and telecommunications technologies will transform the global economy as dramatically as did the first wave (the agricultural revolution) and the second (the Industrial Revolution). If the wave of the future is indeed informa-

tion, those who are highly educated and computer-literate will have the advantage. Those who are not, for reasons of class, race, or location, will find themselves even more disadvantaged as they compete in the twenty-first-century workplace.

Restructuring the Domestic Order: Public Life since 1993

The strong showing of the independent candidate Ross Perot in the 1992 presidential election reflected widespread popular dissatisfaction with the American political system. Like using a remote control device, Americans were clicking off politics as usual. After sixty years of supporting federal activism to combat social ills, the Democratic party found that its core ideology was out of step with a country more concerned with cutting taxes, scaling back government, and balancing the budget. As Democrats abandoned many of their long-held liberal beliefs, the Republican party moved even farther to the right. Looming over all their political debates was the federal deficit.

The Clinton Administration

As William Jefferson Clinton was sworn into office in January 1993, hopes were high that the Democratic Congress and Democratic president would cooperate to pass legislation long stalled by partisan disputes. The first signs were promising. Congress passed the Family and Medical Leave Act in February 1993, providing workers with up to twelve weeks of unpaid leave to tend to a newborn or adopted child or a family medical emergency. President Bush had twice vetoed similar bills. In May, Congress passed the so-called motor-voter bill, which required states to allow citizens to register to vote when they applied for or renewed a driver's license. But Clinton got sidetracked when he tried to implement his campaign promise to lift the ban on gays serving in the armed forces. His compromise policy of "don't ask, don't tell, don't pursue" satisfied no one, and the bungled handling of this emotionally charged issue called into question his willingness to stand firm on issues of principle.

By the time Clinton took office the economy had pulled out of the 1990 recession. He then focused "like a laser" on economic issues, which included crafting trade policies to open foreign markets to U.S. goods. In December 1992 President Bush had signed the North American Free Trade Agreement (NAFTA), an agreement among the United States, Canada, and Mexico to create a free-trade zone covering all of North America, the

Bill Gates: Microsoft's Leader in the Computer Revolution

In the eleventh grade Bill Gates told a friend that he would be a millionaire by the time he was thirty. When Gates went to Harvard two years later, he revised it downward to twenty-five. He was being far too modest. At the age of thirty-one Bill Gates became the youngest self-made billionaire ever. In 1992 *Forbes* magazine named him the richest person in America. What was the source of all this wealth? Microsoft, whose software runs on eight of every ten personal computers in the world. Microsoft is the most successful start-up company in the history of American business.

William Henry Gates III (always called Trey by his family) was born into a wealthy Seattle family in 1955. His father, William Gates, Jr., is a successful corporate lawyer and former president of the Washington State Bar Association; his mother, Mary, was a prominent United Way volunteer who also served as a regent of the University of Washington. Gates attended the exclusive Lakeside School, which was one of the first in the country to offer students computer access through a time-sharing arrangement paid for by the school's mothers' club. The eighth-grader was hooked. Another Lakeside classmate and computer whiz was the tenth-grader Paul Allen, who joined Gates to found a company called Traf-O-Data that counted vehicles at busy intersections by using a rudimentary computer device. In 1975 these two former classmates founded Microsoft. Allen was twenty-one, and Gates, who would soon drop out of Harvard, all of nineteen.

Actually Gates looked even younger. When Miriam Lubow became Microsoft's office manager in 1977, she was appalled when some "kid" whipped by her desk into the office of "Mr. Gates" and began playing with the computer terminal. That kid was Bill Gates. But looks

Microsoft Employees, 1978
This group portrait shows eleven of Microsoft's thirteen employees as the company was about to relocate from Albuquerque to Seattle. Bill Gates is in front row, far left; Paul Allen is in front row, far right.

can be deceiving, as competitors have found out whenever they do business with this formidable entrepreneur.

In certain ways Gates and Allen were classic hackers—nerdy, mathematically inclined, and fascinated by the possibilities for computation (and mischief) that early computers provided. But most hackers saw computers as a hobby or a game. Back then the thought of owning one's own computer seemed as far-fetched as owning a nuclear submarine. But right from the start Gates and Allen saw commercial possibilities in the new field, long before the personal computer revolution of the 1980s. They anticipated that there would be money to be made writing, but especially marketing, software for the new machines. Microsoft's domination has resulted less from developing innovative new products than from anticipating trends in the industry, getting products quickly into the market, and then using its market share to bludgeon the competition. The phenomenal success of products such as MS-DOS and Windows was due as much to Microsoft's relentless marketing barrage as to any inherent technological superiority of its products.

In the early days Microsoft was more like a college dorm than a business. The "Microkids" were barely out of their teens, and some were still in high school. Nobody kept regular hours, and they existed on junk food, rock music, and free Coke (a tradition that Microsoft still maintains). A married employee was an oddity, and almost all the programmers were men. Gates's competitive and confrontational managerial style set the tone: "That's the stupidest thing I ever heard" was a frequently heard comment. But the Microkids thrived under the pressure. As Gates later said, "It's a lot of fun to work with very smart people in a competitive environment."

Gates literally could not sit still, and the Seattle-based Microsoft continued to grow at a fantastic rate. Gates had once thought it might employ 20 people; by 1982, Microsoft had 200 employees and sales of $32 million. In 1985, when the company went public, Gates, Allen (who had left the company in 1983 after a bout with Hodgkin's disease), and many Microsoft employees became overnight millionaires. Allen later cashed in some of his stock to buy the Portland Trailblazers.

Bill Gates does not act like a person with a net worth of approximately $10 billion. He flies coach rather than first class, hates limousines, and is somewhat casual about his appearance. He personally responds to hundreds of E-mail messages a day. He works incredibly long hours and expects his employees to do the same.

However, only billionaires can afford to spend $40 million on a house such as the one that Gates is building on Lake Washington outside Seattle for himself and his wife, Microsoft product manager Melinda French, whom he married on New Year's Day, 1994. The house is a series of interconnected pavilions set deep into a hillside, with its own salmon estuary, a twenty-car subterranean garage, a trampoline room, and video "walls" in every room to display changing electronic images of art (for which Gates has bought the rights from major museums) to suit the mood. "Working for Bill, you design for change," said the architect. That sums up Gates's approach to business as well.

The next step for Gates and Microsoft is onto the information superhighway. The personal computers that he had the vision to see as being part of daily life are evolving into a new kind of machine: a communications device that connects people to the Internet and beyond. Gates wants Microsoft to be part of that connection. Competitors such as Lotus, Sun Microsystems, Novell, and Apple complain that Microsoft has gotten too big, and the Justice Department and the Federal Trade Commission closely monitor its corporate acquisitions. But Gates disputes the notion that he exercises monopoly power over the industry. Why should he be penalized for being the best in a highly competitive market? Gates responds to the "Bill-bashers." Microsoft products are just delivering on the company motto, "We Set the Standard."

When Gates was asked the reasons for his success, he replied (by electronic mail, of course), "Besides a lot of luck, a high energy level and perhaps some IQ I think having an ability to deal with things at a very detailed level and a very broad level and synthesize between them is probably the thing that helps me the most. This allows someone to take deep technical understanding and figure out a business strategy that fits together with it." Friends note his "extraordinary bandwidth," that is, the amount of information he can absorb, but it is his insights into business rather than technology that set Gates apart. His entrepreneurial streak would have made Henry Ford or John D. Rockefeller proud, but Gates keenly worries about being left behind in the next stage of the computer revolution: "It's a little scary that as computer technology has moved ahead there's never been a leader from one era who was also a leader in the next." He takes this as a warning and a challenge: "But I want to defy historical tradition."

"Software is cool," Gates told CNN's Larry King to explain the hoopla surrounding the release of Microsoft's Windows 95. To the computer crowd, cool is the opposite of random, which means out of it, wrong, or inane. No one, especially not his competitors, has ever accused Bill Gates of being random.

Clinton/Gore

Baby boomers Bill Clinton and Al Gore billed themselves as representing a "new generation of leadership." Born in 1946 and 1948 respectively, they came of age in the turbulent 1960s. Vietnam, not World War II or Korea, was the war that defined their generation.

largest such zone in the world. NAFTA was strongly supported by the business community but bitterly opposed by labor unions worried about losing jobs to lower-paid Mexican workers and by environmentalists concerned about weak enforcement of antipollution laws south of the border. In what was seen as a major defeat for labor, a coalition of free-trade Democrats and Republicans narrowly passed NAFTA in November 1993.

Less controversial were the new provisions of the General Agreement on Tariffs and Trade (GATT), the treaty governing most international trade, which was part of the Bretton Woods system created by the major economic powers at the end of World War II. This new round of revisions, the eighth since the 1940s, cut tariffs on many manufactured products and for the first time established regulations protecting intellectual property such as patents, copyrights, and trademarks for software, entertainment, and pharmaceuticals. The U.S. Senate ratified the treaty in December 1994.

With the recession over, crime replaced the economy as a major concern among voters. In 1993 Congress passed the Brady Handgun Violence Prevention Act, named for James Brady, the White House press secretary who was crippled in the 1981 attempted assassination of President Reagan. A much more wide-ranging piece of legislation was the 1994 Omnibus Violent Crime Control and Prevention Act, which authorized $30.2 billion for stepped-up law enforcement, crime prevention, and prison construction and administration; it also expanded the death penalty to cover more than fifty federal crimes and banned the sale and possession of certain kinds of assault weapons.

Health Care. The issue on which Clinton staked his political fortunes was health care. The United States was spending more on health care than any other country in the world: $750 billion in 1991, up 11 percent from the year before. Yet it remained the only major industrialized country not to provide national health insurance, in part because of Roosevelt's decision not to push for a federal health care program in the 1930s. Spiraling medical costs (double the rate of inflation since 1970), rising premiums, and the large number of Americans without health insurance (one-sixth of the population in 1990) had brought the health care system to a crisis.

Despite his slender electoral mandate, the new president felt that his campaign promise to guarantee universal health insurance was finally within reach. He chose his wife, Hillary Rodham Clinton, to head the task force drafting the legislation, a controversial move since no first lady had ever played such a formal role in policy making. The Clinton proposal adopted the idea of *managed competition*: market forces, not the government, would control health care costs and expand access.

It took 1,300 pages to explain all the details when the legislation was submitted to Congress, a symptom of how this complex issue would defy an easy political resolution. Special-interest groups, including the well-financed

A Forceful and Controversial First Lady

Drawing inspiration from Eleanor Roosevelt, Hillary Rodham Clinton hoped the country would be ready for a first lady who could play a role in shaping policy. It wasn't. Throughout her husband's administration, she was subjected to intense criticism for everything from her role in health care reform to the Whitewater land deal to her frequently changing hairstyle.

pharmaceutical and insurance industries, began picking the plan apart. Small business owners argued that the requirement that all but the tiniest firms provide health insurance for their employees would bankrupt them or force them to lay off workers. During the campaign many Americans had expressed support for health care reform, but many began to fear what the changes might bring. In August 1994 the Senate failed to act on the plan, and by September Congressional leaders admitted that health reform was dead.

While the political system dithered, private market forces were already transforming the nation's medical system, replacing the traditional "fee for service" system with managed care plans that limited consumers' choice of doctors and treatments to cut costs. Medical care had become the domain of Wall Street and big business, and growing numbers of Americans had joined health maintenance organizations or looser "preferred provider" networks. While managed care succeeded in curbing the cost of health care premiums, private sector initiatives did nothing to help the unemployed and workers without health insurance, whose numbers continued to grow. An estimated 43.4 million Americans had no health insurance in 1995, almost 20 percent of the population under the age of sixty-five.

Post–Cold War Foreign Policy. One reason why health care reform failed was that President Clinton never devoted his full attention to building a consensus for the plan and shepherding it through Congress. In October 1993, for example, just after Clinton had announced the plan, twelve American soldiers were killed on a United Nations peacekeeping mission in Somalia. Then Clinton had to turn his attention to divisive issues such as the closely contested NAFTA vote, Haiti, and the worsening situation in Bosnia. This patchwork approach to foreign policy added to the perception of Clinton as vacillating, indecisive, and lacking a central vision. Not until 1996 did Clinton's foreign policy team begin to articulate a clear policy on when the United States should intervene in crises overseas.

In the former Soviet Union the increasing unpopularity of the Russian president Boris Yeltsin's efforts to bring about market reforms made American leaders less optimistic about the emergence of democracy within that country. Yeltsin's harsh repression of dissent in the breakaway region of Chechnya strained the already difficult relationship with the United States. In elections held in 1996 Yeltsin struggled to defeat his communist opponent, Gennadi Zyuganov.

Nothing seemed more intractable than the problems engulfing the former state of Yugoslavia, which typified the localized conflicts based on ethnicity, religion, and nationality that replaced the superpower conflicts of the cold war era. In what military analysts call "postmodern" or "future" wars, there is no distinction between armies and people—anybody who gets in the way gets killed. Unlike the Persian Gulf War, these conflicts do not rely on highly sophisticated technology and massive armies, but that does not keep them from being incredibly destructive.

The roots of the Bosnian conflict go back at least as far as the outbreak of World War I, but the immediate backdrop was the breakup of the state of Yugoslavia in 1991 into five independent states in the wake of the collapse of communism in Eastern Europe. Croatia and Slovenia secured their independence from the rump Yugoslavia government in brief, though intense, civil wars. Bosnia was not so lucky. The province of Bosnia and Herzegovina declared its independence in 1992, and its government, made up largely of Muslims and committed to a multiethnic (Serb, Croat, and Muslim) state, was quickly recognized by the United Nations. Bosnian Serbs, supported financially and militarily by Yugoslavia, formed their own breakaway state. They began a siege of the Bosnian capital, Sarajevo, site of the 1984 Winter Olympics, and launched a campaign of "ethnic cleansing" in the countryside. Bosnian Muslims and Croats were driven from their homes, put in concentration camps, or shot to death in mass executions. More than 250,000 people were killed or reported missing after war broke out in April 1992.

After three years of unsuccessful efforts by the European powers to stop the carnage, it was clear that the

Clinton in Bosnia

In his role as commander in chief, President Clinton visited Bosnia in January 1996 to show his support for the peace-keeping mission. Here he salutes American troops in the Bosnian town of Tuzla.

United States still had a critical role to play in guaranteeing European security. In November 1995 President Clinton and Secretary of State Warren Christopher facilitated a peace accord that ended the war, at least temporarily. Only the power of the United States commanded the respect of the three warring factions, and so the United States sent troops to Bosnia as part of a NATO-led force to implement the peace. As the world's only superpower, the United States was compelled to exercise its leadership—backed up by military force—to end the worst conflict in Europe since World War II.

At the same time, the end of cold war superpower rivalry presented unexpected opportunities to resolve other long-standing regional, ethnic, and religious conflicts. In Haiti, the threat of a U.S. invasion in October 1993 led to the restoration of the exiled president, Jean-Bertrand Aristide, who had been ousted by a military coup in 1991. In South Africa, the end of the fifty-year policy of racial separation was capped by the election of Nelson Mandela, who had spent twenty-seven years in prison for challenging apartheid, as the country's first black president in May 1994. With President Clinton proudly looking on, Israeli Prime Minister Yitzhak Rabin and Yasir Arafat, chairman of the Palestine Liberation Organization, signed an agreement in May 1994 allowing limited Palestinian self-rule in the Gaza Strip and Jericho. And in a move that was seen as a symbolic end to the American experience in Vietnam, the United States established diplomatic relations with Hanoi in July 1995, two decades after the fall of Saigon.

With the end of the Cold War, many citizens had hoped for a *peace dividend*, redirecting money from defense to domestic programs. But America's global responsibilities had not declined. Defense spending stayed near its cold war levels even in the Clinton administration. Despite closing up to 130 military bases around the country and making cutbacks in research and development for new weapons systems, the post–cold war defense budget averaged $280 billion, compared with the cold war average of $304 billion (in 1996 dollars). This small peace dividend was swallowed up by the huge deficit.

"The Era of Big Government Is Over"

The 1994 midterm election produced one of the most significant sea changes in recent political history, the culmination of the shift that had begun with Ronald Reagan's election in 1980. Republicans gained 52 seats in the House, giving them control for the first time in forty years; they also retook the Senate for the first time since 1986. The centerpiece of the new Republican majority in the House was the Contract with America, a list of legislation that Newt Gingrich of Georgia, the new Speaker, promised would be voted on in the first 100 days of the session. The key elements of the contract were constitutional amendments to balance the budget and set term limits for Congressional office, $245 billion in tax cuts for individuals and incentives for small businesses, cuts in welfare and other entitlement programs, anticrime initiatives, and cutbacks in federal regulations. Addressing the Republican Congress in his State of the Union message in January 1996, President Clinton acknowledged that "the era of big government is over."

Republicans in Congress
House Speaker Newt Gingrich, shown here in front of the Capitol in 1994, announces the Contract with America, which 73 freshmen Republican candidates rode to victory in the November election. The House's 236-member Republican majority passed many of the contract's planks in 1995, but most either failed to win passage in the Senate or were vetoed by President Clinton. By 1996 the Republican revolution had stalled on Capitol Hill.

Balancing the Budget. The Republicans' commitment to tax cuts *and* a balanced budget by the year 2002 led them to propose much deeper cuts than most Americans would accept. A glance at the major components of the federal budget suggests the difficulty of balancing the budget while also cutting taxes. The budget is divided into five roughly equal parts: interest on the debt; defense; health care costs (Medicare and Medicaid); Social Security; and discretionary spending, that is, everything else. Interest on the debt must be paid. Defense spending in the post–cold war world has declined only slightly. That leaves Medicare and Medicaid, Social Security, and everything else. Since Social Security was considered untouchable, Congress looked for savings in health care and discretionary spending.

Despite the failure of Clinton's health reform bill, by 1995 everyone agreed that it was essential to bring health care costs under control. Medicare, signed into law by President Johnson in 1965, had cost almost $160 billion in 1994, almost 10 percent of the entire federal budget. As new medical technologies proliferated and the number of elderly people increased, expenses were rising at a rate of 10 percent a year. In the fall of 1995 Congress passed a budget cutting $270 billion from projected spending on Medicare and $170 billion from Medicaid over seven years. Other savings came from cuts in various discretionary programs, including education and the environment. Clinton accepted Congress' resolve to balance the budget in seven years, but, vowing to protect the nation from an "extremist" Congress, he vetoed the budget itself. Unfunded departments of the government were forced to shut down twice, and polls showed that a majority of Americans held Congress, not the president, responsible. The budget that Clinton finally signed in April 1996 left Medicare and Social Security intact, though it did meet the Republicans' goal of cutting $23 billion in discretionary spending.

Welfare Reform. Since the Reagan Era, the old argument that the federal government has an obligation to the poor has been supplanted by rhetoric about cost-effectiveness, incentives, personal responsibility, and turning programs over to the states. Although Clinton had promised in the 1992 campaign to "end welfare as we know it," serious debate on the issue did not begin until the Republicans took over Congress in 1995. Welfare, a joint federal-state program, represented a fairly small part of the budget, but to Republicans it had become the prime example of misguided government priorities. The benefits of the main welfare program, AFDC, were far from generous: the average annual welfare payment to families (including Food Stamps) was $7,740, well below the 1995 poverty line of $12,188. In the 1990s both Democratic and Republican statehouses had adopted various financial incentives to try to change welfare beneficiaries' behavior, including setting time limits, imposing work requirements, and denying benefits for additional children born to women on AFDC. After vetoing two earlier versions, in August 1996 President Clinton signed a historic overhaul of the welfare system that ended the federal guarantee of cash assistance to poor children by abolishing AFDC, required most adult recipients to find work within two years, set a five-year limit on payments to any family, and gave states wide discretion in running their welfare programs.

The 1996 Election

The Republican takeover of Congress had one unintended consequence—it unified the usually fractious Democrats behind Bill Clinton. Unopposed in the primaries, Clinton was able to burnish his image as a moderate "New Democrat." His political fortunes were aided by the strong performance of the economy and the unpopularity of the Republican Congress since the government shutdowns.

In the Republican primaries, voters flirted with conservative commentator Pat Buchanan and magazine publisher Steve Forbes before settling on Senate Majority Leader Bob Dole of Kansas as their presidential candidate. Dole was acceptable to both conservative and moderate wings of the party, though his detached campaign style failed to generate much enthusiasm. He made a 15 percent across-the-board tax cut the centerpiece of his campaign, selecting former representative Jack Kemp, a leading proponent of supply-side economics, as his running-mate. Dole and Kemp promised to cut taxes *and* balance the budget by 2002, but their failure to specify what programs they would cut to achieve those goals undermined the credibility of the plan.

Americans seemed to have made up their minds early about the candidates, which made for a rather desultory campaign. Clinton emphasized his success in reducing the budget deficit, raising the minimum wage to $5.15, and reforming welfare, and he took credit for the 10 million new jobs created during his administration. In November, Clinton became the first Democratic president since Franklin Roosevelt to win reelection (see Map 33.6). Voter turnout was the lowest since Calvin Coolidge won in 1924. Despite fears of Democratic coattails, Republicans retained control of the House of Representatives and increased their majority in the Senate; they also maintained control of the majority of statehouses. Among the record number of initiatives on state ballots the most significant to win was California's Proposition 209, which sought to abolish affirmative action in government hiring, contracts, and public college admissions. In general, however, the main lesson of the election was voters' endorsement of the status quo

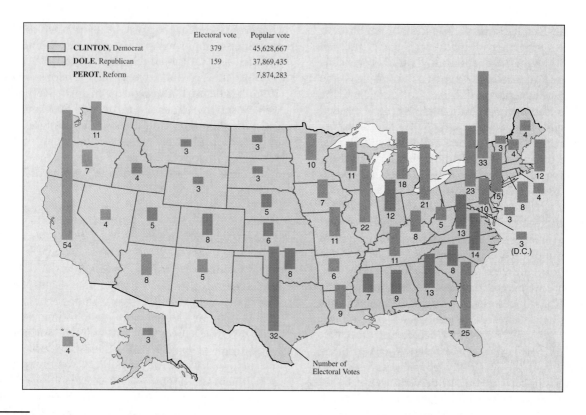

	Electoral vote	Popular vote
CLINTON, Democrat	379	45,628,667
DOLE, Republican	159	37,869,435
PEROT, Reform		7,874,283

MAP 33.6

The Election of 1996
Clinton and Gore broadened their electoral base from 1992, picking up traditional
Republican strongholds like Florida and dominating all regions of the country except
the South and the Great Plains. But with Republicans still in control of both houses of
Congress, Clinton faced uncertain prospects in his second term.

of divided government, with the hope that cooperation, rather than gridlock and paralysis, would characterize the final years of the twentieth century.

The Environmental Movement at Twenty-five, and Still Growing

As Americans came together for the twenty-fifth anniversary of Earth Day on April 26, 1995, they had much to celebrate. The nation's rivers and waterways were cleaner, air pollution had been reduced by a third, and lead emissions from fuel, a cause of retardation in children, had been cut by an astounding 98 percent. The bald eagle and the California condor had come back from the brink of extinction. More than 6,000 communities across the country had recycling programs.

There still was much to be done, activists realized. Despite efforts to reduce urban smog, two of five Americans lived in areas with unhealthy air. Too many rivers and lakes were still unsafe for fishing and swimming. One of four Americans lived within 4 miles of a toxic

waste dump, a trend that disproportionally affected lower-income communities. (This is called *environmental racism*.)

As part of the Contract with America, House Republicans had declared their intention to freeze or roll back environmental initiatives and subject new and existing regulations to a stringent cost-benefit analysis before they could take effect. Although they failed to pass legislation along these lines, they achieved part of their objective by effectively cutting the EPA's funding during the lengthy budget impasse. House Republicans began to moderate their stance only when polls showed strong disapproval for what was seen as their antienvironment position.

Whatever the outcome of the battles over environmental protection in Congress, it is increasingly clear that the environment, like so many other aspects of economics and politics in the 1990s, demands action not just from the United States but from the global community.

Three pressing environmental problems crossed national boundaries and demanded international action: the depletion of the ozone layer, acid rain, and global warming. An important precedent for international action on environmental issues was set by the 1987 Montreal protocol, where thirty-four nations agreed to phase out ozone-damaging chlorofluorocarbons (CFCs) by 1999. In 1991 the United States signed a treaty banning development on the Antarctic continent for fifty years and in 1992 agreed to stop dumping sludge in the ocean, pressing other countries to do the same. In June 1992 a major environmental Earth Summit in Rio de Janeiro adopted a treaty on global warming. In 1994 the United States joined sixty-three other countries in signing the Basel Convention, banning the export of hazardous wastes from industrialized to developing countries.

Making Sense of the Twentieth Century

In 1995 the *New York Times* asked readers to choose a name for the time we are living in. Perhaps not surprisingly, the responses were fairly pessimistic, with words such as *uncertainty, fragmentation, diminished expectations*, and *disillusionment* appearing often. Reflecting the importance of new technology, one reader suggested the Silicone Age; another submitted *Kokusaika* (Japanese for "internationalization"), arguing that a non-English word was appropriate to capture the internationalization of economics, politics, culture, and society. Others took the mandate a little less seriously, submitting "the Gray Nineties" (in deference to aging baby boomers) and "the Age that Even Historians from Harvard Can't Name." Of course eras, unlike people, are named at their deaths, not their births, and so the best thing to call our times is . . . the present.

But the present can be a confusing time. The period since 1980 has brought enormous changes: the end of the four-decade Cold War, a dramatic rethinking of the role of the state in modern American life, the ongoing globalization of political and economic life, and a growing diversity in American culture and public life. The last fifteen years will probably turn out to have been as important a period of realignment as the 1930s and 1940s, when the New Deal state was formed and the United States took on its global responsibilities in World War II and its aftermath. The period is certainly as dramatic as the 1890s, when the country completed the process of industrialization, absorbed a huge wave of immigrants, and secured an overseas empire.

While historians tend to leave the present to journalists, several themes from America's twentieth-century history will certainly influence its twenty-first. First, the United States will continue to be part of an interconnected global economy in which power is shared among multiple players. With trade barriers falling and cyberspace opening the entire world to instant communication, national boundaries and economies will be less important, and decisions made beyond the United States will affect the daily lives of American workers, managers, and consumers.

Second, the United States will continue to play the dominant role in the new world order that is emerging from the end of the Cold War. No other country has the combination of military resources and economic strength to play that role. But this leadership will be quantitatively different from America's role in the Cold War. In the 1990s the world appears to be returning to a situation in which power, both economic and military, is dispersed among a number of key players, of which the United States still is the most important. But also important are Japan, China, Singapore, Hong Kong, and other Pacific Rim countries; Canada and Mexico in North America; and the newly revitalized European Community (EC), with a strong Germany at its heart. Temporarily on the sidelines are the nations of the former Soviet Union and Eastern Europe.

Finally, political decisions made in the mid-1990s probably will ensure that the federal deficit will finally be tamed and the size of government will be reduced. Historians know that the Cold War is over, but it is too soon to tell whether it is time to put an absolute end date to the rise of the state. But a dramatic shift has occurred in the ways that Americans and their leaders seem to be thinking about government and the political system. These emerging domestic and world realities will shape the future of the United States and the globe in the twenty-first century and beyond.

Domestic Terrorism
On April 19, 1995, a powerful car bomb exploded outside the Alfred P. Murrah Federal building in Oklahoma City, killing 168 people, including nineteen children in the building's day care center. Antigovernment hostility was suspected as a possible motive of the two accused bombers, Timothy McVeigh and Terry Nichols.

Summary

Ronald Reagan's administration advocated a smaller role for the federal government in domestic programs and the restoration of American prestige abroad through a massive military buildup. The term *Reaganomics* stood for tax cuts and budget reductions enacted in 1981 and 1982. Reagan's economic policies, notably deregulation and tax cuts, added to the concentration of wealth in the 1980s. Reagan remained enormously popular throughout his two terms but left large budget deficits to his successor, Vice-President George Bush.

The most dramatic change during the Bush administration was the end of the Cold War, which had been the guiding principle of American foreign policy since the end of World War II. The dramatic collapse of communism in the Soviet Union in 1991 further complicated the old truisms. The post–cold war future seemed to promise a fragile world peace that would be vulnerable to regional and ethnic conflicts but in which the United States, as the world's only remaining superpower, would still play the dominant leadership role. The United States also played a leading role in an increasingly global economy but no longer dominated the world economy as it had done during the *Pax Americana* of the immediate postwar world.

American society in the 1980s and 1990s continued to turn inward to address its own needs. Increased immigration, notably from Asia and Latin America, changed the demographic balance of many areas, especially the cities, and the strains of an increasingly diverse society were reflected in debates over affirmative action and multiculturalism. Slow productivity growth, wage stagnation, and growing inequality in income were the major domestic economic trends. Meanwhile, American businesses struggled to compete in an increasingly competitive global marketplace. The information superhighway and cyberspace pointed to a high-tech future.

Soon after the Democrats regained the White House with the election of Bill Clinton in 1992, the Republican landslide of 1994 reshaped politics dramatically by emphasizing a balanced budget, tax cuts, and shrinking the federal government by turning programs over to the states. In January 1996 even President Clinton admitted, "The era of big government is over." In August he signed a welfare reform bill that ended the federal guarantee of cash assistance to the poor. Clinton won reelection to a second term, but continued Republican control of Congress suggested that the long-term trend of federal activism had been reversed.

TIMELINE

1981	Economic Recovery Tax Act Sandra Day O'Connor nominated to Supreme Court MTV premieres Beginning of AIDS epidemic
1982	Recession
1983	Star Wars proposed
1984	Geraldine Ferraro becomes first woman on major party ticket
1985	Gramm-Rudman Balanced Budget Act United States becomes a debtor nation Mikhail Gorbachev takes power in U.S.S.R
1986	Iran-Contra affair Simpson-Mazzoli Immigration Act
1987	Montreal environmental protocol Stock market collapse
1988	George Bush elected president
1989	Savings and loan crisis Political revolutions in Eastern Europe *Webster v. Reproductive Health Services*
1990–1991	Persian Gulf crisis
1990–1992	Recession
1991	Dissolution of Soviet Union ends Cold War Clarence Thomas–Anita Hill hearings
1992	Los Angeles riots Earth Summit at Rio de Janeiro Bill Clinton elected president
1993	Family and Medical Leave Act NAFTA ratified
1994	Omnibus Violent Crime Control and Prevention Act Health care reform fails Republicans gain control of Congress
1995	Congress passes parts of the Contract with America United States establishes diplomatic relations with Vietnam University of California votes to end affirmative action plan Twenty-fifth anniversary of Earth Day U.S. troops enforce peace in Bosnia
1996	Personal Responsibility and Work Opportunity Act (welfare reform) Bill Clinton reelected president

BIBLIOGRAPHY

Few historians have turned their attention to the period after 1980, leaving the field to journalists, economists, and political scientists. The Bureau of the Census offers a fine introduction to the period in its *Statistical Abstract of the United States* (114th ed., 1994). Essays on important issues are available in the *Congressional Quarterly Researcher*. Indexes to newspapers and periodicals point toward stories on major events.

The Reagan Presidency

Haynes Johnson, *Sleepwalking through History* (1991), provides an excellent overview of America in the Reagan years. See also Robert Dallek, *Ronald Reagan: The Politics of Symbolism* (1982); Michael Rogin, *Ronald Reagan: The Movie* (1987); and Lou Cannon, *President Reagan: A Role of a Lifetime* (1991). Nancy Reagan presents her interpretation of the Reagan years in *My Turn* (1989), and the speechwriter Peggy Noonan offers an insider's view in *What I Saw at the Revolution* (1990).

On Reaganomics, George Gilder's *Wealth and Poverty* (1981) represents the views held by many in the Reagan administration, but David Stockman's memoir, *The Triumph of Politics* (1986), is more revealing. See also Benjamin Friedman, *Day of Reckoning: The Consequences of American Economic Policy under Reagan and After* (1988).

For foreign policy, Stephen Ambrose, *Rise to Globalism* (7th ed., 1993), provides a comprehensive overview of the Reagan and Bush years. The Iran-Contra scandal is covered in Jane Hunter et al., *The Iran-Contra Connection* (1987). Good introductions to the United States and Central and South America include Walter LaFeber, *Inevitable Revolutions* (1984); Abraham F. Lowenthal, *Partners in Conflict: The United States and Latin America* (1987); and Kenneth Coleman and George C. Herring, eds., *The Central America Crisis* (1985).

The Bush Presidency and the End of the Cold War

On the Bush administration, see James A. Baker, *The Politics of Diplomacy* (1995); Barbara Bush, *Barbara Bush: A Memoir* (1994); and Stephen R. Graubard, *Mr. Bush's War: Adventures in the Politics of Illusion* (1992). On politics, see E. J. Dionne, *Why Americans Hate Politics* (1992); William Greider, *Who Will Tell the People?* (1992); and Kevin Phillips, *The Politics of Rich and Poor: Wealth and the American Electorate in the Reagan Aftermath* (1990).

The emergence of a new world order has provoked commentary from economists, journalists, and historians, including Paul Kennedy, *The Rise and Fall of the Great Powers* (1987); Joseph Nye, *Bound to Lead: The Changing Nature of American Power* (1990); Robert Kuttner, *The End of Laissez Faire: National Purpose and the Global Economy after the Cold War* (1991); and Henry R. Nau, *The Myth of America's Decline: Leading the World Economy into the 1990s* (1990). Bernard Gwertzman and Michael T. Kaufman, eds., *The Collapse of Communism* (1990), reviews the events of 1989 through articles published in the *New York Times*. See also Michael Beschloss and Strobe Talbott, *At the Highest Levels: The Inside Story of the End of the Cold War* (1994). H. Norman Schwartzkopf's autobiography, *It Doesn't Take a Hero* (1992), recounts the Gulf War, as does former chairman of the Joint Chiefs of Staff Colin Powell in *My American Journey* (1995).

An Age of Anxiety

Paul Krugman provides an overview of economic trends since the 1970s in *Peddling Prosperity: Economic Sense and Nonsense in the Age of Diminished Expectations* (1994); Jeffrey Madrick, *The End of Affluence* (1995), makes similar points. For overviews of U.S. competitiveness in the global marketplace, see Hedrick Smith, *Rethinking America* (1995); Lester Thurow, *Head to Head: The Coming Economic Battle among Japan, Europe, and America* (1992); and Robert B. Reich, *The Work of Nations: Preparing Ourselves for 21st Century Capitalism* (1991). Books that address the growing inequality in American life include William J. Wilson, *The Truly Disadvantaged* (1987); Michael Katz, *The Undeserving Poor: From the War on Poverty to the War on Welfare* (1989); Nicholas Lemann, *The Promised Land* (1989); and Linda Gordon, *Pitied but Not Entitled: Single Mothers and the History of Welfare* (1994).

On the problems of women, work, and families, see Hilda Scott, *Working Your Way to the Bottom: The Feminization of Poverty* (1985); Arlie Hochschild, *The Second Shift: Working Parents and the Revolution at Home* (1989); and Juliet Schor, *The Overworked American* (1991). For feminism and its critics, see Susan Faludi, *Backlash: The Undeclared War on American Women* (1991). Toni Morrison, ed., *Race-ing Justice, En-gendering Power* (1992), covers the Clarence Thomas-Anita Hill hearings.

David Reimers, *Still the Golden Door* (2d ed., 1992), covers immigration policy in the postwar period. Linda Chavez, *Out of the Barrio* (1991), discusses Hispanic assimilation, while Ronald Takaki, *Strangers from a Different Shore* (1989), covers Asian-Americans. Also of interest is Julian Simon, *The Economic Consequences of Immigration* (1989).

Randy Shilts, *And the Band Played On: Politics, People, and the AIDS Epidemic* (1987), is a controversial critique of inaction in the early years of the AIDS epidemic. See also Elinor Burkett, *The Gravest Show on Earth: America in the Age of AIDS* (1995). Allan Bloom, *The Closing of the American Mind* (1987), and E. D. Hirsch, Jr., *Cultural Literacy* (1988), deal with issues of curriculum, learning, and literacy. For differing views on affirmative action, see Stephen L. Carter, *Reflections of an Affirmative Action Baby* (1991), and Gertrude Ezorsky, *Racism and Justice: The Case for Affirmative Action* (1991). For the story of Bill Gates and Microsoft, see Steven Manes, *Gates: How Microsoft's Mogul Reinvented an Industry—and Made Himself the Richest Man in America* (1993); James Wallace, *Hard Drive* (1992); and Gates's own *The Road Ahead* (1995).

Restructuring the Domestic Order

For an excellent overview of Clinton's first year, see Elizabeth Drew, *Finding His Voice* (1994). Other sources include Bob Woodward, *The Agenda* (1994); Roger Morris, *Promises of Change* (1996); and Richard Cohen, *Changing the Guard* (1993). On the Republican agenda, see Newt Gingrich, *To Renew America* (1995).

Gregg Easterbrook provides a general overview of the environment in *A Moment on the Earth* (1995). Al Gore, *Earth in the Balance* (1992), reports on how well or poorly the world is doing on environmental awareness. Daniel Yergin, *The Prize* (1991), chronicles how oil dominates modern life, with both economic and environmental consequences.

The Declaration of Independence

★   ★   ★

The Unanimous Declaration of the Thirteen United States of America

When in the Course of human events, it becomes necessary for one people to dissolve the political bands which have connected them with another, and to assume among the Powers of the earth, the separate and equal station to which the Laws of Nature and of Nature's God entitle them, a decent respect to the opinions of mankind requires that they should declare the causes which impel them to the separation.

We hold these truths to be self-evident, that all men are created equal, that they are endowed by their Creator with certain unalienable rights, that among these are Life, Liberty, and the pursuit of Happiness. That to secure these rights, Governments are instituted among Men, deriving their just powers from the consent of the governed. That whenever any Form of Government becomes destructive of these ends, it is the Right of the People to alter or to abolish it, and to institute new Government, laying its foundation on such principles and organizing its powers in such form, as to them shall seem most likely to effect their Safety and Happiness. Prudence, indeed, will dictate that Governments long established should not be changed for light and transient causes; and accordingly all experience hath shown, that mankind are more disposed to suffer, while evils are sufferable, than to right themselves by abolishing the forms to which they are accustomed. But when a long train of abuses and usurpations, pursuing invariably the same Object evinces a design to reduce them under absolute Despotism, it is their right, it is their duty, to throw off such Government, and to provide new Guards for their future security.—Such has been the patient sufferance of these Colonies; and such is now the necessity which constrains them to alter their former Systems of Government. The history of the present King of Great Britain is a history of repeated injuries and usurpations, all having in direct object the estab-

lishment of an absolute Tyranny over these States. To prove this, let Facts be submitted to a candid world.

He has refused his Assent to Laws, the most wholesome and necessary for the public good.

He has forbidden his Governors to pass Laws of immediate and pressing importance, unless suspended in their operation till his Assent should be obtained; and, when so suspended, he has utterly neglected to attend to them.

He has refused to pass other Laws for the accommodation of large districts of people, unless those people would relinquish the right of Representation in the Legislature, a right inestimable to them and formidable to tyrants only.

He has called together legislative bodies at places unusual, uncomfortable, and distant from the depository of their public Records, for the sole purpose of fatiguing them into compliance with his measures.

He has dissolved Representative Houses repeatedly, for opposing with manly firmness his invasions on the rights of the people.

He has refused for a long time, after such dissolutions, to cause others to be elected; whereby the Legislative powers, incapable of Annihilation, have returned to the People at large for their exercise; the State remaining in the mean time exposed to all the dangers of invasion from without and convulsions within.

He has endeavoured to prevent the population of these States; for that purpose obstructing the Laws of Naturalization of Foreigners; refusing to pass others to encourage their migrations hither, and raising the conditions of new Appropriations of Lands.

He has obstructed the Administration of Justice, by refusing his Assent to Laws for establishing Judiciary powers.

He has made Judges dependent on his Will alone, for the tenure of their offices, and the amount and payment of their salaries.

He has erected a multitude of New Offices, and sent hither swarms of Officers to harass our People, and eat out their substance.

He has kept among us, in times of peace, Standing Armies without the Consent of our legislature.

He has combined with others to subject us to a jurisdiction foreign to our constitution, and unacknowledged by our laws; giving his Assent to their Acts of pretended Legislation:

For quartering large bodies of armed troops among us:

For protecting them, by a mock Trial, from Punishment for any Murders which they should commit on the Inhabitants of these States:

For cutting off our Trade with all parts of the world:

For imposing taxes on us without our Consent:

For depriving us of many cases, of the benefits of Trial by jury:

For transporting us beyond Seas to be tried for pretended offences:

For abolishing the free System of English Laws in a neighbouring Province, establishing therein an Arbitrary government, and enlarging its Boundaries so as to render it at once an example and fit instrument for introducing the same absolute rule into these Colonies;

For taking away our Charters, abolishing our most valuable Laws, and altering fundamentally the Forms of our Governments:

For suspending our own Legislatures, and declaring themselves invested with Power to legislate for us in all cases whatsoever.

He has abdicated Government here, by declaring us out of his Protection and waging War against us.

He has plundered our seas, ravaged our Coasts, burnt our towns, and destroyed the lives of our people.

He is at this time transporting large armies of foreign mercenaries to compleat the works of death, desolation, and tyranny, already begun with circumstances of Cruelty & perfidy scarcely parallelled in the most barbarous ages, and totally unworthy the Head of a civilized nation.

He has constrained our fellow Citizens taken Captive on the high Seas to bear Arms against their Country, to become the executioners of their friends and Brethren, or to fall themselves by their Hands.

He has excited domestic insurrections amongst us, and has endeavoured to bring on the inhabitants of our frontiers, the merciless Indian Savages, whose known rule of warfare, is an undistinguished destruction of all ages, sexes, and conditions.

In every stage of these Oppressions We have Petitioned for Redress in the most humble terms: Our repeated Petitions have been answered only by repeated injury. A Prince, whose character is thus marked by every act which may define a Tyrant, is unfit to be the ruler of a free people.

Nor have We been wanting in attention to our British brethren. We have warned them from time to time of attempts by their legislature to extend an unwarrantable jurisdiction over us. We have reminded them of the circumstances of our emigration and settlement here. We have appealed to their native justice and magnanimity, and we have conjured them by the ties of our common kindred to disavow these usurpations, which, would inevitably interrupt our connections and correspondence. They too have been deaf to the voice of justice and of consanguinity. We must, therefore, acquiesce in the necessity, which denounces our Separation, and hold them, as we hold the rest of mankind, Enemies in War, in Peace Friends.

We, therefore, the Representatives of the United States of America, in General Congress, Assembled, appealing to the Supreme Judge of the world for the rectitude of our intentions, do, in the Name, and by Authority of the good People of these Colonies, solemnly publish and declare, That these United Colonies are, and of Right ought to be FREE AND INDEPENDENT STATES; that they are Absolved from all Allegiance to the British Crown, and that all political connection between them and the State of Great Britain, is and ought to be totally dissolved; and that as Free and Independent States, they have full Power to levy War, conclude Peace, contract Alliances, establish Commerce, and to do all other Acts and Things which Independent States may of right do. And for the support of this Declaration, with a firm reliance on the Protection of Divine Providence, we mutually pledge to each other our Lives, our Fortunes, and our sacred Honor.

John Hancock

Button Gwinnett	George Wythe	James Wilson	Josiah Bartlett
Lyman Hall	Richard Henry Lee	Geo. Ross	Wm. Whipple
Geo. Walton	Th. Jefferson	Caesar Rodney	Saml. Adams
Wm. Hooper	Benja. Harrison	Geo. Read	John Adams
Joseph Hewes	Thos. Nelson, Jr.	Thos. M'Kean	Robt. Treat Paine
John Penn	Francis Lightfoot Lee	Wm. Floyd	Elbridge Gerry
Edward Rutledge	Carter Braxton	Phil. Livingston	Step. Hopkins
Thos. Heyward, Junr.	Robt. Morris	Frans. Lewis	William Ellery
Thomas Lynch, Junr.	Benjamin Rush	Lewis Morris	Roger Sherman
Arthur Middleton	Benja. Franklin	Richd. Stockton	Sam'el Hunington
Samuel Chase	John Morton	Jno. Witherspoon	Wm. Williams
Wm. Paca	Geo. Clymer	Fras. Hopkinson	Oliver Wolcott
Thos. Stone	Jas. Smith	John Hart	Matthew Thornton
Charles Carroll of Carrollton	Geo. Taylor	Abra. Clark	

The Articles of Confederation and Perpetual Union

★   ★   ★

BETWEEN THE STATES OF NEW HAMPSHIRE, MASSACHU-
SETTS BAY, RHODE ISLAND AND PROVIDENCE PLANTA-
TIONS, CONNECTICUT, NEW YORK, NEW JERSEY, PENN-
SYLVANIA, DELAWARE, MARYLAND, VIRGINIA, NORTH
CAROLINA, SOUTH CAROLINA, GEORGIA.*

Article 1.

The stile of this confederacy shall be "The United States of
America."

Article 2.

Each State retains its sovereignty, freedom and independence,
and every power, jurisdiction, and right, which is not by this
confederation expressly delegated to the United States, in
Congress assembled.

Article 3.

The said states hereby severally enter into a firm league of
friendship with each other for their common defence, the security of their liberties and their mutual and general welfare;
binding themselves to assist each other against all force offered to, or attacks made upon them, or any of them, on account of religion, sovereignty, trade, or any other pretence
whatever.

*This copy of the final draft of the Articles of Confederation is taken from
the *Journals*, 9:907–925, November 15, 1777.

Article 4.

The better to secure and perpetuate mutual friendship and intercourse among the people of the different states in this
union, the free inhabitants of each of these states, paupers,
vagabonds, and fugitives from justice excepted, shall be entitled to all privileges and immunities of free citizens in the several states; and the people of each State shall have free ingress
and regress to and from any other State, and shall enjoy
therein all the privileges of trade and commerce, subject to the
same duties, impositions, and restrictions, as the inhabitants
thereof respectively; provided, that such restrictions shall not
extend so far as to prevent the removal of property, imported
into any State, to any other State of which the owner is an inhabitant; provided also, that no imposition, duties, or restriction, shall be laid by any State on the property of the United
States, or either of them.

If any person guilty of, or charged with treason, felony, or
other high misdemeanor in any State, shall flee from justice
and be found in any of the United States, he shall, upon demand of the governor or executive power of the State from
which he fled, be delivered up and removed to the State having
jurisdiction of his offence.

Full faith and credit shall be given in each of these states
to the records, acts, and judicial proceedings of the courts and
magistrates of every other State.

Article 5.

For the more convenient management of the general interests
of the United States, delegates shall be annually appointed, in
such manner as the legislature of each State shall direct, to
meet in Congress, on the 1st Monday in November in every

year, with a power reserved to each State to recal its delegates, or any of them, at any time within the year, and to send others in their stead for the remainder of the year.

No State shall be represented in Congress by less than two, nor by more than seven members; and no person shall be capable of being a delegate for more than three years in any term of six years; nor shall any person, being a delegate, be capable of holding any office under the United States, for which he, or any other for his benefit, receives any salary, fees, or emolument of any kind.

Each State shall maintain its own delegates in a meeting of the states, and while they act as members of the committee of the states.

In determining questions in the United States, in Congress assembled, each State shall have one vote.

Freedom of speech and debate in Congress shall not be impeached or questioned in any court or place out of Congress: and the members of Congress shall be protected in their persons from arrests and imprisonments, during the time of their going to and from, and attendance on Congress, *except for treason*, felony, or breach of the peace.

Article 6.

No State, without the consent of the United States, in Congress assembled, shall send any embassy to, or receive any embassy from, or enter into any conference, agreement, alliance, or treaty with any king, prince, or state; nor shall any person, holding any office of profit or trust under the United States, or any of them, accept of any present, emolument, office or title, of any kind whatever, from any king, prince, or foreign state; nor shall the United States, in Congress assembled, or any of them, grant any title of nobility.

No two or more states shall enter into any treaty, confederation, or alliance, whatever, between them, without the consent of the United States, in Congress assembled, specifying accurately the purposes for which the same is to be entered into, and how long it shall continue.

No state shall lay any imposts or duties which may interfere with any stipulations in treaties entered into by the United States, in Congress assembled, with any king, prince, or state, in pursuance of any treaties already proposed by Congress to the courts of France and Spain.

No vessels of war shall be kept up in time of peace by any State, except such number only as shall be deemed necessary by the United States, in Congress assembled, for the defence of such State or its trade; nor shall any body of forces be kept up by any State, in time of peace, except such number only as, in the judgment of the United States, in Congress assembled, shall be deemed requisite to garrison the forts necessary for the defence of such State; but every State shall always keep up a well regulated and disciplined militia, sufficiently armed and accoutred, and shall provide, and constantly have ready for use, in public stores, a due number of field pieces and tents, and a proper quantity of arms, ammunition and camp equipage.

No State shall engage in any war without the consent of the United States, in Congress assembled, unless such State be actually invaded by enemies, or shall have received certain advice of a resolution being formed by some nation of Indians to invade such State, and the danger is so imminent as not to admit of a delay till the United States, in Congress assembled, can be consulted; nor shall any State grant commissions to any ships or vessels of war, nor letters of marque or reprisal, except it be after a declaration of war by the United States, in Congress assembled, and then only against the kingdom or state, and the subjects thereof, against which war has been so declared, and under such regulations as shall be established by the United States, in Congress assembled, unless such State be infested by pirates, in which case vessels of war may be fitted out for that occasion, and kept so long as the danger shall continue, or until the United States, in Congress assembled, shall determine otherwise.

Article 7.

When land forces are raised by any State for the common defence, all officers of or under the rank of colonel, shall be appointed by the legislature of each State respectively, by whom such forces shall be raised, or in such manner as such State shall direct; and all vacancies shall be filled up by the State which first made the appointment.

Article 8.

All charges of war and all other expences, that shall be incurred for the common defence or general welfare, and allowed by the United States, in Congress assembled, shall be defrayed out of a common treasury, which shall be supplied by the several states, in proportion to the value of all land within each State, granted to or surveyed for any person, as such land and the buildings and improvements thereon shall be estimated according to such mode as the United States, in Congress assembled, shall, from time to time, direct and appoint.

The taxes for paying that proportion shall be laid and levied by the authority and direction of the legislatures of the several states, within the time agreed upon by the United States, in Congress assembled.

Article 9.

The United States, in Congress assembled, shall have the sole and exclusive right and power of determining on peace and war, except in the cases mentioned in the 6th article; of sending and receiving ambassadors; entering into treaties and alliances, provided that no treaty of commerce shall be made, whereby the legislative power of the respective states shall be restrained from imposing such imposts and duties on foreigners as their own people are subjected to, or from prohibiting the exportation or importation of any species of goods or commodities whatsoever; of establishing rules for deciding, in all cases, what captures on land or water shall be legal, and in what manner prizes, taken by land or naval forces in the service of the United States, shall be divided or appropriated; of granting letters of marque and reprisal in times of peace; appointing courts for the trial of piracies and felonies committed on the high seas, and establishing courts for receiving and determining, finally, appeals in all cases of captures; provided, that no member of Congress shall be appointed a judge of any of the said courts.

The United States, in Congress assembled, shall also be the last resort on appeal in all disputes and differences now subsisting, or that hereafter may arise between two or more states concerning boundary, jurisdiction or any other cause whatever; which authority shall always be exercised in the manner following: whenever the legislative or executive authority, or lawful agent of any State, in controversy with another, shall present a petition to Congress, stating the matter in question, and praying for a hearing, notice thereof shall be given, by order of Congress, to the legislative or executive authority of the other State in controversy, and a day assigned for the appearance of the parties by their lawful agents, who shall then be directed to appoint, by joint consent, commissioners or judges to constitute a court for hearing and determining the matter in question; but, if they cannot agree, Congress shall name three persons out of each of the United States, and from the list of such persons each party shall alternately strike out one, the petitioners beginning, until the number shall be reduced to thirteen; and from that number not less than seven, nor more than nine names, as Congress shall direct, shall, in the presence of Congress, be drawn out by lot; and the persons whose names shall be so drawn, or any five of them, shall be commissioners or judges to hear and finally determine the controversy, so always as a major part of the judges who shall hear the cause shall agree in the determination; and if either party shall neglect to attend at the day appointed, without shewing reasons which Congress shall judge sufficient, or, being present, shall refuse to strike, the Congress shall proceed to nominate three persons out of each State, and the secretary of Congress shall strike in behalf of such party absent or refusing; and the judgment and sentence of the court to be appointed, in the manner before prescribed, shall be final and conclusive; and if any of the parties shall refuse to submit to the authority of such court, or to appear or defend their claim or cause, the court shall nevertheless proceed to pronounce sentence or judgment, which shall, in like manner, be final and decisive, the judgment or sentence and other proceedings begin, in either case, transmitted to Congress, and lodged among the acts of Congress for the security of the parties concerned: provided, that every commissioner, before he sits in judgment, shall take an oath, to be administered by one of the judges of the supreme or superior court of the State where the cause shall be tried, "well and truly to hear and determine the matter in question, according to the best of his judgment, without favour, affection, or hope of reward:" provided, also, that no State shall be deprived of territory for the benefit of the United States.

All controversies concerning the private right of soil, claimed under different grants of two or more states, whose jurisdictions, as they may respect such lands and the states which passed such grants, are adjusted, the said grants, or either of them, being at the same time claimed to have originated antecedent to such settlement of jurisdiction, shall, on the petition of either party to the Congress of the United States, be finally determined, as near as may be, in the same manner as is before prescribed for deciding disputes respecting territorial jurisdiction between different states.

The United States, in Congress assembled, shall also have the sole and exclusive right and power of regulating the alloy and value of coin struck by their own authority, or by that of the respective states; fixing the standard of weights and measures throughout the United States; regulating the trade and managing all affairs with the Indians not members of any of the states; provided that the legislative right of any State within its own limits be not infringed or violated; establishing and regulating post offices from one State to another throughout all the United States, and exacting such postage on the papers passing through the same as may be requisite to defray the expences of the said office; appointing all officers of the land forces in the service of the United States, excepting regimental officers; appointing all the officers of the naval forces, and commissioning all officers whatever in the service of the United States; making rules for the government and regulation of the said land and naval forces, and directing their operations.

The United States, in Congress assembled, shall have authority to appoint a committee to sit in the recess of Congress, to be denominated "a Committee of the States," and to consist of one delegate from each State, and to appoint such other committees and civil officers as may be necessary for managing the general affairs of the United States, under their direction; to appoint one of their number to preside; provided that no person be allowed to serve in the office of president more than one year in any term of three years; to ascertain the necessary sums of money to be raised for the service of the United States, and to appropriate and apply the same for defraying the public expences; to borrow money or emit bills on the credit of the United States, transmitting, every half year, to the respective states, an account of the sums of money so borrowed or emitted; to build and equip a navy; to agree upon the number of land forces, and to make requisitions from each State for its quota, in proportion to the number of white inhabitants in such State; which requisitions shall be binding; and thereupon, the legislature of each State shall appoint the regimental officers, raise the men, and cloathe, arm, and equip them in a soldier-like manner, at the expence of the United States; and the officers and men so cloathed, armed, and equipped, shall march to the place appointed and within the time agreed on by the United States, in Congress assembled; but if the United States, in Congress assembled, shall, on consideration of circumstances, judge proper that any State should not raise men, or should raise a smaller number than its quota, and that any other State should raise a greater number of men than the quota thereof, such extra number shall be raised, officered, cloathed, armed, and equipped in the same manner as the quota of such State, unless the legislature of such State shall judge that such extra number cannot be safely spared out of the same, in which case they shall raise, officer, cloathe, arm, and equip as many of such extra number as they judge can be safely spared. And the officers and men so cloathed, armed, and equipped, shall march to the place appointed and within the time agreed on by the United States, in Congress assembled.

The United States, in Congress assembled, shall never engage in a war, nor grant letters of marque and reprisal in time of peace, nor enter into any treaties or alliances, nor coin money, nor regulate the value thereof, nor ascertain the sums and expences necessary for the defence and welfare of the United States, or any of them: nor emit bills, nor borrow money on the credit of the United States, nor appropriate money, nor agree upon the number of vessels of war to be built or purchased, or the number of land or sea forces to be raised, nor appoint a commander in chief of the army or navy, unless nine states assent to the same; nor shall a question on any other point, except for adjourning from day to day, be determined, unless by the votes of a majority of the United States, in Congress assembled.

The Congress of the United States shall have power to adjourn to any time within the year, and to any place within the United States, so that no period of adjournment be for a longer duration than the space of six months, and shall publish the journal of their proceedings monthly, except such parts thereof, relating to treaties, alliances or military operations, as, in their judgment, require secrecy; and the yeas and nays of the delegates of each State on any question shall be entered on the journal, when it is desired by any delegate; and the delegates of a State, or any of them, at his, or their request, shall be furnished with a transcript of the said journal, except such parts as are above excepted, to lay before the legislatures of the several states.

Article 10.

The committee of the states, or any nine of them, shall be authorized to execute, in the recess of Congress, such of the powers of Congress as the United States, in Congress assembled, by the consent of nine states, shall, from time to time, think expedient to vest them with; provided, that no power be delegated to the said committee, for the exercise of which, by the articles of confederation, the voice of nine states, in the Congress of the United States assembled, is requisite.

Article 11.

Canada acceding to this confederation, and joining in the measures of the United States, shall be admitted into and entitled to all the advantages of this union; but no other colony shall be admitted into the same, unless such admission be agreed to by nine states.

Article 12.

All bills of credit emitted, monies borrowed and debts contracted by, or under the authority of Congress before the assembling of the United States, in pursuance of the present confederation, shall be deemed and considered as a charge against the United States, for payment and satisfaction whereof the said United States and the public faith are hereby solemnly pledged.

Article 13.

Every State shall abide by the determinations of the United States, in Congress assembled, on all questions which, by this confederation, are submitted to them. And the articles of this confederation shall be inviolably observed by every State, and the union shall be perpetual; nor shall any alteration at any time hereafter be made in any of them, unless such alteration be agreed to in a Congress of the United States, and be afterwards confirmed by the legislatures of every State.

These articles shall be proposed to the legislatures of all the United States, to be considered, and if approved of by them, they are advised to authorize their delegates to ratify the same in the Congress of the United States; which being done, the same shall become conclusive.

The Constitution of the United States of America

★　　★　　★

We the People of the United States, in Order to form a more perfect Union, establish Justice, insure domestic Tranquility, provide for the common defence, promote the general Welfare, and secure the Blessings of Liberty to ourselves and our Posterity, do ordain and establish this Constitution for the United States of America.

Article I

Section 1 All legislative Powers herein granted shall be vested in a Congress of the United States, which shall consist of a Senate and a House of Representatives.

Section 2 The House of Representatives shall be composed of Members chosen every second Year by the People of the several States, and the Electors in each State shall have the Qualifications requisite for Electors of the most numerous Branch of the State Legislature.

No Person shall be a Representative who shall not have attained to the Age of twenty-five Years, and been seven Years a Citizen of the United States, and who shall not, when elected, be an Inhabitant of that State in which he shall be chosen.

Representatives and direct Taxes shall be apportioned among the several States which may be included within this Union, according to their respective Numbers, *which shall be determined by adding to the whole Number of free Persons, including those bound to Service for a Term of Years, and excluding Indians not taxed, three fifths of all other Persons.* The actual Enumeration shall be made within three Years after the first Meeting of the Congress of the United States, and within every subsequent Term of ten Years, in such Manner as they shall by Law direct. The Number of Representatives shall not exceed one for every thirty Thousand, but each State shall have at Least one Representative; and *until such*

enumeration shall be made, the State of New Hampshire shall be entitled to chuse three, Massachusetts eight, Rhode Island and Providence Plantations one, Connecticut five, New-York six, New Jersey four, Pennsylvania eight, Delaware one, Maryland six, Virginia ten, North Carolina five, South Carolina five, and Georgia three.

When vacancies happen in the Representation from any State, the Executive Authority thereof shall issue Writs of Election to fill such Vacancies.

The House of Representatives shall chuse their Speaker and other Officers; and shall have the sole Power of Impeachment.

Section 3 The Senate of the United States shall be composed of two Senators from each State, *chosen by the Legislature thereof,*[†] for six Years; and each Senator shall have one Vote.

Immediately after they shall be assembled in Consequence of the first Election, they shall be divided as equally as may be into three Classes. The Seats of the Senators of the first Class shall be vacated at the Expiration of the second Year, of the second Class at the Expiration of the fourth Year, and of the third Class at the Expiration of the sixth Year, so that one-third may be chosen every second Year; *and if Vacancies happen by Resignation, or otherwise, during the Recess of the Legislature of any State, the Executive thereof may make temporary Appointments until the next Meeting of the Legislature, which shall then fill such Vacancies.*[‡]

No person shall be a Senator who shall not have attained to the Age of thirty Years, and been nine Years a Citizen of the United States, and who shall not, when elected, be an Inhabitant of that State for which he shall be chosen.

The Vice President of the United States shall be President of the Senate, but shall have no Vote, unless they be equally divided.

Note: The Constitution became effective March 4, 1789. Provisions in italics have been changed by constitutional amendment.

*Changed by Section 2 of the Fourteenth Amendment.

[†]Changed by Section 1 of the Seventeenth Amendment.

[‡]Changed by Clause 2 of the Seventeenth Amendment.

The Senate shall chuse their other Officers, and also a President pro tempore, in the absence of the Vice President, or when he shall exercise the Office of President of the United States.

The Senate shall have the sole Power to try all Impeachments. When sitting for that Purpose, they shall be on Oath or Affirmation. When the President of the United States is tried, the Chief Justice shall preside: And no Person shall be convicted without the Concurrence of two thirds of the Members present.

Judgment in Cases of Impeachment shall not extend further than to removal from Office, and disqualification to hold and enjoy any Office of honor, Trust or Profit under the United States: but the Party convicted shall nevertheless be liable and subject to Indictment, Trial, Judgment and Punishment, according to Law.

Section 4 The Times, Places and Manner of holding Elections for Senators and Representatives, shall be prescribed in each State by the Legislature thereof; but the Congress may at any time by Law make or alter such Regulations, except as to the Places of Chusing Senators.

The Congress shall assemble at least once in every Year, and such Meeting *shall be on the first Monday in December, unless they shall by Law appoint a different Day.**

Section 5 Each House shall be the Judge of the Elections, Returns and Qualifications of its own Members, and a Majority of each shall constitute a Quorum to do Business; but a smaller number may adjourn from day to day, and may be authorized to compel the Attendance of absent Members, in such Manner, and under such Penalties, as each House may provide.

Each House may determine the Rules of its Proceedings, punish its Members for disorderly Behavior, and, with the Concurrence of two thirds, expel a Member.

Each House shall keep a Journal of its Proceedings, and from time to time publish the same, excepting such Parts as may in their Judgment require Secrecy; and the Yeas and Nays of the Members of either House on any question shall, at the Desire of one-fifth of those Present, be entered on the Journal.

Neither House, during the Session of Congress, shall, without the Consent of the other, adjourn for more than three days, nor to any other Place than that in which the two Houses shall be sitting.

Section 6 The Senators and Representatives shall receive a Compensation for their Services, to be ascertained by Law, and paid out of the Treasury of the United States. They shall in all Cases, except Treason, Felony and Breach of the Peace, be privileged from Arrest during their Attendance at the Session of their respective Houses, and in going to and returning from the same; and for any Speech or Debate in either House, they shall not be questioned in any other Place.

No Senator or Representative shall, during the Time for which he was elected, be appointed to any civil Office under the Authority of the United States, which shall have been created, or the Emoluments whereof shall have been increased, during such time; and no Person holding any Office under the United States, shall be a Member of either House during his Continuance in Office.

Section 7 All Bills for raising Revenue shall originate in the House of Representatives; but the Senate may propose or concur with Amendments as on other Bills.

Every Bill which shall have passed the House of Representatives and the Senate, shall, before it becomes a Law, be presented to the President of the United States; If he approve he shall sign it, but if not he shall return it, with his Objections to that House in which it shall have originated, who shall enter the Objections at large on their Journal, and proceed to reconsider it. If after such Reconsideration two thirds of that House shall agree to pass the Bill, it shall be sent, together with the Objections, to the other House, by which it shall likewise be reconsidered, and if approved by two thirds of that House, it shall become a Law. But in all such Cases the Votes of both Houses shall be determined by Yeas and Nays, and the Names of the Persons voting for and against the Bill shall be entered on the Journal of each House respectively. If any Bill shall not be returned by the President within ten Days (Sundays excepted) after it shall have been presented to him, the Same shall be a Law, in like Manner as if he had signed it, unless the Congress by their Adjournment prevent its Return, in which Case it shall not be a Law.

Every Order, Resolution, or Vote to which the Concurrence of the Senate and the House of Representatives may be necessary (except on a question of Adjournment) shall be presented to the President of the United States; and before the Same shall take Effect, shall be approved by him, or being disapproved by him, shall be repassed by two thirds of the Senate and House of Representatives, according to the Rules and Limitations prescribed in the Case of a Bill.

Section 8 The Congress shall have Power To lay and collect Taxes, Duties, Imposts and Excises, to pay the Debts and provide for the common Defence and general Welfare of the United States; but all Duties, Imposts and Excises shall be uniform throughout the United States;

To borrow money on the credit of the United States;

To regulate Commerce with foreign Nations, and among the several States, and with the Indian Tribes;

To establish an uniform Rule of Naturalization, and uniform Laws on the subject of Bankruptcies throughout the United States;

To coin Money, regulate the Value thereof, and of foreign Coin, and fix the Standard of Weights and Measures;

To provide for the Punishment of counterfeiting the Securities and current Coin of the United States;

To establish Post Offices and post Roads;

To promote the Progress of Science and useful Arts, by securing for limited Times to Authors and Inventors the exclusive Right to their respective Writings and Discoveries;

To constitute Tribunals inferior to the supreme Court;

To define and punish Piracies and Felonies committed on the high Seas, and Offenses against the Law of Nations;

To declare War, grant Letters of Marque and Reprisal, and make Rules concerning Captures on Land and Water;

To raise and support Armies, but no Appropriation of Money to that Use shall be for a longer Term than two Years;

To provide and maintain a Navy;

---

*Changed by Section 2 of the Twentieth Amendment.

To make Rules for the Government and Regulation of the land and naval Forces;

To provide for calling forth the Militia to execute the Laws of the Union, suppress Insurrections and repel Invasions;

To provide for organizing, arming, and disciplining the Militia, and for governing such Part of them as may be employed in the Service of the United States, reserving to the States respectively, the Appointment of the Officers, and the Authority of training the Militia according to the discipline prescribed by Congress;

To exercise exclusive Legislation in all Cases whatsoever, over such District (not exceeding ten Miles square) as may, by Cession of particular States, and the acceptance of Congress, become the Seat of Government of the United States, and to exercise like Authority over all Places purchased by the Consent of the Legislature of the State in which the Same shall be, for the Erection of Forts, Magazines, Arsenals, dock-Yards, and other needful Buildings;—And

To make all Laws which shall be necessary and proper for carrying into Execution the foregoing Powers, and all other Powers vested by this Constitution in the Government of the United States, or in any Department or Officer thereof.

Section 9 *The Migration or Importation of such Persons as any of the States now existing shall think proper to admit, shall not be prohibited by the Congress prior to the Year one thousand eight hundred and eight but a tax or duty may be imposed on such Importation, not exceeding ten dollars for each Person.*

The privilege of the Writ of Habeas Corpus shall not be suspended, unless when in Cases of Rebellion or Invasion the public Safety may require it.

No Bill of Attainder or ex post facto Law shall be passed.

No capitation, or other direct, Tax shall be laid, unless in Proportion to the Census or Enumeration herein before directed to be taken.*

No Tax or Duty shall be laid on Articles exported from any State.

No Preference shall be given by any Regulation of Commerce or Revenue to the Ports of one State over those of another: nor shall Vessels bound to, or from, one State, be obliged to enter, clear, or pay Duties in another.

No Money shall be drawn from the Treasury, but in Consequence of Appropriations made by law; and a regular Statement and Account of the Receipts and Expenditures of all public Money shall be published from time to time.

No Title of Nobility shall be granted by the United States: And no Person holding any Office of Profit or Trust under them, shall, without the Consent of the Congress, accept of any present, Emolument, Office, or Title, of any kind whatever, from any King, Prince, or foreign State.

Section 10 No State shall enter into any Treaty, Alliance, or Confederation; grant Letters of Marque and Reprisal; coin Money; emit Bills of Credit; make any Thing but gold and silver Coin a Tender in Payment of Debts; pass any Bill of Attainder, ex post facto Law, or Law impairing the Obligation of Contracts, or grant any Title of Nobility.

No State shall, without the Consent of the Congress, lay any Imposts or Duties on Imports or Exports, except what may be absolutely necessary for executing its inspection Laws: and the net Produce of all Duties and Imposts, laid by any State on Imports or Exports, shall be for the Use of the Treasury of the United States; and all such Laws shall be subject to the Revision and Control of the Congress.

No State shall, without the Consent of the Congress, lay any duty of Tonnage, keep Troops, or Ships of War in time of Peace, enter into any Agreement or Compact with another State, or with a foreign Power, or engage in War, unless actually invaded, or in such imminent Danger as will not admit of delay.

Article II

Section 1 The executive Power shall be vested in a President of the United States of America. He shall hold his Office during the Term of four Years, and, together with the Vice President, chosen for the same Term, be elected, as follows:

Each State shall appoint, in such Manner as the Legislature thereof may direct, a Number of Electors, equal to the whole Number of Senators and Representatives to which the State may be entitled in the Congress; but no Senator or Representative, or Person holding an Office of Trust or Profit under the United States, shall be appointed an Elector.

The Electors shall meet in their respective States, and vote by Ballot for two Persons, of whom one at least shall not be an Inhabitant of the same State with themselves. And they shall make a List of all the Persons voted for, and of the Number of Votes for each; which List they shall sign and certify, and transmit sealed to the Seat of the Government of the United States, directed to the President of the Senate. The President of the Senate shall, in the Presence of the Senate and House of Representatives, open all the Certificates, and the Votes shall then be counted. The Person having the greatest Number of Votes shall be the President, if such Number be a Majority of the whole Number of Electors appointed; and if there be more than one who have such Majority, and have an equal Number of Votes, then the House of Representatives shall immediately chuse by Ballot one of them for President; and if no Person have a Majority, then from the five highest on the List the said House shall in like Manner chuse the President. But in chusing the President, the Votes shall be taken by States, the Representation from each State having one Vote; a quorum for this Purpose shall consist of a Member or Members from two thirds of the States, and a Majority of all the States shall be necessary to a Choice. In every Case, after the Choice of the President, the Person having the greatest Number of Votes of the Electors shall be the Vice President. But if there should remain two or more who have equal Votes, the Senate shall chuse from them by Ballot the Vice President.

The Congress may determine the Time of chusing the Electors, and the Day on which they shall give their Votes; which Day shall be the same throughout the United States.

No Person except a natural born Citizen, or a Citizen of the United States, at the time of the Adoption of this Constitution, shall be eligible to the Office of President; neither shall any Person be eligible to that Office who shall not have at-

*Changed by the Sixteenth Amendment.

*Superseded by the Twelfth Amendment.

tained to the Age of thirty five Years, and been fourteen Years a Resident within the United States.

In Case of the Removal of the President from Office, or of his Death, Resignation, or Inability to discharge the Powers and Duties of the said Office, the same shall devolve on the Vice President, *and the Congress may by Law provide for the Case of Removal, Death, Resignation, or Inability, both of the President and Vice President, declaring what Officer shall then act as President, and such Officer shall act accordingly, until the Disability be removed, or a President shall be elected.**

The President shall, at stated Times, receive for his Services a Compensation, which shall neither be increased nor diminished during the Period for which he shall have been elected, and he shall not receive within that Period any other Emolument from the United States, or any of them.

Before he enter on the Execution of his Office, he shall take the following Oath or Affirmation:—"I do solemnly swear (or affirm) that I will faithfully execute the Office of President of the United States, and will to the best of my Ability, preserve, protect and defend the Constitution of the United States."

Section 2 The President shall be Commander in Chief of the Army and Navy of the United States, and of the Militia of the several States, when called into the actual Service of the United States; he may require the Opinion, in writing, of the principal Officer in each of the executive Departments, upon any Subject relating to the Duties of their respective Offices, and he shall have Power to Grant Reprieves and Pardons for Offences against the United States, except in Cases of Impeachment.

He shall have Power, by and with the Advice and Consent of the Senate, to make Treaties, provided two thirds of the Senators present concur; and he shall nominate, and by and with the Advice and Consent of the Senate, shall appoint Ambassadors, other public Ministers and Consuls, Judges of the supreme Court, and all other Officers of the United States, whose Appointments are not herein otherwise provided for, and which shall be established by Law: but the Congress may by Law vest the Appointment of such inferior Officers, as they think proper, in the President alone, in the Courts of Law, or in the Heads of Departments.

The President shall have Power to fill up all Vacancies that may happen during the Recess of the Senate, by granting Commissions which shall expire at the End of their next Session.

Section 3 He shall from time to time give to the Congress Information of the State of the Union, and recommend to their Consideration such Measures as he shall judge necessary and expedient; he may, on extraordinary Occasions, convene both Houses, or either of them, and in Case of Disagreement between them, with Respect to the Time of Adjournment, he may adjourn them to such Time as he shall think proper; he shall receive Ambassadors and other public Ministers; he shall take Care that the Laws be faithfully executed, and shall Commission all the Officers of the United States.

Section 4 The President, Vice President and all civil Officers of the United States, shall be removed from Office on Impeachment for, and Conviction of, Treason, Bribery, or other high Crimes and Misdemeanors.

Article III

Section 1 The judicial Power of the United States, shall be vested in one supreme Court, and in such inferior Courts as the Congress may from time to time ordain and establish. The Judges, both of the supreme and inferior Courts, shall hold their Offices during good Behaviour, and shall, at stated Times, receive for their Services a Compensation, which shall not be diminished during their Continuance in Office.

Section 2 The judicial Power shall extend to all Cases, in Law and Equity, arising under this Constitution, the Laws of the United States, and Treaties made, or which shall be made, under their Authority;—to all Cases affecting Ambassadors, other public Ministers and Consuls;—to all Cases of admiralty and maritime Jurisdiction;—to Controversies to which the United States shall be a Party;—to Controversies between two or more States;—*between a State and Citizens of another State;**—between Citizens of different States;—between Citizens of the same State claiming Lands under Grants of different States, and between a State, or the Citizens thereof, and foreign States, Citizens or Subjects.

In all Cases affecting Ambassadors, other public Ministers and Consuls, and those in which a State shall be Party, the supreme Court shall have original Jurisdiction. In all the other Cases before mentioned, the supreme Court shall have appellate Jurisdiction, both as to Law and Fact, with such Exceptions, and under such Regulations as the Congress shall make.

The trial of all Crimes, except in Cases of Impeachment, shall be by Jury; and such Trial shall be held in the State where said Crimes shall have been committed; but when not committed within any State, the Trial shall be at such Place or Places as the Congress may by Law have directed.

Section 3 Treason against the United States, shall consist only in levying War against them, or in adhering to their Enemies, giving them Aid and Comfort. No Person shall be convicted of Treason unless on the Testimony of two Witnesses to the same overt Act, or on Confession in open Court.

The Congress shall have Power to declare the Punishment of Treason, but no Attainder of Treason shall work Corruption of Blood, or Forefeiture except during the Life of the Person attainted.

Article IV

Section 1 Full Faith and Credit shall be given in each State to the public Acts, Records, and judicial Proceedings of every other State. And the Congress may by general Laws prescribe the Manner in which such Acts, Records, and Proceedings shall be proved, and the Effect thereof.

Section 2 The Citizens of each State shall be entitled to all Privileges and Immunities of Citizens in the several States.

---

*Modified by the Twenty-Fifth Amendment.

*Restricted by the Eleventh Amendment.

A Person charged in any State with Treason, Felony, or other Crime, who shall flee from Justice, and be found in another State, shall on demand of the executive Authority of the State from which he fled, be delivered up, to be removed to the State having Jurisdiction of the Crime.

No Person held to Service or Labour in one State, under the Laws thereof, escaping into another, shall, in Consequence of any Law or Regulation therein, be discharged from such Service or Labour, but shall be delivered up on Claim of the Party to whom such Service or Labour may be due.*

Section 3 New States may be admitted by the Congress into this Union; but no new State shall be formed or erected within the Jurisdiction of any other State; nor any State be formed by the Junction of two or more States, or parts of States, without the Consent of the Legislatures of the States concerned as well as of the Congress.

The Congress shall have Power to dispose of and make all needful Rules and Regulations respecting the Territory or other Property belonging to the United States; and nothing in this Constitution shall be so construed as to Prejudice any Claims of the United States, or of any particular State.

Section 4 The United States shall guarantee to every State in this Union a Republican Form of Government, and shall protect each of them against Invasion; and on Application of the Legislature, or of the Executive (when the Legislature cannot be convened) against domestic Violence.

Article V

The Congress, whenever two thirds of both Houses shall deem it necessary, shall propose Amendments to this Constitution, or, on the Application of the Legislatures of two thirds of the several States, shall call a Convention for proposing Amendments, which, in either Case, shall be valid to all Intents and Purposes, as Part of this Constitution, when ratified by the Legislatures of three fourths of the several States, or by Conventions in three fourths thereof, as the one or the other Mode of Ratification may be proposed by the Congress; Pro-

vided that no Amendment which may be made prior to the Year One thousand eight hundred and eight shall in any Manner affect the first and fourth Clauses in the Ninth Section of the first Article; and that no State, without its Consent, shall be deprived of its equal Suffrage in the Senate.

Article VI

All Debts contracted and Engagements entered into, before the Adoption of this Constitution, shall be as valid against the United States under this Constitution, as under the Confederation.

This Constitution, and the Laws of the United States which shall be made in Pursuance thereof; and all Treaties made, or which shall be made, under the Authority of the United States, shall be the supreme Law of the Land; and the Judges in every State shall be bound thereby, any Thing in the Constitution or Laws of any State to the Contrary notwithstanding.

The Senators and Representatives before mentioned, and the Members of the several State Legislatures, and all executive and judicial Officers, both of the United States and of the several States, shall be bound by Oath or Affirmation, to support this Constitution; but no religious Test shall ever be required as a Qualification to any Office or public Trust under the United States.

Article VII

The Ratification of the Conventions of nine States shall be sufficient for the Establishment of this Constitution between the States so ratifying the Same.

Done in Convention by the Unanimous Consent of the States present the Seventeenth Day of September in the Year of our Lord one thousand seven hundred and Eighty seven and of the Independence of the United States of America the Twelfth. In Witness whereof We have hereunto subscribed our Names.

---

*Superseded by the Twelfth Amendment.

Go. Washington
President and deputy from Virginia

New Hampshire
John Langdon
Nicholas Gilman

Massachusetts
Nathaniel Gorham
Rufus King

Connecticut
Wm. Saml. Johnson
Roger Sherman

New York
Alexander Hamilton

New Jersey
Wil. Livingston
David Brearley
Wm. Paterson
Jona. Dayton

Pennsylvania
B. Franklin
Thomas Mifflin
Robt. Morris
Geo. Clymer
Thos. FitzSimons
Jared Ingersoll
James Wilson
Gouv. Morris

Delaware
Geo. Read
Gunning Bedford jun
John Dickenson
Richard Bassett
Jaco. Broom

Maryland
James McHenry
Dan. of St. Thos. Jenifer
Danl. Carroll

Virginia
John Blair
James Madison, Jr.

North Carolina
Wm. Blount
Richd. Dobbs Spaight
Hu Williamson

South Carolina
J. Rutledge
Charles Cotesworth Pickney
Pierce Butler

Georgia
William Few
Abr. Baldwin

Amendments to the Constitution

★   ★   ★

Amendment I [1791]*

Congress shall make no law respecting an establishment of religion, or prohibiting the free exercise thereof; or abridging the freedom of speech, or of the press; or the right of the people peaceably to assemble, and to petition the Government for a redress of grievances.

Amendment II [1791]

A well regulated Militia, being necessary to the security of a free State, the right of the people to keep and bear Arms shall not be infringed.

Amendment III [1791]

No Soldier shall, in time of peace, be quartered in any house, without the consent of the Owner, nor in time of war, but in a manner to be prescribed by law.

Amendment IV [1791]

The right of the people to be secure in their persons, houses, papers, and effects, against unreasonable searches and seizures, shall not be violated, and no Warrants shall issue, but upon probable cause, supported by Oath or affirmation, and particularly describing the place to be searched, and the persons or things to be seized.

Amendment V [1791]

No person shall be held to answer for a capital or otherwise infamous crime, unless on a presentment or indictment of a Grand Jury, except in cases arising in the land or naval forces, or in the Militia, when in actual service in time of War or public danger; nor shall any person be subject for the same offence to be twice put in jeopardy of life or limb; nor shall be compelled in any criminal case to be a witness against himself, nor be deprived of life, liberty, or property, without due process of law; nor shall private property be taken for public use, without just compensation.

Amendment VI [1791]

In all criminal prosecutions, the accused shall enjoy the right to a speedy and public trial, by an impartial jury of the State and district wherein the crime shall have been committed, which district shall have been previously ascertained by law, and to be informed of the nature and cause of the accusation; to be confronted with the witnesses against him; to have compulsory process for obtaining witnesses in his favor, and to have the Assistance of Counsel for his defence.

Amendment VII [1791]

In suits at common law, where the value in controversy shall exceed twenty dollars, the right of trail by jury shall be preserved, and no fact tried by a jury, shall be otherwise reexamined in any Court of the United States, than according to the Rules of the common law.

Amendment VIII [1791]

Excessive bail shall not be required, nor excessive fines imposed, nor cruel and unusual punishments inflicted.

Amendment IX [1791]

The enumeration in the Constitution, of certain rights, shall not be construed to deny or disparage others retained by the people.

*The dates in brackets indicate when the amendments were ratified.

Amendment X [1791]

The powers not delegated to the United States by the Constitution, nor prohibited by it to the States, are reserved to the States respectively, or to the people.

Amendment XI [1798]

The Judicial power of the United States shall not be construed to extend to any suit in law or equity, commenced or prosecuted against one of the United States by Citizens of another State, or by Citizens or subjects of any foreign state.

Amendment XII [1804]

The Electors shall meet in their respective States and vote by ballot for President and Vice-President, one of whom, at least, shall not be an inhabitant of the same State with themselves; they shall name in their ballots the person voted for as President, and in distinct ballots the person voted for as Vice-President, and they shall make distinct lists of all persons voted for as President, and of all persons voted for as Vice-President, and of the number of votes for each, which lists they shall sign and certify, and transmit sealed to the seat of the government of the United States, directed to the President of the Senate;—the President of the Senate shall, in the presence of the Senate and House of Representatives, open all the certificates and the votes shall then be counted;—The person having the greatest number of votes for President, shall be the President, if such number be a majority of the whole number of Electors appointed; and if no person have such majority, then from the persons having the highest numbers not exceeding three on the list of those voted for as President, the House of Representatives shall choose immediately, by ballot, the President. But in choosing the President, the votes shall be taken by States, the representation from each State having one vote; a quorum for this purpose shall consist of a member or members from two-thirds of the States, and a majority of all the States shall be necessary to a choice. And if the House of Representatives shall not choose a President whenever the right of choice shall devolve upon them, before *the fourth day of March* next following, then the Vice-President shall act as President, as in the case of the death or other constitutional disability of the President.*—The person having the greatest number of votes as Vice-President, shall be the Vice-President, if such number be a majority of the whole number of Electors appointed, and if no person have a majority, then from the two highest numbers on the list, the Senate shall choose the Vice-President; a quorum for the purpose shall consist of two-thirds of the whole number of Senators, and a majority of the whole number shall be necessary to a choice. But no person constitutionally ineligible to the office of President shall be eligible to that of Vice-President of the United States.

Amendment XIII [1865]

Section 1 Neither slavery nor involuntary servitude, except as a punishment for crime whereof the party shall have been duly convicted, shall exist within the United States, or any place subject to their jurisdiction.

*Superseded by Section 3 of the Twentieth Amendment.

Section 2 Congress shall have power to enforce this article by appropriate legislation.

Amendment XIV [1868]

Section 1 All persons born or naturalized in the United States, and subject to the jurisdiction thereof, are citizens of the United States and of the State wherein they reside. No State shall make or enforce any law which shall abridge the privileges or immunities of citizens of the United States; nor shall any State deprive any person of life, liberty, or property, without due process of law; nor deny to any person within its jurisdiction the equal protection of the laws.

Section 2 Representatives shall be apportioned among the several States according to their respective numbers, counting the whole number of persons in each State, excluding Indians not taxed. But when the right to vote at any election for the choice of electors for President and Vice-President of the United States, Representatives in Congress, the Executive and Judicial officers of a State, or the members of the Legislature thereof, is denied to any of the male inhabitants of such State, being twenty-one years of age, and citizens of the United States, or in any way abridged, except for participation in rebellion, or other crime, the basis of representation therein shall be reduced in the proportion which the number of such male citizens shall bear to the whole number of male citizens twenty-one years of age in such State.

Section 3 No person shall be a Senator or Representative in Congress, or elector of President and Vice-President, or hold any office, civil or military, under the United States, or under any State, who, having previously taken an oath, as a member of Congress, or as an officer of the United States, or as a member of any State legislature, or as an executive or judicial officer of any State, to support the Constitution of the United States, shall have engaged in insurrection or rebellion against the same, or given aid or comfort to the enemies thereof. Congress may by a vote of two-thirds of each house, remove such disability.

Section 4 The validity of the public debt of the United States, authorized by law, including debts incurred for payment of pensions and bounties for services in suppressing insurrection or rebellion, shall not be questioned. But neither the United States nor any State shall assume or pay any debt or obligation incurred in aid of insurrection or rebellion against the United States, or any claim for the loss or emancipation of any slave; but all such debts, obligations and claims shall be held illegal and void.

Section 5 The Congress shall have power to enforce, by appropriate legislation, the provisions of this article.

Amendment XV [1870]

Section 1 The right of citizens of the United States to vote shall not be denied or abridged by the United States or by any State on account of race, color, or previous condition of servitude—

Section 2 The Congress shall have power to enforce this article by appropriate legislation.

Amendment XVI [1913]

The Congress shall have power to lay and collect taxes on incomes, from whatever source derived, without apportionment among the several States, and without regard to any census or enumeration.

Amendment XVII [1913]

The Senate of the United States shall be composed of two Senators from each State, elected by the people thereof, for six years; and each Senator shall have one vote. The electors in each State shall have the qualifications requisite for electors of the most numerous branch of the State legislatures.

When vacancies happen in the representation of any State in the Senate, the executive authority of such State shall issue writs of election to fill such vacancies: *Provided*, That the legislature of any State may empower the executive thereof to make temporary appointments until the people fill the vacancies by election as the legislature may direct.

This amendment shall not be so construed as to affect the election or term of any Senator chosen before it becomes valid as part of the Constitution.

Amendment XVIII [1919]

Section 1 After one year from the ratification of this article the manufacture, sale, or transportation of intoxicating liquors within, the importation thereof into, or the exportation thereof from the United States and all territory subject to the jurisdiction hereof for beverage purposes hereby prohibited.

Section 2 The Congress and the several States shall have concurrent power to enforce this article by appropriate legislation.

Section 3 This article shall be inoperative unless it shall have been ratified as an amendment to the Constitution by the legislatures of the several States, as provided by the Constitution, within seven years from the date of submission hereof to the States by the Congress.*

Amendment XIX [1920]

The right of citizens of the United States to vote shall not be denied or abridged by the United States or by any State on account of sex.

Congress shall have power to enforce this article by appropriate legislation.

Amendment XX [1933]

Section 1 The terms of the President and Vice-President shall end at noon on the 20th day of January, and the terms of Senators and Representatives at noon on the 3d day of January,

---

*Repealed by Section 1 of the Twenty-First Amendment

of the years in which such terms would have ended if this article had not been ratified; and the terms of their successors shall then begin.

Section 2 The Congress shall assemble at least once in every year, and such meeting shall begin at noon on the 3d day of January, unless they shall by law appoint a different day.

Section 3 If, at the time fixed for the beginning of the term of the President, the President elect shall have died, the Vice-President elect shall become President. If a President shall not have been chosen before the time fixed for the beginning of his term, or if the President elect shall have failed to qualify, then the Vice-President elect shall act as President until a President shall have qualified; and the Congress may by law provide for the case wherein neither a President elect nor a Vice-President elect shall have qualified, declaring who shall then act as President, or the manner in which one who is to act shall be selected, and such person shall act accordingly until a President or Vice-President shall have qualified.

Section 4 The Congress may by law provide for the case of the death of any of the persons from whom the House of Representatives may choose a President whenever the right of choice shall have devolved upon them, and for the case of the death of any of the persons from whom the Senate may choose a Vice-President whenever the right of choice shall have devolved upon them.

Section 5 Sections 1 and 2 shall take effect on the 15th day of October following the ratification of this article.

Section 6 This article shall be inoperative unless it shall have been ratified as an amendment to the Constitution by the legislatures of three-fourths of the several States within seven years from the date of its submission.

Amendment XXI [1933]

Section 1 The eighteenth article of amendment to the Constitution of the United States is hereby repealed.

Section 2 The transportation or importation into any State, Territory, or possession of the United States for delivery or use therein of intoxicating liquors, in violation of the laws thereof, is hereby prohibited.

Section 3 This article shall be inoperative unless it shall have been ratified as an amendment to the Constitution by conventions in the several States, as provided in the Constitution, within seven years from the date of submission hereof to the States by the Congress.

Amendment XXII [1951]

Section 1 No person shall be elected to the office of President more than twice, and no person who has held the office of President, or acted as President, for more than two years of a term to which some other person was elected President shall be elected to the office of the President more than once. But this Article shall not apply to any person holding the office of

President when this Article was proposed by the Congress, and shall not prevent any person who may be holding the office of President, or acting as President, during the term within which this Article becomes operative from holding the office of the President or acting as President during the remainder of such term.

Section 2 This article shall be inoperative unless it shall have been ratified as an amendment to the Constitution by the legislatures of three-fourths of the several States within seven years from the date of its submission to the States by the Congress.

Amendment XXIII [1961]

Section 1 The District constituting the seat of Government of the United States shall appoint in such manner as the Congress may direct:

A number of electors of President and Vice-President equal to the whole number of Senators and Representatives in Congress to which the District would be entitled if it were a State, but in no event more than the least populous State; they shall be in addition to those appointed by the States, but they shall be considered, for the purposes of the election of President and Vice-President, to be electors appointed by a State; and they shall meet in the District and perform such duties as provided by the twelfth article of amendment.

Section 2 The Congress shall have power to enforce this article by appropriate legislation.

Amendment XXIV [1964]

Section 1 The right of citizens of the United States to vote in any primary or other election for President or Vice-President, for electors for President or Vice-President, or for Senator or Representative in Congress, shall not be denied or abridged by the United States or any State by reason of failure to pay any poll tax or other tax.

Section 2 The Congress shall have power to enforce this article by appropriate legislation.

Amendment XXV [1967]

Section 1 In case of the removal of the President from office or of his death or resignation, the Vice-President shall become President.

Section 2 Whenever there is a vacancy in the office of the Vice-President, the President shall nominate a Vice-President who shall take office upon confirmation by a majority vote of both houses of Congress.

Section 3 Whenever the President transmits to the President pro tempore of the Senate and the Speaker of the House of Representatives his written declaration that he is unable to discharge the powers and duties of his office, and until he transmits to them a written declaration to the contrary, such powers and duties shall be discharged by the Vice-President as Acting President.

Section 4 Whenever the Vice-President and a majority of either the principal officers of the executive departments or of such other body as Congress may by law provide, transmit to the President pro tempore of the Senate and the Speaker of the House of Representatives their written declaration that the President is unable to discharge the powers and duties of his office, the Vice-President shall immediately assume the powers and duties of the office as Acting President.

Thereafter, when the President transmits to the President pro tempore of the Senate and the Speaker of the House of Representatives his written declaration that no inability exists, he shall resume the powers and duties of his office unless the Vice-President and a majority of either the principal officers of the executive department or of such other body as Congress may by law provide, transmit within four days to the President pro tempore of the Senate and the Speaker of the House of Representatives their written declaration that the President is unable to discharge the powers and duties of his office. Thereupon Congress shall decide the issue, assembling within forty-eight hours for that purpose if not in session. If the Congress, within twenty-one days after receipt of the latter written declaration, or, if Congress is not in session, within twenty-one days after Congress is required to assemble, determines by two-thirds vote of both Houses that the President is unable to discharge the powers and duties of his office, the Vice-President shall continue to discharge the same as Acting President; otherwise, the President shall resume the powers and duties of his office.

Amendment XXVI [1971]

Section 1 The right of citizens of the United States, who are eighteen years of age or older, to vote shall not be denied or abridged by the United States or by any state on account of age.

Section 2 The Congress shall have power to enforce this article by appropriate legislation.

Amendment XXVII [1992]

No law varying the compensation for services of the Senators and Representatives, shall take effect, until an election of Representatives shall have intervened.

The American Nation

Admission of States into the Union

State	Date of Admission	State	Date of Admission	State	Date of Admission
1. Delaware	December 7, 1787	18. Louisiana	April 30, 1812	35. West Virginia	June 20, 1863
2. Pennsylvania	December 12, 1787	19. Indiana	December 11, 1816	36. Nevada	October 31, 1864
3. New Jersey	December 18, 1787	20. Mississippi	December 10, 1817	37. Nebraska	March 1, 1867
4. Georgia	January 2, 1788	21. Illinois	December 3, 1818	38. Colorado	August 1, 1876
5. Connecticut	January 9, 1788	22. Alabama	December 14, 1819	39. North Dakota	November 2, 1889
6. Massachusetts	February 6, 1788	23. Maine	March 15, 1820	40. South Dakota	November 2, 1889
7. Maryland	April 28, 1788	24. Missouri	August 10, 1821	41. Montana	November 8, 1889
8. South Carolina	May 23, 1788	25. Arkansas	June 15, 1836	42. Washington	November 11, 1889
9. New Hampshire	June 21, 1788	26. Michigan	January 26, 1837	43. Idaho	July 3, 1890
10. Virginia	June 25, 1788	27. Florida	March 3, 1845	44. Wyoming	July 10, 1890
11. New York	July 26, 1788	28. Texas	December 29, 1845	45. Utah	January 4, 1896
12. North Carolina	November 21, 1789	29. Iowa	December 28, 1846	46. Oklahoma	November 16, 1907
13. Rhode Island	May 29, 1790	30. Wisconsin	May 29, 1848	47. New Mexico	January 6, 1912
14. Vermont	March 4, 1791	31. California	September 9, 1850	48. Arizona	February 14, 1912
15. Kentucky	June 1, 1792	32. Minnesota	May 11, 1858	49. Alaska	January 3, 1959
16. Tennessee	June 1, 1796	33. Oregon	February 14, 1859	50. Hawaii	August 21, 1959
17. Ohio	March 1, 1803	34. Kansas	January 29, 1861		

Territorial Expansion

Territory	Date Acquired	Square Miles	How Acquired
Original states and territories	1783	888,685	Treaty of Paris
Louisiana Purchase	1803	827,192	Purchased from France
Florida	1819	72,003	Adams-Onís Treaty
Texas	1845	390,143	Annexation of independent country
Oregon	1846	285,580	Oregon Boundary Treaty
Mexican cession	1848	529,017	Treaty of Guadalupe Hidalgo
Gadsden Purchase	1853	29,640	Purchased from Mexico
Midway Islands	1867	2	Annexation of uninhabited islands
Alaska	1867	589,757	Purchased from Russia
Hawaii	1898	6,450	Annexation of independent country
Wake Island	1898	3	Annexation of uninhabited island
Puerto Rico	1899	3,435	Treaty of Paris
Guam	1899	212	Treaty of Paris
The Philippines	1899–1946	115,600	Treaty of Paris; granted independence
American Samoa	1900	76	Treaty with Germany and Great Britain
Panama Canal Zone	1904–1978	553	Hay–Bunau-Varilla Treaty
U.S. Virgin Islands	1917	133	Purchased from Denmark
Trust Territory of the Pacific Islands*	1947	717	United Nations Trusteeship

*A number of these islands have recently been granted independence: Federated States of Micronesia, 1990; Marshall Islands, 1991; Palau, 1994.

Presidential Elections

Year	Candidates	Parties	Percent of Popular Vote	Electoral Vote	Percent Voter Participation
1789	**George Washington**	No party designations	*	69	
	John Adams[†]			34	
	Other candidates			35	
1792	**George Washington**	No party designations		132	
	John Adams			77	
	George Clinton			50	
	Other candidates			5	
1796	**John Adams**	Federalist		71	
	Thomas Jefferson	Democratic-Republican		68	
	Thomas Pinckney	Federalist		59	
	Aaron Burr	Democratic-Republican		30	
	Other candidates			48	
1800	**Thomas Jefferson**	Democratic-Republican		73	
	Aaron Burr	Democratic-Republican		73	
	John Adams	Federalist		65	
	Charles C. Pinckney	Federalist		64	
	John Jay	Federalist		1	
1804	**Thomas Jefferson**	Democratic-Republican		162	
	Charles C. Pinckney	Federalist		14	
1808	**James Madison**	Democratic-Republican		122	
	Charles C. Pinckney	Federalist		47	
	George Clinton	Democratic-Republican		6	
1812	**James Madison**	Democratic-Republican		128	
	DeWitt Clinton	Federalist		89	
1816	**James Monroe**	Democratic-Republican		183	
	Rufus King	Federalist		34	
1820	**James Monroe**	Democratic-Republican		231	
	John Quincy Adams	Independent Republican		1	
1824	**John Quincy Adams**	Democratic-Republican	30.5	84	26.9
	Andrew Jackson	Democratic-Republican	43.1	99	
	Henry Clay	Democratic-Republican	13.2	37	
	William H. Crawford	Democratic-Republican	13.1	41	
1828	**Andrew Jackson**	Democratic	56.0	178	57.6
	John Quincy Adams	National Republican	44.0	83	
1832	**Andrew Jackson**	Democratic	54.5	219	55.4
	Henry Clay	National Republican	37.5	49	
	William Wirt	Anti-Masonic	8.0	7	
	John Floyd	Democratic	[‡]	11	
1836	**Martin Van Buren**	Democratic	50.9	170	57.8
	William H. Harrison	Whig		73	
	Hugh L. White	Whig		26	
	Daniel Webster	Whig	49.1	14	
	W. P. Mangum	Whig		11	
1840	**William H. Harrison**	Whig	53.1	234	80.2
	Martin Van Buren	Democratic	46.9	60	

*Prior to 1824, most presidential electors were chosen by state legislators rather than by popular vote.

[†]Before the Twelfth Amendment was passed in 1804, the electoral college voted for two presidential candidates; the runner-up became vice-president.

[‡]Percentages below 2.5 percent have been omitted. Hence the percentage of popular vote might not total 100 percent.

Year	Candidates	Parties	Percent of Popular Vote	Electoral Vote	Percent Voter Participation
1844	**James K. Polk**	Democratic	49.6	170	78.9
	Henry Clay	Whig	48.1	105	
	James G. Birney	Liberty	2.3		
1848	**Zachary Taylor**	Whig	47.4	163	72.7
	Lewis Cass	Democratic	42.5	127	
	Martin Van Buren	Free Soil	10.1		
1852	**Franklin Pierce**	Democratic	50.9	254	69.6
	Winfield Scott	Whig	44.1	42	
	John P. Hale	Free Soil	5.0		
1856	**James Buchanan**	Democratic	45.3	174	78.9
	John C. Frémont	Republican	33.1	114	
	Millard Fillmore	American	21.6	8	
1860	**Abraham Lincoln**	Republican	39.8	180	81.2
	Stephen A. Douglas	Democratic	29.5	12	
	John C. Breckinridge	Democratic	18.1	72	
	John Bell	Constitutional Union	12.6	39	
1864	**Abraham Lincoln**	Republican	55.0	212	73.8
	George B. McClellan	Democratic	45.0	21	
1868	**Ulysses S. Grant**	Republican	52.7	214	78.1
	Horatio Seymour	Democratic	47.3	80	
1872	**Ulysses S. Grant**	Republican	55.6	286	71.3
	Horace Greeley	Democratic	43.9		
1876	**Rutherford B. Hayes**	Republican	48.0	185	81.8
	Samuel J. Tilden	Democratic	51.0	184	
1880	**James A. Garfield**	Republican	48.5	214	79.4
	Winfield S. Hancock	Democratic	48.1	155	
	James B. Weaver	Greenback-Labor	3.4		
1884	**Grover Cleveland**	Democratic	48.5	219	77.5
	James G. Blaine	Republican	48.2	182	
1888	**Benjamin Harrison**	Republican	47.9	233	79.3
	Grover Cleveland	Democratic	48.6	168	
1892	**Grover Cleveland**	Democratic	46.1	277	74.7
	Benjamin Harrison	Republican	43.0	145	
	James B. Weaver	People's	8.5	22	
1896	**William McKinley**	Republican	51.1	271	79.3
	William J. Bryan	Democratic	47.7	176	
1900	**William McKinley**	Republican	51.7	292	73.2
	William J. Bryan	Democratic; Populist	45.5	155	
1904	**Theodore Roosevelt**	Republican	57.4	336	65.2
	Alton B. Parker	Democratic	37.6	140	
	Eugene V. Debs	Socialist	3.0		
1908	**William H. Taft**	Republican	51.6	321	65.4
	William J. Bryan	Democratic	43.1	162	
	Eugene V. Debs	Socialist	2.8		
1912	**Woodrow Wilson**	Democratic	41.9	435	58.8
	Theodore Roosevelt	Progressive	27.4	88	
	William H. Taft	Republican	23.2	8	
	Eugene V. Debs	Socialist	6.0		

Year	Candidates	Parties	Percent of Popular Vote	Electoral Vote	Percent Voter Participation
1916	Woodrow Wilson	Democratic	49.4	277	61.6
	Charles E. Hughes	Republican	46.2	254	
	A. L. Benson	Socialist	3.2		
1920	Warren G. Harding	Republican	60.4	404	49.2
	James M. Cox	Democratic	34.2	127	
	Eugene V. Debs	Socialist	3.4		
1924	Calvin Coolidge	Republican	54.0	382	48.9
	John W. Davis	Democratic	28.8	136	
	Robert M. LaFollette	Progressive	16.6	13	
1928	Herbert C. Hoover	Republican	58.2	444	56.9
	Alfred E. Smith	Democratic	40.9	87	
1932	Franklin D. Roosevelt	Democratic	57.4	472	56.9
	Herbert C. Hoover	Republican	39.7	59	
1936	Franklin D. Roosevelt	Democratic	60.8	523	61.0
	Alfred M. Landon	Republican	36.5	8	
1940	Franklin D. Roosevelt	Democratic	54.8	449	62.5
	Wendell L. Willkie	Republican	44.8	82	
1944	Franklin D. Roosevelt	Democratic	53.5	432	55.9
	Thomas E. Dewey	Republican	46.0	99	
1948	Harry S. Truman	Democratic	49.6	303	53.0
	Thomas E. Dewey	Republican	45.1	189	
1952	Dwight D. Eisenhower	Republican	55.1	442	63.3
	Adlai E. Stevenson	Democratic	44.4	89	
1956	Dwight D. Eisenhower	Republican	57.6	457	60.6
	Adlai E. Stevenson	Democratic	42.1	73	
1960	John F. Kennedy	Democratic	49.7	303	64.0
	Richard M. Nixon	Republican	49.5	219	
1964	Lyndon B. Johnson	Democratic	61.1	486	61.7
	Barry M. Goldwater	Republican	38.5	52	
1968	Richard M. Nixon	Republican	43.4	301	60.6
	Hubert H. Humphrey	Democratic	42.7	191	
	George C. Wallace	American Independent	13.5	46	
1972	Richard M. Nixon	Republican	60.7	520	55.5
	George S. McGovern	Democratic	37.5	17	
1976	Jimmy Carter	Democratic	50.1	297	54.3
	Gerald R. Ford	Republican	48.0	240	
1980	Ronald W. Reagan	Republican	50.7	489	53.0
	Jimmy Carter	Democratic	41.0	49	
	John B. Anderson	Independent	6.6	0	
1984	Ronald W. Reagan	Republican	58.4	525	52.9
	Walter F. Mondale	Democratic	41.6	13	
1988	George H. W. Bush	Republican	53.4	426	50.3
	Michael Dukakis	Democratic	45.6	111*	
1992	Bill Clinton	Democratic	43.7	370	55.1
	George H. W. Bush	Republican	38.0	168	
	H. Ross Perot	Independent	19.0	0	
1996	Bill Clinton	Democratic	49†	379	49.0†
	Robert J. Dole	Republican	41†	159	
	H. Ross Perot	Reform	8†	0	

*One Dukakis elector cast a vote for Lloyd Bentsen.
†Preliminary figure.

Supreme Court Justices

Name	Terms of Service	Appointed by	Name	Terms of Service	Appointed by
John Jay*, N.Y.	1789–1795	Washington	Joseph McKenna, Cal.	1898–1925	McKinley
James Wilson, Pa.	1789–1798	Washington	Oliver W. Holmes, Mass.	1902–1932	T. Roosevelt
John Rutledge, S.C.	1790–1791	Washington	William R. Day, Ohio	1903–1922	T. Roosevelt
William Cushing, Mass.	1790–1810	Washington	William H. Moody, Mass.	1906–1910	T. Roosevelt
John Blair, Va.	1790–1796	Washington	Horace H. Lurton, Tenn.	1910–1914	Taft
James Iredell, N.C.	1790–1799	Washington	Charles E. Hughes, N.Y.	1910–1916	Taft
Thomas Johnson, Md.	1792–1793	Washington	**Edward D. White**, La.	1910–1921	Taft
William Paterson, N.J.	1793–1806	Washington	Willis Van Devanter, Wy.	1911–1937	Taft
John Rutledge, S.C.	1795	Washington	Joseph R. Lamar, Ga.	1911–1916	Taft
Samuel Chase, Md.	1796–1811	Washington	Mahlon Pitney, N.J.	1912–1922	Taft
Oliver Ellsworth, Conn.	1796–1800	Washington	James C. McReynolds, Tenn.	1914–1941	Wilson
Bushrod Washington, Va.	1799–1829	J. Adams	Louis D. Brandeis, Mass.	1916–1939	Wilson
Alfred Moore, N.C.	1800–1804	J. Adams	John H. Clarke, Ohio	1916–1922	Wilson
John Marshall, Va.	1801–1835	J. Adams	**William H. Taft**, Conn.	1921–1930	Harding
William Johnson, S.C.	1804–1834	Jefferson	George Sutherland, Utah	1922–1938	Harding
Brockholst Livingston, N.Y.	1807–1823	Jefferson	Pierce Butler, Minn.	1923–1939	Harding
Thomas Todd, Ky.	1807–1826	Jefferson	Edward T. Sanford, Tenn.	1923–1930	Harding
Gabriel Duvall, Md.	1811–1835	Madison	Harlan F. Stone, N.Y.	1925–1941	Coolidge
Joseph Story, Mass.	1812–1845	Madison	**Charles E. Hughes**, N.Y.	1930–1941	Hoover
Smith Thompson, N.Y.	1823–1843	Monroe	Owen J. Roberts, Penn.	1930–1945	Hoover
Robert Trimble, Ky.	1826–1828	J. Q. Adams	Benjamin N. Cardozo, N.Y.	1932–1938	Hoover
John McLean, Ohio	1830–1861	Jackson	Hugo L. Black, Ala.	1937–1971	F. Roosevelt
Henry Baldwin, Pa.	1830–1844	Jackson	Stanley F. Reed, Ky.	1938–1957	F. Roosevelt
James M. Wayne, Ga.	1835–1867	Jackson	Felix Frankfurter, Mass.	1939–1962	F. Roosevelt
Roger B. Taney, Md.	1836–1864	Jackson	William O. Douglas, Conn.	1939–1975	F. Roosevelt
Philip P. Barbour, Va.	1836–1841	Jackson	Frank Murphy, Mich.	1940–1949	F. Roosevelt
John Cartron, Tenn.	1837–1865	Van Buren	**Harlan F. Stone**, N.Y.	1941–1946	F. Roosevelt
John McKinley, Ala.	1838–1852	Van Buren	James R. Byrnes, S.C.	1941–1942	F. Roosevelt
Peter V. Daniel, Va.	1842–1860	Van Buren	Robert H. Jackson, N.Y.	1941–1954	F. Roosevelt
Samuel Nelson, N.Y.	1845–1872	Tyler	Wiley B. Rutledge, Iowa	1943–1949	F. Roosevelt
Levi Woodbury, N.H.	1845–1851	Polk	Harold H. Burton, Ohio	1945–1958	Truman
Robert C. Grier, Pa.	1846–1870	Polk	**Frederick M. Vinson**, Ky.	1946–1953	Truman
Benjamin R. Curtis, Mass.	1851–1857	Fillmore	Tom C. Clark, Texas	1949–1967	Truman
John A. Campbell, Ala.	1853–1861	Pierce	Sherman Minton, Ind.	1949–1956	Truman
Nathan Clifford, Me.	1858–1881	Buchanan	**Earl Warren**, Cal.	1953–1969	Eisenhower
Noah H. Swayne, Ohio	1862–1881	Lincoln	John Marshall Harlan, N.Y.	1955–1971	Eisenhower
Samuel F. Miller, Iowa	1862–1890	Lincoln	William J. Brennan, Jr., N.J.	1956–1990	Eisenhower
David Davis, Ill.	1862–1877	Lincoln	Charles E. Whittaker, Mo.	1957–1962	Eisenhower
Stephen J. Field, Cal.	1863–1897	Lincoln	Potter Stewart, Ohio	1958–1981	Eisenhower
Salmon P. Chase, Ohio	1864–1873	Lincoln	Bryon R. White, Colo.	1962–1993	Kennedy
William Strong, Pa.	1870–1880	Grant	Arthur J. Goldberg, Ill.	1962–1965	Kennedy
Joseph P. Bradley, N.J.	1870–1892	Grant	Abe Fortas, Tenn.	1965–1969	Johnson
Ward Hunt, N.Y.	1873–1882	Grant	Thurgood Marshall, Md.	1967–1991	Johnson
Morrison R. Waite, Ohio	1874–1888	Grant	**Warren E. Burger**, Minn.	1969–1986	Nixon
John M. Harlan, Ky.	1877–1911	Hayes	Harry A. Blackmun, Minn.	1970–	Nixon
William B. Woods, Ga.	1881–1887	Hayes	Lewis F. Powell, Jr., Va.	1971–1987	Nixon
Stanley Matthews, Ohio	1881–1889	Garfield	William H. Rehnquist, Ariz.	1971–1986	Nixon
Horace Gray, Mass.	1882–1902	Arthur	John Paul Stevens, Ill.	1975–	Ford
Samuel Blatchford, N.Y.	1882–1893	Arthur	Sandra Day O'Connor, Ariz.	1981–	Reagan
Lucius Q. C. Lamar, Miss.	1888–1893	Cleveland	**William H. Rehnquist**, Ariz.	1986–	Reagan
Melville W. Fuller, Ill.	1888–1910	Cleveland	Antonin Scalia, Va.	1986–	Reagan
David J. Brewer, Kan.	1890–1910	B. Harrison	Anthony M. Kennedy, Cal.	1988–	Reagan
Henry B. Brown, Mich.	1891–1906	B. Harrison	David H. Souter, N.H.	1990	Bush
George Shiras, Jr., Pa.	1892–1903	B. Harrison	Clarence Thomas, Ga.	1991–	Bush
Howell E. Jackson, Tenn.	1893–1895	B. Harrison	Ruth Bader Ginsburg, N.Y.	1993–	Clinton
Edward D. White, La.	1894–1910	Cleveland	Stephen G. Breyer, Mass.	1994–	Clinton
Rufus W. Peckham, N.Y.	1896–1909	Cleveland			

*Chief Justices are printed in bold type.

The American People: A Demographic Survey

★ ★ ★

A Demographic Profile of the American People

Year	Life Expectancy from Birth		Average Age at First Marriage		Number of Children Under 5 (per 1,000 Women Aged 20–44)	Percent of Women in Paid Employment	Percent of Paid Workers Who Are Female
	White	Black	Male	Female			
1820					1,295	6.2%	7.3%
1830					1,145	6.4	7.4
1840					1,085	8.4	9.6
1850					923	10.1	10.8
1860					929	9.7	10.2
1870					839	13.7	14.8
1880					822	14.7	15.2
1890			26.1	22.0	716	18.2	17.0
1900	47.6	33.0	25.9	21.9	688	21.2	18.1
1910	50.3	35.6	25.1	21.6	643	24.8	20.0
1920	54.9	45.3	24.6	21.2	604	23.9	20.4
1930	61.4	48.1	24.3	21.3	511	24.4	21.9
1940	64.2	53.1	24.3	21.5	429	25.4	24.6
1950	69.1	60.8	22.8	20.3	589	29.1	27.8
1960	70.6	63.6	22.8	20.3	737	34.8	32.3
1970	71.7	65.3	22.5	20.6	530	43.3	38.0
1980	74.4	68.1	24.7	22.0	440	51.5	42.6
1990	76.2	71.4	26.1	23.9	377	57.4	45.2

Source: Historical Statistics of the United States, Colonial Times to 1970 (1975); Statistical Abstract of the United States, 1991.

American Population

Year	Population	Percent Increase	Year	Population	Percent Increase
1610	350	—	1810	7,239,881	36.4
1620	2,300	557.1	1820	9,638,453	33.1
1630	4,600	100.0	1830	12,866,020	33.5
1640	26,600	478.3	1840	17,069,453	32.7
1650	50,400	90.8	1850	23,191,876	35.9
1660	75,100	49.0	1860	31,443,321	35.6
1670	111,900	49.0	1870	39,818,449	26.6
1680	151,500	35.4	1880	50,155,783	26.0
1690	210,400	38.9	1890	62,947,714	25.5
1700	250,900	19.2	1900	75,994,575	20.7
1710	331,700	32.2	1910	91,972,266	21.0
1720	466,200	40.5	1920	105,710,620	14.9
1730	629,400	35.0	1930	122,775,046	16.1
1740	905,600	43.9	1940	131,669,275	7.2
1750	1,170,800	29.3	1950	150,697,361	14.5
1760	1,593,600	36.1	1960	179,323,175	19.0
1770	2,148,100	34.8	1970	203,235,298	13.3
1780	2,780,400	29.4	1980	226,545,805	11.5
1790	3,929,214	41.3	1990	248,709,873	9.8
1800	5,308,483	35.1	1993	259,383,000	4.3

Note: These figures largely ignore the native American population. Census takers never made any effort to count the native American population that lived outside their political jurisdictions and compiled only casual and incomplete enumerations of those living within their jurisdictions until 1890. In that year the federal government attempted a full count of the Indian population: the Census found 125,719 Indians in 1890, compared with only 12,543 in 1870 and 33,985 in 1880.
Source: Historical Statistics of the United States, Colonial Times to 1970 (1975); Statistical Abstract of the United States, 1995.

White/Nonwhite Population

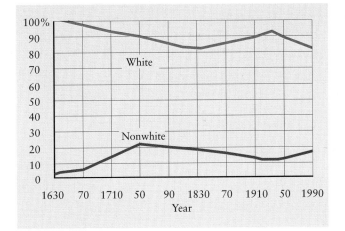

Urban/Rural Population

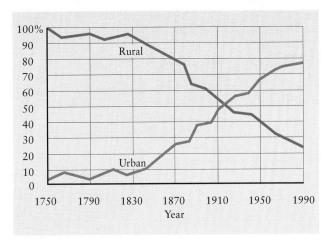

The Ten Largest Cities by Population, 1700–1990

		City	Population				City	Population
1700	1.	Boston	6,700		1910	1.	New York	4,766,883
	2.	New York	4,937*			2.	Chicago	2,185,283
	3.	Philadelphia	4,400†			3.	Philadelphia	1,549,008
						4.	St. Louis	687,029
1790	1.	Philadelphia	42,520			5.	Boston	670,585
	2.	New York	33,131			6.	Cleveland	560,663
	3.	Boston	18,038			7.	Baltimore	558,485
	4.	Charleston, S.C.	16,359			8.	Pittsburgh	533,905
	5.	Baltimore	13,503			9.	Detroit	465,766
	6.	Salem, Mass.	7,921			10.	Buffalo	423,715
	7.	Newport, R.I.	6,716					
	8.	Providence, R.I.	6,380		1930	1.	New York	6,930,446
	9.	Marblehead, Mass.	5,661			2.	Chicago	3,376,438
	10.	Portsmouth, N.H.	4,720			3.	Philadelphia	1,950,961
						4.	Detroit	1,568,662
1830	1.	New York	197,112			5.	Los Angeles	1,238,048
	2.	Philadelphia	161,410			6.	Cleveland	900,429
	3.	Baltimore	80,620			7.	St. Louis	821,960
	4.	Boston	61,392			8.	Baltimore	804,874
	5.	Charleston, S.C.	30,289			9.	Boston	781,188
	6.	New Orleans	29,737			10.	Pittsburgh	669,817
	7.	Cincinnati	24,831					
	8.	Albany, N.Y.	24,209		1950	1.	New York	7,891,957
	9.	Brooklyn, N.Y.	20,535			2.	Chicago	3,620,962
	10.	Washington, D.C.	18,826			3.	Philadelphia	2,071,605
						4.	Los Angeles	1,970,358
1850	1.	New York	515,547			5.	Detroit	1,849,568
	2.	Philadelphia	340,045			6.	Baltimore	949,708
	3.	Baltimore	169,054			7.	Cleveland	914,808
	4.	Boston	136,881			8.	St. Louis	856,796
	5.	New Orleans	116,375			9.	Washington, D.C.	802,178
	6.	Cincinnati	115,435			10.	Boston	801,444
	7.	Brooklyn, N.Y.	96,838					
	8.	St. Louis	77,860		1970	1.	New York	7,895,563
	9.	Albany, N.Y.	50,763			2.	Chicago	3,369,357
	10.	Pittsburgh	46,601			3.	Los Angeles	2,811,801
						4.	Philadelphia	1,949,996
1870	1.	New York	942,292			5.	Detroit	1,514,063
	2.	Philadelphia	674,022			6.	Houston	1,233,535
	3.	Brooklyn, N.Y.	419,921†			7.	Baltimore	905,787
	4.	St. Louis	310,864			8.	Dallas	844,401
	5.	Chicago	298,977			9.	Washington, D.C.	756,668
	6.	Baltimore	267,354			10.	Cleveland	750,879
	7.	Boston	250,526					
	8.	Cincinnati	216,239		1990	1.	New York	7,322,564
	9.	New Orleans	191,418			2.	Los Angeles	3,485,398
	10.	San Francisco	149,473			3.	Chicago	2,783,726
						4.	Houston	1,630,553
						5.	Philadelphia	1,585,577
						6.	San Diego	1,110,549
						7.	Detroit	1,027,974
						8.	Dallas	1,006,877
						9.	Phoenix	983,403
						10.	San Antonio	935,933

*Figure from a census taken in 1698.
†Philadelphia figures include suburbs.
‡Annexed to New York in 1898.
Source: U.S. Census data.

Foreign Origins of the American People

Immigration by Decade

Year	Number	Percent of Total Population	Year	Number	Percent of Total Population
1821–1830	151,824	1.6	1921–1930	4,107,209	3.9
1831–1840	599,125	4.6	1931–1940	528,431	0.4
1841–1850	1,713,251	10.0	1941–1950	1,035,039	0.7
1851–1860	2,598,214	11.2	1951–1960	2,515,479	1.6
1861–1870	2,314,824	7.4	1961–1970	3,321,677	1.8
1871–1880	2,812,191	7.1	1971–1980	4,493,000	2.2
1881–1890	5,246,613	10.5	1981–1990	7,338,000	3.0
1891–1900	3,687,546	5.8	1991–1993	3,705,000	1.4
1901–1910	8,795,386	11.6	Total	27,043,835	
1911–1920	5,735,811	6.2			
Total	33,654,785		1821–1993 Grand Total	60,698,620	

Source: U.S. Bureau of the Census, *Historical Statistics of the United States, Colonial Times to 1970* (1975), Part I, pp. 105–106; *Statistical Abstract of the United States*, 1995.

Regional Origins

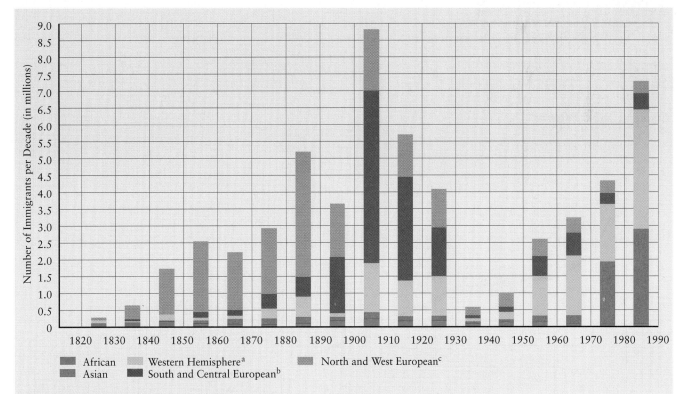

a Canada and all countries in South America and Central America.

b Italy, Spain, Portugal, Greece, Germany (Austria included, 1938–1945), Poland, Czechoslovakia (since 1920), Yugoslavia (since 1920), Hungary (since 1861), Austria (since 1861, except 1938–1945), former U.S.S.R. (excludes Asian U.S.S.R. between 1931 and 1963), Latvia, Estonia, Lithuania, Finland, Romania, Bulgaria, Turkey (in Europe), and other European countries not classified elsewhere.

c Great Britain, Ireland, Norway, Sweden, Denmark, Iceland, Netherlands, Belgium, Luxembourg, Switzerland, France.

Source: Stephan Thernstrom, ed., *Harvard Encyclopedia of American Ethnic Groups* (1980), p. 480; and U.S. Bureau of the Census, *Statistical Abstract of the United States*, 1991.

The Labor Force

(thousands of workers)

Year	Agriculture	Mining	Manufacturing	Construction	Trade	Other	Total
1810	1,950	11	75	—	—	294	2,330
1840	3,570	32	500	290	350	918	5,660
1850	4,520	102	1,200	410	530	1,488	8,250
1860	5,880	176	1,530	520	890	2,114	11,110
1870	6,790	180	2,470	780	1,310	1,400	12,930
1880	8,920	280	3,290	900	1,930	2,070	17,390
1890	9,960	440	4,390	1,510	2,960	4,060	23,320
1900	11,680	637	5,895	1,665	3,970	5,223	29,070
1910	11,770	1,068	8,332	1,949	5,320	9,041	37,480
1920	10,790	1,180	11,190	1,233	5,845	11,372	41,610
1930	10,560	1,009	9,884	1,988	8,122	17,267	48,830
1940	9,575	925	11,309	1,876	9,328	23,277	56,290
1950	7,870	901	15,648	3,029	12,152	25,870	65,470
1960	5,970	709	17,145	3,640	14,051	32,545	74,060
1970	3,463	516	20,746	4,818	15,008	34,127	78,678
1980	3,364	979	21,942	6,215	20,191	46,612	99,303
1990	3,186	730	21,184	7,696	24,269	60,849	117,914
1994	3,409	669	20,157	7,493	25,699	65,633	123,060

Source: Historical Statistics of the United States, Colonial Times to 1970 (1975), 139; Statistical Abstract of the United States, 1995, Table 653.

Changing Labor Patterns

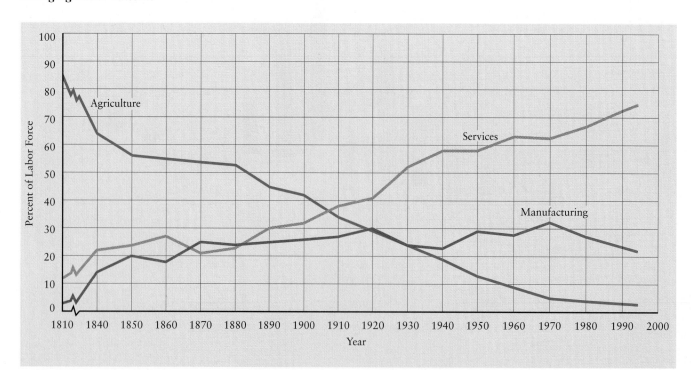

The Aging of the U.S. Population

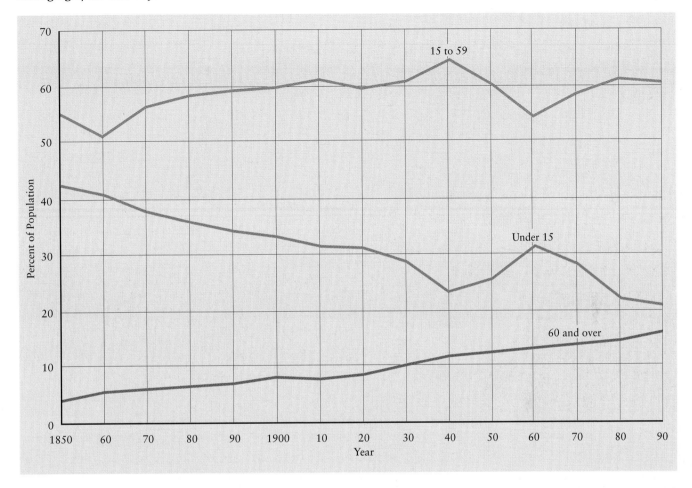

The American Government and Economy

★   ★   ★

The Growth of the Federal Government

| Year | Employees (millions) | | Receipts and Outlays ($ millions) | |
	Civilian	Military	Receipts	Outlays
1900	0.23	0.12	567	521
1910	0.38	0.13	676	694
1920	0.65	0.34	6,649	6,358
1930	0.61	0.25	4,058	3,320
1940	1.04	0.45	6,900	9,600
1950	1.96	1.46	40,900	43,100
1960	2.38	2.47	92,500	92,200
1970	3.00	3.06	193,700	196,600
1980	2.99	2.05	517,112	590,920
1990	3.23	2.04	1,031,321	1,252,705
1993	3.04	1.70	1,153,535	1,408,675

Source: Statistical Profile of the United States, 1900–1980; Statistical Abstract of the United States, 1995.

Gross National Product, 1840–1990

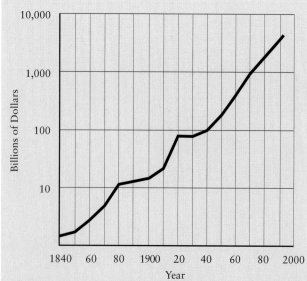

*Note: GNP values have not been adjusted for inflation or deflation. GNP is plotted here on a logarithmic scale.
Source: Statistical Abstract of the United States, 1995.

GNP per Capita, 1840–1990

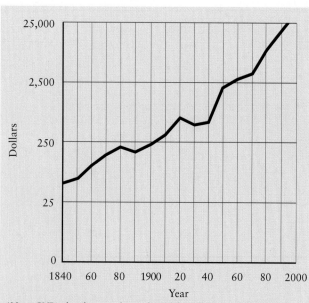

*Note: GNP values have not been adjusted for inflation or deflation. The GNP is plotted here on a logarithmic scale.

Consumer Price Index and Conversion Table

This index estimates how consumer prices changed on the average over ten-year intervals. Such estimates are highly uncertain, particularly when they are used to make comparisons over long periods of time. This is partly because it is extremely difficult to measure how the typical mix of goods (each with its own price) purchased by consumers changes over time.

To convert £ (pounds Sterling, until 1770) or $ (U.S. dollars, beginning in 1780) from any date in the past to the equivalent in 1990 dollars, multiply the historical price by the appropriate number in this column. For example, £10 Sterling in 1730 would equal about $867 in 1990. (£10 × 86.7 = $867); or $10 in 1870 would equal about $99 in 1990 ($10 × 9.9 = $99).

Year	Price Index (1860 = 100)	Conversion Multiplier
1700	130	53.3
1710	100	69.3
1720	76	91.3
1730	80	86.7
1740	66	105.1
1750	84	82.6
1760	96	72.3
1770	100	69.3
1780	165	9.5
1790	148	10.6
1800	151	10.4
1810	148	10.6
1820	141	11.1
1830	111	14.1
1840	104	15.1
1850	94	16.6
1860	100	15.6
1870	157	9.9
1880	123	12.7
1890	109	14.3
1900	101	15.5
1910	114	13.7
1920	240	6.5
1930	200	7.8
1940	168	9.3
1950	288	5.4
1960	354	4.4
1970	464	3.4
1980	985	1.6
1990	1563	1.0

Source: Adapted from John J. McCusker, "How Much Is That in Real Money? A Historical Price Index for Use as a Deflator of Money Value in the Economy of the United States," *Proceedings of the American Antiquarian Society*, Vol. 101, pt. 2, (1991), 297–390.

Illustration Credits

★   ★   ★

Chapter 16   **P. 484:** Chicago Historical Society. **Pp. 486 and 488:** Library of Congress. **P. 489:** Chicago Historical Society. **P. 491:** Collection of The New-York Historical Society. **P. 493:** Library of Congress. **P. 496:** Collection of Mrs. Nancy W. Livingston and Mrs. Elizabeth Livingston Jaeger. Photograph Courtesy of the Los Angeles County Museum of Art. **P. 497:** Corbis-Bettmann. **P. 499:** Library of Congress. **P. 500:** From *Harper's Weekly*, June 23, 1866, Courtesy of the Newberry Library, Chicago. **P. 501:** Rutherford B. Hayes Presidential Center, Spiegel Grove, Freemont, OH. **P. 504:** Collection Tennessee State Museum. Photo by Karina McDaniel. Courtesy Tennessee State Library & Archives, Nashville, TN. **P. 507:** Brown Brothers. **P. 510:** Historical Pictures/Stock Montage, Inc. **P. 513:** *Frank Leslie's Illustrated Newspaper*, Sept. 23, 1876. Courtesy of the Newberry Library, Chicago.

Chapter 17   **P. 518:** Courtesy of the New-York Historical Society, Bella C. Landauer Collection. **P. 521:** America Hurrah, New York City. **P. 523:** North Wind Pictures. **P. 524:** Culver Pictures. **P. 525:** Buffalo Bill Historical Center, Cody, WY. Gift of the Coe Foundation. **P. 526:** Culver Pictures. **P. 527:** The Kansas State Historical Society, Topeka. **P. 529:** Library of Congress. **P. 532:** Archives & Manuscript Division of the Oklahoma Historical Society. **P. 533:** Smithsonian Institution, Photo no. 3200-b-8 (National Anthropological Archives) **P. 536:** The Huntington Library, San Marino, CA. **P. 538:** Courtesy of the Thomas Gilcrease Institute of American History and Art, Tulsa, OK. **P. 540:** Bancroft Library, University of California, Berkeley. **P. 541:** William Hahn, *Market Scene, Sansome Street*, 1872, Oil on canvas, 60 in. × 96 in., Crocker Collection, Crocker Art Museum, Sacramento, CA. **P. 543:** Yosemite National Park Research Library, Yosemite National Park, CA. **P. 545:** Denver Public Library, Western History Division. Photo by Charles Redmond.

Chapter 18   **P. 550:** Chicago Historical Society. **P. 553:** Historical Pictures/Stock Montage, Inc. **Pp. 555 and 558:** Culver Pictures. **P. 562:** National Museum of American History, Smithsonian Institution. **P. 564:** *Harper's Weekly*, vol. 31, 1887, pp. 158–159, Courtesy of the Newberry Library, Chicago. **P. 567** (top): Thomas Anshutz, *The Ironworkers Noontime*, 1880. The Fine Arts Museums of San Francisco, Gift of Mr. and Mrs. John D. Rockefeller 3rd, 1979.7.4. **P. 567** (bottom): International Museum of Photography at George Eastman House, Rochester, NY. **P. 569:** Corbis-Bettmann. **P. 571:** Library of Congress. **P. 572:** Corbis-Bettmann. **P. 575:** Library of Congress. **P. 578:** The George Meany Memorial Archives. Negative # 91 **P. 579:** The Newberry Library.

Chapter 19   **P. 584:** Museum of American Political Life, University of Hartford, West Hartford, CT. Photo: Sally Andersen-Bruce. **P. 586:** Culver Pictures. **P. 589:** Brown Brothers. **P. 591:** Museum of American Political Life, University of Hartford, West Hartford, CT. Photo: Sally Andersen-Bruce. **P. 593:** From the collection of the Newport Historical Society, Newport, RI (P292). **P. 594:** The Kansas State Historical Society, Topeka. **P. 596:** Courtesy Northwestern University Archives/Photograph by Alexander Hesler. **P. 597:** Brown Brothers. **P. 598:** The Kansas State Historical Society, Topeka. **P. 601:** Culver Pictures. **P. 602:** Collection of the New-York Historical Society. **P. 604:** Museum of American Political Life, University of Hartford, West Hartford, CT. Photo: Steven Laschever. **P. 608:** Library of Congress. **P. 610:** General Research Division, New York Public Library, Astor, Lenox and Tilden Foundations.

Chapter 20   **P. 614:** Theodore Groll, *Washington Street, Indianapolis at Dusk*, 1892–1895, Indianapolis Museum of Art, Gift of a Couple of Old Hoosiers. **P. 619** (top): Corbis-Bettmann. **P. 619** (bottom): Andrew Smith Gallery/KEA. **P. 620:** Museum of the City of New York, Gift of Louis Stearns, 1889–1914. **P. 624:** Andrew Smith Gallery/KEA. **P. 625:** New York Public Library, Astor, Lenox, and Tilden Foundations. **P. 628:** Culver Pictures. **P. 629:** W. Louis Sonntag, Jr., *The Bowery at Night*, 1895, Museum of the City of New York, Gift of Mrs. William B. Miles. **P. 631:** Archives of Industrial Society, University Library System, University of Pittsburgh. **P. 632:** Local History and Genealogy Division, New York Public Library, Astor, Lenox and Tilden Foundations. **P. 634:** Culver Pictures. **P. 635** (top): Historical Pictures/Stock Montage, Inc. **P. 635** (bottom): Brown Brothers. **P. 637:** The Preservation Society of Newport County, Newport, RI. **P. 639:** Courtesy of the Cincinnati Historical Society. **P. 640:** Museum of the City of New York, Byron Collection. **P. 641:** John Singer Sargent, *Mr. and Mrs. Isaac Newton Phelps Stokes*, 1897. Oil on canvas, 84¼″ × 39¾″. The Metropolitan Museum of Art, New York. Bequest of Edith Minturn Phelps Stokes (Mrs. I.N.), 1938 (38.104).

Chapter 21   **P. 646:** George Wesley Bellows, *Cliff Dwellers*, 1913. Oil on canvas. 39½″ × 41½″. Los Angeles County Museum of Art, Los Angeles County Fund. **P. 650** (left): Ida M. Tarbell Collection, Reis Library, Allegheny College, Meadville, PA. **P. 650** (right): Culver Pictures. **P. 652:** State Historical Society of Wisconsin, Madison. **P. 653:** Courtesy NAACP National Headquarters. **P. 654:** Schlesinger Library, Radcliffe College, Cambridge, MA. **P. 656:** Chicago Historical Society. **P. 657:** Brown Brothers. **P. 658:** Corbis-Bettmann. **P. 659:** Brown Brothers. **P. 666:** Library of Congress. **P. 667:** Edward Steichen, *J. Pierpont Morgan*, 1903, Plate V from the boxed edition deluxe of the Steichen supplement to *Camera Work*, April 1906. Published simultaneously with XIV April 1906. Gravure, 8⅛ in. × 6¼ in. Collection, The Museum of Modern Art, New York. Gift of A. Conger Goodyear. **P. 668:** Library of Congress. **P. 671:** Woodrow Wilson-Democratic Nominee For President, *Harper's Weekly*, 7/13/12, Courtesy the Newberry Library, Chicago.

Chapter 22   P. 676: James G. Tyler, *Battle of Santiago de Cuba*, 1898, Courtesy Franklin D. Roosevelt Library (#CT79-66(2)). **P. 679:** Hawaii State Archives. **P. 680:** Courtesy of the New-York Historical Society, Bella C. Landauer Collection. **P. 682:** Culver Pictures. **P. 683:** U.S. Naval Historical Center, Washington, D.C. **P. 687:** Archive Photos. **P. 688:** *Destruction of the U.S. Battleship Maine in Havana Harbor, Feb. 15, 1898.* Kurz & Allison Chromolith, Chicago Historical Society. **P. 690:** Library of Congress. **P. 693** (top): National Archives. **P. 693** (bottom): G.W. Peters in *Harper's Weekly*, April 22, 1899, Courtesy of the Newberry Library, Chicago. **P. 694:** Joseph Keppler, Jr., *His 126th Birthday–Gee, but this is an awful stretch!*, from *Puck*, June 29, 1904, Courtesy of the Newberry Library, Chicago. **P. 697:** UPI/Corbis-Bettmann. **P. 700:** The Pat Hathaway Collection of California Views. **P. 702:** Aultman Collection, El Paso Public Library.

Chapter 23   P. 708: The Lester Levy Collection of Sheet Music. Milton S. Eisenhower Library. The Johns Hopkins University, Baltimore, MD. *Oh, How I Hate to Get Up in the Morning* © 1918 by Irving Berlin; © renewed 1945 by Irving Berlin; © assigned to Trustees of God Bless America Fund **P. 710:** Imperial War Museum, London. **P. 713:** Corbis-Bettmann. **P. 714:** UPI/Corbis-Bettmann. **P. 715:** Library of Congress. **P. 719:** Corbis-Bettmann. **Pp. 720 and 721:** UPI/Corbis-Bettmann. **P. 724:** National Archives, photo by M. Rudolph Vetter. **P. 725:** Schlesinger Library, Radcliffe College, Cambridge, MA. **P. 727:** Library of Congress. **P. 728:** Historical Pictures/Stock Montage, Inc. **P. 730:** William Orpen, *The Signing of the Peace in the Hall of Mirrors, Versailles, June 1919*, Imperial War Museum, London. **P. 732**(all): Chicago Historical Society, photo by Jun Fujita. **P. 735:** Ben Shahn. *Bartolomeo Vanzetti and Nicola Sacco*, from the Sacco-Vanzetti series of twenty-three paintings (1931–32). Tempera on paper over composition board, 10½″ × 14½″ (26.7 cm x 36.8 cm). The Museum of Modern Art, New York. Gift of Abby Aldrich Rockefeller. Photograph © 1996 The Museum of Modern Art, New York.

Chapter 24   P. 738: Mazda, General Electric, Courtesy Dartmouth College, Baker Library, Hanover, NH. Photo: © 1992 Jeffrey Nintzel. All rights reserved. **P. 740:** Brown Brothers. **P. 742:** Museum of American Political Life, University of Hartford, West Hartford, CT. Photo: Steven Laschever. **P. 744:** Charles Sheeler, *Untitled (River Rouge Plant)*, 1927, University Art Museum, University of New Mexico, Albuquerque. Gift of Eleanor and Van Deren Coke. **P. 748:** *Portrait of Luisa Ronstadt Espinel*, c. 1921, Arizona Historical Society Library. Gift of Edward Ronstadt, Mexican Heritage Project. **P. 749:** Florine Stettheimer, *Portrait of My Sister Ettie*, 1923. Columbia University in the City of New York, Gift of the Estate of Ettie Stettheimer, 1967. Photo: Gregory W. Schmitz, NYC. **P. 750:** Corbis-Bettmann. **P. 751:** Globe Photos. **P. 752:** Photofest. **P. 753:** Courtesy Christopher Casler. **P. 754:** Kansas City Museum, Kansas City, Missouri. **P. 755:** George Bellows, *Dempsey and Firpo*, 1924, Oil on canvas, 51 in. × 63¼ in., Whitney Museum of American Art, New York City. Purchased with funds from Gertrude Vanderbilt. Whitney 31.95. Photo by Geoffrey Clements. **P. 760:** W.A. Swift Collection, Archives & Special Collections, A.M. Bracken Library, Ball State University, Muncie, IN. **P. 761:** John Sloan, *The Lafayette*, 1928, Oil on canvas, 30½ × 36¼ in., The Metropolitan Museum of Art, New York. Gift of

Friends of John Sloan, 1928 (28.18). **P. 763:** Henry Lee Moon Library and Civil Rights Archive, NAACP, Washington, D.C.

Chapter 25   P. 768: Alexandre Hogue. *Drought-Stricken Area*, 1934. Oil on canvas. 30″ × 42¼″. Dallas Museum of Art, Dallas Art Association Purchase, 1945.6. **P. 770:** UPI/Corbis-Bettmann. **P. 773:** Isaac Soyer, *Employment Agency*. 1937. Oil on canvas, 34¼″ × 45″. Whitney Museum of American Art, New York. Purchase 37.44. Photograph by Geoffrey Clements. **P. 774:** Franklin D. Roosevelt Library, Hyde Park, NY. **P. 778:** UPI/Corbis-Bettmann. **P. 779** (both): Courtesy of Steve Schapiro. **P. 780:** Corbis-Bettmann. **P. 782** (top): UPI/Corbis-Bettmann. **P. 782** (bottom): Schomburg Center for Research in Black Culture, The New York Public Library. Astor, Lenox, and Tilden Foundations. **P. 783:** UPI/Corbis-Bettmann. **P. 786:** Library of Congress. **P. 787:** University of Texas, The Institute of Texan Cultures, *San Antonio Light* Collection. **P. 789:** Courtesy Bert Corona. **P. 791:** Corbis-Bettmann.

Chapter 26   P. 796: Mitchell Wolfson, Jr. Collection, The Wolfsonian, Miami Beach, Florida and Genoa, Italy. **P. 798:** AP/World Wide Photos. **P. 799:** Library of Congress. **P. 801:** Courtesy *Vanity Fair* © 1935 (renewed 1963) by The Condé Nast Publications, Inc. **Pp. 802 and 803:** UPI/Corbis-Bettmann. **P. 804:** Library of Congress. **P. 809:** Brown Brothers. **P. 810:** Franklin D. Roosevelt Library, Hyde Park, NY. **P. 812:** Ben Shahn, *Steel Workers Organizing Committee* Poster, 1930s, Library of Congress. **P. 813** (top): UPI/Corbis-Bettmann. **P. 813** (bottom): William Gropper, *Construction of a Dam*, 1937. (Mural study, Department of the Interior), National Museum of American Art/Art Resource. **P. 817:** Corbis-Bettmann. **P. 818:** Joseph Binder, *World's Fair Poster*, Collection of The Queens Museum of Art, Queens, NY. Gift of Clara Binder. **P. 820:** Louis Guglielmi, *Relief Blues*, c. 1938, National Museum of American Art/Art Resource. **P. 822:** Margaret Bourke-White, *Life Magazine* © 1936 Time Warner, Inc. **P. 823:** Archive Photos.

Chapter 27   P. 826: Courtesy of the War Memorial Museum of Virginia. **P. 829:** UPI/Corbis-Bettmann. **P. 830:** Herbert Hoover Presidential Library. **P. 833:** UPI/Corbis-Bettmann. **P. 835:** Courtesy of the War Memorial Museum of Virginia. **P. 837:** UPI/Corbis-Bettmann. **P. 838** (top): Archive Photos. **P. 838** (bottom): Courtesy of the Dorothea Lange Collection. The City of Oakland, The Oakland Museum. 1982. **P. 841:** Ben Shahn, *For Full Employment After the War Register Vote*, 1944. Offset lithograph, printed in color, 30 in. × 39⅞ in. Collection of the Museum of Modern Art, New York. Gift of the CIO Political Action Committee. **P. 842:** Library of Congress. **P. 843:** Lee Boltin Picture Library. **P. 845:** UPI/Corbis-Bettmann. **P. 846:** Myron Davos, *Life Magazine* © Time Warner, Inc. **P. 850:** UPI/Corbis-Bettmann. **P. 851** (top): Margaret Bourke-White, *Life Magazine* © Time Warner Inc. **P. 851** (bottom): Frank Scherschel, *Life Magazine* © 1942 Time Warner, Inc. **P. 854:** Franklin D. Roosevelt Library, Hyde Park, NY (Photographed by US Army Signal Corps.). **P. 855:** UPI/Corbis-Bettmann.

Chapter 28   P. 860: Los Alamos National Laboratory. **P. 862:** Archive Photos. **P. 865:** UPI/Corbis-Bettmann. **P. 867** (left): UPI/Corbis-Bettmann. **P. 867** (right): AP/World Wide Photos. **P. 868:** Fenno Jacobs/Black Star. **P. 872:** UPI/Corbis-Bettmann. **P. 873:** Wayne Miller/Magnum Pictures, Inc. **P. 874:** Western History Collections, University of Oklahoma Library, The Helen Gahagan Douglas Collection. **P. 875:** AP/Wide World Photos. **P. 876:** UPI/Corbis-Bettmann. **P. 880:** Syracuse University Library, Department of Special Collections. **P. 881:** Robert Phillips/Black Star. **Pp. 882 and 883:** AP/World Wide Photos. **P. 884:** Michael Barson Collection. **P. 886:** FPG International. **P. 887:** Corbis-Bettmann.

Chapter 29   P. 892: 1955 The Curtis Publishing Company. **P. 895:** Tom Wesselmann, *Still Life #24*, 1962, The Nelson-Atkins Museum of

Art, (Gift of the Guild of the Friends of Art) Kansas City, MO. **P. 896:** UPI/Corbis-Bettmann. **P. 898:** Charles Babbage Institute, University of Minnesota. **P. 899:** Photo by Dan Weiner, Courtesy Sarah Weiner. **P. 904** (top): Bern Keating/Black Star. **P. 904** (bottom): The Huntington Library, San Marino, CA. (Whittington Collection). **P. 908:** Globe Photos. **P. 910:** National Archives (HUD Holdings). **P. 911:** AP/World Wide Photos. **P. 912:** From the collections of Henry Ford Museum and Greenfield Village. Courtesy of Franchise Associates, Inc., South Weymouth, MA. **P. 914:** Photofest. **P. 915:** March of Dimes Birth Defects Foundation. **P. 916:** Elliott Erwitt/Magnum Pictures, Inc. **P. 919:** Jackson Pollock, *Autumn Rhythm*, 1950. The Metropolitan Museum of Art, George Hearn Fund, 1957 (57. 92). © 1980 by the Metropolitan Museum of Art. © 1997 The Pollock-Krasner Foundation/Artists Rights Society (ARS), NY. **P. 921:** © 1956 BMG Music.

Chapter 30 **P. 924:** Museum of American Political Life, University of Hartford, West Hartford, CT. Photo: Sally Andersen-Bruce. **P. 926:** AP/Wide World Photos. **P. 929:** Paul Conklin. **P. 930:** UPI/Corbis-Bettmann. **P. 932:** Archive Photos. **P. 933:** Charles Harbutt/Actuality. **Pp. 934 and 935:** Charles Moore/Black Star. **P. 936:** Danny Lyon/Magnum Pictures, Inc. **P. 938:** AP/World Wide Photos. **P. 940:** Andy Warhol, *Red Race Riot*, 1963. Silkscreen ink on synthetic polymer paint on canvas. 137⅞″ × 82¾″. The Andy Warhol Foundation for the Visual Arts. **P. 941:** Eve Arnold/Magnum Pictures, Inc. **P. 942** (top): Dewitt Collection, Museum of American Political Life, University of Hartford, West Hartford, CT. Photographer: Sally Andersen-Bruce. **P. 942** (bottom): George Tames/The New York Times. **P. 945:** George Gardner/The Image Works. **P. 947:** Eve Arnold/Magnum Pictures, Inc. **P. 948:** Michael Alexander/Black Star. **P. 950:** FPG International. **P. 951:** UPI/Corbis-Bettmann. **P. 955:** Bettye Lane.

Chapter 31 **P. 958:** Jim Pickerell/Black Star. **P. 964:** Larry Burrows, *Life Magazine* © Time Warner, Inc. **P. 966:** UPI/Corbis-Bettmann. **P. 967:** AP/World Wide Photos. **P. 968:** UPI/Corbis-Bettmann. **P. 970:** Bancroft Library, University of California, Berkeley. **P. 972** (top): Paul Fusco/Magnum Pictures, Inc. **P. 972** (bottom): © Apple Corps Ltd. **P. 973:** Steve Schapiro/Black Star. **P. 977** (top): AP/Wide World Photos. **P. 977** (bottom): Burt Glinn/Magnum Pictures, Inc. **P. 980:** Michael Abramson/Black Star. **P. 983:** U.S. Army Photo/U.S. Dept. of Defense, Still Media Records Center, Washington, D.C. **P. 984:** Marc Riboud/Magnum Pictures, Inc. **P. 985:** Peter Marlow/Magnum Pictures, Inc. **P. 987:** UPI/Corbis-Bettmann.

Chapter 32 **P. 988:** NASA. **P. 990:** Charles Moore/Black Star. **P. 995:** Dennis Brack/Black Star. **P. 997:** Tony Korody/Sygma. **P. 1001**(top): Michael Philippot/Sygma. **P. 1001** (bottom): Jim Anderson/Black Star. **P. 1002:** UPI/Corbis-Bettmann. **P. 1005:** Bettye Lane. **P. 1008:** Stanley Forman. **P. 1013** (top): D. B. Owen/Black Star. **P. 1013** (bottom): Mingam/Gamma Liaison.

Chapter 33 **P. 1018:** Michael W. Davidson/Photo Researchers, Inc. **P. 1021:** Rick Rickman/Matrix. **P. 1022:** Tannenbaum/Sygma. **P. 1024:** Fred Ward/Black Star. **P. 1026:** Markel/Gamma Liaison. **P. 1027:** Reuters/Corbis-Bettmann. **P. 1028:** Luc Delahaye/SIPA Press. **P. 1034:** Kay Chernush/The Image Bank. **P. 1036:** Sylvie Kreiss/Gamma Liaison. **P. 1038:** Photofest. **P. 1040:** Estate of Keith Haring. **P. 1042:** Photo Courtesy of Bob Wallace. **P. 1044** (top): Sobol/SIPA Press. **P. 1044** (bottom): Robert Trippet/SIPA Press. **P. 1045:** Peterson/Gamma Liaison. **P. 1046:** Erik Freeland/Matrix. **P. 1048:** Dagmar Fabricius/Gamma Liaison. **P. 1049:** Sygma.

Copyright Notices

★   ★   ★

Index